Political Parties and Elections in the United States

AN ENCYCLOPEDIA

Garland Reference Library of the Social Sciences
Volume 498

POLITICAL PARTIES & ELECTIONS *in the* UNITED STATES

A N   E N C Y C L O P E D I A

A–M

GENERAL EDITOR

L. Sandy Maisel

Department of Government
Colby College

ASSOCIATE EDITOR

Charles Bassett

Department of English and American Studies Program
Colby College

GARLAND PUBLISHING, INC.
New York & London
1991

Library of Congress Cataloging-in-Publication Data

Political parties and elections in the United States : an encyclopedia /
     edited by L. Sandy Maisel.
       p. cm. — (Garland reference library of social science:
vol. 498
     Includes index.
     ISBN 0-8240-7975-2
     1. Political parties—United States—Encyclopedias. 2. Elections—
United States—Encyclopedias. I. Maisel, Louis Sandy, 1945– .
II. Series.
JK2261.P633 1991
91-6940
324.273'03—dc20
CIP

Printed on acid-free, 250-year life paper
MANUFACTURED IN THE UNITED STATES OF AMERICA

Contents

Introduction

Political Parties and Elections in the United States is the joint effort of more than 250 scholars—political scientists, historians, students of American culture, sociologists, lawyers, journalists, and others—who share the belief that an obvious and important gap in available reference materials needed to be filled. While various research tools exist to aid students of political parties and elections, no easily accessible source provides a range of materials on a wide variety of subjects. This encyclopedia fills that void.

Broadly defined, the subject matter covered in this work is political parties and elections. Undergraduate and general readers can turn to this source to begin their explorations, to find names and dates, basic data on the history and current operations of political parties, rudimentary information on the individuals who have played and continue to play key roles in the functioning of political parties and the electoral process, and bibliographical information so that they may continue their studies. Graduate students and experienced scholars will draw on the bibliographic references and the discussions of research controversies in the field. All of the users will find lists and tables providing data that have been gathered from a variety of sources and collected so that they are now available from one reference source. I am hopeful—and at the same time confident—that users of this reference work will find it indispensable as they analyze American political parties and elections.

While encyclopedias are meant to be all-inclusive, decisions on which entries should appear and which ones are not necessary must be made. In this encyclopedia specificity was deemed to be important. That is, this is not an encyclopedia about all aspects of American politics, only about political parties and elections. Thus, biographical sketches of all of the chairs of the Democratic and Republican National Committees are included, but users will find entries on members of the Presidents' cabinets and Congressmen and governors only if those individuals were important in the electoral process. James B. Hunt, governor of North Carolina (D, 1977–1985), is included because he chaired an important reform commission in the Democratic Party, but his successor, James G. Martin (R, 1985–1993), is not included—except in the list of all of the governors of all of the states. In a similar vein, the article on Andrew Jackson includes a discussion of his impact on the American party system, but it does not say much about the Battle of New Orleans. The hope is that those who turn to this source will find the material they seek on political parties and elections, and additional sources, but that they will not be distracted by unrelated material.

Even with these general guidelines, decisions were not always easy. Certain individuals were included because of their formal positions—Presidents and Vice Presidents, presidential candidates, Speakers of the House, Majority and Minority Leaders in both houses of Congress, party chairs; but for other individuals judgments were called for—governors and mayors, state and local party officials, feminists, labor leaders, Cabinet members; and the like. The same can be said for organizations. Most political parties were included; only some political action committees were felt to merit inclusion. The same applied to concepts and events. Separate articles were included on most, but not all, presidential elections, but on only a few midterm elections. The criteria included the importance of the election in defining the politics of the time. I am certain that some will feel we made errors of omission. For these I apologize and ask that you communicate with me so that oversights can be corrected in future editions of this work. Perhaps some will feel we have also erred in including some entries that might better have been left out; I hope that readers will understand that the interests of all users of this encyclopedia will not be the same and that what is useless to some might be valuable to others.

What is most apparent is that no one individual could make all of these decisions. As general editor, I compiled a preliminary list of entries. One of the most important roles played by the contributing editors was to review that list and to suggest additions; I would be remiss if I did not single out David Mayhew, whose own encyclopedic knowledge of the important players in the two-century-long game of American politics was invaluable to me as I determined the entries for this work. I am deeply indebted to all of my friends and colleagues who have served as contributing editors, not only for their help in defining the items to be included in this work but also for sharing my commitment to seeing it through to completion. They have each written important articles that are included here; they have provided the valuable bibliographies that accompany their articles; they have helped to select additional authors. They have done this work because they share the view that this work is important, that it will aid our professions in the years ahead, and that work of this sort is appropriate for truly collegial professions. I am extremely grateful to them for all of these things—but mostly for their friendship.

This encyclopedia has also benefited immeasurably from the efforts of my associate editor, Charles Bassett. Put simply, Charles is one of the most exacting professionals I have ever met. He has read and reread every word in these volumes, pointing out flaws in logic, questions left unanswered, stylistic quirks that could cause confusion, errors of fact, and inconsistencies in interpretation. His has been the eye that seeks to make this encyclopedia readable and of interest to all users. For two years Bassett has come into my office marveling at the prose found in some of the articles, despairing at others, fretting that his changes might alter meanings. Each of the authors included in this work shares my debt to Charles, but none is as aware as am I of how much of himself he has put into assuring the quality of the final product.

I would also like to thank my colleagues—here at Colby and at Harvard during the year in which this project was formulated—for allowing me to use them as sounding boards and for reflecting back such beneficial advice. Some are also contributing editors, but I want to note particularly my debt to Al Mavrinac, Roger Bowen, Toni Katz, Cal Mackenzie, Charles Hauss, Beverly Hawk, Tony Corrado, Rob Weisbrot, and especially Chuck Lakin here at Colby College, and to Jim Alt, Gary King, Doug Price, and Ken Shepsle at Harvard.

The efforts of a number of other individuals have also contributed to making this project possible. I have worked with a series of editors at Garland Publishing. This encyclopedia bears the clear stamp of Kennie Lyman, whose sensitivity to me as this work's editor and whose standards of precision and consistency have added greatly to the final product. As an editor she combined enthusiasm for the project and a willingness to let me define its direction with enough of a compassionate but firm guiding hand to allow the project to achieve its final shape. For all of that and much more she has my enduring thanks. Much the same can be said for Chuck Bartelt, whose expertise on computer technology made it possible to produce this manuscript in Waterville, Maine, then refine it in New York City with a minimum of confusion. I am also indebted to Douglas Goertzen for his thorough and professional copyediting, which has improved the quality of this work and saved us from numerous errors, and to Kevin Bradley, the production editor, who combined prodding with patience so that this encyclopedia appeared on time and the editors maintained their sanity.

Patricia Kick, who has served as my secretary for nearly two decades, and Tonya Koenker, who was my secretary at Harvard during the year I began this enterprise, have played critical roles in allowing me to keep track of 250 authors and 1,200 articles over the more than two years this project has taken. I am grateful not only for their organizational skills but for their good natures and their friendship as well. I have also benefitted from excellent student assistants. Gretchen Anglund, Suzanne LaPrade, and Julie Daniele have played critical roles in tracking down missing data, filling in incomplete references, correcting inconsistencies, and developing the cross-references found throughout the text. One of the joys of teaching at Colby has been my ability to work with bright undergraduates on a continuing basis. Gretchen, Suzanne, and Julie are three of the best. In addition I want to acknowledge the hard work and incredible efficiency of those who have typed and incorporated editing into the manuscript: Matt Frymier, Danny Reed, Jill Mongeau, Laura Senier, Missy Ray, and especially Ashley Cornell.

Finally my wife Joyce and my children, Dana, Josh, and Dylan, have borne an unusual brunt of the burden of putting up with me as I have worked on this project. Most projects on which I have worked go on for a while, reach a crescendo, and then are over. This project seemed to have a series of peaks—defining all of the articles, securing all of the authors, receiving all of the articles, reviewing and revising all of the articles, etc.—and at each stage I am certain I reached a state of frenzy that made me less than pleasant to live with. And in each case—as they have in the past—my family tolerated me good-naturedly, chuckling to themselves and hoping that soon I would return to normal. I hope I have, and I hope they all know how much I appreciate their tolerance and love them.

I would like to close this introduction by asking for critical appraisals from those who use this encyclopedia as a resource. A research tool is only valuable if it serves the users. Constructive criticism from you the "consumer" will help me and those who work with me to improve this tool as it goes through subsequent editions.

L. SANDY MAISEL
Waterville, Maine

Bibliographic Note

The professional literature by political scientists, historians, and journalists on the various aspects of American political parties and elections covered in this encyclopedia is rich and voluminous. The authors whose work appears in this work could have cited a great many sources on the subject(s) they cover. In fact, of course, each author made his or her own decision on the number of works to cite. As editors, we made certain decisions beyond those of the individual authors, and our decisions structure the bibliographic references that readers will find below.

First, each of the longer essays, those written by the contributing editors, is supplemented by a long list of references. These references should prove useful to those users of the encyclopedia interested not only in those *particular* subjects but also in many of the more specific subjects involved in these longer essays. Most of the shorter entries refer the reader to other entries in this work, some of which are the longer essays written by the contributing editors. Following these references to other articles is a good strategy for finding additional bibliographical material.

Second, each author has supplied up to five references for each article. Often these references were those employed by the author as he or she prepared the entry. In other cases the references are those that would be useful for readers intending to probe the subject matter in more depth. Some authors provided many more references than we could include. The judgments we made in this area followed the following criteria: books were listed in preference to articles; more recent material was included in preference to that written earlier; standard reference books for political biographies and newspaper obituaries were generally excluded.

Third, footnotes have been excluded from the shorter essays and included in the longer essays only when absolutely essential. Directly quoted material is cited appropriately; it can be assumed that other material drawn from the works cited in the listed references has been used in the shorter articles, even though specific citations are not provided.

Many of the entries that follow are brief biographical sketches of important figures in American political history. In addition to obituaries in the *New York Times*, the *Washington Post,* and local newspapers, which are always good sources of information for figures from the past, we have compiled the following list of standard biographical sources that were used by many of the authors.

Almanac of American Politics. Bi-annual. Edited by Michael Barone and Grant Ujifusa. Washington, DC: National Journal.

Biographical Directory of the Governors of the United States. 1978. Edited by Robert Sobel and John Raimes. Westport, CT: Meckler Books.

Biographical Directory of the United States Congress, 1774–1989. 1989. Prepared for the Joint Committee on Printing of the United States Congress. Washington: DC: U.S. Government Printing Office.

Dictionary of American Biography. 1928. Edited by Allen Johnson. New York: Charles Scribner's Sons.

National Cyclopedia of American Biography. 1898–1984. Clifton, NJ: James T. White & Co.

Political Profiles. Various years. Edited by Eleanora W. Schoenebaum, Nelson Lichtenstein, and Michael L. Levine. New York: Facts on File.

Politics in America. Bi-annual. Edited by Alan Ehrenhalt. Washington, DC: Congressional Quarterly Press.

Who's Who in America. Annual. Wilmette, IL: Marquis Who's Who.

Who's Who in American Politics. Annual. Edited by R. R. Bowker and staff. New York: R. R. Bowker.

List of Contributors

Contributing Editors

Alan I. Abramowitz
Department of Political Science
Emory University

Herbert E. Alexander
Citizens' Research Foundation
University of Southern California

Richard Beeman
Department of History
University of Pennsylvania

William T. Bianco
Department of Political Science
Duke University

John F. Bibby
Department of Political Science
University of Wisconsin, Milwaukee

Allan G. Bogue
Department of History
University of Wisconsin, Madison

David W. Brady
Department of Political Science
Stanford University

Steven J. Brams
Department of Politics
New York University

Charles S. Bullock III
Department of Political Science
University of Georgia

Cornelius P. Cotter
Department of Political Science
University of Wisconsin, Milwaukee

William Crotty
Department of Political Science
Northwestern University

Samuel J. Eldersveld
Department of Political Science
University of Michigan

Leon D. Epstein
Department of Political Science
University of Wisconsin, Madison

Morris P. Fiorina
Department of Government
Harvard University

Linda L. Fowler
Department of Political Science
Syracuse University

Jo Freeman
Brooklyn, NY

James L. Gibson
Department of Political Science
University of Houston

William E. Gienapp
Department of History
Harvard University

Alan R. Gitelson
Department of Political Science
Loyola University of Chicago

Ralph M. Goldman
Senior Consultant
National Democratic Institute for
  International Affairs

Ann D. Gordon
Historical Documents Study
National Historical Publications
    & Records Commission
National Archives

Marjorie Randon Hershey
Department of Political Science
Indiana University

Robert J. Huckshorn
Department of Political Science
Florida Atlantic University

John S. Jackson III
Department of Political Science
Southern Illinois University

Gary C. Jacobson
Department of Political Science
University of California, San Diego

Malcolm E. Jewell
Department of Political Science
University of Kentucky

Charles O. Jones
Department of Political Science
University of Wisconsin, Madison

Ruth S. Jones
Department of Political Science
Arizona State University

John H. Kessel
Department of Political Science
Ohio State University

Kay Lawson
Department of Political Science
San Francisco State University

Lawrence D. Longley
Department of Political Science
Lawrence University

Daniel Hays Lowenstein
School of Law
University of California, Los Angeles

David R. Mayhew
Department of Political Science
Yale University

Daniel A. Mazmanian
Center for Politics and Policy
Claremont Graduate School

Jerome M. Mileur
Department of Political Science
University of Massachusetts, Amherst

Warren E. Miller
Department of Political Science
Arizona State University

Garrison Nelson
Department of Political Science
University of Vermont

Richard G. Niemi
Department of Political Science
University of Rochester

Walter J. Oleszek
Congressional Research Service
Library of Congress

Samuel C. Patterson
Department of Political Science
Ohio State University

Thomas E. Patterson
Department of Political Science
Syracuse University

Ronald M. Peters, Jr.
Carl Albert Center
University of Oklahoma

Gerald M. Pomper
Department of Political Science
Rutgers University

Howard L. Reiter
Department of Political Science
University of Connecticut

Larry J. Sabato
Department of Political Science
University of Virginia

William G. Shade
Department of History
Lehigh University

Joel H. Silbey
Department of History
Cornell University

Barbara Sinclair
Department of Political Science
University of California, Riverside

Frank J. Sorauf
Department of Political Science
University of Minnesota

Harold W. Stanley
Department of Political Science
University of Rochester

John G. Stewart
Tennessee Valley Authority

Walter J. Stone
Department of Political Science
University of Colorado

Martin Tolchin
The New York Times

Susan J. Tolchin
Department of Public Administration
George Washington University

Martin P. Wattenberg
School of Social Science
University of California, Irvine

Contributing Authors

Douglas Carl Abrams
Department of History
Bob Jones University

Roberta S. Alexander
Department of History
University of Dayton

Howard W. Allen
Department of History
Southern Illinois University

Peter H. Argersinger
Department of History
University of Maryland, Baltimore County

Frederick J. Augustyn, Jr.
Department of History
University of Maryland

Denise L. Baer
Department of Political Science
Bliss Institute of Applied Politics
University of Akron

Gary L. Bailey
Department of History
Indiana University of Pennsylvania

Ross K. Baker
Department of Political Science
Rutgers University

Thomas J. Baldino
Department of Political Science
Juniata College

Keith Barnett
Hale and Dorr
Boston, MA

Robert G. Barrows
Department of History
Indiana University—Purdue University,
Indianapolis

Jeffra Becknell
Washington Ethical High School
Washington, DC

Gerald Benjamin
State University of New York
College at New Paltz

John C. Berg
Department of Government
Suffolk University

Geoffrey Blodgett
Department of History
Oberlin College

Frederick J. Blue
Department of History
Youngstown State University

Jon Bond
Department of Political Science
Texas A & M University

Thomas N. Boschert
Department of History
University of Mississippi

David A. Bositis
Joint Center for Political and
    Economic Studies
Washington, DC

Garry Boulard
New Orleans, LA

Morton A. Brody
Supreme Court
State of Maine

Clyde Brown
Department of Political Science
Miami University

Nicholas C. Burckel
Olin Library
Washington University, St. Louis

Richard C. Burnweit
Department of Political Science
Westmont College

Charles W. Calhoun
Department of History
East Carolina University

Scott Cameron
Brownfield, ME

David T. Canon
Department of Political Science
University of Wisconsin, Madison

Gregg Cantrell
Department of History
Sam Houston State University

Richard A. Champagne, Jr.
Department of Political Science
University of Wisconsin, Madison

Hal Chase
Department of History
Des Moines Area Community College

Thomas H. Clapper
Oklahoma State Senate
Oklahoma City, OK

John A. Clark
Department of Political Science
Ohio State University

James C. Clark
The Orlando Sentinel

Paul C. Cline
Department of Political Science
James Madison University

J. Fraser Cocks III
Knight Library, Special Collections
University of Oregon

John F. Coleman
Department of History
St. Francis College

Melissa P. Collie
Department of Government
University of Texas

Patrick T. Conley
Department of History
Providence College

William F. Connelly, Jr.
Department of Politics
Washington & Lee University

M. Margaret Conway
Department of Political Science
University of Florida

William Corbett
Lynn, MA

Anthony J. Corrado
Department of Government
Colby College

Janet L. Coryell
Department of History
Auburn University

Robert E. Craig
Department of Political Science
University of New Hampshire

Mary T. Curtin
Department of State

Lewis A. Dexter
Department of Political Science
University of North Carolina, Charlotte

Matthew J. Dickinson
Department of Government
Harvard University

Richard Digby-Junger
Department of Journalism
Northern Illinois University

Joseph A. Dowling
Department of History
Lehigh University

George C. Edwards III
Department of Political Science
Texas A & M University

Anthony J. Eksterowicz
Department of Political Science
James Madison University

Richard Ellis
Department of Political Science
Willamette University

John Etting
Department of History
University of Houston

Norman B. Ferris
Department of History
Middle Tennessee State University

Phyllis F. Field
Department of History
Ohio University

Terri Susan Fine
Department of Political Science
University of Central Florida

Peter C. Fishburn
AT&T Bell Laboratories
Murry Hill, NJ

Michael W. Fitzgerald
Department of History
St. Olaf College

Richard Fleisher
Department of Political Science
Fordham University

Joseph A. Fry
Department of History
University of Nevada, Las Vegas

R. Kenneth Godwin
Department of Political Science
University of North Texas

Stephen E. Gottlieb
Albany Law School
Union University

Ralph D. Gray
Department of History
Indiana University—Purdue University,
Indianapolis

Michael Green
Department of Political Science
Columbia University

Bernard N. Grofman
School of Social Sciences
University of California, Irvine

David J. Hadley
Department of Political Science
Wabash College

Brian A. Haggerty
Citizens' Research Foundation
Los Angeles, CA

Susan Webb Hammond
Department of Government
American University

Roger D. Hardaway
Division of Social Science
Northwestern Oklahoma State University

Cynthia E. Harrison
Federal Judicial History Program
Federal Judicial Center
Washington, DC

Elinor C. Hartshorn
Department of Government
Western New England College

Charles S. Hauss
Department of Government
Colby College

Kenneth P. Hayes
Department of Political Science
University of Maine

John E. Haynes
20th Century Political History
Library of Congress

Michael Heel
Governor Dummer Academy
Byfield, MA

David Hein
Department of Religion & Philosophy
Hood College

Douglas I. Hodgkin
Department of Political Science
Bates College

William F. Holmes
Department of History
University of Georgia

Margaret Horsnell
Department of History
American International College

R. Douglas Hurt
Graduate Program in Agricultural History
Iowa State University

Reed Hutner
Baltimore, MD

John W. Jeffries
Department of History
University of Maryland, Baltimore County

John R. Johannes
Department of Political Science
Marquette University

Richard R. John
Commonwealth Center for the
    Study of American Culture
College of William and Mary

Loch K. Johnson
Department of Political Science
University of Georgia

Grady L. Johnston
Department of Political Science
Mississippi State University

Gene D. L. Jones
Department of History
Northern Michigan University

Victoria A. A. Kamsler
Harvard University

Tom A. Kazee
Department of Political Science
Davidson College

John G. Kolp
Department of History
U.S. Naval Academy

Steven C. Kottsy
Department of History
University of Cincinnati

Karl A. Lamb
Department of Political Science
U.S. Naval Academy

Lisa G. Langenbach
Department of Government & Law
Lafayette College

Eugene S. Larson
Department of History & Humanities
Pierce College

Jeremy R. T. Lewis
Department of Political Science
University of Northern Iowa

Steve Lilienthal
The Political Report
Washington, DC

Jeffery C. Livingston
Department of History
University of Toledo

Charles Longley
Department of Political Science
Bucknell University

Burdett A. Loomis
Department of Political Science
Kansas University

Richard Lowitt
Department of History
University of Oklahoma

Melissa Ludtke
Time Magazine

James A. McCann
Department of Political Science
University of Colorado

John F. McClymer
Department of History
Assumption College

Scott McDermott
School of Management
Boston College

Stephen Macedo
Department of Government
Harvard University

Mary Ann McHugh
Department of Political Science
Boston College

Clyde D. McKee, Jr.
Department of Political Science
Trinity College

G. Calvin Mackenzie
Department of Government
Colby College

John R. McKivigan
Department of History
West Virginia University

Joan E. McLean
Department of Political Science
Ohio State University

Susan A. MacManus
Department of Public Administration
University of South Florida

Christopher McNickle
New York, NY

Samuel T. McSeveney
Department of History
Vanderbilt University

Joyce McPhetres Maisel
Dean of Students Office
Colby College

Kathryn A. Malone
Brooks School
No. Andover, MA

John W. Malsberger
Department of History
Muhlenberg College

John F. Marszalek
Department of History
Mississippi State University

Thomas A. Mason
Indiana Historical Society
Indianapolis

Brooke A. Masters
The Washington Post

Richard K. Matthews
Department of Government
Lehigh University

Jeffrey G. Mauck
Department of History
University of Texas–Pan American

Sidney Milkis
Department of Politics
Brandeis University

Penny M. Miller
Department of Political Science
University of Kentucky

Robert Earnest Miller
Department of History
University of Cincinnati

Samuel F. Mitchell
Department of Government
Harvard University

Maureen Moakley
Department of Government
Connecticut College

Norman H. Murdoch
Department of Humanities
University College
University of Cincinnati

Charles E. Neu
Department of History
Brown University

Simon P. Newman
Princeton University

Barbara Norrander
Department of Political Science
University of Arizona

Sue C. Patrick
University of Wisconsin Center,
   Barron County

Robert L. Peabody
Department of Political Science
Johns Hopkins University

William David Pederson
American Studies,
Louisiana State University, Shreveport

H. W. Perry, Jr.
Department of Government
Harvard University

Glenn A. Phelps
Department of Political Science
Northern Arizona University

John J. Pitney, Jr.
Department of Government
Claremont McKenna College

Nelson W. Polsby
Institute of Governmental Studies
University of California, Berkeley

H. Douglas Price
Department of Government
Harvard University

Charles L. Prysby
Department of Political Science
University of North Carolina,
   Greensboro

Ronald Rapoport
Department of Political Science
College of William and Mary

David B. Raymond
Northern Maine Technical College
and University of Maine, Presque Isle

Harold B. Raymond
Department of History
Colby College

Reagen Robbins
Elgin, IL

Susan L. Roberts
Department of Political Science
Furman University

Christopher Rogers
Department of Political Science
University of Wisconsin, Madison

Daniel Dean Roland
Claremont Graduate School

W. Mitt Romney
Belmont, MA

Michael C. Ross
Department of Political Science
Loyola University of Chicago

James V. Saturno
Congressional Research Service
Library of Congress

Sean J. Savage
Department of Government
Saint Mary's College

Howard Scarrow
Department of Political Science
State University of New York, Stony Brook

Kay Lehman Schlozman
Department of Political Science
Boston College

John R. Schmidt
Schmidt Associates
Park Ridge, IL

Mildred A. Schwartz
Department of Sociology
University of Illinois, Chicago

Joy A. Scimé
Department of History
Ohio State University

Matthew Seccombe
Cambridge, MA

Stephen D. Shaffer
Department of Political Science
Mississippi State University

James R. Sharp
Department of History
Syracuse University

Martin Shefter
Department of Government
Cornell University

David Sheinin
Department of History
University of Toronto

Hal T. Shelton
Department of History
University of Houston

Kenneth Shepsle
Department of Government
Harvard University

Geoffrey H. Simon
Skadden, Arps, Slate, Meagher and Flom
New York, NY

Brooks Donohue Simpson
Department of History
Arizona State University

Steven E. Siry
Department of History
Baldwin-Wallace College

Raphael J. Sonenshein
Department of Political Science
California State University, Fullerton

Thomas T. Spencer
Department of History
University of Notre Dame

Robert J. Spitzer
Department of Political Science
State University of New York,
    College at Cortland

Charles Stewart III
Department of Political Science
Massachusetts Institute of Technology

David E. Sturrock
Department of Political Science
University of Georgia

Larry E. Sullivan
Rare Book and Special Collections Division
Library of Congress

Elaine K. Swift
Department of Political Science
University of North Carolina, Chapel Hill

Joel A. Tarr
Department of History
Carnegie Mellon University

James A. Thurber
School of Pubic Affairs
American University

C. David Tompkins (dec.)
Department of History
Northeastern Illinois University

Barbara Trish
Department of Political Science
Grinnell College

Gil Troy
Committee on Degrees in History
    & Literature
Harvard University

Nancy C. Unger
Department of History
San Francisco State University

Eric M. Uslaner
Department of Government & Politics
University of Maryland, College Park

Richard M. Valelly
Department of Political Science
Massachusetts Institute of Technology

Karl E. Valois
Department of History
University of Connecticut, Torrington

Vernon L. Volpe
Department of History
Kearney State College

Henry J. Walker, Jr.
Department of History
University of Alabama

John Walsh
Department of Political Science
Claremont Graduate School

Richard L. Watson, Jr.
Department of History
Duke University

Stephen J. Wayne
Department of Government
Georgetown University

John B. Weaver
Department of History
Sinclair Community College

Robert S. Weisbrot
Department of History
Colby College

John K. White
Department of Political Science
Catholic University of America

W. Thomas White
James Jerome Hill Reference Library
St. Paul, MN

Thomas P. Wolf
Department of Political Science
Indiana University Southeast

Gerald W. Wolff
Department of History
University of South Dakota

Robin Bye Wolpert
Department of Political Science
University of Chicago

Gerald Wright
Department of Political Science
Indiana University

Robert F. Zeidel
Department of History
St. Cloud State University

Paul Haskell Zernicke
Department of Political Science
College of the Holy Cross

The Encyclopedia

Abolition Movement

The modern abolition campaign in the United States emerged during the 1830s as a by-product of the upsurge of religious revivalism popularly known as the Second Great Awakening. The original abolitionist principles and objectives revealed a deep influence of evangelical tenets. Revivalistic assumptions led many churchmen to regard slavery as the product of personal sin and to demand emancipation as the cost of repentance. Abolitionists also recognized that slavery received moral support from racial prejudice, and they lobbied the churches to overturn their many discriminatory practices against Blacks.

The rejection of this emancipation and antiracial discrimination program by nearly every major American religious body in the 1830s forced abolitionists to reconsider their church-oriented strategy. Many followed the lead of the Boston abolitionist William Lloyd Garrison and abandoned the churches as hopelessly corrupted by slavery. Many of these Garrisonians also adopted pacifistic or "nonresistant" political practices and counseled northerners to withhold their sanction from the proslavery Constitution by refusing to vote. Many non-Garrisonian abolitionists shared their rivals' hostile attitude toward churches but not toward the government; consequently, they shifted their energies from religious to political antislavery reform.

Beginning in the mid-1830s, abolitionists petitioned legislatures and offered antislavery testimony to any lawmaking body willing to take up the subject. Antislavery groups interro-gated political candidates to determine whether any had acceptable views on slavery-related issues. When no candidate expressed antislavery sentiments, abolitionists often protested by "scattering" their ballots among write-in candidates. When the federal government failed to respond to their petitioning or lobbying, these politically minded abolitionists held a series of conventions that led to the formation of an independent antislavery party in 1840.

The new Liberty Party was launched to allow the advancement of the immediate emancipation program through partisan politics. Although some political abolitionists made efforts to introduce economic considerations into their party's arguments against slavery, the Liberty platform in the 1840 and 1844 presidential elections differed little from those of the old antislavery societies. The abolitionist political party condemned not only slaveholding but also the nation's pervasive racial prejudice as an affront to God's laws. It called for an immediate abolition of slavery wherever constitutionally possible and for the repeal of all racially discriminatory legislation as a religious as well as a political duty.

In the early 1840s, the abolitionists only reluctantly gave public support to the fledgling Liberty Party. Most Garrisonians condemned all political activity, including that of the Liberty Party, as an implied endorsement of the legality of slavery by working under a constitution they branded "a covenant with death and an agreement with Hell." While not philosophically opposed to political institutions as were the Garrisonians, many non-Garrisonian abolitionists shared the widespread antebellum mistrust of politics as sordid and compromising. Another reason for their reluctance to support the Liberty Party was the strong allegiance of most abolitionists and many other reform-minded northerners to the Whig Party. Compared to the laissez faire ideology of the antebellum Democrats, the Whig's moralistic rhetoric and occasional support of Sabbatarian practices and prohibition were highly attractive to the same evangelical voters who were most inclined to abolitionism. Even on issues of slavery and racial discrimination, northern Whig politicians often took positions that won the sympathy of proabolition evangelicals.

By bringing a new ethically defined issue into politics, the Liberty Party challenged the Whig hold on evangelical voters. The support for the Liberty Party presidential candidate James G. Birney—7,000 votes (0.29 percent) in 1840 and 62,000 (2.31 percent) in 1844—however, showed that the single issue of slavery was not yet strong enough to turn a significant number of voters, evangelical or not, away from the Whigs.

Fundamental disagreements over how to build upon the Liberty Party's limited success in the mid-1840s eventually destroyed the unity of the political abolition movement. A faction led by Salmon P. Chase, Gamaliel Bailey, and Henry B. Stanton advocated electoral cooperation with moderate antislavery groups in the major parties. The Mexican War and the subsequent opposition of many northerners to the admission of slavery into the western territories provided a ready issue for the construction of an antiextensionist coalition in the election of 1848. In a complicated series of intraparty battles, the procoalition forces outmaneuvered all opponents and merged the Liberty Party with antiextensionist Whigs and Democrats, creating a new Free Soil Party. Unlike the Liberty Party, the Free Soilers gave no endorsements for immediate abolition or equal rights for Blacks. In fact, many Free Soilers held strong negrophobic sentiments and supported antiextensionism as a means to keep Black labor—free or slave—from the territories. What the Free Soil Party offered in lieu of the Liberty Party's high standards was the chance to expand antislavery influence, albeit of a limited nature, on the political system.

Not all Liberty men could accept the compromised antislavery position of the new party. As early as 1845, Birney, William Goodell, and

Gerrit Smith had proposed to broaden the Liberty Party platform into a program of universal reform. Calling themselves the Liberty League, this faction also advanced the theory that the Constitution did not sanction slavery and that Congress therefore had the power to abolish slavery everywhere in the Union. Although the Liberty League failed to capture control of the Liberty Party or to block the Free Soil merger, they vowed to continue to work for their undiluted abolitionist program. Running candidates until the Civil War, first under the old Liberty Party name and then the Radical Abolition Party label, this tiny abolitionist faction attempted to prod the larger antislavery parties to take a stronger platform position against slavery and racism.

The large majority of political abolitionists were content to work with more moderate antislavery northerners inside first the Free Soil Party and, after 1854, the Republican Party, and even more broadly based antiextensionist coalition. Chase, Bailey, and other former Liberty Party leaders joined forces with "radical" antislavery defectors from the major political parties, such as Joshua Giddings, Charles Sumner, and John P. Hale, to resist efforts by conservative or racist elements in the Free Soil and Republican coalitions to shift the focus of those parties away from moral opposition to the expansion of slavery. These efforts were so successful that by 1860 nearly all political abolitionists and even some Garrisonians endorsed the election of Abraham Lincoln as a principal means of battling slavery. During the Civil War, the abolitionists pressured Lincoln until, it is claimed, he adopted emancipation as a war goal. In the postwar era, surviving abolitionists continued to lobby the federal government to act to protect the rights of the newly freed Blacks. As dedicated agitators for more than 30 years, the abolitionists contributed significantly to moving the political system to act against slavery and racism.

See also: Election of 1844, Free Soil Party, William Lloyd Garrison, Liberty Party, Abraham Lincoln, Mexican War, Prohibition, Slavery

John R. McKivigan

REFERENCES

Blue, Frederick J. 1973. *The Free Soilers: Third Party Politics, 1848–54.* Urbana: U. of Illinois Pr.

Foner, Eric. 1970. *Free Soil, Free Labor, Free Men: The Ideology of the Republican Party before the Civil War.* New York: Oxford U. Pr.

McKivigan, John R. 1984. *The War Against Proslavery Religion: Abolitionism and the Northern Churches, 1830–1865*. Ithaca: Cornell U. Pr.

Sewall, Richard H. 1976. *Ballots for Freedom: Antislavery Politics in the United States, 1837–1860*. New York: Oxford U. Pr.

Abortion and Anti-Abortion Politics

In 1973, the Supreme Court legalized abortion in the U.S. with its ruling in *Roe v. Wade*. Rather than ending the debate over abortion policy, the ruling invigorated the anti-abortion movement. The anti-abortion (or "pro-life") movement involves a number of individuals, interest groups, and political officials who favor a constitutional ban on abortions or, as a second remedy, increased restrictions on the availability of abortions.

Organized anti-abortion groups abound. The major group, the National Right to Life Committee, claims 11 million members and an annual budget of over $1 million. A Right to Life Committee also exists in each state. The National Catholic Conference of Bishops has taken a strong anti-abortion stance, and the Catholic Church has played a pivotal role in the early stages of the anti-abortion movement. In more recent years, the movement has found allies among conservative, religious, and New Right groups.

Anti-abortion activists are typically strongly religious, high-school-educated individuals with families in which the wife does not work outside the home. They believe men and women have different roles in the world, that the most satisfying role for women is raising children and taking care of the home, and that abortion involves the taking of human life.

Anti-abortion activists were slow in organizing to enter electoral politics. Convinced of the correctness of their views on abortion, they felt others would agree with them when presented with the facts. Many of their supporters were also political novices. Some state anti-abortion organizations, however, did develop effective organizations in the mid-1970s. One of the more politically active was Minnesota Citizens Concerned for Life. This group provided money and campaign consulting services to anti-abortion candidates, publishing several candidates' attitudes on abortion. By 1978 the movement claimed, "You can't run for dogcatcher in Minnesota without declaring your position on abortion."

The anti-abortion movement gained national recognition in 1978 for its efforts in Iowa. Anti-abortion activists and single-issue voting were credited with the defeat of Minnette Doderer, a candidate for Lieutenant Governor in the Democratic primary, and of Democratic Senator Dick Clark in the general election. The Iowa Pro-Life Action Council had identified anti-abortion voters and used pamphlets to urge them to vote. For the primary election, a pamphlet with a picture of an unborn child urged Iowans to act: "This little guy wants you to vote in the June 6 primary." For the general election, pro-life activists distributed 300,000 pamphlets in church parking lots the Sunday before the election.

In 1980, anti-abortion groups joined forces with various New Right groups in a national effort to defeat liberal Senators and representatives. The National Right to Life Committee now had someone in each state to identify friendly voters and to organize get-out-the-vote drives. Political action committees also were available to provide financial support for pro-life candidates.

Whether the anti-abortion activists and their New Right allies caused the defeat of liberal candidates is difficult to verify. To be effective, the anti-abortion movement needs to convince candidates that pro-lifers represent a core group of single-issue voters who will consider only a candidate's abortion position when deciding how to vote. The size of this group of single-issue voters does not have to be large; 5 percent could swing many elections. Single-issue voters can be particularly effective in low turnout elections such as primaries and off-year congressional elections.

Presidential politics also has been affected by the abortion controversy. Since 1976, the Republican Party platform has taken an anti-abortion stance, while the Democratic platform has taken a pro-abortion position. In 1972 and 1976, Ellen McCormack ran as an anti-abortion candidate for the Democratic presidential nomination. In 1976, she competed in 18 primary states, qualified for federal matching funds, received 238,000 votes, and won 22 convention delegates. In 1980, Geraldine Ferraro, the Democratic candidate for Vice President, was often heckled at her campaign appearances by anti-abortion activists. Ferraro, an Italian Catholic, had stated that while she personally opposed abortion, she did not support a public ban on abortion. The National Right to Life Committee, meanwhile, endorsed Ronald

Reagan, the Republican nominee for the presidency.

Anti-abortion activists also have become heavily involved in state party politics. In Minnesota, anti-abortion activists teamed up with religious fundamentalists to take over the Republican Party. Anti-abortion activists attended local party caucuses, were elected to the state and national party conventions, and influenced nominations and the party platform. In 1984, these activists were instrumental in nominating two conservative anti-abortion candidates for the U.S. Congress (both subsequently lost to Democratic incumbents). They also altered the Minnesota Republican Party platform, changing the party's previous pro-Equal Rights Amendment stance and calling for the teaching of creationism in public schools.

Moreover, in New York, anti-abortion activists established their own political party. The Right to Life Party (RTLP), with 130,000 votes in the 1978 gubernatorial election, acquired a spot on the New York ballot for subsequent elections. While it sometimes runs its own candidates, the RTLP survives because New York law allows a single candidate to run under several party labels. RTLP candidates usually receive 2 to 3 percent of the vote.

By the mid-1980s the nature of abortion politics had changed. Pro-abortion forces began to become more organized, such that in the 1986 general election they claimed a pickup of five seats in the House and three in the Senate. Additionally, anti-abortion ballot initiatives lost in Massachusetts, Rhode Island, and Oregon.

Another trend was the close alignment of anti-abortion forces with the Republican Party. Much of the original support for the anti-abortion movement came from Democratic voters, since Catholics are often Democratic yet against abortion. The alignment of the anti-abortion forces with the New Right, however, has brought the anti-abortion movement into the Republican Party. Many of the Republicans seeking the 1988 presidential nomination openly sought the support of anti-abortion forces. Some Republican Party activists, however, are uneasy about any close alliance with anti-abortion forces. Noting that most public opinion polls show that the public does not support extremely restrictive abortion laws, moderate Republicans feel the anti-abortion connection could cost the party votes.

Whatever the political fortunes of the pro- or anti-abortion forces in the future, the issue of abortion was clearly one of the most controversial in the 1980s. Massive rallies, protest marches, and the picketing of legislatures and courts underscored the volatility of the disagreement.

See also: Equal Rights Amendment, Geraldine Ferraro, Ellen McCormack, Ronald Reagan, Right to Life Party, Phylis Schlafly

Barbara Norrander

REFERENCES

Conover, Pamela Johnston. 1983. "The Mobilization of the New Right: A Test of Various Explanations." 632 *Western Political Quarterly* 36.

Luker, Kristin. 1984. *Abortion and the Politics of Motherhood.* Berkeley: U. of California Pr.

Paige, Connie. 1983. *The Right to Lifers.* New York: Summit Books.

Spitzer, Robert J. 1984. "A Political Party Is Born: Single-Issue Advocacy and the New York State Election Law." 73 *National Civic Review* 321.

ABSCAM

ABSCAM is the neologism—a combined form of Arab and scam (a confidence artist's trick)—coined to identify an FBI undercover operation that implicated seven members of Congress in criminal actions on the eve of the 1980 elections. The ABSCAM operation involved introducing an undisclosed number of U.S. Representatives and Senators to individuals (actually undercover FBI agents) said to represent wealthy Arabs interested in making investments in businesses in the districts and states of those contacted and in obtaining U.S. residency. Those approached were asked to use their influence in Congress to further the interests of the Arabs, and they were offered money in exchange for their help.

Six members of the House of Representatives—John W. Jenrette, Jr. (D-S.C.), Richard Kelly (R-Fla.), Raymond F. Lederer (D-Pa.), John M. Murphy (D-N.Y.), Michael "Ozzie" Myers (D-Pa.), and Frank Thompson, Jr. (D-N.J.)—and one Senator—Harrison A. Williams, Jr. (D-N.J.)—were indicted, convicted, and eventually served prison sentences for ABSCAM-related crimes.

While some felt that those implicated had been victims of government entrapment, the public and their congressional colleagues were less sympathetic. Of the six Representatives scheduled for reelection, only Lederer was sent back to Congress by his constituents; he was not convicted until well after the fall 1980 elections. Kelly lost a primary in September 1980, and the others were defeated in November. After his conviction, Myers was expelled from the House, the first member of Congress to have been expelled since the Civil War and the only member to have been expelled for a cause other than treason. Jenrette resigned after his defeat and conviction but before his term expired in order to avoid expulsion. Similarly, despite winning reelection, Lederer resigned after his conviction, also to avoid inevitable expulsion.

Senator Williams's term was not up in 1980. He was convicted in May 1981 but held onto his seat until March 1982, finally resigning to avoid a pending vote of expulsion, the first time a Senator would have been expelled since the Civil War.

Taken as a whole, the ABSCAM indictments and convictions (and their impact on the careers of those implicated) demonstrate that ethical scandals have obvious and appropriate consequences on the careers of American politicians. With incumbents increasingly safe from electoral defeat, scandals such as ABSCAM, Koreagate, and the various sexual affairs that have tainted congressional careers in recent years stand as the most frequent causes of the defeat of sitting legislators.

L. Sandy Maisel

Absentee Balloting

The process of casting one's vote at a different time and/or place from one's normal polling place on election day. Regulations governing absentee balloting differ considerably by state of residence, by type of election (federal, state, primary, runoff, general), and by individual circumstance. The trend in recent years has been to ease requirements for obtaining and casting an absentee ballot in order to increase voter participation. At the same time, controls over third-party involvement in the process have been tightened to avoid fraud.

The most frequent absentee balloters are (1) members of the armed forces or merchant marine and their spouses and dependents stationed overseas; (2) certain employees and members of religious or welfare agencies attached to or serving the armed forces living overseas; (3) U.S. citizens who are permanent overseas residents; (4) persons who are away from home on election day owing to employment, student status, or some other circumstance defined as legitimate for eligibility; (5) the elderly or disabled who are physically unable to attend the polls; (6) persons in mental or penal institutions who still retain their voting rights; and (7) those unable to register to vote because they have moved from one state to another within 30 days of a federal election. At least eight states permit ab-

sentee voting for any person who so chooses, regardless of circumstance.

Among the more common permissible ways to cast an absentee ballot are (1) voting in person, usually at a central election office or one of its decentralized sites, during a period prior to election day; (2) voting by mail; (3) voting at an institution (nursing home, mental or penal institution, private residence), usually under the supervision of election office representatives; and (4) voting by way of a third-party courier, usually under emergency conditions.

Methods of applying for an absentee ballot vary considerably. Some states use application systems that make it more difficult for a potential absentee voter to obtain a ballot by requiring completion of detailed written application forms, notarization, or certification; these are known as *frontloaded* systems. While their purpose is to eliminate fraud, frontloaded systems may depress voter participation. *Backloaded* application systems typically require only a signed request for an absentee ballot from the voter and no notarization (and often only a self-administered penalty oath). Backloaded systems transfer the burden of confirming voter eligibility to election officials.

The timing of requests for application and the return and counting of absentee ballots also vary significantly among states. All states use *windows* (opening and closing dates) specifying when requests for absentee ballots must be received and processed. Opening dates may be as long as 90 days before an election. The application deadline for closing dates generally varies from seven days before an election to noon the day before an election. To be counted, ballots must generally be returned by election day or one day before it. However, some states count absentee ballots postmarked on or before election day if they are received within a certain number of days after the election. The counting of ballots may take place as they come in or on the day of the election. Absentee votes totals are either reported in precinct totals, in aggregate election totals, or as a separate category of votes cast.

Absentee voting in federal elections is regulated by Congress. In 1986, Congress passed the Uniformed and Overseas Absentee Voting Act, which consolidated several previous laws and improved absentee voting procedures for uniformed service voters and overseas voters. Among its provisions is authorization of a "write-in" or "blank" ballot in certain situations. Other federal statutes govern absentee voting of the elderly and handicapped (Voting Accessibility for the Elderly and Handicapped Act, 1973) and language minority citizens (The Voting Rights Act of 1965 as amended in 1975 and 1982). *Language minorities* include Native Americans, Asian-Americans, natives of Alaska, and persons of Spanish heritage.

The incidence of absentee balloting is increasing. Estimates are that 8 percent of the ballots cast in presidential general elections in the 1980s were absentee. Absentee voting was estimated to be as high as 33 percent in a San Francisco mayoral recall election. In general, the aging of the population and greater population mobility have contributed to the increase in absentee voting. The higher the political office or the more competitive the contest, the higher the number of absentee ballots cast.

The growing number of absentee voters has made strategies aimed at influencing absentee voters an essential element of political campaigning by parties and candidates. Local election officials often use absentee voter totals as the basis for their election day turnout forecasts. It has changed patterns of campaign spending. "Candidates [can] no longer profitably focus their advertising dollars on the last week of the campaign since many, if not most, of the voters will have returned their absentee ballots by that time." The absentee voter does count.

See also: Voting Rights Act of 1965 and Extensions

Susan A. MacManus

REFERENCES

Crotty, William J. 1977. *Political Reform and the American Experiment*. New York: Crowell.

Feigenbaum, Edward D., and James A. Palmer. 1987. *Absentee Voting: Issues and Options*. Washington: National Clearinghouse on Election Administration, Federal Election Commission.

Kimberling, William C. 1975. *An Analysis of Laws and Procedures Governing Absentee Regulation and Absentee Voting in the United States*. Vol. 1. Summary Report. Washington: U.S. General Accounting Office.

Patterson, Samuel C., and Gregory A. Caldeira. 1985. "Correlates and Consequences of Absentee Voting." 29 *American Journal of Political Science* 766.

Rietman, Alan, and Robert B. Davidson. 1980. *The Election Process: Law of Public Elections and Election Campaigns*. 2nd ed. Dobbs Ferry, NY: Oceana.

Steinbicker, Paul C. 1938. "Absentee Voting in the United States." 32 *American Political Science Review* 898.

Bella S. Abzug (1920–)

One of the most prominent leaders of the women's movement since her first election to Congress in 1970. Bella Savitsky Abzug's initial campaign featured the slogan "This Woman's Place is in the House—the House of Representatives." A practicing lawyer for more than forty years and a member of Congress for six years, she was the first woman to run for the U.S. Senate from New York (in 1976) and for mayor of New York City. Subsequently, Abzug was defeated in two attempts to regain a seat in the House: a 1978 special election in the Fifteenth District, and in 1986 in the Twentieth District.

Abzug courts controversy: she offered a resolution to end the war in Vietnam on her first day in the House, and she was the first in Congress to call for the impeachment of President Nixon. During her tenure in Congress, Abzug cosponsored the Equal Rights Amendment and wrote the first law banning credit discrimination against women and the law authorizing the first federally funded National Women's Conference in Houston, Texas, November 18–21, 1977. Abzug's outspokenness and activism on feminist issues were not without political cost. Appointed by Jimmy Carter as co-chair of the bipartisan National Advisory Committee for Women in 1978, the outspoken Abzug was fired by Carter in 1979, a decision prompting the resignation of a majority of her fellow committee members. She participated in both U.N. Conferences on the Decade for Women, held in Mexico City in 1975 and in Nairobi in 1985. Abzug currently is president of WOMEN USA and secretary of WOMEN USA FUND, founded to mobilize grass-roots feminist activism.

Bella Abzug has been a participant and supporter of party reform since its inception, a history she recounts in *Gender Gap* (1984). She was a founder of the National Women's Political Caucus (NWPC) in 1971, which immediately established delegate selection as a priority issue. With Congresswoman Patsy Mink, Abzug represented the NWPC's "Task Force on Delegate Selection" to the Democratic and Republican national committees. The NWPC Task Force was particularly influential with the McGovern-Fraser Commission, as well as the DNC-initiated extension of the equal division rule to all party committees in 1980. She served on the platform committee at the 1972 Democratic National Convention and has been a delegate to each Democratic convention since 1972. Abzug continues to be a major force in Democratic Party politics. She moderated the debate on platform issues sponsored by the Democratic

National Committee (DNC) Women's Caucus at the 1988 national convention.

See also: Equal Rights Amendment, Gender Gap, McGovern-Fraser Commission, Vietnam as a Political Issue

Denise L. Baer

REFERENCES

Abzug, Bella, and Mim Kelber. 1984. *Gender Gap: Bella Abzug's Guide to Political Power for American Women.* Boston: Houghton Mifflin.

Shafer, Byron E. 1983. *Quiet Revolution: The Struggle for the Democratic Party and the Shaping of Post-Reform Politics.* New York: Russell Sage.

Dean Acheson (1893–1971)

Democratic Secretary of State in the post-World War II era. In his role as author, Dean Acheson published several books, including *A Democrat Looks at His Party* (1955). In this work he sought to repudiate the idea that certain "innate characteristics" differentiated individual Republicans from Democrats. Specifically, he argued that the Republican Party could not be "made up solely of businessmen when, rain or shine, it polls within a few million votes of its rival." His central argument, however, emphasized the role of business interests in the direction of Republican Party politics.

Acheson's view was typified by a letter to a colleague; there he described his view that "the control, the center, the provider of funds, of personnel, the drawer of lines beyond which the politician could not go was, for the Republican party, business. Now this is a very different thing from saying that every Republican holds the same views as Mr. George Humphrey." Acheson asserted that "the controlling interest on which a party may be centered is often quite different from the views of those who vote the ticket." He enumerated "Lincoln, Rum, Romanism and Rebellion, the protective tariff and the full dinner pail" as Republican vote-getters. But the rhetoric of electioneering did not disguise the fact that the Republican Party in power was dominated by the business interest.

On the other hand, Acheson saw the Democratic Party as essentially diverse. Despite the existence of standard Democratic machinery, big city bosses, and southern politicians, Acheson believed that no single interest controlled the party's structure; Democratic politics emphasized the need to harmonize different groups and interests. By contrast, Republican domination by the business interest limited the party's potential for flexibility and experimentation.

With regard to foreign policy, his assessment of both parties was similar. He believed that neither Democrats nor Republicans had shown the necessary degree of imagination in the years leading up to World War II.

Acheson first held national office under Franklin Delano Roosevelt, but his views on parties can be seen in the context of his role as an important member of the Truman administration. In the 1948 presidential campaign Harry Truman's opponent, Thomas E. Dewey, ran on the issue of competence. In response, Truman identified himself as heir to Roosevelt and the New Deal, emphasizing concrete differences between the Democratic and Republican agendas. In line with Truman's approach, Acheson sought to distinguish the national from the business interest without alienating individual voters of either party.

Dean Gooderham Acheson was the first son of Canadian parents who moved to Connecticut a year before his birth when his father, an Episcopalian minister, accepted a rectory in Middletown. Educated at Groton and Yale, he went on to Harvard Law School, where he studied with and was befriended by Felix Frankfurter. One of two early mentors, Frankfurter recommended him for a clerkship with a second mentor, Justice Louis D. Brandeis. After two years with Brandeis, Acheson went to work for the law firm of Covington, Burling in Washington. Appointed Under Secretary of the Treasury under Roosevelt, he resigned and returned to the practice of law. He was subsequently recalled to public office and served as Assistant Secretary of State for Economic Affairs, Under Secretary of State, and Secretary of State, a post he held from 1949 to 1953. His long and distinguished public career included an important role in the Bretton Woods agreement and advocacy of the policy of containment.

See also: Thomas E. Dewey, New Deal, Franklin D. Roosevelt, Harry S Truman

Victoria A. A. Kamsler

REFERENCES

Acheson, Dean. 1955. *A Democrat Looks at His Party.* New York: Harper.

———. 1969. *Present at the Creation: My Years in the State Department.* New York: Norton.

McLellan, David S. 1976. *Dean Acheson: The State Department Years.* New York: Dodd, Mead.

———, and David C. Acheson, eds. 1980. *Among Friends: Personal Letters of Dean Acheson.* New York: Dodd, Mead.

Charles Francis Adams (1807–1886)

Diplomat and statesman. Charles Francis Adams was born into one of the of most remarkable families in the annals of American politics. The grandson of John Adams, the son of John Quincy Adams, and the father of Henry, Charles Francis, Jr., and Brooks, Adams was active as a "Conscience Whig" in the turbulent years before the Civil War. In 1848 the Free Soil Party nominated Adams, one of its founders, as its vice presidential candidate with Martin Van Buren as its presidential standard-bearer. The unsuccessful third-party ticket drew a sufficient number of Democratic votes to swing the election to the Whig candidate, Zachary Taylor.

When the Free Soilers collapsed, Adams drifted into the Republican Party and after Abraham Lincoln's election was appointed minister to Great Britain. Adams arrived in London in May of 1861 to find considerable public sympathy for the Confederacy. His mission was to prevent Britain from recognizing the South as a legally constituted independent nation. Despite the unfavorable climate of opinion in Britain, Adams conducted American affairs with a discretion and self-restraint that won the respect of the British foreign minister, Lord Russell. Once the Emancipation Proclamation was issued in 1863, public opinion in Britain dramatically shifted toward the North and consideration of diplomatic recognition of the South by the British government became unlikely.

Adams spent the last years of his life editing the diaries and papers of his father and his grandfather.

See also: Henry Adams, Conscience Whigs, Emancipation as a Political Issue, Free Soil Party

Margaret Horsnell

REFERENCES

Adams, Ephraim D. 1925. *Great Britain and the American Civil War.* 2 vols. New York: Longmans, Green.
Ford, Worthington C., ed. 1920. *A Cycle of Adams Letters, 1861–1865.* 2 vols. Boston: Houghton Mifflin.
Rayback, Joseph G. 1970. *Free Soil: The Election of 1848.* Lexington: U. Pr. of Kentucky.

Henry B. Adams (1838–1918)

Liberal Republican political journalist. A member of the fourth generation of one of America's political dynasties, Henry Brooks Adams's success as a writer and historian has overshadowed his disappointment in politics. Seeking influence, not position, Adams turned to political journalism as a means through which the intelligentsia could advise those in power. In 1868, after eight years as his father's private secretary, he embarked full time on a career as a political journalist and adviser. His articles on Washington politics and civil service reform, which displayed an antiparty slant, appeared in various journals and periodicals, including the *Nation* and the *North American Review;* he took over as editor of the latter in 1870.

His disillusionment with President Ulysses S. Grant's failure to embrace the causes of civil service and tariff reform led him to assist in the organizing of the Liberal Republican movement, although he was out of the country during the election of 1872. Using the *Review* as a mouthpiece for political reform, he tried but failed to secure the 1876 Republican nomination for Benjamin H. Bristow; afterward he withdrew from politics, although he continued to give advice to John Hay, Theodore Roosevelt, and others from his home overlooking Washington's Lafayette Square.

Three of his later works are of particular political significance: his novel *Democracy* (1880), a witty vignette of Washington politics; the nine-volume *History,* a masterpiece of historical literature, which excoriates the presidencies of Thomas Jefferson and James Madison; and *The Education of Henry Adams* (1918), which, while literarily engaging, quotable, and thoughtful, provides a seriously misleading and warped perspective of politics during the age of Grant.

See also: Charles Francis Adams, John Quincy Adams, Election of 1876, Ulysses S. Grant, Liberal Republican Party

Brooks Donohue Simpson

REFERENCES

Adams, Henry. 1880. *Democracy: An American Novel.* New York: Henry Holt.
———. 1889–1891. *History of the United States During the Administrations of Thomas Jefferson and James Madison.* 9 vols. New York: Scribner's.
———. 1918. *The Education of Henry Adams.* Boston: Houghton Mifflin.
———. 1958. *The Great Secession Winter of 1860–1861 and Other Essays.* George Hochfield, ed. New York: Sycamore Press.
Contosta, David. 1980. *Henry Adams and the American Experiment.* Boston: Little, Brown.
Levenson, J.C., et al., eds. 1982–1988. *The Letters of Henry Adams.* 6 vols. Cambridge: Harvard U. Pr.
Samuels, Ernest. 1948–1964. *Henry Adams.* 3 vols. Cambridge: Harvard U. Pr.

John Adams (1735–1826)

Second President of the United States, John Adams was one of the earliest and most effective supporters of the political rights of American colonists, interpreting the British Constitution to empower Americans with substantial autonomy and personal liberties. But as constitutional solutions became less feasible, Adams was quick to press for independence. As an influential leader in the Continental Congress, he was a key figure in appointing George Washington as commander of the Continental Army and in soliciting Thomas Jefferson to draft the Declaration of Independence. These two actions alone are sufficient to secure Adams's place in American history.

Adams also made important contributions to the development of American political practices as they evolved in the early years of the Republic. Ironically, Adams was no advocate of competitive parties or even of a party system. He believed that the model for American politics should be, in the words of one scholar, a "regal republic." He described this model extensively in his *A Defence of the Constitutions of Government of the United States of America* (1787–1788). The principal purpose of government was to provide a system in which private property was protected and political liberties safeguarded. Because human activity was bound up largely in the pursuit of self-interest, political institutions needed to be carefully constructed so as to protect the liberty and property of each of the social classes. Adams believed that a good constitution was one that balanced these class interests so as to provide peace and stability as well as liberty. Ideally, the people as a whole would be represented in one legislative branch; the aristocracy (which for Adams was based principally on property, education, and talent) would be represented in another. Occupying the critical fulcrum of the constitution would be the executive. A virtuous, public-spirited executive endowed with monarch-like powers would ensure the liberties of all by preventing the exploitation of any one class by the other. This balanced republic took no account of parties that might be organized on some basis other than class.

Adams soon had an opportunity to test his theories. It was a foregone conclusion that George Washington would be elected first President. But the selection of Vice President was not as clear. The Virginia-born Washington believed that an easterner was necessary to balance the new executive branch. John Hancock and Adams were the two most prominent choices, though each carried some liabilities, partly because of the usual animosities generated by long political careers and partly because neither man had been in the forefront of the Federalist (pro-Constitution) fight. Washington's preference for Adams guaranteed that he would receive sufficient votes for the vice presidency.

Like most Vice Presidents, John Adams did not enjoy the office. He was not part of what we would today call the President's "inner circle." Washington preferred to rely on old friends like Alexander Hamilton, James Madison, Henry Knox, and Jefferson for his advice. Adams had hoped that the presidency of the Senate would offer him real opportunities for political leadership, believing the Senate would exemplify what a natural aristocracy could accomplish in a republic. But he quickly found that he was something of an odd man out in the Senate with very little influence even over his fellow Federalists. Like modern Vice Presidents, he served largely to support the President's policies and to be available for key votes. (The Vice President's vote was more critical in a Senate of 26 members than it is today.)

His loyalty was highly regarded by Washington. When the general retired after two terms, he made it clear to his supporters that he wished to see Adams succeed him. Hamilton and his allies, who remained suspicious of Adams's commitment to Federalist programs, tried to undermine his candidacy and to promote Thomas Pinckney, the party's vice presidential candidate (candidates ran as individuals in 1796, not as tickets). Thus, even though the system did not guarantee that a party's presidential nominee would receive more electoral votes than its second choice, Adams easily won the election.

Scholars differ over how effective Adams was as President. What is clear is that those four years featured some of the most vitriolic partisanship ever seen in the United States. The irony is that Adams, like Washington, was a committed antiparty man, deeply suspicious of democracy, believing that government dominated by the poor and uneducated would threaten property and virtue. But unlike many Federalists, he was equally suspicious of the aristocracy because of its arrogance and thirst for power. Thus he found himself conducting a precarious balancing act (much as he had predicted in *Defence*) between the Hamiltonian (High) Federalists and the growing Republican opposition.

As President he was often hampered by his own party. For the most part, Adams vigorously supported Federalist policies (e.g., increased commerce and trade, the Alien and Sedition

Acts, raising an army against France), but most of his own legislative programs were ignored by the Federalist Congress. Some of the resistance was based on personal jealousy: Hamilton and his allies conducted a constant whispering campaign that undermined the President's authority—a campaign based at least in part on Hamilton's own grandiose notions. Some of it also owed to Adams's unwillingness to use an iron glove in suppressing opposition to the federal government (he had pardoned Amos Fries, an important symbol of antifederal rebellion). Adams persisted in hoping for an era of nonpartisanship and thought such gestures necessary, but they only antagonized the High Federalists further.

In fact, the death blow to the Federalist Party was delivered as much by Adams as by the Jeffersonians. Adams had agreed to continue the undeclared naval war with France and to organize a standing army but continued to hope for a peaceful solution to Franco-American tensions. When French diplomatic overtures came in 1799, Adams, over objections from the High Federalists, sent a new mission to France. Even though an honorable peace resulted, the breach in the party became wider than ever. Convinced that Hamilton was undermining his presidency, Adams finally severed his connections with Hamilton and his allies in the Cabinet.

Adams ran again for President in 1800. The successful peace initiative restored enough support from moderate Federalists to garner him the party nomination. Though he lost the election to Jefferson and Aaron Burr by one state (South Carolina), he actually did much better than his party, which was swamped in the congressional elections. The Federalists never again effectively contended for the presidency. But when Adams relinquished the office to Jefferson in 1801, he demonstrated that political power in America was transferable from one party to its former opposition.

See also: Alien and Sedition Acts, Aaron Burr, Elections of 1796 and 1800, Alexander Hamilton, Thomas Jefferson, James Madison, George Washington

Glenn A. Phelps

John Quincy Adams (1767–1848)

Sixth President of the United States. John Quincy Adams is perhaps known best for his contributions to foreign policy during his long career in public service. Son of John Adams, the second U.S. President, young Adams began his professional life in 1781 at the age of fourteen, serving as private secretary to the American envoy to Russia, Francis Dana. Adams also assisted his father in a similar capacity months later in Paris while the U.S. negotiated a peace with Great Britain following the Revolutionary War.

As the son of the last Federalist to serve as President, "Quincy" began his political career as a Federalist himself. Given, however, the growing dissent within the Federalist Party—a split that led to the defeat of his father for reelection—Adams found himself in great disfavor with the bulk of the party with which he identified. Adams served in his father's administration as minister to Russia, then returned to his home state of Massachusetts to serve in the state senate in 1802. Controversial in the legislature for his frequent departure from Federalist Party politics, Adams accepted his selection to the United States Senate the following year, where he found himself as a lone voice within a small minority-party delegation.

In the Senate, Adams's contentiousness emerged freely, and while biographers often hail his predilection for independent thinking, they criticize him for his political ineptitude. Potentially an able young statesman, Adams often expressed his thoughts so forthrightly as to alienate all of his Senate colleagues, regardless of their party designation. Toward the end of his term, Adams dared support a trade embargo proposed by President Thomas Jefferson, a member of the opposition party, and thus ensured the loss of his Senate seat. Adams resigned his seat in June of 1808, nearly a full year before his term was to expire, only to find himself reemployed in March as diplomat for the administration of James Madison, once again in Russia.

The greatest foreign policy achievements of John Quincy Adams followed. As the War of 1812 continued, Madison named Adams as one of five commissioners sent to the city of Ghent to negotiate a peace with Great Britain. The negotiated settlement of the Treaty of Ghent, buttressed by the military success of General Andrew Jackson at the Battle of New Orleans, allowed the commissioners to leave Ghent having saved face for the United States. Adams stayed in London in 1815 as the American minister to Great Britain, second only to the Secretary of State in foreign affairs; he attained the top office during the administration of James Monroe in 1817.

As Secretary of State, John Quincy Adams negotiated a boundary for the Louisiana Territory, established a firm claim for U.S. expansion to the Pacific Northwest, and acquired the Florida Territory from Spain. Most important, however, was Adams's contribution in the construction of the Monroe Doctrine—the acknowledged standard for American foreign policy toward Western Hemisphere nations for over 150 years.

Despite these achievements in foreign policy, John Quincy Adams remained an unpopular figure outside of his native New England, where lack of skill in political affairs hurt him. Adams's election and service as President and his subsequent defeat for reelection illustrate these weaknesses. By 1824, with the withdrawal of President Monroe from office, Adams believed himself the rightful heir to the presidency, but he showed little willingness to work toward that goal. Historical accounts differ, but most agree that Adams did little to facilitate his election until a deadlock in the Electoral College among himself and three rivals encouraged him to strike some political deals. Adams, second to General Jackson but ahead of Senator William Crawford of Georgia and House Speaker Henry Clay of Kentucky, sought to win over support from one or both of his lesser rivals to defeat Jackson.

The degree of bargaining is uncertain, but the results are well known. Crawford, incapacitated by a paralytic stroke, maintained strong support among his following; the four states he carried in the Electoral College also voted for him in the House. Adams, however, received the support of all of his own states, three of those that had supported Jackson, and all three of Clay's. That Adams later appointed Clay as his Secretary of State led to the claims of a "corrupt bargain" and a "bargain and sale"—allegations that Adams and Clay colluded to prevent Jackson from winning the presidency. True or not, these charges helped backers of Jackson's partisans to promote the administration's tainted image. Adams did little to cultivate any positive political relationships or to expand his base of electoral support during his four years in office; the result was a sound electoral defeat in 1828 at the hands of Andrew Jackson.

Adams retired from public life for less than two years. In 1831, he returned to Washington, D.C., as the representative to the U.S. House from Braintree, Massachusetts. From that point until his death in 1848, John Quincy Adams would build a reputation as "Old Man Eloquent." Never previously known for his oratory, Adams used his last 16 years in the Congress to vent frustrations, both personal and political.

He stood as one of the most vocal proponents of the right to petition, and as such, became closely associated with the antislavery movement. He developed the argument that slavery could be addressed by government during any time that Congress utilized its war powers; that argument would later be the cornerstone of Abraham Lincoln's own Emancipation Proclamation. A man who for many years alienated others with his style was finally able to persuade them with substance.

In terms of party politics, Adams was an individualist. A Federalist early in his career, he did little to further the party's ideals. With the withering of the Federalists and the emergence of the Democratic-Republicans as the sole political party, Adams did little to develop, or even encourage, a singular party doctrine. As President, he did nothing to quell regional political pressures, thus ensuring his own eventual defeat. Even at the conclusion of his brilliant public service career, Adams was known more for his individualism than for a commitment to any party or group. Adams was clearly a man whose commitment to policymaking was far greater than his capability in politics.

See also: John Adams, Henry Clay, William Crawford, Elections of 1824 and 1828, Emancipation as a Political Issue, Federalist Party, Andrew Jackson, James Madison

Michael Heel

REFERENCES

Adams, James Truslow. 1930. *The Adams Family*. Boston: Little, Brown.

Bemis, Samuel Flagg. 1956. *John Quincy Adams and the Union*. New York: Knopf.

Clark, Bennet Champ. 1932. *John Quincy Adams*. Boston: Little, Brown.

Seward, William H. 1851. *The Life and Public Services of John Quincy Adams*. Auburn, NY: Derby, Miller.

John T. Adams (1862–1939)

Chairman of the Republican National Committee in the 1920s. John Taylor Adams was an Iowa sash and door manufacturer who was long active in Republican affairs. In 1908, Adams managed William B. Allison's Iowa primary campaign for the United States senatorial nomination, and in 1912, he was a manager of the William Howard Taft forces in Iowa. Adams became a member of the Republican National Committee in 1912.

After the defeat of Charles E. Hughes in the 1916 presidential election, the leaders of the Progressive Party offered to return to the Republican fold if given a voice in national party councils. The conservatives, however, were interested in retaining full control of the national organization. At its January 1917 meeting, the executive committee of the national committee reelected William R. Willcox as chairman but, in a surprise move, chose conservative national committeeman Adams to fill the vacancy of vice-chairman. In part, this was a move to end the practice whereby national chairmen selected their own vice-chairman; the 1916 Republican National Convention had adopted a resolution giving the executive committee sole authority to fill this post.

When Willcox resigned from the chairmanship in January 1918, Adams campaigned to replace him. Theodore Roosevelt and Progressives on the national committee were adamant in their opposition to Adams, charging him with having been pro-German before World War I. As a consequence, Will Hays was elected chairman and Adams continued as vice-chairman. With Hays's resignation in 1921, Adams moved up to become acting chairman and, as President Warren G. Harding's choice, was later confirmed as permanent chairman, which was interpreted as a return to conservative control of the Republican Party. While chairman, however, Adams opposed Harding's efforts to encourage participation in the World Court.

Adams was chairman of Calvin Coolidge's campaign strategy committee in 1924, although not Coolidge's choice for the chairmanship. He returned to his business after the election. In 1928, Adams opened the Washington headquarters for the campaign to nominate Herbert Hoover. From 1931 to 1936, he served as a member of the advisory committee of the U.S. Inland Waterways Commission.

See also: Calvin Coolidge, Warren G. Harding, Herbert Hoover, Progressive Party, Theodore Roosevelt, William Howard Taft

Ralph M. Goldman

REFERENCES

Goldman, Ralph M. 1990. *The National Party Chairmen and Committees: Factionalism at the Top.* Armonk, NY: M. E. Sharpe.

L. Sherman Adams (1899–1986)

Advisor to President Dwight D. Eisenhower. Sherman Adams was born in Vermont, and operated a timberland management business in New Hampshire for 20 years. He was first elected to the New Hampshire House of Representatives in 1941 as a Democrat from the heavily Democratic town of Lincoln, then reelected as both a Democrat and a Republican, and finally became a Republican after being elected by a Republican majority to be Speaker. A "less conservative" Republican, he was elected governor in 1948 on his second try. While in office, he imposed austerity budgets, opposed new taxes, and supported aid to the elderly.

In 1952, Governor Adams chaired New Hampshire's successful Eisenhower-for-President committee and campaigned for him across the country. He was instrumental in the adoption of the Houston Manifesto at the Republican Governor's Conference, which condemned tactics used by the Robert Taft forces in southern states to challenge delegates of Dwight D. Eisenhower; he then successfully served as Eisenhower's convention floor manager. Adams eventually became the campaign chief of staff, mediating among the interests of Eisenhower, the orthodox old-line Republican National Committee, and the progressive independent Citizens-for-Eisenhower groups.

As presidential assistant to Eisenhower (serving as Chief of Staff) from 1953 to 1958, Adams rigidly controlled access to Eisenhower, ensuring that only important matters that could not be resolved at a lower level went to the President in a single-page memorandum with specific recommendations. Eisenhower shared his dreams with Adams about a new political party that would accept U.S. world leadership and liberal human welfare but conservative government spending policies. These Eisenhower policies became known as "Modern Republicanism," and conservative Republicans blamed them on Adams. Adams resigned in 1958 after prominent Republicans feared that allegations of conflicts of interest involving him would become a major political issue in the congressional elections.

See also: Dwight D. Eisenhower

Stephen D. Shaffer

REFERENCES

Adams, Sherman. 1961. *Firsthand Report: The Story of the Eisenhower Administration.* New York: Harper.

Eisenhower, Dwight D. 1965. *Waging Peace: 1956–1961.* Garden City, NY: Doubleday.

Lockard, Duane. 1959. *New England State Politics.* Chicago: Henry Regnery.

Samuel Adams (1722–1803)

Boston politician and theorist of the American Revolution. Samuel Adams was the eldest son of an influential family. After graduation from Harvard and unsuccessful commercial ventures, Adams joined the family malt business, served in minor town offices, and began to write in the Boston anti-British press. He worked as a town tax collector (1756–1765) and was active in his church and in his neighborhood political caucus. As a leading opponent of British domination, he was elected to the legislature in 1765, where he became the assembly's clerk. In the Continental Congress (1774–1781) Adams was a leader of the Massachusetts-Virginia alliance. After assisting in the creation of the Massachusetts state constitution (1779–1780), Adams became a state senator and an executive councilor. Skeptical about the national Constitution, he nevertheless helped to pass the ratification-plus-amendments agreement at the state convention (1788). As lieutenant governor under John Hancock (1789–1793) and as governor (1794–1797), Adams supported the emerging Democratic-Republican Party on the issues of states' rights and support for revolutionary France. His prestige as a revolutionary overcame strong Federalist opposition in the elections of 1794 and 1796. In retirement, he was regarded as a Jeffersonian elder statesman as well as a patriot.

As a party leader, Adams was a mediator among diverse local, state, and American interest groups, an effective committee leader, and a good essayist. He worked well with other leaders and was skilled at building effective coalitions. Without genius or flair, Adams still succeeded through caution, prudent selection of his goals and tactics, and perseverance.

See also: Election of 1796, Jeffersonian Republicans

Matthew Seccombe

REFERENCES

Adams, Samuel. 1904–08. *The Writings of Samuel Adams.* 4 vols. Ed. by Harry A. Cushing. New York: Putnam.

———. 1971. *Samuel Adams Papers.* New York: New York Public Library, Microfilm.

Maier, Pauline. 1980. "A New Englander as Revolutionary: Samuel Adams." In *The Old Revolutionaries: Political Lives in the Age of Samuel Adams.* New York: Knopf.

Miller, John C. 1936. *Sam Adams, Pioneer in Propaganda.* Boston: Little, Brown.

Wells, William V. 1865. *The Life and Public Services of Samuel Adams.* 3 vols. Boston: Little, Brown.

Williams, William A. 1960. "Samuel Adams: Calvinist, Mercantilist, Revolutionary." 1 *Studies on the Left* 47.

Bertha S. Adkins (1906–1983)

A prominent advocate of women's interests in the Republican Party in the 1950s. Active in local party politics in her home state of Maryland, Bertha Sheppard Adkins was named national committeewoman in 1948. Her efforts in drafting the party's declaration of principles (March 1950) led to her appointment as executive director of the Women's Division (1950–1953). In that position, she trained speakers and prepared material to develop women's precinct divisions throughout the nation. She was credited with getting out the women's vote, which contributed to the 1952 victory of Dwight D. Eisenhower. In 1953, she was named assistant chairman of the Republican National Committee, where she urged women to work for equal representation in the party and lobbied for their appointment to government positions. Adkins helped to develop special projects to attract women to the Republican Party and organized national and regional conferences to guide their election activities. As a result, 197 Republican women were elected to state offices in 1953, a gain of 41.

Together with Republican Party officials, she advised Eisenhower on electoral strategy and, after a series of regional meetings in 1957, helped to prepare a report on the GOP's chances in the 1958 elections. It proved to be too optimistic, and the Republicans failed to capture many of the seats predicted.

In 1958, Eisenhower appointed Adkins Under Secretary of the Department of Health, Education and Welfare (HEW) (1958–1961), necessitating her resignation from her party position. In the early 1970s she advised this department on the concerns of older Americans. Later she served as the executive vice-chairman of the Older Americans Advisory Committee to HEW in 1972.

See also: Dwight D. Eisenhower, Election of 1952

Joy A. Scimé

REFERENCES

Cotter, Cornelius P., and Bernard C. Hennessey. 1964. *Politics Without Power.* New York: Atherton.

AFL-CIO COPE

The American Federation of Labor-Congress of Industrial Organizations Committee on Political Education (AFL-CIO COPE) was created on February 14, 1956, by combining Labor's League for Political Education (LLPE) of the AFL and the CIO's Political Action Committee (PAC) after the merger of the parent organizations the previous year. It sought to elect candidates for federal, state, and local offices supportive of organized labor's goals as defined by the policy committee of the AFL-CIO. Present tactics consist of registering voters, educating voters through literature on candidates' records, and conducting get-out-the-vote drives on election day. Officially nonpartisan, COPE ordinarily backs Democratic candidates. As the political arm of the AFL-CIO, COPE must synthesize the interests of particular trades into what is a more generalized policy favorable to labor as a whole. It attempts to coordinate political activity between the international unions and their local affiliates. COPE does not lobby for labor legislation; a special legislative department does that.

The political program evolving since 1956 has been labor specific. COPE seeks to repeal state right-to-work laws authorized by Section 14 (b) of the Taft-Hartley Act, alleviate industrial unemployment and rising living costs by increasing the length and amount of unemployment benefits and by retraining displaced workers, increase the minimum wage and hospital payments under Medicare, support legislation ending discrimination in employment based on race and sex, and support legislation to increase federal aid to education.

The precedent for organized labor's involvement in presidential politics reaches back to 1924. In 1924, the normally nonpartisan AFL first formally endorsed a presidential candidate—Robert M. La Follette—more out of frustration with the two major political parties' platforms than with agreement with the Progressive Party's stance. At that time, the AFL had a policy of voluntarism, viewing state involvement in labor relations as counterproductive. CIO president John L. Lewis's breach with this attitude in 1936 helped to cause the AFL to expel the CIO in 1937. Lewis, together with Sidney Hillman, formed the CIO's Non-Partisan League specifically to assist Franklin Roosevelt in his reelection bid. Lewis accepted the challenge of the politicization of labor relations that began in earnest with an administration favorable to labor.

The 1942 elections were disastrous for labor. In a backlash against the Democrats, 42 pro-labor Congressmen went down in defeat. This debacle allowed Congress to pass the Smith-Connally Act (over the President's veto) in 1943, which required a 30-day cooling-off period during strikes and which empowered the President to seize critical industries that were struck during wartime. The act prompted the CIO in 1943 to create a PAC to raise money, to educate members in politics, and to conduct registration and get-out-the-vote drives. CIO-PAC also began to register to vote Blacks who were not even union members.

The passage of the Taft-Hartley Act in 1947 by a Republican-controlled Congress motivated the AFL to emulate the CIO. In 1947, it created LLPE, with functions roughly similar to CIO-PAC. CIO-PAC was expressly Democratic from the beginning; LLPE was not as Democratic, although it endorsed Adlai Stevenson in 1952. In 1950, CIO-PAC attempted to defeat Robert Taft's Senate reelection bid. The 1952 Republican congressional and presidential victories, plus passage of state right-to-work laws, prompted the AFL and the CIO to consider a merger to protect the labor movement. But the decentralization of authority and resources in a federation that came together for mutual protection rather than natural inclination limited COPE's effectiveness. In the 1956 elections, Democrats maintained control of Congress while the COPE-endorsed Stevenson lost. In many northeastern states, however, AFL and CIO unions backed different candidates.

In 1958, the Republicans made untoward union power a major campaign theme, an issue that unified labor support against the GOP in that recession year. COPE defeated many right-to-work referendums and elected friends of labor but not enough of them. An alliance between southern Democrats and Republicans was able to pass the Landrum-Griffin Act in 1959, which labor regarded as an infringement on autonomy in regulating internal union business.

In 1960, Landrum-Griffin was for COPE the catalyst that Smith-Connally and Taft-Hartley had earlier been for COPE's antecedents. COPE began a national drive for the Democratic Party to recruit voters who were not union members. It endorsed attempts to enroll southern Blacks to undermine conservative strength in Congress. Opposition from some local unions necessitated that this be done discreetly. Organized labor made the difference in the close presidential election, which Richard Nixon himself pointed out.

In 1964, COPE mobilized heavily against Barry Goldwater and helped to elect two-thirds of the congressional candidates that labor promoted. Despite this victory, a filibuster in the new Senate was able to defeat the repeal of Section 14(b) of Taft-Hartley.

In 1966, Democrats lost 47 seats in the House due in part to the absence of an energizing threat to labor as in 1964. It also reflected the beginning of the decline of organized labor as a political power as the work force moved toward the non-unionized service industries and as the New Deal coalition unraveled. In more recent years the AFL-CIO COPE has been an active participant in political action committee funding of congressional campaigns, but it is only one of many such participants.

See also: Business-Industry Political Action Committee, Political Action Committees, Progressive Party

Frederick J. Augustyn, Jr.

REFERENCES

Draper, Alan. 1989. A *Rope of Sand: The AFL-CIO Committee on Political Education, 1955–1967*. Westport, CT: Greenwood.

Spiro T. Agnew (1918–)

Richard Nixon's Vice President who was forced to resign in 1973. Spiro Theodore Agnew was born in Baltimore of a Greek immigrant restaurateur father and attended Johns Hopkins University and the Baltimore Law School, but his education was interrupted by service as a tank commander in Europe. In Towson, a predominantly white Republican suburb of Baltimore, he prospered in banking, real estate, and local politics, becoming county executive in 1962. A progressive Republican in solidly Democratic Maryland, Agnew won the governorship of Maryland in 1966 by an upset. Agnew defeated George Mahoney, a Democratic segregationist who had alienated Blacks and liberals. At first Agnew rewarded liberals with nondiscriminatory open-housing, a graduated income tax, and antipoverty legislation. But in 1968 he denounced demonstrators, won preemptive powers for the National Guard, and cut welfare spending.

Agnew supported Nixon in 1968, eventually winning nomination for Vice President. He campaigned vigorously for the Middle American backlash vote, inveighing against hippies and demonstrators; still, he called for more minority opportunities and fairer racial laws. In office he attacked the press and peace protesters and supported the war in Cambodia and Vietnam; however, he angered his party with his attack on the liberal Republican Senator Charles Goodell of New York. In 1972, he led the Nixon administration's assault on the Democratic candidate George McGovern and on the subsequent Watergate investigation but further soured relations with the press.

Agnew resigned in 1973 in the face of charges of conspiracy, extortion, and bribery; he was fined $10,000 after pleading *nolo contendere* to federal income tax evasion. No longer in politics, he lobbied for oil interests in the 1970s, then retired to Rancho Mirage in the California desert.

See also: George McGovern, Richard Nixon, Vietnam War as a Political Issue, Watergate

Jeremy R. T. Lewis

REFERENCES

Agnew, Spiro T. 1980. *Go Quietly . . . Or Else*. New York: Morrow.

Cohen, Richard M., and Jules Witcover. 1974. *A Heartbeat Away: The Investigation and Resignation of Vice President Spiro T. Agnew*. New York: Viking.

Drew, Elizabeth. 1976. *Washington Journal: The Events of 1973–1974*. New York: Random House.

Witcover, Jules. 1972. *White Knight: The Rise of Spiro Agnew*. New York: Random House.

Agrarianism

The belief that farming is the best way of life and the most important economic endeavor. Although the concept of agrarianism can be traced to the Greek poet Hesiod, it is most commonly associated with Thomas Jefferson, who maintained that agriculture, based on the family farm, provided the most honorable and virtuous life and that the yeoman farmer was the safeguard of freedom and democracy. Although more extreme agrarians advocate the ownership of land as a natural right, a concept that can be traced to John Locke, agrarianism as a political force has most commonly found expression when farmers demand that state and national governments meet their demands. By the late nineteenth century, agrarianism usually involved the use of political means to achieve economic ends.

Agrarianism has been a volatile and sometimes effective political force throughout American history. The first significant expression of agrarianism as a political force occurred among farmers in western Virginia in 1676 under the leadership of Nathaniel Bacon. Unhappy with British land and economic policy as well as with unequal representation in the House of Burgesses and harassed by restrictions on western expansion and by the unwillingness of Governor William Berkeley to provide adequate protection from the Indians, these farmers rebelled. Bacon organized an extra-legal force to pacify the Indians, but he ultimately burned the capital city of Jamestown and forced the governor to flee. Although Bacon soon died and the rebellion ended from lack of leadership, the House of Burgesses responded to this insurrection by approving a series of reforms known as Bacon's Laws, decreasing the authority of the governor and increasing self-government in the counties. Although the governor eventually repealed this legislation, Bacon's Rebellion was a major attempt by small-scale farmers and landless whites to rebel against the planter class and government to improve their economic condition and personal safety. As a result, Bacon's Rebellion became the largest agrarian insurrection against established authority in Colonial America.

In 1786, the second major agrarian revolt, Shays's Rebellion, occurred in Massachusetts. Although an inadequate amount of currency in circulation troubled each state in the new nation, the economic situation was particularly serious in Massachusetts. There, like in other states, the government used a land tax to help finance its administration expenses. The tax had to be paid in specie, and mortgage holders and private creditors also required payment in hard money; as a result, many farmers were unable to meet their debts and faced the loss of their farms. Consequently, they began to advocate the printing of paper money, tax relief, abolition of imprisonment for debt, and a moratorium on payment of debts. When the state legislature failed to provide needed economic relief, Daniel Shays led a group of farmers and other rural citizens from western Massachusetts into Springfield to close the courts and to end the foreclosure of farm mortgages. His force later tried to seize the federal arsenal at Springfield. Although this attack failed, the state legislature soon passed legislation that reduced court fees, provided tax relief and a moratorium for the payment of debts, exempted personal property and tools from seizure for debt, extended the legal tender law, permitted the release of debtors who could not support themselves in jail, and lowered poll and estate taxes. More lasting effects of Shays's Rebellion came with its influence upon the delegates at the Constitutional Convention in Philadelphia. They responded to Shays's threat to civil order by denying the states power to make anything but gold or silver legal tender, by empowering Congress to call out the militia to suppress insurrections, by guarantee-

ing a republican form of government for each state, and by, upon request, providing states with federal protection against domestic violence.

A third major agrarian revolt began in 1867 with the creation of the Patrons of Husbandry, commonly known as the Grange. The Grange, founded by Oliver Hudson Kelley, was an economic, social, and educational organization until the panic of 1873 converted it into an agency for political reform. As a nonpartisan organization that emphasized unity among farmers to achieve economic and social justice, the Grange made many demands upon the Democratic and Republican parties to increase the amount of currency in circulation, to regulate the railroads, and to revise the tariff in favor of farmers. During the late 1880s, Grangers became increasingly political and active in the National Farmers' Alliance and Industrial Union and the National Farmers' Alliance. Although the alliances remained nonpartisan, cooperative organizations, they increasingly acted as political and educational lobbying organizations for the agrarian community. The alliances particularly sought a graduated income tax, the regulation of interstate commerce, the direct election of United States Senators, the inflation of the currency supply, and cheap credit to improve farming economically and as a way of life.

Because the Grange and the farmers' alliances were unable substantially to achieve their desired economic and social reforms through nonpartisan political means, many farmers in the Great Plains and the South, who had economic grievances, organized the People's Party on a national level in 1892. Commonly called the Populist Party, this organization appealed primarily to small-scale farmers and rural businessmen who had little economic security and who felt oppressed by economic forces beyond their control. The farmers in the Populist movement advocated the creation of a subtreasury, a graduated income tax, the government ownership of the railroads and telegraph and telephone systems, and women's suffrage—all designed to weaken corporate-based political and economic power. Although populism failed as an organized reform movement, most of its objectives were achieved during the Progressive period and New Deal years.

During the twentieth century, agrarianism asserted itself most radically as a political force with the creation of the National Farmers' Holiday Association in May 1932. Comprised of members of the Farmers' Union and other agrarian reform groups and led by Milo Reno, the Farmers' Holiday Association (FHA) became a forceful—sometimes violent—and ultimately unsuccessful agrarian reform organization in the Midwest; the FHA advocated the use of a farm strike to achieve its ends and demanded that the federal government guarantee cost-of-production prices plus a small profit. Public rejection of the movement's violent tactics, together with increased federal support for farmers, primarily through the Agricultural Adjustment Administration and the Frazier-Lemke Farm Bankruptcy Act of 1934, helped defuse this radical agrarian political movement.

During the late 1970s, the American Agriculture Movement became another agrarian organization that sought substantive economic change through the political process. Created in 1977, the American Agriculture Movement, primarily strongest in the grain-producing Midwest and Great Plains, advocated a farm strike to achieve economic reform. During a strike, farmers would neither buy nor sell in order to create food shortages and thereby force an increase in agricultural prices. Members wanted the federal government to provide 100 percent parity price supports, and they advocated reducing production by 50 percent unless farmers received parity prices. Higher prices caused by grain shortages abroad helped to defuse this movement and to end its symbolic "tractorcades."

Since the late nineteenth century, agrarianism as a political force essentially has demanded that the federal government do for the individual that which he cannot do for himself or that which others will not do for him on just or equitable terms. As a result, agrarianism as a political force usually has sought increased governmental regulation or control of the economy to enable farmers to earn an adequate return on their investments and labor and to enjoy a comfortable living on the land.

See also: William Jennings Bryan, Thomas Jefferson, National Farmers' Alliance and Industrial Union, New Deal, People's Party, Ben Tillman

R. Douglas Hurt

REFERENCES

Montmarquet, James A. 1987. "Agrarianism, Wealth and Economics." 2 *Agriculture and Human Values* 167.

Shannon, Fred A., ed. 1957. *American Farmers' Movements*. New York: D. Van Nostrand.

Szatmary, David P. 1984. *Shays' Rebellion: The Making of an Agrarian Insurrection*. Amherst: U. of Massachusetts Pr.

Roger Ailes (1940–)

Media consultant to Republican candidates. By the mid-1980s, Roger Ailes had come to be considered one of the country's most successful political strategists. A former producer of television's "Mike Douglas Show," Roger Ailes received his start in political advertising by working on Richard Nixon's 1968 political campaign. Ailes used a "Man in the Arena" concept to project a confident, positive image of the former Vice President. Nixon was shown delivering crisp answers to questions posed by a carefully screened panel in a series of shows broadcast by the campaign. At the end of a program, Nixon, usually considered to be an uncharismatic politician, was mobbed by the studio audience.

Ailes's straightforward style led Republican pollster Lance Tarrance to call him "more of a message communicator than a graphics or technical expert." Ailes played a noteworthy role in the 1984 campaign when he prepared Republican President Ronald Reagan for his second debate with former Democratic Vice President Walter Mondale. Reagan's uninspiring performance in his first encounter with Mondale caused critics to wonder if the President's age had affected his mental acuity. At Ailes's urging, the President charmed viewers by using this line: "I want you to know I will not make age an issue of this campaign. I am not going to exploit for political purposes my opponent's age and inexperience." Ailes played a key role in Vice President George Bush's successful 1988 presidential campaign; his negative commercials were praised for their effectiveness but criticized for the image of politicians they portrayed and because they cynically manipulated public opinion.

Ailes would rather be known for his commercials that have made effective use of humor. A widely acclaimed Ailes commercial for 1984 U.S. Senate candidate Mitch McConnell (Ky.) showed Senator Walter Huddleston (D-Ky.) chased by bloodhounds; the announcer asked where Senator Huddleston was and pointed out how often the incumbent had missed Senate votes.

See also: George Bush; Elections of 1968, 1984, and 1988; Richard Nixon; Ronald Reagan

Steve Lilienthal

Carl B. Albert (1908–)

Democratic Speaker of the United States House of Representatives from 1971 to 1977. Born in Oklahoma, Carl Bert Albert graduated from the University of Oklahoma and was a

Rhodes Scholar to Oxford University. He was first elected to the House in 1946 from the Third District of Oklahoma. Albert strongly supported President Harry Truman, and he advocated agricultural price supports, the expansion of public power, civil rights for Blacks, and strong national defense. A favorite of Speaker Sam Rayburn, Albert was appointed Majority Whip by Rayburn in 1955 and was elected Majority Leader in 1962, defeating Richard Bolling of Missouri.

As Whip and Majority Leader, Albert saw himself as a bridge between the liberal northern and the conservative southern wings of his congressional party. He worked to maintain party unity and to assure the passage of the party's legislative agenda.

Elected Speaker in 1971, Albert witnessed changes in the composition of the House Democratic Party with the election of more liberals and the retirement of conservative members. Albert, never one to seek publicity, toiled effectively within the House to adapt its rules and procedures to accommodate the altered environment. Notably, between 1972 and 1974, he supported Richard Bolling's efforts to reorganize the House committee system. Albert believed the existing system weakened the legislative efficiency of the House and the Speaker's ability to organize business. While he may not be memorialized as a forceful Speaker, his efforts to maintain party unity and congressional integrity in the face of an expanding executive will be remembered by students of Congress.

See also: Samuel T. Rayburn, Speaker of the House, Harry S Truman

Thomas J. Baldino

REFERENCES

Albert, Speaker Carl B., with Danney Goble. 1990. *Little Giant: My Life and Times*. Norman: U. of Oklahoma Pr.

Davidson, Roger H., and Walter J. Oleszek. 1979. *Congress Against Itself*. Bloomington: Indiana U. Pr.

Polsby, Nelson. 1963. "Two Strategies of Influence: Choosing a Majority Leader, 1962." In Robert L. Peabody and Nelson W. Polsby, eds. *New Perspectives on the House of Representatives*. 2nd ed. Chicago: Rand McNally.

Hugh Meade Alcorn, Jr. (1907–)

Republican national chairman during the waning days of the Eisenhower administration. Hugh Meade Alcorn, Jr., was born in Suffield, Connecticut, and was raised in a politically active family; his father was State's attorney for Connecticut and an unsuccessful Republican nominee for governor in 1934. Alcorn graduated from Dartmouth College in 1930 and received a law degree from Yale University three years later. He joined a Hartford law firm in 1933 and is still a member at this writing.

Like his father, Alcorn was interested in politics. During the 1930s, 1940s, and 1950s, Alcorn held a variety of Republican posts. In 1938 he was named chairman of the Suffield Republican Town Committee—a position he held until 1953. He served as a member of the Republican State Committee from 1948 to 1957.

In 1936 Alcorn was elected to the Connecticut House of Representatives. He won reelection twice thereafter. He quickly rose to the top. In 1939 he was made Republican Minority Leader and then Speaker two years after that. From 1935 to 1942 Alcorn also served as an assistant State's attorney for Hartford County. Following in his father's footsteps, Alcorn was named State's attorney in 1942 and held the post for six years. In 1948, he received the Republican nomination for Lieutenant Governor and lost by only 5,000 votes.

In 1952 Alcorn shifted his attention to presidential politics, heading the Connecticut chapter of Citizens for Eisenhower. Following Eisenhower's win, he was named a member of the Republican National Committee. As vice chairman of the 1956 convention arrangements committee, however, Alcorn attracted Eisenhower's serious attention. On January 22, 1957, Alcorn was Eisenhower's personal choice to succeed Leonard Hall as Republican national chairman. That year, the political climate favored Republicans—the GOP had the presidency, money in the bank at its national headquarters, and a well-integrated staff there. Alcorn tried to capitalize on these achievements by creating senior Republican clubs that the elderly could join. He also began "Operation Dixie"—a strategy to woo southern whites to the GOP.

One year later, the political winds had shifted. The Russians launched Sputnik, a severe economic recession hit the United States, and a scandal involving the "sale" of a vicuna coat to the President's Chief of Staff engulfed the White House. The result was a devastating Republican defeat in the 1958 midterm elections. Democrats won a 62 to 34 majority in the Senate—their largest since 1940—and a commanding 282-to-153 majority in the House of Representatives—their largest since 1936.

Despite pleas to continue, Alcorn resigned as chairman of the Republican National Committee on April 1, 1959, citing personal reasons unconnected with politics. Alcorn had been serving as chairman without a salary, and this altruism placed additional burdens on his Hartford law partners. Alcorn returned to politics only briefly thereafter, serving as general counsel to the Republican National Committee from 1960 to 1961 and as Republican floor leader to the Connecticut State Constitutional Convention in 1965.

See also: Dwight D. Eisenhower, Republican National Committee

John K. White

REFERENCES

Goldman, Ralph M. 1990. *The National Party Chairmen and Committees: Factionalism at the Top.* Armonk, NY: M. E. Sharpe.

Nelson W. Aldrich (1841–1915)

Six-term Republican Senator from Rhode Island (1881–1911). Nelson Wilmarth Aldrich became the acknowledged leader of the conservative, business-oriented wing of the national Republican Party during the administrations of William McKinley, Theodore Roosevelt, and William Howard Taft.

A protégé of Henry Bowen Anthony and a partner of Rhode Island Republican boss Charles R. Brayton, Aldrich owed his political longevity to a rural Republican machine that relied upon malapportionment and purchased votes in order to maintain dominance. In 1905 muckraker Lincoln Steffens examined the grass roots of Aldrich's power in his exposé, "Rhode Island, A State for Sale," published first in *McClure's Magazine.*

Had Aldrich been content merely to hold national office (like his sponsor Senator Anthony) rather than wield national power, his association with Brayton would have been sufficient. However, Aldrich was ambitious, relentless, and resourceful in his pursuit of success, both political and financial. He cultivated friendships and business relationships with the great captains of industry and supported their demands for sound money (i.e., the gold standard), high protective tariffs, and minimal governmental interference with private enterprise. They, in turn, provided Aldrich with stock participations, loans, and other business opportunities that enabled the man many called "the General Manager of the United States" to achieve great personal wealth despite his humble beginnings as a grocery clerk in Providence.

Aldrich's most notable alliance was with the Rockefellers when his daughter Abby married John D. Rockefeller, Jr. That union produced several prominent children, the foremost of whom, Nelson Aldrich Rockefeller, became governor of New York (1958–1973) and Vice President of the United States (1974–1977).

The respect that Aldrich commanded from contemporaries is epitomized by the frank admission of Theodore Roosevelt, leader of the Progressive Republicans: "Aldrich is a great man to me," Roosevelt once confided to Lincoln Steffens, "not personally, but as the leader of the Senate. He is the kingpin in my game. Sure, I bow to Aldrich, I talk to Aldrich; I respect him, as he does not respect me. I'm just a president, and he has seen lots of presidents."

Unfortunately for Aldrich, the Progressive tide eroded his influence during his last term. As chairman of the Senate Finance Committee, he failed in his efforts to create a central bank controlled by private banking interests, and his emasculation of the revisionary protectionist Payne Tariff in 1909 helped to set off a wave of insurgent protest from the Midwest that eventually split the Republican Party.

See also: Henry B. Anthony, Charles R. Brayton, William McKinley, Theodore Roosevelt, William Howard Taft

Patrick T. Conley

REFERENCES

Aldrich, Nelson W. 1988. *Old Money.* New York: Knopf.

Merrill, Horace C., and Marion G. Merrill. 1971. *The Republican Command, 1897–1913.* Lexington: U. Pr. of Kentucky.

Stephenson, Nathaniel Wright. 1930. *Nelson W. Aldrich: A Leader in American Politics.* New York: Scribner's.

Sternstein, Jerome L. 1978. "Corruption in the Gilded Age Senate." 6 *Capitol Studies* 13.

Alien and Sedition Acts

The growing partisanship of American politics at the end of the eighteenth century was symbolized by the Alien and Sedition Acts. For a few years after the establishment of the new constitutional government in 1789, the administration of the affairs of state went rather smoothly. Nearly everyone conceded the legitimacy of the new government and, in order to ensure its success, tried to contain differences within a nonpartisan system. But factionalism flared over a series of issues: Hamilton's fiscal policies, centralism versus states' rights, foreign relations toward England and France. Increasingly, partisans of each side began to question the motives and patriotism of the other.

By 1798 these mutual suspicions boiled over into a kind of passion seldom seen before in American politics. Both the Federalists and the Republicans were utterly convinced that their opponents were dedicated to the destruction of the Republic; conspiracy theories abounded on both sides. Each faction sponsored newspapers and pamphlets that printed accusations and rumors of the most scandalous sort. Most Federalists were convinced that their opponents were backed by the French, with whom they expected to be at war at any moment.

That summer, the Federalists enacted four laws intended to stamp out the "French serpent." The Naturalization Act, the Alien Act, and the Enemy Aliens Act were all directed at excising French influence in America. Many Federalists thought the Democratic societies, local groups of pro-French enthusiasts who were usually also Republicans, had already helped to spark the Whiskey Rebellion, a protest against the excise on home-produced liquor. The acts granted the President authority to deport any suspicious aliens. Indeed, many French immigrants returned to France and others applied for citizenship as quickly as possible.

The most controversial law was the Sedition Act. Its passage indicated the growing sectional quality of the period's politics; only two southern Representatives voted for it. The key sections of the act made it unlawful to "write, print, utter, or publish any false, scandalous and malicious writing against the government of the United States . . . the Congress . . . or the President . . . to defame [them] . . . or to bring them into contempt or disrepute; or to excite against them . . . the hatred of the good people of the United States." In effect, it criminalized nearly any sort of dissent against Federalist policy.

Enforcement of the Sedition Act was sporadic. While the times saw numerous individual acts of political suppression, its specter actually did more to increase partisan activity than to reduce it. Thomas Jefferson and James Madison sponsored the Kentucky and Virginia resolutions, which rallied opponents of the measure. The resolutions claimed that the national government had no power to regulate speech—that it was denied to the federal government by the First Amendment. They also asserted a more dubious notion that states could interpose their will against the federal government when the latter acted outside of its constitutional authority. Both of these principles became cornerstones of the Jeffersonian Republican "platform" in 1800.

Thomas Jefferson and his Republicans won the presidency and both Houses of Congress in the election in 1800. True to their word, they allowed the Alien and Sedition Acts to expire in 1801. The Federalists were never again to be a serious force in American national politics.

See also: John Adams, Election of 1800, Alexander Hamilton, Thomas Jefferson, Jeffersonian Republicans, James Madison

Glenn A. Phelps

REFERENCES

Levy, Leonard W. 1985. *Emergence of a Free Press.* New York: Oxford U. Pr.

Smelser, Marshall. 1954. "George Washington and the Alien and Sedition Acts." 322 *American Historical Review* 59.

Smith, James Morton. 1956. *Freedom's Fetters: The Alien and Sedition Laws and American Civil Liberties.* Ithaca: Cornell U. Pr.

Saul D. Alinsky (1909–1972)

Political organizer. Beginning in the late 1930s, the name of Saul David Alinsky became associated with a style of neighborhood organizing that emphasized empowering the poor to achieve radical change by working within the system. Alinsky eventually took his organizing style of radical pragmatism from his native Chicago to communities around the United States.

The son of Orthodox Jews from Russia, Alinsky was born in the Chicago slums. In 1930 he received his B.A. in archeology from the University of Chicago. On a fellowship, he did graduate work in criminology and later worked for the Institute for Criminal Research and the Illinois penitentiary system. His first organizing effort was the "Back of the Yards" movement in which he helped galvanize poor residents of Chicago's old meat-packing district to demand more jobs and improved housing, health care, and schools. Alinsky continued his work as a community organizer by working with the war on poverty in the 1960s.

In his first book, *Reveille for Radicals* (1945), Alinsky set forth his vision of empowering the people, particularly the disinterested and the disenfranchised. Arguing for a people's organization, Alinsky did not dwell on specific programs but focused instead on the interdependent nature of problems facing all communities and the necessity of citizen participation. In *Rules for Radicals* (1971), Alinsky reiterated his pragmatic call for action, stating, "As an organizer I start from where the world is, as it is, not as I would like it to be." Until his death in 1972 Alinsky remained a stalwart of neighborhood organizing.

Susan L. Roberts

REFERENCES

Alinsky, Saul D. 1941. "Community Analysis and Organization.",46 *American Journal of Sociology* 797–808.

———. 1945. *Reveille for Radicals*. Chicago: U. of Chicago Pr.

———. 1971. *Rules for Radicals: A Practical Primer for Realistic Radicals*. New York: Random House.

Alternative Voting Systems

Introduction

The cornerstone of a democracy is fair and periodic elections. The voting procedures used to elect candidates determine to a crucial degree whether elections are considered fair and their outcomes legitimate. *Procedures* here mean the rules that govern how votes in an election are aggregated and how a winner or winners are determined.

Of course, the disembodied study of procedures qua procedures misses the human element that so often enlivens elections—from the struggle by candidates to capitalize on an opponent's weaknesses to the often difficult choice by voters of a preferred candidate who, in addition, can win. Yet this human side of campaigns and elections is inevitably played out against a background of rules—in large part structured by voting procedures—that give election contests their shape and form if not their substance. While the focus here will be on the political-strategic calculations that different procedures engender, the term "voting system" also encompasses the cultural and sociological forces that impinge on and shape election competition.

The two best-known and most commonly used voting procedures in the United States restrict voters to voting for only one candidate, regardless of how many run. They are plurality voting (the candidate with the most votes wins) and plurality voting with a runoff (the two candidates with the most votes are paired against each other in a second, or runoff, election; the candidate with the most votes in the runoff election wins). Runoff elections are held only if the winner in the first election does not receive a majority—or some other designated percentage, such as 40 percent—of the votes.

The ostensible purpose of a runoff election is to prevent a strong minority candidate, who may be preferred by, say, 35 percent of the voters, from defeating majority candidates who might split the remaining 65 percent of the vote. By pairing one of the majority candidates against the minority candidate, runoff elections help to ensure that one of the majority candidates gets elected, providing that most of the supporters of the defeated majority candidate vote for the majority candidate in the runoff.

This analysis also excludes from consideration plurality voting—with or without a runoff—and voting procedures commonly used in legislatures, councils, and other voting bodies, wherein the alternatives that are voted on are not candidates or parties but bills and resolutions. Like the procedures discussed here, these other procedures are vulnerable to *strategic voting*, whereby rational voters vote insincerely (not in accordance with their preferences) to try to obtain a preferred outcome.

If two majority candidates are pitted against a minority candidate, under plurality voting (without a runoff), for example, a voter might vote for the majority candidate who seems to have the better chance of winning—even though this voter might prefer the other majority candidate—to try to prevent the minority candidate from winning. On the other hand, if there were a runoff, supporters of either of the majority candidates would presumably vote sincerely in the first election because at least one of the majority candidates would make the runoff and defeat the minority candidate if that candidate were also in the runoff.

The words *minority* and *majority* are used rather loosely here. The subsequent analysis is more precise about strategic calculations and their effects on outcomes. Analyzing better and worse strategies under alternative procedures not only illuminates their strategic properties but also illustrates paradoxes that can arise under them.

This analysis concentrates on practical voting procedures that have actually been used in elections, including the most prominent ranking procedures and methods of proportional representation. It also discusses an alternative nonranking procedure—*approval voting*. Approval voting is presently used in many universities and several professional societies and has been proposed for public elections, such as party primaries and nonpartisan elections in the United States, that often draw more than two candidates. The article concludes with a brief normative assessment of the alternative voting procedures assayed.

The Hare System of Single Transferable Vote (STV)

First proposed by Thomas Hare in England and Carl George Andrae in Denmark in the 1850s, STV has been adopted throughout the world. It is used in elections of public officials in countries such as Australia (where a special case of it is called the alternative vote), Malta, the Republic of Ireland, and Northern Ireland; in local elections in Cambridge, Massachusetts, and school board elections in New York City; and in elections in numerous private organizations. John Stuart Mill (1862) placed it "among the greatest improvements yet made in the theory and practice of government."

Although STV is known to violate a number of properties of voting systems discussed in the literature on social choice theory, it has a number of strengths as a system of proportional representation. Minorities, in particular, can elect a number of candidates, roughly proportional to their numbers in the electorate, if they rank these candidates at the tops of their lists. Also, if a person's vote does not help to elect his or her first choice, it can still be counted toward lower choices.

To describe how STV works and to illustrate two properties that it fails to satisfy, consider the following examples. The first example shows that STV is vulnerable to "truncation of preferences" when two out of four candidates are to be elected, and the second example shows that it is also vulnerable to "nonmonotonicity" when one candidate is to be elected and there is no transfer of so-called surplus votes.

Example 1. Assume that three classes of voters rank the set of the four candidates x, a, b, c as follows:

    I. 6 voters: *xabc*
    II. 6 voters: *xbca*
    III. 5 voters: *xcab*

Assume also that two of the four candidates are to be elected, and a candidate must receive a quota of six votes to be elected on any round. A *quota* is defined as $(n/(m + 1)) + 1$, where n is the number of voters and m is the number of candidates to be elected.

It is standard procedure to drop any fraction that results from the calculation of the quota; so the quota actually used is $q = [(n/(m + 1)) + 1]$, the integer part of the number in brackets. The integer quota is the smallest number that makes it impossible to elect more than m candidates by first-place votes on the first round. Since $q = 6$ and 17 voters are in our example, at most two

candidates can attain the quota on the first round (18 voters would be required for three candidates to get six first-place votes each). In fact, what happens is as follows:

First round: x receives 17 out of 17 first-place votes and is elected.

Second round: A surplus of 11 votes (above $q = 6$) is transferred in the proportions 6:6:5 to the second choices (a, b, and c, respectively) of the three classes of voters. Since these transfers do not result in at least $q = 6$ for any of the remaining candidates (3.9, 3.9, and 3.2 for a, b, and c, respectively), the candidate with the fewest (transferred) votes (i.e., c) is eliminated under the rules of STV. The supporters of c (class III) transfer their 3.2 votes to their next-highest choice (i.e., a), giving a more than a quota of 7.1. Thus, a is the second candidate elected. Hence, the set of winners is x and a.

Now assume that two of the six class II voters indicate that x is their first choice, but they do not indicate a second or third choice. The new results are

First round: Same as earlier.

Second round: There is a surplus of 11 votes (above $q = 6$) that are transferred in the proportions 6:4:2:5 to the second choices, if any (a, b, no second choice, and c, respectively) of the voters. (The two class II voters do not have their votes transferred to any of the remaining candidates because they indicated no second choice.) Since these transfers do not result in at least $q = 6$ for any of the remaining candidates (3.9, 2.6, and 3.2 for a, b, and c, respectively), the candidate with the fewest transferred votes (i.e., b) is eliminated. The supporters of b (4 voters in class II) transfer their 2.6 votes to their next-highest choice (i.e., c), giving c 5.8, less than the quota of 6. Because a has fewer transferred votes (3.9), a is eliminated, and c is the second candidate elected. Hence, the set of winners is x and c.

Observe that the two class II voters who ranked only x first induced a better social choice for themselves by truncating their ballot ranking of candidates. Thus, it may be advantageous not to rank all candidates in order of preference on one's ballot, contrary to a claim made by a mathematical society that "there is no tactical advantage to be gained by marking few candidates." Put another way, one may do better under the STV preferential system by not expressing preferences—at least beyond first choices.

The reason for this in the example is that the two class II voters, by not ranking *bca* after *x*, prevent *b*'s being paired against *a* (their last choice) on the second round, wherein *a* beats *b*. Instead, *c* (their next-last choice) is paired against *a* and beats him or her, which is better for the class II voters.

Lest one think that an advantage gained by truncation requires the allocation of surplus votes, we next give an example in which only one candidate is to be elected, so the election procedure progressively eliminates candidates until one remaining candidate has a simple majority. This example illustrates a new and potentially more serious problem with STV than its manipulability owing to preference truncation.

Example 2. Assume four candidates, with 21 voters in the following four ranking groups:

    I. 7 voters: *abcd*
    II. 6 voters: *bacd*
    III. 5 voters: *cbad*
    IV. 3 voters: *dcba*

Because no candidate has a simple majority of $q = 11$ first-place votes, the lowest first-choice candidate, *d*, is eliminated on the first round, and class IV's 3 second-place votes go to *c*, giving *c* 8 votes. Because none of the remaining candidates has a majority at this point, *b*, with the new lowest total of 6 votes, is eliminated next, and *b*'s second-place votes go to *a*, who is elected with a total of 13 votes.

Next assume that the three class IV voters indicate only *d* as their first choice. Then *d* is still eliminated on the first round, but since the class IV voters did not indicate a second choice, no votes are transferred. Now, however, *c* is the new lowest candidate, with five votes; *c*'s elimination results in the transfer of his or her supporters' votes to *b*, who is elected with eleven votes. Because the class IV voters prefer *b* to *a*, it is in their interest not to rank candidates below *d* to induce a better outcome for themselves, again illustrating the truncation problem.

Under STV, a first choice can never be hurt by ranking a second choice, a second choice by ranking a third choice, and so on because the higher choices are eliminated before the lower choices can affect them. However, lower choices can affect the order of elimination and hence the transfer of votes. Consequently, a higher choice (e.g., second) can influence whether a lower choice (e.g., third or fourth) is elected.

We wish to make clear that we are not suggesting that voters would routinely make the strategic calculations implicit in these examples. These calculations are not only complex but also might be neutralized by counterstrategic calculations of other voters. Rather, we are saying that to rank *all* candidates for whom one has preferences is not always rational under STV, despite the fact that it is a preferential voting procedure. Interestingly, STV's manipulability in this regard bears on its ability to elect so-called Condorcet candidates (Fishburn and Brams, 1983). We say more about this shortly.

Example 2 illustrates another paradoxical aspect of STV: raising a candidate in one's preference order can actually hurt that candidate. This is referred to as *nonmonotonicity* (Smith, 1973; Doron and Kronick, 1977; Fishburn, 1982; Bolger, 1985). Thus, if the three class IV voters raise *a* from fourth to first place in their rankings—without changing the ordering of the other three candidates—*b* is elected rather than *a*. This is indeed perverse: *a* loses when he or she moves up in the rankings of some voters and thereby receives more first-place votes. Equally strange, candidates may be helped under STV if voters do not show up to vote for them at all, which has been called the "no-show paradox" (Fishburn and Brams, 1983; Moulin, 1986; Ray, 1986; Holzman, 1989).

The fact that more first-place votes, or even no votes, can hurt rather than help a candidate violates what arguably is a fundamental democratic ethic. STV also does not guarantee the election of *Condorcet candidates* (Condorcet, 1785)—those who can defeat all other candidates in separate pairwise contests. Thus in Example 2, *b* is the Condorcet candidate: *b* is preferred to *a* by 14 voters (class II, III, and IV voters), whereas *a* is preferred to *b* by only 7 voters (class I); similarly, *b* is preferred to *c*, 13 to 8, and to *d*, 18 to 3. However, *a* is elected under STV.

The Borda Count

Under a system proposed over 200 years ago (Borda, 1781), points are assigned to candidates so that the lowest-ranked candidate of each voter receives 0 points, the next-lowest 1 point, and so on up to the highest-ranked candidate, who receives $m - 1$ votes if there are m candidates. Points for each candidate are summed across all voters, and the candidate with the most points wins. To the best of our knowledge, the Borda count and similar scoring methods (Young, 1975) are not used to elect candidates in any public elections, but they are used by many private organizations.

Like STV, the Borda count need not elect the Condorcet candidate. This is illustrated by the case of three voters with preference order *abc* and two voters with preference order *bca*. Under the Borda count, *a* receives six points, *b*, seven points, and *c*, two points, making *b* the Borda winner; yet *a* is the Condorcet candidate.

On the other hand, the Borda count would elect the Condorcet candidate (*b*) in Example 2 of the preceding section. This is because *b* occupies the highest position on the average in the rankings of the four sets of voters. Specifically, *b* ranks second in the preference order of 18 voters and third in the order of 3 voters, giving *b* an average ranking of 2.14, which is higher (i.e., closer to 1) than *a*'s average ranking of 2.19 as well as the rankings of *c* and *d*. Having the highest average position is indicative of being broadly acceptable to voters, unlike Condorcet candidate *a* in the preceding paragraph, who is the last choice of two of the five voters.

Unfortunately, the Borda count is readily subject to manipulation. Consider again the example in which three voters have preference order *abc* and two voters have order *bca*. Recognizing the vulnerability of their first choice, *a*, under the Borda count, the three *abc* votes might insincerely rank the candidates *acb*, maximizing the difference between their first choice (*a*) and *a*'s closest competitor (*b*). This would make *a* the winner.

In general, voters can gain under the Borda count by ranking the most serious rival of their favorite candidate last in order to lower his or her point total (Ludwin, 1978). This strategy is relatively easy to effectuate, unlike a manipulative strategy under STV that requires estimating who is likely to be eliminated, and in what order, so as to be able to exploit STV's dependence on sequential eliminations and transfers.

The vulnerability to manipulation of the Borda count led Borda to exclaim, "My scheme is intended only for honest men" (Black, 1958, p. 238). Nurmi (1984) has shown that the Borda count, like STV, is also vulnerable to preference truncation, giving voters an incentive not to rank all candidates in certain situations. However, Chamberlin and Courant (1983) contend that the Borda count would give effective voice to different interests in a representative assembly, if not always ensure their proportional representation.

Another type of paradox that afflicts the Borda count and related point-assignment systems involves manipulability by changing the agenda.

For example, the introduction of a new candidate, who cannot win—and, consequently, would appear irrelevant—can completely reverse the point-total order of the old candidates, even though there are no changes in the voter's rankings of these candidates (Fishburn, 1974). Thus, in the example below, the last-place finisher among three candidates (*a*, with 6 votes) jumps to first place (with 13 votes) when irrelevant candidate *x* is introduced, illustrating the extreme sensitivity of the Borda count to apparently irrelevant alternatives:

3: *cba*	*c* = 8	3: *cbax*	*a* = 13
2: *acb*	*b* = 7	2: *axcb*	*b* = 12
2: *bac*	*a* = 6	2: *baxc*	*c* = 11
			x = 6

Clearly, it would be in the interest of *a*'s supporters to encourage *x* to enter simply to reverse the order of finish.

Cumulative Voting

Cumulative voting is a system in which each voter is given a fixed number of votes to distribute among one or more candidates. This allows voters to express their intensities of preference rather than simply to rank candidates, as under STV and the Borda count. It is a system of proportional representation in which minorities can ensure their approximate proportional representation by concentrating their votes on a subset of candidates commensurate with their size in the electorate.

To illustrate this system and the calculation of optimal strategies under it, assume that there is a single minority position favored by one-third of the electorate and a majority position favored by the remaining two-thirds. Assume further that the electorate comprises 300 voters, who are required to elect a 6-member governing body, and that the 6 candidates with the most votes win.

If each voter has 6 votes to cast for as many as 6 candidates, and if each of the 100 voters in the minority casts 3 votes each for only 2 candidates, then these voters can ensure the election of these two candidates no matter what the 200 voters in the majority do. Each of these 2 minority candidates will get a total of 300 (100 x 3) votes, whereas the two-thirds majority, with a total of 1,200 (200 x 6) votes to allocate, can at best match this sum for its 4 candidates (1,200/4 = 300).

If the two-thirds majority instructs its supporters to distribute their votes equally among five candidates (1,200/5 = 240), then it will not match the vote totals of the two minority candidates (300) but can still ensure the election of four (of its five) candidates—and possibly get its fifth candidate elected if the minority (mistakenly) puts up three candidates and instructs its supporters to distribute their votes equally among the three (giving each 600/3 = 200 votes).

Against these strategies of either the majority (support five candidates) or the minority (support two candidates), it is easy to show that neither side can improve its position. To elect five (instead of four) candidates with 301 votes each, the majority would need 1,505 instead of 1,200 votes, holding constant the 600 votes of the minority; similarly, for the minority to elect three (instead of two) candidates with 241 votes each, it would need 723 instead of 600 votes, holding constant the 1,200 votes of the majority.

It is evident that the optimal strategy for the leaders of both the majority and minority is to instruct their members to allocate their votes as equally as possible among a certain number of candidates. The number of candidates they should support for the elected body should be proportionally about equal to the number of their supporters in the electorate (if known).

Any deviation from this strategy—for example, by putting up a full slate of candidates and by not instructing supporters to vote for only some on this slate—offers the other side the opportunity to capture more than its proportional share of the seats. Clearly, good planning and disciplined supporters are required to be effective under this system.

A systematic analysis of optimal strategies under cumulative voting is given in Brams (1975). These strategies are compared with strategies actually adopted by the Democratic and Republican parties in elections for the Illinois General Assembly, where cumulative voting was used until 1982. This system has been used in elections for some corporate boards of directors. In 1987 cumulative voting was adopted by two cities in the United States (Alamogordo, New Mexico, and Peoria, Illinois) to satisfy court requirements of minority representation in municipal elections.

Additional-Member Systems

In most parliamentary democracies, it is not candidates who run for office but political parties that put up lists of candidates. Under party-list voting, voters vote for the parties, which receive representation in a parliament proportional to the total numbers of votes that they receive. Usually there is a threshold, such as 5 percent, which a party must exceed in order to gain any seats in the parliament.

This is a rather straightforward means of ensuring the proportional representation (PR) of parties that surpass the threshold. More interesting are systems in which some legislators are elected from districts, but new members may be added to the legislature to ensure, insofar as possible, that the parties underrepresented on the basis of their national-vote proportions gain additional seats.

Denmark and Sweden, for example, use total votes, summed over each party's district candidates, as the basis for allocating additional seats. In elections to the Federal Republic of Germany's Bundestag and Iceland's Parliament, voters vote twice, once for district representatives and once for a party. Half of the Bundestag is chosen from party lists, on the basis of the national party vote, with adjustments made to the district results so as to ensure the approximate proportional representation of parties.

In Puerto Rico, no fixed number of seats is added unless the largest party in a house wins more than two-thirds of the seats in district elections. When this happens, that house can be increased by as much as one-third to ameliorate the underrepresentation of minority parties.

To offer some insight into an important strategic feature of additional-member systems, assume, as in Puerto Rico, that additional members can be added to a legislature to adjust for underrepresentation, but this number is variable. More specifically, assume a voting system, called *adjusted district voting*, or ADV (Brams and Fishburn, 1984a, 1984b), that is characterized by the following simplifying assumptions:

1. There is a jurisdiction divided into equal-size districts, each of which elects a single representative to a legislature.
2. There are two main factions in the jurisdiction—one majority and one minority—whose size can be determined. For example, if the factions are represented by political parties, then their respective sizes

can be determined by the votes that each party's candidates, summed across all districts, receive in the jurisdiction.

3. The legislature consists of all representatives who win in the districts plus the largest vote-getters among the losers (necessary to achieve PR if it is not realized in the district elections). Typically, this adjustment would involve adding minority-faction candidates—who lose in the district races—to the legislature, so that it mirrors the majority-minority breakdown in the electorate as closely as possible.

4. The size of the legislature is variable, with a lower bound equal to the number of districts (if no adjustment is necessary to achieve PR), and an upper bound equal to twice the number of districts (if a nearly 50 percent minority wins no district seats).

As an example of ADV, suppose that there are eight districts in a jurisdiction. If there is an 80 percent majority and a 20 percent minority, then the majority is likely to win all the seats unless there is an extreme concentration of the minority in one or two districts.

Suppose the minority wins no seats. Its two biggest vote-getters could be given two extra seats to provide it with representation of 20 percent in a body of ten members—exactly its proportion in the electorate.

Now suppose that the minority wins one seat, which would provide it with representation of $1/8 = 13$ percent. If it were given an extra seat, then its representation would rise to $2/9 = 22$ percent, which would be closer to its 20 percent proportion in the electorate. However, assume that the addition of extra seats can never make the minority's proportion in the legislature exceed its proportion in the electorate.

Paradoxically, the minority would benefit by winning no seats but would then be granted two extra seats to bring its proportion up to exactly 20 percent. To prevent a minority from benefiting by *losing* in district elections, assume the following *no-benefit constraint*: the allocation of extra seats to the minority can never give it a greater proportion in the legislature than it would obtain had it won more district elections.

How would this constraint work in the example? If the minority won no seats in the district elections, then the addition of two extra seats would give it $2/10$ representation in the legislature, exactly its proportion in the electorate. But we just showed that if the minority had

won exactly one seat, then it would *not* be entitled to an extra seat—and $2/9$ representation in the legislature—because this proportion exceeds its 20 percent proportion in the electorate. Hence, its representation would remain at $1/8$ if it won in exactly one district.

Because $2/10 > 1/8$, the no-benefit constraint prevents the minority from gaining two extra seats if it wins no district seats initially. Instead, it would be entitled in this case to only one extra seat because the next-highest ratio below $2/10$ is $1/9$; since $1/9 < 1/8$, the no-benefit constraint is satisfied.

But $1/9 = 11$ percent is only about half of the minority's 20 percent proportion in the electorate. In fact, one can prove in the general case that the no-benefit constraint may prevent a minority from receiving up to about half of the extra seats it would be entitled to—on the basis of its national vote total—were the no-benefit constraint *not* operative and it could therefore get up to this proportion (e.g., two out of ten seats in the example) in the legislature (Brams and Fishburn, 1984b).

This constraint may be interpreted as a kind of "strategyproofness" feature of ADV: it makes it unprofitable for a minority party deliberately to lose in a district election in order to do better after the adjustment that gives it extra seats. But strategyproofness, in precluding any possible advantage that might accrue to the minority from throwing a district election, has a price. As the example demonstrates, it may severely restrict the ability of ADV to satisfy PR, giving the following impossibility result: under ADV, one cannot guarantee a close correspondence between a party's proportion in the electorate and its representation in the legislature if one insists on the no-benefit constraint. Dropping it allows one to approximate PR, but this may give an incentive to the minority party to lose in certain district contests in order to do better after the adjustment.

It is worth pointing out that the second chance for minority candidates afforded by ADV would encourage them to run in the first place. Even if most or all of them are defeated in the district races, their biggest vote-getters would still get a second chance at the (possible) extra seats in the second stage. But these extra seats might be cut by up to a factor of two from the minority's proportion in the electorate should one want to motivate district races with the no-benefit constraint. Indeed, Spafford (1980, p. 393), anticipating this impossibility result, recommended that only a fraction (unspecified) of the seats that the minority is entitled to be allotted to it in the adjustment phase to give it "some incentive to take the single-members contests seriously, . . . though that of course would be giving up strict PR."

Approval Voting

We indicated in the Introduction that a minority candidate, with support from a relatively small percentage of the electorate, can either win a plurality election outright or qualify for a runoff. In the example given in that section, the runoff would deny the election of the minority candidate. On the other hand, a potential defect of runoffs is that a Condorcet candidate may not even make the runoff.

For example, if there are strong minority candidates on both the left and the right, then a moderate candidate in the middle may receive the smallest percentage of the vote. Yet this candidate may in fact be able to defeat each of the minority candidates in separate pairwise contests. Despite being the Condorcet candidate, however, his or her election would be obviated by plurality voting, with or without a runoff.

Approval voting—proposed independently by several analysts in the 1970s (Brams and Fishburn, 1983)—is a voting procedure that is designed in part to prevent the election of minority candidates in multicandidate contests (i.e., contents with three or more candidates). Under approval voting, voters can vote for, or approve of, as many candidates as they wish. Each candidate approved of receives one vote, and the candidate with the most votes wins.

Advantages of approval voting include the following:

1. *It gives voters more flexible options.* They can do everything they can under the plurality system (vote for a single favorite), but if they have no strong preference for one candidate, then they can express this by voting for all candidates that they find acceptable. For instance, if a voter's most preferred candidate has little chance of winning, then that voter could vote for both a first choice *and* a more viable candidate without worrying about wasting his or her vote on the less popular candidate.

2. *It would increase voter turnout.* By being better able to express their preferences, voters would more likely go to the polls in the first place. Voters who think they might be wasting their votes, or who cannot decide which of several candidates best represents their views, would not have to despair about making a choice. By not being forced to make a single—perhaps arbitrary—choice, they would feel that the election system allows them to be more honest, which presumably would make voting more meaningful and would encourage greater participation in elections.

3. *It would help elect the strongest candidate.* Today the candidate supported by the largest minority often wins, or at least makes the runoff. Under approval voting, by contrast, it would be the candidate with the greatest overall support—such as the moderate candidate alluded to above—who would usually win. An additional benefit is that approval voting would induce candidates to try to mirror the views of a majority of voters, not just cater to minorities whose votes could give them a slight edge in a crowded plurality contest.

4. *It would give minority candidates their proper due.* Minority candidates would not suffer under approval voting: their supporters would not be torn away simply because there was another candidate who, though less appealing to them, was generally considered a stronger contender. Because approval voting would allow these supporters to vote for *both* candidates, they would not be tempted to desert the one who is weak in the polls, as under plurality voting. Hence, minority candidates would receive their true level of support under approval voting, even if they could not win.

5. *It is eminently practicable.* Approval voting can readily be implemented on existing voting machines (unlike the preferential systems discussed earlier), and it is simple for voters to understand. Moreover, because it does not violate any state constitutions in the United States (or the constitutions of most countries in the world), it needs only a statute passed by a state legislature to become law.

Although approval voting encourages sincere voting, it does not altogether eliminate strategic calculations. Because approval of a less-preferred candidate could hurt a more-preferred approved candidate, the voter is still faced with the decision of where to draw the line between acceptable and nonacceptable candidates. A rational voter will vote for a second choice if his or her first choice appears to be a long shot—as indicated, for example, by the polls—but the voter's calculus and its effects on outcomes is not yet well understood for either approval voting or the other procedures discussed herein (Nurmi, 1987; Merrill, 1988).

Approval voting is now used in many universities and in several professional societies with collectively over 325,000 members (Brams, 1988; Brams and Fishburn, 1988; Brams and Nagel, 1990; Brams and Fishburn, 1990a). Among other officials, the secretary general of the United Nations is elected by approval voting (Brams and Fishburn, 1983).

Bills to implement approval voting have been introduced in some state legislatures in the United States; in 1987 a bill to mandate approval voting in certain statewide elections passed the senate but not the house in North Dakota. Approval voting has been used in internal elections by the political parties in some states, including Pennsylvania, where a presidential straw poll using approval voting was conducted by the Democratic State Committee in 1983 (Nagel, 1984). In 1990, Oregon used approval voting in a statewide advisory referendum, listing five alternatives on school financing. Beginning in 1987, approval voting has been used in some competitive elections in the Soviet Union (Shabad, 1987) as well as in Poland. Some features of approval voting have been incorporated into two new electoral systems. Constrained approval voting (Brams, 1990) and coalition voting (Brams and Fishburn, 1990b) ensure proportional representation of different groups in an electorate.

Conclusions

There is no perfect voting procedure. But some procedures are clearly superior to others with respect to satisfying certain criteria. Among nonpreferential voting systems, approval voting distinguishes itself as more sincere and more likely to select Condorcet candidates than other systems, including plurality voting and plurality voting with a runoff.

Although preferential systems—notably STV—have been used in public elections to ensure proportional representation of different parties in legislatures, the vulnerability of STV to preference truncation illustrates its manipulability, and its nonmonotonicity casts doubt upon its democratic character. In particular, it

seems bizarre that voters can hurt a candidate's chances by raising him or her in their rankings.

Although the Borda count is monotonic, it is more readily manipulable than STV. Whereas it is difficult to calculate the impact of insincere voting on sequential eliminations and transfers under STV, the strategy of ranking the most serious opponent of one's favorite candidate last is a transparent way of diminishing a rival's chances under the Borda count. Also, the introduction of a new and seemingly irrelevant candidate, as was illustrated, can have a topsy-turvy effect, moving a last-place candidate into first place.

Additional-member systems, and specifically ADV that results in a variable-size legislature, provide a mechanism for approximating PR without the nonmonotonicity of STV or the manipulability of the Borda count. But the no-benefit constraint on the allocation of additional seats to underrepresented parties under ADV—in order to rob them of the incentive to throw district races—vitiates fully satisfying PR. Although cumulative voting offers a means for parties to guarantee their approximate proportional representation, it requires good predictive abilities and considerable organizational efforts on the part of parties to ensure that their supporters concentrate their voters in the proper manner.

Because of the impossibility of satisfying a number of desiderata simultaneously, trade-offs are inevitable in the search for voting procedures that best meet different needs (Niemi and Riker, 1976; Straffin, 1980; Dummett, 1984). We have tried to show how an understanding of certain characteristics of alternative voting procedures—especially those relating to their strategic properties—can facilitate the selection of practical procedures that satisfy the criteria one deems most important.

Steven J. Brams and Peter C. Fishburn

REFERENCES

Black, Duncan. 1958. *The Theory of Committees and Elections*. Cambridge, UK: Cambridge U. Pr.

Bolger, Edward M. 1985. "Monotonicity and Other Paradoxes in Some Proportional Representation Schemes." 6 *SIAM Journal on Algebraic and Discrete Methods* 283

Borda, Jean-Charles de. 1781. "Mémoire sur les élections au scrutin." *Histoire de l'Académie Royale des Sciences*. Paris.

Brams, Steven J. 1975. *Game Theory and Politics*. New York: Free Press.

———. 1982. "The AMS Nomination Procedure Is Vulnerable to 'Truncation of Preferences.'" 29 *Notices of the American Mathematical Society* 136.

———. 1988. "MAA Elections Produce Decisive Winners." 8 *Focus: Newsletter of the Mathematical Association of America* 1.

———. 1990. "Constrained Approval Voting: A System to Elect a Governing Board." 20 *Interfaces*.

———, and Peter C. Fishburn. 1983. *Approval Voting*. Cambridge: Birkhäuser Boston.

———, and ———. 1984a. "A Note on Variable-Size Legislatures to Achieve Proportional Representation." In Arend Lijphart and Bernard Grofman, eds. *Choosing an Electoral System: Issues and Alternatives*. New York: Praeger.

———, and ———. 1984b. "Proportional Representation in Variable-Size Legislatures." 1 *Social Choice and Welfare* 211.

———, and ———. 1984c. "Some Logical Defects of the Single Transferable Vote." In Arend Lijphart and Bernard Grofman, eds. *Choosing an Electoral System: Issues and Alternatives*. New York: Praeger.

———, and ———. 1988. "Does Approval Voting Elect the Lowest Common Denominator?" 21 *PS: Political Science & Politics* 277.

———, and ———. 1990a. "Approval Voting in Scientific and Engineering Societies." Preprint.

———, and ———. 1990b. "Coalition Voting." Preprint.

———, and Jack C. Nagel. 1991. "Approval Voting in Practice." *Public Choice*, forthcoming.

Chamberlin, John R., and Paul N. Courant. 1983. "Representative Deliberations and Representative Decisions: Proportional Representation and the Borda Rule." 77 *American Political Science Review* 718.

Condorcet, Marquis de. 1785. *Essai sur l'application de l'analyse à la probabilité dés decisions rendues à la pluralité des voix*. Paris.

Doron, Gideon, and Richard Kronick. 1977. "Single Transferable Vote: An Example of a Perverse Social Choice Function." 21 *American Journal of Political Science* 301.

Dummett, Michael. 1984. *Voting Procedures*. New York: Oxford U. Pr.

Fishburn, Peter C. 1974. "Paradoxes of Voting." 68 *American Political Science Review* 537.

———. 1982. "Monotonicity Paradoxes in the Theory of Elections." 4 *Discrete Applied Mathematics* 119.

———, and Steven J. Brams. 1983. "Paradoxes of Preferential Voting." 56 *Mathematics Magazine* 207.

Holzman, Ron. 1987. "To Vote or Not to Vote: What Is the Quota?" 22 *Discrete Applied Mathematics 133*.

Kelly, Jerry S. 1987. *Social Choice Theory: An Introduction*. New York: Springer-Verlag.

Ludwin, William G. 1978. "Strategic Voting and the Borda Method." 33 *Public Choice* 85.

Merrill, Samuel, III. 1988. *Making Multicandidate Elections More Democratic*. Princeton: Princeton U. Pr.

Mill, John Stuart. 1862. *Considerations on Representative Government*. New York: Harper.

Moulin, Hervé. 1986. "Condorcet's Principle Implies the No Show Paradox." 45 *Journal of Economic Theory* 53.

Nagel, Jack. 1984. "A Debut for Approval Voting." 17 *PS* 62.

Niemi, Richard G., and William H. Riker. 1976. "The Choice of Voting Systems." 234 *Scientific American* 21.

Nurmi, Hannu. 1984. "On the Strategic Properties of Some Modern Methods of Group Decision Making." 29 *Behavioral Science* 248.

———. 1987. *Comparing Voting Systems*. Dordrecht, Holland: D. Reidel.

Ray, Depankar. 1986. "On the Practical Possibility of a 'No Show Paradox' Under the Single Transferable Vote." 11 *Mathematical Social Sciences* 183.

Riker, William H. 1982. *Liberalism Against Populism: A Confrontation Between the Theory of Democracy and the Theory of Social Choice*. San Francisco: Freeman.

Smith, John H. 1973. "Aggregation of Preferences with Variable Electorate." 47 *Econometrica* 1113.

Spafford, Duff. 1980. "Book Review." 11 *Canadian Journal of Political Science* 392.

Straffin, Philip D. 1980. *Topics in the Theory of Voting*. Cambridge: Birkhäuser Boston.

Young, H. Peyton. 1975. "Social Choice Scoring Functions." 28 *SIAM Journal of Applied Mathematics* 824.

John P. Altgeld (1847–1902)

Reform governor of Illinois in the 1890s. John Peter Altgeld was famous for his pardon of convicted Haymarket rioters, his confrontation with President Grover Cleveland over the use of troops in the Pullman strike, and his advocacy of the free-silver cause.

Born in Prussia, but raised on a farm in Ohio, Altgeld had little formal education. At the age of 16, he served in the Civil War in an Ohio volunteer regiment. After the war, he studied law, moved to Missouri, and, in 1874, won his first political race to become a county prosecuting attorney in Missouri. The following year, Altgeld moved to Chicago.

In Chicago, Altgeld ran for Congress on the Democratic ticket in 1884 but lost. In that same year, he published a book, *Our Penal Machinery and Its Victims*, reflecting his resentment over the legal system's injustices toward the poor. He was elected a superior court judge and served in this position from 1886 to 1891. Meanwhile, he accumulated a fortune in real estate. In 1892, with the support of the farm and labor vote, Altgeld became the first Democratic governor of Illinois since the Civil War. He was a reform governor, lending maximum support to social legislation.

In 1893 Altgeld pardoned three men convicted of complicity in the Haymarket riot, citing evidence for his action that they had not received a fair trial. Nevertheless, the press and the business community attacked him as a friend of anarchists. Later, when he protested President Cleveland's use of federal troops to break the Pullman strike in 1894, he was again condemned as a dangerous radical. He was not reelected in 1896.

Altgeld was a leading advocate of free silver and, despite his foreign birth, was among those considered for the Democratic presidential nomination in 1896. He supported William Jennings Bryan's election campaigns in 1896 and 1900.

See also: Grover Cleveland, Progressivism, Radicalism in American Politics

Ralph M. Goldman

REFERENCES

Altgeld, John P. 1970. *The Mind and Spirit of John Peter Altgeld.* Freeport, NY: Books for Libraries Press.

———. 1973, 1980. *Live Questions.* New York: AMS Press.

———. 1984. *Our Penal Machinery and Its Victims.* Chicago: Janson, A.C. McClurg Publishers.

Barnard, Harry. 1973. *Eagle Forgotten: Life of John Peter Altgeld.* Secaucus, NJ: Lyle Stuart.

Amateurs in the United States Congress

Contrary to common wisdom, the U.S. House and Senate are not exclusively the domain of the politically experienced. Most voters are familiar with celebrities who are elected to Congress without having served in lower office, including former Congressman Jack F. Kemp (R-N.Y.), Senator John H. Glenn (D-Ohio), and Senator Bill Bradley (D-N.J.), who after twelve years is still trying to shake the prefix "former New York Knicks great" from his name. The presence of amateurism, defined here as the lack of prior political experience, is even more widespread than is suggested by these highly visible cases. Over one-fourth of House members and more than 10 percent of Senators in recent years avoid a common apprenticeship in lower office and are elected to Congress with no previous political experience. Amateurs are disproportionately elected during partisan surges, especially in realigning elections such as in the 1930s for the Democrats. This trend also flies in the face of conventional theory, which argues that experienced politicians will run for office and be elected in years when the chances for their success are the highest.

At the individual level, the amateur's path to office is also distinctive. Without the advantage of name recognition and campaign experience that comes with holding office, amateurs often are at a disadvantage in the electoral arena. Experienced politicians generally choose to run in the most attractive races, while amateurs are left to challenge incumbents or other seasoned politicians in open-seat races. To overcome these handicaps, many amateurs rely on attack themes in incumbent races and on issue-based campaigns more generally. Amateurs who already have high name recognition (celebrities), who have already run for Congress, or who have defeated an experienced candidate in their party's primary election are more likely to succeed in the general election.

Are amateurs' careers distinctive once they are in office? Anecdotal evidence abounds. Michael Barone noted that major league pitcher Wilmer "Vinegar Bend" Mizell (R-N.C.), decathlon champ Robert B. Mathias (R-Calif.), and NFL quarterback Jack F. Kemp (R-N.Y.), all elected between 1966 and 1970, were Richard Nixon's "team players," implying a connection between their sports-based loyalties and their political behavior. On the Democratic side, amateurs are not known for their party loyalty. Former Speaker Thomas (Tip) O'Neill (D-Mass.) held amateurs partly responsible for legislative losses in the first year of the Reagan administration, calling the inexperienced legislators "bedwetters."

Another common observation links previous experience and political temperament. The reelection of former talk show host Robert K. Dornan (R-Calif.) in 1984 drew this reaction from the *Almanac of American Politics*: "The interesting question is whether this politician who made his earlier political and media career literally sounding off is now prepared to be a constructive legislator, or will he again be more of a zealot or even zany?" The careers of Congresswoman Bella Abzug (D-N.Y.), Senator Jeremiah Denton (R-Ala.), and Senator Gordon Humphrey (R-N.H.), among others, provide many more anecdotes. Politicians socialized at lower levels of office are not as likely to be as extreme in their behavior.

However, the simple dichotomy between amateurism and political experience generally cannot explain behavioral differences between amateurs and experienced members. David Canon (1990) has presented a typology of amateurism that recognizes differences among amateurs in their electoral and institutional behavior. Canon finds three types: policy, ambitious, and hopeless amateurs. Policy amateurs seek office because they want to effect policy change. Politics is not a career for many of these people; they usually enter politics as an interlude in a career in business or law. Ambitious amateurs resemble their experienced counterparts; they are motivated primarily by their desire to establish a career in politics. Hopeless amateurs are unexpectedly swept into office in landslide elections or in upset victories in non-landslide years. Their relatively short careers will be consumed by the task of remaining in office.

Once elected to office, behavioral differences are evident among the types of amateurs and experienced politicians. Policy amateurs' careers are significantly shorter (3.78 years compared with 5.62 years for ambitious amateurs and 5.35 years for experienced candidates who served between 1972 and 1984); they are more likely to gain policy committee assignments, are more likely to submit amendments on the floor, are more ideologically extreme in their voting behavior, and do not pursue power goals through legislative leadership positions. Hopeless amateurs also have shorter careers (3.93 years); they are more likely to serve on constituency committees, are less likely to be active on the floor, and generally do not win leadership positions. Ambitious amateurs, on the other hand, resemble their experienced counterparts in every regard. Their career patterns are similar, they are more ideologically moderate, and they pursue a variety of goals.

The patterns summarized here generally are more descriptive of the House than the Senate. The typology of amateurism cannot be as readily applied to the Senate because the numbers of each type are too small to allow inferences. Nonetheless, behavioral differences between amateurs and experienced Senators on roll call voting and in the leadership system merit additional attention.

Reaching normative conclusions about the place of amateurs in the political system is not easy, but one point is clear. Amateurs in Congress are not a problem. Policy amateurs often bring with them an ideological fervor that is refreshingly untempered by previous experiences and frustrations in public office. Though the question remains open for systematic study, policy amateurs often appear to serve as an important component of policy change, as in the "Reagan Revolution" in 1981 or the early New Deal days under Franklin D. Roosevelt. Canon and Sousa (1987) argue that the impact of amateurs on the political system during realignments adds an important component to the discussion of the "governing side" of realignments. Hopeless amateurs are elected to Congress to the surprise of most. Without their gutsy campaigns (challenges that most experienced candidates are not willing to accept), incumbents would be even more entrenched. The accountability they help to impose by removing incumbents who are often tainted by scandals helps provide the electoral check that is so central to the democratic process. Thus, presence of amateurs in Congress will continue to be felt, especially in periods of electoral and policy change.

See also: Bella Abzug, Jack Kemp

David T. Canon

REFERENCES

Canon, David T. 1990. *Actors, Athletes, and Astronauts: Political Amateurs in the United States Congress.* Chicago: U. of Chicago Pr.

———, and David J. Sousa. 1987. "Realigning Elections and Political Career Structures in the U.S. Congress." Paper Presented at the Annual Meeting of the American Political Science Association, Chicago.

Dodd, Lawrence C. 1986. "Cycle of Legislative Change: Building a Dynamic Theory." In Herbert F. Weisberg, ed. *Political Science: The Science of Politics.* New York: Agathon.

American Association of Retired Persons

A powerful Washington-based interest group committed to improving the quality of life of older persons in such areas as health care, income maintenance, and employment. Founded in 1958 as an outgrowth of the National Retired Teachers Association (NRTA), the American Association of Retired Persons (AARP) is the country's largest political interest group, with more than 27 million members composed since 1982 of persons 50 years of age or older. The organization has 10 regional offices and 3,600 local groups. It experienced phenomenal growth in the 1980s and is expected to grow significantly as the "baby boom" generation matures. The AARP's political prowess is in part attributed to its large membership and to the high electoral turnout rate among the elderly.

Historically, the AARP has been better known as a service and marketing organization offering members a wide variety of selective material benefits (health insurance, mail discount pharmaceuticals, motor clubs, money market funds) rather than as a political organization. It became politically important in the 1970s and has expanded its political activities since the early 1980s. The AARP avoids partisan identification and is trying to expand beyond the middle-class professional constituency with which it has long been identified. It has had policy differences with the National Council of Senior Citizens (NCSC), another major interest group of the elderly, which is more closely identified with labor and the Democratic Party. While the AARP does not endorse candidates or distribute voting records, it does engage in lobbying and political communication with its members to influence voting behavior.

The elderly are an important constituency in many electoral districts in America, and groups like the AARP have been very successful in promoting the interests of the elderly. Budget constraints and the development of groups like Americans for Generational Equity (AGE), which question growing expenditures for entitlement programs such as Social Security and Medicare, will make issues on the elderly more volatile for candidates and elected officials in the future.

See also: Claude Pepper

Clyde Brown

REFERENCES

Pratt, Henry J. 1976. *The Gray Lobby.* Chicago: U. of Chicago Pr.

American Civil Liberties Union

The preeminent organization in America dedicated to the protection of civil liberties (a legally protected freedom) and civil rights (equal treatment before the law) as defined by the Constitution and statutes. As a public interest group, the American Civil Liberties Union (ACLU) is active in court cases (it is an important source of *amicus curiae* briefs), lobbying, and public protest on issues relating to freedom of speech, press (including censorship and pornography) and assembly, separation of church and state (including opposition to school prayer), due process of law (including the rights of the accused) and fair trial, and equal protection for all before the law.

Since the 1960s the ACLU has been the leading advocate and defender of minority rights. It has also been active in such areas as women's rights, children's rights, victimless crimes, immigration, prisoners' rights, voting rights, capital punishment, national security, and the rights of labor. Founded in 1920, it grew in the mid-1980s to enroll 250,000 members and maintains 50 state organizations and hundreds of local groups, with 5,000 volunteer lawyers. It is affiliated with the American Civil Liberties Union Foundation, which engages in legal defense and research and public education on behalf of civil rights and liberties.

The organization claims an absolute lack of bias and promotes an image of nonpartisanship. It is not involved in "normal" electoral activity. It has been accused by some of having a liberal social agenda that was initially pro-labor and is now pro-equalitarian. Conservative groups and former Attorney General Edwin Meese III have reviled the group as a "criminal lobby" and a "leftist organization." The ACLU responds by claiming that it has protected the civil rights and liberties of all citizens regardless of ideology: Nazis, Communists, Ku Klux Klan members, the business community, and conservative individuals such as Lt. Colonel Oliver North in the Iran-Contra affair.

The ACLU became embroiled in the 1988 presidential election when George Bush repeatedly characterized Michael S. Dukakis as a "card-carrying member of the ACLU," took issue with various positions of the ACLU, and attacked Dukakis as a "strong, liberal Democrat" who was "out of the mainstream." The reference to "card-carrying member" echoes of the Joseph McCarthy hunt for Communists in government in the 1950s and was offensive to supporters of the Democratic candidate. For the first time, the ACLU has become a major issue in national electoral politics, but the effectiveness of the Bush tactic probably guarantees that it will not be the last. Liberal candidates for national office sympathetic with the positions of the ACLU will have to be alert to similar charges from conservative opponents in the future.

See also: Michael Dukakis, Hubert H. Humphrey, Joseph R. McCarthy, McCarthyism, Joseph L. Rauh, Red Scare, Eleanor Roosevelt

Clyde Brown

REFERENCES

Donohue, William A. 1985. *The Politics of the American Civil Liberties Union.* New Brunswick, NJ: Transaction Books.

Markmann, Charles Lam. 1985. *The Noblest Cry.* New York: St. Martin's.

American Farm Bureau Federation

A federation of county farm organizations founded in 1919 to promote the general interests of farmers. Aided by the national preparedness efforts for World War I, the American Farm Bureau Federation (AFBF) grew out of and benefited from a long relationship with the county agent system of the Agriculture Extension Service. Originally an active advocate of government support for agriculture, the AFBF since the 1940s has favored a "free market" approach to agricultural policy.

By the late 1980s, the AFBF had 3.3 million family members concentrated in the Midwest and the South, comprised mainly of prosperous farmers who for the most part grow corn or cotton and raise livestock on large farms; the AFBF's policy positions reflect these economic interests. It has been critical of programs that would help economically marginal farmers, tenant farmers, farm laborers, and migratory farmworkers. Politically, the AFBF has been associated with the Republican Party. As a general farm organization, it has had to compete for members and influence with the more liberal National Farmers Union (NFU) and specific commodity groups.

With the migration of population from the farm since the 1940s and the "reapportionment revolution" of the 1960s, the political power of farmers and rural interests have declined. However, the AFBF is still important politically in rural states and congressional districts and in the crafting of agricultural policy. The jurisdictional organization of Congress into committees and subcommittees guarantees an important role for farm organizations, such as the AFBF, in the development of agricultural policy. Demographic realities, however, have increased the importance of nonfarm groups in passing such legislation.

See also: National Farmers' Alliance and Industrial Union

Clyde Brown

REFERENCES

Anderson, James E., David W. Brady, Charles S. Bullock III, and Joseph Stewart, Jr. 1984. *Public Policy and Politics in America*. Monterey, CA: Brooks/Cole.

Berger, Samuel. 1971. *Dollar Harvest: The Story of the Farm Bureau*. Lexington, MA: Heath.

American Independent Party

American Independent Party was the label used by Alabama governor George Wallace for his third-party presidential campaign in 1968. It also refers to several successor groups.

Charging that "not a dime's worth of difference" separated the Republicans and Democrats, Wallace envisioned a party of populistic, middle-class protest, animated by the issues of taxes, inflation, crime, welfare, the conduct of the Vietnam War, and judicial activism. Looming over these, however, was the issue of race; Wallace aimed his appeals primarily at voters in both the South and the North who were opposed to, or at least wary of, the civil rights movement.

During the 1968 campaign, the American Independent Party was actually a collection of 50 separate state parties, which used 9 different names; 17 went by the name American, and 12 used the American Independent label. AIP held no national convention organization in 1968, and the state parties were largely ignored when Wallace dealt with such party trappings as drafting a platform and choosing his running mate, former Air Force general Curtis LeMay.

Wallace viewed the state parties as flags of personal convenience; he maintained tight control over campaign activities through centralized fundraising and budgeting, and he assigned trusted supporters from Alabama to run many of the state campaigns. Wallace also desired to minimize the influence and visibility of such extremist groups as the John Birch Society in his campaign and, to the extent possible, refused to allow other candidates to run with him, fearing that right-wing ticket-mates would embarrass him and detract from his own campaign. One AIP candidate did run for the U.S. Senate in Oklahoma, and 18 ran for the House of Representatives (14 of them in California) in 1968.

Although he fell short of his goal of denying an Electoral College majority to either major party, Wallace did receive 9.9 million votes (13.5 percent of the total vote) and carried 5 Deep South states with 46 electoral votes. Nearly three-fifths of his national vote came from southern and border states; nearly one-quarter of his votes came from the Deep South. According to the Survey Research Center's 1968 election study, Wallace voters were disproportionately independent southern or southern-born males from farm or rural backgrounds.

In May 1969, delegates from 38 states met in Cincinnati to organize the American Party. A rival group, the National Committee of Autonomous State Parties, attracted delegates from 27 states to a December convention in Indianapolis. The former saw itself as the vehicle for a 1972 Wallace campaign and endorsed the Alabamian's liberal populist economic views, while the latter advocated a strongly conservative program, greater autonomy for the state parties, and a party-centered rather than a candidate-centered orientation. Although Wallace endorsed the American Party as his national political organ, he kept both party groups at arm's length, preferring to speak of the "Wallace Movement" rather than of a party effort per se.

Even as he ran in the 1972 Democratic presidential primaries, Wallace was careful to leave open the possibility of a second third-party campaign later that year. This plan was effectively ended by the attempt on Wallace's life in May 1972, which left him paralyzed. The two organizations, having united under the American Party label (while retaining assorted state party names for ballot status reasons), then nominated Congressman John Schmitz of California, a former Republican, for President.

Schmitz and running mate Thomas Anderson of Tennessee appeared on 34 state ballots, but Wallace refrained from any endorsement, apparently wary of Schmitz's penchant for controversy and advocacy of various conspiracy theories. Although the ticket received more than 1 million votes, it was but a small fraction of the party's 1968 total and came to only 1.4 percent of the national vote.

The party's *raison d'être* as an alternative device for Wallace's national ambitions has been underscored by its sharp decline since formally breaking with Wallace after the 1972 election. The entire history of Wallace-AIP relations is nicely summarized in the words of Wallace aide Mickey Griffin: "When we left the American Party, we left an empty bag. It was a good vehicle while it lasted, but when Wallace left, he took the voters with him."

Schism returned to the party in 1973; driven by power and personality factors, the group broke apart primarily upon the lines of its 1969 division, with William Shearer of California organizing the dissidents as a new American Independent Party, while Anderson retained control of the American Party apparatus.

The two groups fielded separate presidential tickets in 1976. As nominee of the American Party, Anderson was on the ballot in 19 states. The American Independent Party nominated former Georgia governor Lester Maddox, thereby thwarting an attempt by conservative activists to develop the party as a vehicle for Reagan-style conservatism. At least one of the two tickets was on the ballot in 31 states (in eight states, both appeared), but their combined vote total was only 330,000, or 0.4 percent of the national total.

Support for the two parties has continued to dwindle in recent elections. The 1980 nominees ran in only 12 states, and their combined vote total dropped to 55,609, less than one-tenth of 1 percent. In 1984 most of the remaining elements of the AIP supported former Olympic star Bob Richards, nominee of the newly organized Populist Party, but the totals for the American and American Independent parties rose only slightly to 79,497.

Although Wallace threatened at one time to field a full slate of congressional candidates, the AIP never emerged as a significant electoral force below the presidential level. The party's high-water mark for congressional candidates occurred in 1976 (13 Senate, 77 House), while its gubernatorial peak of 16 candidates had come in 1970. Only six of the party's gubernatorial and U.S. Senate candidates have garnered as much as 5 percent of the vote, and a Tennessee state senator elected in 1970 and 1974 appears to have been the only AIP state legislator. In 1986 the AIP fielded only seven gubernatorial and congressional candidates throughout the nation.

See also: Elections of 1968, 1972, and 1976, Electoral College System, Lester Maddox, Populism as a Movement and Party, Third Parties in American Elections, George C. Wallace

David E. Sturrock

American Labor Party

A New York State minor party founded in 1936 with the encouragement of President Franklin D. Roosevelt to provide a means for labor and white collar independent voters to support Roosevelt for his reelection bid without having to rely on the state Democratic Party, controlled by Tammany Hall. Originally called Labor's Non-Partisan League, the party was founded by trade union leaders, including David Dubinsky, Sidney Hillman, Jacob Potofsky, Hyman Blumberg, Luigi Antonini, and Alex Rose (all from garment-related unions). In addition, the party was buttressed by longtime Socialists. With the active support of Roosevelt political lieutenants James Farley and Ed Flynn, the American Labor Party (ALP) gained a spot on the ballot, nominating Roosevelt for President and incumbent Herbert H. Lehman for governor. The new party polled enough votes for governor to establish it as an officially recognized state party. Its base of support was founded primarily in New York City, among union members and old-line Socialists. In 1937 the ALP endorsed Republican incumbent New York City mayor

Fiorello H. LaGuardia for reelection, to the chagrin of some Democratic leaders who had indeed feared that the ALP would stray from Democratic preferences. The ALP endorsement impelled the Republicans to endorse LaGuardia as well, and his margin of victory was exceeded by his ALP vote total. The ALP provided similar key support for LaGuardia in 1941. In 1938 the ALP endorsement of Lehman for governor provided him with the margin of victory over his Republican challenger, Thomas E. Dewey.

At this time, the state's Communist Party had lost its official state designation (such designation is maintained by running a candidate for governor who receives at least 50,000 votes), and members of the Communist Party began to enroll in large numbers in the ALP, while still maintaining the facade of the Communist Party. By 1938 Communists had gained control over the Manhattan ALP. The first major showdown between the Communist and anti-Communist factions came in 1939, precipitated in part by reaction to the Hitler-Stalin nonaggression pact. Over the objections of the Communists, the ALP endorsed Roosevelt for a third term. By 1940 party meetings were so acrimonious that the owners of large meeting facilities in New York were reluctant to rent space for party meetings, and police presence became a necessity. During most of the war years, the factions attempted to minimize their differences, in part because of the American alliance with the Soviet Union. In 1944, however, Rose and Dubinsky pulled their unions out of the ALP and formed the Liberal Party. They did so after rejecting a compromise offered by party leader Sidney Hillman that Communist unions be allowed formal recognition in the party with the understanding that they could not nominate any of their number to office. Following the end of World War II, anti-Communist sentiment intensified in America, thus accelerating the exodus of non-Communist labor from the ALP, mostly to the new Liberal Party. With the availability of a new minor party alternative, the ALP gradually lapsed into nonexistence.

See also: Communism in American Politics, Fiorello H. La Guardia, Liberal Party, Non-Partisan League, Franklin D. Roosevelt, Alex Rose, Socialism in American Politics

Robert J. Spitzer

American Medical Association

A national federation of county medical societies and physicians. Founded in 1847, and with a present membership of some 270,000 members, the American Medical Association's primary activities are scientific, including disseminating information about medicines and medical equipment to health professionals through its many professional journals and over 1,000 meetings annually, setting standards for professional medical education (medical schools, hospitals, residency programs, and continuing education courses), determining questions of medical ethics and quackery, and distributing health information to the public.

Since World War II, the American Medical Association (AMA) has also been a very powerful lobby at the state and national levels on issues of importance to the medical profession. It has consistently opposed efforts to nationalize health care. Originally, the AMA opposed public health care for the elderly (Medicare) and successfully defeated such programs during Harry S Truman's presidency. It has opposed national health insurance and medical cost-containment legislation.

In 1962 the AMA organized the American Medical Political Action Committee (AMPAC), the first major professional PAC. During the 1980s, AMPAC was consistently among the top two or three PACs in terms of both funds raised and money eventually contributed to congressional candidates. Just as important, the AMA is affiliated with state medical associations; the state groups have separate PACs, which are among the largest in the country. The state medical associations often spend heavily on state legislative and executive races and are very important in the politics of their particular states. AMPAC is also one of the largest PACs for independent expenditures. Unlike many PACs, which are reluctant to back challengers in congressional races, AMPAC has shown a willingness to challenge incumbents both as a means of punishing specific congresspersons and as a collective warning to legislators who might oppose the AMA. Most notably, AMPAC spent nearly $600,000 in 1986 to help defeat two liberal Democratic incumbents on the House Ways and Means Committee who were deemed antagonistic to AMA's interests. Although the two incumbents won reelection, the campaigns illustrate the AMA's use of independent expenditures in recent elections.

As a membership organization, the AMA has the advantage of being composed of a relatively small number of wealthy, high-prestige individuals with very well defined interests and wide geographical distribution. As a result it has been and will likely continue to be a very powerful and politically cohesive lobby.

See also: Political Action Committees

Clyde Brown

REFERENCES

Cohen, Richard. 1986. "Spending Independently." 6 *National Journal* 2932.

"*PACs'* Independent Expenditures Slow Down." 1988. 5 *Congressional Quarterly Weekly Report* 3185.

American Party of Texas et al. v. White
415 U.S. 767 (1973)

The American Party of Texas sought access to the general election ballot in 1972 by offering a slate of candidates for various statewide and local offices, including governor and county commissioner. The American Party challenged various provisions of the Texas Election Code, alleging that the restrictive nature of the Code infringed upon their First and Fourteenth Amendment rights to associate for the advancement of political beliefs. The American Party further alleged that the Texas Election Code invidiously discriminated against new or minority political parties as well as against independent candidates. The U.S. District Court decided that the challenged provisions of the Texas Election Code served a compelling state interest and did not inhibit the fair election process. The court denied all relief to the American Party of Texas.

Texas had established a complex and comprehensive scheme for administering the qualifications of political parties for participation in the electoral process. The Texas Election Code provided four methods for a party to gain access to the ballot for the general election. Candidates representing a party whose gubernatorial candidate had received more than 200,000 votes in the previous general election would be nominated by primary election and automatically qualify for a position on the ballot. Candidates of parties whose gubernatorial candidate received less than 200,000 votes, but more than 2 percent of the total votes cast for governor, could be nominated either by a party convention or by primary election. Candidates of the parties whose gubernatorial candidate was less successful, or of parties who did not offer a candidate for governor, were required to hold precinct nominating conventions. If a certain level of support was not exhibited in the local conventions, then these candidates were compelled to circulate petitions for signatures. Unaffiliated or independent candidates would gain access to the ballot only by presentation of a petition containing the signatures of a specific percentage of the vote for governor in the relevant electoral district in the last general election.

The American Party appealed the decision of the U.S. District Court, contending that the preconditions for access to the general election ballot imposed unconstitutional burdens on the First and Fourteenth Amendments and represented invidious discrimination against new and small parties in violation of the equal protection clause.

Affirming the decision of the district court, the Supreme Court recognized the interests advanced by Texas in preserving the integrity of the electoral process by reducing undue voter confusion through the regulation of the number of candidates. The Court concluded that the Texas Election Code afforded minority political parties a reasonably equal opportunity for ballot qualification.

Scott McDermott

The American Voter

The American Voter (1960), by Angus Campbell, Philip E. Converse, Warren E. Miller, and Donald E. Stokes, defined a model of individual voting behavior that structured a generation of work by political scientists interested in how voters reach decisions. Based on surveys conducted by the Survey Research Center at the University of Michigan in 1948, and particularly in 1952 and 1956, *The American Voter* model posits that knowing a voter's political party is the most important means of understanding how Americans evaluate and choose among presidential candidates.

The concept of party identification was first defined in this work. Respondents were asked a series of questions that allowed analysts to classify them on a seven-point scale, ranging from "Strong Republicans," to "Weak Republicans," to "Independents Leaning Republican," through "Independents," to three categories of Democrats paralleling those for Republicans. Party identification was heavily influenced by parental partisanship and by social and economic class identification. Perceptions of candidates and vote, in turn, were heavily influenced by party identification. *The American Voter's* portrait of the electorate was one in which ideology and knowledge of issues played only minor roles.

The American Voter has been criticized both because its interpretation is "time-bound"—that is, the political period in which the investigation was conducted was not one in which issues were salient—and because the implicit demands on citizen knowledge were too rigorous—that is, voters do not need a sophisticated view of issues in order to determine if those in office are acting for or against the evaluator's best interest. However, the work has endured because it is rich in insights and because it highlighted concept after concept that scores of social scientists have been examining and reexamining for 30 years.

See also: Party Identification

L. Sandy Maisel

REFERENCES

Campbell, Angus, Philip E. Converse, Warren E. Miller, and Donald E. Stokes. 1960. *The American Voter.* New York: Wiley.

American Workers Party

Founded in early 1934, the American Workers Party (AWP) proved to be a short-lived and small radical organization of nonaligned, anti-Stalinist, Marxist revolutionaries. Although support for the party was miniscule and the actual duration of its existence but a few months, the AWP nevertheless attracted a number of important, largely New York–based, intellectuals. Led by A. J. Muste, a Dutch-born former minister who had studied at Union Theological Seminary with Norman Thomas and John Dewey, the AWP attracted James Burnham; Edmund Wilson; V. F. Claverton, editor of *Modern Monthly*; James Rorty; and Sidney Hook, a professor of philosophy at New York University and a leading American interpreter of Karl Marx. Hook wrote the AWP's political program but never formally joined the party.

The AWP was organized to rival the Communist Party, which many nonaligned revolutionaries, particularly the Trotskyites, believed to be an ineffectual leader of American workers. Much of the AWP's initial support came from the Conference for Progressive Labor Action, a loose coalition of radical dissidents against the Communist Party's orthodoxy. After only a few months of existence in 1934, the AWP merged with the Trotskyite Communist League of America, under James Cannon's leadership, and formed the Workers Party of the United States.

See also: Communism as a Political Issue, Norman Thomas

John Walsh

Americans for Constitutional Action

In 1958 Senator Karl Mundt (R-S.D.) and retired Admiral Ben Moreell, then chairman of the board of Jones and Laughlin Steel Corporation, established the Americans for Constitutional Action (ACA) as a conservative counterweight to the Americans for Democratic Action (ADA). The ACA's stated purpose was to support candidates who "by their actions, have proved their allegiance to the original spirit and principles of the Constitution" (Koek and Martin, 1987).

At present, the ACA is a small organization that relies on members' financial contributions. The staff numbers five with two professional consultants, and the headquarters is located in Washington, D.C.

The organization is best known for its annual index rating of the roll call voting records of members of Congress. Roll calls are selected according to their importance and their bearing upon issues in six dimensions: (1) sound money and fiscal integrity; (2) private, competitive market (rather than government) price fixing and controls; (3) local self-government and citizen freedom rather than central government intervention; (4) private versus government ownership of enterprise; (5) individual liberty rather than government regulation; and (6) national sovereignty in foreign affairs. Subsidiary indexes are computed on each area as well as an index using all selected votes. The latter is commonly reported in annual newspaper stories.

The group also biennially presents distinguished service awards to selected members of Congress and endorses candidates. Its membership newsletter is the *ACA Congressional Record Digest and Tally*.

Douglas I. Hodgkin

REFERENCES

Koek, Karin E., and Susan Boyles Martin, eds. 1987. *Encyclopedia of Associations 1988.* 22nd ed., Vol. I. Detroit: Gale.

Melia, Thomas O., and Sueanne Pfifferling, eds. 1986. *How They Rate Congress.* Washington: Quadriga Research.

Schapsmeier, Edward L., and Frederick H. Schapsmeier. 1981. *Political Parties and Civic Action Groups.* Westport, CT: Greenwood.

Americans for Democratic Action

An official nonpartisan political action organization that seeks to advance liberal causes and candidacies in the United States. Americans for Democratic Action (ADA) was founded in 1947 by a group of academics, journalists, intellectuals, and politicians who aimed to fulfill the liberal vision of American government at home and to fight totalitarianism from either end of the ideological spectrum abroad. Among its founders were anti-Communist liberals such as Arthur Schlesinger, Jr., Hubert H. Humphrey, Eleanor Roosevelt, Walter Reuther, and then movie actor Ronald Reagan. In recent years, the ADA has pushed for a more restrained U.S. military presence abroad and more government activism in the domestic economy. The 75,000-member organization evaluates politicians with respect to its legislative agenda, and the consequent "ADA rating" is used by both liberals and conservatives as a measure of ideological purity or impurity.

The ADA won its first victories in 1948: the adoption of its alternative civil rights plank by the Democratic convention, a plank that prompted Strom Thurmond's "Dixiecrat" walk-out and also with the election of several of its members to the Senate, the House, and governorships.

About the time of the 1952 Democratic convention, the ADA began to see that the main instrument for realizing its vision in American politics would have to be the Democratic Party. Whereas the group had reluctantly endorsed President Harry S Truman in 1948, it was enthusiastic about Adlai Stevenson's candidacy, though unsuccessful, in both 1952 and 1956. The 1950s were tough times for the ADA, but its unified support for domestic economic growth and U.S. activism internationally held firm.

In 1960, while the ADA preferred Humphrey for President, it supported John F. Kennedy after Humphrey withdrew from the race. The group was subsequently frustrated throughout the 1960s by two Democratic administrations, which failed to live up to their liberal potential at home. Abroad, the Vietnam War was as divisive for the ADA as it was for American society at large. Traditionalists emphasized the need for stopping Communist aggression, while reformers saw little reason for the U.S. to be involved. The antiwar elements prevailed, and in 1968 the ADA endorsed Senator Eugene McCarthy's peace campaign for the presidency.

Within the ADA, the withdrawal of traditional anti-Communist liberals after 1968 meant that moderates and reformers were in control, and the organization made increasingly vehement proposals for fundamental social change and more restrained use of American power abroad. The ADA ultimately supported every Democratic presidential nominee from Truman in 1948 through Walter Mondale in 1984. However, Democratic candidates and platforms have not been all that the ADA hoped for, although even such watered-down progressivism has often been spurned by an increasingly conservative American electorate.

See also: Hubert H. Humphrey, Eugene McCarthy, Joseph R. McCarthy, McCarthyism, Joseph L. Rauh, Ronald Reagan, Walter Reuther, Eleanor Roosevelt, Adlai Stevenson II, Vietnam War as a Political Issue

Samuel F. Mitchell

John B. Anderson (1922–)

Republican Congressman and independent candidate for President in 1980. John Bayard Anderson, lawyer and Republican Congressman from the "good government" northwestern corner of Illinois, started out as a traditionally conservative legislator. He became so independent of the party line, however, that he ran as a third-party candidate for President in 1980. A Phi Beta Kappa at the University of Illinois and a holder of law degrees from the University of Illinois and Harvard University, Anderson was a member of the State Department's Career Diplomatic Service from 1952 to 1955. He was elected State's attorney for Winnebago County (1956–1960) and then served 10 terms in the U.S. House of Representatives (1961–1981).

As an Old Guard Republican, Anderson opposed President John F. Kennedy's plan to create the Department of Housing and Urban Development and opposed all Democratic proposals to expand welfare programs and increase federal assistance to urban areas. In 1964, as a member of the "Paul Revere team" that publicized the Republican platform around the country, Anderson vociferously supported Barry Goldwater. After he garnered an 88 percent American Conservative Union rating for his first three terms, Anderson modified his stance on social issues while he remained a fiscal conservative. He championed more federal aid to education, increased food stamp assistance, advocated consumer protection and gun licensing, and guaranteed housing loans. Coupled with a personal evolution in philosophy no doubt was the influence of demographic changes in his own district as more liberal blue-collar voters moved in from Chicago. In 1968 Anderson, a fine orator, delivered a notable speech on the House floor supporting the open-housing bill, even though in 1966 he had joined with other

Republican House Rules Committee members to defeat a similar proposal.

In 1969 Anderson sought and won and the third most powerful post in the House Republican establishment—the chairmanship of the House Republican Conference—previously held by Melvin Laird. His most significant challenge to this position occurred in January 1971 when Congressman Sam Devine of Ohio, a Nixon loyalist, garnered 81 votes to Anderson's 89; however, Anderson kept this post until he relinquished it in June 1979 to run for the presidency.

Anderson supported Nixon on revenue-sharing and the Vietnam War but not on civil rights, the Cambodian incursion, nor his postponement of the Strategic Arms Limitation Talks (SALT) with the Soviet Union. Anderson favored Nixon's reelection in 1972, but in May 1973 he was one of 18 House Republicans to cosponsor a resolution calling for a special prosecutor to investigate the Watergate scandal.

In May 1974 Anderson called for Nixon to resign. He also cosponsored with Morris Udall what became the presidential campaign financing law to provide matching funds to candidates who raise certain amounts in small contributions.

Winning general elections in his home district rather easily, Anderson in 1978 faced his toughest primary opponent when the Reverend Don Lyon, an evangelist, attacked him as a left-winger. By 1978 Anderson had reached an Americans for Democratic Action rating of 55 percent, which owed in part to his support for the Equal Rights Amendment and government-funded abortions for the poor. Backed by the Gun Owners of America and the National Conservative Political Action Committee, Lyon might have won had it not been for a large Democratic crossover vote to Anderson in the primary.

Anderson pledged not to run for reelection to the House or to try for election to the Senate if he did not win the presidency in 1980. In the Republican primaries, he sought an "issues campaign" and a "Midwest strategy," emphasizing the areas where he was best known. He also aspired to rebuild and broaden the GOP. In the Iowa caucus, he took the politically tough and unpopular positions of suggesting a 50¢ per gallon gasoline tax and supporting the grain embargo against the Soviet Union in retaliation against the invasion of Afghanistan. He also made the memorable quip that the only way

Ronald Reagan could fulfill his promises—balance the budget, cut taxes, and increase defense spending—was with mirrors.

After failing to win a single Republican primary in 1980—although he came close in Vermont and Massachusetts—Anderson conducted a third-party campaign as the candidate of what in some states was called the National Unity Party and in others the Independent Party, with former Wisconsin Democratic governor Patrick J. Lucey as his running mate. He received 7 percent of the vote nationwide, once again doing best in Vermont and Massachusetts (both 15 percent). This total entitled Anderson to federal matching funds in 1984, but he chose not to run again.

See also: Americans for Democratic Action, *Anderson v. Celebrezze*, Election of 1980, Barry Goldwater, National Conservative Political Action Committee, Richard Nixon, Ronald Reagan, Morris Udall

Frederick J. Augustyn, Jr.

Joseph Anderson (1757–1837)

Federal district judge, U.S. Senator from Tennessee, and the first comptroller of the U.S. Treasury. Joseph Anderson was an active member of the post-Revolutionary generation of politicians and officeholders, whose career, typical of many of his contemporaries, spanned several geographical regions and involved changing political identifications and loyalties and a variety of public offices.

Anderson was born in White Marsh, Pennsylvania, outside of Philadelphia. As a young man, he began the study of law, just before the Revolutionary War. He interrupted his studies to serve in the Army, rising from the rank of ensign to that of major by the end of the war. His wartime appointment as regimental paymaster gave early evidence of the financial acumen as well as the confidence he inspired in others, both of which would mark his subsequent career.

After the war, Anderson was admitted to the bar and practiced law in Delaware until he was appointed by President George Washington in 1791 as a federal judge to serve in the western district, which became Tennessee. While still serving as a judge, Anderson played a prominent role in the first Tennessee Constitutional Convention. In 1797 he was chosen by the Tennessee legislature to serve out the uncompleted term of William Blount who had been expelled by the United States Senate. At the end of Blount's term Anderson was again selected to fill a vacancy left by the resignation of Andrew Jackson from his Senate seat.

Anderson served in the Senate from 1797 through 1815, earning a reputation for leadership in financial and economic matters. He was elected by his colleagues to serve as President *pro tempore* on three occasions after Aaron Burr resigned the vice presidency in 1805.

In 1815 Anderson was appointed first comptroller of the Treasury, and he remained in that office despite changing political tides until 1836, thereby enjoying the dubious honor of presiding over the nation's finances during the panic of 1819 and the onset of the panic of 1837.

Joseph Anderson is a relatively obscure but typical figure of his generation of competent, able, astute men who combined politics with public service and who never perceived any conflict between the two. While doing so, he also earned and maintained the confidence of a variety of partisan leaders from George Washington through Andrew Jackson.

See also: Aaron Burr, Andrew Jackson, George Washington

Kathryn A. Malone

Anderson et al. v. Celebreeze
460 U.S. 780 (1982)

In April 1980 Congressman John Anderson announced his intention to seek the presidency as an independent candidate. Anderson had been an early contestant in the Republican presidential primaries, but he had demonstrated only limited strength in races in which Ronald Reagan and George Bush had been the principal contestants. However, John Anderson had attracted substantial support among independent voters and progressive Republicans. Encouraged by this support and by a commitment to the views he had advanced during the primary season, Anderson's campaign workers gathered the signatures, filed the required documents, and paid the filing fees to satisfy the substantive requirements for having his name placed on the ballot in several states for the general election in November 1980. However, by April, Anderson could not qualify for a position on the ballot in Ohio and certain other states because early statutory deadlines for becoming a candidate had already passed.

Anderson contended that early filing deadlines for independent presidential candidates placed an unconstitutional burden on the vot-ing and associational rights of his supporters. In U.S. District Court, he challenged the constitutionality of Ohio's early filing deadline for independent candidates. The court agreed with Anderson, citing the impermissible burden placed on the First Amendment voting and associational rights of Anderson and his Ohio supporters. The court also recognized that a contrary decision could dilute the value of votes cast for Anderson in those states that did not have such restrictive filing deadlines. Additionally, the court cited violations of the equal protection clause of the Constitution because Ohio's filing deadline requirement for independent candidates was not mandated for the nominees of political parties.

While the appeal in the case was pending, voters in Ohio gave John Anderson 5.9 percent of their vote. Nationally, Anderson received over 5.7 million votes—approximately 6.6 percent of the total votes cast in the general election.

The decision of the district court was subsequently reversed by the U.S. Court of Appeals, which held that Ohio's early deadline "ensures that voters making the important choice of their next president have the opportunity for a careful look at the candidates, a chance to see how they withstand the close scrutiny of a political campaign."

In a 5-to-4 decision issued in April 1983, the Supreme Court overturned the court of appeals decision and reinstituted the decision of the district court. The Supreme Court emphasized that its primary concern was not the interest of the candidate, John Anderson, but rather the burden placed on the associational rights of those voters who desired to express their support for Anderson's candidacy and the views he was expressing. The Supreme Court did recognize Ohio's legitimate interests in early filing deadlines for independent presidential candidates, including voter education and political stability. However, when the Supreme Court balanced Ohio's interests against the issues of freedom of choice and freedom of association in an election of nationwide importance, the value of Ohio's early deadline was unquestionably outweighed. Specifically, the Supreme Court found that early deadlines for independent candidates discriminate against those voters whose political preference cannot be filled by candidates in existing political parties. The "Ohio system thus denies the 'disaffected' not only a choice of leadership but a choice on the issues as well," they ruled in *Williams v. Rhodes*, 393 U.S. 23, 33 (1968).

In reaching its decision in this case, the Supreme Court employed an analytical process that compared the character and magnitude of the injury to the First and Fourteenth Amendment rights of Anderson's supporters against the precise interests advanced by Ohio as justification for the burden imposed by its early filing deadline rule. The Court determined that Ohio's rule effectively placed independent candidates at a substantial disadvantage in the competitive environment of the presidential electoral process.

See also: John Anderson, George Bush, Election of 1980, Ronald Reagan, *Williams v. Rhodes*

Scott F. McDermott

Henry B. Anthony (1815–1884)

Rhode Island Republican politician and U.S. Senator. Henry Bowen Anthony served in the United States Senate from 1859 until his death in 1884 and was the principal organizer, publicist, and nurturer of Rhode Island's Republican Party during its formative years.

Of old-line Rhode Island stock, Anthony was born in rural Coventry, a mill village named for his father, a prominent textile manufacturer. At the age of 23, five years after his formal education at Brown, he became the editor of the *Providence Journal*, then a small newspaper with Whig Party affiliations. A skillful and trenchant writer, Anthony held this post until he entered the Senate in 1859. Thereafter he presided as the newspaper's publisher, making the increasingly influential *Journal* the organ of Rhode Island's Republican Party.

Political nativism was one persistent and undistinguished feature of Anthony's long journalistic and governmental career. From the year he assumed the editorship of the *Journal* in 1838, he made war upon "the foreign vagabond" (read "Irish Catholic"), who, he said, "came here uninvited and upon whose departure there is no restraint." Wielding his acid pen during the Dorr Rebellion in 1842, Anthony led the Law and Order Party and zealously supported a real property voting requirement for naturalized citizens. He successfully defended that discriminatory restriction against all challenges (both in Rhode Island and in the U.S. Congress) until his death in 1884, compiling a record of persistence nearly unmatched in the annals of American nativism.

While serving in Washington, Anthony groomed General Charles R. "Boss" Brayton to direct the organizational efforts of Rhode Island's Republican Party. The most notable product of this political coalition (other than its pervasive corruption) was the six-term United States Senator Nelson W. Aldrich (1881–1911).

In Washington, Anthony supported protective tariffs, sound money, and congressional reconstruction of the South. Though he served as President *pro tempore* of the Senate in 1869, 1870, and 1871, he was not a dominant or legislatively productive member of the upper house. Within Rhode Island, however, his political power was unsurpassed. Even Anthony's archfoe, Irish Democratic leader Charles E. Gorman, grudgingly acknowledged in eulogy that Anthony had "possessed in a preeminent degree that peculiar and necessary power in American politics to understand men and to direct their action; to discern the political forces, active and dormant, and to control and bring them into play, so that the political ideas and principles one maintains may be carried to success."

See also: Nelson W. Aldrich, Charles R. Brayton

Patrick T. Conley

References

Byrnes, Garrett D., and Charles H. Spilman. 1980. *The Providence Journal: 150 Years*. Providence: Providence Journal.

Rhode Island General Assembly. 1885. *Henry Bowen Anthony: A Memorial*. Providence: E. L. Freeman.

Tanner, Mary Nelson. 1963. "The Middle Years of the Anthony-Brayton Alliance; or Politics in the Post Office, 1874–1880." 22 *Rhode Island History* 65.

Susan B. Anthony (1820–1906)

Militant leader of the woman suffrage movement. The nineteenth-century women's suffrage campaign owes much of its success to the extraordinary organizational talents of Susan Brownell Anthony. She was attracted to the movement after experiencing discrimination while working for temperance and abolitionism. A meeting with Elizabeth Cady Stanton encouraged her to focus on women's rights. Together the two created an independent suffrage movement with Anthony the strategist and Stanton the writer and orator.

Anthony helped to maintain the movement and attract members by devising unique tactics. She successfully ran door-to-door petition campaigns in New York by innovatively organizing them on a county-by-county basis. When necessary, she was willing to create new alliances. In the 1867 Kansas referendum on women's suffrage, Republicans refused to support Anthony and Stanton, claiming Black suffrage as their primary goal. Anthony then turned to rebel Democrats and allied with the flamboyant Copperhead George F. Train. While she and Stanton were unable to realize the referendum's passage, Anthony did gain new supporters.

Anthony believed the movement had to reach out to women of all backgrounds. She organized the Working Women's Association to work for improved wages and hours, unionization, and suffrage. Even though she failed to convince working women of the overriding importance of the vote, her efforts brought these women and the movement together.

After opposing the Fourteenth and Fifteenth Amendments because they did not include women, she and Stanton formed the National Woman Suffrage Association in 1869. It became her forum to campaign for women's rights and a federal suffrage amendment. Opponents created the American Woman Suffrage Association, which concentrated solely on achieving suffrage but only on a state-by-state basis.

In 1872 she tested the laws by voting in the presidential election. She brought publicity to the cause when she was arrested, tried, and fined. She refused to pay and hoped that the case would be brought to a higher court, but no effort was made at enforcement.

The 1872 election was also important to the movement because it was the last time Anthony took sides in a campaign. (In 1864 she and Stanton had opposed Abraham Lincoln, distrusting his postwar policies.) Anthony supported Ulysses S. Grant because she believed the Republican Party, as the party of reform, was more likely to be sympathetic to women's interests. Afterward, the party ignored the suffragists, which made it apparent that the women had been used simply to gain reform votes.

Anthony continued to acquire supporters by attempting to unify all organized reform-minded women around the vote. The two suffrage organizations united in 1890 as the National American Woman Suffrage Association under Stanton's presidency. Anthony succeeded her in 1892 and kept the organization nonpartisan. She believed the suffrage movement had to be independently run by women, isolated from political alliances and separate from coalition with other reforms. Otherwise, she believed that suffrage would be compromised. This concentration did not keep her from speaking out against other forms of discrimination, and she

vigorously condemned lynchings and race riots. Her labor connections finally came to fruition in 1899 when the American Federation of Labor unanimously adopted a resolution supporting suffrage. She remained active throughout her years and worked for women's suffrage on an international level until her death.

See also: Election of 1872, Fifteenth Amendment, Nineteenth Amendment, Elizabeth Cady Stanton, Suffrage, Woman Suffrage Movement

Joy A. Scimé

REFERENCES

DuBois, Ellen C., ed. 1978. *Feminism and Suffrage: The Emergence of an Independent Women's Movement in America, 1848–1869.* Ithaca: Cornell U. Pr.

———. 1981. *Elizabeth Cady Stanton, Susan B. Anthony: Correspondence, Writings, Speeches.* New York: Schocken Books.

James, Edward T., Janet W. James, and Paul S. Boyer. 1971. *Notable American Women 1607–1950.* Cambridge: Belknap Press.

Scott, Anne F., and Andrew W. Scott. 1975. *One-Half the People: The Fight for Woman Suffrage.* Philadelphia: J. P. Lippincott.

Anti-Federalists

Although they usually did not refer to themselves this way, Anti-Federalists is the negative party label given by the proponents of the Constitution to the diffuse collection of individuals who opposed its adoption during the ratification debates. Given their advocacy of the primacy of the individual states, it was perhaps inevitable that the Anti-Federalists would lack coordination, a unified leadership, and a common positive program. Consequently, it is inappropriate to think of the Anti-Federalists as a bona fide political party, even though the ratification era can be seen as the "seed time" of American political parties. The Federalists, in comparison, were united behind a politically astute leadership armed with a positive vision of a national republic, wisely governed by a centralized political system. Because they usually wrote under pseudonyms, it is impossible to know exactly who many of the Anti-Federalists were; some even switched sides in the course of the debates. Still, among the more prominent were George Mason, Richard Henry Lee, Edmund Randolph, Patrick Henry, Melancton Smith, James Winthrop, and Robert Yates.

While the Anti-Federalists were united primarily through their antagonism to the Constitution, the noted editor of the *Complete Anti-Federalist*, Herbert Storing, claims that finding a single point, including opposition to the Constitution, on which all of the Anti-Federalists agreed is difficult. Still, common elements to the Anti-Federalists position do exist.

Essentially conservative in their orientation, the Anti-Federalists deplored departures from the "good old way" and wanted to preserve the status quo. Historical experience, not reason, was therefore the best guide to designing governments. The proposed system was a novelty that had yet to be tested by history. Hence these "men of little faith" did not share with the Federalist framers the vision of a strong, central government uniting a powerful nation, even though they did share their essentially negative view of humanity. The Anti-Federalists believed that, with some modifications, the Articles of Confederation could continue to serve as the governing instrument for the nation. They viewed the proposed Constitution as an attack on four cherished values: law, political stability, federalism, and the Declaration of Independence. They argued that the new, untried system of government would inevitably lead to a "consolidated system" of government that would destroy republican government, the independence of the states, and individual liberty.

The new system was designed, in their view, to select the most talented to rule rather than to be truly representative of the people; the small number of representatives in the legislative branch would lead to the creation of a distant and despotic aristocracy. Empowered to levy and collect its own taxes and to regulate interstate commerce, the new "Federalist" government insured the destruction of state sovereignty. Lacking mandatory rotation in office, the President was a king in all but name. The legally oriented Anti-Federalists argued that both the Constitution itself, as well as its method of ratification, were illegal. Many argued that the Constitution was a betrayal of the Declaration of Independence and the Revolutionary War: it made the state governments subservient to another government that, in time, would degenerate into tyranny. But their most telling charge was the failure of the Constitution to include a specific bill of rights—a protection the Anti-Federalists believed every people deserve against every government. The Federalists conceded this point and promised the addition of a bill of rights immediately upon ratification. In this sense, it is possible to see the Anti-Federalists as contributors to the creation of the Constitution: the document that began the ratification process was not the same document that emerged from that process.

See also: Federalist Party, Patrick Henry, George Mason, George Washington

Richard K. Matthews

REFERENCES

Jensen, Merrill. 1948. *The Articles of Confederation.* Madison: U. of Wisconsin Pr.

McDonald, Forrest. 1958. *We the People: The Economic Origins of the Constitution.* Chicago: U. of Chicago Pr.

Main, Jackson Turner. 1961. *The Anti-Federalists: Critics of the Constitution.* Chapel Hill: U. of North Carolina Pr.

Pole, J.R,. ed. 1987. *The American Constitution: For and Against.* New York: Hill and Wang.

Rutland, Robert. 1966. *The Ordeal of the Constitution: The Anti-Federalists and the Ratification Struggle of 1787–1788.* Norman: U. of Oklahoma Pr.

Storing, Herbert J. 1981. *The Complete Anti-Federalists.* 7 vols. Chicago: U. of Chicago Pr.

———. 1981. *What the Anti-Federalists Were For.* Chicago: U. of Chicago Pr.

Anti-Imperialist League

In the fall of 1898, a loose grouping of dissenters from both major political parties gave coherent voice to a policy of anti-imperialism in the United States with the formation of a network of anti-imperialist leagues in major northeastern cities. Subsequently termed the Anti-Imperialist League, this association of critics of American foreign policy objected on moral grounds to American expansionism. In their stress on the territorial colony as an imperial injustice, members of the league also expressed a limited understanding of American imperialism, which was now shifting from the formal political controls of the nineteenth century to the informal economic relationships of twentieth-century dominance abroad.

Those who founded the league represented a wide range of political backgrounds; many, however, practiced an underlying and shared conservatism. League members were united for the most part not only in their anxiety over American expansionism but also in their dissatisfaction with political corruption among both Democrats and Republicans, in their unease over the growing numbers of immigrants from central and eastern Europe, as well as in their aversion to radical trade union activity. Among the original vice presidents of the league were Andrew Carnegie, Samuel Gompers, Grover Cleveland, and Carl Schurz.

Schurz was the most prominent anti-imperialist voice among the league's creators. The former Interior Secretary's political trajectory symbolized that of many in the league who could not find expression in mainstream politics. As did many antislavery Republicans who joined the Anti-Imperialist League, Schurz became disillusioned with the party in the 1870s and 1880s, especially on issues of territorial expansion. Schurz and other league founders had led the political fight against the annexation of the Dominican Republic during Ulysses S. Grant's administration and against the proposed annexation of Hawaii in 1893. The urgency of the league's formation in 1898 was based on the potential annexation of Cuba, Puerto Rico, and the Philippines as a result of the war with Spain.

Aside from the Liberal Republican and Mugwump representation, the league was also composed of Republicans such as Carnegie and John C. Bullitt, more firmly associated with turn-of-the-century Republican Party politics. Cleveland typified the conservative Democratic membership of the league, while a fourth broad sector of members were political independents.

Where the anti-imperial objective was the same for all the league founders, motivations varied. Schurz employed racist arguments against the inclusion of tropical inhabitants in the national polity, warning of their purported degeneracy. Samuel Gompers feared a massive influx of cheap foreign labor in the event of annexation. All league members adhered to a founding political statement decrying imperial control, with specific reference to the Spanish-American War, as anathema to American democracy.

During 1899 the league spread to other important cities across the country. Its principal political activity over the long term was organizing public protests and the publishing of pamphlets describing the anti-imperialist cause. Although the impact of these actions are difficult to measure, the Anti-Imperialist League fared poorly on specific political battles. Unsuccessful in their efforts to prevent the annexation of the Hawaiian Islands and the spoils of the war with Spain, league members mounted a failed national opposition to William McKinley's candidacy in the election of 1900.

After Theodore Roosevelt's brusque appropriation of the Panamanian isthmus in 1903, the league tried once again to channel popular opposition to American imperialism. Joined in Congress by such long-term supporters of its cause as Senators George F. Hoar and Edmund W. Pettus, the league was nonetheless unable to mount a strong political opposition. Americans had already begun to accept the nation's new imperial role, and in the first decade of the new century, the Anti-Imperialist League's membership began to drop.

The final annual report of the Anti-Imperialist League was issued in 1920. Even though the organization continued to argue against American imperialism through the 1910s, its political efficacy had ended during Theodore Roosevelt's presidency. Some local chapter leagues continued to function sporadically during the 1920s, joining with other critics of the American presence in Nicaragua. Curiously, the final influence of the league on American politics was through Latin American chapters that had followed the American organization's lead. During the mid-1920s, the administrations of Calvin Coolidge and Herbert Hoover voiced repeated concerns through the Department of State at the burgeoning strength of the Mexico City and Buenos Aires chapters of the Anti-Imperialist League.

See also: Grover Cleveland, Election of 1900, Samuel Gompers, William McKinley, Mugwumps, Theodore Roosevelt, Carl Schurz

David Sheinin

REFERENCES

Anderson, David L. 1985. *Imperialism and Idealism.* Bloomington: Indiana U. Pr.

Beisner, Robert L. 1968. *Twelve Against Empire.* New York: McGraw-Hill.

Bryan, William Jennings. 1900. *Bryan on Imperialism: Speeches, Newspaper Articles and Interviews.* Chicago: Bentley.

Healy, David. 1970. *Expansionism.* Madison: U. of Wisconsin Pr.

LaFeber, Walter. 1963. *The New Empire.* Ithaca: Cornell U. Pr.

Paterson, Thomas G., ed. 1974. *American Imperialism and Anti-Imperialism.* New York: Crowell.

Rystad, Goran. 1975. *Ambiguous Imperialism.* Lund, Sweden: Esselte Studium.

Tompkins, E. Berkeley. 1970. *Anti-Imperialism in the United States: The Great Debate, 1890–1920.* Philadelphia: U. of Pennsylvania Pr.

Welch, Richard E., Jr. 1979. *Response to Imperialism: The United States and the Philippine-American War, 1899–1902.* Chapel Hill: U. of North Carolina Pr.

Antimasons

Representatives of a social and political movement of the 1820s and 1830s directed initially against the Order of Freemasons and then against the Jacksonian Democrats on the state and national level. Originating in New York following the mysterious disappearance and probable murder in 1826 of an obscure Mason, William Morgan, who had threatened to reveal the secret rituals of the group, the Antimason movement was quickly taken over by those recognizing its political potential.

Opposition to Masonry had a long history even before the Morgan case in New York. Because of their secret oaths and rituals, Masons were accused of elitism and involvement in a conspiracy against the lower classes as well as advocating infidelity, irreligion, and intemperance. Originating in western New York, an area of religious fundamentalism given to support of emotional reform movements, Antimasons believed that a conspiratorial effort by Masons controlled politicians and courts to subvert justice in the Morgan case.

Because many New York Democratic leaders were Masons, the opposition quickly recognized the political potential of Antimasonry. Building on the issue of rooting out a privileged class, political pragmatists—led by Thurlow Weed and William H. Seward—and moralistic idealists combined in an effort to oppose New York Democrats dominated by Martin Van Buren and the national party controlled by Andrew Jackson. With the National Republican Party ineffective in New York, a third party was seen by Weed as a more effective avenue to power. By 1830 the Antimasons had replaced the National Republicans as the second in the state with growing power in the state legislature. Two years later the party won eight New York seats in Congress and came close to capturing the governorship.

Nationally, the Antimasons met first in convention in Philadelphia in 1830 and again in Baltimore in September 1831. The latter meeting—the first presidential nominating convention ever held—chose former Attorney General William Wirt as its candidate. Party leaders hoped to combine with National Republicans in opposition to Andrew Jackson. When that coalition failed to materialize, Wirt, an ineffective campaigner at best, remained in the race and finished a poor third behind Jackson and Henry Clay. He did carry Vermont, the first American third-party candidate ever to win electoral votes. In the ensuing months, the Antimasons gave up their separate identity to combine with National Republicans in forming the new Whig Party in 1833.

Although the party ceased to operate as a separate organization after 1833, it continued in several other northern states, often successfully using coalition politics as a vehicle to power.

In Vermont, the party was dominant by 1831, controlling the governorship under William Palmer between 1831 and 1835 and electing several members to Congress. Antimasons secured passage of laws outlawing extra-judicial oaths and otherwise weakened the Masonic movement. In Pennsylvania, it controlled the governorship briefly in the mid-1830s and remained influential through the crusading efforts of Thaddeus Stevens. The party was also important in Rhode Island, Connecticut, and Ohio. John Quincy Adams identified briefly with the Antimasonic Party and was thus the most prominent member of Congress associated with it.

See also: Jacksonian Democrats, National Republicans, Presidential Nominating Conventions, Thaddeus Stevens, Third Parties in American Elections, Martin Van Buren, Thurlow Weed, William Wirt

Frederick J. Blue

REFERENCES

Cross, Whitney R. 1950. The *Burned Over District: The Social and Intellectual History of Enthusiastic Religion in Western New York, 1800–1850*. Ithaca: Cornell U. Pr.

Formisano, Ronald P., and Kathleen S. Kutolowski. 1977. "Anti-masonry and Masonry: The Genesis of Protest, 1826–1827." 29 *American Quarterly* 139.

Holt, Michael F. 1973. "The Antimasonic and Know Nothing Parties." In Arthur M. Schlesinger, Jr. et al., eds. *History of United States Political Parties*. New York: Chelsea House.

Ratner, Lorman. 1969. *Antimasonry: The Crusade and the Party*. Englewood Cliffs, NJ: Prentice-Hall.

Remini, Robert. 1971. "Election of 1832." In Arthur M. Schlesinger, Jr., and Fred L. Israel, eds. *History of American Presidential Elections, 1789–1968*. New York: Chelsea House.

Vaughn, William P. 1983. *The Antimasonic Party in the United States 1826–1843*. Lexington: U. Pr. of Kentucky.

Anti-Saloon League

Possibly the most successful lobbying effort in American history, the Anti-Saloon League was an organization whose success was based on a multipartisan appeal; a paid, full-time staff; a pledge system that produced weekly contributions; and a constituency of over 50,000 churches. Howard Hyde Russell (1855–1946), a Congregational minister and lawyer, organized the league in Ohio in May 1893 for the purpose of ending people's use of alcoholic beverages. In 1895 the league became a national organization. As its general superintendent, Russell opened branches in 36 states between 1895 and 1903.

Sentiment favoring prohibition rose and fell with native-Protestant attitudes toward immigrants. During the Know-Nothing era of the 1850s, 13 states passed local-option laws, but by the time the league organized, there were only 3 local-option states. Much of the league's appeal in the 46 states that ratified the Eighteenth Amendment in 1919 focused on World War I anti-German and antibrewery attitudes.

The league reached its zenith under the guidance of Wayne B. Wheeler (1869–1927), a lawyer who served as its Ohio superintendent (1904–1915), and then as the league's general counsel in Washington (1915–1927), where he worked to end liquor traffic through local and state option bills, and to establish national prohibition. Passage of the Prohibition (Eighteenth) Amendment in 1919 owed largely to his efforts as the era's leading single issue exponent. The amendment went into effect on January 16, 1920. Then Wheeler wrote the law, introduced by Congressman Andrew Volstead, to enforce it. Senator Warren G. Harding, hardly a teetotaler himself, was Wheeler's agent for guiding the Volstead Act through the Senate. Led by Methodist bishop James Cannon, Jr., the league opposed Alfred E. Smith's candidacy for President in 1928. The U.S. rescinded the Eighteenth Amendment in 1933, when the states ratified the Twenty-first Amendment.

Since 1964 the Anti-Saloon League has been renamed the American Council on Alcohol Problems.

See also: Election of 1928, Warren Harding, Know Nothings, Prohibition, Alfred E. Smith

Norman H. Murdoch

Chester A. Arthur (1829–1886)

Eighteenth President of the United States. Chester Alan Arthur was born and raised in Vermont, the son of a Baptist minister. He attended Albany, New York's Union College and began his political career in the Whig Party under the tutelage of leading politician Thurlow Weed. In 1861 he was appointed New York's Quartermaster General and soon became the chief operative for New York's Republican political boss, Roscoe Conkling. His 1871 appointment by President Ulysses S. Grant to be Collector of the Port of New York allowed him to control the main patronage plum of the Conkling empire.

When James A. Garfield won the Republican presidential nomination in 1880, he chose Arthur as his running mate in order to appease the losing Conkling faction. Garfield died at the hands of a disappointed office seeker, however; and Arthur, universally regarded as nothing but a political hack, became President.

His one term proved to be a pleasant surprise to his critics; Arthur seemed to prove the adage that the office can make the man. Hardly an activist President in twentieth-century terms, he proved to be an honest, efficient administrator. He did not favor his old political cronies; in fact, he signed the Pendleton Civil Service bill that they opposed. Arthur began the modernization of the Navy, supported a reasonable tariff, and sought overseas markets for American products. Finally, his vetoing of such bills as an unnecessary $18 million rivers and harbors authorization asserted executive prerogative—an important precedent for future Presidents.

Still, his insistence on privacy and his failure to achieve anything outstanding doomed any chance he might have had for renomination and reelection. By that time, however, Arthur was suffering from Bright's disease and died soon after he left office.

See also: Roscoe Conkling, James A. Garfield, Ulysses S. Grant, Thurlow Weed

John F. Marszalek

Jacob M. Arvey (1895–1977)

Chicago machine politician. Jacob M. Arvey was a powerful political figure from a classic American big-city machine. Arvey was the first child born to his Polish-Jewish parents in the New World. They had come to America in the early 1890s with four children. After his father died, Arvey's family moved to the Twenty-fourth Ward in Chicago, which became Arvey's base of power. (In later years, the Twenty-fourth Ward was famous for its huge pluralities in support of Franklin D. Roosevelt.) Arvey left school to help his family, but he later attended night school, made up his lost credits, and eventually passed the bar.

Arvey first became an alderman and later a ward committeeman in the 1930s. Along with his party work, Arvey was closely associated with a large number of local and national Jewish organizations. Interrupting his political career, Arvey served in the 33rd Infantry during World War II, leaving the Army with the rank of lieutenant colonel. After the war, Arvey replaced Ed Kelly as Chicago's Democratic Party boss. In that role, Arvey also found it necessary to have Kelly replaced as mayor (the corruption of his administration was becoming an embarrassment to the machine). He was instrumental in slating Martin Kennelly for mayor, Paul Douglas for U.S. Senate, and Adlai Stevenson II for governor in 1948, and subsequently was hailed as a genius for his slate making.

Arvey was a longtime member of the Democratic National Committee. In his later years, he was closely associated with Richard J. Daley, a man whose career was promoted by Jake Arvey and who followed him into the position of Chicago Democratic Party boss in 1954.

See also: Richard J. Daley, Democratic National Committee, Paul Douglas, Edward Kelly, Franklin Roosevelt, Adlai Stevenson II

David A. Bositis

REFERENCES

Crotty, William J. 1986. "Local Parties in Chicago: The Machine in Transition." In William J. Crotty, ed. *Political Parties in Local Areas.* Knoxville: U. of Tennessee Pr.

Rakove, Milton. 1979. *We Don't Want Nobody Sent.* Bloomington: Indiana U. Pr.

Royko, Mike. 1971. *Boss.* New York: E. P. Dutton.

Australian Ballot

Also known as a secret ballot, a ballot that is prepared, distributed, and tabulated by government officials at public expense. It was an electoral reform advocated by the Progressives near the end of the nineteenth century. The secret ballot was designed to increase popular government while weakening the control of partisan political machines over the electoral process. (Other Progressive reforms of this type were the direct primary, and the initiative, referendum, and recall.)

The adoption of the Australian ballot in all states by 1888 represented one of the most dramatic changes in the balloting system in American electoral history. Before the 1880s, ballots were cast orally or printed by political parties and candidates in varying colors and sizes. Thus, voters found it difficult to cast ballots secretly for a candidate of their own choice, especially one running as a minority or third-party candidate. Use of oral declarations and colored ballots printed by political parties also made split-ticket voting (voting for members of different parties for different offices) nearly impossible. Split-ticket voting in general elections increased sharply after the adoption of the Australian ballot.

See also: Progressive Party, Split-Ticket Voting

Susan A. MacManus

REFERENCES

Hofstader, Richard. 1955. *The Age of Reform: From Bryan to F.D.R.* New York: Vintage Books.

White, William Allen. 1910. *The Old Order Changeth.* New York.

B

Augustus Octavius Bacon (1835–1914)

United States Senator from Georgia (1895–1914). Augustus Bacon was a leading Democratic politician. After receiving his B.A. from the University of Georgia, he was a lawyer in Atlanta for a brief time and then served in the Confederate Army. After the Civil War, he moved to Macon and entered politics, serving in the state House of Representatives for 14 years—8 years as its Speaker. During his years in the United States Senate, he served on the powerful Rules, Judiciary, and Foreign Relations committees (chairman of the latter, 1913–1914). During the Sixty-second Congress he was President *pro tempore*, the first Georgian to hold that post since William Henry Crawford in 1818.

Bacon was an anti-imperialist who offered an unsuccessful amendment to the 1899 Treaty of Paris with Spain that attempted to assure the Philippine Islands of eventual independence. He fought the protectionist Dingley Tariff and Payne-Aldrich Tariff bills unsuccessfully. A noted debater, he made his greatest impact in 1906 when he spoke out against what he considered to be the unconstitutional expansion of executive power by Theodore Roosevelt. He protested against the President's involvement of the United States in any treaty agreement without the Senate's advice at all stages and not simply when the treaty was complete. Bacon's death in 1914 prevented him from seeing a President from his own party (Woodrow Wilson) ignore the very senatorial rights (and national isolation) he had argued for.

See also: Theodore Roosevelt

John F. Marszalek

REFERENCES

Boifeuillet, John T. 1921. "Senator A. O. Bacon of Georgia." 5 *Georgia Historical Quarterly* 16.

Jones, R.L. 1930. "Senator A. O. Bacon, Champion of the Constitutional Division of Powers." 14 *Georgia Historical Quarterly* 202.

Steelman, Lela Carr. 1950. "The Public Career of Augustus Octavius Bacon." Ph.D. dissertation. University of North Carolina.

Douglas Bailey and John Deardourff

Consulting team to Republican candidates. Douglas Bailey and John Deardourff worked on the staff of Governor Nelson Rockefeller (R-N.Y.) in the 1960s and were involved with his 1964 and 1968 presidential campaigns. They formed a campaign consulting firm in the mid-1960s, concentrating their efforts on behalf of moderate-liberal Republican candidates. Bailey and Deardourff came eventually to be viewed as strategists as much as political advertising experts.

Frequently, the Bailey-Deardourff team would begin a campaign by running positive commercials about their candidate's background and personal qualities. Later spots would lay out the candidate's stands on issues. Shortly before the election, comparative or negative advertising would be employed to develop strong contrasts with the opponent.

However, the firm would make notable departures from the orthodox rules of political advertising.

In 1974 Bailey and Deardourff represented former Republican governor Jim Rhodes of Ohio in his successful attempt to make a political comeback. The firm surprised Democratic strategists by making unusually heavy buys in the Democratic Cleveland media market. However, Bailey-Deardourff aired negative spots that criticized the record of Democratic governor John Gilligan and held the Democratic vote down. Rhodes's victory in 1974 represented one of the few bright spots in a dismal Republican year.

Bailey-Deardourff played a key role in the 1976 campaign of President Gerald Ford. Polls taken during the summer showed that Ford trailed the Democratic nominee, former Georgia governor Jimmy Carter, by a wide margin. Ford was viewed by critics as only a caretaker President, and he had to fight a tough battle with former California governor Ronald Reagan for the presidential nomination.

Bailey-Deardourff successfully promoted Ford's positive attributes in commercials that took advantage of the country's recovery in spirit from the Watergate affair. "There's a change that's come over America. A change that's great to see," the lyrics ran in one effective Ford commercial. Ford was promoted as a solid, trustworthy leader. Bailey-Deardourff used man-in-the-street interviews with Georgians to raise doubts about Carter's ability to govern effectively. Ford narrowly lost the race, but the campaign aired original, memorable advertising.

Bailey-Deardourff's brand of Republicanism lost its appeal with the ascendency of Ronald Reagan and more conservative Republicans. In fact, the firm's candidates usually had trouble winning primary elections that were dominated by ideologically committed voters. The partners are still active in politics, but the firm's profile has been reduced in recent years.

See also: Election of 1976, Gerald Ford, Media and Presidential Campaigns, Ronald Reagan, Nelson Rockefeller

Steve Lilienthal

Gamaliel Bailey (1807–1859)

Leading journalist of the abolitionist movement. Gamaliel Bailey was born in Mount Holly, New Jersey, but his father, the Reverend Gamaliel Bailey, soon moved the family to Philadelphia where he took up a new post with the Methodist church. Young Bailey proved an avid student, graduating from Jefferson Medical College in 1827. Frequently in poor health, Bailey taught school briefly before sailing to China as part of his medical recovery. Once home again, Bailey began his medical practice, and he also soon

accepted the duties of editor of the *Methodist Protestant* in Baltimore. This publication quickly failed, however, and the young doctor headed west. His arrival in Cincinnati in 1831 coincided with an outbreak of cholera during which he secured his reputation as a physician.

Bailey's career began to take a new course in 1834 when he witnessed the Lane Seminary debates on slavery. By 1836 he had firmly allied himself with James G. Birney, editor of the *Cincinnati Philanthropist*, the leading abolitionist journal of the West. In 1837 Bailey purchased the paper, becoming its owner-editor. His Methodist upbringing and the fact that Cincinnati was the center of Methodist publishing in the West may have molded his views; nevertheless, Cincinnati was also commercially linked with the South, and Bailey's energetic stance against slavery alienated many residents. Angry mobs twice destroyed his offices and were stopped on another occasion only by the efforts of police.

In 1847 the American and Foreign Anti-Slavery Society asked Bailey to serve as editor of the newly created *National Era*, a weekly based in Washington, D.C. The paper became a leading antislavery journal, presenting works by abolitionists such as John Greenleaf Whittier and Theodore Parker and was first to publish Harriet Beecher Stowe's *Uncle Tom's Cabin*. Although plagued by illness, Bailey edited the journal for 12 years. In 1853 he went to sea again because of his health, this time to Europe. He died in 1859 while on another recuperative voyage to Europe.

See also: Abolition Movement, James Birney, Slavery

Steven C. Kottsy

REFERENCES

Harrold, Stanley. 1986. *Gamaliel Bailey and Antislavery Union.* Kent, OH: Kent State U. Pr.

John M. Bailey (1905–1975)

Connecticut political leader and chairman of the Democratic National Committee in the 1960s. John Moran Bailey was chairman of the Connecticut Democratic Party from 1946 to 1975; owing in part to longevity, he became one of the most powerful state party bosses in the country. Starting as a Young Democrat, he became Democratic leader of Connecticut's largest city, Hartford. Picked by powerful Senator Brian McMahon as state party chairman, Bailey became the most powerful Democrat in the state after McMahon's death in 1952.

With statewide nominations usually made by conventions and elections influenced by the straight-party lever, Bailey was able to groom, handpick, and elect most Democratic candidates for governor and the Senate by slating carefully balanced tickets. Democratic governors elected with his help included such diverse politicians as Chester Bowles (a liberal), Abraham Ribicoff (a Jew), John Dempsey (an Irishman), and Ella Grasso (a female). Bailey maintained his power by forging alliances with city bosses and by granting and refusing patronage. Never an autocratic party boss, he was very willing to compromise in order to be victorious.

Bailey was also a legislative leader who was in constant attendance at legislative leadership meetings. Serving as a critical link between Democratic governors and Democrats in the legislature, he was very supportive of administration proposals, which even included Bowles's progressive policies. Senate Democrats especially became very cohesive in roll-call voting during major portions of his tenure. Bailey supported John F. Kennedy's vice presidential bid in 1956 by circulating a memo about the importance of the Catholic vote in the key industrial states. He was a key member of the Kennedy campaign team in 1960: the "regional man" who focused on New England and upstate New York and recruited hesitant big-city bosses. While retaining his state party chairmanship, Bailey also served as chairman of the Democratic National Committee (DNC) from 1961 to 1968. After playing a key role in the campaign of Lyndon Johnson in 1964, the DNC was nevertheless downgraded by Johnson in 1966. Bailey's death in 1975 is associated with a decline in the power of the state Democratic Party in Connecticut because of his reputation for effective personal leadership.

See also: Bosses, Democratic National Committee, Thomas Dodd, Elections of 1960 and 1964, Ella Grasso, Lyndon B. Johnson, John F. Kennedy

Stephen D. Shaffer

REFERENCES

Goldman, Ralph M. 1990. *The National Party Chairmen and Committees: Factionalism at the Top.* Armonk, NY: M. E. Sharpe.

Huckshorn, Robert. 1976. *Party Leadership in the States.* Amherst: U. of Massachusetts Pr.

Jeffries, John W. 1979. *Testing the Roosevelt Coalition: Connecticut Society and Politics in the Era of World War II.* Knoxville: U. of Tennessee Pr.

Lockard, Duane. 1959. *New England State Politics.* Chicago: Henry Regnery.

White, Theodore H. 1961. *The Making of the President 1960.* New York: New American Library.

Howard H. Baker, Jr. (1925–)

Republican leader of the United States Senate and White House Chief of Staff. Howard H. Baker, Jr., is a Republican from Tennessee who has been his party's floor leader in the Senate, a presidential hopeful, and Ronald Reagan's White House Chief of Staff. Baker's father, Howard Baker, Sr., was a member of the House of Representatives from 1951 until his death in 1964, and his father-in-law, Senator Everett McKinley Dirksen, was a longtime Republican leader from Illinois.

Baker lost a special election for a Senate seat in 1964 but won a full term two years later. With only three years' experience, he challenged incumbent whip Hugh Scott for the minority leadership following Dirksen's death in 1969. Baker was defeated, and Scott won a rematch for that position in 1971.

Baker shot into the national spotlight during the televised Watergate hearings in 1973. As the ranking Republican on the Senate Select Committee on Presidential Campaign Activities, he asked the now-famous question, "What did the President know, and when did he know it?"

Following Scott's retirement, Baker was elected Minority Leader in 1977 by a single vote. In that position, Baker worked to strengthen the Senate party while earning a reputation as a master of political compromises. He met with Republican committee leaders on a weekly basis and attempted to incorporate freshmen Republicans into the Senate party. He teamed with Majority Leader Robert Byrd to push ratification of the Panama Canal Treaty in 1978. Baker became Majority Leader when the Republicans took control of the Senate in 1981. He was able to deliver consistent Senate majorities for Ronald Reagan during the early years of his administration.

Baker had run for the Republican presidential nomination in 1980 without success. He opted not to run for reelection to the Senate in 1984 and instead formed an exploratory committee to consider the 1988 presidential race. He never declared an active candidacy, however, as he was tapped to replace Donald Regan as Reagan's chief of staff on February 27, 1987. By the time he left that post on July 1, 1988, most Washington insiders agreed that Baker had helped to restore credibility to the administration.

See also: Robert Byrd, Everett Dirksen, Minority Party Leadership in Congress, Ronald Reagan, Watergate

John A. Clark

Robert Gene (Bobby) Baker (1928–)

Political "fixer" for Lyndon Johnson. Born in Pickens, South Carolina, Robert Gene Baker became an energetic congressional page at age 15. He earned degrees from George Washington and American universities while he worked for the Senate Democratic leadership. He served Robert Kerr (D-Okla.) and Lyndon Johnson as Senate Majority Secretary from 1955 until 1963, when his career was ended by scandal.

Baker knew Senators and procedures so thoroughly that his head counts were legendary. President Lyndon Johnson described him as "my strong right arm," and Baker was thus nicknamed "Lyndon Junior." Liberals resented his control of the Democratic campaign chest, and after 1961, he seemed to serve Kerr more loyally than he served Mike Mansfield, the new Majority Leader.

Baker was forced to resign in 1963 when it became known that he was a millionaire despite his modest government salary. An associate alleged that Baker "conspired maliciously" against his business. The Senate Rules Committee found Baker had a million-dollar stake in a vending corporation, Serv-U, with clients in the aerospace industry overseen by Senator Kerr's committee. He had also dealt in insider stock trading and received fees for favors from lobbyists, which included "party girls," bank charters, and product licenses.

Barry Goldwater attacked Johnson on the Baker scandal in the 1964 presidential campaign, until Johnson denied that Baker had been his protégé. Baker survived two bitter, partisan investigations but was convicted and imprisoned in 1971 for tax evasion, theft, and conspiracy to defraud the government, having demanded campaign contributions and lobbying fees. On at least three occasions during the Johnson administration, the Senate failed to pass amendments that would have required financial disclosure by Senators and federal employees—legislation known as "Bobby Baker amendments."

See also: Election of 1964, Barry Goldwater, Lyndon B. Johnson, Majority Party Leadership in Congress

Jeremy R. T. Lewis

REFERENCES

Baker, Robert Gene, and Larry L. King. 1978. Wheeling and Dealing: Confessions of a Capitol Hill Operator. New York: Norton.

Kearns, Doris. 1977. Lyndon Johnson and the American Dream. New York: New American Library.

White, Theodore H. 1965. The Making of the President, 1964. New York: Atheneum.

Wicker, Tom. 1968. JFK and LBJ: The Influence of Personality upon Politics. New York: Penguin.

Baker v. Carr
369 U.S. 186 (1962)

This 1961 Supreme Court case centered around an apportionment struggle in the Tennessee State Legislature. The boundaries for districts that had been established by a statute in 1901 had never been amended to reflect Tennessee's changing demographics. This civil action had been brought to redress alleged deprivations of constitutional rights guaranteed by the equal protection clause. The Tennessee Federal District Court dismissed the case on procedural grounds, asserting that it lacked jurisdiction on the subject matter and that the interested voters failed to state a claim under which relief could be granted.

The Supreme Court, in an opinion by Justice William Brennan, reversed the decision of the district court. The Court decided that the appellants had standing to sue because they were able to allege facts showing that the Tennessee system disadvantaged their electoral influence. The Supreme Court also held that the case did not present a nonjusticiable "political question." The Court admitted that claims that depended on the Constitution's guarantee of a "republican form of government" for their constitutional link were incapable of resolution by the courts. However, contrary to the claim of the state and the decision of the court below, the Supreme Court asserted that the case neither rested upon nor implicated the guarantee clause.

The majority opinion contained a long analysis of the historical development of the doctrine of nonjusticiable "political questions" and reached the conclusion that the types of cases forbidden by this doctrine were essentially questions that related to the separation of powers. The Court said that it was the relationship between the judiciary and the coordinate branches of the federal government and not the judiciary's relationship to states that gave rise to political questions. The Court further distinguished political questions from political cases. Although Baker was undeniably a political case, the Court did not see any of the traditional characteristics of a political question. The Court did not make a decision on the merits of the case, but by asserting that the political question doctrine did not apply, appellants were able to bring the case back to the district court for a decision on the merits.

Baker occasioned many separate opinions: Justice William Douglas emphasized that he thought the basic issue was the extent to which a state could weigh one person's vote more heavily than another's; Justice Tom Clark wanted the Court to make a decision on the merits or at least give the district court more guidance for fashioning proper relief. Justice Felix Frankfurter, however, wrote a long and bitter dissent; he considered the case to be nonjusticiable under the political question doctrine, and he believed that *Baker* was essentially a guarantee clause claim "masquerading under a different label." Justice John Harlan also dissented, arguing that a state's choice to distribute electoral strength among geographic units rather than according to a census of population was not only a common practice but also a completely rational one.

Scott Cameron

Ballot Access

When asked to explain why the United States has a two-party rather than a multiparty system, scholars commonly refer to the single-member district electoral system, to the workings of the Electoral College, and to the fact that the United States is so heterogeneous that only large "catch-all" parties are capable of amassing sufficient votes to win elections. There is, however, another reason: getting a new party on the ballot is very difficult.

How a new party gets its name on the ballot varies from state to state. In 1971 the U.S. Supreme Court ruled that a state may require a separate petition for every candidate of a new party; further, states may require that each petition have a number of signatures equal to 5 percent of the number of voters registered when the previous election was held for the office in question (*Jenness v. Fortson*, 403 U.S. 432 [1971]). In practice, states more commonly require 1 percent of the previous gubernatorial or presidential vote for each candidate; the median state requirement works out to be 0.43 percent of all registered voters. Only Arkansas, Louisiana, and Michigan require no signatures whatsoever; the states requiring the highest percentage of registered voters in signatures are Oregon, Montana, and Wyoming. Although most states do not require as many signatures as they legally could, in 1989 a total of nearly 620,000 signatures was required to get a new party's presidential candidate on the ballot of all 50 states (Winger, 1989: p. 3–4).

In addition, a number of laws restrict how signatures may be gathered. A state may require that a certain portion of qualifying signatures be gathered in each congressional district of a state (*Libertarian Party of Virginia v. Davis*, 766 F. 2d 865 [1985]). States may prohibit those who voted in either of the major party primaries from signing a petition to get a new party on the ballot and may also impose restrictions on who may circulate petitions for signatures (for example, in Virginia no one may circulate a petition outside his or her own congressional district). (See *American Party of Texas v. White*, 415 U.S. 767 [1974] and *Storer v. Brown*, 415 U.S. 724 [1985].) In some states voters must furnish their registration numbers on such petitions; in others they must give their precinct numbers, although very few voters, of course, are prepared to provide such numbers when asked for them. In 15 states signers must declare that they will vote for the party whose petition they are signing or that they are members of that party. As well, 15 states stipulate when signatures must be gathered (and in 3 of these, new parties must qualify by January of the election year). (Lawson, 1987: p. 245–246.)

Once gathered, signatures must be validated; normally the new party must pay the cost of such validation. In Florida, new parties must collect more than 167,000 valid signatures and pay ten cents per signature for their validation. Knowing they must pay at least $16,700 in filing fees discourages many who would otherwise seek to form a new party.

Finally, states may require a new party to continue petitioning until it has polled 20 percent of the national vote for President or 20 percent of the votes cast in state government elections (*Jenness v. Fortson*, 403 U.S. 432 [1971]).

Such laws often keep minor parties off the ballot or compel them to concentrate their energies on a single office or require them to pay such high filing fees that it becomes impossible to meet the costs of effective campaigning. However, the major parties do not always take advantage of their own well-established access to the ballot. In 1988 only one major party candidate ran in one-sixth of all congressional districts and only one major candidate in three-eighths of the state legislative contests. The Republicans did not bother to field candidates for the ballot in 56 of the 435 districts; the Democrats defaulted in 19. Easier access to the ballot could conceivably give minor parties the opportunity to fill such gaps in competitiveness in the American political system.

See also: American Party of Texas v. White, Electoral College System, *Jenness v. Fortson*, Single Member Districts, *Storer v. Brown*

Kay Lawson

REFERENCES

Lawson, Kay. 1987. "How State Laws Undermine Parties." In A. James Reichley, ed. *Elections American Style*. Washington: Brookings.

Winger, Richard. 1989. "Number of Signatures to Qualify a New Party or Independent Presidential Candidate in 1988." *Ballot Access News*. February 27.

William B. Bankhead (1874–1940)

Southern champion of the New Deal in the United States House. As a U.S. Congressman from northern Alabama from 1916 to 1940, William Brockman Bankhead worked to maintain Democratic unity in his state and strongly supported the New Deal. In 1928 conservative Democrats in Alabama wanted the state party to join with five other southern states in bolting the national party because of its nomination of Alfred E. Smith, a Catholic and an anti-Prohibitionist, for President. With his popularity and influence, Bankhead defeated this movement and then worked to reunite the hostile factions of the state's party.

With the election of Franklin D. Roosevelt in 1932, Bankhead became a legislative champion of the New Deal. In 1934 he and his brother, Senator John Bankhead, Jr., coauthored the Cotton Control Act, which financially penalized cotton farmers who exceeded their assigned quotas. William Bankhead's importance, however, was not in drafting bills but in using his power in the House to help the administration's programs. As chairman of the Rules Committee in 1932, House Majority Leader in 1934, and Speaker of the House in 1936, he consistently facilitated the passage of New Deal legislation.

In 1940 many of his fellow Democrats urged Bankhead to run for President, but he refused to oppose Roosevelt. However, that year at the Democratic National Convention, he unsuccessfully challenged Roosevelt's man, Henry A. Wallace, for the vice presidential nomination. Shortly after this convention, Bankhead died at age 66.

See also: Election of 1928, Majority Party Leadership in Congress, New Deal, Franklin Roosevelt, Alfred E. Smith, Speaker of the House, Henry Wallace

Henry J. Walker, Jr.

REFERENCES

Heacock, Walter J. 1952. "William B. Bankhead: A Biography." Ph.D. dissertation. University of Wisconsin.

———. 1955. "William B. Bankhead and the New Deal." 21 *Journal of Southern History* 347.

Owens, Marie. 1949. *The Story of Alabama: A History of the State*. 5 vols. New York: Lewis Historical Publishing.

William Brockman Bankhead: Late a Representative from Alabama, Memorial Address Delivered in Congress. 1942. Washington: U.S. Government Printing Office.

Banking and Monetary Policy in the Nineteenth Century

Debates over banking and money have affected political parties from the beginning of the nation. Four controversies have been particularly important: the First Bank of the United States, the "Bank War" of the 1830s, and the agitation over the greenback and free-silver issues.

Treasury Secretary Alexander Hamilton proposed the First Bank of the United States to collect taxes, issue money, and lend funds. Hamilton thought it would promote strong national government and economic development, and he believed opposition equaled government subversion. Thomas Jefferson opposed the bank's creation, complaining that incorporation was not a right that the Constitution gave Congress. He also was suspicious of the bank directors' power, since only one-fifth would be government chosen. Thus, the issue helped define the division between the Federalists and the Jeffersonian Republicans. Jefferson's constitutional argument did not prevent the bank's establishment, but his opposition began a legacy of agrarian distrust of banks that persisted throughout the nineteenth century.

Before the bank's charter expired, President James Madison suggested renewal mainly because the bank was valuable. However, many in Congress still considered the bank unconstitutional and allowed it to close. As a result, public finance was disorganized during the War of 1812. Congress chartered the Second Bank of the United States in 1816, which the Supreme Court declared constitutional in 1819.

Agrarian dislike of the bank reemerged during Andrew Jackson's presidency. In 1829 he claimed the institution had not established sound or uniform currency, and he questioned its constitutionality. This began a "Bank War" that led to its demise.

The bank's president tried to deflect Jackson's attack through congressional support. In 1832 he requested the charter's immediate renewal, which Congress approved. Jackson's veto claimed that the bank fulfilled no necessary function, endangered democracy, and invaded states' rights.

The bank became the primary issue of the 1832 presidential campaign. To oppose Jackson, National Republicans nominated Henry Clay. Clay argued that the bank was useful, but antibank sentiment among agrarians and mechanics reelected Jackson, who withdrew federal deposits. The bank later closed.

Debates about money reemerged after 1865. Initially, argument concerned repayment of U.S. Government bonds for Civil War debts. Prior to 1861, the nation had been officially bimetallic but effectively on a gold standard. During the war, specie payments halted, and the Treasury issued nearly $500,000 of legal-tender notes (greenbacks) that had a value below the prewar ratio of dollars to gold. To repay bonds in currency would thus net investors less purchasing power than would gold. Republicans advocated repayment in gold, while Democrats favored greenbacks. In 1869 a Republican Congress approved repayment in coin and eventual resumption of specie payments.

After depression began in 1873, agrarian and labor groups favoring inflation formed the Greenback Party. Nominating presidential candidates from 1876 to 1884, the party peaked in 1878 when it won 14 congressional seats. Greenback sentiment also penetrated both Democrat and Republican parties, creating factions favoring inflation and postponement of specie resumption.

After 1876 inflationists also focused on silver. Passed without controversy, the Coinage Act of 1873 demonetized silver, establishing the gold standard to prevent rising silver supplies from flooding the Treasury and driving gold out of circulation. By 1877 many favored inflation through remonetizing silver and coining it at a ratio of 16 ounces of silver to 1 ounce of gold, although such a silver dollar would equal less than 90 cents in gold. In 1877 the Democratic House passed the free-silver Bland Bill. The Republican Senate approved the Allison Bill, which made silver dollars legal tender but limited coinage to $2 million to $4 million a month. The House accepted this measure, and in 1878, Congress overrode President Rutherford Hayes's veto. Because it limited coinage, the Bland-Allison Act did not threaten gold resumption.

A separate House measure would have repealed the Specie Resumption Act of 1875, which required resumption to begin in 1879. Congress ultimately approved a substitute that fixed greenback circulation at $346 million and returned to circulation greenbacks that had been redeemed in gold. This act repealed the part of the Resumption Act that contracted greenback circulation to $300 million for a greenbackers' promise to cease agitation on resumption. Gold convertibility began on schedule.

Prosperity returned in 1879, and silver agitation receded until agricultural prices collapsed in 1888. In 1890 farm and silver state representatives agreed to the McKinley Tariff in exchange for the Sherman Silver Purchase Act, which authorized the Treasury to purchase 4.5 million ounces of silver a month to be stored as bullion. To pay for silver, the Treasury issued silver certificates redeemable in gold or silver. Silver and agricultural prices continued to decline.

Agrarian discontent led to formation of the Populist Party in 1892: currency expansion and free silver were important Populist proposals. The party's presidential candidate, James Weaver, polled more than 1 million votes. Populist support came mainly from southern Democrats who could not accept their party's gold-standard nominee, Grover Cleveland, and from western Republicans who felt that their party had ignored economic distress.

During 1893, depression began. President Cleveland decided to save the gold standard and end depression by asking Congress to repeal the Sherman Silver Act's purchase clause. Ruthlessly using patronage, Cleveland forced Democrats to join Republicans in repeal. The repeal did not, however, end depression nor did it rescue the gold standard, since silver certificates and greenbacks previously issued still could be redeemed in gold. The Treasury maintained its gold reserve only by issuing new bonds, and Cleveland made permanent enemies among Democrats.

In 1896 the parties presented clear choices. The Republicans upheld the gold standard until international bimetallism could be established. Southern and western Democrats controlled their party's convention, declaring in favor of free silver and other Populist reforms. The Populists adopted a fusion ticket with the Democratic nominee, William Jennings Bryan. Bryan campaigned solely on the basis of free silver, while Republican William McKinley emphasized gold and protective tariffs.

Party realignment occurred as gold Democrats refused to support Bryan and silver Republicans abandoned McKinley. The South supported Bryan, the North supported McKinley, and the West was divided. Bryan's loss destroyed the Populist Party and the silver issue. McKinley's victory made the Republican Party the nation's majority for decades to come. Never again has money assumed such importance in partisan politics.

See also: Agrarianism as a Political Force, Bland-Allison Act, William Jennings Bryan, Henry Clay, Elections of 1832 and 1896, Federalist Party, First Bank of the United States, Greenbacks, Alexander Hamilton, Rutherford Hayes, Andrew Jackson, Thomas Jefferson, Jeffersonian Republicans, James Madison, New Deal, National Republicans, Populist Party, Franklin D. Roosevelt, Second Bank of the United States

Sue C. Patrick

REFERENCES

Cunningham, Noble E., Jr. 1957. *The Jeffersonian Republicans: The Formation of Party Organization, 1789–1801.* Chapel Hill: U. of North Carolina Pr.

Curtis, James C. 1976. *Andrew Jackson and the Search for Vindication.* Boston: Little, Brown.

Govan, Thomas P. 1959. *Nicholas Biddle: Nationalist and Public Banker, 1786–1844.* Chicago: U. of Chicago Pr.

Hammond, Bray. 1957. *Banks and Politics in America from the Revolution to the Civil War.* Princeton: Princeton U. Pr.

McFaul, John M. 1972. *The Politics of Jacksonian Finance.* Ithaca: Cornell U. Pr.

Nugent, Walter T.K. 1968. *Money and American Society, 1865–1880.* New York: Free Press.

Remini, Robert V. 1967. *Andrew Jackson and the Bank War.* New York: Norton.

Sharkey, Robert P. 1959. *Money, Class, and Party: An Economic Study of Civil War and Reconstruction.* Baltimore: Johns Hopkins U. Pr.

Unger, Irwin. 1964. *The Greenback Era: A Social and Political History of American Finance, 1865–1879.* Princeton: Princeton U. Pr.

Weinstein, Allen. 1970. *Prelude to Populism: Origins of the Silver Issue, 1867–1878.* New Haven: Yale U. Pr.

Nathaniel P. Banks (1816–1894)

Congressman and governor of Massachusetts in the mid-nineteenth century. Nathaniel Prentice Banks was a coalition builder in a period of party redefinition. Born in Waltham, Massachusetts, Banks was the oldest son of Nathaniel (a mill foreman) and Rebecca Banks. Primarily self-educated, he went to work in the mills as a child. A good speaker with a flair for the dramatic, he stumped for the Democrats and was rewarded with a customshouse appointment in 1843. The decline of the Massachusetts Whigs allowed him to win a seat in the legislature in 1849 after numerous defeats. Reelected through 1852, he was twice speaker. In 1853, he chaired the state constitutional convention.

Elected to Congress in 1853, he broke with the Democrats on the Kansas-Nebraska Act. Reelected as an American (Know-Nothing), he was chosen Speaker on the one hundred thirty-third ballot over strenuous southern objections. Having rejected a presidential nomination from the northern wing of the American Party in 1856, he was elected Republican governor of Massachusetts in 1857. Republican radicals detested him as an antislavery moderate and nativist, but in three terms as governor, he enacted significant educational and humanitarian reforms.

Appointed a major general for political reasons in 1861, the militarily inexperienced Banks proved predictably inept in battle. Stonewall Jackson defeated him in his famous Valley Campaign and again at Cedar Mountain, both in 1862. Banks's Red River Campaign in Louisiana (1864) was one of the most disastrous of the war. As commanding general in Louisiana (1862–1864), he put his political skills to work and built a white unionist party premised on making slavery's demise gradual enough to reassure whites. A dearth of white moderates doomed such efforts.

Banks returned to Congress in 1865, serving a working-class district. He was defeated once in 1872, when he ran as a Liberal Republican, but otherwise served until 1879. President Rutherford Hayes appointed him a U.S. marshall (1879–1888), and he served a final House term from 1889 to 1891. Banks died three years later, one of the most politically experienced men of his era.

See also: Kansas-Nebraska Act, Know-Nothings, Liberal Republicans, Speaker of the House

Phyllis F. Field

James Barbour (1775–1842)

Governor of Virginia and United States Senator in the Era of Good Feelings. A Jeffersonian Republican turned Whig, James Barbour was a political bellwether who led the conversion of many Jeffersonians to nationalist public policies. He later became a prominent National Republican and Whig.

Barbour was born in Orange County, Virginia. Educated mainly by a local minister, he became a lawyer and planter. Between 1798 and 1812, he intermittently was elected to the Virginia House of Delegates, the governorship of Virginia (1812–1815), and the U.S. Senate (1815–1824). During the John Quincy Adams administration (1825–1829), Barbour was appointed Secretary of War and later minister to England. After Andrew Jackson's election in 1828, Barbour joined the short-lived National Republican Party and later the Whig Party.

For Barbour, the British invasion of Virginia and nearby Washington, D.C., during the War of 1812 exposed the perils of the Jeffersonian belief in limited national government. As Senator and Secretary of War, he either authored or rallied support for such nationalizing measures as establishment of a new national bank, federal sponsorship of public works, and strengthened military services.

Barbour's nationalism led him naturally to oppose Andrew Jackson and his policies of decentralization. Barbour played a prominent role in the National Republican Party; he chaired its 1832 presidential convention and actively supported its candidate, Henry Clay. With the formation of the Whig Party, Barbour backed state and national Whigs and chaired that party's famous 1840 presidential convention when it nominated William Henry Harrison.

See also: Elections of 1832 and 1840, Jeffersonian Republicans, National Republicans

Elaine K. Swift

REFERENCES

Lowery, Charles D. 1984. *James Barbour, A Jeffersonian Republican.* University: U. of Alabama Pr.

Swift, Elaine K. 1989. "Reconstitutive Change in the United States Congress: The Transformation of the Senate, 1789–1841." Ph.D. dissertation, Harvard University.

Philip P. Barbour (1783–1841)

Speaker of the United States House of Representatives and Associate Justice of the U.S. Supreme Court. Philip Pendleton Barbour of Virginia served as Speaker of the U.S. House in the Seventeenth Congress (1821–1823) during one of Henry Clay's absences from the speakership. He was the only Speaker ever to be appointed to the U.S. Supreme Court.

Barbour was born at Frascati, a plantation near Gordonsville, Virginia. The son of a planter and an alumnus of the College of William and Mary, he began his career as a lawyer in Kentucky. When he returned to Virginia, he was elected to the Virginia House of Delegates in 1812. Two years later, Barbour was elected to the U.S. House to fill a vacancy and served as a Democratic-Republican from 1814 to 1825. He left the House for two years to serve as a state judge, only to return as a Jackson Democrat in 1827; he served until 1830 when President Andrew Jackson elevated him to the Supreme Court where he served until his death.

Barbour's only election as Speaker occurred in 1821 when he bested John W. Taylor of New York, who had presided over the previous House. Barbour entered the contest on the eighth ballot and quickly gained his majority on the twelfth ballot by a vote of 88 to 67.

Politically, Barbour was a slaveholder who opposed the philosophy of Henry Clay's "American System" and the Missouri Compromise. He seemed more suited to judicial life than to legislative life and enjoyed the Supreme Court far more than he did the House.

See also: Henry Clay, Andrew Jackson, Jacksonian Democracy, Missouri Compromise, Speaker of the House

Garrison Nelson

REFERENCES

Gatell, Frank Otto. 1969. "Philip Pendleton Barbour, 1789–1841." In Leon Friedman and Fred L. Israel, eds. *The Justices of the United States Supreme Court, 1789–1989: Their Lives and Major Opinions.* Vol. I. New York: Chelsea House.

Smith, William Henry. 1971. *Speakers of the House of Representatives of the United States.* New York: AMS Press.

Alben W. Barkley (1877–1956)

A longtime Democratic U.S. Senator from Kentucky (1927–1949), a Majority Leader of the Senate (1937–1947), and a successful Vice President under President Harry Truman (1949–1953).

Born in a log cabin in Lowes, Kentucky, to a tenant tobacco farmer, Alben William Barkley attended nearby Marvin College, Emory College, and the University of Virginia Law School. Admitted to the bar in 1901, he established practice in Paducah, Kentucky, and won election to several county posts, including a judgeship of the county court. Elected to the U.S. House of Representatives in 1912, Barkley, a loyal follower of Woodrow Wilson, served seven terms. Unsuccessful in the Kentucky gubernatorial primary in 1923, Barkley was subsequently elected to the U.S. Senate in 1926.

A strong supporter of Franklin D. Roosevelt's New Deal, Barkley won election to the Senate leadership with a nod from FDR and then snarled with the Senate in his attempt to "pack" the Supreme Court through the Judiciary Reorganization bill. Barkley, a supporter of the measure, defeated the more conservative Mississippian Byron "Pat" Harrison by a 38-to-37 vote, a narrow victory interpreted by some as a mild rebuff to Roosevelt. Loyal both to the White House and the Senate, Barkley surprised the President by resigning the leadership when, in 1944, Roosevelt insisted on vetoing a revenue bill against the advice of Barkley and other congressional leaders. Barkley was immediately reelected in Kentucky. Famed as an orator and raconteur, Barkley was keynote speaker at the Democratic National Convention, in 1932, 1936, and 1940. In that capacity in 1948, Barkley reportedly "set the place on fire" securing the vice presidential nod when President Truman outwardly turned the decision over to the delegates. Affectionately called the "Veeps," Barkley assisted the White House with congressional liaison but was thwarted because of the age issue (he was then 75) in a bid for the presidential nomination in 1952. He returned to serve in the Senate in 1954 and died in 1956.

See also: Election of 1952, Byron P. Harrison, New Deal, Franklin D. Roosevelt, Harry S Truman

Richard C. Burnweit

REFERENCES

Barkley, Alben W. 1954. *That Reminds Me.* Garden City, NY: Doubleday.

Davis, Polly. 1979. *Alben Barkley: Senate Majority Leader and Vice President.* New York: Garland.

Barnburners

A faction that made up the antislavery wing of the New York Democratic Party in the 1840s, the Barnburners bolted to help form the Free Soil Party. Their origins involved the complexities of New York politics as well as a growing desire to resist the territorial expansion of slavery.

The immediate cause of division in New York Democratic ranks centered on the anger of supporters of Martin Van Buren over President James K. Polk's patronage policies. When Polk ignored their claims in favor of those of their New York rivals, the followers of William L. Marcy, already existing factionalism intensified. The introduction by David Wilmot in 1846 of a proposal to ban slavery in any territories acquired from Mexico produced national ramifications in the feud. The Van Burenites, led in Congress by Preston King, now demanded that support of the Wilmot Proviso become the test of Democratic Party regularity.

By 1847 the bickering groups had received revealing nicknames. The Marcy faction was said to be more concerned with Polk's patronage than any issue of principle—that is, they "hunkered" after office. Hence, they were called the Hunkers. The Van Buren group, now willing to split the party and even secede to get its way, was compared to a Dutch farmer who supposedly burned down his barn to get rid of the rats inside. The Barnburners adopted the name with pride, identifying it with antislavery principle. On the other hand, some felt that the name referred to contemporary incendiarism practiced by the followers of Thomas Dorr in Rhode Island.

The clash climaxed in the fall of 1847 when, in separate meetings, each faction proclaimed itself to be the true Democrats and promised to seek sole recognition at the party's national convention the following spring. By early 1848 the Barnburners began considering a third-party movement with such leaders as Martin Van Buren and his son John, Preston King, and Samuel Tilden. When the Democratic convention nominated Lewis Cass, rejected the Wilmot Proviso, and voted to divide the New York delegation between the Hunkers and the Barnburners, the Van Burenites made their decision to secede. Motivated as much by a desire to regain control of the Democratic Party as by antislavery principle, they met in Utica, New York, in June and chose the elder Van Buren as their standard-bearer.

Later that summer, the new Free Soil Party was formed at a Buffalo convention, bringing together the Liberty Party, antislavery Democrats led by the Barnburners, and antislavery Whigs led by the Conscience Whig element from Massachusetts. At Barnburner insistence, the new party nominated Van Buren for President. The platform endorsed the Wilmot Proviso, and the party chose Charles Francis Adams as its vice presidential candidate. The Barnburners took a leading role in the campaign that followed but were disappointed not only by the national Free Soil vote but also by the Whig victory in New York.

Their point having been made, most Barnburners beat a hasty retreat back to the Democratic Party in 1849. To do so they were forced to abandon their demand that the party endorse the Wilmot Proviso, but regaining political position was a more persuasive lure. The independent Free Soil movement thus lost an important element as the Barnburners were content to be Democrats again. Most agreed to accept the Compromise of 1850, which rejected the Wilmot Proviso principle.

See also: Charles Francis Adams, Lewis Cass, Conscience Whigs, Free Soil Party, Hunkers, Liberty Party, James K. Polk, Secession, Martin Van Buren, Wilmot Proviso

Frederick J. Blue

REFERENCES

Blue, Frederick J. 1973. *The Free Soilers: Third Party Politics, 1848–54.* Urbana: U. of Illinois Pr.

Donovan, Herbert. 1925. *The Barnburners: A Study of the Internal Movements in the Political History of New York and of Resulting Changes in Political Affiliations.* New York: New York U. Pr.

Morrison, Chaplain W. 1967. *Democratic Politics and Sectionalism: The Wilmot Proviso Controversy.* Chapel Hill: U. of North Carolina Pr.

Rayback, Joseph G. 1970. *Free Soil: The Election of 1848.* Lexington: U. Pr. of Kentucky.

Wilson, Henry. 1872. *History of the Rise and Fall of the Slave Power in America.* Vol. I. Boston: Houghton Mifflin

William H. Barnum (1818–1889)

Connecticut politician and chairman of the Democratic National Committee. William Henry Barnum was a leader of the Connecticut Democratic Party who served as national party chairman from 1877 to 1889

Barnum was one of Connecticut's richest men, with vast interests in iron, manufacturing, and railroads. He served briefly in the state legislature (1851–1852) and attended Andrew Johnson's National Union ("arm-in-arm") convention in 1866, but he first achieved national notice the next year when he defeated showman P. T. Barnum (no relation) for a seat in Congress. After nine years in the House, he won election to complete an unexpired Senate term and served from 1876 to 1879.

A capable organizer and a mainstay of the northeastern Democrats, Barnum gave early support to Samuel J. Tilden and played a leading part in Tilden's presidential campaign in 1876. Barnum's election as national chairman in 1877 showed Tilden's lingering party power. In subsequent years, some considered Barnum a natural heir to Tilden strength for the presidency, but he preferred the behind-the-scenes managerial role. Republican opponents considered him a ruthless combatant who freely spent money—his own and others'—in his own successful races for Congress and in behalf of Democratic presidential nominees.

After Grover Cleveland's election in 1884, speculation placed Barnum in the Cabinet, but he received no appointment. Four years later, though still party chairman, he played a reduced role in the President's 1888 reelection bid. His tariff views did not square with Cleveland's call for substantial reduction of duties. Moreover, in the middle of the contest, he fell ill and never really recovered before his death the following spring.

See also: Grover Cleveland, Democratic National Committee, Election of 1876, Samuel J. Tilden

Charles W. Calhoun

REFERENCES

Katz, Irving. 1968. *August Belmont: A Political Biography.* New York: Columbia U. Pr.

McFarland, Gerald W. 1969. "The Breakdown of Deadlock: The Cleveland Democracy in Connecticut, 1884–1894." 31 *The Historian* 381.

Nevins, Allan. 1932. *Grover Cleveland: A Study in Courage.* New York: Dodd, Mead.

Marion S. Barry (1936–)

African-American political leader and mayor of Washington, D.C. Marion Barry began his political career as a leader of the Student Nonviolent Coordinating Committee (SNCC) and eventually became the second elected mayor of Washington, D.C. Barry was first elected as an activist, with broad support from labor, feminists, Washington's Black community, and gay and lesbian organizations. Under his administration, the city gave strong support to social welfare programs and other progressive causes. In the late 1980s, Barry became the center of controversy owing to his lavish spending on personal travel expenses and charges of corruption by his appointees.

Barry was born in Mississippi and grew up in Tennessee. A chemist, he dropped out of a doctoral program to work full time in the civil rights movement, becoming chairman of SNCC in 1960. By 1965 he was directing SNCC's Washington office; he founded the Free D.C. Movement and Youth Pride, a job-training program. He was elected to the D.C. Board of Education in 1971. When Washington, D.C., regained the right to elect its local government (Congress had removed it in 1874), Barry was elected to the first city council in 1974. He was first elected mayor in 1978 and then reelected in 1982 and 1986.

Barry has been credited with improving Washington's financial administration, with passage of strong gay rights and women's rights laws, and with a good record of service delivery. At the same time, he has been accused of filling city jobs with personal friends—some of them corrupt—and associating with drug dealers. His former wife, Mary Treadwell, was convicted of fraud in 1983, but he was not implicated. For several years Barry was able to convince many of Washington's Black voters that he was the victim of racist political harassment, but in 1990 federal agents videotaped and arrested him for using cocaine. Barry then entered a drug treatment program and announced that he would not seek reelection as mayor. After a Washington jury failed in 1990 to convict him of all save one minor offense, Barry resigned his membership in the Democratic Party and unsuccessfully sought election to the city council as an independent.

See also: Student Non-Violent Coordinating Committee

John C. Berg

REFERENCES

Elliot, Jeffrey M. 1986. "Marion S. Barry, Jr.; A Time to Act." In Jeffrey M. Elliot, ed. *Black Voices in American Politics.* New York: Harcourt Brace Jovanovich.

Nocera, Joseph. 1979. "Barry in Africa: How Washington's Mayor Got a Free Ride." 11 *Washington Monthly* No. 9, 12.

———. 1981. "The Nashville Sit-ins: Nonviolence Emerges." 9 *Southern Exposure* No. 1, 30.

Williams, Juan. 1986. "A Dream Deferred." 18 *Washington Monthly* No. 6–7, 24.

Birch E. Bayh, Jr. (1928–)

Liberal Democratic Indiana United States Senator. First elected in 1962 to the Senate as a 34-year-old lawyer and farmer from his home state of Indiana, Birch Evans Bayh, Jr., quickly established himself as an able politician capable of balancing hometown politics with national policymaking. At home, Bayh served for three terms as a stalwart liberal Democrat for a state with strong conservative tendencies and a competitive Republican Party. In Washington, the Senator took advantage of several opportunities to emerge as a key Democratic leader and spokesman for liberal and constitutional causes.

Birch Bayh's overall legislative record was not a particularly strong one. Impressive, however, was his quick success in his role as chairman of the Judiciary Committee's Constitutional Amendments Subcommittee. Bayh transformed what had been an inactive and unimportant committee into a fountainhead of legislative change during the late 1960s and early 1970s. Bayh was the chief author of the Twenty-fifth Amendment, modifying the presidential succession process, and he developed the Twenty-sixth Amendment, establishing the vote for 18 year olds. Bayh's work also included sponsoring the Equal Rights Amendment and an amendment to establish direct election of the President; however, both of these efforts failed.

Bayh's effort on the Judiciary Committee was not limited to his subcommittee assignment. In his second term, the Senator led the opposition to Richard Nixon's selection of Judge Clement Haynsworth for the Supreme Court. After successfully defeating Haynsworth's nomination, Bayh also led the successful fight against the follow-up Nixon nominee, Judge Harrold Carswell. Popular among his cohorts for his strong support for Democratic Party liberal policies and popular at home for his "folksy" manner, Bayh decided in 1971 to test his campaigning abilities on a run for the presidency. Bayh withdrew from the campaign early when his wife, Marvella, underwent cancer surgery late that same year.

After a close reelection campaign for the Senate in 1974, Bayh returned to the national scene in 1976 for a second run for the presidency. Entering late into what was already a crowded Democratic field, Bayh was unable to catch up to his rivals in fundraising or media exposure. Once again, he ended his campaign early, turning the focus of his attention to his Senate duties and his 1980 reelection campaign.

In 1980, a political action committee, a landslide presidential election, and his own liberal voting record combined to defeat Birch Bayh's bid to become Indiana's first four-term Senator. Bayh, along with five other Senate Democratic colleagues, came under criticism from a well-funded, highly critical campaign organized by the National Conservative Political Action Committee (NCPAC). NCPAC charged that Bayh's liberal voting record was a misrepresentation of what Indiana voters wanted, and it contributed thousands of dollars to a negative media campaign designed to defeat Bayh. In his other three campaigns Bayh never managed 52 percent of the vote, and against a young conservative Republican opponent, J. Danforth Quayle, he proved vulnerable. In a year when Ronald Reagan bested Jimmy Carter by a margin of 56 percent to 38 percent in Indiana, Dan Quayle defeated Birch Bayh 54 percent to 46 percent. Thus, Bayh's Senate career ended in much the same way that it began: 18 years earlier, as a young man and a member of a resurgent political party, Birch Bayh had defeated a popular Indiana Senator who was seeking his fourth term. Bayh's defeat contributed to the loss of Senate control by the Democrats in 1980 and spurred an investigation of independent political contributions of the sort used by NCPAC.

See also: Elections of 1972, 1976, and 1980; Equal Rights Amendment; National Conservative Political Action Committee; Twenty-sixth Amendment

Michael Heel

REFERENCES

Sorauf, Frank J. 1984. *What Price Pacs?* New York: Twentieth Century Fund.

John Beckley (1757–1807)

Behind-the-scenes operative in early American politics. John James Beckley was never elected to any office of significance, but his name appears often in the accounts of many of the most prominent political leaders of the early Republic. His importance rests with his efforts on behalf of the Democratic-Republican Party in its formative years.

Beckley was perhaps the first campaign manager to emerge under the new system established by the 1787 Constitution. He had established a reputation as a meticulous and reliable clerk of the Virginia House of Delegates and of its ratifying convention in 1788. Thus, it was no surprise when James Madison used his influence to obtain a similar position for Beckley with the newly forming U.S. House of Representatives.

He quickly became an unending source of inside information for the Republican faction. He despised all Federalists—especially Alexander Hamilton—and was always willing to pass on critical pieces of information from his many contacts to his Republican allies or to leak embarrassing accusations to newspapers and pamphleteers.

In 1796 Beckley determined that Pennsylvania would be the key to Republican success in the presidential election. He underwrote the printing of thousands of "tickets" with the names of the 15 Jeffersonian electors (voters had to be able to write the names of each elector) that he then distributed to his many friends in the state. Beckley urged them to get the tickets into the hands of all the right people. Part of his strategy was also to distribute these tickets in western parts of the state first, hoping to give the Federalists little time to respond. In addition to planting the usual newspaper essays about the evil Federalists and virtuous Republicans, he had hundreds of handbills distributed across

the state. The Republicans lost the national election but won 14 of Pennsylvania's 15 electors. Federalists were aghast at Beckley's grassroots electioneering, but Republicans hailed him as an organizational genius.

Not surprisingly, the Federalist House of Representatives turned him out of office in 1797. When Thomas Jefferson attained the presidency in 1801 he rewarded Beckley's devoted and effective partisanship. He was named clerk of the House and first head of the Library of Congress.

See also: Election of 1796, Federalist Party, Alexander Hamilton, Thomas Jefferson, Jeffersonian Republicans, James Madison

Glenn A. Phelps

REFERENCES

Cunningham, Noble E., Jr. 1956. "John Beckley: An Early American Party Manager." 13 *William and Mary Quarterly* 40.

Marsh, Philip M. 1948. "John Beckley, Mystery Man of the Early Jeffersonians." 72 *Pennsylvania Magazine of History and Biography* 54.

Henry Ward Beecher (1813–1887)

Prominent abolitionist. Henry Ward Beecher was a liberal Congregational minister and, from 1850 until his death, one of the most popular and influential public figures in America. Beecher was the first clergyman with a national following to speak out regularly on every major political and social issue of the day. Famous for his oratory, he gave over 100 speeches a year on the lyceum lecture circuit, and he preached to congregations at Plymouth Church (Brooklyn) that regularly numbered between 2,000 and 3,000. Beecher reached many more people through his columns in religious and secular periodicals. Millions heeded his pronouncements as he spoke out against slavery, advocated women's rights, endorsed the theory of evolution, and supported various political candidates. In 1856 Beecher worked for the Republican, John C. Frémont, and in 1860 threw his energies into the campaign for Abraham Lincoln. He continued to back Republican candidates until the presidential election of 1884, when he finally decided to come out in favor of the Democrat, Grover Cleveland. Beecher's attitude was ecumenical: he sought to unite Americans in love of God and country. He saw the cause of the North in the Civil War as a holy crusade to defend the principles of republican government, which in his view represented the highest stage in the evolution of civilization. Lincoln recognized Beecher's unique position as spokesman for American civil religion when he asked the minister to deliver the chief address when the Stars and Stripes were once again raised over Fort Sumter, South Carolina, on April 14, 1865, at the end of the Civil War.

See also: Elections of 1860 and 1884, John Frémont

David Hein

Martin Behrman (1864–1926)

Democratic political leader of New Orleans in the early twentieth century. Martin Behrman was born in New York City of German-Jewish parents and was less than a year old when the family moved to New Orleans. Shortly thereafter, his father died, and his mother opened a dry goods stand in the French Quarter. In school he learned to speak both French and German and helped his classmates, many of whom were recent immigrants attending public school. Orphaned at the age of 12, he got a job in a small department store as assistant cashier.

For the next dozen years he changed jobs several times: he was a grocery store clerk, a traveling salesman, and a member of the voluntary fire department. In 1887 he married Julia Collins, a Roman Catholic. It may have been at that time that he became a Roman Catholic.

As an articulate, intelligent young man, he became deputy assessor for Algiers (1888–1892), then assessor (1896–1904), and finally census taker in 1890 and 1900. He was also a member of the school board. By 1892 he was also "the recognized leader of the fifteenth ward," clerk of various city council committees, and a charter member of the Choctaw Club—the regular Democratic organization of New Orleans.

By 1904 significant change had taken place in the state's political machinery. The Constitutional Convention of 1898 had imposed voting restrictions on Blacks, thus establishing the supremacy of the Democratic Party in the state. The institution of the primary system in 1906 also controlled the franchise, since the party, at that time, determined who voted in the primary. In the primary, however, political factions fought it out, and the Choctaws (or Ring or Old Regulars) were the most powerful faction in the largest city in the state.

By 1904 Behrman was well known in New Orleans and was elected to the position of state auditor and eventually mayor. He was reelected three times—each election victory solidifying Choctaw control of the city's political machinery—but lost in 1920 when a reform ticket defeated him.

Behrman was too much of a professional to retire at this point. Whereas the Orleans Democratic Association tore itself apart in factional squabbles after its victory, the Choctaws survived their defeat almost intact. By 1924 Behrman had reestablished his power and was chosen to be permanent chairman of the Democratic State Convention. He had also regained enough prestige to be chosen by the Choctaws as their candidate for mayor, and he returned to office in a bitter partisan fight. Within a year, however, Behrman died.

Martin Behrman was undoubtedly proud to be considered a patronage-dispensing political boss, critical of amateur political reformers. Rarely accused of corruption himself, he winked at petty graft in New Orleans; as a result, the Home Rulers, the Good Government League, and the Orleans Democratic Association all opposed him at various times. Still, the long reign of Behrman in the city was accounted successful. He improved the city in many ways—economically and physically—even if he was highhanded on occasion. Behrman *was* New Orleans for over 25 years.

Richard L. Watson, Jr.

REFERENCES

Howard, Perry H. 1957. *Political Tendencies in Louisiana, 1812–1952.* Baton Rouge: Louisiana State U. Pr.

Kemp, John R., ed. 1977. *Martin Behrman of New Orleans: Memoirs of a City Boss.* Baton Rouge: Louisiana State U. Pr.

Reynolds, George M. 1957. *Machine Politics in New Orleans, 1897–1926.* New York: Columbia U. Pr.

Schott, Matthew J. 1983. "The New Orleans Machine and Progressivism." 24 *Louisiana History* 141.

Williams, Robert W., Jr. 1961. "Martin Behrman and New Orleans Civic Development, 1904–1920." 2 *Louisiana History* 373.

Williams, T. Harry. 1969. *Huey Long.* New York: Knopf.

John Bell (1797–1869)

Constitutional Union Party candidate for President in 1860. Speaker of the U.S. House in the Second Session of the Twenty-third Congress (1834–1835), John Bell of Tennessee was elected when Andrew Stevenson of Virginia retired from the House. Bell was a Whig in a Congress that was controlled by Democrats. He had the unique distinction of presiding over a House that his party did not control.

Bell was born near Nashville, Tennessee. The son of a farmer and a graduate of the University of Nashville, Bell passed the bar at age 19 and was elected to the state senate a year later in 1817. He left politics to establish his law practice but was induced to run for the U.S. House in 1826. He served in the House until 1841 when he left to serve as Secretary of War for President William Henry Harrison. He served in that capacity for six months until he and four others quit the Cabinet of President John Tyler, who had succeeded Harrison.

Bell's minority party speakership in 1834 was made possible when five Democrats split the vote among themselves. Bell got a majority on the tenth ballot by defeating James K. Polk, also of Tennessee, 114 to 78. In the next Congress, the Democrats regrouped around Polk to defeat Bell 132 to 84 on the first ballot. Bell had held prominent committee chairs prior to his speakership (e.g., Indian Affairs and Judiciary), but his leadership of the Whigs denied him of such positions later. He left the House in 1841 but returned to Washington as a U.S. Senator in 1847. Bell served in the Senate as a Whig from 1847 to 1859.

Bell's most notable political accomplishment probably came in the presidential contest of 1860 when he ran as the presidential candidate of the Constitutional Union Party. This party was formed by southern Whigs who tolerated slavery and did not wish to leave the Union. Senator Bell and Edward Everett of Massachusetts, his vice presidential candidate, finished fourth in the election. They received only 12.6 percent of the national vote, but they carried three states with 39 electoral votes. Owing to the peculiar character of this four-way race for the presidency, they were the major opposition to John Breckinridge of the secessionist southern Democrats in all 14 of the southern and Border States. Following the election, Bell retired from politics again, and during the Civil War, he spent his time out of political life.

See also: Constitutional Union Party, Election of 1860, William Henry Harrison, James K. Polk, Andrew Stevenson, John Tyler

Garrison Nelson

REFERENCES

Parks, Joseph H. 1950. *John Bell of Tennessee.* Baton Rouge: Louisiana State U. Pr.

Smith, William H. 1971. *Speakers of the House of Representatives of the United States.* New York: AMS Press.

August H. Belmont (1816–1890)

Powerful chairman of the Democratic National Committee from 1860 to 1872. Although never elected to public office, wealthy financier August Belmont wielded enormous behind-the-scenes influence in the mid-nineteenth-century Democratic Party. Son of a prosperous Jewish landowner from the Rhenish Palatinate, Belmont went to work for the Frankfurt branch of the House of Rothschild at the age of 14. He became the Rothschilds' American agent in 1837 when he established his own New York City investment firm.

In 1844 he became a naturalized United States citizen and a committed Democrat. Franklin Pierce rewarded Belmont with a diplomatic post in Holland for his generous financial contributions to the 1852 presidential campaign. Belmont backed Stephen A. Douglas for the presidency in 1860 and was chosen chairman of the Democratic National Committee. He held that post until 1872 and directed most of the party's national fundraising and propaganda operations.

After Douglas's death in June 1861, Belmont became titular head of the party during the Civil War. He supported the Union military effort, especially by discouraging European financiers from investing in Confederate bonds. Belmont played a major part in recruiting General George B. McClellan as the 1864 Democratic presidential candidate and largely directed the party's unsuccessful campaign.

After the war, Belmont favored reconciliation with the South and opposed inflationary fiscal policies popular among midwestern Democrats. He disapproved of the selections of Horatio Seymour in 1868 and Horace Greeley in 1872 as presidential candidates and resigned as party chair rather than campaign for the latter. Belmont's political power subsequently waned, and in 1876, 1880, and 1884 he failed to win the presidential nomination for his close friend, Senator Thomas F. Bayard of Delaware.

See also: Democratic National Committee, Stephen Douglas, Elections of 1860 and 1864, Titular Head of Party

John R. McKivigan

REFERENCES

Black, David. 1981. *The King of Fifth Avenue: The Fortunes of August Belmont.* New York: Dial Press.

Goldman, Ralph M. 1990. *The National Party Chairmen and Committees: Factionalism at the Top.* Armonk, NY: M. E. Sharpe.

Katz, Irving. 1968. *August Belmont: A Political Biography.* New York: Columbia U. Pr.

Silbey, Joel H. 1977. *A Respectable Minority: The Democratic Party in the Civil War Era, 1860–1868.* New York: Norton.

Judah P. Benjamin (1811–1884)

Prominent Jewish political leader in the pre–Civil War South and the Confederacy. Judah

Philip Benjamin was the first acknowledged Jew elected to the United States Senate, and his senatorial career, combined with his subsequent service as the Confederate Attorney General, Secretary of War, and Secretary of State, made Benjamin the most prominent and powerful Jew in nineteenth-century American politics.

Born on St. Croix in the British West Indies, Benjamin migrated with his family to Fayetteville, North Carolina, in 1813 and then on to Charleston, South Carolina, seven years later. After graduating from Yale University, he moved to New Orleans and was admitted to the Louisiana bar in 1832. A brilliant and influential attorney, Benjamin parlayed his marriage into an important Creole family and his association with John Slidell's political machine into increased political influence.

First elected to the state legislature as a Whig in 1842, he subsequently served as a delegate to the Louisiana Constitutional Convention from 1844 to 1845 and as a presidential elector for Zachary Taylor in 1848. The Louisiana legislature rewarded his service with election to the United States Senate in 1852, and he was reelected in 1858 after switching to the Democratic Party. During his senatorial career, Benjamin distinguished himself as a learned lawyer and an eloquent defender of southern interests.

With the South's secession, he became Jefferson Davis's Attorney General and later Secretary of War (1861) and Secretary of State (1862). Throughout the war, Benjamin functioned as the Confederate President's closest confidant and adviser and in so doing became the public target of much of the South's frustration and disillusionment at being unable to win independence from the North. Following the war, he escaped to Great Britain where he practiced international law very successfully until his death.

See also: Jefferson Davis, John Slidell

Joseph A. Fry

REFERENCES

Evans, Eli N. 1988. *Judah P. Benjamin: The Jewish Confederate.* New York: Free Press.

Meade, Robert Douthat. 1943. *Judah P. Benjamin: Confederate Statesman.* New York: Oxford U. Pr.

Thomas, Emory M. 1979. *The Confederate Nation, 1861–1865.* New York: Harper & Row.

Thomas Hart Benton (1782–1858)

Powerful United States Senator from Missouri from 1821 to 1850. Considered one of the premier political orators of his time, Thomas Hart Benton was a spokesman of the "New West" and an unabashed proponent of a number of controversial political causes. Born in North Carolina, young Benton moved with his family to Tennessee where he acquired the values of a western frontiersman. After earning his law degree and entering the Tennessee bar, Benton began his political career in 1811 as a one-term member of the Tennessee state legislature.

Following the War of 1812—a conflict he heartily supported—Benton relocated to the territory of Missouri, where he rose to prominence in the debate over restriction of slavery as a condition for Missouri's admission into the Union. Benton addressed the issue as a question of restrictiveness, rather than as a point of morality. With the Missouri Compromise in 1821 came the state's admission to the Union (as a slaveholding, and thereby nonrestrictive, state) and Benton's election to the U.S. Senate.

By 1828 Benton had become a staunch popular Democrat. His support of Andrew Jackson was unstinting, which served to reinforce his position in the West as an heir apparent to the presidency. He spoke passionately on support of the hard money policy (for which he was nicknamed "Old Bullion Benton"), the settlement of the Oregon Territory, and the relocation/removal of Indian tribes from western territories.

Mentioned as a vice presidential candidate on the ballot with Martin Van Buren in 1836, Benton chose to remain in the Senate. Hard economic times and a growing organized opposition from the newly formed Whig Party led to the defeat of Van Buren for reelection in 1840. While Thomas Hart Benton continued to be one of the most powerful and influential men in the Senate throughout the decade, he lost his bid for a sixth term in 1850. Elected to the House of Representatives almost immediately in 1852, he retired from politics in 1854 when his second bid for reelection to the Senate failed.

See also: Andrew Jackson, Missouri Compromise, Slavery, Martin Van Buren

Michael Heel

REFERENCES

Chambers, William Nisbet. 1956. *Old Bullion Benton, Senator from the New West.* Boston: Little, Brown.

Magoon, E.L. 1851. *Living Orators in America.* New York: Scribner's.

Ray, P. Orman. 1909. *The Repeal of the Missouri Compromise.* Cleveland: Arthur H. Clark.

Roosevelt, Theodore. 1887. *Thomas Hart Benton.* Boston: Houghton Mifflin.

Lloyd M. Bentsen (1921–)

Democratic United States Senator and candidate for Vice President in 1988. The senior Senator from Texas and longtime chairman of the Senate Finance Committee, Lloyd Millard Bentsen was first elected to the Senate in 1970 after a bitter Democratic primary in which he defeated the incumbent Ralph Yarborough. In the general election, Bentsen defeated a Houston Congressman, George Bush, by a 54 percent to 46 percent margin. He was elected to a fourth term in 1988.

Born in Mission, Texas, Bentsen attended the University of Texas School of Law, receiving a J.D. degree in 1942. After graduation, he enlisted in the Army where he served as a bomber pilot flying missions over Europe. He rose to the rank of major and was a B-24 squadron commander.

After World War II, Bentsen returned to the Rio Grande valley of Texas where he was elected Hidalgo County judge. Elected to the U.S. House of Representatives in 1948, he served three terms but chose not to seek reelection in 1954. He moved to Houston in 1955 to enter business. By 1970, when he decided to run for the Senate, he was president of Lincoln Consolidated, a financial holding company.

Bentsen has had a reputation of being among the most powerful and effective politicians in Washington. His voting record in Congress has tended to be moderately conservative. He has staunchly supported the oil industry, and he has tended to be hawkish on defense and national security issues. Bentsen, however, has been a consistent supporter of civil rights legislation to protect minorities, and he opposed President Ronald Reagan's nomination of Robert Bork to the U.S. Supreme Court in 1987.

Michael Dukakis, the Democratic nominee for President in 1988, tapped Bentsen as his vice presidential running mate. Dukakis's choice of Bentsen seemed to be an attempt to balance the ticket with another "Boston-Austin" axis that elected John F. Kennedy and Lyndon Johnson in 1960. Bentsen also took advantage of the "Johnson law" that was enacted by the Texas legislature to allow Johnson to run simultaneously for national office and reelection to his Senate seat in 1960. While Johnson won both races in 1960, Bentsen was successful only in his bid for reelection to the Senate. When asked why he was unable to swing Texas for the presidential ticket as Johnson did, Bentsen quipped that he just could not convince Texans that Dukakis was really Greek for "Bubba."

See also: George Bush, Michael Dukakis, Lyndon B. Johnson

Jon Bond

Victor L. Berger (1860–1929)

American Socialist Party leader. A politician, trade unionist, journalist, and longtime leader of the moderate ("constructivist") wing of the Socialist Party of America (SPA), Victor Louis Berger believed that Socialist cooperation would come to America through peaceful democratic means—not through revolution—and argued that Socialist theory ought to be responsive to American conditions and pragmatic political considerations.

Born in 1860 in Transylvania (now Romania), Berger was educated at universities in Vienna and Budapest. He emigrated to America in 1878, lived in Bridgeport, Connecticut, and later moved to Milwaukee, Wisconsin. At first he taught German in Milwaukee, but in 1892, he quit to devote his full energies to radical journalism and the Socialist movement.

No great theoretician, Berger was a follower of Eduard Bernstein's reformist brand of socialism, which stressed the efficacy of concrete political action within capitalist political systems. In the early twentieth century, Berger built the heavily ethnic city of Milwaukee into the greatest stronghold of Socialist Party politics. He contended that Socialists must work with existing trade unions. A defender of the conservative American Federation of Labor (AFL) against acrimonious attacks by other Socialists, Berger was the leading SPA foe of the syndicalist Industrial Workers of the World (IWW).

In 1910 Victor Berger became the first Socialist elected to Congress, taking as his mission the task of making the SPA respectable in the eyes of the nation. He publicly announced that he would support any effort from any quarter to alleviate bad industrial conditions for workers. He proposed an old-age pension bill (bitterly criticized as woefully inadequate by several Socialists) and legislation limiting working hours for women and children in Washington, D.C.

Berger's opposition to World War I undid his political career. As did a majority in the SPA, he asserted that the war was an imperialistic struggle. Indicted under the Espionage Act in February 1918 for remarks he made in a Milwaukee newspaper, Berger nonetheless was elected to Congress in the same year. Congress refused to seat him. A special election was then called for December 1919, and Berger, who by then had been convicted of sedition and sentenced to 20 years in prison, was once again elected and once again denied a congressional seat. In January 1921 the Supreme Court overturned the sentence, and he was released. In 1923 Berger was elected to Congress and seated, a position he held until 1928.

See also: Socialist Party of America

John Walsh

Albert J. Beveridge (1862–1927)

"Turncoat" Indiana Republican United States Senator. Although he served two terms in the U.S. Senate as a Republican from Indiana (1899–1911), Albert Jeremiah Beveridge is perhaps best remembered politically for his bolt from the GOP to the Progressive Party in 1912.

Born in Ohio, Beveridge moved with his family to Illinois in 1866. Following his 1885 graduation from DePauw University—where he had honed his considerable oratorical skills—he moved to Indianapolis, read law, and was admitted to the bar in 1887. Both his legal practice and his political ambitions grew during the 1890s, culminating with his election to the Senate by the Republican-controlled state legislature in 1899. He was reelected in 1905.

Beveridge came to the Senate a stalwart apologist for business America. Gradually, however, he moved toward the progressive Theodore Roosevelt wing of the Republican Party and away from the conservative majority of William Howard Taft. Defeated for reelection after the state legislature went Democratic in 1910, Beveridge cast his lot with the Roosevelt insurgents in 1912. When Taft won renomination at the Republican National Convention, Beveridge joined Roosevelt's Progressive ("Bull Moose") Party. He delivered the keynote address at the Progressive National Convention, served as the convention's permanent chairman, and accepted nomination as the Progressive candidate for governor in Indiana.

The GOP-Progressive split in 1912 resulted in Democratic victories that fall; Beveridge, like Roosevelt, finished second in his contest. Twice again he sought a Senate seat—as a Progressive in 1914 and as a Republican in 1922—but he was unable to revive his political career. His later years were spent with literary and historical projects, most notable of which were his biographies of John Marshall and Abraham Lincoln.

See also: Bull Moose Party, Progressive Party, Theodore Roosevelt, William Howard Taft

Robert G. Barrows

REFERENCES

Bowers, Claude G. 1932. *Beveridge and the Progressive Era.* Cambridge: Riverside Press.

Braeman, John. 1971. *Albert J. Beveridge: American Nationalist.* Chicago: U. of Chicago Pr.

Dunn, Jacob Piatt. 1919. *Indiana and Indianans.* Vol. 4, 1862–1863. Chicago: American Historical Society.

Seeds, Russel M. 1899. *History of the Republican Party of Indiana.* Indianapolis, IN: Indiana History Co.

Theodore G. Bilbo (1877–1947)

Race-baiting United States Senator from Mississippi. "The Man Bilbo," as he called himself, had many labels—"Prince of the Peckerwoods," "Bilbonic Plague." Always embroiled in controversy, Theodore Gilmore Bilbo basked in the limelight of Mississippi's politics for four decades and received national notoriety in the Senate in the 1940s. Bilbo epitomized the rank demagogue to many—particularly Blacks. To others—particularly less-affluent whites in the grip of rural poverty—he became an idol because he knew how to articulate their grievances and exploit their prejudices.

Bilbo knew disgrace and defeat as often as triumph, but he never fled a fight, often posing as martyr to find victory anew. The national press made Bilbo a whipping boy by 1944 because of his coarse racial slurs against Blacks in the Senate. In reaction, Mississippi's white Democratic voters gave Bilbo their greatest support in 1946, his last campaign. However, accusations against Bilbo of having accepted illegal favors from war contractors and of having intimidated Blacks at the polls led the Senate to delay Bilbo's seating in January 1947. He left Washington ill with cancer and died with the dispute unresolved.

From the Piney Woods of southern Mississippi, Bilbo came from obscurity to the state senate in 1908, and because of allegations of scandal in the legislature, he skyrocketed to statewide recognition. He served as lieutenant governor (1912–1916), and as governor (1916–1920). Although he logged a progressive record of gubernatorial accomplishments, voters turned down his try for Congress in 1918 and for governor in 1923. Winning a second term as governor four years later, Bilbo's fortunes ebbed by the end of his second administration in 1932. He bounced back and won all of his races for U.S. Senate, where his tenure began in 1935, and supported New Deal legislation with regularity.

On the stump in Mississippi, Bilbo combined biblical quotations with slang, hymn singing with off-color jokes, throughout his political career. As trademarks he sported a loud-checked suit, snap-brimmed hat, diamond horseshoe stickpin along with red necktie, socks, and suspenders. He preferred to drive Cadillacs, built a $75,000 home in the 1930s, and always admitted a weakness for women. A longtime advocate of Black migration to Africa, Bilbo's invectives against Blacks intensified during World War II and eclipsed any positive aspects of his controversial career.

See also: New Deal, Race and Racial Politics

Thomas N. Boschert

REFERENCES

Garson, Robert A. 1974. *The Democratic Party and the Politics of Sectionalism, 1941–1948.* Baton Rouge: Louisiana State U. Pr.

Green, A. Wigfall. 1963. *The Man Bilbo.* Baton Rouge: Louisiana State U. Pr.

Key, V.O., Jr. 1949. *Southern Politics in State and Nation.* New York: Knopf.

Morgan, Chester M. 1985. *Redneck Liberal.* Baton Rouge: Louisiana State U. Pr.

Percy, William A. 1941. *Lanterns on the Levee.* New York: Knopf.

Bipartisanship in Foreign Policy

Bitter partisanship has characterized most of the history of American foreign policy. Starting with the differences between the Federalists and the Jeffersonians, foreign policy disagreements between the administration and members of Congress have been a source of deep conflict. During World War II, active efforts on the part of the State Department and both parties in Congress led to a model period of bipartisan foreign policy.

Bipartisanship may be considered the active cooperation of the administration with both parties' leadership in Congress to seek agreement on the broad outlines of policy under the direction of the President, to compromise differences, and to conduct the country's affairs abroad with a united voice. Working primarily with the members of the Senate Committee on Foreign Policy to prevent differences from becoming the basis of strong partisan differences, the State Department maintains full communication with key Senators and, during presidential campaigns, with the leaders of both parties. The net result should be a firmer, better-conceived policy that Congress will support, especially with funds and troops if necessary.

During World War II both houses of Congress enacted resolutions calling for the participation of the United States in a postwar international peace-keeping organization. The Fulbright and Connally resolutions were enacted to prevent the faux pas of 1919–1920 that kept the United States out of the League of Nations. The model for bipartisan cooperation was hammered out during consideration of the United Nations Relief and Rehabilitation Administration when, after some Senators objected to participation through an executive agreement, Assistant Secretary Dean Acheson met with a Senate subcommittee headed by Senator Arthur Vandenberg (Mich.) to work out legislation requiring approval by both houses. A subcommittee of eight Senators met with Secretary Cordell Hull to support State Department planning for the Dumbarton Oaks Conference to organize the United Nations. To ensure bipartisan support, President Franklin Roosevelt appointed Senators Tom Connally (Tex.) and Vandenberg as delegates to help write the UN Charter at San Francisco. The Senate approved the Charter overwhelmingly.

President Harry Truman named Connally and Vandenberg as delegates to the UN, and they attended the Foreign Ministers Conference to write peace treaties. Vandenberg, as chairman (1947–1948) of the Foreign Relations Committee, won unanimous committee approval for aid to Greece and Turkey, the Marshall Plan of economic assistance to Europe, the Rio Treaty of mutual defense assistance, and the Vandenberg Resolution, which resulted in the North Atlantic Treaty Organization (NATO) and the Military Assistance Program. Republicans kept foreign policy out of the 1948 presidential campaign despite Truman's vicious attacks on the Republican-controlled Eightieth Congress.

Bipartisanship began its gradual decline in late 1949 because of Vandenberg's loss of the chairmanship, the fall of China, McCarthyism, the outbreak of the Korean War, and Dean Acheson's controversial decisions as Secretary of State. Still, bipartisanship generally characterized foreign policy until the mid-1960s when the Vietnam War destroyed the consensus. Recent Presidents have paid lip service to the concept but have neglected to build a working relationship with Congress. In June 1975 the Commission on the Organization of Government for the Conduct of Foreign Policy urged a return to the bipartisanship of 1947 and 1948 but with little appreciable results. President Ronald Reagan ignored cooperation with Congress and the Democrats; President George Bush promised to reestablish bipartisanship but has followed his promise with no serious efforts.

See also: Dean Acheson, George Bush, Federalist Party, Jeffersonian Republicans, League of Nations, McCarthyism, Ronald Reagan, Arthur Vandenberg, Franklin D. Roosevelt, United Nations

C. David Tompkins

Biracial Urban Coalitions

The powerful Black political assertions of the 1960s, expressed first through civil disorder and then through independent Black mayoral candidacies, polarized America's cities. They also forced Democratic Party organizations, which had included both Blacks and whites, to choose racial sides. They generally chose preservation of white hegemony. In Chicago, for example, Mayor Richard J. Daley came out strongly against the Black protest movement and against the redistribution of resources and attention to the Black community.

As urban Black populations increased and as Black links to party organizations eroded, the movement to elect Black mayors gathered strength. In Gary, Indiana, and Cleveland, Ohio (1967); Newark, New Jersey (1970); and Chicago, Illinois (1983), local Democratic Party organizations constituted the main obstacles to Black victories. Black Democrats running for mayor generally faced the opposition of the majority of white Democrats and of their party leaders. Black Democrats concentrated on mobilizing the Black community and searching for new allies not tied to the traditional party organizations.

Hispanics were open to biracial alliance in Chicago but less so in Los Angeles and were clearly opposed in Miami. Blacks and poor whites were even less likely to cohere. The most common alliance took place between Blacks and middle-class white reformers, themselves alienated from party machines and ideologically liberal on racial issues. Black mayoral candidates generally received unified Black support and the votes of well-educated, liberal whites, especially Jews.

Elements of the earlier civil rights coalition in the 1960s were thus applied to practical urban politics. This liberal alliance emerged even in cities without Black mayors. The belief that Black-liberal coalitions died with the civil rights movement has been challenged by the persistence of these alliances.

Once in power, liberal biracial regimes became vehicles for achieving some of the goals of racial equality. Black mayors especially have been active in affirmative action, in the redevelopment of declining downtown areas, and in the search for federal aid. Like the party machines before them, stable Black mayoral regimes have become vehicles for sustaining a city's political order.

The most fully biracial Black mayoral coalition formed in Los Angeles around Tom Bradley. In a city with a Black population of only 16 percent, a tightly knit network of Blacks and white liberals—principally Jews—won power in 1973 and held it without serious challenge until the late 1980s. While the Los Angeles coalition has expanded to accommodate Latinos, Asians, and business interests, the maintenance of amicable relations between Blacks and Jews has remained crucial to its survival. The Los Angeles case suggests the viability of a crossover model of racial politics, in which Black unity and white liberal support are complementary.

Liberal biracial coalitions, especially in Black mayor regimes, have represented an important electoral "solution" to the challenge of incorporating Blacks as full partners in the governance of cities—a role that traditional party organizations have seemed unwilling or unable to play.

See also: Tom Bradley, Civil Rights Legislation and Southern Politics

Raphael J. Sonenshein

REFERENCES

Browning, Rufus, Dale R. Marshall, and David Tabb. 1984. *Protest Is Not Enough: The Struggle of Blacks and Hispanics for Equality in Urban Politics.* Berkeley: U. of California Pr.

———, ———, and ———, eds. 1990. *Racial Politics in American Cities.* New York: Longman.

Erie, Steven P. 1980. "Two Faces of Ethnic Power: Comparing the Irish and Black Experiences." 13 *Polity* 261.

Kleppner, Paul. 1985. *Chicago Divided: The Making of a Black Mayor.* DeKalb: Northern Illinois U. Pr.

Murray, Richard, and Arnold Vedlitz. 1978. "Racial Voting Patterns in the South: An Analysis of Major Elections from 1960 to 1977 in Five Cities." 439 *Annals* 29.

Pettigrew, Thomas. 1971. "When a Black Candidate Runs for Mayor: Race and Voting Behavior." In Harlan Hahn, ed. *People and Politics in Urban Society.* Beverly Hills, CA: Sage.

Ransom, Bruce. 1987. "Black Independent Electoral Politics in Philadelphia: The Election of Mayor W. Wilson Goode." In Michael B. Preston, Lenneal J. Henderson, Jr., and Paul L. Puryear, eds. *The New Black Politics.* New York: Longman.

Sonenshein, Raphael J. 1989. "The Dynamics of Bira-cial Coalitions: Crossover Politics in Los Angeles." 42 *Western Political Quarterly* 333.

———. 1990. "Biracial Coalitions in Big Cities: Why They Succeed, Why They Fail." In Rufus Browning, Dale R. Marshall, and David Tabb, eds. *Racial Politics in American Cities*. New York: Longman.

Warren, Christopher L., John F. Stack, Jr., and John G. Corbett. 1986. "Minority Mobilization in an International City: Rivalry and Conflict in Miami." 19 *PS* 626.

James G. Birney (1792–1857)

Abolitionist politician in the 1830s and 1840s. An antislavery activist, politician, and lawyer, James Gillespie Birney was born in Kentucky, educated at Transylvania University and the College of New Jersey, and read law and began his public career in Alabama, where he was first elected to the state assembly in 1816. Although then not a full-fledged abolitionist, Birney pushed unsuccessfully for state laws allowing for gradual emancipation and a ban on interstate slave sales in Alabama.

In 1832 Birney became a member of the American Colonization Society, a group that sought to resettle slaves in Africa; he traveled throughout the South on the society's behalf, using Danville, Kentucky, as his new base. During the 1830s Birney was involved in numerous antislavery organizations, attended abolitionist meetings in New York and New England, and spoke and wrote prolifically on behalf of legal abolitionism. He was threatened for his views on several occasions but escaped injury each time.

After the 1837 American Anti-Slavery Society (AAS) meeting in New York, Birney soon emerged as an important AAS figure and an outspoken critic of the ultra-radicals, led by William Lloyd Garrison. A firm believer that the North was superior to the South, Birney advocated moral suasion and practical political solutions, within the bounds of constitutional law, to end American slavery. Birney received the newly formed Liberty Party's presidential nomination in 1840 and 1844, gaining 7,000 and 62,000 votes respectively in the two elections. He was also chosen as one of the vice presidents of the World Anti-Slavery Convention and attended its first London meeting in 1840.

A fall from a horse made Birney an invalid in 1845 and forced him to retire from public life.

See also: Abolition Movement, Election of 1844, Emancipation as a Political Issue, William Lloyd Garrison, Liberty Party, Slavery

John Walsh

Alice Stone Blackwell (1857–1950)

Suffragist leader. Alice Stone Blackwell, a feminist and humanitarian, was a vigorous journalistic champion of the cause of women's suffrage during the four decades leading to its fulfillment. The only child of the famous suffragist Lucy Stone, Alice absorbed the fervor of her mother's mission while growing up in suburban Boston, and she became known as the "daughter of the regiment." After graduating Phi Beta Kappa from Boston University in 1881, she carried for the next 35 years the main burden of editing the *Woman's Journal*, which her mother had founded in Boston in 1870 to promote the views of the American Woman Suffrage Association.

Blackwell had a knack for crisp, provocative prose, and she grounded her arguments for female enfranchisement in reformist realism. If women had the vote, she held, they could more forcefully assert their collective interest in improving the status and treatment of women of all classes and occupations. She played an important part in bringing about the 1890 merger of the Stone family's American Woman Suffrage Association with Susan B. Anthony's rival organization, the National Woman Suffrage Association; Blackwell served as secretary of the new National American Woman Suffrage Association for the next 20 years.

Meanwhile she devoted much energy to aiding Armenian refugees and publicizing the plight of other persecuted groups. Her reform commitments grew more expansive as she aged. Calling herself a Socialist radical, she remained a familiar figure at Boston protest rallies well into the 1930s, when failing eyesight forced her into retirement.

See also: Susan B. Anthony, National American Woman Suffrage Association, Elizabeth Cady Stanton, Lucy Stone, Woman Suffrage Movement

Geoffrey Blodgett

REFERENCES

Blodgett, Geoffrey. 1971. "Alice Stone Blackwell." In Edward T. James, ed. *Notable American Women*. Cambridge: Harvard U. Pr.

Hays, Elinor Rice. 1961. *Morning Star: A Biography of Lucy Stone, 1818–1893*. New York: Harcourt, Brace & World.

Merrill, Marlene Deahl. 1990. *Growing Up in Boston's Gilded Age: The Journal of Alice Stone Blackwell, 1872–1874*. New Haven: Yale U. Pr.

James G. Blaine (1830–1893)

Powerful Republican politician and candidate for President in 1888. James Gillespie Blaine was the most dynamic leader of the Republican Party in the era between Abraham Lincoln and Theodore Roosevelt in the late-nineteenth-century "Gilded Age." Although he never won the presidency and was his party's presidential candidate only once, Blaine played a major role in every presidential contest from 1876 to 1892. Moreover, he helped to shape American foreign policy by serving as Secretary of State in two administrations. Plagued by charges of political corruption, Blaine nonetheless had a tremendous appeal to millions of Republicans throughout the nation in an age when most politicians had only regional recognition and appeal.

Blaine was a native of western Pennsylvania and taught school in Kentucky before moving to Maine in 1854. His wife's relatives helped to establish him as editor and publisher of the *Kennebec Journal* in Augusta, the state capital. He became an early supporter of the Republican Party and from 1859 to 1881 was chairman of the Maine State Republican committee. In 1862 he entered into the U.S. House of Representatives and from 1868 to 1875 was Speaker of the House. From 1876 to 1881 he represented Maine in the U.S. Senate. In the early 1870s, Republicans split into two factions—Stalwarts and Halfbreeds—partly over policies of Ulysses S. Grant's administration and partly over personal rivalries among politicians. Blaine became the acknowledged leader of the Halfbreeds, the group chary of Grant and eager to shift the party from Reconstruction-related issues and toward economic matters such as the protectionist tariff. A bitter personal animosity between Blaine and Stalwart leader Roscoe Conkling defined the factional split and probably exaggerated its real significance.

In 1876 Blaine's first try for the presidency was overshadowed by revelation of the "Mulligan letters," detailing his financial relationship with a railroad for whom he had obtained favorable treatment. In 1880 Blaine was the leading Halfbreed candidate against General Ulysses S. Grant, who was seeking an unprecedented third term, but the national convention finally settled on a dark-horse candidate, James A. Garfield. The assassination of Garfield, Conkling's fall from power, and lack of enthusiasm for President Chester A. Arthur made Blaine's nomination in 1884 all but inevitable. It was his misfortune that the revolt of the "mugwumps"—independent-minded Republicans who regarded Blaine as corrupt—and the

"rum, romanism, and rebellion" remark on the eve of the election combined to bring about the first Democratic presidential victory since 1856. Blaine had not immediately disavowed a comment by one of his supporters that the Democrats were the party of the liquor interests, Catholic immigrants, and ex-Confederates. Yet so popular was Blaine among Republicans that his name dominated much of the 1888 convention, despite his repeated denials of availability, until his followers finally turned to Benjamin Harrison. The incumbent Harrison forced an unenthusiastic party to renominate him in 1892, but some even then looked hopefully to Blaine, who days before had suddenly resigned as Secretary of State.

Although denied the presidency, Blaine played a leading role in Garfield's brief administration. As Secretary of State, he advised the President on both diplomatic and domestic political matters. In his second period at the State Department (1889–1892), he had more time to begin to develop policies, especially commercial expansion and increased involvement in Latin America. A tall, dignified appearance and a brilliant oratorical ability gave Blaine an attractive political personality that his contemporaries called "magnetic." Although his political views and standards of ethical conduct largely reflected the tenor of the times, James G. Blaine was an important and constructive leader in an age not remembered for high statesmanship.

See also: Elections of 1876, 1880, 1884, 1888, and 1892; James A. Garfield; Ulysses S. Grant; Stalwarts (and Half-Breeds); Benjamin Harrison; Mugwumps; Theodore Roosevelt

John B. Weaver

REFERENCES

Blaine, James G. 1884. *Twenty Years of Congress: From Lincoln to Garfield.* Norwich, CT: Henry Bill Publishing.

Marcus, Robert D. 1971. *Grand Old Party: Political Structure in the Gilded Age, 1880–1896.* New York: Oxford U. Pr.

Morgan, M. Wayne. 1969. *From Hayes to McKinley: National Party Politics, 1877–1896.* Syracuse, NY: Syracuse U. Pr.

Muzzey, David S. 1934. *James G. Blaine: A Political Idol of Other Days.* New York: Dodd, Mead.

Bland-Allison Act

An important incident in 1878 in the evolving currency question in the last third of the nineteenth century. After the Civil War, the economy entered a decades-long deflationary spiral that debtors, many farmers, and others sought to reverse through the expansion of the currency. Opposing them, advocates of "sound money" clung to a gold standard and viewed inflation as immoral. Because these groups divided along class and sectional lines rather than partisan lines, national party leaders found the currency issue enormously vexing.

Inflationists first fought for the retention and expansion of greenbacks in circulation inconvertible with gold, but they lost that battle with the passage of the Resumption Act of 1875 and the beginning of Treasury gold payment for greenbacks in 1879. Alternatively, inflationists turned to silver and were joined by western mining interests in advocating its free coinage. The severe depression of the mid-1870s added urgency to the inflationists' argument for silver's remonetization.

In 1877 Missouri Democrat Richard Bland secured House passage of a free-coinage bill. Republican leaders who opposed free coinage but who were eager to quiet an issue that threatened to cause defections, especially from the party's western wing, followed Iowa Senator William Allison in amending the bill to limit the silver purchased for coinage each month. A bipartisan vote passed the act over President Rutherford B. Hayes's veto. Returning prosperity in the late 1870s blunted the currency issue for a time, but agricultural depression sparked it again until it reached a climax in the 1890s.

See also: Banking and Monetary Policy in the Nineteenth Century, Greenback Party, Rutherford Hayes
Charles W. Calhoun

REFERENCES

Nugent, Walter T.K. 1967. *The Money Question During Reconstruction.* New York: Norton.

———. 1968. *Money and American Society, 1865–1880.* New York: Free Press.

Unger, Irwin. 1964. *The Greenback Era: A Social and Political History of American Finance, 1865–1879.* Princeton: Princeton U. Pr.

Weinstein, Allen. 1970. *Prelude to Populism: Origins of the Silver Issue, 1867–1878.* New Haven: Yale U. Pr.

Blanket Primaries

An extreme variant of the open primary. As in open primaries, voters need not disclose their party affiliation. However, the blanket primary provides further freedom: the voter can choose among all candidates, regardless of party, for each office. Thus, an individual can select a Democratic candidate for one office and a Republican candidate for another. Two states, Alaska and Washington, use a pure blanket primary to select party nominees for state and local offices; Louisiana's unitary primary is in fact a unique case of the blanket primary.

The birth of the blanket primary can be traced to the state of Washington in the 1930s. With a closed primary system in place, the Washington State Grange undertook a campaign to replace the closed primary with the blanket system. Although the motivation underlying Grange support is not clear, Depression-era farmers, relying on governmental services and fearing reprisal for supporting the losing candidate or party, clearly placed a premium on partisan anonymity. A closed primary system makes it easy to trace the partisanship of the voter, so the blanket primary provided an appealing alternative.

In 1935 the Grange succeeded in guiding an initiative to establish the blanket primary through the Washington legislature. Regular party leaders opposed the new system and sought to abolish it by means of a referendum as well as by challenging it in the courts. The blanket primary system, however, withstood this opposition and is still in place today in Washington. Alaska's blanket primary, closely resembling Washington's, facilitates primary election participation of the large nonpartisan contingent of Alaska's voters.

The system established by Louisiana in 1978 is a blanket primary with two oddities: there are no party labels on the ballot, and any candidate receiving majority support in the primary is elected. The general election in Louisiana, then, serves as a runoff election between the top two candidates for each office for which no primary election candidate received majority support.

The blanket primary offers distinct opportunities to voters. Under its rules, an individual can, in essence, participate in the primary of more than one party. Party leaders, however, perceive this opportunity as a barrier to their organizational integrity. They argue that party control over nominations is reduced when partisans of the opposing party can readily affect nominations.

Party leaders also criticize the blanket primary—as they do open primaries—because they render party affiliation insignificant. The partisan anonymity afforded by blanket systems diminishes the instrumental value of party affiliation. Whereas the voter needs to disclose his partisanship in a closed primary, party affiliation has no bearing on participation in a blanket system. Party leaders contend that this process subverts party loyalty.

In general, the blanket primary offers tremendous freedom to the voter, freedom that is potentially at the expense of the political parties. It is precisely for this reason that the national parties have resisted the adoption of blanket primaries in presidential nomination races. Thus the controversy surrounding blanket primaries appears destined to remain active only for nominations for state and local offices.

See also: Closed Primary, Louisiana's Nonpartisan Primary, Open Primary

Barbara Trish

REFERENCES

Bone, Hugh A. 1961. "Washington State: Free Style Politics." In Frank H. Jonas, ed. *Western Politics*. Salt Lake City: U. of Utah Pr.

Sorauf, Frank J., and Paul Allen Beck. 1988. *Party Politics in America*. Boston: Scott, Foresman.

Ray C. Bliss (1907–1981)

Chairman of the Republican National Committee (RNC) in the 1960s. Ray C. Bliss was the chairman of the RNC from January 1965 to February 1969 and the national committeeman for Ohio from 1952 to 1980. As national chairman, he has been widely credited with rebuilding the party organization after its 1964 electoral disaster and with developing the organizational framework and strategy used by his successors to create a strong national party organization.

Senator Robert A. Taft recruited Bliss, an Akron insurance executive and Summit County chairman (1942–1964), to rebuild the Ohio GOP after the 1948 elections. As the chairman of the Republican State Central Committee of Ohio (1949–1965), Bliss was a paid, full-time, professional party executive who stressed organizational development, fundraising, professional headquarters staffing, candidate recruitment, and use of the latest techniques and technology in campaigning.

After his election as RNC chairman, Bliss sought to implement his Ohio system at the national level. As a paid, full-time chairman, he expanded a fledgling direct mail operation into a highly effective fundraising program while increasing revenues from solicitations of large contributors. He also initiated a series of RNC-sponsored training programs for 20,000 state party leaders, staff personnel, candidates, and volunteers. These training seminars dealt with political research, public relations, campaign management, fundraising, computer technology, and big-city operations.

Bliss was a shy and self-effacing person who considered himself an "office" or "nuts-and-bolts" chairman attending to the organizational dimensions of party activity. He believed that elected officials, not the national chairman, should serve as the party's spokespersons on policy issues. He did, however, recognize the importance of issue development and committed substantial national committee resources to the Republican Coordinating Committee, a policy development body composed of prominent party leaders.

Although credited with making a major contribution to Republican electoral successes in 1968, Bliss was forced out of the national chairmanship in February 1969 after President-elect Richard Nixon sought to restructure the RNC in a manner that would have undermined Bliss's status and independence. Bliss did, however, continue to serve as the national committeeman from Ohio until his retirement in 1980.

See also: Richard Nixon, Republican National Committee, Robert A. Taft

John F. Bibby

REFERENCES

Bibby, John F., and Robert J. Huckshorn. 1968. "Out-Party Strategy: Republican National Committee Rebuilding Politics, 1964–1966." In Bernard Cosman and Robert J. Huckshorn, eds. *Republican Politics: The 1964 Campaign and Its Aftermath for the Party*. New York: Praeger.

Broder, David S. 1981. "Bliss Remembered." *The Washington Post*. Aug. 12: A25.

Bloody Shirt

After the Civil War, Republican speakers and politicians attempted to stigmatize their Democratic opposition by reviving wartime antagonism. Hatched during Andrew Johnson's administration, the bloody shirt theme was first presented in its full glory during the 1868 presidential race featuring war hero Ulysses S. Grant versus Democrat Horatio Seymour; it proved so successful that it became a staple of Republican stump speeches and campaign rhetoric for decades, but it declined in effectiveness in the late 1880s. Republican spokesmen charged that disloyal white southerners and their northern Democratic allies were seeking to overturn the results of a bloody and hard-won Union victory. The South's rebellious and unrepentant spirit had not died; it had merely been subsumed by the untrustworthy Democrats, who, according to Republicans, had sought to destroy the Union. The victory at Appomattox, Virginia, had to be preserved at the polls by the election of representatives of the party that saved the nation—the Republican Party. Most prominent among these superpatriots were Senator Oliver P. Morton of Indiana, Representative James G. Blaine of Maine, and cartoonist Thomas Nast of *Harper's Weekly.*

If the tactic was cynical, it was nevertheless effective; its use reflected the northern electorate's willingness to support antisouthern policies, which was not always forthcoming from Republican policies to protect Black civil and political equality. In some ways it was a rejoinder in kind to Democratic efforts to play on white racism in order to gain support. Although the term "bloody shirt" is commonly associated with Republican campaign oratory, southern Democrats also kept wartime memories alive in their attacks on Republican candidates as representatives of continued Yankee oppression. Moreover, Republican charges were not without some foundation. The Democrats' success in regaining power and office in the South was made possible in part by violence and terrorism against both Blacks and white Republicans, a tactic that many observers took to be a revival of the spirit of the Confederacy.

See also: Election of 1868, Reconstruction

Brooks Donohue Simpson

REFERENCES

Buck, Paul H. 1938. *The Road to Reunion, 1865–1900.* Boston: Little, Brown.

DeSantis, Vincent P. 1959. *Republicans Face the Southern Question: The New Departure Years, 1877–1897.* Baltimore: Johns Hopkins U. Pr.

Hirshson, Stanley P. 1962. *Farewell to the Bloody Shirt: Northern Republicans and the Southern Negro, 1877–1893.* Bloomington: Indiana U. Pr.

Winton M. Blount (1921–)

Moderate Republican politician in the 1950s and 1960s. Shortly after World War II, Winton Malcolm Blount founded Blount Brothers, a construction and manufacturing company responsible for building projects ranging from the Louisiana Superdome to missile and rocket launch equipment. "Red," a nickname he acquired because of the flaming red hair of his youth, served as president and chairman of the board of Blount Brothers from 1948 to 1968.

Red Blount's involvement in Republican politics dates from 1952 when he left the Democratic Party to chair the Alabama Citizens for Eisenhower organization. In addition, Blount headed Volunteers for Nixon-Lodge in the South in 1960.

In 1969 President Richard Nixon appointed 47-year-old Blount to the post of U.S. Postmaster General. The appointment of Blount as the only southerner to President Nixon's Cabinet initially caused apprehension among the many Black postal workers in the North. However, in this capacity, Blount established a good record of advocacy for racial equality. Some observers have said that he played this role despite his own personal feelings toward Blacks. Yet before serving in the Nixon Cabinet, Blount took the initiative in the desegregation of the school system in his home town of Montgomery, Alabama, and he was among the first to condemn violent actions against Black "freedom fighters" who sought to desegregate Alabama's mass transit system in 1961.

In addition to racial reform, Blount restructured the U.S. Postal Department. He followed the principle of proposing business solutions for postal problems; under Blount's leadership, this politicized department was replaced in 1971 by the United States Postal Service, an independent federal agency.

In 1971 Red Blount resigned in order to challenge Alabama's incumbent Senator, John Sparkman. Unsuccessful in this race, Blount then returned to his business. In 1980 Blount returned to politics as the national chairman of John Connolly's short-lived presidential campaign.

See also: Dwight Eisenhower, Richard Nixon

Reagan Robbins

REFERENCES

Blount, Winton M. 1980. *The Blount Story: American Enterprise at Its Best.* New York: Newcowen Society in North America.

Bode v. National Democratic Party
452 F.2d 1302 (1971)

This challenge to the delegate apportionment formula for the 1972 Democratic National Convention failed to prove to the U. S. District Court of Appeals for the District of Columbia that a violation of the equal protection clause of the Fourteenth Amendment had occurred. The Democratic National Committee had decided to allocate 46 percent of 3,000 delegates on the basis of average Democratic voting strength in the last three presidential elections in each state. Remaining delegates were awarded to each state by multiplying each state's Electoral College vote by three. An additional 16 delegates were distributed among the territories.

In a series of decisions following *Baker v. Carr*, 369 U.S. 186 (1962), the court had applied the one-person, one-vote standard to representation in the state legislatures, in the United States House of Representatives, and in local government legislative bodies. This case represented an attempt to extend the doctrine to national party conventions. In *Bode*, the court did agree that the apportionment formula was subject to constitutional equal protection requirements. However, the particular formula of the Democrats did not violate the standard.

Party liberals, including Kenneth A. Bode, the director of the Center for Political Reform, argued that the apportionment should be based upon the principle of one Democrat, one vote as measured by past voting strength. The district court agreed, but the court of appeals found two problems with this approach. First, it argued that the constituency for the Democratic National Convention did not consist solely of Democrats; since all voters have a stake in the outcome of the nominating process of both parties, to a certain degree the national convention's constituency is the entire electorate. Second, it is impossible to identify current Democrats as a body to be represented, and it is questionable whether past voters constitute the current population to be represented.

The court's analysis of the formula focused on the portion based upon the Electoral College. Although it had rejected the federal analogy in cases involving state legislatures, it concluded that the analogy is permissible here because of the context. The Democrats were selecting delegates to a national convention—the purpose of which is to select candidates capable of carrying enough states to win the election—and thus stimulating efforts to enlarge the party's appeal beyond its Democratic base. Finally, the majority found no demonstration that the plan would dilute the vote of any qualified voter nor concentrate power in the convention in an unrepresentative manner.

The 16 votes awarded to the territories were "an appropriate recognition of the interest of the territorial citizens in who are to be the candidates for their President and Vice-President, notwithstanding they have no vote in the election" (p. 1310). Bode's appeal to the Supreme Court was denied certiorari (404 U.S. 1019, 1972), thereby allowing the appeals court decision to stand.

See also: Baker v. Carr, Democratic National Committee, Electoral College System, Presidential Nominating Politics

Douglas I. Hodgkin

Richard Bolling (1916–)

Influential Missouri Democratic member of the U.S. House of Representatives. A Democrat from the Fifth District of Missouri and a member of the House of Representatives from 1949 to 1983, Richard Bolling served 24 years on the Joint Economic Committee, was chairman of the House Select Committee on Committees (1973–1974), member (1955–1983) and chairman of the House Rules Committee (1979–1983), and a scholar of Congress. A protégé of Speaker Sam Rayburn, Bolling was an influential member of the Democratic Party's congressional leadership. His powerful intellect, Rayburn's early sponsorship, and his later formal positions of authority made him an influential power in the House.

A superb legislative strategist, he coordinated efforts to achieve major legislative initiatives during his tenure. Bolling was an expert parliamentarian and student of the rules and procedures of the House. His books—*House Out of Order* and *Power in the House*—analyze House party leadership and indict the old-style House for its decentralized committee fiefdoms chaired by members who often operated independent of party and party leaders. He was instrumental in designing and achieving the reforms of the 1970s, including the Budget Act and Democratic Caucus and House rules changes.

After Rayburn's death in November 1961, Bolling challenged Carl Albert (D-Okla.), the party whip, for Majority Leader. Reserved and somewhat aloof, and bearer of the onus of a lieutenant who had often performed unpleasant tasks for the Speaker, he withdrew after his extra-congressional strategy failed to win him enough support. In 1976 he lost a very close three-way race for Majority Leader against Philip Burton (Calif.) and the eventual winner, Jim Wright (Tex.).

The reform proposals developed by the 1973–1974 House Select Committee on Committees (the Bolling Committee) under his chairmanship were considered too extreme by many of his party colleagues. Subsequently modified by a Democratic Caucus task force, many of the reforms were nevertheless eventually adopted. After his retirement from the House, Bolling remained influential in House reform efforts.

See also: Carl B. Albert, Party Rules in Congress, Sam Rayburn, Jim Wright

Susan Webb Hammond

REFERENCES

Bolling, Richard. 1965. *House Out of Order.* New York: E. P. Dutton.

———. 1968, and 2d ed. 1974. *Power in the House.* New York: Capricorn.

Davidson, Roger H., and Walter J. Oleszek. 1976. "Adaptation and Consolidation: Structural Innovation in the U.S. House of Representatives." 1 *Legislative Studies Quarterly* 37.

———, and ———. 1977. *Congress Against Itself.* Bloomington: Indiana U. Pr.

Hardeman, D.B., and Donald C. Bacon. 1987. *Rayburn: A Biography.* Austin: Texas Monthly Press.

Peabody, Robert L. 1976. *Leadership in Congress: Stability, Succession, and Change.* Boston: Little, Brown.

Polsby, Nelson W. 1977. "Two Strategies of Influence: Choosing a Majority Leader, 1962." In Robert L. Peabody and Nelson W. Polsby, eds. *New Perspectives on the House of Representatives.* Chicago: Rand McNally.

Julian Bond (1940–)

African-American civil rights leader and Georgia politician. Julian Bond is one of the best known and most respected of the civil rights leaders who came to national attention in the 1960s. A graduate of Morehouse College, he is a founder of the Student Nonviolent Coordinating Committee. Elected to the Georgia House in 1965, he was refused his seat because of his antiwar activities (and probably his race). A U.S. Supreme Court decision seated him in 1967, and he eventually served there for 20 years.

Julian Bond was a leader of the successful challenge to the Georgia delegation at the Democratic National Convention in Chicago in 1968; he received national attention after he appeared on television (and received a vote for Vice President). Bond's young and handsome telegenic image made a lasting impression on many viewers. In 1972 Bond was a member of the Georgia delegation to the Democratic National Convention. In recent years, he has been much in demand for antiwar and civil rights speaking engagements.

The most damaging period in Julian Bond's political career was his bruising and ultimately unsuccessful 1986 Democratic primary battle with John Lewis for the congressional seat that was vacated when Wyche Fowler (D-Ga.) ran for the U.S. Senate. Although better financed and strongly supported by Atlanta's Black elite, Bond was defeated by Lewis, who had more grassroots support in the Democratic primary. Worse still for Bond, the campaign generated allegations of drug use that have lingered. While Bond continues to lecture as before, he clearly was hurt by the 1986 campaign.

See also: Civil Rights Legislation and Southern Politics, Race and Racial Politics, Student Non-Violent Coordinating Committee

David A. Bositis

REFERENCES

Bond, Julian. 1972. *A Time to Speak, A Time to Act.* New York: Simon & Schuster.

Neary, John. 1971. *Julian Bond: Black Rebel.* New York: William Morrow.

William E. Borah (1865–1940)

Liberal Republican U.S. Senator from Idaho from 1907 until his death. William Edgar Borah served as chairman of the Foreign Relations Committee from 1924 until 1933 and was a major voice in American foreign policy between the two world wars. He established himself in Idaho, earning stature as a lawyer. In 1896 Borah lost a race for Congress as a "silver" Republican after backing William Jennings Bryan on the free-silver issue. Failing in a bid for the Senate in 1902, he finally won a seat in 1906 as an avowed admirer of Theodore Roosevelt. A gifted orator, Borah achieved rapid prominence, and despite frequent disagreements with the Idaho Republican Party, he easily won reelection thereafter.

As a loner, an individualist, and a nineteenth-century Jeffersonian, Borah opposed both business monopoly and government bureaucracy. He claimed to base his principles on the Constitution and on the principles of the Founding Fathers, but he contradicted himself by supporting amendments for the direct election of Senators, the income tax, and prohibition while opposing women's suffrage and child labor amendments. Borah frequently accused the Republican Party of being too conservative; despite his backing of Republican nominees during "normalcy," he was quick to quarrel with them. He refused Calvin Coolidge's offer of a vice presidential nomination in 1924; in 1932 he maintained his silence. Borah favored many New Deal measures but not those that he feared would encourage monopoly or centralization. Borah sought the Republican presidential nomination in 1936, but his maverick record won him little support.

Borah's influence turned out to be greatest in foreign policy. In 1919 he directed the isolationists' attack against the League of Nations. Instead, he advocated a disarmament conference, initiating the Washington Conference of 1921. Opposed to U.S. participation in the World Court, he early supported recognition of the USSR and the legal abolition of war, which led to the Kellogg-Briand Pact. As a major isolationist critic of Roosevelt's foreign policy in the 1930s, he was unable to prevent revision of the Neutrality Act on the eve of World War II. By the time of his death, his influence had waned.

See also: William Jennings Bryan; Calvin Coolidge; Elections of 1924, 1932, and 1936; Isolationism in American Politics; League of Nations; New Deal; Prohibition; Theodore Roosevelt; Suffrage

Eugene S. Larson

REFERENCES

Ashby, LeRoy. 1972. *The Spearless Leader.* Urbana: U. of Illinois Pr.

McKenna, Marian C. 1961. *Borah.* Ann Arbor: U. of Michigan Pr.

Maddox, Robert J. 1969. *William E. Borah and American Foreign Policy.* Baton Rouge: Louisiana State U. Pr.

David L. Boren (1941–)

Oklahoma U.S. Senator and advocate of campaign finance reform. Senator David L. Boren emerged in the mid-1980s as a leading proponent of campaign finance reform. The former Rhodes scholar won his state's governorship in 1974 after a campaign stressing reform of welfare and campaign spending. Elected to a vacant Senate seat in 1978 at age 37, David L. Boren won seats on the Agriculture and Finance committees, where he proved to be a staunch supporter of the oil industry and of farmers. Among the strongest Democratic backers of President Ronald Reagan, he was a leading sponsor of the balanced budget amendment that passed the Senate in 1982. In 1987 Boren became chairman of the Senate Intelligence Committee.

Refusing to accept contributions from political action committees (PACs) for his own campaign, Boren emerged as the Senate Democrats' leader in election campaign finance reform efforts when he sponsored a series of bills in 1985, 1987, and 1990. Each was different, as Boren sought to find a formula that would please his fellow Democrats, pick up sufficient Republican support in the Senate, meet House objections, and avoid a presidential veto. The bills included provisions for campaign contribution limits by PACs, free media coverage to candidates attacked by groups that used "independent expenditures," overall campaign spending limits, public funding for candidates agreeing to those limits and for candidates attacked by independent expen-

ditures, disclosure of "soft" money spending, matching funds, and higher limits on individual contributions. The 1985 bill was shelved; the 1987 version died when attempts to invoke cloture against the GOP filibuster failed a record-setting seven times; and in 1988, a scaled-down version again fell victim to a filibuster. Finally, on August 1, 1990, amid the savings-and-loan crisis and a series of scandals involving congressional ethics, and after accepting an outright ban on PAC contributions advocated by Republicans, S-137 passed by a near part-line vote of 59 to 40. A very different House bill also passed at the same time, but inter-chamber negotiations never succeeded in producing the needed compromise.

See also: Robert Byrd, Campaign Finance and the Constitution, Political Action Committees, Ronald Reagan, Soft Money in Presidential Campaigns

John R. Johannes

REFERENCES

Hook, Janet. 1988. "Stalemated Senate Shelves Campaign Measure." 46 *Congressional Quarterly Weekly Report* 485.

Bosses

The preeminent leaders of traditional party organizations or political machines—organizations that relied upon the distribution of patronage as a reward to party workers. When such an organization controlled a majority of offices within a political jurisdiction, its boss would be in a position to exercise substantial influence over the government of that jurisdiction.

The label "boss" was often employed as a pejorative; nonetheless, the term points to an underlying reality. In traditional party organizations, the leader's discretion in distributing patronage was largely unconstrained by formal rules or procedures. The boss allocated benefits in accord with his judgment regarding the loyalty of subordinate politicians to his leadership, the contribution of individual party workers to the organization, or the personal need of supplicants. This exercise enabled the leaders of many patronage-oriented party organizations to centralize power in their own hands. One indication that personalized leadership was characteristic of traditional party organizations was the general practice of referring to these groups by the name of their preeminent leader or leadership team (e.g., the "Pendergast machine" or the "Gorman-Rasin organization").

The leaders of political machines within urban neighborhoods were known as "ward bosses," and in some cities, no higher authority was able to assert control over these local leaders. For example, the most powerful politicians in Boston at the turn of the century were such Democratic ward bosses as Martin Lomasney and John F. Fitzgerald. In other cities, a single boss sometimes managed to establish his hegemony over local machine politicians. In the late nineteenth and early twentieth centuries, some political bosses also established their dominance at the state level.

The heyday of urban political bosses extended roughly from the 1870s through the 1940s. Brown and Halaby (*Journal of Interdisciplinary History*, 1987) found evidence of organized machine politics in 22 of the 30 largest American cities at some point during the years between 1870 and 1945. In 17 of these cities, the machine achieved relatively stable dominance, controlling the executive and a majority of the local legislature for at least three consecutive elections. Machines most commonly achieved such citywide dominance in the 1920s and 1930s. The urban bosses of this period included Edward Crump in Memphis, Tennessee; Frank Hague in Jersey City, New Jersey; Charles Murphy in New York City; Daniel O'Connell in Albany, New York; Thomas Pendergast in Kansas City, Missouri; and William Vare in Philadelphia.

On the state level, dominant machines and their political bosses emerged in the 1870s, reached their peak of influence in 1900, and largely disappeared by 1912. The most powerful state party bosses of this era were Simon Cameron, Matthew Quay, and Boies Penrose in Pennsylvania; Thomas C. Platt in New York; Charles R. Brayton in Rhode Island; Arthur Pue Gorman in Maryland; Stephen B. Elkins in West Virginia; Thomas Martin in Virginia; and Alexander McKenzie in North Dakota. After World War I, the only state party bosses to achieve such dominance were Harry F. Byrd, Sr. in Virginia and J. Henry Roraback and John M. Bailey in Connecticut.

At the turn of the century, most state party bosses were U.S. Senators. The practice of senatorial courtesy gave members of the upper chamber influence over the distribution of federal patronage in their states, and the dependence of Senators upon state legislatures for their election and reelection provided them with an incentive to assert control over state party organizations. Urban bosses, by contrast, characteristically did not occupy public office. Over the course of the twentieth century, however, the formal authority and resources controlled by mayors increased, enabling a number of occupants of that office to take control of the party organizations in their cities. Politicians who simultaneously served as mayors and political bosses included Anton Cermak, Edward Kelly, and Richard Daley of Chicago; David Lawrence of Pittsburgh; and during his last years in office (1977–1983), Erastus Corning II of Albany, New York.

Many urban bosses were Irish-Americans, and often the subordinate politicians and voters who supported them were first- or second-generation immigrants, leading some scholars to locate the source of machine politics and boss rule in an Irish cultural tradition of respect for hierarchy or in a private-regarding political ethos of immigrant groups. However, on the state level, old-stock Protestants predominated among the bosses, politicians, and voters who supported political machines; even on the municipal level, they predominated among the machine's leaders and supporters in a sufficient number of cities (e.g., Philadelphia, Cincinnati, Kansas City) to raise questions about this line of analysis.

The geographic distribution of patronage-oriented party organizations suggests that the sources of machine politics and its associated style of leadership are more probably to be found in patterns of political development than in ethnic cultures. As David Mayhew has observed, powerful political machines and bosses emerged almost exclusively in cities and states that had been settled by the eve of the Jacksonian era. Political parties in these cities and states participated in the extensive popular mobilization and organization that characterized the second and third American party systems. In many of these jurisdictions, patronage-oriented party organizations managed to establish a base for themselves during the nineteenth century—one that was sufficiently strong to withstand the assaults to which they were subject during and after the Progressive era. By the 1980s, however, traditional machine politicians had largely succumbed to the innovations in communications technologies and to changes in political and governmental organization that in recent decades have transformed the conduct of electoral politics and the character of political leadership in the United States.

See also: Individual Party Leaders, Jacksonian Democracy, Progressive Party, Tammany Hall

Martin Shefter

REFERENCES

Banfield, Edward, and James Q. Wilson. 1963. *City Politics*. Cambridge: Harvard U. Pr.

Bridges, Amy. 1984. *A City in the Republic: Antebellum New York and the Origins of Machine Politics*. Cambridge, UK: Cambridge U. Pr.

Brown, M. Craig, and Charles N. Halaby. 1987. "Machine Politics in America, 1870–1945." 17 *Journal of Interdisciplinary History* 587.

Erie, Steven. 1988. *Rainbow's End: Irish-Americans and the Dilemmas of Urban Machine Politics, 1840–1985*. Berkeley: U. of California Pr.

Mayhew, David. 1986. *Placing Parties in American Politics*. Princeton: Princeton U. Pr.

Shefter, Martin. 1983. "Regional Receptivity to Reform." 98 *Political Science Quarterly* 459.

Wilson, James Q. 1973. *Political Organizations*. New York: Basic Books.

Zink, Harold. 1930. *City Bosses in the United States*. Durham, NC: Duke U. Pr.

John Minor Botts (1802–1869)

Pro-Unionist politician of the pre–Civil War era. John Minor Botts was less a Whig, a Know-Nothing, and a Constitutional Unionist during his long political career than an anti-Democrat. The Democrats, he believed, were power-hungry sycophants of John C. Calhoun who continually agitated the slavery question in order to maintain their place in American politics. He was determined to defeat them.

Botts served in Congress from 1839 to 1843 and from 1847 to 1849. His positions were Unionist: he opposed the abolition of slavery and the annexation of Texas, which he saw as the "first entering wedge of disunion." He supported the Compromise of 1850 as the final solution to the slavery problem and, in the 1852 Whig Convention, cast the sole southern vote for Winfield Scott's nomination for President because of Scott's support for the Compromise.

The breakup of the Whig Party disgusted Botts, who called those who left "rats in a sinking ship." He joined the Know-Nothing Party, where he continued to attack the Democrats and even accused them of secretly supporting John Brown's raid on Harper's Ferry. In 1859 Anna Ella Carroll, a leading Know-Nothing writer, promoted Botts as a fusion candidate for the Republicans and Know-Nothings. Botts, however, would not compromise over the Republican plank calling for no extention of slavery

in the territories. He preferred a form of popular sovereignty.

Botts's name came before the Constitutional Union Party's nominating convention in May 1860 for Vice President with Judge John McLean leading the ticket, but they lost the nomination to John Bell and Edward Everett. When the Civil War loomed, Botts maintained his Border State Unionism: he fought against Virginia's secession until it was fact and then proposed a constitutional amendment that would allow the southern states to withdraw, arguing that such an amendment would keep the Border States with the Union. During Reconstruction, he supported the conservatives in Virginia but called for the disfranchisement of anyone who had supported secession in any form. When the radicals took power, Botts shifted his allegiance to them—an act that marked his political suicide.

See also: Abolition Movement, Constitutional Union Party, Know-Nothings, Reconstruction, Slavery

Janet L. Coryell

REFERENCES

Botts, John Minor. 1866. *The Great Rebellion: Its Secret History, Rise, Progress, and Disastrous Failure*. New York: Harper.

Greeley, Horace, and John F. Cleveland. 1860. *A Political Textbook for 1860*. New York: Tribune Association.

Webster, Clyde C. 1915. "John Minor Botts, Anti-Secessionist." 1 *Richmond College Historical Papers* 9.

Chester Bowles (1901–1985)

Connecticut Democratic politician and influential foreign affairs expert. Chester Bowles, advertising executive, public administrator, U.S. diplomat, governor, Congressman, ambassador, and author, was born into a prominent Republican publishing family but served four Democratic Presidents (Franklin D. Roosevelt, Harry S Truman, John F. Kennedy, and Lyndon Johnson). Best known in Connecticut as the state's most liberal and progressive chief executive (1949–1951), Bowles's greatest and most satisfying contributions were in foreign affairs during his second diplomatic post as ambassador to India (1963–1969)—his last public assignment before Parkinson's disease forced him to retire.

After graduating from Yale in the early 1920s, he entered advertising, created his own agency, Benton and Bowles, in New York City, and retired from private enterprise a millionaire at the age of 40. His second career as a public official lasted 28 years during which he was a consistent advocate for traditional liberal values that challenged the political status quo and set goals for broader distribution of social, political, and economic justice.

Bowles's public career was filled with so much controversy and political conflict that he was compelled to resign from Truman's Office of Economic Stabilization (1946), was denied his party's nomination in his first quest for governor of Connecticut (1946), was limited to only two years as Connecticut's seventy-sixth governor, was blocked as Secretary of State in the Kennedy administration, and was unacceptable to party leaders as a nominee for U.S. President.

Symbolic of his refusal to accept partisan and governmental institutions as givens was his antagonistic relationship with state and national Democratic chairman John M. Bailey. Nevertheless, Bowles's 1948 gubernatorial campaign platform, which called for abolition of the sales tax, creation of a state income tax, comprehensive reorganization of state governmental structure, construction of 65,000 low-income housing units, and direct primaries for election of state and local officials, represented the zenith of progressive liberal thinking in a state best known for its steady habits and political conservatism. At the national and international levels, he is remembered best for his service as a creative and compassionate foreign policy planner and administrator.

See also: Lyndon Johnson, John F. Kennedy, Franklin D. Roosevelt, Harry S Truman

Clyde D. McKee, Jr.

REFERENCES

Lieberman, Joseph I. 1966. *The Power Broker.* Boston: Houghton Mifflin.

Linn Boyd (1800–1859)

Kentucky politician instrumental in the Compromise of 1850. A pro-southern Jacksonian Congressman from Kentucky and a two-term House Speaker, Linn Boyd was a nationalist during the sectional conflict and a participant in many important antebellum congressional actions.

The son of poor parents, Boyd was born in Nashville, Tennessee. After prep school, he moved to Kentucky and later farmed in Calloway County. He served in the Kentucky General Assembly (1827–1832) and first came to Congress in 1835 as a Jacksonian Unionist, losing his reelection bid when the Whigs coalesced around fellow Kentuckian Henry Clay. Boyd returned to Congress in 1839 and was Speaker from 1851 to 1855.

Boyd worked closely with Speaker Howell Cobb, Illinois Senator Stephen Douglas, and other congressional leaders to pass the Compromise of 1850. As chairman of the House Committee on Territories and the Committee of the Whole, he helped to break the deadlock over the omnibus by pushing through the bill that tied together New Mexico's territorial status with the Texas boundary and debt. Boyd, a Unionist, was one of the few southern or Border State Congressmen who did not sign the inflammatory "Southern Address," which attacked the Compromise. A rumored dark horse at the 1852 Democratic National Convention that nominated Franklin Pierce, Boyd, whose superb parliamentary strategy had been honed as Speaker the previous term, instead returned to that post and helped the Pierce administration move the Kansas-Nebraska Act through the House in 1854.

Boyd left Congress in 1855, only to be elected lieutenant governor of Kentucky in 1859. By that time, however, he was too ill to perform his duties and died in Paducah, Kentucky, that year.

See also: Henry Clay, Jacksonian Democracy, Kansas-Nebraska Act, Franklin Pierce, Speaker of the House

Michael Green

REFERENCES

Hamilton, Holman. 1957. "Kentucky's Linn Boyd and the Dramatic Days of 1850." 55 *Kentucky Historical Society Register* 185.

———. 1964. *Prologue to Conflict: The Crisis and Compromise of 1850.* New York: Norton.

Jennings, Thelma. 1980. *The Nashville Convention: Southern Movement for Unity, 1848–1851.* Memphis, TN: Memphis State U. Pr.

William M. Boyle, Jr. (1902–1961)

Chairman of the Democratic National Committee in the Truman era. When Senator J. Howard McGrath prepared to resign from the Democratic National Committee chairmanship in order to accept an appointment in President Harry Truman's Cabinet, the President asked William Marshall Boyle, Jr., to leave his Washington law practice to take over the management of national headquarters as executive vice-chairman. Six months later, Boyle was elected national chairman and served from August 24, 1949, to November 1, 1951.

Boyle was born in Leavenworth, Kansas, and attended Kansas City Junior College. At age 16, he successfully organized a Young Democrats' Club in the "silk stocking" ward of Kansas City and subsequently became a ward chairman. In 1922 he began studying at Georgetown University Law School but completed his training at the Kansas City School of Law in 1926. During the late 1930s he worked in the prosecuting attorney's office.

Boyle's family had become acquainted with the Trumans in the early 1930s. In 1941 Truman invited Boyle to come to Washington as assistant counsel to the Truman Committee investigating wartime defense spending. Boyle also assisted National Chairman Robert E. Hannegan during the 1944 campaign. After the election, Boyle opened a law office in Washington. When Truman succeeded to the presidency, he asked Boyle to take over at Democratic national headquarters.

Subsequently, politicians were turning to the prospects for the 1952 presidential race. During 1951 there was much doubt about President Truman's intentions. A probe of these intentions came in the form of an attack on National Chairman Boyle. In August 1951, the *St. Louis Post-Dispatch* charged Boyle with having received a fee of $8,000 for inducing the Reconstruction Finance Corporation to lend $565,000 to the American Lithofold Company of St. Louis while he served as an official of the Democratic National Committee.

Boyle denied having had anything to do with the application for a loan. After conducting an independent investigation of the circumstances surrounding the loan, Truman expressed full confidence in his national chairman. The anti-Truman leaders interpreted Truman's loyalty to Boyle as evidence that the President would seek another nomination.

A Senate investigation, led by Senator Richard M. Nixon of California, turned up evidence of possible influence peddling in the 1940s and 1950s by Boyle; he resigned as national chairman in 1951, still defending his conduct.

See also: Robert E. Hannegan, Richard Nixon, Harry S Truman

Ralph M. Goldman

John Brademas (1927–)

Longtime Indiana U.S. Congressman. A former Democratic Congressman from Indiana, John Brademas served in the House of Representatives from 1959 to 1981, the last four years as Majority Whip. Brademas moved to New York City to become president of New York University after his defeat in the 1980 Republican landslide. Such a transition was hardly unusual. In his congressional career, Brademas was widely known as "Mr. Education," a title bestowed upon him by *Look* magazine in 1968.

Brademas graduated from Harvard University in 1949 and attended Oxford University on a Rhodes scholarship. He received a Ph.D. in political science there in 1954. Returning to Indiana, he ran twice unsuccessfully for Congress, then came to Washington to work on the staffs of Senator Pat McNamara (D-Mich.), Congressman Thomas Ludlow Ashley (D-Ohio), and Adlai Stevenson in Stevenson's unsuccessful presidential campaign in 1956. Brademas went back to Indiana to teach at St. Mary's College in 1957 and 1958 and was elected to Congress in 1958 from South Bend. His district was never secure, and he continually had close races for reelection. In 1976 Brademas admitted receiving a small campaign contribution from Korean lobbyist Tongsun Park, whose influence peddling led to the "Koreagate" miniscandal. While no evidence of any wrongdoing by Brademas appeared, the simple linkage, together with his increasing attention to Washington business, exacerbated his electoral difficulties at home. As Majority Whip, Brademas's liberalism became much more prominent. He won by less than 60 percent in both 1976 and 1978, and in the Republican landslide of 1980, Brademas lost to 27-year-old businessman John Hiler.

In the House, Brademas served on the Education and Labor Committee, rising to third-ranking Democrat. In the 1960s he was the leading advocate in Congress of federal aid to education and a major advocate of the 1975 Education for All Handicapped Children Act. He also worked on legislation to benefit the elderly, on foreign policy issues relating to education, and on legislation to benefit Greece (Brademas is of Greek background). In 1975 columnist Jack Anderson cited him as one of the "ten best" members of Congress, and he was placed on President Richard Nixon's "enemies list" during the Watergate scandal. As House Majority Whip, he was loyal to Speaker Thomas P. O'Neill and Majority Leader Jim Wright, but he also expanded the whip system to provide greater opportunities for participation by junior members.

See also: Majority Party Leadership in Congress, Richard Nixon, Thomas P. O'Neill, Adlai Stevenson II, Watergate, Jim Wright

Eric. M. Uslaner

William Bradford (1729–1808)

Rhode Island politician of the early national period. A Rhode Island physician, lawyer, and politician whose brief service in the U.S. Senate accurately reflected his home state's ambivalence about the value of joining the Union, William Bradford was a direct descendent of Governor William Bradford of Plymouth, Massachusetts. Born and educated in Massachusetts, he moved to Rhode Island where he began the practice of medicine in Warren; he then moved to Bristol, Connecticut, and took up law. After admission to the bar, he began a successful practice and established himself as a prominent member of the community. Bradford achieved some fame during the Revolutionary War by taking a personal role in attempting to halt the British bombardment of Bristol.

Bradford was a member of the Rhode Island legislature in 1764 and 1765, and he served as the speaker of the Rhode Island Committee of Correspondence in 1773. He was the deputy governor of the newly independent state from November 1775 to May 1778. Bradford was elected to represent Rhode Island in the Continental Congress but never served.

After Rhode Island's reluctant acquiescence in joining the Union, he was chosen as one of its first U.S. Senators, serving from 1793 to 1797, when he resigned. He was chosen by his colleagues in the Senate as President *pro tempore* in July 1797. Bradford appears to be typical of those provincial politicians of the Revolutionary era whose loyalties and orientation were to their home districts; he never identified with the new nation as a whole. On the other hand, he would hardly have been chosen to represent chauvinist Rhode Island in any capacity had the situation been otherwise. Bradford's limited national role may well be responsible for the dearth of material about him.

Kathryn A. Malone

Stephen R. Bradley (1754–1830)

Early Republican U.S. Senate leader from Vermont. A Jeffersonian Republican from New England, Stephen Bradley represented Vermont in the United States Senate from the time of its admission to statehood through the outbreak of the War of 1812. Bradley graduated from Yale College in 1776 and studied law at Litchfield, Connecticut. He was admitted to the bar in 1779 although he also saw active military service during the ongoing Revolutionary War.

In 1779 Bradley chose to join the settlers of the disputed region soon to become Vermont and immediately became active in the statehood movement, as demonstrated by his authorship of *Vermont's Appeal to the Candid and Impartial World*, in which he made the case for control of the territory still claimed by New York before the Continental Congress.

Bradley, one of the first two lawyers admitted to the Vermont bar, served in almost every possible state and local office in his time. He was a member of the Vermont legislature and was its speaker; an associate judge of the Vermont Supreme Court; and a member of the commission that reached a final border settlement with New York allowing for final admission to statehood. Bradley was a Federalist delegate to the Vermont Ratification Convention, State's attorney of Cumberland County, register of probate and of the city council of Winchester, in 1782 and 1798 respectively, and a judge of Windham County in 1783.

Chosen as one of Vermont's first U.S. Senators, Bradley drew a four-year term. He was defeated for reelection in 1794 but returned to the Senate to fill a vacancy after the Jeffersonian triumph in 1801. Bradley served in the U.S. Senate from 1801 to 1813 and was elected President *pro tempore* in 1802 and 1803.

Bradley enjoyed a prominent role as a New England Republican. He was selected by James Madison to chair the congressional caucus that renominated Thomas Jefferson in 1804, and he called and presided over the caucus that selected Madison in 1808. Although a loyal Republican, Bradley acted independently, and his vote to acquit Justice Salmon P. Chase at his impeachment trial in the Senate signaled Jefferson's failure to turn his attack on the federal judiciary into a successful partisan movement.

The War of 1812 finally caused Bradley to desert the Republican administration. On April 25, 1812, he delivered a Senate speech protesting against a declaration of war, which had been issued before the Army had been organized. His retirement from public life the following year was attributed to his unhappiness with the war policy.

See also: Jeffersonian Republicans

Kathryn A. Malone

Thomas Bradley (1917–)

African-American mayor of Los Angeles. Since 1973, Tom Bradley has been the only Black mayor elected in a major city with a small Black population—in 1982 Bradley nearly became the first elected Black governor, losing the California race to George Deukmejian by fewer than

100,000 votes out of over 14 million cast. Among Black politicians, he has been a pioneer.

Tom Bradley was born in Calvert, Texas—one of seven children of sharecropper parents. Difficult work in the cotton fields led the Bradleys to Los Angeles in 1924.

In 1940 Bradley joined the Los Angeles Police Department, rising to the rank of lieutenant. He attended night school and earned a law degree before retiring from the police force in 1961. When Bradley defeated a white incumbent for a city council seat in 1963, he became the first Black ever elected to office in Los Angeles. In 1969 Bradley challenged conservative Mayor Sam Yorty. After leading in the nonpartisan primary, Bradley was defeated by Yorty's race-baiting campaign. Four years later, Bradley defeated Yorty by a large margin, and he won reelection in 1977, 1981, 1985, and 1989.

Bradley has appealed to a united Black community, to highly politicized Jews and other white liberals, to a less well-organized Latino community, and to downtown businessmen. Bradley's conciliatory style, quiet leadership, and symbolic appeal as the city's first Black mayor have combined to lend stability to the liberal biracial regime.

See also: Biracial Urban Coalitions

Raphael J. Sonenshein

REFERENCES

Patterson, Beeman. 1969. "Political Action of Negroes in Los Angeles: A Case Study in the Attainment of Councilmanic Representation." 30 *Phylon* 170.

Payne, J. Gregory, and Scott C. Ratzan. 1986. *Tom Bradley: The Impossible Dream.* Santa Monica, CA: Roundtable Publishing.

Robinson, James Lee. 1976. "Tom Bradley: Los Angeles' First Black Mayor." Ph.D. thesis, University of California, Los Angeles.

Sonenshein, Raphael J. 1989. "The Dynamics of Biracial Coalitions: Crossover Politics in Los Angeles." 42 *Western Political Quarterly* 333.

John Branch (1782–1863)

Influential North Carolina politician of the pre-Civil War period. John Branch had a long and varied political career, which included service as a state senator (1811, 1813–1817, 1822, 1834), a speaker of the state senate (1815–1817), a governor of North Carolina (1817–1820), a United States Senator (1823–1829), a Secretary of the Navy (1829–1831), a Representative in Congress (1831–1833), a member of the North Carolina Constitutional Convention (1835), and a governor of the Florida Territory (1834–1845).

When he was governor of North Carolina, Branch advocated state aid to education, internal improvements, reorganization of the state supreme court, adoption of a less severe penal code (which reduced the number of capital offenses and abolished imprisonment for debt), and elimination and punishment of impostors in the medical profession.

In 1819 Branch also presided over the North Carolina branch of the American Colonization Society, which supported the resettlement of emancipated slaves in Africa. In 1820 he resisted local public sentiment by refusing to grant clemency to a white man sentenced to die for murdering a slave. After serving the constitutional limit of three one-year terms as governor, Branch won reelection to the state senate and was later elevated by the legislature to the United States Senate. As a U.S. Senator, he allied himself with the Jacksonians and was subsequently appointed by President Andrew Jackson as Secretary of the Navy. Thus, Branch became the first North Carolinian to be appointed to the federal Cabinet and the first of five North Carolinians to hold this office.

In 1831 he resigned and severed relations with Jackson. Branch was part of a feud involving the wives of Cabinet members over the social acceptability of Secretary of War John H. Eaton's bride, Peggy O'Neill—the so-called "Eaton Affair." Branch remained a Democrat and secured political offices in the U.S. and state legislatures. As a state delegate to the Constitutional Convention, he urged repeal of the religious test for public officeholders and spoke out against the voting disenfranchisement of free, landholding Blacks. President John Tyler appointed Branch as governor of the Florida Territory; he was the last man to hold that office before Florida's statehood.

See also: John H. Eaton, Andrew Jackson, Jacksonian Democracy, John Tyler

Hal T. Shelton

REFERENCES

Ashe, Samuel A' Court. 1925. *History of North Carolina.* Vol. 2. Raleigh, NC: Edwards and Broughton.

Haywood, Marshall D. 1915. "John Branch, 1782–1863." 15 *The North Carolina Booklet* 50.

Hoffman, William S. 1958. "John Branch and the Origins of the Whig Party in North Carolina." 35 *The North Carolina Historical Review* 299.

Frank B. Brandegee (1864–1924)

Conservative Connecticut politician. Born in New London, Connecticut, Frank Bosworth

Brandegee was the son of Augustus Brandegee, who, like his father, became a leader of the Republican Party in Connecticut with a long career as a public servant. After graduating from Yale College in 1885, he studied law and was admitted to the bar in 1888.

Active as a state Republican leader, Brandegee served as a delegate to the Republican National Convention in 1888, 1892, 1900, and 1904 and was chairman of the Republican State Convention in 1904.

Brandegee took public office when he was elected to the state House of Representatives in 1888. He was later elected to the post of corporation counsel of New London, which he held from 1889 to 1893 and from 1894 to 1897. Brandegee returned to the state House of Representatives after the election of 1898, serving as speaker during the 1899 session. Later, he again held the post of corporation counsel for New London (1901–1902), resigning to become a member of Congress following the death of Charles A. Russell.

He remained in the House of Representatives from 1902 to 1905 when he was elected to the U.S. Senate to fill the vacancy left by Orville H. Platt when he died. A defender of the Old Guard, he opposed the League of Nations as well as a number of other progressive reforms, such as the direct election of Senators, the regulation of child labor, the graduated income tax, and women's suffrage. Reelected in 1908, 1914, and 1920, his Senate career lasted over 19 years until his suicide in Washington, D.C.

See also: League of Nations, Woman's Suffrage Movement

James V. Saturno

Louis D. Brandeis (1856–1941)

Liberal Supreme Court Justice appointed by Woodrow Wilson. Woodrow Wilson's January 1916 decision to name Louis Dembitz Brandeis to the Supreme Court was widely regarded as politically motivated. The Jewish Bostonian had already gained national fame as a Progressive attorney. In his most famous case, *Muller v. Oregon* (1908), Brandeis used scientific studies to persuade the Supreme Court to uphold a state law that set maximum working hours for women. Brandeis's nomination was both unexpected and frightening to many Americans. Conservative Republicans around the country, especially those in Boston, decried the appointment and speculated that the choice represented an attempt to win Jewish votes in crucial states

like New York in the upcoming presidential election.

Progressives too saw the nomination as related to the election. Wilson was elected in 1912 because Teddy Roosevelt ran as the choice of the Bull Moose Party, thus taking Progressive votes away from William Howard Taft, the regular Republican candidate. For Wilson to win in a normal two-candidate race, he had to earn the votes of some of the Progressives who had defected from Taft to Roosevelt. The Brandeis nomination therefore was an attempt to win liberal approbation—and votes—for Wilson.

The confirmation battle lasted six months as Brandeis's opponents attacked his personal and professional morals in hearings before a subcommittee of the Senate Judiciary Committee. The subcommittee and the Judiciary Committee both voted along partisan lines to approve the appointment, and the roll call vote was 47 to 22. Only one Democrat voted against Brandeis, and three Progressive Republicans voted for him.

In the 1916 campaign, Wilson pointed to his selection of Brandeis as evidence that he was accomplishing Progressive goals. Wilson's victory over Charles Evans Hughes owed largely to his ability to woo traditionally Republican liberal voters in western states like California and New Mexico. The Brandeis nomination did not, however, win New York for Wilson because the state went solidly Republican.

See also: Bull Moose Party, Theodore Roosevelt, William Howard Taft, Woodrow Wilson

Brooke A. Masters

REFERENCES

Lovell, S.D. 1980. *The Presidential Election of 1916.* Carbondale and Edwardsville: Southern Illinois U. Pr.

Mason, Alpheus T. 1946. *Brandeis: A Free Man's Life.* New York: Viking.

Todd, A.L. 1964. *Justice on Trial.* New York: McGraw-Hill.

Charles R. Brayton (1840–1910)

Rhode Island Republican political boss. During four decades, between 1870 and 1910, Charles Ray Brayton manipulated the politics of Rhode Island as the prototypical boss of a highly successful rural-based political machine. Brayton, a Brown University graduate with a distinguished Civil War career during which he was capped as a brevet brigadier general of volunteers, traced his Rhode Island ancestry to the founding of his native town of Warwick. His father, William, served as a Republican Congressman from 1857 to 1861.

Shortly after the Civil War, General Brayton became the chief political lieutenant of U.S. Senator Henry Bowen Anthony, the principal organizer of Rhode Island's Republican Party. Anthony secured for his protégé such politically sensitive positions as those of United States pension agent for Rhode Island (1870–1874) and U.S. postmaster for Providence (1874–1880). In 1876 Brayton began his long tenure as chairman of the state Republican Party, whose members he addressed as "fellow machinists."

The controversial Brayton resigned from the post office under fire in 1880 for allegedly using the mails to distribute fixed ballots and for converting postal funds to party purposes. When he was stoutly defended by most of the state's elected Republicans and was allowed to maintain his party position, the situation gave credence to this lament of a contemporary reformer: "If a man is an expert in all the deviltry known to politics, in Rhode Island he is made chairman of the Republican State Committee instead of being sent to jail."

For the next three decades, Brayton survived repeated political scandals. After Senator Anthony's death in 1884, Brayton concerned himself chiefly with the longevity, and hence the seniority, of U.S. Senator Nelson W. Aldrich. Both men weathered a 1905 exposé in an article by muckraker Lincoln Steffens, "Rhode Island: A State for Sale."

The key to Brayton's success, in addition to his leadership abilities and his deserved reputation as a stern disciplinarian, was his ability to control the Rhode Island General Assembly through old-stock rural legislators from the country towns because each of the state's municipalities, regardless of size, had one vote in the senate. Cynically remarking that "an honest voter is one that stays bought," Brayton used the contributions of Providence businessmen to pay off voters in these small towns. This practice prompted Steffens to allege that "the political system in Rhode Island . . . is grounded on the lowest layer of corruption that I have found thus far—the bribery of voters with cash at the polls."

When growing Democratic strength rendered the office of governor politically insecure, "the Boss" sponsored a law—the so-called Brayton Act of 1901—that placed the appointive and budgetary powers of the state in the hands of the rotten borough Republican senate. Though not a member of the legislature, Brayton maintained an office in the new Statehouse. In a cause célèbre, the general was finally ousted from this command post in 1907 by James H. Higgins, the first Irish-Catholic Democrat to win Rhode Island's governorship. A loss of sight in 1903 diminished Brayton's effectiveness, but only his sudden death in 1910 broke his grip on the reins of power in Rhode Island.

See also: Nelson Aldrich, Henry Bowen Anthony

Patrick T. Conley

REFERENCES

Buenker, John D. 1974. "The Politics of Resistance: The Rural-Based Yankee Republican Machines of Connecticut and Rhode Island." 47 *New England Quarterly* 212.

Gersuny, Carl. 1980. "Uphill Battle: Lucius F. C. Garvin's Crusade for Political Reform." 39 *Rhode Island History* 57.

Tanner, Mary Nelson. 1963. "The Middle Years of the Anthony-Brayton Alliance; or Politics in Post-Office, 1874–1880." 22 *Rhode Island History* 65.

John C. Breckinridge (1821–1875)

Pro-southern Kentucky politician of the 1850s. A contender for the presidency who received 72 electoral votes in 1860, John Cabell Breckinridge finished second to Abraham Lincoln. Running as the southern states' rights candidate within a badly divided Democratic Party, Breckinridge was only 39 years old. He had previously served during the presidency of James Buchanan as Vice President of the United States, the youngest man ever to hold that position.

Born near Lexington, Kentucky, Breckinridge benefited from his ancestry, which included distinguished lawyers and statesmen. A precocious graduate of Centre College, he later studied at Princeton and completed his law education at the Transylvania Institute, gaining admission to the bar at the age of 20. During the Mexican War he left his Lexington law practice to enlist as a major of volunteers, and in 1849, he was a member of the Kentucky House of Representatives. A U.S. Congressman from 1851 to 1855, he declined a mission to Spain in 1854 only to receive the vice presidential nomination of the Democratic Party two years later.

Breckinridge represented Kentucky in the U.S. Senate for only nine months in 1861 when he was expelled for pro-southern activities. In the Confederate Army he rose to the rank of major general and served as Jefferson Davis's Secretary of War from January until April of 1865, when he fled to Europe. Later resuming law practice in Lexington and serving also as a railroad executive, he died there in relative obscurity.

See also: James Buchanan, Jefferson Davis, Election of 1860, Abraham Lincoln

Norman B. Ferris

REFERENCES

Davis, William C. 1974. *Breckinridge: Statesman, Soldier, Symbol*. Baton Rouge: Louisiana State U. Pr.

Calvin S. Brice (1845–1898)

Ohio Democratic politician and chairman of the Democratic National Committee. Calvin Stewart Brice was elected national committee chairman of the Democratic Party (1889–1892) to complete the term of Chairman William H. Barnum who died in office. Brice had been chairman of Grover Cleveland's campaign committee in 1884 and appeared to be a moderate in the tariff protectionist-reductionist factionalism of the party at that time. He won the United States Senate seat from Ohio in 1890. Once in the Senate, he became an outspoken protectionist and one Democratic leader who resisted a Cleveland renomination in 1892.

The son of a Presbyterian minister, Brice took up a career in corporation law and, even before he had reached his mid-twenties, earned a reputation as an outstanding and wealthy Cincinnati lawyer. Brice had participated only occasionally in Ohio politics before 1888.

In 1884 the Democratic National Committee chose Brice, then Ohio's national committeeman, as the chairman of its first separate campaign committee. Grover Cleveland's advisers were right to doubt that Brice would give much attention to the menial tasks of a campaign publicity bureau or handle the tariff issue well. Brice established and then neglected the management of the campaign's office in New York. Since he shared the general protectionist attitudes of the majority of business leaders of his day, he did little to advance Cleveland's reductionist position.

By 1888 Brice had become keenly interested in holding public office. He was encouraged by his longtime Ohio business associate, vice presidential nominee Allen G. Thurman, and by William C. Whitney, one of President Cleveland's closest advisers as well as the son-in-law of Ohio's Senator Henry B. Payne. Payne (on the verge of retiring) and Thurman agreed that Brice should inherit the senatorial seat.

Although assuming the Democratic national chairmanship in June 1889, Brice immediately turned to his successful campaign for the Senate. Because Brice spent most of his year at his New York City home, the Republican press referred to him as "New York's third Senator." Brice never relinquished his activities as a railroad promoter and executive.

See also: William H. Barnum, Grover Cleveland, Democratic National Committee

Ralph M. Goldman

REFERENCES

Goldman, Ralph M. 1990. *The National Party Chairmen and Committees: Factionalism at the Top*. Armonk,

John W. Bricker (1893–1986)

Conservative Ohio U.S. Senator of the 1950s. As an influential Republican conservative nationalist and, in 1944, Thomas E. Dewey's running mate, the sonorous John W. Bricker gained national prominence as a three-time governor of Ohio from 1939 to 1945. There he proved himself an able, budget-minded administrator and a successful vote-getter. After seeking the 1944 presidential nomination as a favorite son, Bricker was the GOP convention's unanimous choice for second slot on the ticket. Republicans believed Bricker's midwestern isolationism, anti-New Deal record, and his defense of states' rights balanced Dewey's Eastern internationalism and moderate domestic policies. Throughout the subsequent campaign, Bricker foreshadowed Republican cold war red-baiting by alleging ties between communism, the New Deal, and organized labor. Though in the election Bricker helped Dewey capture Ohio, which had gone for Franklin D. Roosevelt in 1940, the President won his fourth term.

Bricker is remembered more for his attempts to limit the treaty power of the executive and the Senate. A Senator from 1947 to 1959, he aligned himself with the conservative Republican Old Guard. Bricker worried that treaties (especially those with the United Nations) might subvert the U.S. Constitution and influence American domestic policy. During the early 1950s the Ohioan sponsored several versions of the Bricker Amendment, which would have forbidden treaty provisions that conflicted with the Constitution and would have allowed Congress to regulate executive agreements. The Bricker Amendment attracted national grassroots support from isolationists and conservatives. Concerned that the proposal would hamper presidential foreign policymaking, Dwight Eisenhower's administration opposed it. After the Senate defeated the amendment 42 to 50 in 1954, Bricker abandoned meaningful efforts to secure its passage.

See also: Communism as a Political Issue, Thomas Dewey, Dwight Eisenhower, Election of 1984, Isolationism in American Politics, New Deal, Franklin Roosevelt, United Nations

Jeffery C. Livingston

REFERENCES

Miles, Michael W. 1980. *The Odyssey of the American Right.* New York: Oxford U. Pr.

Seasongood, Murray. 1946. "John W. Bricker: 'Personally Honest.'" In J. T. Salter, ed. *Public Men In and Out of Office.* Chapel Hill: U. of North Carolina Pr.

Tananbaum, Duane A. 1985. "The Bricker Amendment Controversy: Its Origins and Eisenhower's Role." 9 *Diplomatic History* 73.

Zahniser, Marvin R., ed. 1978. "John W. Bricker Reflects Upon the Fight for the Bricker Amendment." 87 *Ohio History* 322.

H. Styles Bridges (1898–1961)

Reactionary Republican Senator from New Hampshire. As a Republican Senator from New Hampshire who helped to keep ultra-conservatism alive during New Deal liberalism's zenith in the middle third of the twentieth century and a powerful figure in the federal government and in his party, H. Styles Bridges fought the welfare state, big spending, and domestic and foreign communism. Labeled a genuine American Tory, Bridges represented a link between Old Guard Republicanism and the modern Far Right.

Bridges never lost an election. He became New Hampshire's governor in 1934 at age 36. Two years later, after consideration for the vice presidential nomination, he was elected to the U.S. Senate for the first of five consecutive times. From 1947 to 1948 and from 1953 to 1954 he chaired the important Senate Appropriations Committee. Bridges was Republican floor leader from 1952 to 1953, and was President *pro tempore* from 1953 to 1955.

Best known for his stands on American foreign relations, Bridges supported overseas intervention before World War II. He became a vociferous critic of Democrat cold war policy. The leading Senate supporter of Joseph R. McCarthy and a prominent "China Lobby" member, Bridges accused the Democrats and the State Department of "selling out" to Soviet-led communism. He denounced President Harry S Truman for firing hard-liner General Douglas MacArthur in 1951. Bridges battled to cut foreign aid, especially to Communist and non-aligned nations.

Though illness reduced Bridges's influence in the 1950s, he remained a leader of the Republican Right. From 1955 to 1961 he chaired the Senate Republican Policy Committee. Bridges pressed Dwight Eisenhower's administration to adopt more conservative policies, and he distrusted Eisenhower's summit meetings with the Soviets. Bridges backed Richard M. Nixon's presidential candidacy in 1960. Until his death in November 1961, he criticized President John F. Kennedy for naive anti-Communist policies.

See also: Communism as a Political Issue, Dwight Eisenhower, Election of 1936, New Deal, Harry S Truman

Jeffery C. Livingston

REFERENCES

Griffith, Robert. 1970. *The Politics of Fear: Joseph R. McCarthy and the Senate.* Lexington: U. Pr. of Kentucky.

Grimmett, Richard F. 1973. "Who Were the Senate Isolationists?" 421 *Pacific Historical Review* 479.

Horn, Stephen. 1970. *Unused Power: The Work of the Senate Committee on Appropriations.* Washington: Brookings.

Miles, Michael W. 1980. *The Odyssey of the American Right.* New York: Oxford U. Pr.

Jesse D. Bright (1812–1875)

Proslavery Indiana Democratic Senator of the 1850s. Referred to by his contemporaries as a "dough face"—a northern man with southern principles—Jesse David Bright owned a farm and slaves in Kentucky long after moving to Indiana. He held minor offices in Indiana for a decade before being elected lieutenant governor in 1843 as a spokesman for the "Hunker," or proslavery, faction of the Democratic Party. He was then three times elected to the United States Senate (1845–1862). With little reputation as an orator or statesman, Bright showed great skill at the rougher organizational side of politics. By the ruthless use of patronage, he built a political machine that for a time made Indiana Democratic politics his personal domain. As the most reliable northern ally of the dominant southern wing, he also exercised great influence on the National Democratic Party and administrations.

Bright was one of the inner circle of Senators credited with the nomination of James Buchanan in 1856 and with the destruction of Stephen Douglas's presidential ambitions in 1856 and 1860. A bitter feud with Douglas, a tainted re-election to the Senate in 1857, and his dough face reputation cost Bright control of the Democratic National Convention delegation in 1860, and his influence was undermined when he bolted the Douglas ticket in a futile support of John Breckinridge. When secession came, he refused to commit himself to the Union cause even when questioned by the Indiana legislature. In 1861 it was revealed that Bright had written to "His Honor Jefferson Davis President of the Confederate States" recommending a friend with arms for sale. This resulted in his expulsion from the Senate by a partisan Republican majority in 1862. After failing to rally the Indiana Democrats to his aid, Bright withdrew to his Kentucky farm.

See also: James Buchanan, Copperheads, Jefferson Davis, Election of 1860, Hunkers

Harold B. Raymond

REFERENCES

Dunn, J. P. 1905. *Indiana: A Redemption from Slavery.* Boston: Houghton Mifflin.

Stamp, Kenneth. 1949. *Indiana Politics During the Civil War.* Bloomington: Indiana U. Pr.

Benjamin H. Bristow (1832–1896)

Reformist Republican politician of the 1870s. A leading contender for the Republican presidential nomination in 1876, Benjamin Helm Bristow was the favorite of the party's reform wing. Although he lost the nomination, his supporters confounded the blatant spoilsmen and helped nominate Rutherford B. Hayes.

Raised in western Kentucky, Bristow, originally a Whig, was an ardent Unionist and a colonel in the Union Army. From 1866 to 1870, as U.S. district attorney for Kentucky, he distinguished himself by vigorous prosecution of the Ku Klux Klan. In 1870 Ulysses S. Grant appointed him to the newly created post of Solicitor General, and he continued his crusading legal work until resigning in 1872. Two years later he became Secretary of the Treasury and commenced his most noted public service: prosecution of the Whiskey Ring, a notorious conspiracy of tax evaders.

Anti-Grant reformers such as Carl Schurz saw Bristow as the only hope for the party's salvation in 1876. They believed that a Bristow administration would represent clean government, civil service reform, and a "conciliatory" policy toward the conservative white South. At first reluctant, Bristow showed more interest in the nomination as his relations with the suspicious Grant deteriorated, especially after the unsuccessful Whiskey Ring prosecution of Grant's secretary, Orville Babcock. Anathema to most regular Republicans, Bristow had no real chance of nomination. At the national convention, he received 126 of the total 756 votes, and his supporters led the movement to Rutherford B.

Hayes to forestall the nomination of Maine's tainted James G. Blaine.

After the convention, Bristow resigned from the Treasury Department, moved to New York, and practiced law with only a tangential interest in politics.

See also: Election of 1876, Ulysses S. Grant, Rutherford B. Hayes, Ku Klux Klan, Union Party

Charles W. Calhoun

REFERENCES

Nevins, Allan. 1937. *Hamilton Fish: The Inner History of the Grant Administration.* New York: Dodd, Mead.

Polakoff, Keith I. 1973. *The Politics of Inertia: The Election of 1876 and the End of Reconstruction.* Baton Rouge: Louisiana State U. Pr.

Thompson, E. Bruce. 1945. "The Bristow Presidential Boom of 1876." 32 *Mississippi Valley Historical Review* 3.

Webb, Ross A. 1969. *Benjamin Helm Bristow: Border State Politician.* Lexington: U. Pr. of Kentucky.

Broadcast Media Regulations

Federal law governing candidates' use of broadcast media to appeal to the electorate is embodied in the Communications Act of 1934, administered by the Federal Communications Commission (FCC). Section 315 of the act regulates political broadcasting. "If any licensee shall permit any person who is a legally qualified candidate for any public office to use a broadcasting station," states Section 315, "he shall afford equal opportunities to all other such candidates for that office in the use of such broadcasting station." Only when the candidate himself or herself appears on a broadcast is Section 315 operative. Appearances by spokespersons for candidates generally have been covered by the FCC's "Zapple Doctrine," described below.

The equal opportunities requirement of Section 315 is triggered when the identity of a candidate who appears on a broadcast can reasonably be presumed to be known by the audience and when the appearance is of sufficient magnitude to be considered an integral part of the broadcast. The appearance does not necessarily have to be related to or make mention of an individual's candidacy in order to be considered a "use" entitling a political opponent to an equal opportunity to appear. A classic example is the appearance of Ronald Reagan in television broadcasts of the films he made during his career as a screen actor before he entered politics. Because any such appearance would have entitled political opponents to equal opportunities to appear, television stations, for the duration of

Reagan's campaigns, refrained from showing films in which the former film actor appeared.

The equal opportunities requirement, conversely, is not absolute. In 1959 Congress amended the law, exempting candidate appearances in four news situations from the requirement: newscasts; news interviews; news documentaries, provided the candidate's appearance is incidental to the subject matter of the documentary; and on-the-spot coverage of news events. In 1960 Section 315 was suspended as it applied to presidential and vice presidential nominees. This unique suspension permitted John Kennedy and Richard Nixon to appear in a series of broadcast debates without broadcasters being required to provide equal opportunities for candidates from minor parties. Similar attempts to suspend Section 315 to allow presidential debates in 1964, 1968, and 1972 failed. In 1975, however, the FCC, in response to a petition filed by the Aspen Institute Program on Communications and Society, ruled that broadcast political debates qualified as exempt, on-the-spot coverage of news events provided that they were sponsored by outside parties and were covered contemporaneously. This administrative ruling permitted presidential debates sponsored by the League of Women Voters to be broadcast both in 1976 and 1980.

In November 1983 the FCC relaxed its 1975 ruling regarding broadcast-debate sponsorship. It ruled that broadcasters may stage their own debates, inviting political candidates of their choice to participate, without violating Section 315, provided that broadcasters do not favor or disfavor any particular candidate.

The League of Women Voters, an organization that had sponsored presidential forums and debates during the prenomination and general election campaigns in 1976 and 1980 and that had already launched similar plans for 1984, strongly objected to the FCC decision. The League appealed the decision, but in March 1984, the U.S. Court of Appeals in Washington issued a brief, unsigned, unanimous judgment affirming the FCC's ruling. The court held that the commission's decision was a legitimate exercise of its discretion.

The Zapple Doctrine

Section 315 of the Communications Act does not cover broadcast appearances by supporters of political candidates. Rather, the "Zapple Doctrine," sometimes called the "quasi-equal opportunities doctrine," has applied to such appearances. Under this rule, if a broadcast station sells time to supporters or spokespersons of a candidate during an election campaign, it must make comparable time available for sale to supporters or spokespersons of the candidate's opponent. If a candidate's supporters are given free broadcast time, then free time also must be given to the supporters of the candidate's opponent. This doctrine, however, has not required broadcast stations to provide "fringe candidates and minor parties" with broadcast time.

The Zapple Doctrine combines elements of the equal opportunities doctrine with those of the Fairness Doctrine, which was repealed by the FCC in mid-1987 after operating for some 38 years. The Fairness Doctrine, already codified in provisions of Section 315, required broadcasters to operate in the public interest and to afford reasonable opportunity for the discussion of conflicting views on issues of public importance. It did not require broadcast licensees to provide equal time to coverage of both sides of relevant issues, nor, with one exception, did it require them to grant time to particular persons or groups who wished to offer viewpoints opposing those presented in a broadcast. The licensee did have a positive duty to encourage the presentation of opposing viewpoints on matters of public controversy and to seek out responsible spokespersons to present those viewpoints.

Moreover, the FCC's "Cullman Doctrine" has required broadcast licensees who have sold broadcast time to spokespersons of one side of a controversial issue to provide free time for response if those with contrasting viewpoints cannot afford to purchase time. Under the personal attack rule, which was part of the Fairness Doctrine, licensees had been required to offer individuals and groups whose honesty, character, integrity, or similar personal qualities were attacked during the presentation of views on a controversial issue of public importance a reasonable opportunity to respond using the licensee's facilities. The rule, however, did not apply to newscasts, news interviews, or coverage of news events. Nor did it apply to attacks made by legally qualified candidates, their authorized spokespersons, or persons associated with them. But if a broadcast licensee either endorsed or opposed a legally qualified candidate, the licensee has been required to give the candidate's opponent a reasonable opportunity to respond.

Immediately after the FCC decided to repeal the Fairness Doctrine, congressional supporters of the doctrine vowed to pass legislation placing it into law. Whether Congress will ever succeed in doing so is not certain; neither is it certain how the courts might respond to such legislation. In the meantime, the effect of the FCC decision on associated doctrines such as the Zapple and Cullman doctrines remained untested in the period before the 1988 general election.

Reasonable Access

Although Section 315 of the Communications Act requires broadcast stations to afford political candidates equal opportunities to appear or to respond in the circumstances described, it does not require stations to allow any candidates to appear in the first place. Section 312(a)(7) of the act, however, warns licensees that among grounds for revocation of license is the "willful or repeated failure to allow reasonable access to or to permit purchase of reasonable amounts of time for the use of a broadcasting station by a legally qualified candidate for Federal elective office on behalf of his candidacy." State and local candidates are not mentioned in this section, but the FCC interprets Section 307 of the act, which grants licenses only "if the public convenience, interest or necessity will be served thereby," to mean, among other things, that stations cannot choose to avoid equal opportunities requirements simply by refusing to provide political candidates with any access to their broadcasting facilities. Even state and local candidates must be provided with access, although no fixed formula measures reasonableness in that case.

Section 312(a)(7) does not require broadcast licensees to sell broadcast time to candidates at any level. Rather, licensees may fulfill the requirement that this provision imposes by inviting candidates for specific offices to participate in forums and debates. The requirement is that some broadcast time, whether purchased or free, must be made available, a provision that became a matter of litigation during the 1980 presidential campaign. The three major commercial television networks late in 1979 refused to sell candidates Ronald Reagan, Jimmy Carter, and John Connally broadcast time to announce and promote their presidential candidacies, maintaining that such advertisements came much too early. When the FCC sided with the Carter campaign committee, which had filed a complaint based on the reasonable access provision of the law, the networks brought suit against the FCC. The matter was carried to the Supreme Court, which ruled in July 1981 that the First Amendment rights of candidates to present their views and of voters to obtain information outweigh the constitutional rights of broadcasters.

Lowest Unit Rate

If a broadcast licensee does sell time to a candidate, the licensee must do so in accordance with a provision of the Federal Election Campaign Act (FECA), according to which Section 315(b) of the Communications Act was amended. Under this provision, the broadcast media cannot charge political candidates more than the lowest unit rate charged to any other advertiser for the same class and amount of time for a period extending 45 days before a primary election and 60 days before a general or special election. At other times rates cannot exceed the charges made for comparable use for other purposes. Thus, during the designated campaign period, political candidates are to be given the same discounts as a broadcast station's most-favored advertiser. Some broadcasters, however, have interpreted the lowest-unit-rate rule to mean that they may offer candidates the lowest rate on an immediately preemptible basis—that is, with no guarantee of airing. Thus, despite the lowest-unit-rate provision, candidates who feel strongly that their advertising must air at specific times in the weeks before an election often have no choice but to pay the high rates for fixed time charged by the stations.

See also: Election of 1960, Federal Communications Commission, Federal Election Campaign Act of 1971, John F. Kennedy, League of Woman Voters, Richard Nixon

Brian A. Haggerty

William E. Brock III (1930–)

Politician, Cabinet member, and Republican National Committee chairman from Tennessee. Born in Chattanooga, Tennessee, and heir to the Brock candy fortune, William Emerson Brock III served with the Navy in the mid-1950s after his education at Washington and Lee University. He scored an upset Republican victory in Tennessee's Third Congressional District in 1962 in his maiden political adventure. Early in his first House term, Brock helped launch the 1964 Barry Goldwater presidential campaign, a crusade that proved ironic in light of Brock's later reputation as a moderate.

In 1970 he challenged incumbent Democratic Senator Albert Gore, Sr. Portraying Gore as a supporter of racial-balance busing, a foe of school prayer, and an absentee from the state, Brock won with 52 percent. Six years later, Brock himself felt the lash of a negative campaign. His opponent, State Democratic chairman James Sasser, taunted the millionaire Senator for paying only $2,000 in federal income tax in 1975 and for refusing to release his 1974 return. The state was filled with Democratic buttons and bumper stickers proclaiming, "I paid more tax than Brock." Sasser won with 53 percent. Campaign professionals now use the Brock defeat as a "horror story" when they advise candidates to shun even the appearance of financial finagling.

Brock did not leave politics, however. Having chaired the National Republican Senatorial Committee, he was elected chairman of the Republican National Committee in January 1977. The party had not recovered from Watergate; it controlled only one-third of House seats and a handful of governorships and state legislatures. Brock then made the national committee a prime instrument of the party's revival. He started a hugely successful direct mail program that yielded a list of more than two million contributors. The donations supported a number of party-building operations: financial and organizational aid to state and local parties; "generic" television spots urging viewers to "vote Republican, for a change"; data-processing services; and advisory councils to develop and promote such Republican "new ideas" as the Kemp-Roth tax cut.

During the 1980s, the Democrats worked hard to catch up to the Republican effort. Largely because of Brock, national party organizations have changed from sleepy irrelevancies to major suppliers of campaign resources.

In 1981 President Ronald Reagan appointed Brock U.S. Trade Representative. In 1985 he became Secretary of Labor. In that post, Brock angered some conservative groups because they thought he failed to consult with them on labor issues.

In 1987 Brock resigned his Cabinet job to take charge of Senator Robert Dole's 1988 presidential campaign. He could not, however, get Dole to delegate enough authority, nor could he curb bickering within the campaign. This disunity kept Dole from capitalizing on his victory in the Iowa caucuses. George Bush won handily in the New Hampshire and "Super Tuesday" primaries, effectively ending Dole's candidacy and damaging Brock's reputation as a political miracle worker.

See also: George Bush, Direct Mail, Robert Dole, Barry Goldwater, Ronald Reagan, Republican National Committee, Watergate

John J. Pitney, Jr.

REFERENCES

Bibby, John F. 1980. "Party Renewal in the National Republican Party." In Gerald Pomper, ed. *Party Renewal in America: Theory and Practice.* New York: Praeger.

Herrnson, Paul. 1988. *Party Campaigning in the 1980s.* Cambridge: Harvard U. Pr.

Reichley, James A. 1985. "The Rise of National Parties." In John E. Chubb and Paul E. Peterson, eds. *The New Direction in American Politics.* Washington: Brookings.

David S. Broder (1929–)

Political journalist and commentator. On any list of the most important American political journalists, the name of David Broder would be near, if not at, the top. As the national political correspondent for the *Washington Post,* Broder's by-line lends immediate legitimacy to any story and thus gives him uncommon influence over developing political events. Timothy Crouse, author of *The Boys on the Bus,* a book about the reporters who covered the 1972 presidential election, has called Broder the "high priest of political journalism." And Hunter Thompson— the so-called "gonzo" journalist from *Rolling Stone* magazine and harsh critic of the press— described Broder in *Fear and Loathing on the Campaign Trail '72* as "the ranking wizard" of the campaign press corps.

Broder's column for the *Washington Post* is syndicated twice weekly to more than 260 newspapers in the United States and abroad. In 1973 Broder won the Pulitzer Prize for Distinguished Commentary. He is the author of four books about American politics: *The Republican Establishment: The Present and Future of the GOP* (1967, with coauthor Stephen Hess); *The Party's Over: The Failure of Politics in America* (1972); *Changing of the Guard: Power and Leadership in America* (1980); and *Behind the Front Page: A Candid Look at How News Is Made* (1987).

Before coming to the *Washington Post* in 1966, Broder wrote for the Bloomington, Illinois, *Daily Pentagraph, Congressional Quarterly,* the *Washington Star,* and the *New York Times.* He has contributed articles to various magazines and appears often as a commentator on television programs such as *Meet the Press* and *Washington Week in Review.*

Tom A. Kazee

REFERENCES

Broder, David S. 1972. *The Party's Over: The Failure of Politics in America.* New York: Harper & Row.

———. 1987. *Behind the Front Page: A Candid Look at How News Is Made.* New York: Simon & Schuster.

Crouse, Timothy. 1972. *The Boys on the Bus.* New York: Random House.

Hess, Steven. 1981. *The Washington Reporters.* Washington: Brookings.

Thompson, Hunter. 1973. *Fear and Loathing on the Campaign Trail '72.* New York: Warner Books.

REFERENCES

Brooke, Edward W. 1966. *The Challenge of Change: Crisis in Our Two Party System.* Boston: Little, Brown.

Cutler, John Henry. 1972. *Ed Brooke: Biography of a Senator.* Chicago: Bobbs-Merrill.

Hartshorn, Elinor C. 1973. "The Quiet Campaigner: Edward W. Brooke in Massachusetts." Ph.D. dissertation, University of Massachusetts, Amherst.

———. 1979. "The Election and the Defeat of Senator Brooke." Paper presented at the Annual Meeting of the Northeastern Political Science Association, Newark.

Edward W. Brooke (1919–)

African-American Protestant Republican Senator from Massachusetts. In 1962, Edward W. Brooke became attorney general of the Commonwealth of Massachusetts. He was the first Black man ever to win a statewide election in Massachusetts. Four years later, he scored another electoral breakthrough by becoming the nation's first popularly elected African-American Senator. At the time, Massachusetts was predominantly white (97 percent), predominantly Catholic (62 percent), and predominantly Democratic (66 percent).

Brooke, born in Washington, D.C., graduated from Howard University in 1941. He served for five years in the Army, emerging at war's end with a captain's bars, the Combat Infantryman's Badge, and a Bronze Star. He received an LL.B. and an LL.M. from Boston University Law School in 1948 and 1949 respectively. He ran unsuccessfully for Massachusetts state representative in 1950 and 1952 and for secretary of state of the commonwealth in 1960. His first success came in 1962.

Brooke served in the Senate from 1967 to 1979. Although he campaigned for the Nixon-Agnew ticket in 1968, he subsequently opposed Richard Nixon on a number of important issues, including several Supreme Court appointments and the Nixon record on civil rights. While in the Senate he worked for the passage of a number of bills providing for housing for low and moderate income persons. An opponent of involvement in the Vietnam War, Brooke was author of a 1972 amendment adopted by the Senate, which called for the withdrawal of U.S. troops in Vietnam.

After losing his Senate seat to Paul Tsongas in 1978, Brooke returned to Washington, D.C., where he joined the law firm of O'Connor and Hannon.

See also: Election of 1968, Richard Nixon, Vietnam War as a Political Issue

Elinor C. Hartshorn

Earl R. Browder (1891–1973)

Influential American Communist of the 1920s and 1930s. Earl Russell Browder was one of the two most prominent leaders of the Communist Party of the United States of America (CPUSA) during the inter-war years.

Browder was born in Wichita, Kansas, where his father, a Methodist minister, was first a Populist and later a Socialist. The younger Browder followed in his father's footsteps by joining the Socialist Party at the age of 15 but then quit the party seven years later, criticizing it for being too reformist. Browder refused to register for and actively campaigned against the draft during World War I and was sentenced to three years in prison.

In 1921 Browder joined the Communist Party. He was an officer of Profintern, the international Communist labor organization, and spent 1926 until 1929 working for that organization in China. He quickly rose to prominence in the Communist Party and by 1930 had become its general secretary and its second most important leader.

When Comintern, the international organization of Communist parties, adopted its popular front line in early 1935, Browder became leader of the American Party and its presidential candidate in 1936. Like Communists everywhere, Browder championed alliances with all pro-democratic forces, socioeconomic reform, and the struggle against fascism. He got 80,160 votes.

Browder was the CPUSA candidate again in 1940, this time supporting Moscow's new line following the signing of its pact with Germany in 1939. After Soviet and American entry into World War II, Browder advocated the early opening of a "second front" in Western Europe to take pressure off the beleaguered Soviet forces.

During the war, he actively advocated continued cooperation between the United States and the Soviet Union. With the onset of the cold war, that position became untenable within the CPUSA, and he was stripped of his leadership positions in 1945 and expelled from the party the following year.

See also: Communist Party of the United States, Election of 1936, Socialist Party of America

Charles S. Hauss

Edmund G. (Jerry) Brown, Jr. (1938–)

Controversial two-term Democratic governor of California. Twice an aspirant for the Democratic Party's presidential nomination, Edmund G. ("Jerry") Brown, Jr., was born in San Francisco, the son of Edmund G. ("Pat") Brown. Pat Brown was a longtime Democratic politician whose twenty-three-year electoral career included eight years as California's attorney general and culminated in his election to governor for two terms (1959–1966).

Jerry Brown attended the University of Santa Clara for one year (1955–1956) after which he entered Sacred Heart Novitiate, a Jesuit seminary, for three and a half years. He subsequently enrolled and graduated from the University of California at Berkeley (1961) and received a law degree from Yale University in 1964. After clerking on the state level, Brown entered private practice in Los Angeles.

Although an alternate Eugene McCarthy delegate at the 1968 Democratic National Convention, Jerry Brown's own political career began in 1969 when he was elected to the newly established Los Angeles Junior College Board. A year later, Brown successfully sought election as secretary of state. In 1974, at age 36, Jerry Brown was elected California's youngest-ever governor by a narrow 3 percent margin.

As governor, Brown quickly earned a distinctive reputation as one who disdained conventional political norms. He chose, for example, to reside in his own apartment rather than the governor's mansion. The new governor also appointed increased numbers of women and racial minorities to public office, many of them drawn from public-interest law backgrounds. In so doing, Brown signified his commitment to those traditionally underrepresented in political life. More generally, the governor gave widespread voice to British economist E. F. Schumacher's "small is beautiful" aphorism and heralded an era of limitations and lowered expectations.

Brown's first term saw some significant legislative accomplishment: enactment of the Agricultural Labor Relations Act (1975), which gave farmworkers collective bargaining protection and the California Coastal Act (1976), which established land development strictures. Although opposed to capital punishment, Brown approved mandatory sentencing legislation for those convicted of violent crimes. He also signed legislation ending the indeterminate sentence.

In 1976 Brown belatedly entered his party's presidential nomination contest. He recorded several surprise performances and convincingly won his own state's primary, but his campaign was characterized by a lack of organization and planning. Brown's interest in the investigation of space colonization, as well as his use of Zen-based metaphors, did little to offset his press characterization as "Governor Moonbeam."

When he sought reelection in 1978, Brown overcame a "flip-flop" on California's controversial Proposition 13 initiative, which imposed a limit on property taxes, and was an easy victor. Brown's second term also saw a second attempt to gain his party's presidential nomination. This time, however, his candidacy generated little national enthusiasm, and by the time of the late California primary, he was able to get only 4 percent of the vote. In 1981 Brown was widely criticized for his delay in handling the Mediterranean fruit fly crisis in California's groves and fields. Even so, the two-term governor captured the 1982 Democratic Senate nomination. In the general election, however, Brown was soundly defeated (52 percent–45 percent) by San Diego mayor Pete Wilson. Since 1982 Jerry Brown has practiced law while also traveling and commenting on social and global policy. In 1989 he made a comeback of sorts, being selected as chair of the California Democratic Party.

Governor Brown's popularity derived from careful orchestration and use of political language. Symbolic manipulation was especially important, given the media-based, nonparty politics of California. Critics, however, believed that Brown was more adept at rhetorical posturing than actual governing. To them, Brown's self-styled "creative inaction" demonstrated nothing more than an inability to act, much less decisively to lead the state. Eventually California's voters as well came to have doubts about Jerry Brown.

The governor's penchant for solitude, his preference for nonpolitical friendships, and his conception of politics as an evolutionary process not easily subjected to public fiat, all have contributed to his unique but ultimately less-than-significant place in American politics.

See also: Election of 1976, Race and Racial Politics

Charles Longley

REFERENCES

Lorenz, J.J. 1978. *Jerry Brown, The Man on the White Horse*. Boston: Houghton Mifflin.

Pack, Robert. 1978. *Jerry Brown, The Philosopher-Prince*. New York: Stein and Day.

Edmund G. (Pat) Brown (1905–)

Popular Democratic governor of California. Born in San Francisco, Edmund Gerald "Pat" Brown earned his law degree in 1927 and was admitted to the California bar. In the following year, he launched his career in politics as a Republican in an unsuccessful bid for the California state assembly. After practicing law and switching his party affiliation, he served as San Francisco's Democratic district attorney and was twice elected attorney general of California (1950, 1954) on the Democratic ticket.

Capitalizing on Republican disunity and promising liberal reforms, Brown in 1958 became only the second Democrat in the twentieth century to capture the governorship of California in a crushing victory over Republican William Knowland by more than 1 million votes. Four years later, Brown defeated former Vice President Richard Nixon in a much closer election (3,037,109 votes to 2,740,351) that prompted Nixon's celebrated but premature retirement from politics.

As governor, Brown sought solutions to the problems caused by California's population explosion and persuaded the legislature to enact huge taxing and spending programs. By the close of his second term, he counted among his accomplishments various reforms in higher education, water resource development, and expanded social services. Seeking a third term in 1966, he faced a conservative Republican who was making his first bid for elective office—Ronald Reagan. On election day, Reagan won a smashing victory at the polls, beating Brown by 1 million votes of the 6.5 million cast. Following this defeat, Brown returned to his law practice and has remained active in Democratic politics. Brown's son, E. G. "Jerry" Brown, also served two terms as governor of California in the 1970s.

See also: California Democratic Council, William Knowland, Richard Nixon, Ronald Reagan

Karl E. Valois

REFERENCES

Brown, Edmund G. 1970. *Reagan and Reality: The Two Californias*. New York: Praeger.

Delatier, Roger D., Clarence F. McIntosh, and Earl G. Waters, eds. 1970. *The Rumble of California Politics, 1848–1970*. New York: Wiley.

Melendy, H. Brett, and Benjamin F. Gilbert. 1965. *Governors of California*. Georgetown, CA: Talisman.

Robin, Michael P., and John Shover. 1970. *Political Change in California: Critical Elections and Social Movements, 1890–1966*. Westport, CT: Greenwood.

H. (Rap) Brown (1943–)

African-American civil rights leader. Hubert "Rap" Brown (Jamil Abdullah al-Amin) is best known for his involvement in the Student Non-violent Coordinating Committee (SNCC) and as a militant spokesperson for radical Black concerns. Brown is the author of *Die Nigger Die* (1969), an affecting autobiography and revolutionary statement.

Brown, who acquired his nickname from his reputed ability to "rap" with poor Blacks, was born in Louisiana and attended Southern University for three years, quitting in order to devote himself full time to the civil rights struggle. In Washington, D.C., he worked with his brother Ed in the Non-Violent Action Group (NAG), eventually becoming its chairman.

Brown became a full-time SNCC worker in 1966, replacing Stokely Carmichael as its chairman in 1967. This position put him in the spotlight as the new spokesperson and national symbol of Black militancy. In his fiery public orations, he generated fear and reaction in the white community.

Brown, despite his affiliation with SNCC, never accepted nonviolence as a tactic and often carried a gun, believing that whites respected firepower. He believed that armed self-defense was necessary and racial violence was inevitable. In *Die Nigger Die*, Brown said, "If America chooses to play Nazi, black folks ain't going to play Jews." His speeches often were incitements to violence, urging burning and looting. For this, he was pursued by authorities in several states.

Brown's outspoken militancy and encouragement of young Blacks to rebel against white authority earned him the wrath of millions of whites and played into the hands of law-and-order presidential candidates like Richard Nixon and George Wallace. Thus, Brown can be credited with stimulating a white reaction and backlash to civil rights and Black militancy that indirectly helped elect in 1968 even less understanding white authorities.

See also: Stokely Carmichael, Civil Rights Legislation and Southern Politics, Election of 1968, Race and Racial Politics, Student Non-Violent Coordinating Committee

Lisa G. Langenbach

REFERENCES

Brown, H. Rap. 1969. *Die Nigger Die.* New York: Dial Press.

Carson, Clayborne. 1981. *In Struggle: SNCC and the Black Awakening in the 1960s.* Cambridge: Harvard U. Pr.

Killian, Lewis. 1968. *The Impossible Revolution? Black Power and the American Dream.* New York: Random House.

John Brown (1757–1837)

Early Kentucky political leader. A Republican Senator from Kentucky, John Brown's Virginia origins and subsequent western loyalties were emblematic of the differences in orientation and interests that eventually split the Agrarian Jeffersonians of the Seaboard South from their western colleagues who were increasingly more interested in nationalistic development during the early decades of the 1800s.

Born in Staunton, Virginia, Brown grew to be one of three distinguished sons of a prominent Presbyterian clergyman. He was a student at Princeton, leaving to join the Revolutionary Army. After the war, he continued his studies at Washington College and later studied law under Thomas Jefferson.

Brown moved to Kentucky in 1782, settling first at Danville and then permanently at Frankfort, becoming an active promoter of Kentucky development and statehood. Brown's absorption with Kentucky's interests embroiled him in Spanish efforts to use passage of the Mississippi River to separate the recently settled areas west of the Appalachians from the new United States.

Brown was chosen to represent Kentucky in the Virginia Assembly in 1787, and that body, in turn, sent him to Philadelphia as one of Virginia's representatives to the Confederation Congress. Upon his return in 1788 to Kentucky, he was selected as a delegate to the Virginia Ratification Convention, where he voted against accepting the new Constitution. He also sat at Kentucky's own Constitutional Convention.

In 1789 Brown represented the district of Kentucky in the U.S. House of Representatives and was reelected to a second term. When Kentucky became a state in 1792, Brown was chosen as one of her first U.S. Senators. He remained in office through 1805 and was elected President *pro tempore* in 1803 and 1804.

Brown's behavior is illustrative of the complicated personal ties that characterized early national politics. He had maintained close ties with his mentor Jefferson, who drew the plans for Brown's Frankfort home, Liberty Hall. It was in that home that Aaron Burr, another close friend, stayed during his mysterious western trip, which gave rise to Burr's eventual indictment for treason by the Jefferson administration.

Brown was a progressive thinker as were his brothers, James Brown, a U.S. Senator from Louisiana, and Samuel Brown, a physician and distinguished medical educator. The three Browns joined young Henry Clay in 1799 in advocating the abolition of slavery in Kentucky through gradual emancipation.

After leaving the Senate, Brown resumed his law practice in Frankfort, where he died in 1837, the last member of the Confederation Congress.

See also: Abolition Movement, Agrarianism, Aaron Burr, Henry Clay, Thomas Jefferson, Kentucky Resolutions

Kathryn A. Malone

John Brown (1800–1859)

Radical abolitionist activist of the 1850s. On the night of May 24, 1856, near Pottawatomie Creek in Kansas, John Brown and a small band of men seized and hacked to death five proslavery settlers. Their actions were, ostensibly, in retaliation for the sack of Lawrence, Kansas, by proslavery forces. The massacre gained national notoriety for Brown and thrust the issue of "Bleeding Kansas" into the presidential campaign of 1856.

Born in Torrington, Connecticut, Brown grew up in Hudson, Ohio, in an atmosphere of deep religious fervor and militant abolitionism. He lived most of his life in obscurity. His role in the antislavery crusade, however, earned him a permanent place in the public consciousness.

Brown developed a preoccupation with the abolition of slavery and believed that he was God's chosen instrument to achieve that end through any means including violence—an eye for an eye. The Pottawatomie Creek massacre was an outgrowth of that thought.

By then, however, Brown had developed a grander vision: to establish an armed base in the mountains of Virginia and, from it, to liberate slaves in an ever-widening area, eventually to become a free state. After Kansas, his plans were encouraged and some financial support came from prominent eastern abolitionists. Then, on October 16, 1859, with an army of 21 men (including 3 of his sons), Brown seized the federal armory at Harper's Ferry, Virginia, and spread the promise of freedom to the slaves in the surrounding countryside, but few came. Instead, militia swarmed into the town sniping at Brown's men. Finally, the U.S. Cavalry under Colonel Robert E. Lee arrived and, on October 18, stormed the engine house of the armory and captured a wounded John Brown. In all, 15 persons died, including 8 of Brown's men and 2 of his sons. Tried by the state of Virginia for murder, treason, and conspiracy, Brown was convicted and hanged on December 2, 1859.

In death, Brown became one of the most powerful symbols in the nation's history. He confirmed southerners' worst suspicions about abolitionists and Black Republicans, and they carried this perception to the presidential election of 1860 and to Fort Sumter. To many in the North, forgetting Brown's deeds but remembering his goals and his serenity and eloquence through his trial and execution, he became a martyr. Shortly thereafter, Union soldiers would march to battle singing "John Brown's Body."

See also: Abolition Movement, Election of 1860

John F. Coleman

REFERENCES

Furnas, Joseph C. 1959. *The Road to Harper's Ferry.* New York: William Sloane.

Malin, James C. 1970. *John Brown and the Legend of Fifty-Six.* 2 vols. New York: Haskell House.

Oates, Stephen B. 1984. *To Purge This Land with Blood: A Biography of John Brown,* 2nd. ed. Amherst: U. of Massachusetts Pr.

Brown v. Thomson
462 U.S. 835 (1983)

In this case, the Supreme Court ruled that Wyoming did not "violate the equal protection clause by allocating one seat in its legislature to a county with small population." Following provisions in the state constitution, the 1981 Wyoming apportionment statute allocated one state representative to Niobrara County, the least populous county in the state. As a result, the 64-seat apportionment plan had a maximum deviation of 89 percent from population equality. The legislation also provided that if the statute was declared unconstitutional, Niobrara County would be combined with a neighboring county to form a state representative district in a 63-seat apportionment plan with a maximum de-

viation of 66 percent from population equality. Appellants specifically challenged representation for Niobrara County, contending that it diluted their voting power and represented a violation of the the equal protection clause of the U.S. Constitution.

While generally finding that state apportionment plans must provide for districts of equal population, the Supreme Court has not demanded mathematical precision, instead allowing for some population deviation if it can be shown to further some rational state policy and to be free of discrimination. The Court has previously suggested in *Reynolds v. Sims*, 377 U.S. 533 (1964), that providing representation for existing political subdivisions could be considered a rational state policy as long as it was not carried to such an extreme that the "one man, one vote" principle was excessively diluted.

Brown was a narrowly defined case focusing not on the entire state reapportionment plan but instead only on the appellants' voting power under the 64-seat House of Representatives (which granted Niobrara County its own state representation) as compared to the 63-seat House of Representatives (which did not). The Court found little impact on the voting power of the appellants when the two plans were contrasted. Since the Court's majority restricted its consideration to a comparison of the two plans, the question became whether Wyoming's policy of granting representation to existing political subdivisions justified the additional population deviation contained in the 64-seat plan. Because significant population deviations would remain even under the 63-seat plan, the Court reasoned that representation for Niobrara County was not a major cause of the population deviation that existed in Wyoming. Furthermore, the Court found that the policy of granting representation to all counties in the state was a longstanding one and that it had been applied consistently and without discrimination. In the end, the Court concluded, "This case presents an unusually strong example of an apportionment plan the population variations of which are entirely the result of the consistent and nondiscriminatory application of a legitimate state policy."

The case is significant because it indicates clearly that the Court is not slavishly attached to the equal population criteria in state legislative districts and will allow population deviations that can be justified by other considerations. Also, the case illustrates the risk involved in challenging only a portion of a reapportionment plan rather than the entire plan.

Clyde Brown

REFERENCES

Wells, David I. 1984. "The 1983 Redistricting Decisions: What People Think the Court Said . . . What the Court Really Said." 73–4 *National Civic Review* 181.

Herbert Brownell, Jr. (1904–)

Prominent Republican politician and Cabinet member. Herbert Brownell, Jr., served as Republican National Committee chairman during and after Thomas E. Dewey's unsuccessful campaign for President in 1944 until 1946. He was also President Dwight D. Eisenhower's Attorney General from 1953 to 1957.

Brownell was a native of Peru, Nebraska. His family moved to Lincoln, where his father was a member of the University of Nebraska faculty. Brownell received his degree from the University of Nebraska in 1924 and a law degree from Yale in 1927. After two years of service as a law clerk in a New York City firm, he became a member of the firm Lord, Day and Lord, an association that lasted until 1977.

Brownell's first efforts as a Republican Party worker were in the Tenth Manhattan Assembly District, which housed the headquarters of Tammany Hall. Then working in a neighboring district was district captain Thomas E. Dewey; the two became close friends. When Brownell ran for election to the New York State Assembly in 1931, Dewey was his campaign manager. Their assault on Tammany's stronghold was innovative but not easy. Among their campaign innovations was a phonograph record that included music, an introduction by Dewey, and a speech by Brownell. The record went to every voter in the district. Although he lost in 1931, Brownell repeated the race in 1932 and was elected. He served five one-year terms in the state assembly before returning to his law practice in 1937.

As a fighting district attorney, Dewey had by this time achieved national fame for his racketbusting investigations begun in 1935. By 1938 Dewey's popularity made him the unanimous choice of the Republican state convention for the gubernatorial race against Herbert Lehman. Losing a close race to Lehman, Dewey was promoted by state leaders for the 1940 presidential nomination. At about this time, Brownell began again to take part in party affairs, managing the successful campaign of the party's nominee for Manhattan borough president in 1941. Brownell

ran two other major campaigns successfully: Dewey's for governor in 1942 and Hanley's for lieutenant governor in 1943. These experiences prepared him for his 1944 management of Dewey's presidential campaign.

In his losing race against Franklin D. Roosevelt, Dewey's defeat was considered honorable by most Republican leaders. As Republican national chairman, Brownell's management was thought to be outstanding. In an unusual move, Republican leaders in Congress took the initiative in arranging for the continuation of a full-time national headquarters with Brownell at its head. Working without pay and on a part-time basis, Brownell launched an eight-point program of headquarters reorganization. Within the year, he insisted that he be relieved so that he could return to his lucrative law practice.

When Dewey was renominated in 1948, Republican national chairman Hugh D. Scott, Jr., named Brownell manager of the campaign, in keeping with the nominee's wishes. Again in 1952, Brownell played a leading role in the successful preconvention campaign for Dwight D. Eisenhower. He took leave from Lord, Day and Lord to serve as Attorney General in Eisenhower's first administration.

See also: Thomas Dewey, Dwight Eisenhower, Election of 1944, Republican National Committee, Tammany Hall

Ralph M. Goldman

REFERENCES

Abels, Jules. 1959. *Out of the Jaws of Victory.* New York: Holt.

Goldman, Ralph M. 1990. *The National Party Chairmen and Committees: Factionalism at the Top.* Armonk, NY: M. E. Sharpe.

William Jennings Bryan (1860–1925)

Perennial Democratic candidate for President. Best known as the standard-bearer of the Democratic Party in the late nineteenth and early twentieth centuries and as the man who recharted his party's direction, William Jennings Bryan served as a delegate to Democratic National Conventions in 1896, 1904, 1912, 1920, and 1924 and was three times nominated for the presidency. In both 1896 and 1900 he lost to William McKinley and in 1908, to William Howard Taft.

Bryan was born in Salem, Illinois, and raised in Jacksonville, where he graduated from Illinois College in 1881. He studied law at Union College in Chicago and graduated in 1883 and then returned to Jacksonville to practice law. In

1887 he moved to Lincoln, Nebraska, where he continued to practice law and became active in Democratic Party politics, first serving as a delegate to the Democratic State Convention in 1888.

In 1890 he became only the second Democrat from Nebraska to be elected to Congress. Reelected in 1892, he established his reputation as an orator and a representative of agrarian interests with his numerous speeches in favor of tariff reform, the income tax, and, especially, the free coinage of silver. He declined to run for a third term in 1894 in order to seek nomination to the U.S. Senate. Unsuccessful in his attempt to be elected to the Senate, he continued to make his views known through public speaking (he was called "The Boy Orator of the Platte") and through his duties as editor of the *Omaha World-Herald.*

He served as a delegate to the Democratic National Convention in Chicago in 1896. There he was able to use his famous "Cross of Gold" speech to mobilize convention support and became the youngest ever presidential nominee of a major political party, at the age of 36. He subsequently obtained the nominations of three other parties (People's [Populist], National Silver, and Silver Republican). Despite this support, and a campaign unprecedented in its scope, he lost the election to William McKinley.

During the Spanish-American War he helped to raise the Third Regiment, Nebraska Volunteer Infantry, and was commissioned a colonel but did not see action. Following the signing of the peace treaty, he resigned his commission to begin his second quest for the presidency.

At the 1900 Democratic Convention in Kansas City, Bryan expanded his 1896 platform to include anti-imperialist and antitrust planks. Although he again received the endorsements of the Populists and the Silver Republicans, he again lost to McKinley in November.

Following his second defeat, Bryan returned to Lincoln to establish and edit *The Commoner,* a weekly political journal. Although conservative forces within the Democratic Party succeeded in replacing Bryan as leader of the party and in nominating Alton B. Parker at the St. Louis convention in 1904, Parker's defeat allowed Bryan to recapture the leadership, and he received his third nomination for the presidency in 1908 in Denver. Despite losing the presidency for a third time, he continued to play a prominent role in the Democratic Party, helping

to secure Woodrow Wilson's nomination for the presidency in 1912.

Following Wilson's victory, Bryan served as Secretary of State, using his office as a platform to advocate world peace and international arbitration. On June 9, 1915, he resigned because of his disagreement with the President over the tone of the second *Lusitania* note. Although he remained active in party politics after that, his influence was no longer decisive.

Bryan devoted the remainder of his life to writing and lecturing, especially against Darwinism, which he blamed as the cause of World War I. His last appearance on the national scene was his assistance in the famous "Monkey Trial" to prosecute John T. Scopes for teaching evolution. Soon after the trial, Bryan fell ill and died in Dayton, Tennessee.

See also: Elections of 1896 and 1908, William McKinley, National Silver Party, Populist (People's) Party, William Howard Taft, Tariffs and Trade

James V. Saturno

REFERENCES

Ashby, LeRoy. 1987. *William Jennings Bryan: Champion of Democracy.* Boston: Twayne.

Bryan, William Jennings, and Mary Baird Bryan. 1925. *The Memoirs of William Jennings Bryan.* Chicago: John C. Winston.

Glad, Paul W. 1960. *The Trumpet Soundeth: William Jennings Bryan and his Democracy, 1896–1912.* Lincoln: U. of Nebraska Pr.

———. 1968. *William Jennings Bryan: A Profile.* New York: Hill and Wang.

Koenig, Louis W. 1971. *Bryan: A Political Biography.* New York: Putnam.

Benjamin C. Bubar (1918–)

Maine Prohibitionist leader. The presidential nominee of the Prohibition Party in 1976 and 1980 (known as the National Statesman Party in 1980), Benjamin Bubar has been a life-long resident of Maine. His political career began in 1938 when he ran for the state legislature as a Republican at the age of 20. Elected in that year, he served until 1945, the youngest person ever to have served in the Maine legislature.

Bubar's father and grandfather were both members of the Prohibition Party, which had strong roots in the movement (Maine first enacted prohibition in 1856). Bubar's father was a clergyman and sometimes an officeholder. Beginning in 1952 Bubar served for many years as executive director of the Christian Civic League (based in Waterville, Maine). Although not related to the Prohibition Party, the league shares similar social and political concerns, including opposition to abortion, gambling, drugs, and alcohol.

Bubar became involved with the Prohibition Party in the 1950s and attended several party conventions. In 1976 Bubar ran for President in 14 states, receiving some 16,000 votes on a campaign budget of $15,000 (most went to travel expenses). In 1980 Bubar ran in 8 states, garnering about 7,200 votes. The conservative multi-issue concerns of party leaders like Bubar led to the renaming of the Prohibition Party after the 1976 election. The change was reversed after 1980, however, as many traditional party supporters were confused by the change. Bubar claims no false hopes that the party will become a major force in national politics, but he has devoted himself to promoting the party's conservative Christian-oriented social and political agenda. He has vowed not to run for President again, hoping instead to see younger people become active in politics.

See also: Elections of 1976 and 1980, Prohibition Party

Robert J. Spitzer

REFERENCES

Smallwood, Frank. 1983. *The Other Candidates: Third Parties in Presidential Elections.* Hanover, NH: U. Pr. of New England.

James Buchanan (1791–1868)

President of the United States on the eve of the Civil War. After a long career in Congress and the executive branch, James Buchanan became the fifteenth President of the United States in 1857. Son of a prosperous merchant from Mercersberg, Pennsylvania, Buchanan graduated from Dickinson College in 1809 and then studied law. After just two years of practice, he began his political career with election to the state legislature as a Federalist in 1814. Buchanan served ten years in the U.S. House of Representatives (1821–1831), shifting allegiances from the dying Federalist Party to the new Democratic Party headed by Andrew Jackson. Jackson made him ambassador to Russia (1831–1833), and in 1834 Buchanan was elected to the U.S. Senate, where he stayed until 1845.

Pennsylvania supporters first boomed Buchanan as a presidential candidate in 1844. After Tennessee Democrat James K. Polk won the nomination and the presidency, he selected Buchanan to be his Secretary of State (1845–1849). In that post, Buchanan strongly supported Polk's expansionist program, guiding the final steps of Texas annexation and the resolu-tion of the Oregon territorial dispute with Great Britain. His offer to purchase Cuba, however, was rebuffed by Spain. After the U.S. had defeated Mexico, Buchanan favored major territorial concessions. Despite his enhanced popularity, Buchanan finished second to Lewis Cass in the balloting for the Democratic nomination at the 1848 convention. His efforts four years later also failed.

President Franklin Pierce appointed Buchanan ambassador to Great Britain (1853–1856), where he again pressed for the annexation of Cuba by helping two other U.S. ambassadors to draw up the avidly expansionist Ostend Manifesto. In 1856 his long search for the Democratic presidential nomination finally succeeded. He did little active campaigning except to issue statements that denounced abolitionism and endorsed the nonintervention of Congress in the issue of the westward expansion of slavery. Although he received only a plurality of votes in a three-way race, Buchanan handily defeated Republican John C. Frémont and the American Party's Millard Fillmore in the Electoral College.

Committed to a single term, Buchanan devoted his energy to foreign policy and to resolving the perplexing issue of slavery in the western territories. Once again he tried but failed to purchase Cuba from Spain. He claimed to oppose slavery on moral grounds. His efforts to bring Kansas into the Union as a state also were frustrated. The dispute in Congress over admitting the territory under the proposed Lecompton Constitution (which would have made Kansas a slave state) deeply divided the President's own party. Buchanan made the issue a test of party loyalty and bitterly feuded with Senator Stephen A. Douglas, the leading Democratic anti-Lecomptonite. In 1860 Buchanan supported the presidential candidate of southern Democratic bolters rather than Douglas, the party's regular nominee.

After Abraham Lincoln's election, Buchanan backed the unsuccessful efforts to arrange a sectional compromise to prevent civil war. He denied the right of southern states to secede but claimed to be powerless to use force to prevent them from doing so. His essentially defensive policy prevented the outbreak of actual warfare until Lincoln succeeded him as President.

See also: Lewis Cass, Stephen Douglas, Electoral College System, Federalist Party, Millard Fillmore, John C. Frémont, Andrew Jackson, Abraham Lincoln, Franklin Pierce, James Polk

John R. McKivigan

REFERENCES

Klein, Philip Shriver. 1962. *President James Buchanan, A Biography*. University Park: Pennsylvania State U. Pr.

Nichols, Roy Franklin. 1948. *The Disruption of American Democracy*. New York: Macmillan.

Rawley, James A. 1969. *Race and Politics: "Bleeding Kansas" and the Coming of the Civil War*. Philadelphia: J. B. Lippincott.

Charles A. Buckley (1890–1967)

Machine politician in New York City and U.S. Congressman. A bricklayer and construction company owner, Charles Anthony Buckley became one of the most significant political bosses in the country as Bronx County, New York, leader and chair of the Public Works Committee of the U.S. Congress. He ruled the nation's best-disciplined machine from 1953 through 1966, although the reform insurgents of Mayor Robert Wagner managed to defeat him for Congress in 1964. He spread patronage jobs to the precincts, though not to his family; he was a tenacious negotiator who snarled obscenities at the press; he never campaigned on the hustings, let alone on television. Yet he won 15 House elections as an Irishman in the half-Jewish Bronx.

Buckley was an old-fashioned professional who dealt quietly and only in private. He played a major role in the success of John F. Kennedy in the 1960 presidential convention, swinging New York delegates to the son of his old friend, Joseph Kennedy. He supported Kennedy's Appalachian program by selective distribution of public works and federal office buildings to key districts, and in the early days of his rule, he supported the young Congressman Robert Wagner. Robert Kennedy, the Attorney General and senatorial candidate from New York, supported Buckley over the reform forces of Wagner from 1962 to 1964 but announced that he would be neutral when Buckley's machine began to decline. Buckley was defeated in the House Twenty-third District primary of June 1964 (despite the mysterious breakdown of voting machines) by patrician reformer Jonathan B. Bingham.

In 1966 he joined forces at the last minute with the northern Manhattan machine to defeat the reformers' choices for judicial positions—his last hurrah.

It was the end of an era when he died. He had lived modestly in the Bronx district (with a stud farm in Rockland County), surviving countless charges of graft and absenteeism from the Congress.

See also: Bosses, Election of 1960, John F. Kennedy

Jeremy Lewis

James L. Buckley (1923–)

Conservative Party Senator from New York. James Lane Buckley was the son of wealthy Catholic parents; he graduated from Yale Law School following wartime service in the Navy. He entered politics by managing his brother William's unsuccessful campaign for mayor of New York in 1965. He then ran twice for the Senate from New York as a Conservative. Supported by President Richard Nixon, he was seated in 1970—the winner of 38.7 percent of the vote against Republican and Democratic candidates.

Buckley was an outspoken, independent conservative New York Senator in foreign and domestic policy who opposed the welfare state and government intervention in the economy. He held to this principle even in opposing assistance to Lockheed, the military contractor; he opposed federal child-care centers, the minimum wage bill, rehabilitation for the handicapped, the Equal Rights Amendment, abortion, and federal loan guarantees to New York. He favored anticrime and antidrug abuse laws, supported the Nixon administration's Vietnam policy and high defense appropriations, and opposed the War Powers Resolution. He was also unafraid to oppose social security benefit increases.

The Supreme Court ruled in *Buckley v. Valeo* that limits on campaign spending violated the First Amendment, although public financing of campaigns in the 1974 Federal Election Amendments was upheld. Then the Buckley Amendment of 1976 gave adults the privacy and inspection rights over student files. Finally, Buckley became the first conservative to call for President Nixon's resignation after the Watergate scandal broke. Buckley was unseated by Daniel Patrick Moynihan in 1976.

See also: Buckley v. Valeo, Equal Rights Amendment, Federal Election Campaign Amendments, Richard Nixon, Watergate

Jeremy R. T. Lewis

REFERENCES

Buckley, James L. 1975. *If Men Were Angels: A View From the Senate*. New York: Putnam.

Markmann, Charles L. 1973. *The Buckleys: A Family Examined*. New York: Morrow.

William F. Buckley, Jr. (1925–)

Conservative political commentator and media figure. A major figure in the post-World War II conservative political renascence that culminated in the election of Ronald Reagan in 1980, William Frank Buckley, Jr., is the son of a wealthy oil baron. He was early imbued with the essential characteristics of a twentieth-century conservative: faith in God, a capitalist approach to the economy, and an antipathy toward the restrictive power of big government. Buckley's most enduring contribution to postwar conservative politics has been his efforts to bridge the gap between conservative intellectuals and ordinary politicians.

He has accomplished his goal in two ways: by providing the intellectual capital to be used by conservative candidates for office and by his own efforts as political activist. The intellectual capital was provided by the journal that Buckley has edited since its inception in 1955, the *National Review*. Over the years the *National Review* has served as a public forum for the discussion of conservative ideology and political solutions to contemporary problems. Buckley has also endeavored to translate his conservative ideas into political action. With L. Brent Bozell, Buckley wrote an intellectual defense of Joseph McCarthy, founded a political organization for university students known as the Young Americans for Freedom (1960), was co-founder of New York's Conservative Party (1961), ran for mayor of New York City (1965), and served as the United States delegate to the United Nations General Assembly (1973). He has also moderated a popular television talk show, *Firing Line*, for many years.

See also: Joseph McCarthy, McCarthyism, Ronald Reagan, United Nations, Young Americans for Freedom

David B. Raymond

REFERENCES

Buckley, William F., Jr., and L. Brent Bozell. 1954. *McCarthy and His Enemies: The Record and Its Meaning.* Chicago: H. Regnery.

———. 1962. *The Committee and Its Critics; A Calm Revue of the House Committee on Un-American Activities.* New York: Putnam.

———. 1966. *The Unmaking of a Mayor.* New York: Viking.

———. 1974. *UN Journal: A Delegate's Odyssey.* New York: Putnam.

Nash, George H. 1976. *The Conservative Intellectual Movement in America Since 1945.* New York: Basic Books.

Buckley v. Valeo
424 U.S. 1 (1976)

A case that arose out of a set of challenges to the recently enacted provisions of a federal campaign law that limited the amount of campaign contributions and expenditures, required extensive disclosure of contributions and expenditures for campaigning, provided public financing of presidential election campaigns, and set up a Federal Election Commission.

The Supreme Court in *Buckley v. Valeo* judged the statute under First Amendment principles that protect speech unless the regulation or restriction is essential to the accomplishment of a compelling governmental interest (a standard often called strict scrutiny) and prohibits restrictions on speech that discriminate among messages or speakers (known as the requirement of neutrality).

The statute at issue in *Buckley* made extensive distinctions among parties, candidates, political action committees (PACs), and others. *Buckley* sustained portions of the statute that included those distinctions on the basis of an analysis that assumed that all involved were being treated alike or comparably. As a result, the status of parties after *Buckley* is unclear.

Expenditure Limitations

The Court held that expenditure limitations impermissibly diminished the quantity of speech, in conflict with the First Amendment. Thus Congress could not constitutionally restrict the sums spent on campaigning except in exchange for public financing of a campaign. The Court found unconstitutional all other restrictions on expenditures by candidates and independent political committees.

Underlying the Court's elaboration of the First Amendment are significant effects on campaigning. Without enough funds, candidates may not be able to achieve even name recognition, let alone communicate a message to or achieve a responsible evaluation by the public. Insufficient funds may well determine the winner of the contest, particularly when unknowns are pitted against famous candidates or incumbents who benefit from many forms of exposure not counted within campaign restrictions. Those possibilities implicate basic First Amendment values.

The Court's holding gave renewed life to independent expenditures. The statute would have prohibited campaign expenditures in excess of $1,000 by any person or group other than the candidate, the press, and the parties. Holding that all political discussion would have an impact on elections, the Court defined the statute quite narrowly, limiting it to speech expressly advocating the election or defeat of a candidate. Even limited as such, the Court struck those provisions of the act that would have restricted noncandidate speech that had not been pre–arranged with the candidates. In accord with these rulings, the federal statute was subsequently amended to define an "independent expenditure" as "an expenditure by a person expressly advocating the election or defeat of a clearly identified candidate which is made without cooperation or consultation with any candidate" or agent and not at their suggestion or "in concert" with a candidate. Such expenditures are not limited by the act.

While holding that other political actors could not be excluded, the Court left standing the specific expenditure levels in the statute directed to political parties. *Buckley* thus sanctioned the trend toward candidate-centered (rather than party-centered) campaigns without explicitly abandoning its demand for neutrality in treatment of speech under the First Amendment.

Contribution Limits

In its treatment of contribution limits, the Court ignored the comparative impact of the statute on political parties and other political organizations.

The Court held that contributions could be limited because the statute treated all candidates and contributors alike."[T]he Act applies the same limitations on contributions to all candidates regardless of their present occupations, ideological views, or party affiliations." Thus, the First Amendment requirement of neutrality toward speech appeared unoffended.

The Court then clarified the factual basis of its holding: "Absent record evidence of invidious discrimination against challengers as a class, a court should generally be hesitant to invalidate legislation which on its face imposes evenhanded restrictions." The Court found no evidence and "little indication" that the limitations on contributions to candidates or organizations would give incumbents an added advantage and found no support in the record for the claim that the statute would disadvantage fledgling parties in their search for seed money.

The factual nature of the *Buckley* holding suggests the possibility that contribution limitations may not survive. Evidence has accumu-

lated that contribution limitations alter the course of political campaigns. The crucial issue does not appear to be the relative financial means of competing candidates but rather the ability of challengers to meet significant thresholds of public awareness. Restraints on campaign finance reduce the amount that can be raised and spent on campaigning. Gary Jacobson, on the basis of an elaborate study, concluded that many candidates had been and would be deprived of adequate funding by the contribution limits. The Court has not confronted the significance of research showing the importance of the level of funding and the tie between the levels and the limitations on contributions. Nor did the Court address the impact of the contribution limitations in shifting the weight of political muscle among various political actors, early contributors, and others.

The contribution rules themselves make significant distinctions among political actors. The maximum contributions that may be directed toward the parties are somewhat greater than those that may be directed to the candidates. But the parties are more strictly limited in what they can contribute to or spend on individual campaigns, which must be run by the candidate through separate committees to receive and spend campaign funds. *Buckley* also left these standing despite the requirement of neutrality.

Reporting and Disclosure

The Court held that the value of disclosure to the public exceeds the costs in loss of privacy except when a reasonable probability of threats, harassment, or retaliation exists. The Court believed that most would suffer little probability of such adverse consequences. Thus, in general, there was little harm to be compared to the value of disclosure to the public. Specific groups may be exempted, however, where a reasonable probability of threats, harassment, or retaliation seems likely.

The Court found it unnecessary and therefore unconstitutional to subject speech to reporting and disclosure when that speech, while relevant to campaigns, is not explicitly for or against a candidate. All discussion of public issues is relevant to campaigns. The more controversial the issue and the more public figures have taken positions, the greater the effect of commentary on the electoral chances of those who have taken positions or acted on those issues. To subject all such speech to the regulation designed for elections, however, could squelch a good deal of commentary by disclosing the membership lists of groups opposing popular feelings. The Court concluded that a definition of speech intended to influence political campaigns that subjected most political speech to campaign requirements would sweep far too broadly and cut too deeply into discussion of public affairs. Thus, only financial transactions in relation to speech that expressly advocates the election or defeat of a candidate are subject to reporting and disclosure requirements.

Public Funding

The requirement of neutrality poses many problems with respect to public funding. First are the relationships among the parties. In *Williams v. Rhodes*, the Court wrote, "There is, of course, no reason why two parties should retain a permanent monopoly on the right to have people vote for or against them. Competition in ideas and governmental policies is at the core of our electoral process and of the First Amendment freedoms." The Court reiterated that language in *Buckley v. Valeo* and in *Anderson v. Celebrezze*.

Thus, campaign-funding legislation must treat the parties in the same way. The Court found acceptable funding that is roughly proportional to support for the parties and does not exclude third parties.

Second, commensurate treatment of candidates raises particular difficulties with respect to primaries. The statute, with the blessing of *Buckley*, matches contributions according to a formula but at the cost of exaggerating some of the early differences among the candidates.

Third, the relation between parties and candidates is troublesome. Public funding of campaign expenses has been directed to the candidates. Specifying candidate control over public funds increases factionalism and may exacerbate a cult of personality. Public funding of conventions has been directed to the parties. Funding the parties could decrease popular control over nominations. Both alternatives conflict with the neutrality principle affirmed in *Buckley*, which delegates to the people the choice of whether to support the candidate, the party, or other institutions.

Buckley saw little difficulty in this area. The Court held that, because public financing enhances speech, it does not abridge the First Amendment. Whatever burdens are imposed on those who do not receive public financing are minimal, and whatever benefits public financing offers to some political actors are balanced by the burden of refusing private contributions and justified by compelling interests. Thus, the Court found no violation of the obligation of equal protection imposed by the Fifth Amendment

Justifications for Regulation

Buckley demonstrates that the Supreme Court has permitted some constrictions of speech (e.g., contribution limits, if enacted for sufficiently good reasons), which are often described as compelling governmental interests. The question, then, is whether the Constitution has sufficient justifications for campaign regulation.

In *Buckley*, the Court accepted the *appearance* of corruption as a rationale justifying that portion of the federal scheme that it held constitutional. Deference to appearances implies that the First Amendment can be overruled by opinion polls.

Buckley also recognized actual corruption as a justification for campaign regulation. Corruption defeats the expression of popular will through the election process as it does the obligation of the representative to serve the public. Campaign finance legislation may also implicate those same values by decreasing campaign funding, increasing the complexity of campaigning, and restricting entry into the campaign field, channeling dollars among organizations, and subjecting the entire process to administrative supervision. The question is whether more is sacrificed than gained.

That problem is cast in bolder relief by yet another justification the Court has used to sustain electoral regulation—the mitigation of factionalism. Campaign finance legislation can significantly increase factionalism.

Decided in haste, *Buckley* has had a powerful impact on American election law. Insofar as it has sustained federal campaign laws, it seems to have won considerable popular support. It is, nevertheless, internally inconsistent and factually insupportable. How those conflicts will be resolved in the future is unclear.

See also: James L. Buckley, Contribution Limits and Presidential Nominating Campaigns, Federal Election Commission, Financing Presidential Elections, Political Action Committees

Stephen E. Gottlieb

REFERENCES

ACLU v. Jennings, 366 F. Supp. 1041 (D.D.C. 1973).
FEC v. Central Long Island T.R.I.M., 616 F. 2d 45 (2 Cir. 1980).

FEC v. Massachusetts Citizens for Life, 107 S. Ct. 616 (1986).

Gottlieb, Stephen E. 1985. "Fleshing Out the Right of Association: The Problem of the Contribution Limits of the Federal Election Campaign Act." 49 *Albany Law Review* 825.

Storer v. Brown, 415 U.S. 724 (1974).

Bull Moose Party

The popular name for the short-lived United States Progressive Party, or National Progressive Party, that was organized in 1912 with headquarters in New York City. It was a tool to facilitate Theodore Roosevelt's return to the White House after the 1912 Republican convention rejected his bid to replace William Howard Taft as the nominee. The party soon dissolved after 1916 when Roosevelt returned to the Republican Party. Newspapers coined the popular name for the party after Roosevelt's remark early in the campaign that he felt as fit as a bull moose.

After William Howard Taft alienated the Progressive Republicans during his administration by seemingly siding with the ultraconservatives, Theodore Roosevelt decided to challenge him for the Republican presidential nomination. During his years in the White House, Roosevelt had carefully maneuvered between Progressive and conservative factions within the party. Although he captured 51 percent of the popular vote in the 13 states holding primaries (compared to Taft's 34 percent and Senator Robert M. La Follette's 15 percent), Roosevelt was defeated at the Republican National Convention in Chicago. Conservative forces controlled the party organization, and they refused to bargain with Roosevelt.

After obtaining financial backing, Roosevelt bolted the party to form the Bull Moose Party. The August convention met in Chicago, where every state but South Carolina was represented. Women predominated among the delegates. The amateurs selected Roosevelt for President and Hiram W. Johnson of California for Vice President, but clearly, the Bull Moose Party was largely a vehicle of its energetic and charismatic leader. It marked the first minor party challenge in American history to focus more on the personality of the leader than the principles of the party.

In addition to setting the American record of producing the best-financed third-party candidate in comparison to major party expenditures, the 1912 presidential campaign was marked by major political conflict, including an assassination attempt on Roosevelt in Milwaukee. On October 14, 1912, an assailant shot Roosevelt who insisted on delivering a speech even as he bled under his coat. After a member of the audience questioned Roosevelt's veracity about the attempted assassination, he flung his coat open to reveal the blood to the frenzy of the crowd. A folded 50-page speech and glass case in his breast pocket deflected the bullet.

Roosevelt's 1912 campaign for the "New Nationalism" has been characterized as one of the most radical in American history. The Bull Moose platform reflected the values of the Progressives. It called for a variety of political, judicial, economic, and social reforms: the direct election of Senators; popular control of state government through the initiative, referendum, and recall; women's suffrage; minimum-wage and child-labor legislation; social insurance against industrial accidents, unemployment, sickness, and old age; convict leasing; monopoly-control laws; tariff reform; and the suggestion of graduated income and inheritance taxes.

Woodrow Wilson won the 1912 election with a minority of the popular vote (42 percent, 435 electoral votes), fewer than William Jennings Bryan had pulled in the 1896, 1900, and 1908 elections. Roosevelt was second with 27 percent of the popular vote (88 electoral votes), and Taft was third with 23 percent of the popular vote (8 electoral votes). Taft made history as the only major-party candidate for President to ever finish in third place. Socialist Eugene V. Debs was fourth with 6 percent of the popular vote.

The Bull Moose Party disappeared in 1916 after Roosevelt turned down their nomination. He was again the most prominent Republican Party leader by 1918, and the likely nominee of the Republicans in 1920, but he died on January 6, 1919. Unfortunately, the Bull Moose Party gave the Republican Party to the conservatives, who eventually turned it into the minority party for half a century. On the other hand, most of the Bull Moose Party platform eventually became law.

See also: Election of 1912, Robert La Follette, Progressive Party, Theodore Roosevelt, William Howard Taft, Third Parties in American Elections

William David Pederson

REFERENCES

Barber, James David. 1980. *The Pulse of Politics*. New York: Norton.

Burdette, Franklin L. 1972. *The Republican Party*. New York: D. Van Nostrand.

Gable, John Allen. 1978. *The Bull Moose Party: Theodore Roosevelt and the Progressive Party*. Port Washington, NY: Kennikat.

Rosenstone, Steven J., Roy L. Behr, and Edward H. Lazarus. 1984. *Third Parties in America*. Princeton: Princeton U. Pr.

Bullet Voting

Also known as single-shot voting, bullet voting occurs when a voter casts fewer votes than he or she is entitled to cast in a multimember district election. The phenomenon is of most interest when employed as strategic behavior as a group, usually defined in racial or ethnic terms.

Bullet voting may allow numbers of a minority group to elect a legislative or council member they otherwise would not be able to elect. For example, consider a city with a five-member council elected at large. The Black minority in the city might target their vote on one or two Black candidates, withholding support for all other candidates. As a result, the one or two Black candidates may place in the top five, even if unsupported by white voters. However, this strategy is sometimes ruled out by full-slate laws, found primarily in southern cities. Such laws invalidate ballots in which fewer than the full number of votes have been cast for an office.

The use of bullet voting by minority groups has been cited as one reason multimember legislative or council districts should be replaced by single-member districts. In *Thornburg v. Gingles*, 478 U.S. 30 (1986), the plaintiffs argued that Blacks had to engage in bullet voting in order to elect Black legislators to the North Carolina legislature and thus were effectively forced to forfeit their right to vote for a full slate of candidates, an argument accepted in part by the district court.

See also: Single-Member Districts, *Thornburg v. Gingles*

Charles L. Prysby

REFERENCES

Engstrom, Richard L., and Michael D. McDonald. 1987. "The Election of Blacks to Southern City Councils: The Dominant Impact of Electorial Arrangements." In Laurence W. Moreland, Robert P. Steed, and Tod A. Baker, eds. *Blacks in Southern Politics*. New York: Praeger.

Grofman, Bernard. 1985. "Criteria for Redistricting: A Social Science Perspective." 33 *UCLA Law Review* 77.

Thernstrom, Abigail M. 1987. *Whose Votes Count?* Cambridge: Harvard U. Pr.

Bullock v. Carter

405 U.S. 134 (1972)

In this case, the Supreme Court held that a filing fee requirement for candidates in the Texas Democratic primary for county offices was unconstitutional. The Court did not find, however, that all filing fees are prohibited.

Under a Texas statute, the executive committees of county political parties were to estimate the total cost of primaries and then apportion the cost "among the various candidates, 'as in their judgment is just and equitable.'" "Justness" was determined by such variables as the importance of the office and its emolument. Filing fees, therefore, could be as high as $8,900. Paying a filing fee was the only way to gain access to the ballot; no alternative means, such as petitions or write-in votes, existed in Texas. Writing for a unanimous Court (Justices William Rehnquist and Lewis Powell did not participate), Chief Justice Warren Burger declared the Texas scheme a violation of the equal protection clause of the Fourteenth Amendment.

As with all equal protection claims, the Court first had to decide what level of scrutiny to apply before deciding the case. Normally for a statute to withstand a constitutional challenge, a state need only show that its purposes are legitimate and its means rational (deferential scrutiny). If, however, the constitutional claim involves a "fundamental right," a more rigorous standard of review than rationality is triggered. With "heightened scrutiny," it becomes very difficult for a state to show that its challenged scheme is "necessary" (rather than rational) to accomplish the legitimate state objective. The Court determined that heightened scrutiny was appropriate in this case. The fundamental interest involved was not the right to be a candidate but rather that the scheme impinged on the fundamental rights of voters.

States have a legitimate interest in being able to control access to the ballot so as to maintain the integrity of the electoral process. Likewise, states have a legitimate interest in regulating the process so that the cost is reasonable. Finally, there is no constitutional right per se to be a candidate. But, according to Chief Justice Burger, "the rights of voters and the rights of candidates do not lend themselves to neat separation." The Texas filing fee impermissibly limited the field of candidates from which the voters might choose. Burger noted that the size of the fees and the lack of alternate means of access to the ballot "would fall more heavily on the less affluent segment of the community . . . [which would] deny some voters the opportunity to vote for a candidate of their choosing; at the same time it gives the affluent the power to place on the ballot their own names or the names of the persons they favor . . . [therefore] the scheme has a real and appreciable impact on the exercise of the franchise. . . ."

In *Bullock*, the Court noted that "reasonable filing fees" were not precluded but that a system that required candidates to "shoulder the costs of conducting primary elections" with no alternative of ballot access was not acceptable.

H. W. Perry, Jr.

Dean Burch (1927–)

Republican National Committee chairman in the Goldwater era. An Arizona attorney originally from Enid, Oklahoma, Dean Burch graduated from the University of Arizona Law School in 1953.

Early in 1964, William Miller, New York Congressman and chairman of the Republican National Committee, obtained a commitment from each prospective Republican presidential nominee that, if nominated, he would direct the campaign through RNC headquarters. This strategy was designed to reassure the Republican stalwarts who claimed that Richard Nixon's narrow defeat in 1960 happened because Nixon's personal organization bypassed the regular party machinery.

Barry Goldwater secured the nomination and named his youthful former administrative assistant, Phoenix attorney Dean Burch, as the RNC chairman. Burch spent weeks remodeling the party headquarters and reorganizing the staff. William Miller, by then the vice presidential nominee, made no effort to guide Burch's efforts. By bringing the National Draft Goldwater Committee staff into the headquarters, Burch offended many veteran employees, several of whom resigned. Some of the preparations for the ensuing campaign made prior to the national convention were discarded.

While no degree of headquarters efficiency could have reversed Lyndon Johnson's landslide victory, Burch became a scapegoat for the party regulars. He was replaced by Ohio Republican chairman Ray Bliss in January 1965.

Dean Burch managed Goldwater's successful 1968 campaign for the Arizona seat in the U.S. Senate, then served the first Nixon administration as chairman of the Federal Communications Commission. In 1973 and 1974, he led a White House group that coordinated Richard Nixon's political defense against the Watergate charges. Burch then practiced law in Washing-

ton and has since moved in and out of campaigns and government appointments.

See also: Election of 1964, Federal Communications Commission, Barry Goldwater, Lyndon Johnson, Richard Nixon, Republican National Committee

Karl A. Lamb

REFERENCES

Cosman, Bernard, and Robert J. Huckshorn, eds. 1968. *Republican Politics: The 1964 Campaign and Its Aftermath for the Republican Party*. New York: Praeger.

Lamb, Karl A., and Paul A. Smith. 1968. *Campaign Decision-Making: The Presidential Election of 1964*. Belmont, CA: Wadsworth.

John A. Burns (1909–1975)

Liberal Democratic Hawaiian politician and governor. John Anthony Burns was born in Montana and moved with his family when he was four years old to the islands of Hawaii. He spent his childhood in the tough Hawaiian neighborhood known as the Kalihi District. His father, Jack Burns, is credited with building the Democratic Party in Hawaii from practical nonexistence to supremacy. While his involvement in politics did not begin until the late 1940s, Burns remained active in Hawaii's government until his death.

In the years before his public service, Burns farmed, operated a liquor store, and served on the police force. As a police captain during World War II, Burns was in charge of the espionage division before the Japanese attack on Pearl Harbor. Burns nevertheless defended the loyalty of thousands of Americans of Japanese ancestry and assisted many in avoiding incarceration.

As a delegate to Congress from the Territory of Hawaii from 1956 to 1959, Burns was instrumental in Hawaii's eventual statehood. However, Burns lost his first bid for governor in 1960 immediately following his successful effort at gaining statehood for Hawaii. A Democrat, he was subsequently elected governor three times (1962, 1966, and 1970).

As governor, his chief goal centered on equality of opportunity in the Islands. A related goal for Burns was the improvement of public education. He earned a reputation for consensus government, much in the style of his friend and colleague in Washington, D.C., Lyndon Johnson. Burns, a man with liberal social views, turned out to be a fiscal conservative with the ability to work with the businessmen of Hawaii, who initially were apprehensive about his election to the governorship.

Reagan Robbins

REFERENCES

Amalu, Samuel. 1974. *Jack Burns: A Portrait in Transition*. Honolulu: Mamalohoa Foundation.

Coffman, Tom. 1973. *Catch a Wave: A Case Study of Hawaii's New Politics*. Honolulu: U. of Hawaii Pr.

Aaron Burr (1756–1836)

Controversial politician of the early Republic and third Vice President of the United States. A powerful political leader in New York in the 1790s and later the third Vice President of the United States, Aaron Burr had a genius for political organization that greatly contributed to the Republican victory in the presidential election of 1800. Born in Newark, New Jersey, Burr was a bright student at Princeton and a young officer in the Continental Army before he studied law. In 1783 he moved to New York City where he rose to the top of the legal profession and entered politics.

In 1789 Governor George Clinton appointed Burr as attorney general of New York. The following year he won election to the United States Senate by defeating Alexander Hamilton's father-in-law, General Philip Schuyler. Burr failed to win reelection in 1796, but the next year he was elected to the New York assembly. After his involvement in several allegedly corrupt business deals cost him reelection in 1799, Burr helped organize the Republican forces in New York City around a social club called the Society of St. Tammany. With this group as his base of power, Burr organized the voters of the city, and in April 1800, they selected a Republican delegation to the state assembly. This triumph gave the party control of the legislature and thus guaranteed it the entire electoral vote of New York in the presidential election. Then Burr engineered his own endorsement as Vice President on the ticket with Thomas Jefferson.

In the presidential election of 1800, Jefferson and Burr defeated the Federalist Party's candidates. But under the election system of that time (before the passage of the Twelfth Amendment), Burr and Jefferson received the same number of votes in the Electoral College. Despite Burr's immediate disclaimer for the highest office, deadlock and confusion developed. The contest went to the House of Representatives where the Federalists controlled the votes of enough states to block the election of Jefferson. Partly owing to Hamilton's influence, Jefferson was eventually selected as President on the thirty-sixth ballot. Burr became Vice President.

In 1804, however, the New Yorker was dropped from the presidential ticket because Jefferson now distrusted Burr and wanted James Madison to be the heir apparent. That same year, Burr was defeated for the governorship of New York, and he blamed the loss on Hamilton's continued opposition. As a result, Burr killed Hamilton in a duel at Weehawken, New Jersey, on July 11, 1804. Since duels were officially banned in New York and New Jersey, both states charged Burr with murder. He returned to Washington to finish his term as Vice President, and later the murder charges were dropped. The duel, however, had ended his political career.

After he left office, Burr became involved in organizing an expedition into the Southwest. He was arrested and charged with attempting to split off a part of the Louisiana Territory from the United States. Despite a strenuous effort by the Jefferson administration, Burr was acquitted. In debt and with his reputation ruined, Burr went to Europe. For several years he unsuccessfully tried to enlist the British and French in schemes against the United States Government. He returned to New York in 1812 and resumed his legal practice, his political life effectively at an end.

See also: George Clinton, Election of 1800, Electoral College System, Federalist Party, Alexander Hamilton, Thomas Jefferson, James Madison, Twelfth Amendment

Steven E. Siry

REFERENCES

Adams, Henry. 1889–1891. *History of the United States During the Administrations of Jefferson and Madison.* 9 vols. New York: Macmillan.

Kline, Mary-Jo, ed. 1983. *Political Correspondence and Public Papers of Aaron Burr.* 2 vols. Princeton: Princeton U. Pr.

Lomask, Milton. 1979, 1982. *Aaron Burr.* 2 vols. New York: Farrar, Straus & Giroux.

Burroughs v. United States
290 U.S. 534 (1934)

Prior to *Buckley v. Valeo*, *Burroughs* was the most important case involving the right of government to regulate campaign finances. *Burroughs* upheld portions of the Federal Corrupt Practices Act of 1925. The relevant sections of the act required that political committees on behalf of presidential and vice presidential candidates keep detailed records of contributions and expenditures, including the amount contributed, name and address of contributors, and the recipients of the funds.

The Supreme Court rejected the argument that congressional authority was limited because the Constitution only gives Congress explicit control over the day and time of choosing electors. For the majority, Justice George Sutherland wrote, "The congressional act under review seeks to preserve the purity of presidential and vice presidential elections. . . . To say that congress is without power to pass appropriate legislation to safeguard such an election from the improper use of money to influence the result is to deny to the nation in a vital particular the power of self protection." Justice Sutherland went on to quote extensively from *Ex parte Yarbrough*, which had justified the need for a republican government to protect itself from violence, corruption, and bribery. In addition to obvious impediments such as violence, the author argued that "the free use of money in elections, arising from the vast growth of recent wealth in other quarters, presents equal cause for anxiety."

Burroughs is a good starting place for the student of election financing. It is a short, comprehensible opinion that details the principles involved in the protection of the integrity of elections generally and the regulation of campaign finances specifically.

See also: Campaign Finance and the Constitution, Federal Corrupt Practices Act of 1925, Political Action Committees

H. W. Perry, Jr.

George H. W. Bush (1924–)

The forty-first President of the United States. George Herbert Walker Bush was born in Milton, Massachusetts, and grew up in Greenwich, Connecticut. He is the second son of Prescott Bush, a partner in Brown Brothers, Harriman investment bankers of New York, and Dorothy Walker Bush, whose family holds extensive summer property in Kennebunkport, Maine, and who were donors of the leading Anglo-American trophy in amateur golf, the Walker Cup. While George Bush and his siblings were growing up, Prescott Bush was moderator of the Representative Town Meeting of Greenwich; later (1952–1963) he was a middle-of-the-road Republican U.S. Senator from Connecticut.

George Bush attended Greenwich Country Day School, prepped at Andover, and, like his father, went to Yale where he was Phi Beta Kappa, captain of the baseball team, and a member of the most socially elite secret society, Skull and Bones. Before entering Yale, Bush served with distinction in World War II as a Navy pilot and married Barbara Pierce, a Smith College student whose father was a magazine publisher from Rye, New York.

After Yale (B.A., 1948), Bush went to work for Dresser Industries in Texas and California to learn the oil business. In 1950 he started a partnership in Midland, Texas, dealing in oil and gas properties. A successor company—Zapata Offshore Company—of which he was president, moved to Houston in 1958. Since 1950 he has considered himself a Texan, although his family origins and ties, his education, his summers in Kennebunkport, his habits of speech, and his religious affiliation (Episcopalian) remind many observers of his firm roots in the upper-class metropolitan Northeast.

In Houston, Bush became active in Republican politics. In 1964 he received the Republican nomination for the Senate but was beaten by the incumbent, Ralph Yarborough. In 1966 he was elected to Congress to represent Houston's wealthier neighborhoods, and he was reelected in 1968. He served on the Ways and Means Committee in 1970 and once again ran for the Senate and was once more defeated, this time by Lloyd Bentsen.

Presidents Richard Nixon and Gerald Ford appointed him thereafter to a succession of positions requiring a high degree of visibility, acquiescence, and team play: Permanent Representative of the U.S. to the U.N. (1971–1972); chairman of the Republican National Committee (1973–1974); Chief of the U.S. Liaison Office in the People's Republic of China (1974–1975); and Director of the Central Intelligence Agency (1976–1977). The conditions of his Senate confirmation to the CIA post precluded his being considered for the vice presidency on the Ford ticket in 1976. Bush left his fingerprints on none of these jobs. This was notably the case with respect to the Republican National Committee, which he led during the height of the Watergate scandal without embarrassment to the Nixon administration but also without insulating the party from the ill effects of the scandal.

Bush began to campaign for President soon after he left the government in 1977. In the 1980 nomination battle, he was defeated by Ronald Reagan despite some early primary victories. His departure from the race in late May was soon enough and was managed with sufficient adroitness by his manager, James Baker, so as not to spoil his chances to be picked as Reagan's running mate.

As Vice President, Bush continued to exercise his by-then extraordinarily well-practiced capacities for loyal self-effacement, leaving the limelight for eight years to the President. He traveled extensively, attended state funerals abroad, and presided over various task forces at the President's pleasure.

His reward finally came in the Republican presidential nomination in 1988 when he was able to outdistance a crowded field of challengers, confident that President Reagan would do nothing to undercut him, as Lyndon Johnson had undercut Hubert Humphrey in 1968 and Dwight Eisenhower had undercut Nixon in 1960. Indeed, where Reagan was especially popular with Republican primary electorates, Bush did particularly well.

His presidential effort against Michael Dukakis benefited from ugly negative campaigning that seemed to some observers out of keeping with Bush's gentlemanly personal style but entirely congruent with emerging doctrines among hardnosed campaign professionals about how to win elections.

Bush's early presidency was likewise marked by a high degree of professionalism and reliance more on appointments of experienced Republican operators to staff Cabinet positions than had been the case with his predecessor. Bush also moved swiftly to establish cooperative relations with Congress, of which both houses were led by the Democratic Party. Not only was Bush more conciliatory toward Congress than Ronald Reagan but he was also far more respectful than Reagan of conventional wisdom about the probable outcomes of various policy options.

See also: Lloyd Bentsen, Michael Dukakis, Election of 1980, Gerald Ford, Richard Nixon, Ronald Reagan, Republican National Committee, United Nations, Watergate

Nelson W. Polsby

Business-Industry Political Action Committee

Established in 1963, the Business-Industry Political Action Committee (BIPAC) is both the longest-lived and most important business group in contemporary electoral politics. Formed by high officials in the National Association of Manufacturers as a counterweight to labor's political action committees—especially the AFL-CIO's Committee on Political Education (COPE)—BIPAC has metamorphosed from a small, little-known organization to a crucial force in orienting the political involvement of large segments of the American corporate community.

The history of BIPAC can be divided into two eras: before and after the 1974–1976 period when amendments to the Federal Election Campaign Act (FECA) were passed and key regulations written. Before the 1974–1976 period, BIPAC operated with a minimal staff and handed out modest amounts of cash to Republicans and to a few conservative Democrats ($1 million between 1963 and 1970). The organization survived on relatively small contributions; in 1969, for example, only 142 donations exceeded $100 and just two surpassed $1,000. During its early years, BIPAC was neither a major force in congressional elections nor was it within the Washington campaign community. Indeed, from 1963 to 1970, the organization's headquarters were located in New York. Its contribution patterns favored incumbent Republicans, challenging Republicans, and southern Democratic incumbents, respectively.

As one of the few business PACs in operation when the FECA amendments were adopted, BIPAC was in an excellent position to influence the development of the wave of corporate and trade PACs that were organized in the wake of the campaign law changes. In the 1970s and 1980s, BIPAC's own fundraising increased but more important has been its encouragement of PACs among various industries and its central role in providing contribution cues to these and other PACs. BIPAC represents the most popular source of electoral intelligence within the business community. In practice, this means that BIPAC often makes early contributions to favored candidates, thus signaling a positive assessment of the candidates' ideologies and issue positions by business. Moreover, BIPAC provides frequent briefings for more than 100 PAC managers during the campaign season. In its own giving patterns, BIPAC has retained its bipartisan flavor, with significant numbers of conservative incumbent Democrats receiving contributions.

Organized to counteract labor influence in politics, BIPAC has fulfilled and surpassed its original mission by becoming the central voice of business and industry in the campaign arena of American politics.

See also: AFL-CIO COPE, Federal Election Campaign Act of 1971, National Association of Manufacturers, Political Action Committees

Burdett A. Loomis

REFERENCES

Budde, Bernadette. 1980. "Business Political Action Committees." In Michael Malbin, ed. *Parties, Interest Groups, and Campaign Finance Laws.* Washington: American Enterprise Institute.

Cottin, Jonathan. 1972. "Business-Industry Political Action Committee." In Judith Smith, ed. *Political Brokers.* New York: Liveright.

Sabato, Larry J. 1984. *PAC Power.* New York: Norton.

Benjamin F. Butler (1818–1893)

Controversial Civil War military officer and Massachusetts politician. One of the most famous "political generals" of the Civil War, Benjamin Franklin Butler left his native New Hampshire to establish a prosperous law practice in Massachusetts in the antebellum years. An active Democrat, Butler supported Jefferson Davis for his party's presidential nomination in 1860. At the start of the Civil War, Butler won national prominence for leading the Massachusetts militia troops that pacified pro-Confederate Baltimore and thereby reopened Washington's communications with the North. While commander of Union forces at Fortress Monroe in Virginia in the summer of 1861, he began the policy of sheltering runaway slaves within his lines as "contrabands of war." For all that, Butler later demonstrated a conspicuous lack of military talent in field commands in Louisiana and Virginia. When Abraham Lincoln's reelection made Butler's political support for the administration no longer crucial, he was finally relieved from active duty.

After the war, Butler served six terms as a Republican Congressman from Massachusetts and was a leader in the impeachment effort against Andrew Johnson. He returned to the Democratic Party in 1878 and won election as Massachusetts governor in 1882. Butler played a leading role in the Democratic National Convention of 1884 when he unsuccessfully fought to add planks favoring currency inflation and a protective tariff to the platform. When the Democrats nominated Grover Cleveland of New York, Butler bolted the party and accepted the presidential nominations of both the Greenback-Labor Party and the Anti-Monopoly Party. In a number of states, Butler attempted to fuse his electoral slate with the weaker of the two major parties. When these efforts failed, he concentrated on courting Democrats unhappy with Cleveland and almost brought the Tammany Hall machine into his camp. On election day 1884, Butler received a disappointing 175,000 votes out of 10 million cast.

See also: Grover Cleveland, Jefferson Davis, Elections of 1860 and 1884, Greenback Party, Tammany Hall, Andrew Johnson, Abraham Lincoln

John R. McKivigan

REFERENCES

Holzman, Robert S. 1954. *Stormy Ben Butler.* New York: Macmillan.

Nash, Howard P., Jr. 1969. *Stormy Petrel: The Life and Times of Benjamin F. Butler, 1818–1893.* Rutherford, NJ: Fairleigh Dickinson U. Pr.

West, Richard S., Jr. 1965. *Lincoln's Scapegoat General: A Life of Benjamin F. Butler, 1818–1893.* Boston: Houghton Mifflin.

Marion Butler (1863–1938)

Populist North Carolina governor and U.S. Senator. Born on a farm in southeastern North Carolina, Marion Butler graduated from the University of North Carolina in 1885 and, upon the death of his father, returned to the farm to support his family, serving as well as a principal of the nearby Salem High School. A Democrat, he became president of the county Farmer's Alliance from 1887 to 1888. That same year, he became editor of the Clinton *Caucasian* and made it the voice of the Farmer's Alliance. In 1893 he began to publish an edition of the paper in Goldsboro and, in 1894, in Raleigh. In 1890 he was elected state senator and, in the Senate, supported educational and legal reforms and the establishment of a railway commission. His efforts led to his election to president of the state Farmer's Alliance in 1891.

In 1892 he opposed Grover Cleveland for President but supported Democratic candidates in the state. Such a stand was considered unacceptable by the Democratic State Committee, and Butler reluctantly joined the Populist Party. Within a week, he was elected state party chairman. In the same year he was elected national vice president of the Farmer's Alliance and in 1894, he was elected president.

In that year, completely disillusioned by the Democratic Party, he was largely responsible for persuading the leaders of the Populists and Republicans to cooperate (to "fuse"). They were able to elect the governor and a majority of the legislature. This legislature promptly sent Butler to the U.S. Senate. In 1896 he became the national chairman of the Populist Party and persuaded that party to support the Democrat, William Jennings Bryan, for the presidency while at the same time endorsing the Republican-Populist fusion in North Carolina.

In the Senate, he was known as a vigorous advocate of the cause of free silver and was largely responsible for establishing the rural free postal delivery system. He also supported postal savings banks, a postal telegraph, and a parcel post system. While he was Senator, he had time to complete a law course at the University of North Carolina and to serve actively on the university's board of trustees.

With the notorious "white supremacy" elections of 1898 and 1900, Democrats returned to power in North Carolina, and Butler lost his seat in the Senate in 1902. However, he continued as national chairman of the Populist Party until 1904. He then became a Republican and set up law offices in Raleigh, North Carolina, and Washington, D.C., and became associated with mining corporations in Alaska and the Southwest.

See also: Grover Cleveland, National Farmers' Alliance and Industrial Union, Populist (People's) Party

Richard L. Watson, Jr.

REFERENCES

Durden, Robert F. 1965. *Climax of Populism: The Election of 1896.* Lexington: U. Pr. of Kentucky.

Goodwyn, Lawrence. 1976. *Democratic Promise: The Populist Movement in America.* New York: Oxford U. Pr.

Steelman, Lala Carr. 1985. *The North Carolina Farmer's Alliance: A Political History, 1887–1893.* Greenville, NC: East Carolina U. Publications.

The Marion Butler Papers are in the Southern Historical Collection at the University of North Carolina, Chapel Hill.

Nicholas Murray Butler (1862–1947)

Educator and Republican politician. Republican Vice President John S. Sherman died just before the 1912 election. He had been renominated with President William Howard Taft, who won only 8 electoral votes to Democrat Woodrow Wilson's 485 and Progressive Theodore Roosevelt's 88. The Republican National Committee decided that the electoral votes for Vice President should go to Nicholas Murray Butler, president of Columbia University. The selection was a tribute both to Butler's prestige and his support for Taft, whose nomination he had seconded at the 1912 GOP convention.

Butler took part in Republican politics from the late 1900s through the early 1930s. In 1900 he served as Theodore Roosevelt's emissary to Republican chairman Mark Hanna in Roosevelt's attempt to forswear interest in the vice presidential nomination. During the 1912 Taft-Roosevelt split, his link to Roosevelt made his backing for Taft all the more prominent. In 1920 he made a forlorn run at the GOP presidential nomination under the slogan "Pick Nick for President and Pic-Nic in November." He passed up many chances to run for lesser offices.

Butler was born in New Jersey and studied philosophy at Columbia University and in Europe. He helped found the Teachers College at Columbia University, and he served as president of Columbia from 1902 to 1945. He established the Carnegie Endowment for International Peace and shared the 1931 Nobel Peace Prize with Jane Addams.

See also: Progressive Party, Republican National Committee, Theodore Roosevelt, William Howard Taft

John J. Pitney, Jr.

REFERENCES

Bain, Richard C. 1960. *Convention Decisions and Voting Records.* Washington: Brookings.

Butler, Nicholas. 1939. *Across the Busy Years, Recollections and Reflections.* 2 vols. New York: Scribner's.

Martin, Ralph G. 1964. *Ballots and Bandwagons.* Chicago: Rand McNally.

Paul M. Butler (1906–1961)

Democratic National Committee chairman in the 1950s. A corporation lawyer from South Bend, Indiana, who was born in that city, Paul Mulholland Butler received a law degree from the University of Notre Dame Law School in 1927 while working as a part-time reporter for the *South Bend Tribune.* Thereafter, his legal practice and work for the Democratic Party consumed most of his time.

Butler began his party work by managing a friend's unsuccessful campaign, then became a loyal Democratic district chairman and a friend of H. F. Schricker whose successful gubernatorial bid Butler promoted. Butler's record was the Democratic national committeeman's post from Indiana in 1952, and the Schricker-Butler support went to Adlai E. Stevenson II.

Butler aided Stephen Mitchell, the Democratic national chairman, in reorganizing the party after Stevenson's defeat, and he became Mitchell's chosen successor for national chairman in 1954 (despite opposition from ex-President Harry Truman). Butler's success in helping the Democrats to regain control of Congress in 1954 and an uneasy reconciliation with Truman won him the job as Democratic national chairman.

As chair, Butler stressed party loyalty, especially support of national Democratic nominees. He also sought to regularize and coordinate the relationship between the Democratic congressional leaders and the party itself. Congressional power brokers like Sam Rayburn and Lyndon Johnson tended toward independence, and Butler (reelected national chairman in 1956) sought to organize policy and strategy at all levels of the party through a Democratic advisory council. When the congressional leaders chose not to participate, the council eventually became the voice of the liberal wing of the party.

Butler retired after the 1960 convention, which nominated John F. Kennedy.

See also: Democratic National Committee, Lyndon B. Johnson, John F. Kennedy, Adlai Stevenson II, Harry S Truman

Ralph M. Goldman

REFERENCES

Goldman, Ralph M. 1990. *The National Party Chairmen and Committees: Factionalism at the Top.* Armonk, NY: M. E. Sharpe.

Roberts, George C. 1987. *Paul M. Butler, Hoosier Politician and National Political Leader.* Lanham, MD: U. Pr. of America.

William M. Butler (1861–1937)

Republican National Committee chairman under Calvin Coolidge. A Massachusetts textile manufacturer who was one of President Calvin Coolidge's closest advisers, William Morgan Butler was elected Republican national chairman (1924–1928) as Coolidge's personal choice and appointed United States Senator from Massachusetts in 1924.

Born in New Bedford, Massachusetts, and educated in its public schools, Butler worked as a clerk in a shoe manufacturing firm and at the same time studied law at Boston University, beginning practice in 1884.

Butler was elected to two terms in the Massachusetts House of Representatives and to four terms to its Senate, becoming president of the Senate in his last two terms. During this tenure, he became an ally and protégé of the state's leading organization Republican, W. Murray Crane.

In 1902 Butler built his own textile mill and thereafter acquired other manufacturing properties. He also maintained his friendship with Senator Crane, also becoming a friend of another Crane protégé, Calvin Coolidge. Coolidge advanced through Massachusetts politics along the same route as Butler but continued on to the offices of lieutenant governor and governor.

As Vice President, Coolidge was able to remain untainted by the Teapot Dome scandals of Warren Harding's administration. He maintained close touch with Massachusetts politics and was pleased when his good friend, Butler, became the state's Republican national committeeman. Butler ran Coolidge's preconvention campaign in 1924.

Although Coolidge made it clear long before the convention that Butler was his national chairman, most members of the national committee would have preferred to have had someone else. Coolidge insisted, and Butler was elected. He ran a highly decentralized election campaign in which most fundraising was left to the state organizations. What distinguished the campaign was Coolidge's occasional use of a new communication medium, radio.

After the election, Butler was appointed to the United States Senate to fill out the term of the recently deceased Henry Cabot Lodge. The Republican Senate leadership was hostile to Butler and to the President for whom he spoke. While retaining the national chairmanship, Butler served in the Senate until 1926, losing a hard-fought campaign for reelection. Herbert Hoover tried to get Butler to stay on as national chairman in 1928, but he declined in order to return to his legal and manufacturing interests.

See also: Calvin Coolidge, Warren G. Harding, Republican National Committee

Ralph M. Goldman

REFERENCES

Fuess, Claude M. 1965. *Calvin Coolidge, The Man from Vermont.* Hamden, CT: Archon Books.

Harry F. Byrd, Jr. (1914–)

Independent U.S. Senator from Virginia from 1965 to 1983. The second person in the history of the Senate to be elected as an Independent, Harry Flood Byrd, Jr., was educated at Virginia Military Institute and the University of Virginia. He served with the U.S. Navy during World War II. Under the tutelage of his father, who was U.S. Senator and head of the party machine that controlled postwar Virginia politics, Harry, Jr., entered politics in 1947 upon his election from Winchester to the state senate; he held the seat until 1965. He also was a member of the Democratic State Central Committee from 1948 to 1965. Byrd's politics reflected those of the machine he perpetuated, most notably in supporting "massive resistance" (the Byrd Machine's program of opposing racial desegregation) and favoring severe limitations on government spending, known as "pay as you go."

With his father's resignation because of ill health from the Senate in 1965, Byrd was appointed to fill the seat; he won a special election in 1966 to complete the remaining four years of the term. In the Senate, Byrd was one of the more conservative Democrats. In 1970, fearing a difficult Democratic primary, Byrd declared himself an Independent, bypassed the primary, and defeated all of the other candidates in the general election. Byrd's public reason for this action was a Democratic "loyalty oath" requiring that he support the 1972 presidential nominee, the liberal George McGovern. As an Independent, Byrd chose to sit with the Democrats, and the party allowed him to retain his seniority and his committee assignments on Armed Services and Finance. Despite occasional rumblings about switching parties, Byrd continued his ties with the Democrats until his retirement in 1983.

See also: Harry F. Byrd, Sr., Race and Racial Politics, Third Parties in American Politics

Thomas J. Baldino

REFERENCES

Bass, Jack, and Walter DeVries. 1976. *The Transformation of Southern Politics*. New York: Basic Books.
Key, V. O., Jr. 1949. *Southern Politics in State and Nation*. New York: Knopf.

Harry F. Byrd, Sr. (1887–1966)

Conservative U.S. Senator from Virginia. Harry Flood Byrd, Sr., headed the Democratic organization that dominated Virginia politics for 40 years while he served as governor and then as United States Senator. He was known for his economy-oriented "pay-as-you-go" point of view.

Byrd was born in Martinsburg, West Virginia, of an old Virginia political family. He quit school at age 15 and took over his father's bankrupt Winchester, Virginia, newspaper, turning it into a profitable enterprise. He was also a successful apple orchardist.

Elected to the state senate in 1915, he attained statewide prominence in 1923 for his successful referendum against a road bond issue. In his term as governor from 1926 to 1930, he advocated curbs on lynching, voting and tax reforms, rural electrification, and support for tourism. In addition, he streamlined the organization of state government.

The Byrd political organization was characterized by its conservative economic philosophy and its support for rural interests. Despite claims that they were dictatorial in nature, Byrd's lieutenants always heeded the opinions of local courthouse personnel in making decisions.

Byrd was appointed to the United States Senate in 1933 where he served until just before his death. He was chairman of the Finance Committee and the Joint Committee on Reduction of Nonessential Federal Expenditures. His opposition was an obstacle to both New Deal and New Frontier legislation. In his later years, the power of the Byrd organization on Virginia's politics waned largely because of the changes in attitudes that occurred as the state became more urban.

See also: Harry F. Byrd, Jr., New Deal, Race and Racial Politics

Paul C. Cline

REFERENCES

Heinemann, Ronald L. 1983. *Depression and New Deal in Virginia*. Charlottesville: U. Pr. of Virginia.
Wilkinson, J. Harvie, III. 1968. *Harry Byrd and the Changing Face of Virginia Politics, 1945–1966*. Charlottesville: U. Pr. of Virginia.

Robert C. Byrd (1917–)

West Virginia Democratic U.S. Senate leader. Robert Carlyle Byrd was an able floor leader who led Senate Democrats for 12 years (1977–1988), a record of longevity exceeded by only two other Democrats: Michael J. Mansfield of Montana (1961–1976) and Joseph T. Robinson of Arkansas (1923–1937) and matched by Alben W. Barkley of Kentucky (1937–1948). Byrd's performance compares favorably with these other strong floor leaders, a Senate position formally created in 1910. Byrd's effective, if sometimes controversial, discharge of his duties has been excelled by only Lyndon B. Johnson of Texas (1953–1960), generally acknowledged as the most successful Senate Majority Leader.

Byrd's style of leadership was based on indefatigable effort, attention to detail, the wide dispensation of favors, and above all, mastery of the Senate's arcane rules and folkways. Criticized both in the media and by his Senate colleagues for a less-than-effective television presence, Byrd nevertheless was instrumental in bringing television coverage of floor proceedings to that body. Byrd is the first man in Senate history to hold the job of Majority Leader (1977–1980), drop down to Minority Leader (the first six years of Ronald Reagan's administration, 1981–1986), and then to regain the majority leadership (1987–1988).

Before his election to a sixth Senate term in 1988, Byrd, in another unprecedented move, resigned from the majority leadership. In the One Hundred First Congress (1989–1990) Byrd's seniority propelled him into the position of President *pro tempore* of the Senate and chairman of its powerful Appropriations Committee.

Born Robert Carlyle Sale in North Carolina, Byrd was adopted by his uncle Titus Byrd and grew up in the coal-mining country of West Virginia. His rise to high political office is a classic poverty-to-power story. First elected to the U.S. Senate in 1968, Byrd previously served in the West Virginia House of Delegates (1946–1950), the state senate (1950–1952), and the U.S. House of Representatives (1953–1958). As a former secretary of the Senate Democratic Conference (1967–1970) and Majority Whip (1971–1976), Byrd has already sustained a more varied and longer party leadership role than any Senator in history.

See also: Majority Party Leadership in Congress, Michael J. Mansfield, Minority Party Leadership in Congress

Robert L. Peabody

REFERENCES

Hook, Janet. 1988. "The Byrd Years." 46 *Congressional Quarterly Weekly Report* 976.

Peabody, Robert L. 1976. *Leadership in Congress.* Boston: Little, Brown.

———. 1981. "Senate Party Leadership: From the 1950s to the 1980s." In Frank H. Mackaman, ed. *Understanding Congressional Leadership.* Washington: Congressional Quarterly.

Jane Byrne (1933–)

First female mayor of Chicago. Jane Byrne (born Margaret Jane Burke), while still a young widow in the early 1960s, entered local Democratic politics on a volunteer basis. Her work caught the eye of Mayor Richard J. Daley, who took a fatherly interest in promoting her career. Byrne spent almost eight years in Daley's municipal cabinet, also serving as his nominal equal in her position as co-chair of the Cook County Democratic Party. After Daley's death in 1976, however, her influence waned. Byrne eventually broke with the machine and adopted a reform stance, becoming an insurgent Democratic candidate for mayor in 1979. Her campaign was given little chance for success until inept snow removal after a storm convinced voters that the regular Democratic organization had lost its ability to make the city work. Byrne's coalition of reformers, Blacks, and disgruntled snow victims won a narrow victory, and their candidate became the first person to defeat the Chicago machine in a mayoral primary.

Byrne quickly made peace with the conquered regulars and won election as mayor with 82 percent of the vote—the highest percentage in the city's history. As mayor, Byrne's record was mixed, her grand public works projects often overshadowed by confrontationist politics. Many of her reformist and Black allies eventually deserted her. Within the party, she was challenged by State's attorney Richard M. Daley, the son of her onetime mentor. The Byrne-Daley schism split the party regulars in the 1983 mayoral primary, allowing Blacks and reformers to win the nomination for Congressman Harold Washington. Byrne flirted with the idea of a write-in campaign then dropped it. In 1987 she opposed Washington in the Democratic mayoral primary; after losing again, she supported him in the general election. Jane Byrne's most recent political foray was an unsuccessful primary campaign for clerk of Cook County in 1988.

See also: Richard J. Daley, Harold Washington

John R. Schmidt

REFERENCES

Fitzgerald, Kathleen W. 1981. *Brass: Jane Byrne and the Pursuit of Power.* Chicago: Contemporary Books.

Granger, Bill, and Lori Granger. 1980. *Fighting Jane.* New York: Dial Press.

Green, Paul M., and Melvin G. Holli, eds. 1987. *The Mayors: The Chicago Political Tradition.* Carbondale: Southern Illinois U. Pr.

Holli, Melvin G., and Paul M. Green, eds. 1984. *The Making of the Mayor: Chicago, 1983.* Grand Rapids: Eerdmans.

James F. Byrnes (1879–1972)

South Carolina politician, Cabinet member, and Supreme Court Associate Justice. As Congressman, Senator, Supreme Court justice, World War II "assistant President," Secretary of State, and governor of South Carolina, James Francis "Jimmy" Byrnes had a remarkable public career that spanned nearly half a century. He was born of Irish immigrant parents in Charleston, South Carolina, and left school at age 14 to help support his family. A self-taught lawyer, Byrnes began his political career by winning election to public prosecutor in 1908; two years later he won the first of seven consecutive elections to the U.S. House of Representatives. After losing a U.S. Senate race in 1924 and practicing law for several years, Byrnes was elected Senator from South Carolina in 1930 and again in 1936.

His close association with Franklin D. Roosevelt, begun during the Woodrow Wilson era, brought him his greatest prominence and power. An early proponent of Roosevelt's nomination in 1932, Byrnes, despite his own more conservative views, became known as the President's "legislative ball carrier" for effectively advancing administration programs on Capitol Hill early in Roosevelt's presidency. Though increasingly at odds with New Deal liberalism by the late 1930s, Byrnes remained on good personal terms with Roosevelt and provided important support on key administration foreign-policy and defense measures.

In 1941 Roosevelt nominated Byrnes to the Supreme Court and then in 1942 asked Byrnes to leave the Court in order to help manage the war effort. Byrnes gladly did so, becoming, in FDR's words, "assistant President" for the homefront as the powerful director of the Office of War Mobilization from 1943 to 1945. In 1944 Byrnes pursued the Democratic vice presidential nomination (which he had sought more hesitantly in 1940), but his labor and civil rights record and his status as an apostate Catholic proved insuperable obstacles. Byrnes next served as a foreign-policy assistant and spokesman for Roosevelt and then as Harry Truman's Secretary of State from 1945 until 1947. In 1949 Byrnes broke publicly with Truman over domestic issues and, beginning in 1952, consistently supported Republican candidates for the presidency. Byrnes concluded his political career as South Carolina's conservative and segregationist Democratic governor from 1951 to 1955.

See also: New Deal, Franklin Roosevelt, Harry S Truman

John W. Jeffries

REFERENCES

Byrnes, James F. 1958. *All in One Lifetime*. New York: Harper and Bros.

Moore, Winfred B., Jr. 1976. "New South Statesman: The Political Career of James Francis Byrnes, 1911–1941." Ph.D. dissertation, Duke University.

Joseph W. Byrns (1869–1936)

Loyalist Democratic U.S. Congressman from Tennessee. Joseph Wellington Byrns, a conservative southern Democrat, was Speaker of the U.S. House of Representatives (1934–1936) and Majority Leader (1932–1934) during the early days of the New Deal. By placing party loyalty above ideology, Byrns guided all of Franklin D. Roosevelt's legislation through the House.

Born near Cedar Hill, Tennessee, Byrns graduated from Vanderbilt University in 1890. After establishing a law practice, Byrns was elected to the lower house of the Tennessee legislature in 1894, serving three terms. Elected Speaker in the 1899 session, Byrns went on to the state senate for a term the following year. In 1908 he won election to the U.S. House of Representatives.

In his service on the House Appropriations Committee, Byrns developed a reputation as a fiscal watchdog, and, as senior Democrat, Byrns chaired the committee when Democrats took control of Congress in 1930. Among Byrns's many cost-cutting proposals was the consolidation of the War and Navy departments into a department of defense (an idea that came true only after World War II).

A member of the House Democratic leadership as chairman of the Democratic Congressional Campaign Committee (which assists Democratic congressional nominees in electoral campaigns) since 1928, Byrns was elected majority leader in 1932. Having resigned the Appropriations Committee chair, Byrns exerted party leadership through a geographically representative whip organization. Legislative leadership and strategy in the early New Deal years, however, came primarily from the President, not the Speaker or Majority Leader, who were, in terms of personal authority, closer to being figureheads.

Elected Speaker when Henry T. Rainey died in 1934, Byrns defeated Sam Rayburn and William Bankhead, both of whom the President preferred over Byrns, as he believed the Tennessean was unwilling and/or unable to control the unruly House. Byrns's brief tenure as Speaker disproved Roosevelt's fears, as Byrns remained steadfastly loyal to the President and his party.

See also: Majority Party Leadership in Congress, New Deal, Sam Rayburn, Franklin Roosevelt, Speaker of the House

Richard C. Burnweit

REFERENCES

Ripley, Randall B. 1967. *Party Leaders in the House of Representatives*. Washington: Brookings.

Galloway, J. M. 1966. "Speaker Joseph W. Byrns: Party Leader in the New Deal." 25 *Tennessee Historical Quarterly* 63.

C

George Cabot (1751–1823)

Federalist statesman of the early national period. A sea captain, merchant, banker, businessman, and a leading Federalist politician from Massachusetts, George Cabot was a member of the "Essex Junto" (political organization) during its most powerful era. Cabot was born in Salem and attended Harvard University, resigning shortly before being expelled. His two older brothers promptly sent him to sea in one of the ships owned by their firm in Beverly, Massachusetts. He was an immediate success and became master of his own ship before he reached age 20. During the Revolutionary War Cabot retired from sailing to become a member of his brothers' firm, which profited enormously from the war by operating at least 40 privateers to capitalize on the conflict.

Cabot was an adventurous businessman. Beginning in 1784 he served as a director of the Massachusetts Bank—the commonwealth's earliest bank—promoting both the Essex Bridge Corporation and the Beverly Cotton Manufactory in 1788. Three years earlier, in partnership with his brother-in-law, Joseph Lee, he made so much money that he was able to retire comfortably in 1795 at the age of 43.

Cabot became politically active in 1778, helping to form the nucleus of the dominant Essex Junto. He was a delegate to the state constitutional convention and helped engineer the ratification of the relatively conservative document ultimately approved for the commonwealth in 1780. After serving in the ratification convention in 1788, he was elected as a Federalist Senator in the First Congress and served from 1791 until his resignation in 1796. As a close ally of Alexander Hamilton, Cabot was considered an expert on economic and commercial matters. He was chairman of the Committee on Appropriations from 1792 to 1794. True to his Federalist ideology, he supported the Jay Treaty, deplored the French Revolution, and advocated stronger ties with Great Britain.

Cabot considered that he had retired from public life when he resigned from the Senate. In 1803 he moved into the city of Boston and became president of the Boston Marine Insurance Company in 1809. Cabot remained active in Federalist politics as an adviser, taking a dim view of the nation's prospects after Thomas Jefferson's election to the presidency in 1801. Even so, his was a moderating influence compared to the reaction of Timothy Pickering, John Adams's Secretary of State, to such events as the Embargo Act, which forbade foreign commerce, and the presidential elections of 1808 and 1812. Cabot's greatest moment may well have come when, serving as president of the Hartford Convention (1814), he used all his influence to ward off militant efforts aimed at secession. He was a man of integrity and vision who served his society well.

See also: Alexander Hamilton, Jay Treaty

Kathryn A. Malone

John C. Calhoun (1782–1850)

Major American political theorist and politician of the 1820s. John C. Calhoun played a leading role in the transformation of the Republican Party of Thomas Jefferson and James

Madison into the National Republican Party of the 1820s. Calhoun then led the southern agrarian revolt against the Jacksonians, first in the Nullification controversy, and then through the formation of the Whig Party, and finally in the development of theoretical and structural defenses of slavery. Calhoun was one of the principal architects of the Second American Party System, whose own activities and work played a central role in its destruction.

Calhoun was born in the Abbeville district of South Carolina. He graduated from Yale College in 1804 and attended Tapping Reeve's Law School in Litchfield, Connecticut. He was admitted to the bar and went back to practice law in Abbeville in 1807. In 1808 and 1809 he represented his home district in the South Carolina legislature.

Calhoun was elected to Congress in 1810 and served in the House of Representatives as one of the "War Hawks" until 1817. He married his wealthy cousin, placing himself, politically and socially, among the Low Country aristocracy. House Speaker Henry Clay appointed Calhoun to the Committee on Foreign Affairs, where they worked together successfully to bring about war with Great Britain. Along with his support for the war, Calhoun endorsed the other nationalist policies that came to be identified with Clay's "American Plan," including federally funded internal improvements and protective tariffs.

In 1817 Calhoun became President James Monroe's Secretary of War, and he remained in that office throughout Monroe's presidency. As the presidential election of 1824 approached, Calhoun, along with Clay, John Quincy Adams, William Crawford, and Andrew Jackson, was expected to compete for the honor of being the first non-Virginian in the White House since 1801. Ironically, Calhoun's weakness was in the South where his nationalism was viewed with much suspicion by the traditional Jeffersonians in Virginia. Calhoun emerged as a consensus vice presidential candidate and was elected to that office in the disputed election of 1824. Calhoun served as Adams's Vice President, but managed to keep sufficiently above the fray to be elected in 1828 to serve Andrew Jackson in the same capacity. Calhoun's relations with Jackson grew increasingly strained, but the final break came over Nullification when Calhoun resigned the vice presidency in 1832 and returned to the Senate to lead South Carolina's fight against the protective tariff.

During the 1820s, as the agrarian South grew increasingly hostile to economic nationalism and focused particular ire on protective tariffs, Calhoun constructed a constitutional defense of the rights or interests of a regional minority against majority will. The tariff was the immediate concern of the arguments presented during Nullification, but Calhoun drew on the states' rights theories of Madison that covered a variety of "municipal" matters, including slavery.

After Jackson's reelection in 1832, Calhoun devoted his energies to opposing Jackson and Martin Van Buren and to the development of states' rights constitutional theory. He was briefly considered as a Whig candidate for President in 1844 but declined to run. President John Tyler named him Secretary of State, and he served in that office until March 1845. He then returned to the Senate where he remained until his death. In the Senate, Calhoun was the chief spokesman for the South, insisting on the gag rule to control abolitionist petitions to Congress and strenuously denouncing the Wilmot Proviso. He died in the midst of the slavery crisis of 1850, uncompromising to the end.

See also: John Quincy Adams, Henry Clay, Election of 1824, Federalist Party, Gag Rule, Andrew Jackson, Jacksonian Democrats, James Monroe, National Republican Party, Nullification, Wilmot Proviso

Kathryn A. Malone

REFERENCES

Hopkins, James F. 1971. "Election of 1824." In Arthur M. Schlesinger, Jr., et al., eds. *History of American Presidential Elections, 1789–1968.* New York: McGraw-Hill.

Niven, John. 1988. *John C. Calhoun and the Price of Union.* Baton Rouge: Louisiana State U. Pr.

Peterson, Merrill D. 1987. *The Great Triumvirate: Webster, Clay, and Calhoun.* New York: Oxford U. Pr.

California Democratic Council

A federation of local volunteer clubs established in 1953. Modeled after the California Republican Assembly, the California Democratic Council (CDC) sought to reestablish party control over the nominating process through preprimary endorsements. Cross-filing, a Progressive-era reform, had enabled many Republican incumbents routinely to capture Democratic nominations.

Drawing heavily from activists first attracted to politics by the 1952 Adlai Stevenson campaign, the CDC worked to develop a distinctly liberal program for the Democratic Party. Under the direction of founding president (and later U.S. Senator) Alan Cranston, the CDC was at first able to balance its electoral and legislative goals. In 1954 CDC endorsements and active campaign support led to the nomination of the first full statewide slate of Democrats in 40 years. The CDC also figured importantly in the election of Edmund G. "Pat" Brown as governor in 1958 as well as in that year's Democratic capture of the state legislature and most state offices.

After the 1958 Democratic landslide, however, the CDC's focus became increasingly ideological, aggravating already existing tensions among party regulars, organized labor, and minority groups. Elected officials, most notably Jesse Unruh, Speaker of the California Assembly, were especially resentful (and fearful) of the CDC's claims to policy leadership. These tensions led to a steady decline in the CDC's influence and stature, and by the early 1970s, it was no longer considered a major force in California Democratic politics. CDC membership, which peaked at a reported 75,000 in 1964, today totals only 2,000.

See also: Edmund G. Brown, Sr., California Republican Assembly, Jesse Unruh

David E. Sturrock

REFERENCES

Carney, Francis. 1958. *The Rise of the Democratic Clubs in California*. New York: Henry Holt.

Fowle, Eleanor Cranston. 1984. *Cranston: The Senator from California*. Boston: Houghton Mifflin.

Rowe, Leonard. 1961. *Preprimary Endorsements in California Politics*. Berkeley: Bureau of Public Administration, University of California.

Wilson, James Q. 1962. *The Amateur Democrat*. Chicago: U. of Chicago Pr.

California Medical Association v. Federal Election Commission
453 U.S. 182 (1981)

This Supreme Court case, involving the California Medical Association (CMA), held that it is not a denial of equal protection of the laws for Congress to restrict the amount that an unincorporated association can contribute to a multicandidate political action committee when it has not restricted the contribution amount of a corporation to a segregated political fund. CMA also held that the contribution limit is not a violation of the First Amendment.

The Federal Election Campaign Act of 1971 prohibits individuals and unincorporated associations from contributing more than $5,000 a year to any multicandidate political committee. The Federal Election Commission (FEC) claimed that the CMA, an unincorporated association of doctors, violated this provision by contributions to the California Medical Political Action Committee (CALPAC).

Writing for the majority, Justice Thurgood Marshall rejected the Fifth Amendment equal protection claim, noting that the act as a whole places far fewer restrictions on unincorporated associations and individuals than it did on unions and corporations. The differing treatment reflects "a judgment by Congress that these entities have differing structures and purposes, and that they therefore may require different forms of regulations in order to protect the integrity of the election process."

Moreover, Justice Marshall rejected the First Amendment claim as well. CMA had argued that the restriction was, in effect, a limit on expenditures rather than contributions because CMA spoke through CALPAC; and even if the Supreme Court saw it as a contribution, it was quite different from that discussed in *Buckley v. Valeo*. The Court was not persuaded. Marshall argued that the expenditures protected in Buckley "were those made independently by a candidate, individual, or group in order to engage directly in political speech. Nothing in [the statute] limits the amount CMA or any of its members may independently expend in order to advocate political views; rather, the statute restrains only the amount that CMA may contribute to CALPAC." The Court found untenable the claim that CALPAC was simply the "mouthpiece of CMA," and it stated that, though it merited some First Amendment protection, "the 'speech by proxy' that CMA seeks to achieve through its contributions to CALPAC is not the sort of political advocacy that this Court in Buckley found entitled to full First Amendment protection."

See also: Buckley v. Valeo, Federal Election Campaign Act, Political Action Committees

H. W. Perry, Jr.

California Republican Assembly

A statewide volunteer organization founded in 1934 for the purpose of furnishing Republican candidates with preprimary endorsements and financial and volunteer support, prerogatives denied to official party organizations by the Progressive reforms of Governor Hiram Johnson (1911–1917).

During its heyday, the California Republican Assembly (CRA) was the preeminent force in California Republican politics. From 1942 through 1952, each of its 22 endorsed statewide candidates was nominated, with nonendorsed candidates often withdrawing. Local CRA endorsements were frequently decisive in congressional and legislative primaries. The CRA also dominated California's state party committee and national convention delegations during this period. The CRA's ability to promote strong Republican candidates helped the GOP prevail in most statewide, congressional, and state legislative elections for a quarter century, despite a large Democratic voter registration advantage.

The CRA's electoral influence has declined to minimal levels since the late 1950s because of the prohibition of cross-filing (whereby a candidate could run in both the Republican and Democratic primaries) and because candidates have developed a large contingent of nonparty sources of financial and volunteer support. The CRA became dominated by the party's conservative wing in the early 1960s (and remains so today), a domination that led to the formation of competing groups by both ultraconservative and moderate factions. CRA membership, nearly 20,000 in the 1960s, now runs between 5,000 and 10,000.

The CRA has exerted a major influence on modern American politics by serving as a model for other party auxiliaries (see California Democratic Council), and through its support of such Republican leaders as Earl Warren, Thomas Kuchel, Goodwin Knight, William Knowland, Richard Nixon, Barry Goldwater, and Ronald Reagan.

See also: California Democratic Council, Barry Goldwater, William Knowland, Richard Nixon, Ronald Reagan, Earl Warren

David E. Sturrock

REFERENCES

Baer, Markell C. 1957. *Story of the California Republican Assembly*. Vacaville, CA: Reporter Publishing.

Rowe, Leonard. 1961. *Preprimary Endorsements in California Politics*. Berkeley: Bureau of Public Administration, University of California.

James Donald Cameron (1833–1918)

Pennsylvania politician and chairman of the Republican National Committee after the Civil War. James Donald Cameron (called Don) was a United States Senator from Pennsylvania, Secretary of War for a brief period for President Ulysses S. Grant, and chairman of the Republican National Committee (1879–1880). With his father, Simon, Don Cameron headed a powerful Pennsylvania party machine that endured from the post-Civil War period into the twentieth century.

Simon Cameron had been a leader of the Radical Republicans and later the Stalwarts in the United States Senate. He continued in office until his resignation in 1877 in favor of Don. Don Cameron was reelected for a full term in January 1879.

The Stalwarts were the Old Guard Republican leadership in Congress during the 1870s and 1880s. The Stalwarts were for the most part cut off from patronage by Rutherford B. Hayes. Unhappy, the Stalwarts joined forces to prevent a Hayes renomination and to capture control of the national party machinery in 1880. Their strategy included a third-term nomination for former President Grant. The choice of a Republican national chairman in 1879 was looked upon as a test of the influence of the Grant coalition, and Don Cameron became their candidate for the chairmanship. He was elected by a bare majority.

The powerful role of a national chairman in the handling of national convention preparations was demonstrated in 1880. The Republicans having dropped the unit rule at the 1876 convention, Cameron and his allies pushed through resolutions at their respective state conventions recommending a return to the rule. Had this recommendation prevailed at the national convention, the machine coalition could indeed have renominated Grant.

The day after the 1880 Republican convention adjourned, National Chairman Cameron called a "snap" meeting of the national committee; only the Stalwarts had been informed of the call. His intention was to choose the officers of the national committee without regard to nominee James A. Garfield's wishes. Cameron hoped to continue in the chairmanship so as to keep the national organization under the control of the coalition of bosses. The maneuver was discovered and forestalled, disgracing Cameron.

Cameron was reelected to the Senate in 1885 and 1891 but declined to be a candidate in 1897.

See also: Simon Cameron, Radical Republicans, Republican National Committee, Stalwarts (and Half-Breeds), Unit Rule

Ralph M. Goldman

REFERENCES

Crippen, Lee F. 1942. *Simon Cameron: Ante-Bellum Years*. Oxford, OH: Mississippi Valley Press.

Goldman, Ralph M. 1990. *The National Party Chairmen and Committees: Factionalism at the Top*. Armonk, NY: M. E. Sharpe.

Simon Cameron Papers, Library of Congress.

Simon Cameron (1799–1889)

Conservative Pennsylvania Republican leader. Simon Cameron was Abraham Lincoln's first Secretary of War. More importantly, his long political career in Pennsylvania culminated in the establishment of a durable Republican Party political machine that lasted into the twentieth century. Born in Lancaster, Pennsylvania, the young Cameron was apprenticed as a printer. Working successively in Harrisburg, Pennsylvania, and Washington, D.C., Cameron engaged in a number of business pursuits, among them canal and railroad construction, banking, and publishing. As a newspaperman, Cameron espoused the protective tariff, and, through contacts with key leaders, he earned a reputation as a skillful political manipulator. Appointed commissioner to settle the claims of the Winnebago Indians, Cameron earned a reputation for corruption in mishandling the funds and was known thereafter as "The Great Winnebago Chieftain."

Nominally a Democrat, Cameron won election to the United States Senate in 1845 by assembling a coalition of Whigs, Nativists, and Protectionist Democrats, defeating the regular Democratic nominee in the state legislature. Cameron's maneuvering led to a break with Democratic party leader, James Buchanan. The belief in party circles was that Cameron was an opportunistic bolter. Consequently, Cameron failed for reelection to the Senate in 1849 and 1855. Nevertheless, Cameron's skill in dispensing federal patronage enabled him to maintain a personal political machine through the politically chaotic 1850s. The rallying point for a sizable faction of Pennsylvania Democrats disenchanted with Buchanan's presidential aspirations, Cameron provided not only leadership but also campaign funds to his supporters in the legislature. By throwing in his lot with the emergent People's (Republican) Party in 1856, Cameron won election to the Senate in 1857.

His elevation to the leadership of the Republican Party spurred Cameron's own presidential aspirations in 1860, though, in Pennsylvania, Cameron was opposed by a powerful faction of former Whigs. Although Cameron's candidacy received little support outside the state, he sought to induce Abraham Lincoln to take the vice presidential spot on his ticket. At the Chicago national party convention, Cameron bargained his "uncommitted" support between the two major contenders, Lincoln and William Seward. Lincoln's managers traded a place at the President's council table for Pennsylvania's timely support. Consequently, because of the agreement and to reward Pennsylvania for its support in the election, Lincoln offered Cameron the secretaryship of the War Department, despite his misgivings over Cameron's reputation for chicanery.

Marked by charges of cronyism, contract scandals and profiteering, and gross ineptitude on his part in organization of the war effort, Cameron's tenure as Secretary of War lasted but a year. While not previously a staunch antislavery man, Cameron sought to shore up his political support by urging the creation of a slave army in his annual report to Congress in December 1861, a position that placed Cameron in direct opposition to Lincoln's war policy. Subsequently, Lincoln removed him from the Cabinet by naming him minister to Russia.

Cameron's diplomatic career was brief as he shortly returned to Pennsylvania to run for the Senate and to reinvigorate his political machine. Cameron was reelected to the Senate in 1867, marking the establishment of the Cameron Dynasty. Simon's son, James Donald Cameron, long involved in his father's business interests, increasingly oversaw patronage in the state during Simon's remaining Senate tenure. When he resigned from the Senate in 1877, Simon was succeeded, in turn, by his son, who served until 1897. To many, Simon Cameron's career was epitomized by his famed observation that "an honest politician is one who, once he is bought, will stay bought."

See also: James Buchanan, James Donald Cameron, Abraham Lincoln, William Seward

Richard C. Burnweit

REFERENCES

Bradley, Erwin Stanley. 1964. *The Triumph of Militant Republicanism: A Study of Pennsylvania and Politics, 1860–1872.* Philadelphia: U. of Pennsylvania Pr.

———. 1966. *Simon Cameron: Lincoln's Secretary of War.* Philadelphia: U. of Pennsylvania Pr.

Crippen, Lee F. 1942. *Simon Cameron: Ante Bellum Years.* Oxford, OH: Mississippi Valley Press.

Campaign Finance and the Constitution

The United States Supreme Court has intervened more actively and more decisively in the regulation of campaign finance than in any other aspect of the political process, excepting only reapportionment. Yet, before the enactment of the 1974 amendments to the Federal Election Campaign Act (FECA), the Court had gone to great lengths to avoid deciding to what extent or even whether the First Amendment protects the raising and spending of money in election campaigns.

Prior to the 1970s, regulation of campaign finance consisted primarily of (1) prohibition of campaign contributions by corporations and labor unions (largely ineffective), and (2) disclosure requirements and limits on spending (totally ineffective). Federal election laws, particularly those restricting labor unions, were challenged repeatedly, but in each case the Supreme Court dodged the constitutional question.

In 1971 Congress enacted the original FECA. Although this act contained several novel provisions, only newly strengthened disclosure requirements were destined to go into effect. The Nixon reelection committee's scramble to raise money before the effective date of these requirements constituted a major element of the Watergate scandal; in turn, this maneuvering prompted Congress to enact the 1974 FECA amendments.

In addition to the disclosure requirements, the amended FECA limited the amount that could be spent in campaigns for federal office; limited the size of contributions to federal candidates ($5,000 for contributions by "multiple-candidate committees," more popularly known as political action committees, or PACs; larger amounts for political party organizations; and $1,000 for other organizations and for individuals); limited the amount that candidates could spend from their personal funds in their own behalf; limited amounts that could be spent independently to support or oppose a federal candidate; and provided for public financing of presidential campaigns. The prohibition of contributions and expenditures by corporations and labor unions was carried over from previous law. Finally, the 1974 amendments created the Federal Election Commission (FEC) to administer the act.

Buckley v. Valeo

Congress has made relatively minor adjustments, but since 1974, the direction of change in campaign finance regulation has been set primarily by the Supreme Court. The first and still the most important campaign finance decision was *Buckley v. Valeo* (1976). In sharp contrast to its earlier efforts to avoid constitutional decision making on issues of campaign finance, in *Buckley* the Court was willing to consider every challenge presented against the FECA by an ideologically diverse group of plaintiffs. This rush to decision was all the more striking given the abstract setting, none of the provisions under challenge having yet undergone the practical test of being applied in an election.

The resulting treatise-in-the-guise-of-a-judicial-opinion was prepared under unusual time pressure, resulting from the perceived need to decide the case in time to let the candidates in the 1976 election know the ground rules and to permit the public financing machinery to go into effect. Running to 138 pages, *Buckley* is probably the longest *per curiam* decision in the Court's history. (*Per curiam* is the term used to describe an opinion "by the Court," i.e., not signed by any one Justice. Appendices, notes and separate opinions by five Justices, each of whom dissented from one or another portion of the *per curiam* decision, brought the grand total to 294 pages.)

One portion of *Buckley* required a restructuring of the FEC on grounds that as originally constituted it violated the principle of separation of powers. Beyond this, and despite vigorous argument to the contrary from defenders of the legislation, *Buckley* established that regulation of the contributing and spending of money in election campaigns affects rights of speech and association protected by the First Amendment. Such regulation is therefore subject to judicial review, although it will be upheld if the government's reasons for regulating are sufficient. The Court's campaign finance doctrine, as laid down in *Buckley* and in subsequent cases—the limits within which the Court will permit regulation of campaign finance at the federal, state, and local levels—may be stated fairly simply, though some unanswered questions remain, and as is usually the case with constitutional doctrine, even the answers that have been provided are subject to change.

Provisions that do not directly restrict the flow of campaign money—in particular, disclosure requirements and public financing of election campaigns—are relatively free of constitutional limitation. The Court did express a willingness in *Buckley*, and acted upon it in *Brown v. Socialist Workers '74 Campaign Committee* (1982), to intervene when such provisions clearly impose serious hardships on third parties or independent candidates, a ruling that has not prevented some commentators from criticizing the Court for insufficient protection of minor candidacies. So far as nonrestrictive campaign finance provisions affect the major parties, the

Court has given Congress and the state legislatures a free hand.

Contribution and Expenditure Limits

In the case of direct restrictions on the flow of campaign money, the Court has relied on three sharp distinctions. The first and most fundamental, originating in *Buckley*, differentiates between restrictions on expenditures and restrictions on contributions. The *Buckley* Court stated that limits on the size of contributions were permissible so long as they could be justified as measures to prevent corruption or the appearance of corruption. On this basis, the contribution limits in the 1974 FECA amendments were upheld. Expenditure limits were struck down across the board—not only the overall campaign spending limits, which were said to be redundant of the contribution limits so far as the prevention of corruption is concerned, but also the limits on spending of candidates' personal funds and on independent spending.

Limits on contributions were found in *Buckley* to restrict rights of association protected by the First Amendment, but limits on expenditures were a direct restriction of speech, and therefore more suspect. In comparison with the spending of money in a campaign, a contribution was merely "speech by proxy," as Justice Thurgood Marshall later said (*California Medical Assn. v. Federal Election Commission*, 1981). The Court dismissed rather casually the objection that a candidate's ability to spend, and therefore under the Court's premises, to speak, would be limited to the extent that contribution restrictions limited his or her ability to raise funds. In addition to their lesser infringement on First Amendment rights, contribution limits were favored by the Court relative to spending limits because limiting contributions avoids the undue influence of large contributors over public officials. Informed observers have disagreed over the seriousness of corruption resulting from campaign contributions, but the electoral advantage that derives from the ability to raise large amounts of money is real. Accordingly, those who would deny the pressure that campaign contributors can bring to bear on officials must maintain either that officials are indifferent to their prospects for reelection or that they consistently set aside their political ambitions when engaging in their official activities. Generally, political science has proceeded on opposite assumptions. In any event, the *Buckley* Court

sought to avoid this question by asserting that it would be sufficient justification for contribution limits that they avoid the mere appearance of undue influence.

In contrast, the *Buckley* majority maintained, the various expenditure limits could not be justified as anticorruption measures, most clearly in the case of limits on spending of candidates' personal funds. The majority did not entertain the suggestion that such a limit might overcome the unfair advantage contribution limits give to a wealthy candidate whose less fortunate opponents must raise funds in small increments.

The anticorruption potential of limits on independent spending was more controversial. Supporters of FECA had regarded these limits as a corollary to the contribution limits, but the *Buckley* Court maintained that independent spending did not have the same potential as contributions for undue influence. The Court's observation that spending uncoordinated with the candidate's own campaign may not be helpful to the candidate is true but of dubious relevance, since the reformers were concerned about influence in the cases in which independent spending *is* helpful. The Court's argument that by definition the independent spender is not able to consult with the candidate in advance and that corruption therefore is unlikely is also flawed, because corrupt influence is possible without any advance agreement.

Whatever the merits of the Court's logic, it is doubtful that widespread independent spending has been used as a means of evading the contribution limits, as some reformers had feared. True, the success attributed to conservative independent spending committees in defeating several incumbent Democratic Senators in the 1978 and 1980 elections stimulated controversy and renewed attempts to establish the validity of regulating at least some independent spending. However, these committees were more ideological than interest based, and their money came primarily from small contributors. Concern over the issue subsided after most of the incumbents targeted by the conservative committees in the 1982 elections were reelected, and the Supreme Court reaffirmed the immunity of independent spending from limitation in 1985.

Independent spending is unlikely to reemerge as a major constitutional issue until and unless business and professional groups turn to independent spending in behalf of candidates as a means of gaining influence over elected officials. Significant subsidiary questions, especially regarding how much coordination with the candidate's campaign may exist before spending loses its character as "independent" and is treated as an in-kind contribution subject to limitation, have gone unresolved, primarily because of the FEC's passive enforcement policies.

Finally, the Court found that overall limits on how much a candidate's campaign could spend were unnecessary for the prevention of corruption or its appearance. Congress had limited contributions to a size that would pose no such danger, the Court reasoned. Given such limits, the ability of a candidate to raise large amounts of campaign funds would reflect widespread support, rather than posing a danger of undue influence.

The Court's reasoning fails to recognize that Congress had to trade off conflicting goals when it enacted and amended the FECA. Contribution limits could not be set single-mindedly with the intent of preventing the possibility of corrupt influence, because setting the limits too low might prevent candidates from mounting effective campaigns. Contribution limits would prevent the most flagrant instances of corruption, but expenditure limits would eliminate the need for candidates to raise large amounts, thereby reducing the pressure that derives from contributions generally and from any particular contribution.

Despite its assertions that expenditure limits greatly infringed on First Amendment freedoms and served no legitimate purpose, the *Buckley* Court added in a footnote that the government could validly require that a candidate accepting public financing agree to limit his or her overall campaign spending. The Court offered no explanation—if expenditure limits were so grave an intrusion against freedom of speech and so lacking in their justification—of why their imposition was not an unconstitutional condition on receipt of public financing. Perhaps some members of the Court hoped Congress would adopt public financing in House and Senate races if doing so were the only way to preserve spending limits. If so, these hopes have not come to fruition. Political scientists have found that challengers tend to gain relative to incumbents as more money is spent in a campaign. By prohibiting spending limits in the absence of public financing, the Court, purposefully or not, may have deprived incumbent legislators of one potent means of self-preservation.

Ballot Measure Elections

The second of the major distinctions that the Court has drawn in campaign finance cases is between elections for public office and ballot measure elections. *Buckley*, of course, was limited to the former, since the statute under challenge (the FECA) applied only to federal elections, while ballot measure elections occur only at the state and local levels. Nevertheless, many states and localities have applied their campaign finance restrictions to ballot measure elections, and these were brought before the Court in *First National Bank of Boston v. Bellotti* (1978) and *Citizens Against Rent Control v. City of Berkeley* (1981) (*CARC*).

Bellotti was a challenge to a Massachusetts statute prohibiting corporations from contributing to certain ballot measure campaigns and *CARC* was a challenge to a local ordinance limiting to $250 the contributions that anyone could make to a ballot measure campaign committee. Despite the favorable reception given by the Court to contribution restrictions in *Buckley* and in *California Medical Association*, the restrictions in both *Bellotti* and *CARC* were struck down.

The infringement of First Amendment interests resulting from restricting contributions to ballot measures is neither greater nor less than instances when contributions to candidates are limited. Therefore, the results in *Bellotti* and *CARC* must be explained on the basis of the strength of the state's interest in imposing the restrictions. In *Buckley*, the Court had upheld the restrictions as a means to avoid corruption or undue influence on elected officials. The same state interest could not be asserted in *Bellotti* and *CARC*, since there was no candidate to be corrupted.

The argument in favor of controlling contributions in ballot measure elections is that the political system is distorted, if not "corrupted," not only when undue pressure is brought to bear on candidates through campaign contributions but also when enormous corporate contributions, unrelated to any widespread popular support for the corporate position, can skew election results by sponsoring an unfair and one-sided public debate. The Court proved unreceptive to this sort of argument in *Bellotti* and *CARC* but hedged its position by relying in part on the lack of evidence in the record of each case that any such skewing actually exists. Precisely what evidence, if any, could have persuaded the majority in *Bellotti* or *CARC* to uphold the restrictions is uncertain, but some research suggests that one-sided spending resulting from corporate contributions in certain ballot measure elections, especially in opposition to measures, can be extremely potent.

Restrictions on Corporations

The third and last major distinction in the Court's campaign finance doctrine emerged later than those between expenditure and contribution limits and between candidate and ballot measure elections. In recent cases, the Court has made it clear that restrictions may be imposed on business corporations that would not be permitted against individuals or other kinds of organizations.

It is true that in *Bellotti* the Court upheld restrictions applicable only to corporations. Confronted with the assertion that corporations are not protected by the freedom of speech guarantee of the First Amendment, the majority responded (somewhat evasively) that it was sufficient that the speech itself was directed to current political issues and deserved protection. Relying on the distinction between ballot measures and elections for public office, the majority stated it was not ruling on the validity of bans on corporate participation in elections for public office.

The Court first confronted the latter question in *FEC v. National Right to Work Committee*, in which it upheld the federal prohibition on corporate contributions. As in *Buckley* and *California Medical Association*, the Court relied on the government's purpose of preventing corrupt influence.

More far-reaching in its implications were *FEC v. Massachusetts Citizens for Life* (MCFL) and *Austin v. Michigan Chamber of Commerce*, which involved the federal prohibition of independent spending by corporations. The Court previously had barred limits on noncorporate independent spenders, even in behalf of a candidate who accepts public financing (*FEC v. National Conservative Political Action Committee*). The independent spender in *MCFL* was a nonprofit corporation formed primarily for the purpose of political advocacy. The Court held that independent spending by such a group was protected by the Constitution. This holding in itself was unremarkable, although four justices dissented from it. More significant was an extended dictum in which the majority stated that the prohibition of independent spending would be upheld as applied to business corpo-

rations operated for profit. The Court so held four years later in *Austin.*

We may now summarize the Court's current campaign finance doctrine, bearing in mind the three major distinctions around which it has been organized:

1. Nonrestrictive interventions into the campaign finance system, such as disclosure requirements and public financing, are valid except to the extent that they are shown concretely to prejudice seriously the interests of third parties or independent candidates.
2. Limits on the size of contributions to candidates for public office are generally valid, if the limits can be justified reasonably as efforts to prevent undue influence of officials or the appearance of such undue influence.
3. Subject to the single exception in the next paragraph, all limits on spending in connection with elections for public office are unconstitutional. This doctrine applies to overall campaign expenditures, independent spending in behalf of a candidate, and spending of the candidate's own money in his or her behalf.
4. Restrictions on spending in behalf of candidates by business corporations operated for profit are constitutional.
5. In ballot measure campaigns, limits on both contributions and expenditures, even those of business corporations, are unconstitutional in the absence of a showing, the requirements of which are vaguely defined, that the practices in question jeopardize the democratic process.

Unanswered Questions

As major areas of constitutional law go, doctrine in the campaign finance area is thus reasonably well elaborated, whatever may be said for or against the doctrine as a matter of logic or policy. Nevertheless, a number of questions remain. Among the more important issues likely to be presented to the Court in the foreseeable future are the following:

1. Will the Court's tolerance for regulation of campaign finance activity by corporations be extended to labor unions? Much of the Court's rationale for singling out corporations is either inapplicable to unions, or applicable to them to a much lesser extent. For example, in *MCFL* the majority relied

in part on "the prospect that resources amassed in the economic marketplace may be used to provide an unfair advantage in the political marketplace." The same prospect does not exist in the case of unions, especially since the Court does not permit the union dues of objecting members to be used for political purposes. Furthermore, it is feasible for affluent corporate managers to make substantial political contributions as individuals, while union members may need the collective vehicle of the union if they are to contribute effectively at all.

On the other hand, it has been the tradition for half a century at the federal level and in many states to apply similar restrictions to corporations and to unions. Constitutionally mandated differential treatment may be perceived as unfairly favoring the economic and ideological position of labor against that of business. In addition, many would regard it as unfair from a partisan standpoint to provide constitutional protection to the political activity of a traditionally Democratic group while withdrawing such protection from a more Republican group.

2. Will the Court permit "aggregate" contribution limits? In recent years reform proposals have sought to restrict the amount a candidate may accept from sources or in amounts likely to represent "special interests." These may be defined variously as contributions from PACs, from any source other than an individual, or from any source in an amount above a specified figure.

Aggregate contribution limits may be vulnerable to constitutional attack on the theory that once the recipient has reached the limit, new would-be contributors are completely barred from contributing, rather than merely being limited in amount. Furthermore, the connection between an aggregate contribution limit and the amount the candidate can spend might seem more direct to the Court than in the case of the individual contribution limits that were upheld in *Buckley*.

Nevertheless, where public financing and the concomitant possibility of expenditure limits are not politically feasible, aggregate contribution limits may be the only effective means of limiting political pressures generated by campaign financing. Their constitutional prospects may be enhanced by the fact that in form, at least, they are contribution limits rather than expenditure limits, and that only specified types of contributions come within the aggregate limits. The possibility of a candidate with widespread support spending an unlimited amount is therefore retained.

3. What are the limits on the incentives that may be created to induce candidates to accept spending limits "voluntarily"? In *Buckley*, as we have seen, the Court offered no explanation for its conclusion that expenditure limits could be imposed on a candidate as a condition of his or her accepting public financing. This lack of explanation makes it especially difficult to predict whether additional incentives for the voluntary acceptance of spending limits would be acceptable. For example, would it be constitutional to impose contribution limits, but waive them for Candidate A if his or her opponent, Candidate B, refused to agree to spending limits? The "benefit" offered to Candidate B on the condition of assent to expenditure limits would consist not of public funding but of the imposition of a limitation on Candidate A. If such an arrangement were unconstitutional, then would the result change if, by agreeing to the expenditure limits, Candidate B would receive public financing in addition to contribution limits being made applicable to Candidate A?

Elected legislators tend to favor expenditure limits, and many particularly fear opponents who can spend unlimited amounts from their own personal funds. Given the reluctance of legislatures to adopt public financing—or if they do adopt it to fund it to the point that they can be confident that all candidates will accept it—then it is likely that experimental new incentives to accept spending limits will arise and sooner or later will be tested in the Supreme Court.

Competing Visions

In addition to noting the existence of these and other unanswered questions, one may question the long-term stability of the Court's campaign finance doctrine. The three central distinctions upon which the Court has relied have generated answers to the questions the Court has had to decide, but they lack such far-reaching validity that they can easily support the weight that the Court has placed on them.

Thus, the Court's distinction between contribution limits and expenditure limits is supported by recognition that contributions are the direct source of political pressure that the regulator seeks to control, while the expenditures are directly associated with the political expression that the civil libertarian seeks to protect. Nevertheless, neither contributions nor expenditures have meaning without regard to the other. It is the need or the desire to spend that creates the demand for contributions. So long as we continue to finance campaigns privately, we cannot enjoy the benefit of unlimited speech without the social cost of considerable corrupt influence, and we cannot substantially control corrupt influence without some limits on speech.

The distinction between elections for public office and elections on ballot propositions holds up if the only concern is corruption defined narrowly as unacceptable influence on public officials derived from campaign contributions. The distinction breaks down when the concern is broadened to include broad structural inequality in influence over the political process, especially given that the main purpose for adopting the initiative process in many states during the Progressive era was to provide ordinary citizens with a device for overcoming the perceived domination of legislatures by special interests.

Finally, the business corporation is the paradigm of massive financial resources that are accumulated for nonpolitical and nonideological purposes, and the infusion of which into election campaigns may bear little relation to the distribution or intensity of political support. Nevertheless, while the corporation stands at one end of the spectrum in this regard, it is not sharply separated from other political contributors and spenders. Contributions by individuals give disproportionate influence to the affluent, and even noncorporate groups that are well organized (such as unions and professional trade groups) have an advantage over relatively unorganized groups (such as ordinary taxpayers, consumers, and the poor).

Some observers have regarded the campaign finance controversy as reflecting two competing visions of the government's rights and obligations with respect to the political process. In one vision, emphasis is placed on the individual's or group's right to be free from government interference with political participation. Vast inequalities in resources that may be available for such participation, by reason of unequal distribution of wealth or of relative structural advantages and disadvantages in the ability of different interests to organize, are either regarded as benign or accepted as the possibly unavoidable cost of protecting rights of speech and association.

In the opposing vision, the right to political participation may be infringed not only by government suppression but also by structural inequalities in access to the resources that are necessary for effective participation. In this vision, government intervention to offset such inequalities is permissible if not obligatory, because an individual's or group's good fortune in the economic sector does not create a right to a corresponding advantage in the political sector.

Though these visions are largely incompatible with each other, each plainly has substantial grounding in American political thought and practice. *Buckley v. Valeo* and other of the Supreme Court's earlier campaign finance decisions may be seen as an attempt to impose a moderate version of the first vision. Inequality of political resources could be assuaged only by nonrestrictive measures or as a by-product of regulations aimed at unethical methods of exercising influence. Even these approaches were qualified by the right to deploy economic or organizational advantages to gain political influence.

Viewed from this perspective, *MCFL* may represent a major departure from the earlier campaign finance cases. Statements in that decision that "concern over the corrosive influence of concentrated corporate wealth reflects the conviction that it is important to protect the integrity of the marketplace of political ideas" do more than underscore the Court's distinction between corporations and other types of contributors and spenders. In the context of a case involving independent spending, the Court's use of the term "integrity" goes beyond concern for unethical practices. Rather, the term expresses a systemic concern that elections not be dominated by those whose overwhelming resources "are not an indication of popular support" for their political ideas.

Ideological movement by the Court along the path suggested by the language of *MCFL* could upset existing campaign finance doctrine. *Bellotti*'s holding that states may not regulate corporate participation in ballot measure elections seems most vulnerable. So long as the issue was corruption, narrowly conceived, the Court could distinguish corporate participation in ballot propositions from elections for public office. If the issue is domination of the process by wealth unrelated to public support, the distinction vanishes.

The Court is not likely ever to accept fully and permanently one of the competing visions described above to the exclusion of the other. *MCFL* suggests some movement away from the laissez faire end of the spectrum toward toleration of some affirmative government action in pursuit of more equal political participation. The extent and duration of that movement cannot be predicted.

See also: Buckley v. Valeo, Federal Election Campaign Act and Amendments, Richard Nixon, Political Action Committees, Third Parties in American Elections, Watergate

Daniel Hays Lowenstein

REFERENCES

Drew, Elizabeth. 1983. *Politics and Money: The New Road to Corruption.* New York: Macmillan.

Fiss, Owne M. 1986. "Free Speech and Social Structure." 71 *Iowa Law Review* 1405.

Jacobson, Gary C. 1980. *Money in Congressional Elections.* New Haven: Yale U. Pr.

Lowenstein, Daniel H. 1982. "Campaign Spending and Ballot Propositions: Recent Experience, Public Choice Theory and the First Amendment." 29 *UCLA Law Review* 505.

———. 1985. "Political Bribery and the Intermediate Theory of Politics." 32 *UCLA Law Review* 784.

Mayhew, David R. 1974. *Congress: The Electoral Connection.* New Haven: Yale U. Pr.

Nicholson, Marlene Arnold. 1987–88. "Basic Principles or Theoretical Tangles: Analyzing the Constitutionality of Government Regulation of Campaign Finance." 38 *Case Western Reserve Law Review* 589.

Note. 1978. "Campaign Contributions and Federal Bribery Law." 92 *Harvard Law Review* 451.

Polsby, Daniel. 1976. "Buckley v. Valeo: The Special Nature of Political Speech." 1976 *Supreme Court Review* 1.

Schneider, Carl E. 1986. "Free Speech and Corporate Freedom: A Comment on First National Bank of Boston v. Bellotti." 59 *Southern California Law Review* 1227.

Shockley, John S. 1980. "The Initiative Process in Colorado Politics: An Assessment." Boulder: Bureau of Governmental Research & Service, University of Colorado.

———. 1985. "Direct Democracy, Campaign Finance, and the Courts: Can Corruption, Undue Influence, and Declining Voter Confidence Be Found?" 39 *University of Miami Law Review* 377.

Sorauf, Frank. 1988. *Money in American Elections.* Glenview, IL: Scott, Foresman.

Van Alstyne, William W. 1968. "The Demise of the Right/Privilege Distinction in Constitutional Law." 81 *Harvard Law Review* 1439.

Wright, Skelly. 1976. "Politics and the Constitution: Is Money Speech?" 85 *Yale Law Review* 1001.

CASES

Abood v. Detroit Board of Education, 431 U.S. 209 (1977).

Brown v. Socialist Workers '74 Campaign Committee, 459 U.S. 87 (1982).

Buckley v. Valeo, 424 U.S. 1 (1976).

California Medical Association v. Federal Election Commission, 453 U.S. 290 (1981).

Citizens Against Rent Control v. Berkeley, 454 U.S. 197 (1981).

FEC v. Massachusetts Citizens for Life, 479 U.S. 238, 107 S. Ct. 616 (1986).

FEC v. National Conservative Political Action Committee, 470 U.S. 480 (1985).

FEC v. National Right to Work Committee, 459 U.S. 197 (1982).

First National Bank of Boston v. Bellotti, 435 U.S. 765 (1978).

Pipefitters v. United States, 407 U.S. 385 (1972).

United States v. CIO, 335 U.S. 106 (1948).

United States v. UAW-CIO, 352 U.S. 567 (1957).

Joseph G. Cannon (1836–1926)

Powerful Speaker of the U.S. House of Representatives in the early twentieth century. As Republican Speaker of the U.S. House of Representatives from 1903 to 1911, Joseph G. Cannon used his power in ways that stirred revolt even within his own party. As a result, the House changed its rules to decentralize authority. For decades, no other Speaker would have the clout that Cannon enjoyed—and lost.

Cannon was born to a Quaker family in New Garden, North Carolina. After studying at Cincinnati Law School, he practiced law in Illinois. From 1861 to 1868, he served as State's attorney for the Twenty-seventh Judicial District of Illinois. He lost his first bid for the House in 1870 but won in 1872.

In his fourth term, Speaker Samuel Randall named Cannon to the Appropriations Committee. In his eighth term, Speaker John Carlisle named him to the Rules Committee. When the Republican caucus of the Fifty-first Congress met in December 1889, he ran against Thomas B. Reed and William McKinley for the speakership. Reed won but made Cannon his parliamentary lieutenant.

In 1890 he defended a controversial Reed decision. To block action on an election dispute, House Democrats tried to prevent a quorum by refusing to vote. Breaking with tradition, Reed counted as present all those who were in the chamber, whether or not they voted. When Democrats noted that Reed himself had once argued against the kind of action he had now taken, Cannon responded: "I say that a majority under the Constitution is entitled to legislate, and that, if a contrary practice has grown up, such practice is unrepublican, undemocratic, against sound policy and contrary to the Constitution." The Republican position prevailed. The House then adopted rules that formalized the chair's power to count a quorum and empowered the Rules Committee to write for each bill a rule setting the conditions of debate. The latter change made the Rules Committee a power center in the House, and so it remains today. It also strengthened the Speaker's hand because he chaired the Rules Committee.

In 1890 Republicans lost 85 House seats, including Cannon's. In addition to running in a bad year for Republicans, Cannon had other handicaps. The public disliked his support for Reed's rule and was offended by a floor speech in which he denounced a colleague in scatological terms. Cannon regained his seat in 1892, and his party regained its majority two years later.

Back in power, Reed appointed Cannon to head the Appropriations Committee. As chairman, he made a point of thrift. "You may think my business is to make appropriations," he once said, "but it is not. It is to prevent their being made." But in 1898, his long-time colleague, President William McKinley, asked him to secure passage of a $50 million appropriation for the war with Spain. He then drafted an appropriation bill that won quick approval. Nineteen years later, Cannon's bill served as the model for early appropriations for World War I.

Reed retired in 1899. Cannon ran for Speaker again, but lost to David Henderson of Iowa. Henderson retired after two terms, and Cannon finally won the speakership.

Thinking that America was already "a hell of a success," Cannon used the Rules Committee to hinder Theodore Roosevelt's reform proposals. Speaking for the President's supporters within the House GOP, John Nelson of Wisconsin said in 1908 that Roosevelt "has been trying to cultivate oranges for many years in the frigid climate of the Committee of Rules, but what has he gotten but the proverbial lemons?"

Cannon had the power to appoint committees. During his first three terms, he used this power within certain restraints: he generally held to the custom that seniority should weigh heavily in committee assignments, and he allowed the minority leader to make assignments for the Democrats. In 1909, however, several Republicans did not vote for Cannon for Speaker; despite their seniority, he punished them with unfavorable assignments. And after a partisan dispute over a tariff bill, he took back the authority to name Democrats to committees. Now, both Democrats and insurgent Republicans were gunning for Cannon.

The revolt against Cannon started on March 16, 1910. Through a series of parliamentary maneuvers, insurgents led by George Norris of Nebraska brought to the floor a rules change that would remove the Speaker from the Rules Committee and enlarge its membership. Despite their understanding that the rules change would strip the Speaker of much of his power, Cannon's supporters lacked the votes to win. On March 19 an amended version of the Norris resolution passed 193 to 153, with 43 Republicans voting against Cannon's position. Cannon then invited a resolution to declare the speakership vacant. This maneuver saved face: as Cannon knew, most members of his party did not want to oust a Republican from the chair. The resolution lost 192 to 155, with only 8 Republicans voting against Cannon.

In spite of the personal blow to Cannon, the House then carried out reforms that further weakened the speakership. A new discharge rule let any member supported by a majority vote to take bills from committees that did not report them.

In 1910 Democrats won control of the House. In organizing the chamber, they acted to keep a 1908 platform promise to "enable a majority of the [House's] members to direct its deliberations and control legislation." Among other things, the Democratic caucus voted to strip the speakership of its power to make committee assignments. For many years thereafter, real power in the House would lie less in the speakership than in the committee chairs.

In 1912 Cannon lost his seat, but he regained it two years later. As well liked as he was now powerless, he remained in the House until he retired in 1923 at the age of 87.

See also: William McKinley, Thomas B. Reed, Theodore Roosevelt, Speaker of the House

John J. Pitney, Jr.

REFERENCES

Bolling, Richard. 1968. *Power in the House: A History of the Leadership in the House of Representatives.* New York: E. P. Dutton.

Busbey, L. White. 1927. *Uncle Joe Cannon: The Story of a Pioneer American.* New York: Henry Holt.

Cheney, Richard B., and Lynne V. Cheney. 1983. *Kings of the Hill: Power and Personality in the House of Representatives.* New York: Continuum.

Jones, Charles O. 1971. "Joseph G. Cannon and Howard Smith: An Essay on the Limits of Leadership in the House of Representatives." In Nelson Polsby, ed. *Congressional Behavior.* New York: Random House.

Kennon, Donald R. 1986. *The Speakers of the House of Representatives.* Baltimore: Johns Hopkins U. Pr.

Hattie W. Caraway (1878–1950)

First woman elected to the U.S. Senate. The second woman to serve in the United States Senate, Hattie Caraway was first appointed to fill the vacancy left by the death of her husband, populistic Arkansas Democrat Thaddeus Caraway; in January 1932 she won a special election for the remaining year of his term with the backing of Democratic party leaders, who saw her as a safe place-holder who would not interfere with the election to the full term. When local officials said they could not afford a special election, the newly formed Arkansas Women's Democratic Club recruited women as volunteer election judges in 72 of the state's 75 counties.

Caraway unexpectedly sought and won re-election, in defiance of those same leaders. She won a second full term in 1938, defeating John McClellan, whose slogan was, "Arkansas needs another man in the Senate." In 1944, however, she lost the Democratic primary to J. William Fulbright.

Caraway made only 15 speeches in her 13 years in the Senate; she was called "Silent Hattie" and was portrayed as "a housewife among politicians." Her view of debate was that "we could have much less of it and get more done and save lots of money." Her journal, *Silent Hattie Speaks* (1979), shows that she was sometimes bewildered by legislation but grounded her votes in firm populistic beliefs.

Caraway's electoral victories have been described as fortuitous, owing either to the voters' sympathy for her widowhood or to the support of her by Louisiana Democrat Huey Long. But she campaigned hard and twice defeated capable male politicians. Long's support, while important, was based on their voting alliance in the Senate, not on whim or personal friendship. Long was particularly appreciative of Caraway's

support for him against the wishes of her senior Arkansas colleague, Minority Leader Joseph T. Robinson.

After Caraway's 1944 defeat, she served on the federal Employees Compensation Commission and later the Employees Compensation Appeals Board.

See also: J. William Fulbright, Huey Long

John C. Berg

REFERENCES

Caraway, Hattie W. 1979. *Silent Hattie Speaks: The Personal Journal of Senator Hattie Caraway.* Ed. by Diane D. Kincaid. Westport, CT: Greenwood.

Towns, Stuart. 1966. "A Louisiana Medicine Show: The Kingfish Elects an Arkansas Senator." 25 *Arkansas Historical Quarterly* 117.

John G. Carlisle (1835–1910)

Powerful Democratic Speaker of the U.S. House of Representatives in the 1880s. Born in Campbell (now Kenton) County, Kentucky, John Griffin Carlisle spent his career as a public servant in a wide variety of positions. As a young man he taught school and later studied law. Admitted to the bar in 1858, he practiced law in Covington, Kentucky, and was elected to the Kentucky House of Representatives, where he served from 1859 to 1861. He returned to elective politics in 1866 when he became a member of the state senate. Reelected in 1869, he served until 1871 when he resigned following his nomination for lieutenant governor. While he was lieutenant governor (1871–1875), he also worked as editor of the *Louisville Daily Ledger* in 1872.

Carlisle entered national politics in 1868 when he was a delegate-at-large from Kentucky to the Democratic National Convention in New York. He was also an alternate presidential elector for the state at large in 1876. His larger impact on national politics was as a member of the House of Representatives from 1877 to 1890. He was a party leader on the issues of revenue and tariff reform. Although he was not regarded as an advocate of free trade, he was a determined antiprotectionist.

Carlisle is most famous for his tenure as Speaker of the House. A return to Democratic control of the House allowed him to be elected Speaker in 1883 over former Speaker Samuel J. Randall. He was reelected in 1885 and 1887. During his tenure he was regarded as absolute leader of the House. Carlisle considered it to be the Speaker's duty to lead Congress, rather than his party, and he used his recognition powers toward that end by sometimes refusing to recognize members who opposed his views, regardless of partisanship. He was noted for his judicious adherence to parliamentary law and to the Speaker's powers over partisanship, as well as for his generous treatment of the minority and his use of his role as chairman of the Rules Committee to use special orders to control the consideration of legislation.

He resigned his House seat in 1890 when he was elected to fill a vacancy in the U.S. Senate. Immediately taking a position on the powerful Finance Committee, he played a major, if brief, role in the Senate, serving only until 1893, when he resigned to become Secretary of the Treasury under Grover Cleveland (1893–1897). As Secretary, he put his sound money views to work to preserve the gold standard after the panic of 1893. The ascendancy of the free-silver wing of the Democratic Party after 1896 helped to bring him and other Gold Democrats into disrepute, and he retired from politics.

See also: Grover Cleveland, Gold Democrats, Speaker of the House

James V. Saturno

REFERENCES

Barnes, James A. 1967. *John G. Carlisle: Financial Statesman.* Gloucester, MA: Peter Smith (orig. pub. New York: Dodd, Mead, 1931).

Follett, Mary Parker. 1974. *The Speaker of the House of Representatives.* New York: Lenox Hill.

Stokely Carmichael (1941–)

African-American civil rights leader. Stokely Carmichael is known primarily as a leading spokesperson for "Black Power," a philosophy of assertive Black self-determination in a white racist society. He co-authored (with Charles V. Hamilton) *Black Power: The Politics of Liberation in America* (1967).

Carmichael graduated from Howard University in 1964 with a degree in philosophy. While at Howard, Carmichael participated in civil rights movement activities, for which he was arrested many times. He became the leader of the Nonviolent Action Group (NAG), a Student Nonviolent Coordinating Committee (SNCC) affiliate at Howard. After graduation, Carmichael became a full-time SNCC worker and, in 1966 and 1967, SNCC chairman.

Carmichael is noted for his great talents as an organizer and orator, his astute political awareness, and his ability to communicate with less well educated people. During his tenure as chairman of SNCC, the organization shifted from a policy of nonviolence to one of support for the Black Power movement.

While in Africa on a four-month tour in 1967, Carmichael established a close relationship with both exiled Ghanaian leader Kwame Nkrumah and Guinean president Sekou Toure. He strengthened his reputation as the most vocal of America's Black leaders by his association with Third World leaders, condemnation of the United States, and calls for revolutionary violence.

Shortly after returning from Africa, Carmichael met with two leaders of the new Black Panther Party (BPP) and agreed to become the Party's prime minister. Although Carmichael's Pan-African ideology differed from the Marxism of the BPP, he proved useful to them. Differences in ideology and personality disputes between SNCC and the BPP led to the eventual rupture of relations between the two groups in the spring of 1968. Carmichael was expelled from SNCC but continued to work for the BPP. However, he resigned in July 1969, citing disagreement with the BPP's association with white radicals.

Carmichael is one of a small handful of Black activists who can be credited with setting the tone and tenor of a movement that was to have significant impact on the 1968 presidential election. In this election, independent candidate George Wallace, and later Republican Richard Nixon (in his "Southern Strategy"), played upon white fears of Black revolt and Black Power popularized by Carmichael. On the heels of major urban riots and violent inflammatory rhetoric by Carmichael and other Black Power and Black Panther spokespersons, white reaction was galvanized, feeding the successes of Wallace, and ultimately, the election of Nixon.

See also: Election of 1968, Richard M. Nixon, Race and Racial Politics, Student Non-Violent Coordinating Committee, George Wallace

Lisa G. Langenbach

REFERENCES

Carmichael, Stokely. 1965. *Stokely Speaks.* New York: Random House.

———. 1969. "Pan-Africanism—Land and Power." 1 (November) *The Black Scholar* 36.

———, and Charles Hamilton. 1967. *Black Power: The Politics of Liberation in America.* New York: Random House.

Carson, Clayborne. 1981. *In Struggle: SNCC and the Black Awakening of the 1960s.* Cambridge: Harvard U. Pr.

Scott, Robert L., and Wayne Brockriede. 1969. *The Rhetoric of Black Power.* New York: Harper & Row.

Carpetbaggers

Southern conservatives used this term to vilify northerners who participated in southern politics as Republicans during Reconstruction. Even northerners came to accept this characterization of impecunious northerners, carrying their worldly possessions in carpetbags and using southern political office to enrich themselves at public expense.

Ironically, few northerners came to the South with ideas of political officeholding. At the Civil War's close, northern editors, hoping to spur reunion by "northernizing" the South, stressed the opportunities offered by high cotton prices and low land prices in the defeated section. Northern migrants who responded were typically former Union Army officers or Freedmen's Bureau officers who brought with them capital to invest. Although they were resented by southerners for their assumption that their ways were superior, northerners did find limited acceptance because their investments helped to stabilize the economic position of the southern landed class. Northerners were never numerous. No southern state had more than 2 percent northern-born residents.

With the passage in 1867 of the Reconstruction Acts, which granted Blacks the right to vote, a southern Republican Party became feasible and northerners were often the catalysts for its organization. White conservative hostility increased proportionately. About one-sixth of the delegates to the new constitutional conventions held in the South were northerners. They were the best educated and wealthiest of the delegates and often chaired the key committees and drafted large sections of the new state constitutions. Under those new rules, northerners, representing chiefly Black Belt counties, won elective office far in excess of their proportion of the Republican electorate. Some 60 northerners served in Congress during Reconstruction; South Carolina, Florida, Mississippi, Louisiana, Georgia, and Arkansas elected northern-born governors. Many appointive positions went to northerners too, as declining cotton prices and conservative boycotts of northern-born businessmen and professionals weakened the migrants' economic position.

Through the Republican Party northerners hoped to democratize and modernize the South. They typically favored equality before the law, economic development (especially railroads), and public (rather than private) responsibility for education and charity. Southern conserva-tives and some native white Republicans bristled at the racial program and at the cost of social services in a still-impoverished section while better educated and more successful Blacks resented the white northerners' monopolization of political offices in Black communities. Bitter conflict characterized intraparty factional squabbles as well as those between Republican and southern conservatives. Charges of official malfeasance and financial extravagance, sometimes accurate but often exaggerated, flourished in such a climate. Bloodshed accompanied most elections. Even many northerners came to believe that only the South's "natural" (i.e., white conservative) leaders could restore order.

As conservatives returned to power in the 1870s, some northerners, such as Marshall Twitchell of Louisiana who lost his property, most of his family, two arms, and the use of a leg to conservative vengeance, returned to the North; others remained in the South, sometimes assisted by federal patronage positions. Some individuals who went back, such as Albion Tourgée, once a North Carolina judge, remained true to their ideals for a lifetime. He helped to organize a forerunner of the National Association for the Advancement of Colored People and argued the unconstitutionality of segregation in the famous 1896 Supreme Court case *Plessy v. Ferguson*.

See also: Reconstruction

Phyllis F. Field

REFERENCES

Current, Richard N. 1988. *Those Terrible Carpetbaggers: A Reinterpretation.* New York: Oxford U. Pr.

Hume, Richard L. 1977. "Carpetbaggers in the Reconstruction South: A Group Portrait of Outside Whites in the 'Black and Tan' Constitutional Conventions." 64 *Journal of American History* 313.

Anna Ella Carroll (1815–1894)

Nativist political propagandist of the 1850s. Anna Ella Carroll of Maryland, a mid-nineteenth-century pamphleteer and lobbyist, spent much of her career in the 1850s writing on behalf of the American, or Know-Nothing Party. Carroll's massive tome, *The Great American Battle; or, the Contest Between Christianity and Political Romanticism*, could be viewed as the American Party bible, so accurately did it delineate the party and its dictates. *The Great American Battle* served as an 1856 election year statement of the principles of the more moderate wing of the Know-Nothings: Carroll argued for the inclusion by the party of native-born Catholics—an essential concession for victory in her native state and in Louisiana, where Know-Nothings were also popular.

In fact, the party split over the slavery issue, not over its anti-Catholic stance. *The Union of the States* and *Review of Pierce's Administration; Showing Its Only Popular Measures to Have Originated with the Executive of Millard Fillmore*, both written by Carroll during the campaign, are clear examples of the Know-Nothings' decision to avoid the divisive slavery issue by emphasizing the nationalism of Millard Fillmore, the party's presidential nominee in 1856.

Fillmore lost the election and, in 1858, Carroll began working as a campaign manager for Virginian John Minor Botts. She wrote countless letters to newspapers promoting Botts's candidacy as a fusion candidate for the Know-Nothings and the Republicans and describing him as a man who could "harmonize and unite the contending influences" in a divided country. She tried to persuade New York Republican leader Thurlow Weed to take Botts over William Seward; when that failed, she pushed Judge John McLean as a candidate for the Constitutional Union Party's nomination in May 1860, provided Botts could be his running mate.

The McLean-Botts combination did not win at the Constitutional Union Party's nominating convention in 1860, and Carroll, who supported herself with her pen, agreed orally with the War Department soon after the outbreak of the Civil War to write on behalf of Abraham Lincoln's administration. The government distributed several of her pamphlets supporting Lincoln's actions in the early days of the war, but it failed to pay her for her work and reneged on the oral contract. She spent the last 30 years of her life in Washington petitioning Congress for payment for her Civil War work as well as publishing occasional articles on the glories of American history and life.

See also: John Minor Botts, Constitutional Union Party, Election of 1856, Know-Nothings, Slavery, Thurlow Weed

Janet L. Coryell

REFERENCES

Basler, Roy P. 1979. "Lincoln, Blacks, and Women." In *The Public and Private Lincoln: Contemporary Perspectives*. Carbondale: Southern Illinois U. Pr.

Carroll, Anna Ella. 1856. *The Great American Battle; or the Contest Between Christianity and Political Romanticism*. New York: Miller, Orton & Mulligan.

———. 1856. *The Union of the States*. Boston: James French.

———. 1856. *Review of Pierce's Administration; Showing Its Only Popular Measures to Have Originated with the Executive of Millard Fillmore*. Boston: James French.

———. 1856. *Which? Fillmore or Buchanan*. Boston: James French.

———. 1856. *Who Shall Be President? An Appeal to the People*. Boston: James French.

Coryell, Janet L. 1990. *Neither Heroine Nor Fool: Anna Ella Carroll of Maryland*. Kent, OH: Kent State U. Pr.

Jimmy Carter (1924–)

Thirty-ninth President of the United States. James Earl Carter, Jr., a Democrat from Georgia who prefers the more informal nickname "Jimmy," defeated incumbent Republican President Gerald R. Ford in 1976 to become President of the United States (1977–1981). His victory capped an extraordinary political rise from relative obscurity.

Though Carter had served two terms in the Georgia state senate (1962–1970) and, after losing on the first attempt (1968), went on to serve as governor of Georgia for one term (1971–1975), he remained virtually unknown outside the state. In December 1973 Carter made a guest appearance on the television panel show "What's My Line?" and none of the panelists was able to identify him. In October 1975 Carter failed even to be mentioned in a national public opinion poll ranking of presidential contenders. "Jimmy Who?" became the standard media appellation that greeted his presidential candidacy in 1976.

His staff in Georgia, however, had long been convinced that Carter possessed the makings of a presidential candidate. Born in Plains, Georgia (population: 550)—the first American President born in a hospital—he has excelled throughout his life. In 1946 Carter graduated from the Naval Academy in the top 10 percent of his class; he served with distinction on battleships and nuclear submarines and, when he left the Navy in 1953 to manage the Carter family peanut business upon his father's death, he turned the ailing farm and warehouse into a million dollar enterprise.

As a successful businessman, Carter was soon drawn into community affairs, first as a leader in the Baptist Church and as chairman of the Sumter County Board of Education (1955–1962) and then as a spokesman for the economic development of southern and central Georgia. In his first try at electoral office in 1962, he won the Quitman County state senate seat—though only after local attorney and subsequent confidant Charles Kirbo won a suit on Carter's behalf that reversed the initial vote tally on grounds of ballot-stuffing by Carter's opponent. As a state senator, Carter resisted pressures to become involved in a local prosegregation White Citizen's Council and, despite racist opposition to his reelection, managed in 1964 to win another term in the state senate. He continued to speak out against segregation laws that separated Blacks and whites in schools and other public facilities, and he encouraged Black membership in the Plains Baptist Church.

Carter's only setback in this early period came in 1966, when he finished third in a six-man Georgia gubernatorial contest that was won by the flamboyant segregationist Lester Maddox. Depressed by his lackluster showing, Carter entered a period of introspection and, influenced by his evangelist sister, emerged the next year as a born-again Christian. With renewed self-confidence and determination, Carter set out again to become governor of Georgia, delivering some eighteen hundred speeches across the state in the next two years. In the 1970 Democratic primary, Carter confronted the darling of the Atlanta establishment, the politically moderate and well-heeled attorney Carl E. Sanders—known as "Cuff Links Carl" to rural Georgians who distrusted Atlanta's urbane elite.

Compared to Sanders, voters saw Carter as the conservative candidate. Backing up this perception, Carter declared that he was against busing to achieve racial balance in the schools and advocated other positions with appeal to Georgians beyond the Atlanta beltway. The *Atlanta Constitution* concluded that the candidate from Plains was nothing more than an "ignorant, racist, backward, ultra-conservative, rednecked South Georgia peanut farmer."

Carter won the primary and the general election and no doubt shocked conservative supporters by declaring in his inaugural address: "I say to you quite frankly that the time for racial discrimination is over." He created another stir in 1974 when he hung a portrait of Black civil rights leader Martin Luther King, Jr., in the state capitol. Carter was dubbed the archetype of a "new style" southern governor and, as such, appeared on the cover of *Time* in May 1971.

While governor, Carter increasingly became involved in national politics: he joined the Trilateral Commission in 1972, an organization of business and political leaders interested in improved relations among the United States, Japan, and the nations of Western Europe; he chaired the Democratic Governor's Campaign Committee in 1972; and he served as campaign chairman for the Democratic National Committee in 1974—positions that allied him with leading thinkers and doers in the party.

With these achievements in mind, well aware of Carter's personal charm and determination, his staff began to lay plans for a presidential bid. His top political aide, Hamilton Jordan (pronounced Ger-din), wrote Carter a lengthy memorandum in 1972 outlining how he might successfully run for the presidency. With remarkable prescience, Jordan emphasized the growing dissatisfaction of the American public with professional politicians in Washington and foresaw how voters might prefer the candidacy of an outsider like Carter. The Watergate scandal would soon strengthen the validity of this hypothesis. Jordan also stressed the importance that Iowa would play in the 1976 presidential elections. For the first time, this state would hold its initial presidential delegate selection caucuses in January of the election year, making it the first contest in the series of caucus and primary battles on the way to the nominating convention in the summer. Whoever won the early skirmish in Iowa, Jordan reasoned, would draw the attention of the media across the nation. Here was a chance to turn "Jimmy Who" into "Jimmy Carter, Winner!"

Governor Carter quietly began to prepare himself. As early as 1973 Jordan and other staff aides combed Iowa in search of supporters, and Carter frequently traveled the state, increasing his Atlanta–Des Moines shuttles when his term as governor expired in January 1975—recording 110 visits in all. The strategy paid off: when the ballots in the Iowa primary were counted on January 19, 1976, Carter stood first in a crowded field of Democrats. The extensive media coverage of his surprise victory helped carry him on to another win in the crucial New Hampshire primary. Carter now had the national credibility he needed to raise funds for the rest of the campaign. Putting together a string of additional victories (among a few losses), Carter—campaigning on an anti-Washington platform—won his party's nomination on the first ballot. He went on to defeat President Gerald Ford by a narrow margin, as the incumbent's popularity ebbed because of his Watergate pardon of former President Richard M. Nixon and because of the 8 percent unemployment rate in the nation.

Having brilliantly won the presidency, Carter now faced an even more difficult challenge—governing the country in constitutional harness with the Washington legislators whom he had just spent months attacking on the campaign circuit. His relations with Congress soured, outsider that he was and wished to remain. Nevertheless, the new President did manage to pass some significant domestic legislation, including measures designed to consolidate government agencies and a spate of energy bills. His major achievements, though, came in the realm of foreign policy. Here he expressed a strong concern for morality in America's foreign affairs and championed human rights in the small and poor nations. He also led the fight for passage of the Panama Canal treaties, which improved U.S. relations with Central America. And, as the centerpiece of his foreign policy, he guided to fruition the Camp David Accords—the first peace treaty ever between Israel and an Arab state (Egypt).

Despite these accomplishments, his standing in the polls plummeted as inflation spiraled to 15 percent, unemployment figures rose above 6 percent, and American diplomats in Iran remained hostage for over a year. By July 1980 Carter's popularity had dipped to a 21 percent approval rating in the polls—the lowest ever for a President. In November GOP conservative Ronald Reagan, a former film actor and governor of California, defeated Carter's reelection bid, with the incumbent carrying only six states. Carter then returned to Georgia and has since taken an active role as political pundit, citizen activist, and campaigner for Democratic candidates.

See also: Democratic National Committee, Elections of 1976 and 1980, Gerald Ford, Martin Luther King, Jr., Lester Maddox, Ronald Reagan, Watergate

Loch K. Johnson

REFERENCES

Carter, Jimmy. 1982. *Keeping Faith: Memoirs of a President*. New York: Bantam Books.

Carter, Rosalynn. 1984. *First Lady from Plains*. Boston: Houghton Mifflin.

Glad, Betty. 1980. *Jimmy Carter: In Search of the Great White House*. New York: Norton.

Germond, Jack W., and Jules Witcover. 1981. *Blue Smoke and Mirrors: How Reagan Won and How Carter Lost the Election of 1980*. New York: Viking.

Johnson, Haynes. 1980. *In the Absence of Power: Governing America*. New York: Viking.

Jones, Charles O. 1988. *The Trusteeship Presidency: Jimmy Carter and the United States Congress*. Baton Rouge: Louisiana State U. Pr.

Jordan, Hamilton. 1982. *Crisis: The Last Year of the Carter Presidency*. New York: Putnam.

Witcover, Jules. 1977. *Marathon: The Pursuit of the Presidency, 1972–1976*. New York: Viking.

Thomas H. Carter (1854–1911)

Chairman of the Republican National Committee at the end of the nineteenth century. Thomas Henry Carter, United States Senator from Montana, was a Republican national chairman (1892–1896) and an ardent advocate of free silver at a time when most Republican leaders favored a gold-standard currency policy.

Born and educated in Illinois, Carter settled in Montana, where he specialized in mining law. Although the Montana Territory was Democratic, he won election as its representative to Congress in 1888. Carter developed a strong friendship with Speaker Thomas B. Reed, who appointed him chairman of the Committee on Mines despite his junior status as a freshman Congressman. In 1890 Carter was secretary of the Republican congressional campaign committee, although he himself failed reelection that year.

President Benjamin Harrison, as a gesture to the silver Republicans of the Northwest, appointed Carter head of the Land Office of the Department of the Interior. Carter resigned from this position just prior to the 1892 Republican National Convention, which he attended as a Harrison manager. President Harrison, James G. Blaine, and William McKinley were the three names before the convention. Louis T. Michener was Harrison's personal manager, and his most frequent adviser was Carter.

At Harrison's request, the national committee elected William J. Campbell, a Chicago lawyer and a supporter of Blaine's candidacies in 1880 and 1884, as national chairman. Carter was chosen secretary. Within two weeks, Campbell resigned for business reasons. The executive committee of the national committee, after several inquiries to others, unanimously elected Secretary Carter to the chairmanship. Not a member of the national committee, Carter was the first outsider to hold the Republican chairmanship.

During his tenure as chairman, Carter led the first serious discussion about establishing a permanent Republican national headquarters. He was the only leading silver Republican to refrain from bolting the party when it adopted a gold-standard plank in 1896. Carter's political career concluded with his election as Senator from Montana in 1895 and again in 1905.

See also: James G. Blaine, Benjamin Harrison, William McKinley, Thomas B. Reed, Silver Republicans

Ralph M. Goldman

REFERENCES

Goldman, Ralph M. 1990. *The National Party Chairmen and Committees: Factionalism at the Top.* Armonk, NY: M. E. Sharpe.

Benjamin Harrison Papers, Library of Congress.

William McKinley Papers, Library of Congress.

Lewis Cass (1782–1866)

Perennial Democratic presidential aspirant. Lewis Cass was the Democratic nominee for President in 1848. He had an impressive résumé—war hero in 1812, governor of the Michigan Territory, Secretary of War under Andrew Jackson, and minister to France. In 1844, championing the annexation of Texas, Cass fought Martin Van Buren for the Democratic nomination. The divided Democrats compromised on James Polk.

In December 1847, now serving as a United States Senator from Michigan, Cass again sought the Democratic nomination. He advocated popular sovereignty—the notion that the people of each territory should decide the slavery question for themselves. This position solidified the Michigan Senator's reputation as a "doughface"—a northern man with southern principles—essential to gaining a national Democratic following. Cass was nominated for President. Disgruntled Democrats, known as Barnburners, joined with antislavery Conscience Whigs and nominated Martin Van Buren to run on the Free Soil ticket. The regular Whigs nominated the Mexican War hero Zachary Taylor.

In keeping with custom—and Democratic wishes—Cass embraced the party platform, resigned from the Senate, and made few appearances during the campaign. Exploiting their candidate's reticence and ambiguous positions, the Democrats circulated one campaign biography of Cass in the North and a second one in the South. When election day came, Cass had done everything right except to win. The Free Soil Party split the Democrats' vote in New York City, swinging New York State and the election to Taylor. Cass returned to the Senate in 1849, resigning in 1857 to become James Buchanan's Secretary of State.

See also: Barnburners, James Buchanan, Conscience Whigs, Free Soil Party, Andrew Jackson, Mexican War, James Polk, Zachary Taylor, Martin Van Buren

Gil Troy

REFERENCES

McLaughlin, Andrew C. 1899. "Lewis Cass." In John T. Morse, Jr., ed. *American Statesmen.* Boston: Houghton Mifflin.

Potter, David M. 1976. *The Impending Crisis, 1848–1861.* New York: Harper & Row.

Rayback, Joseph G. 1970. *Free Soil: The Election of 1848.* Lexington: U. Pr. of Kentucky.

Woodford, Frank B. 1950. *Lewis Cass: The Last Jeffersonian.* New Brunswick: Rutgers U. Pr. (orig. pub. New York: Octagon Books, 1973).

Carrie Chapman Catt (1859–1947)

Leading suffragist. Carrie Chapman Catt was born in Ripon, Wisconsin, and educated at the state college of Iowa at Ames, receiving her undergraduate degree in 1880. After a year's training in the law, she moved into the field of education, first as principal of the Mason City High School and, after 1883, as superintendent of schools.

Carrie Chapman Catt was a major contributor to the twentieth-century women's suffrage movement. Her talent as an orator was matched by her skill as an organizer. After joining the Iowa Women Suffrage Association in 1887, her skill in attracting new members to the National American Women Suffrage Association (NAWSA) encouraged its president, Susan B. Anthony, to choose Catt as her successor in 1900. Catt resigned in 1904 when her husband became ill. After his death, she resumed her work. She successfully brought together diverse New York City groups, leading to the 1910 creation of the Woman Suffrage Party.

Admired for her skill as a detailed organizer, a careful planner, and an efficient administrator, she was reelected to the presidency of NAWSA in 1915. The organization was under challenge by militants who campaigned for a federal amendment by holding the Democrats in power responsible for the failure of woman suffrage. Led by Alice Paul, they left NAWSA and subsequently formed the National Woman's Party in 1916. Their radical methods resulted in their arrests and gained them publicity. In opposition, Catt devised a "Winning Plan," which combined support for a federal amendment with efforts to achieve state suffrage. Her goal was to pressure federal legislators by first achieving state suffrage. Catt carefully courted both parties, gaining their endorsement of a constitutional amendment in 1916.

Though a pacifist who had helped found the Woman's Peace Party in 1915, she believed women's contributions to World War I would demonstrate the justice of their demand. Women's war efforts, combined with a string of suffrage victories in the states, finally gained them Woodrow Wilson's personal support. The

Nineteenth Amendment ultimately was ratified because she and others were able to convince men that it was to their own political benefit to do so.

After victory, she urged the establishment of the League of Women Voters as a nonpartisan organization to replace NAWSA. She continued her international work on behalf of suffrage and peace throughout her remaining years.

See also: League of Woman Voters, National American Woman Suffrage Association, Nineteenth Amendment, Woodrow Wilson, Woman Suffrage Movement, Women's Peace Party.

Joy A. Scimé

REFERENCES

Fowler, Robert Booth. 1986. *Carrie Catt, Feminist Politician.* Boston: Northeastern U. Pr.

Scott, Anne F., and Andrew M. Scott. 1975. *One Half the People: The Fight for Woman Suffrage.* Philadelphia: J. P. Lippincott.

James, Edward T., Janet W. James, and Paul S. Boyer. 1971. *Notable American Women 1607–1950.* Cambridge: Belknap Press.

Caucuses

A meeting of party members called to decide on matters affecting the political party. Caucuses are the traditional means of party decision-making. However, caucus decision-making is tainted because few citizens know what really goes on at a caucus.

In the early nineteenth century, presidential nominations were determined in congressional caucuses, that is, in meetings of like-minded members of Congress who decided on presidential candidates. "King Caucus" dominated presidential politics; but when caucus selections met with popular dissatisfaction, as happened in 1824 (when the caucus nominated William Crawford of Georgia and ignored the growing popularity of Andrew Jackson), the caucus as a nominating tool fell into disuse. The term came to imply secretive, antidemocratic decision-making. Eventually, congressional nominating caucuses were replaced by "popular conventions," meetings of active partisans, as the means for selecting presidential candidates.

Still, caucuses persisted in one form or another, often far removed from public view. Before the advent of direct primary elections in the early twentieth century, most party decisions, including selections of national convention delegates and nominees for local offices, were made at caucuses, frequently at those to which only a select few were invited. The public knew little about the mechanisms of party decision-making in the time of powerful political machines and their dominant bosses. After the introduction of direct primaries, caucuses were used less and less in deciding on local nominations. By the mid-1950s, primaries in some form or another in every state had replaced the caucus as the key nominating tool, even though in a number of states, with Connecticut as the prime example, local caucuses and conventions still play a prominent role. As caucus and convention nomination for state and local office declined, however, many states still selected delegates to national nominating conventions far from the public view.

After the Democratic National Convention in 1968, the national party established a reform commission to study the nominating process in detail. The Commission on Party Structure and Delegate Selection (the McGovern-Fraser Commission) spelled out in detail how caucuses had been used (and abused) in the presidential nominating process. The commission report demonstrated how many delegates were chosen at caucuses closed to the public and conducted autocratically by local party officials. The commission recommendations, which were ultimately implemented by the Democratic National Committee, specified that caucuses were a legitimate means through which party members could select candidates to presidential nominating conventions, if, and only if, they were run openly and democratically. Before the McGovern-Fraser reforms, more than half of the delegates to national nominating conventions were chosen in states that used a caucus system rather than a primary system. These reforms made caucus systems more cumbersome to implement and less advantageous for party officials. Nevertheless, even though states change their rules from election to election, the number of states using caucuses has declined precipitously since 1968. In that year, Vice President Hubert Humphrey won a first ballot nomination at the Democratic National Convention without winning a single primary. By 1988 only about one-quarter of the delegates to the nominating conventions were chosen in caucus states.

The current caucus procedure is a multistage process, usually beginning at the town or rural precinct level. The precise caucus rules vary between the two major political parties. Democratic Party rules are established by the national party and are more constricting than are Republican Party rules, which allow a good deal of local autonomy.

Democratic Party rules require that all caucuses in a state be held at the same time, that they be publicized in prescribed ways, and that the meetings be run in precisely the same manner. The charge of each local caucus is to elect delegates to the next highest level of party decision-making (county conventions in some states, congressional district conventions or state conventions in others) in proportion to the number of supporters that each presidential candidate has at the local caucus. (Party rules deal with fractional representation in ways that allow for no local leeway.) At each subsequent stage in the process, until delegates to the national convention are selected, the proportional representation of presidential candidate preference must be maintained.

In contrast, the local option for Republican Party rules allows for a wide variety of experiences, from those similar to the Democrats to situations in which none of those attending a caucus are even asked their presidential preference. In those cases, local party officials run on their own and are allowed to support whichever candidate they choose.

Those who favor caucus decision-making point out that the modern caucus requires personal contact and offers the potential for discussing issues before selecting delegates representing presidential candidates. While the caucuses in Iowa (the most widely publicized) have been described as the functional equivalent of a primary since candidates invest so much time and effort in that state and because so many people participate in the caucuses every four years, in most states caucuses attract fewer participants and are dominated by party leaders and other political activists. Caucus supporters claim that those more directly involved in the process know more about the candidates and are capable of making more informed judgments.

Caucus opponents claim that this method of decision-making is inherently undemocratic, particularly in comparison to presidential preference primaries. They point to the extreme differences in participation rates, even between Iowa and other states but more pointedly in states with small caucus attendance. (Only about 2 percent of the eligible electorate attends party caucuses in those states that select delegates using this method; in primary states the voter turnout, while still small, normally exceeds 20 percent.) Furthermore, opponents show that caucuses are more easily dominated by fringe elements, as was demonstrated by the successes

enjoyed in early caucus states by Republican Pat Robertson in 1988. While Robertson failed to do well in any Republican presidential primaries, he either won or finished well in seven caucus contests.

Caucus contests reflect the intensity of support for a candidate but not necessarily the breadth of that support. Campaign organization can make a critical difference in a caucus contest, particularly one in which no candidate has an overwhelmingly enthusiastic following. Caucuses are often seen as party-building devices. Party leaders can use caucuses and subsequent delegate selection to encourage the party faithful, to reward their workers and supporters, and to build enthusiasm for active participation in party politics. Thus, caucuses continue as an important feature of American political life, not the dominating force they once were, but as a factor politicians must be aware of in planning presidential campaign strategies.

See also: Bosses, William Crawford, Democratic National Committee, Direct Primary, Elections of 1824 and 1968, Hubert Humphrey, Andrew Jackson, McGovern-Fraser Commission, Presidential Nominating Politics

Michael Heel

REFERENCES

Aldrich, John H. 1980. *Before the Convention: Strategies and Choices in Presidential Nomination Campaigns.* Chicago: U. of Chicago Pr.

Ceaser, James W. 1982. *Reforming the Reforms: A Critical Analysis of the Presidential Selection Process.* Cambridge: Ballinger.

Crotty, William, and John S. Jackson III. 1985. *Presidential Primaries and Nominations.* Washington: Congressional Quarterly.

DiClerico, Robert, and Eric Uslaner. 1984. *Few Are Chosen: Problems in Presidential Selection.* New York: McGraw-Hill.

Anton J. Cermak (1873–1933)

Boss of Chicago Democratic machine. Mayor of Chicago from 1931 until his death in 1933, Anton J. Cermak played a central role in reinvigorating the Democratic Party of Chicago in the 1930s and forged Chicago's first political machine from its diverse ethnic groups. His short tenure as mayor, but lengthy political career, laid the basis for the rise of the Democratic Party's legendary political machine that has dominated Chicago politics for decades.

Cermak held a succession of public offices (state representative, 1902–1909; city alderman, 1909–1912; and court bailiff, 1912–1918) before his first electoral defeat in 1918 in his race for Cook County sheriff. He returned to the city council and remained there until 1922 when he became president of the Cook County Board of Commissioners. In 1928 he became chair of the Cook County Democratic Party. He was a leading spokesperson against Prohibition.

Born in Prague, Czechoslovakia, Cermak was brought to Illinois by his immigrant parents as an infant. In 1889 he went to Chicago and quickly became a successful businessman. Well acquainted with the life of the city's numerous immigrants, he used patronage and public works contracts to tie them to the Democratic machine that he was building. Cermak became the archetypal political boss who dispensed favors in return for political loyalty. He was also, however, a master at the political process of compromise and adjustment. His 1930 electoral challenge against the incumbent Republican mayor, William Hale Thompson, had the support not only of the Democratic Party but also of various reform groups determined to be rid of the scandal-plagued Thompson administration. Cermak's mobilization of the ethnic vote was facilitated by Thompson's open disdain for immigrants, but he also rallied business, women, and other interest groups to his campaign. He was endorsed by both of the city's major newspapers and was swept into office in 1931 with the largest majority ever.

Cermak's Democratic mayoral victory displaced the entrenched Republican Party just as the city was entering the economic crisis of the Great Depression. With unemployment mounting and the city close to bankruptcy, Cermak was unsuccessful in getting state aid for the unemployed. He was successful in making radical cuts in Chicago's budget and in reforming the tax collection process.

Using his considerable statewide political power, Cermak helped Franklin D. Roosevelt win the presidency with a sweeping Illinois victory in 1932. On February 15, 1933, while visiting the President in Miami, Florida, to consult about federal patronage for Chicago, Cermak was shot in an assassination attempt on Roosevelt. He died shortly afterward.

See also: Election of 1932, Prohibition, Franklin Roosevelt

Michael C. Ross

REFERENCES

Gottfried, Alex. 1962. *Boss Cermak of Chicago: A Study of Political Leadership*. Seattle: U. of Washington Pr.

George Chacharis (1908–)

Gary, Indiana, political organizer. Born in Greece, George "Cha Cha" Chacharis and his family subsequently lived in Italy before moving to Gary, Indiana, in 1918. Already familiar with Turkish and Italian, in addition to his native tongue, George learned English and had a childhood that touched key American institutions of that era: altar boy (Greek Orthodox), manager of high school athletic teams, participant in school plays, newspaper delivery boy (Greek language press), and sports stringer for the *Post-Tribune*, Gary's newspaper.

Chacharis went to work in the steel mills, where he would be employed until the mid-1940s and where his ambition and leadership made him chief project engineer. At about the same time, he organized Club SAR, devoted to social, athletic, and recreational activities in his neighborhood, Gary's Central District. From an initial membership of 22, Club SAR became the base of Chacharis's political influence. It operated in the prototypical style of urban political machines—favors for votes.

An avid supporter of Franklin D. Roosevelt, Chacharis found his political strength culminating in the post-1945 period. At first successful in winning minor public offices, Club SAR candidates gained control of city hall when Pete Mandich was elected mayor of Gary in 1951. Mandich appointed Chacharis to key posts from whence the latter's influence was second only to that of the mayor. In 1958 Mandich resigned as mayor permitting Chacharis to become Gary's first foreign-born mayor. The new mayor, a bachelor, became even more visible at community activities and was returned as mayor in 1959 with 72 percent of the vote.

In a way, that victory was his last hurrah. Chacharis launched what seemed to be a popular move to have the city purchase the water company that it had sold in 1932. Opposed in this effort by the *Post-Tribune*, the chamber of commerce, United States Steel, and the utility, Chacharis turned to the public with a referendum. Following a well-financed campaign by his opponents, the voters rejected Chacharis's proposal by a massive majority.

By that time, Chacharis was an enthusiastic backer of John F. Kennedy's bid for the presidency. Soon after Kennedy took office, the President's brother, the U.S. Attorney General, sent Justice Department officials to investigate possible violations of federal law during the Mandich mayoralty. As the inquiry developed,

Chacharis became a principal target. In early 1962, he was indicted on tax evasion charges. In the midst of the trial, he pleaded guilty and resigned as mayor. In January 1963 he was fined $10,000 and sentenced to three years in prison. He was paroled in December 1964 and then returned to Gary where he subsequently held a staff job in an assessor's office until 1977.

Thomas P. Wolf

REFERENCES

Lane, James B. 1978. *"City of the Century": A History of Gary, Indiana.* Bloomington: Indiana U. Pr.

Navasky, Victor. 1971. *Kennedy Justice.* New York: Atheneum.

Whittaker Chambers (1901–1961)

Controversial witness against Communists in the 1950s. Whitaker Chambers, a journalist, grew up on Long Island, New York, attended Columbia University but did not graduate, and then turned instead to the life of a bohemian writer. He gained a minor reputation as a translator of German (translating *Bambi* in 1928) and as a poet.

He joined the Communist Party in 1925 and in 1932 began clandestine Communist work. From 1934 until 1938, Chambers acted as the contact ("cutout") between Soviet agents and undercover American Communists employed by government agencies in Washington. Chambers delivered instructions to the domestic Communists and collected their reports and documents for his Soviet superiors. In 1938 Chambers broke with Communism and started a new life, becoming a writer for *Time* magazine and rising to a senior editor's post at that influential news magazine.

In 1948, in testimony to the House Un-American Activities Committee (HUAC), Chambers named Alger Hiss, a respected diplomat then with the Carnegie Endowment for Peace, as a Communist. When Hiss sued, Chambers produced documents indicating that Hiss had been part of Chambers's spy ring. Despite continued denials, Hiss was convicted of perjury. The Hiss-Chambers case gave a major boost to the career of Congressman Richard M. Nixon (R-Calif.), the HUAC member who pursued the affair, and to the growth of public and political concern with domestic communism in the late 1940s and 1950s. In 1988 Chambers's Maryland farm, where the Hiss-Chambers documents (known as the "pumpkin papers") were hidden for a time, was designated a national historical landmark.

See also: Communism as a Political Issue, House Un-American Activities Committee, Richard Nixon

John E. Haynes

REFERENCES

Weinstein, Allen. 1978. *Perjury: The Hiss-Chambers Case.* New York: Knopf.

A. B. (Happy) Chandler (1898–)

Kentucky politician and baseball commissioner. Between 1931 and 1963, Albert Benjamin "Happy" Chandler was a central figure in Kentucky's Democratic Party. Happy appealed to legions of voters with his friendly demeanor and populist touch.

Chandler grew up poor in rural Kentucky and was educated at Transylvania College, Harvard Law School, and the University of Kentucky Law School. He began his political career when he was appointed to the position of master commissioner of his county's circuit court. He was subsequently elected to a term in the state senate. He was then tabbed by Kentucky's Democratic boss to be the party's candidate for lieutenant governor in 1931. After four years as lieutenant governor, Chandler rebelled, challenged the machine, and won the governorship in 1935.

In 1939 he was appointed to the U.S. Senate to fill a seat left vacant. One year earlier, Chandler's challenge to Senator Alben Barkley had been turned back in the 1938 primary. Chandler was elected to the Senate to fill the remaining years of Marvel Logan's term in 1940 and was reelected in 1942.

In 1943 Chandler rose to national prominence when he led the "Beat Japan First" movement in Congress, implicitly criticizing President Franklin D. Roosevelt's war policies. This prominence led to talk that Chandler might become Roosevelt's running mate in 1944, but he was passed over for Harry Truman.

In 1945 Chandler abruptly resigned from the Senate to take a higher paying job as commissioner of baseball. After six years in that post he resigned and returned to Kentucky, where, in 1955, he again ran a successful gubernatorial campaign against the state's Democratic establishment. As governor, Chandler was a favorite son candidate for the presidency in 1956. Ineligible to run for reelection in 1959, Chandler's next gubernatorial campaign was in 1963. He was defeated badly in the primary by a young Democrat preaching efficiency, and his political career effectively came to an end.

See also: Election of 1956, Franklin Roosevelt, Harry S Truman

Keith Barnett

REFERENCES

Jewel, Malcolm E., and Everett W. Cunningham. 1968. *Kentucky Politics*. Lexington: Kentucky U. Pr.

Miller, Penny M., and Malcolm E. Jewel. 1990. *Political Parties and Primaries in Kentucky*. Lexington: Kentucky U. Pr.

Zachariah Chandler (1813–1879)

Chairman of the Republican National Committee in the 1870s. Zachariah Chandler was a United States Senator from Michigan, a leader of the Radical Republicans during the administrations of Abraham Lincoln and Andrew Johnson, and chairman of the Republican National Committee (1876–1879) during the disputed Hayes-Tilden presidential election. A "fire-eating" politician, Chandler favored the abolition of slavery, the defense of the Union, and punishment for the South following the Civil War.

Chandler's story is rags to riches. Staked by his father, Chandler ran $1,000 into great wealth in wholesale dry goods in Detroit. He had begun his political career as a Whig, and he was a significant contributor to the Whig Party. In 1851 Chandler was the Whig candidate for mayor of Detroit. Both the city and the state were Democratic strongholds, but Chandler won narrowly. A year later he was the Whig nominee for governor, defeated by a margin of only 8,000 votes.

Chandler was one of the founders of the Republican Party in Michigan in 1854 and became its first national committeeman. Two years later, he was a successful candidate for the United States Senate. Older states of the Midwest like Illinois were reluctant to deal severely with the South, as expressed in Lincoln's policies. From the newer states came the populism and demagoguery of the Radical Republicans; the two most radical of the congressional Republicans during the critical winter of 1860–1861 were "Zack" Chandler and Benjamin Wade of Ohio.

When Congress met in December 1861, Chandler proposed a committee of three to investigate the Civil War defeats at Bull Run and Edward's Ferry. The committee consisted of Republicans Chandler and Wade and Democrat Andrew Johnson. Thus began a vendetta that lasted until Johnson's impeachment and near removal from the presidency in 1867 and 1868. The original committee of three eventually became the Radical-controlled Committee on the Conduct of the War that harassed Lincoln throughout the Civil War and Johnson afterward.

During his many years in national politics, Chandler was nearly always at the center of Radical Republican operations, a vigorous and skillful organizer and campaigner. His success continued during the years of the Ulysses S. Grant's administration when Chandler was one of "The Directory," the ruling clique in Congress. His handling of the disputed presidential election in 1876 kept the presidency in Republican hands but opened the South to the racist politics he abhorred.

See also: Election of 1876, Andrew Johnson, Abraham Lincoln

Ralph M. Goldman

REFERENCES

Detroit Post and Tribune. 1880. *Zachariah Chandler: His Life and Public Service*. Detroit: Post and Tribune.

Harris, Wilmer C. 1917. *Public Life of Zachariah Chandler*. Lansing: Michigan Historical Commission.

Salmon P. Chase (1808–1873)

Important antislavery politician of the Civil War era. Chief Justice of the Supreme Court and Secretary of the Treasury under Abraham Lincoln, Salmon Portland Chase was one of the most enduring and important political figures of the mid-nineteenth century. Self-righteous yet ambitious, Chase predicated his political career on the principle of antislavery, a position that led him into the Liberty, Free Soil, Democratic, and Republican parties, and into numerous political combinations.

Born in New Hampshire, Chase grew up in Ohio. He graduated from Dartmouth College in 1826, then studied law under William Wirt. He began practicing law in Cincinnati in 1829.

Chase first made his presence felt in the antislavery movement as a lawyer willing to defend slaves and abolitionists. He enunciated in court a key principle of the political antislavery movement: no law of the federal government, including the 1798 Fugitive Slave Act, could enforce slavery.

In the 1840s Chase also became involved in party politics. A member first of the Liberty Party, Chase tried to move this antislavery party in a more moderate direction; he believed the Liberty Party should restrict slavery in the territories, a policy he carried with him into the initial Free Soil Party convention in Buffalo, New York. Owing to a peculiar balance of power between state Democrats and Free Soilers, Chase was chosen Democratic U.S. Senator for Ohio in 1848. In the Senate, Chase dissented from the Compromise of 1850 and spoke out against fellow Democrat Stephen Douglas's doctrine of popular sovereignty.

By the mid-1850s Chase had become a nationally known critic of slavery, standing very far from the mainstream of the Democratic Party. Thus, early on Chase jumped to the emerging Republican Party. Twice an unsuccessful candidate for the Republican presidential nomination, Chase lost out to John C. Frémont in 1856, and Lincoln in 1860.

Lincoln chose Chase to become Secretary of the Treasury, a post that the Civil War's outbreak made immensely important. Chase was faced with the task of financing the Union's war effort, and, with the assistance of Jay Cooke, the Philadelphia financier, he carried out the task ably. Public credit was sustained through high interest government loans and bonds. Paper currency ("greenbacks") was then issued, a policy which Chase at first did not support. Chase's greatest achievement as Secretary of the Treasury was his creation of the national bank system, designed to increase government bond sales and to protect the value of federal currency.

Able as he was at the Treasury, Chase ran into political difficulties and unintentionally resigned from the Cabinet in 1864. Throughout the war, Chase had sided with the Radical Republicans, a faction within the party that was impatient with Lincoln's military leadership. Chase himself found Lincoln a slow administrator and thought him too heavily influenced by William Seward, Chase's chief Cabinet rival. A movement among the Radical Republicans to stop Lincoln's renomination in 1864 engendered a Chase boom. Senator Samuel C. Pomeroy of Kansas distributed a circular calling for Chase to replace Lincoln on the ticket. The "Pomeroy Circular" became publicly known and was an embarrassment to Chase, who offered his resignation, as he had done in several instances in the past. This time, much to Chase's surprise, Lincoln accepted the resignation, and Chase was removed from the Cabinet.

Lincoln appointed Chase Chief Justice of the Supreme Court in 1864, following Roger Taney's death. The Chase Court was forced to rule on a number of important Reconstruction issues: the meaning of the Fourteenth Amendment, whether Congress or the executive should administer to Reconstruction, and the degree of civil rights protection afforded ex-slaves and former Confederates. In *Mississippi v. Johnson, Georgia v. Stanton*, and *Ex parte McCardle*, pivotal cases in which southern whites or white-controlled governments sought to use the Court to limit the federal government's power over Reconstruction, the Court refused to enjoin the federal government from enforcing the Reconstruction acts, calling these acts political questions beyond the Court's preview.

Though on the Supreme Court and in poor health, Chase continued throughout the postwar era to intrigue for a presidential nomination. In 1868 he considered switching back to the Democratic Party as their nominee against Ulysses S. Grant. As late as 1872, Chase was being considered for President by the Liberal Republicans.

See also: Free Soil Party, John Frémont, Ulysses S. Grant, Liberal Republican Party, Liberty Party, Abraham Lincoln

John Walsh

REFERENCES

Blue, Frederick J. 1987. *Salmon P. Chase: A Life in Politics*. Kent, OH: Kent State U. Pr.

Gienapp, William E. 1987. *The Origins of the Republican Party, 1852–1856*. New York: Oxford U. Pr.

Holt, Michael F. 1978. *The Political Crisis of the 1850s*. New York: Wiley.

Roseboom, Eugene H. 1938. "Salmon P. Chase and the Know-Nothings." 25 *Mississippi Valley Historical Review* 335.

Cesar Chávez (1927–)

Organizer of migrant farmworkers. Cesar Estrada Chávez was born in Yuma, Arizona, and as a child was forced to wander throughout the Southwest with his family during the Great Depression. He experienced firsthand the economic and ethnic prejudices against migrant Mexican-Americans. It was the memory of this prejudice that led Chávez into his fight for workers' rights.

Chavez first became involved in organizing farm unions in Delano, California, in 1962. There he helped form the National Farm Workers Association, a union that the agricultural producers tried to break. This tension led to the Delano grape fields strike of September 1965 and launched Chávez into national prominence. Many liberals understood the strike as a symbol of the Mexican-American fight for social justice and human dignity. During the strike, Chávez advocated nonviolent actions such as widespread appeals to sympathizers nationwide to boycott table grapes. This boycott spread across the country and brought victory and concessions to the union. Chávez personally achieved success when his political agitation led to the passage of the California Agriculture Labor Relations Act of 1975. This act gave farmworkers the right to use the secret ballot in union elections.

Chávez continues to use nonviolent protest to challenge the agriculture producers and their insistence on exploiting the seemingly unlimited supply of indigent and vulnerable Mexican workers as cheap and disposable labor. Cesar Chávez is both a hero to and a symbol for the Mexican-American movement for equality and human rights.

Mary Ann McHugh

REFERENCES

Taylor, Ronald B. 1975. *Chavez and the Farm Workers.* Boston: Beacon.

Check-off

This term refers to an administrative mechanism whereby taxpayers check a box on their income tax returns thereby designating a portion of their tax payment for the financing of political campaigns. Check-off funds are the primary source of public campaign financing in the United States. Money derived from the $1 ($2 on a joint return) check-off (Federal Revenue Act of 1971) on the federal tax return provides matching funds (up to $11.5 million in 1988, with block grants up to $42.6 million in 1988) to qualified presidential primary candidates.

State income tax check-offs (varying from $1 to $5 in different states) have been used in about one-third of the states to generate campaign funds that, in 1988, were allocated to political parties (e.g., Idaho, Iowa, Kentucky, North Carolina, Ohio, Rhode Island, and Utah), to gubernatorial candidates (New Jersey and Michigan), to all statewide candidates (Hawaii) as well as to state legislative candidates (Minnesota and Wisconsin). Average taxpayer participation in state check-off programs has varied from 9 percent in North Carolina to 39 percent in New Jersey; participation in the federal check-off program has averaged about 25 percent.

Use of check-off funds is voluntary but candidates who accept check-off money also accept a limit on their total expenditures and agree to specific reporting and expenditure rules. The check-off, which does *not* increase the taxpayer's tax liability, is often confused with the "add-on" mechanism that enables taxpayers to agree to increase their tax liability by a specified amount. The "contribution" is collected by the state revenue department but is then transferred either to the political parties or to a state-administered election fund that ultimately allocates money to qualified candidates.

Ruth S. Jones

Richard B. Cheney (1941–)

Dick Cheney's co-authorship with his wife of *Kings of the Hill*, profiling eight House Speakers, says a lot about his roots and aspirations. Cheney came to Washington in 1968 while still a graduate student to work as a Congressional Fellow for Congressman William A. Steiger (R-Wisc.). He remained to become Gerald Ford's White House Chief of Staff at age 34 and a House Republican leader only two years after his 1978 election to Congress from Wyoming. The Congressional Fellowship was a turning point marking the end of his academic and the beginning of his political career. True to his roots and ambitions, Cheney's style remains that of the thoughtful academic, including while he advanced seemingly inexorably through House Republican leadership ranks.

Following his Congressional Fellowship year, Cheney served as special assistant to the director of the Office of Economic Opportunity, as deputy to White House Counsel Donald Rumsfeld, and as assistant director of the Cost of Living Council. Along with Rumsfeld, Cheney worked on Ford's transition team, only to be appointed deputy assistant to the President, and eventually, White House Chief of Staff. Cheney's self-effacing yet self-confident and determined manner earned for him the respect of his White House colleagues as well as the Secret Service code name "Back Seat." As one observer noted, "By avoiding the appearance of power and potency, he actually increased his influence."

Cheney's manner continued to serve him well in Congress. As a member of the House Interior, Select Intelligence, and 1987–88 Iran/Contra Investigation committees, Cheney proved to be more a pragmatic "institutionalist" than a partisan obstructionist. Cheney's love of politics and others' respect for his political judgment sustained him as he advanced from his election as Republican Policy Committee chairman in 1980 to becoming Republican whip in 1988. Cheney seemed destined to continue his move up the Republican leadership ladder to become minority leader someday. However, in 1989 he left Congress to serve as President George Bush's Secretary of Defense. Thus, it seems less likely that he will have an opportunity to become the kind of historically successful Speaker he describes in *Kings of the Hill*.

See also: George Bush, Gerald Ford, Minority Party Leadership in Congress

William F. Connelly, Jr.

REFERENCES

Bullock, Charles S., and Burdett A. Loomis. 1985. "The Changing Congressional Career." In Lawrence C. Dodd and Bruce I. Oppenheimer, eds. *Congress Reconsidered*. Washington: Congressional Quarterly.

Cheney, Richard B., and Lynne V. Cheney. 1983. *Kings of the Hill*. New York: Continuum.

Medved, Michael. 1979. *The Shadow Presidents*. New York: Times Books.

Langdon Cheves (1776–1857)

South Carolina politician. Langdon Cheves was a Congressman, Senator, and financier who was one of those fascinating politicians from South Carolina who played a central role in national affairs during the early decades of the nineteenth century. Cheves was distinctive as one of the few southern Jeffersonians who understood and was sympathetic to the interests of banking and finance. Born and educated in South Carolina where he began the practice of law in 1797, he held local office and served in the state legislature from 1802 to 1810. Cheves was elected to the Twelfth Congress, but he began serving during the Eleventh Congress as an appointed replacement. The respect in which he was held from the beginning in Washington was evident when he was elected to replace Henry Clay as Speaker of the House when Clay resigned during the Thirteenth Congress.

Cheves joined Clay, John C. Calhoun, and the other "War Hawks" in pursuing a war with Britain and overseeing its prosecution. Cheves served as chairman of both the House Ways and Means and Naval Affairs committees during the war period. But as the war was ending he declined reelection in 1814 and President James Madison's offer to appoint him Secretary of the Treasury.

Madison's offer was an expression of the esteem in which Cheves's financial judgment was held. It was that which brought him back into national service in 1819 when he was called upon to become the president of the Second Bank of the United States in order to rescue it from the dire straits that it was in after less than two years in operation. Cheves saved the faltering bank but at enormous cost to its reputation and political support in regions apart from the nation's financial centers. He remained president until 1822 when he was succeeded by Nicholas Biddle.

Cheves remained in the North, living variously in Pennsylvania and Washington, D.C., until 1829 when he returned to South Carolina and his farm. While in the North he had practiced law and served as a commissioner of the Treaty of Ghent. After his return to South Carolina, Cheves was steadfast in his refusal of further public office, including the offer that he succeed Calhoun in the Senate after the latter's death in 1852. Cheves did have some problems in South Carolina politics, in spite of the respect in which he was held, because he had been an opponent of Nullification, and he remained firmly opposed to action by any single state throughout the rest of his life. He was a South Carolinian and a nationalist; a Jeffersonian and a banker.

See also: John C. Calhoun, Henry Clay, Jeffersonian Republicans, Second Bank of the United States, Speaker of the House

Kathryn A. Malone

Shirley Chisholm (1924–)

First Black woman elected to the United States Congress. Shirley Chisholm was born to Barbadian immigrant parents in Brooklyn, New York, and graduated cum laude from Brooklyn College in 1946. She earned her M.A. degree from Columbia University in 1952.

Having organized Black student organizations while in college, Chisholm later was instrumental in challenging the white, male leadership of Brooklyn's Democratic political clubs during the 1950s and 1960s. Chisholm's early successes eventually led to election to the New York State Assembly in 1964 where she specialized in education-related legislation. In 1968 Chisholm was elected to the U.S. House of Representatives. She continued her assault on sexism and racism in the House, acknowledging that she found gender discrimination a greater political handicap than her race. "Unbought and unbossed," Democratic Congresswoman Chisholm practiced what she termed "principled coalition politics" and endorsed the successful New York City mayoral candidacy of Liberal (formerly Republican) John Lindsay in 1969.

Although unsuccessful, Chisholm in 1972 became the first Black woman to contest seriously for her party's presidential nomination. In Congress Chisholm successfully rebuffed the traditional committee assignment process. At the time of her retirement in 1982, however, she was a member of the Rules Committee, following extensive service on the Education and Labor Committee. Although criticized during her early years in Congress as a "show horse," Chisholm was instrumental in adoption of legislation extending employment protection to domestic workers. More generally, Congresswoman Chisholm focused on child and education reform while maintaining a consistently liberal human rights voting record, and she was an early practitioner of "constituent services" politics. Since retirement from Congress, Chisholm has continued to write and speak on public matters. She is a member of the faculty at Mount Holyoke College in Massachusetts.

See also: Election of 1972, John Lindsay, Race and Racial Politics

Charles Longley

REFERENCES

Chisholm, Shirley. 1970. *Unbought and Unbossed*. Boston: Houghton Mifflin.

———. 1973. *The Good Fight*. New York: Harper & Row.

Haskins, James. 1987. *Fighting Shirley Chisholm*. New York: Dial.

Chowder and Marching Club

The oldest and most exclusive social organization of Republican members of the United States House of Representatives. Meeting every Wednesday afternoon in a member's office, the Chowder and Marching Club serves as a forum for sharing information and planning strategy in a relaxed atmosphere. Its 20 to 30 members are thereby able to pool resources and exert collective influence in a large body such as the House, especially important for members of the minority party.

The club was born when Congressmen Glenn R. Davis of Wisconsin and Donald Jackson of California invited 13 other Republicans to meet with them in March 1949 to discuss strategy for defeating a veterans' pension bill that they believed had been rammed through committee. Among the founders was future President Richard Nixon. The group name harkens back to the social clubs of the nineteenth century.

The club has no officers or bylaws. Election of new members is by secret ballot. Criteria for election have never been stated, but observers note the selection of those with promising careers. Members have included Presidents Nixon and Gerald R. Ford, Vice President Dan Quayle, and several other Representatives who became Senators, governors, Cabinet secretaries, ambassadors, and holders of other high offices. Often members of the House Republican leadership have been members, including minority leader Robert H. Michel.

See also: Gerald Ford, Richard Nixon, J. Danforth Quayle

Douglas I. Hodgkin

Winston Churchill (1871–1947)

Best-selling American historical novelist of the early twentieth century. The American Winston Churchill (not to be confused with the British politician of the same name) was also active, as a friend and follower of Theodore Roosevelt, in launching New Hampshire's version of progressive reform. Born in St. Louis, he was raised in a genteel middle-class home. Soon after graduating from the Naval Academy at Annapolis, Maryland, in 1890, he resigned his commission and turned to a career in writing. In 1898 he moved to New Hampshire, building a country home near Cornish, the center for a colony of artists and writers, one of whom was the political analyst Herbert Croly.

A growing interest in the orderly development of New Hampshire's rural economy, together with his novelist's curiosity about the workings of practical politics, led Churchill to run for a seat in the state legislature in 1902. His election began a swift education in the process by which Republican statehouse politicians ran the state in dutiful subservience to the Boston & Maine Railroad. In 1906 he decided to challenge party regulars by running for governor. His campaign for the Republican nomination, though finally unsuccessful, won wide press attention and galvanized reform elements in the state. Thereafter New Hampshire insurgents managed to break the grip of the regular organization on legislative outcomes and party nominations.

Meanwhile Churchill returned to writing novels, including a fictionalized account of his campaign in *Mr. Crewe's Career* (1908). In 1912, inspired by the themes of Roosevelt's New Nationalism, he ran for governor, again unsuccessfully, as the Progressive Party nominee. Thereafter he sank into political obscurity.

See also: Herbert Croly, Election of 1912, Progressive Party, Theodore Roosevelt

Geoffrey Blodgett

REFERENCES

Blodgett, Geoffrey. 1974. "Winston Churchill: The Novelist as Reformer." 47 *New England Quarterly* 495.

Schneider, Robert W. 1976. *Novelist to a Generation: The Life and Thought of Winston Churchill.* Bowling Green, OH: Bowling Green State U. Popular Pr.

Wright, James. 1987. *The Progressive Yankees: Republican Reformers in New Hampshire, 1906–1916.* Hanover, NH: U. Pr. of New England.

Henry G. Cisneros (1947–)

Prominent Latino politician of the 1980s. Henry G. Cisneros, mayor of San Antonio, Texas, was born in San Antonio. After graduating from Texas A & M University, he became San Antonio's assistant director of Model Cities, left to study at Harvard, and then returned to his home city to teach at the University of Texas.

At the age of 27, Cisneros was elected to the city council as the leading candidate of the powerful Good Government League (GGL). When the GGL collapsed soon thereafter, Cisneros emerged as the favorite politician of the rising Latino community, liberal reformers, and new business interests. In 1977 the city council moved to a district system, and minority candidates, among them Cisneros, won a majority of the 10 seats. Cisneros got his chance to run for mayor in 1981 when the incumbent stepped down. He built a formidable coalition and won 61.8 percent of the vote, including 45 percent of the white vote. He was easily reelected in 1983, 1985, and 1987.

As mayor, Cisneros focused on the city's economic development. The young mayor received national recognition in 1983 when he was appointed to the Kissinger Commission on Central America and when Walter Mondale interviewed him for the Democratic vice presidential slot in 1984.

Cisneros surprised many when he announced that he would leave office after his third term. In October 1988, he acknowledged rumors of an affair with a married woman and strains in his marriage. But at the age of 41, he remained a potentially powerful leader for the future.

See also: Ethnic Voting, Walter Mondale

Raphael J. Sonenshein

REFERENCES

Diehl, Kemper, and Jan Jarboe. 1985. *Cisneros: Portrait of a New American.* San Antonio, TX: Corona Publishing.

Munos, Carlos, Jr., and Charles P. Henry. 1986. "Rainbow Coalitions in Four Big Cities: San Antonio, Denver, Chicago and Philadelphia." 19 *PS* 598.

Citizens Against Rent Control v. City of Berkeley
454 U.S. 290 (1981)

The Supreme Court's decision in this case prohibits state and local governments from imposing contribution limitations in referendum and initiative campaigns. It extends the decisions in *Buckley v. Valeo* (424 U.S. 1, 1976) and in *First National Bank v. Bellotti* (435 U.S. 765, 1978) to make it more difficult to find a compelling state interest in regulating First Amendment freedoms.

In 1974 the voters in Berkeley, California, adopted a comprehensive election reform ordinance that included a limit of $250 on contributions to committees formed to contest ballot questions. Citizens Against Rent Control accepted nine contributions over the limit during its campaign against a rent control ballot measure.

The United States Supreme Court ruled in this case that the contribution limit impinged upon the rights of political association and political expression as protected by the First Amendment. It placed a limit on the ability of persons to band together to participate in a campaign on ballot questions, while still permitting unlimited individual expenditures. Moreover, placing limits on contributions in turn limits expenditures, thereby impairing freedom of expression.

Only the existence of a compelling state interest allows a state or locality to regulate such First Amendment rights. For the majority of the Court in the *CARC* case, the only compelling interest was protection against corruption. The undue influence of the contributor upon the recipient is a danger when candidate elections are involved, so limits on contributions were upheld in the *Buckley* case. However, as the *Bellotti* case showed, because initiatives and referenda involve issues, the risk of corruption simply is not present, so prohibitions on corporate contributions and expenditures in ballot measure campaigns were struck down.

Justice Byron White, the only dissenter in *CARC*, argued that an additional state interest was to protect public confidence in the referendum process. If one side can dominate the debate through heavy campaign spending, the outcome can be skewed. White maintained, moreover, that free speech could be enhanced by preventing dominance by special interests. On the other hand, Chief Justice Burger, writing for the majority, responded that disclosure requirements provided sufficient protection for the integrity of the system.

As a result of this decision, it appears that no interest is sufficient to justify any state and local contribution limits or spending limitations for noncandidate elections.

See also: Buckley v. Valeo, Campaign Finance and the Constitution, First National Bank v. Bellotti

Douglas I. Hodgkin

REFERENCES

Citizens Against Rent Control v. City of Berkeley, 454 U.S. 290 (1981).

1982. "Right to Contribute in Ballot Measure Elections, The Supreme Court, 1981 Term." 96 *Harvard Law Review* 161.

Citizens for the Republic

A political action committee (PAC) dedicated to the election of conservative candidates to public office, Citizens for the Republic (CFTR) was organized in 1977 with the nearly $1 million remaining in Ronald Reagan's campaign treasury after his unsuccessful bid for the Republican presidential nomination. In terms of fundraising, CFTR has been the most effective nonparty PAC, raising $2.1 million for 1977 and the first half of 1978. A review of CFTR's financial activities in 1980 and in 1984 by the Federal Election Commission led to an imposition of penalties of $500 and $1,000 for violations of the federal election laws—in the first instance for accepting checks drawn on corporate accounts and in the latter instance for contributing more than the statutory limit of $5,000 to the Reagan campaign. Aside from the funding of campaigns, the most important function performed by the CFTR was keeping Ronald Reagan in the public eye and in the minds of his fellow Republicans as the future President bided his time waiting for the 1980 campaign and the opportunity to run again for the Republican nomination.

See also: Elections of 1976 and 1980, Federal Election Commission, Political Action Committees, Ronald Reagan

David B. Raymond

Citizens Party

One of the many, largely unsuccessful, third or minor parties in American electoral history. From the mid-1960s on, a number of activists in the civil rights, feminist, antiwar, and environmental movements regularly tried to create new parties to contest what they thought to be the failure of the Democrats and the Republicans to address adequately the issues of concern to them. The concern led to campaigns by Eldridge

Cleaver and Dick Gregory in 1968 and by Dr. Benjamin Spock in 1972.

In 1980, the noted environmental scientist Dr. Barry Commoner brought together what he hoped to be an even larger coalition in a new effort—the Citizens Party. The new party was best known for its strong stands on behalf of environmental protection. It also supported the Equal Rights Amendment and sharply increased spending for social services. Finally, the party advocated steps to enhance economic democracy, including nationalizing private oil companies, involving workers in the management of major corporations, and guaranteeing full employment. The party nominated Commoner to be its standard bearer that fall. Native American activist La Donna Harris (then wife of U.S. Senator Fred Harris, D-Okla.) ran as the vice presidential candidate.

The party appeared on the ballot in 31 states. It won 221,083 votes and did not exceed 1 percent of the vote in any state. However, the party did do well enough to become the first third party to win United States government matching funds (about $157,000) for the 1984 elections. The party nominated Sonia Johnson, a radical feminist and an excommunicated Mormon, for President; she got 72,153 votes.

See also: Eldridge Cleaver, Barry Commoner, Equal Rights Amendment, Benjamin Spock, Third Parties in American Elections

Charles S. Hauss

Civil Rights Legislation and Southern Politics

In 1949 V. O. Key noted the following characteristics of southern politics: the Democratic Party was dominant, voter turnout was low, and the electorate was overwhelmingly white. Now, four decades later, just over three decades after passage of the first civil rights bill of the twentieth century, Democratic control has been broken as the Republicans have become adept at capitalizing on Democratic weaknesses. Regional disparities in registration and turnout largely have been eliminated. These changes are related to the enfranchisement of hundreds of thousands of Blacks.

In addition to growing Republican power and heightened rates of participation, the Democratic Party has undergone major modifications. While the Democrats remain the party to beat—except at the presidential level where Republicans have dominated for the last generation—the bedrock of Democratic strength is now the Black electorate. Blacks (who, through Democratic-led efforts, had been removed from the electorate at the turn of the century) have become the party's most loyal supporters in the South just as they are in the rest of the country. Many southern Democrats owe their elections to the near-unanimous support of their Black constituents. If the electorate today were as white as it was in 1957 and if the white voters split along party lines as they do today, most southern Senators would probably be Republicans.

Barriers to Black Voting

Beginning with the Mississippi Constitution of 1890, the South executed a remarkably thorough purge of Black voters. Central to Black disenfranchisement were obstacles to registration that included literacy tests, poll taxes, cutoff dates for registration many months in advance of the election, and lengthy residency requirements.

When the Populist challenge waned, the South, except for a few counties in Appalachia, became one-party Democratic. The absence of a serious Republican challenge meant that the identity of officeholders were invariably determined in the Democratic primary. Black influence could be eliminated by restricting the Democratic primary to white voters, so states established white-only Democratic primaries.

The first major obstacle to Black political influence to be successfully challenged was the white primary. In 1944 the Supreme Court (in *Smith v. Allwright*) ruled that primaries were so central to the electoral process that their sponsor, the Democratic Party, could not be regarded as simply another private organization able to set standards for membership or participation.

Other impediments to Black participation persisted until Congress acted. The first modern civil rights act, passed in 1957, sought to overcome the blatantly discriminatory features that accompanied voter registration in many southern communities. All too often, local election officials stepped forward to prevent even Blacks who met the various standards from registering. For example, literate Blacks failed literacy tests because of the discriminatory fashion in which they were graded. Officials often simply refused to process Blacks' applications. Elsewhere, prospective Black registrants met physical or economic intimidation. Authorizing the Justice Department to bring suit on behalf of qualified Blacks who had not been allowed to register was ultimately to prove very beneficial, but in the

short run, the legislation had little impact. Thus, in 1960, Congress acted to close some of the loopholes in the earlier legislation.

Black registration grew as the civil rights movement spread. Organizations such as the Voter Education Project, the Southern Christian Leadership Conference, and the Student Nonviolent Coordinating Committee sent scores of volunteers into southern communities. These activists prepared Black applicants to pass the literacy and understanding tests. They also encouraged applicants to try to register (after generations of politics as "white folks' business," many rural Blacks hesitated to challenge the white establishment).

Despite impressive gains compared to the levels of Black registration in the 1940s, Blacks in the mid-1960s were still substantially less likely to register than were whites. Reliable data for the early 1960s show the white registration rate to exceed the Black registration rate by at least a factor of two.

The Voting Rights Act of 1965 was critical in narrowing the Black-white registration disparity. This legislation singled out six southern states and part of a seventh where Black political participation was particularly low (less than 50 percent of the voting age population turned out or registered in 1964) and where registration was contingent on passing a test (e.g., literacy or good character tests). The legislation authorized the Attorney General to send out federal registrars to sign up voters, bypassing obdurate local officials. It also charged the Justice Department with appointing election-day monitors to see if newly registered Blacks were kept from voting. The legislation included a provision designed to thwart future discriminatory maneuvers. Changes affecting the electoral systems in the covered jurisdictions had to be approved by the Justice Department or the federal district court sitting in Washington, D.C., before taking effect. The 1965 legislation reduced local and state autonomy in two critical ways: it permitted removing the voter registration function from local officials, and it allowed the Justice Department to overrule local and state officials when they modified their electoral systems.

Immediately upon enactment, federal registrars were dispatched to a number of southern counties, and much of the resistance to Black registration was broken. In order to retain control of the registration process, most southern communities ceased discriminatory application of registration requirements. In the covered jurisdictions, the literacy tests, understanding tests, and good character tests no longer blocked Black registration.

Table 1 shows the changes in registration rates during this period. Black and white registration rates in the South have become quite similar, and regional differences in registration have largely been attenuated.

By facilitating registration, the Voting Rights Act encouraged more participation by both races (Stanley, 1987). Particularly during 1984, conservative groups endeavored to counterbalance Jesse Jackson–inspired Black registration. Given the traditionally low levels of registration in the South and the region's much larger white than Black population, some observers estimate that,

despite Jackson's efforts, the southern electorate is becoming increasingly white.

Registration is only the prelude to meaningful participation. Registrants who do not vote have little impact upon the shaping of public policy (there may, of course, be some anticipatory action by policymakers in the face of a particular registration configuration). Table 2 demonstrates that the racial gap in southern turnout has been largely eliminated. And, as with registration, the southern deficit has also been substantially reduced. More similarity than dissimilarity now exists in the rates at which the Black and white voting-age populations translate into registration which, in turn, translates into voting.

Table 1

Proportion of the Voting Age Population Registered by Race and Region, 1966–1988

	1966	1968	1970	1972	1974	1976	1978	1980	1982	1984	1986	1988
South												
White	64.3	70.8	65.1	69.8	61.0	66.7	61.2	66.2	63.2	67.8	63.2	66.6
Black	52.9	61.6	57.5	64.0	55.5	56.4	56.2	59.3	56.9	65.6	64.6	63.3
Disparity	11.4	9.2	7.6	5.8	5.5	10.3	5.0	6.9	6.3	2.2	-1.4	3.3
North												
White	74.5	77.2	70.8	74.9	64.6	69.0	64.9	69.3	66.7	70.5	66.2	68.5
Black	68.8	71.8	64.5	67.0	54.2	60.9	58.0	60.6	61.7	67.2	63.1	65.9
Disparity	5.7	5.4	6.3	7.9	10.4	8.1	6.9	8.7	5.0	3.3	3.1	2.6

Source: Bureau of the Census, *Voting and Registration in the Election of November, 1986*
(Washington: U.S. Government Printing Office, 1989), p. 3.

Table 2

Proportion of the Voting Age Population That Turned Out by Race and Region, 1964–1988

	1964	1966	1968	1970	1972	1974	1976	1978	1980	1982	1984	1986	1988
South													
White	59.5	45.1	61.9	46.4	57.0	37.4	57.1	41.1	57.4	42.9	58.1	43.5	56.4
Black	44.0	32.9	51.6	36.8	47.8	30.0	45.7	33.5	48.2	38.3	53.2	42.5	48.0
Disparity	15.5	12.2	10.3	9.6	9.2	7.4	11.4	7.6	9.2	4.6	4.9	1.0	8.4
North													
White	74.0	61.7	71.8	59.8	67.5	50.0	62.6	50.0	62.4	53.1	63.0	48.7	60.4
Black	72.7	52.1	64.8	51.4	56.7	37.9	52.2	41.3	52.8	48.5	58.9	44.2	55.6
Disparity	1.3	9.6	7.0	8.4	10.8	12.1	10.4	8.7	9.6	4.6	4.1	4.5	4.8

Source: Bureau of the Census, *Voting and Registration in the Election of November, 1986*
(Washington: U.S. Government Printing Office, 1989), p. 1.

Partisan Composition

The transformation of the electorate has been accompanied by a transformation in the partisan distribution of the electorate. Republicans have won the hearts and votes of millions of white southerners, and this allegiance—which has varied across time as well as across offices—has changed the composition of what political scientist Frank Sorauf calls the party in the electorate.

Party in the Electorate

In southern states that maintain registration figures by party, Republicans, while remaining the minority, have made striking advances. From 1976 to 1986 the proportion of Republicans among registered voters rose from 28 percent to 36 percent in Florida, while in Louisiana the increase was from 3 percent to 13 percent. Recent polls in South Carolina show the Republicans holding a two-to-one edge in white voters' loyalties.

Easier to change than party registration is one's partisan identification. For some share of the electorate, the response to a question about party identification may reflect little thought and even less commitment. The share of the electorate identifying with the GOP has fluctuated, with some recent polls reporting equal numbers of Republican and Democratic loyalists among the white respondents. President Reagan's popularity coupled with the weakness of the Mondale-Ferraro ticket resulted in Republican strength being particularly pronounced at the time of the 1984 election. Poll data from CBS News/*New York Times* showed the shift among whites continuing beyond 1984. From 1980 to 1986 the share of southern white registered voters professing GOP loyalties rose from 19 percent to 36 percent while Democrats declined from 52 percent to 33 percent.

Whatever the current level of Republican Party affiliation, some GOP candidates have polled not only the votes of their identifiers but also have made serious inroads among Independents and Democrats. Particularly successful were Richard Nixon in 1972, Ronald Reagan in 1980 and 1984, and George Bush in 1988. These campaigns revealed the total demise of what once constituted the solid Democratic South. In 1952, 68 percent of the southerners identified with the Democratic Party; by 1976 that figure had dropped to 51 percent: from 1952 to 1984, GOP identifiers grew from 14 to 39 percent. Political scientist Harold Stanley points out that GOP victories are increasingly due to loyal Republican voters and are less the product of Democratic defections.

Blacks

As the white electorate has become increasingly infatuated with the Republican Party and particularly with Republican presidential candidates, Blacks have become the bulwark of the Democratic party. The New Deal realignment that found northern Blacks leaving the Republican Party was not replicated in the South until 1964. Democrats in the South were the party of white supremacy while the Republicans made some largely ineffectual overtures to Blacks—such as sending a few people of color to their national party conventions.

The Republican Party lost its southern Black contingent in 1964. The nomination of Barry Goldwater, one of the few northern Senators to vote against the 1964 Civil Rights Act, and the concomitant conversion of racially conservative whites into Republicans drove out Black members. The leadership that Lyndon Johnson had given to the 1964 Civil Rights Act sufficed to win the allegiance of southern Blacks to the Democratic Party despite the presence of George Wallace and his admirers in high offices in most other southern states.

Over the last quarter century, southern Blacks have regularly given at least 80 percent of their votes to Democratic presidential candidates. They have also played critical roles in the election of many Democrats in statewide contests. In Senate and gubernatorial contests in 1986, whites voted GOP (according to Petrocik) while sizable margins of Blacks backed the Democrats.

Civil rights legislation unquestionably is the major factor in bringing Blacks to the Democratic Party in the South. Scholars are less uniform in their assessment of the impact of civil rights on white partisanship. Carmines and Stimson (1982) identify civil rights issues as critical in the changes in the political alignments that occurred during the 1960s. On the other hand, Wolfinger and Hagen (1985) find little evidence that the strength enjoyed by the Republican Party today is derived from party differences on racial matters. Van Winger and Valentine (1988) report that civil rights issues are not important to younger southern voters. With the passing of race as an issue with flash-point potential, increasingly class-based coalitions have emerged in competing partisan camps.

It would not be surprising that even if many of those who first voted Republican in 1964 did so because of Goldwater's civil rights stand, opposition to civil rights may explain the behavior of a declining share of the electorate. The Republican Party is particularly attractive to well-educated, younger, white voters for whom civil rights is hardly a burning issue. It is, of course, possible that the willingness of these new electors to support Republican candidates derives, in part, from the weakening of their parents' commitment to the Democratic Party that began when Goldwater and Nixon distanced themselves from the Johnson administration's civil rights programs. And in that fashion, civil rights may continue to underlie the racial cleavage that often parallels party lines.

The Party in Office

At every level, the GOP has scored gains, its success most pronounced at the presidential level and generally tapering off in the lower offices. Nonetheless, the Republican Party in the 1980s is at its strongest in more than a century. Civil rights legislation has contributed to GOP electoral success in two ways: first, particularly in the 1960s and early 1970s when the initial Republican gains were made, the victors vowed opposition to Democratic civil rights initiatives; subsequently, where Blacks are a significant component of the Democratic Party, they have pulled southern Democratic candidates to the left on various social issues.

When party competition was first spreading into the South in the 1960s, Democrats and Republicans often took positions within a narrow band on the right of the ideological spectrum. Today the options offered southern voters have begun to approximate the partisan positions in the rest of the country. When candidates' stands have differed most, Republicans have generally benefited. Until after the mid-1950s, the promise of the Democratic Party as the protector against congressional challenges to white supremacy kept the South in bondage to the Democratic Party despite the ideological rift that began in the 1940s. Once this incentive to stay Democratic passed, the region's conservatism allowed the politically ambitious to seek office as Republicans.

Partisan choices have been most dissimilar at the presidential level. Consequently, throughout the 1970s and 1980s, with the exception of 1976, the GOP's share of the electoral votes varied little between the South and the rest of the country. For other offices, candidates have run as Georgia Democrats or Alabama Democrats in order to emphasize their commitment to the principles traditionally associated with the Democratic Party in the South. These principles were more conservative than those now dominating the national Democratic Party.

Republicans have enjoyed their greatest successes below the presidential level when they have come upon Democrats in disarray. Democratic susceptibility increases if an incumbent is involved in scandal or when multiple candidates struggle through a prolonged, bitter nominating campaign. For example, in 1980, Mack Mattingly became Georgia's first Republican Senator after the incumbent, Herman Talmadge, withstood a challenge led by the lieutenant governor, who used Talmadge's reputed alcoholism and denouncement by his Senate colleagues. A year earlier, Louisiana elected its first Republican governor following a primary in which a Republican faced multiple Democrats. The Republican emerged as the leader in Louisiana's unique open primary with 22 percent of the vote, with three Democrats finishing within four percentage points of the leader.

From 1970 to 1986, when there have been open seats, 84 percent of all Democratic nominations and 64 percent of the senatorial nominations have necessitated a runoff. The heightened stakes that accompany a prolonged nomination struggle improve the chances for a breach that the Republican nominee can exploit.

Despite occasional setbacks, Republican strength in southern congressional delegations has crept upward. The first popularly elected Republican Senator from the South in this century, John Tower of Texas, won the special election to fill the vacancy created by Lyndon Johnson's accession to the vice presidency. Within the next few years, Tower was joined by Howard Baker and Bill Brock (Tenn.), Jesse Helms (N.C.), and Strom Thurmond (S.C.) who switched parties. The 1980 Reagan sweep of all southern states except Jimmy Carter's Georgia produced the first Republican Senators from Georgia and Alabama, along with new Republicans in Florida and North Carolina. When Paul Trible was elected in Virginia in 1982, Republicans held half of the South's Senate seats. The Republican gains of the early 1980s did not persist, however, as vigorous Democratic campaigns defeated the entire southern Republican Senate class in 1986.

The Republican gains have been more consistent in the House of Representatives. Beginning with the traditional Republican enclave of two seats in the mountains of eastern Tennessee, the GOP has come to hold more than a third of the seats with consistency. They broke out of their mountain stronghold to win seats in the Rim South during the Dwight Eisenhower years. Initial Deep South victories came on the Goldwater coattails. The popularity of Presidents Nixon and Reagan promoted the candidacies of a number of Republican congressional aspirants. In 1990, 41 Republicans compare with 75 Democrats from the South.

Democrats have held on more tenaciously to state legislative seats. Republican challengers have found it tough to convince the electorate that the same cookie cutter produced local good-old-boy Democrats running for the state legislature and liberals such as George McGovern and Walter Mondale. State legislators, with their smaller constituencies, are more familiar to their constituents and less likely to be seen as out of step on policy matters. As of 1989, Republicans held a quarter of the southern state legislative seats, a figure ten percentage points above their level of success in the U.S. House.

Republican successes have fluctuated more in gubernatorial elections than in the four sets of legislative offices. In 1990, Republican governors served in Alabama, Florida, North Carolina, Texas, and South Carolina. Four years earlier the South had only two Republican governors.

A major obstacle to consistent gubernatorial victories has been the limitation on incumbency. Most southern states restrict governors to two consecutive terms. Republicans who win are quickly pushed out of office. Not so in the legislature where incumbency has proven to have no more than a moderate pro-Democratic bias, with many GOP officeholders successfully winning additional terms like their Democratic counterparts. Also important is the fact that (except in North Carolina) the election of southern governors is insulated from presidential coattails. Seven states choose their governors in the middle of a presidential term while Louisiana, Mississippi, and Virginia hold elections separate from any national elections. These conditions may help explain why even very popular Republican governors have not been succeeded by fellow partisans. Only in Virginia— arguably the most Republican state in the South—where Republicans held the governor's office from 1969 to 1981, has a GOP chief executive been succeeded by another Republican.

Usually overlooked have been partisan shifts at the local level: suburban communities have been most receptive to GOP candidacies for local and state legislative positions. Some metropolitan counties are so dominated by Republicans that Democratic nominations go begging. Just the opposite, however, obtains in many rural areas.

Policy Consequences

During the 1930s and 1940s national civil rights legislation could not be enacted. Even a national law against lynching was defeated by a southern filibuster in the Senate. In 1957 when a civil rights act was finally passed, southern Democrats diluted it before acquiescing without a filibuster. While southern Senators did not block enactment, only 5 of 22 voted for it. In the House, only one southerner—a Republican— voted yes.

When the Voting Rights Act was initially passed in 1965, it was opposed by southerners in the House 76 to 23 and on the Senate side 19 to 3. Seventeen years later when that legislation, which had been beefed up through congressional amendment and judicial interpretation, was rechartered for 25 years, it was approved by southern House members by a margin of 85 to 19. Southern Senators supported it by a vote of 18 to 4.

Hidden within the overall vote on the 1982 Voting Rights Act extension are partisan differences. The Democrats in the House favored the legislation by 62 to 6 while southern Republicans were less cohesive, supporting enactment by 23 to 13. The Republican Party has persisted in opposing civil rights bills much as southern Democrats did in the past. Conversion of congressional southern Democrats signifies the importance of Black votes for Democratic candidates. Successful Democrats build biracial coalitions of moderate to liberal whites plus Blacks.

While the most dramatic demonstration of the consequences of the Democrats' biracial coalition appears in the Voting Rights Act, the coalition has left its imprint on other areas. Sinclair (1985) shows that, beginning in the early 1970s, southern Democrats in the House became more liberal on social welfare and government management issues.

The long decline in southern Democrats' support for liberal programs that began as the crisis of the Great Depression receded, bottomed out during the latter half of the 1960s. Barry

Goldwater's popularity, augmented by President Nixon's opposition to school desegregation, led many southern Democrats to foresee an imminent political realignment of sweeping proportions. If few Democratic officeholders converted to the Republican Party, many heeded their constituents' criticisms of the Great Society's programs. Others doubtless recalled the defeats of southern incumbents who had failed to pledge unswerving fealty to segregation. From the mid-1970s, however, the size and commitment of the Black vote to responsive Democrats coupled with an awareness that many Great Society programs were color-blind and helped large numbers of poor whites, led many southern Democrats to vote with their northern brethren.

The Black vote has been significant on two levels. In the primary, the Black-supported candidate has a substantial leg-up on the nomination. Since crowded primary fields have been most common when no incumbent is running, the importance of the Black vote is highlighted at the recruitment stage. Even if the Black preference is not nominated, Blacks often can determine the outcome of the general election. While not many Republicans have enjoyed enthusiastic Black support, Democrats who have alienated Blacks have often been defeated. In Mississippi, several white Democrats have faced Black independent candidates in the general election. When the Black vote was diverted in that fashion, Republicans were elected. A more common phenomenon in the South has been for alienated Blacks to sit out the election. The Republican Party is now strong enough that if the Democratic Party is deprived of Black support, the GOP nominee may well win, particularly in statewide contests in the Deep South.

Districting Configurations

The configuration of the districts from which southern officeholders run has undergone major changes, particularly following the 1982 Voting Rights Act. A major modification in that legislation was to rewrite Section II so that Black plaintiffs need only show that election procedures had a discriminatory impact. If Black political influence is diluted, then even if that were not the intent of the policy, the policy is illegal. In assessing the effect of multimember districts, if it is possible to create a district from which the election of a Black seems likely, then that outcome has usually been mandated.

Multimember electoral districts for state legislatures and local governments have been suc-cessfully attacked wherever the Black population is sufficiently large and concentrated to create a district with a Black voting age majority and in which Blacks have historically coalesced behind one set of candidates who are usually defeated by a white bloc vote. The civil rights revolution has also forced jurisdictions using single-member districts to increase the proportion of Blacks in some districts. Jurisdictions subject to Justice Department preclearance may have to redraw their districts so as to create one or more in which Blacks will have an election-day majority. Furthermore, it is impermissible to reduce the proportion of Blacks in a district that already has a substantial Black population.

Creating majority Black districts has increased the number of Black elected officials. While there has been a gain in the Black symbolic representation, the implications for substantive representation are less clear. At the local level, where most of the predominantly Black districts have been created, frequently one Black member represents an overwhelmingly Black district while the remainder of the collegial body consists of whites with few Black constituents. White council or school board members have little electoral incentive to be responsive to Black concerns when Blacks have been withdrawn from their districts, just as GOP members of Congress who get little Black support less often vote for Black initiatives than do Democrats. Indeed, the electoral incentives would be for the bulk of the council to oppose those Black-backed initiatives that were unpopular with the white electorate.

Districting designed to elect Blacks often benefits Republicans. Creating Black districts results in even more heavily white districts. And white districts which are higher in socioeconomic status are likely to elect Republicans. Because Blacks are among the most liberal southern legislators and because Republicans dominate the right end of the spectrum, redistricting has been one of the few issues that has united these two groups against the dominant white Democrats.

Immediately after a race-conscious redistricting, more Blacks may be elected. However, once Blacks are "ghettoized" into Black districts, there are a limited number of districts in which they have any chance of being elected. Therefore, Republicans have a greater potential for growth: since its growth is not tied to the birth rate, the Republican Party can hope to control a majority of the seats on collegial bodies. The post-1980 census redistricting resulted in a greater increase in new Republican members than in Black members in state houses but with the opposite pattern for the senates.

White Swing Votes

Another side effect of creating predominantly Black districts is that the number of polities in which whites hold the balance of power will grow. The potential was most clearly demonstrated in the 1986 Fifth Congressional District of Georgia and in the 1986 New Orleans mayoral election. Both of those political units have Black majorities, and in those elections, the candidates in the critical runoff election were both Black. Neither winner, on the other hand, was the candidate of choice in the Black community. Victory was achieved when a minority of the Black voters combined with an overwhelming majority of white voters. Thus, in some predominantly Black areas, the roles played by the races have reversed. For many years the Black vote was critical in choosing more liberal whites. Now the white vote elects the less liberal from among competing Black candidates.

Summary

Since the 1957 Civil Rights Act was passed, the politics of the South has been transformed. The Democratic Party no longer occupies a position of unchallenged hegemony. The GOP has dominated the presidential elections during the 1970s and 1980s. In Virginia, Democrats have held fewer than half of the congressional seats during the 1980s and were shut out of the governor's mansion in the 1970s. In Tennessee, Republicans have won three of the last five gubernatorial elections. While no state legislature has yet been organized by Republicans, that may change with the redistricting in 1991, particularly if the Republican presidential nominee in 1992 runs well in the South.

Paralleling the growth in the Republican Party has been increased political participation by southern Blacks. Their rates of registration and turnout now differ little from those of whites. As Black participation has grown, so has the share of offices filled by Blacks or by whites sympathetic to Black concerns. Receipt of strong Black support has become critical to Democratic success in both the primary and subsequent general elections.

The enfranchisement of Blacks has done much to offset the traditionally lower levels of participation found in the South. The region's improved economic conditions and heightened partisan competition have provided incentives for new whites to enter the political arena. Registration, turnout, and, to a lesser degree, the distribution of southern votes between the parties, have become increasingly similar to the patterns found in other parts of the country.

See also: George Bush, Jimmy Carter, Barry Goldwater, Jesse Jackson, Lyndon B. Johnson, Abraham Lincoln, Literacy Tests, New Deal, Richard Nixon, Ronald Reagan, *Smith v. Allwright*, Student Non-Violent Coordinating Committee, Voting Rights Act of 1965 and Extensions

Charles S. Bullock III

REFERENCES

Abramson, Paul R., and William Claaggett. 1984. "Race-Related Differences in Self-Reported and Validated Turnout." 46 *Journal of Politics* 719.

Bass, Jack, and Walter DeVries. 1976. *The Transformation of Southern Politics.* New York: New American Library.

Beck, Paul Allen, and Paul Lopatto. 1982. "The End of Southern Distinctiveness." In Laurence W. Moreland, Tod A. Baker, and Robert T. Stead, eds. *Contemporary Southern Attitudes and Behavior.* New York: Praeger.

Black, Earl. 1976. *Southern Governors and Civil Rights: Racial Segregation as a Campaign Issue in the Second Reconstruction.* Cambridge: Harvard U. Pr.

———, and Merle Black. 1987. *Politics and Society in the South.* Cambridge: Harvard U. Pr.

Bullock, Charles S., III. 1987. "Redistricting and Changes in the Partisan and Racial Composition of Southern Legislatures." 19 *State and Local Government Review* 62.

———. 1988. "Regional Realignment from an Officeholding Perspective." 50 *Journal of Politics* 553.

———. 1991. "Creeping Realignment in the South." In Robert H. Swansborough and David M. Brodsky, eds. *Party Realignment and Dealignment in the South.* Columbia: U. of South Carolina Pr.

———, and Loch K. Johnson. 1991. *Runoff Elections in the United States.* Knoxville: U. of Tennessee Pr.

Carmines, Edward G., and James A. Stimson. 1982. "Racial Issues and Structure of Mass Belief Systems." 44 *Journal of Politics* 2.

Key, V. O., Jr. 1949. *Southern Politics in State and Nation.* New York: Knopf.

Kousser, J. Morgan. 1974. *The Shaping of Southern Politics.* New Haven: Yale U. Pr.

Perry, Huey L., and Alfred Stokes. 1987. "Politics and Power in the Sunbelt: Mayor Morial of New Orleans." In Michael B. Preston, Lenneal J. Henderson, Jr., and Paul L. Puryear, eds. *The New Black Politics,* 2nd ed. New York: Longman.

Petrocik, John R. 1987. "Realignment: New Party Coalitions and the Nationalization of the South." 49 *Journal of Politics* 347.

Rodgers, Harrell R., Jr., and Charles S. Bullock III. 1972. *Law and Social Change.* New York: McGraw-Hill.

Silver, Brian D., Barbara A. Anderson, and Paul R. Abramson. 1986. "Who Over-reports Voting?" 80 *American Political Science Review* 613.

Sinclair, Barbara. 1985. "Agenda, Policy, and Alignment Change from Coolidge to Reagan." In Lawrence C. Dodd and Bruce I. Oppenheimer, eds. *Congress Reconsidered*, 3rd ed. Washington: Congressional Quarterly.

Smith v. Allwright. 1944. 321 U.S. 649.

Sorauf, Frank J. 1984. *Party Politics in America.* Boston: Little, Brown.

Stanley, Harold W. 1987. *Voter Mobilization and the Politics of Race.* New York: Praeger.

———. 1988. "Southern Partisan Changes: Dealignment, Realignment, or Both." 50 *Journal of Politics* 64.

Sundquist, James L. 1983. *Dynamics of the Party System*, rev. ed. Washington: Brookings.

U.S. Commission on Civil Rights. 1968. *Political Participation.* Washington: U.S. Government Printing Office.

Van Winger, John, and David Valentine. 1988. "Partisan Politics: A One-and-a-Half, No-Party System." In James F. Lea, ed. *Contemporary Southern Politics*. Baton Rouge: Louisiana State U. Pr.

Williams, Linda F. 1987. "Blacks and the 1984 Elections in the South: Racial Polarization and Regional Congruence." In Laurence W. Moreland, Robert P. Stead, and Tod A. Baker, eds. *Blacks in Southern Politics*. New York: Praeger.

Wolfinger, Raymond, and Michael G. Hagen. 1985. "Republican Prospects: Southern Comfort." 8 *Public Opinion* 8.

Civil Service Reforms

The post-Civil War drive for reform of the American civil service, which was inspired in part by British example, aimed at a revamping of hiring practices at the lower levels of federal and state bureaucracies by replacing party loyalty with merit as the main criterion for appointment.

Party loyalty had been the linchpin of the spoils system that governed the distribution of public jobs since the age of Andrew Jackson. This system, euphemistically called "rotation in office," used places on the public payroll as patronage to reward supporters of the party currently in power. In turn, job holders were expected to fuel the party's campaign needs with assessments from their salaries. In practice the spoils system operated in Washington and in public agencies across the country to decentralize political power among politicians with local influence, to hamstring national executive authority, and to diminish the chances for longevity, experience, and competence among appointed officeholders.

The dismantling of this system was a precondition for the development of a modern and reasonably efficient bureaucracy to administer centralized policy decisions about outstanding public problems. The sudden expansion of the federal bureaucracy during the Civil War dramatized the drawbacks of the spoils system and—together with revelations of postwar corruption—inspired a search for remedies. Prominent in the agitation for change were genteel liberal reformers like George W. Curtis, Edwin L. Godkin, and Dorman Eaton, who gained growing support from businessmen whose interests were affected by dealings with governmental agencies.

Despite the creation in 1871 of a federal Civil Service Commission to formulate rules for screening job seekers through competitive exams, congressional spoilsmen resisted threats to their traditional control of federal patronage, and Presidents wobbled in their efforts at change. But President James Garfield's assassination by a frustrated office seeker in 1881 mobilized national sentiment behind the Pendleton bill, a reform measure largely written by Eaton. A skeptical Congress passed the bill into law in 1883. The Pendleton Civil Service Act, mandating competitive exams for positions on the classified "merit" list and outlawing political assessments, was designed to be incremental in its impact, with the classified list expanding gradually at a pace to be determined by the President.

In effect the law engendered a slow shift in control over the federal bureaucracy from the legislative to the executive branch. Presidents Grover Cleveland, who as governor of New York had signed the first state civil service reform measure in 1883, and Theodore Roosevelt, a vigorous exponent of the reform cause, were instrumental in launching the Pendleton Act on a strong course. When Cleveland took office in 1885, 11 percent of the service was classified. When Roosevelt left office in 1909, the figure had reached 66 percent, and it continued to climb thereafter. The rising percentage was buoyed by a rhythm in which outgoing Presidents added large numbers of their partisan appointees to the classified list to protect them from subsequent removal.

In the twentieth century, as the new bureaucracy created by the Pendleton Act matured and sprawled, it became itself the object of reform. The Hatch Act of 1939 prohibited political activity among civil servants. Changes recommended by the Hoover Commission reports after World War II were implemented for greater administrative efficiency. The Civil Service Reform Act of 1978 introduced sweeping rearrangements to make the civil service as a whole more responsive to political winds while maintaining the security of its individual personnel.

See also: Grover Cleveland, James Garfield, Hatch Acts of 1939 and 1940, Theodore Roosevelt

Geoffrey Blodgett

REFERENCES

Hoogenboom, Ari. 1961. *Outlawing the Spoils: A History of the Civil Service Reform Movement, 1865–1883.* Urbana: U. of Illinois Pr.

Ingraham, Patricia, and Carolyn Ban, eds. 1984. *Legislating Bureaucratic Change: The Civil Service Reform Act of 1978.* Albany: State U. of New York Pr.

Skowronek, Stephen. 1982. *Building a New Administrative State: The Expansion of National Administrative Capacities, 1877–1920.* New York: Cambridge U. Pr.

Van Riper, Paul. 1958. *History of the United States Civil Service.* Evanston, IL: Row, Peterson.

White, Leonard D. 1958. *The Republican Era, 1869–1901: A Study in Administrative History.* New York: Macmillan.

William Claflin (1818–1905)

Chairman of the Republican National Committee under President Grant. William Claflin was the son of a Massachusetts boot and shoe manufacturer. With help from his father, Claflin went into this same business and was so successful that he became a wealthy leader of Boston society from the late 1840s until his death. His political activities started in 1848, when he was one of the founding members of the Free Soil Party of Massachusetts and was elected to the lower house of the Massachusetts legislature. He served in the legislature from 1849 to 1853 as a Free Soiler and in the state senate from 1859 to 1861 as a Republican.

Claflin held no public office between 1861 and 1866, when he began three consecutive one-year terms as lieutenant governor. Also during this time, he was a member of the Republican National Committee. His most important political activity was serving as chairman of the National Committee during Ulysses S. Grant's presidential campaign in 1868. Claflin was governor of Massachusetts from 1869 to 1871, during which time legislation was passed extending the rights of women. He was the first Massachusetts governor to favor female suffrage. He ended his political service by serving two terms in the U.S. House of Representatives from 1877 to 1881.

See also: Free Soil Party, Election of 1868, Republican National Committee

Reed Hutner

REFERENCES

Goldman, Ralph M. 1990. *The National Party Chairmen and Committees: Factionalism at the Top.* Armonk, NY: M. E. Sharpe.

James B. (Champ) Clark (1850–1921)

Democratic Speaker of the U.S. House of Representatives. James Beauchamp Clark was a member of the U.S. House of Representatives from Missouri and Speaker of the House from 1911 to 1919. Clark was born in Anderson County, Kentucky, and attended Kentucky University (1867–1870) until he was expelled for firing a pistol at a fellow student. He graduated from Bethany College in West Virginia in 1873 and Cincinnati Law School in 1875. While a law student he took Champ as his given name and was so known for the rest of his life. At age 23 he served one year as president of Marshall College, Huntington, West Virginia (1873–1874). He moved to Missouri in 1875.

Clark held several local and state offices in Louisiana and then in Bowling Green, Missouri, including deputy prosecuting attorney and prosecuting attorney of Pike County (1885–1889), Democratic presidential elector in 1880, and from 1889 to 1891 a seat in the lower house of the Missouri state legislature. He was elected as a Democrat to the United States House of Representatives from the Ninth Congressional District in 1892, lost his seat in the Republican landslide of 1894, and was reelected in 1896. Thereafter he served in the House without interruption until his final defeat in 1920. He was elected Minority Leader of the Democratic Party in the House in 1908 and Speaker in 1911 when the Democrats gained control.

Clark consistently associated himself with the issues that William Jennings Bryan championed in the election of 1896; he could be described as a progressive Democrat. As Minority Leader, Clark played the key role in the reform of the rules of the House of Representatives in 1909 and 1910 (the 1910 Revolt), and most of the votes cast in favor of the reforms that drastically reduced the powers of Speaker Joseph G. Cannon of Illinois were provided by Clark and the Democrats. Clark was a leading candidate for the Democratic nomination for President in 1912, and, for several ballots, he received the support of a solid majority of the delegates. Only the Democratic rule requiring a two-thirds majority prevented Clark from capturing the nomination and, probably, the presidency. Woodrow Wilson ultimately won the nomination and the election in 1912, and Clark served as Speaker of the House from 1911 until the Republicans regained control in the Sixty-sixth Congress in 1919.

In the Wilson years Clark's role as Speaker was less influential than had been that of his immediate predecessors partly because Wilson himself played a very active role in the legislative process and at times overshadowed the Speaker. Clark was the presidential spokesman, much involved in the enactment of most of the significant legislation of the Progressive era, including the Underwood Tariff, the Progressive income tax, the Federal Reserve Act, the Clayton Antitrust Act, and the Federal Trade Commission Act. Clark supported his country's entry into World War I, and on most issues he loyally supported Wilson's conduct of the war, although in 1917 he refused to vote for military conscription. Clark lost his seat in the election of 1920. The veteran of 26 years in the House of Representatives was turned out by the postwar Republican landslide.

See also: William Jennings Bryan, Majority Party Leadership in Congress, Minority Party Leadership in Congress, Speaker of the House, Woodrow Wilson

Howard W. Allen

REFERENCES

Clark, Champ. 1920. *My Quarter Century of American Politics*. New York: Harper.

Morrison, George F. 1965. "A Political Biography of Champ Clark," Ph.D. dissertation, St. Louis University.

Joseph S. Clark (1901–1990)

Democratic reform politician from Pennsylvania. An activist in both local and national politics, Joseph Sill Clark served as Democratic mayor of Philadelphia and U.S. Senator from Pennsylvania. Earning his undergraduate degree at Harvard, Clark received a law degree from the University of Pennsylvania and then worked as an attorney. Reared as a Republican, Clark left the GOP when he chose to support Al Smith for President in 1928. In 1947 he served as campaign manager for Richardson Dilworth, a Democratic reform candidate for mayor of Philadelphia seeking to dislodge the corrupt Republican machine controlling the city. Though Dilworth lost, both men were successful in 1949, when Clark was elected city controller and Dilworth County treasurer. Grand jury investigations of city government contributed to the final demise of the Republican machine in 1951 when Clark was elected the first Democratic mayor

since 1884 (Dilworth was elected district attorney). With a broom as a campaign symbol (sweeping corruption out of the city), Clark defeated the Reverend Daniel A. Poling despite a nearly two-to-one Republican registration advantage.

During his one term in office, Clark oversaw the merging of the city and county governments of Philadelphia and the implementation of a new home rule charter for the city. In 1956 Clark ran for the U.S. Senate, winning by a narrow margin. Clark had a liberal voting record during his two terms but became widely recognized as a critic of the congressional establishment, advocating reforms strengthening the Congress but also weakening centralized party control. Clark was defeated for reelection in 1968 by four-term Congressman Richard Schweiker.

See also: Richardson Dilworth, Election of 1928, Alfred E. Smith

Thomas J. Baldino

REFERENCES

Clark, Joseph S. 1963. *The Senate Establishment*. New York: Hill and Wang.

———. 1964. *Congress, the Sapless Branch*. New York: Harper & Row.

———, ed. 1965. *Congressional Reform: Problems and Prospects*. New York: Crowell.

Petshek, Kirk R. 1973. *The Challenge of Urban Reform*. Philadelphia: Temple U. Pr.

Reichley, James. 1959. *The Art of Government: Reforms and Organization Politics in Philadelphia*. New York: The Fund for the Republic.

James P. Clarke (1854–1926)

Democratic Congressman and U.S. Senator from Arkansas. James P. Clarke was a prominent Arkansas Democrat who left the Arkansas House of Representatives to become the President *pro tempore* of the U.S. Senate. Clarke's rise within Arkansas state politics took a steady course: he served in the state house of representatives (1886–1888), the state senate (1888–1892), as attorney general (1892–1894), and governor (1895–1896). Although defeated in his first try for the U.S. Senate in 1897, Clarke was elected to the Senate in 1903 and reelected in 1909 and 1915.

The zenith of Clarke's career came in 1913, when he was elected President *pro tempore* of the Senate. Clarke's election as President *pro tempore* created considerable controversy, because it came with the defeat of Augustus O. Bacon (Georgia) for the position. Bacon was the most senior Democratic Senator at the time and had shared the presiding role with Jacob H. Gallinger, a Republican, during the Sixty-second Congress (1911–1913) in a power-sharing arrangement between the two parties that was designed to overcome the progressive insurgency. Bacon was nominated in the Democratic caucus of 1913 to become President *pro tempore*, but Clarke's name was also placed in nomination by a coalition of progressive Democrats.

Clarke was nominated by the caucus in a 17-to-14 vote. The motivations of the progressive Senators who sought to elevate Clarke to the position of President *pro tempore* have never been clear; their actions are especially vexing to liberals since Clarke was well known as a conservative Democrat. Explanations offered at the time included a desire to limit Bacon to only one powerful position in the Senate (he also chaired the Foreign Relations Committee), a concern that Bacon had lacked decisiveness in his previous actions as the Senate presiding officer, and an interest in bolstering Clarke's prestige to aid in his upcoming reelection. Regardless of his progressive sponsorship, Clarke remained a reactionary for the remainder of his career, often relinquishing the chair when the Senate passed progressive legislation so that he would not have to sign it.

Charles Stewart III

James S. Clarkson (1842–1918)

Republican National Committee chairman in the 1890s. James S. "Ret" Clarkson was elected Republican National Committee chairman (1891–1892) when Matthew S. Quay resigned. He had been vice chairman of the committee to that time. Clarkson worked on his father's Iowa farm and attended nearby schools until age 17 when he began to teach school. He became a champion of civil rights for Blacks, an active worker in the "Underground Railroad," and a founder of the Republican Party in Iowa. By 1866 he was elected chairman of the Iowa Republican state committee. Clarkson became city editor of the Des Moines *Register*, which, three years later, he and members of his family purchased.

President Ulysses S. Grant appointed Clarkson postmaster of Des Moines in 1871, from which he resigned in 1877 in protest of President Rutherford B. Hayes's southern policy. In 1880 he became a member of the Republican National Committee. Clarkson was particularly active in the James Blaine campaign of 1884, spending most of his time in New York in constant consultation with Blaine's managers.

At the 1888 Republican National Convention, Iowa's was a critical delegation, led by Clarkson and pledged to its favorite son, Senator William B. Allison. Clarkson's timing of Allison's withdrawal on the eighth ballot helped swing the nomination to Benjamin Harrison. When Harrison asked him to serve as national chairman, Clarkson declined, suggesting that the position go to Matthew Quay as a gesture to "the Grant crowd," that is, the network of eastern state bosses. Instead, Clarkson was elected to fill the new office of vice chairman.

Chairman Quay urged President Harrison to appoint Clarkson as Postmaster General, but, for reasons of factional accommodation, Harrison appointed him First Assistant Postmaster General (the position with greatest responsibility for distributing the vast post office patronage). Clarkson became an outspoken opponent of civil service reform and an advocate of federal election reforms intended to halt the southern drift to a one-party system. When Chairman Quay resigned in 1891, Clarkson was promptly chosen to take his place.

Clarkson, by now a Blaine supporter, was not President Harrison's choice for national chairman following the 1892 national convention. Although continuing as Iowa's member of the national committee until 1896, Clarkson in effect retired from politics in 1893 to return to his business interests.

See also: Civil Service Reforms, Ulysses S. Grant, Benjamin Harrison, Republican National Committee

Ralph M. Goldman

REFERENCES

Kleeberg, Gordon S. P. 1911. *The Formation of the Republican Party as a National Political Organization.* New York: Moody Publishing.

Louis T. Michener Papers, Library of Congress.

Henry Clay (1777–1852)

United States Senator, Speaker of the U.S House of Representatives, presidential candidate, and Secretary of State. Henry Clay was one of the dominant forces in American electoral and legislative politics from his election to the U.S. House of Representatives in 1810 to his death in 1852. As Speaker of the House, he transformed the office from impartial arbiter to partisan pulpit; as a leading nationalist, he was at the forefront of efforts to find room for compromise in the bitter sectional clashes of the day; and as part of the "great triumvirate" (with John C.

Calhoun and Daniel Webster), he was among the most significant of the first generation of post-revolutionary American politicians.

Clay was born poor in Virginia, never receiving a formal education. However, he did study law under a number of eminent Richmond attorneys and was admitted into the Richmond bar at the age of 20. Kentucky had been admitted to the Union in 1792, and one consequence of the massive migration into the new state and the uncertainties of pre-revolutionary land claims was a lucrative market for the service of attorneys in the new state capital. Thus, Clay moved to Lexington, Kentucky, in 1797 to practice law, handling land claims and criminal matters.

Clay gradually immersed himself in the politics of the new state. Traveling in circuit with the state courts, he developed contacts with many influential citizens and became a forceful speaker. Clay entered politics by winning election to the Kentucky legislature in 1803. Clay's early career was typical of many state and national politicians in the early years of the Republic, as he served intermittent terms in both Lexington and Washington.

In the Kentucky legislature, Clay immediately began to exert considerable influence, and in 1806 he was selected by the state legislature to serve out the unexpired term of John Adair in the U.S. Senate. His election at the age of 29 clearly contravened the constitutional requirement that U.S. Senators be 30 years of age, but apparently no member of the Senate challenged Clay. He returned to the Kentucky House of Representatives in 1808 and was elected speaker in 1809. Once again the legislature in 1810 sent Clay to serve out another unexpired Senate term, this time that of Bucker Thrunston.

At the expiration of this tour of duty in the Senate, Clay did not return to the Kentucky state legislature. He had already become established as the leader of a group of politicians, mostly from the South and West, who were known as the War Hawks. These public men, reflecting widespread sentiments in their home regions, were strongly nationalistic, especially taking offense at British interference with American shipping and demanding military retaliation. Presidents Thomas Jefferson and James Madison resisted these calls to arms. But, western and southern opinion was eventually rallied to the side of military action, leading to the election of a large contingent of War Hawks to the House of Representatives in 1810, among whose numbers was Henry Clay.

Clay emerged as the leader of the War Hawks and subsequently was elected Speaker of the House. As Speaker, Clay used the powers of his office and his own political skills to pursue an aggressive foreign policy. He was also a strong advocate of protective tariffs. Clay became the first truly "modern" speaker, using his power to make appointments so as to insure that key committees (such as Foreign Affairs, Military Affairs, and Ways and Means) shared his policy views. He also developed the parliamentary mechanism of the "previous question" to shut off debate on the floor and bring issues to a vote.

Following the War of 1812 (he was a member of the negotiating team that produced the Treaty of Ghent in 1814), Clay served off and on in the House from 1815 to 1825, was President John Quincy Adams's Secretary of State from 1825 to 1829, and served in the Senate from 1831 to 1842 and from 1849 to 1852. Interruptions to his public service in Washington, D.C., owed to numerous matters, running from personal business to exploratory presidential campaigns.

Clay ran for President in 1824, 1832, 1844, and 1848, in a series of campaigns that were typical for Whigs at the time: the campaigns were primarily regional and were conducted among an elite group of politicians. Clay doubted he could ever win a majority of the electoral vote outright, but if he could force the election into the House of Representatives, then he would have a good chance at victory. The 1824 election was in fact decided by the House, over which Clay was presiding as Speaker, but he had already been eliminated from consideration by finishing fourth in the Electoral College. Clay's influence was felt in the proceedings on the House floor, however, with some attributing Adams's final victory to Clay's ability to round up support on Adams's behalf.

As a national politician, Clay was an ardent advocate of his "national system," an attempt to tie various regions of the country together, with the federal government financing the elements necessary to create a national economy (such as roads, railroads, and canals). Though ultimately unsuccessful in fully implementing his system in antebellum America, Clay would have been pleased to see his ideas carried through in post-Civil War efforts by the federal government to undergird America's industrial and agricultural infrastructure. Another of Clay's significant contributions toward regional integration was his effort at piloting the Missouri Compromise through the House in 1820.

See also: John Quincy Adams; John C. Calhoun, Elections of 1824, 1844, and 1848; Electoral College System; Thomas Jefferson; James Madison; Missouri Compromise; Speaker of the House; Daniel Webster

Charles Stewart III

REFERENCES

Eaton, Clement. 1957. *Henry Clay and the Art of American Politics*. Boston: Little, Brown.

Mayo, Bernard. 1937. *Henry Clay: Spokesman of the New West*. Boston: Houghton Mifflin.

Peterson, Merrill D. 1987. *The Great Triumvirate: Webster, Clay, and Calhoun*. New York: Oxford U. Pr.

Eldridge Cleaver (1935–)

African-American political author and activist. Eldridge Cleaver has been a thief, a rapist, a convict, a writer, a leader of the revolutionary Black Panther Party, a presidential candidate, a political fugitive and exile, and a conservative Christian. Born in Wabbaseka, Arkansas, Cleaver grew up in Phoenix and Los Angeles. He began the first of several prison terms at the age of 12. In prison he wrote the essays later published as *Soul on Ice* and became a follower of Malcolm X; after his release in 1966 he met leaders of the Black Panther Party (BPP) and decided that it was the best vehicle for reviving the tradition of Malcolm's Organization of Afro-American Unity. Cleaver became the BPP's minister of information and editor of its newspaper, *The Black Panther*. He argued that the U.S. Black community is an internal colony of the white imperialist country, the theoretical basis for the Panther's program.

Cleaver helped to negotiate a coalition between the BPP and the radical Peace and Freedom Party (PFP), helping the PFP register 100,000 voters to qualify for California ballot position. The PFP in turn endorsed the BPP program and eventually chose Cleaver as its presidential candidate in 1968. Cleaver finished seventh, with 36,533 votes, although he was not yet old enough to be eligible for the office, and California and Utah refused to print his name on their ballots.

Cleaver was wounded in a gunfight with Oakland police in 1969; another BPP member, Bobby Hutton, was killed. Charged with attempted murder, he posted $50,000 bail, fled, and took asylum in Algeria. Cleaver returned to the U.S. in 1975, announcing that he was now a devout Christian and conservative. He pled guilty to a reduced charge in 1979, and was sentenced to probation. He became a supporter of Sun Myung Moon's Unification Church in 1979, and endorsed Ronald Reagan for President in 1980. Cleaver sought the Republican nomination for U.S. Senator from California in 1986, finishing ninth in the primary with 23,152 votes.

See also: Election of 1980, Race and Racial Politics, Ronald Reagan

John C. Berg

REFERENCES

Anderson, Jervis. 1968. "Race, Rage & Eldridge Cleaver." 6 *Commentary* 63.

Bronstein, Phil. 1977. "Eldridge Cleaver-Reborn." 23 *Midstream* 57.

Cleaver, Eldridge. 1968. *Soul on Ice.* New York: McGraw-Hill.

———. 1969. *Post-Prison Writings and Speeches.* Robert Scheer, ed. New York: Random House.

———, Bill Kauffman, and Lynn Scarlett. 1986. "Eldridge Cleaver." 17 (9) *Reason* 22.

Heath, G. Louis, ed. 1976. *The Black Panther Leaders Speak; Huey P. Newton, Bobby Seale, Eldridge Cleaver and Company Speak Out Through the Black Panther Party's Official Newspaper*. Metuchen, NJ: Scarecrow Press.

Marine, Gene. 1969. *The Black Panthers.* New York: New American Library.

Earle C. Clements (1896–1985)

Kentucky governor and U.S. Senator. Earle Chester Clements was born and reared in Morganfield, Kentucky, only a few miles from where two other famous Kentucky politicians, Albert B. "Happy" Chandler and John Y. Brown, Sr., grew up. The three would be youthful friends, athletic rivals, and, eventually, political foes. Clements followed a successful high school record as an athlete and student leader with a brief period at the University of Kentucky and then served as an Army captain (1917–1919). Clements's political career began in 1922 when he became deputy to his father, the county sheriff. Upon his father's death, he served as acting sheriff and then was successively chosen by the Union County voters to be county clerk, county judge (chief county executive), and state senator.

Unlike Chandler, renowned as a colorful stump speaker, Clements was, at best, a nondescript orator. His talent was in administration, not in campaigning. Once he exercised that talent at the state level, the effect was remarkable and beneficial for Kentucky. Elected to the state senate in 1941, Clements was majority leader in less than three years. His success in that role in pushing through a progressive budget while opposed by a Republican governor was a prelude to his election in 1944 to the U.S. House of Representatives. Reelected in 1946, after declining overtures to run for the U.S. Senate, Clements instead was elected governor in 1947.

As chief executive in Frankfort, Clements made his indelible mark on Kentucky. In what has been termed "foundation legislation," he created or expanded the infrastructure that is crucial to a modern state and economy: repair and construction of roads and highways, expansion of the state park system (only New York spent more on parks at that time), reorganization of the state insurance commission, establishment of a professional state police and a legislative research commission, and promotion of rural economic development.

Constitutionally denied a second term, Governor Clements resigned in 1950 to capture the U.S. Senate seat formerly held by Vice President Alben Barkley. By the end of his first year in the Capitol, he was assistant majority leader to Lyndon B. Johnson of Texas. Handicapped by the opposition of Governor Chandler's faction and by increased Senate duties that fell to him after Johnson's major illness, Clements was narrowly denied reelection by Thruston B. Morton in 1956. At Johnson's request, Clements was appointed to the new position of executive director for the Senate Democratic Re-election Committee. In that post (1957–1959), he oversaw a Democratic gain of 14 seats that was not eroded until the 1980 elections.

Except for brief service as Kentucky highway commissioner, Clements spent the 1960s and 1970s in Washington as either a consultant or a lobbyist. Throughout that period, he returned regularly to Kentucky where he retired in 1981.

See also: Albert B. Chandler, Lyndon Johnson, Thruston B. Morton.

Thomas P. Wolf

REFERENCES

Jewell, Malcolm E., and Everett W. Cunningham. 1968. *Kentucky Politics.* Lexington: U. Pr. of Kentucky.

Luhr, Gary. 1983. "The Governor Who Broke New Ground." 37 *Rural Kentuckian* 8.

Pearce, John Ed. 1987. *Divide and Dissent: Kentucky Politics, 1930–1963.* Lexington: U. Pr. of Kentucky.

Syvertsen, Thomas H. 1985. "Earle Chester Clements, 1947–1950." In Lowell H. Harrison, ed. *Kentucky's Governors, 1792–1985.* Lexington: U. Pr. of Kentucky.

Grover Cleveland (1837–1908)

Only U.S. President to serve two nonconsecutive terms. Stephen Grover Cleveland, an iron-willed, conservative Democrat who served as President from 1885 to 1889 and from 1893 to 1897, asserted the independent authority of that office over Congress more forcefully than had any President since the Civil War. His narrow win in 1884 over James G. Blaine, after one of the dirtiest campaigns in history, climaxed his sudden ascent from political obscurity. A blunt, methodical lawyer from western New York, Cleveland drew national attention as a reform mayor in Buffalo in 1882, winning the New York governorship later that year. In both offices his executive habits anticipated his presidential style, turning on prudent administration, a close watch over patronage, and a knack for startling, caustic veto messages. His passion for political restraint (which contrasted with the fleshly indulgences of his early private life in Buffalo) attracted businessmen, Mugwump civil service reformers, and a substantial constituency of ordinary voters wearied by the political excesses of the late-nineteenth-century Gilded Age.

Cleveland's White House years turned him into a national sheriff of law and order, determined to sanitize the sorry reputation of both the postwar Democratic Party and the federal bureaucracy in Washington. During his first term he administrated the Pendleton Civil Service Act, which had recently been passed by a dubious Congress, with sufficient zeal to guarantee its long-term success through steady expansion of the classified list. Meanwhile Cleveland labored endlessly to improve the calibre of presidential patronage appointments in the teeth of fierce partisan pressures from job-hungry Democrats. His frequent vetoes of private pension bills for Civil War veterans—vetoes inspired by his stern mistrust of dependence on federal welfare support among needy citizens—became legendary. Less well remembered were his efforts to impose restraint on the private exploitation of land resources in the West.

In a notable message to Congress in 1887, Cleveland called for comprehensive downward tariff revision, an issue he would pursue doggedly for years thereafter. In so doing, he became the first President to identify tariff reform with the interests of wage earners and other consumer citizens benefiting from low prices. He justified his opposition to currency inflation in similar terms. In the presidential contest of 1888, Cleveland won a slightly wider national popular plurality than in 1884; however, he failed to carry New York's crucial electoral votes and thus lost to Benjamin Harrison in the Electoral College. A rematch four years later restored Cleveland to the White House by an ample margin, just on the eve of the worst depression of the nineteenth century.

The President's response to hard times was unyielding, consistently conservative, and politically disastrous for Cleveland and the Democrats. His refusal to compromise with both western silver inflationists and eastern high-tariff defenders in Congress alienated important segments of his 1892 coalition, as did his reliance on the House of Morgan banking firm to float gold-bond issues on the European market. His decision to break the Chicago Pullman strike of 1894 by means of a court injunction and the dispatch of federal troops, though widely supported in the press and pulpit at the time, damaged his reputation among liberal critics later on. The Democratic convention of 1896 repudiated Cleveland's leadership in open revolt against the astringency of the values he clung to and the policies he pursued. His two presidencies make a vivid contrast between early promise and ultimate failure.

See also: John G. Blaine; Elections of 1884, 1888, and 1892; Electoral College System; Benjamin Harrison; Mugwumps

Geoffrey Blodgett

REFERENCES

Blodgett, Geoffrey. 1983. "The Political Leadership of Grover Cleveland." 82 *South Atlantic Quarterly* 288.

Kelley, Robert. 1969. *The Transatlantic Persuasion: The Liberal-Democratic Mind in the Age of Gladstone.* New York: Knopf.

Merrill, Horace. 1957. *Bourbon Leader: Grover Cleveland and the Democratic Party.* Boston: Little, Brown.

Nevins, Allan. 1932. *Grover Cleveland: A Study in Courage.* New York: Dodd, Mead.

Welch, Richard E., Jr. 1988. *The Presidencies of Grover Cleveland.* Lawrence: U. Pr. of Kansas.

Clark M. Clifford (1906–)

Influential statesman of the Democratic Party. Clark McAdams Clifford is perhaps best known for his role in President Harry Truman's upset victory over Thomas Dewey in the 1948 presidential race and for working to reverse escalation of the Vietnam War by the U.S. while serving as President Lyndon Johnson's Secretary of Defense.

Clifford spent his formative years in the Midwest, attending school in St. Louis and receiving his law degree from Washington University in 1928. After more than a decade practicing law in a St. Louis firm, Clifford in 1944 was commissioned a lieutenant in the Naval Reserve. It was here that he became assistant to Truman's naval aide and subsequently was appointed White House special counsel in 1946.

Clifford served a multipurpose role in the Truman White House. Arguing for a tough line toward the Soviet Union, he helped draft the 1947 National Security Act and position papers on aid to Greece and Turkey. Domestically Clifford led a faction of advisors who steered Truman in a more liberal policy direction. "Well, it was two forces fighting for the mind of the President, that's really what it was. It was completely unpublicized, and I don't think Mr. Truman ever realized it was going on," Clifford once recalled.

Clifford also served as a campaign strategist, writing a 43-page memorandum that outlined the coming 1948 election with remarkable prescience, thus helping Truman win. But by 1950, Clifford, tired of the White House, resigned to become a senior partner for a Washington, D.C., law firm. Clifford's subsequent legal work advising corporations on tax and legal policy made him a millionaire.

Although a supporter of the presidential candidacy of Senator Stuart Symington (D-Mo.) in 1960, Clifford drafted a number of transition memos for John F. Kennedy when JFK won the presidency. In 1961 Kennedy named Clifford to the Foreign Intelligence Advisory Board. Clifford continued to advise Kennedy and his successor, Lyndon Johnson, although he turned down high-ranking appointments in both administrations.

In his capacity as a member of the Foreign Intelligence Advisory Board, Clifford made several trips to Southeast Asia. A committed hawk, Clifford later recalled that during the summer of 1967 he began to have doubts about America's Vietnam policy after noticing that America's Asian allies seemed less concerned about Communist aggression in Vietnam than did the United States. However, when he was appointed as Johnson's Secretary of Defense in 1968, observers generally considered him a hard-liner. Clifford's appointment came on the heels of the North Vietnamese 1968 Tet Offensive, which seemed to many to discredit the Johnson administration's claims of progress in winning the war. Then, during high-level talks on increasing the number of American soldiers in Vietnam in light of the Tet Offensive, Clifford voiced objections about the open-ended nature of the American military commitment. After a long and bitter internal debate at the upper echelon of the Johnson administration, Clifford was instrumental in convincing President Johnson to order a total halt to the bombing of North Vietnam, although his efforts cost Clifford the close friendship of Johnson. Johnson subsequently decided not to seek reelection.

In January 1969, Clifford left office and returned to his legal practice. He continued to serve in an advisory capacity to various Democratic Party political leaders. In 1972 he played the part of secretary of state in Edmund Muskie's "shadow cabinet" during Muskie's failed bid for the presidency. Clifford later went on a special diplomatic mission to Cyprus during the initial days of the Carter administration and served as counsel for Carter's ill-fated budget director Bert Lance during the latter's testimony before a congressional investigating committee.

See also: Jimmy Carter, Thomas Dewey, Election of 1948, Lyndon B. Johnson, John F. Kennedy, Harry S Truman

Matthew J. Dickinson

REFERENCES

Anderson, Patrick. 1968. *The President's Men: White House Assistants of Franklin D. Roosevelt, Harry S Truman, Dwight D. Eisenhower, John F. Kennedy, and Lyndon B. Johnson.* Garden City, NY: Doubleday.

Halberstam, David. 1984. *The Best and the Brightest.* New York: Penguin.

Heller, Francis H., ed. 1980. *The Truman White House (The Administration of the Presidency 1945–1953).* Lawrence: Regents Pr. of Kansas.

Medved, Michael. 1979. *The Shadow Presidents: The Secret History of Chief Executives and Their Top Aides.* New York: Times Books.

DeWitt Clinton (1769–1828)

Important Republican politician of the early nineteenth century. Initially an Anti-Federalist, DeWitt Clinton emerged as a leading Republican who promoted northern interests that he believed the politicians who dominated the post-Revolutionary period—known as the Virginia Dynasty—neglected. Clinton was born in Little Britain, New York, and after graduating from Columbia College, he served as secretary to his uncle, George Clinton, the governor of New York. DeWitt was a Republican member of the state legislature (1797–1802) and in 1801 and 1802 he gained enormous power while serving on the four-member council of appointment.

Appointed to the United States Senate in 1802, he introduced the Twelfth Amendment to the Constitution, establishing the present method of electing the President and Vice President. In 1803 he resigned to become mayor of New York City, and he simultaneously served in the state senate (1806–1811) where he introduced a significant amount of reform legislation. He was mayor of New York City from 1803 to 1815 with the exception of two annual terms in 1807–1808 and 1810–1811. He is credited with helping to establish the public school system of New York City. After 1803 Clinton vigorously disagreed with Thomas Jefferson's administration over maritime issues and other related matters. In 1808 he helped organize George Clinton's unsuccessful campaign for the presidency. Four years later DeWitt Clinton forged an alliance of discontented Republicans and Federalists, a coalition that almost enabled him to defeat James Madison in the presidential election of 1812.

In 1815 Van Burenites, stressing Clinton's Federalist connections, removed him from the mayoralty of New York City. Clinton then devoted himself to promoting the construction of a state canal from the Great Lakes to the Hudson River. Successfully campaigning on the Erie Canal issue, Clinton was elected in 1817 to the first of four terms as governor of New York. He was chiefly responsible for completion of the Erie Canal and served as its commissioner.

See also: Anti-Federalists, George Clinton, Election of 1812, Thomas Jefferson, James Madison, Twelfth Amendment, Martin Van Buren

Steven E. Siry

REFERENCES

Lagana, Michael P. 1972. "DeWitt Clinton, Politician Toward a New Political Order, 1769–1802." Ph.D. dissertation, Columbia University.

Siry, Steven E. 1989. *De Witt Clinton and the American Political Economy: Sectionalism, Politics, and Republican Ideology, 1787–1828.* New York: Peter Lang.

George Clinton (1739–1812)

Governor of New York and Vice President of the United States under Jefferson and Madison. Vice President of the United States from 1805 to 1812, George Clinton was a veteran of the French and Indian War. Although he served as a brigadier general during the American Revolution, he was more effective in the political arena than in the military arena. In an upset election, he defeated Philip Schuyler to become the first governor of New York (1777–1795) and then served again from 1801 to 1804. Clinton vigorously opposed ratification of the federal Constitution and was a minor vice presidential candidate in the 1789, 1792, and 1796 elections. An advocate of personal liberty and states' rights, he, like most Anti-Federalists, became a Republican during the partisan realignment of the early 1790s. In 1804 President Thomas Jefferson declined to support the reelection of Vice President Aaron Burr, Clinton's protégé. The congressional caucus nominated Clinton in Burr's place, thus continuing the New York–Virginia alliance of Republican strongholds. Jefferson and Clinton defeated Federalists Charles Cotesworth Pinckney and Rufus King by 162 to 14 electoral votes. In 1808 Clinton was both a presidential and a vice presidential candidate. With support from Republican opponents of Jefferson's trade embargo, he challenged James Madison for the presidency. A coalition with the Federalists that Clinton hoped for failed to materialize, and he received only New York's six electoral votes. (Interestingly, his nephew, DeWitt Clinton, lost to Madison in the presidential election of 1812.) But he easily retained the vice presidency, defeating Federalist Rufus King by 113 to 47 electoral votes. His relations with Madison were understandably strained. True to his Republican principles, Clinton exercised his tie-breaking vote in the Senate against the bill to recharter the Bank of the United States in 1811. He died in office the following year.

See also: Anti Federalists; Aaron Burr; DeWitt Clinton; Elections of 1792 and 1796; Federalist Party; First Bank of the United States; Thomas Jefferson; James Madison

Thomas A. Mason

REFERENCES

Hastings, Hugh, and J. A. Holden, eds. 1899–1914. *Public Papers of George Clinton, First Governor of New York, 1777–1795, 1801–1804.* 10 vols. New York: State of New York.

Kaminski, John P. 1990. *George Clinton: Yeoman Politician of the New Republic.* Madison, WI: Madison House.

Closed Primary

A closed primary is a primary election that limits participation in a party's nominating election to those voters who are enrolled in or pledged to that particular political party. The purposes of the closed primary are to close the nomination process to nonparty members and to prevent nonparty members from participating in a primary with the intent of upending the opposition's normal political balance.

Voters demonstrate their allegiance to the party either at the time of registration or at the primary election. Most of the 38 closed primary states rely on prior registration, so that voters are enrolled in the party of their choice when they register to vote. In some closed primary states, voters declare their party preference at the time of the primary, subject to challenge by party poll observers. Challenged voters may then be required to take a party loyalty oath or otherwise affirm loyalty based on past allegiance, present affiliation, or future intention. In practice, the statement of affiliation is rarely challenged and difficult to verify.

Party leaders often prefer a closed system, as it invokes cloture on the electorate and allows for the creation and maintenance of lists of enrolled voters—rosters that can be used by party leaders and candidates for establishing direct contact with sympathetic voters. Closed primary states that rely on voter statements of loyalty, or states that allow voters to change their party enrollment just before or at the primary election (Iowa and Wyoming, for example, allow voters to change enrollment on primary day), are often thought to be similar to open primary states.

See also: Open Primary, Party Identification

Robert J. Spitzer

REFERENCES

Bibby, John F. 1987. *Politics, Parties, and Elections in America.* Chicago: Nelson-Hall.

Coalition for a Democratic Majority

The Coalition for a Democratic Majority (CDM) was organized in 1972 as an antireform group of prominent moderate to conservative Democrats, many of whom supported the presidential aspirations of Senator Henry M. Jackson. Ben J. Wattenberg, Jackson's 1972 campaign manager, was the founder of CDM. Congressman James O'Hara (Mich.), Rules Commission chairman in the Democratic Party, presented a draft charter to the 1972 convention and co-chaired the CDM. In its first mail solicitation for funds, the CDM sought to return the party to the New Deal–Fair Deal alliance of labor, ethnic groups, the elderly, and small farmers, arguing in a 1973 *Washington Post* manifesto that George McGovern's defeat was a repudiation of Democratic Party reforms. Not surprisingly, the CDM was initially supported by the AFL-CIO, which opposed McGovern and felt slighted by the affirmative action guidelines; support as well came from regulars whose control of the party had been constrained by the procedural reforms.

The CDM sought representation on both the Mikulski and the Sanford commissions charged with implementing reforms in the operating procedures of the party. The key reforms attacked by the group were the mandatory quotas for women, blacks, and youths—deemed "arbitrary biological categories." The CDM has been very successful in achieving its aims: the Mikulski Commission banned quotas, and later, reform commissions have provided for *ex officio* delegate status for public and party officials (the "superdelegates"). The major defeat was the exemption of the equal division for women in the party chamber and the extension of the fifty-fifty gender rule to convention delegates.

The coalition developed a systematic critique of the McGovern-Fraser reforms, and more recently, it has produced position papers on national security and the proposed texts for Democratic Party platforms. It is better known, however, through the writings of its more prominent members. Wattenberg, in a widely read book, *The Real Majority*, co-authored with Richard Scammon in 1970, argued that the Democrats should focus on the "unyoung, unpoor, and unblack." Political scientist Austin Ranney, who had served on the McGovern-Fraser Commission, soon became a prominent CDM spokesman in the popular media. Credited by Theodore White (1972) as responsible for the onerous McGovern-Fraser quotas, Ranney argued in *Curing the Mischiefs of Faction* (1975) that reform has had deleterious, unanticipated consequences. Jeane Kirkpatrick, who served on the first Winograd Commission wrote two trenchant scholarly critiques of reform: *The New Presidential Elite* (1976) presents evidence that the 1972 Democratic delegates were unrepresentative of the electorate, while *Dismantling the Parties* (1979) argues that reform rules had led to the decline of parties and the rise of a "new class" of ideological-issue activists whose class interests are advanced to the detriment of traditional Democrats.

See also: AFL-CIO COPE, Fifty-Fifty Rule, Jeane Kirkpatrick, McGovern-Fraser Commission, New Deal Coalition, Sanford Commission, Superdelegates

Denise L. Baer

REFERENCES

Baer, Denise L., and David A. Bositis. 1988. *Elite Cadres and Party Coalition: Representing the Public in Party Politics.* Westport, CT: Greenwood.

Crotty, William J. 1978. *Decision for the Democrats.* Baltimore: Johns Hopkins U. Pr.

———. 1983. *Party Reform.* New York: Longman.

Kirkpatrick, Jeane J. 1976. *The New Presidential Elite.* New York: Russell Sage.

———. 1979. *Dismantling the Parties: Reflections on Party Reform and Decomposition.* Washington: American Enterprise Institute.

Ranney, Austin. 1975. *Curing the Mischiefs of Faction.* Berkeley: U. of California Pr.

Scammon, Richard M., and Ben J. Wattenberg. 1970. *The Real Majority.* New York: Coward, McCann, and Geoghegan.

Coattails

Presidential coattails are part of the lore of American politics. Politicians project them, journalists attribute them, historians recount them, and political scientists analyze them. Yet we really know little about coattails. Most significantly, we have a limited understanding of how they affect the outcomes of congressional elections.

Coattail votes occur when voters cast their ballots for congressional candidates of the President's party because they support the President. Most recent studies show a diminishing connection between presidential and congressional voting. One indicator is the great increase in split-ticket voting. Nevertheless, the percentage of the congressional vote attributable to the President's coattails is not insignificant.

A coattail victory is one for a candidate of the President's party in which presidential coattail votes provide the increment of the necessary to win a seat. If coattail votes determine which candidate wins a seat, then they will be more significant than if they only raise a winner's percentage by a few points.

If a large number of seats are determined by presidential coattails, the implications for public policy can be substantial. New members of Congress, who might be brought in on a President's coattails, are primary agents of policy change, because incumbents tend not to alter the voting patterns that they have established in previous years. Whether they bring in new members or preserve the seats of incumbents, coattail victories are important because representatives of the President's party generally support the administration's programs more loyally than do opposition party members. Moreover, these members of the President's party who win close elections may provide him an extra increment of support out of a sense of gratitude for the votes they perceive they receive as a result of the President's coattails, and members of both parties may be interested in responding tangible indicators of public support for the President.

The effects of coattails on individual voters do not translate into aggregate election results in any straightforward manner. To have influence on congressional elections, presidential coattails have to be quite strong (i.e., a large number of coattail votes must occur in any one constituency). However, most congressional seats are safe for one party because of the balance of party identifiers in the constituency and the power of incumbency. The only way a President's coattail vote can influence election outcomes in these instances is usually for a large number of affiliates of the other party to vote for both the President and a nonincumbent candidate of the President's party, based on their support for the President. This number must be large enough to win the seat from the dominant party.

A President's coattails may also save a seat for a representative of his party who previously won an election in a constituency in which the other party was dominant in terms of party identifiers. Finally, presidential coattails may make a difference in a highly competitive race in a constituency with a close balance between the parties. Since these conditions do not occur very often, we can point to relatively few presidential coattail victories. Presidents, therefore, cannot expect their coattails to carry many like-minded running mates into office to provide additional support for their programs.

See also: Party Identification, Split-Ticket Voting

George C. Edwards III

REFERENCES

Edwards, George C., III. 1980. *Presidential Influence in Congress.* San Francisco: W. H. Freeman.

——. 1983. *The Public Presidency.* New York: St. Martin's.

Howell Cobb (1815–1868)

Antebellum Democratic Speaker of the U.S. House of Representatives. A Unionist, Howell Cobb helped pass the Compromise of 1850. In 1857 he became James Buchanan's Secretary of the Treasury (pro-Compromise until Abraham Lincoln's election made him a secessionist) and then became a Confederate politician and military leader.

A Georgia lawyer, Cobb served in the House from 1843 to 1851 and from 1855 to 1857, and then as governor from 1851 to 1853. Fifty-nine ballots were necessary to elect Cobb as Speaker in 1849, because northern Democrats would not support a southerner; an agreement to require a plurality for victory put him over.

Cobb at first tried to ease sectional tensions by backing the Compromise of 1850, and he fought secessionist "fire-eaters" at the Nashville convention. After beating secessionist Democrats for governor of Georgia as a Constitutional Unionist in 1851, Cobb rejoined the Democratic Party in 1853 when he failed reelection. Cobb campaigned in 1856 for James Buchanan, who named him Secretary of the Treasury. He helped Buchanan battle Stephen Douglas after their fight over the admission of Kansas as a slave state and briefly ran for President in 1860. Pro-Compromise until Lincoln won the presidency, Cobb resigned and urged secession. He chaired the convention that organized the Confederacy. Although he had support for President of the Confederacy, Cobb professed disinterest and backed Jefferson Davis; he instead became Speaker of the Provisional Congress. Cobb was made angry at the selection of Georgia foe Alexander Stephens as Vice President of the Confederate States of America.

Cobb served in the Confederate military, rising to major general. Head of the Georgia and Florida District, he first proposed establishing the prison camp at Andersonville, Georgia, and opposed arming slaves. During Reconstruction, Cobb practiced law and opposed the Radical Republicans.

See also: James Buchanan, Constitutional Union Party, Jefferson Davis, Stephen Douglas, Election of 1860, Abraham Lincoln, Radical Republicans, Reconstruction, Secession, Speaker of the House

Michael Green

REFERENCES

Johnson, Michael P. 1977. *Toward a Patriarchal Republic: The Secession of Georgia.* Baton Rouge: Louisiana State U. Pr.

Johnson, Zachary. 1929. *Political Policies of Howell Cobb.* Nashville, TN: Vanderbilt U. Pr.

Montgomery, Horace. 1959. *Howell Cobb's Confederate Career.* Tuscaloosa: U. of Alabama Pr.

Phillips, Ulrich B., ed. 1913. *The Correspondence of Robert Toombs, Alexander H. Stephens, and Howell Cobb.* 2 vols. Washington: American Historical Association.

Simpson, John E. 1973. *Howell Cobb: The Politics of Ambition.* Chicago: Adams Press.

Tony Coelho (1942–)

Architect of a rejuvenated Democratic Congressional Campaign Committee in the 1980s. A Congressman from the Central Valley of California in the House of Representatives from 1979 to 1989, Tony Coelho rose rapidly in the ranks of the House Democratic leadership, only to be forced to resign from Congress on the heels of a series of financial scandals that also saw the downfall of Speaker Jim Wright in 1989.

Coelho began his political career working as a staff assistant to Congressman B. F. Sisk (D-Calif.). When Sisk retired from the House, Coelho ran for the seat in the 1978 election, winning the general election with 60 percent of the vote. Like most House members of this era, his hold on this congressional seat only strengthened with tenure, and Coelho never received less than 64 percent of the vote in subsequent elections.

Coelho was elected to chair the Democratic Congressional Campaign Committee (DCCC) following the 1980 election. At the time, the Democratic Party was reeling from a series of dramatic defeats in 1980: the loss of the presidency, loss of control of the Senate for the first time in 26 years, and the loss of 35 House seats. The Republican Party was widely acknowledged to have a great advantage over the Democrats in both fundraising and grass-roots organizing. Coelho's task as DCCC chair was to revitalize the Democratic campaign effort, moving it from a moribund effort to a state-of-the-art operation.

Tony Coelho has been credited more than any other elected politician with expanding the Democrats' ability to raise money, especially among political action committees (PACs), and to plan congressional campaign strategy. His fundraising prowess became legendary, but critics began audibly to wonder whether the improvement in House Democratic fundraising chances owed to Coelho's special skills or to increased prospects for the Democratic Party compared to an abysmal recent past. For instance, during Coelho's tenure as chair, DCCC revenues rose 500 percent (from $2.08 million to $12.47 million), compared to a drop of 35 percent for the Republican National Congressional Committee (from $53.3 million to $34.5 million); yet the Democratic Senatorial Campaign Committee's (DSCC) revenues increased by an even more staggering 888 percent during the same period while the revenue of the National Republican Senatorial Committee (NRSC) increased 58 percent. PAC contributions, in which Coelho was reputed to be especially gifted, reveal similar trends; PAC contributions to the DCCC rose a total of 1,500 percent (from $167,000 to $2.79 million), but this total paled in comparison to the DSCC's increase of 2,600 percent and even the NRSC's total 2,000 percent improvement.

Regardless of Coelho's independent contribution to the Democrats' better fundraising fortunes during the 1980s, his election to the post of House Majority Whip following the 1986 general election was widely attributed to services he had performed on behalf of House Democratic candidates. Coelho was the first Democratic whip to be elected by his peers; all previous whips had been appointed by the Majority Leader and the Speaker. Coelho's margin in the Democratic Caucus was indicative of the support he had attracted over the years as DCCC chair: Coelho received 167 votes, compared to 78 for Charles B. Rangel (N.Y.) and 15 for W. G. Hefner (N.C.).

Although Coelho had not been previously known as a particularly skilled legislative operative, his tenure as Majority Whip helped to vitalize the Democratic side of the House aisle. Coelho's ambition and tactical sense brought reports that he might try to challenge Majority Leader Thomas Foley or even Speaker Jim Wright for leadership positions, but nothing ever came of these rumors.

Coelho's rapid rise to the top of the Democratic Party in the House came to an abrupt halt in 1989 when he was charged with ethical violations stemming from a "junk bond" deal he had negotiated with a savings and loan executive in California. Coupled with the concurrent ethical troubles faced by Speaker Wright, Coelho announced his resignation from the House in the late spring of 1989.

See also: Democratic Congressional Campaign Committee, Thomas Foley, Majority Party Leadership in Congress, Political Action Committees, Jim Wright

Charles Stewart III

David Cohen (1936–)

President of Common Cause. David Cohen, born in Philadelphia, was best known as the president of Common Cause (1975–1981) but is still widely regarded in the Washington community as his generation's leading public interest congressional lobbyist and mentor of lobbyists. Of modest origins and educated at Temple University (B.A., 1957), after a brief fling at law school he became an employee of an upholsterers union in Philadelphia. In 1958 he married Carla Furstenberg, a city planner and bookstore owner of the prominent liberal and philanthropic Baltimore Hollander clan, and moved to Washington in 1963 where he became legislative representative for Americans for Democratic Action. Very soon he established a reputation for balanced judgment, scrupulous dealing, unrelenting patience, and a gift for forming legislative coalitions, thus greatly multiplying the influence of his small liberal organization. He followed labor leader Jack Conway into the industrial union department of the AFL-CIO in 1967 and 1968 and then into the Center for Community Change from 1968 to 1971. He joined Common Cause in 1971 and since 1985 has been co-director with Michael Pertschuk of the Advocacy Institute, a training organization for lobbyists, predominantly liberal, for not-for-profit causes.

In his 1986 book, *Giant Killers*, Pertschuk refers to Cohen as the dean of Washington's public interest lobbyists. Cohen's concerns have always run far beyond any particular legislative campaign that has engaged his formidable strategic skills. His dedication to liberal causes is founded on desires to build large communities of interest and to improve the effectiveness of democratic institutions. He never, in consequence, cuts corners in legislative combat, genuinely respecting and winning respect from those who disagree with him. He seeks to find just balances of interest in society. Thus, Cohen is a highly credible fighter no matter how unfashionable his cause. His causes have been popular for the most part within the liberal mainstream, but his reputation for probity and statesmanship extends far beyond his liberal constituency.

See also: Common Cause, John Gardner, Fred Wertheimer

Nelson W. Polsby

REFERENCES

McFarland, Andrew S. 1984. *Common Cause: Lobbying in the Public Interest*. Chatham, NJ: Chatham House.
Pertschuk, Michael. 1986. *Giant Killers*. New York: Norton.

Colegrove v. Green
328 U.S. 549 (1946)

This Supreme Court decision let stand a Federal District Court dismissal of a suit challenging an Illinois law that established the boundaries for congressional districts. The suit contended that because of shifts in population over time in the state, congressional districts in Illinois lacked "compactness of territory and approximate equality of population" and that the state should be enjoined from using the extant congressional districts for the upcoming election. Although a majority of the Court could not agree about why the Federal District Court should be sustained, the decision nevertheless had an important political impact because it was generally interpreted for the next decade and a half as permitting malapportionment of electoral districts.

In announcing the decision of the Court, Justice Felix Frankfurter asserted that "Courts ought not to enter [the] political thicket [of congressional redistricting] because due regard for the effective working of government revealed this issue to be of a peculiarly political nature and therefore not meat for judicial determination." The judgment of the Court in this case was that congressional malapportionment constitutes a "political question" (i.e., a doctrine used by the Court at times to avoid deciding constitutional issues by claiming that the issues need to be resolved instead by the legislative or executive branches). By stating that the case was not justiciable, the Court took the position that the state's establishment of congressional district lines was not an issue subject to adjudication by the federal courts. Because of the Court's decision not be involved, state legislatures were thought to be absolved from the responsibility to reform malapportionment plans for congressional and state legislative districts. As a consequence of this position, for many years, electoral districts in many states remained grossly malapportioned, and rural interests were often favored over urban and suburban interests.

Baker v. Carr, 369 U.S. 186 (1962), represents a reversal of the Court's position in *Colegrove v. Green* on the issue of the justiciability of state apportionment plans. In *Baker* the Court decided that it could consider suits challenging the constitutionality of malapportioned districts since such plans might violate the equal protection clause of the Fourteenth Amendment. Later, in *Wesberry v. Sanders*, 376 U.S. 1 (1964), the Court would also cite Article I, section 2, of the Constitution as grounds for reviewing congressional apportionment. As a consequence of subsequent Court rulings, inequalities in the population of various federal and state electoral districts have been substantially reduced.

See also: Baker v. Carr, Legislative Districting, *Wesberry v. Sanders*

Clyde Brown

REFERENCES

Hacker, Andrew. 1963. *Congressional Districting: The Issue of Equal Representation*. Washington: Brookings.
McKay, Robert B. 1965. *Reapportionment: The Law and Politics of Equal Representation*. New York: Clarion.

Schuyler Colfax (1823–1885)

U. S. Grant's Vice President. Schuyler Colfax, Vice President of the United States during Ulysses S. Grant's first term (1869–1873), was inextricably linked with the Credit Mobilier affair that came to light in 1872, even though his involvement in it was minimal or (some say) nonexistent. Neither was the possible taint of this railroad scandal responsible for Colfax's failure to be renominated, for its exposure came following the Republican convention of 1872. Colfax was welcomed back home to South Bend, Indiana, as a celebrity, and for the remaining 12 years of his life he was a highly successful public speaker, lecturing throughout the country on either the Great West or the life and death (which Colfax had witnessed) of Abraham Lincoln. Colfax died in Minnesota on the way to a speaking engagement.

Colfax was born in New York City but moved with his mother and stepfather to Indiana in 1836. There he graduated from farm work to a career in journalism and politics, appointed by his stepfather to a minor political office even before he was old enough to vote. As a reporter for and then as an editor of Indiana newspapers, Colfax was a staunch Whig and often covered legislative sessions in Indianapolis himself. In the mid-1850s, when the Whig Party disintegrated over slavery, Colfax flirted with the Know-Nothing Party and then joined the Republicans. A loyal party man, he entered Congress in 1855 and remained in Washington for 18 years. His affability (he was known as "Smiler" Colfax) and party regularity made him the Speaker of the House of Representatives for 6 years during much of the Civil War.

See also: Credit Mobilier, Ulysses S. Grant, Know-Nothings, Abraham Lincoln, Speaker of the House

Ralph D. Gray

REFERENCES

Furlong, Patrick J., and Gerald E. Hartdagen. 1977. "Schuyler Colfax: A Reputation Tarnished." In Ralph D. Gray, ed. *Gentlemen from Indiana: National Party Candidates, 1836–1940.* Indianapolis: Indiana Historical Bureau.

Kleppner, Paul D. 1970. *The Cross of Culture: A Social Analysis of Midwestern Politics, 1850–1900.* New York: Free Press.

Smith, Willard H. 1952. *Schuyler Colfax: The Changing Fortunes of a Political Idol.* Indianapolis: Indiana Historical Bureau.

Colonial Electoral Competition

Popular elections were used primarily to select members for the lower houses of assembly in each of the British North American colonies, although the governor and upper house were chosen by this method in two colonies and some local offices were filled by an election. The diverse political cultures of the colonies and the local socioeconomic structure combined to determine the level of competitive electoral activity in each colony at various times and even within the local electoral districts of a single colony. Assessing such competition involves understanding the length of the campaign, the frequency of campaign gatherings, and the presence of certain types of campaign literature. Limited statistical evidence from the period on the number of candidates running, voter turnout, and defeat of incumbents provides the most precise data upon which to judge the competitive nature of colonial elections.

Electoral competition only existed in those colonial elections in which the voters had to make a choice between two or more candidates vying for the same office. Where there was no choice on election day, the voters were completely removed from the selection process and the election was uncontested. If the voters had a choice—no matter how similar in background and ideology the candidates appear to the modern observer—then there was competition and the election was contested. In eighteenth-century New York, Pennsylvania, Rhode Island, and Connecticut, colonywide factions dominated political activity, and it was not uncommon to find two opposing slates of candidates who had been nominated by caucuses or political clubs running against each other in elections. Eight of the Quaker Party opposed eight of the Proprietary Party in several Pennsylvania county contests while in colonywide races in Connecticut as early as the 1740s printed paper ballots were prepared with the names of each faction's nominees listed for the voters. In the southern colonies where provincial factions were less important, candidates for legislative seats tended to run as individuals or occasionally joined forces for one or two contests. Eight unconnected candidates once vied for two Virginia House of Burgesses seats from Halifax County in 1765, but, on average, just three candidates competed in the two-member constituencies of Virginia. Conversely, in many colonial American towns and counties, candidates regularly ran unopposed, sometimes as a result of the political power of a single landowner, often because the local gentry had decided on candidates in advance or occasionally because the elite and the commoners of a community were entirely satisfied with their present representation.

Where election totals for the period are known and the size of the adult male population estimated, voter turnout can be calculated and used to judge the competitive nature of elections. Turnout among adult males averaged from 10 percent to 25 percent in New England, between 20 percent and 40 percent in New York and Pennsylvania, and probably over 40 percent in Virginia. Where more precise estimates of the number of eligible voters can be made, both very high and very low rates as well as substantial variation have been noted. Turnout ran from 30 percent to 80 percent in different parts of Virginia; it may have been over 95 percent in one Massachusetts town in 1757; and in George Washington's home county in Virginia the turnout declined gradually from 75 percent to 50 percent over a 25-year period. Turnout at Rhode Island gubernatorial races also declined from about 45 percent to about 33 percent during the 1760s while rates fluctuated wildly in Philadelphia during the same period. Among contested colonial elections, voter turnout rates have been used to determine the intensity of electoral competition.

The extent to which incumbents were able to retain their legislative seats is another measure of the degree of competition in colonial elections. Incumbency was a powerful political asset in most colonies as, for example, in Connecticut where between 1730 and 1774 only 4 percent of the members of the upper house were defeated in bids for reelection. On the other hand, veteran politicians were thrown out of office with some regularity in some colonies. Limited data in Virginia suggest that over one-third of the incumbent legislators were routinely being defeated between 1725 and 1745. Yet in Virginia and elsewhere, the struggles with Britain beginning in the 1760s fostered a kind of "patriotic solidarity" that reduced incumbent losses to less than 10 percent.

Although observers have noted substantial variation within colonies and over time, electoral competition was probably highest in the middle colonies and the upper South, less so in New England, and lowest in the Deep South.

John G. Kolp

REFERENCES

Dinkin, Robert J. 1977. *Voting in Provincial America: A Study of Elections in the Thirteen Colonies, 1689–1776.* Westport, CT: Greenwood.

Kolp, John G. 1988. "The Flame of Burgessing: Elections and the Political Communities of Colonial Virginia, 1728–1775." Ph.D. dissertation, University of Iowa.

Tully, Alan. 1977. *William Penn's Legacy: Politics and Social Structure in Provincial Pennsylvania, 1726–1755.* Baltimore: Johns Hopkins U. Pr.

Colonial Franchise

Each of the British North American colonies established a popularly elected representative assembly within 20 years of the first settlement, and each eventually developed a fairly specific set of laws governing the selection of representatives to those assemblies. Although Britain imposed no uniform franchise upon her colonial possessions, similarities existed nonetheless: (1) colonial electoral laws were based upon English models but blended developments in the mother country with the particular circumstances of each province; (2) requirements for participation in elections were either nonexistent or loosely defined early in each colony's history and became more rigorously specified as small homogeneous settlements developed into large heterogeneous societies; and (3) there was general agreement that certain types of personal attributes defined membership in the electorate.

The evolution of the colonial franchise was based upon a growing awareness that only those with some kind of stake in society could be counted upon to act as responsible electors. During Virginia's first 30 years, for example, the terms "inhabitants" or "freemen" were apparently adequate to describe voters. By the 1650s, however, a more diverse population brought with it a requirement that a person had to be a "householder," while in 1670 it was thought necessary to restrict voting to "freeholders and householders" who paid public levies. Although the taxation qualification was lifted briefly during Bacon's Rebellion (1676), it was reinstated shortly thereafter and some kind of property-based requirement remained a part of Virginia law until the nineteenth century. Not until 1736 was the amount of property necessary for voting specified as either 100 acres of unimproved land or 25 acres improved with a house or a lot and house in town.

Most colonies developed similar requirements: New York and New England restricted voting according to the *value* of the land, while colonies to the south described the amount of land in acres. An estate worth £50 was required to vote in New Hampshire. Rhode Island, Massachusetts, Connecticut, and New York law harkened back to the original English county franchise requiring possession of lands that produced an income of at least 40 shillings per year. New Jersey laws talked only of "inhabitants, freeholders, and freemen" until 1701 when ownership of 100 acres was specified. North Carolina, Pennsylvania, Maryland, Delaware, and Georgia had a 50-acre minimum.

Although a "stake-in-society" concept based upon either wealth or land came to dominate voting requirements in the American colonies, such personal characteristics as sex, age, religion, and race were used to restrict the electorate further. A few wealthy widows may have voted in New England and New York, but in general, women were barred from most public activity, and colonies took it for granted that women were excluded from the voting process as well. Virginia was the only colony explicitly to forbid women from voting (1699), although three colonies restricted the franchise to males. Religious affiliation also limited the suffrage in most colonies. In the Massachusetts Bay Colony, voting was initially restricted to "freemen," and all freemen had to be members of the Puritan church. In predominantly Anglican colonies, adherents of all other religions were denied the vote in the seventeenth century. After the passage of the English Toleration Act (1689), most restrictions against Protestant sects were lifted, but in the early decades of the eighteenth century, more stringent limits were placed upon Roman Catholics. Jews were excluded from voting in about half of the colonies.

Age limitations, like those related to sex, were often taken for granted, as it was universally recognized that 21 years marked the beginning of adult responsibilities. A Virginia law of 1705, for example, simply denied the vote to those "under age." Puritan Massachusetts required for a time that nonchurch members be 24 years old to vote, but minors who had assumed adult roles were occasionally allowed to vote in a some colonies. Race further defined the electorate, although restrictions were generally a product of the eighteenth century, not the seventeenth century. Indians did vote in Massachusetts in the 1730s, free Blacks voted in Virginia and the Carolinas in the seventeenth century, and mulattoes probably voted in a number of colonies throughout the period. As the Black population grew and the fear of slave insurrections mounted in the eighteenth century, laws specifically excluding free Blacks and others began to appear on the books of the southern colonies.

The percentage of the white adult male population that was actually eligible to vote under these laws varied considerably by colony and has been the subject of considerable debate among historians. Recent tabulations suggest that only 25 percent of the adult males could vote in rural New York, less than 50 percent in Maryland, about 50 percent throughout Pennsylvania and in the Connecticut seaports, 70 percent in New York City and Rhode Island, and 75 percent or higher in many of Virginia's counties.

John G. Kolp

REFERENCES

Dinkin, Robert J. 1977. *Voting in Provincial America: A Study of Elections in the Thirteen Colonies, 1689–1776.* Westport, CT: Greenwood.

Kammen, Michael. 1969. *Deputyes & Libertyes: The Origins of Representative Government in Colonial America.* New York: Knopf.

Kolp, John G. 1988. "The Flame of Burgessing: Elections and the Political Communities of Colonial Virginia, 1728–1775." Ph.D. dissertation, University of Iowa.

Williamson, Chilton. 1960. *American Suffrage from Property to Democracy, 1760–1860.* Princeton: Princeton U. Pr.

Colored Farmers' National Alliance and Co-operative Union

Founded in Houston County, Texas, in 1886, the Colored Alliance spread through the South and reached its peak in 1891. At a time when most African-Americans lived in the rural South, the Alliance attempted to help its members improve their status in a variety of ways: through cooperatives and exchanges, it sold goods at reduced prices; it solicited funds to help sick and disabled members; and it called for improved public schools and more effective ways to disseminate knowledge of better farming techniques.

Although the Colored Alliance occasionally cooperated with the all-white Southern Alliance, the two organizations had sharp differences as they revealed in their stands on the Lodge Election Bill (1890), a measure designed to provide federal protection for voting rights. The Colored Alliance supported it, but the Southern Alliance condemned it. The Southern Farmers' Alliance also opposed the Colored Alliance's 1891 call for a cotton pickers strike. With a membership consisting of many landless people, the Colored Alliance tried to assist them by demanding higher wages for cotton pickers. The failure of that strike to materialize, combined with the collapse of the cooperative ventures by 1891, contributed to the Colored Alliance's rapid demise. The experiences generated by the Colored Alliance prepared some of its members to support the People's Party in the 1890s.

See also: Agrarianism as a Political Force, Lodge Force Bill, People's Party, Populism as a Movement and Party, Race and Racial Politics

William F. Holmes

REFERENCES

Gaither, Gerald. 1977. *Blacks and the Populist Revolt: Ballots and Bigotry in the "New South."* University: U. of Alabama Pr.

Holmes, William. 1975. "The Demise of the Colored Farmers' Alliance." 41 *Journal of Southern History* 187.

Miller, Floyd J. 1972. "Black Protest and White Leadership: A Note on the Colored Farmers' Alliance." 33 *Phylon* 169.

Committee to Reelect the President

The Federal Election Campaign Act of 1971 required that all subsequent presidential campaigns identify one central committee as the repository of campaign funds so that the reporting and disclosure provisions of that act could be effective. The Committee to Reelect the President, headed by former Attorney General John Mitchell, was the committee so designated for President Richard Nixon's 1972 bid to retain the White House.

The Committee to Reelect the President, which came to be known by the uncomplimentary acronym CREEP, would barely rate a footnote in history were it not for the June 7, 1972, break-in at the headquarters of the Democratic National Committee in the Watergate office complex. One of those arrested shortly after the bungled burglary was James W. McCord, Jr., the security coordinator for CREEP. The McCord connection to Nixon's reelection campaign, and subsequent leads to E. Howard Hunt at the White House, and G. Gordon Liddy, finance counsel to CREEP, raised suspicions that the Watergate break-in was more than a petty burglary. Subsequent investigations revealed that the Committee to Reelect the President had raised huge sums of money—approximately $20 million of it just before the new disclosure law went into effect, some of it in cash and much of the rest laundered through various accounts. This money was used for political "dirty tricks." Nearly $500,000, in fact, was paid to the defendants in the Watergate burglary for support and their legal fees. Thus, CREEP came to be memorialized as the committee that funded the Watergate episode, leading to the only resignation of a President in American history.

See also: John Mitchell, Richard Nixon, Watergate

L. Sandy Maisel

REFERENCES

Bernstein, Carl, and Bob Woodward. 1974. *All the President's Men.* New York: Simon & Schuster.

Drew, Elizabeth. 1974. *Washington Journal: The Events of 1973–1974.* New York: Random House.

Ervin, Sam J., Jr. 1980. *The Whole Truth: The Watergate Conspiracy.* New York: Random House.

White, Theodore H. 1975. *Breach of Faith: The Fall of Richard Nixon.* New York: Atheneum.

Common Cause

Common Cause is a public-interest organization founded as a "people's lobby" in 1970 by John W. Gardner. From the outset Gardner conceived it as an activist organization rather than as an educational organization. Although Common Cause does engage in research and occasionally gets involved in litigation, its principal strategies of influence have been direct access to public officials and the mobilization of its membership in grass-roots lobbying. A national organization with state affiliates, Common Cause is active at both the national and state levels.

Although Common Cause is part of a strong tradition in American politics of middle-class reform, Gardner sought self-consciously to avoid the mistakes of the Progressives. In contrast to his Progressive forebears, Gardner did not wish his organization to be above politics, unwilling to engage in political bargaining, or inflexible in its choice of specific allies. Consonant with these principles, Common Cause has, by and large, eschewed schemes that ignore the necessity for politics in favor of "scientific administration" in the name of the public interest. Indeed, Gardner did not consider Common Cause to represent the public interest but rather as providing a countervailing force to balance the well-organized special interests.

Although Common Cause has taken positions on a number of domestic and foreign policy issues, it has concentrated most heavily on reform of the governmental process. A major supporter of Federal Election Campaign Amendments of 1974, Common Cause has had an ongoing concern with campaign finance reform. Its 1990 agenda includes support for the federal financing of congressional campaigns. Common Cause has also advocated such procedural reforms as sunshine laws that open up government meetings to the public, requirements for financial disclosure by public officials, and, often without success, stronger lobbying disclosure legislation. The focus on procedural reform is reflected even in some of the non-governmental issues on which Common Cause has taken stands, especially when the power of the special interests is thought to be at stake (such as with respect to the oil depletion allowance and subsidies to milk and sugar producers).

In the 1980s, the membership of Common Cause has remained somewhere between 200,000 and 250,000. Typical of such organizations, its membership is heavily weighted toward the upper middle class and the very well educated. Appropriate to its goals, the membership leans strongly in a liberal—although not a uniformly Democratic—direction. Indeed, Gardner was himself a liberal Republican. Like all organizations that represent broad publics, Common Cause makes continuing efforts to find new members. Although Common Cause has experimented with various methods of recruitment, it relies most heavily on direct mail, which is responsible for over 70 percent of new memberships.

Consistent with the principles it champions, Common Cause subsists on small contributions: 90 percent of its income is derived from donations (including dues) under $100. Because it is not a tax-exempt organization and does not coexist with a separate tax-exempt educational arm as do many similar organizations, it does not look to foundations for support. Common Cause also has rules of limiting the size of contributions it will accept from unions or corporations, though it is unlikely that many sizable donations from these sources would be forthcoming.

Sensitive to the frequently made charge that mass-membership checkbook organizations are themselves oligarchical, Common Cause has instituted democratic procedures that are unusual for an organization of its kind: board members are elected by the rank and file in open elections, and rank-and-file members are polled regularly for their responses to proposed new additions to the Common Cause agenda. Whether adherence to such procedural niceties guarantees membership control over the leadership and staff of Common Cause is not clear; Common Cause is clearly not a participatory democracy. Still, the threat of massive exit by members is probably the most powerful force ensuring the responsiveness of Common Cause leaders.

See also: Campaign Finance and the Constitution, David Cohen, Direct Mail, Federal Election Campaign Act of 1971 and Amendments, John Gardner, Fred Wertheimer

Kay Lehman Schlozman

REFERENCES

Berry, Jeffrey M. 1977. *Lobbying for the People.* Princeton: Princeton U. Pr.

———. 1984. *The Interest Group Society.* Boston: Little, Brown.

McFarland, Andrew S. 1984. *Common Cause.* Chatham, NJ: Chatham House.

Schlozman, Kay Lehman, and John T. Tierney. 1986. *Organized Interests and American Democracy.* New York: Harper & Row.

Barry Commoner (1917–)

Environmental activist. Barry Commoner, one of the pioneers of the modern environmental movement, ran for President on the Citizens Party ticket in 1980. Born in Brooklyn, New York, Commoner received his B.A. from Columbia and his graduate degrees from Harvard. He then embarked on a career as a botanist, spending the bulk of his career at Washington University (St. Louis). In 1989 he was professor at the Center for Biology of Natural Systems, Queens College (New York).

In the mid-1960s, Commoner began writing and lecturing extensively on environmental issues and is widely known for three of his books: *Science and Survival* (1966), *The Closing Circle* (1971), *The Politics of Energy* (1979). He also served as an advisor to numerous governmental agencies, scientific organizations, and environmental groups.

During the 1960s and 1970s, Commoner became increasingly convinced that as a scientist he had to be politically involved. He therefore participated actively in a number of organizations committed to ending the war in Vietnam and was one of most effective and vocal advocates of the new environmental protection movement that emerged toward the end of the 1960s.

In 1980 Commoner was one of the founders of the Citizens Party and ran as its candidate for President that fall. The party was known primarily for its strong stands on ecological issues but also advocated sharp increases in spending for social services and a 30 to 50 percent decrease in military expenditures. Commoner and his running mate, La Donna Harris, won over 200,000 votes.

Commoner remains active in a variety of organizations that are trying to increase awareness and change American public policy about the environment.

See also: Third Parties in American Elections, Vietnam War as a Political Issue

Charles S. Hauss

Communism as a Political Issue

Although Americans welcomed the overthrow of the Russian czar in 1917, the November Bolshevik coup was a different matter. The Bolsheviks' withdrawal of Russia from the war freed German divisions to face American soldiers just joining the fighting in France. Further, American radicals who welcomed the Bolshevik revolution were vocal opponents of American participation in the war and already the object of patriotic scorn.

Many Americans blamed communism for the chaos that followed World War I when the Communist International promoted world revolution, Soviet armies advanced into Poland, and Bolshevik regimes came to power in Hungary and Bavaria. In America, the dislocations of the war's end and pent up demands led to widespread labor unrest in 1919, including a nationwide steel strike, the Seattle general strike, and the Boston police strike. Radical terrorists nearly assassinated Seattle's mayor as well as U.S. Attorney General A. Mitchell Palmer, set off bombs in 8 cities on one day in 1919, and in 1920 killed 33 persons on a New York street. For a brief time radicals hoped (and their opponents feared) that Communist revolution might sweep the world, America included.

In response, thousands of radical aliens were rounded up in the "Palmer raids" and deported. Additional thousands of citizen radicals were arrested but released shortly; several hundred, however, were imprisoned under federal or state sedition laws. Attorney General A. Mitchell Palmer made his leadership of the anti-Red campaign the center of his campaign for the Democratic Party's presidential nomination in 1920. Political concern with the radical menace encouraged many states to enact new sedition or criminal syndicalism laws. With the eventual recession of the Bolshevik tide in Europe in the early 1920s, concern with the Red menace subsided.

During the 1930s, the Communist Party of the United States of America (CPUSA) benefited from the leftward shift of politics and, in its popular front stance, downplayed revolutionary Marxism–Leninism to seek a role in the left wing of Franklin Roosevelt's New Deal. By the late 1930s, CPUSA had won a significant role in labor's Committee for Industrial Organization (CIO), acceptance in literary and artistic circles, and a toehold in mainstream politics in a few states. This limited but real growth of American communism did not go unnoticed or unprotested. Twice in the early 1930s the U.S. House of Representatives launched special investigations of communism and in 1938 established the Committee on Un-American Activities that would remain active in investigating communism until 1975. Some conservative critics of the New Deal maintained that President Roosevelt's policies were communistic or that FDR's administration was infiltrated by Communists. The role of Communists in unions and in public agencies became a political issue in several states in the late 1930s, particularly California, Washington, and Minnesota.

President Roosevelt repudiated CPUSA support but regarded communism as of little public interest; he treated conservative charges about Communists in the New Deal as just another political calumny. After the Nazi–Soviet Pact and the beginning of World War II, Communists became vocal opponents of Roosevelt's policies of assisting nations fighting the Nazis, opposed Roosevelt's reelection in 1940, and urged noncooperation with his rearmament program. FDR then dropped his indifference and authorized federal actions against Communist activity. The government, for example, imprisoned Earl Browder, CPUSA's general secretary, for use of a false passport. Encouraged by federal action, a dozen states also undertook prosecution of Communists. In 1940 Roosevelt signed the Smith Act, making illegal the advocacy of overthrowing the government. The first Smith Act prosecutions were directed at Trotskyists of the Socialist Workers Party.

After the Nazi attack on the USSR, CPUSA supported Roosevelt's policy of aid to anti-Nazi belligerents. After America entered the war and the USSR became an ally, CPUSA urged cooperation with the war effort and renewed its popular front stance. Communist support of the war and American admiration for the Red Army's fight against the Nazis reduced public hostility, and CPUSA regained the limited acceptance it had achieved in the late 1930s. FDR, in a gesture welcoming the visit of Soviet foreign minister Vyacheslav Molotov, freed Earl Browder from prison. Even so, many conservatives remained hostile, and Congress forced the discharge of some government employees linked to CPUSA. In 1944 Republican presidential candidate Thomas Dewey occasionally made an issue of Communist support for FDR.

After World War II, Soviet suzerainty in Eastern Europe and its support for aggressive Communist movements in Greece, Italy, and France alarmed Americans. CPUSA adopted a more aggressive stance, supporting Henry Wallace's attempt to defeat President Harry Truman and establish a new Progressive Party supporting an American foreign policy compatible with Soviet goals. Growing Cold War tensions along with dramatic espionage cases linking American Communists with Soviet spying dissipated the public's wartime tolerance for the Soviet Union and its friends.

In 1947 President Truman ordered the creation of a loyalty program to eliminate Communists from government employment. In 1948 the government began to deport alien Communist leaders and indicted CPUSA leaders under the Smith Act. In 1947 Congress enacted a law denying labor law coverage to unions with Communist officials. A 1950 internal security law required organizations deemed subversive to provide membership lists to the government and authorized mass arrest of subversives in time of war.

Among liberals and labor unionists an ideological civil war developed between popular front liberals (organized as the Progressive Citizens of America) who backed Henry Wallace and did not object to cooperation with CPUSA and anti-Communist liberals (organized as the Americans for Democratic Action) who supported Truman's cold war policies and opposed CPUSA. The 1948 election of Truman and the defeat of Wallace signaled the triumph of anti-Communist liberalism. During 1949 and 1950, the CIO replaced or expelled union officials and unions associated with CPUSA. By 1950 an anti-Communist consensus dominated the Democratic Party and the unions of the American Federation of Labor (AFL), and the Congress of Industrial Organizations (CIO). Nonetheless, the defeat of popular pront liberals in 1948 and Truman's leadership in the Cold War did not prevent communism from becoming a partisan issue.

Republicans called Democrats to account for the late 1930s and 1940s when the popular pront had been part of the New Deal coalition in some states. Further, more partisan Republicans vehemently insisted that nothing had changed. The latter charged that Communists and their friends were still a hidden influence in the Democratic Party. Senator Joseph McCarthy became the most prominent of those who denounced the New Deal's heroes as front men or worse for a Communist conspiracy.

Throughout the 1950s, congressional investigations of domestic communism demonstrated the political salience of the issue and kept the subject before the public. CPUSA, already in retreat, nearly disintegrated in 1956 and 1957 from the twin blows of Khrushchev's confirmation of Stalin's crimes and the Hungarian revolution. CPUSA's weakness and the lessening of Cold War tensions in the late 1950s reduced political interest in domestic communism. In the late 1960s, opponents of American involvement in the Vietnam War blamed the war in part on excessive anti-communism. In the 1970s anti-Communist liberalism ceased to dominate the Democratic Party although anti-communism remained a prominent part of Republican doctrine.

See also: AFL-CIO COPE, Americans for Democratic Action, John W. Bricker, Earl Broder, Whittaker Chambers, Communist Party of the United States, Thomas Dewey, Helen Gahagan Douglas, John Foster Dulles, Gus Hall, Alger Hiss, House Un-American Activities Committee, Joseph McCarthy, McCarthyism, New Deal, Richard M. Nixon, A. Mitchell Palmer, Radicalism in American Politics, Red Scare, Socialist Workers Party, Vietnam War as a Political Issue, Henry A. Wallace

John E. Haynes

REFERENCES

Caute, David. 1978. *The Great Fear: The Anti-Communist Purge Under Truman and Eisenhower.* New York: Simon & Schuster.

Fried, Richard M. 1990. *Nightmare in Red: The McCarthy Era in Perspective.* New York: Oxford U. Pr.

Gillon, Steven M. 1973. *Politics and Vision: The ADA and American Liberalism, 1947–1985.* New York: Oxford U. Pr.

Hamby, Alonzo. 1987. *Beyond the New Deal: Harry S Truman and American Liberalism.* New York: Columbia U. Pr.

Harper, Alan D. 1969. *The Politics of Loyalty; The White House and the Communist Issue, 1946–1952.* Westport, CT: Greenwood.

Haynes, John Earl. 1986. "The New History of the Communist Party in State Politics: The Implications for Mainstream Political History." 27 *Labor History* 4.

——. 1987. *Communism and Anti-Communism in the United States: An Annotated Guide to Historical Writings.* New York: Garland.

Latham, Earl. 1966. *The Communist Controversy in Washington: From the New Deal to McCarthy.* Cambridge: Harvard U. Pr.

McAuliffe, Mary Sperling. 1978. *Crisis on the Left: Cold War Politics and American Liberals, 1947–1954.* Amherst: U. of Massachusetts Pr.

Murray, Robert K. 1955. *Red Scare: A Study in National Hysteria, 1919–1920.* New York: McGraw-Hill.

O'Neill, William L. 1982. *A Better World, The Great Schism: Stalinism and the American Intellectuals.* New York: Simon & Schuster.

Saposs, David. 1960. *Communism in American Politics.* Washington: Public Affairs Press.

Theoharis, Athan G. 1971. *Seeds of Repression: Harry S Truman and the Origins of McCarthyism.* Chicago: Quadrangle Books.

Communist Labor Party

The Communist Labor Party (CLP) was one of two parties (the other was the Communist Party of America, or CPA) founded in Chicago in 1919 by the left wing of the Socialist Party (SP). Both parties had either quit or been expelled by the SP leadership and ultimately combined to form the Communist Party of the United States of America (CPUSA).

Aided by widespread enthusiasm for the Bolshevik Revolution in Russia as well as by a wave of strikes involving 25 percent of the industrial working class in one year, the left wing of the SP appeared to have the support of a majority of members by the summer of 1919, but the right wing kept a solid grip on the party by bureaucratic manipulation. The left then divided over a purely tactical issue—whether to stage a fight at the SP convention in Chicago, or to simply announce the formation of a new party. The group that was to become the CPA consisted of the SP's Michigan branch, led by Dennis Batt, and seven foreign-language federations (Russian, Lithuanian, Polish, Lettish, Hungarian, Ukrainian, and South Slav), which the SP leadership had expelled in May; it was later joined by Charles Ruthenberg of the Ohio SP, who had first sided with the other group. This group wanted to launch a new communist party immediately and called a convention to do so (also in Chicago) on September 1, 1919. The future CLP, led by John Reed, Alfred Wagenknecht, Alexander Bittleman, and others, thought it important to go to the SP convention. While they expected to lose, they hoped to gain supporters among the SP rank and file.

Reed's delegation was barred from the SP convention at the door. After a fistfight, they withdrew to a nearby hall and held a convention of their own. Two left-wing Socialist conventions were now taking place in the same city at the same time, with 82 delegates at Reed's and 128 at the other. Several delegates attended both meetings alternately. Efforts to unify the two groups, particularly by Ruthenberg, failed; two competing parties were formed, both of which applied to join the Communist International.

The political stance of the CLP differed little from that of the CPA. Both believed the country to be in a revolutionary situation and condemned electoral politics (although the CLP did campaign for some of its Ohio members who had been nominated as SP candidates before the split). The real differences were organizational and cultural. The CPA's membership was largely foreign born, and it was made up of nearly autonomous language federations; the CLP was more centralized and most of its members had been born in America. The CPA was much larger; it started with some 50,000 members to CLP's 15,000. But most scholars have felt that the CLP was more in tune with American idiom.

Like the CPA, the CLP was hit hard by the wave of repression in 1919 and 1920, which later became known as the Red Scare. Many of its leaders were convicted and imprisoned on purely political grounds, and the party was forced to operate covertly—a mode in which it was ineffective.

Most of the CLP's attention during its brief existence was on the attempt to achieve Communist unity. The main obstacle was the attitude of the CPA's language federations, which insisted on a high measure of autonomy. The CPA itself split over this issue, with Ruthenberg's faction leaving to unite with the CLP in a new United Communist Party (UCP) in May 1920. Not until May 1921, under pressure from the Communist International, was unity between the UCP and the CPA achieved, with the federations brought firmly under central control. The CLP had few concrete achievements during its brief life but is remembered for such illustrious members as Reed and Benjamin Gitlow and for the unrealized hope of a less dogmatic communism that some saw in it.

See also: Communism Party of the United States, Radicalism in American Politics, Red Scare, Socialist Party of America, Socialist Workers Party

John C. Berg

REFERENCES

Foster, William Z. 1952. *History of the Communist Party of the United States.* New York: International Publishers.

Howe, Irving, and Lewis Coser. 1962. *The American Communist Party: A Critical History*. 2nd ed. New York: Praeger.

Communist Party of the United States of America

Since its founding in 1921 the Communist Party of the United States of America (CPUSA) has usually run candidates for President and, occasionally, for other offices. But these electoral efforts have been a relatively insignificant component of its influence on American politics, which has been much greater in the labor movement, the civil rights movement, mass protest, and, for a time, in intellectual activity. The party's size and influence declined drastically during the 1950s as it faced a massive government repression that drove it underground and sent many of its leaders to prison. The party was further disoriented by the outbreak of divisions in the international Communist movement. It eventually won the legal right to exist through court action but has not yet regained its strength of earlier decades.

The major controversy generated by the Communist Party has always been its relationship to the Soviet Union. The right has portrayed it as no more than a piece of a Soviet-controlled spy and sabotage apparatus, while the party itself has insisted that it is an expression of indigenous American radicalism. In fact, few if any serious historians believe that the party had any connection with espionage; its adhesion to the political line of the Soviet leadership was more a matter of its own leaders' convictions than of string pulling from Moscow. At the same time, the CPUSA has been less independent in its thinking than virtually any other member of the international Communist movement.

This dependence was evident in the party's founding. In America, as elsewhere, the Russian Revolution and Lenin's call for a party of a new type inspired a split in the old Socialist Party; but the U.S. saw the rise of, not one, but two new organizations, divided both by minor political differences and by ethnicity. The Communist Party of America was based on the foreign-language federations of the Socialist Party, while the Communist Labor Party was composed mainly of native-born Americans. Despite insistence of both sides that unity was needed, it took pressure from the Communist International—after some further splits and reunifications—to bring about the final merger into the Communist Party of the United States of America in 1921.

Driven largely underground by the Red Scare of 1920, the Communist Party concentrated with little success on organizing independent revolutionary labor unions during the 1920s. It ran its leader, William Z. Foster, for President in 1924, 1928, and 1932, achieving little impact on the Progressive or Farmer–Labor movements. It was only in the mid-1930s that it began to grow in numbers and influence, owing particularly to its role in the union organizing struggles of the Committee for Industrial Organization (CIO) of which it was one of the two major components (the other was United Mine Workers Union of John L. Lewis). Additional important activities included support for the Loyalists in the Spanish Civil War of 1936–1939, for which 3,000 volunteer soldiers were recruited in the United States; organizing unemployed councils; and agitation in the *Scottsboro* case, a national legal campaign to defend nine young Black men who had been framed on rape charges in 1931. The party grew rapidly during this period, with 75,000 members on its rolls by its tenth convention in 1938. As a rule, actual members of the party were dedicated activists, so that this number represented much more influence than would an equal number of registered Democrats or Republicans.

Party historian William Z. Foster described the party's position in the 1936 election as "one of objective, but not official support for Roosevelt." The party ran Earl Browder for President but did so in a campaign that stressed "the defeat of Landon at all costs."

Despite shock and confusion among its members when the party blindly followed the Soviet Communists in supporting the Hitler–Stalin Pact, it reached its high point in numbers and influence during World War II. The alliance of the USA and the USSR helped overcome public anti-communism, and Browder confidently proclaimed that "Communism is twentieth century Americanism." Seeking to enter the political mainstream, in May 1944 Browder formally dissolved the Communist Party, and reorganized it as the Communist Political Association (CPA). But this change lasted barely a year; following an attack on Browder's policy by French Communist leader Jacques Duclos, who was thought to represent the views of the Communist Party of the Soviet Union, Browder was suspended as CPA leader and later expelled;

the Communist Party of the United States of America was formally reestablished in July 1945.

The party's growth during the late 1930s and early 1940s had come not only from its grass-roots activity but also from its tacit alliance with the Roosevelt administration. The outbreak of the cold war changed everything. Despite the wave of postwar labor militancy and its involvement in Henry Wallace's third-party presidential campaign in 1948, the party staggered under the legal and political assaults made on it. Several of its leaders were convicted and sent to prison under the Smith Act, which made it a crime to advocate the overthrow of the United States Government. The Taft-Hartley Act banned Communists from holding office in labor unions, while Senator Joseph McCarthy (R-Wis.) and others popularized the idea that Communists were inherently disloyal to the United States. These attacks kept the party from growing; but its real decline came after Nikita Khrushchev denounced Stalin in a secret speech to the Twentieth Congress of the Communist Party of the Soviet Union in 1956. CPUSA members who had defended the party line loyally through all the changes over the years felt disillusioned and betrayed, and many left the party.

The party joined in the civil rights and anti-war movements of the 1950s, 1960s, and 1970s; but while it succeeded in recruiting a few prominent individuals—most notably Angela Davis—it never regained either the numbers or influence it had had in the earlier decades. The "new left" defined itself in part by its belief that the CPUSA had become irrelevant. The Communist Party today is generally believed to have somewhere between 6,000 and 12,000 members, but many are no longer active. Although it has failed to grow, it maintains some level of activity in the labor unions, the civil rights movement, and the movements for disarmament and against intervention in the Third World.

Electorally, the party either abstained or joined in coalition campaigns in every presidential election from 1940 to 1968. It has placed the name of its leader, Gus Hall, on the presidential ballot every four years since 1972 but has failed to generate any excitement around his campaigns, even among party members. In 1972 Hall was said to have accused some members of the party's national committee of having voted for George McGovern rather than for him.

See also: Earl Browder, Communist Labor Party, Election of 1936, Gus Hall, Red Scare, Socialist Party of America, Henry Wallace

John C. Berg

REFERENCES

Dyson, Lowell K. 1982. *Red Harvest: The Communist Party and American Farmers.* Lincoln: U. of Nebraska Pr.

Foster, William Z. 1952. *History of the Communist Party of the United States.* New York: International Publishers.

Howe, Irving, and Lewis Coser. 1962. *The American Communist Party: A Critical History.* 2nd ed. New York: Praeger.

Isserman, Maurice. 1982. *Which Side Were You On? The American Communist Party During the Second World War.* Middletown, CT: Wesleyan U. Pr.

Keeran, Roger. 1980. *The Communist Party and the Auto Workers Unions.* Bloomington: Indiana U. Pr.

Klehr, Harvey. 1984. *The Heyday of American Communism: The Depression Decade.* New York: Basic Books.

———. 1988. *The American Radical Left.* New Brunswick, NJ: Transaction.

Kraditor, Aileen S. 1988. *"Jimmy Higgins": The Mental World of the American Rank-and-File Communist, 1930–1958.* Westport, CT: Greenwood.

Naison, Mark. 1983. *Communists in Harlem During the Depression.* Urbana: U. of Illinois Pr.

Record, Wilson. 1951. *The Negro and the Communist Party.* Westport, CT: Greenwood.

Schwartz, Lawrence H. 1980. *Marxism and Culture: The CPUSA and Aesthetics in the 1930s.* Port Washington, NY: Kennikat Press.

Starobin, Joseph R. 1972. *American Communism in Crisis, 1943–1957.* Cambridge: Harvard U. Pr.

Compliance Review Commission of the Democratic Party

The Compliance Review Commission is a manifestation of the Democratic Party's two-decade long struggle with a fundamental dilemma: how can the party ensure meaningful grass-roots participation in decision-making, particularly by activists and ideologues outside the formal organization, yet nominate presidential candidates who have broad-based appeal to a largely nonideological electorate? On the Republican side, party outsiders played a significant role in the nomination of Barry Goldwater in 1964; Democratic amateur activists, however, were frustrated in the 1960s by the party professionals' control of presidential nomination politics. The nomination of Minnesota Senator Hubert Humphrey in 1968, the choice of the professionals but a candidate who entered no state primary elections, erased any doubts about the locus of control within the party.

Revisions of the delegate selection process have thus been adopted by the Democrats in the aftermath of every presidential nomination since 1968. After the 1968 convention, the party implemented the McGovern-Fraser reforms, a highly structured set of rules regarding delegate selection, conduct of the national convention, and representation of women, minorities, and young people. Subsequent rules revisions occurred in 1974 (the Mikulski Commission), in 1978 (the Winograd Commission), in 1982 (the Hunt Commission), and in 1986 (the Fairness Commission). Much of the revision since 1968 has represented an attempt to relax the McGovern-Fraser rules, including the elimination of mandatory quotas for representation of various groups in state delegations and restrictions on the scheduling of primaries and caucuses. Other changes have increased the participation of elected officials in party conventions.

To ensure enforcement of the Mikulski rules, the party created the Compliance Review Commission (CRC). The 25-member CRC, which began work in 1974, was charged with assisting the state parties in developing delegate selection and affirmative action plans and to hear challenges alleging noncompliance with the new rules. The CRC issued a number of rulings before to the 1976 convention (e.g., granting a waiver to Wisconsin allowing that state to use the crossover primary in 1976). Though the CRC was to cease operations after the 1976 convention, the Winograd Commission recommended its reestablishment in 1978. The newly constituted CRC issued various rulings prior to the 1980 convention, in several cases allowing exceptions to party rules, such as those mandating a three-month "window" for primaries and caucuses and those prohibiting "loophole" primaries.

See also: Democratic National Committee, Hubert Humphrey, McGovern-Fraser Commission, Winograd Commission

Tom A. Kazee

REFERENCES

Conway, Margaret, Frank B. Feigert, and Alan R. Gitelson. 1984. *American Political Parties: Stability and Change.* Boston: Houghton Mifflin.

Polsby, Nelson. 1983. *Consequences of Party Reform.* New York: Oxford U. Pr.

Price, David E. 1984. *Bringing Back the Parties.* Washington: Congressional Quarterly.

Congressional Black Caucus

The Congressional Black Caucus (CBC), founded in 1971, is one of nearly 100 informal organizations that the House of Representatives designates as "legislative service organizations." The membership of the CBC consists of all the Black members of Congress; the CBC had 26 members—all in the House of Representatives—at the start of the One Hundred Second Congress (1991–1992). Although the CBC is not a partisan organization, all but one of its members are Democrats, all score high on liberal policy scales, and all have traditionally represented largely urban, minority districts. The policy aims of the CBC are twofold: to represent the district interest of CBC members and to serve as spokespersons for the Black community at large, promoting a policy agenda that will better the economic and social condition of Blacks in the United States.

As one of the oldest informal organizations in Congress, the CBC's legislative roles have evolved and changed since its founding in 1971. In its earliest years, the CBC adopted a "collective" model of group action, engaging in such symbolic political action as boycotting Richard Nixon's 1971 State of the Union address and attempting to champion the broader interests of the national Black community. In the middle 1970s, the CBC adopted an "ethnic" model of group action, following the example of other ethnic groups in the Congress by attempting to expand and consolidate its authority with the normal legislative process by securing positions in the party leadership and by actively lobbying for assignments to powerful congressional committees. Since the late 1970s, the CBC has adopted a "synthesis" model of group action, in which it both represents national African-American interests and tries to secure leadership positions in the Congress.

The CBC has been extremely successful in getting these positions of authority. Because CBC members generally represent "safe" congressional districts in which they are assured reelection by large majorities, they have slowly acquired the seniority necessary to move up into positions of authority in the congressional committee system as well as into the ranks of the Democratic Party leadership. In the 101st Congress, the CBC's 24 members chaired 4 committees and 17 subcommittees, were represented on the powerful Steering and Policy Committee, and had positions in the Democratic Party whip system. William Gray (D-Penn.)

chaired the powerful Budget Committee and in 1989 was elected Majority Whip, the first Afro-American to hold such a high position in House party leadership. Although the number of Blacks in Congress remains disproportionately low in comparison to the percentage of Blacks as a proportion of the total population in the United States, African-American Congressmen in the CBC have clearly emerged as a powerful force in Congress in the 1980s.

See also: William Gray, Race and Racial Politics

Richard A. Champagne, Jr.

REFERENCES

Barnett, M. R. 1975. "The Congressional Black Caucus." In Harvey Mansfield, ed. *Congress Against the President*. New York: Praeger.

————. 1982. "The Congressional Black Caucus." In Michael B. Preston, Lenned J. Henderson, Jr., and Paul L. Puryear, eds. *The New Black Politics*. New York: Longman.

Champagne, Richard A., and Leroy N. Rieselbach. 1990. "Blacks in Congress." In Huey L. Perry and Wayne Parent, eds. *Blacks and the American Political System*. Lexington: U. Pr. of Kentucky.

Henry, Charles. 1977. "Legitimizing Race in Congressional Politics." 5 *American Politics Quarterly* 149.

Congressional Elections

To look at congressional elections in the 1990s is to see the product of tremendous change. Congressional campaigns are now candidate centered, in sharp contrast to the party-centered campaigns of the last century. Incumbents have gotten better at, and more interested in, campaigning for reelection than they were early in the life of the Republic. Before the Civil War, about half the membership of the House of Representatives were rookies after each election, along with one-quarter to one-third of the Senate membership. In the 1990s, campaigning has become a full-time job, closely intertwined with almost full-time fundraising, especially in the House. The result is that the turnover rate from election to election, again especially in the House, is extremely low. These changes—candidate-centered races, high reelection rates, dramatic shifts in the methods for reaching voters—have important consequences for the American parties and for the making of public policy.

This article will explore these broad changes and chart the major influences on congressional elections. Throughout, however, readers will see ways in which the term "congressional elections" covers two very different types of races: House and Senate. As the founders intended, these two institutions are structured differently, work differently (though in some ways they are becoming more alike), and have different electoral arrangements. As one example, the simple fact that in any given congressional election year voters are choosing 435 House members but only 33 or 34 Senators means that, inevitably, an individual Senate race will have a greater share of media prominence than will the average House contest. The greater visibility of Senate elections makes a difference in how much the voters know about things, the role of issues in the race, and the electability of incumbents.

The Institutional Environment of Congressional Elections

Political Parties. Party organizations ran their candidates' congressional campaigns until late in the nineteenth century. The parties controlled the nomination of candidates, financed their campaigns, distributed ballots, and dominated the channels through which voters learned about the election. During the first half of the twentieth century, however, a transition took place from party-centered to candidate-centered campaigns. At present normally, the candidate's own organization, not the party's, which chooses the campaign themes, contracts with a pollster, mobilizes volunteers, and contacts the voters. Local parties, in particular, tend to play a very limited role in congressional campaigns.

But party activity has recently resurfaced in some congressional races, primarily at the national level. The Republicans led the way, reorienting their national party to undo the damage left by the Watergate political scandals in the early 1970s. This revitalized national party role in congressional campaigns includes recruitment of candidates, funding, and provision of services to carefully targeted Senate and House contests.

Republican national committees have worked in some election years to recruit strong congressional candidates, offering the lure of adequate party resources to convince them to run. The national Republican Party also helped fund state legislative races in 1978 and again in the late 1980s, in part to gain control of more state legislatures in time for the 1990 congressional redistricting and in part to groom promising local candidates who could later be recruited to run for the U.S. House or Senate. Once these and other candidates have agreed to run, both national parties hold "candidate schools" to improve their campaign skills, and both offer field advisers to help guide the graduates.

The campaign finance reforms of the 1970s have further encouraged the national parties to provide services to congressional candidates. Under these finance laws, a party's national, state, and congressional campaign committees are each allowed to contribute a maximum of $10,000 directly to each House race ($5,000 per election, counting the primary and general elections as separate contests, and another $5,000 if there is a runoff)—only a small fraction of a viable campaign budget. The maximum contribution to a general election Senate candidate from all national party sources combined is $17,500 a year, plus $5,000 from the state party. But using the provision known as "coordinated spending," national party committees and state parties could each spend up to an additional $23,050 in most House races and between $46,100 and $938,688 (depending on the state's population) per Senate contest in 1988 to buy services such as polling for the campaign. For the parties, then, coordinated spending offers both an expanded opportunity to contribute and a greater chance to enhance the technological sophistication of the campaign.

As a result of its intensive use of direct mail fundraising, the national Republican Party has been able to "max out" (give the maximum) on each Republican Senate candidate in recent elections. The GOP could also do so in House races, but instead it concentrates its spending on contests targeted for special effort because they are winnable but close. The national and state Democrats have lagged far behind, having developed their direct mail program later and less fully.

Republicans have taken the lead in other services as well. The national Republican committees conduct daily tracking polls just before the election in close congressional races. They run generic pro-Republican or anti-Democratic ads in congressional districts. The party works with like-minded interest groups to channel their contributions into races targeted by the party. Both national parties offer complete media production services to targeted campaigns, and they will conduct drives to register likely supporters of their party. These registration drives can be vital, since turnout rates in midterm elections average only about 35 percent of registered voters.

But all these new or expanded party activities, according to Stephen and Barbara Salmore do not really succeed in making congressional campaigns more party centered. Rather, they simply expand the technologies and the finances of candidate-centered campaigns. Parties continue to remain part of the environment of the congressional campaign, not part of the campaign itself.

Interest Groups. Stronger and more numerous now than they were 20 years ago, interest groups are increasingly important actors in congressional races. One major reason is that citizen activists are now more likely to be found in interest groups than in the parties. It is a new form of activism: not so much face-to-face participation as the writing of letters to public officials and the sending of checks in response to direct mail appeals. Nevertheless, when congressional candidates need to mobilize activists, interest groups are where they must look.

The campaign finance reforms have had a hand here too. These reforms legitimized the role of political action committees (PACs), fundraising groups sponsored by interest groups or set up independently, as contributors to campaigns. As a result, the number of PACs has increased from 608 in 1974 to over 4,000 in 1988. PACs are permitted to give $5,000 to a congressional candidate in each election, while an individual citizen's contributions are limited to $1,000. An ambitious candidate, then, taps as many PACs as possible. Individual citizens still account for the biggest share of congressional campaign funds, but PAC money has expanded greatly as a proportion of the typical congressional candidate's campaign budget, especially in House races. Among PACs, the corporate committees are the ones whose numbers and contributions are expanding most rapidly.

How influential is PAC money in congressional races? The answer is not clear. The dramatic claims of some single-issue PACs to have defeated incumbent House and Senate members cannot be taken at face value (though reporters have sometimes believed PAC boasts). PAC spending in a race, however, can make a candidate more visible and the election more competitive. But most PAC money goes into races that are either sure bets or already very competitive: House incumbents and open seats (those with no incumbent running) in both houses. PACs' concerns can affect the discourse of congressional campaigns, for example, by injecting national issues of special interest to the PAC. And some ideological PACs have been a source of highly negative campaigning in some congressional races.

Media Coverage. Public visibility is a matter of life or death to congressional candidates, especially to challengers and open-seat candidates who have not had as much officeholding and campaigning experience as their opponents. In the absence of armies of party volunteers going door to door, the mass media are the main—if not the only—means of gaining that visibility.

But the media spotlight does not shine on all congressional campaigns equally. Senate races are more important to the media than are House races. In particular, Senate challengers attract much more press attention than House challengers do; House incumbents get a lot more media coverage than do House challengers. Each of these tendencies has a big impact on the results of congressional elections. Each will be explored below in the section on incumbency.

What Influences Voters' Choices in Congressional Elections?

Party Identification. The decline in voter partisanship in the United States has been as well documented as any trend in recent American political history. It encompasses less straight-ticket and more split-ticket voting in elections, a decrease in the percentage of Americans who say they identify with a party, and a decline in the influence of people's party identifications on their voting behavior. The decline in partisanship leaves voters open to other cues in congressional elections, including incumbency, candidates' characteristics, national issues, the state of the economy, and the President's popularity.

Nevertheless, party identification remains the major influence on some voters' choices in congressional races. Its effects can be seen especially clearly when the competing effect of incumbency is absent (in open seat elections). Further, at the aggregate level, the distribution of party loyalties in a district also affects the extent to which national tides will be felt in that district's voting choices.

Incumbency. In the 1990 midterm election, fully 96 percent of those House members who chose to run again were reelected, along with 31 of 32 Senators who sought reelection. During the period 1970–1990, an average of 93 percent of all House members seeking reelection were victorious, compared with 78 percent of Senators. So the only genuinely competitive races, in the House at least, are in districts with open seats.

One measure of the electoral advantage of being an incumbent is the phenomenon called "sophomore surge": the increase in a candidate's percentage of the vote between his or her first victory and the first reelection as an incumbent. In House races during the 1950s and early 1960s, that increase averaged less than 2 percent. Since 1966 the "sophomore surge" has jumped to about 6 percent.

What has made incumbents, especially in the House, so hard to beat? Numerous explanations have been offered. Some start with the structure of Congress itself. David Mayhew has pointed out that the houses of Congress, as institutions, have been structured very effectively to serve members' reelection needs. The committee and subcommittee system allows members to spend much of their time on questions especially important to their district or state. Weak party leaders in Congress can only wink at members who vote against their party's position on issues, in favor of what they see as their district or state's preference. Prevailing congressional norms encourage support for projects that members feel will help them win reelection.

In addition, incumbents often come from districts or states where their party is in the majority among voters. And to have become an incumbent, the House member or Senator is likely to have good campaigning skills and practice in building supportive coalitions, while most House challengers, at least, have had little or no officeholding and campaigning experience. Richard Fenno has noted that the "home styles" that members of Congress build—the ways they allocate resources, present themselves, and explain their Washington activity—are meant to help them cultivate and hold that support.

Incumbents of both chambers can also benefit from the resources of their office in the period between campaigns. They have large staffs whose members can be used to do constituent service ("casework") and to work in the incumbent's campaign. Incumbents get a travel allowance to make trips home between elections, trips that allow them to meet constituents, hold news conferences, and carry on other activities that would be rightly called "campaigning" if they took place just before to an election. They have unlimited free mailing privileges except for the 60 days just before election day. Because they are national policymakers, incumbents find it much easier than challengers, at least in House races, to attract media attention on their own terms (i.e., to get their press releases printed).

But how great are these benefits of officeholding? Congressional incumbents do seem to believe that paying close attention to district needs pays off in votes at election time; consequently, the use of congressional resources for constituent service expands. For example, the number of pieces of mail sent by congressional offices has increased enormously: from 43.5 million in 1954 to about three-quarters of a billion in 1986. Yet research on House elections by political scientists J. C. McAdams and J. R. Johannes turns up no evidence of a significant relationship between such service activities as allocating staff members to district offices (rather than Washington) and deterring a high-spending challenger in the next election. Nor are voters' choices in House elections more than only slightly related to the amount of constituent service they remember receiving from the incumbent according to Ragsdale and Cook.

The "casework connection," then, can be only a partial explanation of the advantages possessed by incumbents in congressional elections. We can draw the same conclusion about another common explanation: incumbents have a great advantage over challengers in campaign fundraising. It is true that under normal circumstances, incumbents can raise as much money as they want. Interestingly, though, lots of money may not help them. Researchers (e.g., Abramowitz on the Senate and Jacobson on the House) have found, in both House and Senate races involving incumbents, that the most significant influence on the election result is the amount that the *challenger* spends on the campaign.

The money that challengers spend, especially in House races, must work to solve a key problem. Although almost 90 percent of all Americans claim to recognize the name of their House member, Erikson and Wright show that House challengers are often all but anonymous to the voters. Furthermore, voter recognition of most House incumbents is both positive and unencumbered by much substantive information; only a minority of Americans say they have heard or read anything about the incumbent whose name they recognize. Unless the challenger can spend enough to compete with the name recognition and positive image of the incumbent, the election is over before the campaign starts.

Incumbents' spending, Jacobson argues, is mainly reactive. Incumbents spend a lot when they feel their challenger is a real threat. They may even raise money preemptively, either to try to deter a strong challenger or to mask their own vulnerability. By tapping their tested sources of funding, incumbents can build campaign war chests of awesome proportions, in the hope that a politically astute challenger would be loathe to run against someone with so big a bankroll so early in the election cycle. And campaign funds can accumulate over time; congressional incumbents have voted to allow themselves to carry over unused campaign money from one election to the next, on the assumption, as House Ways and Means chairman Dan Rostenkowski (D-Ill.) puts it, that "when you need the money, it's too late to raise it." Some incumbents may feel a great need for that bankroll if they have appeared weak in the previous election (for example, if they won by a smaller margin than usual). Looking weak in one election is likely to bring a strong challenger in the next. An incumbent coming off a narrow victory may try to ward off the inevitable by raising big money early in the next election cycle.

Perhaps one of the two safest conclusions here is that incumbency has a multifaceted, rather than a simple, effect on voters' choices in congressional elections. The other is that incumbents' most effective campaigning is done between elections; money spent by incumbents during the formal campaign period adds little to their voter support.

House-Senate Differences in the Incumbency Advantage. Incumbency is clearly a substantial advantage, even more in House than in Senate elections. Why are House seats more secure? First, House districts can be custom tailored for an incumbent; Senate districts cannot. State legislatures frequently draw congressional district lines to protect incumbent House members of the majority party; Senators are stuck with their state lines. Moreover, state electorates tend to be more varied, more heterogeneous than the typical House district, and therefore more difficult to please. Second, most Senate elections attract more media attention than the great majority of House races do. The Senate is a smaller institution than the House but is considered more prestigious; its purview includes lofty matters of war and peace and major presidential appointments, while the House is more closely tethered to dams, highways, and local politics. Unsurprisingly, then, many Senators become players on the national stage; few House members do.

But Carmines and Dodd show that this media spotlight is as much a hazard as a blessing to Senators. The more visible a Senate race is, the more interested reporters will be in the legislative votes cast by the incumbent—particularly on controversial bills—and in the issue-oriented attacks of the challenger. Media coverage of Senate races, then, is more heavily laced with national issues (and less with local politics) than is the coverage given House contests. As a result, Alan Abramowitz argues, "voters' ideological preferences appear to have a significant influence on their voting decisions in Senate elections"— a situation that poses significant risks for the Senate incumbent.

Because Senators are more often in the media's eye than are House members, they can exercise less control over what their constituents learn about them. And because their constituency is usually much bigger, incumbent Senators have a harder time spreading their own message to voters through personal meetings. In contrast, in the quieter media environment of House campaigns, the incumbents are more likely to control the content of their media coverage. It is to the incumbent's advantage to focus that coverage, using press releases and other devices, on constituent service to the district, not on controversial issues. Thus a House member may sometimes be able to escape the electoral consequences of an unpopular vote or stance because reporters are not watching or because the press is content to print the incumbent's press releases on local projects. A Senator really can never count on this sloth.

Even worse for Senate incumbents, when a race is exciting (as Senate races are more likely to be), press coverage is not limited to the incumbent. The challenger also basks in (or shrinks from) the media glow. Senate challengers can often gain visibility, and the concomitant name recognition, nearly comparable to that of their incumbent opponent, thus erasing one of an incumbent's most powerful advantages. Most House challengers, all but ignored by the media, have to struggle much harder to get media attention for their name and good qualities; issues on which voters may disagree with the incumbent are even more difficult to spotlight.

Because of these forces undermining the security of Senate incumbents, and because of the Senate's greater prestige, Senate races are more likely than House elections to attract strong challengers: people who have previously held major public office or acquired fame in other fields, people who have the requisite name recognition, and people who can raise the money needed for a successful campaign. Again, the quality of the challenger, even more than that of the incumbent, determines the competitiveness of the race.

Note, however, that this distinction between Senate and House races can sometimes become blurred. Some Senate contests resemble House races in their low visibility. These contests, often in smaller states, involve an incumbent who is so entrenched that potentially strong challengers decline to run, contributors find other uses for their money, and the media look elsewhere for an exciting story.

The Case of the Not-So-Vanishing Marginals. The dazzling reelection rate of House incumbents has led many observers to conclude that competition in House races has been dwindling: the number of House seats vulnerable to defeat in the next election has declined ("marginal" seats). And in fact the share of the vote won by incumbent House candidates increased from 61 percent to about 65 percent during the 1960s, remaining at the higher level since then. Some argue that this increase is evidence of the "vanishing marginals" among House districts.

Gary Jacobson has disputed this hypothesis. Though the typical House incumbent's victory has gotten bigger, the percentage of incumbents *defeated* for reelection has not gone down significantly in the last 35 years. The reason for this is that declining voter partisanship has made elections more unpredictable and more unstable over time. Voters liberated from the party habit may be more open to the charms (and constituent service) of a House incumbent of the other party. But by the same token, incumbents can expect to get fewer votes simply because of their party affiliation. The vote for the incumbent can swing more widely now from one election to the next. Strong national tides can wash over districts formerly safe for the incumbent.

The result is that the increasing margin of victory is a hollow comfort; incumbents who won with 60 percent to 65 percent of the vote in the 1970s were as likely to lose the next race as were their colleagues in the 1950s who were winning by margins of 55 percent to 60 percent. The marginal districts are, therefore, not vanishing. Rather, they are coming in disguise—an unsettling prospect for House members. Incumbents struggle mightily to hold on to one of these marginal seats to increase their use of the perquisites—the frank, travel allowances, district offices, larger staffs—that permit extensive constituent service.

In sum, incumbency, even in the House, is not a ticket to reelection. But House incumbents can reassure themselves that if they keep working diligently to maintain their district support, they are very likely to succeed. Incumbency, in House races, stands for a series of ingredients—name recognition, media visibility, fundraising capacity, proven campaigning skill, an edge in the district's partisan balance—that, more than nine times out of ten, add up to reelection. House challengers, normally unable to attract enough contributions to look like a threat, do not attract much media attention either. So their name recognition remains low, their support does not grow, and their funding fades even more rapidly. They might as well have stayed home. The only major disruption in this smooth pattern occurs when a challenger is able to raise enough money to match the incumbent's visibility. When that happens, the seat becomes competitive. Big money challenges happen rarely, however, and typically only when one or more of the incumbency advantages is absent. Still, because competition does happen, House incumbents usually campaign on a continuous basis, between elections as well as during campaigns.

Senate incumbents can have even less assurance of their chances of reelection. Incumbency does not provide Senators as many unique advantages as it does House members. Most Senate challengers are more comparable to their incumbent opponents in campaign experience, media coverage, name recognition, and fundraising ability than are House challengers to House incumbents. Even so, in a typical election year, three-quarters of Senators who choose to run again will win.

Candidates' Characteristics. The public's assessment of the candidates—how effectively they campaign, how trustworthy they seem, how close they come to matching the district or state's vision of what it is and would like to be—can make a substantial difference in the election results. Recall, however, that especially in House races, voters may have an assessment of one candidate only—normally the incumbent.

National Issues. Issues play a larger role in voters' choices among Senate candidates than in House races, probably because competing factors—incumbency, candidate visibility, officeholding advantages—play a lesser role in Senate races. Voters' positions on the issues are especially influential when a great ideological distance separates Senate candidates. Issues can at times make a difference in House races as well. Although most voters do not know where their House member stands on major issues, a small group of informed voters may affect the outcome of the occasional close House race.

State of the Economy and the President's Popularity. At the aggregate level, voting in congressional elections is strongly related to change in the state of the national economy and the President's popularity. Because of that, midterm elections often have been described as referenda on the President and his handling of the economy. Yet at the level of the individual voter, these relationships are weak.

Gary Jacobson and Samuel Kernell offer a possible explanation. National economic conditions and the President's popularity, they argue, affect the choices made by prospective congressional challengers. When the economy is strong and the President's job rating high, potentially attractive candidates of the presidential party are more likely to decide to run, because they feel their party's prospects look good in the upcoming election. Prospective contributors to that party are more likely to put their money into these challengers' campaigns. When the economy and the President's popularity are declining, the other party will be better able to field an attractive and well-funded group of challengers.

Voters respond to that choice at the local level. The result is that the favored party is in fact more likely to do well nationally, but the direct cause is the decisions made by prospective challengers and contributors and only indirectly the choices made by voters.

This "strategic politicians" argument cannot completely explain the effects of presidential popularity and the national economy on congressional races; if it did, then the party favored by national conditions would have all the attractive challengers in an election and the other party none. Yet it is a valuable reminder of the vital role played by political elites, their perceptions and their behavior, in determining the results of congressional races.

Internal Dynamics of the Congressional Campaign

A congressional candidate faces three major tasks. The first is to select the campaign's main themes: the agenda that the candidate will use to persuade the voters. The second is to put in place a campaign organization (including a manager and people to deal with the media) empowered to raise money, research issues and the opponent's record, organize volunteers, analyze public opinion, write speeches, turn out voters, and make sure the campaign complies with federal election laws. The third task is to choose the tools with which the campaign's message will be presented: the kinds of media, types of ad presentations, scheduling of the candidate's appearances, contacts with interest groups.

But beyond these common tasks, almost everything else about the campaign depends upon whether the candidate is an incumbent or a nonincumbent (challenger or open-seat candidate). With respect to the campaign's main themes, for example, incumbents have the advantage of time. In advance of the campaign, incumbents can try to pinpoint their own weaknesses and find ways to neutralize these faults before the challenger can make use of them. Efforts to immunize incumbents against later attack can best take place between campaigns, when they are seen by voters as public officials rather than mere candidates.

Congressional incumbents normally campaign on their record in the most general sense: they have served constituents well, they are one with their district or state, they can be trusted, among other things. Challengers start with too many handicaps to be able to campaign in such an affirmative style. They have to take pains to show that they are a vigorous alternative to the incumbent, but they must also show, especially in House races, that something is very wrong with the incumbent. Otherwise, voters have little reason to consider a change. The problem is that people who run negative campaigns are often viewed with distaste by the public. The ideal situation for a challenger, then, is for some third party to make the negative points about the incumbent so that the challenger can wage a positive campaign. Sometimes this strategy if successful when the local media investigate a scandal involving the incumbent. At other times ideological PACs conduct their own, highly negative campaign against the incumbent. In such cases the challenger reaps the benefit but does not bear the blame.

Similarly, in setting up the campaign organization, incumbents face a very different situation from nonincumbents. The incumbent has run at least once before, with a campaign staff tested in that race. (More of it may remain currently available to House incumbents, whose last race was only two years earlier, than to Senators, who last ran six years before.) He or she also has a Washington and a district or state staff, whose work is at least indirectly related to the campaign and is very likely indistinguishable from it. The incumbent's knowledge of these people's skills, and their interrelationships as a working team, often will help to reduce the uncertainty that pervades the campaign environment.

Challengers must also set up a campaign organization, but typically they have much less protection against uncertainty. Those who have run a previous race may be in better shape, but the fact remains that they have not run a successful campaign for the office they seek, and the incumbent has. One logical approach to dealing with this uncertainty is to hire one or more consultants—experts who can bring to the campaign both experienced political skills and an established organization. But consultants are out of the reach of many challengers because their price is too high and because consultants do not like to take on likely losers—a description that fits most Senate and almost all House challengers.

Finally, candidates must select their tools. The expense of television limits its usefulness in House races, especially because media markets often do not coincide with House district lines and thus candidates would be paying to reach viewers who do not vote in their districts. That makes personal campaigning more useful to House candidates. Television is very useful in a statewide race, however. Because of the greater size of Senate districts, candidates are unlikely to come into direct touch with more than a tiny proportion of their constituents.

Computerized direct mail has been employed increasingly in congressional races. The great value of direct mail is that unlike network television, it can be targeted to particular audiences rather than to the general public and to carry messages that other people might consider at best boring and at worst offensive.

Professionally conducted polls can limit uncertainty by uncovering the strengths and weaknesses, in the voters' eyes, of the candidate, the opponent, and various possible campaign themes. But polls cost money. They are very often used by candidates with big campaign budgets, especially in Senate races, and seldom used by typically underfinanced House challengers.

Observers must remember, however, in the face of all these high-tech marvels, that one of the most important tools for communicating the campaign's message is the candidate. Here again, the congressional incumbent has a real edge—and a potential vulnerability. In many ways, incumbents have a better chance than challengers to keep learning how to improve their campaign skills. Incumbents have more time, more exposure to constituents through their activities in office, and more experience in the campaign situation to help them adapt to its demands. Without an already successful strategy, with little time to learn from experience, challengers typically face a much more frustrating and less effective situation. The danger for incumbents, however, is that years of reward for their campaign strategies, in the form of election victories, tend to harden those strategies into habits. These habits can be time-savers as long as the current campaign situation closely resembles the last one. But when the situation changes, habits can hamper an incumbent's ability to adapt to that change.

Conclusion

Perhaps the most ubiquitous finding in the analysis of congressional elections is that incumbents have tremendous advantages. It is a finding with major implications for an understanding of American politics.

"Permanent incumbency" is particularly accurate at the level of the individual House member; the result is limited turnover in the institution as a whole. In some election years retirements combine with strong national forces to produce more change than usual. Yet the generally low turnover raises some serious concerns about the openness of the House to new ideas and about its accountability to the voters. In author David Broder's words, "The part of the federal government which the Founders intended to be most sensitive to shifts in political climate has instead become the most immune to change."

But has it really? Certainly the House is relatively immune to change in its membership. A major reason, however, is the local orientation of so many of those members, a focus that the founders might well have applauded. Their emphasis on constituent service, on being (or at least seeming to be) one with the district, on personal campaigning, helps get House members reelected. It is an emphasis that Senators are adopting increasingly, in the hope of winning similarly high reelection rates. Election results suggest, then, that voters do not mind low turnover in their own congressional district or state, though, somewhat illogically, they are often dissatisfied with the performance of the Congress as a whole.

The risk many observers see is that by satisfying the voters' needs for service and trust, members of Congress gain more leeway to act as they choose on issues of national import. In short, their success in dealing with constituent requests can allow them to be less accountable to the district and the nation as a whole on vital matters of national policy.

Not everyone agrees that the relatively low turnover exacts a price in terms of accountability. Studies show that voters do have a choice offered them, in both House and Senate elections. For example, G. C. Wright and M. B. Berkman find that Republican and Democratic Senate candidates take different positions on issues, in part because candidates work to appeal to their own party's activists and primary voters, who are often more ideologically polarized than are other citizens. And in state-level data, Wright has found that candidates' issue positions have a stronger impact on election outcomes than has been found in analyses of individuals' voting choices.

Central to an accountable system, however, is a credible challenger. In Senate races (and probably in most House elections as well), the challenger is the one who stakes out the clearer policy position; incumbents tend to moderate their stance in time for the campaign. An effective challenger, then, is the voter's insurance that elections will involve choices and not just rituals of public reassurance.

The problem with all of this, of course, is that most incumbent candidates face an all-but-invisible opponent. As voters' party loyalties fade, challengers lose a reliable cushion of support; to reconstruct that support, they need money. Under the present system, they are unlikely to raise enough to run an effective race. The dilemma of congressional elections (House elections in particular) then is the existence of a genuine choice between policies in a situation that allows many or most voters to be unaware of it.

See also: Direct Mail, Negative Advertising, Party Identification, Political Action Committees, Republican National Committee, Split-Ticket Voting, Watergate

Marjorie Randon Hershey

REFERENCES

Abramowitz, Alan I. 1988. "Explaining Senate Election Outcomes." 82 American Political Science Review 385.

Carmines, Edward G., and Lawrence C. Dodd. 1985. "Bicameralism in Congress: The Changing Partnership." In Lawrence C. Dodd and Bruce I. Oppenheimer, eds. Congress Reconsidered. 3rd ed. Washington: Congressional Quarterly.

Erikson, Robert S., and Gerald C. Wright. 1985. "Voters, Candidates, and Issues in Congressional Elections." In Lawrence C. Dodd and Bruce I. Oppenheimer, eds. Congress Reconsidered. 3rd ed. Washington: Congressional Quarterly.

Fenno, Richard F., Jr. 1978. Home Style: House Members in Their Districts. Boston: Little, Brown.

Goldenberg, Edie N., and Michael W. Traugott. 1984. Campaigning for Congress. Washington: Congressional Quarterly.

Hershey, Marjorie Randon. 1984. Running for Office: The Political Education of Campaigners. Chatham, NJ: Chatham House.

Hinckley, Barbara. 1981. Congressional Elections. Washington: Congressional Quarterly.

Jacobson, Gary C. 1987a. The Politics of Congressional Elections. 2nd ed. Boston: Little, Brown.

———. 1987b. "The Marginals Never Vanished: Incumbency and Competition in Elections to the U.S. House of Representatives, 1952–1982." 31 American Journal of Political Science 126.

———, and Samuel Kernell. 1981. Strategy and Choice in Congressional Elections. New Haven: Yale U. Pr.

McAdams, John C., and John R. Johannes. 1987. "Determinants of Spending by House Challengers, 1974–1984." 31 American Journal of Political Science 457.

Maisel, Louis Sandy. 1982. From Obscurity to Oblivion: Running in the Congressional Primary. Knoxville: U. of Tennessee Pr.

Mann, Thomas E. 1978. Unsafe at Any Margin: Interpreting Congressional Elections. Washington: American Enterprise Institute.

Mayhew, David R. 1974. Congress: The Electoral Connection. New Haven: Yale U. Pr.

Ragsdale, Lyn, and Timothy E. Cook. 1987. "Representatives' Actions and Challengers' Reactions: Limits to Candidate Connections in the House." 31 American Journal of Political Science 45.

Salmore, Stephen A., and Barbara G. Salmore. 1985. Candidates, Parties, and Campaigns: Electoral Politics in America. Washington: Congressional Quarterly.

Tufte, Edward R. 1978. Political Control of the Economy. Princeton: Princeton U. Pr.

Westlye, Mark C. 1983. "Competitiveness of Senate Seats and Voting Behavior in Senate Elections." 27 American Journal of Political Science 253.

Wright, Gerald C., and Michael B. Berkman. 1986. "Candidates and Policy in United States Senate Elections." 80 American Political Science Review 567.

Roscoe Conkling (1828–1888)

Leader of the "Stalwart" faction of the Republican Party during the late nineteenth century. The son of a federal judge, Roscoe Conkling became involved in Republican Party politics at an early age. Before he reached the age of 21 he was named district attorney for upstate New York's Oneida County. In 1857 he was elected mayor of Utica. A year later he was elected to the U.S. House of Representatives. He was reelected in 1860 but defeated in the midterm elections of 1862. Conkling briefly returned to private life, but in 1864 he reentered politics, winning back the congressional seat that he had lost two years before.

He was reelected to the House of Representatives in 1866, but before he could take his seat, the New York State Legislature appointed Conkling to the United States Senate. Twice thereafter, he was returned to the U.S. Senate.

Conkling's rise to political power came with the presidency of Ulysses S. Grant. Conkling was a protégé of William H. Seward, the Republican boss of New York State and Secretary of State during the Civil War. Seward was a leader of the Radical Republicans—those who wanted federal troops to remain in the defeated states of the Old Confederacy and to continue the carpetbagger form of government there. Conkling inherited Seward's supporters, and called his backers "Stalwarts," while Conkling's opponents—including Rutherford B. Hayes, James G. Blaine, John Sherman, and James A. Garfield—were dubbed by Conkling as the "Halfbreeds." In addition to favoring removal of federal troops from the South, the Halfbreeds wanted enactment of a federal civil service.

Conkling and his Stalwarts opposed the Halfbreeds chiefly on these issues. Conkling's power base resided in the support he received from major Republican party figures in the industrial states: General Ben Butler of Massachusetts, Simon and James Cameron (father and son) of Pennsylvania, and John Logan of Illinois.

Together these Stalwarts presided over immense kickback and patronage schemes: for example, the Railroad Ring in which members of Congress got free shares in the Credit Mobilier, a scheme that financed government subsidies for the building of the Union Pacific Railroad; the Whiskey Ring, in which distillers paid either no tax or a small fraction of the excise tax on their product and contributed some of the remainder to the Stalwarts; or the Star Postal Ring—a scheme by which the mail contracts went to a fraudulent low bidder who later, with the collusion of the Post Office Department, charged huge amounts for purely fictitious extra services.

But the most profitable of these scams was the Customhouse Ring. At that time, customs officers received no salary. Instead they got a percentage of the fines levied on violators plus one-half the value of goods confiscated for nonpayment or false declaration of duty. The Boston Customhouse, for example, generated hundreds of thousands of dollars that went into Stalwart coffers.

These rings thrived during Ulysses S. Grant's administration. But Grant's successor, Rutherford B. Hayes, removed the federal troops from the Old Confederacy and abolished the percentage system for customs officers, giving them a straight salary of $12,000 per year.

Hayes thus earned the enmity of Conkling, who had supported Grant for President in 1880. Grant was opposed by Halfbreeds James G. Blaine and John Sherman. Sherman's campaign manager, James A. Garfield, eventually won the Republican nomination over Conkling's opposition. Stalwart Chester A. Arthur, a New York customs officer and one of Conkling's most trusted lieutenants, was chosen as Vice President.

The Garfield–Arthur ticket prevailed, thanks to Stalwart backing in the key industrial states. But when President Garfield appointed someone to the New York Customhouse without consulting Conkling, he resigned his Senate seat in protest. Conkling felt the Republican-controlled New York legislature would reinstate him, but to his surprise it did not. Garfield, meanwhile, was assassinated by a Stalwart job seeker, and Arthur became President. Garfield's death resulted in the enactment of a federal civil service system—a law that Conkling opposed, but Arthur signed anyway. Relations between Arthur and Conkling deteriorated. Out of office, Conkling lived in relative obscurity.

See also: Chester Arthur, James Blaine, Carpetbaggers, Credit Mobilier, James Garfield, Ulysses S. Grant, Rutherford Hayes, Radical Republicans, William Seward, John Sherman, Stalwarts (and Halfbreeds), Whiskey Ring

John K. White

REFERENCES

Conkling, A. R. 1889. *The Life and Letters of Roscoe Conkling.* New York: C. L. Webster.

DiSalle, Michael V., with Lawrence G. Blochman. 1966. *Second Choice.* New York: Hawthorn Books.

John B. Connally, Jr. (1917–)

Texas politician, Cabinet officer, and presidential aspirant. John Bowden Connally, Jr., was an influential figure in the politics of the Democratic and Republican parties—in his home state of Texas and in the nation—for more than three decades. At every stage in Connally's career, he demonstrated remarkable political skills. At the University of Texas, he managed the campaign of his friend J. J. Pickle who later was to represent Texas in the United States Congress for Student Assembly president. The next year, Connally used the political apparatus he had built for Pickle to win the office himself. In the Navy during World War II, he worked his way onto the staffs of Under Secretary James V. Forrestal and later General Dwight Eisenhower.

Returning to civilian life after the war, Connally went to work on the staff of Congressman Lyndon B. Johnson, a connection he maintained until Johnson's death. He managed the senatorial campaign of 1948 in which Johnson won by fewer than 100 votes and served as LBJ's administrative assistant in the Senate. When he returned to Texas, Connally was part of Johnson's political advisory network. In 1960 he managed Johnson's campaign for the Democratic nomination for President and was involved in his friend's decision to accept John F. Kennedy's request that Johnson accept the vice presidential nomination.

Connally served as Secretary of the Navy for the first two years of the Kennedy administration. He left that position to return to Texas and then ran successfully for governor. As the host governor, Connally was riding in the limousine on November 22, 1963, when President Kennedy was assassinated in Dallas; Connally himself was wounded by one of the bullets that took the President's life. The attention he received after the Dallas assassination thrust him into national prominence.

In 1968 Connally tested the waters as a possible presidential candidate on the Democratic ticket, but his overtures were not warmly received. In 1971 President Richard Nixon asked Connally to serve as his Secretary of the Treasury; he soon became one of the President's most valued policy and political advisers.

Connally played an important role in Nixon's reelection campaign, heading Democrats for Nixon and raising significant amounts of money for the President's campaign. Connally, who officially joined the Republican Party in 1973, was touched by the Watergate scandal. He was tried and acquitted of charges that he had accepted a bribe from the American Milk Producers in exchange for increasing price supports for the dairy industry.

But even the taint of Watergate could not dispel Connally's political ambitions. In 1980 he reentered national politics as a candidate for the Republican presidential nomination. His campaign is the only one since the implementation of the Federal Election Campaign Act that refused to accept federal matching funds for campaign expenditures. (Those campaigns that accept federal money must comply with spending limitations.) The Connally strategy held that he could raise the money without federal assistance and that he would need to outspend his opponents in order to have a chance. He was accurate in determining that he could raise campaign money, but the $12 million that he spent during the campaign resulted in only one convention delegate—probably the most expensive failure in American political history.

In the 1980s John Connally, who had amassed millions of dollars investing in Texas' booming oil economy, faced financial ruin when the bottom fell out of the domestic oil market and with all aspects of the Texas economy suffering accordingly. But even as he declared bankruptcy and auctioned off his personal possessions in 1987, John Connally stood tall and told the media to witness the fall of this proud man and that he would recover.

See also: Elections of 1960, 1968, and 1980; Federal Election Campaign Act of 1971; Lyndon Johnson; John F. Kennedy; Richard Nixon; Party Switchers; Watergate

Reagan Robbins

REFERENCES

Birmingham, Frederic A. 1979. *John Connally: The Man Who Would Be President.* Indianapolis, IN: Curtis Publishing.

Crawford, Ann Fears, and Jack Keever. 1973. *John B. Connally: Portrait in Power.* Austin, TX: Jenkins Publishing.

Connecticut's Challenge Primary

The challenge primary in Connecticut is a method of selecting candidates for state and district offices in the event that one or more candidates for these offices receives at least 20 percent of the vote at the state's nominating convention. Should one or more candidates receive at least 20 percent of delegate support, he or she is entitled to challenge the party-endorsed candidate in a primary election. In order to obtain the party endorsement, the candidate must receive at least 50 percent of the votes at the nominating convention.

This law, enacted in 1955, currently stands as amended in 1981. "Within fourteen days following the close of the state convention, a candidacy for nomination by a political party to a state office may be filed by, or on behalf of any person . . . who has received at least twenty percent of the votes of the convention delegates present and voting on any roll-call vote taken on the endorsement or proposed endorsement of a candidate for such state office . . . with the secretary of state. . . ." These provisions also apply to district offices.

This law, Public Act 9–400 of the Connecticut General Statutes, was last exercised in 1986 by the gubernatorial candidates for the Republican Party nomination. Julie Belaga and Gerald Labriola received 22 percent and 23 percent respectively at the convention. Richard Bozzuto received 55 percent of the vote at the state nominating convention and therefore received the party's endorsement, yet Belaga and Labriola retained their right to challenge in a primary. Belaga was the victor, hence she received the Republican Party nomination.

Candidates for office also retain the right to challenge in a primary when there is no party-endorsed candidate. Provided a candidate receives at least 20 percent of the convention vote, and one of the candidates has not received at least 50 percent of the convention vote, then no candidate receives the party endorsement, regardless of who wins the plurality of votes. In the event of a tie vote, no party endorsement is declared, and all candidates retain the option to challenge. Not all candidates, however, choose to challenge. When all candidates but one choose not to challenge, the remaining candidate wins the party endorsement and no primary is held. The primary election, unlike the convention vote, is decided on a plurality basis, and the candidate with the most votes wins the nomination.

Challenge primaries are held on the fifty-sixth day preceding the general election, which is held on the Tuesday following the first Monday of November. The primary cannot be held if the fifty-sixth day preceding the general election is a Sunday or legal holiday, in which case it is "held on the next succeeding day, other than a Sunday or a legal or such religious holiday."

The Connecticut challenge primary is a primary held following the nominating convention in the event that one or more candidates receives at least 20 percent of the convention vote and chooses to challenge the party-endorsed candidate should one be selected. This gives candidates a second opportunity to compete for the nomination in the event that at least one-fifth of the delegation gives them support.

Terri Susan Fine

Conscience Whigs

A faction that made up the antislavery wing of the Massachusetts Whig Party in the 1840s, the Conscience Whigs eventually bolted to help form the Free Soil Party. Their origins involved the complexities of Massachusetts politics as well as a firm devotion to containing slavery within the existing states.

As sectionalism intensified in the early 1840s, most Massachusetts Whigs agreed that the annexation of Texas as a slave state had to be resisted. But the manufacturing commercial wing of the party was eager to maintain its southern alliance and source of cotton for its textile industry. By 1845, the year of Texas annexation, a group of younger Whigs led by Charles Sumner, John G. Palfrey, and Charles Francis Adams grew increasingly restless over the older, more conservative group's domination of the state party and its willingness to retreat from antislavery concerns to keep their allies in the South content. At this point, however, the young Whigs had no interest in a third-party movement and resisted Liberty Party overtures to that effect.

The introduction in 1846 of the Wilmot Proviso banning slavery in any territory acquired from Mexico gave antislavery Whigs an opportunity to renew their anti-extension movement. It also led to the naming of the two factions—the Conscience Whigs and the dominant conservative group known as the Cotton Whigs. When a member of the younger group claimed that the party had to represent the conscience as well as the cotton of the state, the antislavery faction quickly adopted the name Conscience Whigs. At the state party convention, the Cotton Whigs blocked a Wilmot Proviso resolution and a complete break looked possible. The Cotton Whigs, led by manufacturers Abbott

Lawrence and Nathan Appleton and their key congressional spokesmen Daniel Webster and Robert Winthrop, were determined not to upset national Whig harmony. Conscience men, on the other hand, sought a presidential nominee for 1848 who would back the Wilmot Proviso.

In June 1848, the Whig Party nominated Louisiana slaveholder Zachary Taylor and blocked consideration of the Wilmot Proviso, thus cementing the Conscience men's decision to bolt. Meeting later in the month at Worcester, Massachusetts, they chose delegates to the Buffalo convention of the new Free Soil Party. At that meeting, the Conscience Whigs were one of three elements, the others being the Liberty Party and antislavery Democrats, dominated by the New York Barnburners. The latter, the most numerous, insisted on Martin Van Buren's nomination for President. The Conscience men were somewhat pacified with Adams's nomination for Vice President, with a platform endorsing the Wilmot Proviso.

Following the election and Taylor's victory, the Conscience Whigs remained loyal to their new party and their antislavery principles even as the Barnburners returned en masse to the Democrats. Conscience Whig power in the legislature allowed these men to form a temporary coalition with Massachusetts Democrats and to place Charles Sumner in the Senate in 1851. As a more important element in the smaller third-party movement in 1852, Conscience Whigs led by Adams and Sumner willingly joined the new Republican Party in 1854.

See also: Charles Francis Adams, Barnburners, Cotton Whigs, Elections of 1848 and 1852, Free Soil Party, Liberty Party, Charles Sumner, Zachary Taylor, Third Parties in American Elections, Martin Van Buren, Daniel Webster, Wilmot Proviso

Frederick J. Blue

REFERENCES

Blue, Frederick J. 1973. *The Free Soilers: Third Party Politics, 1848–54.* Urbana: U. of Illinois Pr.

Brauer, Kinley J. 1967. *Cotton Versus Conscience: Massachusetts Politics and Southwestern Expansion, 1843–1848.* Lexington: U. Pr. of Kentucky.

Darling, Arthur B. 1925. *Political Changes in Massachusetts, 1824–1848: A Study of Liberal Movements in Politics.* New Haven: Yale U. Pr.

Donald, David. 1960. *Charles Sumner and the Coming of the Civil War.* New York: Knopf.

Duberman, Martin B. 1960. *Charles Francis Adams, 1807–1886.* Boston: Houghton Mifflin.

Wilson, Henry. 1872. *History of the Rise and Fall of the Slave Power in America.* Vol. I. Boston: Houghton Mifflin.

Conservative Coalition

The "Conservative Coalition" has been the most significant voting bloc in the U.S. Congress since the 1930s. The Coalition can be defined as a loose confederation of Republicans and southern Democrats who originally joined together to oppose New Deal economic legislation. Over time, programs influenced by Conservative Coalition activity have expanded to include military, foreign, civil rights, and social policies.

While few would doubt that the Conservative Coalition has been a mighty force in the evolution of congressional politics in the middle and late twentieth century, the very nature of the Coalition makes problematic a precise delineation of what that role has been. The Coalition has never employed a paid or centralized staff, nor has it had a formal whip organization. Unlike most formal coalitions, its effectiveness has derived almost solely from the shared values of its members rather than from active mobilization. In addition, the Conservative Coalition has rarely come together for the positive enactment of a legislative program; instead, it has mainly served as a blocking coalition.

Because the Conservative Coalition has never had much of a formal organization, identifying clearly the date of its establishment is impossible. Organizational histories of Congress attribute the rise of the Conservative Coalition to Roosevelt's "court-packing" plan in 1937 as well as to southern disillusionment with New Deal economic policies.

However, attempts to quantify the rise and ongoing activity of the Coalition do not find an abrupt shift in behavior after Roosevelt's first reelection. Rather, it appears that the Conservative Coalition rose gradually as a presence on the House and Senate floors in the middle 1930s, reaching its peak of power in the 1940s and 1950s. During these years the Coalition operated through continual, informal contacts among prominent Republicans and southern Democrats. The most famous of these networks was in the House, where Republican leaders, such as Joseph W. Martin and Charles A. Halleck, informally coordinated their activities with southern Democrats, most notably Chairman Howard W. Smith, on the Rules Committee. The Coalition began to forfeit much of its strength in the early 1960s, losing assaults on the Rules Committee's conservative dominance in 1961 and 1963 and falling before the Great Society juggernaut after the election of 1964.

Thoughts of a resurgence of the Conservative Coalition occurred in 1981, the first year of Ronald Reagan's presidency. In that year, Republicans and southern Democrats in the House formed a working majority that enabled the passage of several important budgetary proposals favored by the Reagan administration. What made 1981 so unusual was that the Coalition was active in the passing of conservative legislation, rather than simply opposing proposed liberal legislation. Related to this resurgence, many southern Democrats moved to strengthen a loose, preexisting organization called the "Boll Weevils," which had formed the nucleus of Democratic support for conservative activism.

The resurgence of the Conservative Coalition was short-lived, however. First, federal policy had been pushed so far to the right that many southern Democrats simply believed things had progressed far enough; thus they refused to support actively further efforts to push the conservative agenda. Second, several southern Democratic seats switched hands to the Republican Party; the southern seats that remained Democratic increasingly fell into the hands of Democrats who were nearly as liberal on average as their northern counterparts. Third, dissatisfaction among northern Democrats with southern defections in 1981 produced calls for stricter party discipline coupled with demands that committee assignments be used more aggresively to reward loyalty and punish disloyalty. While only one House Democrat was overtly punished because of his active support of coalition activity in 1981 (Philip Gramm, Tex.), some southern Democrats may have moderated their stances, fearing that further overt coordination with Republicans would bring sanctions from the Democratic Caucus.

The activity and success of the Conservative Coalition has been subjected to frequent quantitative analysis, and three measures of the Coalition's activity and success are most frequently used. The first measures the number of times a year that the Conservative Coalition "appears" in roll-call votes; this is the basis of the *Conservative Coalition Appearance Index*. The Conservative Coalition appearance index records the percentage of times in a year when a majority of Republicans and southern Democrats vote on the same side of an issue against a majority of non-southern Democrats. The second measure is the *Conservative Coalition Victory Index*. This is the percentage of times in a year when the Conservative Coalition won the roll-call votes on which it was "active." The third measure is the *Conservative Coalition Support Score*. This index is different from the first two because it measures the degree to which individual Senators and House members support the Conservative Coalition in a particular year. For any individual member of Congress, the Conservative Coalition Support Score is the percentage of times that the member voted on the same side as the Conservative Coalition each time the coalition appeared in a roll-call vote. A *Conservative Coalition Opposition Score* is defined analogously.

The Conservative Coalition support score is frequently used as a general measure of individual left–right ideology. The first two measures frequently are used to summarize how liberal or conservative particular years or Congresses were or how successful the Conservative Coalition was in reaching its legislative goals. The standard reference source for these scores is in the annual voting studies of the *Congressional Quarterly Weekly Report*.

Although these numerical measures of coalition activity, strength, and support are commonly used in academic research, a number of dangers attend their use. In brief, these measures are very sensitive to the number and nature of issues that actually come to a floor vote. They also appear to be sensitive to whether nearly unanimous votes are excluded from the analysis. In addition, the definition of the measures ensures that the Conservative Coalition success rates will always be fairly high and that southern Democrats will always have relatively high support scores, even when they are judged fairly liberal by other indices. Finally, the objective measure overlooks the original definition of the Coalition as being a loose confederation that operates through the informal interaction of a few legislators. Such a loose confederation may be successful in blocking liberal legislation even when a majority of southern Democrats vote in a liberal direction.

See also: Franklin Roosevelt

Charles Stewart III

REFERENCES

Brady, David W., and Charles S. Bullock III. 1981. "Coalition Politics in the House of Representatives." In Lawrence C. Dodd and Bruce I. Oppenheimer, eds. *Congress Reconsidered*. 2nd ed. Washington: Congressional Quarterly.

Fraser, James M., and Thomas H. Hammond. 1982. "What Roll Calls Should We Exclude from Conservative Coalition Calculations?" 7 *Legislative Studies Quarterly* 423.

Manley, John W. 1973. "The Conservative Coalition in Congress." 17 *American Behavioral Scientist* 223.

Weisberg, Herbert. 1978. "Evaluating Theories of Congressional Roll-Call Voting." 22 *American Journal of Political Science* 554.

Conservative Opportunity Society

The Conservative Opportunity Society (COS) is an organization of House Republicans that was formed in 1983 with the express goal of leading the Republicans to majority status in the House. The group, first chaired by Georgia Congressman Newt Gingrich, is comprised of so-called "new conservatives" or "conservative populists" who have been critical of more established Republican conservative leadership as too willing to compromise and too accepting of minority status. The COS began with a dozen members in 1983 but had grown strong enough to elect Gingrich as Republican whip at the beginning of the George Bush administration.

With respect to issues, the Conservative Opportunity Society emphasizes traditional conservative Republican positions—a strong defense (e.g., support for President Ronald Reagan's Strategic Defense Initiative) and opposition to the Soviet Union; policies to stimulate economic growth in the private sector without undue government regulation; strong commitment to traditional social policies such as opposition to abortion and permitting prayers in the schools. With regard to tactics, the COS stressed confrontation with the Democrats; in fact the group formed largely out of concern that traditional Republicans were too willing to compromise with the Democrats of the issue of raising taxes to fight the deficit. Gingrich pioneered the use of C-SPAN telecasts to attack Democratic policies and Democratic politicians. He played a central role in instigating the investigation that led to the resignation of Speaker Jim Wright.

The Conservative Opportunity Society is a prime example of an informal caucus within one of the major parties, formed to push the party in a particular policy direction. As such it is a descendent of the Democratic Study Group (liberal Democrats), the Republican Study Group (traditional conservative Republicans), and the Wednesday Group (moderate Republicans). It differs, however, in the extent to which its goals are electoral as well as legislative and procedural.

L. Sandy Maisel

REFERENCES

Pitney, John J. 1988a. "The Conservative Opportunity Society." Paper presented at the Annual Meeting of the Western Political Science Association, San Francisco.

———. 1988b. "The War on the Floor: Partisan Conflict in the U.S. House of Representatives." Paper presented at the Annual Meeting of the American Political Science Association, Washington.

Rohde, David W. 1991. *Parties and Leaders in the Post-Reform House.* Chicago: University of Chicago Press.

Conservative Party of New York State

The New York State Conservative Party was formed in 1961 by a group of conservative professionals, including journalists, business-men, and intellectuals who sought to provide a conservative alternative to the seemingly more moderate-to-liberal Republican Party, then dominated by Governor Nelson Rockefeller. Conservative Party leaders wanted to provide a ballot counterpart to the state's Liberal Party and hoped to pressure the Republicans to move to the right.

Recognizing the difficulty of challenging Rockefeller within the Republican Party, the Conservatives ran David Jacquith for governor in 1962. He garnered 141,877 votes, thereby gaining official ballot recognition for the party (New York parties gain ballot recognition by running a gubernatorial candidate who receives at least 50,000 votes). The party's 1966 guber-natorial candidate, Paul Adams, received over half a million votes. The Conservative-Rockefeller feud lasted until the mid-1970s, when Rockefeller was compelled to make peace with the Conservatives out of loyalty to the national Republican Party, in conjunction with Rockefeller's selection to serve as Vice President under Gerald Ford.

The Conservative Party's greatest statewide successes came in senatorial races. They consis-tently declined to endorse Republican Jacob Javits (a Rockefeller ally who was endorsed in each of his races by the Liberal Party), and in 1968 nominated James Buckley, who received over a million votes in a losing effort. Two years later, Buckley was elected to the Senate solely on the Conservative line, defeating an anti-Vietnam War Republican, Charles Goodell, and Democrat Richard Ottinger. Buckley's race was buttressed by unofficial support from the Rich-ard Nixon administration. Buckley lost in his 1976 reelection bid (despite a joint Republican-Conservative endorsement) to Democrat Daniel Patrick Moynihan.

In 1980 the Conservative Party gave a critical boost to the senatorial campaign of an unknown Hempstead town supervisor, Alphonse D'Amato,

by endorsing him before the Republican pri-mary. In a stunning upset, D'Amato beat Javits out of the Republican nod. With combined Re-publican-Conservative-Right to Life Party (RTLP) endorsements, D'Amato went on to defeat Democrat Elizabeth Holtzman and Javits (run-ning solely on the Liberal line).

As is true of other New York minor parties, the Conservatives have been able to bargain with the major parties by offering an endorse-ment in exchange for ideological or material concessions. In 1978, for example, Republican gubernatorial nominee Perry Duryea sought the Conservative endorsement in his race against Democratic-Liberal nominee Hugh Carey. Since Duryea's conservative credentials were less than sterling (he was a Rockefeller protégé), he struck a deal with Conservative Party leaders that al-lowed them to nominate one of their own (William Carney), for the U.S. Congress from the First Congressional District (Duryea's home area) in exchange for granting Duryea the Conservative nod.

The Conservative Party has generally outpolled the Liberals, even after the establish-ment of the RTLP in 1978. Despite the apparently similar interests of the Conservatives and the RTLP, they have relied on different constituen-cies and have avoided public squabbling. Whereas the Conservatives are more strictly upper middle class and business oriented (the *National Review* was an early supporter), the RTLP has drawn more from working-class, blue-collar ethnic sectors.

See also: Charles Goodell, Liberal Party of New York, Richard Nixon, Right to Life Party, Nelson Rockefeller

Robert J. Spitzer

REFERENCES

Schoenberger, Robert A. 1968. "Conservatism, Per-sonality and Political Extremism." 62 *American Po-litical Science Review* 868.

Spitzer, Robert J. 1989. "The Tail Wagging the Dog: Multi-Party Politics." In Peter W. Colby and John K. White, eds. *New York State Today.* Albany: State U. of New York Pr.

Constituency Service and Congressional Elections

Well over 90 percent of incumbents in the House of Representatives regularly win reelec-tion, and three-fourths of them do so with at least 60 percent of the vote. Obvious reasons are that incumbents are widely recognized; they receive comfortable, and mostly favorable, press attention; they are well liked and favorably evaluated by their constituents; and their election campaigns are incredibly well funded. For the House, but less so for the Senate, challengers lack these advantages, generally leading to electoral defeat.

Political scientist David Mayhew has tried to explain this incumbency advantage: Congressmen behave in ways designed to allow them to engage in advertising themselves—credit claiming and position taking. These goals are easily achieved by frequent travel to their home areas, ready access to local media, the use of the franking privilege, and constant attentiveness to constituents. Other credit is earned by steering (or appearing to steer) federal contracts and grants to their states and districts, by providing information and small favors, and especially by helping constituents in their dealings with the federal bureaucracy; thus, incumbents seem to be able to endear themselves to enough voters to make a difference. Since Representatives receive somewhere near 100 constituent requests for help each week (Senators receive more), and since services are provided in a nonpartisan manner, the numbers of grateful constituents of all political persuasions could rise rapidly.

This explanation for electoral success, stressing service to constituents (especially pork barreling and casework) rather than policy, has long been conventional wisdom in Washington. A survey in 1978 revealed that over four-fifths of a sample of Congressmen and staffs agreed that voters who receive casework help from their Representatives would vote for them at the next election. No wonder that virtually all House and Senate incumbents aggressively seek casework requests from constituents!

Since most members of Congress rarely alter their policy views or voting patterns much, the primary mechanism available to voters for affecting public policy is to replace their Representatives. To the extent that constituency service might influence electoral results and protect incumbents, members of Congress could gain a wide measure of policy freedom from their constituents. Policy responsiveness could decline, and representative democracy could be threatened.

But does constituency service buy votes? Political scientists are divided on this question, in part because the necessary data (a panel study of voters before and after they received assistance from their Congressmen) are lacking and in part because ascertaining and measuring causality are so difficult. The strongest arguments come from survey research; yet studies yield contradictory results. It certainly seems clear that, because constituents certainly expect Congressmen to be of service, any Senator or Representative who violates such expectations will be in trouble. Since none do, however, no one can tell what would happen if they did. On the other hand, no scholar using either individual or aggregate-level data has proved that seeking out ever more constituent requests for help, or providing services to more and more citizens, actually produces votes. Nor has there been evidence that incumbents can scare away strong challengers by attending assiduously to constituent's wants. The reasons may be that most people who seek help from an incumbent either do not vote or already are supporters; others are ungrateful, believing that it is a politician's job to help if asked and that no special rewards are in order; and the remaining cases are too few to matter.

John R. Johannes

REFERENCES

Bond, Jon, Cary Covington, and Richard Fleisher. 1985. "Explaining Challenger Quality in Congressional Elections." 47 *Journal of Politics* 510.

Cain, Bruce, John Ferejohn, and Morris Fiorina. 1987. *The Personal Vote: Constituency Service and Electoral Independence.* Cambridge: Harvard U. Pr.

Feldman, Paul, and James Jondrow. 1984. "Congressional Elections and Local Federal Spending." 28 *American Journal of Political Science* 147.

Fiorina, Morris P. 1977. *Congress: The Keystone of the Washington Establishment.* New Haven: Yale U. Pr.

Hinckley, Barbara. 1981. *Congressional Elections.* Washington: Congressional Quarterly.

Jacobson, Gary C. 1987. *The Politics of Congressional Elections.* 2d ed. Boston: Little, Brown.

Johannes, John R. 1984. *To Serve the People: Congress and Constituency Service.* Lincoln: U. of Nebraska Pr.

———, and John McAdams. 1981. "The Congressional Incumbency Effect: Is It Casework, Policy Compatibility, or Something Else?" 25 *American Journal of Political Science* 512.

McAdams, John C., and John R. Johannes. 1987. "Determinants of Spending by House Challengers, 1974–84." 31 *American Journal of Political Science* 457.

———, and ———. 1988. "Congressmen, Perquisites, and Elections." 50 *Journal of Politics* 412.

Mayhew, David R. 1974. *Congress: The Electoral Connection.* New Haven: Yale U. Pr.

Constitutional Union Party

During the presidential election of 1860, conservative Whigs, alienated by the emergence of Abraham Lincoln as the leader of the Republican Party, assembled in Baltimore to form the Constitutional Union Party. This group decided that the best way to avoid the collapse of the Union was to take no stand on the hotly contested political issue of the role of the federal government in the expansion of slavery into the territories.

The Constitutional Union Party was organized without a platform other than to recognize the Constitution of the country, the union of the states, and the enforcement of the laws. Most of the convention delegates were men in their sixties. Their opponents derisively referred to the party as either the "Old Gentlemen's Party" or as the "Do Nothing Party" because it made no statement on the vital issue of slavery.

The convention nominated John B. Bell, a wealthy slaveholder from Tennessee and a former Whig, as its presidential candidate and a well-known Cotton Whig, Edward Everett, from Massachusetts, for the vice presidency. At the time of his nomination Bell (age 64) was universally acknowledged to be a man of character and patriotism. Everett, 3 years older than Bell, was a man respected among supporters of the old Whig Party but one lacking political appeal. The ticket had intellectual distinction but inspired no great enthusiasm. The basic message of the party was that the election of Lincoln would drive southerners into secession because the ultimate aim of the Republican Party was not merely to keep slavery out of the territories but to put slavery on the road to extinction.

The Constitutional Unionists did not expect to win the election, but they did hope to prevent a Republican victory by carrying enough electoral votes in the South to throw the election into the House of Representatives. In the House no party had a majority of the votes, thus giving the Constitutional Unionists the potential to combine with various factions of the Democratic Party to prevent Lincoln's election.

The willingness of Constitutional Union leaders to trade votes with both the Stephen Douglas-led Democrats as well as the John Breckinridge-led Democrats made the party appear to be equivocal and without principle. The election of 1860 clearly demonstrated that the slavery issue could not be settled by ignoring it. In that election, the Bell-Everett ticket carried only the three Border States of Tennessee, Kentucky, and Virginia and in the North the ticket won less than 3 percent of the vote and took no states away from Lincoln.

See also: John Breckinridge, Cotton Whig, Stephen Douglas, Election of 1860, Abraham Lincoln, Secession, Slavery

Margaret Horsnell

REFERENCES

Baum, Dale. 1984. *The Civil War Party System: The Case of Massachusetts, 1848–1876.* Chapel Hill: U. of North Carolina Pr.

Crenshaw, Ollinger. 1945. *The Slave States in the Presidential Election of 1860.* Baltimore: Johns Hopkins U. Pr.

Mering, John V. 1977. "The Slave-State Constitutional Unionist and the Politics of Consensus." 43 *Journal of Southern History* 395.

Contribution Limits and Presidential Prenomination Campaigns

In 1974 Congress incorporated individual and political action committee contribution limits into the Federal Election Campaign Act (FECA), largely to prevent contributors of large amounts from playing a dominant role in future federal election campaigns. Campaign reform advocates were concerned that such contributors ("fat cats") could exercise undue influence over candidates and officeholders. They also were concerned that candidates with access to wealth enjoyed an unfair advantage over other candidates in funding their campaigns.

Under the 1974 FECA Amendments, candidates for the presidential nomination are permitted to accept no more than $1,000 from any individual contributor, nor any more than $5,000 from any multicandidate committee. The candidates are allowed to contribute an unlimited amount to their own campaigns, unless they accept public funding. In that case they are permitted to contribute a maximum of $50,000 in personal or family funds.

Public matching funds are available to candidates who raise $5,000 in each of 20 states in contributions from individuals of $250 or less. The federal government matches each contribution to qualified candidates up to $250 per contributor, but the total federal subsidy to any candidate may not exceed one-half the presidential prenomination campaign spending limit: $20.2 million in 1984 and about $23 million in 1988.

Although several means have been developed to circumvent the presidential prenomination campaign contribution limits, for the most part the limits have succeeded in eliminating donors of large amounts from the process of directly funding federal election campaigns. No longer do wealthy individuals using their own funds play the prominent role they once played in funding campaigns for presidential nominations.

Bases of Financial Support

The contribution limits, in combination with the provision of matching funds and of tax credits for relatively small contributions, were meant to force candidates to broaden their bases of support and thereby give donors of modest sums an opportunity to play a meaningful role in campaign financing. In this regard the law also appears to have succeeded. During the 1972 prenomination and general elections, the last to be conducted before the new campaign law took effect, both Richard Nixon's and George McGovern's campaigns claimed about 600,000 contributors each. The Nixon list of contributors, however, was dominated by givers of large amounts. The McGovern campaign was more dependent on donors of small amounts, most of them giving in response to mass mail appeals.

In the 1984 prenomination campaigns, candidates submitted almost 800,000 contributions eligible for matching funds. That figure does not necessarily mean that a like number contributed to all those campaigns; some individuals may have made more than one matchable contribution, either to the same candidate or to various candidates. On the other hand, some modest contributions may not have been submitted for matching, such as the large number of small cash contributions reportedly collected by Jesse Jackson's campaign on the occasion of the candidate's campaign appearances in Black churches and other gatherings.

Electoral Competition

The contribution limit and matching fund provisions of the FECA also were intended to open up the electoral process to candidates whose lack of access to wealthy donors would have prevented them, under the previous campaign financing system, from being influential factors in that process. In 1976 contribution limits and public funding permitted Jimmy Carter—a Washington outsider, a regional candidate—to break into the field and establish his candidacy. In 1980 those provisions helped George Bush establish himself as Ronald Reagan's major competitor and helped him stay the course of the primaries and caucuses. They also helped John Anderson become an influential factor in some early Republican primaries and, more significant, allowed him to start building the name recognition and national organization that he needed in order to launch his independent candidacy for the presidency.

In 1984 the contribution limit and matching fund provisions were particularly helpful to Senator Gary Hart. Hart began his campaign as a little-known Senator from a relatively small western state and did not enjoy ready access to large amounts of private money. At least twice in his campaign Hart used either matching funds he had qualified to receive or the prospect of future public funds as collateral for bank loans he needed to remain competitive. And after his unexpected success in early prenomination contests, the combination of private contributions and public matching funds he received permitted him to finance an expensive media campaign to maintain his momentum over his principal rival, Walter Mondale. No one doubts that Hart's impact on the Democratic campaign would have been far less—perhaps even negligible—if public funds had not been available at critical points in his campaign's development.

Unintended Consequences

Although the contribution limits and matching fund provisions have achieved some of their initial purposes, they also have had some unforeseen, and not always salutary, consequences for the prenomination campaign process. These limits have contributed to an increase in the length of the season of active campaigning and have caused wealthy contributors to be replaced by well-connected solicitors and other types of fundraisers in positions of financial influence in campaigns. The limits have also rigidified the campaign process by virtually eliminating the possibility of late candidacies by insurgent candidates and have made it difficult for many candidates to raise adequate funds.

Lengthening the Campaign Season

Many observers considered the $1,000 individual contribution limit restrictively low when Congress enacted it in 1974. Since that time inflation has eroded the value of contributions, reducing a $1,000 contribution in 1984, for example, to a value of less than $500 expressed in 1974 dollars. Accordingly, prospective candidates in 1984, believing that they probably would have to raise between $15 million and $20 million in private contributions and matching funds to wage competitive campaigns, were required to begin their fundraising as early as feasible. No longer could they depend on a few wealthy backers to provide seed money, as well-connected pre-1976 candidates could.

The advantage in the fundraising process now belongs to well-known candidates with abundant time to devote to fundraising coupled with an ability to tap into networks of proven contributors. Officeholders, particularly those in congressional and state-level leadership positions, are handicapped because they often are unable to devote the time needed to raise campaign money. Also disadvantaged are little-known candidates without established donor bases.

The need to spend many months developing a donor base and collecting sufficient money to establish a presence at least in states with important early primary and caucus contests also eliminates the possibility of successful late candidacies. In 1968 New York Senator Robert Kennedy entered the primaries in March of the election year after Senator Eugene McCarthy had demonstrated that incumbent President Lyndon Johnson was vulnerable to challenge. Unhindered by contribution limits, Kennedy was able to raise sufficient money quickly from contributors of large amounts and from creditors to fund a highly competitive campaign in the primary contests that followed. In all, the Kennedy campaign spent about $9 million in 11 weeks. In comparison, in 1976 Governor Edmund G. "Jerry" Brown, Jr., of California entered the Democratic nomination contest in mid-March of the election year, and his campaign, operating under FECA restraints, spent only $1.9 million in a four-month-long period leading up to the nominating convention. In March 1980 many Republicans speculated that former President Gerald Ford would enter the Republican nomination race. By that time GOP front-runner Ronald Reagan had already spent a substantial portion of the amount he was permitted under the national spending limit. Undoubtedly Reagan would have been hard pressed to counter a well-financed challenge by Ford in the remaining primaries. But the $1,000 individual contribution limit would have made it difficult for Ford to raise sufficient funds to mount an effective challenge. Therefore, he chose not to join the competition.

The matching fund provisions also contribute to lengthier campaigns. Journalists have found attainment of the threshold required to qualify for public funds a useful measure in determining whether candidates deserve to be considered as "serious" contenders. The quicker a candidate reaches the threshold, the sooner he may receive favorable news coverage. Qualifying for matching funds has become what one former Democratic candidate called a "license to practice" that few candidates can afford to delay obtaining.

Finally, matching funds may prolong the campaigns of some candidates who have no real chance of winning the nomination by providing them with the money needed to carry on. Without such funds many such candidates would be required to withdraw from the race leaving the field to the front-runners.

Altering Fundraising Patterns

The FECA's individual contribution limit prevents wealthy individuals from bankrolling a candidate's campaign, but that limit does not prevent individuals from occupying positions of great financial influence in campaigns. In fact the fundraising void created by the elimination of fat-cat contributors has been filled by a variety of fundraising entrepreneurs—some volunteers and others paid professionals. Most notable among these entrepreneurs are numerous well-connected individuals with the time, energy, and commitment to raise a large number of contributions from $250 to $1,000 for their favored candidates from persons who belong to their business and social networks. Often these "elite solicitors" are involved in investment banking, real estate, insurance, law firms, stocks and bonds, venture capital, or lobbying; these endeavors put them in touch with large numbers of affluent persons. Elite political financiers appeal to prospective donors in person or through telephone calls or put together fundraising luncheons and dinners to which they invite their clients and associates.

Most of the 1984 presidential campaigns depended in part on the efforts of at least some members of this new campaign elite. Attorney and art collector Duane B. Garrett and real estate developer Nathan Landow, for example, had each collected about $700,000 for Walter Mondale's campaign by mid-May 1984. Hart campaign money specialists included Mike Medavoy, an executive vice president of Orion Pictures. By midway through the primary campaign season, Medavoy, according to his own estimate, had been involved in raising between $400,000 and $500,000 for Hart, about half from the entertainment industry and another substantial portion from young lawyers.

The contribution limits have given rise to other new forms of fundraising as well. Entertainers and artists may play influential roles in presidential candidate fundraising because their volunteered services—time, effort, talents—are exempt from the contribution limits. Several 1980 presidential candidates enlisted a variety of entertainers to appear at benefit concerts for their campaigns. The 1980 Kennedy campaign prevailed on a number of artists to donate works to be used at raffles and as door prizes at fundraising events and to be offered as inducements to potential contributors. The 1984 Mondale campaign sold artworks donated by artists including Claes Oldenburg, George Segal, and Richard Estes as part of the campaign's debt-retirement program.

Direct mail appeals have been used effectively by some presidential candidates to reach large numbers of small contributors—precisely what the framers of the 1974 FECA Amendments set out to accomplish. Large-scale mail appeals, however, generally are productive only for candidates who are clearly identified as liberal or conservative or for candidates who have the time available to develop a list of proven contributors. Moreover, mass mail solicitations can be costly, requiring candidates to spend large sums early in the campaign or to find a direct mail firm willing to extend credit. In 1984, Ronald Reagan used mail solicitations to raise three-fourths of the approximately $16 million he received from private donors to his prenomination campaign. Unlike his Democratic counterparts, he was well-positioned to use this method, which helped him collect the maximum amount of matching funds. Reagan has long been identified as an ideological conservative and had used direct mail with notable success in earlier campaigns.

Candidate Debts

Despite the matching fund provision of the FECA, intended in part to make up for the campaign money taken out of the system by the individual contribution limit, every 1984 Democratic candidate who received matching funds ended his prenomination campaign in debt. At one point the total indebtedness of those candidates reached more than $15 million. Prenomination debt reduction activities continued throughout the general election period, distracting attention and draining resources from the Democratic election campaign. Presidential candidate debt certainly is not a creature of the FECA, since some candidates in earlier, non-FECA regulated campaigns also finished their campaigns in the red. But the fact that so many

candidates in 1980 and in 1984 were in debt at the conclusion of their campaigns suggests that the $1,000 individual contribution limit has not kept pace with increases in campaign costs. Many candidates appear to find it increasingly difficult, under the limit, to raise sufficient money to conduct their campaigns.

See also: John Anderson, Edmund G. Brown, Jr., George Bush, Jimmy Carter, Direct Mail, Elections of 1976, 1980 and 1984, Federal Election Campaign Act of 1971 and Amendments, Gerald Ford, Jesse Jackson, Walter Mondale, Richard Nixon, Political Action Committees, Ronald Reagan

Brian A. Haggerty

REFERENCES

Alexander, Herbert E. 1976. *Financing the 1972 Election.* Lexington, MA: Heath.

———. 1979. *Financing the 1976 Election.* Washington: Congressional Quarterly.

———, and Brian A. Haggerty. 1987. *Financing the 1984 Election.* Lexington, MA: Heath.

———, with Brian A. Haggerty. 1983. *Financing the 1980 Election.* Lexington, MA: Heath.

Cheney, Richard B. 1980. "The Law's Impact on Presidential and Congressional Election Campaigns." In Michael J. Malbin, ed. *Parties, Interest Groups, and Campaign Finance Laws.* Washington: American Enterprise Institute.

Financing Presidential Campaigns: An Examination of the Ongoing Effects of the Federal Election Campaign Laws Upon the Conduct of Presidential Campaigns. 1982. A Research Report by the Campaign Finance Study Group to the Committee on Rules and Administration of the United States Senate. Cambridge: Institute of Politics, John F. Kennedy School of Government, Harvard University.

Calvin Coolidge (1872–1933)

Thirtieth President of the United States. Elected as Vice President on the Republican ticket in 1920, Calvin Coolidge became President upon the death of President Warren G. Harding on August 2, 1923. With his election to the presidency in 1924, Coolidge joined Theodore Roosevelt as the second President to succeed himself after completing the term of another President.

Coolidge's climb to the presidency was relatively uneventful. Following his service as lieutenant governor in the Commonwealth of Massachusetts, Coolidge was elected governor in 1919. After only eight months in office, he faced a police strike in Boston on September 11 which paralyzed the city for three days. On September 14, in defense of his actions to call out the state militia to restore order, Governor Coolidge sent a telegram to AFL president Samuel Gompers asserting that "[t]here is no right to strike against the public safety by anybody, anywhere, any time." Almost overnight, in a period when many Americans feared bolshevism, Calvin Coolidge became a national figure.

Coolidge's seeming hard line on law and order and his solid record on fiscal matters earned him the Republican vice presidential nomination in 1920. As President in 1923, Coolidge presided over a country experiencing broad economic growth and prosperity and enjoying great stature in world affairs. During his nearly six years as President, Coolidge followed a strict laissez faire policy toward business affairs. His general attitude that everyone should "keep his own house in order" also extended into foreign policy, where the President opposed the formation of the League of Nations.

Even though he won election to the presidency in 1924 by a landslide over Democrat John Davis and Progressive Robert La Follette, Coolidge was popular neither among the public nor among members of Congress. Known as "Silent Cal" because of his taciturn manner, Coolidge lacked skill at building congressional coalitions. Progressive Republicans in the Senate often voted with Democrats to upset the tenuous Republican voting majority in that house. Despite Republican majorities in both houses of Congress, Coolidge had to employ his veto power 50 times during his tenure—equal to the total that Presidents Woodrow Wilson and Warren G. Harding had used in previous terms.

Regardless of the split between traditional and progressive Republicans, party leaders expected that Coolidge would run for and win reelection in 1928. On the fourth anniversary of his accession to the presidency, Coolidge announced: "I do not choose to run for President in nineteen twenty-eight." Suspecting that Coolidge hoped for a draft for the nomination, prospective Republican opponents remained wary for several months. While Republican leaders gradually recognized Coolidge's sincerity in not running, the President remained carefully neutral throughout the ensuing campaign, neither endorsing nor showing opposition to any other Republican's candidacy.

Coolidge's hands-off policy in government represented the prevailing attitude of a dominant Republican Party devoted to business as the guiding force in America's political economy. Because Coolidge, his successor Herbert Hoover, and the Republican Party in general continually ran election campaigns on the basis of eco-

nomic prosperity, the oncoming depression in 1929 would spell political doom for the Republicans. Just as the GOP stood on its economic record in times of prosperity, so too did it have to stand on its record in the economically depressed era of the 1930s. Calvin Coolidge, however, managed to escape the wrath bestowed on his successor Hoover. Coolidge "got out in time."

See also: Elections of 1920, 1924, and 1928; Samuel Gompers; Warren Harding; Herbert Hoover; Robert La Follette; League of Nations; Theodore Roosevelt; Woodrow Wilson

Michael Heel

REFERENCES

Dumond, Dwight Lowell. 1947. *America in Our Time.* New York: Henry Holt.

McCoy, Donald R. 1967. *Calvin Coolidge: The Quiet President.* New York: Macmillan.

Whiting, Edward Elwell. 1924. *Calvin Coolidge: His Ideals of Citizenship.* Boston: W. A. Wilde.

Peter Cooper (1791–1883)

Greenback Party candidate for President. Peter Cooper, one of the most successful businessmen in nineteenth-century America, became a patron of the Independent or National Greenback Party and ran for President as its first nominee in 1876. Cooper was born in New York City, and by 1828 he had helped to establish the Canton Iron Works in Baltimore. In 1829 and 1830 Cooper designed and built "Tom Thumb," the first American railway locomotive. With the locomotive he saved the Baltimore & Ohio Railroad from bankruptcy and thus greatly increased the value of the Canton Iron Works. He sold this property in 1836 and rapidly expanded his financial investments. In 1854, in his Trenton, New Jersey, factory, the first structural iron for fireproof buildings was rolled. In addition, he was the chief supporter of Cyrus Field's successful effort to lay a transatlantic cable. As one of the theater's principal benefactors, he was called "the patriarch of Broadway."

Having amassed great wealth, Cooper became a philanthropist. His greatest monument is the Cooper Union for the Advancement of Science and Art in New York City to which he contributed over $600,000 for its construction. Furthermore, he advocated a number of economic and social reforms, including a civil service, government aid to the unemployed, government owned and operated railroads, and a wider distribution of wealth. In 1876 Cooper accepted the Greenback Party's presidential nomination, even though he did not support the inflationist views of many western leaders. Instead, Cooper advocated a managed currency that would be limited according to population and trade. He believed such a currency would be a mortgage upon the nation's entire wealth and that it would put all the useful labor to work. In the presidential election, however, Cooper polled only 81,737 votes. At the end of his life, he was the leader of the Anti-Monopoly League, a strong opponent of trusts.

See also: Greenback Party, Railroads

Steven E. Siry

REFERENCES

Mack, Edward Clarence. 1949. *Peter Cooper: Citizen of New York.* New York: Duell, Sloan & Pearce.

Nevins, Allan. 1935. *Abraham S. Hewitt, with some Account of Peter Cooper.* New York: Harper.

Unger, Irwin. 1964. *The Greenback Era: A Social and Political History of American Finance, 1865–1879.* Princeton: Princeton U. Pr.

Cooper Union Speeches

For almost a century and a half, Cooper Union's Great Hall has served New York City and the nation as a center for discussing public issues through speeches and debates. Cooper Union for the Advancement of Science and Art was established to disseminate "useful" knowledge to the practical New Yorker. In 1859, at a personal cost of $630,000, business leader and philanthropist Peter Cooper completed the building that houses the Great Hall. Mark Twain delivered the institution's inaugural lecture and soon Henry Ward Beecher, William Cullen Bryant, William Lloyd Garrison, and others used the magnificent auditorium to speak out against slavery. But on February 27, 1860, Abraham Lincoln delivered probably the institution's most famous speech. He was the third lecturer in a series arranged by the Young Men's Republican Union of New York. The Illinois politician's fame had preceded him. Thus, the Great Hall was crowded to overflowing. As the New York *Tribune* noted, no one since the days of Henry Clay and Daniel Webster had spoken to a larger body of the city's intellectual elite. The audience warmly received Lincoln's closely reasoned argument against the extension of slavery. Furthermore, Republican Party leaders considered the "Right makes Might" speech a major address, and it convinced many that Lincoln was presidential timber after all.

After the Civil War, reformers often met at Cooper Union to express their dissatisfaction against corrupt city administrations. Moreover, it became a tradition that lasted up to Woodrow Wilson for every President to deliver a speech in the Great Hall. By the end of the nineteenth century, Cooper Union functioned in close association with the People's Institute, the most notable public forum in New York City. Throughout the twentieth century the Great Hall has continued to serve as a center for discussion and debate.

See also: Henry Clay, William Lloyd Garrison, Abraham Lincoln, Daniel Webster, Woodrow Wilson

Steven E. Siry

REFERENCES

Bender, Thomas. 1987. *New York Intellect: A History of Intellectual Life in New York City, From 1750 to the Beginnings of Our Own Time.* Baltimore: Johns Hopkins U. Pr.

Wolfe, Gerald R. 1975. *New York: A Guide to the Metropolis.* New York: New York U. Pr.

Copperheads (Peace Democrats)

During the Civil War the Democratic Party gradually divided into "war" and "peace" factions. The War Democrats usually supported whatever military measures were necessary to defeat the Confederacy. The Peace Democrats called for the restoration of the Union through negotiation and compromise, tending to believe that the Republican Party's policies had driven the South into secession.

The Republican opposition derogatorily termed the Peace Democrats, "Copperheads," a term with an otherwise unclear origin. One authority, James McPherson, believes that the name first appeared in a Republican newspaper in Ohio 1861; there the Peace Democrats were compared to poisonous copperhead snakes. Allan Nevins writes that the term was used at least as early as July 30, 1862, to stigmatize Democrats at the Indiana State Convention. According to Nevins the Democrats, seeking to render the unfavorable epithet a mark of distinction, wore identifying badges of heads of Liberty punched from big copper cents as a means of illustrating their unity and loyalty.

The Peace Democrats, associated with various secret antiwar societies such as the Knights of the Golden Circle, the Order of American Knights, and the Sons of Liberty, were scattered throughout the North but tended to be concentrated in the Midwest, a region that had strong economic and cultural ties with the South. This group also drew their support from the immigrant Catholic population of the cities. The Peace Democrats adamantly opposed the

Emancipation Proclamation, which they believed would result in a mass migration of Blacks into the Midwest. Fearing the radical social changes set in motion by the Republican Party's war policies, the Peace Democrats took as their slogan "The Constitution as it is and the Union as it was."

A series of bizarre plots allegedly linking the Confederate government to the Peace Democrats as well as the statements made by their more outspoken members opposing the draft and urging recruits in the army to desert fueled the suspicions of the Lincoln administration that these northern sympathizers for the South posed a threat to the successful completion of the war.

No doubt the activities of the Peace Democrats contributed to Abraham Lincoln's arbitrary treatment of dissenters during the Civil War. In the fall of 1862, Lincoln suspended the writ of habeas corpus in part as a means of containing opposition to the draft. In some areas of the Midwest, military commissions were set up to try civilians. During the war, Union authorities arrested at least 15,000 civilians, including newspaper editors as well as public officials.

The movement's influence peaked at the Democratic convention of 1864 when Clement Vallandigham, one of the leaders of the Peace faction, persuaded the party to adopt a resolution declaring the war a failure and demanding an immediate end to hostilities. However, the Democratic presidential candidate, George McClellan, repudiated that plank of the party's platform. With the North victorious at Appomattox, the Peace Democrats collapsed.

See also: Emancipation as a Political Issue, Abraham Lincoln, Secession, Clement Vallandigham

Margaret Horsnell

REFERENCES

Gray, Wood. 1964. *The Hidden Civil War: The Story of the Copperheads.* New York: Viking.

Klement, Frank L. 1960. *The Copperheads in the Middle West.* Chicago: U. of Chicago Pr.

———. 1970. *The Limits of Dissent: Clement L. Vallandigham.* Lexington: U. Pr. of Kentucky.

Nevins, Allan. 1960. *The War for the Union.* New York: Scribner's.

Thomas G. Corcoran (1900–1981)

Architect of the New Deal of the 1930s. Nicknamed "Tommy the Cork," Thomas Gardiner Corcoran was instrumental in drafting and facilitating the enactment of much major New Deal legislation. Born in Pawtucket, Rhode Island, Corcoran earned two degrees from Brown University in 1922 and law degrees from Harvard University in 1925 and 1926. After clerking for Justice Oliver Wendell Holmes, he joined the law firm of Cotton and Franklin in New York City.

Through his law firm's relationship with Herbert Hoover's administration, Corcoran was appointed counsel to the Reconstruction Finance Corporation in 1932. During Franklin Roosevelt's administration, Corcoran retained this position until 1941 as at the same time he was performing other duties and briefly filling other positions. From 1932 until 1935, Corcoran served as special assistant to the Attorney General. In 1933 he served as an assistant to the Secretary of the Treasury.

Regardless of his official positions, Corcoran gained prominence and power as a legislative draftsman and as Roosevelt's chief liaison with Congress. With Benjamin Cohen, General Counsel for the National Power Policy Committee, Corcoran drafted the Securities Act of 1933, the Federal Housing Act of 1933, the Securities Exchange Act of 1934, the Public Utility Holding Company Act of 1935, and the Fair Labor Standards Act of 1938.

As Corcoran's power as a political operative for the White House declined, he entered private law practice in 1941, forming the firm of Corcoran, Youngman, and Rowe in Washington. He was soon called before a Senate investigating committee to answer charges of influence-peddling on behalf of his firm's clients. These charges were dismissed, but Corcoran was investigated again in 1969 by a panel of the District of Columbia bar for allegedly lobbying the Supreme Court for a rehearing of one of his client's antitrust case. These charges were also dismissed. In his later years he became prominent in alumni affairs for Brown University.

See also: New Deal, Franklin Roosevelt

Sean J. Savage

REFERENCES

Anderson, Patrick. 1968. *The Presidents' Men.* New York: Doubleday.

Koenig, Louis. 1960. *The Invisible Presidency.* New York: Rinehart.

Niznik, Monica L. 1981. *Thomas G. Corcoran: The Public Service of Franklin Roosevelt's "Tommy the Cork."* Notre Dame, IN: U. of Notre Dame Pr.

Erastus Corning II (1909–1983)

The longest-serving mayor in U.S. history. The scion of one of New York State's oldest Dutch families, Erastus Corning II was reared in

Albany; he graduated from Albany Academy, Groton, and Yale. Corning hailed from a Democratic background—his father was a lieutenant governor under Alfred E. Smith and his great-grandfather was an Albany mayor—and he quickly entered politics as a state assemblyman and state senator.

In 1941, one month before the Japanese attack on Pearl Harbor, Corning was elected mayor of Albany. He was subsequently reelected to ten four-year terms, usually winning 70 percent of the vote. While serving as an Army private in Europe during World War II, Corning continued as mayor and was reelected while abroad. Except for a single run for lieutenant governor in 1946, Corning sought no other political office.

During most of Corning's mayoral years, political power in Albany rested in the hands of Daniel P. O'Connell, boss of the Democratic machine. Corning was O'Connell's candidate for mayor. A 1972–1973 State Commission on Investigation charged the O'Connell machine with exercising "over-riding power that controls hiring, firing, raises, promotions, contracts, purchases and prices and probably every other activity in the City of Albany." The result was considerable "mismanagement" and "waste of public funds." Corning responded, "This city is as political as any in the state." One politician described the tall and courtly Corning as "the ideal guy to have out front."

Corning's political longevity was legendary. After Daniel O'Connell's death in 1977, Corning faced opposition from within the Democratic Party for the first time in 36 years. In 1977 he won the primary by a two-to-one margin and was easily reelected in the fall. His closest call came in 1973 when Corning faced a Republican businessman, Carl Tuohey. Corning won that race with just 53 percent of the vote. In his last contest from his hospital bed in 1981, Corning defeated Tuohey's son, Charles, by a two-to-one margin, indicating his political strength and popularity.

See also: Bosses, Alfred E. Smith

John K. White

REFERENCES

Farber, M. A. 1983. "Erastus Corning II, Albany Mayor Since '42, Dies." *New York Times.* 29 May.

George B. Cortelyou (1862–1940)

Republican National Committee chairman and holder of three Cabinet offices. George Bruce Cortelyou was national chairman of the Republican Party, Postmaster General, Secretary of Commerce and Labor, and Secretary of the Treasury during Theodore Roosevelt's administration. In 1908 he was considered a serious contender for the Republican presidential nomination. Son of a successful businessman, Cortelyou's education was largely in literature and music at private schools, but at age 20, the need for practical skills sent him to a stenographic school—a decision that subsequently proved to be of great importance.

In 1884 he was appointed stenographer and private secretary to the Republican appraiser of the port of New York and was active in James Blaine's campaign. After Blaine's defeat, Cortelyou became a stenographer in the New York superior court where he achieved a reputation as a medical as well as a legal stenographer.

From 1889 to 1891 Cortelyou was private secretary to the Post Office Department's inspector in charge of the New York area. In spring of 1891, he became private secretary to President Benjamin Harrison's fourth Assistant Postmaster General. Cortelyou performed his official duties with such skill that, although known to be a Republican and active in the Harrison campaigns, he was requested to stay on to manage the fourth assistant's office after President Grover Cleveland's reelection. Hearing of Cortelyou's reputation for efficiency, Cleveland in 1895 appointed him presidential stenographer and, later, executive clerk. Cortelyou continued in this position under President William McKinley, while earning an LL.B., an LL.M., and an LL.D. at various District of Columbia law schools.

President Theodore Roosevelt retained Cortelyou as presidential executive clerk and in February 1903 elevated him to the Cabinet position of Secretary of the new Department of Commerce and Labor; Cortelyou also managed Roosevelt's 1904 preconvention nomination effort. Thus, when the time came to select a new national party chairman, Roosevelt insisted on Cortelyou despite the objections of most national committeemen. As Republican national chairman, Cortelyou began to appoint a new generation of Republican politicians to strategic positions in the national party.

After the election, Roosevelt appointed Cortelyou Postmaster General in 1905 and Secretary of the Treasury in 1907. Cortelyou did not resign from the national chairmanship at the time he became Postmaster General, thus setting a custom that prevailed for the next half-century. However, Cortelyou did resign when he became Secretary of the Treasury, in part to free himself for a run for the Republican presidential nomination in 1908. However, Roosevelt favored William Howard Taft, who received the nomination. In 1909 Cortelyou became president of the Consolidated Gas Company of New York, a position he held until 1935.

See also: Grover Cleveland, Election of 1908, Benjamin Harrison, William McKinley, Republican National Committee, Theodore Roosevelt, William Howard Taft

Ralph M. Goldman

REFERENCES

Dawes, Charles G. 1950. *A Journal of the McKinley Days.* Chicago: Lakeside Press.

Halstead, Albert. 1904. "Chairman Cortelyou and the Republican Campaign." *American Monthly Review of Reviews* 294.

Cotton Whigs

The Cotton Whigs were the dominant faction in the Massachusetts Whig Party from 1830 to 1852. Their name originated in their support of close cooperation at the national level with the Whigs from the cotton states of the South and because several of their leaders were wealthy cotton manufacturers like Abbot Lawrence and Nathan Appleton. As an analogy the term was occasionally applied to northern Whigs in other states who stressed party unity and compromise with slavery.

The Whig Party, largely controlled by the cotton faction, was dominant in Massachusetts politics in this period. It lost the governorship in only two elections and regularly carried the state in presidential elections. The Cotton Whigs represented a powerful coalition of Boston aristocrats, textile manufacturers, and bankers who combined social, economic, and political power. In national politics they tended to favor Henry Clay and later Zachary Taylor. This predilection, plus Abbot Lawrence's ambition for national office, brought the faction into intermittent conflict with the followers of Daniel Webster and the antislavery radicals.

Nearly all Massachusetts Whigs were against slavery, but in the view of the dominant oligarchy, abolitionist and "Conscience Whigs" within their own party carried this hostility much too far. The Cotton Whigs desired close cooperation with southern Whigs in order to secure support for a protective tariff and other legislation that they believed essential to the Massachusetts economy. They also placed party loyalty, moderation, and the Union at the center of their ideology. Radical antislavery men seemed to endanger all of these concerns and to introduce an unwelcome element of egalitarian demagoguery into politics.

Divisions in the party became acute in the 1840s as the Conscience Whigs vehemently attacked the annexation of Texas and the Mexican War as manifestations of a "slave power conspiracy." The cotton faction opposed both annexation and war but based their opposition on constitutional grounds that would not offend their southern allies. Once Texas was annexed and war had begun, they felt opposition should cease. The Conscience Whigs responded by a full-scale attack on the Boston oligarchs and the national alliance of "lords of the lash and the loom." Their goal was to remake the Whigs into a primarily antislavery party while the Cotton Whigs insisted on preserving the Union and the primacy of traditional economic issues. When the cotton faction successfully promoted the presidential candidacy of Zachary Taylor in 1848, the Conscience Whigs bolted to the Free Soil Party.

By a combination of social ostracism and appeals for party unity, the Cotton Whigs retained control of the party and briefly of the Massachusetts state government. Their triumph was a hollow one, however, as they had chosen commitment to national party solidarity at the expense of neglecting new interests and attitudes in Massachusetts. In 1852 they were defeated by a Democratic Free Soil coalition and in 1854 and 1856 the Whigs were overwhelmed by landslides by the new American and then the Republican parties. The Cotton Whig leaders tended to back Millard Fillmore's American Party candidacy in 1856 and the Constitutional Union ticket in 1860. Their share of the vote fell to under 15 percent, and the Massachusetts Whigs disappeared. They had dominated the state for 20 years, but the cotton lords and Boston aristocrats had failed to adapt to the new issues that emerged in the 1840s.

See also: Abolition Movement; Henry Clay; Conscience Whigs; Constitutional Union Party; Elections of 1848, 1852, 1856, and 1860; Free Soil Party; Mexican War; Zachary Taylor; Daniel Webster

Harold B. Raymond

REFERENCES

Baum, Dale. 1984. *The Civil War Party System.* Chapel Hill: U. of North Carolina Pr.

Brauer, Kinley. 1967. *Cotton Versus Conscience: Massachusetts Politics and Southern Expansion 1843–1848.* Lexington: U. Pr. of Kentucky.

Darling, Arthur. 1925 Reprint 1969. *Political Change in Massachusetts 1824–1848: A Study of Liberal Movements in Politics*. New Haven: Yale U. Pr.

Formisano, Ronald. 1983. *The Transformation of Political Culture: Massachusetts Politics 1790–1840*. New York: Oxford U. Pr.

Gatell, Frank Otto. 1958. "Conscience and Judgment: The Bolt of the Conscience Whigs." 21 *The Historian* 18.

Gienapp, William. 1987. *Origins of the Republican Party*. New York: Oxford U. Pr.

Howe, David W. 1979. *The Political Culture of the American Whigs*. Chicago: U. of Chicago Pr.

O'Connor, Thomas. 1968. *Lords of the Loom: The Cotton Whigs and the Coming of the Civil War*. New York: Scribner's.

Charles E. Coughlin (1891–1979)

Conservative Catholic radio priest of the 1930s. Father Charles Edward Coughlin gained prominence as an early supporter and later an antagonist of Franklin Roosevelt. Born in Hamilton, Ontario, he studied theology at the University of Toronto and entered the Roman Catholic priesthood in 1916. After seven years of teaching at Assumption College in Windsor, Ontario, he moved to Michigan and in 1926 was assigned to work as a parish priest in the Detroit suburb of Royal Oak.

During his first months in Royal Oak, Father Coughlin was harassed by the local chapter of the Ku Klux Klan and troubled by the financial insolvency of his new church, the Shrine of the Little Flower. In an effort to solicit support for the church, he began in October 1926 to broadcast his Sunday sermons on a local radio station. Favorable response encouraged him to continue and, when his sermons began in 1930 to include warnings about the dangers of communism and attacks on international bankers, Coughlin's popularity soared. The phenomenal success of these broadcasts, called "The Golden Hour of the Little Flower," led to a nationwide contract with CBS. Coughlin became a leading radio personality, and by 1933 his estimated weekly audience of 30 million listeners was contributing approximately $5 million a year to his Radio League of the Little Flower.

In 1932 Father Coughlin began his relationship with Franklin Roosevelt by using his radio rostrum to endorse Roosevelt's election. Coughlin denounced Herbert Hoover, assailing him as "the banker's friend" and "the Holy Ghost of the Rich," and told his listeners that the election was a choice between "Roosevelt or ruin." He continued to support Roosevelt throughout 1933 and early 1934, claiming that "the New Deal is Christ's Deal." Throughout this period, he envisioned himself as an important ally of the President and anticipated an offer to serve in the administration. Roosevelt accepted Coughlin's support but never regarded him as more than an influential advocate. Coughlin's boasts of his relationship with the President soon became a source of embarrassment to the White House, and the President began to distance himself from the priest.

In the spring of 1934, Coughlin began to criticize individual New Deal measures, and by 1935 he was stridently attacking the administration. He described the New Deal as "the Jew Deal" and spoke of Roosevelt as an "anti-God." At this time he also announced the formation of the National Union for Social Justice. The avowed purpose of this organization was to promote social and economic reforms to benefit the poor and the downtrodden masses, but its actual goal was to support Coughlin's financial proposals, which included an inflationary monetary policy, income redistribution, and widespread welfare measures. At its peak, the National Union for Social Justice had an estimated one million members and was active in 26 states.

This political base helped Coughlin establish the groundwork for the Union Party. He joined with other New Deal critics, especially Gerald L. K. Smith, an associate of Senator Huey P. Long, and Dr. Francis Townsend, the pension crusader, to form this third party in 1936. Soon thereafter, the party nominated Congressman William Lemke of North Dakota for the presidency. Coughlin pledged to attract 9 million votes for Lemke or he would retire from public broadcasting. When Lemke polled less than a million votes, Coughlin announced the end of his radio career. But he resumed his weekly "sermons" early in 1937.

After the 1936 election, Coughlin's speeches were little more than reactionary statements riddled with hate, suspicion, and prejudice. He began to express admiration for the fascist regimes of Hitler and Mussolini and became increasingly anti-Semitic and pro-isolationist. His popularity declined rapidly and his radio broadcasts ceased in 1940. Early in 1942, the Catholic Church ordered him to end his political activities, and two years later the National Union for Social Justice officially disbanded. For the next 24 years, Coughlin worked quietly as a parish priest at the Shrine of the Little Flower.

See also: Communism as a Political Issue, Elections of 1932 and 1936, Herbert Hoover, Ku Klux Klan, Huey Long, New Deal, Isolationism in American Politics, Franklin Roosevelt, Union Party

Anthony J. Corrado

REFERENCES

Bennett, David H. 1969. *Demagogues of the Depression.* New Brunswick, NJ: Rutgers U. Pr.

Brinkley, Alan. 1982. *Voices of Protest: Huey Long, Father Coughlin, and the Great Depression.* New York: Knopf.

Tull, Charles J. 1965. *Father Coughlin and the New Deal.* Syracuse, NY: Syracuse U. Pr.

County Party Organizations

Political parties in the United States are typically organized at four geographical levels: the apex of the party is the national party committee; below the national parties are state party organizations; within each state are county party organizations; and within counties are precinct or ward organizations. This article will consider the *county party organizations.* Though they may appear to reside near the bottom of the party hierarchy, these organizations are of substantial significance within the party and political systems.

The Structure of County Party Organizations

In most parts of the country, if one were to try to visit the local county party organization, some difficulty would arise. County party organizations typically do not exist within an office or a building. Indeed, it is uncommon to find even a listing in the telephone book for many county parties. Instead, these organizations are frequently little more than the homes or offices of their county chairpersons. As physical structures, county parties in the U.S. are elusive at best.

At the same time, county party organizations do have many of the attributes of "real" organizations. Most have a constitution or a set of bylaws, and county committees meet fairly regularly. Most are able to fill their leadership positions on both the county and precinct levels. And during the election season, a majority of the county parties opens a campaign office. Thus, in many meaningful ways, these county party organizations do exist.

County party organizations typically are led by a county chairperson and are governed by the chair and a party central committee. The chairperson is usually selected by a vote of the party faithful (although party primaries increasingly are used to select county chairs).

County chairs are overwhelmingly white, middle aged, and male (Gibson, et al., 1985: 142). They tend to be longtime residents of their counties and tend to have held other party offices prior to assuming the position of county chair. Thus, most county chairs are party "insiders."

County-level political parties are accountable to the state party organization. The basic organizational structure of the county parties is mandated by state party regulations, which frequently have the full force of law. Although, in practice, county party organizations have been quite independent of state party guidance, the two layers of party organization are formally related in a hierarchical fashion.

County party organizations are generally volunteer organizations. That is, they rely upon party activists to come forward and donate their efforts. Only the most highly developed (and wealthy) party organizations have paid permanent party staffs. This heavy dependence on volunteers makes it difficult to maintain a standardized structure or a regularized schedule of activities. Because the county party organizations are personalized in the sense that they are the products of the party leaders, the relatively rapid turnover of party leaders deprives these parties of stability and continuity. Indeed, the diversity of motives, ideologies, skills, and party commitments of these volunteers generates considerable organizational difficulty.

The Activity of County Party Organizations

Though they are not imposing physical structures, the county party organizations can play a vital role in local politics. The major activities of these parties include organization building (e.g., establishing precinct-level organizations), fundraising, candidate recruitment and de-recruitment, involvement in the nomination process (e.g., preprimary endorsements), campaigning (e.g., get-out-the-vote drives), coordinating candidate campaign organizations, and patronage. Not all county party organizations perform all of these functions, but it is rare to find organizations that conduct none of these activities.

It is in the election season that the county party organizations bloom. Parties perform a variety of activities, ranging from distributing campaign literature to contributing money to candidates and conducting voter registration drives. An increasing number of these organizations is even engaged in fairly sophisticated, and costly, activities such as public opinion polling. With a variety of candidates standing for office within the county, the party organization often plays an important role in coordinating campaign activity. The county party organization is frequently found right in the center of the electoral maelstrom.

Much of this activity is focused on state and local (not national) politics. For instance, the chairs of these organizations report that they are most involved in recruitment of candidates for state legislative office rather than recruitment of candidates for national offices. This in part reflects the fact that national elections (especially presidential) are held less often than local elections, but is also reflects the domination by candidate campaign organizations in national campaigns. County and state legislative offices are the primary (though not exclusive) focus of county party organizations.

One of the reasons that county party organizations are able to engage in so many campaign activities is that they increasingly share resources with the state and national party organizations. For instance, nearly two-thirds of the county party organizations in the country now have joint state–county voter registration drives. The sharing of resources of different levels of the party organizations provides significant impetus for the strengthening of the campaign activities of county party organizations.

The primary business of political parties is contesting elections. Thus, campaign activity is perhaps the most important job of county party organizations. Survey evidence reveals that most county parties are reasonably active in this regard.

The Impact of County Party Organizations

Perhaps the acid test of the importance of county party organizations is whether they have any impact on politics. Some observers believe that the electoral relevance of county party organizations is declining. Evidence for this may be the demise of urban party "machines"—the hierarchically organized county party fueled by patronage and an ability to deliver the vote for candidates. As well, the increasing obsolescence of party resources such as volunteers and the rise of significant competitors to party influence may also have an adverse effect on the impact of county party organizations. This has led some to question the relevance of county party organizations, which is the classic question of whether parties matter. We can consider evidence on the relevance of party organizations along several distinct dimensions.

The Electoral Relevance of Parties

Conventional wisdom asserts that county party organizations have become less influential in delivering the vote. The model of ultimate electoral relevance is the urban party machine. It is thought that in the heyday of the machine, the party organization could virtually control elections due to its ability to turn out voters. Compared to this model of organization, county party organizations today are generally not relevant.

On the other hand, research has shown that strong county party organizations have some impact on election returns. Even with fairly rigorous statistical controls, it has been shown that strong party organizations are somewhat successful at raising the party's vote total. The effect is not great, but in some elections, the contributions of county party organizations do make a difference.

Traditionally, the electoral strength of county party organizations has been its volunteers. The party organization mobilizes volunteers for purposes of voter registration, canvassing, distribution of campaign literature, among other things. When campaigns involved greater interpersonal contact with the community, resources of this sort were quite attractive to candidates. Much of the historical influence of county party organizations on elections has been their ability to provide "people" resources to candidates.

Campaigning, however, has evolved from a primary focus on labor-intensive activity to the inclusion of more capital-intensive activities. This means that people resources have become somewhat less important than financial, organizational, and technological resources. Access to media has become more important than door-to-door canvassing. Thus, the challenge to county party organizations is to provide resources that candidates desire.

Political action committees (PACs) have been increasingly successful in attracting the allegiance of candidates by providing these services and resources. To the extent that candidates owe allegiance to these nonparty organizations, the party's influence declines. The independence in candidates' campaign strategies and the increase in PACs have brought about major changes in the environment of county party organizations.

Even during the electoral period, county party organizations are not completely undermined by their competitors. An increasingly important role of county party organizations is the coordination of campaigns. Since county party organizations do not have the monetary resources of PACs they must play a coordinating role in local politics. For instance, while the local party may not be able to pay for a public opinion survey, it can organize the various campaigns for an omnibus survey. Coordinated fundraising and making sure that all candidates appear at party-sponsored events are other such examples. Since there can be several candidates standing for office in each election held in the counties, the task of coordination is of considerable importance. And since one of the consequences of the ever-increasing technological sophistication of national campaigns is that what is expected of candidates for local offices has risen, county party organizations are provided an important opportunity. To the extent that county party organizations can provide these resources—even if they are shared by a variety of candidate campaign organizations—they are becoming increasingly important for local electoral politics.

Thus, county party organizations do not dominate electoral politics. Indeed, even strong county party organizations have only a small direct effect on the electoral success of the party. Too many other factors influence election outcomes for party organizations to have much of a direct effect.

Election day is not, however, the point at which county party organizations have their only impact. During the campaign season there are simply too many actors (individuals and groups) seeking to influence the outcome for any single agency to make much difference. The relevance of party organizations is to be found in their activities that are preparatory to the actual election.

County party organizations may be able to influence elections by their activities months and even years prior to election day. While we are accustomed to seeing dozens of candidates for important national and state offices, candidates for local offices are sometimes difficult to find. The recruitment activity of the county party organizations can be quite important for electoral success. After all, the first step toward winning an election is fielding a candidate. Frendreis, Gibson, and Vertz found that where county party organizations were stronger, it was more likely that there was a complete slate of candidates for congressional and state legislative offices. Party organizations seem to be successful at encouraging reticent potential candidates to stand for public office. This function is not only important just in terms of recruiting candidates who are likely to win elections but also in recruiting candidates even when they are highly unlikely to win. The ability of a party to put forth a full slate of candidates is useful in preserving the party's image among voters as a viable alternative. De-recruitment is also frequently necessary in order to avoid bitter and divisive intraparty struggles over nominations.

The nomination process is another point at which county party organizations can become influential. The party may offer preprimary endorsements and may make significant resources available to candidates. The contribution of the party organizations can be more influential at this stage of the process because resources of any sort are usually quite scarce and because voter participation is usually quite limited. Moreover, in primary elections or conventions, the party cue cannot provide the information for voters that it does in the general elections. Since all candidates running in the Republican primary are Republicans, endorsements can be of considerable importance. Though only about one-third of county party organizations in the U.S. now issue endorsements prior to the primary, this practice seems to be growing. The extent to which the party organization backs candidates at the primary stage is an extremely important resource. While the trend toward greater use of relatively open primaries to nominate candidates certainly reduces the role of the county party organizations, there are ample opportunities for the party to have an impact on who is nominated.

County party organizations can also affect electoral outcomes through a variety of activities outside the immediate campaign period. Voter registration drives, research, and public opinion polls can all contribute to laying the groundwork for a successful electoral challenge. Only a minority of county party organizations engages in this sort of "off-year" activity, but those that do have a significant impact on the futures of the party's candidates.

As the importance of state politics has increased, the importance of county party organizations has increased as well. There are many reasons that state politics has increased in importance, including the role that state legislatures play in reapportionment of electoral districts.

Since nearly all electoral districts are subject to reapportionment after each census, the party that controls the state legislature has a great opportunity to shape its own electoral destiny for the ensuing decade. The national parties in particular have recognized this and have made a concerted effort to build county party organizations in order to influence the reapportionment process.

At the same time, county party organizations are playing an increasingly important role in national politics. This is reflected in part by the attention given to these organizations by the national parties. The Republicans have been especially interested in building strong county party organizations and have devoted considerable resources toward that goal. Part of the motivation for this is the belief that strong local parties can benefit the national party.

The Policy Relevance of
County Party Organizations
Much less is known about how county party organizations affect public policy. This in part reflects a presumption made long ago that ideological activity on the part of local party leaders is inimical to party success and in part reflects the reality of nonpartisanship in many local public offices. Party leaders who are motivated by ideology generally are not willing to make compromises that are essential in politics, they are not sufficiently committed to the party to maintain allegiance to it when they disagree with party policy positions, and they do not have the requisite organizational and technological skills to build and maintain party organizations. All of these attributes are captured in the term applied to these party activists—they are "amateurs."

Once they assume their positions, it is highly doubtful that county party organizations have much of an ideological affect on higher public officeholders. Mayors, county officials, and even state legislators are required to make a variety of nonideological decisions, and when ideology is important, they are much more influenced by other political actors than by county party officials.

At the same time, however, evidence has accumulated that some ideologically motivated party leaders have been able to build strong county party organizations. Gibson, Frendreis, and Vertz have argued that while ideology may provide the goals for the party, organization provides the means. Moreover, to the extent that party leaders influence candidate recruit-

ment, party nominations, and election day activity, opportunities for getting the "right" candidates into office exist. Those active in county party organizations often scorn ideology, but ideological aspiration can be achieved through some local party organizations.

The Democratic Relevance of
County Party Organizations
Some observers have been eager to ascribe to county party organizations a role in the democratization of politics. Within this perspective, party organizations can provide opportunities for political participation that not only give citizens a greater voice in controlling their government but also give them a greater *sense* of control.

Once more, the empirical evidence on the democratic relevance of county party organizations is fairly limited. It is clear that the nomination process in most states has become more open to participation by ordinary citizens. Whether this has enhanced democracy is less clear. However, to the extent that county party organizations lose control over nominations, culpability and accountability are lost. Thus, there is some tension between opening party processes to widespread political participation and maintaining any sort of responsibility of parties for their candidates and policies.

At the same time, there has been a much greater effort by party organizations—national, state, and local—to reach out to party supporters than ever before. The bulk of this activity is in fundraising. The advent of direct mail, telephone campaigns, among other things, has given the ordinary voter a much greater sense of reality of political parties and has provided more opportunity than ever before for citizens to participate.

*Party Integration and the
Nationalization of Politics*
The national and state party organizations have recognized the increasing importance of county party organizations and have taken many steps to strengthen them. In a 1984 survey, county party leaders reported that the most important factor strengthening their organizations was assistance from the state and national party organizations. For instance, in 1984 the Republican National Committee provided $400,000 in grants to 615 county party organizations, and in 1985 another $400,000 to 214 key counties. To county party organizations that have extremely limited budgets, these are fairly

large and important amounts of money. Joint state-local or even national-local activities (e.g., joint get-out-the-vote drives) have become quite common. There has never been a time in American political history when the national, state, and local party organizations have worked so closely together.

An important consequence of this party-building activity is greater intraparty integration. Samuel Eldersveld, one of the most insightful observers of county party organizations, long ago coined the term "stratarchy" to describe the absence of hierarchy within party organizations. Stratarchy implies that the parties are organized at various strata (national, state, and local) and that the strata are not connected in any sort of hierarchical fashion—the national party cannot *command* the state parties and the state parties cannot *command* the local parties. Integration of parties in the past has been due to a commonalty of self interests—a commonalty that has often been ephemeral.

Transfers of resources to county organizations from the state and national parties have done much to increase the dependence on the local parties. This integration means greater coordination of effort; it means that county party organizations have resources they can contribute to candidates for local offices; it means that politics has to some degree become "nationalized."

The nationalization of partisan and organizational politics may have a significant impact on the structure of politics in the United States. Nationalization could result in a de-emphasis on local political issues and an increase in attention to nationally, and perhaps more ideologically, grounded issues. To the extent that parties and candidates become dependent upon nonlocal sources for resources, opportunities for national issues to affect local campaigns increase. Therefore, regional differences in political issues may become less significant. At the same time, the importance of politics to ordinary voters may decline since most voters are more concerned with local issues than national issues. A host of ramifications may emerge from the increasing confluence of national, state, and local politics.

County Party Organization and
Party System Change

Many observers of the American party system perceive a basic change in the structure of politics. The change is sometimes termed "dealignment." The basic elements of this theory are that the primary party attachments of American voters have weakened and that basic party functions are being assumed by nonparty organizations and groups. Since many scholars view political parties as essential to democracy, this dealignment has given rise to considerable consternation.

Evidence for such a view is easy to assemble. Parties are said to be no longer able to control access to the ballot, mainly due to the rise of direct primaries. Candidates and officeholders are no longer beholden to the party organizations for resources because the resources that parties can provide (mainly people) are no longer so important and because the rise of PACs that are willing to spend large amounts of money on politics has made candidates more dependent upon interest groups than on party organizations. Voters who are no longer persuaded by party-based messages believe that county party organizations have become largely irrelevant to politics.

Yet at the same time that party organizations are buffeted by the antiparty tides, new opportunities have arisen. All organizations are continually faced with changing environmental circumstances, some of which are threatening to the basic structure and function of the organization. Parties are no different. Yet there is evidence that these changes have not undermined county party organizations. Instead, the party organizations are devising new strategies for coping with change. For instance, as the number of organizational players proliferates, the need for a coordinating role becomes all the more important. The county party organization is ideally situated to perform such a function. As the cost of campaigning skyrockets, the need to have cooperative efforts (e.g., surveys for a variety of candidates) increases. While it may be true that party organizations do not dictate local politics the way they once did, party organizations can persuade, organize, and coordinate.

Party organizations are generally active (or potentially active) outside the campaign season. As noted above, not all county party organizations are active year round, but those that are find few competitors. Off-year activities such as recruitment, research, organization, and planning can be an important means for extending party organization influence.

Indeed, it might be argued that the uncertainty of the political environment has contributed to the strengthening of party organizations. The weakening of party attachments in the South, for instance, has provided new opportunities for Republicans. Especially at the early stages of party development, strong local and state organizations can make a great deal of difference: Recruiting candidates and showing the party flag in hopeless elections, encouraging candidates and officeholders to switch their party affiliations, and even legal challenges to the practices of the dominant party are all activities for which party organizations have few competitors. At a minimum, it is obvious that party organizations are not helplessly swept along by changing tides in the party system. Instead, party organizations are significant independent forces that affect the transformation of the party system. This may ultimately be the most important function of county party organizations.

See also: Direct Mail, Political Action Committees

James L. Gibson

REFERENCES

Beck, Paul Allen. 1974. "Environment and Party: The Impact of Political and Demographic County Characteristics on Party Behavior." 68 *American Political Science Review* 1229.

Bibby, John F. 1987. *Politics, Parties, and Elections in America*. Chicago: Nelson-Hall.

Conway, M. Margaret. 1984. "Republican Political Party Nationalization, Campaign Activities, and Their Implications for the Party System." 14 *Publius* 2.

Cotter, Cornelius P., James L. Gibson, John F. Bibby, and Robert M. Huckshorn. 1984. *Party Organizations in American Politics*. New York: Praeger.

Crotty, William. 1971. "Party Effort and Its Impact on the Vote." 65 *American Political Science Review* 439.

———, ed. 1986. *Political Parties in Local Areas*. Knoxville: U. of Tennessee Pr.

Eldersveld, Samuel J. 1964. *Political Parties: A Behavioral Analysis*. Chicago: Rand McNally.

Frendreis, John P., James L. Gibson, and Laura L. Verta. 1990. "The Electoral Relevance of Local Party Organizations." 84 *American Political Science Review* 226.

Gibson, James L., Cornelius P. Cotter, John F. Bibby, and Robert J. Huckshorn. 1985. "Whither the Local Parties?: A Cross-Sectional and Longitudinal Analysis of the Strength of Party Organizations." 29 *American Journal of Political Science* 139.

———, John P. Frendreis, and Laura L. Vertz. 1989. "Party Dynamics in the 1980s: Change in County Party Organizational Strength, 1980–84." 33 *American Journal of Political Science* 67.

Maggiotto, Michael A., and Ronald E. Weber. 1986. "The Impact of Organizational Incentives on County Party Chairpersons." 14 *American Politics Quarterly* 201.

Mayhew, David R. 1986. *Placing Parties in American Politics: Organization, Electoral Settings, and Government*

Activity the Twentieth Century. Princeton: Princeton U. Pr.

Wekkin, Gary D. 1984. "National-State Party Relations: The Democrats' New Federal Structure." 99 *Political Science Quarterly* 45.

Wilson, James Q. 1962. *The Amateur Democrat: Club Politics in Three Cities*. Chicago: U. of Chicago Pr.

Cousins v. Wigoda
419 U.S. 477 (1974)

This 1974 Supreme Court case involved a dispute over the selection and seating of Illinois delegates at the 1972 Democratic National Convention. The Wigoda delegates were those elected by voters in the Illinois primary. The Cousins delegates asserted that the selection of the Wigoda delegates violated Democratic Party guidelines. The national convention's Credentials Committee agreed with the Cousins delegates. The national convention accepted the Credentials Committee's recommendations and seated the Cousins delegates as the convention's representatives from Illinois.

The Illinois State Appellate Court asserted that the right to sit as representatives of Illinois was governed exclusively by the Illinois Election Code. The court declared that the law of the state was supreme and that any party rules to the contrary were of no effect.

The Supreme Court, in an opinion by Justice William Brennan, reversed the decision of the Illinois court. The Supreme Court asserted that the National Democratic Party enjoyed a constitutionally protected right of political association and that it could seat whatever delegates it chose or even leave seats vacant. The court said that the interests of the state must be "compelling" to justify an abridgement of the exercise of the party's constitutionally protected rights of association. The Supreme Court asserted that the role of the national party was more important than that of any individual state in the selection of candidates for national office and that the party's internal rules took precedence over state regulations. The court concluded that Illinois' declared interest in protecting the integrity of the political process could not be deemed compelling considering the context of the selection of delegates to the national party convention.

Justice William Rehnquist wrote an opinion concurring in the result, which was joined by Chief Justice Warren Burger and Justice Potter Stewart. The justices agreed that the interests of Illinois were insufficient in this case, but thought that the language of the majority opinion was unnecessarily broad.

Justice Lewis Powell wrote a partial dissent. He agreed with the assertion of the Illinois State Appellate Court that the Democratic Party should not be able to seat delegates of its own choice and force those representatives upon the people of Illinois. He believed that Illinois had a legitimate and compelling interest in protecting its citizens from being represented by delegates who had been previously rejected by those citizens in a democratic election.

Scott Cameron

George B. Cox (1853–1916)

The Republican boss of Cincinnati politics for more than 30 years. George Barnsdale Cox started out as a newspaper delivery boy earning money for his widowed mother during the Civil War. The adolescent Cox then worked as a dealer in his brother-in-law's gambling house in Cincinnati. In 1880, at the age of 27, Cox won his first race for political office with his election to Cincinnati's city council. While a councilman, Cox also was elected to the Decennial Board of Equalization, which reappraised all property in the city every 10 years. Cox quickly learned his way around the city's political circles, and by 1884 he managed several successful Ohio Republican congressional campaigns as well as the state effort of Republican presidential elections. Cox traveled to New York to take lessons from the powerful political machine boss William M. Tweed of Tammany Hall. After his return, Cox backed a series of successful candidates for a variety of state and city offices. He also made an alliance with Cincinnati's business community, providing lucrative tax breaks in return for political and financial support. By the early 1890s, Cox was the undisputed boss of Cincinnati; his candidates regularly won elections while the city's payroll was loaded with Cox loyalists. In the 1905 election, however, a fusion ticket of Cox opponents won a number of important offices. Cox was further hurt by prosecuting attorney Henry T. Hunt's investigation of practices under Cox's rule. Cox was never convicted of any of these charges, but his reputation was greatly damaged nonetheless. In 1911 Cox lost a majority on the city council. In 1915 his candidates returned triumphant, although the known public scandals of Cox's rule left his power diminished in his final years.

Garry Boulard

REFERENCES

Miller, Zane L. 1968. *Boss Cox's Cincinnati-Urban Politics in the Progressive Era.* New York: Oxford U. Pr.
Warner, Hoyt Landon. 1964. *Progressivism in Ohio, 1897–1917.* Columbus: Ohio State U. Pr.

James M. Cox (1870–1957)

Newspaperman, governor of Ohio, and Democratic candidate for President. James Middleton Cox was born on a farm near Jacksonburg, a small town in southwestern Ohio. Although never a high school graduate, Cox taught school briefly before becoming a newspaper reporter. Building upon his practical newspaper experience and a brief tenure as a congressional assistant, Cox purchased the struggling *Dayton News* in 1898. After he took control of several other newspapers, his entry into politics was not difficult.

Running as a Democrat in 1908, Cox won the U.S. House seat in Ohio's Third District, a Republican stronghold. Voters returned him in the next two elections. In 1912 he was elected governor of Ohio, only to be defeated in 1914. Subsequently he won in 1916 and 1918, making him the state's first three-term governor. In 1920 Cox emerged on the national scene as the Democratic nominee for President on the forty-fourth ballot. In spite of strong urban support and his reputation as the champion of labor, education, and social programs that foreshadowed the New Deal, Cox and the Democrats lost the election. Few voters could see beyond Cox's support of Wilson's unpopular plan for joining the League of Nations. Republican (and fellow Ohioan) Warren G. Harding won by a popular margin of almost two to one.

After his defeat in 1920 Cox devoted most of his energies to his journalistic empire, adding newspapers in Ohio, Florida, and Georgia. His commitment to education, however, led him to help establish Florida's University of Miami in 1925. He stepped forward again in 1933, agreeing to serve as vice president of U.S. delegation to the World Monetary and Economic Conference. In the 1930s Cox got involved in the new field of radio, acquiring stations in Ohio and Florida, and in the late 1940s he became a pioneer owner of television stations. At his death, he was a wealthy and respected media giant.

See also: Election of 1920, Warren Harding, League of Nations, New Deal

Steven C. Kottsy

REFERENCES

Cebula, James E. 1985. *James M. Cox: Journalist and Politician*. New York: Garland.

Rhodes, Benjamin D. 1982–1983. "Harding v. Cox: The 'Ohio Election' of 1920 as Viewed from the British Embassy at Washington." 55 *Northwest Ohio Quarterly* 17.

Samuel S. Cox (1824–1889)

Scion of the pro-Union Democrats during the Civil War era. Samuel Sullivan Cox established his reputation as an author, lawyer, editor, and newspaper owner before becoming Ohio's Democratic chairman in 1852. He was elected to the U.S. House of Representatives in 1856 where he opposed the proslavery "Lecompton Constitution" for Kansas and supported all efforts for sectional peace and compromise. Withdrawal of southern secessionist Congressmen in 1861 left Cox as one of the leaders of the Democratic minority. While personally friendly with such peace Democrats as Clement Vallandigham and while occasionally indulging in sectional rhetoric against New England "puritan tyranny," Cox was one of the few western Democrats determined to preserve a pro-Union, constitutionally correct image for his party.

He worked with eastern "legitimist" Democrats to find a middle position between all-out support of Abraham Lincoln by war Democrats and the "purist" peace faction, which refused to vote for military appropriations. With this goal in mind, Cox futilely urged General George McClellan to oppose Vallandigham's candidacy for governor of Ohio. In 1864 he was one of the managers of McClellan's presidential nomination by the Democratic convention. This success was undermined, however, when the peace faction wrote the platform and in the election a Republican landslide swept Cox and the Ohio Democrats out of office. In the lame duck session of Congress in 1865, he helped promote the futile Hampton Road peace conference between Lincoln and Confederate leaders and urged his party to finally get rid of the slavery issue by moderating its resistance to the Thirteenth Amendment. Cox moved to New York and was again elected to Congress in 1868 and 1887. Under President Grover Cleveland he served briefly as American minister to Turkey.

See also: Election of 1864, Abraham Lincoln, George McClellan, Slavery, Clement Vallandigham

Harold B. Raymond

REFERENCES

Cox, Samuel Sullivan. 1885. *Union-Disunion-Reunion*. San Francisco: Occidental Publishing.

Cox, William Van Zandt, and Milton H. Northrop. 1899. *The Life of Samuel Sullivan Cox*. Syracuse, NY.

Klement, Frank. 1984. *Dark Lanterns, Secret Political Societies and Conspiracies and Treason Trials in the Civil War*. Baton Rouge: Louisiana State U. Pr.

Lindsey, David. 1959. *Sunset Cox: Irrepressible Democrat*. Detroit: Wayne St. U. Pr.

Porter, George H. 1911. *Ohio Politics in the Civil War Period*. New York: Columbia U. Pr.

Silbey, Joel H. 1977. *A Respectable Minority: The Democratic Party in the Civil War Era, 1860–1868*. New York: Norton.

Joseph F. Crangle (1932–)

Last powerful leader of the Erie County (N.Y.) Democratic machine. Joseph F. Crangle, a three-time candidate for Democratic national chairman, entered politics in 1958 as a committeeman in Buffalo, New York. He was the handpicked successor to the Erie County chairman in 1965 and won his first victory when his candidate was elected mayor of Buffalo. Crangle quickly solidified his position by means of city hall patronage. He gained access to state patronage as chairman of the New York State Democratic Party (1971–1975), and through a series of posts he held with the state legislature (1966–1987). As chief of staff to the speaker (1976–1987), he was responsible for attracting programs to help the economically depressed Buffalo area.

Crangle's influence extended to the national scene when he delivered the only minority report adopted by the Democratic National Convention in 1968. It was a Rules Committee report that reformed the manner in which delegates were chosen, making the process more democratic; and providing for quotas to allow those previously denied access a place in the convention process. He came within one vote of winning the position of Democratic national chairman in 1970.

Crangle actively worked for the presidential candidacy of Robert F. Kennedy in 1968, attempted an unsuccessful draft of Hubert H. Humphrey in 1976, and in 1980 supported Edward M. Kennedy's efforts to dump President Jimmy Carter. Crangle's last major electoral victory occurred in 1976 when he persuaded United Nations ambassador Daniel P. Moynihan to run for the U.S. Senate.

A series of losses, beginning with the 1977 Buffalo mayor's race and his failure in the 1982 primary to support Mario Cuomo's successful run for governor, weakened Crangle and ultimately led to his retirement as Erie County chairman in 1987.

Joy A. Scimé

William H. Crawford (1772–1834)

Republican Cabinet officer who was a leading presidential contender in 1824. William H. Crawford was the man that most of his contemporaries expected would have the honor of succeeding James Monroe in the White House when the Virginia Dynasty finally retired from the field in 1825. It was not to be because he suffered a stroke in 1823. However, the difficulty that the Jeffersonian Republicans had in finding a consensus candidate after Crawford became ill was testimony to Crawford's reputation and signaled an end to the Era of Good Feelings.

Crawford was born in Virginia, and following a common migration pattern of the time, he moved first to South Carolina and then to Georgia while still a child. He was educated in Georgia where he began to practice law in Lexington in 1799, then to become a member of the state legislature from 1803 to 1807 when he was elected to fill a vacancy in the United States Senate. Crawford remained in the Senate until 1813 and was elected President *pro tempore* in 1812. In 1813 he declined an offer from President Madison to serve as Secretary of War, a position of no little significance during the war with Great Britain. Crawford chose instead to represent the United States as a minister to France, where he served from 1813 until 1815, when he returned to become Secretary of War. In 1816 he moved from the War Department to the Treasury Department where he remained as Secretary until 1825, when he cited ill health as his reason for declining John Quincy Adams's request that he continue in office.

During his nine years as Secretary of the Treasury, Crawford earned the confidence and respect of Republican politicians in search of a successor to the Virginians. His name came up in the presidential sweepstakes as early as 1816, and after Monroe's reelection in 1820, Crawford was conceded to be the leading candidate. He enjoyed the support of the crucial Virginia Republicans of the Richmond "Junto" as the man who could best represent and protect the "Fundamental Principles" of Jeffersonian Republicanism. Crawford had their support in spite of his conservative financial credentials which had caused him to favor rechartering the First Bank of the United States in 1811. In spite of his close association with finance and commerce, he was considered ideologically sound by such convinced agrarian ideologues as John Randolph and Nathaniel Macon, as well as by the two most astute politicians of the time, Martin Van Buren and James Madison.

Until his stroke, Crawford's ability to combine financial and administrative sophistication with agrarian ideology made him the favorite presidential candidate over Henry Clay, John Quincy Adams, Andrew Jackson, and John C. Calhoun. Crawford's political ties and ideological finesse may have enabled him to have held the increasingly disparate Republican coalition together a bit longer. His illness both destroyed the coalition and laid the ground work for the age of Jackson to succeed to that of Jefferson. Desperate Jeffersonian efforts to keep his candidacy alive in 1824 testify not only to the importance of his role in the political world of his time but also to the bitter realization of the Jeffersonian Republicans that their time was coming to an end.

See also: John Quincy Adams, Henry Clay, First Bank of the United States, Andrew Jackson, Jeffersonian Republicans, James Madison, James Monroe, Martin Van Buren

Kathryn A. Malone

REFERENCES

Remini, Robert. 1963. *The Election of Andrew Jackson.* Philadelphia: Lippincott.

———. 1971. "Election of 1828." In Arthur M. Schlesinger, Jr., et al., eds. *History of American Presidential Elections, 1789–1968.* New York: McGraw-Hill.

———. 1981. *Andrew Jackson and the Course of American Freedom, 1822–1832.* New York: Harper & Row.

Credit Mobilier

Post-Civil War investors in the Union Pacific Railroad sought to take advantage of federal subsidies for the building of this transcontinental railroad to line their own pockets with sums estimated to total at least $20 million. Funneling the money through a construction company christened "Credit Mobilier," Union Pacific promoters diverted profits to themselves. In 1867, to ward off a possible congressional investigation, company director and Massachusetts Congressman Oakes Ames distributed at least 160 shares of Credit Mobilier stock among Senators and Congressmen, selling it at par instead of its substantially higher market value and allowing many of the recipients to defer immediate payment by applying the large future dividends to the purchase price. Many Congressmen, suspicious of the tremendous dividends yielded by the stock, subsequently withdrew from the transaction.

During the election of 1872, the *New York Sun* published reports revealing Ames's activities and naming the recipients of the Credit Mobilier stock, most of them Republicans. Among those implicated during the ensuing investigation conducted by Congress in the winter of 1872–1873 were outgoing Vice President Schuyler Colfax, Republican vice presidential nominee Henry Wilson, future President and then Ohio Congressman James A. Garfield, and Maine's James G. Blaine, the Speaker of the House, who ran for President in 1884. None of them (except for Blaine) was able to give fully satisfactory explanations, although Wilson's testimony virtually exonerated him. The investigating committee recommended expulsion for Ames, Democratic Congressman James Brooks of New York, and Republican Senator James W. Patterson of New Hampshire; Ames and Brooks were censured, while Patterson was allow to retire at the expiration of his term in 1873.

Credit Mobilier is usually cited as one of the scandals associated with Ulysses S. Grant's administration. However, the scandal occurred during Andrew Johnson's administration and involved Congress, not President Grant. Although Colfax and Wilson served under Grant as Vice President, they had been selected by the party—not by Grant—for the second spot on the Republican ticket. The Credit Mobilier scandal, along with an effort by Congress to pass a retroactive pay raise for itself in an incident known as the Salary Grab, shook public confidence in the ethics of the federal government and damaged the reputation of several Republican notables.

See also: James G. Blaine, Schuyler Colfax, Election of 1872, James Garfield, Ulysses S. Grant, Railroads, Scandals and Scandalizing

Brooks Donohue Simpson

REFERENCES

Abbott, Richard H. 1972. *Cobbler in Congress: The Life of Henry Wilson, 1812–1875.* Lexington: U. Pr. of Kentucky.

Peskin, Allan. 1978. *Garfield.* Kent, OH: Kent State U. Pr.

Woodward, C. Vann, ed. 1974. *Responses of the Presidents to Charges of Misconduct.* New York: Dell Publishing.

Charles F. Crisp (1845–1896)

Speaker of the U.S. House of Representatives in the 1890s. Charles Frederick Crisp was born in Sheffield, England, while his actor parents were there on tour. Returning to the United States, the family settled in Georgia. Crisp entered the Confederate Army in 1861 and served until 1864 when he was taken prisoner of war. After his release from Fort Delaware in 1865, he returned to Georgia where he studied law and was admitted to the bar in 1866.

Taking up the practice of law in Ellaville, he was appointed solicitor general of the southwestern Georgia judicial circuit in 1872 and reappointed in 1873. In June 1877 he was appointed judge of the superior court of this circuit and then was elected by the general assembly to remain in office in 1878 and 1880. He resigned in September 1882 to accept the nomination of the Democratic Party to Congress. As a member of the House of Representatives, he was known as an advocate of low tariffs, a champion of the free coinage of silver, and one of the chief legislative supporters of the Interstate Commerce Act of 1887.

When the Democratic Party regained the majority in the House following the election of 1890, Crisp was selected as Speaker of the House after a protracted fight. A diligent and forceful Speaker during the era when the Rules Committee was controlled by the Speaker, he helped increase the power of both positions through innovative use of the committee's powers.

He was nominated for U.S. Senator in the Georgia primary of 1896 but died at his home in Atlanta before the election.

See also: Speaker of the House

James V. Saturno

REFERENCES

Follett, Mary Parker. 1974. *The Speaker of the House of Representatives.* New York: Lenox Hill. (Orig. pub. New York: Longmans, Green, 1902.)

U.S. Congress. 1897. *Memorial Addresses on the Life and Character of Charles Frederick Crisp.* 54th Congress, 2nd Session. Washington: U.S. Govt. Printing Office.

Critical Elections

In a seminal article in 1955, V. O. Key, Jr., the preeminent theorist of American voting behavior, theorized that certain elections distinguish themselves from others because they result in an enduring shift in the social forces that support the competing political parties. Critical elections are characterized by a high degree of voter interest, a high level of concern over the outcome of the election, and a high voter turnout. In critical elections, significant issues divide the parties; many voters switch allegiance from one party to the other (and new voters form party allegiances for the first time) on the basis of policy concerns, not personalities. These elections are deemed critical because, according to Key's theory, loyalties formed during these election campaigns tend to persist for a significant period of time.

Following Key, scholars at the University of Michigan devised a theory for classifying presidential elections. Campbell, Converse, Miller and Stokes (1960) categorize elections as *realigning* if the party holding power is replaced by another (e.g., in 1932); *maintaining*, if electoral coalitions are maintained (e.g., in 1940); or *deviating*, if the party which holds the allegiance of a minority of the voters prevails because of short-term forces such as the personality of the presidential candidates (e.g., in 1952). In a later article, Gerald Pomper elaborated on this scheme, noting that scholars had elected for analysis two aspects of presidential elections—whether or not the majority party retained power or not and whether or not coalitions in place were maintained. In a maintaining election, the coalition remains the same, and the majority party retains power. In a deviating election, the majority party loses power, usually temporarily, as the coalitions are not changed. In a realigning election, the coalitions change and a new majority comes to power. Pomper noted the existence of a fourth possibility: a *converting* election in which the coalitions change, but the same majority party remains in power. He offered the election of 1896 as an example of this electoral result.

The theory of critical elections holds that major shifts in party affiliation happen quickly as a result of significant differences in the body politic over how to respond to serious situations. Key also noted the possibility of *secular* realignments—gradual realignments over a period of years, not caused by specific issues or noted after particular elections. In addition, scholars have recently detected a trend toward dealignment: a decline of commitment among voters to either of the major political parties. Taken together, these concepts provide the agenda for scholars and the tools for understanding the importance of individual elections within the context of the American two-party system.

See also: Elections of 1860, 1896, and 1932; V. O. Key

Jeremy R. T. Lewis

REFERENCES

Campbell, Angus, Philip E. Converse, Warren E. Miller, and Donald E. Stokes. 1960. *The American Voter.* New York: Wiley.

Key, V. O., Jr. 1955. "A Theory of Critical Elections." 17 *Journal of Politics* 3.

———. 1959. "Secular Realignment and the Party System." 21 *Journal of Politics* 198.

Pomper, Gerald M. 1967. "Classification of Presidential Elections." 29 *Journal of Politics* 535.

David Crockett (1786–1836)

"King of the Wild Frontier" and Whig politician. "Davy" Crockett was neither the gargantuan frontier superman of legend nor the oafish dupe of Whig politicians. He was, on a small scale, the owner of land, slaves, mills, and distilleries who, despite minimal formal education, was a respected, and when he wished, "gentle and quiet" frontier community leader. He served as justice of the peace, militia officer, member of the Tennessee legislature, and three terms in the U.S. Congress (1827–1831, 1833–1835). Crockett was a champion for the small slaveholders and frontier farmers against such established planter leaders as Andrew Jackson. He did support Jackson for President in 1832 but soon broke with the administration when it opposed Crockett's bill legalizing squatters' land claims. He then joined with John Bell and Hugh White to form the Tennessee Whig Coalition.

In Washington the new party was delighted to tout a frontier politician who fiercely opposed Jackson and who enjoyed being promoted as the Whig embodiment of the western common man. Crockett's much-publicized tour of the Northeast and four colorful books bearing his name were largely the work of party managers and propagandists. The Davy Crockett legend grew, but Crockett, an indifferent businessman who was assailed by Jackson's followers, lost most of his property and then his seat in Congress. In 1835 he migrated to Texas and soon met a hero's death at the Alamo.

Crockett, a minor but genuine spokesman for the Tennessee "plain folk," became an early example of a legendary character largely created by party propaganda to fit an age of mass democracy. Numerous politicians adopted "the Crockett line," which achieved its greatest triumph in the "log cabin campaign" that made Benjamin Harrison President in 1840. The Crockett legend soon become part of American folklore and frontier humor.

See also: Election of 1828, Andrew Jackson, Jacksonian Democracy

Harold B. Raymond

REFERENCES

Abernathy, Thomas. 1932. *From Frontier to Plantation in Tennessee.* Chapel Hill: U. of North Carolina Pr.

Arped, Joseph J., ed. 1972. *A Narrative of the Life of David Crockett.* New Haven: Yale U. Pr.

Crockett, David. 1833. *Sketches and Eccentricities of Colonel David Crockett of West Tennessee.* New York: Harper.

———. 1834. *A Narrative of the Life of David Crockett of the State of Tennessee.* Philadelphia: E. L. Carey and A. Hart.

———. 1835. *An Account of Colonel Crockett's Tour of the North and Down East.* Philadelphia: E. L. Carey and A. Hart.

———. 1836. *Colonel Crockett's Exploits and Adventures in Texas.* Philadelphia: T. K. and P. G. Collins.

Lofaro, Michael, and Joseph Cummings. 1989. *Crockett at Two Hundred: New Perspectives on the Main and the Myth.* Knoxville: U. of Tennessee Pr.

Null, Marion. 1954. *Forgotten Pioneer: The Life of Davy Crockett.* New York: Vantage Pr.

Shackford, James Atkins. 1956. *David Crockett: The Man and the Legend.* Chapel Hill: U. of North Carolina Pr.

Herbert Croly (1869–1930)

American philosopher and journalist. Herbert Croly was one of the major American philosophers of the twentieth century, best known for his "national progressivism." Educated at Harvard in philosophy, he studied under William James, Josiah Royce, and George Santayana. At Harvard, Croly experienced a crisis of faith and revolted against the positivism of Comte after being exposed to the pragmatism of James, the Hegelian idealism of Royce, and the naturalism of Santayana. Herbert Croly was a friend to Theodore Roosevelt (who was influenced by his philosophy) and together with Walter Lippmann and Walter Weyl, he founded *The New Republic*. Among his other friends and colleagues were Supreme Court leaders Louis Brandeis, Felix Frankfurter and Rexford Tugwell of the New Deal.

Croly was at the height of his powers during the period when progressivism was likewise at the peak of its influence (1902–1917), and (as some argue) the middle class was at the height of its anxiety. Croly was the prophet of a new sort of liberalism. Unlike the followers of Jeffersonian liberalism, he believed in an inherent conflict between liberty and equality. A product of his times, he was a nationalist and an advocate of American culture (unlike Theodore Roosevelt and Alfred Thayer Mahan, who were advocates of American power). Like other progressives, he was distrustful of big business and organized labor; however, he was not as egregiously hostile to foreign immigrants (and cultures) as other progressive nationalists of his time such as William Alan White. Unlike some progressives, he was deeply committed to the Republican Party.

Croly, like Santayana, believed in rule by a nonhereditary elite. He was distrustful of mass culture and politics despite his view (and in this Lippmann, Weyl, and *The New Republic* concurred) of the consumer as a promising recruit to the progressive movement. Croly's most important work was *The Promise of American Life* (1909), considered by many to be the most influential book of its time (Frankfurter said that to omit it "from any list of half dozen books on American politics since 1900 would be grotesque").

After the failures of Woodrow Wilson and the return to power of Warren Harding and traditional (big business) Republicanism, Croly spent his waning years in deep pessimism. He especially regretted the lack of religious and moral emphasis in his major work. Croly did not live to see the rise of fascism in Germany and Italy and the consequences there of (an admittedly twisted) nationalism and strong executive leadership.

See also: Theodore Roosevelt, Progressive Party

David A. Bositis

REFERENCES

Croly, Herbert. 1909. *The Promise of American Life.* New York: Macmillan.

———. 1912. *Marcus Alonzo Hanna.* New York: Macmillan.

Forcey, Charles. 1961. *The Crossroads of Liberalism.* New York: Oxford U. Pr.

Levy, David W. 1985. *Herbert Croly of The New Republic.* Princeton: Princeton U. Pr.

Wilbur L. Cross (1862–1948)

Democratic governor of Connecticut in the 1930s. Wilbur Lucius Cross, "The Connecticut Yankee," was born in Mansfield, Connecticut, and received both his B.A. and his Ph.D. from Yale University. An educator and a writer, Cross was known as an authority on eighteenth-century English literature. He joined the faculty at Yale after graduation and remained there from 1894 until 1930 as a professor of English, as the dean of the Graduate School, and as editor of the *Yale Review.*

Upon his retirement from Yale in 1930, Cross moved into politics. As a Democrat, he was elected governor of Connecticut in 1931 and was reelected for four terms, finally suffering defeat in the general election of 1938. Cross, a warm and genial man, was a popular governor and attracted wide support from people across the state. His administration was characterized as progressive, and clean, and he maintained high standards for public service. After his defeat, Wilbur Cross kept politically active by serving on many boards and associations across Connecticut. He also continued his life-long involvement with Yale University until his death at the age of 86. A major Connecticut highway is named in his honor.

Mary Ann McHugh

REFERENCES

Burpee's: The Story of Connecticut. Vol. III. New York: The American Historical Company. 1939.
Devane, William Clyde. 1948. *The Yale Review.*

Cross-Endorsement Rule

The cross-endorsement rule is a provision found in New York State election law allowing political parties to nominate candidates already endorsed by other parties. The votes a candidate receives on his/her lines are then added together in the final count to determine the winner. This provision allows state minor parties to sustain themselves without actually winning elections on their own, as voters can demonstrate support for minor parties and not "waste" their votes on minor party candidates. Major party candidates typically seek multiple party endorsements as a means of appearing on the ballot more than once in order to improve their electability.

The cross-endorsement provision gives minor parties some bargaining ability, as they can exchange their endorsement for ideological or material concessions. Members of New York's Liberal Party, for example, received substantial patronage rewards when New York City mayor John Lindsay won reelection in 1969 solely on the Liberal line. The state's Right to Life Party exchanges its ballot endorsement for pledges by candidates to oppose abortion. Minor parties can also punish the major parties by withholding endorsements or by running their own candidates, thus drawing votes from major party contenders. The Liberal Party expressed its displeasure with the state Democratic Party's nomination of Frank O'Connor for governor in 1966 by nominating Franklin D. Roosevelt, Jr. This tactic split the Democratic-Liberal vote,

allowing the reelection of Nelson Rockefeller. The minor parties can also influence major party nominations by holding nominations first, forcing the major parties to avoid a situation in which major-minor nominations differ between otherwise allied parties. Vermont and Connecticut also have cross-endorsement provisions, but the lack of close party competition in Vermont and the difficulty in getting recognition for new parties in Connecticut undercut the provision's impact.

See also: Liberal Party of New York, John Lindsay, Right to Life Party, Nelson Rockefeller, Franklin Roosevelt

Robert J. Spitzer

REFERENCES

Spitzer, Robert J. 1989. "The Tail Wagging the Dog: Multi-Party Politics." In Peter W. Colby and John K. White, eds. *New York State Today.* Albany: State U. of New York Pr.

Crossover Voting

Crossover voting occurs when voters who identify with one party participate in the primary election of the other party. The motivation for such behavior can be either benign or malevolent—voters may cross over because they are more enthusiastic about a candidate in the opposite camp or because they want to weaken the other party by nominating a less competitive candidate. This second possibility, in which individuals cast a primary ballot for a candidate who they really oppose, often is termed "raiding," especially if carried out in an organized fashion. While raiding sometimes occurs, most crossover voting appears to represent genuine support for a primary candidate by voters outside the party.

Crossover voting basically is restricted to states with open primaries, although voters in states with closed primaries can cross over by switching their party registration (usually 30 days prior to the election)—an event that rarely happens. Presidential primaries, especially when held separately, stimulate the greatest amount of crossover voting. At lower levels, primaries for several offices occur together, so crossing over for one primary means doing so for others on the ballot as well (unless the voter is in Washington State or Alaska, which hold blanket primaries).

Proponents of strong, responsible parties favor closed primaries on the grounds that crossover voting weakens the nomination process as a *party* activity. Raiding is most strongly condemned, naturally, but even benign forms of crossover voting are denounced as limiting the influence of party leaders, activists, and members on nominations. Crossover voting can be both substantial in amount and significant in impact, as illustrated by data from Wisconsin, which has one of the most studied open primaries. In several recent Wisconsin presidential primaries, a majority of the participants were independents or supporters of the opposite party, and these crossover voters often differed greatly from loyal partisans in their presidential preferences.

See also: Blanket Primaries, Closed Primary, Open Primary

Charles L. Prysby

REFERENCES

Adamany, David. 1976. "Cross-over Voting and the Democratic Party's Reform Rules." 70 *American Political Science Review* 536.

Eldersveld, Samuel. 1982. *Political Parties in America.* New York: Basic Books.

Hedland, Ronald D., and Meredith W. Watts. 1986. "The Wisconsin Open Primary." 14 *American Politics Quarterly* 55.

Price, David E. 1984. *Bringing Back the Parties.* Washington: Congressional Quarterly.

Sorauf, Frank, and Paul Allen Beck. 1988. *Party Politics in America.* 6th ed. Glenview, IL: Scott, Foresman.

Edward Crump (1874–1954)

Legendary Tennessee political boss. Edward H. "Boss" Crump is regarded as one of the last of the old-time urban bosses. With his power in Memphis and Shelby County, Tennessee Democrat Crump maintained absolute control from the late 1920s to 1948. During this period the Crump ticket was virtually guaranteed success in local races, and Crump himself could deliver the city and county in statewide contests.

Crump was born of meager means in 1874 but established himself as a successful businessman, eventually amassing considerable personal wealth. In 1909 he was elected mayor of Memphis, a city plagued by a sordid political history, on a reform ticket; Crump was then able to assemble a model urban organization. But in 1915, at the beginning of his third mayoral term, he resigned from office when confronted with an impending court removal for not enforcing a Tennessee prohibition law. Some believe, however, that the conditions leading to Crump's departure may have been engineered by the electric light company in Memphis, which was threatened by the mayor's plan for municipal ownership of utilities.

Regardless of Crump's ill-fated mayoral tenure, he was essentially able to pick his successor and was soon elected to the coveted position of county treasurer. Over the course of his political career, Crump would hold a variety of elected offices, including U.S. Representative from Tennessee. In an unconventional move to secure the Memphis mayoral seat for his candidate in 1939, Crump ran himself, assured of success, and was elected. Then he immediately resigned and appointed his chosen candidate.

Boss Crump and his Memphis machine are credited with a number of accomplishments: securing public ownership of utilities, lowering Memphis's crime rate, and improving the city's public health program. Crump considered himself a benevolent leader, and his allies lauded Memphis' clean government. Yet adversaries of the machine, while acknowledging the efficiency with which Memphis was governed, pointed to election fraud, graft, and Crump's iron hand used to maintain absolute control of the machine.

Although enduring until his death, Crump's power was significantly diminished in 1948 when the Crump ticket failed in a statewide primary. But Crump remained an outspoken and flamboyant figure in Memphis politics until his death at age 80.

See also: Bosses

Barbara Trish

REFERENCES

Caspers, Gerald M. 1947. "Memphis, Tennessee: Satrapy of a Benevolent Despot." In Robert S. Allen, ed. *Our Fair City.* New York: Vanguard.

Coppock, Paul R. 1980. *Memphis Memoirs.* Memphis, TN: Memphis State U. Pr.

Miller, William D. 1964. *Mr. Crump of Memphis.* Baton Rouge: Louisiana State U. Pr.

Shelby M. Cullom (1829–1914)

Republican Party leader in Illinois for 50 years after the Civil War. After an inauspicious start as an unsuccessful candidate for presidential elector on the Millard Fillmore ticket in 1852 and election on that ticket to the Illinois legislature (1856), Shelby Moore Cullom's political career altered when he followed Abraham Lincoln in 1858, in his own words, "firmly and without mental reservation into the ranks of the Republican Party." He then stood as witness to and beneficiary of the Midwest's realignment into the Republican camp, and was reelected to the legislature (1860–1861, 1872, 1873–1874), then subsequently elected a Representative in

Congress (1865–1871), governor of Illinois (1867–1883), and finally U.S. Senator (1883–1913). As a loyal party man, Cullom was inspired to seek the presidential nomination, first in 1888 and then in 1892. Ironically his aspirations were never taken seriously since his greatest asset was to be known as "the man who looks like Lincoln." Party loyalty helped put an end to his senatorial career when he resigned after defeat in the 1912 party primary, apparently a victim of ill feelings that were aroused by his support for William Lorimer, the other Republican Senator from Illinois, against charges disputing the latter's election.

Living through times of major social change, Cullom was a compromiser rather than a leader or innovator, demonstrated most clearly in his sponsorship of legislation establishing the Interstate Commerce Commission (1887) and in his proposals for annexing Hawaii. His sympathy for agrarian interests and suspicion of railroad barons clearly present in Cullom's advocacy of transportation regulation was not extended, however, to the Republican Party's progressive wing, which he perceived to be destructive of party unity.

See also: Election of 1852, Millard Fillmore, Abraham Lincoln, Railroads

Mildred A. Schwartz

REFERENCES

Cullom, Shelby M. 1911. *Fifty Years of Public Service.* 2nd ed. Chicago: McClurg.

Mayer, George H. 1967. *The Republican Party. 1854–1966.* 2nd ed. New York: Oxford U. Pr.

Neilson, James W. 1962. *Shelby M. Cullom: Prairie State Republican.* Illinois Studies in the Social Sciences, No. 51. Urbana: U. of Illinois.

Pitkin, William A. 1956. "Shelby M. Cullom: Presidential Prospect." 49 *Journal of the Illinois State Historical Society* 375.

Sundquist, James L. 1973. *Dynamics of the Party System. Alignment and Realignment of Political Parties in the United States.* Washington: Brookings.

Homer S. Cummings (1870–1956)

Democratic National Committee chairman in the Woodrow Wilson administration. When Democratic National Chairman Vance C. McCormick became heavily involved in peace negotiations in 1918, Vice Chairman Cummings bore the main burden of directing the midterm congressional campaign in that year. After McCormick's resignation in 1919, Cummings was elevated to national chairman to fill out the term (1919–1920).

Homer Stile Cummings, born in Chicago, was the son of an inventor, cement manufacturer, and Lincoln Republican. From the Heathcote School in Buffalo, the youth entered the Sheffield Scientific School of Yale University, receiving his bachelor's degree in 1891 and a Yale law degree two years later. Upon admission to the Connecticut bar in 1893, he joined a partnership with Samuel Fessenden and G. A. Carter in Stamford, both eminent in the state's politics.

An active Democrat, Cummings was elected mayor of Stamford three times beginning in 1900. He was also chosen Democratic national committeeman for Connecticut, a position he held from 1900 to 1925. At the end of his second term as mayor, he made an unsuccessful race for Congressman-at-large, returning in 1904 to serve his final term as mayor. In 1908 Cummings became corporation counsel and rose rapidly to a position of leadership in the New England bar.

Cummings became vice chairman of the Democratic National Committee in 1913. When Vance C. McCormick became national chairman in 1916, Cummings was reelected as vice chairman and then elevated to the chairmanship in 1919.

Cummings was active in Democratic national affairs throughout the 1920s, often in close cooperation with Franklin D. Roosevelt. In 1932 he was one of Roosevelt's principal national convention floor leaders. After Roosevelt's election, Cummings served as United States Attorney General from 1933 to 1939. He also found time to write four books on legal issues.

See also: Democratic National Committee, Franklin Roosevelt, Woodrow Wilson

Ralph M. Goldman

REFERENCES

Goldman, Ralph M. 1990. *The National Party Chairmen and Committees: Factionalism at the Top.* Armonk, NY: M. E. Sharpe.

Link, Arthur S. 1947. *Wilson: The Road to the White House.* 3 vols. Princeton: Princeton U. Pr.

The Cummings File, in the Papers of Ray Stannard Baker, Library of Congress, particularly during 1920.

Albert B. Cummins (1850–1926)

Iowa U.S. Senator in the early twentieth century. Albert Baird Cummins, Iowa Republican, served from 1908 to 1925 in the Senate, where he was President *pro tempore* from 1919 to 1925. Born in Pennsylvania, he practiced law in Iowa, winning fame with a suit against the barbed-wire trust. In 1894 and 1900 he lost bids for Senate as a reform Republican but was elected governor of Iowa in 1901.

In 1908 Governor Cummins challenged the incumbent Republican Senator William Boyd Allison. When Allison died shortly after winning the primary, the Iowa legislature selected Cummins to replace him. During the William Howard Taft and Woodrow Wilson years Cummins was an insurgent, dissenting from the Republican Old Guard and Wilson's New Freedom in hopes of making the Republican Party the true party of reform. In 1912 he supported Theodore Roosevelt but remained within the Republican Party.

In 1916 Cummins sought the Republican presidential nomination, moderating his progressivism to broaden his appeal. Even though he got support in the midwestern primaries, he lost to Charles Evans Hughes in Oregon, effectively ending his campaign.

Cummins played a major role in postwar reconstruction. As chairman of the Senate Committee on Interstate Commerce, he co-authored the Esch-Cummins bill, returning the railroads to private control with financial guarantees despite progressives' demands for continued government operation and/or ownership. Cummins also advocated compulsory arbitration in labor disputes, a measure unpopular with organized labor. In Iowa's 1920 Senate race, Cummins defeated Smith W. Brookhart, a radical progressive.

In 1919, as an Old Guard sop to the progressives, Cummins became President *pro tempore* of the Senate. During Normalcy, Cummins generally supported both Warren Harding and Calvin Coolidge, an indication either of Cummins's conservatism or of reform's changing nature. In 1926 Smith W. Brookhart defeated him in the primary, and he died soon afterward.

See also: Theodore Roosevelt, William Howard Taft, Woodrow Wilson

Eugene S. Larson

REFERENCES

Holt, James. 1967. *Congressional Insurgents and the Party System, 1909–1916.* Cambridge: Harvard U. Pr.
Robertson, James Oliver. 1983. *No Third Choice: Progressives in Republican Politics, 1916–1921.* New York: Garland.

Mario M. Cuomo (1932–)

Three-term New York governor. Born to poor, immigrant parents in New York City, Mario

Matthew Cuomo has lived the American dream, rising to prominence through intelligence and hard work yet never forgetting his roots.

A graduate (B.A., LL.B.) of St. John's University and a successful lawyer, Cuomo was drawn to public service by New York City reform mayor John Lindsay, who asked him to mediate a dispute over placing low-income housing in the middle-class Forest Hills neighborhood. His electoral career began inauspiciously, with losing campaigns for the Democratic nomination for lieutenant governor of New York (1974) and mayor of New York City (1977). However, New York governor Hugh Carey tapped Cuomo, his appointed secretary of state, as his running mate when he sought reelection in 1978, leading to Cuomo's first successful election. In 1982, Cuomo upset New York City Mayor Ed Koch in the Democratic gubernatorial primary and then beat conservative businessmen Lew Lehrman in November. Extremely popular in his first term as governor, Cuomo was reelected by a landslide in 1986. However, he won reelection in 1990 more narrowly despite mediocre competition.

New York's Democratic governors are traditionally mentioned as presidential contenders. One of his generation's most eloquent political orators, Cuomo abets such speculation by speaking out often on key national concerns: the need for two Americas—one rich and sated, the other poor and needy—to unite (the 1984 Democratic convention keynote address); church-state relations; international and economic affairs. Still claiming no need to be President, he remained above the nominating fray in 1984 and 1988. Despite continued disclaimers, his name remains high on the list of potential presidential contenders.

See also: Elections of 1984 and 1988, Ed Koch, John Lindsay

L. Sandy Maisel

REFERENCES

McElvaine, Robert S. 1988. *Mario Cuomo: A Biography.* New York: Scribner's.

James Michael Curley (1874–1958)

Massachusetts Democratic political legend. The political career of James Michael Curley was popularized in Edwin O'Connor's *The Last Hurrah.* This novel claimed that local machine politics died because of New Deal welfare programs. This thesis was widely accepted until cumulative research on urban machines discredited it.

Theories aside, the story of Curley's political life reads like fiction. Colorful, relentless, even devious, he first won a seat on the Boston Common Council in 1900. In 1955, he lost his last mayoral election. In the intervening years Curley served one or more terms as state representative, city councilman, U.S. Congressman, mayor of Boston (the office for which he is best remembered), and governor of Massachusetts. He also was an alderman early in his career and much later became a Democratic national committeeman.

Although intermittently successful over a long period, Curley was never able to construct an organization on the Tammany model. The son of Irish immigrants, he had substantial support in Boston's Irish wards and among the working class, and his campaigns always featured heavy doses of anti-upper class rhetoric. He was, however, a maverick Democrat who had to contend with an opposing Irish faction within the regular state organization. As a result, he resorted to rough-and-tumble campaigning, charismatic posturing, and occasionally, dirty tricks.

In 1932 Curley decided to support New York governor Franklin D. Roosevelt as the Democratic nominee for President while the regular Massachusetts organization favored Alfred E. Smith. Thereafter, Curley clung to Roosevelt's coattails even though the President tried repeatedly to shake him loose. In office Curley employed typical machine strategy: patronage for the faithful, services for the needy, and projects with visibility to gain prestige. He was indicted in 1943 and later convicted for mail fraud in a questionable case, believed by some to have been a vendetta by President Roosevelt. Pardoned by Harry Truman, Curley closed his long career with three unsuccessful attempts to return to city hall.

See also: Bosses, New Deal, Franklin Roosevelt, Tammany Hall, Harry S Truman

Gene D. L. Jones

REFERENCES

Steinberg, Alfred. 1972. *The Bosses.* New York: Macmillan.

Charles Curtis (1860–1936)

Kansas Congressman and U.S. Senator and Herbert Hoover's Vice President. Charles Curtis of Kansas served eight terms in the U.S. House of Representatives, and from 1907 to 1913 and from 1915 to 1928 he sat in the U.S. Senate. After 1915 he acted as Senate representative whip, until he became Majority Leader in 1924.

The strength of Curtis lay not in his ideas but in personal politics. A critic charged that for Curtis, a supreme regular, "the trinity meant the Republican party, the high protective tariff, and the Grand Army of the Republic." But Curtis built model relations with his constituents. He was a classic Senate insider who, though not imaginative or a good speaker, excelled at private negotiations and mediation.

In the mid-1920s Curtis developed higher political ambitions, but Calvin Coolidge rejected his bid for the vice presidency in 1924. Curtis contended as a favorite son for the presidential nomination in 1928, but he could not overcome support for Hoover. Moreover, Curtis lacked the necessary skills for a national campaign. Despite his disparagement of Hoover's qualifications before the convention, the GOP selected him for Vice President to reward his party loyalty. In addition, Republicans that believed Curtis's support for limited farm relief would attract discontented midwestern farmers.

The Hoover-Curtis ticket was the first in American history to feature two candidates from states west of the Mississippi. An awkward stump orator, Curtis contributed little to Hoover's victory, which was almost certain anyway. He exercised little influence in the Hoover administration. Against opposition within the GOP, the President nonetheless retained Curtis as running mate in his unsuccessful 1932 campaign.

See also: Calvin Coolidge, Elections of 1928 and 1932, Herbert Hoover

Jeffery C. Livingston

REFERENCES

Ewy, Marvin. 1961. *Charles Curtis of Kansas: Vice President of the United States, 1929–1933.* Emporia: Kansas State Teachers College.

Seitz, Don C. 1928. *From Kaw Teepee to Capital: The Life Story of Charles Curtis, Indian, Who Has Risen to High Estate.* New York: Frederick A. Stokes.

Unrau, William E. 1989. *Mixed-Bloods and Tribal Dissolution: Charles Curtis and the Quest for Indian Identity.* Lawrence: U. Pr. of Kansas.

Young, Klyde, and Lamar Middleton. 1948. *Heirs Apparent: The Vice Presidents of the United States.* New York: Prentice-Hall.

George W. Curtis (1824–1892)

Abolitionist and journalist. A popular nineteenth-century author and lecturer, George William Curtis was a literary man who used his talents to advocate reforms ranging from abolition of slavery to women's suffrage. Born in Providence, Rhode Island, Curtis spent much of his youth in boarding school before his family moved to New York. At age 18 he left New York for Brook Farm in Massachusetts, where he began an association with the Transcendental Movement, an association that introduced him to such notables as Henry David Thoreau and Ralph Waldo Emerson, which strengthened his idealistic bent.

A prolific author, he published a number of nonfiction books beginning with *Nile Notes of a Hawadji* in 1851. As well, he became a frequent contributor to several major periodicals. His work as editor for *Putnam's Monthly*, and later *Harper's Weekly*, afforded him the opportunity to make his views known on myriad subjects. Curtis's varied career also included terms as chancellor of the University of the State of New York and director of the Metropolitan Museum of Art, but he was best known for his advocacy of what he called "civic virtue."

A strong early supporter of the Republican Party, Curtis was a delegate to the Republican national conventions of 1860 and 1864 as well as a presidential elector in 1868. His one attempt at elective office ended when he was defeated for Congress in 1864. Although he declined appointive positions offered by Presidents Abraham Lincoln and Rutherford B. Hayes, Curtis accepted a post under President Ulysses S. Grant as a member of a commission on civil service reform, and later he helped form the National Civil Service Reform League in 1881.

See also: Abolition Movement, Civil Service Reforms, Ulysses S. Grant, Abraham Lincoln, Women's Suffrage

James V. Saturno

Kenneth M. Curtis (1931–)

Governor of Maine and chairman of the Democratic National Committee. Kenneth Curtis served as the sixty-sixth governor of Maine, from 1967 until 1974. He was elected governor after an unsuccessful race for Congress in 1964 and a two-year term as Maine's Secretary of State—at that time a largely ceremonial position whose occupant was chosen by the majority party in the legislature. His political style was new for Maine, spotlighting his charisma and his willingness to confront controversial social and environmental issues. He was the first Maine governor to televise major addresses. Despite vehement opposition to the war in Vietnam and advocacy of social welfare programs, he was able to work closely with the Republican Party, which controlled the state

legislature, and to pass important programs. He was the first Democratic governor to serve a four-year term; his reelection in 1970 guaranteed him the distinction of serving as governor of Maine for the longest continuous term possible under Maine law.

While serving as Maine's chief executive, Curtis successfully reorganized and modernized the state's bureaucracy, including a major reduction of the number of separate departments and commissions, consolidating over 200 into 10 major departments. He developed a personal friendship with Jimmy Carter, the governor of Georgia, who was facing similar problems. In 1976 Curtis assumed a major role in Carter's presidential campaign. Following his election, Carter asked Curtis to serve as chairman of the Democratic National Committee (DNC). Curtis did so for 2 years, during which he fought constantly with Carter loyalists in the White House, whose interests were dedicated more to President Carter's renomination than to building the party. In 1978 Ken Curtis left the DNC. President Carter than appointed him ambassador to Canada, a position he held with distinction until 1982.

Curtis returned to his native Maine and the practice of law. While he has frequently been mentioned as a candidate for statewide office in Maine since his return, he has stayed out of public life, serving as the president of the Maine Maritime Academy.

See also: Jimmy Carter, Democratic National Committee, Election of 1976, Vietnam War as a Political Issue

Kenneth P. Haynes

REFERENCES

Lipez, Kermit. 1974. *Kenneth Curtis of Maine.* Brunswick, ME: Harpswell Press.

Bronson M. Cutting (1888–1935)

Republican Senator from New Mexico. Selected to replace the deceased Andrieus A. Jones as United States Senator from New Mexico in 1927, Bronson Murray Cutting was elected in his own right on the Republican ticket in 1928 by the largest plurality then accorded a senatorial candidate. He was reelected in 1934, but the result was contested.

Born to wealth on Long Island, New York, Cutting went to Groton and then on to Harvard, where his severe tuberculosis cut short his academic career. Cutting settled in Santa Fe for his health, and in 1913 he purchased the *Santa Fe New Mexican* and its weekly Spanish edition *El*

Nuevo Mexicano. Following a family tradition, he enlisted his papers in the cause of good government, supporting individuals more than parties in championing progressive reform and criticizing public officials. As a result he was soon involved in a lengthy battle over freedom of the press, which was not fully resolved until after World War I.

Cutting was a reformer, once treasurer of the Progressive Party of New Mexico, and he often deserted the progressive wing of the Republican Party to support Democratic candidates for governor of his state. Still, Republican New Mexico governor Richard Dillon appointed Cutting to the U.S. Senate in 1926.

During World War I he served as an assistant military attaché at the U.S. embassy in London as a liaison with British military intelligence. After the war, Cutting helped organize the American Legion and became closely involved with native Spanish-speaking inhabitants. In promoting veteran's benefits the Legion found itself involved in politics; Cutting soon became the don of a nonpartisan organization of Hispanic voters, veterans, organized labor, and progressive-minded citizens. By 1930 Cutting was the most powerful politician in New Mexico. In 1932, when he endorsed Franklin D. Roosevelt for President, he organized a fusion ticket and supported the Democratic incumbent for a second term as governor.

Roosevelt, a family friend, offered Cutting the post of Secretary of the Interior, which he refused. In the Senate he advocated the immediate payment of the bonus to veterans, but he first got national attention by opposing the censorship of foreign literature by custom's officials. He cosponsored a Philippine Independence bill, which met a presidential veto. While he supported most of the New Deal measures, he incurred Roosevelt's wrath when he got veteran's benefits reinstated in the 1933 Economy Act. As a result, in his reelection campaign in 1934, the administration endorsed his opponent.

Cutting was the only Republican seeking a major office in New Mexico to win in 1934. His election was immediately challenged by his opponent, Dennis Chavis. Having returned to New Mexico to insure that ballots were not tampered with, Cutting died in a plane crash in northeastern Missouri on his way back to Washington.

See also: Election of 1932, Herbert Hoover, New Deal, Progressive Party, Franklin Roosevelt, Theodore Roosevelt

Richard Lowitt

REFERENCES

Armstrong, Patricia. 1959. *A Portrait of Bronson Cutting Through His Papers, 1910–1927.* Albuquerque: Division of Research, Department of Government, University of New Mexico.

Pickens, William H. 1971. "Bronson Cutting vs. Dennis Chavis: Battle of the Patrones in New Mexico, 1934." 46 *New Mexico Historical Review* 5.

Seligmann, Gustav L. 1971. "Bronson Cutting, Politician." In Richard N. Ellis, ed. *New Mexico, Past and Present.* Albuquerque: U. of New Mexico Pr.

———. 1972. "The Purge That Failed: The 1934 Senatorial Election in New Mexico, Yet Another View." 47 *New Mexico Historical Review* 361.

D

Richard J. Daley (1902–1976)

Quintessential boss of an urban political machine. Richard J. Daley, mayor of Chicago from 1955 until his death in 1976, built the Cook County Democratic Party into the most powerful big city political organization of its time. Because of his dual role as chairman of the party organization and mayor, Daley became the strongest mayor in Chicago history and a significant political actor on a national scale. He led and shaped Chicago politics for more than two decades through his administration of "the city that works" as well as through his political acumen. The political machine that bore so much of his personal imprint was split into several factions after his death and was almost killed by the 1983 mayoral victory of Harold Washington's insurgent political movement.

Daley began in Chicago politics as a precinct worker in his home eleventh ward. Practicing the political ethos that would characterize the political organization he created, Daley loyally supported Democrats while he steadily and slowly rose in the hierarchy: ward secretary, ward committeeman, and then the pivotal position of chairman of the Cook County Democratic Party in 1953. His first elected position in government was to the Illinois House of Representatives in 1936. From 1938 to 1946 he served in the state senate, in 1949 was appointed the state director of revenue by Governor Adlai Stevenson, and from 1950 to 1955 was county clerk of Cook County. During this career in public office, his only electoral defeat came when he was aced in 1946 for Cook County sheriff.

Before his mayoral victory in 1955, Daley captured leadership in the party with his victory over incumbent Martin Kennelly in the 1955 mayoral primary.

Daley easily won succeeding mayoral elections. The emaciated Chicago Republican Party had not mounted a serious challenge to Chicago Democrats since the early 1930s. Daley's only close contests were the first and a 1963 race against a popular Polish candidate who drew heavy support from the city's large Polish population.

Under Daley, Chicago government was efficient, effective, and innovative. Enjoying a broad consensus from labor, business, and other major interest groups, the mayor renewed the central business district, constructed a web of highways, maintained a high level of city services, provided a generally well functioning public transportation system, and encouraged lakefront development. Maintaining the city's financial health did not preclude a rapid pace of urban renewal and construction of public housing. Not a cultured man, Daley nevertheless oversaw the improvement of Chicago's cultural life through programs such as symphony concerts in the parks and commissions of major artworks. Although scandals of fiscal malfeasance and other improprieties frequently made news, Daley himself was never implicated and kept a reputation of being a hard and honest administrator.

Richard J. Daley's impact reached beyond Chicago. A powerful figure in the state Democratic Party, his ability to deliver large number of votes in presidential races made him popular among aspiring presidential nominees. Daley's critical help in John Kennedy's narrow victory over Richard Nixon in 1960 helped establish Daley as a Democratic kingmaker.

He also gained notoriety during the turmoil of the 1960s protest movements. During the riots following Martin Luther King's assassination, he told the Chicago police to shoot to kill. That same year, at the 1968 Democratic National Convention in Chicago, his police were condemned across the country for taking part in a "police riot" against demonstrators. At the 1972 Democratic convention, Daley's delegation was denied credentials by the George McGovern leadership.

Despite these difficulties, Daley won an unprecedented sixth four-year term as mayor in 1975, only to die in office the next year. Although condemned by many as an anachronistic machine boss insensitive to the needs and aspirations of the city's Blacks and other minorities, some observers praised Daley as one of the best big city mayors in American history.

See also: Bosses, John F. Kennedy, Richard Nixon, Adlai Stevenson, Harold Washington

Michael C. Ross

REFERENCES

Royko, Mike. 1971. *Boss.* New York: E. P. Dutton.

George M. Dallas (1792–1864)

Jacksonian era politician and diplomat from Pennsylvania. Jacksonian Democrat George Mifflin Dallas was a politician, an attorney, and a diplomat whose activities spanned half a century. Secretary to the minister to Russia and, later, Philadelphia mayor, Dallas won a Senate seat in 1831 when his "Family" group beat James Buchanan's "Amalgamators" for political primacy in Pennsylvania. He agreed with Andrew Jackson's opposition to the U.S. Bank but split with him on other issues. Declining to run again, he vented his antibank views and came home as Pennsylvania's attorney general.

To ease state in-fighting, Martin Van Buren named Dallas minister to Russia in 1837; he served until 1839. Dallas quietly broke with Van Buren in 1844 over the annexation of Texas. Being chosen as James Polk's running mate placated Van Buren and Pennsylvania and gave Polk a fellow Jacksonian expansionist.

Although a high-tariff man, Dallas broke the votes in the Senate in favor of the tariff cuts that Polk sought in 1846. Dallas backed Polk over annexations in Oregon and Mexico, yet patronage fights involving Secretary of State

Buchanan left Dallas and Polk barely speaking. Buchanan blocked Dallas from the 1848 ticket, but their split enabled Dallas to help Lewis Cass win nomination.

The first to urge popular sovereignty, Dallas backed the Compromise of 1850. In 1856 Franklin Pierce, mentioned in 1852 and 1856 for President, named Dallas minister to England. Buchanan retained his old foe, Dallas, as minister to England in order to shelve him politically and to please the English, among whom Dallas was popular. As minister, he negotiated the Dallas-Clarendon Convention to settle boundary disputes. The Senate rejected it, but it helped promote Anglo-American cooperation.

Dallas returned to Philadelphia in 1861, spending his last years as a lawyer and a Unionist.

See also: James Buchanan, Lewis Cass, Election of 1848, Andrew Jackson, Jacksonian Democracy, Franklin Pierce, Second Bank of the United States, Martin Van Buren

Michael Green

REFERENCES

Belohlavek, John M. 1977. *George Mifflin Dallas: Jacksonian Patrician.* University Park: Pennsylvania State U. Pr.

Klein, Philip S. 1962. *President James Buchanan.* University Park: Pennsylvania State U. Pr.

Sellers, Charles G. 1966. *James K. Polk: Continentalist, 1843–1846.* Princeton: Princeton U. Pr.

Shenton, James P. 1961. *Robert John Walker.* New York: Columbia U. Pr.

Van Deusen, Glyndon G. 1959. *The Jacksonian Era, 1828–1848.* New York: Harper and Row.

Harry M. Daugherty (1860–1941)

Ohio Republican politician and Warren Harding's Attorney General. A longtime cog in the Ohio Republican Party, Harry Daugherty won his greatest prominence as President Warren G. Harding's disgraced Attorney General. Daugherty was born and raised in Washington Court House, Ohio, and after receiving his law degree from the University of Michigan in 1881, he quickly became involved in Ohio Republican politics. He served two terms in the Ohio House of Representatives in the early 1890s but thereafter met failure in seeking elective office, in part because of his deserved reputation as a self-serving politician and lobbyist. Nonetheless, Daugherty was a good speaker and organizer who for a quarter-century helped manage Republican campaigns in Ohio; eventually, he became an important, though not always successful, power broker in the state GOP. His fleeting national power and lasting notoriety came after he was named U.S. Attorney General as a reward for his management of Warren Harding's campaign for the presidency in 1920. Part of the "Ohio Gang" that plundered the government during the Harding administration, Daugherty proved an inept Attorney General and perhaps a corrupt one as well. His friend and Washington apartmentmate, Jesse Smith, peddled jobs, pardons, and protection from the Justice Department, and Daugherty refused to cooperate with the investigation of his department. Daugherty's chief accomplishment of substance—a dubious one—was the famous 1922 railroad strike injunction that deeply antagonized organized labor. After Harding's death, new President Calvin Coolidge removed Daugherty. He spent his remaining 20 years vainly trying to salvage his reputation.

See also: Calvin Coolidge, Election of 1920, Warren G. Harding.

John W. Jeffries

REFERENCES

Giglio, James N. 1968. "The Political Career of Harry M. Daugherty." Ph.D. dissertation, Ohio State University.

David Davis (1815–1886)

Lincoln's 1860 campaign manager and later Supreme Court Justice. David Davis, jurist and politician, was born in Maryland and educated at Kenyon College and the Yale Law School, graduating in 1835 and relocating to Illinois, where he pursued his law practice. In 1844 he was a successful Whig candidate for the state legislature and four years later was elected to the circuit court, serving for 14 years (1848–1862). Davis associated with many of the prominent public figures in antebellum Illinois, especially Abraham Lincoln with whom he struck an intimate and lifelong friendship. A man of outsized proportions, Davis was well respected by both the public and the bar.

Davis's political importance stems from two critical episodes in his career. In the Republican National Convention in 1860, he directed the Lincoln campaign for the nomination with enormous energy and skill and was widely regarded as the most significant contributor to Lincoln's nomination. Whether, despite Lincoln's prohibition, he traded Cabinet seats and other offices for delegate votes has since become an issue among historians. In 1862 Lincoln appointed his friend Davis to the Supreme Court. There he remained for 15 years; however, he was a serious but unsuccessful

contender for the Liberal Republican Party nomination for President in 1872.

Partly owing to the excesses of Ulysses S. Grant's administration, Davis became an independent. During the disputed presidential election of 1876, he was expected to occupy the crucial fifteenth seat on the Electoral Commission. When, instead, he declined the appointment, resigned his court position, and accepted election to the U.S. Senate from Illinois, he was the object, probably unjustly, of widespread accusation and innuendo.

See also: Liberal Republican Party, Abraham Lincoln

John F. Coleman

REFERENCES

King, Willard L. 1960. *Lincoln's Manager: David Davis.* Cambridge: Harvard U. Pr.

Kutler, Stanley I. 1969. "David Davis." In Leon Friedman and Fred L. Israel, eds. *The Justices of the United States, 1789–1969: Their Lives and Major Opinions.* New York: Chelsea House.

Henry G. Davis (1823–1916)

Democratic candidate for Vice President in 1904. Henry G. Davis was a self-made businessman and a two-term Senator from West Virginia who was an unsuccessful Democratic vice presidential nominee on the ticket with Judge Alton B. Parker in 1904. Davis began his working life as a brakeman on the Baltimore & Ohio Railroad in 1842. After marriage he moved to Piedmont, Virginia (now West Virginia) and started a general store. His growing business permitted him to undertake lumbering and railroading on a large scale.

Davis combined his business success with an active political career, beginning with his election to the West Virginia House of Delegates as a Union-Conservative candidate in 1865, followed by two terms in the state senate. Beginning in 1868 he represented West Virginia at Democratic national conventions for 20 years. He served two terms in the United States Senate beginning in 1871 but declined to stand for a third term, preferring instead to return to his railroads. While in the Senate his committee service included the Appropriations Committee (two years as chairman), Committee on Claims, and the Select Committee on Transportation. He supported the General Amnesty Bill that enabled ex-Confederates to hold elective office; the Inflation Bill that increased the national bank circulation following the panic of 1873; and the Bland-Allison Bill that included the remonetization of silver. Davis also advocated the establishment of a Department of Agriculture, a Department of Commerce, and a moderate protective tariff. Although he did not seek a third term, he remained active in politics while pursuing his considerable business interests. At the age of 81 he accepted the Democratic nomination for Vice President, losing in the landslide election of 1904.

See also: Bland-Allison Act, Alton Parker, Railroads

Nicholas C. Burckel

REFERENCES

Pepper, Charles M. 1920. *The Life and Times of Henry Gassaway Davis*. New York: Century.

Jefferson Davis (1808–1889)

President of the Confederate States of America. Born in Kentucky, Jefferson Davis grew up on a small farm in Mississippi. First a student at Kentucky's Transylvania University (1821–1824), he graduated from the U.S. Military Academy at West Point in 1828. He participated in the Black Hawk War in 1832, resigning his commission in 1835 to marry Zachary Taylor's daughter, Sarah Knox. When his bride died from malaria after only three months of marriage, a depressed Davis returned to Mississippi where his brother Joseph took care of him until his marriage to Varina Howell in 1845.

That same year, Mississippians elected Davis to a two-year term in the U.S. House of Representatives and then, in 1847, to the Senate. He served in the Mexican War and then returned to the Senate, and during the 1850s he was Franklin Pierce's Secretary of War, becoming the driving force in the Pierce administration. In 1857 he went back to the Senate where he defended the South's right to introduce slavery into the territories. When secession came, he resigned and returned to Mississippi to become commander of its state militia.

The Provisional Confederate Congress elected him President, and he took office on February 22, 1861. Davis faced a difficult task, which his truculent personality and lack of political skills made more difficult. He attempted to control everything in both military and civilian spheres, often alienating subordinates and fellow politicians because of his unbending insistence that he was always right. Davis failed to provide effective leadership for the Confederate Congress, was constantly embroiled in national–state government controversies, and interfered with his generals in the field.

Still most historians agree that he was the best man the South had available for the position; he did indeed help sustain the Confederacy through four difficult years of war. Later, his determined effort to escape Union capture and to keep the Confederacy afloat and his two-year prison term after the war won him southern admiration and a place in the pantheon of "Lost Cause" heroes. He maintained the correctness of secession until the day he died, his two-volume *The Rise and Fall of the Confederate Government* (1878–1881) stubbornly insisting upon this contention.

See also: Mexican War, Franklin Pierce, Secession, Zachary Taylor

John F. Marszalek

REFERENCES

Ballard, Michael B. 1987. *The Long Shadow: Jefferson Davis and the Last Days of the Confederacy.* Jackson: U. Pr. of Mississippi.

Eaton, Clement. 1977. *Jefferson Davis.* New York: Free Press.

McElroy, Robert M. 1937. *Jefferson Davis: The Unreal and the Real.* New York: Harper.

Strode, Hudson. 1955–1964. *Jefferson Davis.* 3 vols. New York: Harcourt Brace Jovanovich.

John W. Davis (1799–1859)

Indiana politician and Speaker of the U.S. House of Representatives. Dr. John Wesley Davis brought to the speakership previous experience as he had twice served as the presiding officer of the Indiana House of Representatives.

Born in Pennsylvania, at the close of the eighteenth century, Davis completed medical studies at Baltimore in 1821 and established a practice at Carlisle, Indiana, two years later. Service as a sergeant-at-arms in the state senate in 1828 and election as a county probate judge in 1829 inaugurated a political career that spanned the next 30 years. Six terms as a Democrat in the Indiana House of Representatives (speaker in 1832–1833, 1841–1842, and 1851–1852) were interspersed with four nonconsecutive terms in the U.S. House during the years 1835 to 1847. Besides his term as Speaker in 1845–1847, the capstone of his political service was selection as chairman of the chaotic 1852 Democratic National Convention that required 49 ballots to nominate Franklin Pierce. Few Democrats have had so exhausting a pinnacle.

In addition to his elective positions, Davis was appointed commissioner to China (1848–1850) by President James Polk, governor of Oregon Territory (1853–1854) by Pierce, and was a member of the U.S. Military Academy's board of visitors (1858).

See also: Franklin Pierce, James K. Polk, Speaker of the House

Robert G. Barrows

REFERENCES

Who Was Who in America: Historical Volume. Chicago, 1963.

A Biographical Directory of the Indiana General Assembly. 2 vols., Indianapolis, 1980, 1984, I, 94.

Biographical Directory of the American Congress.

Wollen, William Wesley. 1883. *Biographical and Historical Sketches of Early Indiana.* Indianapolis: 233–240.

John Wesley Davis (1873–1955)

Democratic candidate for President in 1924. The title of his biography, *Lawyer's Lawyer*, asserts his reputation as a lawyer, but John Wesley Davis's best-known political venture was as Democratic candidate for President in 1924. Some 103 ballots were needed to nominate Davis as a compromise selection to face the Republican incumbent, Calvin Coolidge, and the Progressive Party nominee, Robert M. La Follette.

Born in Clarksburg, West Virginia, Davis took undergraduate and law degrees at Washington and Lee University. He began the practice of law in Clarksburg in 1895, and in 1899 he was elected to the West Virginia House of Delegates. In 1910 and 1912 he was elected to the United States House of Representatives.

Davis was Woodrow Wilson's Solicitor General in 1913, and he served with distinction at this post until 1919 when the President appointed him ambassador to Great Britain. He became head of a Wall Street law firm in 1921, representing numerous large corporations. Davis was very active as an appellate lawyer, arguing numerous cases before the United States Supreme Court. Late in life, he represented the steel industry in its 1952 suit to overturn President Harry Truman's emergency takeover of the industry. And he defended South Carolina in *Brown v. Board of Education* (1954).

A political conservative, he differed little in viewpoint from Calvin Coolidge in 1924 but received only 136 electoral votes. He helped to establish the Liberty League in order to counter the harm he believed the New Deal of President Franklin Roosevelt was causing to individualism. Although Davis remained nominally a Democrat, he supported Republican candidates for President, beginning with Alfred M. Landon in 1936.

See also: Calvin Coolidge, Robert La Follette, New Deal

Paul C. Cline

REFERENCES

Harbaugh, William H. 1973. *Lawyer's Lawyer: The Life of John W. Davis.* New York: Oxford U. Pr.

Davis v. Brandemer
106 S.Ct. 2797 (1986)

This suit challenged the 1981 reapportionment for the Indiana state legislature on the grounds that the plan was a political gerrymander that disadvantaged Democratic voters, thereby violating their right to equal protection under the Fourteenth Amendment. Specifically, Democrats pointed to the 1982 election in which Democratic candidates for the state house of representatives received 51.9 percent of the vote cast but only won 43 of the 100 seats at stake (for the senate, they received 53.1 percent of the popular vote and won 13 of 25 seats) as proof of gerrymandering. In urban multimember House districts, Democrats were even more grossly underrepresented in this regard. The district court had concluded that the redistricting plan indicated "an intentional effort to favor Republican incumbents and candidates and to disadvantage Democratic voters" and had enjoined its use. The U.S. Supreme Court found insufficient evidence of equal protection violations and allowed the plan to stand. The case is significant because it represents the first substantial ruling by the Court on the issue of political gerrymandering.

Drawing parallels to racial gerrymandering decisions in which the Court considered the invidiously discriminatory impact of reapportionment plans in addition to the "one man, one vote" criterion, the Court ruled that political gerrymandering was a justiciable question. In this case, however, the Court found no prima facie evidence of an equal protection violation of the Democrats' rights. A threshold showing of discriminatory vote dilution, according to the Court, requires more than demonstrating that a plan makes it more difficult for some groups to elect their candidates or that proportional representation of election outcomes is not achieved. The intention to political gerrymander is not a constitutional violation in and of itself; proof of electoral disadvantage resulting from the gerrymander must be evident at the polls. In stating the Court's opinion, Justice Byron White wrote: "unconstitutional discrimination occurs only when the electoral system is arranged in a manner that will consistently degrade a voter's or a group of voters'

influence on the political process as a whole."
The Court concluded here that a history of discriminatory results, in which a political group has been denied opportunities to influence the political process generally, must occur before a threshold finding of equal protection violations can be sustained. In particular, one election under the new plan or the results from one set of election districts did not prove such a history. Because the Court did not find an equal protection violation, it did not need to judge the constitutionality of the apportionment plan in Indiana.

The significance of the case is that it seems to invite political gerrymandering for state legislative districts as long as they meet equal population and nonracial discrimination standards. Because they have to prove the existence of a consistent pattern or history of degrading voters' influence on the political process as a whole, disadvantaged groups are without short-term recourse to the courts for protection. This approach by the Court would not seem to be a deterrent to political parties and politicians interested in maximizing present political power.

See also: Gerrymandering

Clyde Brown

REFERENCES
Brace, Kimball W., and John P. Katosh. 1986. "From the Political Thicket to a Political Swamp." 59 *Journal of State Government* 104.

Charles G. Dawes (1865–1951)

Calvin Coolidge's Vice President. Charles Gates Dawes was born in Marietta, Ohio, the son of Rufus Dawes, a prominent businessman, Civil War colonel, and future member of Congress. Dawes graduated from Marietta College in 1884 and from Cincinnati Law School in 1886 before taking up the practice of law in Nebraska. There his interest in business eventually led him to become involved with banking, which he made his career.

His involvement with politics was generally appointive and managerial, beginning with his appointment as Comptroller of the Currency after he successfully managed William McKinley's 1896 presidential campaign in Illinois. Dawes served in that position from 1897 to 1902 when he resigned to run unsuccessfully for the U.S. Senate from Illinois. He then turned his attention back to business, organizing the Central Trust Company of Illinois.

During World War I, Dawes served in the Army, rising from major to brigadier general.

After the war his managerial expertise earned him appointment as the first director of the Bureau of the Budget, a position he held in 1921. Dawes was later appointed by the Allied Reparations Commission to find a solution to the Germany's financial problems. For his 1924 "Dawes Plan" he was a co-recipient of the Nobel Peace Prize in 1925.

His only election to office was as Vice President under Calvin Coolidge from 1925 to 1929. He later served as ambassador to Great Britain from 1929 to 1932 and briefly served as director of the Reconstruction Finance Corporation but resigned to return to banking and business in 1932. Dawes was also a prolific author, writing books about his experiences in several of his posts.

See also: Calvin Coolidge, William McKinley

James V. Saturno

Jonathan Dayton (1760–1824)

Federalist politician and co-conspirator with Aaron Burr. Jonathan Dayton was a Federalist delegate, Representative, and Senator from New Jersey whose active public career ended when he was indicted for treason in connection with the Aaron Burr conspiracy to split off the Louisiana Territory from the U.S. Born in New Jersey, Dayton graduated from Princeton University in 1776 and then studied law. During the Revolutionary War, he served in a variety of capacities under his father, Elias. After the war, he was elected to the New Jersey assembly in 1786, 1787, and 1790, serving as speaker during his last term. Elias Dayton had been selected as a delegate to the Constitutional Convention in 1787, but he declined the appointment in favor of his son, who became the youngest signer of the Constitution. Johnathan also represented New Jersey in the Continental Congress in 1787 and 1788, and he was elected to the New Jersey Council in 1790.

Once the new government was established, Dayton was elected to Congress, serving as a Federalist Representative in the second, third, fourth, and fifth Congresses. He was the Speaker of the House during his second two terms. In 1798 he did not run for reelection to the House because he was a candidate for one of New Jersey's United States Senate seats—an office to which he was elected; he remained in the Senate until 1805. Dayton was a loyal Federalist who supported the formation of a regular army, as opposed to reliance on militia. He consistently supported Alexander Hamilton's financial policies and took a leading role in supporting the suppression of the Whiskey Rebellion. His influence as Speaker buoyed Federalist efforts to prevent the House from opposing the Jay Treaty.

In the Senate, Dayton opposed the repeal of the Judiciary Act in 1801, endorsed the Louisiana Purchase, opposed the Twelfth Amendment, and voted against the impeachment of Supreme Court Justice Salmon Chase. His active interest in promoting the settlement of the Ohio region earned him both fame (as the namesake of Dayton, Ohio) and infamy (as a co-conspirator of Aaron Burr). Dayton was one of the first generation of "professional" politicians produced by the new American system, and as such, with all his flaws, he represented the future of United States politics more accurately than did his aristocratic contemporaries.

See also: Aaron Burr, Federalist Party, Alexander Hamilton, Jay Treaty, Speaker of the House, Twelfth Amendment

Kathryn A. Malone

William L. Dayton (1807–1864)

First Republican Party candidate for Vice President. Although handicapped by an inability to speak or to understand French, William Lewis Dayton served creditably as U.S. minister at the Court of Napoleon III of France during the American Civil War. Ably supported by John Bigelow, the American consul in Paris, and wisely guided by Secretary of State William H. Seward, Dayton helped fend off European intervention on the side of the Confederacy—intervention that could have permanently divided the Union. Among Dayton's most serious problems were Louis Napoleon's sponsorship of Maximilian's puppet government in Mexico, French support for Confederate blockade running, southern efforts to build warships in French shipyards, and the cotton shortage in Europe, which provided a major pretext for Anglo-French intervention in the American conflict.

Born in New Jersey, Dayton graduated from Princeton College in 1825 and was admitted to the bar in 1830. After serving as an associate justice of the New Jersey Supreme Court from 1838 to 1841, he was a Whig U.S. Senator from 1842 to 1851 and the first vice presidential candidate of the Republican Party in 1856. During James Buchanan's administration he served as attorney general of New Jersey, before receiving President Abraham's Lincoln's appointment as American envoy in Paris early in 1861.

See also: William H. Seward

Norman B. Ferris

REFERENCES

Bigelow, John. 1909. *Retrospections of An Active Life.* New York: Baker and Taylor.

Case, Lynn M., and Warren F. Spencer. 1970. *The United States and France: Civil War Diplomacy.* Philadelphia: U. of Pennsylvania Pr.

Dealignment in the American Electorate

For decades now scholars of American political parties have anxiously searched polls and electoral results for signs of a critical realignment. Given the regular historic patterns of party system change, such a realignment seems long overdue. The last major restructuring of the party system occurred in the 1930s, and many once-controversial aspects of government involvement in the economy have become institutionalized and widely accepted by both parties. At the same time, since the New Deal, new issues have divided the electorate in ways that could potentially realign American voters. None of these issues, however, has had more than a marginal impact on the overall distribution of party identification.

Waiting for a major realignment has been much like waiting for Godot. While many of the signs seem to indicate that it should surely come along any time now, that promise remains unfulfilled. Perhaps the most important sign has been the gradual decaying of the existing party system. As James Sundquist has told us: "fluidity, independence, and party-switching—those marks of the turbulent 1960s—also characterized the prealignment and realignment eras of the past." Therefore, much of our initial interest in and theorizing about the movement away from the parties in the late 1960s and early 1970s has centered on how such a development might facilitate a new partisan alignment. In order for the system to realign, it would first have to dealign, and such a process was clearly taking place.

The term "dealignment" was apparently first used in print by Ronald Inglehart and Avram Hochstein in their article, "Alignment and Dealignment of the Electorate in France and the United States." In this 1972 essay Inglehart and Hochstein contrasted the relationship between age and strength of partisan identification in a decaying American system to that of a rapidly developing French partisan alignment.

However, Inglehart and Hochstein's article was preceded by two years by the publication of

Walter Burnham's seminal book *Critical Elections and the Mainsprings of American Politics*. Here, Burnham analyzed what he called the "long-term electoral disaggregation" and "party decomposition" in the United States. While neither of these terms made much of a dent in the common parlance of scholarship on political parties, "dealignment" stuck almost immediately. In contrast to realignment—which refers to a durable change in the distribution of partisan attachments and hence political behavior—dealignment involves a movement away from party affiliation and guidance. Dealignment is thus characterized by a weakening of party identification and a decline in the role of partisanship in shaping individual voting decisions.

What was initially seen as a temporary development, opening the way for a new partisan alignment has since come to be viewed as an enduring feature of American party politics by many analysts. Burnham has recently gone so far as to label the dealignment period since 1968 as the sixth American party system.

> In retrospect, the critical realignment that so many people looked for around 1968 actually happened around that date, but in the "wrong" place. Instead of producing an emergent Republican (or any other) majority, parties themselves were decisively replaced at the margins by the impact of the "permanent campaign." (Burnham, 1985, p. 248)

While the old party alignment continues to fade away, Burnham and others believe that a new alignment will find it very difficult to put down roots in the current dealigned era. Any realignment that does occur will be hollow as long as political parties continue to have a weak image in the public mind and an uncertain role in the future of American government.

The evidence for dealignment can be classified into three broad categories. The first to be addressed here concerns normative attitudes toward the role of political parties in the United States. Second is trends in party-line and split-ticket voting. And third, we look at the decline of party identification and party images

American Attitudes Toward Political Parties

Americans have traditionally maintained an ambivalent attitude toward political parties. The founders wished to avoid the establishment of parties but at the same time viewed them as necessary evils. Initially, they established parties not with the view of creating long-term organizations to compete for power but rather as a means of permanently defeating the opposition. To them, political parties were needed only until a national consensus could be attained. Even after the acceptance of regularized opposition parties in the mid-nineteenth century, Congress was able to weaken the role of parties in American political life. For example, the power of patronage was greatly limited by the implementation of merit-based civil service in the 1880s. Furthermore, the nomination function was largely taken away from parties with the introduction of direct primaries at the turn of the century.

Ironically, in a nation that founded the world's first political party system, parties have been looked upon with such suspicion. As the first to experiment with democratic political parties, the American ethos has apparently gotten an indelible imprint. Whereas other countries have consciously adopted a political party system in light of experience elsewhere, for the U.S., parties were a risky adventure in the then-uncharted waters of democratic development. As a consequence, in no other western country are parties as tightly regulated and constrained as they are in the United States. From the European perspective, observers such as Philip Williams are often left wondering "how in the 1980s American political parties can be said to have lost power when they hardly ever had any."

Extensive survey evidence exists to document Americans' lack of concern with partisanship and the role of political parties in U.S. Government. Most pervasive is most Americans' belief that they should vote for the man, not the party. Even in 1956, when most voters were in fact voting straight party tickets, 74 percent of respondents in a Gallup poll agreed with this general belief; by 1968 this figure had risen to 84 percent. Most recently, a survey by Sabato found 92 percent agreeing with this statement: "I always vote for the person who I think is best, regardless of what party they belong to."

On the other side of the coin, only 14 percent in Sabato's 1986 survey agreed with the statement that "I always support the candidates of just one party." Such feelings have been shown to be particularly weak in the younger generation. For example, Beck's 1984 analysis of the 1973 wave of the Jennings-Niemi socialization study, found that 18 percent of the parents felt "it is better to vote a straight ticket than to divide your votes between the parties" compared to a mere 8 percent of their 25-year-old offspring.

Using such public opinion data, we can now safely say that putting candidate considerations ahead of party considerations in voting has become a part of the American creed. One reason for this consensus has been a sense that political parties are not very meaningful in today's political world. For example, in the Jennings-Niemi socialization study, 86 percent of the parents and 92 percent of their children agreed with this statement: "A candidate's party label does not really tell a person what the candidate's stand will be on the issues." Similarly, the 1980 National Election Study found that 52 percent of the public agreed that "the parties do more to confuse the issues than to provide a clear choice."

The most potentially damaging attitude to the political parties' future, however, is the large percentage of the population that sees little need for parties altogether. For example, 45 percent of the 1980 election study sample agreed that "it would be better if, in all elections, we put no party labels on the ballot." An astonishing 30 percent agreed with the extreme statement that "the truth is we probably don't need political parties anymore." And similarly, 37 percent in Sabato's 1986 survey agreed that "political parties don't really make any difference anymore." Indeed, by a 45 percent to a 34 percent margin more people see interest groups as better representatives of their political needs than either of the political parties, according to a 1983 Gallup poll. Patterns such as these have prompted Jack Dennis to write that "we may be called upon in the not so distant future to witness the demise of a once prominent institution of American government and politics," that is, the political party.

In stark contrast to political scientists' handwringing about party decline, the public seems blithely unaware of the parties' plight. A December 1985 *New York Times* poll asked people the following question: "Think about how much influence political parties have today. Do they have more influence than they had twenty years ago, less influence, or about the same influence as they had twenty years ago?" The results revealed that 50 percent actually thought the parties have more influence today, compared to 24 percent who thought their influence was less, 18 percent who said it was about the same, and 8 percent who didn't know. Because the public is so unaware of the problem of party decline, the task of educating people on the need for party revitalization takes on greater importance as well as difficulty. To make people

care once again about political parties will require a public conviction that parties can and do fill an important institutional role.

The Decline of Party-Line Voting

Analysis of American voting patterns in the twentieth century clearly reveals a steady trend away from straight party-line voting. Although sample survey evidence is necessarily limited to the relatively recent period for which data are available, we can get a far more extended historical perspective on dealignment and the relationship of partisanship to the vote by examining aggregate election returns over time. We can expect that if party loyalties are closely related to the vote, the results for different offices in the same election will tally faithfully. Therefore, if a Democratic candidate wins the presidential race in a given district, then other Democratic candidates in the district should also win. If, however, voters are casting their ballots on the basis of variables other than party, ticket-splitting may result in victories for some candidates on the ticket and losses for others.

As Burnham (1985) has shown, the squared correlation between a nonsouthern state's vote for President and its vote for Senate, House, and for governor has declined continuously throughout this century. The degree of shared variance with the presidential vote for every fifth election year from 1900 to 1980 plus 1988 is presented below:

	Senate	House	Governor
1900	—	.97	.94
1920	.80	.70	.55
1940	.76	.66	.61
1960	.43	.55	.36
1980	.24	.06	.00
1988	.09	.00	.09

In simple terms, these squared correlations indicate that at the turn of the century, observers could predict almost perfectly how a state would vote for Congress and governor by its vote for President. By mid-century a state would often follow the same pattern in voting for President as for other offices, but with a fair number of exceptions. Finally, knowing a state's presidential vote in 1988 was of virtually no help in predicting its vote for other offices, as the voting patterns were hardly correlated at all.

The results of these patterns have distinct political significance. They clearly demonstrate the unprecedented level of split-party control of both the federal and state governments in recent years. Most visible, of course, has been the division between partisan control of the presidency and the Congress from 1952 to 1992. During this 40-year period, the same party has controlled the presidency and the House for just 14 years. In addition, for the period between 1981 and 1986, different parties controlled the House and Senate for the first time since 1916.

On another level, as of 1988, in only 18 states was one party in control of both houses of the legislature as well as the governor's office. Not since the formation of the Republican Party in the 1850s can one find anything like this split in the history of state politics. And, as Sabato points out, the link between state and national party politics has also weakened. Between 1880 and 1956 only 17 percent of states electing their governor in a presidential year went in opposite directions for the two executive offices—compared to 40 percent from 1960 to 1984.

While such patterns have clear substantive significance, they are somewhat less than definitive indicators of split-ticket voting because of the possibility of aggregate fallacy. Only through analysis of individual-level survey data is it feasible to actually gauge the scope and nature of party-line voting. Examinations of the National Election Study data from 1952 to 1984 confirm the conclusion from the aggregate election returns that the degree of cross-party voting has risen quite sharply over the last few decades. Listed below are the percentages over time for ticket-splitting between (1) President and House votes; (2) House and Senate votes; and (3) votes for other state and local offices.

It is thus readily apparent that split-ticket voting has at least doubled in every respect over the last three decades. During the 1952–1960 period ticket-splitting was relatively rare as well as fairly stable. Over the next twenty years, however, a steady increase is apparent, with the 1980 election recording the highest levels to date.

To recapitulate, one prominent sign of dealignment has been the decline of the parties' ability to structure the vote. Division of party control of both the federal and state governments has become common as split-ticket voting has increased greatly over the last quarter of a century. Furthermore, given the current state of public attitudes about voting the man rather than the party, we have good reason to expect that this element of dealignment will continue for some time to come. Because the potential for ticket-splitting has consistently been greater than its incidence, we can reasonably interpret recent trends as reflecting the tendency for behaviors eventually to come into line with attitudes.

The Decline of Party Identification and Partisan Images

Accompanying the trend toward greater split-ticket voting has also been a decline in party identification. Election studies during the period from 1952 to 1964 consistently found that approximately 75 percent of the electorate identified themselves as either Democrats or Republicans, and roughly half of these identifiers considered themselves to be strong partisans. The similarity in party identification margins from one sample survey to another during this period led Philip Converse (1966) to write of the "serene stability in the distribution of party loyalties," and later (1976) to call these years the "steady state period" of party identification. However, after 1964 the picture changed significantly. By 1972 the percentage of respondents identifying with one of the parties had dropped from 77 percent to 64 percent, and the proportion of strong partisans declined from 38 percent to 25 percent.

At first, these changes in the distribution of party loyalties were seen as quite a revolutionary development. For example, Burnham (1970) has argued that the losses in identification for both parties could very well represent "a disso-

	1952	1956	1960	1964	1968	1972	1976	1980	1984	1988
President-House	12	16	14	15	26	30	25	34	25	25
Senate-House	9	10	9	18	22	23	23	31	20	27
Local	27	30	27	41	48	56	NA	59	52	NA

lution of the parties as action intermediaries in electoral choice and other politically relevant acts." In addition, the rise of a "mass base for independent political movements of ideological tone and considerable long-term staying power" seemed to be one possible consequence of the decline, according to Burnham. Similarly, Gerald Pomper wrote that the continuation of such a trend "may eventually bring the nation to a free-floating politics, in which prediction is hazardous, continuities are absent and governmental responsibility is impossible to fix."

More recently, however, revisionist views interpret the decline in party identification as far less cataclysmic. To begin with, the downward trend no longer seems to be a trend at all, but rather a limited period effect in which a rapid decline was followed by the development of a new, somewhat lower level of stability. Since 1972 the proportion of the population identifying with one of the parties during presidential election years has held steady at between 63 percent and 65 percent. In retrospect, the period of most seriously weakened party loyalties—1964 to 1972—seems to be an unusually tumultuous epoch in the history of American politics, which may well never again be duplicated in the severity of the shocks (Vietnam, racial unrest, etc.) felt by the electorate.

Perhaps more important is the analytic argument by Keith et al. (1977) that the decline in party identification has been greatly inflated by classifying as "nonpartisans" those Independents reporting themselves as "closer" to one of the two parties. These so-called "Independent leaners" are not an uncommitted and unmobilized bloc but are instead largely "closet" Democrats or Republicans. Although they may prefer to call themselves Independents rather than Democrats or Republicans, their voting behavior in presidential elections show them to be just as partisan as weak party identifiers. Between 1952 and 1988 the mean defection rate for weak Democrats was 34 percent, compared to 31 percent for Independent Democrats; likewise, weak Republicans defected 15 percent of time on the average, compared to 14 percent for Independent Republicans. If Independent leaners are simply partisans by another name, then the proportion of the population identifying with a party can hardly be said to have declined at all over the years. As Keith et al. tells us, "Most of the growth in Independents has occurred among the hidden partisans, while the high-level speculations

have concerned the genuine Independents, whose increase has been rather modest."

On the other hand, as Sabato has maintained, "the reluctance of 'leaners' to admit their real party identification in itself is worrisome because it reveals a sea change in attitudes about political parties and their proper role in our society." Even if increased independence is little more than a movement of partisans into the closet, the question of what is particularly attractive about the closet at present must be addressed. In the 1980 National Election Study, respondents who called themselves Independents were handed a list of 11 statements and asked which ones best described why they so identified themselves. The percentages follow:

74.7%	I decide on the person not the party.
59.0%	I decide on the issue not the party label.
36.3%	The parties almost never deliver on their promises.
29.5%	I support both Democrats and Republicans.
20.2%	I'm not much interested in politics.
17.0%	I don't know enough to make a choice.
14.8%	Neither party stands for what I think is important.
13.5%	I like both parties about the same.
12.6%	I'm Independent because of the way I feel about what Jimmy Carter has been doing.
4.7%	My parents were Independent and I am too.
4.2%	I dislike both parties.

The primary reasons are thus normative values: voters should decide on the basis of person and issues rather than on the party. Such findings support the notion that parties are presently seen as lacking in relevance to the large majority of Independents.

In contrast, we have relatively little evidence for Nie, Verba, and Petrocik's hypothesis postulating a lack of voter confidence in the parties. The negative statement most frequently mentioned was that "the parties almost never deliver on their promises," checked by slightly over one-third of the Independents. Yet such an opinion could conceivably reflect a perception that parties have become so institutionally irrelevant that they no longer have the power to keep their promises. A far better test of the alienation hypothesis is the statement that "neither party stands for what I think is important," checked by only 14.8 percent of the

Independents. And finally, the purest measure of dissatisfaction with the parties follows from the statement that "I dislike both parties," checked by a mere 4.2 percent. All told, even if we accept a party's inability to deliver on promises as a negative performance statement, less than 20 percent of the reasons checked for independence indicate a lack of satisfaction with the two political parties.

Indeed, when asked what they like and dislike about the two major political parties in an open-ended fashion, very few Americans make an overall negative evaluation of both parties. Even at the high point of negative feelings toward the parties in 1968, only 10 percent of the public expressed more dislikes than likes about both the Republicans and Democrats. For 1984 and 1988 this figure was down to a miniscule 3 percent—just what it was in 1952 and 1956.

Rather than expressing negative attitudes toward the parties, the dealignment era has been characterized by an increasing proportion of the mass public—that is, neutral toward both parties. From 1952 to 1984 the percentage who can be classified as neutral toward both parties gradually increased from 13.0 percent to 35.8 percent. Virtually all of these "neutrals" exhibit this response pattern to the four open-ended questions about the parties in the National Election studies:

Q. Is there anything in particular that you like about the Democratic Party?
A. No.
Q. Is there anything in particular that you don't like about the Democratic Party?
A. No.
Q. Is there anything in particular that you like about the Republican Party?
A. No.
Q. Is there anything in particular that you don't like about the Republican Party?
A. No.

In the 1950s such a response pattern reflected general political ignorance. Most of these "neutrals" had little to say about candidates as well and were of little political importance because of their apathy and consequent low turnout. Today this group is apathetic about parties, but not about candidates and politics in general. Indeed, these "neutrals" are often considered the most important group in American electoral politics, and they are known collectively as "the floating voters."

Compared to the decline of party identification, the rise of neutrality in party images has occurred over a much longer period of time and has been a far more pronounced trend. This discrepancy occurs because party identification involves a process of self-labeling and is thus likely to be far more stable than most other political attitudes. Yet such stability can be seen as a theoretical weakness of the measure as well as a strength. While the label may survive intact from year to year, the meaning associated with it may change considerably over time. If parties have become less relevant to the public in recent decades, then attitudes toward people's support of one party and/or opposition to the other will have become less clear—even among those whose party affiliation remains unchanged.

The best possible test for this hypothesis requires an examination of what people have replied to the party "likes/dislikes" questions over time, controlling for party identification. The following comparison of the level of neutrality toward the parties in 1952 and 1984 reveals that the increase is evident for each category of the party-identification scale:

	1952	1984
Strong Democrats	4.8%	14.2%
Weak Democrats	14.5	37.4
Independent Democrats	13.3	38.0
Pure Independents	23.3	70.2
Independent Republicans	9.5	40.8
Weak Republicans	13.5	36.8
Strong Republicans	4.6	14.4

In particular, the proportion of weak partisans and Independent leaners who can be classified as neutral toward both parties has increased from hardly more than one-tenth in 1952 to nearly two-fifths by 1984. The similarity over time between the two supports the contention of Keith et al. that Independent leaners are generally quite similar to weak partisans. However, their basic point is to show that the decline of party identification is not so serious as some maintain, whereas the above data indicate just the reverse. Indeed we know of little reason to be alarmed that more people are calling themselves Independent leaners given their similarity to weak partisans. However, the fact that both categories are now far more neutral toward the parties themselves is cause for genuine concern.

Thus, the rise of neutrality does not really account for the decline of party identification: rather it indicates that the decline in party relevance is even sharper than the rise in independence would lead us to expect. The "likes/dislikes" measure reveals greater neutrality over time among strong partisans, weak partisans, Independent leaners, and pure Independents alike, thereby showing that strength of party identification no longer has the depth of meaning attached to it that it once did.

Conclusion

Evidence of dealignment, then, is readily apparent most everywhere one looks in public attitudes and behavior. The belief that one should vote the man and not the party has now become part of the American consensus, and split-ticket voting has risen markedly. Fewer people now identify with parties, and the percentage who have neither likes nor dislikes for the two parties has more than tripled since the 1950s. As the candidate-centered age reaches maturity, these dealigning trends will probably not be substantially reversed in the near future. Even the Reagan–Mondale contest of 1984, pitting a traditional Democrat against the most partisan President in recent memory, did little to undo the dealigned state of the American electorate.

During the early stages of the dealignment, many analysts were concerned that parties were on the verge of disappearing from the political scene. As dealignment has progressed, however, a more realistic view has been that parties will continue to play an important but significantly diminished role in American electoral politics. For example, Leon Epstein writes that "frayed" strikes him as "an apt word for what has happened to party identification during the last three decades. . . . The word connotes a wearing that need not mean disintegration or abandonment." Epstein concludes that the parties will "survive and even moderately prosper in a society evidently unreceptive to strong parties and yet unready, and probably unable, to abandon parties altogether."

The data concerning normative attitudes toward the parties reviewed in this article indicate that most voters now view parties as a convenience rather than a necessity. However, regardless of whether the public recognizes it or not, the fact of the matter is that parties are necessary for structuring the vote. Political scientists have long recognized the indispensable functions performed by parties, and dealignment has not changed this view. As Dalton, Flanagan, and Beck tell us, "Unless elections become purely contests of personalities, parties are likely to continue to play an important role in structuring political choices, even in a purely dealigned and issue-oriented electorate."

Consequently, political parties will doubtless survive in an atmosphere of dealignment, but will parties still be able to perform many of their key functions in such an environment? If many voters no longer pay much attention to party labels, why should elites pay more than lip service to the concept of party unity in government? As Burnham (1985) writes, "[the dealigned electorate] can and does elect people, but it cannot and does not give them the power to govern with the kind of coherence and cross-institutional will that effective state action will come to require." If a political party wants to play like a team in office, then they must achieve office as a team. The crucial point to note about dealignment is therefore that such a scenario has become increasingly unlikely.

See also: New Deal, Party Identification, Split-Ticket Voting, Third Parties in American Elections

Martin P. Wattenberg

REFERENCES

Beck, Paul Allen. 1984. "The Dealignment Era in America." In Russell J. Dalton et al., eds. *Electoral Change in Advanced Industrial Democracies: Realignment or Dealignment?* Princeton: Princeton U. Pr.

Burnham, Walter Dean. 1970. *Critical Elections and the Mainsprings of American Politics.* New York: Norton.

———. 1985. "The 1984 Elections and the Future of American Politics." In Ellis Sandoz and Cecil V. Crabb, Jr., eds. *Election 84: Landslide Without a Mandate?* New York: Mentor.

———. 1987. "Elections as Democratic Institutions." In Kay Lehman Schlozman, ed. *Elections in America.* Boston: Allen and Unwin.

Converse, Philip E. 1966. "The Concept of a Normal Vote." In Angus Campbell et al., eds. *Elections and the Political Order.* New York: Wiley.

———. 1976. *The Dynamics of Party Support: Cohort-Analyzing Party Identification.* Beverly Hills, CA: Sage.

———, and Gregory B. Markus. 1979. "Plus ca change . . . The New CPS Election Study Panel." 73 *American Political Science Review* 32.

Dalton, Russel J., Scott C. Flanagan, and Paul Allen Beck, eds. 1984. *Electoral Change in Advanced Industrial Societies.* Princeton: Princeton U. Pr.

Dennis, Jack. 1975. "Trends in Public Support for the American Party System." 5 *British Journal of Political Science* 187.

Epstein, Leon D. 1986. *Political Parties in the American Mold.* Madison: U. of Wisconsin Pr.

Inglehart, Ronald, and Avram Hochstein. 1972. "Alignment and Dealignment of the Electorate in France and the United States." 5 *Comparative Political Studies* 343.

Jennings, M. Kent, and Gregory B. Markus. 1984. "Partisan Orientations over the Long Haul: Results from the Three-Wave Political Socialization Study." 78 *American Political Science Review* 1000.

Keith, Bruce E., David B. Magleby, Candice J. Nelson, Elizabeth Orr, Mark Westlye, and Raymond E. Wolfinger. 1977. "The Myth of the Independent Voter." Paper presented at the Annual Meeting of the American Political Science Association.

———, et al. 1986. "The Partisan Attitudes of Independent Leaners." 16 *British Journal of Political Science* 155.

Nie, Norman H., Sidney Verba, and John R. Petrocik. 1976. *The Changing American Voter*. Cambridge: Harvard U. Pr.

Pomper, Gerald. 1975. *Voter's Choice: Varieties of American Electoral Behavior*. New York: Dodd, Mead.

Sabato, Larry J. 1988. *The Party's Just Begun: Shaping Political Parties for America's Future*. Glenview, IL: Scott, Foresman.

Sundquist, James L. 1983. *Dynamics of the Party System: Alignment and Realignment of Political Parties in the U.S.* Rev. ed. Washington: Brookings.

Wattenberg, Martin P. 1990. *The Decline of American Political Parties, 1952–1988*. Cambridge: Harvard U. Pr.

———. 1987. "The Hollow Realignment: Partisan Change in a Candidate-Centered Era." 51 *Public Opinion Quarterly* 58.

Eugene V. Debs (1855–1926)

A radical who expressed the hopes and promise of American socialism. Eugene Victor Debs was a trade unionist, a Democratic Party politician, a social activist, a journalist, and a presidential candidate of the Socialist Party of America (SPA) who drew attention to the moral difficulties posed by the emerging industrial-capitalistic social order. The mature Debs wedded the principles of socialism to an older American ideology that stressed community, the dignity of workers, and democracy.

Born in Terre Haute, Indiana, of German and Alsatian heritage, Debs entered the working world at age 14. Joining a local lodge of the Brotherhood of Locomotive Engineers in 1875, he quickly rose through the ranks, becoming secretary of the union, assistant editor of the locomotive engineers newspaper, and finally in 1880, national secretary and treasurer of the trade union. Although active on behalf of workers as a town clerk in Terre Haute and as a Democratic representative in the Ohio legislature, the young Debs was actually a conservative unionist. He disliked strikes and favored genial agreement between capital and labor.

Troubled by business and government actions during the great strikes of the mid-1880s, Debs abandoned hope for industrial harmony and became a forceful working-class partisan. In 1893 Debs was chosen leader of the newly formed industrial American Railway Union (ARU), and he gained credibility for himself and the new union by winning a strike the following year against the Great Northern Railroad in Minnesota.

Debs and the ARU first rose to national prominence in the famous Chicago Pullman strike of 1894. Initially against going out in sympathy for the Chicago Pullman workers, Debs finally took on a leading role in the strike. Pullman suppressed the strike, largely because of the federal troops sent by President Grover Cleveland; Debs was sentenced to six months in prison for violating a court injunction. Debs later asserted that he converted to socialism in jail, and, although the suddenness of this political radicalization is doubtful, from the mid-1890s onward, he emphasized political action over strict unionism.

The remnants of Debs's ARU eventually merged with the followers of Victor Berger to form the Social Democracy Party of America in 1897. Against the personal wishes of Debs and Berger, the seceded "kangaroo" faction of the Social Labor Party, under Morris Hillquit, combined with the Social Democracy Party to create the Socialist Party of America (SPA) in 1900. The SPA was never a unified party, in part owing to a personal antagonism between Berger and Debs, both of whom claimed political and intellectual leadership of the party. Trade union policy was another contentious issue. The conservative Berger and Hillquit favored "boring from within" the American Federation of Labor (AFL) and securing that trade union federation's support. Debs, who disliked the proclaimed anti-Socialist Samuel Gompers, president of the AFL, first stressed the primacy of political organization, then supported the syndicalist Industrial Workers of the World (IWW), and finally in 1912 renounced IWW members (Wobblies) and their leader William Haywood. Debs's vacillation on the trade union question and his inability early on to perceive the IWW's political liabilities cost the SPA valuable union support. Debs never mounted a sustained challenge to Gompers, and the early union movement remained largely outside Socialist hands.

Tactical deficiencies notwithstanding, Debs's most important contribution to the SPA was his public speaking. Easily the most visible of American Socialists, Debs attracted attention wherever he spoke, countering with his own Indiana accent the claim that socialism was only a foreign importation. Four times his party's candidate for President, Debs's greatest success came in 1912 when he got 900,000 votes—over twice his 1908 total and fully nine times the vote he received in 1900.

The most obvious sign of Debs's personal magnetism, however, showed in the presidential campaign of 1920. He did not run in the 1916 election, but he still became an outspoken critic of the wartime administration and its prosecutions of antiwar radicals under the Espionage Act. Following a speech in Canton, Ohio, on June 16, 1918, Debs was arrested and sentenced to a ten-year prison term for sedition. While still a prisoner in an Atlanta penitentiary during the 1920 election, Debs received 920,000 votes for President. President Harding ordered Debs released on December 25, 1921, although the old Socialist's citizenship was never restored. Debs remained active in radical politics in the 1920s, writing a book on prison conditions entitled *Walls and Bars*. At his death, he was America's best-known "radical."

See also: Election of 1920, Social Democratic Party, Socialism in American Politics

John Walsh

Delegates to State Nominating Conventions

One of the most complex and enduring problems in American political history involves the selection of presidential candidates. Nominations are critically important because they drastically narrow the field of choice in the general election. Controversy has focused on the procedures to be followed by parties in nominating candidates and who should participate. The Constitution, that document most commonly cited in times of political controversy, is silent on this topic. The Founders believed that men of great reputation would present themselves as candidates every four years, and they made no provisions for parties, caucuses, primary elections, or nominating conventions. Not long after the founding, however, some nomination procedures clearly were essential. But a sustained consensus on how to go about nominating presidential candidates remains elusive. Controversy and reform, consequently, have characterized the history of presidential nominations.

State nominating conventions, where delegates meet to pledge their support for a candidate, conclude the sometimes lengthy and complex state process that begins with local caucus meetings and concludes with state conventions. The question we address relates to the problem of political representation among state convention delegates—an important problem since "representativeness" and "openness" have often stimulated reforms of the process, including the most recent round following the 1968 election. Despite the ready use of the concept by critics, a simple application of principles of political representation to presidential nominations is not possible. In a legislature, the natural habitat of the concept, members are elected by popular constituencies and regularly must face the prospect of reelection or defeat, thus becoming formally accountable to those who selected them and on whose behalf they govern. These conditions do not pertain to convention delegates. Delegates are selected by activists who attend local caucuses or county conventions, but their selection is an informal process rather than an extended campaign that invites broad and informed participation. And, of course, delegates are not accountable for their actions once they reach the nominating conventions in their states. This lack of formal accountability is crucial in the nomination campaign because the state convention often takes place months after the start of the process. Much can change in those intervening months, including the field of candidates competing for the nomination. The simple reflection of preferences as expressed earlier in the campaign, therefore, is often impossible.

Despite the complexities, the claim that the nomination process is unrepresentative has fueled major reform movements. Take, for example, the transition from the congressional caucus method of presidential candidate selection to state and local nominating conventions. In the early part of the nineteenth century, presidential nominations were decided by the mutual agreement of members of the House of Representatives. This method saw the nominations of Thomas Jefferson, James Monroe, and James Madison. During the early 1820s, however, opponents of the congressional caucus system successfully challenged the system's legitimacy by charging that it excluded the public. An 1823 newspaper editorial voices the opponents' concerns in proclaiming that the congressional caucus was "a nocturnal assembly convoked at short notice . . . bound by no rule, acting without authority." By this time, state legislatures and party organizations were beginning to conduct their own presidential nominations, thus making the congressional caucus increasingly irrelevant. As a result, the final caucus meeting of 1824 was sparsely attended by members of Congress, and the candidate selected through the declining system, William H. Crawford, had little popular following.

Perhaps inevitably, reforms of nomination processes have been sensitive to national concerns about making them more democratic and representative. The Progressive era of the early twentieth century ushered in the direct primary, which some states adopted as an alternative to less open and "democratic" party conventions. In the reforms of the Democratic Party following the 1968 presidential election, even greater concern with openness and representation was evident.

The concern with the procedures used to nominate our President is well placed. The presidency is the one office with a national constituency, and its increasing visibility and power make it the centerpiece of American national government. The nomination of presidential candidates is inevitably a federal process with substantial variation among the states. Today, state parties follow one of two general paths in selecting national convention delegates: the primary method or the caucus-convention method. Our focus here is on assessing representativeness among state nominating convention delegates. Direct primaries cannot be faulted for failing to be open to rank-and-file participation, although they may have a number of other unfortunate consequences. Still, even if the caucus-convention method is less open, we contend it is not necessarily unrepresentative.

The process of delegate selection in caucus-convention states involves at least two stages: a caucus or mass meeting takes place at the precinct, municipal, county, or congressional district level; then a state convention follows several weeks or months later. In 1988, the Democrats in Idaho and Hawaii, the Republicans in Arizona, and both parties in Delaware and Maine relied upon some version of this two-step process. A more common variant of the caucus-convention system uses one or two intermediate steps between the local caucus and the state convention. In Iowa, for example, the precinct caucuses occur very early in the campaign. The more than 2,000 precinct caucuses select delegates to 99 county conventions that meet a month or more later. These county meetings, in turn, select delegates to congressional district and state conventions that meet in June. Similar procedures were followed in 1988 by Republicans in Wyoming and Virginia, by Democrats in Arizona and North Dakota, and by both parties in Alaska, Colorado, Minnesota, Kansas, Nevada, and Washington.

One of the major reasons for anxiety about representation among state convention delegates is that participating in the process is necessarily costly in time and effort. Those who eventually become delegates are likely to be unusually committed to politics and to their parties, and the self-selection involved may yield a cast of characters quite out of step with the party rank and file and the general electorate participating in the fall. If this is the case, participants may select candidates with outlooks incompatible with mainstream America. The Republican National Convention that nominated Barry Goldwater in 1964 and the Democratic National Convention that selected George McGovern in 1972 are contemporary examples of national conventions unrepresentative both in their makeup and in their selection of a party standard-bearer.

Assessments of representation in the presidential nomination process must recognize two dimensions of the problem. The first is descriptive, while the second takes into account relevant political action. Determining the quality of descriptive representation involves comparing the demographic and attitudinal characteristics of convention delegates with these same characteristics among the presumed "constituency." These comparisons must be given meaning in the realm of action. If it can be shown that state convention delegates are descriptively unrepresentative, what follows? Our explicit consideration of the active side of representation in presidential nominations deals with that question.

Our evidence shows that state nominating convention delegates are descriptively unrepresentative of the popular bases of their political parties. These findings are consistent with similar research on descriptive representation comparing those actively participating in the nominating process with those who affiliate with the parties in the general population. We then show that state convention delegates are aware of the most important ways in which they differ from the electorate and that their action—that is to say, their choice of a nominee to head their party's presidential campaign—

takes that difference into explicit account. In choosing a candidate to represent their party against the opposition in the fall campaign, state convention delegates act in ways that mitigate the biases and misrepresentations that creep in as a result of their failure to achieve a descriptive watch with the party rank and file.

The Data

The primary data source for this report is a series of surveys of state convention delegates conducted during the presidential nomination campaigns of 1980, 1984, and 1988. These surveys were supported by grants from the National Science Foundation. The samples are not from identical states year to year, so comparisons across time must be made with caution. A brief description of each year's delegate sample follows:

1980: This sample is the most extensive of the three years included. It is based upon surveys of some 17,628 Democratic and Republican delegates in 11 caucus-convention states. The states included in the survey are not a random sample of all states, so the comparisons we make with the national electorate in 1980 must be taken as illustrative only.

1984: Since no Republican contested for the nomination in 1984, we surveyed only Democratic state convention delegates. Moreover, because of other requirements of the design, we included only 2 states from the 11 surveyed in 1980 (Iowa and Virginia). Thus, our sample is very much smaller both in the number of states included, and in the number of respondents surveyed (N = 1,998). Once again, we must caution against concluding too much from the comparisons either with the national sample of partisan identifiers in 1984 or with the larger 1980 sample of delegates.

1988: This sample also includes only the two states of Iowa and Virginia, although in 1988 we surveyed both Democrats and Republicans at the state nominating conventions (N = 2,835).

The national data on the American public result from the 1980 and 1984 National Election Study surveys. At this writing, the 1988 data are not available. The comparisons we draw, as we have said, are purely illustrative of the pattern we believe would emerge with strictly compa-

rable samples. We can say this with some confidence because a number of excellent studies have compared statistically parallel samples of national convention delegates and the national electorate. Where the concern is with descriptive comparisons between delegates and partisans in the public, and where equivalent analyses have been undertaken, the findings of our research comport very well with those of previous studies.

Patterns of Descriptive Representation

Table 1 presents selected demographic and attitudinal comparisons between our state convention delegate surveys and samples of partisan identifiers in the national electorate. In 1980 comparisons between Democratic and Republican delegates and the relevant partisans in the public can be made, whereas in 1984 only the Democratic comparisons are possible.

The major point is a simple one: on purely descriptive grounds, state convention delegates, like their colleagues one step higher at the national conventions, are not typical of partisans in the electorate. There are three important areas where this lack of representation manifests itself: on demographic characteristics, especially those related to socioeconomic status; on degree of commitment to the political party; and on ideology.

Socioeconomic differences between an active elite like state convention delegates and the mass public are so regular as to verge on an iron law. Our data are not exceptional. Table 1 shows that delegates are consistently more likely to have completed college and to earn higher incomes than partisans in the general public nationwide. The available evidence strongly reinforces this finding where comparable data on the public in specific states is available. Other variables such as sex, age, and race also show a bias. Women, Blacks, and those from the youngest age groups tend to be represented in smaller proportions than the partisan bases of the parties in the public.

Despite the existence of clear biases common to the parties when their active and mass strata are compared, differences between the parties are also captured in the data. For example, Blacks and labor union members are traditionally firm members of the Democratic coalition. In 1980, both groups are prominent among Democratic identifiers in the public. And, although Blacks and union members are underrepresented in our convention delegate samples (in part at least

Table 1

Comparisons of State Convention Delegates and Public on Indicators of Descriptive Representation ("D" = Delegates, "P" = Public)

	1980				1984		1988	
	Democrats		Republicans		Democrats		Democratic	Republican
	D	P[a]	D	P[a]	D	P[a]	D	D
	%	%	%	%	%	%	%	%
Demographics								
College Graduates	53	15	54	22	52	15	54	58
High Income[b]	26	12	38	20	16	7	34	35
Member Labor Union	16	29	3	18	13	25	34	13
Female	50	60	40	55	50	58	48	42
Black	8	18	1	3	8	18	12	1
Born Again	22	25	31	24	23	24	26	55
Age								
under 25	8	12	7	14	7	13	7	5
over 40	50	56	62	56	54	53	62	65
Religion								
Catholic	23	24	10	20	27	31	24	10
Protestant	64	60	86	69	55	63	57	79
Jewish	2	5	1	1	2	4	2	–
Attitudes								
Strongly Identified with Party	72	34	84	26	76	35	82	82
Ideology								
Liberal	59	38	4	10	72	40	68	2
Middle	22	34	9	23	15	38	19	6
Conservative	19	28	87	67	13	22	13	92
Smallest N =	*(6145)*	*(515)*	*(4946)*	*(377)*	*(1553)*	*(722)*	*(1119)*	*(1112)*

[a] Partisan identifiers (including independents who lean toward a party) in National Election Surveys.
[b] High income in 1980 is $35,000 or more per year; in 1984 and 1988, high income is $50,000 or more per year.

because they are underrepresented in states in our sample and in caucus-convention states generally), the partisan differences in our delegate samples are quite evident. Both Blacks and union members captured a larger share of Democratic than Republican delegate samples. Likewise, Republicans have recently appealed in visible ways to the Christian Right, perhaps explaining why a majority of the 1988 Republican delegate samples indicated that they were born-again Christians. The point is important: despite the fact that some demographic groups may be underrepresented in the delegate stratum, party differences in the public are nonetheless reflected among state convention delegates.

In Table 1 we present two attitudinal measures that capture additional differences between delegates and partisans in the public. Again, these differences are quite consistent with our expectations from previous research on national convention delegates. Indeed, these differences are of perhaps greater magnitude and importance than those reflected in the demographic data.

Consider the fact that delegates are consistently far more strongly identified with their party than are partisans in the public. This strong identification is not at all surprising. Running for convention delegate requires a high degree of interest in the party because of the effort required to get chosen. And because of the inherently partisan character of nomination campaigns, a strong commitment to the party is present among those who are extraordinarily active. Our research shows that those who attend those caucuses that start the process in caucus-convention states are also far more likely strongly to identify with their party than does the average partisan in the electorate at large. On a host of other indicators measuring party commitment—from holding various party offices to working in campaigns—state convention delegates show up as more committed to the party than identifiers in the public.

The final point to be made from Table 1 is also a regular pattern in descriptive comparisons between convention delegates and the public. In general, party activists are both more likely to have an ideology and more "extreme" in their ideological preferences than are members of the public. For example, in 1984 only 21 percent of Democrats in the public were either "extremely liberal" or "liberal," but 51 percent of our 1984 Democratic delegate sample identified themselves in this way. Thus, identifiers in the electorate as a whole are more likely to adopt a "middle" position on an ideological scale than are state convention delegates. This pattern holds on a number of specific issue questions as well (not shown). That is, delegates both are less likely to adopt a middle position on issues and are more consistent in their answers than are voters in the same party.

All of these findings from Table 1—the greater socioeconomic status of delegates, their stronger identification with their party, and their greater ideological consistency—demonstrate that delegates are not typical of their larger partisan bases in the electorate. All three findings also make perfect sense given the nature of the contemporary presidential nomination process. State convention delegates must negotiate a protracted and sometimes competitive process in order to attend the state conventions. The effort and skills necessary to get to the state convention are most likely to be present among those of relatively high status. Those who are wealthier and better educated are more likely to have the time and the interest to pursue voluntary political action. The nomination process is also a highly partisan one, so it is natural to find that those most active in it are strongly committed to their party. Moreover, those most interested in politics who are willing and able to become

involved in extraordinary ways are likely to adopt firmly held ideological stands on issues.

The upshot of this analysis, then, is that participants at or near the top are not descriptively typical of those whom they represent. The implications for assessments of the process are not altogether clear. Similar patterns show up when members of legislatures are compared with the public, but in that case a mechanism promotes accountability—regular elections. Convention delegates are not linked to the public bases of their party in the same fashion. Does it follow, therefore, that the variables that distinguish them from the public have the effect of distorting the nomination process and undermining the interests and preferences of the general public?

Representation As Action

A complete assessment of representation in the nomination process must take into account the actions of participants such as state convention delegates. By analyzing the descriptive side of representation, we have established the possibility of distorting effects. For example, we have seen that delegates are not ideologically representative of co-partisans in the electorate. Democratic delegates are more liberal and Republican delegates more conservative than their parties' supporters—perhaps the most significant difference between convention delegates and partisans in the public because ideology is most likely to have a direct effect on the the actions of state convention delegates. In particular, we are interested in delegates' candidate support. If, when delegates support a nominee, they act solely on their own ideological preferences, they will support a candidate significantly at odds with the interests of partisans generally. Likewise, demographic differences between delegates and rank-and-file partisans could be significant if it can be shown that these factors have an important effect on delegates' candidate choice.

Several conditions must be present in order to avoid the distorting effects of ideology in delegates' nomination choices: (1) delegates must have an incentive to depart from their personal ideological interests and to act on behalf of the larger electorate; (2) delegates must be aware that their ideological preferences differ from those of the electorate; and (3) delegates' actual candidate support must reflect the interests of a constituency broader than their ideological concerns would normally encompass.

Incentives. The imperatives of the presidential selection process create a powerful incentive for delegates to think beyond their own personal preferences. The nomination stage typically offers a field of two or more candidates competing to be each party's general election nominee. If the nomination race were the whole story, then we could reasonably expect participants to pursue their personal ideological (and other) goals by supporting the candidate who best represents those interests. But, of course, the nomination race is only the first of two stages. Followed as it is by the general election, those making choices during the nomination campaign must anticipate the interests of the fall electorate. In selecting a candidate to stand for their party, convention delegates and other nomination activists must inevitably ask how that candidate will fare against the opposition party.

Because delegates are strongly committed to their party, they generally would prefer any of the nomination contenders in their party to any of those competing for the other party's nomination. In 1980, for example, almost all Democratic delegates preferred Jimmy Carter to Ronald Reagan or George Bush, even if they strongly supported Senator Edward Kennedy's insurgent attempt to unseat the incumbent Democratic President. The strong partisanship of delegates means that they consider not merely the ideological and issue positions of nomination candidates, but ultimately how electable these candidates are vis-à-vis the opposite party's. We contend that delegates have powerful incentives to consider candidate electability as they decide whom to support precisely because they are strongly committed to the ideological and issue stands common to their party: without an electable candidate, the opposition party (with its contrary ideological and issue stands) will win.

This concern with candidate electability creates a kind of accountability to the broader electorate arising from the delegates' anticipation of the reactions (and therefore the preferences) of general election voters. A delegate wishing to promote the liberal ideals of Senator Kennedy in 1980 had to decide whether he or President Carter was more likely to win against the Republicans in the fall. If Carter was judged more electable, the delegate may have compromised his ideological principles by supporting the less consistently liberal (but more popular) Carter. In considering the tradeoff between his own ideological preferences and candidate electability, he is inevitably introducing the interests of others in his choice of candidates. In that sense, he is "accountable" to them, and the distortions that might possibly result from the failure of delegates to be typical of the broader party electorate are reduced.

Delegates' Ideological Perceptions. Having established that delegates have an incentive to depart from their own ideological interests in deciding whom to support for their party's nomination, we must show that delegates are aware that their ideological positions differ from those of the general electorate. Without that awareness, delegates might reasonably select a candidate who represents their own views in the mistaken belief that the public shares them. Figure 1 presents data on delegates' ideological perceptions in 1988 that are consistent with our findings from earlier years. We include delegates' perceptions of themselves, of the "average American voter," of both political parties, and of the major nomination contenders in both parties.

Delegates in both parties see the average voter as being very close to the center of the ideological spectrum. And indeed, delegates are accurate in perceiving the average voter as just to the right of center. Delegates from both parties also see themselves ("self-identification" in the figure) as distinctly off-center. Democratic delegates collectively identify themselves as one unit to the left of the center ("slightly liberal"), while Republicans see themselves as almost two units to the right. Delegates' perceptions of their parties closely approximate their own average position on the scale.

These results indicate a realistic mapping of the ideological placement of parties, voters, and candidates. The parties and those active in the presidential nomination process are ideologically distant both from each other and from the American electorate. That our data from 1984 and 1980 reveal a similar understanding by state convention delegates reinforces the accuracy of this fundamental picture. Certainly delegates understand that their ideological preferences are not entirely shared by the electorate.

To say that delegates have a reasonably accurate picture of the ideological space of American politics is not to say that no distortions are evident. Most obviously from Figure 1, a clear partisan bias shows up in the perception of candidates and parties. Democrats tend to see Republican candidates as more extreme than

Figure 1

Delegates' Ideological Perceptions, 1988

	DEMOCRATS	REPUBLICANS
EXTREMELY LIBERAL		Jackson
	Jackson	Dukakis
		Democratic Party
LIBERAL		
		Gore
	Democratic Party	
SLIGHTLY LIBERAL	Self-Identification	
	Dukakis	
MIDDLE-OF-THE-ROAD	Gore	
	American Voter	
SLIGHTLY CONSERVATIVE		American Voter
		Bush
		Dole
		Republican Party
	Dole	
		Self-Identification
CONSERVATIVE	Republican Party	
	Bush	Reagan
	Reagan	Robertson
	Robertson	
EXTREMELY CONSERVATIVE		

Republicans do, and Republicans see Democratic candidates as more extreme than do Democrats. Thus, Democrats regarded Albert Gore as a centrist candidate, but Republicans saw him as firmly in the liberal camp. In relative terms, however, delegates in both parties placed Gore to the right of his party by roughly the same amount.

Delegates' ideological mapping does not translate directly into perceptions of a candidate's electability. For example, Republicans and Democrats alike in 1980 very strongly believed that Ronald Reagan was more electable than George Bush, but they also were aware that Reagan was considerably to the right of his principal rival for the nomination. By the same token, Democrats and Republicans in 1988 saw Michael Dukakis as the most electable Democratic contender in the field, despite the fact that Dukakis was seen as further from the electorate on the ideological scale than the relatively moderate Albert Gore. By differentiating candidate electability from ideological centrism, therefore, delegates recognize that a great deal more than ideological compatibility goes in to a winning presidential candidacy.

Candidate Support. Analysis of representation-as-action in the nomination process must consider the choices of candidates made by delegates. If delegates' candidate choices are driven by personal preferences, the evidence will suggest a process unrepresentative in both descriptive and active terms. If, however, electability is a powerful motivator, we have good reason to believe that delegates depart from their personal preferences in favor of the broader interests of the general electorate in their support of a candidate.

Table 2 addresses the "active" side of representation directly by considering the factors that explain candidate choice among convention delegates in the three presidential campaigns of the 1980s. Candidate choice, we have argued, need not simply reflect the personal preferences of delegates. Indeed, we suggest that party activists have a powerful incentive to anticipate the interests of the general electorate, and to take their perceptions of how well candidates will fare in the fall election into account as they choose among candidates competing for their party's nomination.

The analysis of candidate choice in Table 2 is based upon the variables included in our discussion of the descriptive side of representation. In particular, delegates differ from partisans generally in their level of education, income, and the like; they are much more likely to identify strongly with their party than do their counterparts in the electorate; and they are more likely to adopt ideological views off-center to the left or right depending upon the party. We examine the independent effect of each of these variables on nomination candidate preference in each year. The entries in Table 2 are standardized regression coefficients that measure the effect of the variable on candidate preference, controlling for the effects of the other variables included in the analysis. The larger the coefficient, the greater the impact. An "NS" entry means the effect was not statistically significant, and the effect of the variable should be considered zero.

The unique constituencies of Jesse Jackson among Democrats in 1984 and 1988, and Pat Robertson among Republicans in 1988 appear in the demographic analysis in Table 2. Race had a clear effect on candidate choice among Democrats when Jesse Jackson is compared with Mondale in 1984, or with Michael Dukakis in 1988. Likewise, born-again Christian delegates in 1988 showed a strong tendency to support Pat Robertson. That race had an effect indepen-

Table 2

Explaining Candidate Choice, 1980–1988[a]

	1980		1984		1988		
	Carter/ Kennedy	Reagan/ Bush	Mondale/ Hart	Mondale/ Jackson	Dukakis/ Jackson	Bush/ Dole	Bush/ Robertson
Education	.044	−.037	NS	NS	NS	NS	NS
Income	NS	NS	NS	−.094	−.076	.070	.069
Labor Union Member	NS	NS	NS	NS	NS	NS	NS
Sex	NS	−.112	NS	NS	NS	−.071	−.060
Race	NS	.040	NS	−.223	−.124	NS	NS
Born-Again Christian	NS	.036	NS	NS	NS	−.071	−.344
Age	.064	NS	NS	−.084	NS	NS	−.057
Party Identification	NS	.057	−.159	−.099	NS	NS	NS
Ideological Proximity to Candidates	.235	.241	.216	.273	.291	.320	.294
Candidate Electability	.590	.430	.532	.355	.434	.447	.353
R^2	.579	.342	.464	.373	.439	.359	.636
N(3565)	(3089)	(980)	(950)	(684)	(670)	(643)	

[a]We require a coefficient to be significant at the .05 level. In 1984 and 1988, the candidate preference variable is measured by (at least) a ten-point comparative ranking measure. In 1980, however, the candidate preference measure is a simple dichotomy that violates rather badly the assumptions of Ordinary Least Squares. We have replicated the analysis using the more appropriate logit analysis in 1980, and the findings are entirely consistent with those reported. Therefore, in the interest of consistency, we report the OLS for all three years.

dent of other factors such as income or ideology, an effect that also motivated support of Jackson, has implications for the representativeness of process. Had Blacks been proportionally represented among Democratic convention delegates, we can presume that Jackson would have realized significant gains in his support.

With the exceptions of the Jackson and Robertson candidacies, the effect of demographic variables on nomination preferences are modest to nonexistent. Most of the effects do not achieve statistical significance, but several have possible implications for the representativeness of the process. For example, the fact that sex had a significant effect among 1980 and 1988 Republicans indicates a kind of "gender gap" that might undermine the representativeness of delegates in the GOP. Particularly in 1980 when Reagan opposed the Equal Rights Amendment and Bush favored it, policy implications may result. That, coupled with the fact that women were underrepresented among Republican delegates, suggests the possibility of genuine distortion in the process.

With respect to strength of party identification, again some potential for distortion exists. For example, Senator Gary Hart's campaign against Walter Mondale in 1984 attracted those less attached to the Democratic Party. And we have seen that the delegate stratum of the party in 1984 significantly underrepresents Democrats weakly affiliated with their party. This result gives an advantage to party "insiders" like Walter Mondale over candidates whose appeal is to those less committed to the party. The fact that many national convention delegates are chosen in primary states may minimize this effect in the process as a whole.

The variables with the most powerful effects on nomination preference are also the most interesting: ideology and electability. It is here that the question of representation is most directly confronted. We have seen that ideology rather sharply differentiates delegates from the public at large and that the personal ideological preferences of these delegates have a consistently strong effect on nomination preference. If these influences were the whole story, then we could conclude that delegates are "purists" intent upon supporting a candidate most compatible with their (unrepresentative) ideological views. The result of a nomination process dominated by such activists would regularly be a Democratic nominee markedly off-center to the left and a Republican nominee even further to the right of center.

Because the force of candidate electability regularly outweighs that of ideological preferences, the nomination process works in ways more subtle than simply registering the issue and ideological preferences of the activist participants. It is clear from Table 2 that delegates are inclined to nominate the most electable candidate over the candidate who best conforms to their personal ideological preferences, when there is a conflict. This conclusion can be illustrated with simple percentages. For example, among Republican delegates who were closer on the ideological scale to a candidate whom they believed to be less electable than his opposition in 1980, fully 82 percent went against their ideological preferences and supported the more electable candidate. In 1988, ideology exerted a somewhat stronger pull among Republican delegates: only 55 percent of those pulled in opposite directions with respect to their ideology and their judgments of candidate electability supported the more electable candidate. We would expect the relative effects of ideology and electability to vary from year to year and among candidates. But our major point is that delegates have a strong incentive to think about the interests of the November electorate in choosing a nominee, and the analysis of their choices indicates that they do exactly that.

We have shown that delegates differ from the public in their ideological interests, that they are aware of these differences, and that they are ready and willing to depart from their own interests in nominating a candidate who they believe can win in the fall election. This flexibility, we contend, produces a kind of accountability through anticipated reactions that may mitigate the absence of descriptive representation among delegates. However, we do not claim that delegates' interest in candidate electability motivates them to nominate a moderate who necessarily reflects the ideological preferences of the general electorate. Recent experience provides ample evidence that nomination activists do not equate candidate electability with philosophical compatibility with the electorate. In 1980, for example, Republican and Democratic delegates alike perceived Ronald Reagan as simultaneously the most extreme and yet the most electable of the GOP nomination contenders. As a result, many relatively moderate Republican delegates deserted the more compatible George Bush or John

Anderson in favor of the more electable Reagan. Likewise, Democrats in 1988 passed over a candidate (Senator Albert Gore) whom they viewed as closest to the electorate on the ideological scale for Michael Dukakis, considered both more liberal and more electable.

Conclusion

In part because ideological centrism does not translate into candidate electability in any simple or straightforward manner, the problem of representation in the presidential nomination process surely cannot be laid to rest by this analysis. The candidate sought by delegates and other nomination activists is some combination of one who appeals to their ideological preferences and yet one who can win in the fall campaign. Delegates understand that appeal to the general electorate only very loosely depends upon ideological affinity. The "accountability" that we have argued exists in the process, then, is not one strictly tied to matters of political philosophy and issue preferences. Our primary point is that a perception that delegates and other nomination activists (including primary voters) are not representative in the descriptive sense does not close the door on the question of representation in the process.

The finding that state convention delegates do not merely act on their personal preferences must be taken into account in assessments of the nominating process. It reflects the much broader fact that the political parties must always face the electoral imperative in one way or another. If precedent is any guide, then we will continue to reform the way we nominate presidential candidates, and these reforms may have far-reaching and unforeseen consequences for the political parties. But as we debate reform proposals, we would do well to remember that parties are unique among political organizations in their interest in mobilizing and responding to broad electoral coalitions. We should not, therefore, rob them of their control over presidential and other nominations because of their failure to meet simple criteria of descriptive representation. When we watch what they do, we find good reason to believe they are motivated to respond to interests well beyond those that differentiate them from the public at large.

See also: Individual presidential candidates, individual elections, Presidential Nominating Conventions, Presidential Nominating Politics.

Walter J. Stone
James A. McCann

REFERENCES

Abramowitz, Alan I., and Walter J. Stone. 1984. *Nomination Politics: Party Activists and Presidential Choice.* New York: Praeger.

Axelrod, Robert. 1986. "Presidential Election Coalitions in 1984." 80 *American Political Science Review* 281.

Dallinger, Frederick W. 1887. *Nominations for Elective Office.* New York: Longmans, Green.

Kirkpatrick, Jeane. 1975. "Representation in the American National Conventions: The Case of 1972." 5 *British Journal of Political Science* 265.

———. 1976. *The New Presidential Elite.* New York: Russell Sage.

McClosky, Herbert, Paul J. Hoffman, and Rosemary O'Hara. 1960. "Issue Conflict and Consensus Among Party Leaders and Followers." 54 *American Political Science Review* 406.

Miller, Warren E. 1988. *Without Consent: Mass-Elite Linkages in Presidential Politics.* Lexington: U. Pr. of Kentucky.

———, and M. Kent Jennings. 1986. *Parties in Transition.* New York: Russell Sage

Pitkin, Hannah F. 1967. *The Concept of Representation.* Berkeley: U. of California Pr.

Polsby, Nelson W. 1983. *Consequences of Party Reform.* New York: Oxford U. Pr.

Rapoport, Ronald B., Alan I. Abramowitz, and John McGlennon, eds. 1986. *The Life of the Parties.* Lexington: U. Pr. of Kentucky.

———, Walter J. Stone, and Alan I. Abramowitz. 1990. "Sex and the Caucus Participant: The Gender Gap and Presidential Nominations." 34 *American Journal of Political Science* 725.

Stone, Walter J., and Alan I. Abramowitz. 1983. "Winning May Not Be Everything, But It's More than We Thought." 77 *American Political Science Review* 945.

———, ———, and Ronald B. Rapoport. 1989. "How Representative Are the Iowa Caucuses?" In Peverill Squire, ed. *The Iowa Caucuses and the Presidential Nominating Process.* Boulder: Westview.

Wildavsky, Aaron. 1965. "The Goldwater Phenomenon: Purists, Politicians, and the Two-Party System." 17 *Review of Politics* 386.

Daniel De Leon (1852–1910)

The American Lenin. A stern, fractious, doctrinaire man, Daniel De Leon was trained as a lawyer and embraced Marxian socialism as an intellectual, not as a worker. His continued insistence upon an orthodox revolutionary creed, however, isolated him in Socialist and trade union circles.

Born to a Dutch Jewish family, perhaps in Curaçao, Venezuela, but more probably in New York City, De Leon early established his intellectual abilities by winning a fellowship to teach international diplomacy at Columbia University. His fellowship lapsed because of his public support of radical causes, and De Leon drifted through New York City politics, first involving himself with Henry George's 1886 mayoral campaign, then with the Knights of Labor, and finally with Edward Bellamy's National Clubs. De Leon joined the Socialist Labor Party (SLP) in 1890, quickly becoming its leader and editor of the party's newspaper, *The People*.

De Leon refashioned the SLP into a top-down political organization espousing revolution. Initially he had hoped to capture for socialism the moribund Knights of Labor and afterward the American Federation of Labor. Failing in his power struggle with these established unions, he formed the Socialist Trades and Labor Alliance (STLA). Eschewing immediatism (i.e., immediate material benefits for the Alliance's membership), De Leon projected the STLA as a revolutionary appendage of the SLP. But the STLA failed miserably, and De Leon abandoned trade unionism until the formation of the Industrial Workers of the World (IWW) in 1905.

De Leon's unswerving insistence upon revolutionary Marxism and his unwillingness to fight for better working conditions within the capitalist system placed him at odds with most in the emerging American Socialist movement. Frustrated with De Leon's labor policy, in 1900 Morris Hillquit and others from the SLP's "kangaroo" faction broke ranks and formed the Socialist Party of America (SPA) with Eugene Debs and Victor Berger. De Leon became an outspoken critic of the SPA and Debsian Socialism. Although he was one of the founders of the IWW, De Leon never gained control of the syndicalist union. IWW organizers had little in common with the austere New York Socialist intellectual. De Leon died in 1910, having never inspired the Socialist revolution he had sought for so long.

See also: Eugene V. Debs, Henry George, Socialist Labor Party

John Walsh

REFERENCES

Coleman, Stephen. 1990. *Daniel De Leon*. Manchester, UK: Manchester U. Pr.

Democratic Advisory Council

In the wake of the Republican landslide that returned President Dwight Eisenhower to office in 1956, Democratic national chairman Paul Butler sought to organize an advisory body on national policymaking for the party. Congressional Democratic leaders saw such an organization as a threat to their own status as the focal point of the opposition party. Resistance from Senate Majority Leader Lyndon Johnson and Speaker of the House Sam Rayburn, who represented the moderate-to-conservative wing of the Democrats, prompted the liberals to create the Democratic Advisory Council (DAC) as "an all-northern and -western [body]," which would reflect the wishes of the liberal, presidential wing of the Democratic Party.

In the remaining years of the 1950s, the DAC, as the Democrats' official policymaking body, issued a series of statements setting out a liberal agenda on major issues of the day—especially civil rights and an activist economic policy. With such luminaries as former New York governor Herbert Lehman and economist John Galbraith in its ranks, DAC attracted substantial media attention and quickened the pace of the articulation of liberal policy proposals. Thus, the 1960 Democratic convention could incorporate many of the DAC's proposals in its platform. In concert with growing numbers (especially after the 1958 elections) of congressional liberals, the DAC helped to shape a coherent agenda on Medicare, federal aid to education, tax cuts, and civil rights, among other central elements of the Kennedy-Johnson presidency.

In the wake of the election of John F. Kennedy in 1960, the DAC no longer had a reason to exist, given that the party's presidential wing had both captured the White House and developed a liberal agenda. Even though it never won the support of the entire Democratic establishment, the DAC did succeed in promoting its favored policies. In many ways, it served as a model for the moderate-to-conservative Democratic Leadership Council of the 1980s.

See also: Paul Butler, Democratic National Committee, John F. Kennedy, Herbert Lehman, Eleanor Roosevelt, Speaker of the House

Burdett A. Loomis

REFERENCES

Bailey, Steven K. 1966. "The Condition of Our National Parties." In Donald Herzberg and Gerald M. Pomper, eds. *American Party Politics*. New York: Holt, Rinehart, Winston.

Sundquist, James L. 1968. *Politics and Policy: The Eisenhower, Kennedy and Johnson Years*. Washington: Brookings.

Democratic Congressional Campaign Committees

Although congressional candidates rely heavily on their own efforts to raise campaign funds, both major parties have maintained committees in each house of Congress to provide technical assistance and financial support for congressional candidates. For the Democratic Party those committees are the Democratic Congressional Campaign Committee (DCCC), which handles House elections, and the Democratic Senatorial Campaign Committee (DSCC), which assists senatorial candidates. Membership on each committee is drawn from the party membership in the respective chamber, with the chair of the committee serving as a major party official in that chamber.

These committees originated in the era between the Civil War and World War I when political parties were the principal direct and indirect sources of campaign support; the DCCC was founded in 1882 and the DSCC in 1916. Campaign finance during this period was dominated by party committees, with local committees playing a much more significant role than in the 1980s. The congressional committees, which were and continue to be separate from the Democratic National Committee (DNC), were useful because they were removed from direct concern with presidential elections.

With the passage of the Federal Election Campaign Act and its amendments in the 1970s, information about the activity of these campaign committees became more widely publicized as the quality of the information improved. Data detailing the funds raised and spent by the committees is periodically published by the Federal Election Commission. For the 1988 election, the DSCC contributed approximately $400,000 to Democratic senatorial candidates and the DCCC contributed $670,000 to House candidates. Overall, Democratic Senate candidates spent $96.5 million in 1986, while Democratic House candidates spent a total of $242.6 million. While these figures suggest that the committees do not play a significant part in congressional campaign finance, their roles have been critical in certain situations. And the congressional candidates who stand to gain by their activity have paid close attention to their actions. First, while direct contributions to campaigns may be relatively small, "indirect expenditures," such as providing research on incumbent Republicans, on the behalf of candidates are much larger. Second, these indirect expenditures tend to be used late in the campaign, providing a key boost to candidates close to election day. Third, while the committees may contribute small amounts overall, they may choose to disburse their funds unevenly among candidates, thus helping a few campaigns significantly.

In the 1970s the Democratic committees were more likely to contribute funds to incumbent members of each chamber. In the 1980s, however, distributional strategies changed, so that candidates in open seat races and candidates in close races were more likely to be the beneficiaries of the committees' largess.

The future direction of the influence of these committees is open to speculation. With congressional campaigns growing increasingly expensive, the congressional campaign committees could become more important. Some believe committee prestige to have elevated Tony Coelho (Calif.) from the chair of the DCCC to the House Majority Leader's post in 1987 and to have elected George Mitchell (Me.) to the position of Senate Majority Leader in 1989, following Mitchell's service as DSCC chair between 1985 and 1987. However, individual members of both chambers have established political action committees as a way of channeling money to colleagues, circumventing traditional party channels and the congressional campaign committees.

See also: Tony Coelho, Democratic National Committee, Federal Election Campaign Act of 1971 and Amendments, Federal Election Commission, George Mitchell

Charles Stewart III

REFERENCES

Alexander, Herbert A. 1972. *Money in Politics.* Washington: Public Affairs Press.

Jackson, Brooks. 1988. *Honest Graft: Big Money and the American Political Process.* New York: Knopf.

Jacobson, Gary. 1980. *Money in Congressional Elections.* New Haven: Yale U. Pr.

———. 1985/1986. "Party Organization and Distribution of Campaign Resources: Republicans and Democrats in 1982" 100 *Political Science Quarterly* 603.

Overaker, Louise. 1932. *Money in Elections.* New York: Macmillan.

Sorauf, Frank J. 1988. *Money in American Elections.* Glenview, IL: Scott, Foresman.

Democratic Farmer–Labor Party of Minnesota

The two national parties, Democratic and Republican, were once viewed as uneasy federations of state-level parties. Each state-level component of a national party was seen as having its own unique history that made its leadership ideologically and organizationally different from—and potentially hostile to—the other 47 to 49 parties with which it was nominally affiliated. While this understanding is now passé (for a variety of reasons), the Minnesota Democratic Farmer-Labor Party's ideological and organizational distinctiveness after its establishment in 1944 demonstrates the plausibility of the earlier hypothesis. Indeed, Hubert Humphrey's 1948 civil rights speech at the Democratic convention—one which threatened to divide the southern parties from the national Democratic Party—is an event that seems to fit the model well.

The ideological distinctiveness of the DFL Party was partly evident in the policy and coalitional stances of its most famous leaders—Hubert Humphrey and his protégé, Walter Mondale. During their active political careers both men were—relative to other national Democratic politicians—strongly social Democratic politicians. Among Humphrey's last political acts was co-authorship of legislation calling for full employment; among Mondale's last political acts was securing a rare preconvention endorsement by the AFL-CIO for the 1984 Democratic presidential nomination.

This social Democratic distinctiveness can be traced to the ideological and organizational consequences of the DFL Party's "founding." The Democratic Farmer-Labor Party is the only Democratic party in the Union whose name reflects a merger between a third party and the state-level affiliate of one of the two major national parties. The DFL Party's name results from the merger in 1944 of, on the one hand, a once very weak but increasingly powerful Democratic party and, on the other hand, a once very powerful but increasingly weak third party, the Farmer-Labor Party.

At the merger, the Democrats, in order to retain the loyalties of Farmer-Labor voters and activists, agreed to keep "Farmer-Labor" in the new party's name. The DFL Party was anchored, by choice, on the left of the ideological spectrum. This ideological positioning continued to shape the party's policy stances even after many Farmer-Labor activists, particularly those close to the Communist Party, were purged from the party during the internal split created by Henry Wallace's 1948 presidential campaign.

The DFL Party also inherited the Farmer-Labor Party's historic and unusually strong ties to the labor movement. The Farmer-Labor Party had initially been founded and financed in large part by trade unions, city central bodies, and the Minnesota State Federation of Labor.

Since its founding, the DFL Party has become increasingly like other state Democratic parties in all but name, and by now there are no Farmer-Laborites in the Minnesota electorate. Nevertheless, the DFL Party has not changed its name. Because the party's resources have been invested for several decades in advertising its unusual name, the party's leaders might face high exit costs from their electoral market if they wished to adapt to a regular name (i.e., the Democratic Party). The DFL Party's leaders probably will continue cherishing their unique linguistic link to Minnesota's political past.

See also: AFL-CIO COPE, Election of 1948, Hubert Humphrey, Walter Mondale, Henry Wallace

Richard M. Valelly

REFERENCES:

Mitau, G. Theodore. 1970. *Politics in Minnesota.* Minneapolis: U. of Minnesota Pr.

Democratic National Committee

Formally created in 1848 by the Democratic National Convention "to promote the Democratic cause" between the quadrennial nominating gatherings and to prepare for the next convention. The Democratic National Committee (DNC) has existed continuously since that time, making it the country's oldest national party institution.

Like its counterpart, the Republican National Committee (established in 1856), the DNC for more than a century reflected the largely local and decentralized nature of American politics. The power to control internal party affairs, especially the nominating process, resided principally with state and local Democratic organizations. In this political environment, the national Democratic Party was an undisciplined collection of autonomous state and territorial parties that displayed little inclination to relinquish authority or power to a national organization. This arrangement prompted an apt description of national party committees by Cotter and Hennessy: "National Committees themselves are large groups of people, variously selected, representing different amounts and kinds of local political interests, who come together now and then to vote on matters of undifferentiated triviality or importance, about which they are largely uninformed and in which they are often uninterested."

During its first 100 or so years, the DNC was concerned with preparing for and managing the quadrennial presidential nominating convention and, at times, helping to conduct the presidential campaign itself and the midterm congressional campaigns. In between campaigns, the DNC usually would meet twice a year, provide a forum for internal party communication, discuss current political problems or opportunities, and occasionally vote on internal party issues. The DNC itself was controlled by a handful of prominent Democrats, usually from states with large numbers of votes in the Electoral College, and other committee members chosen in recognition of their long years of loyal service at the state or local level. Some national chairmen, such as James Farley of New York during the presidency of Franklin D. Roosevelt, also served as national party advocates and spokesmen. But until the post-World War II years, the DNC was a drifting organization of only marginal importance to political matters of national significance. Indeed, Democrats did not open a full-time national committee office until 1928 after the defeat of presidential nominee Governor Al Smith of New York.

Beginning in the mid-1950s, however, the DNC assumed a more prominent role in the party's affairs than could have been imagined during its first 100 years. Today, the DNC is the focal point for much of the interparty turmoil that has characterized the national Democratic Party as it has struggled to define its purpose and direction in the post-New Deal era. The DNC has continued to execute the routine tasks of internal party organization, such as issuing the call for and managing the next national nominating convention. In more recent years, it also has followed the Republican example of helping build a grass-roots base for party fundraising and of assisting local and state candidates and organizations understand and use current campaign technology.

Beyond these traditional activities, however, the DNC has transformed itself from a largely passive and politically irrelevant symbol of party government to an institution that essentially dictates the role and duties of state parties in choosing the Democratic presidential nominee. In so doing, the DNC has fundamentally altered the nature of the nominating process itself. In the 1970s, when the DNC's membership grew in number and diversity, political control of the national party shifted from the "regulars"—state party leaders and prominent elected officials— to a multitude of shifting coalitions of party activists, many of whom were introduced to grass-roots Democratic politics through the civil rights and antiwar movements of the 1960s and

1970s. Moreover, in those years, the DNC wrote and adopted a national Charter and Bylaws of the Democratic Party. But, in a paradoxical shift, having spent the early years of the 1970s striving to diminish the authority and power of regular Democrats, the DNC closed out the decade and continued through the 1980s looking for ways to bring back the regulars. Indeed, the DNC is today what it always has been—a bundle of paradoxes that accurately reflects the paradoxical nature of American politics.

Duties and Powers. As spelled out in the Charter and Bylaws of the Democratic Party, as amended October 7, 1987, the national convention is the highest authority of the Democratic Party (subject to the provisions of the Charter itself), and the DNC is responsible for Democratic Party matters between conventions. Among the more important responsibilities identified are issuing the call to the national convention, conducting the presidential campaign, filling vacancies in the nominations for President and Vice President, electing DNC officers, assisting state and local party organizations in electing Democrats, issuing policy statements and conducting public relations, operating a national headquarters, raising money, and approving budgets. To carry out this program, the DNC has a permanent staff of about 80, augmented during campaigns, and an annual operating budget of approximately $8 million. In addition, the DNC raised approximately $59 million in support of the 1988 presidential and congressional campaigns, almost twice the previous record of $30 million raised during 1984.

Membership. At the time of its creation in 1848, the Democratic National Committee was composed of one member from each state and each territory and one from the District of Columbia. After adoption of universal women suffrage, the membership was doubled in size to include one man and one woman from each jurisdiction. Nominations for membership were made by state committees or corresponding state conventions and confirmed by the national convention, usually a noncontested action. In fewer cases, representation was determined by contested primaries or by the national convention delegation. In many instances, DNC selections were used to reward state party members and carried little authority or importance within the state party itself.

These various methods of selection were superseded in 1972 by provisions initially approved by the national convention and then included in the national Charter and Bylaws adopted in 1974. The simple formula of one man and one woman from each state or similar jurisdiction was changed to encompass a broader cross section of party activists as DNC members and, at the same time, to enlarge the total membership. Included as members were Democratic state chairpersons (and the highest ranking party officer of the opposite sex), 200 additional members apportioned among the states according to population and Democratic vote in the last presidential election, the chairperson of the Democratic Governors' Association and two additional governors, the Democratic leaders of the U.S. Senate and House of Representatives and one additional person from each body, the DNC officers, along with representatives of Democratic mayors, county officials, state legislators, Young Democrats, National Federation of Democratic Women, and no more than 25 at-large members. In 1988 the DNC added 2 vice chairs and 20 at-large members primarily to accommodate supporters of presidential candidate Jesse Jackson. Total membership now stands at 404.

Officers and Executive Committee. Officers selected by the DNC include the chairperson, five vice chairpersons, a treasurer, a secretary, and "other appropriate officers." Until 1892 national chairmen were selected from among committee members. Since then, this requirement no longer exists. On the day following adjournment of the national nominating convention, the DNC usually selects for the duration of the campaign a leader chosen by the presidential nominee, although even this tradition was violated in 1984 when the committee rebelled against Walter Mondale's putative choice of Georgia chair Bert Lance. Rejection led Mondale to accede to the committee's desire that Charles Manatt remain chair. Following the presidential election, the post is filled again. If the Democratic nominee has won, the decision again is normally one of personal designation by the successful presidential candidate. In defeat, the chairmanship is more likely to be openly contested. The normal term of office is through the next national nominating convention when the selection process begins again. Given the large size of the DNC, the Charter and Bylaws also establish an executive committee that meets at least every quarter. The executive committee comprises, in essence, a microcosm of the full DNC since its members are drawn from all

principal constituent groups, including representatives from the DNC's four regional caucuses. It is charged with conducting party business between semi-annual meetings of the DNC.

Location. Franklin D. Roosevelt once described the party's national headquarters as "two ladies occupying one room in a Washington office building." Until recently, the Democrats occupied a series of somewhat larger rented offices in Washington, D.C. The most famous of these accommodations was the DNC's office in the Watergate Office Building in 1972, the site of the break-in by agents of the Committee to Reelect the President (Nixon); this blunder eventually led to President Richard Nixon's resignation. Finally in 1984, following the example of the Republicans who had built a large headquarters complex on Capitol Hill in the 1960s, the Democrats in collaboration with the House and Senate Democratic Campaign Committees, built a comparable four-story structure on Capitol Hill at the corner of South Capitol and Ivy Streets, S.E. The new building provides offices, computer facilities, and a media center.

Transforming the Democratic National Committee

A combination of factors brought about the DNC's striking transformation over the past three decades: (1) the emergence of galvanizing national political issues, especially civil rights and the Vietnam War—issues that caused activists to regard national party mechanisms and institutions as vehicles for advancing their causes; (2) the rise of a new technology of campaigning that swept away the largely local and personal techniques that had worked effectively in the states and localities; and (3) the related high monetary costs of maintaining a successful presence on the American political science.

Democratic Advisory Council. Paul Butler of Indiana, national chairman from 1955 to 1960, initiated the departure from the DNC's accustomed posture that emphasized low-key fundraising and public relations, an avoidance of involvement with substantive political questions, along with acceptance of state organizations and leaders as the foundation on which the DNC itself rested. Butler began this evolution toward nationalizing and increasing the visibility of internal Democratic Party affairs by creating the national Democratic Advisory Council (DAC), an appointed body of national leaders who sought to define what they portrayed as "national" party positions on a host of domestic and international issues.

The Democratic Advisory Council's agenda was broad in scope, liberal in tone, and presidential in character. It directly challenged the more conservative, southern-dominated views of the party's elected congressional leadership, best embodied in Senate Majority Leader Lyndon B. Johnson (Tex.) and House Speaker Sam Rayburn (Tex.). The congressional leadership turned down Butler's efforts to include them as DAC members and publicly rejected the notion that such a body had either the wisdom or authority to speak for the Democratic Party. But Butler persisted, organized the DAC principally with noncongressional members, and began an active program of criticizing the Eisenhower administration and, on occasion, those congressional leaders who leaned toward cooperation rather than confrontation with the administration. The controversy continued during the 1950s until the DAC itself was disbanded upon John F. Kennedy's nomination as the party's presidential candidate and Butler's departure from the DNC's chairmanship.

Whether the DAC's pronouncements helped define Kennedy's presidential agenda, as Butler and some of his DAC members claimed, is a matter of opinion. Not open to dispute is the fact that Butler's efforts had thrust an arm of the DNC into the unaccustomed role of proclaiming what Democrats were said to believe on controversial national issues, even though the DAC's views were consistently those of the party's more northern and predominantly urban constituencies. Butler's initiative has been replicated by the DNC in various forms—for example, the Democratic Policy Council (1969–1972), the Democratic Advisory Council of Elected Officials (1973–1976), the DNC Strategy Council (1983–1985), and the Democratic Policy Commission (1985–1988). However, events external to the DNC provided the political momentum that ultimately thrust the DNC itself into the center of the nation's two most controversial issues of the past three decades.

Civil Rights. Mayor Hubert H. Humphrey of Minneapolis made the civil rights issue crucial at the 1948 Democratic National Convention in Philadelphia. Adoption of the minority platform plank on civil rights produced a walkout of most delegates from the South and formation of the Dixiecrat Party in the presidential election. But these dramatic events did not lead directly to any structural or procedural changes within the DNC itself.

A different result and one of more lasting importance to the DNC took place at the 1964 Democratic National Convention in Atlantic City. The regular Mississippi delegation was challenged by members of the largely African-American Mississippi Freedom Democratic Party on the basis that they had been excluded from the delegate selection process through deception and, at times, physical intimidation. Although the regulars correctly pointed to the absence of any national standards by which to judge the procedural "fairness" of the delegate selection process, the Freedom Democrats dominated national media coverage with moving accounts of the intimidation and violence that had kept them on the sidelines in selecting the Mississippi delegation.

President Lyndon Johnson feared a southern walkout similar to 1948. On his direct instructions, a compromise was engineered by Senator Humphrey, United Auto Workers president Walter Reuther, and then Minnesota attorney general Walter Mondale. It called for (1) the Mississippi regulars to sign a stringent loyalty oath to support the national ticket; (2) the Freedom Democrats to receive two symbolic at-large delegate seats in the Mississippi delegation; (3) the call for the 1968 Democratic National Convention to include new language guaranteeing that "voters in the States(s), regardless of race, color, creed, or national origin, will have the opportunity to participate fully in Party affairs"; and (4) a Special Equal Rights Committee of the DNC to be established to assist the states in meeting these new requirements. Both contending parties—the regulars and the Freedom Democrats—rejected the compromise. But the convention adopted it enthusiastically, and the feared southern exodus was averted. Of greater significance, a procedure was established for the national Democrats at future conventions to reject any delegation selected by discriminatory or exclusionary procedures. The DNC was given the responsibility for carrying out this historic commitment.

By 1968 this commitment to nondiscrimination in delegate selection had been implemented, and New Jersey governor Richard J. Hughes became chair of the DNC's Special Equal Rights Committee. In July 1967 the Committee advised all Democratic state chairpersons and DNC members of the six criteria—the "six basic elements" as they came to be known—that would have to be observed by state parties in choosing delegations to the 1968 convention.

Although the six basic elements were designed primarily to eliminate *racial* discrimination in delegate selection, these procedural guarantees soon were extended to delegate selection generally. In addition, this agenda of delegate selection reforms dominated the activities of the DNC for the next two decades. At the end of those 20 years, the party's structure and its operating rules and procedures had been radically transformed. Moreover, as the closing decade of the century begins, there is no reason to believe that the simmering controversy over how the Democrats nominate their presidential candidate will disappear.

Antiwar Activism. Between Atlantic City in 1964 and the 1968 National convention in Chicago, the focus of concern shifted dramatically from civil rights to the Vietnam War protest movement. Culminating in violent confrontation between antiwar activists and the Chicago police, the efforts to change U.S. policy in Vietnam by capturing the Democratic Party's presidential nomination failed (even though President Johnson decided not to run for a full second term). Although severely tested by the antiwar forces of Senators Eugene McCarthy, Robert F. Kennedy and, in the aftermath of Senator Kennedy's assassination, George McGovern, regular party forces won a first-ballot victory for Vice President Hubert H. Humphrey. In conjunction with this triumph, however, the "regulars," as they had done in 1964, set in motion a process to examine and presumably change a delegate selection process that appeared to be insulated from popular sentiment that was expressed outside established party channels and institutions.

This pattern of change mandated by the conventions and implemented by special DNC commissions was to be repeated every four years—1964, 1968, 1972, 1976, 1980, and 1984—until the 1988 national convention adjourned without creating a new commission (but approving two changes in delegate selection rules worked out before the convention by the Michael Dukakis/Jesse Jackson camps). The work of the respective commissions, along with various offshoots of the commissions (such as the midterm national party conferences of 1974, 1978, and 1982) obsessed the DNC and its leadership during the administrations of Richard Nixon, Gerald Ford, Jimmy Carter, and Ronald Reagan.

Party Reform in the 1970s. Three separate DNC commissions grappled with the delegate-selection issue during the 1970s: the Commission on Party Structure and Delegate Selection, chaired by Senator George McGovern of South Dakota and, subsequently, Congressman Donald Fraser of Minnesota (1969–1971); the Commission on Delegate Selection, chaired by Baltimore City Council member Barbara Mikulski (1973); and the Commission on Presidential Nominations and Party Structure, chaired by Michigan State Democratic chair Morley A. Winograd (1977–1978). A fourth commission, the Commission on Rules, chaired by Congressman James O'Hara of Michigan (1969–1971), focused on the apportionment of delegates and a streamlining of the rules, procedures, and conduct of the national convention to make it more "representative, open, deliberative, and fair." Finally, the Charter Commission, chaired by former North Carolina governor Terry Sanford (1973–1974), examined the entire structure of national party institutions, particularly the DNC, in the context of drafting a permanent charter for the Democratic Party of the United States.

With the turmoil of the 1968 presidential nominating process and the Chicago convention as a backdrop, the commissions on delegate selection understood their fundamental mission to be "democratizing" the nominating process by promulgating national procedural standards that would transform (1) traditional party caucuses of established state Democratic leaders into participatory conventions open to all; and (2) delegate primaries that routinely ratified the selection of familiar Democratic leaders, into highly charged popular elections among contending presidential candidates. By the end of the decade, state and local party leaders, along with elected Democratic officials, were, in essence, either bypassed or driven out of the presidential nominating process. These radical changes, moreover, were adopted by the DNC and simply imposed on the state parties—a far cry from the traditional state and local domination of such matters. One observer of the process has characterized the transformation as "centrally planned, nationally imposed, and historically unprecedented."

These changes in the structure and character of the national party have been described as "the diminution, the constriction, at times the elimination, of the regular party in the politics of presidential selection." Thus, their relatively quiet, almost anticlimatic acceptance by such regular party stalwarts as Lawrence F. O'Brien of Massachusetts, national chairperson (1970–1972), and his successor, Robert S. Strauss of Texas (1972–1976), illustrates another DNC paradox.

The reforms themselves consisted of guidelines or rules designed to give "all Democratic voters . . . a full, meaningful, and timely opportunity to participate" in the delegate-selection process. Some rules were noncontroversial, such as requirements for adequate public notice of meetings, written rules, and elimination of proxy voting. Others, however, were controversial, such as the imposition of de facto quotas for minorities, women, and young people—the groups allegedly discriminated against in 1964 and 1968—for slots on national convention delegations. The McGovern-Fraser Commission (1969–1971) guidelines resulted in the imposition of such de facto quotas. The successor Mikulski Commission (1973) then flatly rejected quotas but instituted rigorous state compliance standards and a DNC Compliance Review Commission to enforce the standards. The Winograd Commission (1977–1978) next decided that all delegations should be equally divided between men and women and also set aside 10 percent of the delegate slots for state Democratic leaders and elected officials. These and other changes in the delegate-selection rules had a direct and profound effect not only on how the party selected its presidential nominee but also on who the nominee was likely to be. As Professor Nelson Polsby (1985: p. 57) pointed out, "the rules of the presidential nominating process continue to have a strong impact on political outcomes." During this period, the DNC found itself in the unfamiliar and often uncomfortable role as arbiter and enforcer of this redistribution of power in selecting the party's presidential nominee.

A direct outgrowth of the delegate-selection struggle was the decision by the DNC and the 1972 national convention to adopt a national Charter and Bylaws for the Democratic Party, a step that, in effect, officially recognized the demise of the loosely structured, highly decentralized arrangements that had traditionally characterized the DNC's functions. The Charter Commission produced a draft that affirmed significant changes in the structure, composition, and size of the DNC itself (changes in the size and structure of the DNC had been previously adopted by the 1972 convention). In addition, a number of new national party institutions were proposed, such as a Judicial Council to adjudicate disputes over "national party law," an array of national finance organizations to help lift the DNC out of its chronic funding problems, and a National Education and Training Council to help upgrade the political skills of Democratic workers across the country. The Charter also proposed that DNC members apportioned to the states be selected in a way that assured all interested persons a "full, timely, and equal opportunity" to participate. Primacy of national party rules over state law in selecting DNC members, as well as national convention delegates, had been established. The Charter and Bylaws were adopted in 1974 by the DNC's first midterm national party conference.

Party Reform in the 1980s. Having spent most of the 1970s devising procedures that reduced or eliminated the role of state and local party leaders and elected officials in selecting convention delegates, the DNC spent the 1980s underscoring the importance of bringing these political actors back into national party circles and processes. The Winograd Commission presaged this effort by setting aside 10 percent of the 1980 convention delegates for party leaders, a provision that had limited practical effect. In the 1980s, two additional DNC commissions were established: the Commission on Presidential Nominations, chaired by Governor James B. Hunt of North Carolina (1981–1982), and the Fairness Commission, chaired by DNC Executive Committee member Donald L. Fowler of South Carolina (1985–1986). The principal device for reinvolving party and elected leaders (without significantly changing other elements of the nominating process) was the creation by the Hunt Commission of the category of "superdelegates"—a 568-member group comprised of members of Congress, governors, mayors, and state and local party leaders—who would become delegates to the 1984 convention through appointment rather than in contested election. Officially uncommitted at the time of appointment, the superdelegates presumably would play a significant role in choosing the nominee at the convention (a presumption that has not worked out in practice). Another 305 delegates' slots were set aside for committed party and elected officials. The commissions of the 1980s also adjusted other rules dealing with the nature and extent of proportional representation in delegate selection as opposed to the more traditional winner-take-all procedures.

Political Effectiveness. The DNC was the principal forum and battleground during these years of reform and restructuring. Its primacy in internal party matters, surpassed only by the quadrennial national convention, grew accordingly. The continuing efforts to change the delegate-selection process, reform the conduct of national conventions, create a national party Charter and Bylaws, conduct midterm party conferences, and sponsor numerous policy and specialized commissions required extraordinary expenditures of money, time, and attention by the party's most active adherents.

At the same time, the Democrats lost the presidential elections of 1968, 1972, 1980, 1984, and 1988. To the extent that the DNC's overriding purpose was winning presidential elections—an assumption that has prevailed since 1848—observers inevitably began to question the relationship between the party's extensive internal changes and its political effectiveness.

The victory of Ronald Reagan in the 1980 presidential election and the loss of the U.S. Senate to the Republicans brought the issue of political effectiveness to the top of the DNC's agenda. Charles T. Manatt of California, elected DNC chairperson in February 1981, charged the DNC and its staff with bringing established party leaders and elected officials back into national party affairs and with strengthening state parties by providing year-round assistance in the new technology of winning elections. To support these initiatives, Manatt also worked to escape from the DNC's chronic budget problems, principally by expanding the DNC's direct-mail fundraising capabilities targeted at individual contributors.

By early 1982 Manatt achieved a major milestone by paying off the last remnant of the 1968 $9.3 million campaign debt of Hubert Humphrey and Robert Kennedy that had been assumed by the DNC. The Democratic National Training Academy was established to train party workers and candidates. By 1983 a direct-mail campaign had identified 300,000 active contributors, up from 25,000 in 1981. This effort directed at small contributors was linked to an expanded structure to enroll larger contributors through a Business Council, a Democratic Labor Council, Finance Council, and a network of constituent groups representing agriculture, seniors, women, small business, ethnic, and young leaders. In 1984 more than $30 million was raised through these various sources, compared to $13 million in 1980.

These efforts were intensified by Manatt's successor, Paul G. Kirk, Jr., of Massachusetts, elected in 1985 after yet another losing presidential campaign. In response to the concern that the national party had become too beholden to "special interest," Kirk abolished the formal DNC caucuses of Blacks, women, labor, Hispanics, and Asian-Americans. He canceled the midterm party conference in order to save $2 million and to avoid a potentially divisive forum on the eve of the race for the 1988 presidential nomination. He established a DNC Democratic Policy Commission (one of several successors to Butler's Democratic Advisory Council) of current and former officeholders to define middle-of-the-road approaches to defense, foreign policy, family and community, international trade, and rural issues. Ties with state Democratic parties were strengthened through creation of regional "desks" at the DNC to work directly with state leaders. Training seminars in campaign techniques and fundraising were continued. Eighty percent of the DNC's political division's budget of $3.8 million in 1986 was channeled directly to state parties and individual candidates. Another $500,000 was earmarked for research into ways of recapturing traditional Democratic voters who had voted Republican in recent presidential elections. Additional funds were invested in direct-mail appeals.

These efforts at rebuilding party institutions and capabilities appeared to pay off in the 1986 midterm elections when Democrats strengthened their control of Congress and continued to win a majority of gubernatorial and state legislative races. DNC members looked with new optimism toward the 1988 presidential campaign.

Despite a successful national convention, the final result in 1988 echoed 1984, 1980, 1972, and 1968. Although the level of controversy over delegate-selection rules had subsided greatly from the mid-1970s, the Dukakis and Jackson campaigns kept alive the dispute over the proper balance between established party leaders and grass-roots participants as national convention delegates. In a preconvention compromise later ratified by the convention, Dukakis and Jackson agreed to a reduction of one-third of the "superdelegates" at the 1992 convention and a more strictly proportional awarding of delegate slots reflecting percentages of popular votes won in primaries and caucuses. It turned out that the superdelegates who lost their seats in the compromise were DNC members.

The events of 1988 demonstrated anew the paradoxical and unsettled nature of the national Democratic Party, culminating in the election of Ron Brown as DNC chair in 1989. Brown became the first African-American to chair the national committee. An early supporter of Jesse Jackson, Brown was elected because he alone of the active candidates seemed capable of continuing the progress made by Manatt and Kirk—if the very symbolism of his election did not further divide the party. As the party's struggle for definition and electoral success continues in the future, one certainty is that the DNC will serve as a principal battleground.

See also: Individual chairs of the Democratic National Committee, Compliance Review Commission of the Democratic Party, Democratic Advisory Council, Direct Mail, Donald Fraser, James B. Hunt, McGovern-Fraser Commission, National Federation of Democratic Women, Republican National Committee, Superdelegates, Winograd Commission, Young Democrats

John G. Stewart

REFERENCES

Bone, Hugh A. 1968. *Party Committees and National Politics.* Seattle: U. of Washington Pr.

Bonafede, Dom. 1983. "Democratic Party Takes Some Strides Down the Comeback Trail." 15 *National Journal* 2053.

Cotter, Cornelius P. 1969. "The National Committees and Their Constituencies." In Cornelius P. Cotter, ed. *Practical Politics in the United States.* Boston: Allyn and Bacon.

——, and Bernard C. Hennessy. 1964. *Politics Without Power: The National Committees.* New York: Atherton Press.

Democratic National Committee. 1970. *Mandate for Reform: A Report of the Commission on Party Structure and Delegate Selection.* Washington: Democratic National Committee.

Harmel, Robert, and Kenneth Janda. 1982. *Parties and Their Environments.* New York: Longman.

Mann, Thomas E. 1985. "Elected Officials and the Politics of Presidential Selection." In Austin Ranney, ed. *The American Election of 1984.* Durham, NC: Duke U. Pr.

Polsby, Nelson W. 1985. "The Democratic Nomination and the Evolution of the Party System." In Austin Ranney, ed. *The American Election of 1984.* Durham, NC: Duke U. Pr.

Shafer, Byron E. 1983. *Quiet Revolution: The Struggle for the Democratic Party and the Shaping of Post-Reform Politics.* New York: Russell Sage.

Stewart, John G. 1974. *One Last Chance: The Democratic Party, 1974–76.* New York: Praeger.

Democratic Party Finance Council

When the Democrats met in Chicago during the summer of 1968 to nominate a presidential candidate, party activists could not have realized that a lengthy period of painful introspection and fundamental reform of the party machinery was at hand. Vice President Hubert Humphrey ran in no primaries, yet he won the presidential nomination; his subsequent loss in the general election and the creation of the Commission on Party Structure and Delegate Selection—the McGovern-Fraser Commission—initiated a series of events that culminated in the writing of a charter for the Democratic Party.

Reformers at the 1968 convention had asked for a clear set of party rules, including a charter, and the McGovern-Fraser Commission along with the Rules (O'Hara) Commission had produced a draft to present to the 1972 convention. The charter was not brought up for discussion, however: "the issues were too complex, the document too controversial, and the party's divisions too deep to permit the convention to deal with the proposal." Instead, the party formed another group, the Charter Commission, headed by former North Carolina governor Terry Sanford. The Charter Commission produced a document that addressed various party functions, including policy formulation, national leadership selection, fundraising and allocation, national influence on state and local parties, and communications. It was, according to some, an important step toward a "more authoritative national Democratic Party organization."

One element of the charter was the creation of a National Finance Council. The national Democratic Party had employed various ad hoc mechanisms during the years before the charter in order to coordinate and centralize the effort to fund party affairs, and the National Finance Council simply institutionalized that vehicle (emulating earlier Republican Party efforts). Specifically, the charter stated that the Council "shall raise funds to support the Democratic Party and shall advise and assist state Democratic Parties and candidates in securing funds for their purposes." The chairman of the Finance Council is selected by the Democratic National Committee.

See also: Democratic National Committee, Hubert Humphrey, McGovern-Fraser Commission, Terry Sanford

Tom A. Kazee

REFERENCES

Crotty, William J. 1977. *Political Reform and the American Experiment.* New York: Crowell.

——. 1978. *Decision for the Democrats.* Baltimore: Johns Hopkins U. Pr.

Democratic National Committee. 1974. *Charter of the Democratic Party*. Washington: Democratic National Committee.

Harmel, Robert, and Kenneth Janda. 1982. *Parties and Their Environments: Limits to Reform*. New York: Longman.

Polsby, Nelson. 1983. *Consequences of Party Reform*. New York: Oxford U. Pr.

Price, David E. 1984. *Bringing Back the Parties*. Washington: Congressional Quarterly.

Ranney, Austin. 1975. *Curing the Mischiefs of Faction: Party Reform in America*. Berkeley: U. of California Pr.

Democratic Party National Education and Training Council

Beginning in 1968 with the Commission on Party Structure and Delegate Selection (the McGovern-Fraser Commission), the Democratic Party established a series of reform commissions designed to review and, as it turned out, remake the rules of the party. McGovern-Fraser operated simultaneously with the Commission on Rules (the O'Hara Commission), which was, among other things, given the responsibility to revise the formula allocating convention votes to the states. Both commissions claimed the authority to deal with a topic left over from the 1968 convention—writing a party charter. On the eve of the 1972 convention, McGovern-Fraser and O'Hara produced a charter draft, though the complexity and contentiousness of the issues facing the party conspired to force the charter issue off the convention agenda.

The Democrats then formed a Charter Commission, chaired by former North Carolina governor Terry Sanford, to write a party constitution and submit it to a midterm convention to be convened in 1974. The document that resulted covered many areas, including national leadership selection, fundraising and allocation, policy formulation, national party influence on state and local parties, and communications. The charter established several new party organs, including a Judicial Council, a National Finance Council, and a National Education and Training Council. The latter group was created to implement "education and training programs for the Democratic Party in furtherance of its objectives."

The grant of authority to the National Education and Training Council was broad and vague; indeed, critics complained of the "Europeanizing" of the party, arguing that the new councils, responsible to the Executive Committee of the Democratic National Committee, created a centralized party system similar to those of many European democratic parties. The Education and Training Council is composed of eight members selected by the Executive Committee of the DNC, operating with an annual budget prepared by the national committee one year in advance—"a most unusual occurrence for the normally penurious Democrats," in the words of author William Crotty. According to the charter, such budgeting allows the Council to prepare a systematic plan "to reach every young citizen as they enter the electorate at eighteen years of age [in order to] encourage a lifetime of meaningful participation."

See also: Democratic National Committee, McGovern-Fraser Commission

Tom A. Kazee

REFERENCES

Crotty, William J. 1977. *Political Reform and the American Experiment*. New York: Crowell.

———. 1978. *Decision for the Democrats*. Baltimore: Johns Hopkins U. Pr.

Democratic National Committee. 1974. *Charter of the Democratic Party*. Washington: Democratic National Committee.

Harmel, Robert, and Kenneth Janda. 1982. *Parties and Their Environments: Limits to Reform*. New York: Longman.

Polsby, Nelson. 1983. *Consequences of Party Reform*. New York: Oxford U. Pr.

Price, David E. 1984. *Bringing Back the Parties*. Washington: Congressional Quarterly.

Ranney, Austin. 1975. *Curing the Mischiefs of Faction: Party Reform in America*. Berkeley: U. of California Pr.

Democratic Party of the United States v. Wisconsin
450 U.S. 107 (1980)

This 1980 Supreme Court case involved a dispute over Wisconsin's open primary system. In Wisconsin's open primary, each voter was given a ballot listing candidates from all parties. The voter could make the decision of which party's candidates to vote for in the secrecy of the voting booth and need not declare an affiliation with either party. The state's actual delegates would be chosen later at party caucuses, but the delegates chosen there were required to vote in accordance with the results of the open primary. The charter of the Democratic Party provided that delegates to its national convention were to be chosen through procedures in which only Democrats could participate. The Democratic Party did not want its delegates to be selected through Wisconsin's system.

The Supreme Court, in an opinion by Justice Potter Stewart summarized the problem as follows: Could Wisconsin successfully insist that its delegates to the convention be seated even though those delegates were chosen through a process that included a binding state preference primary election in which voters did not declare their party affiliation? The Wisconsin Supreme Court held that the state's delegate selection system was binding on the party. The Supreme Court reversed.

In 1972 the Democratic Party had hoped to magnify the role of rank-and-file Democrats, assuring that all Democrats who wanted to could participate in the candidate selection process. However, the party was disturbed by the role of crossover voting in open primaries such as Wisconsin's, and it wanted to minimize the influence non-Democrats had in the party's selection process. The Supreme Court recognized that the inclusion of persons unaffiliated with a political party could seriously distort its collective decisions. The Court considered it reasonable and justifiable for a political party to protect itself from intrusion by those with adverse political principles.

The Supreme Court held that a political party's choice among the various methods of determining the formation of a state's delegation to the party's national convention was protected by the Constitution. The Court did not believe that the interests advanced by Wisconsin were sufficient to override the party's interest. Wisconsin could still have an open primary, but it could not force delegates to follow the primary's results if this would violate party rules.

Justice Lewis Powell wrote a dissenting opinion that was joined by Justices William Rehnquist and Harry Blackmun. The dissent declared that Wisconsin's open primary system had long been used without any complaints from the Democratic Party, and that the national party failed to show a sufficient burden on its associational rights. The dissenters considered it sufficient that people chose to vote for the candidates of the Democratic Party. Any public avowal of affiliation was not necessary for participation in the selection process.

See also: Crossover Voting, Open Primary

Scott Cameron

REFERENCES

Crotty, William J. 1977. *Political Reform and the American Experiment*. New York: Crowell.

———. 1978. *Decision for the Democrats*. Baltimore: Johns Hopkins U. Pr.

Democratic National Committee. 1974. *Charter of the Democratic Party*. Washington: Democratic National Comm.

Harmel, Robert, and Kenneth Janda. 1982. *Parties and Their Environments: Limits to Reform*. New York: Longman.

Polsby, Nelson. 1983. *Consequences of Party Reform*. New York: Oxford U. Pr.

Price, David E. 1984. *Bringing Back the Parties*. Washington: Congressional Quarterly.

Ranney, Austin. 1975. *Curing the Mischiefs of Faction: Party Reform in America*. Berkeley: U. of California Pr.

Democratic Study Group

The Democratic Study Group (DSG) is among the most important unofficial organizations for members of the Democratic Party in the House of Representatives. It was founded primarily to further the passage of liberal legislation in the House. Over time it has developed such a strong reputation for delivering useful information to its members that even conservative Democratic members of the House are reputed to have joined simply to be able to receive its legislative reports and whip notices.

The DSG was founded between 1957 and 1959 by a group of northern liberal House members who had grown impatient with the dominance of the "conservative coalition" in blocking liberal legislation. Although the House leadership at the time was at least nominally in favor of extending the legislative promises of Franklin Roosevelt's New Deal, they proved either unwilling or unable to overcome the opposition of conservative southern Democrats in order actually to pass legislation. In the 1940s and 1950s southern Democrats had been effective in blocking liberal legislation for a number of reasons: they frequently could form a working conservative majority by voting with House Republicans on the floor, they usually comprised a voting majority with the Republicans on the Rules Committee, and southern Democrats tended to spend more time mastering parliamentary maneuvers.

To overcome what were perceived to be the advantages maintained by the Conservative Coalition, a group of House Democrats, led by Eugene McCarthy (Minn.), issued a "liberal manifesto" in 1957 (Eighty-fifth Congress) as a call to organize. Liberals were unsuccessful in pushing their program in the Eighty-fifth Congress. Responding to their own ineffectiveness in enacting a legislative program, this group of liberals moved to formalize their organization. In a series of meetings held after the 1958 election, chaired by Lee Metcalf (Mont.), liberal Democrats created a formal organization to coordinate research, communication, and legislative tactics. This organization became the Democratic Study Group, and Metcalf was installed as its first chair.

Much of the DSG's early activity was spent in trying to reform internal procedures of the House, mainly in the Rules Committee. Later, in the 1960s and early 1970s, it was instrumental in passing a number of internal reforms in the House and its Democratic Caucus, including the Legislative Reorganization Act of 1970, the requirement that the Democratic Caucus meet regularly, the institution of ballots to elect Democratic chairs to legislative committees, and the election of the Democratic whip.

Throughout its existence, the success of the DSG has fluctuated considerably. Its numbers steadily expanded throughout the 1960s and 1970s, reaching approximately 250 by 1979; following the Republican resurgence in 1980, its membership declined to approximately 220. In addition to the added conservative strength in Congress during the 1980s, the independent effectiveness of the DSG has surely been affected, ironically enough, by the infusion of liberals into the upper ranks of House Democratic leadership. Speaker Tip O'Neill (Mass.) was an early member of the DSG. Tom Foley (Wash.), elected Democratic whip in 1981 and Majority Leader in 1987, served as the DSG's chair in the early 1970s, and as Speaker in 1989. And Philip Burton (Calif.), who chaired the Democratic Caucus during 1975 and 1976, also had served as the DSG chair. With party leadership now much more sympathetic to liberal causes than was the case in the 1950s, the opportunity for the DSG independently to affect the passage of liberal legislation has surely declined.

See also: Thomas Foley, Eugene McCarthy, New Deal, Thomas O'Neill

Charles Stewart III

REFERENCES

Ferber, Mark F. 1971. "The Formation of the Democratic Study Group." In Nelson W. Polsby, ed. *Congressional Behavior.* New York: Random House.

Ornstein, Norman J., and David W. Rohde. 1976. "Congressional Reform and Political Parties in the U.S. House of Representatives." In Jeff Fishel, ed. *Parties and Elections in an Anti-Party Age.* Bloomington: Indiana U. Pr.

Stevens, Arthur G., Jr., Arthur H. Miller, and Thomas E. Mann. 1974. "Mobilization of Liberal Strength in the House, 1955–1970: The Democratic Study Group." 68 *American Political Science Review* 667.

Democratic-Republican Societies

In 1793 the German Republican Society was formed in Philadelphia—its name reflecting the origins of most of its members; it was the first Democratic-Republican society to appear. By 1798 at least 43 of these popular societies had been established in every state except New Hampshire and Georgia. These associations, which resembled clubs more than political parties, went by various names, but most members called their societies either Democratic or Republican.

They were formed by people who were convinced that the American Revolution was losing its steam and that certain political figures (principally Federalists) were threatening the promise of democracy for which they believed the Revolution had been fought. These men admired the French Revolution and enthusiastically followed its progress; they actively opposed many of the policies of the federal government, particularly the Jay Treaty and Alexander Hamilton's fiscal programs. Their dissent was often pointed and passionate. Federalists became sufficiently alarmed by the activities of the clubs that they enacted the Alien and Sedition Acts in 1798. Ironically, the clubs were already in decline, partly over growing disillusionment with the French Revolution, partly from growing acceptance of the Jay Treaty, and partly because some of the most active members were becoming more directly involved in the nascent Democratic-Republican Party.

This last factor has led some to believe that the societies were stalking-horses for the party organization that was beginning to coalesce around Thomas Jefferson at the century's end. While the claim cannot be wholly dismissed, it should be noted that the societies originated as clubs dedicated to discussing public issues, albeit with a particular ideological slant. They had an active communications network but rarely offered their own candidates for office. A modern analogy is not wholly apt, but the societies more closely resembled an ideological political action committee than a political party.

See also: Federalist Party, Alexander Hamilton, Jay Treaty

Glenn A. Phelps

REFERENCES

Link, Eugene Perry. 1973. *Democratic-Republican Societies, 1790–1800.* New York: Octagon.

Miller, John C. 1960. *The Federalist Era: 1789–1801.* New York: Harper.

Eugene Dennis (1904–1961)

Political leader of America's Far Left. Born Francis Waldron in Seattle, Washington, Eugene Dennis used several aliases in his early life, which remains shrouded in mystery. He joined the Communist Party of the United States of America (CPUSA) in 1926. In 1930 Los Angeles authorities arrested Dennis at an unemployment demonstration, but he escaped prosecution, went to New York, and then left for the Soviet Union. There, he worked for the Communist International (Comintern), spending some time in China and the Philippines. In 1928 Dennis entered into a common-law marriage with Regina "Peggy" Karacick, the daughter of radical exiles from tsarist Russia. She joined Dennis in exile, and their son Tim remained in the Soviet Union after the couple returned to the United States in 1935. Eugene and Peggy then undertook party work in Wisconsin and New York City, interspersed with additional trips abroad. Dennis, considered indecisive by some, served the CPUSA as an organizer, lobbyist, and in 1946 he became the secretary general of the National Committee. In 1947 a federal district court in Washington, D.C., convicted Dennis of contempt of Congress for refusing to testify before the House Un-American Activities Committee (HUAC), and between 1951 and 1955, at the height of the Cold War, he and other party leaders went to prison for violating the Smith Act, which made it illegal to conspire to overthrow violently the government of the United States. The Supreme Court upheld the convictions, concurring that the CPUSA had advocated violent revolution.

In 1956 Dennis led the efforts to try to revive the Communist Party after a five-year hiatus, but he faced numerous difficulties. Internal confusion, brought on by prosecutions under the Smith Act and different opinions as to doctrine and conciliation with other leftist groups, doomed Dennis's attempts at party rejuvenation. Even though after 1958 the CPUSA existed as little more than a sect, Dennis remained an active member and won the presidency of the National Committee in 1959.

See also: Communist Party of the United States

Robert F. Zeidel

REFERENCES

Dennis, Peggy. 1977. *The Autobiography of an American Communist: A Personal View of Political Life.* Westport, CT: L. Hill.

Isserman, Maurice. 1982. *Which Side Were You On? The American Communist Party During the Second World War.* Middletown, CT: Wesleyan U. Pr.

Starobin, Joseph R. 1972. *American Communism in Crisis, 1943–1957.* Cambridge: Harvard U. Pr.

George Dent (1756–1813)

Early leader of the American Congress. George Dent was a Republican member of the House of Representatives from Charles County, Maryland. After serving in the military during the Revolutionary War, Dent was elected to the Maryland General Assembly, where he remained from 1782 to 1790. He was elected Speaker *pro tempore* of that body in 1788, Speaker in 1789, and unanimously reelected to that post in 1790. During 1791 and 1792 he was a member of the Maryland Senate, as well as a justice of the Charles County Court. He resigned from the Maryland Senate in 1792 to take a seat in the United States Congress. He was a Representative from Maryland during the Third, Fourth, Fifth, and Sixth Congresses, from March 1793 to March 1801. Dent served as Speaker *pro tempore* of the House of Representatives on various occasions from 1797 to 1799. After he left Congress, he was appointed United States marshal for the Potomac District by President Thomas Jefferson in 1801. Dent's public career ended in 1802 when he emigrated to Georgia, where he resided outside of Augusta until his death.

See also: Thomas Jefferson, Speaker of the House

Kathryn A. Malone

Carmine DeSapio (1908–)

The first Italian-American boss of Tammany Hall. Characteristic of the old-style political chiefs, Carmine DeSapio has been called the "last boss," a title that more aptly belonged to Richard J. Daley of Chicago. Unlike most of the old-style party bosses, DeSapio was indicted and convicted of activities that were only hinted at in other cities.

DeSapio, who became party boss in the late 1940s, stayed in power in New York for almost 20 years. Two periods in Carmine DeSapio's political life are particularly noteworthy: first, he was part of the Stop-Kennedy movement in 1960, but as described in Theodore White's *The Making of the President, 1960*, DeSapio was outmaneuvered in New York by the John F. Kennedy forces (John Bailey, Charles Buckley, Eugene Keogh, Peter Crotty, and the candidate's father, Joseph P. Kennedy). Starting in upstate New York, the Kennedy forces had achieved so much political momentum that they were guaranteed New York's votes without having to curry favor from and thus incur a debt to DeSapio and the machine forces in New York. Eventually DeSapio and Prendergast had to accept a *fait accompli*, and when Kennedy became the party's nominee, they had to come to terms with him.

Carmine DeSapio's second brush with fame was even more inglorious than the first. In the late 1960s, DeSapio was convicted of bribing a former city commissioner and of shaking down utility company Consolidated Edison on construction contracts. He was sentenced to two years in Lewisberg Federal Penitentiary and fined $4,500. DeSapio served his time and was released. "The Boss" is still active in the insurance business, and at public functions he is still surrounded by politicians.

See also: Bosses, John Bailey, Charles Buckley, Richard Daley, James Farley, Frank Hague, John F. Kennedy, Tammany Hall, Theodore White

David A. Bositis

REFERENCES

Moscow, Warren. 1971. *The Last of the Big Time Bosses.* New York: Stein and Day.

White, Theodore H. 1961. *The Making of the President, 1960.* New York: Atheneum.

Thomas E. Dewey (1902–1971)

Republican governor of New York and twice presidential candidate. Thomas E. Dewey, born in Owosso, Michigan, and educated at the University of Michigan and Columbia University, achieved national prominence in the 1930s as the elected district attorney of New York County crusading against organized crime. Dewey was denied the 1940 Republican presidential nomination because of the Wendell Willkie boom in public support and because Dewey's youth and inexperience were clear weaknesses at a time of developing war in Europe. After easily winning election as governor of New York in 1942, Dewey became the front-runner for the 1944 Republican presidential nomination in opinion polls. Because of his pledge to serve four years as governor, Dewey did not announce his candidacy before the convention, declined to campaign outside New York, and refused to alienate potential supporters by speaking out on issues. Dewey's two strongest opponents, Robert A. Taft and Arthur H. Vandenberg, withdrew in favor of weaker candidates (John Bricker, Douglas MacArthur), and Willkie was defeated by Dewey supporters in the Wisconsin primary. Dewey received the presidential nomination with only one opposing vote—the greatest victory margin by a nonincumbent in the history of the Republican Party.

Characteristic of his rural, small-town background, Dewey's pragmatic political philosophy was based on self-reliance, individual initiative and freedom, and the belief that state government could best provide the active and creative solutions needed to promote individual welfare, initiative, and freedom. Dewey strongly supported the two-party system, which he felt increased governmental efficiency because the "loyal opposition" party served as a watchdog of the majority party holding office, offered constructive alternative policies, and offered voters a choice of different leadership. He also urged discipline, harmony, and unity among Republicans and in the nation as a whole. Because of Dewey's support for the New Deal programs and internationalism, his presidential nominations in 1944 and 1948 seemed to mark the continued domination of the Republican presidential party by the eastern "liberal" establishment.

Dewey lost the 1944 election because of Americans' unwillingness to turn away from incumbent President Franklin Roosevelt during a time of war and because of public concern over his attacks on the New Deal as an all-inclusive government that destroyed self-reliant individualism. Despite an issueless campaign in 1948 stressing national unity, Dewey again lost, as Harry Truman stressed the Democratic track record of support for the New Deal and Republican identification with the rich and big business. The nomination by Republicans of a more liberal presidential candidate who nevertheless lost two successive presidential elections demonstrated that the Democratic Party had become the majority party in America in terms of the partisan identifications of the public.

See also: Elections of 1948 and 1952, Franklin Roosevelt, Robert A. Taft, Harry S Truman, Arthur W. Vandenberg

Stephen D. Shaffer

REFERENCES

Beyer, Barry. 1979. *Thomas E. Dewey, 1937–1947: A Study in Political Leadership.* New York: Garland.

Dewey, Thomas. 1952. *Journey to the Far Pacific.* Garden City, NY: Doubleday.

Keech, William R., and Donald R. Matthews. 1977. *The Party's Choice.* Washington: Brookings.

Smith, Richard. 1984. *Thomas E. Dewey and His Times.* New York: Touchstone.

Mary W. (Molly) Dewson (1874–1962)

Leading Democratic female politician in the New Deal. During a time when few women were active in national politics, Mary "Molly"

Dewson was an influential national figure working to gain more political opportunity for American women. Mary William Dewson was born in Quincy, Massachusetts, and graduated from Wellesley College in 1897. In 1928 she began to be recognized for her efforts, with Eleanor Roosevelt, to develop the Democratic Party's organization of women in every state of the Union.

In 1933 Dewson was named the vice chairman of the Democratic National Committee. She spearheaded the women's division of the national committee during Franklin Delano Roosevelt's 1936 presidential campaign. Dewson gained notoriety for her wit, which was demonstrated in the "Rainbow Flyer" pamphlets she produced to inform women about the aims of the New Deal. In fact, these pamphlets worked so well in 1932, the male leadership of FDR's 1936 campaign committee had the women comprise the bulk of their campaign literature, distributing more than one million to both women and men across the nation.

Dewson worked well with the men in the Democratic Party. They like her down-East saltiness and admired her political savvy. Dewson's influence owed also, in part, to her close working relationship with FDR's wife, Eleanor. Together they were instrumental in achieving the appointment of women to high-ranking positions in the Roosevelt administration.

Throughout her life, Dewson was active in a myriad of other political areas. Prior to the Nineteenth Amendment's passage, Dewson worked for the right for women to vote. When she was 26, she became the superintendent of parole at the Massachusetts State Industrial School for Girls. She also served as secretary for the State Commission on Minimum Wage. During World War I she traveled to France with the American Red Cross. In addition, Dewson, at various times, served on the Social Security Board, acted as president of the Consumer's League of New York, and was appointed to the President's Advisory Committee on Economic Security.

In her later years, Molly Dewson operated a scientific dairy farm in Massachusetts and served as a director of the Franklin D. Roosevelt Foundation and the International Migration Service.

See also: Democratic National Committee, New Deal, Nineteenth Amendment, Eleanor Roosevelt, Franklin D. Roosevelt

Reagan Robbins

REFERENCES

Lash, Joseph P. 1971. *Eleanor and Franklin.* New York: Norton.

Ware, Susan. 1987. *Partner and I: Molly Dewson, Feminism, and New Deal Politics.* New Haven: Yale U. Pr.

Richardson Dilworth (1898–1974)

Liberal Pennsylvania Democratic reformer. As district attorney and mayor of Philadelphia in the 1950s, Richardson Dilworth helped rid the city of much of its political corruption. Born to a wealthy Pittsburgh family, Dilworth, after graduation from Yale Law School in 1926, moved to Philadelphia where he became one of the city's most respected trial lawyers. Drawn initially into Democratic Party politics by his support of Al Smith for President in 1928, Dilworth eventually focused his attention on corruption in Philadelphia where local politics had been controlled by a Republican machine since the late-nineteenth century. Spearheading a reform movement of liberal Democrats, which also included Joseph Clark, Dilworth ran unsuccessfully for mayor in 1947; but as evidence of political corruption mounted, he was elected city treasurer two years later. In 1951 the Democratic reform group wrested political control of Philadelphia from the GOP in an election that elevated Dilworth to district attorney and Clark to mayor. Over the next five years Dilworth and Clark succeeded in reforming Philadelphia's government, and in 1956 when Clark moved on to the U.S. Senate, Dilworth was elected to the first of two terms as mayor.

Dilworth's tenure as mayor was marked by dedication to public housing, desegregation of the city's schools, expansion of labor's rights, as well as industrial development and renovation of the city's historic areas. In the early 1960s, moreover, he became a nationally prominent reformer when, as president of the U.S. Conference of Mayors, he campaigned for expanded public housing programs and increased federal aid for cities to counter the urban blight created by postwar suburbanization. In 1962 Dilworth resigned as mayor in an unsuccessful bid to become governor of Pennsylvania. Following his defeat he remained active in public affairs, serving as president of Philadelphia's school board where he continued to speak in behalf of liberal reform.

See also: Joseph Clark

John W. Malsberger

REFERENCES

Kraft, Joseph. 1958. "Pennsylvania's New Breed of Politicians." 217 (October) *Harper's* 46.

Petshek, Kirk R. 1973. *The Challenge of Urban Reform: Policies and Programs in Philadelphia.* Philadelphia: Temple U. Pr.

Reichley, James. 1955. "Clean-cut Reformers of Philadelphia." 133 (October 24) *New Republic* 7.

Direct Mail

With the passage of the Federal Election Campaign Act in 1971 and the subsequent amendments in 1974, the era of the "fat cat" contributor ended and preeminence of direct mail fundraising began. Political parties are the largest beneficiary of this change in campaign financing, but individual candidates and various organizations also heavily rely on mail solicitation.

In 1972, in the last few weeks before the reporting requirements for campaign financing were implemented, Richard Nixon raised millions of dollars from wealthy donors, including $2.1 million from one person. Today, contributors are limited to $1,000 per candidate in each election, and $25,000 overall in each calendar year. The Republican Party was the first to recognize the significance of the changed rules: parties, with their less restrictive limits, were a logical outlet for money that could no longer go directly to candidates. Under the leadership of William Brock in the early 1970s, the Republican National Committee (RNC) developed computer-based lists of proven contributors, increased efforts to recruit candidates, and strengthened party organizations at all levels.

Within a few years Brock proved to the skeptics that broad-based mail appeals could work. In 1974 he raised $6.3 million, $17 million in 1979, and $37 million in 1980 for the Republican Party. Ninety-two percent of the $84 million that the RNC raised from 1985 to 1986 came from individuals; about three-fourths of those contributions came from direct mail appeals. The successful fundraising allowed parties to provide many "in kind" services such as voter registration and get-out-the-vote drives, phone banks, and polling, as well as direct contributions to candidates. The Democratic Party was late in developing the same technology; from 1985 to 1986 Democrats were outpaced in fundraising by Republicans by a four-to-one margin.

The increasingly competitive world of direct mail has created an environment best summarized as "let the contributor beware." As one observer has noted, with direct mail "political candidates and causes suspend any concern they might have for truth, integrity, and your own intelligence in order to shake you down for the money." Some of the practices are relatively harmless, such as using "live stamps" rather than bulk-mail indicia (some even pay extra to have the stamp affixed slightly crookedly by the machine), "handwritten" notes on irregularly sized pieces of paper or faked hotel stationery, and return addresses as the candidate's home rather than campaign headquarters—all to give a personal, human touch. Other tactics are more pernicious as they play on fear and emotion. Direct mail is primarily targeted at older Americans because, as one fundraiser put it, "This is the age when people start to scare easily." A recent mailing of the Republican National Committee posed as official government business with "PENALTY FOR UNAUTHORIZED USE" and "BUY U.S. SAVINGS BONDS" stamped on the envelope and "Congress of the United States" as the return address (the RNC was forced to change the mailing by outraged Democrats).

Direct mail fundraising may have reached its saturation point in the mid-1980s. Though a return rate of only 2 percent is needed to make a direct mail effort successful (5 percent is "striking gold"), the initial successes and proven donor lists have given way to "prospecting" and falling returns. Some drives are still fruitful (the "Stop [Robert] Bork for the [Supreme] Court" campaign raised $12 million nationally), but parties complained of donor fatigue, or "burnout," as contributions fell by a third from 1984 to 1986.

As proven donors become reluctant to give, some organizations and candidates become dedicated to "prospecting for new gold," spending as much as 98 cents for every dollar they raise. Jack Kemp sent 5.5 million letters early in the 1988 presidential campaign, at a cost of $1.4 million, but he only raised $1.2 million (though the matching federal funds turned the $200,000 loss into a $1 million profit). The most successful fundraisers in the late 1980s have avoided direct mail. George Bush and Michael Dukakis kept their costs to less than 20 percent of revenue in 1988 by holding $1,000-a-plate dinners and soliciting large contributions from groups.

Direct mail is also used for political advertising in some congressional campaigns when television use is inefficient. In the 1984 campaign between Congressman Jerry Patterson and former Congressman Robert K. Dornan in Orange County, California, each candidate sent 20 mailings to every voter in the district! This use of direct mail remains the exception; fundraising is still the most common aim.

See also: William Brock, George Bush, Michael Dukakis, Federal Election Campaign Act of 1971 and Amendments, Jack Kemp, Richard Nixon, Republican National Committee

David T. Canon

REFERENCES

Jacobson, Gary C. 1985. "The Republican Advantage in Campaign Finance." *New Directions in American Politics.* Washington: Brookings.

Kayden, Xandra. 1980. "The Nationalization of the Party System." In Michael J. Malbin, ed. *Parties, Interest Groups, and Campaign Finance Laws.* Washington: American Enterprise Institute.

Price, David E. 1984. *Bringing Back the Parties.* Washington: Congressional Quarterly.

Sorauf, Frank J. 1988. *Money in American Politics.* Glenview, IL: Scott, Foresman.

Everett McKinley Dirksen (1896–1969)

Leading Republican Senator of the 1950s. Everett McKinley Dirksen was an extremely successful Republican politician from Illinois. When he first ran for a U.S. House seat in 1932, Dirksen downplayed his Republicanism, thus kicking off his vaunted pragmatism. ("I am a man of principle," he once said, "and one of my main principles is flexibility.") In 1948 an eye ailment forced him to leave Congress. After recovering, he won a 1950 Senate race against Democrat Scott Lucas, then Senate Majority Leader. At the 1952 Republican convention, he nominated Robert Taft. He blasted Dwight Eisenhower's main backer, Thomas Dewey, with this famous lament: "We followed you before, and you took us down the path to defeat!"

For the next few years, GOP moderates shunned him, but by the mid-1950s he had regained their respect by backing Eisenhower initiatives on civil rights and foreign aid. In 1957, he became the Senate Republican whip. Two years later, he succeeded William Knowland as Minority Leader.

Delighting in his visibility, he held weekly press conferences with his House counterpart, Charles Halleck, and then with Halleck's successor, Gerald Ford. Dirksen's trademarks were his carefully mussed hair and his hoarse-voiced but florid oratory. (When he was a boy, William Jennings Bryan gave him speech advice.) Though still a conservative—he nominated Barry Goldwater at the 1964 GOP convention—he

supplied crucial support for the 1963 Test-Ban Treaty and for the 1964 Civil Rights Act.

See also: Civil Rights Legislation and Southern Politics, Dwight Eisenhower, Gerald Ford, Thomas Dewey, Barry Goldwater, Minority Party Leadership in Congress

John J. Pitney, Jr.

REFERENCES

MacNeil, Neil. 1970. *Dirksen: Portrait of a Public Man.* New York: World.

Pearson, Drew, and Jack Anderson. 1969. *The Case Against Congress.* New York: Pocket Books.

Schapsmeier, Edward L., and Frederick H. Schapsmeier. 1985. *Dirksen of Illinois: Senatorial Statesman.* Urbana: U. of Illinois Pr.

Frank M. Dixon (1892–1965)

Leader of the Dixiecrat movement. In the vanguard of southern Democrats who fomented revolt against the national party, Frank Murray Dixon of Alabama played a key role in the Dixiecrat movement in 1948. Active in veterans' organizations after World War I, Dixon stumped Alabama for Al Smith in 1928. Having failed four years earlier, he eventually won election as governor in 1938, serving until 1943. As chairman of the Southern Governors' Conference (1941–1942), Dixon spoke out against New Deal encroachment upon the power of the states. In 1943, he and Sam Jones of Louisiana failed to interest other southern governors in forming an independent, regional Democratic Party.

Later a corporate lawyer in Birmingham, Dixon led conservative Alabama Democrats who wanted to reverse the trend of New Deal economics and abort the liberalized racial proposals advocated by Harry Truman's administration. Dixon joined other southern Democratic bolters in organizing the Dixiecrat convention in Birmingham in July 1948 and delivered a keynote address in which he dramatized the perceived threat to traditional social customs and white political control throughout the South. Rejecting the group's offer to become its presidential nominee, he delivered speeches and planned strategy during the canvass. He remained an intellectual leader of the conservative Democratic faction in Alabama throughout the 1950s, and Dixon's last major political effort resulted in his selection as a Democratic presidential elector in 1960. Along with five other Alabama electors and eight from Mississippi, Dixon cast his electoral vote for Harry F. Byrd, Sr., conservative Democrat of Virginia, in protest against the national Democratic platform and the victorious nominee, John F. Kennedy.

See also: Harry F. Byrd, Sr.

Thomas N. Boschert

REFERENCES

Barnard, William D. 1974. *Dixiecrats and Democrats: Alabama Politics, 1942–1950.* University: U. of Alabama Pr.

Garson, Robert A. 1974. *The Democratic Party and the Politics of Sectionalism, 1941–1948.* Baton Rouge: Louisiana State U. Pr.

Hamilton, Virginia Van der Veer. 1987. *Lister Hill: Statesman from the South.* Chapel Hill: U. of North Carolina Pr.

Key, V. O., Jr. 1949. *Southern Politics in State and Nation.* New York: Knopf.

Joseph M. Dixon (1867–1934)

Leading Montana Republican of the early twentieth century. The son of cotton machinery manufacturer Hugh W. and Flora A. (Murchison) Dixon, Joseph Moore Dixon was born a Quaker in Snow Camp, North Carolina, and was educated at Guilford College. Following graduation, Dixon moved to Missoula, Montana, in 1891, where he studied law and was admitted to the bar the following year. There, he served as assistant county prosecutor (1893–1895) and prosecutor (1895–1897).

In 1900 Dixon was elected to the state house of representatives, and two years later, he emerged as the state's leading progressive, serving as Montana's only Congressman from 1903 to 1907. Within the Republican Party he challenged Old Guard conservatives and in 1906 was elected to the United States Senate where he served until 1912. During that tumultuous election year, Dixon, who already had distinguished himself as a progressive opponent of the railroads and the powerful Anaconda Copper Company and as a champion of the direct primary and other reforms, served as chairman of the Progressive (or Bull Moose) Party convention in Chicago. Following the convention, he was Theodore Roosevelt's national campaign manager in the three-way presidential race that pitted Roosevelt against William Howard Taft and Woodrow Wilson.

Following Theodore Roosevelt's defeat, Dixon continued his business activities, which included newspaper publishing and dairy farming. He was elected governor of Montana in 1920. However, as governor he once again infuriated the Anaconda Company and other conservative interests by championing a series of tax reforms and an old age pension program. Consequently, he was defeated in his 1924 bid for reelection and, four years later, ran unsuccessfully for the U.S. Senate. President Herbert Hoover named Dixon First Assistant Secretary of the Interior in 1929, a post that he held until the onset of the New Deal.

See also: Herbert Hoover, New Deal, Progressive Party, Railroads, Theodore Roosevelt, William Howard Taft, Woodrow Wilson

W. Thomas White

REFERENCES

Karlin, Jules A. 1957. "Congressman Joseph M. Dixon and the Miles City Land Office, 1903: A Study in Political Patronage." In J. W. Smurr and K. R. Toole, eds. *Historical Essays on Montana and the Northwest.* Helena, MT: Western Press.

———. 1974. *Joseph M. Dixon of Montana.* 2 vols. Missoula: U. of Montana Publications in History.

Malone, Michael P., and Richard B. Roeder. 1976. *Montana: A History of Two Centuries.* Seattle: U. of Washington Pr.

Thomas J. Dodd (1907–1971)

Democratic Senator from Connecticut. Thomas J. Dodd was the first Senator to be investigated by the Senate's Select Committee on Standards and Conduct. Beginning in 1966, the committee examined charges that Dodd had used campaign funds for personal expenses, double-billed the government for the cost of several trips, and improperly used his position to help friends. The committee recommended that Dodd be censured on the first two charges. On June 23, 1967, the Senate censured Dodd on the charge of misusing campaign funds. Dodd served out the remainder of his term, but he was defeated for reelection in 1970.

Thomas Dodd was employed by the Justice Department as a special assistant to five Attorneys General between 1938 and 1945. He received several citations for his work with the prosecution at the Nuremberg War Trials (1945–1946). Dodd was a candidate for the Democratic gubernatorial nomination in Connecticut in 1946 and 1948 before being elected to Congress in 1952. He was reelected in 1954. After mounting an unsuccessful run for the Senate in 1956, Dodd won election to that body in 1958. He was rewarded for his support of the party leadership with assignments to the prestigious Appropriations, Judiciary, and Aeronautics and Space committees. Dodd was elected to a second term in 1964 before his defeat as an independent candidate in 1970.

Dodd's son, Christopher J. Dodd, served in the U.S. House of Representatives from 1975 to 1981 and has been a Senator from Connecticut since 1981.

John A. Clark

Robert J. Dole

Kansas Republican Senator, national party chairman, and presidential hopeful. Robert J. Dole was born in Russell, Kansas. In political speeches, he would note his Depression up-bringing: "American voters want someone [who] understands hard knocks and understands the problems of real people."

In 1942 he left the University of Kansas to join the Army, and in 1945, while serving in Italy, he was badly wounded by shrapnel or machine gun fire. Even after months in hospitals, he never regained the use of his right arm and had little feeling in his left. Explaining his political drive, he said, "Much of my life since April, 1945, has been an exercise in compensation." According to associates, his handicap has also led him to hate dependency, making it hard for him to delegate authority.

Dole went back to school as soon as his health allowed. In 1950, while still a law student at Topeka's Washburn University, he was elected as a Republican to the Kansas House of Representatives. After a two-year term in the house, he was elected Russell County attorney in 1952. In that job, he had to sign welfare checks for his grandparents. That experience, he said, heightened his concern for the poor.

In 1960 he was elected to the U.S. House of Representatives, where he stressed farm issues. In 1968 he won a seat in the U.S. Senate. In floor debate, Dole used his sharp wit to back Richard Nixon's policies, support that the President appreciated. In 1971 Nixon named him to head the Republican National Committee, while he kept his Senate seat. Dole sought to broaden the GOP's voter appeal, but Nixon's reelection committee kept Dole from having much effect. In 1973 he resigned as party chairman. Although he had no role in Watergate—he said that the break-in had "occurred on my night off"—its fallout nearly cost him his Senate seat in 1974.

In 1976 Gerald Ford tapped him as the GOP vice presidential candidate. In a debate with Walter Mondale, he insisted that 1.6 million Americans had died in "Democrat wars." Some called Dole a "hatchet man" and a GOP liability, but he probably helped Ford carry several midwestern states.

In 1980 Dole lost the race for the GOP presidential nomination but won the chairmanship of the Senate Finance Committee when the GOP took control of the upper chamber. His accomplishments as chairman included the indexation of income tax brackets. In 1984 Dole succeeded Howard Baker as Senate Majority Leader. Two years later, when the Democrats retook the Senate, he became Minority Leader.

In 1988 Bob Dole again ran for President. He won the Iowa GOP caucuses, but his hopes were ruined by primary election losses to George Bush. Some political analysts blamed his defeat on poor organization stemming from his reluctance to delegate.

His second wife, Elizabeth Hanford Dole, served as U.S. Secretary of Transportation from 1983 to 1987 and as Secretary of Labor from 1989 to 1990.

See also: Howard Baker, Minority Party Leadership in Congress, Walter Mondale, Republican National Committee, Watergate

John J. Pitney, Jr.

REFERENCES

Dole, Robert, Elizabeth Dole, and Richard Norton Smith. 1988. *The Doles: Unlimited Partners.* New York: Simon and Schuster.

Taylor, Paul. 1990. *See How They Run: Electing the President in an Age of Mediaocracy.* New York: Knopf.

Witcover, Jules. 1977. *Marathon: The Pursuit of the Presidency, 1972–1976.* New York: Viking.

Ignatius Donnelly (1831–1901)

Populist Party leader from Minnesota. The son of an Irish-American physician and Catharine Frances (Gavin) Donnelly, Ignatius Donnelly was born in Philadelphia. He graduated from Central High School and read law in the office of future United States Attorney General Benjamin Harris Brewster. In 1856 he moved to Nininger, Minnesota, where he speculated in land development until the panic of 1857 left him heavily burdened with debt.

Donnelly then turned actively to politics, winning election as lieutenant governor at the age of 28, serving from 1859 to 1863. He then served three terms in Congress (1863–1869), where he was an outspoken Republican proponent of the war effort, abolitionism, and federal land grants for Minnesota's railroads; he later advocated a lenient policy toward the defeated Confederate states. Disillusioned with the Republican Party following his reelection defeat in 1868, Donnelly returned to Minnesota where he became a Liberal Republican, then a Granger, and finally a Greenbacker. He served in the state senate from 1874 to 1878 and was a perennial candidate for other offices, while he edited the *Anti-Monopolist* and was a constant speaker and author.

Subsequently, Donnelly wrote a number of books, including *Atlantis: The Antediluvian World* (1882), *Ragnarok: The Age of Fire and Gravel* (1883), and *The Great Cryptogram* (1888). His most famous work, *Caesar's Column: A Story of the Twentieth Century* (1891), predicted the destruction of modern civilization and proved important in the Populist Revolt. In the late 1880s he became the leader of Minnesota's Farmers' Alliance and led it into the national People's Party. At the Populists' 1892 Omaha convention, Donnelly authored its famous preamble, declaring, "we meet in the midst of a nation brought to the verge of moral, political, and material ruin. Corruption dominates the ballot-box, the legislatures, the Congress, and touches even the ermine of the bench." That same year he ran for governor of Minnesota on the Populist ticket but was defeated. In 1900, the "Sage of Nininger" was the People's Party's unsuccessful candidate for Vice President. Two months after the election, Ignatius Donnelly died shortly after midnight on the first day of the twentieth century.

See also: Greenback Party, People's Party

W. Thomas White

REFERENCES

Abrahams, Edward H. 1978 "Ignatius Donnelly and the Apocalyptic Style." 46 *Minnesota History* 102.

Anderson, David D. 1980. *Ignatius Donnelly.* Boston: Twayne Publishers.

Axelrad, Allan M. 1971. "Ideology and Utopia in the Works of Ignatius Donnelly." 12 *American Studies* 47.

Bovee, John R. 1969. "'Doctor Huguet': Donnelly on Being Black." 41 *Minnesota History* 286.

Pollack, Norman. 1965. "Ignatius Donnelly on Human Rights: A Study of Two Novels." 47 *Mid-America* 99.

Ridge, Martin. 1962. *Ignatius Donnelly: The Portrait of a Politician.* Chicago: U. of Chicago Pr.

Thomas W. Dorr (1805–1854)

Mid-nineteenth-century Rhode Island political reformer. Thomas Wilson Dorr's campaign for equal rights (the Dorr Rebellion) produced a major realignment of his state's party system. Dorr, the eldest child of a prominent Providence merchant, graduated from Harvard and studied law in New York City under Chancellor James Kent before entering politics in 1834 as a state representative from Providence. Though originally a Whig, he supported bank regulation and the liberalization of suffrage, thus estranging himself from that party.

In 1834 he was a major force in the formation of the Constitutional Party, an effort aimed at replacing Rhode Island's colonial charter of 1663 with a popularly written state constitution. With the demise of that unsuccessful group in 1838, Dorr became a Democrat, affiliating himself with the equal rights, or the "Locofoco," wing of that organization.

In 1841, after Rhode Island's disfranchised males had launched a campaign to achieve the vote through constitutional reform, Dorr joined them and quickly became a leader of their movement. These reformers, calling themselves the Rhode Island Suffrage Association, convened their own constitutional convention because they felt that the existing government was insincere in dealing with reform demands. Their November 1841 conclave produced the "People's Constitution," with Dorr as its principal draftsman. This remarkably progressive document was approved in a three-day referendum by a majority of Rhode Island's free white adult males. In April 1842 Dorr was elected the "people's governor" under this new regime, and the state was confronted with two rival governments.

Generally, urban Whigs and rural Democrats opposed the Dorrites and united to form the Law and Order Party. These conservatives prevailed, and Dorr, after surrendering to them, was tried and convicted for treason against the state. The Whig-led Law and Order coalition dominated state politics for the remainder of the 1840s, despite a brief intraparty dispute in 1845 over whether or not to liberate Dorr.

Beginning in 1851, the equal rights Democrats captured the governorship for three successive years, owing to the defection of the rural Democrats from the Law and Order Party. When the liberals (called "Dorr Democrats") pardoned Dorr, reversed his conviction, and attempted to reenact the People's Constitution, the agrarians again defected. At this juncture Know-Nothingism and the rise of the Republican Party produced a major political realignment in Rhode Island. By the end of the decade, the Republicans, who had revived the Law and Order coalition, completely dominated state politics (and would continue that domination until the New Deal). Dorr's urban wing of the Democratic Party, appealing mainly to equal rights advocates and Irish Catholics, was consigned to minority status until well into the twentieth century.

See also: Know-Nothings

Patrick T. Conley

REFERENCES

Conley, Patrick T. 1976. *The Dorr Rebellion: Rhode Island's Crisis in Constitutional Government.* Providence: R.I. Bicentennial Foundation.

————. 1977. *Democracy in Decline: Rhode Island's Constitutional Development, 1776–1841*. Providence: Rhode Island Historical Society.

Dennison, George M. 1976. *The Dorr War: Republicanism on Trial, 1831–1861*. Lexington: U. Pr. of Kentucky

Gettleman, Marvin E. 1973. *The Dorr Rebellion: A Study in American Radicalism*. New York: Random House.

Mowry, Arthur May. 1901. *The Dorr War*. Providence: Preston and Rounds.

Helen Gahagan Douglas (1900–1980)

California Democratic politician dubbed "The Pink Lady" by Richard Nixon. Helen Gahagan Douglas was born in Boonton, New Jersey, the daughter of a wealthy builder and financier. As a sophomore at Barnard College, she first appeared on Broadway and later combined careers as an actress and opera singer. She married actor Melvyn Douglas in 1931. The couple moved to California and both became involved in supporting New Deal programs. She joined the Steinbeck Committee to aid residents of migrant camps, and Franklin Roosevelt named her to an advisory committee for the Works Progress Administration.

In 1940 Douglas was elected Democratic national committeewoman from California and appointed vice chairman of the state party. With her financial resources, ties to Hollywood, and friendship with President Roosevelt, she became a major figure in the party. In 1944 she was elected to the United States House of Representatives from the Fourteenth District with 51 percent of the votes. In 1946 and 1948 she was reelected by wider margins.

In 1950 she challenged incumbent U.S. Senator Sheridan Downey for the Democratic nomination. Downey withdrew, and Douglas won the nomination. In the general election she ran against two-term Republican Congressman Richard M. Nixon. The campaign became famous because of the use of political innuendo by Nixon and his supporters. Douglas was accused of not being a strong anti-Communist, and Nixon referred to her as the "Pink Lady." Her support for liberal causes, including opposition to the House Un-American Activities Committee, was used against her. During the campaign, the phrase "Tricky Dick" was coined for Nixon for the first time by a California newspaper. Nixon was elected with 59 percent of the vote.

Douglas returned to the stage but remained active in politics, frequently campaigning for Democratic candidates. She was especially active in the 1960 and 1972 campaigns in which Nixon was the Republican presidential candidate.

See also: House Un-American Activities Committee, New Deal, Richard Nixon, Franklin Roosevelt

James C. Clark

REFERENCES

Ambrose, Stephen E. 1987. *Nixon: The Education of a Politician, 1913–1952*. New York: Simon and Schuster.

Douglas, Helen Gahagan. 1982. *A Full Life*. Garden City, NY: Doubleday.

Paul H. Douglas (1892–1976)

Author, educator, and Democratic politician from Illinois. Paul Howard Douglas was born in 1892 and was reared by his mother in Maine. After working his way through Bowdoin College, Douglas went on to teach economics at several universities and to earn his Ph.D. from Columbia University.

In 1925, Douglas, by now a professor at the University of Chicago, received nationwide recognition for his book, *Wages of the Family*. Another work, *Real Wages in the United States (1890–1926)*, published in 1930, paved the way for numerous governmental and academic appointments. *Theory of Wages*, often regarded as his most distinguished work and for which he received a $5,000 prize in an international competition, appeared in 1934. During the Depression, Douglas also helped draft the legislation that became the Social Security Act. Douglas favored the formation of a national Labor Party, a subject that he addressed in *The Coming of a New Party* (1931).

While his pacifism and problems with his eyes allowed Douglas to escape fighting in World War I, he voluntarily enlisted as a private in the Marines during World War II after losing the 1942 Democratic Senate primary in Illinois. Douglas fought in the Pacific and earned a Bronze Star.

In 1938 Douglas had first been elected to public office as an alderman for the Fifth Ward of Chicago. It was while running for this office that he pledged to reveal his income publicly if elected. By this uncommon and then-voluntary action, Douglas sought to demonstrate that he considered the post of alderman to be one of public trust. Ten years after his election as alderman, Douglas was successful in a second try for the Senate seat from Illinois. Douglas continued the practice of annually publishing his income while in the Senate. He also vowed that neither he nor his staff would accept any gift worth more than $2.50. Among his primary legislative goals as a Senator were the advancement of civil rights, the closing of tax loopholes, and the increasing of social security and minimum-wage coverage. Douglas was a strong proponent of the Great Society Legislation. He favored the Vietnam War policy of President Lyndon Johnson, although he would later, after the release of the *Pentagon Papers*, revise his view.

Douglas served in the Senate until his defeat in 1966 by Charles Percy. Douglas lost votes, in part, because of his record of strong support for civil rights and for his defense of the Vietnam War. After Douglas left the Senate, President Johnson appointed him chairman of the National Commission on Urban Problems, which found Johnson's administration to be remiss for not fulfilling its promise to provide low-cost housing. Douglas also returned to teaching and published his memoirs, *In The Fullness of Time*, in 1972.

See also: Lyndon Johnson

Reagan Robbins

REFERENCES

Burns, James MacGregor. 1972. "Endless Decency and Humanity." (June 3) *New Republic*.

Kaiser, Charles. 1976. "Former Sen. Paul H. Douglas Dies; Liberal Illinois Democrat was 84." (September 25) *New York Times*. p. C 24.

Lichtenstein, Nelson, ed. 1976. *Political Profiles, the Kennedy Years*. New York: Facts on File.

———. 1976. *Political Profiles, the Johnson Years*. New York: Facts on File.

McGaffin, William. 1962. "'Ferocious Independent' at 70." (March 25) *The New York Times Magazine* 36+.

McGrory, Mary. 1966. "The Liberal Loner from Illinois." (December 4) *Washington Star*. p. c1.

1976. "Paul H. Douglas" (obituary). Chicago Tribune. (Sept. 26) sec. 1, p. 25.

Schoenebaum, Eleanora W., ed. 1977. *Political Profiles, the Eisenhower Years*. New York: Facts on File.

Warden, Rob. 1978. "Paul Douglas on FBI War Detention List." (November 1) *Chicago Tribune*, sec. 1, p. 3.

1970. "Where Are They Now?" (November 16) *Newsweek*. p. 21.

Rothe, Anna, ed. 1950. *Current Biography 1949*. New York: H. W. Wilson.

Smith, Terence. 1967. "Douglas Returns As A Professor." (February 15) *New York Times*: p. 30.

Stephen A. Douglas (1813–1861)

Presidential candidate of the northern wing of the pre-Civil War Democratic Party. Stephen Arnold Douglas was a central figure in the political controversies over slavery during the 1840s and 1850s. Born in Brandon, Vermont, Douglas moved to Illinois in 1834. There he became a lawyer and a successful Democratic Party politician, winning election to the U.S. House of Representatives (1843–1847) and to the Senate (1847–1861).

Douglas took a leading role in securing passage of the Compromise of 1850 after the Senate initially dismembered Henry Clay's "omnibus bill" in July 1850. As chair of the Senate Committee on Territories, he served as floor manager for the separate bills and rallied pro-Compromise congressional majorities, mainly northern Democrats and southern Whigs, for the passage of each by that September.

In January 1854 Douglas introduced a bill to organize the territories of Kansas and Nebraska. In line with the principle of "popular sovereignty," this legislation granted settlers of those territories the right to decide whether or not to permit slavery there. Most of the controversy over the Kansas-Nebraska bill stemmed from its implicit repeal of the Missouri Compromise's prohibitions against slavery in the Louisiana Purchase territory north of the 36°30' line. Widespread opposition in the North to Douglas's bill was largely responsible for the formation of the Republican Party on a platform opposing the westward extension of slavery.

The competition between proslavery and antislavery settlers for control of Kansas kept the territorial issue at the forefront of national politics for the remainder of the decade. Adherence to the principles of popular sovereignty led Douglas to oppose the efforts of President James Buchanan and a majority of his party in 1858 to get Congress to admit Kansas as a state under the proslavery Lecompton Constitution, which a large majority of Kansans had rejected in a referendum. Over Douglas's opposition, Congress finally passed a compromise measure, the English Bill, which attempted to bribe Kansas voters by extensive land grants to approve the Lecompton Constitution. Kansans, however, turned down the constitution by a heavy margin in a new referendum, vindicating Douglas.

During the bitter congressional battle, Douglas had allied with Republicans to fight the admission of Kansas, and some eastern Republican leaders, such as Horace Greeley, proposed a coalition of Douglas's Democratic followers with their own young party. Illinois Republicans strongly opposed any such merger, however, and ran Abraham Lincoln against Douglas for the Senate that year. Although Douglas ultimately triumphed, the seven well-publicized debates between the two men made Lincoln a nationally known figure.

In 1860 Douglas won a bitter contest for the Democratic presidential nomination in the face of defection by most southern Democrats who believed he would not aggressively defend the rights of slaveholders. In the four-way race that fall, Douglas finished second in the popular vote to Lincoln, the Republicans' victorious candidate, but received only twelve electoral votes from Missouri and New Jersey. After Lincoln's election, Douglas supported unsuccessful attempts in Congress to arrange a new sectional compromise to placate the South. Opposed to secession, he died shortly after the firing on Fort Sumter while rallying northern Democrats behind the Union war effort.

See also: Election of 1860, Kansas-Nebraska Act, Abraham Lincoln, Missouri Compromise, Secession

John R. McKivigan

REFERENCES

Johannsen, Robert W. 1973. *Stephen Arnold Douglas.* New York: Oxford U. Pr.

Potter, David M. 1976. *The Impending Crisis, 1848–1861.* New York: Harper and Row.

Silbey, Joel H. 1977. *A Respectable Minority: The Democratic Party in the Civil War Era, 1860–1868.* New York: W. W. Norton.

Frederick Douglass (1818–1895)

Eloquent African-American reformer and abolitionist. Born a Maryland slave with the name Frederick Augustus Washington Bailey, Frederick Douglass became one of the best-known and most politically influential African-Americans of the nineteenth century. Douglass's treatment as a slave was relatively "mild," and he even managed to learn to read. In 1838 he escaped from his master and settled in New Bedford, Massachusetts.

Recruited into the abolitionist movement in 1841, Douglass became one of its most effective orators. In 1845 he published the first of three autobiographies, *The Narrative of the Life of Frederick Douglass*, which recounted his experiences as a slave. His identity as a fugitive slave now public, Douglass fled to Great Britain to avoid recapture. Sympathizers there purchased his freedom and gave him funds to return to the United States and to start his own newspaper.

The founding of the *North Star* (later the *Frederick Douglass' Paper*) in Rochester, New York, in 1847 marked the beginning of Douglass's development of a personal political ideology. Originally a follower of abolitionist William Lloyd Garrison, Douglass espoused the Garrisonian tenets that the Constitution was a proslavery document, and that voting, therefore, lent moral sanction to slavery. He condemned not only the two major political parties, the Whigs and the Democrats, but also the small Liberty Party, founded by abolitionist opponents of Garrison in 1840.

In 1851, however, Douglass merged his financially struggling new paper with a Liberty Party publication underwritten by wealthy abolitionist Gerrit Smith. The move marked Douglass's defection from the Garrisonians to the political antislavery camp. In 1848, Douglass had attended the national convention in Buffalo, New York, that founded the Free Soil Party and had given a qualified endorsement to its platform opposing the extension of slavery into western territories. Throughout the 1850s, Douglass wavered between support for the anti-extensionist Free Soilers and their Republican successors and Smith's tiny political abolitionist faction that claimed that the federal government had the constitutional power to abolish slavery.

During the Civil War, Douglass spoke several times with President Abraham Lincoln, who held his advice in high regard. Such treatment, coupled with the Republicans' support for the Thirteenth, Fourteenth, and Fifteenth amendments, made Douglass a staunch supporter of the party for the remainder of his life. As a powerful orator with a large following among both African-Americans and white abolitionists, Douglass was recruited by the Republicans to stump in both presidential and state election campaigns. A loyal party worker, and an acknowledged leading Black Republican, Douglass received a number of political appointments in the post-bellum years, including the offices of the U.S. marshal (1877–1881) and recorder of deeds (1881–1886) for the District of Columbia and minister resident to the Republic of Haiti (1889–1891).

Inside the Republican Party, Douglass aligned with the Stalwart faction, believing that white politicians such as Ulysses S. Grant, John A. Logan, and Roscoe Conkling, had the stronger record of support for civil rights than competing Republican leaders. Douglass particularly was displeased with the relative indifference that Rutherford B. Hayes, James A. Garfield, and James G. Blaine displayed toward Black rights. Nonetheless, Douglass fought against any suggestion that the African-Americans split their votes between the two major parties to gain more leverage with each. Douglass's post-Civil War political creed is summed up in his statement that for Black voters, "The Republican party is the ship and all else the sea."

See also: Abolition Movement, Fifteenth Amendment, Free Soil Party, Liberty Party, Stalwarts (and Half-Breeds)

John R. McKivigan

REFERENCES

Clontz, William H. 1976. "An Analysis of the Political Career of Frederick Douglass, 1865–1895." Ph.D. dissertation, University of Idaho.

Martin, Waldo. 1984. *The Mind of Frederick Douglass.* Chapel Hill: U. of North Carolina Pr.

Pitre, Merline. 1976. "Frederick Douglass: Party Loyalist." Ph.D. dissertation, Temple University.

Quarles, Benjamin. 1948. *Frederick Douglass.* New York: Associated Publishers.

Drop-off

Voter turnout in American elections varies widely across years and offices. Various descriptions (such as drop-off, roll-off, and fall-off) have been used to characterize different aspects of turnout variations. Although the terms are inconsistently used, the concepts they refer to are clear.

Drop-off generally denotes the decline in turnout that occurs from presidential to off-year elections. Drop-off between the presidential election and the following off-year congressional elections has averaged around 20 percentage points in recent years. For example, 53 percent of the voting age population voted in the 1984 presidential contest, but only 33 percent did so in the 1986 congressional elections. The drop-off is somewhat less if we compare congressional elections in both years, but it is still around 15 points. Even greater drop-off exists if we compare presidential elections to primaries or to state and local elections held separately from national elections.

Roll-off usually refers to the decline in turnout that regularly occurs between the top and the bottom of the ticket. Although occasionally a lower-level contest will produce a higher turnout than one at the top of the ticket, in the usual pattern a roll-off of two to ten points takes place from the top to the bottom of the ballot. Roll-off varies considerably across states, being affected by a variety of factors, including ballot length and form. Competition can also be a factor. The presidential contest is always at least moderately competitive, but lower-level offices in many states may often be very uncompetitive or even uncontested.

These definitions represent the most common usage of drop-off and roll-off, but the terms sometimes are used interchangeably; another term, *fall-off*, is also used to designate one or both of these phenomena. The common denominator for all these concepts is that voter inclinations to cast a ballot vary across elections. Turnout is stimulated by high visibility and exciting races. That explains both why more citizens bother to vote in presidential election years, and why those who do go to the polls sometimes fail to vote for races further down on the ballot.

See also: Presidential Nominating Politics

Charles L. Prysby

REFERENCES

Burnham, Walter Dean. 1965. "The Changing Shape of the American Political Universe." 59 *American Political Science Review* 7.

Sorauf, Frank, and Paul Allen Beck. 1988. *Party Politics in America.* 6th ed. Glenview, IL: Scott, Foresman.

W. E. B. Du Bois (1868–1963)

African-American theoretician and political leader. Political activist, founder of the NAACP and the Pan-African Congress, historian, sociologist, and novelist, William Edward Burghardt Du Bois was the leading African-American intellectual of the twentieth century. Born in Great Barrington, Massachusetts, Du Bois graduated from Harvard in 1895. From 1897 to 1910, Du Bois taught at Atlanta University, published often (including *The Souls of Black Folks* and *John Brown*), and headed a pioneering sociological project on living conditions in Black America.

Du Bois split with Booker T. Washington's accommodationist approach to race relations and became a political activist early in the new century. He argued that the "talented tenth" of Black America ought to lead the race to political equality. Du Bois helped found the Niagara Movement in 1905, and in 1910 co-founded the National Association for the Advancement of Colored People (NAACP). From 1910 to 1934 Du Bois edited the NAACP's journal, *The Crisis*, making the magazine a political forum for African-American intellectuals. Attaining a subscription of 100,000 at its peak in 1918, *The Crisis* was an important journal of social criticism and a spokespiece for racial equality.

In 1919 Du Bois traveled to the Peace Conference in Paris and organized the Pan-African Congress, an international conference of Black leaders from America, the Caribbean, and Africa. Four more congresses took place in the next 26 years, and although politically ineffectual, they marked the first international attempt by Black leaders to solve political problems commonly, and revealed Du Bois's own sense of the Black race's commonality. Du Bois was hailed as the father of Pan-Africanism.

In 1934 Du Bois resigned from the NAACP because of political differences with the leadership and the NAACP's conservative approach to the Depression. Returning to Atlanta University and scholarship, he published *Black Reconstruction* (1935), a Marxist-influenced analysis of Reconstruction, and in 1939 published *Black Folk Then and Now*.

Atlanta University retired Du Bois in 1945, and he returned for a short time to the NAACP. The bulk of his postwar years, however, were devoted to socialism and questions of African colonialism. Du Bois ran for office in New York on the American Labor Party ticket in 1950. After visiting the Soviet Union in 1926, he had expressed admiration for the new Communist regime. In 1951 Du Bois was indicted for failing to register as a foreign agent, but the case against him was dismissed. Nonetheless, McCarthyites in the federal government continued to harass Du Bois in the 1950s, denying him a passport to travel for much of the decade. He defiantly became a member of the Communist Party of America in 1961. He died in Ghana, a newly made citizen of that nation, in 1963.

See also: National Association for the Advancement of Colored People, Socialism in American Politics

John Walsh

REFERENCES

Du Bois, W. E. B. 1968. *The Autobiography of W. E. B. Du Bois.* New York: International Publishers.

Michael S. Dukakis (1933–)

Massachusetts Democratic governor and candidate for President. Michael Stanley Dukakis was born in Boston, Massachusetts, the second son of a successful doctor and a schoolteacher, both immigrants from Greece. He graduated from Brookline High School, took an honors degree at Swarthmore College, and graduated from Harvard Law School in 1960. Always interested in civic questions and in good management of government, Dukakis began his political career as an activist on his local school board, represented Brookline in the state assembly, and in 1971 ran unsuccessfully for lieutenant governor on the Democratic ticket. In the ensuing

four years, he practiced law in Boston and served as moderator on the public affairs television program *The Advocates*.

In 1975 he ran for governor of Massachusetts, winning a four-year term. Great difficulties with the legislature controlled by his own Democratic Party ensued. The legislature found him hard to work with, headstrong, and self-righteous. He exercised his veto on 35 bills; two-thirds of the vetoes were overridden. In 1979 he was defeated in the Democratic primary for renomination by Edward King, who ran as a more conservative candidate and went on to win the election. This defeat shocked Dukakis and caused him to reevaluate his style of operation in which political accommodation had been given such short shrift. He taught intergovernmental relations during this period at the John F. Kennedy School of Government at Harvard University and planned a political comeback.

Remarkably, he pulled it off. Dukakis defeated King in the 1982 Democratic gubernatorial primary and went on in overwhelmingly Democratic Massachusetts to be elected governor for a second term. He won a third term handily in 1986. He is widely credited during this period with having mastered a more cooperative approach to government and with successfully managing a "Massachusetts miracle" in which high employment—sparked in great measure by federal contracts to Massachusetts industry—was spread to low income parts of the state. He sponsored an amnesty for tax evaders that boosted tax revenues and an employment training program for welfare recipients.

His greatest claim to national fame was his successful quest for the Democratic presidential nomination in 1988, in which he outdistanced a large field of competitors. Dukakis drew upon the financial support of Greek-Americans nationwide and built skillfully on his Massachusetts base to raise more money than any of his competitors. Early successes in New England primary elections gave him adequate momentum to win the nomination. In the general election campaign, however, Dukakis, for the first time in his life, faced an electorate that was not mostly or entirely Democratic. He refused to answer (as beneath notice) George Bush's well-orchestrated attacks on him and on selected aspects of his record. In other respects his campaign was not well organized or well executed and, although he did far better on election day than had any Democrat running for President since 1976, he nonetheless lost and turned his attention once again to the govenorship.

See also: George Bush, Election of 1976, John F. Kennedy

Nelson W. Polsby

John Foster Dulles (1888–1959)

Secretary of State during the Eisenhower administration. John Foster Dulles was born in Washington, D.C., and educated at Princeton University, the Sorbonne, and the George Washington University Law School. His grandfather was John W. Foster and his uncle, Robert Lansing, both Secretaries of State—a position held by John Foster Dulles himself in the 1950s. He joined the distinguished law firm of Sullivan and Cromwell and launched his diplomatic career. The son of a Presbyterian clergyman, Dulles remained active in the Federal Council of Churches and served as the chairman of the Commission on a Just and Durable Peace. Following several minor diplomatic activities, Dulles attended the Versailles Peace Conference after World War I to draft reparations sections. An admirer of Woodrow Wilson, both as his Princeton teacher and for his moralism in international affairs, Dulles wrote with the distinct didactic tone of Presbyterianism. Through his diplomatic efforts and legal work, he became a renowned expert on international relations.

Dulles helped guide the Republican Party toward internationalism during World War II, advised the American delegation to the United Nations Conference at San Francisco, was appointed delegate to the United Nations, served as a Republican adviser to Secretaries of State Edward Stettinius, James Byrnes, George Marshall, and Dean Acheson, and negotiated the Japanese Peace Treaty. Following a brief stint in the Senate, to which he was not reelected, Dulles became Secretary of State for President Dwight D. Eisenhower in 1953.

Dulles's service as Secretary was largely as a caretaker of the Cold War. He called for the liberation of Eastern European satellites but did nothing in the face of the East German revolt or the movement of Russian troops into Hungary to crush a rebellion there. He advocated "brinkmanship," or the use of atomic diplomacy, to soften Eisenhower's reduction of the defense budget, but the affect was to increase the threat of nuclear war. He acted frequently in America's interest without consulting her allies. He negotiated the Southeast Asia Treaty Organization and paved the way for the Vietnam War by lack of realism in Indo-China. He betrayed France, Great Britain, and Israel by demanding withdrawal of their troops from Egypt; then pushed Egypt to the Russian side by refusing to finance the Aswan Dam. He ignored the needs of the Third World and supported colonialism. His moralism fueled his extreme position as a cold warrior, and instead of finding areas of agreement and negotiation with the Soviets, he intensified differences, leaving an undistinguished record.

See also: Dwight D. Eisenhower, United Nations

C. David Tompkins

REFERENCES

Beal, John Robinson. 1957. *John Foster Dulles.* New York: Harper.

Dulles, John Foster. 1939. *War, Peace, and Change.* New York: Macmillan.

———. 1950. *War or Peace.* New York: Macmillan.

Gerson, Louis L. 1967. *John Foster Dulles.* New York: Cooper Square Publishers.

Hoopes, Townsend. 1973. *The Devil and John Foster Dulles.* Boston: Little, Brown.

Pruessen, Ronald W. 1982. *John Foster Dulles: The Road to Power.* New York: Free Press.

Dunn v. Blumstein
405 U.S. 355 (1972)

In *Dunn v. Blumstein*, the Supreme Court invalidated state-imposed durational residency requirements for residents who wished to vote in state and local elections. The Court found that durational residency requirements force a choice between exercising the right to vote and the right to unimpeded interstate travel—rights that the Court had previously determined in *Reynolds v. Sims* [377 U.S. 533 (1964)] and *Shapiro v. Thompson* [394 U.S. 6181 (1969)] to be fundamental. The Court ruled that citizens should not be forced to choose between fundamental rights unless there exists an overriding state interest that cannot be achieved by any less restrictive means.

In *Dunn*, a new resident of Tennessee was prohibited from registering to vote because Tennessee law required a resident to live in the state for one year prior to the election in which he wished to participate. The plaintiff in *Dunn* challenged the state's authority to restrict access to the ballot box by treading on the fundamental right to unrestricted interstate travel. The Supreme Court determined that if the residency requirement were to pass constitutional muster, the state had to demonstrate that the requirement served a significant state interest with the least possible restriction on the exercise of fundamental rights.

While the *Dunn* Court did not doubt that the states could impose certain reasonable restrictions on the electoral franchise, it found that the durational residency requirements exceeded the permissible latitude. The requirements discriminated against new residents by denying citizens the right to vote based entirely upon the length of their stay within the state. The *Dunn* Court made clear that it was not calling into question the ability of a state to require that voters be bona fide residents of that state, but rather, it was the requirement that bona fide residents live in the state for a pre-ordained period of time that was suspect.

In support of its requirement, Tennessee asserted that it had important interests in preventing electoral fraud and in assuring that the electorate be informed and knowledgeable about community matters. The *Dunn* Court agreed that the state's interest in preventing electoral fraud was indeed significant; nonetheless, the Court invalidated the law based upon its finding that the means employed to achieve the interest were unrefined and imprecise.

If the *Dunn* Court was unpersuaded by the state's proposition that purity at the ballot box could only be maintained by durational residency requirements, it was moved even less by the state's alleged interest in assuring that the electorate be informed and knowledgeable. The state claimed that the durational residency requirement was a mechanism to assure that new voters were adequately sensitized to local issues and points of view, and hence more likely to cast a knowledgeable ballot. The *Dunn* Court found that not only was the state interest in assuring an informed electorate not compelling but also that such an interest was tantamount to requiring that voters have a common viewpoint on community matters. The Court found that such an interest was impermissible and insignificant. Even if the state's interests were significant, the Court held that the durational residency requirements had to be invalidated because it was a crude means of achieving those interests.

Dunn made clear that legislation which restricts fundamental rights is constitutionally defective unless the state enacting the legislation can establish that the legislation is the only reasonable method of achieving an overriding government interest. Since *Dunn*, states have been prevented from restricting access to the ballot box based upon the length of a bona fide resident's stay in a given state. States may close voter registration to *all* residents far enough in advance of an election to afford ample opportunity to verify questionable voter registrations. The Supreme Court, while not prescribing specific periods of time, has indicated that 30 to 50 days would be appropriate.

Dunn establishes the high priority that the Court places on the right to vote and the right to move freely across state lines. More significantly, *Dunn* makes clear that states may not enact laws forcing citizens to have to choose between fundamental rights.

Morton A. Brody

Maurice Duverger (1917–)

French student of political parties. Maurice Duverger was professor of political sociology at the University of Paris from 1955 to 1985 and the founder and director of the Center for the Comparative Analysis of Political Systems at the Sorbonne. Author of numerous books on comparative and French government and politics, Duverger is best known for his seminal study *Les Partis Politiques* published in 1951 and translated into English in 1954. In that pioneering work, Duverger developed broad categories for the study of parties and party systems, identified the various factors that affected their development, and toward both objectives, drew illustrations from a wide range of political systems, both democratic and nondemocratic.

In addition to the "law" that bears his name, Duverger's work is perhaps best known for distinctions drawn between political parties according to the nature of their organization. Central to that discussion is the contrast between loosely structured "cadre-type" organizations (characteristic of parties in the United States and of conservative and liberal parties in Europe) and the highly structured working-class, Socialist parties. Duverger regarded the latter type of party as the most modern, developed type, and he predicted that this organizational form would be the one that other democratic parties would be forced to adopt out of necessity ("contagion from the left").

See also: Duverger's Law

Howard Scarrow

REFERENCES

Duverger, Maurice. 1954. *Political Parties*. New York: Wiley.

Epstein, Leon. 1967. *Political Parties in Western Democracies*. New York: Praeger .

Duverger's Law

In his book *Political Parties* (first published in 1951 as *Les Partis Politiques*), Maurice Duverger hypothesized that the single-member district plurality system of legislative elections "favors the two-party system." He referred to the relationship as one that "approaches" a "sociological law." Duverger contrasted the plurality system with two other election systems: proportional representation and second-ballot run-off systems. Both systems, he argued, "favored" a multiparty system. Although Duverger did not, in his initial volume, use the term "law" to describe these latter two relationships, he made clear in later writings that he considered all three relationships to constitute a "threefold sociological law"; each, he argued, "tends to lead to the formation of" a particular type of party system. Many political scientists before Duverger had observed the relationships between election systems and party systems, but Duverger was the first to use the term "law" to describe them.

As will be seen by the words he chose, Duverger stated the three relationships in cautious terms, making no attempt to identify conditions that may be necessary or sufficient for particular types of party systems to arise or for them to be maintained. Instead, he emphasized that many factors affect the nature of a nation's party system.

Cross-national testing has confirmed the strong relationship between the plurality system and the two-party system; among modern democracies only Canada and India present major exceptions. In addition to these macro-level studies, students of rational-choice theory have explained the relationship in terms of incentives and disincentives offered by the plurality system to voters and to party leaders.

See also: Single-Member District

Howard Scarrow

REFERENCES

Duverger, Maurice. 1954. *Political Parties*. New York: Wiley.

———. 1986. "Duverger's Law: Forty Years Later." In Bernard Grofman and Arend Lijphart, eds. *Electoral Laws and Their Political Consequences*. New York: Agathon Press.

Rae, Douglas. 1971. *The Political Consequences of Electoral Laws*. New Haven: Yale U. Pr.

Riker, William. 1982. "The Two-Party System and Duverger's Law: An Essay on the History of Political Science." 76 *American Political Science Review* 753.

E

Eagle Forum

Founded in 1975, this conservative organization is perhaps best known for its opposition to the Equal Rights Amendment (ERA) and for its outspoken founder and president, Phyllis Schlafly. The Eagle Forum, with a membership of about 80,000, is part of a larger family of like-minded groups, including the Eagle Forum Education and Legal Defense Fund, Stop ERA, and the Eagle Forum Political Action Committee. These groups support private enterprise, a strong national defense, and "pro-family" issues, including increases in tax exemptions for children, unfair tax discrimination against the "traditional" family, and strengthening parents' and pupils' rights in education. The Forum also bestows a "Fulltime Homemaker Award" and publishes the *Phyllis Schlafly Report*.

The origins and prominence of the Eagle Forum can be traced to the rise, fall, and rise again of conservatives in the Republican Party. An early 1960s conservative tide in the GOP, which resulted in the nomination of Barry Goldwater for President in 1964, also carried Phyllis Schlafly to the first vice presidency of the National Federation of Republican Women. (Schlafly authored *A Choice Not an Echo*, a book supporting Goldwater's candidacy.) Goldwater's overwhelming defeat, however, weakened the position of conservatives within the party hierarchy; Schlafly eventually lost a bitterly contested floor fight for the Federation's presidency at its 1967 convention. Schlafly then established a new, more conservative group called The Eagles Are Flying. She also founded the Eagles Trust Fund, and later the Eagle Forum.

Schlafly and the Eagles vigorously opposed the Equal Rights Amendment. The organization claimed ERA would require women to serve in the armed forces in combat, make a wife responsible for providing 50 percent of the financial support for her family, legalize homosexual marriages, and require unisex toilets in public places. The time limit for approval of the amendment by the states, set to expire in 1979 but extended by Congress, eventually ran out in 1982 three states short of the 38 necessary for ratification. The Eagles took some of the credit for its defeat.

See also: Election of 1964, Equal Rights Amendment, Barry Goldwater, National Federation of Republican Women, Political Action Committees, Phyllis Schlafly

Tom A. Kazee

REFERENCES

Boles, Janet K. 1979. *The Politics of the Equal Rights Amendment*. White Plains, NY: Longman.

Schlafly, Phyllis. 1977. *The Power of the Positive Woman*. New Rochelle, NY: Arlington House.

Thomas F. Eagleton (1929–)

Three-term Democratic Senator from Missouri. Thomas Francis Eagleton was the first vice presidential candidate to withdraw from a presidential campaign. Eagleton received a B.A. from Amherst College in 1950 and a law degree from Harvard University in 1953. Running as a Democrat in 1956, he was elected prosecutor in St. Louis. From 1961 to 1968, he was lieutenant governor of the state. In 1968 Eagleton ran for the Senate, defeating incumbent Senator Edward V. Long in the Democratic primary, and then with a campaign based on opposition to the Vietnam War, he bested nine-term Republican

Congressman Thomas Curtis in the general election. During his Senate career, Eagleton opposed increases in military expenditures and supported the causes of organized labor and increased federal spending for education and health programs. At the Democratic convention in July 1972, Eagleton was selected by George McGovern, the Democratic presidential nominee, to be his Vice President even though McGovern's advisers knew that Eagleton had been treated for depression. When this information was made public, McGovern said that he was "1,000 per cent for Tom Eagleton and I have no intention of dropping him from the ticket." But on July 31, with controversy surrounding Eagleton's competence supposedly jeopardizing the McGovern campaign, Eagleton resigned from the ticket. He was never damaged in Missouri or in the Senate. He co-sponsored the War Powers Act of in 1973, and by his retirement in 1987, he had earned the respect of his Senate colleagues for his honesty and integrity.

See also: George McGovern, Vietnam War as a Political Issue

Thomas J. Baldino

REFERENCES

Eagleton, Thomas F. 1974. *War and Presidential Power.* New York: Liveright.

White, Theodore H. 1973. *The Making of the President 1972.* New York: Bantam Books.

James O. Eastland (1904–1986)

Six-term Senator from Mississippi. James O. Eastland led southern resistance against civil rights for Blacks for nearly 40 years. He began this resistance at the 1944 Democratic National Convention by protesting the party's promise of equal rights for African-Americans. Four years later, he and other southerners bolted the party because of the inclusion of a civil rights plank in the platform. These bolters (called Dixiecrats) held a convention in 1948 in Birmingham at which they nominated South Carolina's Strom Thurmond for President and Mississippi's Frank Wright for Vice President. Eastland accompanied Wright to Birmingham and played an important role in the convention.

In the 1950s, southern politics turned even more resolutely on the issue of race. In 1954 Eastland and other segregationists organized the Federation for Constitutional Government Convention in Memphis where they planned their opposition to integration. The same year Eastland supported the formation of the Citi-

zens' Council in Indianola, Mississippi. This organization soon spread across the South, leading white opposition to Black protest. Two years later, he became chairman of the Senate Judiciary Committee, from whose leadership he defeated many civil rights bills.

Even with the increase of African-American protest in the 1960s, Eastland encouraged (white) Citizens' Councils to continue opposing integration locally while he fought it in the Senate. Taking this stand, he won reelection in 1966 and 1972. Eastland retired in 1978 after completing his sixth consecutive Senate term.

See also: Strom Thurmond

Henry J. Walker, Jr.

REFERENCES

Lamis, Alexander P. 1984. *The Two-Party South.* New York: Oxford U. Pr.

Sherrill, Robert. 1968. "Jim Eastland: Child of Scorn." In *Gothic Politics in the Deep South: Stars of the New Confederacy.* New York: Grossman.

John Henry Eaton (1790–1856)

A strategist, organizer, and propagandist for Andrew Jackson. Born near Scotland Neck, North Carolina, John Henry Eaton settled in Tennessee, was admitted to the state bar, and was elected to the state legislature in 1815 and 1816. From 1821 to 1829, he served as a U.S. Senator and thereafter held office as Secretary of War (1829–1831), territorial governor of Florida (1834–1836), and minister to Spain (1836–1840).

Early on, Eaton devoted his talents to furthering the career of General Andrew Jackson, completing a laudatory biography of Jackson in 1817 and helping to engineer the general's 1823 election to the Senate and his 1824 presidential campaign. Although Jackson won the popular vote, the Electoral College results threw the election into the U.S. House, which selected John Quincy Adams. In the wake of Jackson's controversial defeat, Eaton and others formed a campaign organization that would not only elect Jackson in 1828 but lay the foundation for the Democratic Party. Eaton wrote political propaganda; assisted in buying a newspaper for use as a campaign organ; and helped to build a sophisticated, centrally coordinated network of state and local Jackson supporters around the country.

Rewarded by Jackson with a Cabinet position as Secretary of War, Eaton ran afoul of the political struggle between President Jackson and Vice President John Calhoun. Peggy Eaton, John's wife, suffered systematic snubs by all the ladies of the administration—Mrs. Calhoun leading the pack. Mrs. Eaton allegedly had an affair with John Eaton while still married to another man. Jackson defended Peggy Eaton's good name, but Eaton was forced to resign as Secretary of War in 1831.

See also: John Quincy Adams, John Calhoun, Elections of 1824 and 1828, Electoral College System, Andrew Jackson

Elaine K. Swift

REFERENCES

Remini, Robert V. 1977. *Andrew Jackson and the Course of American Empire, 1767–1821*. New York: Harper & Row.

———. 1981. *Andrew Jackson and the Course of American Freedom, 1822–1832*. New York: Harper & Row.

———. 1984. *Andrew Jackson and the Course of American Democracy, 1833–1845*. New York: Harper & Row.

George F. Edmunds (1828–1919)

United States Senator from Vermont. George Franklin Edmunds was born in Richmond, Vermont, of Quaker parentage. Because of childhood ill health, he was educated by private tutors and, later, largely by his own direction. He read law, was admitted to the Vermont bar in 1849, and subsequently relocated to Burlington where he maintained a home for many years.

Entering politics, Edmunds served for five years (1854–1859) in Vermont's lower house and for two years (1861–1862) in the state senate. When Vermont's incumbent U.S. Senator Solomon Foot died in March 1866, Edmunds, a Republican, was appointed to complete the term. He remained in the Senate for 25 years.

During Edmunds's tenure, Congress confronted momentous issues, and Edmunds played important roles in several of them. On his second day in office, he cast the deciding vote to override Andrew Johnson's veto of the Civil Rights Act of 1866. He chaired the committee on procedure for Johnson's impeachment trial and, subsequently, voted for conviction. During the disputed election of 1876, he authored the bill establishing the Electoral Commission. He also authored or helped secure enactment of other key measures of the era including the Ku Klux Klan Act (1872), the Civil Rights Act (1875), the Electoral Count Act (1887), and the Sherman Antitrust Act (1890), of which he was the principal author.

Edmunds's impressive skills as a constitutional lawyer earned him the respect of his colleagues, but his sharp tongue and aloof demeanor denied him their affection.

See also: Solomon Foot, Andrew Johnson, Ku Klux Klan, Sherman Antitrust Act

John F. Coleman

REFERENCES

Benedict, Michael Les. 1973. *The Impeachment and Trial of Andrew Johnson*. New York: Norton.

India Edwards (1895–1990)

Leader of the Women's Division of the Democratic National Committee. India Edwards became a model to subsequent generations of Democratic and Republican party women because of her success in securing presidential appointments of women.

Edwards's effectiveness stemmed from President Truman's trust in her loyalty to him. During the 1944 campaign, when Truman ran as Franklin D. Roosevelt's vice presidential candidate, Edwards was one of the few DNC workers who included Truman's name in speeches and publicity releases. When political pundits deemed Truman a sure loser in his 1948 race for President, Edwards steadfastly voiced her certainty that he would win. In the 1948 campaign, Edwards mobilized the women's vote for the Democrats through campaign schools for women volunteers, which included "Housewives for Truman" trailers and the widespread distribution of literature. In October 1951 Truman offered to name her chair of the DNC—a first for a woman of either party—but Edwards declined, believing that she would be more effective in the Women's Division. She later characterized the decision as "one of the great mistakes of my life."

Indeed, acting on behalf of Democratic Party women who viewed appointments as the crucial reward and incentive for loyal party service, Edwards saw to it that Truman surpassed Franklin Roosevelt in his appointments of women. Her tactics included proposing an exceptionally well qualified woman for almost every specific vacant post, getting the requisite political clearances herself, and then, after the appointment was made, ensuring that the President received publicity for having done it. During Truman's 8 years in office, he named 18 women to Senate-confirmed appointments (15 of them after 1948), including 9 to posts never before held by women, among them Assistant Secretary of Defense Anna Rosenberg and Ambassador to Denmark Eugenie Anderson. In addition, Truman placed 200 women in posts that did not require Senate confirmation.

A Tennessee native, Edwards worked as a reporter in Chicago for many years before moving to Washington and entering politics. Edwards began work with the DNC as a volunteer at the Women's Division during World War II, becoming the division's executive secretary in 1945 and its executive director in 1948. Edwards was elected vice chair of the DNC in 1950 (a post she held until 1956), but she left the staff of the DNC in 1953 after the Women's Division (over her objections) was abolished.

Edwards remained active in Democratic politics for two decades more, becoming campaign director for Averell Harriman's try for the Democratic nomination for President in 1956. In the 1960 primary campaign, during which she supported Lyndon Johnson, Edwards made herself persona non grata by announcing to the press that John Kennedy had Addison's disease. When Johnson became President, he had her named special consultant to the Secretary of Labor for youth employment, and Edwards regained some of her access to the White House, using it to continue her championship of appointments for Democratic women. In 1972 she chaired a fundraising committee for the Democratic candidate, George McGovern. Edwards married three times and raised two children, one of whom died in World War II.

Throughout her career, Edwards saw her mission as twofold: electing Democrats and raising the status of women within the party. Edwards displayed less interest in specific policy issues concerning women than in the appointment of women to government posts. In pursuing this tack, India Edwards won the support and affection of women throughout the Democratic Party and the respect of women Republicans as well.

See also: Lyndon B. Johnson, John F. Kennedy, Franklin D. Roosevelt, Harry S Truman

Cynthia A. Harrison

REFERENCES

Edwards, India. 1977. *Pulling No Punches: Memoirs of a Woman in Politics.* New York: Putnam.

Harrison, Cynthia. 1988. *On Account of Sex: The Politics of Women's Issues, 1945–1968.* Berkeley: U. of California Pr.

"India Edwards' Oral History Interview." 1969. Harry S Truman Library, Independence, Missouri.

"India Edwards' Oral History Interview." 1969. Lyndon Baines Johnson Library, Austin, Texas.

Dwight D. Eisenhower (1890–1969)

Military hero in World War II and twice President of the United States. From Abilene, Kansas, to the heights of military and political authority, Dwight David Eisenhower had a public career that reads like a storybook. Until he was 50 years old, Eisenhower's life attracted little notice. A student of more athletic than academic skills at West Point, "Ike" served as a junior officer in World War I and toiled through a typical variety of assignments in the scaled-down Army between the wars. In 1941 he achieved some notice for his role in war-game exercises in Louisiana and then his military/political career rocket took off.

Eisenhower's reputation as a skillful organizer of military campaigns and his special skills in the politics of military alliances brought him increasingly broad responsibilities after the United States entered World War II. President Franklin Roosevelt placed him in charge of the planning and execution of the allied invasion of France, and his name and face quickly became important national symbols. Eisenhower emerged from Wold War II a general of the Army and a great American hero.

In the immediate postwar years, he served as Army chief of staff. In the early months of 1948, a possible presidential candidacy for Eisenhower seemed likely. But Eisenhower had no political record, nor at that point any political aspirations. He made it clear before the 1948 primaries that he would not run for President that year and shortly thereafter accepted an invitation to become president of Columbia University.

After two and a half years at Columbia and a year as supreme commander of NATO forces in Europe, Eisenhower was more receptive to renewed appeals to be a presidential candidate in 1952. Without actively campaigning for the Republican nomination, Eisenhower won a narrow victory over Senator Robert Taft (R-Ohio) at the Republican National Convention.

His nomination secured, Eisenhower selected the young California Senator Richard M. Nixon as his running mate. Their campaign was a call for the country to return to the Republican "middle way" after 20 years of Democratic leadership. Eisenhower was especially effective in playing upon national fatigue with American involvement in the war in Korea. He pledged that, if elected, "I will go to Korea." No further details of the Korean itinerary emerged, but given the state of Eisenhower's reputation, his pledge was enough to lead many Americans to believe that his election would bring a swift resolution of the conflict there.

Eisenhower and Nixon won a decisive victory over their Democratic opponents, Governor Adlai Stevenson of Illinois and Senator John Sparkman of Alabama, garnering 55 percent of the popular vote and 442 of the 531 electoral votes. Eisenhower ran strongly everywhere, even showing surprising strength for a Republican in what had long been regarded as the solid Democratic South. Eisenhower's victory also helped Republicans win control of both houses of Congress. "I like Ike" was the national watchword.

The first Eisenhower term was marked by an end to the war in Korea; the rise and fall of Senator Joseph McCarthy (R-Wisc.) and his attacks on Communists in government; new crises abroad in Indochina, Formosa, and the Suez Canal; and the granting of statehood to Alaska and Hawaii.

Eisenhower's decision to run for reelection was delayed by a heart attack that he suffered in September 1955. His recovery was swift, however, and he and Nixon ran for reelection in 1956, this time facing Stevenson and Senator Estes Kefauver of Tennessee. The President was reelected in a landslide of enormous proportions, winning 57 percent of the popular vote and 457 of the 531 electoral votes.

Eisenhower was the first President affected by the Twenty-second Amendment, limiting Presidents to two elected terms. Hence he began his second term knowing it would be his last. The lame duck status that that restriction created, combined with the President's advancing age, recurring health problems, and lack of an ambitious political agenda, all resulted in the emergence of few significant political initiatives from the White House. New civil rights acts in 1957 and 1960 were stimulated largely by congressional action. So, too, was the landmark National Aeronautics and Space Act of 1958.

The last two years of Eisenhower's presidency were a time of uncommon congressional activism. The Democrats gained 15 seats in the Senate in the 1958 midterm elections. A number of Democratic Senators were positioning themselves for presidential candidacies in 1960, and observers pointed to a significant leadership vacuum in the White House. All of this executive inactivity gave new energy to the Congress and made the late 1950s a time in which the Congress played an unusually important role in setting the national agenda.

Eisenhower left the presidency in 1961 with his national popularity largely intact. Historians of his era often described his administration as a time when little of consequence occurred and have characterized Eisenhower's approach to the presidency as inactive and detached. More recent revisionism has suggested that Eisenhower's unique political style was more engaged and effective than it appeared, that he was especially skilled at initiating actions or preventing problems while letting others get the credit. Fred Greenstein has labeled Eisenhower's style the "hidden hand presidency."

The debate goes on, and Eisenhower's reputation as President is far from settled. Nobody doubts, however, Ike's contemporary popularity; few national figures in the twentieth century have been able to match the breadth or the depth of the affection in which Eisenhower was held by the American people. His electoral successes were a tribute less to his mastery of political strategy than to a reputation and a personality that swept traditional political obstacles aside.

See also: L. Sherman Adams, Civil Rights Legislation, Election of 1952, Joseph McCarthy, Richard Nixon, Adlai Stevenson II, Robert Taft

G. Calvin Mackenzie

REFERENCES

Adams, Sherman. 1961. *Firsthand Report.* New York: Harper.

Ambrose, Stephen. 1984. *Eisenhower, The President.* New York: Simon & Schuster.

Eisenhower, Dwight D. 1963. *Mandate for Change, 1953–1956.* New York: Doubleday.

———. 1965. *Waging Peace, 1956–1961.* New York: Doubleday.

Greenstein, Fred I. 1982. *The Hidden-Hand Presidency.* New York: Basic Books.

Election of 1792

In this election, the first party system was in the process of formation. During President George Washington's first term, Secretary of the Treasury Alexander Hamilton's program for the funding and assumption of state and national debts and his establishment of a national bank had been strongly opposed in the Cabinet by Secretary of State Thomas Jefferson. These issues, together with the problem of evolving a sound foreign policy in the wake of the French Revolution and subsequent European wars, generated considerable social, sectional, and political disagreement in the nation at large.

Washington continued to think of politics in classical, Whig terms; the policy depended upon the virtue of its citizenry, and thus warring political factions espousing interest above virtue endangered the young Republic. While no institutional parties or campaigns emerged in the months before the election, the nation was clearly moving toward a more modern political system. Unwilling to preside over a divided nation that could not be relied upon to rally behind his administration, Washington wished to retire. But leaders from both sides begged him to remain, legitimately arguing that his absence would widen divisions and polarize factions in a nation still too weak to withstand such pressures. Washington won all of the presidential votes in all 15 states, but nascent party divisions were reflected in the votes for Vice President: John Adams won a clear majority and held New England and Pennsylvania, but Virginia, North Carolina, New York, and Rhode Island backed either DeWitt Clinton or Thomas Jefferson.

See also: John Adams, DeWitt Clinton, Alexander Hamilton, Thomas Jefferson, George Washington

Simon P. Newman

REFERENCES

Chambers, William N. 1963. *Political Parties in a New Nation: The American Experience, 1776–1809.* New York: Oxford U. Pr.

Charles, Joseph E. 1956. *The Origins of the American Party System: Three Essays.* Williamsburg, VA: Institute of Early American History and Culture.

Cunliffe, Marcus. 1971. "Elections of 1789 and 1792." In Arthur M. Schlesinger, Jr., and Fred L. Israel, eds. *History of American Presidential Elections, 1789–1968.* New York: Chelsea House.

Cunningham, Nobel E., Jr. 1965. *The Making of the American Party System, 1789–1809.* Englewood Cliffs, NJ: Prentice-Hall.

Formisano, Ronald. 1974. "Deferential-Participant Politics: The Early Republic's Political Culture, 1789–1840." 68 *American Political Science Review* 473–487.

Election of 1796

It was during George Washington's second term as President that the first American party system was born. When the wars of the French Revolution began in 1793, Washington adhered to Alexander Hamilton's Federalist policy, which proposed an American neutrality that, in terms of trade, tended to favor Great Britain above France. Democrats firmly resisted the abandonment of America's revolutionary ally, now a sister republic, and unprecedented criticism of Washington mounted, reaching its highest level when arch-Federalist John Jay negotiated a commercial treaty with Great Britain in 1795.

In an attempt to avoid a divisive contested election, Washington delayed announcing his decision not to seek reelection until mid-September 1796. Nevertheless, campaigning was fierce, with Democratic societies and newspapers actively supporting Thomas Jefferson and Aaron Burr. These opponents criticized Washington and the Federalists for pursuing aristocratic and undemocratic policies, arguing that they had betrayed the ideals of the American Revolution. Vice President John Adams and Thomas Pinckney were the Federalist candidates. They saw in the raucous campaigning and crowd actions of the Democrats the threat of anarchy and the demise of the Republic.

The issues, policies, and sectional and class affiliations that were to distinguish the parties were revealed in the election of 1796. Drawing much of their support from the rural South and West and from the laborers and mechanics of the urban East, the Democrats celebrated the rights of the "independent" American citizen. Opposing entrenched financial and political interests, they favored small government, low tariffs, and support of the French republic. The Federalists had a more traditional, elitist conception of government by the "natural elite" of society, and the radical French Revolution had increased their fears of democracy. They favored a strong central government, one that would encourage the development of national commerce and industry with the aid of protective tariffs and good relations with Great Britain. Most of their support came from the mercantile and professional interests in large towns and cities, although traditional loyalty to Washington, who clearly identified himself with the Federalists in his Farewell Address, won the party votes from all quarters.

In was unclear to contemporaries—who were not yet willing to think of opposition as a legitimate activity in American politics—whether the Republic could survive the transfer of the presidency from Washington to a successor. In an attempt to divert Electoral College votes from his rival John Adams to the more amenable Pinckney, Hamilton succeeded in weakening his party's hold on power, causing dissension within its ranks and enabling a Democrat to win the vice presidency. Adams won the election with 71 votes, Jefferson the vice presidency with 68 votes, followed by Pinckney with 59, Burr with 30, and 48 votes were split among other candidates. The final result did much to encourage a smooth transfer of power: Jefferson assured Adams of his support, and the two parties were temporarily united in one administration. The issues that separated them, however, were not so easily dismissed and would plague the new nation for the next four years.

See also: John Adams, Aaron Burr, Federalist Party, Alexander Hamilton, Charles Pinckney

Simon P. Newman

REFERENCES

Ames, William E., and S. Dean Olson. 1963. "Washington's Farewell, the French Alliance, and the Election of 1796." 63 *Mississippi Valley Historical Review* 641.

Hofstadter, Richard. 1969. *The Idea of a Party System: The Rise of Legitimate Opposition in the United States, 1780–1840*. Berkeley: U. of California Pr.

Link, Eugene P. 1942. *Democratic-Republican Societies, 1790–1800*. New York: Columbia U. Pr.

Young, Alfred F. 1964. "The Mechanics and the Jeffersonians: New York, 1789–1801." 5 *Labor History* 247–276.

Election of 1800

This election, between Federalist John Adams and Republican Thomas Jefferson, was one of the two most critical presidential elections in American history; it was second only to the election of 1860 that polarized the nation and sent Abraham Lincoln to the presidency and Americans off to fight a bloody civil war. Both elections occurred during times of extreme sectional hostilities and reflected an acutely divided polity along sectional lines. Both were also surrounded with rumors of violence and the dismemberment of the Union.

Jefferson's victory reflected the extreme sectional polarization in 1800, with the Virginian and his running mate Aaron Burr of New York receiving 53 of their 73 votes (72.6 percent) from the South, and 20 (27.4 percent) of their votes from the Middle Atlantic States of New York and Pennsylvania. Of Adams's 65 electoral votes, 56 (82.6 percent) were from New England and Middle Atlantic States, while only 9 (13.8 percent) were from the South.

Bred by mutual animus and mistrust, this political polarization was aggravated and intensified: the election of 1800 was the first time in American history that political power was to be transferred from one proto-party to another. One political scientist has called "the voluntary, peaceful transfer of vast powers from one set of committed leaders to another who by definition are adversaries . . . one of the most complex and mysterious phenomena in political life." Certainly, the questions raised by the prospect of the transfer of power in 1800 created among the participants a terrible uncertainty and anxiety about the future. Indeed, the British foreign minister wrote in the spring of 1800 that the "whole system of the American Government seems to me to be tottering to its foundations, and so far from being able to enforce upon the country good faith towards foreign powers, I much doubt their power of maintaining internal tranquility." With such a stark confrontation between the two sectionally based proto-parties, the conventional historical wisdom that holds that the "first national parties . . . brought new order into the conduct of government" simply misreads the case.

The tie vote in the Electoral College between Jefferson and his running mate, Burr, further aggravated the crisis. Burr infuriated his Republican allies by refusing to disavow presidential ambitions, and the Federalists manipulated events in a desperate effort to retain power. Finally, after 36 ballots in the House of Representatives, Jefferson was chosen President because a number of Federalists, fearing political chaos and possible civil war if the deadlock were to be continued, withdrew their support from Burr.

Jefferson and the Republicans' accession to power in 1801 did not really mark "the growing acceptance of the legitimacy of opposition and idea of party." It was not until the Federalists had disappeared, the Republicans had established a national political hegemony, and mass democratic politics had been introduced during the Jacksonian era, that Americans finally accepted the legitimacy of opposition and the positive virtues of two-party politics.

See also: John Adams, Aaron Burr, Election of 1860, Electoral College, Federalist Party, Thomas Jefferson

James R. Sharp

REFERENCES

Banning, Lance. 1980. *The Jeffersonian Persuasion: Evolution of a Party Ideology*. Ithaca: Cornell U. Pr.

Chambers, William N. 1963. *Political Parties in the New Nation: The American Experiences, 1776–1809*. New York: Oxford U. Pr.

Cunningham, Noble E., Jr. 1957. *The Jeffersonian Republicans: The Formation of Party Organization, 1789–1801*. Chapel Hill: U. of North Carolina Pr.

Goodman, Paul. 1967. "The First American Party System." In William Nesbit Chambers and Walter Dean Burnham, eds. *The American Party Systems: Stages of Political Development*. New York: Oxford U. Pr.

Grodzins, Morton. 1966. "Political Parties and the Crisis of Succession in the United States: The Case of 1800." In Joseph LaPalombara and Myron Weiner, eds. *Political Parties and Political Development*. Princeton: Princeton U. Pr.

Hoadley, John F. 1986. *Origins of American Political Parties, 1789–1803*. Lexington: U. Pr. of Kentucky.

Hofstadter, Richard. 1969. *The Idea of a Party System: The Rise of Legitimate Opposition in the United States, 1780–1840*. Berkeley: U. of California Pr.

Lipset, Seymour Martin. 1963. *The First New Nation: The United States in Historical and Comparative Perspective*. New York: Basic Books.

Election of 1812

The presidential election of 1812 was the nation's first wartime contest. Furthermore, it was the closest election since 1800 and the most partisan in sectional divisions before 1860. In 1812 the Virginia–New York alliance that had dominated Republican nominations for national office since 1796 had temporarily ended. DeWitt Clinton, mayor of New York City and lieutenant governor of the Empire State, led the opposition against President James Madison. The opposition resulted from growing northern disenchantment with the South's domination of the presidency and the resulting limited support for merchant and manufacturing interests. Basically, the sectional discontent arose from a growing conflict between two diverging political cultures. In the North this split manifested itself in a reinterpreted Republican ideology. Refuting a traditional Republican agrarian tenet, Clinton and his supporters believed commerce, manufacturing, and agriculture were equally important for the economic growth and prosperity of New York and the nation. Clinton's reinterpreted Republicanism primarily developed from the special social and economic conditions of New York and was at variance with the southern Republicans' belief that an agrarian-dominated society could best preserve public virtue.

Clinton's campaign strategy required support from Federalists and dissident Republicans. He did not receive the outright endorsement of the Federalist Party. But in September the Federalists convened a national convention in New York City to consider the selection of a presidential nominee. The Massachusetts Federalists led by Harrison Gray Otis maintained that no hope existed of electing a presidential candidate unless Federalists combined with dissident Republicans. Otis managed to get a resolution adopted opposing the nomination of a Federalist, and the delegates then agreed to give Clinton secret support instead of an outright endorsement. They further decided that the Federalist state organizations had to incite support for his candidacy. To Clinton, who might have alienated some dissident Republicans if he had associated himself too closely with Federalist policies, the convention's position gave him all that he could desire.

In comparison to Clinton's aggressive campaign, Madison's efforts seemed to lack vitality. The President principally relied on Republican newspapers to state his policies and differentiate him from Clinton. In particular, Madison believed the election would be a referendum on the war. The Madisonian press argued that only the reelection of the President could ensure the defense of the nation's honor by continuing the war against Great Britain.

The election involved 18 states with no uniform date for voting and no uniform method of choosing presidential electors. Clinton won impressive victories in seven states and split the vote in Maryland. But his failure to win Pennsylvania, Ohio, and North Carolina guaranteed his defeat in the closely contested and sectionally oriented election. Nationally, Madison won 128 electoral votes to Clinton's 89. Eighty of Clinton's electoral votes came from states north and east of the Delaware River, and 120 of Madison's were from states south and west of the Delaware.

See also: DeWitt Clinton, Federalist Party, James Madison

Steven E. Siry

REFERENCES

Risjord, Norman K. 1971. "Election of 1812." In Arthur M. Schlesinger, Jr., et al., eds. *History of American Presidential Elections, 1789–1968*. New York: McGraw-Hill.

Siry, Steven E. 1989. *DeWitt Clinton and the American Political Economy: Sectionalism, Politics, and Republican Ideology, 1787–1828*. New York: Peter Lang.

Election of 1824

This election marked the demise of the congressional caucus as the means for selecting candidates for the presidency. In addition, it was the second—and probably the last—to be decided by the House of Representatives in keeping with the provisions of the Twelfth Amendment.

The campaign began with President James Monroe's decision not to nominate a successor. At this point, three members of Monroe's Cabinet—Secretary of the Treasury William H. Crawford of Georgia, Secretary of War John C. Calhoun of South Carolina, and Secretary of State John Quincy Adams of Massachusetts—indicated their willingness to run, as did House

Speaker Henry Clay of Kentucky. A fifth candidate, Andrew Jackson of Tennessee, was nominated by various southerners and westerners even though the notoriously hot-tempered military hero lacked the administrative experience that before 1824 had been presumed a prerequisite for the office. No previous presidential campaign had involved so many prominent men.

Since the Federalist Party was now moribund, all of the candidates proclaimed themselves Republicans. In February 1824 the Virginia-born Crawford, heir to the so-called "Virginia Dynasty"—the clique of slaveholding planter-politicians that, with the single exception of John Adams, had controlled the presidency ever since the ratification of the Constitution—was officially nominated by a caucus of like-minded Congressmen. Since the caucus had come to be regarded as undemocratic, it was purposely avoided by many congressional Republicans. Its significance was further limited by Crawford's serious illness of the previous September; the caucus would remain insignificant throughout the campaign. Predictably, Crawford's nomination was opposed by the many newspaper editors opposed to his election and by all the other candidates. These criticisms would prove so effective that the caucus, previously the preferred device for selecting presidential candidates, was never revived. Each of the other candidates was nominated by locally based popular assemblies of one sort or another, a strategy greatly facilitated by the rapid improvements in communications and transportation, and, specifically, by the expansion of the postal system, the press, and the network of roads and canals.

The election had a largely sectional cast. Crawford and Calhoun were strongest in the South Atlantic states, Clay and Jackson in the Southwest, and Adams in New England. Frustrated by Jackson's popularity as a fellow southerner, Calhoun withdrew before the election, deciding instead to run as the vice presidential candidate for both Jackson and Adams. Predictably, the vote in the electoral college was sharply divided, with Jackson receiving 99 votes, Adams 84, Crawford 41, and Clay 37.

Since no candidate received a majority of the electoral votes, the election was thrown into the House, with Clay eliminated. Under the provisions of the Constitution, each state had a single vote, regardless of population. Unsurprisingly, Clay threw his support to Adams, who shared Clay's commitment to federally

sponsored internal improvements (the so-called "American System") and Adams won on the first ballot, with 13 votes to Jackson's 7 and Crawford's 4. Nonetheless, opposition Congressmen and editors, as well as Jackson himself, soon popularized the unsubstantiated charge that Adams and Clay had engaged in a "corrupt bargain," a charge that gained much of its force from Adams's decision to appoint Clay his Secretary of State. In the language of classical Republicanism, Adams had used his executive patronage to buy off the Speaker of the House—just as, in the eighteenth century, English prime minister Robert Walpole had "corrupted" Parliament.

Above all, the 1824 election illustrated the collapse of the gentry-based political order of the Founding Fathers. The revolutions in communications and transportation had rendered the caucus obsolete, creating the technical preconditions for the mass-based political order of the 1830s and beyond. Henceforth, all presidential campaigns acquired an ostensibly "popular" cast, a development that would culminate in the celebrated "log cabin and hard cider" campaign of 1840.

See also: John Quincy Adams, John C. Calhoun, Henry Clay, William H. Crawford, Andrew Jackson, James Monroe, Twelfth Amendment

Richard R. John

REFERENCES

Ames, William E., and S. Dean Olson. 1963. "Washington's Political Press and the Election of 1824." 40 *Journalism Quarterly* 343.

Formisano, Ronald P. 1974. "Deferential-Participant Politics: The Early Republic's Political Culture, 1789–1840." 68 *American Political Science Review* 437.

Hargreaves, Mary W. M. 1985. *The Presidency of John Quincy Adams.* Lawrence: U. Pr. of Kansas.

Hopkins, James F. 1971. "Election of 1824." In Arthur M. Schlesinger, Jr., et al., eds. *History of American Presidential Elections, 1789–1968.* New York: McGraw-Hill.

Morgan, William G. 1967. "John Quincy Adams Versus Andrew Jackson: Their Biographers and the 'Corrupt Bargain' Charge." 26 *Tennessee Historical Quarterly* 43.

Election of 1828

This presidential election marked a major turning point in American politics. On the surface, the campaign was perhaps the most vulgar and acrimonious in American history. The candidates—President John Quincy Adams of Massachusetts and popular military hero Andrew Jackson of Tennessee—were vilified by a partisan press more intent on exploiting scandal than on exploring the issues. Trumped-up charges of sexual impropriety figured prominently in the campaign: the church-going Jackson was unjustly branded a bigamist while, even more incredibly, the staid and moralistic Adams was portrayed as a pimp to the tsar of Russia.

But the campaign was hardly devoid of issues. Jackson's began in 1824, when he lost the presidency despite having won a plurality of both the electoral and popular vote. Drawing on the eighteenth-century classical Republican tradition, with its preoccupation with patronage and executive tyranny, pro-Jackson publicists Duff Green, Amos Kendall, and Isaac Hill, charged Adams with having made a "corrupt bargain" with Henry Clay and ridiculed the Adams administration's bold commitment to public works and energetic government. Though later historians have often termed Jackson in 1828 a "Democrat," his official campaign organ, Green's *United States Telegraph*, labeled him and his running mate, John C. Calhoun of South Carolina, the true "republican ticket." (The term "Democratic Party" was not regularly used until 1832.) Like Ronald Reagan in 1980, Jackson considered the incumbent government the problem, his election the solution.

Jackson won the election in a landslide, garnering 178 electoral votes to Adams's 83, and sweeping every state south of the Potomac and west of New Jersey. Jackson's percentage of the popular vote was unequaled by any presidential candidate in the nineteenth century. The social origins of Jackson's popularity have been a source of continuing controversy among historians. Frederick Jackson Turner thought him a westerner; Arthur Schlesinger, Jr., found him an ally of organized labor, small farmers, and immigrants with strong support in the eastern cities. Most recently, Edward Pessen and others have stressed Jackson's close ties to the slaveholding South Atlantic and Southwest. Significantly, Jackson publicist Duff Green was a rabidly proslavery Missourian with close ties to Calhoun, and the Jackson-Calhoun coalition marked the first (and only) time in American history that two major southern slaveholders ran together on the same ticket.

Jackson's victory owed much to basic changes in American society: new voting requirements increasing the size of the electorate; and, even more important, the nineteenth-century revolution in communications and transportation. Taking advantage of improvements in the postal

system, the press, and the road and canal network, Jackson's supporters established an unprecedented number of organizing committees and state nominating conventions. Probably the most important single accomplishment of the new party was its creation of an impressive array of newspapers designed to keep the electorate informed about national affairs—and, of course, to boost party-backed candidates.

Robert Remini, the leading student of this election, has estimated that his supporters had to raise approximately $1 million to elect Jackson President; Remini attributes Jackson's victory primarily to superior organization. Perhaps the most important organizer was Martin Van Buren of New York, a crafty and ambitious political strategist who successfully adapted the traditional gentry-based alliance of southern planters and so-called "plain republicans" of the North to the new circumstances of mass politics. The emergent two-party system, as Ronald Formisano has persuasively argued, was quite different from the two-party competition of Federalists and Republicans. Thus, the 1828 election marked the beginning of what historian Richard L. McCormick has termed the "party period" in American politics.

See also: John Quincy Adams, John C. Calhoun, Henry Clay, William Crawford, Andrew Jackson, Jacksonian Democracy, Martin Van Buren

Richard R. John

REFERENCES

Formisano, Ronald P. 1980. "Federalists and Republicans: Parties, Yes—System, No." In Paul Kleppner, ed. *The Evolution of American Electoral Systems.* Westport, CT: Greenwood.

Latner, Richard B. 1979. *The Presidency of Andrew Jackson: White House Politics, 1829–1838.* Athens: U. of Georgia Pr.

McCormick, Richard L. 1986. "The Party Period and Public Policy: An Exploratory Hypothesis." In *The Party Period and Public Policy: American Politics from the Age of Jackson to the Progressive Era.* New York: Oxford U. Pr.

Remini, Robert. 1963. *The Election of Andrew Jackson.* Philadelphia: Lippincott.

———. 1971. "Election of 1828." In Arthur M. Schlesinger, Jr., et al., eds. *History of American Presidential Elections, 1789–1968.* New York: McGraw-Hill.

Smith, Culver H. 1934. "Propaganda Techniques in the Jackson Campaign of 1828." 6 *East Tennessee Historical Society Publications* 44.

Election of 1844

One of the closest contests in American presidential history, the election of 1844 nonetheless carried serious consequences for the young American nation steadily dividing itself between the free and slave states. Democratic candidates James K. Polk and George M. Dallas defeated Whigs Henry Clay and Theodore Frelinghuysen by 170 to 105 electoral votes, winning a popular majority of just 38,181 of nearly 2.7 million votes cast. Polk lost his home state of Tennessee by 113 votes, reflecting the importance of party loyalties in antebellum American society.

Also noteworthy in this election is the nomination of slaveholders to the presidency by both major political parties. Rejecting the nominal Whig President John Tyler, the Whig convention meeting in Baltimore in May instead nominated party leader Henry Clay, a Kentucky slaveholder. Later in May in the same city, Democrats likewise passed over their former President, Martin Van Buren of New York, and selected instead the Tennessee slaveholder James K. Polk. Even the Liberty Party nominee, James G. Birney, had once been an Alabama slaveholder, although this abolitionist party candidate had voluntarily freed his slaves several years earlier.

Birney's presence on the northern ballot may have contributed to Polk's victory in the critical state of New York (with 36 electoral votes). Polk carried the Empire State by only 5,106 votes, while Birney won 15,812 New York votes. Most Liberty Party voters were former Whigs who might have been expected to favor Clay, although many abolitionists no doubt would have refused to support *any* slaveholder. Nearly as important as New York, Pennsylvania too went for Polk, but without help from the Liberty Party. During the campaign Polk wisely supported a "judicious" tariff, thus helping to secure the 26 electoral votes of protectionist Pennsylvania.

The most important national issue of the 1844 campaign was the westward expansion of the United States. Settlement of the Oregon boundary dispute with Great Britain proved less controversial than the issue of annexation of the slaveholding Texas Republic. Before the nominating conventions Clay and Democratic hopeful Van Buren had agreed to avoid the divisive issue, a joint decision that ultimately contributed to Van Buren's rejection by southern and western expansionists at the Democratic convention and Clay's subsequent defeat in the general election.

The Democratic call for the "reoccupation of Oregon and the reannexation of Texas" left Clay in a vulnerable position, fearful of losing support among either antislavery voters or proslavery forces favoring the annexation of Texas. In contrast to Polk's adept handling of the tariff issue and cautious silence on other matters, the effusive Clay uncharacteristically bungled the Texas question in a series of public letters first rejecting annexation, then seemingly reversing himself, before finally returning to his original position of opposing immediate annexation. In this case the famous orator and Whig Party leader fell victim to his own mistakes, boosting the chances of the lesser-known Polk, a former governor twice denied reelection.

Polk's victory ensured that the annexation of Texas would proceed and that the United States would pressure Great Britain into a settlement of the Oregon dispute. Although President Tyler initiated annexation of Texas, Polk's insistence on honoring Texas' claim of a border at the Rio Grande provoked war with Mexico. Because slaveholders had been so prominent in the efforts to gain Texas, antislavery forces in the North insisted on the Wilmot Proviso, a failed attempt to prohibit slavery's spread into the southwestern domain taken from Mexico. Southerners responded angrily to the Wilmot proposal, provoking a sectional debate in the late 1840s and early 1850s over the expansion of slavery to the western territories, a debate that contributed to the disruption of the nationally balanced Jacksonian party system, thus ultimately helping to trigger the Civil War.

See also: James G. Birney, Henry Clay, George Dallas, Liberty Party, James K. Polk, John Tyler, Martin Van Buren, Wilmot Proviso

Vernon L. Volpe

REFERENCES

Eaton, Clement. 1957. *Henry Clay and the Art of American Politics*. Boston: Little, Brown.

Fladeland, Betty L. 1955. *James Gillespie Birney: Slaveholder to Abolitionist*. Ithaca: Cornell U. Pr.

Merk, Frederick. 1972. *Slavery and the Annexation of Texas*. New York: Knopf.

Sellers, Charles. 1966. *James K. Polk: Continentalist*. Princeton: Princeton U. Pr.

———. 1985. "Election of 1844." In Arthur M. Schlesinger, Jr., et al., eds. *History of American Presidential Elections, 1789–1968*. New York: Chelsea House.

Election of 1848

The triumph of American arms in the Mexican War (1846–1848) yielded bountiful fruits of victory—an enormous expanse of land stretching from Texas to California. Yet this territorial acquisition also rekindled the issue of the expansion of slavery and threatened to splinter the major political parties along sectional lines. To preserve unity, Whigs and Democrats alike muddied the political waters in the presidential election of 1848.

Bypassing President James K. Polk, who had pledged himself to a single term, southern and western Democrats engineered the presidential and vice presidential nominations for Senator Lewis Cass of Michigan and General William Butler of Kentucky. Cass, a seasoned politician and clever opportunist, was widely known as the father of "squatter sovereignty" (later to be called "popular sovereignty"), a scheme whereby the settlers of a territory would themselves decide the question of the legality of slavery in that territory. Deliberately vague in details, it was equally alluring to both North and South. But while the Democrats endorsed Cass (distributing different campaign biographies in each section), the party platform stopped short of endorsing the plan and remained silent on the slavery issue.

Such confusion, evasiveness, and irony was matched, if not exceeded, by the Whigs. In selecting General Zachary Taylor for President, they nominated a hero of the recent war that most Whigs had excoriated. Careless in appearance, "Old Rough and Ready" was a wealthy Louisiana plantation owner (with over 100 slaves) who had neither held civil office nor ever voted in a national election. Meanwhile, northern Whigs arranged the vice presidential spot for New Yorker Millard Fillmore. Eager to dodge all troublesome issues, the Whigs adopted no platform, and Taylor steadfastly refused to comment on any current topics.

As a result, the time was ripe for a third-party coalition of antislavery forces. "Barnburning" Democrats, "Conscience" Whigs, and disaffected Liberty Party men all combined to support ex-President Martin Van Buren in the newly created Free Soil Party. With Charles Francis Adams as his running mate, Van Buren presided over an odd amalgam of negrophobes and racial equalitarians who unequivocally advocated the exclusion of slavery from the territories. Its slogan of "free soil, free speech, free labor, and free men" would soon be appropriated by a major new antislavery coalition—the Republican Party.

On election day, Taylor swept to victory by capturing 163 electoral votes and 1,360,967 popular votes to Cass's 127 electoral votes and 1,222,342 popular votes. Van Buren failed to carry any states while receiving 291,263 votes nationwide.

See also: Charles Francis Adams, Barnburners, William Butler, Lewis Cass, Conscience Whigs, Millard Fillmore, Free Soil Party, Liberty Party, James K. Polk, Zachary Taylor, Martin Van Buren

Karl E. Valois

REFERENCES

Blue, Frederick J. 1973. *The Free Soilers: Third Party Politics, 1848–1854.* Urbana: U. of Illinois Pr.

Hamilton, Holman. 1971. "Election of 1848." In Arthur M. Schlesinger, Jr., et al., eds. *History of American Presidential Elections, 1789–1968.* New York: Chelsea House.

Nevins, Allan. 1947. *Ordeal of the Union: Fruits of Manifest Destiny, 1847–1852.* New York: Scribner's.

Potter, David M. 1976. *The Impending Crisis, 1848–1861.* New York: Harper & Row.

Rayback, Joseph G. 1970. *Free Soil: The Election of 1848.* Lexington: U. Pr. of Kentucky.

Sewell, Richard H. 1976. *Ballots for Freedom: Antislavery Politics in the United States, 1837–1860.* New York: Oxford U. Pr.

Election of 1852

This presidential election was held against the backdrop of a tenuous national harmony. The Compromise of 1850 had succeeded in reducing some of the sectional antagonisms generated by the volatile issue of slavery. As northern and southern politicians prepared for the upcoming campaign, experienced leaders of both major parties resolved to maintain the fragile peace.

Assembling in Baltimore, the Democratic convention was hopelessly deadlocked through 48 roll calls. At one time or another, Lewis Cass, Stephen Douglas, and James Buchanan all held a lead. But none could muster a majority of the delegates, much less the two-thirds needed for the presidential nomination. On the next ballot, however, the Democrats shocked the nation by nominating the second "dark horse" candidate in American history—Franklin Pierce of New Hampshire. William R. King, a Senator from Alabama, was chosen as his running mate.

A former Senator and undistinguished veteran of the Mexican War, Pierce ("The Young Hickory of the Granite Hills") was handsome, amiable, and without enemies. Moreover, as a reputed "doughface"—a northerner with southern principles—he enjoyed widespread support below the Mason-Dixon line. With the acquiescence of many northern members, the Democrats once again became a united, intersectional party.

In what would be their last national convention, the Whigs, also meeting in Baltimore, faced a similar dilemma. Pushing aside President Millard Fillmore and Daniel Webster, they finally settled on a military hero of the Mexican War, General Winfield Scott, on the fifty-third ballot. William A. Graham of North Carolina received the vice presidential nomination. Pompous, vain, and haughty, Scott ("Old Fuss and Feathers") suffered greatly from his own political ineptitude. Although a Virginian—but not a slaveholder—he was unable to forestall a massive desertion of southern Whigs who questioned his devotion to southern interests. Clearly, the disorganized Whigs were on the brink of disaster.

The campaign itself was marked by a general disposition in both parties to avoid sectional controversy. The platforms of the Whigs and Democrats each endorsed the Compromise of 1850. As a result, the contest degenerated into a mudslinging attack on the candidates. Pierce was portrayed as a drunkard and a coward; Democrats , on the other hand, mocked Scott's pomposity while declaring, "We Polked 'em in '44, we'll Pierce 'em in '52." More noteworthy, the Whigs, branded with nativism, made their first concerted effort to court the German and Irish Catholic vote. For the most part, however, Catholic immigrants remained solidly in the ranks of the Democrats.

On election day, Pierce trounced Scott in the Electoral College, 254 to 42; the popular vote was closer, 1,601,117 to 1,385,453. Meanwhile, John P. Hale and the Free Soil Party, a coalition of antislavery forces, received 155,825 votes. The real significance of the election, however, lay not in Scott's personal defeat but in the nascent disintegration of the Whig Party. In its failure to unite both northern and southern wings, the Whig Party would soon vanish from the political scene.

See also: James Buchanan, Lewis Cass, Stephen Douglas, Millard Fillmore, Free Soil Party, John P. Hale, William R. King, Franklin Pierce, Winfield Scott, Daniel Webster

Karl E. Valois

REFERENCES

Blue, Frederick J. 1973. *The Free Soilers: Third Party Politics, 1848–1854.* Urbana: U. of Illinois Pr.

Holt, Michael F. 1978. *The Political Crisis of the 1850s.* New York: Wiley.

Nevins, Allan. 1947. *Ordeal of the Union: A House Dividing, 1852–1857.* New York: Scribner's.

Nichols, Roy. 1958. *Franklin Pierce: Young Hickory of the Granite Hills.* Philadelphia: U. of Pennsylvania Pr.

Nichols, Roy, and Jeannette Nichols. 1971. "The Election of 1852." In Arthur M. Schlesinger, Jr., et al., eds. *History of American Presidential Elections, 1789–1968.* New York: Chelsea House.

Potter, David M. 1976. *The Impending Crisis, 1848–1861.* New York: Harper & Row.

Sewell, Richard H. 1976. *Ballots for Freedom: Antislavery Politics in the United States, 1837–1860.* New York: Oxford U. Pr.

Election of 1860

Triggering as it did the secession crisis—a paroxysm that eventually led to the founding of the Confederacy and the outbreak of the American Civil War—the presidential election of 1860 obviously ranks among the most critical in the nation's history. From its very beginning, the national political campaign of 1860 was waged against a backdrop of sectional strife, which had grown worse since John Brown's raid on Harper's Ferry late the previous year. The Thirty-sixth Congress, which met shortly after Brown's execution, witnessed a protracted controversy in the House over the selection of a Speaker, during which southerners condemned Republican Congressmen who had endorsed Hinton R. Helper's *The Impending Crisis of the South* and debate in the Senate over resolutions introduced by Senator Jefferson Davis (D-Miss.) affirming not only that the national government could not close the federal territories to property in slaves but also that it must protect slaveholders' property rights therein.

The campaign of 1860 developed into a four-way race, the first such contest since the 1830s. The Democrats contributed to this confusion by twice dividing at their national convention: first in Charleston, South Carolina, where many southerners bolted because the northern majority refused to commit the Democratic Party to federal protection of slavery in the territories; then in Baltimore, where the adjourned convention reconvened, only to split more deeply over the seating of contested delegations from those slave states that had withdrawn from the earlier gathering. Senator Stephen Douglas (Illinois), who had failed to win nomination on fifty-seven roll calls in Charleston, was declared the party nominee in Baltimore after two roll calls, although he was still short of the usually required two-thirds support. When Benjamin Fitzpatrick (Alabama) subsequently declined the vice presidential nomination, Herschel Johnson (Georgia) ran in his stead. Baltimore bolters, nearly four-fifths from the South, nominated Vice President John Breckinridge (Kentucky) for President and Senator Joseph Lane (Oregon) as his running mate.

Between the Democratic donnybrooks, the new Constitutional Union Party—made up of Whigs, Oppositionists, Americans (Know-Nothings), and others opposed to both the major parties—quietly nominated its bisectional ticket of John Bell (Tennessee) and Edward Everett (Massachusetts). The party sought to counter sectional extremists, North and South, who threatened the Union.

The Republicans convened shortly after the Constitutional Unionists. Their hopes ran high: they had, after all, won a plurality (45 percent) of the North's popular vote and eleven free states in their first presidential bid in 1856. (The Democrats had captured 41 percent and five northern states, the American-Whigs 14 percent and none.) Still, to win the presidency the Republicans would have to gain the requisite number of electoral votes from among New Jersey, Pennsylvania, Indiana, Illinois, and California and hold their own states, especially closely contested New York and Ohio. Accordingly, the party drafted a platform that appealed to key groups and states on economic issues (support for protective tariff and homestead legislation); sought in various ways to woo both Know-Nothings and Protestant immigrants, especially Germans; arraigned the Slave Power and Democratic corruption; and tried to assuage the fears of conservative northerners that the radicalism of this sectional party threatened disunion. The nomination of Abraham Lincoln over William Seward reflected such considerations: "Honest Abe," "the Railsplitter," hailed from a key state, was deemed an antislavery moderate, and, although antinativist, he was acceptable to many Know-Nothings as well as to Protestant Germans. (Seward was identified as an antislavery radical; as a Whig, he had sought to reach out to Roman Catholics, earning him the enduring enmity of nativists. His delegate strength lay largely in solidly Republican districts, not in doubtful areas that the party had to capture or hold to win in 1860.) Hannibal Hamlin (Maine), a former Democrat, joined Lincoln, a former Whig, on the Republicans' national ticket.

Stephen Douglas alone departed from tradition by campaigning on the road, warning northerners of the threat of secession and southerners of its unacceptability. In some northern states, parties attempting to defeat the Republicans formed fusion tickets. In Texas, Bell and Douglas's supporters did likewise against Breckinridge's party.

The election brought victory to the Republicans, in reality the most sectional of the parties. Lincoln received some votes in but five slave states, of which only one later seceded. The concentration of his popular support in the North meant that he would have won the presidency (with only 40 percent of the national popular vote) even if his three foes had combined against him. Lincoln polled majorities in all but three free states—New Jersey (where he trailed Douglas), California, and Oregon. The northern states that he carried by popular majorities controlled more than the 152 electoral votes needed for election.

Douglas ran second in the North but a weak third in the South. He led only in New Jersey and Missouri. Breckinridge triumphed in eleven slave states (including South Carolina, whose legislature chose the electors), six by majority popular vote. Bell won three Upper South states, all by pluralities, two narrowly. Both Breckinridge and Bell received small popular votes in the North. Douglas, whose popular support was second only to Lincoln's, fared worst in the Electoral College, which rewards first-place finishers only.

Within the North, where the election was decided, Republicans and Democrats largely reaffirmed their 1856 decisions to vote and for whom to vote; abstentions and shifts, primarily toward the Republicans, were more characteristic of 1856 Whig-Americans. These shifts, together with disproportionate support from new voters and 1856 nonvoters put the Republicans over the top. Compared with the 1856 election then, Lincoln received his strongest support in Republican bailiwicks but scored his largest gains in Whig-American areas, especially in the southern Midwest.

The Republicans' capture of the presidency without the support of a single slave state was to contribute to the success of secessionists in convincing southerners that they and their "Peculiar Institution" were now at unacceptable risk within the Union.

See also: John Bell, John C. Breckinridge, John Brown, Constitutional Union Party, Stephen A. Douglas,

Electoral College System, Know-Nothings, Abraham Lincoln, Secession

Samuel T. McSeveney

REFERENCES

Gienapp, William E. 1986. "Who Voted for Lincoln?" In John L. Thomas, ed. *Abraham Lincoln and the American Political Tradition*. Amherst: U. of Massachusetts Pr.

———. 1987. *The Origins of the Republican Party, 1852–1856*. New York: Oxford U. Pr.

Holt, Michael F. 1978. *The Political Crisis of the 1850s*. New York: Wiley.

Nichols, Roy F. 1948. *The Disruption of American Democracy*. New York: Macmillan.

Potter, David M. 1976. *The Impending Crisis, 1848–1861*. New York: Harper & Row.

Election of 1868

Republican setbacks in the off-year elections of 1867 and the incidents leading to the impeachment of President Andrew Johnson in February 1868 ensured the nomination of war hero and general-in-chief Ulysses S. Grant by the Republican Party in its convention in Chicago in May. Grant, widely viewed as moderate on Reconstruction issues, had reassured Radicals of his support for congressional Reconstruction by making public his break with President Johnson. Advocates of contraction and of repaying war loans in gold—fearing that Senator Benjamin Wade of Ohio, who favored inflation, might sneak into the Presidency upon Johnson's conviction—also lined up behind the general. Speaker of the House Schuyler Colfax rounded out the ticket as the vice presidential nominee; the platform endorsed the principles of sound money and equivocated on the issue of Black suffrage, deeming it mandatory for the South but optional in the northern states. In his acceptance letter, Grant sounded the memorable phrase, "Let us have peace," which set the tone for a Republican campaign that promised to end political squabbling and secure the fruits of northern victory under the leadership of the hero of Appomattox.

The contest for the Democratic nomination was more heated. Chief Justice Salmon P. Chase, frustrated in his ever-present desire to win the Republican nomination, wooed Democratic delegates. So too did Ohio Senator George H. Pendleton, whose plan to repay the war debt in greenbacks split the party along east/west lines. Both of these candidates promised to shift the presidential contest away from a referendum on Reconstruction. But at their convention in New York in July, the Democrats chose instead to make the war and Reconstruction the central issues of the campaign. Bypassing military leaders George B. McClellan and Winfield Scott Hancock as well as the acquitted Andrew Johnson and Senator Thomas A. Hendricks, the convention named former New York governor Horatio Seymour to head the ticket, with Francis P. Blair as his running mate. Seymour had addressed draft rioters during the war as "my friends"; Blair had declared the Reconstruction Acts unconstitutional and called for their overthrow. This ticket, by promising to revive wartime emotions, played right into the hands of the Republicans.

The campaign was marked by violent rhetoric in the North and violence in the South. Republicans gleefully compared Grant's promise of peace, law, order, and prosperity with the turmoil and upheaval that would accompany a Democratic triumph. Waving "the bloody shirt" to recall wartime emotions, they pointed to the activities of the Ku Klux Klan as proof that white southerners had yet to accept the verdict of the battlefield. Only Grant of Appomattox could bring an end to such resistance. Although northern Democrats played upon the repetitions of racism and constitutionalism, they were embarrassed by the activities of their southern brethren. In October, following Republican victories in Ohio, Indiana, and Pennsylvania, Democratic leaders discussed the possibility of sacking Seymour; however, they abandoned such an idea as futile in the face of the growing probability of Grant's victory.

A superficial examination of the election results suggests that Grant beat Seymour rather handily, capturing 26 of 34 states with 214 electoral votes to the Democrat's 80. But Grant's popular vote majority of only 306,000 out of some 5,715,000 ballots cast was made possible by the vote of approximately 500,000 recently enfranchised southern Blacks. Three southern states (Virginia, Mississippi, and Texas) were barred from the election because of their failure to adopt new state constitutions in accordance with the Reconstruction Acts; fraud and violence characterized the contests in New York and Georgia, where fair counts probably would have resulted in Republican wins. Some historians have mistakenly suggested that Seymour would have won if the election had been limited to white voters alone; even had Seymour carried the seven southern states won by Grant whose votes were counted by Congress, Grant would have retained a majority in the electoral college

(162 to 132). More importantly, Grant ran ahead of the Republican ticket by over 100,000 votes, and the party improved upon its performance in the 1867 elections. Without Grant as its standard bearer, the Republican Party might well have lost the election.

See also: Bloody Shirt, Salmon P. Chase, Schuyler Colfax, Ulysses S. Grant, Andrew Johnson, Race and Racial Politics, Reconstruction, Horatio Seymour, Suffrage, Benjamin Wade

Brooks Donohue Simpson

REFERENCES

Benedict, Michael Les. 1974. *A Compromise of Principle: Congressional Republicans and Reconstruction 1863–1869.* New York: Norton.

Coleman, Charles H. 1933. *The Election of 1868.* New York: Columbia U. Pr.

Franklin, John Hope. 1971. "Election of 1868." In Arthur M. Schlesinger, Jr., et al., eds. *History of American Presidential Elections, 1789–1968.* New York: Chelsea House.

Sibley, Joel H. 1977. *A Respectable Minority: The Democratic Party in the Civil War Era, 1860–1868.* New York: Norton.

Election of 1872

During Ulysses S. Grant's first administration, divisions appeared among Republicans over the party's mission and positions on major issues. The declining significance of Reconstruction in American politics revealed anew the old differences over other issues—especially economic ones—which Republicans had subordinated in creating an antislavery, antisouthern, and anti–Andrew Johnson coalition. With the war won, slavery destroyed, and Johnson replaced, GOP leaders struggled to define a common vision of the party's position on the issues confronting the postwar polity. Tariff reform, monetary policy, civil service reform, federal intervention to protect Black voters, foreign policy, and territorial expansion, among other things, were issues on which Republicans had yet to form a solid front. In part, these cleavages resulted from generational differences between veterans of the party's early years and those who gained political prominence during and after the Civil War; in part they were sparked by President Grant's programs, most notably his ambition to annex Santo Domingo, his desire to protect the free exercise of the suffrage in the South, and his distribution of patronage among Republican factions. As the party struggled to define itself, ruptures were inevitable.

By 1871 several powerful Republicans were thoroughly disenchanted with the President.

Senator Charles Sumner battled the annexation effort; his colleague, Carl Schurz, attacked other foreign policy measures and called for a reform of the civil service; another Senator, Lyman Trumbull, joined Schurz in attacking Grant's Reconstruction policy. Others, notably editor Horace Greeley, journalist Henry Adams, former Cabinet member Jacob D. Cox, and Senator Reuben Fenton, were alienated by disputes over patronage and policy. These men sought to deny Grant renomination; failing that, they contemplated the idea of establishing a new party (soon christened the Liberal Republican movement). Other Republicans, although not enthusiastic about Grant's renomination, regarded it as inevitable and decided to remain within the party.

The early momentum of the dissident movement was soon spent, owing in part to Grant's crafty efforts to strip it of several issues, including tariff reduction, civil service reform, and amnesty to former Confederates, by adopting his opponents' position as administration policy. Foreign policy triumphs—most notably the agreement with Great Britain to arbitrate the so-called "Alabama Claims" and other disputes—enhanced Grant's standing. The Liberals also were hard-pressed to find issues upon which to unite other than their heartfelt desire to beat Grant. A rather heterogeneous group assembled at Cincinnati in May 1872 to select a nominee. Although Trumbull, Supreme Court Associate Justice David Davis, and Charles Francis Adams, Sr., were all mentioned for the top slot, the prize went eventually on the fifth ballot to Greeley, much to the chagrin of Schurz and others, for Greeley supported neither tariff reductions nor civil service reform, both chief party tenets; indeed, several members either rejoined the Republican party or sat out the contest. The Democrats, perceiving no other way to wrest the White House from Grant, endorsed the Liberals' nomination, although a splinter ticket (labeled the Straight-Out Democrats) also appeared on the ballot.

Grant won renomination unanimously in June, although Sumner's Senate colleague from Massachusetts, Henry Wilson, replaced Schuyler Colfax as his running mate. In the ensuing campaign, personalities, not policies, dominated, as the political cartoons of Thomas Nast of *Harper's Weekly* on behalf of Grant revealed. Greeley even took to the stump on his own behalf, but it was soon evident that he was no match for the man who saved the Union. Grant's final victory was overwhelming: with nearly 3.6

million popular votes to Greeley's 2,834,000, Grant carried 31 states with 286 electoral votes, while his opponent won but 6 states with 66 electoral votes.

Tragically, Greeley, depressed by the death of his wife and the attacks upon him during the campaign, died on November 29; his electoral votes were scattered among several Democrats. The returns in several states were disputed; eventually Congress chose not to count the results in Arkansas and Louisiana. To Grant, the victory meant vindication in the face of slurs cast upon his character and motives during his first term. It was in part a tribute to his ability to defuse the Liberal Republican movement, although that coalition's self-destructive tendencies and the continuing identification of the Democratic Party with disunion and the Confederacy also contributed to the outcome. But the political events of the next four years suggest that the Republican landslide of 1872 represented a short-lived majority.

See also: Charles Francis Adams, Henry Adams, Bloody Shirt, Civil Service Reforms, Ulysses S. Grant, Horace Greeley, Andrew Johnson, Liberal Republican Party, Thomas Nast, Reconstruction, Carl Schurz, Charles Sumner

Brooks Donohue Simpson

REFERENCES

Downey, Matthew T. 1967. "Horace Greeley and the Politicians: The Liberal Republican Convention in 1872." 53 *Journal of American History* 727.

Gerber, Richard A. 1975. "The Liberal Republicans of 1872 in Historigraphical Perspective." 62 *Journal of American History* 40.

Gillette, William. 1971. "Election of 1872." In Arthur M. Schlesinger, Jr., et al., eds. *History of American Presidential Elections, 1789–1968*. New York: Chelsea House.

———. 1979. *Retreat from Reconstruction, 1869–1879*. Baton Rouge: Louisiana State U. Pr.

Election of 1876

No presidential election in American history was as tarnished by fraud as the election of 1876. This one pitted Ohio's Republican governor Rutherford B. Hayes against New York's Democratic governor Samuel J. Tilden. By the time that Hayes was inaugurated in 1877, the country had seen an apparent victory by Tilden nullified by vote fraud in three states and the election decided by an electoral commission, the one and only time such a device had been used to settle a disputed presidential election. Behind the scenes, however, a political deal really put Hayes in the White House—a deal involving nothing less than the removal of U.S.

troops from the three remaining southern states where they had been stationed at the end of the Civil War. By removing them, the Republican Hayes put an end to Reconstruction in the South and with it the protection of the civil and political rights of the Black citizens of the former Confederacy.

The campaign of 1876 was one of the five post-Civil War contests profoundly and directly influenced by "The Rebellion." The passions that had been inflamed by the war were still intense—so much so that Republican orators could, with great effect, fan the fires of its strength from the hated South. Such oratory typically involved tales of southern violence against African-Americans or northern whites who assisted them after the war; these speeches were so stylized that they became known as "waving the bloody shirt."

The use of "bloody shirt" rhetoric in the 1876 campaign was intensified because of the natures and backgrounds of the two candidates. Hayes had served as an officer in the Union Army from 1861 to 1865, leaving the service with the temporary rank of major general. He had been wounded at the battle of South Mountain and was cited for gallantry at the battles of Fisher's Hill and Cedar Creek. The father of eight children, Hayes had the reputation of being a steady and honest man, which was particularly important to Republicans in the aftermath of the scandal-ridden administration of Ulysses S. Grant.

Tilden was a 62-year-old bachelor called by his friends "The Sage of Gramercy Park" and by his detractors "Whispering Sammy." A figure out of a Dickensian counting house, Tilden was once described as "a sallow faced, dried up old man." But he was also a political manager and practitioner of systematic political analysis that made him a precursor of contemporary campaign professionals. He pioneered in the use of straw polls to determine voter attitudes and even applied a primitive kind of content analysis to college commencement speeches to identify the issues that he would stress in the 1876 campaign. The key issue was political reform, one that Tilden was admirably qualified to emphasize given his role as an antagonist of the infamous Tweed Ring in New York City. He correctly saw the advantages in a Democrat rooting out Democratic corruption. But his great wealth and lack of a war record opened him to charges of being a plutocrat and even a southern sympathizer.

The Cincinnati convention of the Republicans that nominated Hayes on the seventh ballot and the St. Louis Democratic convention that chose Tilden on the second ballot were confident that both men would appeal to the spirit of reform. But despite the apparent high-mindedness of both candidates, the campaign degenerated into mudslinging. By October, a trend toward Tilden was detectable.

When the first returns came in on November 7, they seemed to confirm the political hunches. New York, New Jersey, and Connecticut had gone for Tilden, and it was reported that Hayes went to bed that night believing that Samuel J. Tilden had been selected as the nineteenth President. But on the morning of November 8, John C. Reid, managing editor of the pro-Republican *New York Times*, was asked by the New York state Democratic chairman for his estimate of the electoral vote. For a Democratic official to ask a Republican editor for vote totals suggested to Reid that the Democrats were unsure of the outcome in a number of states, and that Tilden was short of the 185 electoral votes he needed. Three of these still had federal troops and Republican governors. Reid and Republican National Chairman Zachariah Chandler sent telegrams to Republican leaders in the 3 doubtful states—Florida, Louisiana, and South Carolina—telling them not to report their vote totals. Agents with valises full of cash were then dispatched to the disputed states. Through the use of bribery, the Republicans' "visiting statesmen" managed to overturn apparent Tilden popular vote majorities.

These and other disputed state election returns caused the Democratic House and Republican Senate to create a fifteen-member Electoral Commission consisting of five Senators, five Representatives, and five justices of the Supreme Court to rule on which candidate should receive the electoral votes for those states whose returns were in dispute. Democrats were confident that since Tilden needed only one vote to win, the Commission would almost surely award him at least that much from the 19 votes of the disputed states. There were seven Democrats and seven Republicans on the commission plus one neutral member, Associate Justice Joseph J. Bradley.

Just prior to the announcement of the commission's findings, one of Tilden's campaign managers secured a copy of Bradley's opinion, which awarded Florida's votes to Tilden. But sometime between then and the formal announcement of the decision, a Republican Senator from Bradley's own state of New Jersey, a Cabinet member of the Ulysses Grant administration, and Mrs. Bradley convinced the jurist to rule in favor of Hayes. The other contested electoral votes of Louisiana, South Carolina, and Oregon were likewise given to Hayes.

Despite public threats by Democrats of efforts to block Hayes's inauguration, behind-the-scenes negotiations were taking place between Hayes's managers and southern conservatives. In return for not blocking the inauguration, Hayes promised to withdraw federal troops from the South. The deal was clinched at a meeting at Wormley's Hotel in Washington in late February 1877. Although Hayes's agents were said to have extracted from the southern conservatives the promise of equal rights, the removal of federal troops eliminated the guarantee that Black voters would be able to exercise their new-won freedoms.

Tilden refused to carry the fight beyond the Electoral Commission for fear that it might plunge the country into civil war. He had finished with 4.3 million popular votes to Hayes's 4 million. Hayes received 50.4 percent of the electoral vote (185 votes from 21 states) and Tilden received 49.86 percent (184 votes from 17 states). Without the chicanery in the disputed states, Tilden certainly would have been the winner.

See also: Bloody Shirt, Zachariah Chandler, Ulysses S. Grant, Greenback Party, Rutherford B. Hayes, Reconstruction, Samuel J. Tilden

Ross K. Baker

REFERENCES

Blaine, James G. 1884. *Twenty Years of Congress, 1861–1881*. 2 vols. Norwich, CT: Henry Bill.

Cox, S. S. 1888. *Three Decades of Federal Legislation*. Providence, RI: Reid.

Josephson, Matthew. 1938. *The Politicos*. New York: Harcourt-Brace.

Stoddard, Henry L. 1927. *As I Knew Them*. New York: Harper.

Election of 1884

This presidential election was a contest between two men of extraordinary political accomplishments, both of whose careers were tarnished by accusations of moral turpitude. In both cases the allegations were true and served as ammunition in a close and rancorous campaign.

The two men were Speaker of the House James G. Blaine of Maine, the Republican, and Grover Cleveland, Democratic governor of New

York. Blaine was a kind of political chameleon whose only consistent set of principles involved the acquisition of personal wealth. He sought out the company of wealthy individuals who were only too happy to reward him financially if Blaine would use his official position to advance their interests in Congress. When asked about the propriety of appearing to be the instrument of powerful and arrogant railroad magnates, Blaine replied ingenuously "I like rich people."

But Blaine was no minor corrupt official. He was blessed with a magnetic personality and a remarkable photographic memory that enabled him to greet thousands of voters by name based upon only one introduction. He was a powerful speaker who tended to let his sarcasm get out of hand, thus causing his enemies to be legion. But it was Blaine's incredible moral obtuseness that resulted in his acceptance of loans, gratuities, and insider deals with the Union Pacific Railroad that helped bring him to grief in 1884.

A packet of letters written by Blaine was turned over to a congressional committee investigating Blaine's railroad activities while he was serving as Speaker of the House. These "Mulligan letters," produced by a James Mulligan who had served as bookkeeper for the man with whom Blaine negotiated a shady stock deal, dogged Blaine's steps through the campaign.

Cleveland's problems were of a more personal nature. As a bachelor living in Buffalo, New York, he boarded with a widow named Maria Halpin who subsequently gave birth to a child. While Mrs. Halpin was involved with other men at the time of her relationship with him, Cleveland acknowledged patrimony and supported the woman and the child. These facts came out only after Cleveland had received the nomination of the second ballot at the Democratic convention in Chicago. Had they been revealed earlier, his nomination would have been doubtful.

Because of these scandals, the campaign took on a highly personal and negative tone, with Democrats taunting Blaine for denying that he had been corrupted by the railroads with the couplet, "Blaine, Blaine, James G. Blaine / The continental liar from the state of Maine." Republicans shot back with "Ma, ma, where's my pa? Gone to the White House, Ha, ha, ha."

Influential Republican reformers who had come to be known as "Mugwumps" deserted Blaine. The 1882 elections had given the Democrats control of the House of Representa-tives; all of the states of the solidly Democratic South had been reconstructed and would participate fully in the election. As the contest was nearing its close, Republican Party leaders saw disaster looming for the candidate, so they dispatched Blaine on a speaking tour of the states of the Middle West. Blaine lifted the sagging spirits of midwestern Republicans. For the most part, Blaine took the high road, refraining from personal attacks on Cleveland. He emphasized that the main issue of the campaign was the tariff and urged a protective wall against imports. Despite his history of "waving the bloody shirt" of antisouthern feeling, Blaine preached reconciliation with the former rebels. It was almost as if he were truly the "Plumed Knight"—an adoring term used by orator Robert Ingersoll to describe Blaine. His anti-British diatribes brought him support from Irish voters. Of particular importance was the Irish-led Tammany Hall machine of New York that despised Cleveland for his efforts at political reform. It was characteristic of this topsy-turvy election that the solidly Democratic Irish Catholics were straying from Cleveland and the normally Republican temperance forces were on the verge of deserting Blaine over a rebuff that had taken place at the Republican National Convention.

The decisive battleground was New York with its 36 electoral votes. No other state had even half the total of the Empire State. Although Cleveland was its governor, his victory in New York was not automatic. Accordingly, it was to New York that Blaine came in late October, and it was there that his campaign received two wounds that turned out to be mortal.

On the morning of October 29, Blaine was visited at the Fifth Avenue Hotel by a delegation of Protestant ministers. In endorsing Blaine, the Reverend Samuel D. Burchard, a Presbyterian minister from Brooklyn, uttered a sentence that probably cost Blaine thousands of Catholic votes. "We are Republicans," Burchard told Blaine, "and don't propose to leave our party and identify with the party whose antecedents have been rum, Romanism, and rebellion." In a single alliterative phrase, Burchard had consigned to political perdition consumers of alcoholic beverages (rum), Catholics (Romanism), and southerners (rebellion). Burchard was too clever by half, and his endorsement was strongly counterproductive for Blaine.

But it was Blaine himself with his attraction to the company of rich men who administered the final blow. The very evening after the

Burchard gaffe, Blaine attended a sumptuous banquet and Delmonico's Restaurant hosted by New York's wealthiest men—people who would later be called "robber barons." The year 1884 was a period of hard economic times, and the image of Blaine seated at a luxurious banquet table confirmed in the mind of the public a man callous to the needs of the poor, at ease only in the company of the wealthy. Dubbed "Belshazzar's Feast" by New York Democratic newspapers after the biblical orgy, the testimonial dinner turned out to be a political fiasco. It was too late for Blaine to undo the damage done by the two incidents of October 29. On November 4, Cleveland took New York by 1,149 votes of a total of 1.7 million cast. He captured the solid South, New Jersey, Connecticut, and Indiana for a total of 219 electoral votes. Blaine captured the Republican heartland of New England and the Midwest and Plains States (save Indiana) but came up short with 182 electoral votes in the 18 states he won.

The outcome of the election of 1884 demonstrated that the personal negatives of the candidates canceled each other out. More decisive were the economic hard times for which any Republican candidate would have been held responsible. Given the severity of the recession, it is remarkable that the election was so close and that Blaine and Cleveland spent so little time discussing the economy. Another important factor in the outcome was the wholesale defection of the liberal Republican reformers. The split between the conservative "stalwart" wing of the party and the "Mugwumps" probably contributed to Cleveland's strong showing in the four northern states he won. Finally, nature smiled on Cleveland. November 4 was a day of Democratic weather. Driving rains in upstate New York made it difficult for pro-Blaine farmers to get to the polls over muddy roads while Cleveland voters strolled to vote under clear skies.

Grover Cleveland became the first Democrat since James Buchanan in 1856 to win the White House. Cleveland would win it again in 1892 after failing to earn a second term in 1888.

See also: James G. Blaine, Bloody Shirt, Benjamin F. Butler, Grover Cleveland, Greenback Party, Mugwumps, Railroads, Stalwarts (and Half-Breeds), Tammany Hall

Ross K. Baker

REFERENCES

Blaine, James G. 1884. *Twenty Years of Congress, 1861–1881.* Norwich, CT: Henry Bill.

Hoyt, Edwin Palmer, Jr. 1960. *Jumbos and Jackasses.* Garden City, NY: Doubleday.

Lambert, John R. 1953. *Arthur Pue Gorman.* Baton Rouge: Louisiana State U. Pr.

Porter, Kirk, and Donald Bruce Johnson. 1956. *National Party Platforms.* Urbana: U. of Illinois Pr.

Roseboom, Eugene H. 1964. *A History of Presidential Elections.* New York: Macmillan.

Election of 1888

This presidential campaign got under way in December 1887 when Democratic President Grover Cleveland startled politicians in both parties by devoting his entire annual message to Congress to a call for tariff reform. High tariff protection had, since the 1860s, been the keystone of Republican Party economic policy. Protectionists argued that tariff barriers against foreign competition promoted national industrial growth and kept up wage levels among American workers. Cleveland's message promoted the rival view that tariff taxation burdened workers and all other consumers with high prices and that it fostered the spread of corporate monopoly. Although low-tariff Democrats promptly introduced a bill for downward revision in response to the presidential call, a divided Congress postponed legislative action and insured that the tariff issue would dominate campaign rhetoric in the coming presidential contest. Republicans seized the issue eagerly, sure that it improved their chances for regaining the White House. GOP spokesmen caricatured tariff reform as "free trade" and stigmatized it as "pro-British"—a threat to the security of factory owners and factory workers alike.

These tactics forced Cleveland into defensive retreat, and he quietly arranged for moderate tariff language in his party's platform. Following renomination he took little part in the campaign, leaving the main burden of stump speaking to his elderly running mate Allen Thurman. Mismanagement and disunity dogged efforts to rally the eclectic Democratic coalition behind the President, especially in the crucial state of New York where Cleveland characteristically shunned Tammany Hall and the reelection bid of his party rival, Governor David B. Hill.

The Republican campaign turned out to be a much smoother operation. When the party's perennial favorite, James G. Blaine, declined to run again, half a dozen fresh prospects vied to take his place. From this pack, Indiana's Benjamin Harrison, a Civil War veteran with an honored name, a modest political record, and a rather frosty intelligence, gained Blaine's favor and emerged with the nomination. Party managers, led by Pennsylvania's Matthew Quay, arranged a well-synchronized and lavishly financed campaign effort around Harrison's front porch performances in Indianapolis. Massive GOP pamphleteering on the tariff issue smothered Cleveland's early hopes for an educational campaign for lower rates. Meanwhile partisans for both tickets mobilized voters by staging military-style political party spectacles featuring torchlight parades with brass bands and uniformed clubs.

The election itself was the last presidential contest before the introduction of the secret ballot. The November results, with turnout over 75 percent, enforced the stable two-party equilibrium and narrow margins of possibility in the politics of that era. As in the three previous national elections, Democrats won big in the South and carried most Border States, while Republicans swept Pennsylvania, most of New England, and most of the Middle West. New York and Indiana were, as usual, the main swing states, inspiring intense efforts at voter manipulation and accompanying charges of bribery and fraud. While Cleveland's southern strength gained him a national plurality of the popular vote, Harrison carried both New York and Indiana and won the electoral vote, 233 to 168. Republicans gained clear control of Congress for the first time in 14 years; high on the agenda of its next session was upward revision of the tariff.

See also: James G. Blaine, Grover Cleveland, Benjamin Harrison, Matthew Quay, Tammany Hall

Geoffrey Blodgett

REFERENCES

Jensen, Richard. 1971. *The Winning of the Midwest: Social and Political Conflict, 1888–1896.* Chicago: U. of Chicago Pr.

Marcus, Robert D. 1971. *Grand Old Party: Political Structure in the Gilded Age.* New York: Oxford U. Pr.

Morgan, H. Wayne. 1969. *From Hayes to McKinley: National Party Politics, 1877–1896.* Syracuse, NY: Syracuse U. Pr.

Election of 1892

This presidential election, coming on the heels of a startling Democratic landslide in the congressional elections of 1890, signaled the beginning of the end of the tightly balanced party system of the Gilded Age. The major parties waged an oddly quiet campaign, marked on both sides by anxious foreboding about the country's political future. A primary reason for their anxiety was the advent of populism as a national third-party alternative, growing out of farmers' alliances in the impoverished rural South and West. The Populists' Omaha platform called for economic and political reforms reaching far beyond the agendas of both major parties, whose leaders regarded populism as a dangerous heresy. However, the Populist demand for currency inflation through silver coinage won widespread if guarded support among party regulars of both persuasions.

Former Democratic President Grover Cleveland's "silver letter" of February 1891 reasserted his longstanding opposition to silver inflation and positioned him for renewed leadership of his party's conservative wing. Both Cleveland and incumbent Republican President Benjamin Harrison won first-ballot nominations at their respective conventions, but enthusiasm for these choices was well controlled. Despite the remarkable legislative productivity of Congress during Harrison's White House years, his administration of public affairs chilled his relations with many powerful party leaders who had rallied to his cause in 1888. His wife's fatal illness in 1892 limited Harrison's personal involvement in the campaign. The Homestead steel strike in the summer of 1892 further damaged his chances by dramatizing the potential for labor strife in an industrial economy heavily subsidized by Republican-sponsored high-tariff protection, a point that Cleveland underscored in one of his rare campaign appearances.

The Democratic campaign was managed effectively by New York City capitalist William C. Whitney. His fundraising efforts outdid the GOP, and he forcefully mediated Cleveland's perennial differences with Tammany Hall. The Cleveland camp, striving to pull together the multiple factions in the party's national coalition, was greatly concerned over the prospect of Populist inroads in the Democratic South. In midwestern states like Illinois and Wisconsin, Democrats worked to exploit cultural resentments among ethnic Republicans over prohibition and school regulation. In many states of the trans-Mississippi West, Democrats expediently searched for votes by fusing their tickets with the Populists.

Election day results were sobering on all sides. Cleveland gained his third straight national plurality, winning 277 electoral votes to Harrison's 145, with Wisconsin and Illinois going Democratic for the first time since the Civil War. But Democrats lost 17 House seats—a prelude, as it turned out, to their huge losses 2 years later. The potential for discord in the Democratic coalition is suggested by the fact that Cleveland's supporters in 1892 included John Peter Altgeld, William Jennings Bryan, Eugene V. Debs, and Henry George. The Populist ticket, headed by General James B. Weaver, polled over a million popular votes but only 22 electoral votes, none of them in the South. The patterns in the 1892 outcome indicated a restless electorate on the move, but its vectors remained unfixed, awaiting the onset of a national depression just six months later.

See also: William Jennings Bryan, Grover Cleveland, Henry George, Benjamin Harrison, Populism as a Movement and Party, Tammany Hall, James B. Weaver

Geoffrey Blodgett

REFERENCES

Hicks, John D. 1931. *The Populist Revolt: A History of the Farmers' Alliance and the Peoples' Party.* Minneapolis: U. of Minnesota Pr.

Knoles, George H. 1942. *The Presidential Campaign and Election of 1892.* Stanford, CA: Stanford U. Pr.

Marcus, Robert D. 1971. *Grand Old Party: Political Structure in the Gilded Age.* New York: Oxford U. Pr.

Morgan, H. Wayne. 1969. *From Hayes to McKinley: National Party Politics, 1877–1896.* Syracuse, NY: Syracuse U. Pr.

Election of 1896

Generally regarded as one of the most heated of presidential contests, the election of 1896 is also regarded as a significant turning point in American party politics. Party loyalties that had existed since the Civil War were widely supplanted by new ones.

The panic of 1893, and the ensuing depression, brought about widespread economic hardship and a general increase in the unrest felt in many agrarian parts of the country. Increasingly, the unlimited coinage of silver was touted by William Jennings Bryan and others as a way of expanding the economy so as to help the great body of farmers and workers. The gold standard and President Grover Cleveland's monetary policies were portrayed, even by fellow Democrats, as oppressing the masses by robbing them for the benefit of the rich.

The free-silver forces in the Democratic Party worked for commitments by convention delegates to a "Principles First" platform and the nomination of a prosilver candidate at their Chicago convention. Bryan was able to use these commitments and his famous "Cross of Gold" speech to mobilize convention support and be-

come the youngest presidential nominee of a major political party at the age of 36.

For the Populists, the campaign proved to be less about silver and more about the question of fusion with the Democrats or independence as a third party. Subsuming their other concerns, they accepted Bryan and the primacy of the silver issue at their St. Louis convention. In a futile attempt to maintain a distinct identity, they nominated Thomas E. Watson, an antifusionist, for Vice President.

Disappointment and disaffection spawned splinter groups within both the Democratic and Republican parties. Dissident Democrats held a rump convention in Indianapolis. Calling themselves the National Democratic Party, they drew up a platform defending Cleveland's gold policy and deploring the "grave departures from Democratic principles" in Chicago. For President they selected Senator John M. Palmer, a 70-year-old political maverick and former governor of Illinois. Because their party had failed to include a prosilver plank in their platform, a group of Republicans formed the Silver Republican Party. Along with the National Silver Party, they supported Bryan.

The Republicans waged a well-managed and well-financed campaign. Their platform endorsed sound money policies but emphasized a protective tariff. The nominee at their St. Louis convention, William McKinley, was portrayed in terms of institutional and social stability, as opposed to Bryan's perceived radicalism. McKinley conducted a front porch campaign in which an estimated 750,000 people of all stripes traveled to his Canton, Ohio, home to meet the candidate. This parade was supplemented by the efforts of McKinley's friend and manager, Cleveland businessman Mark Hanna, and the Republican National Committee to distribute millions of pages of campaign literature throughout the country.

Despite the fact that Bryan traveled throughout the country and made over 600 speeches in a campaign unprecedented in its scope, he lost the election in close balloting. Although he lost the electoral vote, 271 to 176, a shift of only 20,396 votes (of 13,630,456 cast) in six states (Ind., Ky., Calif., W.Va., Ore., and Del.) would have made Bryan President.

See also: William Jennings Bryan, Grover Cleveland, Mark Hanna, William McKinley, Populism as a Movement and Party, Silver Republicans, Thomas E. Watson

James V. Saturno

REFERENCES

Burnham, Walter Dean. 1970. *Critical Elections and the Mainsprings of American Politics*. New York: Norton

Goodwyn, Lawrence. 1976. *Democratic Promise: The Populist Moment in America*. New York: Oxford U. Pr.

Kleppner, Paul, ed. 1981. *The Evolution of American Electoral Systems*. Westport, CT: Greenwood.

Petersen, Svend. 1963. *A Statistical History of the American Presidential Elections*. New York: Ungar.

Polakoff, Keith I. 1981. *Political Parties in American History*. New York: Wiley.

Schlesinger, Arthur M., Jr., ed. 1972. *The Coming to Power: Critical Presidential Elections in American History*. New York: Chelsea House/McGraw-Hill.

Sundquist, James L. 1983. *Dynamics of the Party System*. Rev. ed. Washington: Brookings.

Election of 1908

In the 1908 presidential campaign, William Howard Taft, Theodore Roosevelt's designated successor, defeated William Jennings Bryan. For the first time in American history, both major party nominees took to the stump. The election illustrated Roosevelt's continuing popularity and marked the third and final repudiation of Bryan as the Democratic nominee.

At the Republican National Convention, Roosevelt ignored the pleas to run again. Displaying uncharacteristic self-control, the President engineered the nomination of his Secretary of War, William Howard Taft of Ohio. Taft's political inexperience guaranteed a continuing campaign role for Roosevelt. Pundits scoffed that T.A.F.T. stood for "Take Advice from Theodore."

Taft dutifully followed his mentor's lead. He ran on a compromise platform uniting congressional conservatives and the increasingly progressive President in favor of tariff revision, antitrust enforcement, and conservation. Although preferring a quiet, traditional front porch campaign, Taft obliged Roosevelt by taking to the stump.

The Democratic opposition, heartened by Theodore Roosevelt's retirement and Taft's inexperience, nominated William Jennings Bryan for the third time. The Nebraska Populist hoped to avoid another marathon rear platform campaign. In his notification speech he introduced the "over-shadowing" question of the campaign: "Shall the People Rule?" He promised to address the "'various' economic questions" in a few major speeches calling for tariff reduction, strict antitrust enforcement, and greater government regulation of railroads and banks. After that, he would write articles and give interviews. But he would stay at home.

Bryan, however, could not abide the calm, nor could his devotees. The new expectations he helped to create imprisoned him. By mid-September he was stumping. Bryan cast the election as a crusade to free the government from the corporations and their patronage-wielding political lackeys. The Republicans responded by branding Bryan a Socialist, excoriating his advocacy in 1906 of government ownership of railroads.

As the campaign heated up, Republicans begged for the President's involvement. Roosevelt's opportunity came when the publisher William Randolph Hearst accused Standard Oil of bribing Republican Senator Joseph B. Foraker and Democratic National Committee treasurer C. N. Haskell, among others. Long hostile to Foraker, eager to embarrass the Democrats, and anxious to "put a little vim into the campaign," the President repudiated Foraker and attacked Bryan for not firing Haskell. Bryan responded by accusing Roosevelt of taking corporate campaign contributions. As Bryan and Roosevelt clashed in public letters and interviews, Americans debated the propriety of the President's unprecedented involvement in a campaign.

On November 3, Taft and his running mate, James S. Sherman of New York, received 7,679,006 popular votes and 321 electoral votes. Bryan and John W. Kern of Indiana received 6,409,106 popular votes and only 162 electoral votes. A host of minor party candidates, including Eugene V. Debs of the Socialist Party, Thomas E. Watson of the Populist Party, and Eugene W. Chafin of the Prohibition Party, received approximately 800,000 popular votes combined, but no electoral votes. "We have beaten them to a frazzle," Roosevelt exulted. For weeks after the election, a baffled Bryan asked readers of his weekly, *The Commoner*, to help explain "THE MYSTERY OF 1908." This time, Bryan had really thought he would win.

See also: William Jennings Bryan, Eugene V. Debs, Populist Party, Prohibition Party, Railroads, Theodore Roosevelt, Socialist Party of America, William Howard Taft, Thomas E. Watson

Gil Troy

REFERENCES

Abbott, Lawrence F., ed. 1924. *The Letters of Archie Butt, Personal Aide to President Roosevelt*. Garden City, NY: Doubleday, Page.

Anderson, Judith I. 1981. *William Howard Taft: An Intimate History*. New York: Norton.

Hibben, Paxton. 1967. *The Peerless Leader: William Jennings Bryan*. New York: Farrar and Rinehart.

Pringle, Henry F. 1939. *The Life and Times of William Howard Taft: A Biography*. 2 vols. New York: Farrar & Rinehart.

Roseboom, Eugene H. 1956. *Theodore Roosevelt: A Biography*. Rev. ed. New York: Harcourt, Brace and World.

———. 1957. *A History of Presidential Elections*. New York: Macmillan.

Election of 1912

The Democratic Party attained the White House for only the third time since the Civil War in the election of 1912. Woodrow Wilson won a majority of the vote in 11 southern states and a plurality of the vote in 29 other states to achieve an electoral landslide over his two Republican opponents, incumbent President William Howard Taft and former President Theodore Roosevelt. Wilson's victory was not entirely impressive. Although his plurality over the second-placed Roosevelt was fully 2 million votes out of 15 million cast, Wilson managed only 42 percent of all the ballots.

The events leading up to the election foretold of trouble for the Republican Party. After the midterm congressional elections gave control of the House to the Democrats, Theodore Roosevelt and the Republican Party's progressive wing began contemplating a challenge to the conservative President Taft. The President, recognizing the threat from his friend and predecessor, chose to run for reelection despite the progressive insurgency. Although Roosevelt beat Taft repeatedly in the Republican primaries, allowing the incumbent only a slim victory in the state of Massachusetts, Taft controlled the party's national committee and machinery. At the Chicago convention, on the strength of his organization and the support of the southern delegations, Taft won the Republican nomination on the first ballot. Roosevelt and his supporters split with the mainstream Republicans to form the new Progressive Party, known also as the "Bull Moose Party," which immediately nominated Roosevelt as its candidate for President.

The Democratic Party was no less divided, but personalities rather than ideology marked the split here. Chief among the contenders for the Democratic nomination were Champ Clark, Speaker of the House from Missouri, and New Jersey governor Woodrow Wilson. After splitting the primaries between them, Clark and Wilson were virtually deadlocked until, after 46 ballots, the governor secured the required two-thirds majority of delegates for nomination.

With two candidates opposing him, President Taft himself doubted that he would win reelection. Roosevelt took away some of Taft's Republican Party support but could not entice many Democrats to his candidacy, as Wilson was also Progressive. In an election when Socialist Party candidate Eugene V. Debs polled 6 percent of the vote—a higher portion than in any previous election—Progressives polled collectively over 75 percent of the vote. Given the electorate's predilection for reform at the time, Taft probably could not have won, even without the third-party candidacy of Roosevelt. In a contest involving Wilson against Taft and Debs alone, Wilson would have needed to garner only 30 percent of Progressive Roosevelt's actual vote to have won 50.1 percent of the popular vote, including majorities in 29 out of 48 states with 355 electoral votes—89 more than needed for election.

The Democratic Party also managed to increase its majority in the House and win control of the Senate. In successive years, Wilson demonstrated just how close his progressivism was to Roosevelt's, as his administration and Congress adopted nearly all of the proposed reforms stated in the Roosevelt platform.

See also: Bull Moose Party, Champ Clark, Eugene V. Debs, Progressive Party, Theodore Roosevelt, Socialist Party of America, William Howard Taft, Woodrow Wilson

Michael Heel

REFERENCES

Anderson, Donald F. 1973. *William Howard Taft*. Ithaca: Cornell U. Pr.

Coletta, Paolo E. 1973. *The Presidency of William Howard Taft*. Lawrence: U. Pr. of Kansas.

Cooper, John Milton, Jr. 1983. *The Warrior and the Priest*. Cambridge: Belknap Press.

Elletson, D. H. 1965. *Roosevelt and Wilson*. London: John Murray.

Kleppner, Paul. 1987. *Continuity and Change in Electoral Politics, 1893–1928*. Westport, CT: Greenwood.

Link, Arthur S. 1947. *Wilson: The Road to the White House*. Princeton: Princeton U. Pr.

Mowry, George E. 1958. *The Era of Theodore Roosevelt*. New York: Harper.

National Portrait Gallery. 1972. *If Elected. . . .* Washington: Smithsonian Institution Press.

Petersen, Svend. 1967. *A Statistical History of the American Presidential Elections*. New York: Ungar.

Election of 1920

The presidential campaign and election of 1920 were influenced by dispute over America's involvement in World War I and by domestic turmoil following the war. Controversy over ratification of the Versailles Treaty and membership in the League of Nations was accompanied by other conflicts: the achievement of nationwide prohibition and women's suffrage; racial strife; concern over renewed large-scale immigration from Europe; fear of radicalism and protest against the violation of civil liberties during the resultant Red Scare; opposition to the militancy of labor and workers' frustration over their postwar setbacks; inflation, followed by a sharp decline in farm prices; and disputes arising out of wartime government economic policies and the reconversion of the American economy to peacetime operation and relations with government.

The Democrats entered 1920 in disarray, vulnerable to a Republican campaign that would capitalize on voters' discontents by arraigning the administration of President Woodrow Wilson, who was now ill, as well as in public disfavor. Although the Democrats had captured the two most recent presidential elections, they now clearly stood on the defensive. After reaching peak strength in Congress in the elections of 1912, they had lost ground in 1914, 1916 (even as Wilson won reelection), and 1918: control of both houses rested in GOP hands. No Democrat commanded broad enough support to dominate the party's national convention. William Gibbs McAdoo led a large field on the first ballot. Thereafter, he and James M. Cox, three-term governor of Ohio, fought it out until the Ohioan was declared the unanimous winner after the forty-fourth roll call. The Democrats nominated Assistant Secretary of the Navy Franklin D. Roosevelt (New York) for Vice President; their platform called for ratification of the Versailles Treaty, with noncrippling reservations if need be.

The Republicans also lacked a dominant contender for the presidential nomination. In their case, none of the early front-runners—General Leonard Wood (New Hampshire), Governor Frank Lowden (Illinois), and Senator Hiram Johnson (California)—won the nomination, which fell to Senator Warren Harding (Ohio) on the tenth roll call. Governor Calvin Coolidge of Massachusetts, who had made a name for himself during the strike of Boston policemen the previous year, easily won nomination for Vice President on the first ballot. The GOP platform criticized the Wilson administration's preparedness and peace policies, praised the Senate for

rejecting Wilson's League of Nations position, and fudged by pledging to seek agreement with other nations without surrendering America's freedom of action.

The Democrats suffered a crushing defeat in the elections of 1920. The Republican national ticket easily broke the record (56.4 percent, 1904) for popular support in a presidential contest, polling 60.3 percent of the total vote, a mark exceeded (narrowly) only 3 times—in 1936, 1964, and 1972. By carrying Tennessee, the Republicans won the electoral votes of an ex-Confederate state for the first time since 1876. Cox and Roosevelt salvaged only one Border State, Kentucky. County-level returns starkly revealed the contraction of Democratic support. In 1916 Wilson had carried 2,039 counties nationwide; in 1920 Cox led in 1,096. Outside of the southern and Border States, the Democrats declined from 784 to only 42 counties. Despite the considerable enlargement of the electorate, the consequence of nationwide women's suffrage, the total Democratic vote for President rose by fewer than 15,000 (and fell off in the North), while the Republican vote jumped by more than 7.5 million. Turnout increased, but the turnout rate declined. Almost all Democratic senatorial candidates ran ahead of the national ticket, more markedly in the South than elsewhere, though most fell short of victory. Democratic gubernatorial nominees generally registered lower percentages than Cox-Roosevelt, but all outside the former Confederate states went down to defeat. Democratic congressional strength ebbed again, to all intents and purposes reducing the House party to its southern base. (Barely one-tenth of nonsouthern Congressmen were Democrats.) Democratic delegations in northern state legislatures were likewise weakened.

The Socialist Party also contested for the presidency in 1920, with Eugene V. Debs (Indiana), who was in federal prison for violating the wartime Espionage Act, running for the fifth and last time. Debs polled over 900,000 votes, the Socialists' largest total, but his percentage (3.4) was closer to that of 1916 (3.2) than to the party's high (6.0) of 1912. The Socialists showed best in Wisconsin and Minnesota, where antiwar ethnic support aided their totals, but Debs lost ground in his earlier strongholds in the Southwest and West.

The elections of 1918 and 1920 terminated a Democratic interlude (1910–1916) within a Republican era. Competing in a generally prosperous nation and themselves divided, the Democrats did not regain strength during the period 1922–1926. In 1928 Al Smith's presidential candidacy partially revived the party in some areas but produced defections elsewhere. Not until the Great Depression and New Deal would the Democrats regain national power.

See also: Calvin Coolidge, James M. Cox, Eugene V. Debs, Warren G. Harding, League of Nations, Prohibition, Red Scare, Franklin D. Roosevelt, Socialist Party of America, Woodrow Wilson, Woman's Suffrage Movement

Samuel T. McSeveney

REFERENCES

Bagby, Wesley M. 1962. *The Road to Normalcy: The Presidential Campaign and Election of 1920.* Baltimore: Johns Hopkins U. Pr.

Burner, David. 1968. *The Politics of Provincialism: The Democratic Party in Transition, 1918–1932.* New York: Knopf.

Ferrell, Robert H. 1985. *Woodrow Wilson & World War I, 1917–1921.* New York: Harper & Row.

Kleppner, Paul. 1987. *Continuity and Change in Electoral Politics, 1893–1928.* Westport, CT: Greenwood.

Election of 1928

This presidential election was a watershed in American politics. For the first time, a major party nominated a Roman Catholic for the presidency of the United States.

Alfred E. Smith, the Democratic nominee for President, personified the eastern "wet," urban, and Catholic, elements of his party. A Roman Catholic he was born on New York City's East Side, the son of an Irish immigrant. He ran for governor of New York State five times from 1918 to 1926, losing only in the Republican landslide of 1920. His presidential nomination was more than a personal triumph; it signified acceptance of the hyphenated immigrant groups, like the Irish-Americans of Smith's heritage. As the *New Republic* observed, "For the first time a representative of the unpedigreed, foreign-born, city-bred, many-tongued recent arrivals on the American scene has knocked on the door and aspired seriously to the presidency of the national council chamber."

Smith's opponent was Herbert Hoover, wartime food administrator and Secretary of Commerce in Calvin Coolidge's administration. Hoover received the 1928 Republican presidential nomination after Calvin Coolidge stunned reporters at a 1927 news conference with the statement, "I do not choose to run for President in 1928."

Alfred E. Smith lost the presidency to Herbert Hoover in one of the great landslides in American political history. Hoover amassed 21,392,190 votes, or 58.2 percent of the total, to 15,016,443 ballots for 40.8 percent. In the Electoral College, Smith won 8 states: Alabama, Arkansas, Georgia, Louisiana, Massachusetts, Mississippi, Rhode Island, and South Carolina for 87 ballots to Hoover's 40 states and 444 electoral votes. The nation's economic prosperity, and the fact that many voters believed the Republican Party was responsible for it, made Smith's chance to win slim. Richard Hofsteader maintains, "There was not a Democrat alive, Protestant or Catholic, who could have beaten Hoover in 1928." Scholar Ruth Silva notes that Smith's membership in the Democratic Party was his greatest liability.

Smith's Catholicism and his opposition of prohibition made winning even more difficult. Smith was unacceptable to many white Protestant southerners and became the first Democrat since the Civil War to lose several Border States, carrying only a few in the Deep South.

But Smith made gains among immigrant voters, winning the heavily Catholic states of Massachusetts and Rhode Island, marking only the second time since the founding of the Republican Party that these two states had gone Democratic—the first was in 1912 when Theodore Roosevelt's Bull Moose candidacy split the Republican vote. Together, these states along with the industrial Northeast and the South were to become reliable Democratic strongholds during the New Deal era.

The industrial Northeast had a sizable Catholic population, most of whom sided in large numbers with Smith. Boston, for example, gave the Democratic candidate a 100,000 vote plurality—enough to tip the state into the Democratic column. Urban ethnic neighborhoods voted overwhelmingly for Smith. In an Irish stronghold of Boston, Smith received 91 percent of the votes; an Italian neighborhood cast 82 percent of their votes for the Catholic Democrat. Nationally, Smith won majorities in the nation's industrial cities—a first.

Alfred E. Smith unleashed strong emotions in 1928. Campaigning in southern New England, the Democratic nominee drew crowds that surpassed not only those gathered to hear previous presidential candidates but also the mobs at the welcomes extended to the current folk hero, Charles Lindbergh: 750,000 in Boston; 100,000 in Hartford; 40,000 in Providence. Smith later wrote of his Boston reception: "So intense was the feeling, so large the throng, that at times I feared for the safety of Mrs. Smith riding with me in the automobile."

On election day, the size of the crowds and the political speeches mattered little. What counted was how one felt toward the candidates. The *Springfield Republican*, a Massachusetts newspaper, reported that when voters talked politics they spoke in "terms of French, Irish, Pole, and Yankee or Catholic and non-Catholic." The paper concluded, "Votes will undoubtedly be cast on other issues, particularly prohibition and prosperity, but when you get down to the ground there's dirt." When the "dirt" was analyzed, Catholic immigrants empathized with Smith; White Anglo Saxon Protestants preferred Hoover. This basic division—along ethnic and religious lines—formed the basis of the New Deal coalition established by Franklin D. Roosevelt. It adhered for more than a generation until it unraveled in the wake of the political explosions of the 1960s and 1970s.

See also: Calvin Coolidge, Herbert Hoover, Prohibition, Franklin Roosevelt, Alfred E. Smith, Norman Thomas

John K. White

REFERENCES

Burner, David. 1968. *The Politics of Provincialism: The Democratic Party in Transition, 1918–1932.* New York: Knopf.

Handlin, Oscar. 1958. *Al Smith and His America.* Boston: Little, Brown.

Huthmacher, J. Joseph. 1967. *A Nation of Newcomers: Ethnic Minorities in American History.* New York: Delacorte Press.

Lichtman, Allan J. 1979. *Prejudice and the Old Politics: The Presidential Election of 1928.* Chapel Hill: U. of North Carolina Pr.

Lubell, Samuel. 1965. *The Future of American Politics.* New York: Harper & Row.

Silva, Ruth. 1962. *Rum, Religion and Votes: 1928 Reexamined.* University Park: Pennsylvania State U. Pr.

Smith, Alfred E. 1929. *Up to Now: An Autobiography.* New York: Viking.

White, John Kenneth. 1983. *The Fractured Electorate: Political Parties and Social Change in Southern New England.* Hanover, NH: U. Pr. of New England.

Election of 1932

Occurring in the depths of the Great Depression, this election was an overwhelming victory for Franklin D. Roosevelt and the Democratic Party. Yet while it ended an era of Republican hegemony dating back to the 1890s and began a long period of Democratic domination of national politics, the election was more a repudiation of Republican President

Herbert Hoover and the GOP than an affirmation of Roosevelt or the Democrats. It did, however, provide a mandate for change and a transfer of power that enabled implementation of the New Deal and facilitated the political realignment of the 1930s.

In the election, Governor Franklin D. Roosevelt of New York and Speaker of the House John Nance Garner from Texas ran against Republican incumbents Herbert C. Hoover and Charles Curtis. Nominated because of his progressive record and vote-getting prowess in New York and his ability to attract support from both urban and rural Democrats, Roosevelt dramatically broke tradition by traveling to the convention to accept his nomination in person. He called on Democrats to be the "party of liberal thought, of planned action . . . and of the greatest good to the greatest number of our citizens," and said, "I pledge you, I pledge myself, to a new deal for the American people." On the hustings, however, candidate Roosevelt was more consistent about attacking Hoover and supporting the repeal of prohibition than about propounding a clear liberal program, and he adumbrated only part of what would be the New Deal. Receiving sometimes conflicting advice from his academic "Brains Trust" and supported by the carefully orchestrated efforts of the Democratic National Committee directed by New York's James Farley, Roosevelt campaigned more as a Progressive than a New Dealer and more as a canny politician than anything else. Still, a clear contrast did emerge between the buoyant Roosevelt, with his commitment of active, responsive governmental programs to attack economic ills and alleviate human distress; and the dour Hoover, who doggedly defended his policies and denounced FDR as a dangerous radical.

Roosevelt and the Democrats won in a landslide. With Roosevelt capturing 57.4 percent of the vote and every state except for 6 in the Northeast, the presidential returns marked the greatest 4-year reversal ever. (Democrat Al Smith had won just 40.9 percent of the vote in 1928. Roosevelt in fact was the first Democrat in 80 years to be elected President with a majority of the popular vote.) Producing Democratic gains of some 70 Congressmen and 13 Senators, the voters' anti-Republican animus also gave the Democrats commanding control of the Congress, with margins of nearly three to one in the House and two to one in the Senate. Despite the Great Depression, Socialist nominee Norman

Thomas won but 2.2 percent of the vote. Turnout was roughly the same (about 57 percent of the potential electorate) as in 1928; thus while Democratic totals in 1928 and 1936 were swelled by millions of new voters, massive switching from the GOP evidently lay behind the Democratic gains of 1932. In particular, Roosevelt added important new strength among old-stock lower-middle-class, working-class, and farm voters to the Democrats' traditional urban, ethnic, and white southern bastions. As compared to the full-blown Roosevelt coalition of 1936, the 1932 returns showed relatively more Democratic support in nonsouthern farm areas, less in northeastern urban, ethnic, Black, and working-class areas. In its outcome and voting patterns, the 1932 election was nonetheless an important part of the realignment producing the New Deal party system that was for decades central to American politics.

See also: Charles Curtis, John Nance Garner, Herbert Hoover, New Deal, Franklin Roosevelt, Socialist Party of America

John W. Jeffries

REFERENCES

Allswang, John. 1978. *The New Deal and American Politics*. New York: Wiley.

Freidel, Frank. 1971. "Election of 1932." In Arthur M. Schlesinger, Jr., and Fred L. Israel, eds. *History of American Presidential Elections, 1789–1968*. New York: McGraw-Hill.

Election of 1936

This presidential election confirmed what the 1932 election suggested: these were critical elections marking the emergence of a new majority party. The Republicans had been the "normal" national majority since 1896, but the Democrats became the majority party after 1936 and retained that status for more than three decades.

The critical nature of an election is clear only in retrospect, however. Despite the inspired activity of Roosevelt's first term, millions remained unemployed in 1936, farmers were being driven from the land, and the big-business community was united in opposition to the New Deal. Opportunity seemed open to the Republicans.

The Republican Party, however, was in a state of disarray. In the midterm election of 1934 the party holding the White House, for the first, time increased its congressional representation, while only 7 of 48 governors were adherents of the GOP. The Republican organization withered; many counties had no Republican chairman, and the big-city organizations ("machines") were

entirely Democratic. Democratic candidate Al Smith first cracked the Republican big-city vote in 1928; this popularity became the base of Democratic national majorities with Roosevelt.

Meeting in June in Cleveland, the Republican National Convention selected Governor Alfred M. Landon of Kansas. Colonel Frank Knox, a Chicago publisher, became his running mate. Landon was a millionaire oil man, presumably able to soothe the nerves of eastern business; but he was a midwestern supporter of Theodore Roosevelt. Landon was neither "mugwump" nor "stalwart." First elected to the state house in 1932, he was the only Republican governor reelected in 1934. However, Landon's raspy midwestern voice was no match for Roosevelt's patrician tones on the radio.

The Democrats convened in Philadelphia two weeks later, renominating Roosevelt and Vice President John Nance Garner. Landon began his campaign in August, but Roosevelt, to the consternation of his associates, made no response until September. His campaign trips then became triumphal processions. Landon was accused of sounding progressive in the West and conservative in the East. Roosevelt ran on his record, offering no specifics as to the policies his second term might bring. He would be unable to claim a mandate for his 1937 proposal to "pack" the Supreme Court.

Franklin D. Roosevelt was reelected in a stunning landslide by a majority of 10 million votes. Landon carried only Maine and Vermont, for a total of 8 electoral votes. Roosevelt won in the face of the editorial opposition of 80 percent of the newspapers by appealing directly to voters over the radio (the predominant mass medium of the time) and by winning the allegiance of the reporters. The "Roosevelt coalition" was formed—an imposing combination of the Democratic solid South, big-city residents, Catholics, intellectuals and, above all, the working man.

See also: John Nance Garner, New Deal, Franklin Roosevelt, Frank Knox, Alfred M. Landon

Karl A. Lamb

REFERENCES

Burnham, Walter Dean. 1970. *Critical Elections and the Mainsprings of American Politics*. New York: Norton.

Ickes, Harold L. 1953. *The Secret Diary of Harold L. Ickes*. New York: Simon & Schuster.

Lubell, Samuel. 1952. *The Future of American Politics*. New York: Harper.

White, William Allen. 1936. *What Its All About: Being a Reporter's Story of the Early Campaign of 1936*. New York: Macmillan.

Election of 1940

In the spring of 1940, Hitler's conquest of Western Europe made isolationism impractical and unpopular. The international crisis accounted for the election's two unique features: Franklin D. Roosevelt's unprecedented third term and the Republican nomination of utility magnate Wendell L. Willkie, a lifelong Democrat.

When Alfred Landon, the 1936 Republican candidate, carried only Maine and Vermont, the Republican Party's demise seemed likely. In 1938, vigorous Republican candidates, aided by economic recession and FDR's abortive plan to "pack" the Supreme Court, recaptured 81 House seats and 8 in the Senate. But no obvious Republican nominee emerged for 1940. The aspirants ranged from former President Herbert Hoover to newcomers like New York attorney general Thomas Dewey and Ohio's freshman Senator, Robert Taft. Such candidates were deemed too closely associated with isolationist positions.

For nearly two years, Wendell Willkie had been winning public notice for his acceptance of many New Deal goals and for his belief that they could be achieved only by unshackled free enterprise. Willkie supported the draft and rearmament and saw the need for national unity in foreign relations. He announced his candidacy 12 days before the Philadelphia convention. Many delegates were uncommitted and those sent to the convention by the few primary elections were bound only on the first ballot.

The Republican delegates were bombarded by telegrams—many of them phony—supporting Willkie and loud chants of "We want Willkie" from the galleries. The leadership of the convention favored Willkie, and his image as the "people's choice" was a triumph of public relations. He won the nomination on the sixth ballot and then accepted Charles McNary of Oregon, isolationist Minority Leader of the U.S. Senate, as his running mate.

Franklin D. Roosevelt did not seek renomination, but he did nothing to anoint a successor. The Chicago Democratic convention was designed as a "draft" of the incumbent. Its least attractive tactic was the famous "voice from the sewer," as a Chicago machine politician in the basement chanted Roosevelt slogans for an hour, while other microphones went dead.

Democratic delegates initially balked at FDR's choice of Secretary of Agriculture Henry A. Wallace as vice presidential nominee. But the party's leaders worked privately to soothe ruffled feelings, and Eleanor Roosevelt was flown to the convention to deliver a unifying speech.

Willkie won the nomination as an independent above partisanship, but he embraced the tactical suggestions of established party leaders. Clumsily, they over-scheduled him; his voice became strained and his speeches increasingly strident. Willkie eventually challenged FDR to guarantee that the U.S. would not enter the war. For his part, President Roosevelt traveled around the country, dedicating federal projects. In the final ten days, stung by Willkie's charges, he delivered rousing campaign speeches.

Willkie carried 8 midwestern states plus faithful Maine and Vermont for 82 electoral votes and 45 percent of the popular vote. The election confirmed the nature of the Roosevelt coalition formed in 1932 and 1936. The Roosevelt vote was based more upon increasingly positive economic conditions than on foreign affairs.

See also: Thomas Dewey, Herbert Hoover, Isolationism in American Politics, Franklin Roosevelt, Robert Taft, Henry A. Wallace, Wendell Willkie

Karl A. Lamb

REFERENCES

Barnard, Ellsworth. 1966. *Wendell Willkie: Fighter for Freedom*. Marquette: Northern Michigan U. Pr.

Moscow, Warren. 1968. *Roosevelt and Willkie*. Englewood Cliffs, NJ: Prentice-Hall.

Election of 1946

From the outset of the 1946 congressional elections campaign the Democrats were in serious trouble. Much of the early praise for President Harry Truman had faded and his shortcomings had surfaced. American voters, tired of wartime controls, wanted to get on with their lives without governmental interference. In blunt terms, people were tired by the fights over reform legislation and the regimentation necessitated by World War II. To exploit this malaise, the Republicans used the slogans "Had enough" and "It's time for a change." Truman had fired Henry Wallace, the last of the New Dealers, for delivering a speech, read and approved by the President, in which Wallace criticized the foreign policy of Secretary of State James F. Byrnes as being too anti-Russian. Subsequently, the Republicans branded anyone supported by Wallace a "red"—a tag meant to associate radicals with Democrats. Truman's unpopularity stemmed from administrative bungling, inflation, and the shortage of meat; compounding these trends, the President refused to campaign and remained relatively quiet during the campaign.

The Democratic National Committee conducted a poorly focused and poorly organized campaign. Instead of vigorous speeches by the President, they played old Franklin D. Roosevelt recordings, which only reminded the voters of the way things had changed under Truman. The frail charge that the election of Republicans would result in large profits for a few left the voters unmoved. The campaign's best efforts were made by the political action committee of the Congress of Industrial Organizations (CIO). The Republicans, on the other hand, conducted a vigorous campaign with exciting new faces who were primarily conservatives who appealed to old values and virtues—the politics of "normalcy." The Republican national chairman promised to clean up the mess in Washington with a Republican-controlled Congress that would end "controls, confusion, corruption, and communism."

As expected, the GOP scored massive victories beyond their wildest expectations. The Republicans won both houses of Congress and swept a majority of governorships and state legislatures as well as county and township positions—the best they had done since the 1920s. They also shifted political power at all levels of government—a seizure of control that would not be overturned by the Democrats until the 1958 elections. Republicans increased their Senate seats from 38 to 51, a feat most political analysts considered impossible. The new Republican-controlled Senate included such future newsmakers as John W. Bricker of Ohio, William Jenner of Indiana, William Knowland of California, George W. Malone of Nevada, Joseph R. McCarthy of Wisconsin, Arthur V. Watkins of Utah, and John J. Williams of New Jersey—all conservatives who would strengthen the conservative coalition of southern Democrats and northern Republicans, which applied a hammerlock to liberal legislation until 1964. Only Irving M. Ives of New York was elected as a Republican moderate liberal.

In the House, the Republicans won 56 new seats, leaving the Democrats with the fewest members that they had had since 1928. Among GOP House winners was Richard Nixon of California. Voters elected 25 Republican governors, including such luminaries as Thomas E. Dewey of New York and Earl Warren of California. When President Truman returned to Washington, only Under Secretary Dean Acheson greeted him; some Democrats suggested that Truman appoint a Republican Secretary of State and then resign. Instead Truman, his fighting instincts aroused, began his efforts to insure that the same fate would not befall him in 1948.

See also: Thomas Dewey, Joseph McCarthy, Richard Nixon, Franklin D. Roosevelt, Robert Taft, Harry S Truman, Henry A. Wallace

C. David Tompkins

Election of 1948

An important component of the political environment in 1948 was the putative weakness of Democratic President Harry Truman. In the 1946 elections, public dissatisfaction with economic conditions gave the Republicans control of both houses of Congress for the first time since 1930. Liberal dissatisfaction with Truman intensified as the President clashed with organized labor and the Soviet Union, causing many New Deal liberals like Henry Wallace, who in fact was fired, to leave the administration. Southerners were concerned about their declining influence in a national Democratic Party that was increasingly sympathetic to organized labor and to the cause of Blacks. Southern Democrats formally protested after Truman's Committee on Civil Rights in October 1947 came out strongly for greater civil liberties. By April 1948 only 36 percent of Americans approved of Truman's job performance, prompting a "non-political" national speech-making tour by Truman in June.

Dissatisfaction with Truman and concern with his slim chances for election led some Democrats to search for an alternative candidate. Out of desperation the liberal Americans for Democratic Action (ADA) headed an effort to draft Dwight Eisenhower, the hero of World War II. Eisenhower's great public popularity as well as his vagueness on issues attracted support from diverse groups, among them southerners and big-city bosses. After Eisenhower refused to run, Democratic Party leaders backed incumbent Truman at the Democratic National Convention. He won on the first ballot with 75 percent of the vote.

At the convention, liberal ADA delegates, led by Andrew Biemiller of Wisconsin and Hubert Humphrey of Minnesota, inserted an aggressive civil rights plank into the platform to replace the more moderate and vague plank found in the 1944 platform that Truman endorsed. Thirty-five delegates from Mississippi and Alabama immediately withdrew from the convention in protest, and all except 13 of the remaining southern delegates supported Georgia Senator Richard Russell for the presidential nomination. Truman's effort to unify the party by selecting a liberal running mate failed as Supreme Court Justice William Douglas refused the offer, and the delegates selected as Vice President moderate Senate Minority Leader Alben Barkley of Kentucky, who had delivered a rousing keynote address. In his acceptance speech, Truman attacked the "rotten record" of the Republican-controlled Congress and challenged them to enact the GOP's fairly liberal platform by calling a special session of Congress.

For the Republican presidential nomination, two strong candidates had emerged by 1947. Clearly ahead was the moderate governor of New York, Thomas Dewey, who had been the party's unsuccessful presidential nominee in 1944 and was supported among the rank and file. A strong challenger was conservative Ohio Senator Robert Taft, his party's congressional leader on domestic issues, popular chiefly among conservative GOP professionals. Other Republican hopefuls included former Minnesota governor Harold Stassen, California Senator Arthur Vandenberg, California governor Earl Warren, and General Douglas MacArthur. Some Republican professionals were concerned that a relative newcomer like Stassen could hurt their chances in the November general election, but Stassen's support among the party rank and file seemed to be growing after victories in the Wisconsin and Nebraska primaries. Victories by Taft in Ohio and Dewey in Oregon ended the Stassen bandwagon, and Dewey entered the convention as the front-runner.

A "Stop Dewey" movement failed after it was unable to unify behind one candidate, and Dewey won the nomination unanimously on the third ballot. Dewey's victory was attributed to five factors: (1) polls indicating that Republican identifiers in the public preferred his nomination; (2) polls showing him leading Truman by a larger margin than Taft among the voting public; (3) a strong first ballot showing, when Dewey received 434 of the 548 delegate votes required for nomination; (4) his popularity among all ideological elements of the party with special strength in eastern liberal states (Taft's support was concentrated in conservative states); and (5) the efficiency of the Dewey organization, which assigned liaison men to every delegation and kept file cards on individual

delegates. The liberal and internationalist platform reflected the dominant wing of the party that had nominated Dewey. Earl Warren, who had administrative experience as governor of California, received the vice presidential nomination and balanced the ticket geographically.

Truman's election was threatened by defections on the left and right extremes of the Democratic Party. The leftist Progressive Party nominated Henry Wallace for President and the singing cowboy and Idaho Democratic Senator Glen Taylor as Vice President. The Progressive platform's opposition to Truman's policy of containment of communism led to active support of Wallace by the Communist Party, support that he refused to repudiate. Some southern conservatives formed the States' Rights Party dedicated to upholding racial segregation and nominated South Carolina governor Strom Thurmond for President and Mississippi governor Fielding Wright for Vice President. They expected at least to effect Truman's defeat, which would serve to make the national Democratic Party more responsive to white southerners in the future. At best, southerners would hold the balance of power if the election were thrown into the House of Representatives.

Truman pursued a liberal strategy, vetoing the antilabor Taft-Hartley Act and attacking the Republican Congress for failing to enact the liberal domestic programs in its own platform. In an aggressive old-style whistle-stop campaign, Truman made over 250 speeches while traveling over 20,000 miles after Labor Day. The President continually pointed to the help that domestic New Deal programs had given average Americans. He charged that the Republicans wanted to repeal the New Deal and cared only about "special interests" and "gluttons of privilege" like the rich and big business. Polls consistently showed a significant Dewey lead, and Dewey became overconfident. In an issueless campaign that sought to avoid alienating anyone, Dewey acted like a statesman who had already won the election, stressing the need for national unity. As the campaign progressed, many labor unions endorsed Truman, and the ADA mobilized liberal support behind him.

In a stunning comeback that confounded the pollsters, Truman won the election with 49.5 percent of the popular vote, compared to 45 percent for Dewey. Truman carried 28 states from all regions, while Dewey carried 16 states primarily in the Northeast and Midwest. Thurmond won only the Deep South states of

Alabama, Louisiana, Mississippi, and South Carolina, which were the only states to list him on the ballot as the official Democratic Party nominee. Truman was helped because his party was in the majority in terms of the partisan identifications of the public; his aggressive campaign that stressed popular Democratic positions on New Deal economic issues caused many undecided Democrats to return to the party fold. Despite the endorsement of most of the nation's newspapers, Dewey nevertheless was hurt by the GOP's identification with narrow interests like the rich and big business as well as by the impression he gave of being cold, smug, complacent, and patronizing.

The election of 1948 has been labeled a "maintaining" election, since short-term factors like issues and candidate attributes were not strong enough to outweigh long-term Democratic Party dominance. Low voter turnout in 1948 suggests that neither candidate was extremely popular. The dominance of the Democratic Party showed when it regained control of both chambers of Congress as well as by maintaining control of the presidency after the death of charismatic Franklin Roosevelt.

See also: Alben Barkley, Bosses, Civil Rights and Southern Politics, Thomas E. Dewey, Dwight D. Eisenhower, Hubert Humphrey, Media and Presidential Campaigns, New Deal, Franklin Roosevelt, Robert A. Taft, Strom Thurmond, Harry S Truman, Henry A. Wallace, Earl Warren

Stephen D. Shaffer

REFERENCES

Berelson, Bernard, Paul Lazarsfeld, and William McPhee. 1954. *Voting.* Chicago: U. of Chicago Pr.

Divine, Robert. 1974. *Foreign Policy and U.S. Presidential Elections.* New York: Franklin Watts.

Keech, William R., and Donald R. Matthews. 1977. *The Party's Choice.* Washington: Brookings.

Mosteller, Frederick, Herbert Hyman, Philip McCarthy, Eli Marks, and David Truman. 1949. *The Pre-Election Polls of 1948.* New York: Social Science Research Council.

Ross, Irwin. 1968. *The Loneliest Campaign: The Truman Victory of 1948.* New York: New American Library.

Election of 1952

Of the presidential election of 1952 the *Manchester Guardian*'s correspondent, Max Freedman, said, "You cannot defeat a beatitude with an aphorism." Adlai Stevenson, in whom many Americans of that year discovered a most extraordinary eloquence, was nevertheless pitted against Dwight David Eisenhower, the most popular American soldier to emerge from the very recently concluded World War II.

Stevenson was a reluctant candidate. In 1948 he had been plucked from a Chicago law practice by Colonel Jack Arvey, mastermind of the Chicago Democratic machine, and run successfully for governor in a year in which Democrats were not expected to do well. His administration was a success. And so Harry Truman (who decided not to push the astounding good fortune of his 1948 victory by standing for reelection) and other Democratic leaders identified Stevenson as their candidate. Stevenson responded standoffishly and would not declare his candidacy until very late in the preconvention process.

Given Stevenson's genuine reluctance, numerous other Democrats jumped into the race. Alben Barkley, Truman's popular "Veep" was, at age 74, considered too old. Richard Russell of Georgia, one of the ornaments of the Senate, was too southern. Averell Harriman of New York, then Mutual Security director in the Truman administration, had never run for any other elective office. Bob Kerr, rough-tongued Senator from Oklahoma, was regarded by party leaders as far too much of an "acquired" taste. Senator Estes Kefauver of Tennessee had become something of a national hero as the result of his 1951 investigatory hearings on organized crime, and he announced early that he would contest the primary elections. Party leaders around the country, and in the Senate, disliked him, however, in part because these very same hearings brought some urban Democrats into disrepute. It was Kefauver's candidacy that inspired President Truman to characterize primaries as "eyewash."

Stevenson, as host governor, gave a superb speech to open the Chicago Democratic National Convention. By virtue of his primary-won delegates, Kefauver led the field on the first ballot with 340 votes, to 273 for Stevenson, 268 for Russell, 123 1/2 for Harriman, 65 for Kerr, and 48 1/2 for Barkley, with 111 going to others. On the second ballot, Stevenson picked up significant strength, and on the third ballot Harriman (121 votes on the second ballot) withdrew in Stevenson's favor and the convention nominated Stevenson.

On the Republican side, there was also a reluctant candidate in Dwight ("Ike") Eisenhower. In early 1952 General Eisenhower was on duty in Paris as commander at Supreme Headquarters, Allied Powers in Europe, and nobody was sure that he was a registered voter, let alone a Republican. Senator Henry Cabot Lodge of Massachusetts and others of the so-called Dewey (internationalist, East Coast oriented) wing of the party in January obtained Ike's consent to enter his name in primaries. Leading a predominantly Midwest, isolationist bloc of the party was Ohio Senator Robert A. Taft, "Mr. Republican." Earl Warren, governor of California, and Harold Stassen of Minnesota were also candidates.

The main battle was between Taft and Eisenhower. As a practical matter, although Taft called up deep and sincere loyalties within the party, the nomination contest was over when in the March Minnesota primary—in Harold Stassen's home state—over 100,000 Republican voters wrote Eisenhower's name in on their ballots. Taft battled Eisenhower's juggernaut down to the wire, notably, at the convention, in a contest involving the seating of the Texas delegates. Eisenhower won the nomination on the first ballot.

Eisenhower won the election handily by garnering 442 electoral votes to Stevenson's 89. In the popular vote Ike won 55 percent or 34 million votes to Stevenson's 27 million out of 62 million cast. Ike's coattails also elected a Republican House—adding 22 Republican members—but Republicans were less successful in the narrowly divided Senate, adding only one member. Of the three Republican issues, "Communism, Corruption, and Korea," disaffection with the prolongation of the Korean War seemed to resonate most strongly with public opinion. General Eisenhower's pledge to "go to Korea" was therefore a useful campaign weapon. Notable also was Eisenhower's decision to remove from a speech in Wisconsin a short defense of his mentor, General George Marshall, who had been scurrilously attacked by Wisconsin Republican Senator Joseph McCarthy.

The Stevenson campaign was inefficient and hampered by tension between the candidate and the outgoing Truman administration. Stevenson's speeches, following the theme of "talking sense to the American people," met a level of oratorical excellence unique in the twentieth century. Later in his life, when asked to give advice to young politicians, Stevenson said, "Never run against a war hero."

See also: Dwight D. Eisenhower, Henry Cabot Lodge, Joseph McCarthy, Richard M. Nixon, Adlai Stevenson II, Robert A. Taft

Nelson W. Polsby

REFERENCES

Campbell, Angus, et al. 1960. *The American Voter.* New York: Wiley.

David, Ralph T., Malcolm C. Moos, and Ralph M. Goldman. 1954. *Presidential Nominating Politics in 1952.* Baltimore: Johns Hopkins U. Pr.

Johnson, Walter. 1955. *How We Drafted Adlai Stevenson.* New York: Knopf.

Stevenson, Adlai E. 1952. *Speeches.* New York: Random House.

Election of 1960

This presidential election would have been noteworthy under any circumstances because of the closeness of its outcome. But it was also an election of historical significance in the development of the American electoral process. In several important ways, it helped to define enduring new directions in presidential campaigns.

The Democratic ticket of Senator John F. Kennedy of Massachusetts and Senator Lyndon B. Johnson of Texas defeated their Republican opponents, Vice President Richard M. Nixon and Ambassador Henry Cabot Lodge, by only 115,000 popular votes among 68.8 million cast. Kennedy received 49.72 percent of the popular vote to Nixon's 49.55 percent. The narrow margin between the candidates was consistent across the country. In only four states did Kennedy receive more than 55 percent of the popular vote; Nixon received more than 55 percent in only nine.

With very narrow victories in the critical states of Texas and Illinois, Kennedy was able to win by a larger margin in the Electoral College. He polled 303 electoral votes to 219 for Nixon. In addition, Senator Harry Byrd, Sr. of Virginia received 15 electoral votes. The division of candidate support adhered closely to the patterns typical for the time. Kennedy won majorities in most of the southern states and in most of the Plains States and Mountain States and the three states on the West Coast. He also won victories in Florida, the upper South, and Indiana, Ohio, and Wisconsin.

Nixon's path to the Republican nomination was uncluttered. He had spent his years as Vice President assiduously building support among Republicans around the country. His intention to seek the presidency when Dwight D. Eisenhower left office was never in doubt, and all of his potential opponents in the Republican Party declined to run against him. Nixon won almost 90 percent of the votes cast in the primary elections.

The race for the Democratic nomination was significantly different. After eight years of waiting for Eisenhower to leave, many Democrats were anxious to run for President. Some support remained for Adlai Stevenson, who had been the party's nominee in 1952 and 1956, but Stevenson never undertook a formal candidacy. Among the announced candidates, the leaders were all Senators: Hubert Humphrey of Minnesota, Johnson of Texas, Kennedy of Massachusetts, and Stuart Symington of Missouri.

Johnson and Symington adopted strategies that focused on state and local party leaders; they largely avoided the 16 presidential primaries scheduled in 1960. Kennedy and Humphrey chose to build their campaigns on primary victories. Kennedy started the campaign with substantial liabilities: at 42, he was unusually young; though he had served 14 years in Congress, he could claim little legislative accomplishment; he was not well known nationally; and he was Catholic in a nation that had never had a Catholic President. He and his advisers believed that the primaries would allow him to lay those liabilities to rest by demonstrating broad popular appeal.

Kennedy's March victory in the New Hampshire primary counted for little because he drew no real opposition. The first critical test was the April primary in Wisconsin where Humphrey had mounted a major effort in the state next to his own. Kennedy won the Wisconsin primary, however, with 56.5 percent of the Democratic vote.

The next critical test was in West Virginia in May. Humphrey's wounded candidacy was nonetheless still alive, and West Virginia was a poor and heavily Protestant state. It provided an important and visible test of the extent to which Kennedy's religion was a handicap to his hopes for the nomination. Kennedy won the West Virginia primary with almost 61 percent of the Democratic vote, and Humphrey withdrew from the race.

At the Democratic convention, the principal contestants were Kennedy and Johnson, though Kennedy came to Los Angeles with delegate support approaching the total needed for nomination. He won nomination on the first ballot and, despite some personal antipathy between Kennedy and Johnson partisans, Kennedy offered the vice presidential nomination to Johnson, who quickly accepted.

The general election campaign focused on several substantive and candidate issues. Kennedy avoided any personal criticism of Eisenhower, still the most popular political figure of his time. But he tried to portray the Eisenhower years as a time of drift and immobility. His repeated theme was "It's time to get the country moving again." He spoke often of a "missile gap," claiming that American lethargy had allowed the Soviet Union to make important military gains. He called for the creation of a Peace Corps, a minimum wage, more coherent agricultural policies, and better educational opportunities. His convention acceptance speech had referred to the 1960s as a "new frontier—a frontier of unknown opportunities and perils— a frontier of unfulfilled hopes and threats . . . a set of challenges." He sought to turn his relative youth into an asset, emphasizing his vigor and the contrast between the generation he represented and the one of which Eisenhower was the symbol.

Nixon's campaign emphasized his own strengths—the experience he had gained in eight years as Vice President, particularly his experience in foreign affairs; his affiliation with Eisenhower's popular support; the peace and prosperity of the times—and the traditional Republican belief in private enterprise and fiscal conservatism. Nixon sought to build his campaign on a broad national base and pledged to appear in all fifty states.

Religion remained an important subtext of the election, though Nixon never raised it. In September, Kennedy decided to face it head-on in a speech before a group of Protestant clergymen in Houston. By defining what he viewed as a clear separation between his personal faith and his public duties, he helped to allay the worst fears of those who felt any Catholic would have to commit higher loyalty to church than to country.

The 1960 campaign featured the first nationally televised debates between major party presidential candidates. Kennedy and Nixon had four debates altogether, with the first occurring in Chicago in September. It attracted an audience of 70 million viewers. Most students of the election regard that first debate as a turning point for Kennedy. No clear winner or loser emerged, but Kennedy was able to demonstrate that there was no significant contrast between the candidates in age or in understanding of issues. In appearance and style, Nixon was not Kennedy's equal before the television cameras, and the debate helped to put to rest some of the concerns about Kennedy's age and experience.

The closeness of the final result raised questions about possible improprieties in vote counting in Illinois and Texas, where Kennedy narrowly won. Some supporters urged Nixon to demand recounts in those states. But Nixon, not wishing to provoke a constitutional crisis, declined to do so.

The election of 1960 marked no critical realignment of voter loyalties or partisan divisions. Kennedy's support came primarily from the traditional elements of the New Deal coalition, and Nixon's came from traditional Republican sources of strength. Nixon fared somewhat better among Protestants and somewhat worse among Catholics than had Republicans in previous elections, but 1960 provided no profound evidence that Americans base their votes on religious considerations. In fact, the principal significance of the election in religious terms was that Americans elected their first Catholic President and thus effectively put to rest the traditional political "wisdom" that no Catholic could be elected President.

Of more lasting importance from the 1960 election were two emerging changes in the electoral process itself. The first was the importance of primaries in the nominating process. Kennedy had demonstrated how critical primary election success could be as a means of building support for the nomination. In the years that followed, more states adopted primaries as their principal means of selecting delegates, and competing for popular support in the primaries quickly became the principal route to nomination in both parties.

A second landmark of the 1960 election was the emergence of televised debates. Such debates did not immediately become a norm of presidential elections; indeed the next ones did not occur until 1976. But the visible importance of the Kennedy-Nixon debates was long remembered and set a standard that, by the 1980s, seemed to have become a routine feature of presidential campaigns.

See also: Dwight D. Eisenhower, Lyndon B. Johnson, John F. Kennedy, Henry Cabot Lodge, Media and Presidential Campaigns, Richard M. Nixon

G. Calvin Mackenzie

REFERENCES

Campbell, Angus, et al. 1966. *Elections and the Political Order.* New York: Wiley.

Nixon, Richard. 1978. *RN: The Memoirs of Richard Nixon.* New York: Warner Books.

Schlesinger, Arthur M., Jr. *A Thousand Days.* Boston: Houghton Mifflin.

Sorenson, Theodore. 1965. *Kennedy.* New York: Harper & Row.

White, Theodore. 1961. *The Making of the President— 1960.* New York: Atheneum.

Election of 1964

The single event that determined the nature of this presidential election was the assassination of President John F. Kennedy in November 1963. Because the nation was plunged into grief by the sudden loss, the presidential election season was suspended until the new year. Suddenly thrust into the Oval Office, Lyndon Johnson, with his sure instinct for power, took firm command of the government and began to pass legislation that Congress had resisted when proposed by John Kennedy. No one doubted that Lyndon Johnson would be the Democratic nominee.

The Republicans nominated Arizona Senator Barry Goldwater, who had little instinct for power. Not personally ambitious, Goldwater was drafted as the spokesman for a grass-roots conservative movement, a putative American majority that was never activated by liberal Republican candidates. In 1964 the eastern liberal Republican establishment was led by New York governor Nelson Rockefeller, who in early 1963 led Republican opinion polls as the most-favored presidential nominee. Conservative Republicans felt the party's candidate should directly confront the liberal propensity for ever-growing government, with its presumed threat to individual liberties, and the liberal "softness" in foreign affairs. A corollary argument was that the Republicans could build an organization and a following in the South based on conservatism rather than racism.

Barry Goldwater attacked Democratic policies and practices with blunt, colorful, and sometimes frightening phrases. His Republican rivals for the nomination pictured him as a radical extremist, setting the theme for the later Democratic campaign. The bruising Republican primary contests were nearly irrelevant: Goldwater's nomination had been all but locked up through the selection of national convention delegates in state conventions by F. Clifton White's conservative Republican activists. White began operations without Goldwater's permission in 1961 and publicly launched the National Draft Goldwater Committee with a massive rally in the Washington Armory on July 4, 1963. By then, public reaction to Rockefeller's remarriage had destroyed his lead in the polls; Goldwater had to take the movement seriously. He announced his candidacy on January 3, 1964.

Sixteen states held primary elections in 1964. Goldwater planned to confront Rockefeller directly in three of them. In the folksy atmosphere of New Hampshire, Goldwater made off-the-cuff suggestions (e.g., social security should be made voluntary and NATO commanders should decide whether to employ atomic weapons) that plagued him the rest of the year. Scared of Goldwater, New Hampshire voters were even more suspicious of Rockefeller's huge New York budgets; the primary was won (in absentia) by Ambassador Henry Cabot Lodge. Goldwater withdrew from the Oregon primary to regroup; it was won by Nelson ("He cared enough to come") Rockefeller. Barry Goldwater clinched the nomination by narrowly winning the California primary only hours after Rockefeller's young wife gave birth to their first child.

Offended by the charges of "extremism" made by members of his own party, Goldwater decided against any gesture of unity at the national convention in San Francisco. Accepting the nomination, he declared, "Extremism in the defense of liberty is no vice! . . . Moderation in the pursuit of justice is no virtue!" As running mate he chose a little-known, but very conservative, New York Congressman, William Miller. A scant 22 percent of voters identifying themselves as Republicans favored Goldwater as their candidate.

Meanwhile, Lyndon Johnson, disclaiming any interest in politics, kept his image before the public by traveling around the nation being President. His chief political decision was to choose a running mate. Johnson wanted the opportunity to be elected President in his own right; only the Kennedy magic had made Johnson the Vice President. Striving to show his independence of that magic, Johnson eliminated then Attorney General Robert Kennedy from consideration but told the public that no member of the Cabinet should be considered. When Goldwater's nomination indicated that no easterner was needed to balance the ticket (Goldwater once suggested that the eastern states should be cut adrift), Johnson settled on liberal Senator Hubert Humphrey of Minnesota.

The Democratic convention in Atlantic City produced three days of drama focused on the contest over the seating of the Mississippi Freedom Democratic Party—the hard-won stepchild of the drive to register Black voters. The Black delegation had an impeccable moral right to convention seats, but the regular (read "white") delegates had the legal right. Hubert Humphrey worked out the compromise: two of the sixty-eight Black delegates would be seated, and the rules changed so that, in 1968 and thereafter,

no delegates would be seated from states in which the political process excluded citizens on account of race. This provision eventually led to racially integrated Democratic parties in the South; in 1964 southern Republican parties broke their historic allegiances with Black voters.

Goldwater's managers felt he should give half-hour television broadcasts to make his positions fully clear. His audiences were comprised mainly of those already convinced, but their flood of small campaign contributions suggested that millions more would at least vote for the Republican. The Democrats threw Goldwater off balance with the single showing of a television advertisement. It showed a little girl picking petals from a daisy. As she counted, the numbers became a countdown, and a nuclear mushroom cloud filled the screen while the announcer suggested voting for someone who would protect our children from the dangers of nuclear war. Although the commercial appeared only once, its message was widely disseminated. For domestic policy, the Democrats filled every available time slot with an eloquent picture of two hands tearing apart a social security card.

Lyndon Johnson won the election in a historic landslide, capturing 61 percent of the vote. Goldwater won only six states: Arizona, Alabama, Georgia, Louisiana, Mississippi, and South Carolina. Yet he paved the way for a conservative candidate less frightening and more polished in public speech—Ronald Reagan.

See also: Barry Goldwater, Hubert Humphrey, Lyndon B. Johnson, John F. Kennedy, Robert F. Kennedy, Ronald Reagan, Nelson Rockefeller, F. Clifton White

Karl A. Lamb

REFERENCES

Ladd, Everett Carll, Jr., with Charles D. Hadley. 1975. *Transformations of the American Party System.* New York: Norton.

Lamb, Karl A., and Paul A. Smith. 1968. *Campaign Decision-Making: The Presidential Election of 1964.* Belmont, CA: Wadsworth.

White, F. Clifton. 1967. *Suite 3505: The Story of the Draft Goldwater Movement.* New Rochelle, NY: Arlington House.

White, Theodore H. 1965. *The Making of the President—1964.* New York: Atheneum.

Election of 1968

This election changed the manner in which our Presidents are nominated and elected more dramatically than any other election in the twentieth century. The riotous Democratic National Convention in Chicago, the subsequent reforms of Democratic politics by the McGovern-

Fraser Commission, and a revolution in campaign technology and in the use of television permanently altered the political terrain.

Early in 1968 the Democratic Party was torn apart by the increasingly unpopular war in Vietnam. In March, President Lyndon Johnson announced that he would not run for reelection after his poor showing in the New Hampshire primary against the antiwar candidate, Senator Eugene McCarthy (Minn.). In April, civil rights leader Martin Luther King, Jr., was assassinated in Memphis; tension mounted and cities burned as the nation dealt with its grief and anger. Senator Robert F. Kennedy (N.Y.) moved to the front in the presidential race with victories in three primaries and strong showing in two others as a write-in candidate. Kennedy was assassinated following his victory in California in June and Vice President Hubert Humphrey positioned himself to claim the nomination, though he had not won a single primary. The Democratic nomination process culminated with the violent clashes between war protesters and Chicago police and between McCarthy and Humphrey delegates on the convention floor as the world watched. Humphrey won the nomination on the first ballot with 67 percent of the delegates.

In contrast, the Republicans had a relatively calm summer with the "new" Richard Nixon emerging as the nominee. Nixon easily won all the primaries he entered, but at the convention Governors Ronald Reagan (Calif.) and Nelson Rockefeller (N.Y.), and "favorite son" candidates Governor George Romney (Mich.) and Governor James Rhodes (Ohio) won nearly enough votes to deny Nixon a first-ballot nomination. Nixon was a narrow victor with 51.9 percent of the delegates.

In the general election campaign, Nixon started with a huge lead, which he maintained with a conservative front-runner strategy, using frequent television spots and staged question-and-answer sessions to present himself in the best light. Another key decision was to concede the South to George Wallace, who was running as an Independent, while trying to capture the Border States. The strategy worked as Wallace carried five southern states, with Nixon picking off five Border States and Florida. Interestingly, the Vietnam War did not play a pivotal role in deciding whether those who voted preferred Humphrey or Nixon. Rather, the alienated Kennedy and McCarthy supporters who sat out the election may have been decisive in the razor-thin Nixon victory (a 0.7 percent popular vote margin over Humphrey and 56 percent of the electoral votes).

In the wake of the Chicago debacle, Democrats vowed "never again" and moved to reform the nomination process. The central point of contention was the closed nature of delegate selection procedures. McCarthy and Kennedy supporters were often excluded from those caucuses that were controlled by local party leaders who were strong supporters of Humphrey. To reform these procedures, the 1968 convention created two commissions—the Commission on Party Structure and Delegate Selection (popularly known as the McGovern-Fraser Commission) and the Commission on Rules (the O'Hara Commission).

The McGovern-Fraser Commission recommended a set of rules and guidelines that were subsequently adopted by the party. They abolished the unit rule, required that delegate selection meetings be open and publicized, reduced the role played by party leaders and elected officials, provided for opportunities to challenge delegate slates, and mandated that women, Blacks, and young people receive delegate slots in proportion to their size in the state population. Rather than contend with the myriad of rules, many state parties decided to choose delegates chosen in fair and open primaries. The number of states selecting their delegates in Democratic presidential primaries increased from 17 to 30 from 1968 to 1976 (16 to 28 for Republicans). Subsequent party reforms changed some of the McGovern-Fraser rules, but the nature of the nomination process would never be the same. Today it is impossible for a presidential candidate to pursue Humphrey's strategy and still be nominated on the first ballot. Candidates *must* run in a full slate of presidential primaries.

The 1968 presidential election also saw the development of modern campaign technology and tactics. While the adversary commercial in politics was not invented by the Nixon campaign, his handlers raised it to an art form. Using an ad agency to package a politician is taken for granted today, but in 1968 it was daring and controversial for both Humphrey and Nixon. Joe McGinnis argues that Nixon would not have been elected in 1968 had it not been for his effective use of television.

The reporting of presidential campaigns also changed in three important ways in 1968: (1) Theodore White maintains that conventions first became a television producer's showcase in 1968. The violent images of the Chicago demonstrations and riots that were played and replayed and interspersed between convention floor footage may have sunk the Humphrey campaign. (2) CBS introduced exit polling to gain an edge in the hyper-competitive "calling" of races. (3) "Pack" coverage of candidates by journalists replaced the traditional method of home-city reporting.

Wallace's victories in five southern states nearly threw the election into the U.S. House and heightened the quadrennial calls for direct popular election of the President. In September 1969 the House passed (by 339–70) a bill that provided for the direct election of Presidents with a 40 percent plurality runoff provision, but the measure failed to clear the Senate.

See also: Spiro Agnew, Hubert Humphrey, Lyndon B. Johnson, Robert F. Kennedy, Martin Luther King, Jr., Eugene McCarthy, McGovern-Fraser Commission, Media and Presidential campaigns, Edmund S. Muskie, Richard M. Nixon, Presidential Nominating Conventions, Nelson Rockefeller, Vietnam War as a Political Issue, George C. Wallace

David T. Canon

REFERENCES

Longley, Lawrence, and Alan G. Braun. 1975. *The Politics of Electoral College Reform.* New Haven: Yale U. Pr.

McGinniss, Joe. 1969. *The Selling of the President.* New York: Trident Press.

Polsby, Nelson W. 1983. *Consequences of Party Reform.* New York: Oxford U. Pr.

White, Theodore. 1969. *The Making of the President— 1968.* New York: Atheneum.

Wills, Garry. 1970. *Nixon Agonistes: The Crisis of the Self-Made Man.* Boston: Houghton Mifflin.

Election of 1972

This presidential election produced one of the greatest landslides and one of the greatest scandals in American political history. In the November balloting, Republican incumbent Richard Nixon crushed his Democratic challenger, Senator George McGovern of South Dakota. Nixon received almost 61 percent of the national popular vote compared with less than 38 percent for McGovern; former Congressman John Schmitz of California, running as the candidate of the American Party, got just over 1 percent of the popular vote. George McGovern carried only Massachusetts and the District of Columbia, for a total of 17 electoral votes, compared with 520 for Richard Nixon. (One Nixon elector from Virginia cast his ballot for the Libertarian presidential candidate, John Hospers.)

Although the 1972 presidential campaign ended with a landslide victory for Richard Nixon

and his Vice President, Spiro Agnew, such an outcome did not appear likely when the campaign began. During 1971, President Nixon faced serious problems with inflation at home and an unpopular war in Southeast Asia. The early front-runner for the Democratic presidential nomination was Senator Edmund Muskie of Maine, a moderate liberal who had performed admirably as Hubert Humphrey's running mate in 1968. National polls during late 1971 and early 1972 showed Muskie giving Nixon a close race. However, Edmund Muskie's candidacy would not survive the new presidential nominating process that had emerged as a result of the Democratic Party's reformed rules.

At their tumultuous 1968 nominating convention in Chicago, the Democratic delegates had voted to create a commission to recommend changes in the party's nomination process. The commission, appointed by Democratic National Committee chair Fred Harris, was chaired initially by Senator McGovern and later by Congressman Donald Fraser of Minnesota.

The McGovern-Fraser Commission's recommendations led to major changes in the Democratic presidential nominating process, including a greatly reduced role for party leaders and elected officials and a greatly increased importance for presidential primaries.

In the first presidential primary of 1972, held in New Hampshire, George McGovern achieved what the news media described as a much "better than expected" second place finish to Senator Muskie. After several setbacks in later primaries, Muskie eventually dropped out of the race for the Democratic nomination. McGovern's success reflected his ability to understand and exploit the party's new rules and his strong appeal to liberal party activists because of his opposition to the war in Vietnam. After Muskie's withdrawal from the race, McGovern's principal opponents for the Democratic nomination were Governor George Wallace of Alabama, whose campaign faltered after he was shot and seriously injured at a campaign rally in Maryland, and Hubert Humphrey, the party's 1968 standard-bearer.

George McGovern won the Democratic nomination on the first ballot at the party's nominating convention in Miami. However, McGovern's extremely liberal positions on issues ranging from Vietnam to welfare reform and busing made him an easy target for the Republicans in the fall.

McGovern's problems were compounded by his inept handling of the vice presidential nomination. After reports surfaced that his first running mate, Senator Thomas Eagleton of Missouri, had received electroshock therapy for depression, McGovern announced that he was "one thousand percent" behind Eagleton while his aides tried to convince the Missouri Senator to withdraw from the ticket. After Eagleton finally did step down, McGovern was rejected by several prospective running mates, including Senator Edward Kennedy of Massachusetts, before he finally found a willing candidate—former Peace Corps director (and Kennedy in-law) Sargent Shriver.

The McGovern-Shriver ticket started the fall campaign with a huge deficit that it never made up. The contest between Nixon and McGovern did, however, provide voters with a clear choice on a wide range of issues. Even the candidates' television ads, for once, emphasized their contrasting issue positions. The result was an election marked by an extraordinarily high level of issue voting and massive defections to the Republican ticket by moderate-to-conservative Democrats.

Perhaps the most significant event of the 1972 presidential campaign was what appeared at the time to be a minor incident—the break-in at the headquarters of the Democratic National Committee (DNC) in the Watergate complex. Several burglars were arrested attempting to remove documents from the files of DNC chairman Larry O'Brien. Although George McGovern tried to link the break-in to Richard Nixon's presidential campaign, the incident received little attention from the media until many months after the election when the burglars began to talk about their White House connections.

What came to be known as the Watergate scandal eventually involved much more than the break-in itself. The investigation of the break-in led to revelations concerning efforts by Richard Nixon and his close advisers to subvert the Democratic Party, intimidate the news media, and extort campaign funds from individuals and businesses interested in federal appointments or contracts. In August of 1974, Richard Nixon was forced to resign from the presidency after transcripts based on White House tape recordings revealed that the President had been directly involved in planning the cover-up of the Watergate break-in. Nixon was succeeded by Vice President Gerald Ford whom Nixon himself had appointed to replace Spiro Agnew after Agnew had pleaded no contest to

charges of accepting payoffs from government contractors in Maryland.

The Watergate scandal led to major reforms of the campaign finance laws, including the public financing of presidential election campaigns. The scandal, along with President Ford's later decision to pardon former President Nixon, also contributed greatly to the Republican loss of 49 House and 4 Senate seats in the 1974 midterm election and to Ford's defeat at the hands of Jimmy Carter in the 1976 presidential election.

See also: Spiro Agnew, Thomas Eagleton, George McGovern, Edmund Muskie, Richard Nixon, Scandals and Scandalizing, R. Sargent Shriver, Watergate

Alan I. Abramowitz

REFERENCES

Asher, Herbert B. 1988. *Presidential Elections and American Politics.* 4th ed. Chicago: Dorsey.

Congressional Quarterly. 1974. *Watergate: Chronology of a Crisis.* Washington: Congressional Quarterly.

Kirkpatrick, Jeane. 1976. *The New Presidential Elite.* New York: Russell Sage.

Miller, Arthur H., Warren E. Miller, Alden S. Raine, and Thad A. Brown. 1976. "A Majority Party in Disarray: Policy Polarization in the 1972 Election." 70 *American Political Science Review* 753.

Patterson, Thomas E., and Robert D. McClure. 1976. *The Unseeing Eye.* New York: Putnam.

Polsby, Nelson W. 1983. *Consequences of Party Reform.* New York: Oxford U. Pr.

Shafer, Byron E. 1983. *Quiet Revolution.* New York: Russell Sage.

Election of 1976

This presidential election represented an opportunity for the Democratic Party to reassert itself on the national level after George McGovern's devastating loss to Richard Nixon in 1972. With the midterm congressional election of 1974 and the denouement of Watergate signaling renewed support for the Democrats, unseating incumbent Gerald R. Ford seemed at the beginning of 1976 to be a task of relative ease.

Ford, the only President to reach that office without having been elected, faced a strong challenge within the Republican Party from Ronald Reagan, former governor of California and leader of the party's conservative wing. Even at the Republican National Convention in August, the outcome of the party's nomination process was not certain until the eve of the roll-call vote for President. In the end, the party opted for the more moderate incumbent, as the delegate vote went to Ford 1,187 to 1,070 in one of the most divisive Republican conventions in history.

The Democrats, by contrast, were surprisingly united behind a relative political unknown, former Georgia governor Jimmy Carter. Carter, mastering the new rules that dominated the Democratic delegate selection process, charged to an early lead with wins over a crowded candidate field in the Iowa caucuses and the New Hampshire primary. He later won close victories over Arizona Congressman Morris Udall in other primaries. the early publicity combined with his appeal to his own native South allowed Carter to fend off late challenges by California governor Edmund G. (Jerry) Brown and Idaho Senator Frank Church. With Senators Edward (Ted) Kennedy and Hubert Humphrey presenting no challenge to the Carter candidacy, Jimmy Carter was nominated by a unified convention.

In the months preceding the general election, President Ford managed to close a 33-point deficit in the preference polls to make the election a toss-up in the closing weeks. Ford put Carter on the defensive by charging that his opponent was too inexperienced to be President. Carter, who tried to make the election a choice between corrupt Washington politics and honest government, reminded voters of the Watergate scandal: public opinion had turned against Ford two years earlier when he had unconditionally pardoned former President Nixon. Ford himself would later attribute his loss to Carter to "the Nixon issue."

The actual vote demonstrated that, while the Nixon pardon may have had some impact, Carter capably brought together much of the old Roosevelt coalition to win election. Post-election polls indicated that voters preferred Carter to Ford on domestic and economic issues, and a vote largely along party lines fell in Carter's favor. Carter won all states in the "Solid South" except Virginia and forged enough victories in key eastern and midwestern industrial states to get 297 electoral votes to Ford's 240. Despite a plurality in the popular vote of nearly 2 million, Carter could have lost the election in the Electoral College with a switch of under 8,500 votes to Ford in Ohio and Hawaii.

In the end, Carter owed his election not only to a strong southern preference for a "native son" but also in particular to labor unions and Blacks. In the Northeast and Midwest, labor union organization delivered Pennsylvania and insured New York. Blacks, who voted for Carter in proportions of nine to one nationally, turned Ford majorities among white voters in seven states into Carter victories. Those 7 states, comprised of 117 of Carter's 297 electoral votes, meant that the new President would have to balance the wishes of the strongly conservative white South with the more liberal wing of his party represented predominantly by southern and urban African-Americans in order to achieve unity in his own party.

Despite a large turnover of membership in the Senate, Democratic control of that chamber remained frozen at 62 to 38. A similar status quo in the House elections meant that more than 30 freshman Democrats from 1974 were able to retain their seats. Democratic Senators and Representatives for the most part ran even or ahead of President-elect Carter, indicating that no coattail effect was present.

See also: Jerry Brown, Jimmy Carter, Robert Dole, Gerald Ford, Walter Mondale, Richard M. Nixon, Ronald Reagan, Morris Udall, Watergate

Michael Heel

REFERENCES

Asher, Herbert B. 1980. *Presidential Elections and American Politics.* Homewood, IL: Dorsey.

Keeter, Scott, and Cliff Zukin. 1983. *Uninformed Choice: The Failure of the New Presidential Nominating System.* New York: Praeger.

Williams, Philip, and Graham K. Wilson. 1978. "The 1976 Election and the American Political System." 25 *Political Studies* 182.

Election of 1980

This presidential election was a watershed in American political history. For the first time since 1932, an incumbent President seeking re-election was rejected by the voters. Jimmy Carter won just 6 states and the District of Columbia for 49 electoral votes, while Ronald Reagan captured 44 states and 489 electors. An Independent candidate, John Anderson, won no electors.

Other measures were equally lopsided. Reagan got 43,901,812 votes for 50.7 percent of the total; Carter, 35,483,820 votes for 41.0 percent; Anderson, 5,720,060 for 6.6 percent. Moreover, the Republicans gained 12 U.S. Senate seats, winning control of that body for the first time since 1952: 53 Republicans to 47 Democrats. Democrats maintained their majority in the House of Representatives: 243 Democrats to 192 Republicans. But the election dealt the Democratic Party a severe blow—one that crippled it in subsequent presidential contests in the 1980s.

Ronald Reagan began his 1980 quest for the presidency with a severe partisan disadvantage.

Fifty-one percent of voters called themselves Democrats; only 30 percent said they were Republicans and 19 percent were Independents. To win, Reagan had to get a massive majority of the Republican vote, large numbers of Independents, and cut substantially into Carter's Democratic base.

Carter's record and a conjuncture of foreign and domestic disasters allowed Reagan to do that. Elected in 1976, Carter entered office with high expectations. But these hopes were quickly dashed upon the shoals of a battered economy and foreign setbacks. Economically, the United States was plagued by double-digit inflation and high unemployment. Campaigning against Gerald R. Ford in 1976, Carter devised the "misery index," a figure arrived at by adding the rates of inflation and unemployment. In 1976 the misery index stood at 12.5 percent; by 1980, it was nearly 20 percent.

Overseas, Americans were fixated on the fate of the hostages in Iran. On November 4, 1979, militant Iranian students stormed the United States embassy in Teheran and captured 63 Americans working there. The hostages were held for 444 days, finally winning their freedom on January 20, 1981—the day Reagan took office.

These misfortunes raised doubts about Carter that he acknowledged in a 1979 address known as the "malaise speech": "[T]he public acknowledged my intelligence and integrity, my ability to articulate problems and to devise good solutions to them, but doubted my capacity to follow through with a strong enough thrust to succeed."

The American lack of confidence in Carter extended to the action itself. Carter's presidency came on the heels of John F. Kennedy's assassination, the loss of the Vietnam War, and the Watergate scandal. From 1973 to 1980, less than 20 percent of survey respondents thought the nation was on the "right track"; 75 percent believed it was in disarray. Moreover, many began to question the quality of their own lives and the prospect that their children's would be better. Patrick Caddell, Jimmy Carter's pollster, found in the late spring of 1979 that most Americans believed they would be "worse off" five years hence than they were then.

Perhaps the best-remembered line of the campaign came from Reagan. In a final debate with Carter the Republican candidate asked voters, "Are you better off than you were four years ago?" Voters decisively answered "no." In fact, opinions about Carter were so negative that he received the smallest percentage of the popular vote of any Democratic President seeking reelection. That, coupled with the Democrats' loss of the United States Senate, prompted pollster Peter D. Hart to remark that "voters saw the Democrats as ineffective stewards of the nation's affairs, whose underlying agenda related to the past rather than to the present or future, and whose approach lacked the balance necessary to keep America on an even keel."

Voters did more than reject Carter in electing Reagan. They wanted renewed confidence in heretofore unchallenged American values: the sanctity of family, the importance of community, the merits of hard work, and the reverence for freedom. The basic thrust of Reagan's strategy was to appeal to these values and highlight their restoration through strong leadership. Hence, throughout the campaign Reagan pledged his fidelity to tradition, promising "an era of national renewal," one that "will revitalize the values of family, work, and neighborhood." From this ethos sprang other principles that were a subliminal part of the Reagan message: self-esteem, patriotism, self-realization, and religiosity.

In choosing Reagan, Americans were optimistic that they had found the right man with the right message. Sixty-one percent believed that Reagan "has the strong leadership qualities the nation needs"; 71 percent said that he "offers the single best hope to reduce inflation"; 69 percent thought he "has a highly attractive personality and will inspire confidence in the White House"; 53 percent cited economic improvement or reduced inflation rates as "one good thing that will happen to American families" now that Reagan was President.

One analyst said of Reagan's 1980 win, "It appears that our society is at a transition point, and that the public may be willing, under almost imperceptible influences, to throw its entire weight behind a leader who strikes the correct 'moral' or 'reaffirming' tone." Reaffirming faith in the American values was to be Reagan's mandate.

See also: John Anderson, George H. W. Bush, Jimmy Carter, Electoral College System, Gerald Ford, Walter Mondale, Ronald Reagan, Vietnam War as a Political Issue, Watergate

John K. White

REFERENCES

Barrett, Laurence I. 1983. *Gambling with History: Reagan in the White House.* Garden City, NY: Doubleday

Broder, David, et al. 1980. *The Pursuit of the Presidency 1980.* New York: Berkely Books.

Carter, Jimmy. 1982. *Keeping Faith*. New York: Bantam Books.

Chubb, John E., and Paul E. Peterson, eds. 1985. *The New Direction in American Politics*. Washington: Brookings.

Connecticut Mutual Life. 1981. *Report on American Values in the '80s: The Impact of Belief*. Lanham, MD: U. Pr. of America.

Duke, Paul, ed. 1986. *Beyond Reagan: The Politics of Upheaval*. New York: Warner Books.

Ferguson, Thomas, and Joel Rogers. 1986. *Right Turn: The Decline of the Democrats and the Future of American Politics*. New York: Hill and Wang.

Germond, Jack, and Jules Witcover. 1981. *Blue Smoke and Mirrors*. New York: Viking Press.

Ladd, Everett Carll. 1982. *Where Have All the Voters Gone?* New York: Norton.

Lipset, Seymour Martin, ed. 1981. *Party Coalitions in the 1980s*. San Francisco: Institute for Contemporary Studies.

Moore, Johnathan, ed. 1982. *The Campaign for President: 1980 in Retrospect*. Cambridge: Ballinger.

Pomper, Gerald M., ed. 1981. *The Election of 1980: Reports and Interpretations*. Chatham, NJ: Chatham House.

Ranney, Austin, ed. 1981. *The American Elections of 1980*. Washington: American Enterprise Institute.

Reagan, Ronald. 1980. "A Vision for America." Television Broadcast. November 3.

White, John Kenneth. 1988. *The New Politics of Old Values*. Hanover, NH: U. Pr. of New England.

White, Theodore H. 1982. *America in Search of Itself: The Making of the President 1956–1980*. New York: Harper & Row.

Wills, Garry. 1981. *Reagan's America: Innocents At Home*. Garden City, NY: Doubleday.

Wirthlin, Richard B. 1980. "Reagan for President: Campaign Action Plan." Richard Wirthlin's Private Papers.

Election of 1984

Some analysts claim that the election of 1984 really need not have been held. Because no Democratic candidate could have beaten Republican Ronald Reagan, Walter Mondale's campaign was then a consummate exercise in futility. Others claim, however, that a great deal can be learned about the two parties and the differences between them—and about the future of American politics—by examining the 1984 election.

The simplest part of the story involves the Republican nomination. No one challenged the Reagan-Bush ticket. But that simplicity hides a more meaningful story. In recent decades, few incumbent Presidents have been renominated without at least token opposition within their own party. The Republican unanimity behind Ronald Reagan revealed the extent to which the conservative wing had captured the GOP. Not only was Reagan renominated without challenge, but other Republicans with aspirations to succeed Reagan—Vice President George Bush chief among them—were recanting moderate views and actively courting the party's right wing.

Because no opposition emerged, the Reagan-Bush campaign was able to use the pre-nomination period to build a significant organizational lead over their general election opponents before those opponents were even chosen. The Reagan campaign was entitled to raise money and to receive federal matching funds during the nomination phase of the campaign. They raised and spent approximately $24 million, approaching the maximum allowable; all of that money was spent laying the groundwork for a unified Republican Party campaign in the fall election.

While the Republican nomination demonstrated the popularity of Ronald Reagan and the ideological coherence of the party, the Democrats' nominating campaign dramatized the lack of popular support for the frontrunner, former Vice President Walter F. (Fritz) Mondale, and the continuing rifts within the party. Mondale began his active campaign for his party's nomination shortly after the 1982 election. His strategy was clear: to claim frontrunner status, to build a formidable organization, to raise a sizable campaign war chest, to garner commitments from organized groups and seasoned politicians, and to wrap up the nomination before any other campaign could get off the ground.

However, while Mondale's advantages were undeniable, they were not enough to deter early opposition. Seven other Democrats—Senators John Glenn of Ohio, Alan Cranston of California, Ernest Hollings of South Carolina, and Gary Hart of Colorado; former Florida governor Reuben Askew; former South Dakota Senator and 1972 presidential nominee George McGovern; and civil rights activist Reverend Jesse Jackson—all joined the fray. From the beginning each of their strategies involved finding a way to emerge from the pack as Mondale's chief rival for the nomination.

The press thought that Glenn was the most likely challenger because of his name recognition and credibility on defense issues, each of which followed from his renown as a military hero and astronaut. But Glenn's candidacy was never to catch fire. After the campaign, Glenn, with a self-deprecating humor that might have helped him overcome his somewhat stiff image, claimed that his candidacy failed because he was too willing to follow the advice of his wife Annie. She told him that she wanted him to run for President in the worst way—and he did. His campaign was poorly organized, poorly conceived, and poorly executed. His 5 percent showing in the first real test of strength, the Iowa caucuses, all but doomed his candidacy; his equally poor showing in New Hampshire assured that no recovery was possible.

Although Mondale won the Iowa caucuses handily, capturing nearly half of the votes, the press played up the second-place showing of Gary Hart, despite the fact that Hart polled only slightly more than 15 percent of the vote, barely getting past George McGovern. The media was looking for a contest and for a credible challenger to Mondale. Hart, speaking about new ideas and a new Democratic party, presented the most likely challenger. Hart's strategy involved a total emphasis on the early contests. The attention his candidacy received after Iowa played to his strength. When he surprised experts by winning the New Hampshire primary and followed that win with others in caucuses in Maine and Wyoming, his position shifted from the challenger to Mondale to that of an emerging frontrunner.

After New Hampshire the contest became a three-way race, with Mondale and Hart joined by Jesse Jackson, whose campaign as the first African-American to contest seriously for a major party presidential nomination was progressing despite the results in the early states. And this three-way contest, which continued on to the convention, revealed a great deal about the Democratic party. First, it demonstrated the importance of organized political groups. Mondale had courted the support of the AFL-CIO, the National Organization for Women, the National Education Association, and other groups early in the contest. They stuck with him and provided important components of his victories in the key primaries in midwestern industrial states. Jackson defined his coalition in terms of demographic groups: the Rainbow Coalition of Black Americans, Hispanic Americans, and others who had not enjoyed the fruits of the American dream. Hart appealed to Yuppies—young, upwardly mobile, urban professionals, first-time political activists tired of the promises of traditional politicians and looking for new voices with new ideas. These groups were all important components of the Democratic party—and they were all separate.

Second, the contest revealed the importance of the rules of the nominating game. After the 1980 election, the Hunt Commission of the Democratic party changed the rules in important ways. Jimmy Carter's two nominations, in 1976 and 1980, had been criticized because elected politicians and party leaders had very little part in selecting the party's nominee; the result was a reinstitution of a type of peer review, over 550 delegate slots (about 14 percent of the total number) being set aside for party professionals, the so-called superdelegates. Second, the Hunt Commission sought to shorten the nomination period, closing the so-called "window" during which states could hold primaries; the states' response to this rule change led to a front-loading of the process with most delegates selected early on, almost half before the end of March. Third, the Commission allowed states greater flexibility in setting primary rules; this flexibility permitted reinstituting winner-take-all primaries at the district level (primaries in which the winner of a district won all of that district's delegates) and introducing "winner-take-more" primaries (in which the winner in a district was given a bonus delegate—above that which his proportion of the vote would have guaranteed him). Finally, the Commission allowed states to require that candidates reach a certain threshold of votes before they were allocated any delegates; thus candidates with few votes in many areas received less delegate support than their proportion of the primary vote would have indicated.

All of these rule changes worked to Mondale's advantage. Approximately 500 of the superdelegates supported Mondale; many of them announced their support early and thus were counted in his ongoing total reported by the media. The front-loading that many thought would help an early leader actually hurt the Hart campaign because it did not have enough time to build an organization that would reap the benefits of the early upsets; Mondale, therefore, could recover because his organization was built, in place, and functioning in states in which Hart was hardly organized. Mondale won six of the seven states with loophole primaries and four of the five with "winner-take-more" systems. Hart won more primaries than Mondale (16 to 11) and more caucuses (13 to 10); Mondale polled only 430,000 more votes than Hart out of the 18 million cast. But because of the bonus rules and the threshold requirement, Mondale converted his 39 percent of the vote into 49 percent of the delegates; Hart received approximately 36 percent of the pledged delegates from about the same percentage of votes; Jackson received only 10 percent of the delegates from 19 percent of the votes.

The nomination went to Mondale with the help of the superdelegates. Hart and Jackson contested to the end, but eventually came together behind the ticket. Demonstrating the power of groups again, Mondale chose New York Congresswoman Geraldine Ferraro as his running mate. The convention ended in unity, but it was a unity that belied serious problems for the Mondale candidacy, problems revealed by his inability to end the contest early, by the lack of enthusiasm that many in the party had for him as a candidate, and by the difficulty he had in bringing the various elements of the party together under one umbrella.

The difficulty faced by the Mondale candidacy was particularly poignant in comparison to the ease with which President Reagan and Vice President Bush were renominated. The general election was clearly Reagan's to lose. The volatility of the lead among the contestants within the Democratic Party contrasted with the relevant constancy of public opinion toward the general election. After the two party conventions, Mondale never drew closer to Reagan than 9 percentage points. The Democratic nominee faced seemingly insurmountable odds. In classic political science terms, President Reagan asked the public to vote retrospectively, to judge the job that he had done. He pointed to decreases in the unemployment rate, the inflation rate, and interest rates; he underlined the contrast between how we as a nation were viewed by foreign nations when Americans were held hostage in Teheran and how we were viewed after standing tall in Grenada. The image of his campaign was that of champion gymnast Mary Lou Retton, of U. S. athletes proudly winning at the Los Angeles Olympics, of "It's morning again in America."

By contrast, the Mondale campaign had to evoke fear for the future. Mondale asked the country to vote prospectively, to see the consequences of the Reagan policies for generations ahead. Mondale wanted Americans to fear the consequences of our rising deficit and our trade imbalance; but these were difficult issues for the public to comprehend when the economy seemed to be going so well. Mondale wanted

Americans to fear a gun-happy president unnecessarily confronting the Soviet Union; but President Reagan was viewed as a confident leader, not an ineffectual old man who still believed in outdated stereotypes of the Soviet Union as the Evil Empire.

Even the few advantages that Mondale seemed to have quickly disappeared. Women's enthusiasm over the Ferraro nomination was lost in questions over her husband's finances. The vaunted organization that won him the nomination made mistake after mistake in the early weeks of the campaign. His "win" in the first televised debate, in which President Reagan appeared old, tired, and uncertain, was wiped out in the second debate in which the President appeared fresh, prepared, and personable. In the end, the American public spoke with a resounding voice. President Reagan won 59 percent of the popular vote, the fifth highest total in the nation's history. He won every electoral vote except for those of Mondale's home state of Minnesota (which Mondale won by a mere 4,000 votes) and those of the District of Columbia.

What did the election mean? At the very least, the contest was a tremendous triumph for Ronald Reagan, one of America's most popular Presidents. The election also showed clearly that the nation looked back on Reagan's first term and approved of what it saw. Beyond that, however, the lessons are not clear. On issue after issue, voters claimed that they favored the positions held by Mondale while deciding to vote for Reagan; this inconsistency was true on social issues such as abortion and the equal rights amendment, on issues relating to the environment and welfare policy, and on the call for a nuclear freeze. The nation favored Reagan, but not his policies. On the other hand, the election seemed to cement a move to the Republican Party that the 1980 election presaged. Not only did Reagan win forty-nine states, but he won many of them by huge margins; he won impressively in those areas of the country gaining in population; and he won by converting most of those who were leaning to the Republican party to his party's cause. Thus, while the election may well have been a foregone conclusion, it also demonstrated impressive changes in the American body politic.

See also: George Bush, Jimmy Carter, Elections of 1976 and 1980, Geraldine Ferraro, Jesse Jackson, George McGovern, Media and Presidential Politics, Walter Mondale, New Hampshire Primary, Politics of Presidential Elections, Presidential Nominating

Politics, Race and Racial Politics, Rainbow Coalition, Ronald Reagan, Retrospective Voting, Winner-Take-All Systems

L. Sandy Maisel

REFERENCES

Ferraro, Geraldine A., with Linda Bird Francke. 1985. *Ferraro: My Story*. New York: Bantam Books.

Germond, Jack, and Jules Witcover. 1985. *Wake Us When It's Over: Presidential Politics in 1984*. New York: Macmillan.

Kessel, John H. 1988. *Presidential Campaign Politics*. 3rd edition. Chicago: Dorsey.

Light, Paul C., and Celinda Lake. 1985. "The Election: Candidates, Strategies, and Decisions." In Michael Nelson, ed. *The Elections of 1984*. Washington: Congressional Quarterly.

Miller, Warren E. 1990. "The Electorate's View of the Parties." In L. Sandy Maisel, ed. *The Parties Respond: Changes in the American Party System*. Boulder, CO: Westview.

Orren, Gary R. 1985. "The Nomination Process: Vicissitudes of Candidate Selection." In Michael Nelson, ed. *The Elections of 1984*. Washington: Congressional Quarterly.

———, and Nelson W. Polsby, eds. 1987. *Media and Momentum: The New Hampshire Primary and Nomination Politics*. Chatham, NJ: Chatham House.

Pomper, Gerald M. 1985. "The Nominations." In Gerald M. Pomper, ed. *The Election of 1984*. Chatham, NJ: Chatham House.

———. 1985. "The Presidential Election." In Gerald M. Pomper, ed. *The Election of 1984*. Chatham, NJ: Chatham House.

Reed, Adolph L., Jr. 1986. *The Jesse Jackson Phenomenon: The Crisis of Purpose in Afro-American Politics*. New Haven: Yale U. Pr.

Election of 1988

The election of 1988 was the first U.S. election since 1960 in which an incumbent President was ineligible to run for re-election; it was the first election since 1968 in which a sitting President's name was not on the November ballot. Yet, despite the fact that Ronald Reagan's forced retirement encouraged six Republicans and eight Democrats actively to seek their parties' nominations—and perhaps a score of other politicians seriously to consider presidential campaigns—in many ways the election of 1988 can be best understood as Ronald Reagan's last hurrah. Both the nomination contests and the general election were political reactions to his two terms in office.

The Republicans sought chiefly an heir to the Reagan legacy. Party leaders understood the contest in those terms; more important, the candidates worked hard to assume Reagan's mantle. Six candidates competed in the early caucuses and primaries. From the start, Vice President George Bush, who had spent eight years courting the conservative wing of his party by trying to shed the image of a moderate who had been Reagan's principal opponent for the 1980 nomination, who had once derided supply-side economics as "voodoo" economics, and who was seen as "soft" on social issues such as abortion or school prayers, was the front-runner.

Bush's main opposition came from two contrasting political camps, one mainstream and predictable, one very much new to Republican politics. Kansas Senator Bob Dole stressed his long and distinguished legislative record, his service to the GOP as its chairman and vice presidential candidate, and his vitality as a campaigner. Dole was the candidate whom political journalists dubbed as the main challenger to Bush's nomination. The unknown factor was the candidacy of televangelist Reverend Marion G. (Pat) Robertson. Robertson appealed to the fundamentalist right wing in the country, his "secret army" of dissatisfied citizens who, he argued, would turn out to vote in Republican caucuses and primaries. Most analysts did not think that Robertson's evangelical cavalry would arrive in time for the battle, but no one was certain.

The other Republican candidates were New York Congressman Jack Kemp and former Delaware Governor Pierre (Pete) DuPont, each of whom stressed that they were more committed to conservative economic policies than were not only the other aspirants but also the policymakers at the end of the Reagan administration, and retired General Alexander Haig, who emphasized his expertise in foreign and military matters. None of these three, however, was ever a serious contender.

The Republican contest had an exciting beginning and a quick ending. Michigan's early caucuses featured intraparty warfare to control state political machinery. The anti-Bush forces of Robertson and Kemp united to deny the Vice President's supporters control of the Michigan party; some felt that these caucuses were the first skirmish for the emerging Robertson army. All of the Bush opponents knew that they would have to capitalize on the Vice President's unpopularity (owing to the Reagan administration's farm policies) in Iowa. Senator Dole staged his major effort in Iowa and won those caucuses; what was most surprising was that Robertson also finished ahead of Bush. The Bush campaign staggered for a moment, but recovery came in New Hampshire.

According to the media—and in this case the media very definitely defined the contest—Dole had to win in New Hampshire to keep his momentum going; Robertson had to win to demonstrate that his forces were strong enough to affect popular voting in primaries, not just in caucuses in which only the most committed participated; Kemp, DuPont, and Haig had to win to gain some semblance of credibility for their campaigns; and Bush had to win to recover from early losses that, while predictable and explainable, gave him the appearance of vulnerability. Dole's momentum gave him the early lead in the New Hampshire polls. The Bush campaign, however, aired a weekend of virtually unanswered negative advertisements just before the voting, and these were credited with reversing the Vice President's campaign fortunes and producing a 10 percentage-point victory over Dole. The others trailed badly, leaving only two contenders going into the March 8 "Super Tuesday" battle in which delegates from twenty states would be chosen.

George Bush swept to victory on Super Tuesday. He won every one of the sixteen Republican primaries held that day; he carried the caucus states as well. The Super Tuesday concept had been the invention of southern Democrats who wanted to reassert influence in their party's nomination contest (fourteen of the twenty states choosing delegates that day were southern or border states); its major impact was to guarantee the Republican nomination for George Bush. Bush's superior organization, his seemingly bottomless campaign war chest, and the good will he had built up campaigning and raising money for Republicans throughout the South during his eight years as Vice President simply overwhelmed Senator Dole. By May 1, Bush had pledged support from more than enough delegates to guarantee his nomination. The heir to Ronald Reagan had secured his title and began preparing for the fall campaign.

If the Republican contest seemed somewhat routine and predictable, nothing was further from the truth for the Democrats. First, four of the party's leading potential candidates—New York Governor Mario Cuomo and U. S. Senators Bill Bradley of New Jersey, Ted Kennedy of Massachusetts, and Sam Nunn of Georgia (who southern political leaders hoped to entice into the race by stacking many of their contests on the early Super Tuesday date)—all decided not

to run. Then the emerging frontrunner, Gary Hart of Colorado, who had not sought re-election to the Senate in 1986 to continue his quest for the presidency begun in the 1984 primaries, self-destructed with a moral peccadillo. Hart's personal eccentricities had attracted some attention in 1984 as first the press and then the Mondale campaign picked up on the facts that he had changed his name from Hartpence to Hart, had altered his signature, and had seemingly "changed" his birthdate during his political career. In 1988, rumors emerged that Hart was having an extra-marital affair. The candidate challenged the press to examine his personal life as closely as they chose; the press did—and discovered an unexplained relationship with model Donna Rice. The negative publicity led Hart to withdraw from the race before the first vote was cast, even though he was still the leader in the polls. He re-entered the contest briefly, after no clear leader emerged; although he again drew support in the public opinion polls, he was never able to convert that support into primary or caucus success.

Hart's departure left the Democrats with six relatively unknown candidates—U. S. Senators Joseph Biden of Delaware, Albert Gore of Tennessee, and Paul Simon of Illinois; Congressman Richard Gephardt of Missouri; former Governor Bruce Babbitt of Arizona; and Governor Michael Dukakis of Massachusetts—and African-American political activist Jesse Jackson. Biden dropped out when, like Hart, his personal integrity came into question; he was first accused of plagiarizing campaign speeches from British Labour Party leader Neil Kinnock and later of exaggerating his academic record during law school.

The remaining candidates faced similar political problems. All except Jackson needed media attention to gain name recognition and to distinguish themselves from the others. All including Jackson had to devise a strategy to deal with Super Tuesday, a day unparalleled in primary history for the number of contests to be held and the number of delegates to be chosen.

From the start, Senator Gore's strategy was a southern one, based on surviving the early contests in Iowa and New Hampshire and winning big in his own political backyard, the states selecting delegates on March 8. The unknown factor was whether he would still be deemed viable by the media as Super Tuesday approached if he was an also-ran in the first contests. As in 1984, Jesse Jackson knew he could survive the early contests; his problem was to expand his base beyond the Black supporters all conceded to him. For the others, the early contests were more critical.

Congressman Gephardt pulled virtually all of his resources out of the southern states to place total emphasis on Iowa, spending more time in Iowa than in his native Missouri in the months before the caucuses. Governor Dukakis concentrated on building a strong organization, raising enough money to contest everywhere over the long haul, assuring a victory in New Hampshire (which was, of course, close to his political base in Massachusetts and whose citizens frequently saw him on the Boston television stations that blanket the southern and most heavily populated parts of the state), and appearing in Iowa enough to exceed the very low expectations of his ability to do well in the farm states. The other candidates seemed to flounder for a strategy, working hard in Iowa but also spreading their time and resources into New Hampshire and into the Super Tuesday states.

The Iowa caucuses went to Gephardt, but he was unable to distance himself from either Senator Simon, who finished a strong second, or Governor Dukakis, who finished a surprisingly strong third. New Hampshire, as expected, went to Dukakis, with Gephardt second and Simon third. The Simon campaign was floundering; and former Governor Babbitt, who appealed to the journalists covering the contests because of his reasoned and forthright positions on the issues, had dropped from sight.

Super Tuesday loomed large, but Super Tuesday was not decisive. The clear loser was Gephardt, who won only in his native Missouri. Gore survived, but did not sweep the South as pundits claimed he had to. The politicians who conceived of a southern-dominated series of primaries on a Tuesday early in the nominating season had assumed this strategy would aid conservative Democratic candidates. Ironically, the two biggest winners were Jesse Jackson, who won five southern primaries on that day by polling huge majorities of the Black vote while the other candidates divided the rest, and Michael Dukakis, who won two southern primaries (Florida and Texas) by concentrating his campaign in specific areas in which he had organizational strength and three other primaries that were held in other areas of the country.

After Super Tuesday the nominating contest assumed a different character. The Dukakis campaign had crucial advantages; the Massa-chusetts governor had enough money and a well enough developed organization to stay the course through the remaining primaries and caucuses. The Jackson campaign was clearly going to persist, though it was unclear if he could turn his Rainbow Coalition into a winning coalition. Each of the remaining candidates needed a critical win to "jump-start" their stalled efforts. Gephardt tried and failed in Michigan, despite a plea to the auto workers on the issue of foreign trade; Simon rallied briefly in his native Illinois, but lost badly in Wisconsin; Gore failed in New York, as did Jackson when he could not add traditional Democratic liberals to his base. Eventually, a consensus emerged behind Michael Dukakis as a competent moderate who was acceptable to liberals and capable of winning throughout the country, especially because no conservative Democrat was running. As the convention approached, no one was in a position to challenge Dukakis, but he still had the problem of what to do with the problematic Jackson candidacy.

In interesting ways, the vice presidential nominations were crucially important for the 1988 election. Governor Dukakis had a unique problem. Jesse Jackson had run a powerful, successful, competent campaign for the nomination. He was clearly the leading spokesperson for an African-American community that comprised a good portion of the Democratic coalition. Dukakis could not afford to alienate either Jackson or his supporters, but he also felt that a Jackson vice presidential nomination would doom his candidacy as too many moderates and independents (and some liberals) feared the flamboyant civil rights activist. And Jackson would not accept this fate. Dukakis chose Texas Senator Lloyd Bentsen, a respected conservative who had obvious appeal in states that Dukakis would need to carry if he were to win the November election. Not until well into the Democratic National Convention did Jackson accept his fate and vow to work for the ticket; it is unclear if he ever did so with enthusiasm and if his supporters ever followed suit.

George Bush had months to make his choice. He settled on two-term Indiana Senator J. Danforth Quayle for reasons that escaped virtually all political analysts. Quayle appealed to party regulars, but he had no national appeal, was inexperienced, and came from a decidedly safe Republican state. At the time of his selection and throughout the fall campaign, the press treated Quayle as roughly as it has any recent candidate, harping on family influence that had gotten him into the National Guard at the time of the Vietnam conflict, and then into law school, and on his relatively undistinguished record as a legislator. During the fall campaign Bentsen was clearly an asset to the Dukakis effort (though in ways far different from those Jackson would have been); the Bush campaign constantly sought to minimize the damage done by Quayle's candidacy.

The general election can be interpreted in a number of ways. On the one hand, the Bush-Dukakis campaign was a referendum on eight years of Ronald Reagan. George Bush campaigned as the heir to the Reagan presidency. He had been the loyal Vice President. He supported the Reagan policies. And 1988 was a time of peace and prosperity. Michael Dukakis had to convince the voters that change was needed at a time when most people were happy with the way things were going.

At another level the election was simply more of the same. The Republicans were emerging as the majority party in presidential elections. They had won four of the last five presidential elections, three of them in landslides. State after state, particularly those south of the Mason-Dixon line and those west of the Mississippi, seemed inexorably locked into Republican presidential majorities. The Democrats had to find a way to break this Electoral College lock—and they were unable to do so. The New Deal Coalition that had brought Democratic Presidents to office so frequently was withering. While more voters identified themselves as Democrats than Republicans, the gap was shrinking, the once-solid Democratic South had disappeared, and many Democratic identifiers (particularly minorities) failed to vote.

And at still another level, the campaign itself was decisive. Public opinion polls showed a volatile electorate. Michael Dukakis had a lead and lost it. Some felt that the Bush won because of an issueless, negative, television-dominated campaign to which Dukakis responded ineffectively. The campaign centered on the Pledge of Allegiance, claims that Dukakis was a liberal card-carrying member of the ACLU, and a furloughed Black life-sentencer named Willie Horton. But others claim that these symbols touched the issues that really had meaning for the public. The Pledge of Allegiance was a surrogate for patriotism; the ACLU supported unpopular causes and their advocacy of unrestrained free speech was turned into a de-fense of purveyors of pornography; the Willie Horton commercials struck a responsive chord with those who feared crime and played into an unspoken but very real racist hysteria.

Michael Dukakis claimed the campaign was not about ideology but about competence. In a sense he was right, in that the two parties were closer together on issues of both domestic and foreign policy than they had been in many years. But in a broader sense the campaign was about leadership. Voters did not question Dukakis' competency—although many did later as his leadership of Massachusetts' economic recovery, the so-called Massachusetts Miracle, seemed to evaporate shortly after the election. But they did question whether he was a leader who understood the American people. George Bush stood for basic American values and for family; Michael Dukakis was a competent technocrat. The low point for Dukakis was his inability to emote in a response to a debate question concerning whether he would not favor the death penalty for someone who raped his wife Kitty. Dukakis never understood that the question was not about his principled opposition to the death penalty; it was about his ability to relate to the emotions of the people he sought to lead.

In the end, George Bush won a relatively easy victory, garnering 54 percent of the vote, nearly 48 million votes compared to about 41 million for Dukakis. The Republican candidate won in the Electoral College by 426 electoral votes to 112. Although this victory was broad, it was not as impressive as those that had preceded it. Bush carried state after state by fewer votes than had Reagan; rarely was Dukakis swamped as Walter Mondale had been. Many traditional Democratic voters came back to the fold—not enough to change the result, but enough to lead analysts to question if the Reagan landslides had signaled a realignment in American politics. The Democratic theme of "fairness" had struck a responsive chord among low income, disadvantaged Democrats who had voted for Reagan in 1984 and even in 1980. Analysis of the 1988 vote revealed a deeper class division than had been the case in the two previous elections. And as the Bush-Quayle administration took office, with Democrats still in control of both houses of Congress, few felt that the shape of American politics in the 1990s had been determined by the election of 1988.

See also: American Civil Liberties Union, Lloyd Bentsen, George Bush, Robert Dole, Michael Dukakis, Elections of 1960, 1968, 1976, 1980, and 1984, Electoral College System, Richard Gephardt, Jesse Jackson, Jack Kemp, Edward Kennedy, Media and Presidential Politics, Walter Mondale, New Hampshire Primary, J. Danforth Quayle, Presidential Nominating Politics, Politics of Presidential Elections, Race and Racial Politics, Ronald Reagan, Marion G. Robertson

L. Sandy Maisel

REFERENCES

Colton, Elizabeth. 1989. *The Jackson Phenomenon: The Man, the Power, the Message.* New York: Doubleday.

Germond, Jack W. and Jules Witcover. 1989. *Whose Broad Stripes and Bright Stars?: The Trivial Pursuit of the Presidency, 1988.* New York: Warner Books.

Lichter, Robert, Daniel Amundson, and Richard Noyes. 1988. *The Video Campaign: Media Coverage of the 1988 Primaries.* Washington: American Enterprise Institute.

Nelson, Michael, ed. 1989. *The Elections of 1988.* Washington: Congressional Quarterly.

Pomper, Gerald M. 1989. "The Presidential Nominations." In Gerald M. Pomper, ed. *The Election of 1988: Reports and Interpretations,* Chatham, NJ: Chatham House.

———. 1989. "The Presidential Election." In Gerald M. Pomper, ed. *The Election of 1988: Reports and Interpretations,* Chatham, NJ: Chatham House.

Electoral College System

The American Electoral College is a curious political institution. Obscure and even unknown to the ordinary U.S. citizen, it nevertheless serves as a crucial mechanism for transforming popular votes cast for President into the electoral votes that actually elect the President. If the Electoral College operated only as a neutral and reliable means for counting and aggregating votes, then it would be the subject of little controversy. The Electoral College, however, is neither certain in its operations nor impartial in its effects. It may fail to produce a winner, generating an extraordinarily awkward contingency. Even when it operates relatively smoothly, the Electoral College does not just tabulate popular votes in the form of electoral votes. Rather, it is an institution that works with noteworthy inequality in favoring some interests and hurting others. In short, the Electoral College is a flawed means of determining the presidency. Its workings at best are neither sure nor smooth and at worse contain the potential for constitutional crisis. Yet it continues to exist as the constitutional mechanism for electing the people's President.

How It Came to Be

The Founding Fathers wrote the Electoral College system into the U.S. Constitution at the Constitutional Convention in 1787 not because they saw it as a particularly desirable means of electing the President but rather because they viewed it as an acceptable compromise; it was the second choice of many delegates though the first choice of few. The Philadelphia delegates were torn and divided, but they finally reached painful agreements on the monumental issues of national-state powers, presidential-congressional relationships, and (most controversial of all) the issue of equal state representation versus representation based on population for the new national legislature. Having weathered these storms, the Founders were determined not to let the Constitutional Convention split anew over the means of presidential election. Some delegates, however, favored election of the President by Congress; others strongly favored a direct election by the people. Even more crucially, each proposal had adamant opponents; adoption of either might mean a breakdown of the emerging convention consensus on the draft Constitution. These concerns resulted in a compromise plan providing for an intermediate electoral body to be called an "electoral college."

Under this plan, each state legislature would choose a method to select "electors" equal in number to the total of that state's congressional Representatives and Senators. The electors would meet in their states on a day chosen by Congress to cast ballots for the presidential candidate of their choice; they would then transmit the record of the vote to the president of the United States Senate, who would tabulate the votes from all the states. In the event of a tie, or the failure of any candidate to gain a majority of the electoral votes, the House of Representatives would immediately make the choice, with each state delegation having a single vote. Central to this complex arrangement was the feeling that the Electoral College, made up of prominent individuals from each state, would act independently and with deliberation in electing the President. Alternatively, should no majority be forthcoming in the Electoral College, the determination of the President would devolve upon the House.

This Electoral College arrangement, awkward as it might appear, had several apparent virtues: it was widely acceptable, it seemed unlikely to give rise to any immediate problem (it was clear to all that George Washington was going to be President, whatever the electoral system), and it appeared—incorrectly, it turned out—to incorporate a certain balance between state and popular interests. Most of all, this compromise plan got the Constitutional Convention over yet another hurdle in its immensely difficult process of constitution making. The result, however, was the creation of a complex and unwieldy multistage mechanism for electing the President. Some allege that the camel resulted from the deliberations of a committee; so the Electoral College can be viewed as born out of immediate political necessity at the Constitutional Convention. As one noted commentator on this period, John Roche, has put it:

> The electoral college was neither an exercise in applied Platonism nor an experiment in indirect government based on elitist distrust of the masses. It was merely a jerry-rigged improvisation which has subsequently been endowed with a high theoretical content. . . . The vital aspect of the electoral college was that it got the Convention over the hurdle and protected everybody's interests. The future was left to cope with the problem of what to do with this . . . mechanism.

To the extent that the Founding Fathers attempted to anticipate how the Electoral College would work, they were wrong. They had assumed that the electors chosen would, in effect, *nominate* a number of prominent individuals, with no one person—because of diverse state and regional interests—usually receiving the specified absolute *majority* of electoral votes. At times, a George Washington might be the unanimous Electoral College choice, but as George Mason of Virginia argued in Philadelphia, nineteen times out of twenty, the final choice of President among the three top contenders would be made not by the Electoral College itself but by the House of Representatives voting as states, with one vote per state.

Inherent in this system, then, was a mechanism for electing the people's President, a mechanism that has not, in fact, operated as the Founders assumed. Unforeseen was the rise of national political parties able to aggregate and focus national support on two, or occasionally three, candidates. Only in 1800 and 1824 did no contender receive a majority of the electoral votes. The House contingency system as the usual means of presidential election has fallen into disuse; instead the President has come to be chosen by the electors. Moreover, the electors themselves are now selected by the voters in a popular election on the basis of which major candidate they are expected to support.

In effect, popular election of the President has replaced a system originally based on presidential selection by independently voting electors. The structure of the original process remains, however, with potentially chaotic consequences should necessity force its use.

Another aspect of the system has also failed to work as its creators had intended. In the assumption of the Founders, the Electoral College—reflecting roughly the varying population sizes of the states—would favor the large states at the expense of the small states (or, more accurately, population rather than equally weighed individual states). When the House contingency procedure went into effect—as it usually would—the voting would be one vote per state delegation, thus favoring individual states regardless of population. This system, then, was a compromise between the principles of *population* and *state interest*, but a balance that rested on the assumption that the House contingency election procedure would normally be used. Since 1824, however, no election has been decided in the House, and the original balance of interests foreseen by the Founders has been destroyed in favor of a representation of population—albeit, at best, a distorted representation.

The historical facts, then, are that the original Electoral College system has not, for nearly 170 years, worked at all as assumed by its creators. It was replaced as a nominating mechanism by national political parties, and it has not provided a balance between state interests and population interests. Furthermore, the Electoral College has undergone a number of crucial changes in its operations since the 1780s. Among these are the Twelfth Amendment, ratified in 1804, which sought to ensure that the Electoral College would elect a President and Vice President of the same party; the development of universal popular election of electors early in the nineteenth century; the emergence of electors pledged to particular parties or candidates; the occurrence, albeit rare, of the curious phenomenon of the "faithless elector" who breaks his pledge or violates expectations by his vote for President; and the emergence of a winner-take-all system for determining each state's bloc of electoral votes. Together, these changes constitute major modifications of the system contemplated and created by the Philadelphia delegates. From an assembly of independent statesmen meeting to nominate three top presidential contenders for a final decision by the House of Representatives, we now have an Electoral College made up of unknown individuals whose only virtue consists of an automatic vote for their party's nominee, and an Electoral College whose only function is to confirm a popular electoral verdict handed down six weeks earlier.

The Flaws of the Contemporary Electoral College

The shortcomings of the contemporary Electoral College are many, but five major flaws stand out. These are the faithless elector, the winner-take-all system, the "constant two" electoral votes, the contingency election procedure, and the uncertainty of victory by the winner.

The Faithless Elector

The first of these flaws is inherent in the contemporary Electoral College: today it is not the assembly of wise and learned elders as assumed by its creators but rather is little more than a state-by-state collection of political hacks and fat cats selected because of their past loyalty and support for the party. Neither in the quality of the electors nor in law do we have any assurance that electors will vote as expected by those who voted for them. State laws requiring electors to vote as they have pledged are in practice unenforceable and almost certainly unconstitutional. The Constitution states that "the electors shall vote," suggesting that electors have discretion about how they cast their votes. As a result, personal pledges—along with party and candidate loyalty—can be seen as the only basis of elector voting consistent with the will of a state's electorate.

The problem of the "faithless elector" is neither theoretical nor unimportant. One Republican elector, Doctor Lloyd W. Bailey of North Carolina, decided to vote for George Wallace after the 1968 election rather than for his "pledged" candidate, Richard Nixon; Bailey decided that Republican nominee Nixon was a Communist. Another Republican elector, Roger MacBride of Virginia, likewise deserted Nixon in 1972 to vote instead for Libertarian Party candidate John Hospers. The 1976 election once again featured a faithless elector—and curiously enough once again a deviant Republican elector. Elector Mike Padden, from the state of Washington, decided, six weeks after the November election, that he preferred not to support the Republican nominee because Gerald Ford had not been forthright enough in denouncing abortion. Instead Padden cast his electoral vote in that year for Ronald Reagan, four years before

Reagan won the Republican nomination and was elected President. Another variant electoral vote was cast in 1988 by a West Virginia Democratic elector who, as a protest against the Electoral College system, cast his presidential vote not for nominee Michael Dukakis but for Democratic vice presidential nominee Lloyd Bentsen. Similar defections from voter expectations also occurred in 1948, 1956, and 1960—in other words, in seven of the twelve most recent U.S. presidential elections.

Even more important is that the likelihood of such deviations occurring on a multiple basis would be greatly heightened should an electoral vote majority rest on only one or two votes, a real possibility in any close presidential election. As a matter of fact, the election returns for the most recent close U.S. election, 1976, show that if 5,560 votes had switched from Jimmy Carter to Ford in Ohio, then Carter would have lost that state and thus received 272 electoral votes, only 2 more than the 270 necessary for election. In that case, two or three individual Democratic electors seeking personal recognition or attention to a pet cause could withhold—or threaten to withhold—their electoral votes from Carter and thus make the election outcome very uncertain.

Republican vice presidential nominee Robert Dole provided evidence of the possibilities inherent in such a close electoral vote election as 1976. Testifying before the Senate Judiciary Committee on January 27, 1977, in favor of abolishing the Electoral College, Senator Dole remarked that in the course of the 1976 election night election count

> We were looking around on the theory that maybe Ohio might turn around because they had an automatic recount. We were shopping— not shopping, excuse me. Looking around for electors. Some took a look at Missouri, some were looking at Louisiana, some in Mississippi, because their laws are a little bit different. And we might have picked up one or two in Louisiana. There were allegations of fraud maybe in Mississippi, and something else in Missouri.
>
> We [would] need to pick up three or four after Ohio. So that may happen in any event.
>
> But it just seems to me that the temptation is there for that elector in a very tight race to really negotiate quite a bunch.

The Winner-Take-All System

The second problem of the contemporary Electoral College system lies in the almost universal state statutory provisions (the sole exception is Maine) giving *all* of a state's electoral votes to the winner of a state's popular vote plurality (not even a majority). This extra-constitutional practice, gradually adopted by all states during the nineteenth century as a means of enhancing state power, can lead to bizarre results: for example, in Arkansas in 1968, where Hubert Humphrey and Richard Nixon together divided slightly over 61 percent of the popular vote, while George Wallace, with less than 39 percent popular support, received 100 percent of the state's electoral votes. More significantly, the winner-take-all determination of slates of state electors tends to magnify tremendously the relative voting power of residents of the largest states. Each of their voters may, by his vote, decide not just 1 electoral vote, but how a bloc of 36 or 47 electoral votes are cast—if electors are faithful.

As a result, the Electoral College has a major impact on candidate strategy—as shown by the concern of Jimmy Carter and Gerald Ford strategists, in the final weeks of the very close and uncertain 1976 campaign, with the 9 big electoral vote states that together had 245 of the 270 electoral votes necessary to win. The vote in seven of these nine megastates proved to be exceedingly close, with both candidates receiving at least a 48 percent share. Similarly, presidential candidates George Bush and Michael Dukakis focused their 1988 campaigns on the largest electoral vote states, which were likewise seen as determinant of the presidential contest's outcome.

The Electoral College does not treat voters alike: a thousand voters in Scranton, Pennsylvania, are far more important strategically than a similar number of voters in Wilmington, Delaware. This inequity also places a premium on the support of key political leaders in large states as could be observed in the 1976 election in the candidates' desperate wooing of Mayors Frank Rizzo of Philadelphia and Richard Daley of Chicago. These political leaders were seen as likely to play a major role in determining the electoral outcome in the large states of Pennsylvania and Illinois and thus the winner of a large bloc of electoral votes. The Electoral College treats political leaders as well as voters unequally; those in large marginal states are vigorously courted.

The Electoral College also encourages fraud—or at least fear and rumor of fraud. In 1976, New York, which by itself had more than enough electoral votes to determine the winner of the presidential contest, went to Carter by 290,000 popular votes. Claims of voting irregularities and calls for a recount were made on election night but were later withdrawn because of Carter's clear national popular vote win. *If* fraud was present in New York, only 290,000 votes determined the 1976 presidential election; under a national direct election plan, at least 1.7 million votes would have had to have been irregular in the same election to have changed the outcome.

The Electoral College at times also provides third-party candidates the opportunity to exercise magnified political influence in the election of the President, when they can gather votes in large and closely contested states. In 1976, third-party candidate Eugene McCarthy, with less than 1 percent of the national popular vote, came close to tilting the election through his strength in close pivotal states. In 4 states (Iowa, Maine, Oklahoma, and Oregon) with a total of 26 electoral votes, McCarthy's popular vote exceeded the margin by which Ford defeated Carter. In those states, McCarthy's candidacy *may* have swung those states to Ford. Even more significantly, had McCarthy been on the New York ballot (he had been ruled off at the last moment on technical grounds), Ford might very well have carried that state with its 41 electoral votes, and with it the election—despite Carter's overall national vote majority and lead of 1.7 million votes.

The "Constant Two" Electoral Votes

A third feature of the Electoral College system lies in the apportionment of electoral votes among the states. The constitutional formula is simple: one vote per state per Senator and Representative. Another distortion from equality appears here because of "the constant two" electoral votes, regardless of population, which correspond to each state's two Senators. Not surprisingly, inhabitants of very small states have an advantage because they "control" three electoral votes (two for the state's two Senators and one for the Representative), while their small population might otherwise entitle them to but one or two votes. The system, then weights by states, not by population; however, the importance of this feature is greatly outweighed by the previously mentioned winner-take-all system. Nevertheless, this feature of the Electoral College—like the preceding one—is yet another distorting factor in the election of the President. These structural components of the Electoral

College ensure that it can never really be a neutral counting device; inherently it contains a variety of biases dependent solely upon the state in which voters cast their ballots. The contemporary Electoral College is not just an archaic mechanism for counting the votes for President; it is also an institution that aggregates popular votes in an inherently imperfect manner.

The Contingency Election Procedure

The fourth feature of the contemporary Electoral College system is the most complex—and probably also the most dangerous for the stability of the political system. The contingency election procedure outlined in the Constitution provides that if no candidate receives an absolute majority of the electoral vote (in recent years, 270 electoral votes) the House of Representatives chooses the President from among the top three candidates. Two questions need to be asked. Is such an Electoral College deadlock likely to occur in contemporary politics? And, would the consequences be likely to be disastrous? A simple answer to both questions is yes.

As an illustrative example, in 1960 a switch of less than 9,000 popular votes from John Kennedy to Richard Nixon in Illinois and Missouri would have prevented either man from receiving an Electoral College majority. Similarly, in 1968, a 53,000 vote shift in New Jersey, Missouri, and New Hampshire would have resulted in an Electoral College deadlock, with Nixon then receiving 269 votes—1 short of a majority. Finally, in the 1976 election, if some 11,950 popular votes in Delaware and Ohio had shifted from Carter to Ford, Ford would have carried these 2 states. The result of the 1976 election would then have been *an exact tie* in electoral votes—269 to 269. The presidency would have been decided *not* on election night but through deals or switches at the Electoral College meetings the following December 13, or alternatively by means of the later uncertainties of the House of Representatives.

What specifically might happen in the case of an apparent Electoral College nonmajority or deadlock? A first possibility, of course, would be that a faithless elector or two, pledged to one candidate, might switch at the time of the actual meetings of the Electoral College so as to create a majority for the other of the presidential candidates. Such an action might resolve the crisis, although it would be sad to think that the President's mandate would be based on such a thin reed of legitimacy.

If, however, no deals at the time of the mid-December meetings of the Electoral College were successful in forming a majority, then the action would shift to the House of Representatives, meeting at noon on January 6, only 14 days before the constitutionally scheduled Inauguration Day for the new President.

The House contingency procedure that would have to be followed is clearly an awkward relic of the compromises of the writing of the new Constitution. Serious problems of equity would exist in the constitutionally prescribed one-vote-per-state procedure. Beyond this problem of fairness lurks an even more serious problem: what if the House itself should deadlock and be unable to agree on a President?

In a two-candidate race, this statement is unlikely to be a real problem; however, in a three-candidate contest, such as the ones in 1968 or 1980, the House would have enormous difficulties in getting a majority of states behind one candidate, as members agonized over choosing between partisan labels and support for the candidate (such as George Wallace or John Anderson) who had carried their district. The result, in 1968 or in 1980, might well have been no immediate majority forthcoming of twenty-six states and political uncertainty and chaos as Americans approached Inauguration Day uncertain of who their President would be.

The Uncertainty of the Winner Winning

Besides these four aspects of the Electoral College system, one last aspect needs to be described. Under the present system, Americans have no assurance that the winner of the popular vote will win the election. This problem is a fundamental one—can a President operate effectively if he has received fewer of the people's votes than the loser? The effect upon the legitimacy of a contemporary American presidency could possibly be disastrous were a President to be elected by an obscure Electoral College after losing in the popular vote.

An American "divided verdict" election *can* happen and *has* in fact occurred two or three times in American history. The most recent undisputable case (the election of 1960 being undeterminable) was the election of 1888, when a popular vote plurality of 100,000 by Grover Cleveland was turned into a losing 42 percent of the electoral vote. A real possibility of such a divided verdict occurred in the last close U.S. election, 1976. An analysis of the election results shows that if 9,245 votes had shifted to

Ford in Ohio and Hawaii, Ford would have been elected President with 270 electoral votes—the absolute minimum—despite Carter's 51 percent of the popular vote and margin of 1.7 million votes. One hesitates to contemplate the political and constitutional consequences had a nonelected President, such as Ford, been inaugurated for four more years despite having been rejected by a majority of the American voters in his only presidential election.

Conclusion

The American Electoral College has disturbing potential as a threat to the certainty of U.S. elections and the legitimacy of the people's President. But even beyond these considerations, the Electoral College—by its very nature—is a distorted counting device for turning popular votes into electoral votes. It can never be a faithful reflection of the popular will and must always stand between the citizen and his or her President.

It is for these reasons that substantial efforts have been made in recent years to reform or abolish the American Electoral College, especially following the close and potentially uncertain presidential elections of 1968 and 1976. These "hairbreadth elections" resulted in the passage by the House of Representative in 1969 of a constitutional amendment abolishing the Electoral College; the U.S. Senate, however, failed to approve the measure in 1970. Similar constitutional proposals were again debated by the Senate during the period of 1977 to 1979, but, despite majority support, they died in July 1979 for want of the necessary two-thirds vote. Inertia, institutional conservatism, and the self-interest of Senators from states perceived as advantaged by the existing Electoral College served to preserve the Electoral College during the debates of the 1970s, despite the concerted efforts of well-organized and persistent electoral reformers.

The fires of Electoral College reform are kindled by close U.S. presidential elections, contests that demonstrate to many the inadequacies of the Electoral College as a means of electing the people's President. Should the 1992 or a subsequent U.S. election prove to be uncertain in outcome or unfairly determined by the special characteristics of the Electoral College, that institution again will become a major target of reformers' efforts. Until that time, the flawed Electoral College will continue as an important aspect of American politics, shaping and in part determining the election of the U.S. President.

See also: John Anderson; Elections of 1824, 1960, and 1968; Hubert Humphrey; John F. Kennedy; Eugene McCarthy; Richard M. Nixon; Ronald Reagan; Third Parties In American Elections; Strom Thurmond; George C. Wallace; Henry A. Wallace; George Washington

Lawrence D. Longley

REFERENCES

Best, Judith. 1975. *The Case Against Direct Election of the President.* Ithaca: Cornell U. Pr.

Keech, William R. 1978. "Background Paper." In *Winner Take All: Report on the Twentieth Century Fund Task Force on Reform of the Presidential Election Process.* New York: Holmes and Meier.

Longley, Lawrence D., and Alan G. Braun. 1975. *The Politics of Electoral College Reform.* 2nd ed. New Haven: Yale U. Pr.

Longley, Lawrence D., and James D. Dana, Jr. 1984. "New Empirical Estimates of the Biases of the Electoral College for the 1980s." 37 *Western Political Quarterly* 157.

Peirce, Neal R., and Lawrence D. Longley. 1981. *The People's President: The Electoral College in American History and the Direct Vote Alternative.* Rev. ed. New Haven: Yale U. Pr.

Zeidenstein, Harvey. 1973. *Direct Election of the President.* Lexington, MA: Heath-Lexington.

Elite Theory

Modern (empirical) elite theory remains, after almost a century, compelling, insightful, and controversial. While almost a thousand works have been written in English alone on the subject of elite theory, most use the term as it has been refined in the works of principal theorists: Gaetano Mosca (1858–1941) wrote *The Ruling Class* (English language edition, 1939); Vilfredo Pareto (1848–1923) wrote *The Mind and Society* (English language edition, 1935); and Robert Michels (1876–1936) wrote *Political Parties* (English language edition, 1915; 1962). Substantial effort has been devoted to the study of elites since the time of these men (especially empirical work), but the most important theoretical formulations are theirs.

The essential elements of elite theory involve the inevitability of elites; the source, recruitment, and socialization of elites and the permeability of elite strata; the variability or uniformity of elites and the issue of circulation of elites versus a *reunion des élites*, or an amalgam; and the nature of elite-nonelite interdependence.

Mosca, Pareto, and Michels each offer a different explanation for the inevitability of elites. For political parties and organizations, Michels's explanation is the more interesting one: organizational needs require task specialization and consequently structural differentiation; further, eventual role differentiation is accompanied by an inevitable psychological transformation. Mosca believes that small groups have inherently better organizing capacities than those of large minorities; Pareto's position is that talent differentiates individuals and that the more talented inevitably dominate.

Mosca, Pareto, and Michels again adopt somewhat different perspectives on the source, recruitment, and socialization of elites and the permeability of elite strata. The source of elites is a less significant issue to Michels since it is organization, per se, that engenders oligarchy. Pareto's imagery of "lions" (i.e., forceful and authoritarian) and "foxes" (i.e., shrewd and guileful) vividly differentiates between those elites arising from more traditional sources (landed aristocracy) rather than from more modern ones (bureaucracy). Mosca identifies the sources of elites in two ways; he identifies the most important "social forces" in a society (land, education, labor, religion, and the military) and then he distinguishes between the "autocratic" and "democratic" principles and two types of ruling classes—one based upon inheritance of power and the other open to talented individuals from the lower classes. Pareto's lions and foxes clearly correspond to Mosca's autocratic and democratic principles. Michels speaks most cogently to the issues of recruitment and socialization—critical for the study of political parties (especially in the reform era). His position is that "in order to avoid having to divide their power with new elements, especially such as are uncongenial . . . , the old leaders tend everywhere with greater or less success, to acquire the right of choosing their own colleagues. . . . In the event they cannot, the old leaders use cooptation or if necessary some other form of accommodation." Once an individual becomes part of an elite stratum, the inevitable psychological metamorphosis begins. Mosca and Pareto seem to agree with Michels, but they offer a more vigorous construction, partly because their analysis is not limited simply to organizations. Established elite ranks must be open to individuals of talent from the lower social strata; otherwise, talented and ambitious individuals will eventually displace the old elites and then become a new elite class. It is far better for the elite classes to recruit these individuals, socialize them (i.e., create an elite consciousness), and use their talents. Mosca holds that the struggle

involved in this process benefits society in stimulating the talents and moral traits of the individuals involved.

The circulation of elites represents a fundamental issue of representative government. Many scholars (e.g., Schattschneider's "opposition party" view) have argued that representative government requires two separate groups of elites and that when one group fails in an electoral context, it is displaced by the other. Michels doubts that elites do indeed circulate. His position is that in "the struggle between the old leaders and the new," the result is "not so much a *circulation des élites* as a *réunion des élites*, an amalgam, that is to say, of the two elements." This issue remains as controversial today as when Michels was writing in the first decades of the twentieth century. Scholars like Cornelius Cotter offer support for Michels's position in observing that the participation of amateurs in the parties has not resulted in circulating elites (and displacement of the old by the new) but rather an amalgam of elite elements: the amateurs are transformed after they enter the leadership ranks of the party, and the old leaders accommodate themselves to the new elements.

The last issue, elite-nonelite interdependence, is a thorny one. The writings of the major elite theorists on the subject are less than clear. Pareto's work is especially difficult to accept because it involves his rather singular notions of "residues" and "derivations." Two points are worth noting: the elite-nonelite interdependence is not simply a matter of "elites versus nonelites"; and, second, this issue is now receiving some long overdue theoretical attention, especially in reference to social movement and other protest groups and their relation to the two major political parties and the party reform movement.

See also: Robert Michels

David A. Bositis

REFERENCES

Baer, Denise L., and David A. Bositis. 1988. *Elite Cadres and Party Coalitions: Representing the Public in Party Politics.* Westport, CT: Greenwood.

Burton, Michael G., and John Higley. 1987. "Invitation to Elite Theory." In G. William Domhaff and Thomas R. Dye, eds. *Power Elites and Organizations.* Beverly Hills, CA: Sage.

Cotter, Cornelius P., James L. Gibson, John F. Bibby, and Robert J. Huckshorn. 1984. *Party Organizations in American Politics.* New York: Praeger.

Duverger, Maurice. 1954. *Political Parties.* New York: Wiley.

Eldersveld, Samuel J. 1982. *Political Parties in American Society.* New York: Basic Books.

Michels, Robert. 1962. *Political Parties*. New York: Collier Books (orig. pub. in German in 1911, 1st English ed. 1915).

Mosca, Gaetano. 1939. *The Ruling Class*. New York: McGraw-Hill.

Pareto, Vilfredo. 1935. *The Mind and Society*. New York: Dover.

Schattschneider, Elmer E. 1942. *Party Government*. New York: Rinehart.

Stephen B. Elkins (1841–1911)

Three-term Republican Senator from West Virginia. Stephen Benton Elkins served as a territorial legislator and attorney general from New Mexico and as Secretary of War under President Benjamin Harrison. Born in Ohio, Elkins received his college education (B.A. and M.A.) at the University of Missouri. Against the wishes of his family he joined the Union Army. After admission to the Missouri bar, he moved to New Mexico where he was elected to the territorial legislature in 1864. He served successively as territorial district attorney (1866), attorney general (1867), United States district attorney (1867–1870), and Republican territorial delegate to Congress (1872–1877). He built sizable businesses in banking, coal mining, and railroads, in addition to establishing an active legal practice. After the death of his first wife, he married the daughter of West Virginia Senator Henry G. Davis, moving to West Virginia and becoming actively involved in business with his father-in-law.

On the national level Elkins acted as an adviser to Republican presidential candidate James G. Blaine and served on the Republican National Committee. In 1891 President Harrison appointed him Secretary of War, and in February 1895, Elkins won the first of three terms as Senator from West Virginia. He chaired the Interstate Commerce Committee (ICC) during an important time of railroad regulation. The Elkins Act of 1903 added teeth to the prohibition against railroad rebates and the Mann-Elkins Act of 1910 expanded the rate-making power of the ICC.

See *also*: Benjamin Harrison, Railroads, Republican National Committee

Nicholas C. Burckel

REFERENCES

Lambert, Oscar Doane. 1955. *Stephen Benton Elkins*. Pittsburgh: U. of Pittsburgh Pr.

Williams, John Alexander. 1976. *West Virginia and the Captains of Industry*. Morgantown: West Virginia U. Library.

Allen J. Ellender (1891–1972)

United States Senator from Louisiana for 35 years. His political career originated in the Huey Long Democratic machine that dominated Louisiana politics for decades. Allen Joseph Ellender's background was solid: he was both a practicing attorney in local government and a successful potato farmer. He then spent 12 years in the state house of representatives, aiming eventually to be Louisiana's governor. After Long's assassination in 1935, Ellender was elected to fill the Senate seat, a post he held until he died.

As a New Deal Democrat from the South, Ellender was curiously both ahead and behind the times. While he supported funds for housing after World War II, for education, and to continue wartime price controls in the postwar period, he also opposed Franklin Roosevelt's antilynch bill, national health care, and the minimum wage. In 1946 Ellender sponsored a bill compensating Japanese-Americans for their forced relocation in World War II, an idea which took 40 years to realize. Senator Ellender chaired the Committee on Agriculture and Forestry until 1971, when he took over the powerful Appropriations Committee. He also gained a certain fame as a watchdog of the Treasury Department in Washington in the 1960s.

See *also*: Hugh P. Long, New Deal, Franklin Roosevelt

Samuel F. Mitchell

REFERENCES

Key, V. O., Jr. 1949. *Southern Politics in State and Nation*. New York: Knopf.

Oliver Ellsworth (1745–1807)

Early Federalist leader of the U.S. Senate. Born in Windsor, Connecticut, Oliver Ellsworth attended Yale and Princeton universities before his legal career. On the state level, Ellsworth's offices included general assembly representative, State's attorney, Governor's Council member, and Superior Court judge. On the national level, he served as a delegate to the Continental Congress (1777–1784), delegate to the Constitutional Convention in 1787, U.S. Senator (1789–1796), U.S. Supreme Court Chief Justice (1796–1799), and envoy to France (1799–1801).

Although the Federalists would not demonstrate the unity of organization that characterizes a congressional party until near the end of Ellsworth's Senate tenure, he was instrumental in that development. From the beginning, he identified with the political vision of a strong central government, governmental economic intervention, and close Senate-executive relations later ascribed to the Federalist Party. Ellsworth worked to realize that vision by helping to draft the organization of the federal judiciary, by strongly backing Treasury Secretary Alexander Hamilton's fiscal plans, and by advising George Washington on foreign relations. Even as opposition to these and other Federalist policies took hold, Ellsworth continued his efforts on their behalf by dominating the Senate select committee system, mastering legislative details, and otherwise trying to rally sympathetic colleagues. Aaron Burr said of his influence, "If Ellsworth had happened to spell the name of the Deity with two d's, it would have taken the Senate three weeks to expunge the superfluous letter." He was a force of some magnitude in the American political scene for 25 years.

See also: John Adams, Aaron Burr, Federalist Party, Alexander Hamilton, George Washington

Elaine K. Swift

REFERENCES

Swanstrom, Roy. 1985. "The United States Senate, 1787–1801." Sen. Doc. 99–19. Washington: U.S. Government Printing Office.

Emancipation as a Political Issue

Now, therefore I, Abraham Lincoln, President of the United States, by virtue of the power in me invested as Commander-in-Chief . . . and as a fit and necessary war measure for suppressing said rebellion, do, on this first day of January, in the year of our Lord, one thousand eight hundred and sixty-three . . . order and declare that all persons held as slaves within said designated states, and parts of states are, and henceforward shall be free. . . .

By signing his name to the Emancipation Proclamation, President Lincoln began a new chapter in the continuing American political saga of "life, liberty, and the pursuit of happiness."

When Thomas Jefferson wrote these words in the first draft of the Declaration of Independence, he also justified armed revolt in order to obtain freedom on the grounds that George III had waged "cruel war against human nature" by promoting and protecting the "execrable commerce" in African slaves. This passage was stricken from the final version because of the insistence of delegates from South Carolina and Georgia and the acquiescence of "northern brethren . . . [who] had been pretty considerable carriers of them [enslaved Africans] to others." This North-South compromise went through

several revisions before Lincoln resolved the emancipation issues with his signature.

Traditionally, emancipation has been discussed as a political struggle between property rights and human rights. To Charles Beard, Staughton Lynd, and others, the interests of property clearly outweighed those of principle among the signers of the Declaration and the Constitution. In the latter, the delegates, and later a majority of those who voted on its adoption, explicitly guaranteed the protection of chattel slavery and the slave trade. Inherent in this approval was the contradiction with the fundamental tenet of a republic, a government based on the consent of all the governed.

The tension generated by this contradiction was heightened by the acquisition of new territory. In the first instance, involving the Northwest Territory, the Confederation and constitutional legislatures voted to prohibit slavery. In 1820, however, when the territorial, and therefore, political stakes were much higher, Congress attempted to resolve the issue by dividing the Louisiana Territory at the 36°30' line in the famous Missouri Compromise.

Neither the advocates of emancipation nor those of slavery were appeased, and the 1830s witnessed the institutional organization of the abolitionists. In November 1839, the issue entered the political arena with the formation of the Liberty Party, which nominated James G. Birney (ex-slaveholder from Kentucky) the next year for President. It did so again in 1844, when his 62,000 votes (2.3 percent of the total) contributed to Henry Clay's (Whig-Ky.) narrow defeat.

When the United States defeated Mexico, the emancipation issue was raised more forcefully in terms of the Wilmot Proviso of 1847; this document stated that "neither slavery nor involuntary servitude shall ever exist in any part of said territory." The Proviso initially passed the House but failed in the Senate, only to become a key issue in the election of 1848. When neither the Democrats nor the Whigs took a stand against slavery, emancipationists in both groups established the Free Soil Party, endorsed the Wilmot Proviso, called for the passage of a homestead act, and nominated Martin Van Buren (N.Y.) and Charles Francis Adams (Mass.). In their first show of real political power, the emancipationists won 10 percent of the popular vote and New York's 36 electoral votes.

The application of California for admission to the United States with a free-soil constitution in March 1850 sparked a national political crisis. The union was evenly divided; 15 free states and 15 slave states, and hence, the famous Compromise of 1850. Both the Democratic and Whig platforms of 1852 endorsed the Compromise, and the Free Soil Party, which condemned it, saw its voter appeal cut in half. This trend was reversed, however, when Senator Stephen A. Douglas (D-Ill.) introduced the Kansas-Nebraska Act in January 1854.

The key political issue was "popular sovereignty," the principle that local inhabitants should determine the free or slave status of their territory through their constitution when they applied for statehood. With the passage of the act in May, dissidents began to hold conventions in hopes of forming a new party. The first of these was held in Ripon, Wisconsin, and its members proposed "Republican" as the name for the new group.

Two years later, popular sovereignty looked more like vigilantism after the "sacking of Lawrence" by proslavery men and, several days later, "the Pottawatomie massacre" by the abolitionist John Brown. "Bleeding Kansas" became the divisive issue of the 1856 election in which James Buchanan (D-Penn.) defeated Colonel John C. Frémont (R-Calif.). The Dred Scott decision by the Supreme Court the following year fanned the emancipation/slavery crisis even further by declaring that African-Americans were not citizens of the U.S. and therefore "had no rights which the white man was bound to respect." In addition, the decision implied that the Missouri Compromise was unconstitutional. The admission of Kansas the following year under the proslavery Lecompton Constitution raised political passions to a fever pitch. It also brought Abraham Lincoln (R-Ill.) national recognition for his denunciation of slavery as "a moral, a social, and a political evil" in his famous debates with the incumbent Senator Stephen A. Douglas (D-Ill.). Although Lincoln lost the election, Republicans were victorious elsewhere and gained control of the House of Representatives.

The polarization of political opinion was advanced in the North by Lincoln's "House Divided" and William Seward's "Irrepressible Conflict" speeches and in the South by George Fitzhugh's *Cannibals All!* Reactions to John Brown's raid on the arsenal at Harper's Ferry in October 1859 widened the split. One of these came in the form of a set of resolutions reaffirming the constitutionality of slavery introduced into the Senate by Jefferson Davis in February 1860. When Douglas (and his "popular sovereignty" position) won the Democratic presidential nomination in June, proslavery Democrats bolted and nominated John C. Breckinridge (Ky.) and Joseph Lane (Ore.). In Chicago, the Republicans nominated Lincoln and Hannibal Hamlin (Maine). The Constitutional Union Party, which attempted to bridge the breech by nominating John Bell (Tenn.) and Edward Everett (Mass.), dramatized the futility of such an effort by finishing a distant fourth in the fall elections. The failure of politicians to resolve the question of free or slave became evident in December 1860 when the South Carolina legislature voted unanimously to secede from the union. Neither secession nor the subsequent attack on Fort Sumter provided sufficient pressure on the new President to support emancipation. This came from the so-called "radical" faction of Republicans in Congress. In the First and Second Confiscation acts of 1861 and 1862, they emancipated enslaved persons owned by those in rebellion. Lincoln followed this lead, justifying both the preliminary and official Emancipation Proclamation in terms of military necessity.

In principle, the proclamation established freedom as the basis of equal citizenship. This development, in turn, removed slavery as a contradiction in a government memorably described by Lincoln as "of the people, by the people, and for the people." The Constitution guaranteed such a republican form of government to every state, and Lincoln cited this guarantee and his powers as Commander-in-Chief to justify his proclamation. The subsequent political struggles over the Thirteenth, Fourteenth, and Fifteenth amendments, the Civil Rights Acts of 1866 and 1875, and the rise and fall of segregation have revealed that emancipation and Black power were perceived by most Americans as separate issues, when in fact freedom and power were, and are, inseparable.

See also: Charles Francis Adams, John Bell, James G. Birney, John C. Breckinridge, John Brown, James Buchanan, Constitutional Union Party, Jefferson Davis, Stephen Douglas, Dred Scott, Election of 1844, 1848, 1856, and 1860, Formation of the Republican Party, Free Soil Party, Kansas-Nebraska Act, Liberty Party, Abraham Lincoln, Missouri Compromise, Secession, Slavery, Wilmot Proviso

Hal S. Chase

REFERENCES

Craven, Avery. 1942. *The Coming of the Civil War.* New York: Scribner's.

Foner, Eric. 1970. *Free Soil, Free Labor, Free Men: The Ideology of the Republican Party Before the Civil War.* New York: Oxford U. Pr.

Franklin, John Hope. 1963. *The Emancipation Proclamation.* Garden City, NY: Doubleday.

Holt, Michael F. 1978. *The Political Crisis of the 1850s.* New York: Wiley.

Nichols, Roy F. 1948. *The Disruption of American Democracy.* New York: Macmillan.

Silbey, Joel H. 1967. *The Shrine of Party: Congressional Voting Behavior, 1841–1852.* Pittsburgh: U. of Pittsburgh Pr.

Williams, T. Harry. 1941. *Lincoln and the Radicals.* Madison: U. of Wisconsin Pr.

Equal Rights Amendment

Had the Equal Rights Amendment (ERA) been ratified and incorporated into the U.S. Constitution, it would have raised almost to the point of prohibition the level of scrutiny to which legal distinctions on the basis of sex are subjected. The entire text of the ERA reads as follows:

1. Equality of rights under the law shall not be denied or abridged by the United States or by any State on account of sex.
2. The Congress shall have the power to enforce, by appropriate legislation, the provisions of this article.
3. This amendment shall take effect two years after the date of ratification.

Since the ERA was designed to constrain governments, it would have neither affected private practices in which legal distinctions are made on the basis of sex—for example, in setting insurance rates—nor rendered unnecessary measures banning discrimination in the private sector.

The ERA has a long history. An early version, drafted by Alice Paul, was first introduced into Congress in 1923. Then, as later, it was women who spearheaded the resistance to the ERA: concerned that passage of the ERA would abrogate protective legislation, social feminists enlisted their allies within Progressive organizations and trade unions in joint opposition to the ERA. The subject of periodic committee hearings, the ERA languished in Congress for several decades, never coming close to passage. (In 1950 and 1953, the Senate did pass the ERA. Because the Senate version included the "Hayden rider," stipulating that the "Amendment shall not be construed to impair any rights, benefits, or exemptions now or hereinafter conferred upon persons of the female sex," ERA supporters were in fact relieved that the House did not do the same.) During this period labor unions, especially union women, were its primary antagonists, a fact that helps to explain why, in a circumstance that was later to be reversed, support for the ERA was stronger within the Republican Party than within the Democratic Party. Indeed, for many years its fate in Congress was determined by the liberal chairman of the House Judiciary Committee, Emanuel Celler (D-N.Y.), whose refusal to schedule hearings on the ERA reflected the opposition of labor.

The rebirth of the women's movement in the late 1960s was accompanied by renewed advocacy on behalf of the ERA. The National Organization for Women (NOW) listed it first on its Bill of Rights for Women. At the same time, the Equal Employment Opportunity Commission (EEOC) and the courts were beginning to interpret Title VII of the Civil Rights Act of 1964, a provision that outlawed discrimination on the basis of gender in employment, as taking precedence over state protective legislation. As the protections contained in such measures began to be extended to men, not withdrawn from women, labor opposition to the ERA began to diminish. In 1970 Martha Griffiths (D-Mich.) extracted the ERA from Celler's committee on a discharge petition. In 1971 the House passed the ERA. The next year, 1972, the Senate followed suit, and the ERA was sent to the states for ratification.

In the immediate aftermath several states ratified the ERA—many of them with little debate and unanimous or lopsided votes. Then, as opposition consolidated in the unratified states under the leadership of Phyllis Schlafly, progress slowed substantially. In the process, the politics of ratification became increasingly acrimonious, and the ERA became invested with additional meanings: the symbols invoked by the contending groups of women resonated with their most deeply held commitments but were often irrelevant to what the ERA might actually accomplish. Debate about serious issues, such as the role of women in the military, was intermingled with rancorous dispute about spurious ones, like unisex toilets.

Throughout the period during which it was being considered (1970–1982), the ERA enjoyed majority support among the public and extremely strong support by women in the state houses. Still, the opposition seized the initiative. ERA advocates were in many ways handicapped:

by their association with "women's liberation," a movement held in public disrepute even though its goals were widely shared; by the potency of the symbols of home, family, and God to which the opposition appealed; by the little-reported ability of ERA opponents to capitalize on the organizational infrastructure and increasing political militancy of fundamentalist Protestant churches; by NOW's ideological inflexibility and failure to build effective coalitions. ERA supporters were also hurt by the nature of the issue in which legislators were being asked to support an irreversible measure of unknown consequences that seemed to hand a blank check to an activist Supreme Court; by the ability of anti-ERA legislators to characterize the ERA, not as a measure that would help women, but as one that divided them; by the incentive given to the risk-averse legislator to sidestep or postpone an increasingly controversial issue; and by the lukewarm support given by Presidents Gerald Ford and Jimmy Carter. In 1976 conservative Republicans nearly succeeded in dropping support for the ERA from their party's platform, a goal they accomplished four years later.

By 1977, with the 7-year limitation on ratification running out, only 35 states had ratified, 3 short of the number needed for the amendment to become part of the Constitution. In 1978, at the behest of ERA supporters, Congress extended the deadline for ratification until 1982—a maneuver that generated controversy among constitutional scholars. None of the remaining states (Alabama, Arizona, Arkansas, Florida, Georgia, Illinois, Louisiana, Mississippi, Missouri, Nevada, North Carolina, Oklahoma, South Carolina, Utah, and Virginia) ratified, however, and the amendment died in 1982. Four months later, the Supreme Court acknowledged the demise of the ERA by declaring moot the case that would have resolved the doubtful status of attempts in several states to rescind ERA ratification. As of the end of the One Hundred First Congress, attempts to reintroduce the ERA into Congress have had no success.

During the 12-year period between the resuscitation of the ERA and its final expiration in 1982, the legal rationale for its passage changed substantially. In 1970 the Supreme Court had never invoked the equal protection clause of the Fourteenth Amendment to invalidate a legal distinction made on the basis of sex. Indeed, as recently as 1961 in the case of *Hoyt v. Florida*, the Supreme Court explicitly refused to do so, upholding a Florida law exempting women from jury duty unless they registered their desire to serve with the clerk of the court. In 1971 (*Reed v. Reed*), the Court began to apply the Fourteenth Amendment to sex-based legal distinctions. While the Court did not declare sex to be a "suspect classification," it did establish an intermediate level of scrutiny for the examination of distinctions made on the basis of sex in *Craig v. Boren* (1976) and had frequently, though not invariably, used that standard to disallow such distinctions. Given the course taken by the Supreme Court, there is now disagreement—even among supporters of equal rights for women—about the legal need for an ERA. Some argue that the legal tools are now in place for accomplishing what the ERA would have done even without its inclusion in the Constitution. Other rejoin that, without a general statement in the Constitution, the establishment of equal rights for women is too dependent upon the sympathies of a particular court. If the future of the ERA seems dim, its supporters have not lost heart, recalling that nearly a century of struggle preceded the passage of the suffrage amendment.

See also: Jimmy Carter, Civil Rights Legislation, Gerald Ford, Alice Paul, Phyllis Schlafly, Woman Suffrage Movement

Kay Lehman Schlozman

REFERENCES

Berry, Mary Frances. 1986. *Why ERA Failed.* Bloomington: Indiana U. Pr.

Boles, Janet K. 1979. *The Politics of the Equal Rights Amendment.* New York: Longman.

Freeman, Jo. 1987. "Whom You Know Versus Whom You Represent: Feminist Influence in the Democratic and Republican Parties." In Mary Fainsod Katzenstein and Carol McClurg Mueller, eds. *The Women's Movements of the United States and Western Europe.* Philadelphia: Temple U. Pr.

Fry, Amelia R. 1986. "Alice Paul and the ERA." In Joan Hoff-Wilson, ed. *Rights of Passage.* Bloomington: Indiana U. Pr.

Mansbridge, Jane J. 1986. *Why We Lost the ERA.* Chicago: U. of Chicago Pr.

Steiner, Gilbert Y. 1985. *Constitutional Inequality.* Washington: Brookings.

Equal Rights Party

The Equal Rights Party was created in 1872 by reformers who believed it to be a necessary alternative to the Republican Party. They condemned the Republicans for failing to support reform causes and for not adequately promoting women's suffrage.

The ERP evolved out of discussions initiated by Victoria Woodhull, leader of the American wing of the First International Workingmen's Association, and members of the National Woman Suffrage Association (NWSA) about the possibility of forming a separate political party. NWSA president Elizabeth Cady Stanton considered the idea a good one because she wanted to make suffrage the center of a comprehensive program of radical social measures designed to alter relations between the sexes. Stanton's positive response to the Internationalists put her at odds with her co-worker, Susan B. Anthony, who believed that suffrage had to be an independent movement. In particular, she feared the loss of women's control over the campaign for suffrage and the adulteration of feminist goals. Anthony distrusted Woodhull not only because Woodhull's colleagues were men but also because she believed suffrage was not Woodhull's main goal, despite past efforts on its behalf. Anthony concluded that any alliance would result in a takeover of NWSA.

Despite her protest, NWSA members agreed to a preliminary meeting the day before a planned joint convention in May 1872. Anthony at first attempted to cancel the hall, then tried to keep Woodhull from speaking, and finally resorted to turning off the gas, leaving delegates in the dark. Even so, Stanton and others attended the convention, where the party was constituted and where Woodhull was nominated as its candidate for President of the United States.

Within weeks, Woodhull's candidacy was subjected to harassment, and the International rejected her women's suffrage/free-love views. In response, she used her newspaper to expose the adulterous affair between prominent preacher Henry Ward Beecher and Elizabeth Tilton, the wife of Beecher's friend, the reformer Theodore Tilton. This scandalous story resulted in Woodhull's arrest under the Comstock obscenity laws and effectively ended her presidential campaign. Though Stanton defended Woodhull, she rejoined Anthony and reluctantly supported Ulysses S. Grant in the 1872 election. Anthony did so with more enthusiasm when the Republicans appeared to be more sympathetic to women's reform interests. However, the Republicans failed them, and the entire episode encouraged many suffragists to avoid alliances of any kind and to refrain from supporting comprehensive reform programs by concentrating solely on the vote.

The Equal Rights Party reappeared in 1884 and 1888 when it nominated for President Belva A. Lockwood, who was active in the peace and temperance movements. In 1884 she ran on a platform that advocated equality and justice for all regardless of sex, color, or nationality and included full citizenship for Native Americans. The ERP supported women's suffrage and defended the need for women's legal equality especially in marriage, divorce, contracts, and property. The party declared that such equity was the only way that women could end dependency and become self-supporting citizens. The platform also called for civil service reform, land distribution to actual settlers, and repression of the liquor traffic. Lockwood was able to poll about 4,000 votes in 1884, fairing little better in 1888.

See also: Susan B. Anthony, Election of 1872, Ulysses S. Grant, Elizabeth Cady Stanton, Woman Suffrage Movement

Joy A. Scimé

REFERENCES

Dubois, Ellen C., ed. 1981. *Elizabeth Cady Stanton and Susan B. Anthony: Correspondence, Writings, Speeches.* New York: Schocken Books.

McKee, Thomas Hudson. 1906. *The National Conventions and Platforms of All Political Parties, 1789–1905.* New York: Burt Franklin.

Woloch, Nancy. 1984. *Women and the American Experience.* New York, Knopf.

Meade H. Esposito (1907–)

Last powerful boss of the Brooklyn Democratic machine. Meade H. Esposito was the owner of printing and insurance businesses, and the last powerful boss of the Brooklyn Democratic machine. He served as Brooklyn County Democratic leader from 1969 until his retirement in 1984, well into the reform era. He "arranged" many favors and enriched himself in the process.

Esposito claimed that after he had supported Abe Beame for mayor in 1973, he got control of six commissionerships in New York City. But Esposito had to be discreet in his support of Ed Koch for the mayoralty since an open endorsement by such a notorious "fixer" would have tarnished Koch. Esposito claimed to have held New York City's Italians back from Koch's opponent, Mario Cuomo.

In 1987 Esposito was found guilty of giving illegal gratuities to Congressman Mario Biaggi (D-N.Y.), including free vacations to Florida. Biaggi had helped the Coastal Dry Dock Corporation of Brooklyn receive payments from the Navy in order to stay in business. Esposito received a suspended two-year sentence and a fine of $500,000. On surveillance tapes he had talked of giving 42 judges their jobs; of being boss of the whole state; of having "invested" the money in helping Congressman Biaggi; of political "contracts" every place he went, even after retirement.

In 1988 he was indicted with his daughter Phyllis Zito, for commercial bribery, tax fraud, and conspiracy in obtaining contracts for his Beaumont Offset Printing Corporation. It was alleged he had given $200,000 in kickbacks and laundered $250,000 in fake invoices.

See also: Mario Cuomo, Edward I. Koch

Jeremy R. T. Lewis

REFERENCES

Koch, Edward I., with William Rauch. 1984. *Mayor.* New York: Bantam.

———, with ———. 1985. *Politics.* New York: Bantam.

Ethnic Voting

Ethnic voting studies focus on the degree to which the ethnic origin of the voter predicts political participation and support for (1) political candidates of the same ethnicity; (2) candidates of other racial and ethnic groups; and (3) political parties. Ethnic voting patterns have also been used to predict electoral outcomes and policy successes. Finally, ethnic voting patterns are a critical element in determining the degree to which various electoral systems are judged fair under the Voting Rights Act (for groups protected under the act).

Much has been made of the differences in the terms "race" and "ethnicity." For example, R. J. Meister "excludes racial groups from the definition of ethnic because nonwhites, especially blacks, have had a historical relationship with white America, that is much different than the relationship that European immigrant groups have had with Anglo-Americans." S. M. Lipset also argues that race and ethnicity are different in the United States: "Race and color clearly are far greater barriers to intimate contact and equal social access than religion or ethnicity."

Others, however, have regarded the terms "race" and "ethnicity" as interchangeable. "Most sociologists use 'ethnic' to include nationality, ethno-religious, and racial groups," claims Richard Meister. And D. L. Horowitz concludes that "comparison is facilitated by an inclusive conception of ethnicity that embraces differences identified by color, language, religion, or some other attribute of common origin."

Yet another view of the distinctions between ethnicity and race is more historically based. Edgar Litt distinguishes between other theories of ethnic politics "based on the examination of European immigrant groups adapting to the urban industrial order" and newer ethnic politics that "involve non-Caucasians dealing with a highly complex urban environment."

Ethnicity is generally found to have an independent effect on political participation, even when social class or socioeconomic status is held constant. In general, participation differentials are explained by assimilation, generational, socioeconomic, cultural, legal, and relative-deprivation theories. Historically, the ethnic groups with the highest level of participation, especially at the local level, have been Irish and Jewish. Newer research (post-1980), focusing on the participation rates of Blacks, Hispanics, and Asians, reports that registration and turnout rates of Blacks are virtually identical to those of whites while those of Asians exceed whites. Hispanic participation rates lag far behind those of the other three groups. Among the common explanations for lower Hispanic participation rates are (1) a higher percentage on noncitizens, many of whom immigrated from countries where they were not socialized to participate; (2) language difficulties; and (3) a disproportionately younger population.

Early studies linking ethnicity with political party identification reported that African-Americans, Jews, the Irish, and some east European immigrant groups identified much more frequently with the Democratic Party than Anglo-Saxons. Today, research shows that of all the racial/ethnic groups in the U.S., Blacks are the most loyally Democratic, followed by Hispanics (although Cubans tend to be Republican), and Asians (split between the two parties). The interactive effects of race, ethnicity, and socioeconomic status still make it difficult to sort out cause-and-effect relationships, however.

The degree to which ethnicity serves as a voting cue, sometimes referred to as *ethnic political consciousness*, is often (in Dale Nelson's words) a function of "(1) a belief that members of the mainstream society discriminate against one's ethnic group, and (2) a positive identification with ethnic group goals and interests." Others have found that ethnic voting is more a function of the size and geographical concentration of the ethnic group. Banfield and Wilson first delineated this theory:

The large city, by concentrating the population, provides a necessary (but not sufficient) condition for ethnic political activity. The various nationality and racial groups are sufficiently large that they believe they 'have some reasonable chances of affecting the outcome of elections; there are enough members of the group to feel a sense of group solidarity and to support their own political leaders and institutions; and they are sufficiently set apart from other groups to stimulate a sense of competition and even conflict.

In summary, the cohesiveness of ethnic groups in their voting patterns is a function of the group's size, geographical concentration, perceptions of discrimination against it, and its ethnic cultural pride. Cohesiveness varies significantly within a group across different electoral contests and issues and changes over time. Generally, African-Americans are regarded as the most cohesive of all racial and ethnic groups. Hispanics are regarded as far less cohesive, owing to differences in length of residence in the U.S., geographical location from which they or their ancestors immigrated (e.g., Cuba, Mexico, Puerto Rico), differing language abilities, and socioeconomic status. Asians, too, tend not to be cohesive for the same reasons as Hispanics. Differences abound among Asians of Japanese, Korean, Filipino, and Chinese descent.

Ethnic electoral successes are frequently contingent upon support from other ethnic groups and whites, especially when the ethnic groups are not a majority of the voting constituency. Some research suggests that Black-Hispanic coalitions are the most plausible since both groups have been discriminated against by whites. The inference is that the common search for more political influence and economic gain is sufficiently strong to stimulate formation of this minority electoral coalition, particularly when minority candidates run against whites. Generally, research has shown that Blacks are more likely to support Hispanic candidates than vice versa.

Other research suggests that ethnic groups sharing common disadvantages may view one another as competitors. For example, in the political machine–dominated cities of the Northeast, the Irish and Italians were frequently political opponents. Today, Blacks and Hispanics are often competitors. Each group's leaders periodically accuse the other of not being genuinely concerned with "minority issues" and of aligning with white voters to get ahead faster. Black-Hispanic coalitions also become more tenuous as the likelihood of electoral success for each group improves. Then each group is more inclined to build electoral coalitions with whites than with the other.

The examination of ethnic voting patterns, particularly the degree of ethnic political cohesiveness and a group's success at electing candidates of its own choice (controlling for the group's size), is an integral element in litigation filed by racial and ethnic groups protected under the Voting Rights Act.

See also: Voting Rights Act of 1965 and Extensions

Susan A. MacManus

REFERENCES

Browning, Rufus P., Dale Rogers Marshall, and David H. Tabb. 1984. *Protest Is Not Enough: The Struggle of Blacks and Hispanics for Equality in Urban Politics.* Berkeley: U. of California Pr.

Bullock, Charles S., III, and Susan A. MacManus. 1990. "Tri-Ethnic Voting." 79 *National Civic Review* 5.

Cain, Bruce, and Roderick Kiewiet. 1986. *Minorities in California.* Pasadena, CA: The Division of Humanities and Social Sciences, California Institute of Technology.

Edds, Margaret. 1987. *Free At Last.* Bethesda, MD: Adler and Adler.

Glazer, Nathan, and Daniel P. Moynihan. 1970. *Beyond the Melting Pot.* Cambridge: MIT Press.

———, eds. 1975. *Ethnicity.* Cambridge: Harvard U. Pr.

Greer, Scott, ed. 1981. *Ethnics, Machines, and the American Urban Future.* Cambridge: Schenkman Publishing.

Horowitz, Donald L. 1985. *Ethnic Groups in Conflict.* Berkeley: U. of California. Pr.

Litt, Edgar. 1970. *Ethnic Politics in America.* Glenview, IL: Scott, Foresman.

MacManus, Susan, and Charles S. Bullock III. 1987. "Race, Ethnicity, and Ancestry as Voting Cues in City Council Elections." Paper presented at the Conference on Ethnic and Racial Minorities in Advanced Industrial Economies, University of Notre Dame, December 3.

Meister, Richard J., ed. 1974. *Race and Ethnicity in Modern America.* Lexington, MA: Heath.

Preston, Michael B. 1987. "The Election of Harold Washington: An Examination of the SES Model in the 1983 Chicago Mayoral Election." In Michael B. Preston, Lenneal, J. Henderson, Jr., and Paul L. Puryear, eds. *The New Black Politics: The Secret for Political Power.* 2nd ed. New York: Longman.

Stone, John. 1985. *Racial Conflict in Contemporary Society.* Cambridge: Harvard U. Pr.

Yetman, Norman R., ed. 1985. *Majority and Minority: The Dynamics of Race and Ethnicity in American Life.* 4th ed. Boston: Allyn and Bacon.

Eu v. San Francisco County Democratic Committee
489 U.S. 214 (1989)

By a vote of eight to zero, in a February 1989

decision with far-reaching national implications, the U.S. Supreme Court declared that several provisions of the California Elections Code were invalid because they "burden the First Amendment rights of political parties and their members without serving a compelling state interest."

In particular, the Court ruled that a ban on primary endorsements was invalid, as were restrictions on the organization and composition of the official governing bodies of political parties, provisions limiting the term of office for state central committee chairs, and the requirement that such chairs rotate between residents of northern and southern California. The Court asserted that the ban on primary endorsements (which included a ban on repudiating as well as on endorsing putative candidates, and had in the past compelled the Democratic Party to accept without demurral the candidacy of a leader of the Ku Klux Klan) violated the rights of parties and their members to free political speech and freedom of association. Freedom of association was construed to include the right to "identify the people who constitute the association and to select a standard bearer who best represents the party's ideology and preferences" as well as to promote candidates "at the crucial primary election juncture." The Court ruled that the laws imposing restrictions on the internal rules and regulations of the parties served to "burden the associational rights of a party and its members by limiting the party's discretion in how to organize itself, conduct its affairs, and select its leaders."

The case, originally organized by the California Committee for Party Renewal, a multipartisan organization composed of political scientists, attorneys, and party politicians and brought to court by the law firm of Morrison and Forester under the direction of Attorney James Brosnahan, established important national precedents. Although before the ruling, New Jersey was the only other state still preventing primary endorsements, almost every state had laws regulating the internal affairs of their political parties (the exceptions were Alaska, Delaware, Hawaii, Kentucky and North Carolina). Thirty-six states regulated the way parties selected the members of their state central committees (and of these, all except Pennsylvania and South Carolina also regulated the choice of members of local party committees). Thirty-two states regulated the composition of the parties' state central committees (and of these, all except

Pennsylvania also regulated the membership of local party committees, as did an additional three states—Connecticut, New York, and Rhode Island—that had nothing to say regarding the composition of state central committees). Twenty-eight states included rules for state party committees in their electoral codes, regulating such matters as when and where the committee had to meet, how it filled vacancies, whether proxies could be used, how members had to be notified in advance of meetings, what constituted a quorum, how and whether executive committees had to be formed, and what were the powers and duties of both officers and members. Similar regulations applied to local party committees.

The unanimous decision and the broad language of the Court in *Eu v. S.F. Democrats*, firmly asserting the First and Fourteenth Amendment rights of political parties and their members, called these laws into question. The Court said that barring a compelling interest "to ensure that elections are fair and honest," a state could not interfere with the right of a political party to conduct its internal affairs and choose its leaders as it alone saw fit. "A State cannot," ruled the Court, "substitute its judgment for that of the party as to desirability of a particular internal party structure, any more than it can tell a party that its proposed communication to party members is unwise . . . a State cannot justify regulating a party's internal affairs without showing that such regulation is necessary to ensure an election that is orderly and fair."

See also: Ku Klux Klan, Party Endorsing Procedures

Kay Lawson

REFERENCES

Eu, Secretary of State of California, et al. v. San Francisco County Democratic Central Committee et al. 87–1269 U.S. Sup. Ct.

Conlan, Timothy. 1986. "State and Local Parties in Contemporary Politics: Decline, Adaptation, and Continuing Legal Constraints." In Advisory Commission on Intergovernmental Relations. *The Transformation in American Politics*. Washington: ACIR.

Evangelicals

The evangelicals are a growing body of conservative Protestants, predominantly white, disproportionately female, and generally older than other religious groups. They are concentrated in rural and small-town regions of the South, the Middle Atlantic States, and west central regions, and in medium-sized cities in the Midwest and South. Generally, evangelicals have slightly lower levels of educational attainment, income, and occupational status than do other "mainstream" religious groups. By party identification, more are Democrats, but most have consistently voted Republican in the past three presidential elections.

In terms of doctrine, evangelicals believe in biblical inerrancy, the divinity of Christ, and salvations of the human soul as demonstrated by the physical resurrection of Jesus Christ.

For political purposes, evangelicalism is seen as religiocultural phenomena centering on the need for the reassertion of traditional values perceived to be lacking in contemporary American society. Evangelicalism became a political force when it joined in the formation of the New Religious Right in the early 1980s. This reactive movement began by calling for the rejection of many social and cultural changes that had begun in the 1960s, particularly women's increasingly active role in society, the legalization of abortion, and the absence of prayer in the public schools.

The evangelicals' emphasis on conservative social issues and on these three bellwether issues in particular are critical to understanding evangelical political motivations. Hence, observers are correct to emphasize that the political interests of the evangelicals and the New Religious Right are largely concerned with family and morality. Convinced that their way of life is under attack, they are determined to regain control of the dominant culture in order to enhance the values they believe have allowed American culture to survive and prevail.

Because their political goals are grounded in conservative Christianity, they perceive life itself as a dichotomy of good and evil and see themselves as an embattled good minority who must eliminate evil infecting American society. In a world of bewildering complexity and startling change, they look for authority and simplicity. The pain of life's ambiguity is banished by their refusal to see grayness in their black-and-white world.

The evangelical movement helped transform the Republican Party into a more conservative organization and boosted its winning margins in presidential elections beginning in 1980. Although the direct impact of evangelicals in the GOP cannot be clearly demonstrated, we know that the entrance into the party of conservative Christians both as delegates to the national nominating convention and in the party-in-the-electorate coincides with the first nomination of Ronald Reagan and subsequent reversal

in party policy on several key social issues, among them legalization of abortion and the Equal Rights Amendment.

One evangelical leader, the religious broadcaster the Reverend Marion G. "Pat" Robertson, ran unsuccessfully for the Republican presidential nomination in 1988.

See also: Equal Rights Amendment, Ronald Reagan, Marion G. Robertson

Lisa G. Langenbach

REFERENCES

Conover, Pamela Johnston, and Virginia Grey. 1983. *Feminism and the New Right: Conflict over the American Family.* New York: Praeger.

Hadden, Jeffrey K., and Anson Shupe. 1988. *Televangelism.* New York: Henry Holt.

Hunter, James Davison. 1983. *American Evangelicalism: Conservative Religion and the Quandary of Modernity.* New Brunswick, NJ: Rutgers U. Pr.

Lienesch, Michael. 1982. "Right Wing Religion: Christian Conservatism as a Political Movement." 97 *Political Science Quarterly* 403.

Charles Evers (1922–)

The first African-American to be elected mayor of a biracial southern town since Reconstruction. Born in Decatur, Mississippi, [James] Charles Evers, along with his brother Medgar, suffered the miseries of racism while growing up in Mississippi. While Charles Evers went into business, Medgar Evers joined the early civil rights movement and worked for the NAACP. When Medgar was killed in 1963, Charles immediately took his brother's place and became a field director for the NAACP in Mississippi.

As a result of his work for the NAACP, Charles Evers became involved in politics. He helped organize the Freedom Democratic Party of Mississippi, which successfully challenged and unseated the all-white Mississippi delegation to the Democratic National Convention in both 1964 and 1968.

Evers entered the political ring in 1968 when he ran, unsuccessfully, for Congress. Defeat never kept Evers down for long; on May 14, 1969, he was elected mayor of Fayette, Mississippi, a town of some 2,000 people. Evers continued to challenge whites for statewide offices but suffered defeat in races for governor in 1972 and for Senator in 1978. Evers remained as mayor of Fayette until 1989 when he was defeated after four terms. In both his mayoral victory and his campaigns for other offices, Charles Evers opened the political doors in Mississippi for African-Americans by being the first to mobilize and utilize the power of Black voting blocs in Mississippi elections.

See also: National Association for the Advancement of Colored People, Race and Racial Politics

Mary Ann McHugh

REFERENCES

Sewell, George Alexander. 1977. *Mississippi Black History Makers.* Jackson: U. Pr. of Mississippi.

Exit Polling

Exit polling, the practice of interviewing voters when they are leaving their polling places, allows the news media to collect information about an election as it takes place. Pollsters ask voters not only to reveal the candidate for whom they cast their ballot but also to explain their reasons for voting as they did. Also sought are demographic characteristics such as religion, party designation, gender, race, and income.

Results gathered from exit polls are used to analyze election outcomes and to verify voting trends in key precincts, allowing the television networks especially to make voter projections about the winner of an election. In 1980 the perceived close presidential election actually turned into a landslide—a fact known by the major television networks early on election day as a result of observed trends in exit polls.

In that election, television viewers nationwide watched as the three major television networks all named Ronald Reagan as the President-elect before 9 P.M. Eastern Standard Time. The polls in many states had not closed when the winner was announced. Local radio and television stations and newspapers reported that, hearing the media projections of Reagan's victory, many prospective voters left voting places before casting their ballots.

In previous elections, analysis of precinct voting and general voting trends had been used to predict election outcomes. This process was slow but reliable, and in 1964 and 1972 it allowed for the early declaration of Lyndon Johnson and Richard Nixon as the election winners. The extended use of exit polling by the news media was relatively new and controversial in 1980 because it allowed the television news media to predict a state's election outcome even before that state's polling places had closed.

The landslide elections for the Republicans in 1980 and 1984 have forced the Democratic Party to be concerned that early pronouncements of election victories work to decrease voter participation, and in particular, to hurt the chances of other candidates in the party of the losing presidential candidate in western states. Their concern is that the use of information generated by exit polls to aid network news analysts in predicting a state's electoral behavior is an inappropriate use of that information.

Exit polling was widely used by the three major news networks in 1988. While it was once again used as a tool to aid the networks in their voter projections, the networks refrained from predicting the outcome in any state until that state's polls had closed. Therefore, the closeness of the election did not create any conflicts with West Coast voting trends.

Those who oppose the extended use of exit polling cite 1980 and 1984 as instances in which too much information released too early could have had an effect on the electoral process. Supporters of the use of exit polling as practiced note that the results of exit polls give the networks a better understanding of the election and that the public has a right to know the results of an election as soon as those results are known.

Discussions on the propriety of exit polling continue. At issue is not the actual practice of exit polling but rather the use of exit poll information and the timing of the release of that information.

See also: Jimmy Carter; Elections of 1964, 1972, and 1980, 1984, and 1988; Lyndon Johnson; Media and Presidential Politics; Richard Nixon; Ronald Reagan

Michael Heel

REFERENCES

Milavsky, J. Ronald. 1985. "Early Calls of Election Results and Exit Polls: Pros, Cons, and Constitutional Considerations." 49 *Public Opinion Quarterly* 1.

Experimental Research on Political Parties

Formal experimental studies are ones in which experimental subjects are randomly assigned to at least two groups, and after assignment, at least one of the two groups is subject to some sort of manipulation by the experimenter. This process attempts to imitate the circumstances described in John Stuart Mill's "method of difference." The first formal experimental studies of political parties and elections occurred in the 1920s, and this method has been associated with some of the most distinguished of American scholars of party, including Harold Gosnell and Samuel J. Eldersveld.

Gosnell performed the first experimental studies on parties and elections in Chicago in the mid-1920s. His experiment tested whether a series of nonpartisan mailings increased registration and voting in both presidential and local elections. Gosnell found that if all adults in Chicago had been properly informed of registration places and procedures, then 10 percent more would have voted.

Samuel Eldersveld extended Gosnell's approach with a series of experiments conducted in Ann Arbor, Michigan, in the 1950s, testing the effects of different contacting modes on the politically apathetic. He was attempting to find out what the best strategies were for party workers seeking increased turnout. One of his findings was that personal appeals were more effective in getting the apathetic to vote than were mail solicitations.

A more recent example of this tradition can be found in the work of John C. Blydenburgh in the early 1970s. He obtained the cooperation of both the Democratic and Republican candidates in a state legislature race in Monroe County, New York. The candidates, according to the dictates of the design, alternated between using personal contact and telephone appeals in their campaigning. Blydenburgh found that personal contacting was the more effective method.

The results of more than 20 experiments have appeared in major political science periodicals on the subject of parties and elections since Eldersveld's work in the 1950s. This method will, without doubt, continue to be represented in research on political parties and elections.

David A. Bositis

REFERENCES

Blydenburgh, John C. 1971. "A Controlled Experiment to Measure the Effects of Personal Contact Campaigning." 15 *Midwest Journal of Political Science* 365.

Bositis, David A. 1990. *Research Designs for Political Science: Contrivance and Demonstration in Theory and Practice.* Carbondale, IL: Southern Illinois U. Pr.

————, and Douglas Steinel. 1987. "A Synoptic History and Typology of Experimental Research in Political Science." 9 *Political Behavior* 263.

Eldersveld, Samuel J. 1956. "Experimental Propaganda Techniques and Voting Behavior." 50 *American Political Science Review* 154.

Gosnell, Harold. 1927. *Getting Out the Vote: An Experiment in the Stimulation of Voting.* Chicago: U. of Chicago Pr.

F

Frank J. Fahrenkopf, Jr. (1939–)

Chairman of the Republican National Committee (RNC) in the middle and late 1980s. Frank J. Fahrenkopf, Jr., an attorney, became Nevada state GOP chairman in 1975. In 1983, another Nevadan, Senator Paul Laxalt, was President Ronald Reagan's personal choice to head the national party. Because party rules required a full-time RNC chair, and Laxalt did not want to leave the Senate, the committee gave Laxalt the new, part-time post of general chairman. On Laxalt's recommendation, the RNC elected Fahrenkopf as its full-time chairman

Under Fahrenkopf, the RNC stressed grass-roots party building. Regional political operatives supplied local party officials with funds, technology, and training. In 1984 the RNC's telemarketing effort helped to register 4 million new Republican voters.

During the 1984 campaign, the RNC also mounted the most sophisticated opposition research effort up to this time. It spent $1.1 million and consulted over 400,000 documents in order to build a computer database on national Democrats such as Walter Mondale and other national Democrats.

By the late 1980s, however, the Iran-Contra scandal had sapped GOP fundraising, and the national Democrats were working hard to close the financial and technological gap with the GOP.

See also: Ronald Reagan, Republican National Committee

John J. Pitney, Jr.

REFERENCES

Advisory Commission on Intergovernmental Relations. 1986. *The Transformation in American Politics: Implications for Federalism.* Washington: ACIR.

Hames, Timothy. 1990. "The Changing Shape of Republican Party Finance in the 1980s." Paper presented at the annual meeting of the American Political Science Association San Francisco.

Fair Reflection of Presidential Preference

The majority of national party conventional delegates are now selected by voters through presidential primaries or caucuses. This process, however, does not guarantee that the candidate preferences of a state's convention delegation will accurately reflect voter preferences. Presidential nomination campaigns often involve numerous candidates. When there are more than two choices, no absolutely fair method can represent voter preferences. All selection rules introduce biases.

Winner-take-all procedures seem especially unfair in the multicandidate races often found in presidential nomination politics. For example, in the 1976 Wisconsin Democratic primary Jimmy Carter received 37 percent of the vote, Morris Udall received 36 percent, and eight other candidates split the remaining vote. If winner-take-all rules had been used, Carter would have claimed all 68 of Wisconsin's delegates. Under proportional representation Carter received 26 and Udall 25.

Recognizing the potential for biases, Democratic reformers in the McGovern-Fraser and Mikulski commissions stressed the use of proportional representation as a system more accurately reflecting voter preferences. Later commissions, however, weakened these provisions by allowing for loophole primaries, in which the winner in a district (but not a state) may win all of that district's delegates.

Whether a state uses proportional representation, winner-take-all, or loophole rules in its primary or caucus will affect which candidates are represented in its convention delegation and, thus, the fairness of the selection process. Even proportional representation rules can produce biased results.

Approval voting has been suggested by some political scientists as a remedy to the fairness problem. Under approval voting, persons may vote for as many candidates as they like but may not vote for any candidate more than once. The total number of votes for candidates would determine how many delegates they received.

See also: Alternative Voting Systems, Jimmy Carter, McGovern-Fraser Commission, Winner-Take-All Systems

Barbara Norrander

REFERENCES

Brams, Steven J., and Peter C. Fishburn. 1978. "Approval Voting." 72 *American Political Science Review* 831.

Hammond, Thomas. 1980. "Another Look at the Role of 'The Rules' in the 1972 Democratic Presidential Primaries." 33 *Western Political Quarterly* 50.

Lengle, James I., and Byron Shafer. 1976. "Primary Rules, Political Power, and Social Change." 70 *American Political Science Review* 40.

Frances (Sissy) Tarlton Farenthold (1926–)

The first woman to be put into nomination as a vice presidential candidate in the Democratic Party. Frances "Sissy" Farenthold, a graduate of Vassar College, received her law degree from the University of Texas and was admitted to the Texas bar in 1949. She served as a member of the Texas House of Representatives (1968–1972); later she was a Democratic candidate for governor of Texas, receiving 46 percent of the vote in a 1972 runoff election. A delegate to the 1972 convention, Farenthold was nominated for Vice President, losing to presidential candidate George McGovern's choice, Senator Thomas Eagleton; still, she received 420 votes. Farenthold's nomination was intended to demonstrate the political strength of the newly formed National Women's Political Caucus (NWPC). The choice of Farenthold, according to Bella Abzug, was a spur-of-the-moment decision, which came after Shirley Chisholm

"turned down a proposal that she run for the post."

After co-chairing the Citizens for McGovern in 1972, Farenthold left electoral politics for an appointment as assistant professor of law at Texas Southern University, and later as president of Wells College (1976–1980). She was elected chair of the National Women's Political Caucus at its first convention in 1973, serving until 1975. Along with other feminist leaders, Farenthold argued in favor of extending the fifty-fifty rule to *all* Democratic Party commissions and committees at a 1976 Democratic National Convention caucus of women delegates. Farenthold now resides in Texas and chairs the Institute for Policy Studies.

See also: Bella Abzug, Shirley Chisholm, Thomas Eagleton, Fifty-Fifty Rule, George McGovern, National Women's Political Caucus

Denise L. Baer

REFERENCES

Abzug, Bella S., and Mim Kelber. 1984. *Gender Gap: Bella Abzug's Guide to Political Power for American Women.* Boston: Houghton Mifflin.

James A. Farley (1888–1976)

Democratic Party leader during the New Deal. Born in New York to second-generation Irish parents, James Aloysius Farley once complained of having only 150,000 patronage positions to dispense. His legendary (legends nurtured in large part by Farley himself) political career began with his first "great American," Al Smith, and like many other Smith supporters, he became closely associated with another New Yorker, Franklin D. Roosevelt.

Highlights of Jim Farley's career included terms as New York state party boss, chairman of the Democratic National Committee (1932–1940), FDR's campaign chairman in 1932 and 1936, and dispenser of patronage as Postmaster General (1933–1940).

Among the legendary episodes of Farley's experience was his travel around the country in 1932 on behalf of FDR's candidacy, where he lined up support from some 50 party bosses. It was supposedly on this trip that Farley negotiated the vice presidency for John Nance Garner of Uvalde, Texas (setting the pattern of a southern Vice President and a northern President on the Democratic ticket).

As DNC chairman, close associate of FDR, and Postmaster General, Farley possessed considerable political power in the 1930s, and his manipulation of patronage was critical to keeping the various elements in the Democratic Party together.

Farley eventually broke with FDR over the President's decision to seek a third term and his attempts to purge 13 anti-New Deal Democrats in the 1938 primaries. Farley wrote two books and was known for a number of pithy quotes, most notably, "The only poll I am interested in is the one to be held on November third."

See also: Bosses, Democratic National Committee, John N. Garner, New Deal, Franklin D. Roosevelt, Al Smith

David A. Bositis

REFERENCES

Cotter, Cornelius P., and Bernard Hennessy. 1964. *Politics Without Power*. New York: Atherton.

Farley, Jim. 1938. *Behind the Ballots*. New York: Harcourt, Brace.

———. 1948. *The Jim Farley Story*. New York: Whittlesey House.

Price, David E. 1984. *Bringing Back the Parties*. Washington: Congressional Quarterly.

Ranney, Austin. 1975. *Curing the Mischiefs of Faction*. Berkeley: U. of California Pr.

Orval E. Faubus (1910–)

Six-term segregationist governor of Arkansas. Born in Combs, Arkansas, Orval Eugene Faubus grew up in the Ozark Mountains. Before entering politics in the 1940s, he was the owner and editor of a weekly county newspaper. He became governor in 1954 after defeating the incumbent.

Faubus became a national figure in 1957 as a result of his reaction to a federal court order that Central High School in Little Rock be racially integrated. Faubus, an ardent opponent of integration, tried to block the order by calling upon the Arkansas National Guard to seize Central High School, citing evidence of possible threats to public safety. A federal judge overruled Faubus, ordered the National Guard out of Little Rock, and prohibited the governor from further interference. When the Black students tried to attend school the next day, they were met by a mob. President Dwight Eisenhower then sent the 101st Airborne Division into Little Rock to restore order. In 1958 Faubus closed all of Little Rock's high schools in an attempt to circumvent the integration order.

As a result of these actions, Governor Faubus enjoyed great popularity among the people of Arkansas. He was reelected easily and remained in office until 1968. Orval Faubus remains a symbol of bigotry and racism resistance that was found in the South during the civil rights movement.

See also: Dwight D. Eisenhower, Race and Racial Politics

Mary Ann McHugh

REFERENCES
Ashmore, Harry S. 1978. *Arkansas*. New York: Norton.

Crystal Bird Fauset (1893–1965)

First Black woman elected to a U.S. state legislature. Born in Princess Anne County, Maryland, one of nine children of Portia and Benjamin Bird, Crystal Dreda Bird Fauset was raised by an aunt in Boston, graduating from racially integrated Boston Normal School in 1914. After teaching in Boston for three years, she became a field secretary for the Young Women's Christian Association (YWCA), where she developed and supervised programs for young Black women. In 1931 she received a B.S. from Teacher's College, Columbia University.

In 1933 she helped found the Institute of Race Relations at Swarthmore College, serving as its first executive secretary. During the New Deal, she headed the Work Progress Administration's Women's and Professional Project in Philadelphia. She also became active in party politics and directed "Colored" Women's Activities for the Democratic National Committee (DNC) in 1936. In 1938, with support from Democratic Party leaders in Philadelphia, she was elected to the Pennsylvania state legislature. Her term as a legislator was brief; she resigned in 1939 to coordinate recreational and educational activities for the WPA in Pennsylvania.

In October 1941, Fauset was appointed Eleanor Roosevelt's special assistant in the Office of Civilian Defense. As one of the agency's chief racial relations advisers, her assignment was to defuse racial tensions on the home front during World War II. In 1944 she resigned her post and devoted her energies to Franklin D. Roosevelt's reelection campaign.

During the course of the campaign, however, Fauset became embittered with the DNC, claiming that it ignored the concerns of Black women. As a result, in September 1944, she left the Democratic Party to publicly support the Republican Thomas E. Dewey for President. During the remainder of her life, her interests shifted away from partisan politics; she helped found the World Affairs Council, traveled extensively in Third World countries, and worked on the YWCA's national board in New York.

See also: Thomas E. Dewey, New Deal, Eleanor Roosevelt, Franklin D. Roosevelt

Robert Earnest Miller

REFERENCES

Bogin, Ruth. 1980. *Notable American Women: The Modern Period*. Cambridge: Harvard U. Pr.

Jones, Jacqueline. 1985. *Labor of Love, Labor of Sorrow: Black Women, Work, and the Family from Slavery to the Present*. New York: Basic Books.

Federal Communications Commission

The Federal Communications Commission (FCC), an independent regulatory body directly responsible to the U.S. Congress, oversees national and international communications by radio, television, wire, cable, and satellite. Established by the Communications Act of 1934, the FCC is composed of five commissioners (not more than three of whom may be of the same political party), appointed to five-year terms by the President of the United States with the approval of the Senate. One commissioner is designated by the President as chairman and serves in that capacity at the pleasure of the President.

The FCC has three major responsibilities: (1) to direct the orderly development of the nation's broadcasting, cable, and communications services in light of technical limitations and economic necessities; (2) to obtain economical, efficient nationwide and worldwide telephone, telegraph, and other common carrier services; and (3) to provide for the safety of life and property and the nation's defense through such facilities.

To carry out its responsibilities, the staff of the FCC is organized into four main bureaus. The Mass Media Bureau authorizes and regulates broadcast and cable services through the allocation of spectrum space for radio and television use, the assignment of frequencies to communities, the granting of licenses to broadcast applicants (usually seven years for radio and five years for television stations), the review of station performance, and the establishment of broad policy for the operations of cable television systems. The scope of responsibilities of the Mass Media Bureau grew considerably with the merger in 1982 of the FCC's previously separate cable and broadcast bureaus and because of the steady growth in recent decades of the number of broadcast outlets and cable systems. Simultaneously, however, the FCC has embarked on a program of deregulation of both broadcast and cable facilities. The Common Carrier Bureau regulates the interstate rates and services of such common carriers as telephone, telegraph, radio, and satellite companies. In the 1980s, this bureau had special responsibilities because of the breaking up of AT&T and the resulting growth of competition among telephone companies. The Private Radio Bureau regulates all radio services other than broadcast, cable, and common carrier. Included are all safety, amateur, commercial and personal radio communication facilities. The Field Operations Bureau monitors broadcast technical operations and examines station equipment. It has a network of 36 field offices and monitoring stations and a nationwide fleet of mobile units.

The FCC was preceded by the Federal Radio Commission, a temporary agency established in 1927. The FRC was able, despite internal and external strife, to alleviate some of the technical problems plaguing broadcasting in its unregulated early years. Creation of the FCC in 1934 consolidated, on a permanent basis, regulatory authority over all interstate communications, including telephone and telegraph.

In the area of broadcast regulation, many of the FCC's actions over the years have precipitated major controversies. These have included early initiatives to regulate network broadcasting, to add radio stations on the "clear channel" AM frequencies, and shift FM radio from the 44-megacycle band to the 98-megacycle band. Later FCC controversies centered on television broadcasting, among them being the initial approval of VHF television service, the struggle among competing color TV systems, and the FCC's efforts to encourage the development of UHF (ultrahigh frequency) television.

In recent years, the FCC has sought to deregulate radio, television, and cable services and to eliminate its Fairness Doctrine, which requires broadcasting outlets mandatorily to present opposing viewpoints on controversial issues. The FCC still enforces the equal time provision, which ensures equal noncommercial broadcast time to candidates for the same political office.

See also: Buckley v. Valeo, Federal Election Campaign Act of 1971 and Amendments, Newton Minow

Lawrence D. Longley

REFERENCES

Congressional Quarterly. 1990. *Federal Regulatory Directory*. 6th ed. Washington: Congressional Quarterly.

Horwitz, Robert Britt. 1988. *The Irony of Regulatory Reform: The Deregulation of American Telecommunications*. New York: Oxford U. Pr.

Krasnow, Erwin G., Lawrence D. Longley, and Herbert A. Terry. 1982. *The Politics of Broadcast Regulation*. 3rd ed. New York: St. Martin's.

Federal Corrupt Practices Act of 1910 and 1911

One of the strategies adopted by the muck-rakers and other political reformers at the beginning of the twentieth century involved limiting excessive political contributions by disclosing their source. This reform effort was most vigorously pursued by the National Publicity Bill Organization (NPBO) after the 1904 election. The NPBO was headed by Perry Belmont, younger brother of Democratic financier August Belmont. Though a bipartisan organization by design, the NPBO was in fact largely dominated by Democrats who opposed the ways in which business interests were influencing politics through their contributions to the majority Republican Party.

The first successful campaign finance reform was the passage of the Tillman Act of 1907, which limited corporate and national bank contributions to candidates in federal campaigns. Even while this bill was being debated, other reformers pushed for publicizing all campaign contributions. This drive was given renewed impetus in the spring of 1907 when it was revealed that E. H. Harriman, the railroad mogul, had contributed $200,000 to President Theodore Roosevelt's 1904 campaign. The vehicle for disclosure reform was a bill, drafted by the NPBO and sponsored by Samuel McCall (R-Mass.), which called for public reporting of contributions and expenditures for any political committee active in federal elections "in two or more states." Thus, this bill called for disclosure by the national party committees and the national party's congressional campaign committees.

Even this modest measure had difficulty achieving passage. Finally, on the eve of the 1910 elections, the Republican majority in the Congress passed the Federal Corrupt Practices Act, also known as the Publicity Act of 1910 (36 Stat. 822). The new law drew heavily on the McCall bill, except that it did not require any reports be filed until after the relevant election was held. In the 1910 election the Democrats took control of the House of Representatives and made significant gains in the Senate. As the Sixty-second Congress convened, they pressed for further reforms, seeking a preelection filing date. Republicans, now the minority in the House, pressed for inclusion of committees operating within a single congressional district and of primary campaigns in the disclosure bill. This effort was aimed at splitting from their

northern copartisans the southern Democrats, who favored states' rights and for whom the primary was the most significant election. The effort nearly succeeded in the House; in the Senate, where the Republicans retained their majority, they not only added these provisions but also set limitations on how much could be spent on a campaign. It seemed that the two parties were involved in an ironic high stakes poker game, upping the ante on campaign finance reform by calling for a limit on bets.

The bill that was accepted by the conference committee was more far-reaching than the reformers could even have hoped when the process began. The 1910 act was amended to include preelection reporting; to require reports for committees working on individual campaigns, including primaries; and to establish spending limits. While this legislation was riddled with loopholes that were soon to become apparent, and while the regulation of primaries was ruled unconstitutional in *Newberry v. United States* in 1921, it stood as a monumental reform effort, clearly laying out the themes that would dominate campaign finance debate for more than 60 years.

See also: August Belmont, *Newberry v. United States*, Theodore Roosevelt, Tillman Act of 1907

L. Sandy Maisel

REFERENCES

Mutch, Robert E. 1988. *Campaigns, Congress, and Courts: The Making of Federal Campaign Finance Law.* Westport, CT: Praeger.

Federal Corrupt Practices Act of 1925

The operative law governing campaign finances from the time of its passage until 1971. That statement says a great deal—and it says nothing. Passed in the wake of the *Newberry v. United States* Supreme Court decision, which invalidated parts of the Federal Corrupt Practices Acts of 1910 and 1911, and of the Teapot Dome scandal, which dramatized how unsuccessful those earlier acts had been in exposing political corruption, the Federal Corrupt Practices Act of 1925 (43 Stat. 1070) was a congressional attempt to give teeth to campaign finance reform. The Act failed because its enforcement mechanisms were not powerful enough to serve its purposes.

The operating principles governing the FCPA of 1925 were that disclosure of expenditures in advance of an election and regulation of the amount that could be spent on an election would keep tainted money out of politics. Those drafting the legislation failed to take into account that publicity of the reports and enforcement of the limitations on expenditures were each essential if the law were to have its desired impact. The law closed the loophole that Teapot Dome had exposed—committees raising money in nonelection years—and required that all political committees doing business in two or more states file quarterly reports, listing all of those who contributed $100 or more, even in nonelection years. The provisions of the law were strongly worded. But they did not specify who would have access to these reports; and they did not require that the reports be published; they did not designate who should examine these reports; and they did not stipulate what would happen if committees failed to comply. Effective publicity and enforcement—absolutely necessary to meet the FCPA's laudable goals—were absent.

The history of the FCPA of 1925 was one of noncompliance and of loophole exploitation. Louise Overacker, the preeminent political scientist studying campaign finance during the early years of this act, found that many of the reports were all but useless. They followed a variety of formats; access through the Clerk of the House and the Secretary of the Senate was difficult; and reports were kept on file only for two years and then destroyed. Even worse, many candidates simply failed to comply with the law, ignoring the necessity of filing quarterly reports at all or spending money in access of the limits. One of the favorite means to get around the law was the establishment of a large number of committees, each of which technically complied with the spending limitation and to each of which individuals could give just under $100 without having to be identified. Wealthy donors gave money through family members; corporations awarded bonuses to executives who passed them on to political campaigns. American politicians' ingenuity in finding ways around the law was seemingly without limit. In the entire history of the Federal Corrupt Practices Act of 1925, no one was prosecuted for failing to comply. Only two persons were excluded for office for exceeding the spending limits; both of these—Republicans William S. Vare of Pennsylvania and Frank L. Smith of Illinois—were excluded by the Senate in 1927, after the first election to which the law applied, for flagrant violations of the letter and intent of the new legislation. Despite well-known, nearly universal violations, no other candidates were punished under this act during its 45 years in effect.

The Federal Corrupt Practices Act of 1925 was a response to scandal, as have been most campaign finance reforms. It represents a further development of the theory of how one must regulate campaign contributions and spending to meet the goals of the reformers in this area. In practice it proved to be more loophole than law, and thus it highlights the difficulty that reformers have faced in seeking to stipulate and apply appropriate and effective regulations in this area of public policy.

See also: Federal Corrupt Practices Act of 1910 and 1911, *Newberry v. United States*

L. Sandy Maisel

REFERENCES

Alexander, Herbert E. 1984. *Financing Politics: Money, Elections, and Political Reform.* 3rd ed. Washington: Congressional Quarterly.

Congressional Quarterly. 1982. *Dollar Politics.* 3rd ed. Washington: Congressional Quarterly.

Mutch, Robert E. 1988. *Campaigns, Congress, and Courts: The Making of Federal Campaign Finance Law.* Westport, CT: Praeger.

Overacker, Louise. 1932. *Money in Politics.* New York: Macmillan.

Federal Elections Bill of 1890 (Lodge Force Bill)

Republican efforts to pass this bill, denounced by Democrats as a "Force" bill, constituted a principal cause of the party's defeat in the 1890 elections, which witnessed one of the largest shifts in party strength in the House of Representatives in history.

Since the fall of the Reconstruction governments in the South, many Republican leaders had condemned the growing suppression of the Black vote. They noted that because the end of slavery had widened the population base in the former slave states, thus affording the South a greater number of Representatives in Congress, the systematic barring of Black suffrage had given the white southern voter much greater influence than his northern counterpart. But Republicans were powerless to redress this wrong until 1889, when in the Benjamin Harrison administration, they controlled both houses of Congress and the presidency for the first time in 14 years.

Introduced in the House by Henry Cabot Lodge, the elections bill called for the policing of congressional elections by the federal courts and by bipartisan supervisory boards. The House passed it by mid-summer 1890, but the Senate postponed consideration until December. Although the bill said nothing of the use of troops or federal marshals and proposed no interference in state or local elections, Democrats charged in the fall campaign that it would bring back "bayonet rule" in the South. In the aftermath of the Republicans' crushing defeat in November, they failed to secure passage of the bill, the last major attempt at civil rights legislation before the mid-twentieth century.

See also: Benjamin Harrison, Henry Cabot Lodge, Suffrage

Charles W. Calhoun

REFERENCES

DeSantis, Vincent P. 1959. *Republicans Face the Southern Question: The New Departure Years, 1877–1897.* Baltimore: Johns Hopkins U. Pr.

Hirshson, Stanley P. 1962. *Farewell to the Bloody Shirt: Northern Republicans and the Southern Negro, 1877–1893.* Bloomington: Indiana U. Pr.

Socolofsky, Homer E., and Allan B. Spetter. 1987. *The Presidency of Benjamin Harrison.* Lawrence: U. Pr. of Kansas.

Welch, Richard E., Jr. 1965. "The Federal Elections Bill of 1890: Postscripts and Prelude." 52 *Journal of American History* 511.

Williams, R. Hal. 1978. *Years of Decision: American Politics in the 1890s.* New York: Wiley.

Federal Election Campaign Act of 1971

The first comprehensive revision of federal campaign finance legislation since the adoption of the Corrupt Practices Act of 1925, the Federal Election Campaign Act of 1971 (Public Law 92-225) was signed into law by President Richard Nixon on February 7, 1972, and went into effect sixty days later. Its purpose was to restrict rising campaign costs and to strengthen the campaign reporting requirements of federal law. It therefore combined two different approaches to reform. The first part of the law established detailed spending limits for all federal campaigns, while the second part imposed strict public disclosure procedures on federal candidates and political committees.

The act resulted from a wave of regulatory reform sweeping the Congress in the late 1960s and early 1970s as members of both parties began to acknowledge the inadequacies and changing realities of the existing campaign finance system. By this time, members of Congress generally agreed that the reporting and disclosure requirements established in 1925 needed to be revised because they were easily circumvented and, as a result, had proven to be wholly ineffective. Legislators also became increasingly concerned with the rising costs of federal campaigns, especially media expenditures. In the 1956 elections, overall campaign spending was estimated at $155 million, $9.8 million of which was used for radio and television broadcasts. During the next decade, however, media advertising became a primary feature of political campaigns, and the costs of running for office skyrocketed. By 1968 overall campaign spending had nearly doubled to an estimated $300 million, but media expenditures had increased sixfold to $58.9 million.

Congressional incumbents feared that if these costs were allowed to rise unabated, they might be unable to finance their campaigns in the future. Legislators were also concerned that, in author Frank Sorauf's words, "challengers with personal fortunes or access to large contributors might unseat them in media-based campaigns." Many Democrats further believed that rising campaign costs would provide Republican candidates with a significant competitive advantage, since Republicans enjoyed a decided advantage in their ability to raise campaign funds.

The Federal Election Campaign Act addressed these concerns by limiting personal contributions, establishing specific ceilings for media expenditures, and requiring full public disclosure of campaign receipts and disbursements. The act imposed a ceiling on personal contributions by candidates and their immediate families of $50,000 for presidential and vice presidential candidates, $35,000 for Senate candidates, and $25,000 for House candidates. The amounts that candidates for federal office could spend on radio, television, cable television, newspapers, magazines, and automated telephone systems in any primary, runoff, special, or general election were limited to the greater sum of $50,000 or 10¢ times the voting-age population of the jurisdiction covered by the election. Finally, the act declared that no more than 60 percent of a candidate's overall media spending could be devoted to radio and television advertising. These limits were to apply separately to primary and general elections and were indexed to reflect increases in the Consumer Price Index.

These ceilings governed all media spending in the 1972 primaries and general elections. In practice, House candidates could spend no more than $52,150 for all media outlays in an election and a maximum of $31,290 on radio and television. Because of the differences in state voting populations, the limits for Senate candidates varied, ranging from $52,150 in sparsely populated states such as Alaska and Montana (where $31,290 could be spent on radio and television) to $1.4 million in California (of which $850,000 could be spent on radio and television). Presidential candidates were limited to $14.3 million in overall expenditures, of which no more than $8.58 million could be spent on radio and television.

In the area of disclosure, the act required every candidate or political committee active in a federal campaign to file a quarterly report of receipts and expenditures. These reports were to list any contribution or expenditure of $100 or more and include the name, address, occupation, and principal place of business of the donor or recipient. During election years, additional reports had to be filed 15 days and 5 days before an election, and any contribution of $5,000 or more had to be reported within 48 hours of its receipt. The reports were to be filed with the secretary of state of the state in which campaign activities took place and with the appropriate federal officer, as established under the act. For the latter purpose, House candidates filed with the Clerk of the House, Senate candidates with the Secretary of the Senate, and presidential candidates with the General Accounting Office. All reports had to be made available for public inspection within 48 hours of being received.

Although the legislation fell short of fulfilling all of its purposes in the 1972 elections, it clearly had a beneficial effect. Sorauf believes that the reporting requirements of the act resulted in "the fullest disclosure of campaign transactions in American history," and the spending limits helped to restrict the use of media advertising, although campaign costs continued to rise. Nevertheless, these successes were overshadowed by the financial abuses of the Nixon campaign and the Watergate scandal, which emerged in the aftermath of the election, partly as a result of the information generated by the new disclosure laws. These excesses highlighted the law's inefficacy in preventing illegal contributions and ensuring proper reporting, thus stimulating a demand for further reform, to which the Congress responded in 1974 by adopting extensive amendments to the 1971 act. These amendments essentially restructured the campaign finance system and left few of the provisions of the 1971 law intact.

See also: Campaign Finance and the Constitution, Media and Presidential Campaigns, Richard Nixon, Political Action Committees, Watergate

Anthony J. Corrado

REFERENCES

Alexander, Herbert E. 1976. *Financing the 1972 Election*. Lexington, MA: Lexington Books.

————. 1984. *Financing Politics: Money, Elections, and Political Reform*. 3rd ed. Washington: Congressional Quarterly.

Cantor, Joseph E. 1986, 1987. *Campaign Financing in Federal Elections: A Guide to the Law and Its Operation*. Washington: Congressional Research Service.

Congressional Quarterly. 1982. *Dollar Politics*. 3rd ed. Washington: Congressional Quarterly.

Sorauf, Frank J. 1988. *Money in American Elections*. Glenview, IL: Scott, Foresman.

Federal Election Campaign Act Amendments of 1974

This bill was signed into law by President Gerald Ford on October 15, 1974, and constituted a landmark in the regulation of political finance in the United States. While technically a set of amendments to the 1971 Federal Election Campaign Act (FECA), the Federal Election Campaign Act Amendments of 1974 (Public Law 93-443) stands as the most comprehensive reform of the campaign finance system ever adopted. It significantly strengthened the disclosure provisions of the 1971 law and enacted unprecedented limits on contributions and expenditures in federal elections. It introduced the first use of public financing at the national level by establishing optional public funding in presidential general election campaigns and a system of federal matching grants in presidential primary campaigns. And it created an independent agency, the Federal Election Commission (FEC), to administer and enforce campaign finance regulations.

The 1974 amendments resulted from renewed pressure for comprehensive reform in the wake of the Watergate scandal and reports of other financial abuses in the 1972 campaign. Detailed investigations of the financial practices of the Committee to Re-elect President Nixon revealed an alarming reliance on large contributions, the use of illegal corporate donations, and other improprieties, such as the "laundering" of campaign funds to circumvent federal laws. The investigations also raised important questions about the influence of money on the political process. Allegations that contributors "bought" ambassadorships, secured special legislative favors in exchange for campaign gifts, or enjoyed other forms of undue influence were common. Charges like these focused congressional attention on the need for fundamental reform and made it clear that specific regulations were required to strengthen disclosure and enforcement procedures and limit the influence of large donors.

The 1972 election also fueled continuing concerns over the rising cost of campaigns. One of the primary reasons that Congress adopted the FECA was to curb rising campaign costs. But the information gathered from disclosure reports demonstrated that the law had failed to achieve this end: total campaign expenditures for all offices rose from an estimated $300 million in 1968 to approximately $425 million in 1972. This increase in spending was especially pronounced in the presidential campaign. President Richard Nixon's reelection committee spent a staggering $56 million, more than twice the amount spent by the 1968 Nixon-Agnew committee, which had spent more than any previous campaign. The George McGovern campaign spent $49 million, or more than four times the amount spent by Hubert Humphrey four years earlier. Congressional campaign spending also increased from an estimated $71.6 million in 1970 to more than $77.2 million in 1972. These spending patterns indicated that the FECA's expenditure limits had had little or no effect on campaign outlays and that more extensive limits would be necessary if costs were to be reduced.

The experience of the 1972 election thus spurred the Congress to make fundamental changes in the campaign finance system. The media spending ceilings established by the 1971 act were abolished and replaced with stringent limits on campaign expenditures. Under the new provisions, Senate candidates could spend no more than the greater amount of $100,000 or 8¢ times the voting-age population of the state in a primary election and no more than the greater amount of $150,000 or 12¢ times the voting-age population in a general election. House candidates in multidistrict states were limited to total expenditures of $70,000 in each primary and general election. Those in states with a single Representative (e.g., South Dakota) were subject to the ceilings established for Senate candidates. Presidential candidates were restricted to $10 million in a nomination campaign and $20 million in a general election. The amount they could spend in a state primary election was also limited to no more than twice the sum that a Senate candidate in that state could spend. All of these ceilings were indexed to reflect increases in the Consumer Price Index, and candidates were allowed to spend an additional sum of up to 20 percent of the spending limit for fundraising costs. This latter provision was instituted in recognition of the added fundraising burden placed on candidates as a result of the act's imposition of contribution limits, which required that they finance their campaigns through small contributions.

The amendments also set limits on the amounts national party committees could expend on behalf of candidates. These organizations were allowed to spend no more than $10,000 per candidate in House general elections; the greater amount of $20,000 or 2¢ times the voting-age population for each candidate in Senate general elections; and 2¢ times the voting-age population (approximately $2.9 million) for their presidential candidate. The amount a party committee could spend on its national nominating convention was also restricted. Each of the major parties (defined as a party whose candidates received more than 25 percent of the popular vote in the previous election) was limited to $2 million in convention expenditures, while minor parties (defined as parties whose candidates received between 5 percent and 25 percent of the popular vote in the previous election) were limited to lesser amounts.

The legislation retained the contribution limits placed on candidates and their immediate families by the FECA and established additional restrictions designed to eliminate the potentially corruptive influence of large donors. An individual was allowed to contribute no more than $1,000 per candidate in any primary, runoff, or general election and could not exceed $25,000 in annual aggregate contributions to all federal candidates. Donations by political committees, in particular the political action committees that the law sanctioned for use by labor unions and corporations, were limited to $5,000 per election for each candidate, with no aggregate limit. Independent expenditures made on behalf of a candidate were limited to $1,000 a year and cash donations in excess of $100 were prohibited.

The most innovative aspect of the 1974 law was its provision instituting a system of public financing in presidential elections. The funds for this program would be drawn from the tax checkoff receipts deposited in the Presidential Election Campaign Fund. The legislation established a program of voluntary public financing for presidential general elections in which major party candidates could receive the full amount authorized by the spending limit ($20 million) if they agreed to forego private donations. Minor party candidates could receive a proportionate share of this amount, with the size of their subsidy determined on the basis of the proportion of the vote they received in the prior election calculated in comparison to the average vote of the major parties. New parties and minor parties could also qualify for post-election funds on the same proportional basis if their percentage of the vote in the current election entitled them to a larger subsidy than the grant generated by their vote in the previous election.

In the primary election, presidential candidates were eligible for public matching funds if they fulfilled certain fundraising requirements. In order to qualify, a candidate had to raise at least $5,000 in contributions of $250 or less in at least 20 states. Eligible candidates would then receive public monies on a dollar-for-dollar basis for the first $250 contributed by an individual, provided that the contribution was received after January 1 of the year before the election year. The maximum amount a candidate could receive in such payments was half of the spending limit, or $5 million under the original terms of the act. In addition, national party committees were given the option of financing their nominating conventions with public funds. Major parties could receive the entire amount authorized by the spending limit ($2 million), while minor parties were eligible for lesser amounts based on their proportion of the vote in the previous election.

Finally, the bill included a number of amendments designed to strengthen the disclosure and enforcement procedures of the 1971 act. The most important of these was the provision creating the Federal Election Commission, a six-member, full-time, bipartisan agency responsible for administering election laws and implementing the public financing program. This agency was empowered to receive all campaign reports, promulgate rules and regulations, make special and regular reports to Congress and the President, conduct audits and investigations, subpoena witnesses and information, and seek civil injunctions to ensure compliance with the law.

To assist the FEC in its task, the amendments tightened the FECA's disclosure and reporting requirements. All candidates were required to establish one central campaign committee through which all contributions and expenditures had to be reported. Candidates were also required to disclose the bank depositories authorized to receive campaign funds. The reporting procedures mandated that each campaign file a complete report of its financial activities with the Federal Election Commission within ten days of the close of each quarter and ten days before and thirty days after every election, unless the committee received or spent less than $1,000 in the quarter. In nonelection years, each committee had to file a year-end report of its receipts and expenditures. Furthermore, contributions of $1,000 or more received within 15 days of an election had to be reported to the FEC within 48 hours.

The initial implementation of the act was complicated first by President Ford's delay in appointing members to the Federal Election Commission and then by the Supreme Court's decision in *Buckley v. Valeo*, which deemed certain provisions unconstitutional and forced Congress to adopt further amendments in the midst of the 1976 elections. In particular, the Court ruled against the spending limits established for House and Senate candidates and the contribution limit for independent expenditures, which substantially weakened the potential efficacy of the act. The decision also inhibited the public matching funds program since no funds could be distributed until the Federal Election Commission was reconstituted in conformance with the Court's opinion. As a result, no public monies were distributed for a two-month period during the middle of the primary campaign.

Despite this unsettled beginning, the 1974 amendments have fulfilled many of the purposes for which they were enacted. The law's contribution limits forced candidates to rely on small contributions in the financing their campaigns. The disclosure and reporting requirements have dramatically improved public access to financial information and have enhanced the ability of federal regulators to uncover improprieties. Public financing has gained widespread acceptance among presidential candidates. Every general election campaign since the provision was adopted has been financed with public money and only one candidate (Republican John Connally in 1980) has chosen not to participate in the primary matching funds program.

Other aspects of the law have not been so successful. The expenditure limits have helped to curb presidential campaign spending, but candidates have responded to these restraints by seeking out legal loopholes through which they could circumvent the law. An important unintended consequence of the law is the proliferation of political action committees. These groups have become a primary source of campaign contributions to House and Senate candidates, and their influence on elections and public policy has become the subject of much debate. The Federal Election Commission has also been the target of criticism, its critics claiming that the FEC is inefficient in discovering violations and ineffective in its enforcement of the law. Nonetheless, the 1974 legislation remains as the foundation of the current system of campaign finance, and its approach to reform continues to shape the patterns of political finance in federal elections.

See also: Buckley v. Valeo, Campaign Finance and the Constitution, Committee to Reelect the President, Contribution Limits and Presidential Nominating Campaigns, Elections of 1972 and 1976, Federal Election Commission, Gerald Ford, Richard Nixon, Watergate

Anthony J. Corrado

REFERENCES

Adamany, David, and George Agree. 1975. "Election Campaign Financing: The 1974 Reforms." 90 *Political Science Quarterly* 201.

Alexander, Herbert E. 1979. *Financing the 1976 Election.* Washington: Congressional Quarterly.

———. 1984. *Financing Politics: Money, Elections, and Political Reform.* 3rd ed. Washington: Congressional Quarterly.

Cantor, Joseph E. 1987. *Campaign Financing in Federal Elections: A Guide to the Law and Its Operation.* Washington: Congressional Research Service.

Congressional Quarterly. 1982. *Dollar Politics.* 3rd ed. Washington: Congressional Quarterly.

Federal Election Commission. 1977. *Legislative History of the Federal Election Campaign Act Amendments of 1974.* Washington: Federal Election Commission.

Institute of Politics, Harvard University. 1979. *An Analysis of the Impact of the Federal Election Campaign Act, 1972–78.* Committee on House Administration. 96th Congress, 1st Session. Washington: U.S. Government Printing Office.

Federal Election Campaign Act Amendments of 1976

In January 1976, the Supreme Court issued its opinion in *Buckley v. Valeo*, ruling unconstitutional several major provisions of the Federal Election Campaign Act Amendments of 1974. Most importantly, the Court struck down the method of appointing Federal Election Commissioners and required that the Federal Election Commission (FEC) be reestablished within constitutional boundaries or that some new method of enforcement be adopted. The Court's decision thus forced Congress to reconsider the campaign finance legislation that it had enacted less than two years earlier.

Since the 1976 election was already underway, President Gerald Ford asked the Congress for a bill that simply reconstituted the FEC. But the legislators, still sensitive to a climate of reform, decided to draft a more extensive bill that included revisions in the public financing program, in contribution limits, and in disclosure procedures established under the 1974 amendments. As a result, new legislation was not adopted within the period mandated by the Court, and the Federal Election Commission was not allowed to exercise its powers for a two-month period. This suspension affected a number of presidential candidates, who had to cut their budgets and alter their strategies because the commission could not approve their requests for public matching funds. The commission was finally reconstituted on May 21, ten days after President Ford signed the new bill into law (Public Law 94-283).

The law's basic provision changed the method of appointing Federal Election Commissioners. The original process gave the President, the Speaker of the House, and President *pro tempore* of the Senate the right to appoint two members apiece, each of different parties, subject to congressional approval. The new legislation called for the appointment of all six members by the President, subject to Senate confirmation. The act also increased the FEC's enforcement powers by granting it the exclusive authority to prosecute civil violations of the law and by giving the FEC jurisdiction over violations previously covered only in the criminal code. At the same time, however, the law checked the FEC's ability to act by requiring the affirmative vote of four members in order to issue regulations and initiate civil actions, by restricting advisory opinions to specific fact situations, and by giving Congress the power to disapprove proposed regulations.

The Court also struck down limits on contributions by candidates and members of their immediate families to their own campaigns, unless a candidate had accepted public funding. In such a case, Congress capped contributions from family at $50,000, a limit that applied only to presidential and vice presidential candidates who had received public funds. The 1976 law also established limits on political contributions that were not considered in previous legislation. Ceilings on individual contributions enacted under the 1974 act were retained, and new limits of $5,000 per year on the amount an individual could donate to a political action committee and of $20,000 per year on the amount that could be given to a national party committee were adopted. The amount a political action committee could donate to a national party committee was set at $15,000 a year and the Democratic and Republican Senatorial Campaign committees were enjoined against giving more than $17,500 per year to a federal candidate. The act further stipulated that all political action committees created by a company or international union would be treated as a single committee for the purpose of the determining compliance with contribution limits; this feature prevented these organizations from circumventing the law by creating multiple committees.

Since the Court struck down the 1974 law's limit on independent expenditures, the 1976 amendments included a number of reporting procedures designed to ensure the disclosure of independent spending. Any committee or individual spending more than $100 independently to advocate the election or defeat of a candidate was required to file a report of this spending with the FEC and declare, under penalty of perjury, that the expenditure was not made in collusion with a candidate. Labor unions, corporations, and membership organizations were required to report expenditures of more than $2,000 per election used for communications to their stockholders or members advocating the election or defeat of a specific candidate. In addition, any independent expenditure of $1,000 or more made within 15 days of an election had to be reported to the FEC within 24 hours.

Other important changes affected the spending limits and public financing program enacted by the 1974 amendments. The earlier Congress had created a minor loophole in the spending limits by exempting payments by candidate committees or national party committees for legal and accounting costs incurred in complying with the law. Now each committee had to list these payments in its disclosure reports. The new act also modified the provisions of the matching funds program in order to ensure that these subsidies did not encourage a losing candidate to remain in the race. Under these provisions, a presidential candidate who received less than 10 percent of the vote in two consecutive primaries would be ineligible for additional matching payments. These subsidies would be restored if that candidate received 20 percent of the vote in a later primary. The law further required that candidates who withdraw from the primary contest after receiving match-

ing funds return any remaining public monies to the Treasury.

With the adoption of these amendments, the period of substantive reform of the political finance regulations came to an end. In 1979 Congress would enact additional amendments designed to resolve problems encountered during the 1976 and 1978 campaigns. But these modifications made only minor adjustments in the law, not a fundamental restructuring of the campaign finance system.

See also: Buckley v. Valeo, Campaign Finance and the Constitution, Contribution Limits and Presidential Nominating Campaigns, Federal Election Campaign Act Amendments of 1974, Gerald Ford, Political Action Committees

Anthony J. Corrado

REFERENCES

Alexander, Herbert E. 1979. *Financing the 1976 Election.* Washington: Congressional Quarterly.

———. 1984. *Financing Politics: Money, Elections, and Political Reform.* 3rd ed. Washington: Congressional Quarterly.

Cantor, Joseph E. 1987. *Campaign Financing in Federal Elections: A Guide to the Law and Its Operation.* Washington: Congressional Research Service.

Congressional Quarterly. 1982. *Dollar Politics.* 3rd ed. Washington: Congressional Quarterly.

Federal Election Commission. 1977. *Legislative History of the Federal Election Campaign Act Amendments of 1976.* Washington: Federal Election Commission.

Federal Election Campaign Act Amendments of 1979

Amendments enacted in response to the criticisms levied against the campaign finance regulations after the 1976 and 1978 elections, critics charged that the detailed reporting requirements forced candidates and political committees to engage in unnecessary and burdensome paperwork. They also noted that the law reduced the role of state and local party committees in presidential elections, since both candidates running in 1976 had chosen to concentrate their legally limited resources on media advertising rather than grass-roots political activities. The Federal Election Campaign Act Amendments of 1979 (Public Law 96-187) was therefore designed to ease the reporting requirements imposed on candidates and political committees and to increase volunteer and grass-roots party activity in presidential campaigns. In order to ensure quick passage, the Congress considered only "non-controversial" reforms acceptable to both Houses. The final bill, which was signed into law by President Jimmy Carter on January 8, 1980, thus contained fewer substantive changes than the previous revisions of the act.

Most of the act's provisions were directed toward reducing the paperwork and financial information required by the law. The maximum number of reports a federal candidate had to file in a 2-year election cycle was reduced from 24 to 9. The maximum number of reports required of a Senate candidate over the 6-year election cycle was reduced from 28 to 17. The act eliminated reporting requirements for candidates who spend or receive less than $5,000. It also eliminated these requirements for those local party committees receiving less than $5,000 a year; spending less than $1,000 a year in contributions or expenditures in connection with a federal election; or spending less than $5,000 a year on certain voluntary activities, such as the purchase of buttons and bumper stickers or voter registration drives. Previously, all candidates and committees involved in federal elections were required to file reports with the Federal Election Commission (FEC). For those candidates and committees not exempted from the disclosure provisions, the threshold amount for reportable contributions and expenditures was increased from $100 or more to $200 or more. This increase substantially reduced the amount of information that they were required to provide to the FEC. The threshold for disclosing independent expenditures was also increased, from $100 to $250.

In order to enhance the role of political parties in presidential general elections, the law exempted certain types of party-related spending from the expenditure ceilings. State and local party committees were allowed to spend unlimited amounts on voter registration and get-out-the-vote activities, provided such activities were primarily conducted on behalf of the party's presidential nominee. These committees were also allowed to spend unlimited amounts on materials related to grass-roots or volunteer activities, such as buttons, bumper stickers, posters, and brochures, provided that the funds used were not drawn from contributions designated for a particular candidate. The amendments sought to encourage volunteer activities further by increasing the amount a volunteer could spend on travel or home entertainment on behalf of a candidate without having to report the expenses from $500 to $1,000 and from $1,000 to $2,000 for expenses incurred through activities undertaken on behalf of a political party.

The act also included a number of miscellaneous changes. It made procedural reforms in the advisory opinion process and clarified certain compliance and enforcement actions. It increased the amount of the public subsidy a major political party could receive to finance its national nominating convention from $2 million to $3 million. More importantly, it prohibited the conversion of excess campaign funds to personal use by any federal candidate or officeholder except for members of Congress holding office at the time the amendments were adopted. This conversion was already prohibited by Senate rules, which disallowed the personal use of campaign funds by both sitting and retired members of the Senate. House rules only disallowed this use of campaign funds for retired members. Individuals serving in the Congress at the time the act was proposed were concerned that the redistricting that would occur after the 1980 election might increase their chances of defeat. Some members were therefore unwilling to extend this prohibition to their own campaign funds; they apparently looked forward to converting excess campaign funds to their own use should they lose their bids for reelection. The House version of the bill thus exempted incumbent members from this prohibition, and this exemption survived in the compromise version of the bill that was finally adopted.

The 1979 amendments resolved several major problems that emerged from the initial experience under the new regulations. But in addressing these concerns, the amendments created two major loopholes in the law. Presidential candidates and party committees have exploited the exemptions established by the act for voluntary activities; they have, moreover, spent millions of dollars on these activities in each of the last two presidential elections. Their efforts have in part been financed by "soft money," that is, by contributions that are not regulated by federal law. The exemption for party-related voluntary activities has thus been used to undermine the contribution and spending limits established for presidential general election campaigns. The provision allowing certain House members to retain any excess campaign funds upon their retirement has also been criticized as violative of the purposes of reform. Some members of Congress have left office with substantial funds as a result of this loophole and, in certain instances, have used these monies for a wide range of noncampaign-related purposes.

The effects of the campaign finance regulations continue to generate debate over the need for more stringent regulations. Still, in recent years, Congress has failed to adopt new legislation, although a number of major proposals have been considered. The primary roadblock to further reform is the demand by some legislators that any bill include public financing for congressional campaigns. Incumbents have been unwilling to accept the limitations that would accompany public subsidies. Consequently, despite the clear need for additional changes, the law has essentially remained unchanged since 1979.

See also: Jimmy Carter, Contribution Limits and Presidential Nominating Campaigns, Election of 1980, Media and Presidential Campaigns, Soft Money in Presidential Elections

Anthony J. Corrado

REFERENCES

Alexander, Herbert E. 1984. *Financing Politics: Money, Elections, and Political Reform.* 3rd ed. Washington: Congressional Quarterly

———. 1986. *"Soft Money" and Campaign Financing.* Washington: Public Affairs Council.

———, and Brian A. Haggerty. 1983. *Financing the 1980 Election.* Lexington, MA: Lexington Books.

Cantor, Joseph E. 1987. *Campaign Financing in Federal Elections: A Guide to the Law and Its Operation.* Washington: Congressional Research Service.

Center for Responsive Politics. 1985. *Soft Money—A Loophole for the '80s.* Washington: Center for Responsive Politics.

Congressional Quarterly. 1982. *Dollar Politics.* 3rd ed. Washington: Congressional Quarterly.

Federal Election Commission. 1983. *The Legislative History of the Federal Election Campaign Act Amendments of 1979.* Washington: Federal Election Commission.

Federal Election Commission

A bipartisan, independent regulatory agency responsible for the administration and enforcement of federal campaign finance laws, the Federal Election Commission (FEC) was established by the Federal Election Campaign Act Amendments of 1974 and formally organized in April 1975. Its membership consists of six voting members appointed by the President with the advice and consent of the Senate and two nonvoting, *ex officio* members, the Clerk of the House of Representatives and the Secretary of the Senate. No more than three of the voting members can be affiliated with the same political party. It performs five major functions: disclosing campaign finance information, administering the public funding program, encourag-

ing compliance with the law, monitoring and enforcing the law, and serving as a clearinghouse for information on election administration.

The Federal Election Campaign Act of 1971 (FECA) did not consolidate administrative and enforcement powers in a single agency. Instead, the Clerk of the House, the Secretary of the Senate, and the Comptroller General of the United States General Accounting Office were authorized to monitor compliance with the 1971 act, and the Justice Department was assigned the responsibility for prosecuting violations of the law. This arrangement proved ineffective during the 1972 campaign and, owing to the abuses documented in the 1972 presidential election, a consensus emerged in Congress for an independent regulatory agency to monitor and enforce the law. The 1974 FECA amendments therefore created the FEC and gave it the administrative functions previously divided between congressional officers and the Comptroller General. The FEC also was given jurisdiction in civil enforcement matters, authority to draft regulations, and responsibility for monitoring compliance. Additionally, it was to serve as a national clearinghouse for information on the administration of elections, a task originally assigned to the General Accounting Office.

Under the 1974 amendments, the President, the Speaker of the House, and the President *pro tempore* of the Senate each appointed two of the six voting commissioners. This method of selecting commissioners was challenged as unconstitutional in *Buckley v. Valeo* (424 U.S. 1). In its 1976 ruling, the Court found that the method of appointment violated the constitutional principle of separation of powers, since four of the commissioners were appointed by Congress and exercised executive powers. Such powers, in the view of the Court, could only be exercised by presidential appointees. As a result, beginning on March 22, 1976, the FEC was prohibited from exercising its executive powers, which meant that it could not enforce the law or certify public matching fund payments to presidential candidates. The 1976 FECA amendments changed the procedure for appointing commissioners, requiring that all six voting members be appointed by the President with the advice and consent of the Senate. The FEC was thus reconstituted and resumed full activity in May 1976.

The FEC's disclosure activities serve a crucial role in informing the public of campaign finance activities and assisting in the enforcement of the law. Federal candidates and political committees are required to register with the FEC and file periodic reports on their financial activity. This information is recorded and made available to the public within 48 hours of receipt through the FEC's Public Records Division. In addition to issuing these reports, the FEC compiles the reported data in a variety of formats to provide the public with summaries of the financial activity of campaigns, party committees, and political action committees.

The FEC administers the FECA's public funding program and certifies payments from the fund, which are made by the U.S. Treasury. Its role is to ensure that presidential candidates requesting funds have met the legal eligibility requirements. It also approves the financial grants given to party presidential nominees in the general election campaign and the monies allocated for national party nominating conventions. All public funding recipients are audited to ensure that monies received from the fund are used solely for purposes allowed under the law.

From its inception, the FEC has encouraged voluntary compliance with the law by offering information, advice, and interpretations of federal statutes. An important means for achieving this end is the advisory opinion process. Through this procedure, a candidate or individual involved in a federal campaign or political committee may request the FEC's advice on a specific proposed activity and receive a binding legal opinion in response from the FEC. These opinions clarify the law and set forth interpretations of particular provisions, as do the written regulations that the agency prescribes when necessary. The FEC also seeks to improve compliance with the law by suggesting statutory changes in its annual reports to Congress.

Federal law also assigns the FEC the duty of determining whether a candidate or political committee has violated the law. Possible violations are identified through the agency's report reviews and audit procedures or through complaints filed by individuals or referred from other government agencies. Before 1979 the FEC could conduct random audits of House and Senate campaigns to determine compliance with the law. This approach was opposed by some legislators, and the 1979 FECA amendments prohibited such audits. Currently the FEC will audit congressional campaigns only after a review

indicates lack of compliance and four commissioners vote to authorize the audit. Once a possible violation is filed, a compliance case (known as a Matter Under Review or MUR) is initiated and pursued in accordance with procedures set forth in the FECA. The FEC also has authority to file suit in order to enforce the law or secure cooperation with an investigation and may be taken to court by an individual or committee challenging an enforcement action.

In contrast to the agency's primary task of regulating campaign finances, its Clearinghouse on Election Administration serves to assist state and local jurisdictions in conducting elections. The Clearinghouse provides information to state and local election agencies to assist them in the administration of elections. For example, in recent years it has published reports on voter registration systems, bilingual election services, and voting machine technology.

Since its creation, the FEC has been a focal point for political controversy. Critics argue that it issues regulations that are too restrictive, tends to favor incumbents in its enforcement actions, is inefficient in its auditing process and in determining offenses, and is too closely tied to Congress to regulate its members effectively. Supporters emphasize the success of disclosure, the FEC's efficiency in issuing advisory opinions and modifying regulations to address new developments, and the large number of audits and compliance actions completed. Whatever the case, the FEC's efforts have significantly improved the administration and enforcement of federal campaign finance regulations.

See also: Buckley v. Valeo, Federal Election Campaign Act of 1971 and Amendments

Anthony J. Corrado

REFERENCES

Baran, Jan W. 1980. "The Federal Election Commission." 22 *Arizona Law Review* 519.

Congressional Quarterly. 1982. *Dollar Politics*. 3rd ed. Washington: Congressional Quarterly.

Federal Election Commission. 1985. *The First 10 Years, 1975–1985*. Washington: Federal Election Commission.

Harvard Campaign Finance Study Group. 1979. *An Analysis of the Impact of the Federal Election Campaign Act, 1972–78*. United States Congress, Committee on House Administration. 96th Cong., 1st Sess. Washington: U.S. Government Printing Office.

Oldaker, William C. 1986. "Of Philosophers, Foxes, and Finances: Can the Federal Election Commission Ever Do An Adequate Job?" 486 *The Annals of the American Academy of Political and Social Science* 132.

Federal Election Commission v. Democratic Senatorial Campaign Committee
454 U.S. 27 (1981)

This case was the first opportunity given the Supreme Court to interpret the application of the Federal Election Campaign Act to political parties. However, the Court backed away from the opportunity, choosing instead to defer to the Federal Election Commission (FEC) and its interpretation of the act. Such deference to administrative agencies is traditional with the judiciary, but it is also used by the courts as a way of avoiding difficult issues that they are not ready to address.

In February 1977, the FEC issued an Advisory Opinion at the request of the National Republican Senatorial Committee (NRSC) that the NRSC could spend its own funds in support of congressional candidates as the designated agent of the Republican National Committee (RNC). This request was a consequence of the NRSC's ability to raise much more money than it could legally spend on or contribute to federal campaigns.

Under the Federal Election Campaign Act, party organizations can make two types of expenditures in federal elections. The first are direct contributions to campaigns; these are limited, as they are for all political committees. The second are coordinated expenditures. Only political party committees can make coordinated expenditures, and the ceilings on them are greater than those on the campaign contributions permitted to other political committees. However, other political committees can only contribute money that they raise; they cannot contribute money raised by other political committees nor can they co-opt the contribution limits of other committees by acting as their agent. The FEC ruling had the effect of raising the expenditure ceiling of the NRSC.

Although the Democratic Senatorial Campaign Committee (DSCC) entered into a similar agreement with the Democratic National Committee (DNC), it complained to the FEC when the Republicans expanded their reach. Without asking the FEC for an additional advisory opinion, in 1978 the NRSC entered into agreements with several state party committees to act as their agent in making coordinated [also known as Section 441(a)(d)(3)] expenditures. The NRSC is the most successful fundraiser of *all* the different party committees and much more effective than any state committee. The agency agreements enabled it to raise and spend up to the limits of all the state and national party committees that it represented.

In 1979 the FEC dismissed the Democrats' complaints. It repeated its action when the DSCC complained again in 1980 that the agency agreements with state parties were contrary to Section 441(a)(d)(3). (It did not object to the agency agreement with the RNC.) The DSCC petitioned the federal court for a review of the FEC's dismissal, and the NRSC intervened. The district court found in favor of the FEC, but the circuit court of appeals reversed its finding. Instead of settling for the traditional review of whether an administrative agency ruling was "arbitrary, capricious, an abuse of discretion or otherwise not in accordance with law," it chose to make an independent analysis. The circuit court (660 F.2nd. 773 [D.C. Cir. 1980]) concluded that the NRSC was not in fact an agent, but a principal, because it was not spending the state party's money but merely using the agency agreements as a cover for raising and spending more of its own money than it would otherwise be allowed to spend by the FECA contribution limits.

The Supreme Court did not address any of these issues when it unanimously reversed the circuit court. Instead it held that Section 441(a)(d)(3) "does not expressly or by necessary implication foreclose the agency agreements," and therefore deferral to the FEC's interpretation was appropriate.

See also: Democratic National Committee, Federal Election Campaign Act of 1971, Federal Election Commission, Republican National Committee

Jo Freeman

Federal Election Commission v. Massachusetts Citizens for Life
479 U.S. 238 (1986)

In this Supreme Court case, Section 316 of the Federal Election Campaign Act (recoded 441b) was held invalid as the section applied to the organization Massachusetts Citizens for Life. The section at issue prohibited a corporation from using treasury funds "in connection with any election to any public office." Such expenditures were to come from a separate segregated fund. Acknowledging that this restriction is appropriate for some corporations, the Court ruled that the statute as applied to MCFL was an unconstitutional burden on free speech.

Massachusetts Citizens for Life (MCFL) was a group set up to promote political ideas; specifically it sought to prevent abortion. It published a special edition of its newsletter that was disseminated widely. The publication gave prominence to the headline "Everything you need to know to vote Pro-Life," and it printed information about who maintained the "correct" position on issues. It featured a clip coupon to take to the polls to remind voters of the identity of pro-life candidates. Photographs of several candidates appeared. The Court held that MCFL clearly violated Section 316 of the act, but that section was unconstitutional as applied because of its burden on free-speech interests. The opinion, written by Justice William Brennan, distinguishes between business corporations and ones such as Massachusetts Citizens for Life that were formed to "disseminate political ideas, not to amass capital." Justice Brennan reasoned that to place the burdens required of business corporations on such a small group could have the effect of stopping speech. He noted, "Detailed record keeping and disclosure obligations along with the duty to appoint a treasurer and custodian of the records, impose administrative costs that many small entities may be unable to bear."

The Court cited three features of MCFL that prevented it from being bound by the statute for constitutional reasons. "First, it was formed for the express purpose of promoting political ideas, and cannot engage in business activities. . . . Second, it has no shareholders or other persons affiliated so as to have a claim on the assets . . . [which] ensures that persons connected with the organization have no economic disincentive for disassociating with it if they disagree with its political activity. Third, MCFL was not established by a business corporation or a labor union, and it is its policy not to accept contributions from such entities. This prevents such corporations from serving as conduits for the type of direct spending that creates a threat to the marketplace."

In many campaign financing cases, the Court has had to try to maintain the spirit of the distinction it created in *Buckley* in the light of increasingly sophisticated financing arrangements. *MCL* is an example of this dilemma.

See also: *Buckley v. Valeo*, Federal Election Campaign Act of 1971 and Amendments

H. W. Perry, Jr.

Federal Election Commission v. National Conservative Political Action Committee
470 U.S. 480 (1985)

In this case the Supreme Court applied the principles it had enunciated in *Buckley v. Valeo* to political action committees (PACs), concluding that they had the same right as individuals and candidates to engage in unlimited independent spending on campaigns.

The case originated in May 1983 when the Democratic Party, its national committee, and an individual eligible to vote for President filed suit against two political action committees who had announced their intention to spend large sums of money in support of President Ronald Reagan's reelection. This spending would have violated Section 9012(f) of the Presidential Election Campaign Fund Act. The plaintiffs asked the Court to make a declaratory judgment that this section was constitutional. (By this action a party asks the courts for a declaration of legal rights or status in advance of any damages or violation of the law.) The Federal Election Commission (FEC) intervened and brought an independent action against the same PACs seeking the same judgment.

However, the three-judge district court ruled otherwise. It decided that the section was unconstitutional on its face as a violation of the First Amendment. The Supreme Court, by a vote of six to two, agreed. It reaffirmed its decision in *Buckley* that "preventing corruption or the appearance of corruption are the only legitimate and compelling government interests thus far identified for restricting campaign finances." In *Buckley* the Court distinguished between contributions to a campaign and expenditures made in support of a candidate independent of the campaign. It concluded that the former could be limited but the latter could not be because they were not tainted with corruption or by the appearance of corruption.

The Court added to this analysis by defining "corruption," which it had not done in *Buckley*:

> Corruption is a subversion of the political process. Elected officials are influenced to act contrary to their obligations of office by the prospect of financial gain to themselves or infusions of money into their campaigns. The hallmark of corruption is the financial quid pro quo; dollars for political favors.

The Court said contributions to PACs are not contributions to candidates, and PAC expenditures are not necessarily coordinated with the campaign of the candidates. The fact that pooling of contributions permitted much larger expenditures and more effective campaign support than most individuals could manage alone was beside the point. "Allowing the presentation of views while forbidding the expenditure of more than $1,000 to present them is much like allowing a speaker in a public hall to express his views while denying him the use of an amplifying system."

See also: Federal Election Campaign Act of 1971 and Amendments

Jo Freeman

REFERENCES

Democratic Party and Democratic National Committee v. National Conservative Action Committee and Fund for a Conservative Majority. 470 U.S. 480 (1985).

Federal Election Commission v. National Right to Work Committee
459 U.S. 197 (1982)

In this case, involving the National Right to Work Committee (NRWC), the Supreme Court ruled that the interpretation of who constitutes a "member" of a corporation or a union, as the term is used in the Federal Election Campaign Act of 1971, can be defined fairly strictly and does not suffer from constitutional infirmity on the basis of associational rights.

Corporations and labor unions are prohibited from making contributions or expenditures in federal elections by the Federal Election Campaign Act of 1971, but they can set up "separate segregated funds" for political purposes. Corporations without capital stock are allowed to solicit contribution only from members of the corporations. At issue in this case was a definition of membership. The National Right to Work Committee was a nonprofit corporation whose stated purpose was to "help make the public aware of the fact that American citizens are being required, against their will, to join and pay dues to labor organizations in order to earn a living." Though the facts in this case are complicated, essentially the NRWC solicited thousands of individuals who at one time had contributed to a separate segregated fund set up by the NRWC. In a merger document, it was stated that the NRWC "shall not have members." The Court held in a unanimous opinion written by Justice William Rehnquist that those solicited in this case were not members.

The NRWC also claimed that the statute impinged upon associational rights guaranteed by the First Amendment. Noting that the right to associate is not absolute, the Court concluded that "the associational rights asserted by [NRWC] may be and are overborne by the interests Congress has sought to protect. . . ." Rehnquist went on to discuss the need to protect elections from corruption or perceived corruption. He concluded that the "careful legislative adjustment of the federal electoral laws . . . warrants considerable deference." However, in *FEC v. Massachusetts Citizens for Life* (479 U.S. 238), the Court was not so deferential. Here the Court ruled that a statute barring political activity by certain "non-business" corporations was an unconstitutional burden on free speech.

NRWC is an important case for federal campaign finance law to the extent that it defines an important statutory term, and it lends support to efforts by Congress to regulate campaign finance. Its discussion of constitutional issues, however, is perfunctory.

See also: *Buckley v. Valeo*, Democratic National Committee, Federal Election Commission, Political Action Committees

H. W. Perry, Jr.

The Federalist Party

Once the federal Constitution of 1787 was accepted as the basic political blueprint for the United States, the framers sought to make policy in an enlightened spirit of cooperation and trust. All agreed at the outset that parties could serve no constructive function in that they tended to produce divisiveness and hostility.

After only a few years, however, virtually all economic and foreign policy matters considered by the George Washington administration elicited great disputes. To what extent should the federal government dominate individual states? What should be done about the debts incurred by the states? What should be the international position of the United States? What should be the citizen's role in the policymaking process? In response to these issues two conflicting political party organizations emerged: the Federalists, under the intellectual leadership of Alexander Hamilton, the first Secretary of the Treasury, and the Republicans (a.k.a. Democrat-Republicans) under Thomas Jefferson and James Madison.

At the heart of the Federalist philosophy was a belief in national political authority. Hamilton believed that states could properly be reduced to no more than administrative districts of the national government. In his words, "American liberty and happiness had much more to fear from the encroachments of the great states, than from those of the general government." The establishment of a central bank and the assumption of state debts by the national government were principal mechanisms whereby state governments were made subordinate. By successfully marshaling support for these measures, Hamilton gave legitimacy to a broad or "loose" reading of the Constitution. Ultimately, the Federalist appeal for national leadership can be traced to a fundamental conception of human nature and citizen action: uneducated individuals without substantial property could not be trusted to act for the benefit of the Republic. Instead, they would seek to advance their own personal or local interests. Only through the reasonable leadership of statesmen at the national level could the established constitutional system prevail.

The Federalists possessed a distinctive vision of America's destiny. If led correctly, the United States could become a powerful commercial nation capable of rivaling the European states. Naturally, then, the Federalist Party favored the development of financial and manufacturing sectors located primarily in the Northeast. Moreover, the party worked toward establishing better relations with Great Britain in pursuit of the economic benefits to be gained through international trade. Such favoritism in foreign policy is evident in the terms of the Jay Treaty of 1794, through which the Washington administration gave its support to the British, who were in conflict with the French.

In contrast to the Federalist platform, Republicans pressed for greater local political autonomy. For Jefferson, the ideal republic would be more egalitarian, with the majority of citizens being gentlemen farmers cultivating small parcels of land. Republicans thus wished to see more restrictions placed on the power of the federal government, and, in that spirit, they opposed the initiatives made by Alexander Hamilton. Republican Party values carried over into foreign policy, where they tended to favor friendlier relations with revolutionary France, given that country's similar ideals of liberty and equality.

The Federalist Party enjoyed its greatest strength during the administrations of George Washington (1789–1797) and John Adams (1797–1801). It was to be, however, a short-lived organization. The party was never able to win a large following among the American public, and during the Adams administration it suffered much from internal dissension. More-over, the Federalists lost many supporters when they championed the Alien and Sedition Acts of 1798. With the election of Thomas Jefferson as President in 1800, the strength and cohesion of the Federalist Party further deteriorated. By 1820 the party was unable to collect even one electoral vote in a presidential contest, and subsequently, it disappeared from national politics.

The brief period of Federalist rule did, however, give the new nation several important political precedents. Though challenged internationally by the French, English, and Spanish, and confronted domestically through outbreaks of civil unrest (notably the Whiskey Rebellion of 1794), the Washington and Adams administrations proved to be remarkably resilient. Potential wars were avoided, and a policy of political neutrality in foreign affairs that would last many generations was established. Furthermore, under the Federalists the executive cabinet system evolved, a federal judiciary was established, and a national debt was created to reinforce national authority and strengthen the economy. Finally, and most importantly, the Federalists were transformed at the turn of the century from the majority party to the opposition without violence or national political disintegration.

See also: John Adams, Alien and Sedition Acts, Alexander Hamilton, Jay Treaty, Thomas Jefferson, James Madison, George Washington

James A. McCann

REFERENCES

Borden, Morten. 1967. *Parties and Politics in the Early Republic, 1789–1815.* New York: Crowell.

Charles, Joseph. 1956. *The Origins of the American Party System.* New York: Harper and Row.

Hofstadter, Richard. 1969. *The Idea of a Party System.* Berkeley: U. of California Pr.

Livermore, Shaw. 1972. *The Twilight of Federalism.* New York: Gordian Press.

Miller, John C. 1960. *The Federalist Era.* New York: Harper and Row.

Dianne Feinstein (1933–)

First female mayor of San Francisco. Dianne Feinstein became the mayor of San Francisco under gruesome circumstances. After the assassination of Mayor George R. Moscone on November 27, 1978, she was elected by her colleagues on San Francisco's Board of Supervisors to fill out the remainder of Moscone's term.

Before being thrust into the position of mayor, Feinstein had run twice for the office, once in 1971 and again in 1975. After her second defeat, she was convinced that she was not electable.

However, having completed Moscone's term, she was elected in her own right in 1979 and once again in 1983. She also successfully beat down a recall election in 1983. Under San Francisco's two-term limit for mayors, Feinstein left office in January of 1988.

During her tenure as mayor, she won a reputation for being a hands-on administrator, with no detail too small for her attention. In addition, her management style for governing was often akin to that of a businesswoman.

Feinstein also has acquired a national reputation, including speculation in 1984 that she would be on the Democratic ticket as Walter Mondale's running mate. In 1990 she ran unsuccessfully for governor of California.

See also: Harvey Milk, Walter Mondale

Reagan Robbins

REFERENCES

Doerner, William. 1984. "The Pride of San Francisco." *Time*, June 4, pp. 26–7.

Moritz, Charles, ed. 1980. *Current Biography Yearbook 1979*. New York: H.W. Wilson.

Ryan, Michael. 1987. "What Makes Dianne Feinstein a Winner?" *Washington Post*. December 13, pp. 20–1.

Sullivan, Cheryl. 1988. "From Mayor to . . . President?" *Christian Science Monitor*. 8 January, pp. 1, 6.

Rebecca Latimer Felton (1835–1930)

The first woman to serve in the U.S. Senate but for only two days in 1922. Rebecca Latimer Felton, a leading Georgia suffragist, was appointed by Governor Thomas Hardwick after the death of Senator Thomas Watson, in part to atone for Hardwick's opposition to the Nineteenth Amendment.

Since Congress had adjourned, Felton was not expected to take her seat; but when President Warren Harding called a special session, she prevailed upon her successor, Walter George, not to present his credentials immediately. After some discussion before galleries packed with militant women, the Senate agreed without objection that she be seated. Felton delivered a speech, cast a vote, and then was replaced by George.

Felton had a long career in Georgia politics. She managed the campaigns of her husband, the Reverend William Felton, who represented Georgia in the House of Representatives as an Independent from 1875 to 1880. She attended political rallies at a time when it was thought improper for women to do so. She advocated prohibition, abolition of the convict lease system, and women's suffrage.

Like many southern feminists, such as Belle Kearney of Mississippi and Kate Gordon of Louisiana, Felton was a racial bigot. She argued that white women had to be protected from rape by Black men by lynching the "ravening beasts a thousand times a week if necessary." She led the campaign that forced Andrew Sledd to resign from the faculty of Emory College after he published an article on southern racial practices, including lynching, in the *Atlantic Monthly*.

See also: Walter George, Warren G. Harding, Prohibition, Thomas Watson, Woman Suffrage Movement

John C. Berg

REFERENCES

Rogers, Evelyna Keadle. 1978. "Famous Georgia Women: Rebecca Latimer Felton." 5 *Georgia Life* 34.

Talmadge, John E. 1960. *Rebecca Latimer Felton; Nine Stormy Decades*. Athens: U. of Georgia Pr.

Warnock, Henry Y. 1965. "Andrew Sledd, Southern Methodists, and the Negro: A Case History." 31 *Journal of Southern History* 251.

Miriam A. (Ma) Ferguson (1875–1961)

First woman governor of Texas. In an era unfavorable to women politicians, Miriam ("Ma") Ferguson was a two-term Democratic governor of Texas, serving from 1925 to 1927 and again from 1933 to 1935. Ferguson was the second woman governor in the United States, having been sworn in a mere 15 days after Governor Nellie T. Ross of Wyoming. As in the case of Ross, Ferguson was the wife of a former governor, a fact instrumental in their elections.

James E. ("Farmer Jim") Ferguson, a dominant figure in Texas politics from the first decade of the twentieth century to the eve of World War II, was elected governor in 1914 and reelected in 1916. However, in 1917, he was impeached and convicted for misappropriations of state funds and removed from office and was barred from holding a future public office. He was to run unsuccessfully for President in 1920 as the candidate of his own American Party and for the Democratic Senate nomination in 1922.

As a result of his prohibition from state office, James Ferguson "conceived the strategy of running his wife for governor" and coined the campaign slogan "Two governors for the price of one." "Ma" Ferguson ran for governor in 1924, 1926, 1930, 1932, and 1940, and was elected in 1924 and 1932. The Fergusons' electoral support came from rural voters, mainly in eastern Texas. During her two terms, "Ma" Ferguson and her husband occupied side-by-side offices, with the "Farmer Jim" functioning as the actual governor.

By Texas standards, the Fergusons' administrations were notable for their liberalism. In the 1924 campaign, the main tenet of the Ferguson campaign was opposition to the Ku Klux Klan. They were also opposed to prohibition and advocated government spending on programs to aid the poor.

"Ma" Ferguson was essentially a surrogate for her husband, whose own political ambitions had been sidetracked but not thwarted in 1917. She must be considered in light of her husband's populist demagoguery and dominance of Texas politics before World War II.

See also: Election of 1920, Ku Klux Klan, Prohibition

Susan L. Roberts

REFERENCES

Key, V. O. 1949. *Southern Politics in State and Nation.* New York: Knopf.

Richardson, Rupert Norval. 1943. *Texas: The Lone Star State.* New York: Prentice-Hall.

Geraldine A. Ferraro (1935–)

First female major party candidate for Vice President of the United States. Geraldine Ferraro was born to Italian immigrants in New York, surviving early deaths in her family to become Walter Mondale's nominee for Vice President, before her political fall as a result of real estate, tax, and drug scandals. Educated at Marymount College and Fordham University Law School, Ferraro worked for a decade in New York Democratic clubs and civic groups: her cousin Nicholas became a state senator in 1974, and she became an assistant district attorney with the Special Victims Bureau. Although a tough prosecutor, she became a liberal while assisting rape victims.

Ferraro won the Ninth Congressional District of Queens (nicknamed "Archie Bunker's district" after the bigoted television character) with 53 percent of the three-way Democratic primary in 1978 and then took a bitter general election by a ten-point margin. The Democratic leadership did not support her, but she succeeded with family help (Geraldine's husband was a wealthy property developer) and a law-and-order platform.

Reelection was assured after Ferraro had pleased Speaker Tip O'Neill, labor unions, and the district, fighting for public works around LaGuardia Airport. She voted the party line except for opposing school busing, supporting tuition tax credits, and opposing some defense projects.

Strongly feminist, she survived cross-pressure by the Catholic Church and her district but supported fairer pensions for women rather than federal funding of abortions for women in limited circumstances.

She served on the Steering and Policy Committee of the House as well as on the Budget Committee. She was also a member of the Hunt Commission (writing the rules for the 1984 Democratic convention) where she helped increase the share of "superdelegates" and served as the chair of the 1984 Democratic platform committee (where she tried to eliminate specific liberal pledges).

The first female nominee for Vice President weakened an already feeble campaign by having to pay back-taxes, return illegal campaign contributions, and list her husband's questionable real estate dealings on financial disclosure forms. The 1984 election was the worst ever Democratic defeat.

See also: Walter Mondale, Thomas P. O'Neill, Superdelegates

Jeremy R. T. Lewis

REFERENCES

Breslin, Rosemary, and Joshua Hammer. 1984. *Gerry: A Woman Making History.* New York: Pinnacle Books.

Ferraro, Geraldine, and Linda Bird Franke. 1985. *Ferraro: My Story.* New York: Bantam.

Simeon D. Fess (1861–1936)

Ohio Republican Congressman, Senator, and national party leader. An Ohio educator turned Republican politician, Simeon Fess held office in both the House of Representatives and the Senate from 1912 to 1934. Born in rural Ohio, he received a B.A. degree in 1889 from what is now Ohio Northern University, subsidizing his prolonged undergraduate program by working as a schoolteacher and university instructor.

Although admitted to the bar in 1894, Fess remained associated with higher education. He was a college professor and dean at his undergraduate institution and later became president of Antioch College from 1907 to 1917. Long active in Ohio Republican circles, Fess unsuccessfully sought election to Congress in 1902. In 1912, however, he won a seat in the House and served there an additional four terms. While a Congressman, Fess focused on educational policy.

In 1922 Congressman Fess became Senator Fess. While in the Senate he co-authored legislation that established the Railway Mediation Board. He continued to promote educational matters and was a prime supporter of various Library of Congress initiatives. An opponent of the League of Nations, Fess did advocate America's membership on the World Court. Although regarded as an "Old Guard" conservative, Fess endorsed policies aimed at enhancing the status of women and protecting child laborers. He also worked on behalf of workman's compensation and minimum wage legislation. Throughout his career Fess was closely identified with the Prohibitionist movement.

Fess also was active in GOP presidential politics. He delivered the keynote address at the 1928 national convention, and he chaired the Republican National Committee from 1930 to 1932. An opponent of most New Deal initiatives, Fess reluctantly ran for reelection in 1934. He was soundly defeated and retired from public life thereafter.

See also: League of Nations, New Deal, Railroads, Republican National Committee

Charles Longley

REFERENCES

Goldman, Ralph M. 1990. *The National Party Chairmen and Committees: Factionalism at the Top.* Armonk, NY: M. E. Sharpe.

William P. Fessenden (1806–1869)

Leading Republican of the Civil War Senate. William Pitt Fessenden earned a deserved reputation as one of the most effective legislators of his time. A Maine native and the godson of Daniel Webster, he embarked upon a legal career after graduating from Bowdoin College. Entering political life in 1832 as a member of the Maine state legislature, he soon joined the Whig Party, winning a term to represent Maine in the House of Representatives (1841–1843) before returning to his legal practice. The Mexican War stirred his partisanship once more, and he became active in Whig politics, losing a congressional contest in 1850 before gaining a seat in the state legislature two years later. Rising to the United States Senate in 1854, Fessenden immediately dove into the debate over the Kansas-Nebraska Act, winning public acclaim as a defender of free soil (antislavery) principles. Instrumental in the formation of Maine's Republican Party in 1855, Fessenden battled southerners and Democrats alike; in the winter of 1860–1861 he resisted efforts at erecting a patchwork compromise to appease southern interests.

During the Civil War Fessenden played a crucial role in passing legislation involving war finance, slavery, and Reconstruction measures as well as appropriation bills, winning plaudits as a sensible legislator who championed moderation, an image furthered by several sharp exchanges with Radical Republican spokesman Charles Sumner. His expertise in financial matters was recognized on July 1, 1864, when President Abraham Lincoln named him Secretary of the Treasury; after some hesitation, Fessenden accepted the position. During his eight months of Cabinet service he raised funds for the Union war effort through loans and bonds before quitting his post at the end of Lincoln's first administration.

Reelected to the Senate in early 1865, Fessenden soon found himself thrust into the maelstrom of Reconstruction politics as head of the Joint Committee on Reconstruction, which eventually framed the Fourteenth Amendment. He also supported, albeit reluctantly, several of Congress's Reconstruction measures, although he favored a more conservative course and opposed the Tenure of Office Act. But the Maine Senator broke with the majority of his party on whether to impeach President Andrew Johnson. Fessenden, who never endorsed impeachment, was one of the seven Republican Senators whose votes secured Johnson's acquittal in May. He died the following year, leaving unanswered the question of how much his opposition to impeachment might have damaged his political future.

See also: Kansas-Nebraska Act, Abraham Lincoln, Mexican War, Reconstruction, Charles Sumner, Daniel Webster

Brooks Donohue Simpson

REFERENCES

Bogue, Allan G. 1981. *The Earnest Men: Republicans of the Civil War Senate.* Ithaca: Cornell U. Pr.

Jellison, Charles A. 1962. *Fessenden of Maine: Civil War Senator.* Syracuse, NY: Syracuse U. Pr.

Fifteenth Amendment

The Right of citizens of the United States to vote shall not be denied or abridged by the United States or by any State on account of race, color, or previous condition of servitude.

The Congress shall have the power to enforce this article by appropriate legislation.

The brevity of the Fifteenth Amendment is a mask that hides some of the most significant realities of American civilization. On the surface, this two-part statement appears to be a clear victory over racism in general and over white racism in particular. That this was not the case is revealed by the facts surrounding its origin, passage, and ratification. These tell a different story, one that lays bare hearts both afraid and fearless of the different and unknown.

The origin of Negro suffrage in the United States can be traced at least to the Northwest Ordinance of 1787, which prohibited slavery in the territories. Three years later, when Vermont entered the Union, its constitution did not exclude Black men from the ballot. More significantly, neither did the constitutions of Kentucky (1792) and Tennessee (1796). An opposing trend, one excluding Blacks from voting, existed simultaneously, and over time it came to dominate: Maryland (1783), Delaware (1792), and Kentucky (1799). After 1800, in both the North and the South, African-Americans lost their right to vote: New Jersey (1807), Mississippi (1808), Tennessee (1834), North Carolina (1835), and Pennsylvania (1838). This trend persisted even in the North despite the abolitionist campaign and Black participation in the Union victory in the Civil War. In 1865 voters in Colorado, Connecticut, Wisconsin, and Michigan all rejected extension of suffrage to African-American men.

So-called "Radical" Republicans were undaunted by such popular sentiment against Black suffrage and started to move against it in December 1864 when the House Committee on Rebellious States, headed by James Ashley (R-Ohio), considered the readmission of Louisiana, Arkansas, and Tennessee. In an apparent compromise with President Abraham Lincoln, the committee agreed to accept the President's 10 percent plan for the three in return for his support of Congress's right to define readmission terms for the remaining eight Confederate states. But Ashley's subsequent proposal for equal suffrage was defeated by moderate Republicans and Democrats. When the Senate tried to readmit Louisiana, Charles Sumner (R-Mass.) and other "Radicals" led a successful filibuster until Congress adjourned March 4, 1865. Their "hard line" against southern whites and for enactment Negro suffrage were significantly strengthened by Lincoln's assassination. The Radical movement to enfranchise Blacks was also enhanced by the publicity campaign George L. Stearns, but in spite of these efforts, President Andrew Johnson issued a proclamation May 29, 1865, for the readmission of North Carolina without any provision for Negro suffrage. When he issued a similar proclamation for Mississippi two weeks later, the political conflict for control of Reconstruction and Black voting rights intensified.

In July 1865 Wendell Phillips, one of the most ardent Radicals, began to suggest that the Clerk of the House exclude the names of southern Representatives from the roll call when Congress reconvened in December, thereby giving Republicans control of the House. In the year-long struggle that ensued, Congress passed legislation requiring territories (Nebraska) and the state of Tennessee to enfranchise African-Americans and then overrode presidential vetoes of these acts. The Radicals case was strengthened by their victories in the November 1866 elections. When Congress reconvened in December, they passed a bill enfranchising Blacks in the District of Columbia and easily overrode a presidential veto in January 1867. A similar process occurred this same month regarding the Nebraska Constitution. But this momentum was slowed by the results of state elections in which Negro suffrage was a major issue. The Radicals suffered their first setback in Connecticut in the spring and suffered others in the fall, most significantly in Ohio and New Jersey. The following spring both Pennsylvania and Michigan rejected Negro suffrage. With such losses in mind, the Republican Party platform straddled the issue in May 1868 calling for preservation of state control (no Negro suffrage) in the North and guaranteed voting for Blacks in the South. Given this ambivalence, General Ulysses S. Grant's relatively narrow popular victory, especially in northern states, provided the context for a renewed and successful campaign by Radicals to pass the Fifteenth Amendment.

George S. Boutwell (R-Mass.) initiated the final phase in the House in early January 1869 by introducing both an amendment and legislation to enfranchise Blacks. This and Samuel Shellabarger's (R-Ohio) affirmative version, which conferred suffrage on all males over 21 except rebels, were defeated. The Senate acted similarly, rejecting Henry Wilson's (R-Mass.) clear and comprehensive version calling for the abolition of all discrimination or qualification for voting or officeholding because of race, color, nativity, property, education, or religious belief. Instead, the Senate passed William M. Stewart's (R-Nev.) version, which had gained Grant's endorsement. When the House rejected this one, a six-member Conference Committee was formed involving John A. Bingham (R-Ohio), George S. Boutwell (R-Mass.), and John A. Logan (R-Ill.)

for the House, and Stewart, Roscoe Conkling (R-N.Y.), and George Edmunds (R-Vt.) for the Senate. Their composite version, the final draft of the amendment, was phrased in the negative—what could not be done—and this restriction was narrowly limited to race, color, and previous condition of servitude. This phrasing constituted a compromise between Radicals who wanted a categorical affirmation of the right to vote for all males over 21 and those whose interests and/or constituents opposed such a change. This negative phrasing also hid the issue of federal versus state priority over voting and the larger issue of federal versus state dominance. Stewart's draft implicitly equalized the two powers and avoided the issue of which had the supreme power on voting. Similarly, outlawing only racially based voter discrimination hid the reality—revealed in the Senate and House debates—that such a singular prescription left many potential loopholes. The final section granting Congress enforcement power masks the need to ameliorate the Radicals' position. Their support was crucial to passage, an eventuality significantly enhanced by Wendell Phillips's endorsement in an *Anti-Slavery Standard* editorial of February 20, 1869. Five days later the Conference Committee report passed the House, and Senate approval followed a day later.

Ratification received a notable boost the next week when, in his inaugural address, President Grant explicitly and strongly called for state approval. Nevertheless, passage was not easy, especially in the Border States. The Kentucky, Delaware, Maryland, and Tennessee legislatures rejected the amendment and so did California's. Passage in Connecticut, New Jersey, Pennsylvania, Ohio, and New York was difficult (New York ratified and then rescinded). Success occurred in Indiana only because Senator Oliver P. Morton (R-Ind.) exerted pressure on the speaker of the house who reversed his previous ruling about a quorum and allowed the house to vote despite the resignation of most of the Democrats. Morton's motion to require ratification by Virginia, Georgia, and Mississippi as a condition for readmission was also crucial, for without those states and Nebraska the necessary 28 assents would not have been attained in February 1870.

When Secretary of State Hamilton Fish issued the proclamation of ratification on March 30, 1870, President Grant sent an unprecedented message to Congress, declaring that ". . . . the adoption of the XVth Amendment to the Con-stitution completes the most important event that has occurred since the nation came into life." The American Anti-Slavery Society, the center of Radical sentiment was no less sanguine, resolving that the Fifteenth Amendment did not abolish racial discrimination in voting, but at least it did so in principle. This conflict between the real and the ideal continues, and if, in hindsight, there seems to be a preponderance of evidence for the conclusion that the Fifteenth Amendment was a compromise, the partial victory of the ideal should be all the more appreciated for the rare, flickering, yet eternal, phenomenon that it is.

See also: Abolition Movement, Roscoe Conkling, George Edmunds, Ulysses S. Grant, Oliver Morton, Race and Racial Politics

Hal Chase

REFERENCES

Gillette, William. 1965. *The Right to Vote: Politics and the Passage of the 15th Amendment.* Baltimore: Johns Hopkins U. Pr.

McPherson, James M. 1964. *The Struggle for Equality: Abolitionists and the Negro in the Civil War and Reconstruction.* Princeton: Princeton U. Pr.

Mathew, John M. 1909. *Legislative and Judicial History of the Fifteenth Amendment.* Baltimore: Johns Hopkins U. Pr.

Rables, George C. 1984. *But There Was No Peace: The Role of Violence in the Politics of Reconstruction.* Athens: U. of Georgia Pr.

Wesley, Charles H. 1970. *The 15th Amendment and Black America 1870–1970.* Washington: Associated Publishers.

Fifty-Fifty Rule

The fifty-fifty rule developed out of efforts by women to secure positions in equal numbers and of equal responsibility with men in the governing committees of the two major parties. Major advances in the implementation of the fifty-fifty rule coincide with the suffrage movement (1890–1925) and with the contemporary women's movement dating from 1966.

Early efforts focused on state regulation of the permanent organization of state and local parties that governed between state conventions. Colorado, the first state to do so, enacted a statute requiring equal representation of men and women on all party committees from the precinct to the state central committee in 1910. Following ratification of the Nineteenth Amendment (August 26, 1920) granting women's suffrage, efforts to compel equal representation increased. By 1947, nine states (Colorado, Florida, Indiana, Iowa, Missouri, Montana, New Jersey, Oregon, and South Dakota) had by state statute provided for full implementation of equal representation provisions for all party committees. Other states had provided for a parallel female vice chair structure without parity on party committees. One survey of state party committee women found that these positions, while fulfilling the equal number goal, were primarily honorific, lacking equality of influence.

Before the ratification of the Nineteenth Amendment, the national Democratic and Republican parties had established liaisons with women active in the suffrage movement and in party politics. The Democratic National Committee (DNC) established a Women's Bureau in 1916 in its campaign division to attract the women's vote in the 11 western states that had already granted women the vote. In 1918 the chairman of the Republican National Committee (RNC) appointed a woman to direct women's activities in connection with the RNC, and in 1919 created a Women's Division and a Republican Women's National Executive Committee. Following the ratification of women's suffrage, both parties adopted the fifty-fifty rule for the national committees.

The 1920 Democratic National Convention adopted a resolution declaring that the DNC was to be composed of one man and one woman from each state and territory. The RNC refused to make such a provision without authorization of the national convention. Instead, in 1921, a "prominent suffrage leader" was appointed vice chairman of the National Republican Executive Committee, with seven other women appointed to serve on the Executive Committee, and the states were directed in 1923 to appoint women as associate members (i.e., without a vote) to the RNC. The 1924 Republican convention reconstituted the RNC, providing that it be composed of one man and one woman from each state. In 1940 the Republican convention passed Rule 29, providing for equal representation of women on all committees of the RNC. The fifty-fifty balance of the RNC itself ended in 1952 with the addition of Republican state chairs to the RNC—an overwhelmingly male group. Through the 1950s, however, female national committee members really had little influence on the national parties.

While the representation of women in state and national conventions increased after 1920, no efforts were made to apple the fifty-fifty rule to the "temporary party organization" of the convention until the McGovern-Fraser Commission, under pressure from newly formed groups like the National Women's Political Caucus, mandated proportional representation for women (and other groups) for the 1972 Democratic convention. The 1974 Democratic Party Charter, which established the supremacy of national party law, banned the McGovern-Fraser "quotas" but expressly exempted equal division of men and women from the ban (Article Ten, Section 11). In 1980 the Democratic Party Charter was amended to provide equal division on "the Democratic National Committee, the Executive Committee, Democratic state central committees, and all official party conventions, committees, commissions, and like bodies" (Article Eleven, Section 16). While all DNC committees are equally divided, the provision for state central committees remains unenforced by the DNC, and the state parties vary in the extent of their voluntary compliance. The 1988 Democratic convention amended the Charter to extend the fifty-fifty rule from the *final* statewide convention delegation to *each* candidate's delegation within each state. By contrast, the national Republican Party has not mandated fifty-fifty division for convention delegates or for the state parties, although several large urban state parties have voluntarily chosen to employ equal division (e.g., the New York state central committee and the 1988 California convention).

See also: Democratic National Committee, McGovern-Fraser Commission, National Women's Political Caucus, Nineteenth Amendment, Republican National Committee, Suffrage, Woman Suffrage Movement

Denise L. Baer

REFERENCES

Breckinridge, Sophonisba P. 1972. *Women in the Twentieth Century: A Study of Their Political, Social, and Economic Activities*. New York: Arno Press.

Cotter, Cornelius P., and Bernard C. Hennessy. 1964. *Politics Without Power: The National Party Committees.* New York: Atherton Press.

Fisher, Marguerite J. 1947. "Women in the Political Parties." *The Annals of the American Academy of Political and Social Science*. Philadelphia: American Academy of Political Social Science.

———, and Betty Whitehead. "Women and National Party Organization." 38 *American Political Science Review* 895.

Millard Fillmore (1800–1874)

Thirteenth President of the United States. Millard Fillmore's work to push through the Compromise of 1850 has been undervalued and overshadowed by his role in the demise of both the Whig Party and the Know-Nothing Party. For both parties, he served as nominal head—first as a Whig President, second as the Know-Nothing presidential nominee. Both parties destroyed themselves over the slavery issue and took Fillmore with them.

On the surface, there appears to be little relationship between Fillmore's principles and the political groups he served. In 1833 he entered the House of Representatives for two years thanks to support from the Antimasons, a political party opposed to secret societies. Twenty-three years later, he became the presidential candidate for the American, or Know-Nothing Party, a political party born from a secret society. But both organizations did in fact have much in common. Both feared secret conspiracies against the middle class by outsiders: Antimasons opposed the political and economic elite who made up the Freemasons as well as their terminology and ritual that smacked of antirepublicanism; the Know-Nothings opposed the corruptive political power of the Democratic-controlled immigrants, their foreign ways, and the terminology and ritual of their Catholicism, which they feared both as a breeding ground for antirepublican sentiment as well as a mechanism with which to overthrow the government.

Fillmore's association with the Whig Party was as an anti-Jackson man. Fearful of the corruption guaranteed by Andrew Jackson's spoils system and later of the Democratic support for the Mexican War, Fillmore fought for internal improvements and against the addition of any lands that could become slave territory. He served in Congress from 1833 to 1835 and from 1837 to 1842. In 1848 the Whigs nominated him as Vice President primarily to pacify northern Whigs enraged by the presidential nomination of slaveholder Zachary Taylor. The sectional appeal worked and Taylor and Fillmore won.

Mexico's cession of land to the United States after the war sparked enormous controversy over the extension of slavery into the territories. A compromise over the issue, provided by Henry Clay's Omnibus Bill, was opposed by Taylor and the issue promised to turn into disunion. But Taylor died unexpectedly on July 9, 1850, and Fillmore was sworn in. He threw his support behind a compromise version of the Omnibus Bill and the crisis over slavery was averted for another ten years.

The intransigence of both sides of the slavery question toward compromise guaranteed Fillmore's repudiation as the Whig nominee in 1852. Northern Whigs, the majority in the convention, viewed Fillmore as unacceptably pro-southern because of his support for the Compromise of 1850; General Winfield Scott replaced him. Four years later, the Know-Nothings drafted Fillmore for the 1856 campaign, promoting him as the only national candidate against the sectional appeals of Democrat James Buchanan and Republican John C. Frémont. His support for his newly adopted party was lukewarm: he refused to campaign as either a nativist or an anti-Catholic. He spoke only of freely adopting the Know-Nothing position and stressed the Union in his campaign speeches.

Fillmore lost the election, carrying only Maryland, a bastion of Know-Nothing sentiment. He won 21.53 percent of the popular vote, a third-party record not even approached until surpassed by the 27.93 percent of the Progressive Party in 1912. But the Know-Nothing party split apart over the slavery issue, and Fillmore retired from active politics. He spent his last years in Buffalo, New York, supporting the Union cause and promoting the interests of the city.

See also: Antimasons, James Buchanan, Henry Clay, Elections of 1848, 1852, and 1856, John C. Frémont, Andrew Jackson, Know-Nothings, Mexican War, Progressive Party, Zachary Taylor

Janet L. Coryell

REFERENCES

Grayson, Benson Lee. 1981. *The Unknown President: The Administration of Millard Fillmore.* Washington: U. Pr. of America.

Rayback, Robert. 1959. *Millard Fillmore: Biography of a President.* Buffalo, NY: Buffalo Historical Society.

Severence, Frank, ed. 1907. *Millard Fillmore Papers.* Buffalo, NY: Buffalo Historical Society.

Smith, Elbert B. 1988. *The Presidencies of Zachary Taylor & Millard Fillmore.* Lawrence: U. Pr. of Kansas.

Financing Congressional Campaigns

Democracy requires competitive elections. Competitive elections for federal office have become unavoidably expensive; voters have little real choice unless candidates of both parties raise and spend the substantial sums it now takes to reach people with campaign messages. But the quality of democracy also depends on how the campaign money is raised, who provides it, and what contributors get in return. The rising cost of competitive campaigns has thus aggravated a basic dilemma. Democratic ideology enshrines a rough political equality: one person, one vote. Money is distributed very unequally, however, and so, when used effectively in politics, it threatens democratic equality. This excites continued controversy as well as considerable scholarly interest in where campaign money comes from, where it goes and for what purposes, and how it affects the way we are governed.

The Federal Election Campaign Act

The congressional campaign finance system—and most of our knowledge about money in congressional elections—is a consequence of the Federal Election Campaign Act (FECA) of 1971 and its 1974 and 1976 amendments. The FECA was enacted in response to a steep increase in campaign spending during the 1960s. Changes in both voting habits and campaign technology had conspired to drive up the costs of campaigning. A decline in party loyalty among voters encouraged a trend toward candidate-centered electoral politics, which was reinforced by the gradual eclipse of party organizations by mass media (radio, television, direct mail, phone banks) as the primary instruments of campaigning. Both trends made campaigns more expensive.

Congress tried to deal with the problem by limiting campaign contributions and expenditures. The Supreme Court, in *Buckley v. Valeo* (424 U.S. 1 (1976)), voided expenditure and some contribution limits as unconstitutional infringements on free political speech, but much of the structure of regulation erected by the FECA remains in force. All contributions to congressional candidates must be reported at regular intervals during the campaign period. "Full disclosure," as it is called, is the principal source of information about campaign finance practices.

Disclosure covers the four major sources of campaign funds: individuals, multicandidate committees, parties, and candidates. Each source is subject to a different set of restrictions. The contribution limit for individuals is $1,000 for each primary, runoff, and general election; a person may give no more than $25,000 in total to candidates or committees in any calendar year. The limit per candidate per election for multicandidate committees, commonly called political action committees (PACs), is $5,000, with no restriction on the total they may contribute to all candidates. To qualify as a multicandidate committee, a PAC has to raise money from at least fifty people and contribute to at least five candidates.

National party committees are subject to the same limits as PACs in making direct contributions to candidates, but they are allowed to spend additional money on behalf of congressional candidates. Coordinated party spending, as it is called, is also limited, but the ceilings rise with inflation. The original limit in 1974 for a House campaign was $10,000; by 1990, inflation had pushed it up to $25,150. The ceiling for Senate campaigns varies with the population of the state (2¢ times the voting-age population, adjusted for inflation since 1974, with a minimum of $20,000, also adjusted). It ranged from $50,280 (in the five least populous states) to $1,073,478 (in California) for the 1990 election. State party committees may also spend up to this ceiling for congressional candidates, but because few of them can afford to do so, national party committees have become their agents for raising and spending the money, doubling, in effect, the amount the national party may spend for its candidates.

The FECA originally forbade candidates and their families to spend more than $35,000 for Senate campaigns and $25,000 for House campaigns. It also limited spending by individuals and committees on behalf of candidates to $1,000. Both restrictions were overturned by the Court; candidates may now spend as much of their own money as they please, and there is no restriction on what individuals and groups may spend "independently" for or against candidates.

The Growth in Campaign Money

Among the FECA's principal goals were capping campaign spending and reducing the financial role of "special interests." The first goal was placed out of reach by the Court. The Court's decision, along with the continued development of expensive new campaign technology, made it impossible to achieve the second goal. As campaign spending has continued to grow, candidates have found it harder to ignore the superior efficiency of soliciting PACs, who can give as much as $10,000 ($5,000 each for the primary and general election campaigns), rather than individuals, who are limited to $2,000. Rising costs have also enhanced the position of party committees, whose coordinated spending limits are indexed against inflation.

The growth in campaign contributions and the increasing financial role of PACs are documented in Table 1. Discounting for inflation, contributions to House candidates increased by

Table 1

Sources of Contributions to House and Senate Candidates, 1972–1986

| | Average Contributions | Percentage of contributions from: | | | |
		Individuals[a]	PACs	Parties[b]	Unknown
HOUSE					
1972	$ 51,752[c]	60	14	17	9
1974	$ 61,084	79	17	4	—
1976	$ 79,421	70	25	8	—
1978	$ 111,232	70	29	5	—
1980	$ 148,268	67	29	4	—
1982	$ 222,620	63	31	6	—
1984	$ 240,722	60	37	3	—
1986	$ 280,260	59	39	2	—
1988	$ 282,949	55	43	2	—
SENATE					
1972	$ 353,933[c]	67	12	14	8
1974	$ 455,515	77	11	6	6
1976	$ 624,094	81	15	4	—
1978	$ 951,930	84	14	2	—
1980	$1,079,346	78	21	2	—
1982	$1,771,167	81	18	1	—
1984	$2,273,635	80	19	1	—
1986	$2,721,793	76	24	1	—
1988	$2,649,492	74	26	1	—

[a] Includes candidates' contributions and loans to their own campaigns.
[b] Does not include party expenditures on behalf of candidates.
[c] Some contributions made before April 7, 1972, may have gone unrecorded.

127 percent, and contributions to Senate candidates increased by 212 percent, between 1974 and 1988. PACs more than doubled their share of contributions over the same period; adjusted for inflation, total PAC contributions grew by 393 percent. Still, contributions from private individuals remain the most important source of funds. Party donations comprise only a small proportion of *direct* contributions to congressional candidates, but most party assistance comes in the form of coordinated spending, which is not included in this table.

Individual Contributors

Whether or not it is forwarded through parties or PACs, all (legal) congressional campaign money originally comes from private individuals. We know something about who the contributors are but much less about why they contribute. About 10 percent of adult Americans report making some sort of campaign contribution in any given election year. Even more

than other political activists, contributors, according to Sorauf (1988) and Jones and Miller (1985), are disproportionately well educated, affluent, partisan, politically involved, white, and Republican. People no doubt contribute for a variety of motives—to further a cause or candidate, to win social approbation, to incur an obligation, or out of a sense of duty—but little is known about the relative importance of different motives. Contributors to PACs appear to be less involved in politics than are contributors to parties and candidates and are thus more willing to leave decisions about who gets the money to PAC managers.

Although congressional candidates continue to get most of their campaign money directly from private individuals, this source of funds has not excited much scholarly or critical attention since the $1,000 limit put the traditional "fat cats" out of business. (The new "fat cats" are those who can persuade other people to give money.) Critics of the current system concentrate their attacks on PACs; individual contributors, because they are not clearly identified with "special interests," are usually treated with benign neglect. Indeed, to the usual critics of the campaign finance system, the individual who supports candidates with small donations is the democratic hero. But the most effective way to raise money on a large scale from individuals is through direct-mail solicitation, and appeals are most successful when they play on emotions of fear, anger, hatred, and frustration. This rewards inflammatory rhetoric and benefits candidates and groups espousing extreme views.

The "Individuals" contributions in Table 1 include donations by candidates to their own campaigns. For some years, the Federal Election Commission (FEC) has reported candidate contributions separately. In 1984, for example, congressional candidates supplied 8.5 percent of all campaign receipts. Normally, candidates are forced to use their own money when their dismal prospects discourage contributions from other sources. For 1984 Sorauf noted that candidates who lost in the primary supplied 31 percent of all the money they reported raising; general election challengers to incumbents provided 14 percent their campaign funds; but incumbents contributed virtually none of their own money to their campaigns.

Although the Court set aside limits on candidate spending, wealthy candidates appear to enjoy little advantage; those who spend large sums of their own money lose elections far more often than they win. Still, most nonincumbent candidates do need to come up with $20,000 to $40,000 of their own money to cover start-up costs; the more successful the subsequent campaign, the more likely they are to be able to pay themselves back with money raised from other courses. In short, "'losers' often are self-financed, and self-financed candidates are losers" (Sorauf, 1988: p. 68).

Political Action Committees

PACs are the second most important source of campaign funds. The category "multicandidate committee" encompasses a diverse set of organizations. The categories used by the Federal Election Commission to report financial activities—labor, corporate, trade/membership/health, nonconnected, cooperative, and corporation without stock—merely hint at the variety. Some amount to little more than an entrepreneur with a mailing list; others are adjuncts of huge corporations or labor unions. In some, decisions

about contributions are made centrally; others encourage extensive input from members. The goals of some are immediate, narrow, and self-interested; others pursue long-term objectives arising from widely shared values. Most PACs just give money; but a few also provide campaign workers, produce advertising, advise on campaign strategy, get out the vote, and recruit and train candidates. Indeed, variety is such that virtually everything said are one time or another about PACs is true of at least *some* PACs.

Between 1974 and 1988, the number of PACs registered with the Federal Election Commission grew from 608 to 4,527. Corporate and nonconnected PACs (PACs that are independent, self-sustaining organizations without any sponsoring organization) multiplied most rapidly, as did their share of PAC contributions. Labor PACs suffered a relative decline. In 1974 labor accounted for half of all PAC contributions; by 1986 their share had fallen to 22 percent, compared to 35 percent for corporate PACs, 25 percent for membership PACs, and 14 percent for nonconnected PACs (Sorauf, 1988: pp. 78–79; Jacobson, 1989a).

These changes initially threatened the Democrats. Typically, 95 percent of labor PAC money goes to Democrats, and the other types of PACs were, at first, more generous to Republicans. Since the early 1980s, however, corporate, membership, and nonconnected PACs have increasingly favored incumbents of both parties. For example, 85 percent of corporate PAC donations to House candidates went to incumbents in 1986, up from 63 percent in 1978; Democratic incumbents received 44 percent of the 1986 total (Jacobson, 1989a). Business PAC generosity to congressional Democrats has provoked frequent complaints by Republican Party officials, who regard business PACs as natural ideological allies. But once the 1982 election made it clear that Democrats would retain control of the House for the foreseeable future, many of these PACs evidently decided that their short-term interest in retaining access to incumbent Democrats outweighed their long-term interest in a more Republican Congress. Certainly Democratic leaders sought to persuade them that this was the case.

One important kind of nonconnected PAC is the personal PAC created and run by a single individual. Most of these PACs are formed by active politicians seeking either the presidency or leadership positions in Congress. Presidential candidates use their PACs as an excuse for traveling around the country, giving speeches, making contacts, and assembling mailing lists while avoiding the campaign spending limits that apply to officially declared presidential candidacies; the money they pass out also presumably encourages endorsements from recipients. Virtually every presidential hopeful in 1988 had his own PAC. Aspiring or current congressional leaders use personal PACs to incur obligations from fellow members of Congress in pursuit of leadership positions or party unity. Personal PACs allow powerful members who do not need much money for their own campaigns to exploit their superior fundraising ability to further other political objectives.

Political Parties

Table 1 shows that the parties have become a trivial source of direct campaign contributions, but party spending on behalf of congressional candidates has increased substantially. Coordinated party spending may cover almost any campaign activity; the only restriction is that the party committee have some control over how the money is spent. Party committees typically pay for conducting polls, producing campaign advertisements, organizing direct mail, and buying media time—expensive activities that require technical expertise. As the data in Table 2 show, Republican Party committees (the National Republican Congressional Committee and the National Republican Senatorial Committee) assumed a large lead in coordinated spending that their Democratic counterparts (the Democratic Congressional Campaign Committee and the Democratic Senatorial Campaign Committee) have only begun to narrow. Their advantage stems from a mature direct mail fundraising system; 75 percent of Republican Party funds are now raised in small sums (less than $100) from regular contributors on their mailing lists. The Democrats have worked to expand their own direct mail system but still have far fewer regular donors; they remain dependent on PACs and other large donors for most of their income.

The money given to, or spent for, congressional candidates represents only one aspect of national party committee activity. Republican Party officials have assembled an extensive organization to pursue a wide range of party-building and electoral activities. The national party maintains a large staff and keeps outside campaign specialties—pollsters, computer vendors, direct-mail firms, stationers, media and advertising professionals—on retainer. It conducts voter registration drives and national advertising campaigns; trains candidates, campaign managers, and party workers in all aspects of campaigning; and coordinates contribution strategies of allied PACs. Democrats have begun to offer some of the same services, though lack of funds has limited their activity; Democratic House and Senate campaign committees had $28.7 million at their disposal for the 1987–1988 election cycle, compared to the Republicans' $100.4 million.

Electoral Strategies and Impact

National party committees and PACs have both thrived under the legal regime established by the FECA. Sometimes they cooperate with one another, as when PACs take cues from party officials in deciding where to place contributions. But in a very basic sense, parties and PACs are natural rivals, because they pursue conflicting goals and follow conflicting electoral strategies. Parties seek to maximize the number of congressional seats they control and prefer campaign money to be distributed efficiently to this end. This means concentrating resources in the tightest races, where the investment might affect the outcome. But many PACs care mainly about policy, often narrowly conceived. They use money not so much to affect election results as to gain access to, and curry favor with, whomever emerges as the winner. PACs of this sort thus contribute to sure winners, to members of both parties sitting on committees dealing with legislation they care about, and to newly elected members after the election. The popularity of this approach explains why PAC contributions as a whole strongly favor incumbents. But money spent on incumbents almost certain to win or on other candidates after they have won is, from the party's perspective, almost entirely wasted.

This is one reason that the expansion of PAC activity has had surprisingly little electoral impact. The injection of ever larger sums of money into congressional campaigns might have enhanced electoral competition substantially—if the money had found its way into the hands of challengers. Money spent by House and Senate challengers has a much larger impact on election outcomes than does money spent by incumbents. The availability of money also helps to attract more talented challengers by offering ambitious career politicians better odds on winning. But as PAC contributions to House

Table 2

Party Contributions and Coordinated Expenditures, 1976–1988 (in dollars)

	Democrats		Republicans	
	Contributions	Expenditures	Contributions	Expenditures
HOUSE				
1976	1,465,629	500	3,658,310	329,583
1978	1,262,298	72,892	3,621,104	1,297,079
1980	1,025,989	256,346	3,498,323	2,203,748
1982	1,052,286	694,321	4,720,959	5,293,260
1984	1,280,672	1,774,452	4,060,120	6,190,309
1986	968,913	1,836,213	2,570,278	4,111,474
1988	1,197,537	2,880,301	2,650,569	4,162,474
SENATE				
1976	468,795	4,359	930,034	113,976
1978	466,683	229,218	703,204	2,723,880
1980	480,464	1,132,912	677,004	5,434,758
1982	579,337	2,265,197	600,221	8,715,761
1984	441,467	3,947,731	590,922	6,518,415
1986	670,832	6,656,286	729,522	10,077,902
1988	488,899	6,692,264	721,237	10,260,600

Source: Norman J. Ornstein, Thomas E. Mann, and Michael J. Malbin, *Vital Statistics on Congress, 1989–1990*. Washington, D.C.: Congressional Quarterly, 1990: 97).

candidates have grown, an increasing share of PAC money has gone to incumbents, and competition has, if anything, declined. PACs have been considerably more generous to nonincumbent Senate candidates, which is one reason that a much larger proportion of Senate contests remain competitive. There is, of course, some circularity here; viable challengers in contests expected to be competitive attract PAC contributions; one reason that business PAC support for Republican House challengers dropped sharply after 1982 was a dearth of viable recipients. Still, the expansion of PACs has more often reinforced than it has challenged existing patterns of electoral competition.

The expansion of national party campaign activity has also had little net electoral impact. Although Republicans have enjoyed a huge advantage in money and organization at the national level for nearly a decade, they have surprisingly little to show for it. After the 1988 election, Republicans held 175 House seats, slightly fewer than their postwar average of 181. And in 1986 they lost the Senate majority they had won in 1980 despite a very large advantage in campaign resources. Explanations for the congressional Republicans' failure to gain much ground during the Ronald Reagan presidency

lie outside the campaign finance system; observers who expected Republicans to translate financial and organizational superiority into congressional seats overestimated the potential effect of national party involvement in congressional elections.

Independent Spending

The Supreme Court declared limits on political spending by individuals or groups independently of official campaigns to be unconstitutional. The freedom to organize independent campaigns leaves a major loophole in any scheme to regulate campaign contributions; anyone feeling constrained by restrictions on donations to campaigns is free to take the independent route. So far, few have chosen to pursue this option, though expensive independent campaigns have been mounted in a small number of contests. The most spent independently in any election cycle was $1.7 million in 1983–1984, about 1 percent of the money spent on congressional campaigns that year.

Independent spending excited considerable attention in 1980, when the National Conservative Political Action Committee (NCPAC) mounted harshly negative independent campaigns against six liberal Democratic Senators, four of whom lost. Though all of the losses could be explained by other factors, negative independent campaigning looked for a moment like the wave of the future. But NCPAC's failure to defeat any of its targets in 1982, amid signs of a backlash against its tactics, halted the trend, at least temporarily. More recent independent campaigns have focused on supporting rather than attacking candidates. Their general failure has probably discouraged imitators; in 1986, for example, the American Medical Association's AMPAC spent $570,000 on behalf of the challengers of House Democrats Andrew Jacobs of Indiana and Fortney Stark of California, both of whom won reelection by the same margin they had won by in 1984. The independent option is important as a constraint on campaign finance regulation, but independent spending remains a very marginal component of congressional campaign finance.

Some money enters congressional campaigns legally without regulation or accounting by the Federal Election Commission. For example, money contributed to state parties to be used for party building, voter registration, and getting out the vote is not regulated. The "soft money," as it is called, is usually deployed by party committees, who use it to cover a variety of their own expenses as well as to help candidates by financing local party work. The legal indulgence of soft campaign money as well as independent spending makes it possible for anyone who wants to put any amount of money into electoral politics to find a legal way to do so.

Consequences for Congress

The workings of Congress are deeply affected by how its members win and hold office. How do present-day campaign finance practices affect congressional behavior? One undeniable consequence of the FECA and its aftermath is that members have come to spend a lot more time worrying about, and pursuing, campaign money. Driven by both supply and demand, campaign costs have continued to rise, while limits on the size of contributions have remained unchanged; thus candidates have had to solicit more contributions to keep up. Aside from taking time from legislative and other duties, some critics charge that the pursuit of campaign money, particularly from PACs, is corrupting the entire political process because campaign contributions purchase votes and policy.

The evidence offered for this charge is largely circumstantial or anecdotal. An investigative reporter or a reform lobby such as Common Cause demonstrates that members taking the position on legislation preferred by some interest group—milk producers, used car dealers, medical doctors, the banking industry, and the National Rifle Association are recent examples—get more campaign money from PACs representing the group than do members taking the contrary position. But unless one expects PACs to distribute money randomly (a bizarre notion), this is hardly conclusive evidence. Recipients of such PAC donations can argue that the PACs are merely helping to reelect legislators who share their conception of the public interest. Any simple matching of contributions to roll-call votes must be inconclusive because the direction of causality is indeterminate.

More carefully specified scholarly studies have uncovered, at most, a rather modest effect of contributions on votes. On some issues attracting little public attention, votes appear to reflect prior PAC contributions even when ideology, party, and district interests are taken into account. The effects of contributions are usually dwarfed by other factors in these studies, but some remain statistically significant. Despite numerous tales of members who vote to please financial backers or who demand money from lobbyists in return for help, there is little systematic evidence that policy is being bought wholesale by special interest.

This is not to say that PAC contributions do not have other effects on congressional behavior. Both members of Congress and PAC officials admit that, at minimum, contributions ensure access—a necessary, if not sufficient, condition for influence. Doors will be open to lobbyists representing groups who have supported members' campaigns. Furthermore, roll-call votes are by no means the only important decisions shaping legislation. Responsibility for the crucial choices made before bills reach the floor is often obscure; we know almost nothing about possible PAC influence in earlier stages of the legislative process. It is doubtful that interest groups would put so much time, energy, and money into PAC activities without some perceived legislative payoff.

Still, there are some formidable barriers to PAC influence. Many important issues produce conflicts among well-organized interests, giving members access to PAC money no matter which side they take and thus freeing them to take whatever side is consistent with their own or their district's preferences. Given the variety of potential sources of campaign money available to incumbents—private individuals and parties as well as the thousands of PACs—most should have little difficulty financing campaigns without putting their principles on the block. Furthermore, the point of campaigns is to win votes, not to raise money. Campaign contributions are a means to an end—winning votes and thus elections—not an end in themselves (except, perhaps, to members of the House elected prior to 1979, who are allowed to keep leftover campaign money when they retire). The marginal return on campaign spending by incumbents is remarkably small; the prospective value, in votes, of even the maximum PAC contribution ($10,000) is tiny. It makes no sense for a member to take a stand that produces even a small net loss in voter's support in order to please a PAC. It is no accident that district sentiment, when it can be estimated, far outweighs campaign contributions in determining roll-call votes.

Proposals for Reform

The growth in campaign spending and the increasing share of funds supplied by PACs has fueled regular demands for reform of the congressional campaign finance system, but strong partisan conflicts have doomed every legislative proposal so far. The solution preferred by liberal Democrats is partial or complete public funding of campaigns, combined with ceilings on contributions from PACs, and a limit on total campaign spending (constitutional if accepted in return for public funds). This would reduce the need to raise funds and diminish the alleged influence of special interests. But unless spending limits were set so high that they scarcely made a difference, they would make it harder for challengers to defeat incumbents.

Republicans, still pursuing majority control of Congress, oppose public funding for this as well as for philosophical reasons (the government should not compel people to pay for the propagation of political views they find repugnant). They advocate reducing the influence of PACs, limiting or banning PAC contributions, and enhancing the financial role of the parties, preferably by doing away with limits on party contribution and coordinated spending. Republicans' enthusiasm for unleashing the parties is understandable, given their advantage in party funds; but so is the Democrats' rejection of this approach, at least as long as the Republican advantage persists.

Aside from issues of partisan advantage, all major proposals for change raise thorny practical and philosophical issues on which there is, at present, little consensus. For example, if PACs were no longer permitted to give money to candidates, they could still spend money independently for or against candidates, with consequences difficult to predict. Less difficult to predict, on the basis of past experience, is that people involved in financing campaigns will discover legal ways to invest in elections under any regulatory system compatible with the First Amendment. Thus the democratic dilemma arising from the fact that competitive elections are expensive and the distribution of money is far from egalitarian is likely to remain unresolved.

See also: Direct Mail, Federal Election Campaign Act of 1971 and Amendments, Federal Election Commission, Political Action Committees

Gary C. Jacobson

REFERENCES

Abramowitz, Alan I. 1988. "Explaining Senate Election Outcomes." 82 *American Political Science Review* 385.

Adamany, David. 1982. "Political Parties in the 1980s." In Michael J. Malbin, ed. *Money and Politics in the United States*. Chatham, NJ: Chatham House.

Brown, Kirk F. 1983. "Campaign Contributions and Congressional Voting." Paper presented at the Annual Meeting of the American Political Science Association, Chicago.

Cantor, Joseph E. 1981. *Political Action Committees: Their Evolution and Growth and Their Implications for the Political System*. U.S. Library of Congress, Congressional Research Service, Report No. 81–246.

Chappell, Henry W. 1982. "Campaign Contributions and Congressional Voting: A Simultaneous Probit-Tobit Model." 64 *Review of Economics and Statistics* 77.

Drew, Elizabeth. 1983. *Politics and Money: The New Road to Corruption*. New York: Macmillan.

Edsall, Thomas B. 1984. "The GOP Money Machine." *Washington Post National Weekly Edition*. July 2.

Eismeier, Theodore J., and Philip H. Pollock III. 1988. *Business, Money, and the Rise of Corporate PACs in American Elections*. New York: Quorum Books.

Frendreis, John P., and Richard W. Waterman. 1985. "PAC Contributions and Legislative Behavior: Senate Voting on Trucking Deregulation." 66 *Social Science Quarterly* 401.

Gopoian, J. David. 1984. "What Make's PACs Tick? An Analysis of the Allocation Patterns of Economic Interest Groups." 28 *American Journal of Political Science* 259.

Green, Donald, and Jonathan Krasno. 1988. "Salvation for the Spendthrift Incumbent: Reestimating the Effects of Campaign Spending in House Elections." 32 *American Journal of Political Science* 884.

Grenzke, Janet M. 1989. "PACs and the Congressional Supermarket: The Currency is Complex." 33 *American Journal of Political Science* 1.

Handler, Edward, and John R. Mulkern. 1982. *Business in Politics*. Lexington, MA: Lexington Books.

Herrnson, Paul S. 1988. *Party Campaigning in the 1980s*. Cambridge: Harvard U. Pr.

Jackson, Brooks. 1988. *Honest Graft: Big Money and the American Political Process*. New York: Knopf.

Jacobson, Gary C. 1979. "Public Funds for Congressional Campaigns: Who Would Benefit?" In Herbert E. Alexander, ed. *Political Finance*. Beverly Hills, CA: Sage.

————. 1980. Money in Congressional Elections. New Haven: Yale U. Pr.

————. 1985a. *"Money and Votes Reconsidered: Congressional Elections, 1972–1982."* 47 *Public Choice* 7.

————. 1985b. "The Republican Advantage in Campaign Finance." In John Chubb and Paul Peterson, eds. *The New Direction in American Politics*. Washington: Brookings.

————. 1987a. *The Politics of Congressional Elections*. 2nd ed. Boston: Little Brown.

————. 1987b. "Enough Is Too Much: Money and Competition in House Elections, 1972–1984." In Kay L. Schlozman, ed. *Elections in America*. New York: Allen and Unwin.

————. 1988. "The Effects of Campaign Spending on Voting Intentions: New Evidence from a Panel Study of the 1986 House Elections." Paper presented at the Annual Meeting of the Midwest Political Science Association, Chicago.

————. 1989a. "Parties and PACs in Congressional Elections." In Lawrence C. Dodd and Bruce I. Oppenheimer, eds. *Congress Reconsidered*. 4th ed. Washington: Congressional Quarterly.

————. 1989b. "Meager Patrimony: Republican Representation in Congress after Reagan." In Larry Berman, ed. *Looking Back on the Reagan Presidency*. Baltimore: Johns Hopkins U. Pr.

Jones, Ruth S., and Warren E. Miller. 1985. "Financing Campaigns: Marco Level Innovation and Micro Level Response."36 *Western Political Quarterly* 187–.

Kau, James, and Paul Rubin. 1982. *Congressmen, Constituents, and Contributors*. Boston: Martinus Nijhoff.

Latus, Margaret Ann. 1984. "Assessing Ideological PACs: From Outrage to Understanding." In Michael J. Malbin, ed. *Money and Politics in the United States*. Chatham, NJ: Chatham House.

Malbin, Michael J. 1982. "Looking Back on the Future of Campaign Finance Reform." In Michael J. Malbin, ed. *Money and Politics in the United States*. Chatham, NJ: Chatham House.

Mayhew, David R. 1974. *Congress: The Electoral Connection*. New Haven: Yale U. Pr.

Nelson, Candice J. 1982. "Counting the Cash. PAC Contributions to Members of the House of Representatives." Paper presented at the Annual Meeting of the American Political Science Association.

Sabato, Larry J. 1984. *PAC Power*. New York: Norton.

Sorauf, Frank J. 1984–85. "Who's in Charge? Accountability in Political Action Committees." 99 *Political Science Quarterly* 591.

————. 1988. *Money in American Elections*. Glenview, IL: Scott, Foresman.

Stern, Philip N. 1988. *The Best Congress Money Can Buy*. New York: Pantheon.

Welch, William P. 1982. "Campaign Contributions and Voting: Milk Money and Dairy Price Supports." 25 *Western Political Quarterly* 478.

Wright, John. 1985. "PACs, Contributions, and Roll Calls: An Organizational Perspective." 75 *American Political Science Review* 400.

Yiannakis, Daina Evans. 1983. "PAC Contributions and House Voting on Conflictual and Consensual Issues: The Windfall Profits Tax and the Chrysler Loan Guarantee." Paper presented at the Annual Meeting of the American Political Science Association, Chicago.

Financing Presidential Campaigns

Modern presidential campaigns are vast and complex operations costing many millions of dollars. Their expense contrasts sharply with the noble conviction expressed in 1828 by the nation's sixth president, John Quincy Adams, that "to pay money for securing [the presidency of the United States] was . . . incorrect in principle." Almost from the beginning, in fact, presidential candidates and their supporters have paid, sometimes dearly, for the privilege of seeking the nation's highest office.

The substantial—and apparently ever-increasing—expense of running for President owes to a variety of factors, many of which did not exist at the time of Adams's presidency: the development of a highly competitive political party system; the gradual democratization of the presidency; the extension of suffrage; the introduction of national nominating conventions and primary elections; and the development of costly communications media and campaign technology with their attendant hosts of expensive specialists—now a standard feature of serious presidential campaigns.

Spending Patterns

In the early years political funds were spent primarily for printing costs. Most presidential campaigning took place in newspapers and pamphlets subsidized by political factions favoring one or another candidate. In time candidates adopted other means of spreading campaign messages, including campaign biographies, buttons and banners, and personal stumping on the campaign trail. Radio was first used in the 1924 campaign, and in 1952 television emerged as a primary means of communicating with voters.

As the size and population of the United States expanded and the means of campaigning for office changed, the costs of campaigning for office grew correspondingly. In 1860 Abraham Lincoln's winning general election campaign reportedly cost about $100,000, and his opponent Stephen Douglas's campaign cost about $50,000. One hundred years later John Kennedy's campaign spent about $9.7 million to defeat Richard Nixon, whose campaign cost about $10.1 million.

In the seven presidential campaigns held since 1960, expenditures have continued to increase. Campaigns have become technologically more sophisticated and thus more expensive. In the 1988 general election campaign, the fourth in which public funds were provided, Republican George Bush had about $93.7 million spent on his behalf, including a public grant of $46.1 million. Democratic Party candidate Michael Dukakis had about $106.5 million spent on his behalf, also including a public grant of $46.1 million.

The total cost of electing the United States President in 1988 was about $500 million. That sum includes not only the $200.2 million spent on behalf of the two major political party candidates in the general election; it also includes funds spent by all the candidates who sought their parties' nominations, by the nominating conventions of the parties, and by third-party and independent campaigns.

Sources of Funds

In the earliest presidential campaigns, collections from candidates and assessments upon officeholders were sufficient to pay the necessary costs. But as campaign costs increased, other sources of funds had to be found.

Andrew Jackson, first elected President in 1828, is generally credited with bringing in the "spoils system"—rewarding with favors and government jobs those who had contributed to campaigns. With the end of the Civil War in 1865, those corporations and individuals who had amassed fortunes from American industry began to pay a major share of presidential campaign costs. Those sources increased in importance when the Congress passed the Civil Service Reform Act of 1883, a law that prohibited officers and employees of the United States from seeking or receiving political contributions from one another. The Hatch Act of 1939 extended to almost all employees in the executive branch of the federal government the restrictions of political activity that the 1883 act imposed on civil service employees.

Reform Efforts

After the turn of the century, concern over the influence of corporations in the federal election process led to the enactment of a number of campaign finance regulations. The first federal prohibition of corporate contributions was enacted in 1907. Forty years later that ban was extended permanently to labor unions. The first federal campaign fund disclosure law was passed in 1910. In 1911 the law was amended to require primary, convention, and preelection financial statements of all candidates for federal office and to limit the amounts that candidates for the House and the Senate were permitted to spend. A subsequent court decision, however, severely diminished the impact of the law. In 1925 federal campaign finance legislation was codified and revised, though without substantial change, in the Federal Corrupt Practices Act, which remained the basic campaign finance law until 1972.

Each time restrictive laws were passed, politicians devised new methods of raising money. As noted, when the assessment of government employees was prohibited, candidates turned to corporate contributions. When corporations were barred from contributing to federal election campaigns, candidates and parties sought gifts from wealthy individuals, including many corporate stockholders and officers. When the size of contributions to political committees was limited by a second Hatch Act, this one of 1940, in an attempt to restrict the influence of wealthy individuals, parties and politicians found other ways of raising funds.

Candidates also have sought small contributions, but until recently systematic efforts to do so did not meet with notable success. In 1964 Republican presidential candidate Barry Goldwater used mass mail solicitations to raise a substantial portion of his campaign funds. Since then several presidential candidates have used that method with good results, notably Democrat Eugene McCarthy and Independent candidate George Wallace in 1968, Democratic nominee George McGovern in 1972, and Ronald Reagan in his 1984 prenomination campaign.

In the 1970s a new wave of political reform swept both the federal and state campaigning. At the federal level the results of those reform efforts—and of subsequent attempts to ease the burdens the laws imposed on candidates and committees—are embodied in the Federal Election Campaign Act of 1971 (FECA), the Revenue Act of 1971, and the FECA amendments of 1974, 1976, and 1979.

Public Funding

In regard to presidential campaigns, the laws provide for optional public matching funds for qualified candidates in the prenomination period. To qualify for the matching funds, candidates seeking their parties' presidential nominations are required to raise $5,000 in private, individual contributions of $250 or less in at least 20 states. The federal government matches each contribution to qualified candidates up to $250, although the federal subsidies may not exceed half the prenomination campaign spending limit, which was $20.2 million in 1984 and $23.1 million in 1988.

The federal government also provides public funds to pay the costs of the national nominating conventions of the two major political parties. In 1984 each of the parties received a grant of about $8.1 million; a cost-of-living increase raised the grant to $9.2 million in 1988. Minor parties are eligible for a partial convention subsidy if their candidates received more than 5 percent of the vote in the previous presidential election.

In the general election, major party presidential nominees are eligible to receive public treasury grants to fund their campaigns. As noted, those grants amounted to $40.4 million for each candidate of the major parties in 1984. In 1988 the grant to each major party nominee totaled $46.1 million. Provisions also are made for partial public funding of qualified minor party and new party candidates.

The public funds provided in presidential campaigns are intended to supply the money that serious candidates need to present themselves and their ideas to the electorate. They also are meant to diminish or eliminate the need for money that formerly was sought from wealthy donors and interest groups.

In a prenomination campaign, public funding is intended to make the process more competitive and to encourage candidates to broaden their bases of support by seeking out large numbers of relatively small contributions. Candidates do so in a variety of ways, including direct-mail appeals, fundraising events (like re-

ceptions and dinners), and one-on-one solicitation of donations by fundraising volunteers.

The feasibility of public financing in the first four publicly funded presidential campaigns depended on the taxpayers' willingness to earmark a small portion of their tax liabilities—$1 for individuals and $2 for married persons filing jointly—for the Presidential Election Campaign Fund by using the federal income tax checkoff on their tax forms. This procedure provided more than enough funds to cover the $70.9 million certified to 1976 presidential prenomination and general election candidates and to the major parties for their national nominating conventions. It also provided ample funds to cover the $100.6 million certified for the same purposes in 1980, the $133.1 million certified in 1984, and the $177.8 million certified in 1988. Although public acceptance of the program started slowly, it grew as taxpayers became more aware of the checkoff procedure. From 1974 through 1989, the approximate percentage of taxpayers using the checkoff has ranged from 20.1 percent to 28.7 percent. Although the amount earmarked for the fund peaked in 1981 at $41 million, and the percentage of tax returns indicating that money should be earmarked has declined since that year, by March 1986 taxpayers had shown sufficient support for the program to provide a fund balance of more that $136 million, ensuring adequate funds for 1988 payouts to eligible candidates and party committee conventions. Because of declining check-offs, sufficient funds may not be available for full financing of the 1992 presidential campaigns.

Contribution and Expenditure Limits

The 1970s reform laws also imposed contribution and expenditure limits on all federal election campaigns, but the Supreme Court subsequently ruled that spending limits are permissible only in publicly financed campaigns (i.e., only presidential campaigns). Individuals may contribute no more than $1,000 per candidate per election, and multicandidate committees may contribute no more than $5,000 per candidate per election. General election candidates who accept public funding, however, may not accept private contributions to further their campaigns, although they may accept private contributions, up to the limits specified, to help defray the costs of complying with the election laws.

The contribution and expenditure limits are intended to control large donations (with their potential for corruption), to minimize financial disparities among candidates, and to reduce opportunities for abuse. Individuals and groups, however, may make unlimited independent expenditures in presidential and other federal election campaigns—that is, they may spend unlimited amounts on communications advocating the election or defeat of any candidate—so long as the spending takes place without consultation or coordination with any candidate's campaign committee. Substantial sums were spent independently in the 1980 presidential prenomination and general election campaigns, leading some campaign participants to challenge the legality and constitutionality of such spending. A Supreme Court ruling, handed down after the 1984 general election, found in favor of those making independent expenditures. While awaiting the outcome of the legal challenge to their activity, groups and individuals spent $17.4 million independently to advocate the election or defeat of presidential candidates in 1984.

Individuals and groups also may contribute to political party committees at various levels. Those committees in turn may spend money on behalf of their parties' presidential tickets. In 1984 Republican Party and Democratic Party committees spent considerable amounts in support of their presidential tickets for such activities as voter registration and turnout drives. Other notable sources of presidential campaign-related spending were labor organizations, which generally favored the Dukakis-Bentsen ticket by publishing favorable communications and conducting voter registration and turnout drives of their own. Thus, even though public funding and the related expenditure limits are intended to control presidential campaign spending, politicians still find numerous legal ways to spend substantial private funds in an attempt to influence the outcome of general elections.

Finally, federal election law requires full and timely disclosure of campaign receipts and expenditures. The disclosure provisions are meant to help voters make informed choices among candidates and to make it possible to monitor compliance with the campaign finance laws.

A Continuing Experiment

The fundamental problem facing those who would design a system of campaign finance regulation for American election campaigns is how to protect the integrity of the election process and yet respect the rights of free speech and free association guaranteed by the First Amendment to the Constitution. The regulatory system that was put in place in the 1970s represents an enormously ambitious effort to achieve that balance. The effort has not always been successful, as the inability of the regulations to control presidential general election campaign spending indicates. But like American democracy itself, the current system of regulating presidential campaign financing is an experiment that will no doubt be subject to modification in the years to come.

See also: Check-Offs, Federal Election Campaign Act and Amendments, Federal Corrupt Practices Acts, Barry Goldwater, Hatch Acts, John F. Kennedy, Eugene McCarthy, George McGovern, Walter Mondale, Richard M. Nixon, Media and Presidential Campaigns, Revenue Act of 1971, George Wallace

Herbert E. Alexander

REFERENCES

Alexander, Herbert E. 1984. *Financing Politics: Money, Elections, and Political Reform.* 3rd ed. Washington: Congressional Quarterly.

——, and Monica Bauer. 1991. *Financing the 1988 Election.* Boulder, CO: Westview.

——, and Brian A. Haggerty. 1983. *Financing the 1980 Election.* Lexington, MA: Heath.

——. 1983. *Financing Presidential Campaigns: A Report of a Conference of Presidential Finance Officers Sponsored by the Citizens' Research Foundation.* 1987. Los Angeles, CA: Citizens' Research Foundation.

——. 1987. *Financing the 1984 Election.* Lexington, MA: Heath.

Heard, Alexander. 1960. *The Costs of Democracy.* Chapel Hill: U. of North Carolina Pr.

Financing State Campaigns

The United States has more than 8,000 elected state officeholders, and almost every one of them is involved in campaign financing. The variation in modes of funding campaign efforts is enormous, reflecting all manners of idiosyncratic variation in the campaigners' experience or their access to resources, differences in the nature of offices sought (executive, legislative, or judicial) or the level of election (district or statewide). The most efficient means of generalizing across the almost infinite variation in the financing of state campaigns is to turn to state regulations for summaries of the constraints imposed on campaign finance.

Although media attention is usually focused on the consequences of federal election campaign legislation enacted in the 1970s, the decades of the 1970s and the 1980s also witnessed extensive change in the financing of state campaigns. Like the federal law, state legislation was, in part, a response to the impact of new technologies, changing patterns of campaign contributions and expenditures, skyrocketing costs of campaigns, and scandals in campaign financing.

Similarities abound in the way states have attempted to address issues of money and campaign politics. For example, every state identifies a particular agency responsible for oversight of campaign finance and requires both some form of registration and some financial reporting by candidates or candidate committees. Yet no two states have the same regulations or identical administrative and enforcement procedures for campaign financing. This variation in type, scope, and nature of state regulation of campaign financing underscores the vitality of federalism in the United States, but it also creates obstacles to generalizing about state-level campaign financing.

State laws differ widely about the identity of those required to report campaign finance activity. For example, in Vermont only statewide candidates or committees, state and local political parties and political action committees (PACs) are subject to extensive regulation. In California, on the other hand, all statewide, legislative, multicounty, single county, and municipal candidates as well as state and local parties, PACs, politically active corporations and labor unions, independent expenditure committees, and major donors must register and report campaign finance activities.

States also vary in their thresholds for reporting contributions as well as expenditures, both in terms of what triggers the reporting requirement and the amount that must be reported. For example, in Connecticut, Idaho, and Louisiana any committee that collects or spends over $500 must file a report; contrarily, the threshold in Rhode Island is $5,000. In Florida, *all* contributions to registered committees must be reported; in Michigan, only contributions in excess of $20 are reported; in Nevada, only individual contributions in excess of $500 must be reported. Similarly, all expenditures must be reported in Alaska, but in Mississippi only expenditures in excess of $250 are subject to disclosure.

States also differ in the kinds of contributions they prohibit or restrict. Almost two-thirds of the states prohibit anonymous gifts and gifts in the name of another; 20 states prohibit direct corporate contributions and/or contributions by state-regulated industries; and 10 states prohibit direct contributions from unions. Iowa, Louisiana, and New Jersey go so far as to prohibit contributions from specified governmental employees; North Carolina and Wisconsin restrict contributions from registered lobbyists. Twenty states set specific limits on how much any individual can contribute to political candidates and committees, restrictions ranging from an aggregate election year contribution limit of $2,000 per individual in Arizona to limits on contributions to individual candidates that range as high as $60,000 per contributor for gubernatorial races in Minnesota. Twenty states limit what PACs can contribute, and ten even restrict how much political parties can contribute to political candidates.

Just as the scope of regulation varies across states, so too do states differ in administrative arrangements and enforcement procedures. For example, 28 states have assigned oversight of campaign finance to established agencies such as the Board of Elections or the Office of the Secretary of State. Since 1969, however, twenty-two states have established special agencies that are assigned to deal solely with one or more of the four major categories of campaign finance-related activities—reporting and disclosure, public ethics, personal financial disclosure, and lobbying regulation. However, in only eight states is oversight of all four of these important dimensions of money in politics placed under a single, independent agency. In all other states, regulatory authority is fragmented.

A few of these independent agencies have extensive investigative and prosecutorial powers, but most are dependent on other (usually elected) governmental offices for formal investigations and sanctions. Thirty-nine states routinely perform desk audits of all campaign finance reports, others conduct desk and field audits on randomly selected reports, while still other agencies review campaign finance reports only after a complaint has been lodged. The record of campaign finance enforcement, prosecutions, and convictions—not surprisingly—varies widely across states; generally, however, states with strong independent administrative agencies have been most diligent in policing the role of money in campaigns.

One consequence of state variation in reporting regulations is variation in the data that are available for analysis of state campaign financing. The number of financial reports a state agency processes in any election year may vary from fewer than 500 to more than 50,000, depending on the particular requirements of state law. Similarly, the level of detail and the comprehensive nature of the picture that the data provide differ from state to state. Moreover, no central repository (comparable to the Federal Election Commission's public information center) collects and disseminates state-level data. Consequently, even though all federal candidates do use a single FEC reporting form and a single set of reporting rules, no common reporting forms or conventions are employed uniformly across the 50 states.

State agencies differ as well in the extent to which they process and publicize campaign finance data. Only half of the states aggregate campaign finance data and produce summary reports that are readily available in printed form. Analysts, therefore, find it difficult to collect and analyze comparative state-level campaign finance information in a way that leads to broad generalizations about state-level campaign financing. Disparate data sources notwithstanding, the issues of campaign finance that states seek to address are indeed comparable across states. Thus, we can identify general trends (though not in exhaustively documentable patterns) of campaign finance activity in the states in terms of costs of campaigns, sources of funding, and problem areas of growing concern to those interested in the financing of election campaigns for state office.

Costs. Traditionally, state-level campaigns were grass-roots, friends-and-neighbors activities. However, modern technology brought direct mail, voter surveys, computer generated databases, WATS telephone banks, and television advertising to state as well as federal election campaigns. The net result, in both instances, has been rapid increases in cost and concomitant needs to raise and spend more money.

Compared to presidential and senatorial campaigns, the costs of individual state level races are not especially impressive. However, compared to the history of state campaign expenditures and the deep-rooted traditions of local electoral activity, the rapid rate of increase—as well as the absolute dollar amounts involved in state campaigns—now demands serious attention. For example, the average cost of a seat in the California legislature increased 4,000 percent in less than 30 years; by 1986 the total amount spent for California legislative campaigns was $57 million. These cost increases,

moreover, are not limited to large states with growing populations. In 1987, in excess of $11 million was spent on New Jersey legislative races, double the amount spent just four years earlier. Between 1974 and 1986, spending on winning a single seat in the Arizona legislature increased 770 percent. In 1983 a Virginia state senate candidate set a state record by spending over $100,000; by 1987, $100,000 was close to the norm in Virginia for spending in contested senate campaigns, and the new Virginia spending record became $600,000 for a single state senate campaign.

Increased costs are even more noticeable at the executive level. In large states such as Texas, California, and New York, total campaign expenditures for the office of governor exceed $25 million to $30 million and individual candidates routinely spend $8 million to $12 million. Even in more sparsely populated states such as Maine and Kansas, total costs of $5 million to $8 million for gubernatorial campaigns are not unusual.

Obviously, campaign expenditures vary widely within as well as among states, but common patterns of state-level expenditures, not unlike those of federal elections, do exist: costs have risen at a rate greater than inflation; costs have increased for both primary and general election campaigns for all state offices; levels of expenditure are related to incumbency and competitiveness; and finally, increased costs have created greater emphasis on money in state campaigns. Emphasis on money in campaigns has been accompanied by increased awareness of the tension generated by an electoral campaign process based on openness, equity, and meaningful choices versus broad-based citizen participation that is at present dominated by highly sophisticated and expensive campaign technology.

Sources. As candidates and party activists recognize the growing importance of campaign financing, fundraising has become central to all campaigns. It remains true that the single greatest source of funds for most state political campaigns is individual members of each state's electorate. Although mass-mail and phone solicitation have become widely used techniques for political fundraising, less than 4 percent of all eligible voters respond to such appeals. Thus, the competition for funds becomes more rigorous as costs increase. The profile of campaign contributors emerging from state-level case studies suggests that contributors tend to be political activists who have clear partisan and ideological preferences; they are middle-aged and relatively wealthy, well-educated and occupationally "powerful"; and they are psychologically predisposed to pay attention to and care about government and politics.

Analyses of contribution records suggest that direct support from individual contributors is the principle source of funds for primary candidates, challengers, and those who run in open-seat races. The central role of the individual contributor is being challenged in state after state, however, as increasing proportions of candidates' funds are provided by political action committees (PACs). Except for some labor union political education activities, PACs were relatively unknown in state politics until the 1970s. By the mid-1980s, PACs were so prominent in legislative campaign financing that one report concluded that the individual citizen who gave a small contribution to his candidate for state legislature was an anachronism, if not an endangered species, in California politics.

In 1988 many state officeholders, like their federal counterparts, received the bulk of their funding from political action committees and—where permitted by state law—corporations, unions, and other special interests. In these states, direct contributions from special interest sources are usually directed to gubernatorial and statewide races while their PAC counterparts target state legislative races. The centrality of PAC contributions to legislative (especially incumbent) campaigns has been widely documented throughout many of the 50 states. In New York, for example, 45 percent to 50 percent of the direct contributions received by state legislative candidates comes from PACs; almost 60 percent of the contributions of general election candidates for the California General Assembly comes from PACs and from special interest groups.

In 1986 more than one-third of Arizona's state senators received more money from PACs alone than they spent on their entire campaigns. PACs have become highly involved in state politics and now compete among themselves for the favor of would-be officeholders. Consequently, PACs are increasingly involved in highly competitive races—especially those involving open seats—and are gradually extending their activity to primary campaigns as a means of solidifying their prominence in the full range of state campaign finance.

Moreover, as state PACs become institutionalized, they are viewed as silent partners of legislative leadership. For example, in his role of legislative party leader, the Speaker of the California General Assembly alone received in excess of $1 million from special interest contributions in a single general election campaign. In the year before the 1988 campaigns, the four party leaders in the Illinois General Assembly received almost $1.5 million in contributions, two-thirds of which came from clearly identifiable special interest groups. The dominance of PAC money in the coffers of partisan leaders raises questions about the autonomy and independence not only of the individuals involved but also of the party they represent.

The involvement of state political party organizations in the financing of political campaigns varies widely from state to state according to the general strength of the party infrastructure, the competitiveness of partisan campaigns, local traditions and party norms, and, of course, the extent of state regulation of party activities and campaign finance. However, the decade of the 1980s witnessed a growing sophistication in partisan state-level campaign financing. Although variations in partisan financing underscore the federated nature of the American party system, attention only to the circumstances of individual state parties overlooks important changes that have implications for partisan politics in all states.

Efforts at the federal level during the 1980s to deregulate public policies and to enhance policymaking the states refocused political interest on state government and thus heightened awareness of the importance of state-level electoral politics. For political parties, the primary impetus for change was a 1979 amendment to the Federal Election Campaign Act (FECA) permitting national party organizations to use their resources to infuse new life into state party organizations as well as partisan election activities. The FECA supported direct allocation of funds for state party-building activities. It also paved the way for national party organizations to enter into agency agreements with the state parties and provide coordinated expenditures for federal candidates in each state. These changes brought to the states not only national party money but also technical expertise and sophistication in the raising and spending of campaign funds. Whether, in the long-run, campaign financing turns out to be the principal vehicle for nationalizing political parties or institutionalizing state party organizations remains to be seen. In the heyday of political machines, most campaign funds were raised by party leaders on behalf of the party's candidates. Analyses of records of direct contributions to candidates reveal that parties are generally the weakest link in the campaign financing chain, often providing less than 1 percent and rarely more than 25 percent of any state candidate's total campaign funds.

However, a very different picture of the role of parties is revealed with attention to indirect contributions and to the in-kind services that state parties provide. Benefiting from the economies of scale, many party activities (voter registration, get-out-the-vote drives, polling, direct mailings, absentee ballot facilitation) aid *all* candidates on the ticket as well as the party organization itself. Moreover, state party leaders have also developed sophisticated strategies for allocating funds and for targeting races where additional resources can be expected to have the greatest impact, usually open-seat and highly competitive campaigns. As state political parties approach the twenty-first century, their future is far from certain. However, national trends in the financing of campaigns would suggest that partisan involvement in state-level campaigns is likely to increase. With such involvement lies the potential to reactivate state political parties for important, but different, roles in state electoral politics.

One recent policy development influencing the campaign financing activities of state political parties has been the enactment of state-level public funding programs. By 1988, 22 states had in place some form of publicly supported subsidy program for election campaigns. The most popular programs provide for a single dollar "check-off" on the state income tax form that allocates tax money to political parties or to individual candidates. About the same number of states operate more or less ineffectual "add-on" programs in which the state uses the tax form to collect voluntary contributions (but not tax dollars) to subsidize election campaigns.

Some state programs—in New Jersey and Michigan for example—are modeled after the Presidential Election Campaign Fund and provide check-off dollars to individual candidates in both the primary and general election. Other check-off programs involve taxpayer designations by which funds are made available to the state party organizations or—as in the case of Oregon and Kentucky—both state and county party organizations. Yet other states (Minnesota

and Rhode Island) have unique public funding systems that allocate check-off dollars both to parties *and* to candidates. Taxpayer participation varies from less than 1 percent in some of the add-on states to as high as 40 percent in check-off states. The check-off programs clearly generate more funds than do add-on programs, and taxpayer participation seems to be higher in candidate- rather than party-oriented programs (although generalizations are tenuous because of differences among the programs).

Notwithstanding voter surveys that seldom reveal majority popular support for the concept of public funding, the use of tax subsidies is viewed as a useful policy option because, in the *Buckley v. Valeo* decision, the U.S. Supreme Court ruled that campaign expenditure limits were unconstitutional unless public money was involved. Therefore, when confronted with the choice of partial public funding *with* spending limits as opposed to uncontrolled spending of private and special interest funds, most citizens as well as state policymakers have reluctantly turned to public financing programs. In all cases, use of public funds is voluntary and neither candidates, parties, nor taxpayers are forced to participate in such programs. However, the general rule has been that once the option of public funding and expenditure controls has become public policy, the majority of eligible candidates and parties participate (even candidates who could raise great sums in private funds or parties that philosophically oppose public subsidies).

The add-on programs are primarily tokenism because no add-on program has generated enough funding to make an impact on campaigns. Many check-off programs, however, have been well received and are viewed as having made a real difference in campaign financing. Generally, strong public funding programs expand the contributor base of electoral financing because people who do not otherwise give to political campaigns do participate in state check-off programs. Moreover, when candidates and parties accept public funds, they agree to specific regulations for the administration (collection, reporting, disclosing, and expenditure) of funds—regulations that are more stringent than would exist otherwise. When candidates receive funds directly, they reduce the burdens of fundraising, know what the expenditure limits are, and can plan a rational campaign strategy. When parties are the recipients of funds, they are as likely to use them for party-building activities (headquarters rent and staff salaries, voter registration, direct-mail fundraising) as for in-kind and direct contributions to candidates. Even when funds are allocated directly to candidates, parties realize an indirect benefit because the party organization is freed from additional, competitive fundraising activities.

Although both check-off and add-on systems slowly continue to be adopted, several states (i.e., Montana, Maryland, Oregon) have radically modified or abandoned existing check-off or add-on systems. All proposals for public subsidy programs give rise to heated partisan, often ideological, debate. Such debate pits concerns about rising campaign costs, equity among candidates, and fairness in election competition against antagonism to expanded governmental regulation and governmental intrusion in the electoral process. Opposition also involves concerns for individualism and free enterprise. These more abstract issues, however, are considered within realistic political contexts that frequently include an advantage for one party (or faction within a party) over another. Still, as long as the constraints imposed by *Buckley* remain in force, public campaign financing will remain a successful policy alternative for state political campaigns.

Ballot-Issue Campaigns. The financing of state-level "ballot-issue" campaigns provides an arena of state election funding that has no parallel at the federal level. The decade of the 1980s witnessed a resurgence of the use of ballot initiatives for state policymaking. Half of the states permit ballot initiatives and referenda, and more than 250 ballot issues were referred to the voters on the November 1988 ballots. California alone presented voters with 29 ballot measures. Political parties seldom get directly involved in ballot-issue campaigns. The major exceptions are when election-process issues, redistricting, or the selection or authority of public officials are involved. Nevertheless, parties are indirectly affected by the competition that ballot-issue campaigns create for campaign finance, media coverage, leadership, and citizen involvement and voter support.

Ballot-issue campaigns can be very expensive. In 1984 more money was spent on a Missouri nuclear power issue than was spent on all the campaigns in the state for statewide offices and state legislative seats combined. The cost of just five California insurance related initiatives in 1988 was almost three times the $25 million

spent in that state's very competitive 1986 U.S. Senate battle.

The sources of money for initiative campaigns are generally quite different from partisan, candidate-centered races. Whereas state regulations of candidate campaigns may limit the amount of money any contributor can give, may prohibit certain "interests" from any financial involvement in election campaigns, or require that sources of campaign funds be disclosed, such restrictions usually do not apply to ballot-issue campaigns. The U.S. Supreme Court has rejected state efforts to limit either contributions or expenditures for ballot propositions. Although agreeing that in election campaigning "money is speech," the Court has reasoned that a rationale for restricting contributions in candidate campaigns (and thereby limiting freedom of speech) is provided by the potential for or the appearance of corrupting influences that contributions pose for individual candidates. No candidates are potentially vulnerable to corruption in ballot-issue campaigns. Thus, in the *First National Bank of Boston v. Bellotti* decision, the Court found no compelling reason to place limits on participation in the financing of ballot-issue campaigns.

Not surprisingly, then, the vast bulk of funding for particular ballot-issue campaigns comes from the industry or industries most likely to be affected (positively or negatively) by the ballot initiatives. Ballot-issue financing comes largely from the coffers of corporate, trade association, labor, and public interest groups either directly, through independent expenditures, or from PAC contributions—often from out of state—as well as from a very few large, individual contributions. Whenever campaigns for bottle bills (calling for deposits on beverage containers coupled with recycling programs) have been waged, the glass and beverage industries have provided 80 percent to 90 percent of the financing for the opposition. Opposition to ballot initiatives related to limits on nuclear power development have been funded almost exclusively by utilities. Ballot issues aimed at tort reform to limit damage awards have pitted trial lawyers against the insurance industry. This kind of campaign, in which two well-financed interests are in competition, often produces extremely expensive contests. A prime example was a 1986 California battle in which trial lawyers spent almost $5 million only to be defeated by the insurance industry, which spent $6 million.

During the post-Watergate reform era, little attention was given to ballot-issue campaigns. However, beginning with the successful 1978 property-tax reduction measure (Proposition 13) in California, the number and costs of ballot-issue campaigns nationwide have increased rapidly, raising important questions about this dimension of state electoral processes. Ballot initiatives were originally adopted (in 1902) to provide an alternative means of influencing public policy by citizens who felt thwarted by established policymaking procedures. Recent ballot-issue campaigns have generated increasing fears that this grass-roots alternative has become perverted in three discernable ways. First, well-funded special interests use the ballot-issue process to bypass duly elected legislative and executive institutions and wage expensive high-tech and media campaigns to win approval for their "legislative interest."

Second, increasing evidence shows that large proportions of the money used to finance ballot campaigns comes from out of state. For example, in the successful Arizona "Official English" campaign in 1988—a campaign requiring that all official state business and documents be only in English—98 percent of the over $300,000 campaign to support official English came from a group called U.S. English, based in Washington, D.C.; opponents raised only half that amount, most of it from in-state contributions.

Finally, special interests that have been successful in protecting their advantages by using the established policymaking procedures are subject to opposition by citizen-sponsored initiatives. The organized interest groups then use vast financial resources to overwhelm the voting public with well-orchestrated campaigns and thereby co-opt the ballot-initiative process to their advantage. Voters, faced with slick, heavily financed campaigns that create a confusing, often conflictual or negative atmosphere, tend to vote against any change, thereby supporting the status quo and indirectly providing greater immunity from future policy change for the special interest.

The electoral advantage does not *always* go to the best funded campaign; very popular issues can overcome even the most well-financed opposition (i.e., toxic waste regulation). Also true is the routine nature of many ballot issues; they are noncontroversial measures, often issues referred by the legislature for approval or constitutionally mandated voter approval measures (i.e., striking gender-biased language from a state constitution).

Research on the impact of spending on ballot success is often based on cross-sectional analyses within a limited time or within single states, and such research frequently produces what appear to be conflicting conclusions. (Similarly, research that treats all ballot issues, referenda, controversial and noncontroversial measures the same often differs in its conclusions from research based only on competitive, highly financed, or highly charged controversial issues.) Analysts generally agree, however, that there are three types of campaigns—low interest, low spending; controversial, highly competitive spending; and controversial, one-sided spending campaigns. While vote outcome in low-spending campaigns is probably not dependent on campaign spending, in the other two kinds of campaigns, spending frequently is related to both voter turnout and voter preferences.

Political parties and elected officials have long been the mainstay of the policymaking process and important components of a political system designed to control the divisive effects of factions. In many ways, the ballot-issue process, intended to involve more citizens, has been stood on its democratic head, becoming a means whereby special interests can thwart the will of political parties, elected officials, and grass-roots citizen efforts. And to the extent that ballot-issue elections are an alternative to the established policymaking procedures, they are competitors not only for campaign resources and citizen involvement, but they also compete with political parties and elected officials for institutional legitimacy in the policymaking process. The ability of some special interests to finance consultant-choreographed media and mass-mail campaigns has called into question the basic premise underlying citizen initiatives and ballot-issue legislation.

Unresolved Issues. Obviously, each state has a unique electoral context within which the issues associated with the financing of state elections are addressed. However, the problems are really quite similar in many states, even when the scope and saliency of any particular issue at a particular time varies considerably across the 50 states. For example, as it becomes more common for PACs and special interest groups to surpass both individual contributors and the political parties as major sources of campaign financing,

PAC activities receive increasingly closer scrutiny.

Observers express growing concern about the relationship of PAC contributions to votes on public policy, that concern generated by the abundant resources and organizational capacities available to PACs for repeatedly making generous contributions to individual policymakers. Moreover, as incumbents are increasingly able to raise very large campaign war chests, primarily from special interests and PACs, evidence mounts that fewer incumbents are defeated and that elections are becoming less competitive.

States have taken different approaches to dealing with the real and perceived problems associated with the dominance of contributions from special interests. Some states, such as Arkansas, have emphasized public disclosure, even to the point of requiring lobbyists to reveal *all* expenditures. Many have sought to limit contributions: for example, Massachusetts limits PAC contributions to $1,000 per candidate; Arizona goes even further and restricts the total amount that any legislative candidate can receive from all PACs to $5,000 per election; Oregon, Texas, and Wisconsin prohibit contributions by lobbyists during the legislative session, while several other states restrict or prohibit officials and their employees from seeking contributions from lobbyists; and several states have even introduced, but not yet passed, legislation to limit contributions from out-of-state or out-of-district PACs.

The states are also beginning to address the issue of independent expenditures. As contribution limits have been imposed, many interest groups have turned to spending unrestricted amounts on behalf of a candidate totally independent of the candidate's campaign committee's activities. Under present U.S. Supreme Court interpretations, however, it is unconstitutional to restrict the amount that any single individual or group can spend independently. Therefore, states have been limited to requiring full disclosure of the sources of funds for independent spending and demanding visible disclaimers and identification on all independent advertising. Given the nature of some independent expenditure campaigns, politicians have even speculated about "remedies" for candidates who have been targets of negative campaigning funded by independent expenditures.

States have also been resourceful in setting boundaries for campaign loans, a frequent ploy in past years to funnel money into campaigns. Similarly, states such as Kentucky have begun to set guidelines for campaign debt retirement by elected public officials and to prescribe narrow uses for excess campaign funds. Other states, such as California, have taken the lead in seeking ways to limit the transfer of campaign funds among legislators, especially members of the legislative leadership.

In recent years, the legislatures in states as diverse as Illinois, California, and Iowa have passed public campaign financing legislation only to encounter a gubernatorial veto. Yet these states are representative of many that are looking for ways to provide a level playing field for competitive elections and to control the spiraling costs of campaigns. Because some states have been particularly innovative in designing public subsidy programs, forms of public financing will likely continue to appeal to those interested in campaign finance reform. In 1988, when the West Virginia legislature refused to enact public financing, the secretary of state called for candidates to agree to voluntary spending limits; some 75 percent of the candidates for the state legislature agreed by signing the "code of fair campaign practices."

Across all states, more and more attention is obviously being given to the administration and enforcement of campaign finance regulations. In some cases this regulation means providing greater autonomy and more prosecutorial powers to an agency; in others it means clarifying the laws and tightening the loopholes. Increasingly, a state's top political leaders are advocating greater attention to the regulation of state campaign financing. New York's Governor Mario Cuomo created the prestigious, independent Commission on Government Integrity, which became the focal point for massive campaign finance reform in New York. In other states, such as Louisiana, the governor cajoled and prodded until the legislature passed a rigorous campaign finance bill. Governor Bill Clinton was not as successful in motivating the Arkansas legislature, but he then supported an initiative petition that led to the restructuring of campaign finance in Arkansas. Thus, as the twentieth century closes, financing of state-level election campaigns continues to be part of the political agenda of almost every state. If the past is any predictor of the future, the expectation must be that states will continue to seek creative and meaningful solutions to problems associated with the financing of state campaign politics.

See also: *First National Bank of Boston v. Bellotti, Buckley v. Valeo*, Check-Offs, Direct Mail, Federal Election Campaign Act and Amendments, Federal Election Commission, Political Action Committees

Ruth S. Jones

REFERENCES

California Commission on Campaign Financing. 1985. *The New Gold Rush: Financing California's Legislative Campaigns*. Los Angeles, CA: Center for Responsive Government.

Commission on Government Integrity. 1988. *The Albany Money Machine: Campaign Financing for New York State Legislative Races*. New York City: State of New York.

Council on Governmental Ethics Laws. 1988. *Campaign Finance, Ethics and Lobby Law: Blue Book 1988–89*. Lexington, KY: Council of State Governments.

Jones, Ruth S. 1984. "Financing State Elections." In Michael J. Malbin, ed. *Money and Politics in the United States: Financing Elections in the 1980s*. Washington, DC: American Enterprise Institute.

Magleby, David B. 1984. *Direct Legislation: Voting on Ballot Propositions in the United States*. Baltimore: Johns Hopkins U. Pr.

Michaelson, Ronald D. 1988. *Campaign Finance Update: Legislation and Litigation*. Presentation at the Council on Governmental Ethics Laws Conference, Orlando, Florida. December.

Sorauf, Frank J. 1988. *Money in American Elections*. Glenview, IL: Scott, Foresman.

First Bank of the United States

As part of his program to strengthen the federal government and to establish national credit, in late 1790 Alexander Hamilton proposed a bank to become the government's fiscal agent, to collect taxes, to issue money, and to lend funds. During debate in Congress, James Madison questioned the bank's constitutionality because delegates at the Constitutional Convention had refused to grant Congress the power to issue charters of incorporation. Madison feared that the bank would provide a precedent that would eliminate barriers to federal action and infringe on state powers. He argued that the bank was not necessary to collect taxes or issue money and that it would merely be more convenient.

President George Washington then asked Cabinet members for opinions about the bank's constitutionality. Secretary of State Thomas Jefferson argued for "strict construction," stating that incorporation was not a delegated power and that Congress could use only those means to carry out a delegated power essential to exercising that power. Hamilton proposed "loose construction," saying that the federal government had a right to use any means suitable to implement delegated powers. In February 1791, Washington signed the bank bill.

The bill had passed Congress with only one northerner opposed and three southerners in favor, and it was among the main contributors to the formation of Jeffersonian and Hamiltonian factions. Hamilton tended to equate opposition to his policies with subversion of the public credit and the federal government, while Jefferson and Madison were convinced that Hamilton and the Federalists wished to make the federal government so strong as to be independent of the people.

See also: Federalist Party, Alexander Hamilton, Thomas Jefferson, James Madison, George Washington

Sue C. Patrick

REFERENCES

Buel, Richard, Jr. 1972. *Securing the Revolution: Ideology in American Politics, 1789–1815*. Ithaca: Cornell U. Pr.

Cunningham, Noble E., Jr. 1957. *The Jeffersonian Republicans: The Formation of Party Organization, 1789–1801*. Chapel Hill: U. of North Carolina Pr.

Hammond, Bray. 1957. *Banks and Politics in America from the Revolution to the Civil War*. Princeton: Princeton U. Pr.

Hoadley, John F. 1959. *Origins of American Political Parties, 1789–1803*. Lexington: U. Pr. of Kentucky.

Miller, John C. 1959. *Alexander Hamilton and the Growth of the New Nation*. New York: Harper & Row.

———. 1960. *The Federalist Era, 1789–1801*. New York: Harper.

Peterson, Merrill D. 1970. *Thomas Jefferson and the New Nation: A Biography*. New York: Oxford U. Pr.

First National Bank of Boston v. Bellotti
435 U.S. 765 (1978)

In a 5-to-4 Supreme Court decision written by Justice Lewis Powell, this case held that "[t]he inherent worth of the speech in terms of its capacity for informing the public does not depend upon the identity of its source, whether corporation, association, union or individual" (435 U.S. 765, 777). Specifically, it declared unconstitutional a state statute prohibiting corporate expenditures in referenda. Expenditure of money is usually seen as speech in this context (see *Buckley v. Valeo*).

A Massachusetts statute forbade corporations from making contributions or expenditures for the purpose of "influencing or affecting the vote on any question submitted to the voters, other than one materially affecting any of the property, business or assets of the corporation." The statute included a statement that "no question submitted to the voters solely concerning the taxation of the income, property, or transactions of individuals shall be deemed materially to affect the property, business or assets of the corporation." At issue was a referendum proposal to amend the Massachusetts Constitution to authorize the legislature to enact a graduated personal income tax. Several corporations opposed the proposal but were prohibited by the statute from spending money to publicize their views.

Justice Powell noted that the Court did not have to examine in this case the "outer boundaries" of First Amendment protection of corporate speech or "the abstract question whether corporations have the full measure of rights that individuals enjoy under the First Amendment." The Court reasoned that the speech here was at the core of First Amendment values because it concerned public affairs and governing. For a state to restrict such speech, it must prove a compelling subordinating interest. The state claimed an interest in preservation of an individual's confidence in government, one that might be eroded by the ability of corporations, with their vast wealth, to bring undue influence on elections. If, Justice Powell reasoned, legislative findings did support this premise, then "these arguments would merit our consideration," but he found no such evidence in Massachusetts. Powell distinguished the potential for corruption in the financing of candidates from a popular vote on a public issue. Corporate ads may persuade the electorate, but persuasion is the purpose of such speech. The Court also rejected the state's claimed interest in protecting the corporate shareholders.

Justice Byron White, joined by Justices William Brennan and Thurgood Marshall, saw *Bellotti* as a case of competing First Amendment values that had to be balanced. He felt that the Massachusetts legislature had balanced them properly. Justice William Rehnquist filed a separate dissent, arguing that corporations do not have the same constitutional protections in political activity that individuals do.

See also: Buckley v. Valeo

H. W. Perry, Jr.

Hamilton Fish (1888–1991)

Conservative Republican Congressman from New York. Hamilton Fish represents the third of four generations elected on the Republican ticket to serve in the U.S. House of Representatives from New York. Fish, a conservative Republican, served in the New York State Legislature from 1914 to 1916 before he began his 25 years in Congress.

During his tenure in the House, Fish was an outspoken opponent of President Franklin Roosevelt's New Deal and a vocal isolationist. Before the Japanese bombing of Pearl Harbor, Fish voted against lend-lease, sought to limit the production of planes and airplane carriers, and opposed implementation of the draft.

By the time of his 1944 reelection bid, Hamilton Fish had lost support from many Republicans who actively sought his defeat in the Republican primary. His opponents claimed that he was unfit and had not upheld principles of the Republican National Committee, which would compel him to work toward preserving freedom and integrity. President Roosevelt, whose residence of Hyde Park made him a constituent of Fish, campaigned actively against him. While Fish did win the Republican primary, he lost in the general election, 25 years after he had first come to Congress.

In 1952 Fish announced his candidacy for the U.S. Senate, this time seeking office as a third-party candidate. Fish described the Constitutional Party on whose ticket he ran as being based upon the "Taft–MacArthur–Hoover–Byrd–Al Smith principles."

Hamilton Fish has been married four times; his most recent marriage took place when he was 99 years old. Fish has remained outspoken into his eleventh decade. In 1988 he actively opposed his grandson and namesake who was defeated in the Democratic primary in a bid for a congressional seat. The elder Hamilton Fish disapproved not only of his grandson's affiliation with the Democratic Party but also of his liberal stands.

See also: Isolationism in the United States, Republican National Committee, Franklin D. Roosevelt

Reagan Robbins

REFERENCES

Alsop, Joseph, and Robert Kintner. 1940. "Activities of His Press Boosters Call for Explanation from Mr. Fish." *Washington Post.*

———. 1989. *Biographical Directory of the United States Congress 1774–1989.* Washington, DC: U.S. Government Printing Office.

Block, Maxine, ed. 1941. *Current Biography Who's News and Why 1941.* New York: H. W. Wilson.

———. 1944. "Defeat Ends Fish's 24-Year Career as Member of House." *Washington Star.*

———. 1967. "Ex-Rep. Fish Marries Russian Born Widow." *Washington Post.*

Ferson, James. 1942. "Fish Denies He Got Fee from Trujillo." *New York Times.*

———. 1952. "Hamilton Fish Out For a Senate Seat." *New York Herald Tribune.*

———. 1987. "Upheaval in the Fish Political Dynasty." *New York Times.*

Pace, Eric. 1942. "Republicans Urge Retirement of Fish." *New York Times.*

———. 1988. "At 100, There's Plenty of Kick in Former Rep. Hamilton Fish." *New York Times.*

John F. Fitzgerald (1863–1950)

Boston Democratic mayor and political boss. The career of John Francis Fitzgerald celebrated the emancipation of Boston's Irish Catholics from the politics of deference toward the city's Yankee elite. Born in a North End tenement in Boston, the son of a prospering fish peddler, Fitzgerald turned from Harvard medical training to North End politics when his father died in 1885. His ascent was swift. After brief service at the Boston Customs House, he won successive elections to the city council (1890), the state senate (1892), and the U.S. Congress (1894 and 1896). His congressional victories, aided by West End ward boss Martin Lomasney, made Fitzgerald the only Democratic member of the House from New England. He exploited close ties with his church, a broad network of hustling young followers, and a flair for campaign pageantry to fuel his rise. Urban playgrounds, protective labor legislation, opposition to immigration restriction, and jobs for friends dominated his political agenda. Acquisition of *The Republic*, a weekly newspaper formerly owned by party leader Patrick Maguire, improved his income and his audience in the city's growing ethnic middle class. Election to city hall in 1905 made him Boston's third Irish Catholic mayor (Hugh O'Brien and Patrick Collins having preceded him) and the first to impose a decisive if fractious Irish-American hegemony on the city's politics. "Honey Fitz" used intense public relations tactics—including motorcades, photographs, and sentimental song solos—to floodlight his presence and to boom Boston. But careless patronage, franchise, and spending policies stained him in the eyes of Boston's Good Government Association. After a searching public investigation of his administration, he suffered his first electoral defeat in 1907. Two years later, however, after a mayoral campaign involving lots of money, slander, and ethnic insults, he unexpectedly trounced Yankee reformer James J. Storrow. His second term at city hall, like the first, was gaudy, energetic, and riven by Irish factional combat. James Michael Curley's insinuations about Honey Fitz's private life discouraged another run, and Curley replaced him as mayor in 1915. Unsuccessful in several subsequent election tries, Fitzgerald lived to watch a grandson, John F. Kennedy, launch his own political ascent.

See also: Edward M. Kennedy, John F. Kennedy, Robert F. Kennedy, Martin Lomasney

Geoffrey Blodgett

REFERENCES

Abrams, Richard M. 1964. *Conservatism in a Progressive Era: Massachusetts Politics, 1900–1912.* Cambridge: Harvard U. Pr.

Blodgett, Geoffrey. 1966. *The Gentle Reformers: Massachusetts Democrats in the Cleveland Era.* Cambridge: Harvard U. Pr.

Cutler, John Henry. 1962. *"Honey Fitz": Three Steps to the White House: The Life and Times of John F. (Honey Fitz) Fitzgerald.* Indianapolis: Bobbs-Merrill.

Goodwin, Doris Kearns. 1987. *The Fitzgeralds and the Kennedys.* New York: Simon & Schuster.

Woods, Robert A. 1902. *Americans in Process, A Settlement Study: North and West Ends, Boston.* Boston: Houghton Mifflin.

Benjamin Fitzpatrick (1802–1869)

Antebellum Alabama Democrat. Benjamin Fitzpatrick, a wealthy planter and staunch Jacksonian Democrat, headed the Montgomery Regency faction that dominated Alabama politics in the two decades before the Civil War. This group—drawing its strength from patronage, close family connections, and disciplined party loyalty—twice secured Benjamin Fitzpatrick's election as governor (1841–1845) and his appointment and subsequent election to the United States Senate (1848, 1853–1861). In Washington he was a moderate who supported southern rights but gave full loyalty and confidence to the national Democratic Party. He was President *pro tempore* of the Senate from 1857 to 1860 and was widely liked and respected without being one of the inner circle of Democratic Senate bosses. By 1859 he was increasingly challenged in Alabama by William Yancey's fire-eaters, who claimed he had betrayed southern interests. The Regency was able to defeat Yancey's bid for Fitzpatrick's Senate seat but lost control of the state convention and delegation to the National Democratic Convention of Charleston in 1860. Its delegates chose Fitzpatrick to be Stephen Douglas's vice presidential running mate, but intense pressure from

Senate colleagues and his wife as well as his own dislike of Douglas's squatter sovereignty platform eventually persuaded him to withdraw. He grudgingly supported John Breckinridge for President and futilely tried to delay the secession of Alabama. He was by then supplanted by Yancey as the major figure in Alabama politics and took no part in Confederate affairs. In 1865 he presided over the state's constitutional convention but was soon defranchised by Reconstruction legislation.

See also: John Breckinridge, Stephen Douglas, Jacksonian Democracy, Reconstruction, Secession

Harold B. Raymond

REFERENCES

Barney, William L. 1974. *The Secessionist Impulse: Alabama and Mississippi, 1860.* Princeton: Princeton U. Pr.

Milton, George Fort. 1934. *The Eve of Conflict: Stephen Douglas and the Needless War.* Boston: Houghton Mifflin.

Thornton, J. Mills. 1978. *Politics and Power in a Slave Society.* Baton Rouge: Louisiana State U. Pr.

Peter F. Flaherty (1925–)

Democratic reform mayor of Pittsburgh. A champion of urban government reform, Peter Francis Flaherty served as mayor of Pittsburgh, Pennsylvania, from 1970 to 1977. Flaherty received a law degree from Notre Dame and an M.P.A. from the University of Pittsburgh. From 1957 to 1964 he was an assistant district attorney for Allegheny County, which includes Pittsburgh. With the support of David Lawrence, Flaherty successfully ran for the Pittsburgh City Council, a seat he held from 1966 to 1969. He established himself as a councilman beyond the control of the Democratic machine. In 1969 Flaherty ran as a reform candidate for mayor, defeating the Democratic machine's candidate, Richard Caliguiri, in the primary and Republican John Tabor in the general election. During his tenure, Flaherty streamlined city services and reduced city expenses while converting many city offices from patronage to merit civil service.

In 1974, while retaining his position as mayor, he ran for the Senate. In the Democratic primary, Flaherty defeated Herb Denenberg, who had resigned as state insurance commissioner, but lost the general election to incumbent Republican Richard Schweiker. During the 1976 presidential campaign, Flaherty supported Jimmy Carter. This position put him at odds with then-Pennsylvania governor Milton Shapp, who was himself a presidential candidate. Flaherty served as vice chairman of the Pennsylvania delegation.

With Carter's election, Flaherty was offered the post of deputy attorney general under Griffin Bell; he resigned as mayor in 1977. He was replaced as mayor by Richard Caliguiri, president of the city council. In 1978 Flaherty returned to Pennsylvania to run for governor but lost the general election to Republican Richard Thornburgh.

See also: David L. Lawrence

Thomas J. Baldino

REFERENCES

Lorant, Stefan. 1978. *Pete: Life of Peter F. Flaherty.* Lenox, MA: Privately printed.

Henry P. Fletcher (1873–1959)

Republican national chairman in the mid-1930s. Henry Prather Fletcher was born in Pennsylvania, graduated from Lafayette College, and became a lawyer in 1894. Fletcher enlisted as a private in the Spanish-American War and served with Theodore Roosevelt's Rough Riders in Cuba and in the Philippines. He entered the diplomatic service in 1902 as a legation secretary in Peking and was promoted to minister to Chile in 1909, the first to that country.

Fletcher's diplomatic career was at all times exemplary. President Woodrow Wilson kept him on as ambassador to Mexico during the period of strained relations with that country. President Warren Harding appointed him Under Secretary of State. He later served as ambassador to Belgium and Italy, resigning from the latter position in 1929. In 1931 President Herbert Hoover called Fletcher back to the public service as chairman of the Tariff Commission.

Much of Fletcher's activity in the Republican Party related to fundraising. In 1932 he became Hoover's chief money-raiser in the East. With the national committee debt still standing at about $200,000, Fletcher's access to sources of funds was undoubtedly a factor in his election as national chairman in 1934. Hoover, no longer in the White House, expressed a preference for a younger leader; the Old Guard had a candidate of their own. In the end, Hoover endorsed compromise candidate Fletcher, who then received a three-to-one majority in the national committee.

As national chairman, Fletcher paid off the 1932 campaign debt, promoted the establishment of a Young Republican National Federation, established the first substantial research division at national headquarters, and fought unsuccessfully with the new radio networks for equal time to respond to President Franklin D.

Roosevelt's annual messages to Congress. Fletcher resigned the national chairmanship before the 1936 election.

See also: Herbert Hoover, Republican National Committee, Young Republicans

Ralph M. Goldman

REFERENCES

Goldman, Ralph M. 1990. *The National Party Chairmen and Committees: Factionalism at the Top.* Armonk, NY: M. E. Sharpe.

Edward J. Flynn (1891–1953)

One of the last modern-day bosses. Edward J. Flynn was chairman of the Bronx County (N.Y.) Democratic Party from 1922 to 1953 and chairman of the Democratic National Committee from July 1940 to January 1943. Born in New York City, Edward J. Flynn was educated at Fordham University and was admitted to the New York State bar in 1913. Elected a member of the New York State Assembly in 1917, he became a powerful figure in New York state politics when he was chosen to head the Bronx County Democratic Party. As a Tammany Hall Democrat, and "Boss" of the Bronx, Flynn wielded enormous influence in state and national party circles.

A loyal supporter of Franklin Roosevelt, Flynn worked tirelessly for him when Roosevelt was governor of New York. With Roosevelt's election as President, Flynn became one of the President's close political advisers. In 1933 Flynn assumed the chairmanship of the Democratic National Committee upon the resignation of James A. Farley and directed Roosevelt's third term campaign. Resigning the chairmanship in 1943, he maintained a close relationship with the President. Roosevelt tried to appoint him minister to Australia in 1943, but he was forced to withdraw the nomination owing to Republican opposition generated by Flynn's many political maneuvers. In February 1945 Flynn accompanied Roosevelt to Yalta. Following Roosevelt's death in April 1945, he returned to his position as Bronx County chairman, which he held until his death.

See also: Bosses, Democratic National Committee, James A. Farley, Franklin D. Roosevelt, Tammany Hall

Thomas T. Spencer

REFERENCES

Dorsett, Lyle W. 1977. *Franklin D. Roosevelt and the City Bosses.* Port Washington, NY: Kennikat Press.

Flynn, Edward. 1947. *You're the Boss.* New York: Viking Press.

Goldman, Ralph M. 1990. *The National Party Chairmen and Committees: Factionalism at the Top.* Armonk, NY: M. E. Sharpe.

Thomas S. Foley (1929–)

Speaker of the House in the One Hundred First Congress. Tom Foley, elected Speaker of the House after the resignation of former Speaker Jim Wright in 1989, has made a career of demonstrating that nice guys can get ahead in politics. Foley was deemed by many to be the precise kind of calming influence necessary to end the acrid partisanship that characterized the end of the Wright speakership.

Raised in Spokane, Washington, in a political family, Foley followed his father into law and thought for a time that he would seek to succeed his father on the superior court bench in the state. In 1961, after briefly serving as a deputy prosecutor and an assistant attorney general in Washington, Foley accepted the offer of his father's friend, Washington's junior Senator Henry M. "Scoop" Jackson, to work as counsel for the Senate Interior Committee. When he returned to his native Spokane after two years, Foley was convinced by local Democratic organizers, who were also family friends, to take on eleven-term incumbent Republican Congressman Walter F. Horan. Though Foley had to borrow money to pay his filing fee, though he barely met the filing deadline, and though he had no personal organization to rely on, Foley pulled off a major upset to win the election. Foley's victory was helped by Jackson and the state's senior Senator, Warren G. Magnuson, and especially by the presidential coattails of Lyndon Johnson's enormous electoral mandate. But more importantly, his election revealed a pattern that has marked Foley's career: he never attacked Walter Horan, and he never viewed his opponent as the enemy but rather as someone with whom he disagreed on important issues.

In his district and in the Congress Foley continued to take strong and clear stands on issues but never to personalize differences. His largely Republican district has reelected him continuously, with no serious competition since 1978. He has mended fences and kept close to his constituents. In the House he developed a reputation as a reform-minded liberal, who did his homework, understood the system, and did not offend his opponents. In 1974 he was elected chair of the Democratic Study Group (DSG), the caucus of Democrats most responsible for congressional reforms to the seniority system. In

1975, using the rules implemented under pressure from the DSG, House Democrats unseated 75-year-old Agriculture Committee Chair W. R. Poage (D-Tex.). Foley was next in seniority to Poage and the likely successor, but he never joined the effort to unseat his senior colleague. As a result, after his defeat, it was Poage who nominated Tom Foley to replace him. With his election, Foley became the youngest member of Congress ever to chair a major committee.

In 1977 Tom Foley was elected chair of the Democratic Caucus; he was viewed as a reformer who would work within the system. In 1981 Speaker Tip O'Neill selected Foley as Majority Whip, recognizing the respect he commanded among all factions in the party and Foley's mastery of parliamentary procedure. In 1986, when O'Neill retired and Wright became Speaker, Foley called every Democratic member seeking support to become Majority Leader; he was unchallenged in that election.

When the extent of Speaker Wright's ethical problems became evident in the spring of 1989, many in Congress began to call for his resignation and Foley's elevation. Consistent with his career-long pattern, Tom Foley remained loyal to his boss. Right up to the eve of Wright's resignation, Foley maintained that the Speaker should see the process through and remain in office if cleared. Foley never joined the cries for Wright's scalp; when Wright did resign, he handed the gavel to his successor as an expression of gratitude, not enmity. As Speaker, the telegenic and articulate Foley joined a new Democratic leadership team. Together with Majority Leader George Mitchell in the Senate, and Majority Leader Richard Gephardt and Caucus Chair William Gray in the House, Foley saw his task as defining a new and appropriate image for the Democratic Party leadership.

See also: Coattails, Richard Gephardt, William H. Gray, Lyndon Johnson, George Mitchell, Tip O'Neill, Speaker of the House, Jim Wright

L. Sandy Maisel

REFERENCES

Mills, Mike. 1989. "Profile: Thomas S. Foley." *Congressional Quarterly Weekly Report*, June 10. p. 1378.
Trescott, Jacqueline. 1989. "The Man Who Will Be Speaker." *Washington Post National Weekly Edition*, June 5–11. pp. 7–8.

Solomon Foot (1802–1866)

Antebellum leader of the Senate. Born in Vermont, Solomon Foot graduated from Middlebury College and taught school before beginning his practice of law in 1831. Elected to the Vermont legislature as a Whig, he served as speaker of the house before being elected to the U.S. House of Representatives in 1842. During his two terms he joined northern Whigs in support of the Wilmot Proviso and denunciation of President James Polk's role in provoking the Mexican War.

In 1850 Foot entered the Senate and began the most prominent phase of his public career. His opposition to the extension of slavery led him to oppose the Kansas-Nebraska Act because of its repeal of the Missouri Compromise line. As a result of the act's passage in 1854, he joined many other northern Whigs and Democrats in preliminary meetings leading to the formation of the Republican Party. In the late 1850s he spoke out strongly in the Senate against the Buchanan-backed proslavery Lecompton Constitution in Kansas. During the Civil War he typically supported President Abraham Lincoln's war and emancipation policies.

Perhaps Foot's greatest contribution was as presiding officer of the Senate during much of the Civil War. A master of parliamentary law, he presided with great fairness in the face of the heated debates during the war years. Never at the center of Whig or Republican Party policymaking decisions nor a great orator, he was nevertheless extremely popular and highly respected among his fellow Senators of whichever party.

See also: James Buchanan, Kansas-Nebraska Act, Mexican War, Missouri Compromise, James Polk, Speaker of the House, Wilmot Proviso

Frederick J. Blue

REFERENCES

Foot, Solomon. 1847. *Speech of Mr. Solomon Foot of Vermont on the Character and Objects of the Mexican War.* Washington: U.S. Government Printing Office.
Mayer, George H. 1964. *The Republican Party, 1854–1964.* New York: Oxford U. Pr.
Trefousse, Hans. 1973. "The Republican Party, 1854–1864." In Arthur M. Schlesinger, Jr., ed. *History of the United States Political Parties.* 4 vols. New York: Chelsea House.
Waite, David H. 1981. *Vermont in the Union: A Study of the Growing Influence of the Concept of Union in Vermont Rhetoric, 1840–1861.* Ann Arbor: University Microfilms.

Joseph B. Foraker (1846–1917)

Ohio jurist, politician, and governor. Joseph Benson Foraker left his imprint on state and national affairs through his terms in office and influence on the Republican Party. Born on a farm in Ohio, Foraker showed little initial interest in school, joining the Union Army in 1862. Rising to the rank of captain, he left the military after the Civil War to attend Ohio Wesleyan University and Cornell University, where he earned his degree in 1869. That same year he became a member of the bar and began a legal practice in Cincinnati.

Involved in Republican campaigns throughout the early 1870s, he ran unsuccessfully for a judgeship in 1876. Three years later he won a position on the superior court. In 1883 he ran unsuccessfully for governor but won the same race two years later and returned the following term as the victorious incumbent only to lose a bid for a third term in 1889. Not content to practice law, Foraker returned to politics in 1896, winning election as U.S. Senator, a seat he defended in 1902. His political career suffered irreparable damage during the presidential campaign of 1908 when newspaper owner William Randolph Hearst published accounts that Foraker had received payments from Standard Oil. He attempted to return to office in 1914 but was defeated in the Republican primary by Warren G. Harding.

As governor, Foraker supported reform of the election and taxation laws. In the Senate he supported intervention on behalf of Cuba, annexation of Hawaii, and retention of Puerto Rico, which came to be governed by legislation he created. As a Republican politician, Foraker commanded national attention, nominating John Sherman for President in 1884 and William McKinley in 1896 and 1900, but never managed to control the Republicans in his own state.

See also: Warren G. Harding, William McKinley, John Sherman

Steven C. Kottsy

REFERENCES

Libby, Justin. 1987. "'Our Plain Duty': Senator Joseph B. Foraker and the First Civil Government of Puerto Rico." 69 *Mid America* 39.

Murray, Percy E. 1983. "Harry C. Smith–Joseph B. Foraker Alliance: Coalition Politics in Ohio." 68 *Journal of Negro History* 171.

Walters, Everett. 1948. *Joseph Benson Foraker: An Uncompromising Republican.* Columbus, OH: The Ohio History Press.

Gerald R. Ford, Jr. (1913–)

First unelected President of the United States. After a long career as a Republican Congressman from Michigan, Gerald Rudolph Ford, Jr., was, after the resignation of Spiro Agnew, selected by Richard Nixon to become Vice President in accordance with the Twenty-fifth Amendment to the Constitution. Ford was elevated to the presidency upon Nixon's resignation less than a year later. His presidential tenure ended after he was defeated by Jimmy Carter in the 1976 general election.

Ford was elected to the House of Representatives in 1948 after defeating the isolationist incumbent in the Republican primary. In 1963 he defeated incumbent Charles B. Hoeven of Iowa for the chairmanship of the Republican Conference, the third-ranking leadership position. Ford challenged Minority Leader Charles Halleck for control of the party two years later. Both men had similar voting records and were ideologically compatible, but Ford's "constructive" leadership style contrasted with Halleck's intransigent opposition to Democratic initiatives. In a close race, House Republicans chose Ford to lead them in the Eighty-ninth and successive Congresses.

Despite these challenges to the Republican hierarchy, Ford was himself a strong partisan. He developed a reputation as a solid leader through hard work and legislative competence. When Spiro Agnew resigned the vice presidency on October 10, 1973, President Richard Nixon turned to Ford. The Minority Leader was overwhelmingly approved by the Senate and the House and sworn in on December 6, 1973.

The Watergate scandal topped the national agenda in 1974. Faced with impeachment proceedings in the House of Representatives, President Nixon announced his resignation on August 8, 1974; Ford took office the following day. Within a month, Ford pardoned Nixon "for all offenses against the United States" that may have been committed by the former President. Subsequent allegations of a deal to grant the pardon in exchange for the presidency somewhat damaged Ford's credibility, and the entire episode may well have cost him the 1976 election.

Ford faced a hostile Congress when he took office, and the 1974 midterm elections made the situation worse. Democrats gained 43 seats in the House and 3 in the Senate to increase their already significant margins. While attempting to work with congressional leaders to advance his legislative goals, Ford did not hesitate to use his veto powers to stop legislation that he did not support. Nearly one-fourth of his vetoes were overridden, but the threat of a possible veto gave Ford a tool for negotiation.

Despite his incumbent status, Ford faced a strong challenge from Ronald Reagan for the

1976 Republican nomination. Reagan had the support of many conservative Republicans. Although Ford won 16 of 26 primaries, the nomination was undecided until the convention where Ford won on the first ballot with 1,187 delegates to Reagan's 1,070.

After securing the nomination, Ford chose Senator Robert Dole of Kansas to be his running mate. The race against Jimmy Carter of Georgia was highlighted by several blunders by Ford, including apparent public confusion on television over the political situation in Poland. Carter won the election with slightly more than 51 percent of the two-party vote and an electoral college margin of 297 to 240.

See also: Spiro Agnew, Jimmy Carter, Robert Dole, Election of 1976, Charles Halleck, Isolationism in American Politics, Richard Nixon, Ronald Reagan, Watergate

John A. Clark

REFERENCES

Ford, Gerald R., Jr. 1979. *A Time to Heal.* New York: Harper & Row.

Peabody, Robert L. 1966. *The Ford-Halleck Minority Leadership Contest.* New York: McGraw-Hill.

Formation of the Republican Party

Since its formation more than a century ago, the Republican Party has earned a durable place in American political life. Born during the political realignment of the 1850s, it was the first antislavery party in American history to win substantial popular support. By the end of 1856, it had assumed the Whig Party's former position as the major opposition party to the Democrats; four years later, in 1860, it had become the strongest party in the nation and elected Abraham Lincoln as its first President. Since then, it has been a fixture in the American two-party system.

Viewed from the perspective of the war that loomed like a dark cloud on the political horizon during the 1850s, the rise of the Republican Party seemed almost predestined. The party's formation, according to the traditional interpretation, was a direct response to the passage in May 1854 by the Democratic-controlled Congress of the Kansas-Nebraska Act, which repealed the 34-year-old Missouri Compromise's ban on slavery in the northern part of the Louisiana Purchase. Angered by this unexpected destruction of the compact of 1820, indignant Whigs, Democrats, and Free Soilers in the North flocked to the new Republican Party, which took as its platform opposition to the expansion of slavery. According to the usual scenario, the party quickly replaced the crumbling Whig organization as the main anti-Democratic party in the nation, and after a narrow defeat in 1856, it swept to victory in 1860. In short, sectionalism, and especially the slavery expansion issue, galvanized by the Kansas-Nebraska Act and reenforced by the ensuing violence in the Kansas Territory, accounts for both the party's formation and its widespread popular support.

In reality, however, the Republican Party had a difficult struggle to survive, and during the first years of its existence, like all previous antislavery parties, it seemed destined for an early death. In 1854 and 1855, in those states where it existed, the party met defeat almost everywhere. Instead, during these years the fastest growing party in the North and in the nation—and the primary rival to the Democrats—was the secret nativist American Party, popularly known as the Know-Nothings. Thus the shift from Whiggery to Republicanism was not a straightforward process, and the formation of the Republican Party was a much more complex, drawn out process than it is usually portrayed.

The rise of the Republican Party occurred in two stages, each of which, while crucial to the party's ultimate success, posed distinctly different problems. In the first stage, which extended from the party's beginning through the presidential election of 1856, the Republicans waged a desperate and, at first, seemingly hopeless battle with the rival American Party to assume the position of the defunct Whig organization as the major anti-Democratic party in the country. The Republicans' amazing showing in that election sealed the doom of the American organization and established the Republican Party as the second party in the two-party system. During the next stage, which extended from the party's defeat in 1856 through the 1860 campaign, leaders sought to broaden the Republican coalition by moderating and expanding the party's appeal and by bringing additional groups into its ranks. Further conversions would occur after 1860, but Abraham Lincoln's victory represented the culmination of the Republicans' rapid rise to power. In many ways, that the Republican Party survived was more remarkable than that it eventually succeeded.

Voting patterns reveal that the realignment in the North began before the Kansas-Nebraska Act was introduced, and it began at the state and local level, not the national. The most important cause of the realignment was the emergence after 1850 of a set of ethnocultural issues, particularly temperance and nativism, that cut across traditional party lines and thus had unusual potential to disrupt the Whig and Democratic coalitions. By the end of 1853, party lines were in complete disarray in many northern states and the process of party decomposition was well advanced. Voters' ties to parties were weaker than observers could ever remember, and party support fluctuated widely from one election to the next.

At this point, Congress passed the Kansas-Nebraska Act. Sensitive that this issue had split northern congressional Democrats down the middle, a number of antislavery leaders believed that the repeal of the Missouri Compromise would at last precipitate the creation of a powerful antislavery sectional party. This expectation was negated, however, by the emergence in the spring of 1854 of the anti-Catholic, anti-immigrant American Party, or Know-Nothings, as a powerful independent organization. Political observers were astounded by this secret society's rapid growth in the summer of 1854, as countless Whigs, Democrats, and Free Soilers joined the new lodges. Combining opposition to the expansion of slavery with virulent anti-Catholicism and support for temperance, the Know-Nothing movement capitalized on the forces that undermined the second-party system and won over many voters discontented with the existing parties and eager for reform, at the same time that it mobilized legions of those who had never voted.

The power of the Know-Nothings, the hostility of eastern Whigs who still clung to their sinking party organization, and the continuing animosity among Whigs, Free Soilers, and anti-Nebraska Democrats blocked formation of the Republican Party in most free states in 1854. Efforts by antislavery men to organize a new party failed in such important states as New York, Pennsylvania, Massachusetts, and Illinois. In Ohio and Indiana, opposition forces combined in a temporary People's Party that was dominated by the Know-Nothings; in Vermont and Iowa, anti-Democratic groups united behind a common ticket but did not organize a new party. Only in Michigan and Wisconsin did the Republican Party take shape in 1854. In both states, the new party adopted a strong antislavery platform that was too extreme for more conservative latitudes.

The 1854 state elections in the North, many of which presented the voters with a bewildering array of choices, were a crushing defeat for the Democratic Party. Yet which party had triumphed in these contests was not clear to contemporaries. Although the Republican Party was victorious in Michigan and Wisconsin, in general the Know-Nothings, by combining nativism, anti-Nebraska sentiment, temperance, and opposition to the existing parties, were the most potent force in the northern elections. Because these other issues—and not just the Nebraska question—were central to the 1854 upheaval, the northern Whig Party, despite its clear anti-Nebraska stance, suffered an even more devastating blow than did the Democrats. Thousands of rank-and-file Whigs abandoned their traditional loyalty for the American Party. After the election, a despondent New York Whig concluded, "This election has demonstrated that, by a majority, Roman Catholicism is feared more than American slavery." Battered first by temperance and then nativism, the Whig Party abruptly collapsed.

With the Know-Nothings riding a crest of popularity, antislavery politicians launched the Republican Party. The Republican movement combined Whigs, anti-Nebraska Democrats, and Free Soilers who wished to make antislavery, not nativism, the dominant element in northern politics. Some of these groups were adamantly hostile to nativism while others, particularly Free Soilers, had previously supported the Know-Nothings; whatever their views on other questions, however, Republican Party members gave greater importance to sectional matters. While the Republican Party confronted a number of major obstacles at its birth, its most serious problem was the power of the Know-Nothings. In most northern states, and especially in the most populous ones with the greatest strength in the Electoral College, the Republican Party could not be victorious without substantial Know-Nothing support. The major task confronting the Republicans, therefore, was to win over the bulk of the northern Know-Nothings and thus replace the American Party as the primary opponent of the Democrats.

Over the next two years, Republicans and Americans battled for control of the anti-Democratic majority in the North. In analyzing the complex maneuvering among anti-Democratic factions during this period, historians have traditionally interpreted this struggle strictly in terms of antislavery versus nativism, seeing it solely as a contest over which idea would prevail and which would be shunted aside politically. Yet antislavery, anti-Catholicism, and hostility to alcohol were not neatly segregated attitudes in the antebellum electorate. In some ways nativism and antislavery competed with each other, but strong links also existed between the movements psychologically and in terms of mass support. For the most part, northern Know-Nothings were anti-Nebraska and opposed the extension of slavery. In addition, Know-Nothings more often than not favored temperance, as referenda in this decade clearly establish. Thus a strong though not perfect congruence existed among these attitudes, an affinity that greatly complicated the process of realignment in general and the formation of the Republican Party in particular. Had a majority of northern voters from the start given greatest priority to the slavery issue or had antislavery voters been indifferent to nativism and temperance, the creation of the Republican Party would have been immensely simplified.

The first significant steps to organize the Republicans occurred in 1855. Hoping to reorient northern politics around sectional questions, party leaders took heart from the disruption of the national American Party in June. When the American Party's national convention adopted a platform endorsing the Kansas-Nebraska Act, a majority of the northern delegates walked out. Even more crucial to Republican hopes was the situation in the territory of Kansas. By the summer of 1855, the rivalry between free state and slave state partisans had led to a complete breakdown of order in the territory. Alarmed by northern efforts to save Kansas for freedom by sending settlers to the territory, proslavery partisans from neighboring Missouri invaded the territory before the March 1855 election, seized control of the polling places, and stuffed the ballot boxes, giving proslavery men firm control of the first territorial legislature. Proslavery leaders in the legislature then made the situation worse by expelling the few legally elected antislavery members and passing a draconian legal code designed to protect the institution of slavery and silence its critics. Antislavery partisans responded by organizing a separate "state" government and petitioning Congress for the admission of Kansas as a free state. With each government denouncing the other and denying the validity of its acts, sporadic fighting soon broke out between proslavery and antislavery partisans. Republican leaders anticipated that affairs in Kansas would significantly strengthen the movement to organize a northern antislavery party.

New York and Ohio offered contrasting visions of how to build a powerful Republican Party. In Ohio, antislavery men, led by Salmon P. Chase, united with the Know-Nothings, who were the strongest element in the Republican coalition. In exchange for Chase's nomination for governor, the Know-Nothings received the remaining seven spots on the Republican ticket. In addition, the Republican platform was silent on the question of nativism, hoping thereby to appeal to both German Protestants and Know-Nothings. In New York, in contrast, the Republican Party under the leadership of William H. Seward and Thurlow Weed, who recognized that the Know-Nothings were controlled by their enemies, assumed a clear antinativist stance. New York's was the only Republican state platform in 1855 to condemn explicitly the Know-Nothings and their proscriptive principles.

Although the Know-Nothing national council in June adopted a pro-Nebraska platform, the American Party in every northern state repudiated this platform and reaffirmed its opposition to the extension of slavery. Thus wherever they ran a separate ticket, the Know-Nothings continued to exploit both nativism and antislavery sentiment. Republican leaders, in contrast, believed that the continuing violence in Kansas between proslavery and antislavery men would enable the party to ride to victory on a strictly antislavery platform. Instead, the 1855 elections documented the continuing power of ethnocultural concerns in northern politics. In Ohio, where the Republican Party won its one significant victory, Republicans had united with the Know-Nothings on a common ticket. In states such as New York and Massachusetts, where the Republicans rejected fusion with the Know-Nothings, the party went down to defeat. In the face of the Republican challenge with its overriding emphasis on the slavery issue, a substantial majority of eastern Know-Nothings remained loyal to the American Party with its more broadly based appeal, a development that doomed the Republicans to defeat. The 1855 results demonstrated that, together, anti-Catholicism and antislavery represented the strongest political program in the North. "The people will not confront the issues we present," one despondent Massachusetts Republican shrewdly observed after the election. "They want a Paddy hunt & on a Paddy hunt they will go."

Chase's victory in Ohio in 1855 was the Republicans' one bright star in an otherwise dismal political sky that year. Bolstered by his narrow victory, Chase launched a movement to organize a national Republican Party on what Seward, an opponent of nativism, scorned as "the Ohio plan, half Republican and half Know-Nothing." As a result of his efforts, Republicans held a national organizing convention in Pittsburgh in February, where they laid the groundwork for a national nominating convention in June. As plans proceeded to field a national ticket, Republican prospects still remained decidedly bleak, for the spring elections produced additional discouraging results. In the most important of these elections in Connecticut, where the Republicans for the first time ran a state ticket, the party polled a discouraging 10 percent of the popular vote. Experienced politicians predicted that the party would finish a distant third in the 1856 presidential election and then quickly fade from the political scene. As one veteran Democratic editor commented, "Nobody believes this Republican movement can prove the basis of a permanent party."

Against this background, the 1856 presidential election produced one of the most remarkable turnarounds in American political history. The weakest party at the beginning of the year and seemingly headed for oblivion, the Republicans were by the time of the election in November the dominant party in the North and the second strongest party in the nation. Several factors contributed to the party's amazing success after two years of frustration. By forming an alliance with northern Know-Nothings and nominating Nathaniel P. Banks, a Massachusetts Know-Nothing–Republican, for Speaker, the Republican minority gained control of the U.S. House of Representatives and forged the first national bonds of union with antislavery Know-Nothings. In addition, the American Party convention ruptured for the second time in two years when the delegates adopted a pro-Nebraska platform and nominated Millard Fillmore to head their national ticket. A majority of northern delegates walked out, repudiating the platform and the ticket. But the most important reason for the Republican Party's sudden growth was two incidents that occurred virtually simultaneously in May at almost opposite ends of the country: the attack on the Lawrence, Kansas, headquarters of the free-state movement by a proslavery mob (Bleeding Kansas); and the caning of Republican Senator Charles Sumner

of Massachusetts, a prominent antislavery spokesman, by Congressman Preston S. Brooks of South Carolina in the Senate Chamber (Bleeding Sumner). Of the two events, the assault on Sumner was decidedly the more important. It inflamed northern public opinion, provided a particularly dramatic example of alleged southern aggression, and brought thousands of moderate and conservative northerners into the Republican ranks.

The Republicans' first national nominating convention met in Philadelphia in June 1856. Stimulated by the recent violence in Kansas and Washington, an atmosphere akin to a religious revival prevailed on the convention floor. The 1856 Republican national platform was largely devoid of the evasions and ambiguities typical of such pronouncements: it clearly focused on the slavery issue. Proclaiming that it was both the right and the duty of Congress to prohibit slavery from all the territories, it denounced slaveholding as "a relic of barbarism." The longest section detailed the violations of the rights of free-state settlers in Kansas and called for the admission of Kansas as a free state. Except for calls for construction of a transcontinental railroad by a northern route and for federal aid to internal improvements, economic issues—over which party members were badly divided—were ignored. A carefully crafted final plank on nativism sought to mollify both former Know-Nothings and naturalized voters.

The convention selected the famous western explorer, John C. Frémont, as the first Republican presidential candidate. Frémont had a rather undistinguished antislavery record, but he enjoyed a popular image as a dashing figure of romance and had a sufficiently malleable record for the party's purposes. Frémont was more a symbol than a real Republican leader; he took no active role in the campaign, which was run by an inner circle.

It was in 1856 that the party's ideology finally crystallized. Republicans continued to emphasize opposition to the expansion of slavery, but they put this question in a larger ideological context. Throughout the decade, some Republican leaders forcefully spoke out against the morality of slavery. In his famous debates with Stephen A. Douglas, Abraham Lincoln declared, "The real issue in this controversy . . . is the sentiment on the part of one class that looks upon the institution of slavery as a *wrong*, and of another class that *does not* look upon it as a wrong. . . . The Republican party . . . look upon it as being a moral, social and political wrong." Other Republicans, exploiting widespread racist sentiment in the northern electorate, denied any humanitarian concern for the welfare of Blacks and advocated preserving the western territories for whites by keeping out all Blacks, free or slave. "The Republicans mean to preserve all of this country that they can from the pestilential presence of the black man," announced the *Hartford Courant*, while in 1860 a Republican banner in Illinois proclaimed, "NO NEGRO EQUALITY IN THE NORTH." More important was the ideal of free labor, which extolled the values of economic opportunity, personal liberty, and social mobility. Portraying the South as an aristocratic and economically stagnant society in which slavery degraded labor, Republicans celebrated the superiority of northern institutions and the North's fluid, progressive society.

Yet none of these ideas stood at the core of the party's ideology, which was more negative than positive in its emphasis and evidenced less concern for the welfare of Blacks than the rights of northern whites. The Lawrence and Sumner incidents, which allowed Republicans to attack the South rather than slavery, provided Republicans with the necessary material to fashion an effective appeal.

Giving less emphasis to the moral question of slavery, Republicans focused on the threat to the liberties of northern whites posed by the aggressive Slave Power, by which they meant the political power of slaveholders. The issues of Bleeding Kansas and Bleeding Sumner were ideal for Republicans' purposes, for they enabled Republicans to agitate the slavery question without addressing the issue of Black rights. Throughout the summer of 1856, Republican spokesmen insisted that slaveowners were engaged in a gigantic conspiracy to expand slavery everywhere and destroy northern white liberties. To northern whites, this threat seemed much more personal than whether slavery would exist in some distant territory. Slaveholders would stop at nothing, Republican leaders cried, to ensure that their power remained supreme, not just in the South but in the nation as well. As the famous Black leader Frederick Douglass aptly noted, "The cry of Free Men was raised, not for the extension of liberty to the black man, but for the protection of the liberty of the white."

In fashioning their ideology, Republicans made use of the tradition of republicanism, which had been central to American politics since the Revolution. While the force of republicanism waned after 1815 in competition with liberalism, which placed economic individualism at the center of society, this body of thought remained influential until at least the end of the Civil War. The ideology of republicanism, as handed down from the Founders, posited that republicanism was a particularly vulnerable form of government and that there always existed conspiracies of those with power to destroy liberty. The raid on Lawrence and the assault on Sumner, like the Kansas-Nebraska Act before them, were pieces of this grand design, Republicans contended, and unless northerners acted quickly, any hope of thwarting the Slave Power would be gone. Following the caning of Sumner, a New Hampshire Republican newspaper declared, "The liberties of our country are in tenfold more danger than they were at the commencement of the American Revolution. We then had a distant foe to contend with. Now the enemy is within our borders."

To the modern observer, such claims seem fantastic, but antebellum Americans were thoroughly accustomed to such rhetoric. Voters *expected* to find conspiracies; they were a political fact of life. Republicans merely modified republican thought to fit the political crisis of the 1850s by identifying the South and more especially slaveowners as the internal threat to the Republic and its promise of liberty and opportunity. In words that echoed those of the 1760s and 1770s, the address of the Ohio Republican State Central Committee following the 1856 presidential election proclaimed, "Every despotism is aggressive, and the despotism of the Slave Power is no exception to the universal rule. The price of Liberty is eternal vigilance."

Republicans also broadened their appeal beyond the slavery issue by catering to nativist (especially anti-Catholic) sentiment in the North. Tactical considerations made an emphasis on opposition to foreigners undesirable, but anti-Catholicism entailed little political risk: the Catholic vote was solidly Democratic and hatred of Catholics was one policy on which both Know-Nothings and Protestant immigrants could unite. Republican newspapers and spokesmen denounced Catholics and linked the Church with the Slave Power in a combined assault on the country's republican heritage. Charging that "Popery and Slavery [had] banded together for a common object—the attainment of political power," the *Chicago Tribune* (February 4, 1856), insisted that "the Republican party, which is the avowed mortal enemy of chattel bondage, is not less the opponent of the partisan schemes of political Catholicism." Republican ideology thus depicted a dual threat to northern whites' liberties—the Slave Power and the Papal Power—and though they gave greater emphasis to the former and considered it the more serious danger, they by no means ignored the latter. Republicans were also careful to reach out to disaffected Americans in 1856. They united with the northern American Party on a national ticket, nominated Know-Nothings for state and local offices, gave them a prominent place in the campaign, and did not require any renunciation of past opinions.

Despite a crusading enthusiasm that recalled the rousing contest of 1840, the first Republican presidential campaign confronted insoluble difficulties. The party was hurt by the fear among conservatives that it was a threat to the Union, but the most damaging accusation brought against it in the 1856 election was that its standard-bearer was a Catholic. In actuality, Frémont was an Episcopalian, but Democrats and American Party leaders never tired of inventing new stories and publishing new testimonials that Frémont was a Catholic. Throughout the campaign, Republicans failed to devise an effective answer to this charge, and to the very end a large number of northern voters remained suspicious of Frémont's true religious affiliation. This accusation was especially damaging among Know-Nothings, who held the key to the 1856 outcome. In the end, the Republican Party was unable to solve this problem, along with the organizational difficulties that any new party confronts.

Even so, aided by the rising sectional animosity, the Republicans' performance in the 1856 election was little short of astounding. Although James Buchanan, the Democratic nominee, was elected, Frémont ran ahead of both Buchanan and Millard Fillmore, the American Party candidate, in the North and carried all but five free states: Pennsylvania, New Jersey, Indiana, Illinois, and California. Despite having virtually no support in the South, Frémont finished second in the Electoral College and polled 33 percent of the popular vote. Had Frémont carried Pennsylvania and one of the other four free states that he lost, or had he carried these four without Pennsylvania, then he would have been elected. In their first national effort, Republicans had come within an eyelash of winning.

The Republican coalition in 1856 was strikingly diverse. The party won the bulk of the former Whigs and all the Free Soilers, a substantial proportion of Know-Nothings (the large majority in some states like Massachusetts, Connecticut, Ohio, and Indiana), a number of Protestant immigrants, and a disproportionate share of young voters and previous nonvoters. In general, Republican strength among Democrats has been exaggerated; only in a few states such as Ohio, Connecticut, and New York did the Republican Party win a significant proportion of former Democrats, and the bulk of these Democratic converts seem to have entered the Republican camp through the secret Know-Nothing lodges rather than the much-emphasized anti-Nebraska movement. Republican strength among the foreign-born also varied from state to state, although everywhere Catholics, and especially Irish Catholics, voted overwhelmingly Democratic. Republicans won lopsided majorities among British, Scandinavian, and Scotch-Irish voters, all of whom had no particular liking for slavery and were also strongly anti-Catholic (many had voted Know-Nothing earlier, though they were ineligible for membership in the order); they adhered to the Republican Party as the enemy of the Irish Democracy as long as it avoided an antiforeign stance. Republicans garnered fewer votes among the Germans, on whom they lavished particular attention, than party leaders had hoped, but in some states such as Illinois, where the party kept free from prohibition and relegated nativism to the background, the Republicans seem to have won a slight majority of German voters.

Among native-born voters, the clearest division was between southern-stock voters and New Englanders. Whereas the Democrats had previously won many Yankee voters, they now swung sharply to the Republicans. After the election, former Senator Daniel S. Dickinson, a prominent New York Democrat, groaned to James Buchanan, "Wherever the *New England* people have sway, they came down like an avalanche,—men, women, and children,—priest, & people, & church, aggregate, and a train of frightened Buffaloes would be no more deaf to reason or argument." At the same time, southern-stock voters in the Ohio valley gave very little support to the Republican Party, which they viewed as a fanatical crusade against their native South and its institutions. Some southern-born Whigs crossed over the Democratic Party, but many more voted for Fillmore. Because of the Republicans' weakness among southern-stock voters, the party did not present a solid evangelical front. In fact, many evangelical voters continued to oppose the party, and Frémont won many votes from those not formally affiliated with any church.

In assuming the Whigs' place in the two-party system, the Republicans did not simply inherit the old Whig voting base. Ethnically the Republican coalition was less homogeneous: while the Republicans had not done as well among the foreign-born as they had hoped, they nevertheless won a greater share of naturalized voters than the Whigs ever had. In addition, a larger proportion of Yankee Protestants voted for Frémont, as Yankee Free Soilers and Democrats switched parties; at the same time, the Republicans won substantially less support among southern-stock voters in the North than the Whigs had, and the Republicans were also weaker among the wealthy business class in large cities. These changes in voting patterns between the second and third party systems produced a fundamentally different anti-Democratic coalition than existed earlier and in the process reduced the Democrats to a minority party in the North.

The Republican Party's remarkable performance in November 1856 marked the close of the first phase of the Civil War realignment: the Whig Party had disappeared, the American Party was on its deathbed, and the Republican Party was the Democrats' primary opponent. Republicans had successfully met their first significant challenge: they had displaced the American Party as the second party in the two-party system. Defeating the Know-Nothings to become the dominant opposition party was the most important victory that the Republican Party would ever win in its long and storied history.

But if the Republican Party were to survive, it had to win national power. For all their postelection elation, Republican leaders remained keenly aware that Frémont had received only a plurality of the vote in the free states, and their next objective was to create a northern Republican majority and elect a President in 1860 by retaining the party's previous supporters while picking up additional support from other groups, particularly the Fillmore voters. As before, Republicans continued to emphasize the threat of the Slave Power. In advancing this argument, the party was immensely aided by

the events of the next four years and by James Buchanan's incompetent leadership.

In Buchanan's star-crossed presidency, the first event that strengthened the Republicans was the Dred Scott decision, rendered by the Supreme Court just two days after Buchanan's inauguration. In this decision, which concerned the status of a Missouri slave named Dred Scott who had lived previously in the free state of Illinois and the free territory of Wisconsin, the Court by a seven-to-two vote declared the Missouri Compromise of 1820 (which had been repealed by the Kansas-Nebraska Act three years earlier) unconstitutional. Congress, the Court declared, had no power to prohibit slavery in the territories, which was the major principle of the Republican Party.

Intended to give additional protection to slavery, the Court's ill-conceived decision instead unleashed a storm of protest. "There is such a thing as the slave power," raged the Republican *Cincinnati Commercial* (March 12, 1857) after the decision was announced. Far from settling the slavery extension question, as the court majority intended, party and sectional differences intensified. More important, Republican leaders now perceived an expanded threat facing the North: they raised the cry that slavery threatened not just the territories, but the free states as well. All that was needed, Lincoln explained, was one more Supreme Court decision that a state could not ban slavery, and it would be a national institution, legal in the North as well as the South. "We shall *lie down* pleasantly dreaming that the people of *Missouri* are on the verge of making their State *free*," he argued, "and we shall *awake* to the *reality*, instead, that the *Supreme* Court has made *Illinois* a *slave* State." At the same time, since all five southern justices had joined in the majority decision, it strengthened northerners' fears of the Slave Power and added credibility to Republican claims that the federal government was entirely controlled by the slaveowning interest.

If the Dred Scott decision were not enough, a financial panic began in October 1857. As the party in power, the Democrats were hurt by the ensuing depression, which lasted until 1861. Seeking to capitalize on the situation, Republicans added several economic planks to their program, including a mildly protective tariff and a homestead law to give free farms to western settlers. Southern opposition in Congress, however, blocked passage of most economic legislation, and Buchanan vetoed a homestead bill in 1860. Economic questions increasingly became sectional rather than partisan issues, and with growing success Republicans appealed to conservative Whig businessmen on economic grounds.

The most important boost that the Republican Party received, however, came from the Kansas controversy, which now entered its final phase. In 1857, in large part because the free-state majority refused to vote, proslavery forces won control of a convention called to draft a state constitution for the territory prior to its admission as a state. This convention, which met at the capital in Lecompton, drafted a constitution recognizing the institution of slavery. Because the delegates were afraid that the free-state majority would reject the constitution, they refused to submit it for popular ratification. Instead, voters were given the choice of voting for the constitution with more slavery or for the constitution with only the slaves already in the territory. They could not vote for the constitution without slavery or reject the constitution entirely. Denouncing this choice as a sham, free-state men again boycotted the election, and the constitution with more slavery was approved.

Warned by the territorial governor that the Lecompton Constitution was a fraud and represented the wishes of only a small minority of the residents of Kansas, James Buchanan nevertheless urged Congress to approve the proposed constitution and admit Kansas as the sixteenth slave state. In the ensuing struggle in Congress, Buchanan pulled out all the stops, including resorting to outright bribery, in an effort to push the Lecompton Constitution through. His efforts split the Democratic Party, as Senator Stephen A. Douglas of Illinois, the leading northern Democrat, broke with the administration and opposed the Lecompton Constitution. Upholding the idea that the residents of a territory should be allowed to decide the status of slavery for themselves without congressional interference, Douglas charged that the Lecompton Constitution made a mockery of this doctrine of popular sovereignty, which the Democrats had endorsed in both the Kansas-Nebraska Act and its 1856 national platform. Ultimately, the House rejected the Lecompton Constitution, and then in a face-saving compromise sent the issue back to the people of Kansas by asking them to vote on whether they would accept admission under the constitution with a reduced land grant. In the election in August 1858, the voters of Kansas overwhelmingly rejected the Lecompton Constitution. This vote, in effect, ended the Kansas controversy. No doubt remained that Kansas would be admitted as a free state as soon as it reached the requisite population, and it entered the Union in January 1861.

The Lecompton struggle left the Democratic Party wrecked beyond repair. Championing the principle of popular sovereignty, Douglas spoke for the northern wing of the Republican Party, while southerners, furious over his apostasy, bitterly denounced him and insisted that they would never accept his nomination as President. Some southern radicals, angry that the Dred Scott decision had given the South no real benefits, now took up the demand for a congressional slave code to protect slavery in the territories, a measure that would surely encourage expansion of the institution. At the same time, Republicans experienced a resurgence in the wake of the popular outcry in the North against this bare-faced attempt to force slavery on the unwilling residents of Kansas. The Lecompton struggle fed northern fears of an aggressive slaveocracy, willing to stop at nothing to protect its power. Here seemed additional direct proof of the existence of a Slave Power conspiracy and its designs on northern liberty. More and more northern conservatives gravitated toward the Republican Party in response to the Buchanan administration's proslavery policies, and also its corruption, which congressional Republicans took great pains to expose and publicize.

Employing various strategies in different states, the Republican Party scored impressive gains in the most populous northern states in the 1858 state elections. It regained power in Ohio and New York, increased its hold on Massachusetts, and added to its vote in New Jersey, Indiana, and Illinois. Moreover, by exploiting the Lecompton controversy and stressing the tariff issue and the need to aid the state's iron and coal industry, a coalition of Republicans and American Party members under the banner the People's Party carried Pennsylvania for the first time with 53 percent of the vote (compared to only 32 percent for Frémont in 1856).

The 1858 contest that attracted the most national attention, however, was the senatorial race between Stephen A. Douglas and Abraham Lincoln. Throughout the campaign, Lincoln hammered away at the idea, developed at length in his famous "House-Divided" speech in June accepting the Republican nomination, that the

Democratic Party was an agent of the Slave Power, committed to spreading slavery throughout the country. He insisted that the crisis between the sections would not end until "either the *opponents* of slavery, will arrest the further spread of it, and place it . . . in course of ultimate extinction; or its *advocates* will push it forward, till it shall become alike lawful in *all* the States, *old* as well as *new—North* as well as *South."*

In the end, the legislature returned Douglas to the Senate, vindicating his opposition to the Lecompton Constitution, but Republicans knew that Lincoln had won a moral triumph: Republicans noted that the total votes cast for candidates pledged to Lincoln exceeded those for Douglas's supporters, and they also believed that Lincoln had bested Douglas in their debates. Douglas's margin of victory rested on Democratic holdovers and a malapportionment of the legislature. Lincoln's strong showing in the 1858 Illinois senatorial contest catapulted him into serious consideration for the Republicans' 1860 presidential nomination.

By 1860 the political tide was running strongly in the Republicans' direction. The Democratic Party split at its national convention in Charleston, unable to agree on a platform or a candidate. In the end, the northern wing nominated Douglas with a platform endorsing popular sovereignty, while most of the southern delegates, joined by supporters of the Buchanan administration, nominated John C. Breckinridge of Kentucky, Buchanan's Vice President, on a platform demanding a congressional slave code for the territories. In addition, a new party, the Constitutional Union Party, which represented another effort to form a national conservative party, selected John Bell of Tennessee as its candidate.

Republicans assembled in Chicago in May for their second national convention. The 1860 Republican platform was evidence of the party's growing moderation. While Republicans continued to oppose the expansion of slavery, the harsh indictment of the institution contained in the 1856 platform was dropped. In addition to reaffirming the party's endorsement of a transcontinental railroad, the Republican platform contained several new economic planks, including a demand for a homestead law and a moderately protective tariff. Finally, with an eye to the foreign vote, the platform opposed any alteration of the naturalization laws.

The front-runner for the presidential nomination was Senator William H. Seward of New York, the most prominent Republican in the country. But a number of Republicans, especially in the doubtful northern states that the party had lost in 1856, believed that Seward could not win. He had a reputation as a radical on the slavery issue and, most important, was bitterly hated by the former Know-Nothings because of his courageous denunciation of nativism earlier in the decade. Seward's major rival was Lincoln, who enjoyed several advantages. He came from a doubtful state, was a moderate on the slavery issue, was acceptable to both the Germans and Know-Nothings, and as a southern-born old Whig could appeal to those conservatives in the lower North who had backed Fillmore in 1856. On the third ballot, Lincoln received the Republican nomination.

A triumph of expediency and availability, Lincoln's nomination represented an act of grave irresponsibility. Dismissing southern threats of secession as mere bluster, Republicans paid little heed to the crisis that was likely to ensue if the party triumphed. The delegates had no way of knowing that Lincoln, who had been out of public office for more than a decade and had never held an administrative office, had the requisite ability to meet the challenge of civil war. Once in office, Lincoln would demonstrate his extraordinary political skills, but of these the delegates were not only blithely ignorant but also unconcerned. To them, Lincoln seemed to have the best chance of winning, and that was sufficient.

With victory seemingly all but certain, Republicans downplayed the issues in the 1860 campaign and conducted what has aptly been called a hurrah campaign. Parades with banners and transparencies saluted Honest Abe and Lincoln the Railsplitter, and campaign pageantry dominated the canvass. The Wide Awake Society, made up primarily of young men who marched with capes and lanterns singing party songs, chanting Republican slogans, and performing intricate maneuvers was the most remembered feature of the campaign.

With the opposition divided, Lincoln easily triumphed in the Electoral College, even though he won less than 40 percent of the popular vote. He carried every free state except New Jersey, whose electoral votes he split with Douglas. Even had the votes for his three opponents been combined, Lincoln would still have been elected, since he had absolute majorities in all the free states except Oregon, California, and New Jersey. He won all the doubtful states that the Republicans lost in 1856, while holding all the states Frémont had carried. Lincoln won 500,000 more votes than the party's total in 1856.

Lincoln's improved showing over Frémont's performance four years earlier stemmed from support from three major groups. First, Lincoln won a number of Fillmore voters, especially in the southern counties of Indiana and Illinois, eastern Pennsylvania, and New Jersey, and in the major metropolitan areas. Many of these midwestern voters had been born in the South, and Lincoln ran much stronger among southern-stock voters than had Frémont. Bell, in contrast, was much weaker in the North compared to Fillmore, winning only one-fifth as many votes. Lincoln also did better among foreign-born voters, especially Germans. Republican efforts to woo immigrant voters paid dividends in 1860, especially in states like Pennsylvania where the so-called Pennsylvania Dutch now swung to the Republicans. Finally, Lincoln did especially well among young men, many of whom cast their first presidential vote in 1860, after having been mobilized by the Wide Awake clubs. Together, these three groups, coupled with the party's retention of most of Frémont's supporters, provided the Republicans' margin of victory.

Having elected their first President in 1860, Republicans had no idea what they would do with their new-won power. Since its founding, the party had emphasized the necessity of displacing the South from control of the federal government as the way to preserve republicanism, and following Lincoln's victory, Seward announced that "the battle for Freedom had been fought and won." Party members were deeply divided over the slavery issue and economic matters. Moreover, the party did not control either house of Congress and had only one member of the Supreme Court. But the secession of the Deep South in response to Lincoln's election drastically altered the political situation. Lincoln took office determined to maintain the Union, and six weeks after his inauguration, the Civil War began.

Secession and war would convert the Republican Party into the party of the Union and of emancipation. Under Lincoln's leadership, the Republicans would abolish slavery, push the military struggle through to victory, and preserve the Union. After 1865, the party was tied increasingly to northern industrial and corporate interests and promoted quite different policies than it had in 1860, when the Republicans' main principles had been to stop the expansion of slavery and check the South's political power.

In the short span of six years, the Republican Party had gained national power and established itself as the most powerful party in the nation. It was a truly remarkable achievement. Perhaps the clearest measurement of the Republican Party's accomplishment is that it was the last new party to carry a presidential election in American history.

See also: Abolition Movement, Salmon Chase, Constitutional Union Party, Frederick Douglass, Emancipation as a Political Issue, Free Soil Party, John C. Frémont, Kansas-Nebraska Act, Know-Nothings, Abraham Lincoln, Missouri Compromise, Secession, William H. Seward, Slavery, Charles Sumner, Thurlow Weed

William E. Gienapp

REFERENCES

Baringer, William E. 1937. *Lincoln's Rise to Power.* Boston: Little, Brown.

Basler, Roy, ed. 1953. *The Collected Works of Abraham Lincoln.* 8 vols. New Brunswick, NJ: Rutgers U. Pr.

Baum, Dale. 1984. *The Civil War Party System: The Case of Massachusetts, 1848–1876.* Chapel Hill: U. of North Carolina Pr.

Berwanger, Eugene H. 1967. *The Frontier Against Slavery: Western Anti-Negro Prejudice and the Slavery Expansion Controversy.* Urbana: U. of Illinois Pr.

Booraem, Hendrik. 1983. *The Formation of the Republican Party in New York: Politics and Conscience in the Antebellum North.* New York: New York U. Pr.

Crandall, Andrew Wallace. 1930. *The Early History of the Republican Party 1854–1856.* Boston: Gorham Press.

Crenshaw, Ollinger. 1941. "Urban and Rural Voting in the Election of 1860." In Eric F. Goldman, ed. *Historiography and Urbanization: Essays in American History in Honor of W. Stull Holt.* Baltimore: Johns Hopkins U. Pr.

Fehrenbacher, Don E. 1961. "The Republican Decision at Chicago." In Norman A. Graebner, ed. *Politics and the Crisis of 1860.* Urbana: U. of Illinois Pr.

———. 1962. *Prelude to Greatness: Lincoln in the 1850s.* Stanford, CA: Stanford U. Pr.

———. 1965. "Comment on Why the Republican Party Came to Power." In George H. Knoles, ed. *The Crisis of the Union, 1860–1861.* Baton Rouge: Louisiana State U. Pr.

———. 1978. *The Dred Scott Case: Its Significance in American Law and Politics.* New York: Oxford U. Pr.

Foner, Eric. 1970. *Free Soil, Free Labor, Free Men: The Ideology of the Republican Party Before the Civil War.* New York: Oxford U. Pr.

Formisano, Ronald P. 1971. *The Birth of Mass Political Parties: Michigan, 1827–1861.* Princeton: Princeton U. Pr.

Gara, Larry. 1969. "Slavery and the Slave Power: A Crucial Distinction," 15 *Civil War History* 5.

Gienapp, William E. 1979. "The Crime Against Sumner: The Caning of Charles Sumner and the Rise of the Republican Party." 25 *Civil War History* 218.

———. 1986a. "The Republican Party and the Slave Power." In Robert H. Abzug and Stephen E. Maizlish, eds. *New Perspectives on Race and Slavery in America: Essays in Honor of Kenneth M. Stampp.* Lexington: U. Pr. of Kentucky.

———. 1986b. "Who Voted for Lincoln?" In John L. Thomas, ed. *Abraham Lincoln and the American Political Tradition.* Amherst: U. of Massachusetts Pr.

———. 1987. *The Origins of the Republican Party, 1852–1856.* New York: Oxford U. Pr.

Holt, Michael F. 1969. *Forging a Majority: The Formation of the Republican Party in Pittsburgh, 1848–1860.* New Haven: Yale U. Pr.

———. 1978. *The Political Crisis of the 1850s.* New York: Wiley.

Huston, James L. 1987. *The Panic of 1857 and the Coming of the Civil War.* Baton Rouge: Louisiana State U. Pr.

Kleppner, Paul. 1979. *The Third Electoral System, 1853–1892: Parties, Voters, and Political Cultures.* Chapel Hill: U. of North Carolina Pr.

Luebke, Frederick C., ed. 1971. *Ethnic Voters and the Election of Lincoln.* Lincoln: U. of Nebraska Pr.

Luthin, Reinhard H. 1944. *The First Lincoln Campaign.* Cambridge: Harvard U. Pr.

Maizlish, Stephen E. 1983. *The Triumph of Sectionalism: The Transformation of Ohio Politics, 1844–1856.* Kent, OH: Kent State U. Pr.

Meerse, David E. 1966. "Buchanan, Corruption, and the Election of 1860." 12 *Civil War History* 116.

Nevins, Allan. 1947. *Ordeal of the Union.* 2 vols. New York: Scribner's.

———. 1950. *The Emergence of Lincoln.* 2 vols. New York: Scribner's.

Nichols, Roy F. 1948. *The Disruption of American Democracy.* New York: Macmillan.

Nye, Russel B. 1963. *Fettered Freedom: Civil Liberties and the Slavery Controversy, 1830–1860.* Rev. ed. East Lansing: Michigan State U. Pr.

Potter, David M. 1976. *The Impending Crisis, 1848–1861.* New York: Harper & Row.

Rawley, James A. 1969. *Race and Politics: "Bleeding Kansas" and the Coming of the Civil War.* Philadelphia: J. P. Lippincott.

Roseboom, Eugene H. 1938. "Salmon P. Chase and the Know-Nothings." 25 *Mississippi Valley Historical Review* 335.

Sewell, Richard H. 1976. *Ballots for Freedom: Antislavery Politics in the United States, 1837–1860.* New York: Oxford U. Pr.

Sibley, Joel H. 1985. *The Partisan Imperative: The Dynamics of American Politics Before the Civil War.* New York: Oxford U. Pr.

Stampp, Kenneth M. 1980. *The Imperiled Union: Essays on the Background of the Civil War.* New York: Oxford U. Pr.

———. 1990. *America in 1857: A Nation on the Brink.* New York: Oxford U. Pr.

Jesse Franklin (1760–1823)

A Jeffersonian politician from Georgia. Jesse Franklin served in a variety of state and federal offices during the early national period. Like many of his generation, he followed a common migration pattern from his native Orange County, Virginia, to North Carolina where he moved with his parents in 1774. He fought in the Revolutionary War, rising to the rank of major.

Franklin was elected to the North Carolina state legislature in 1793, 1794, 1797, and 1798, as well as to the state senate in 1805 and 1806. Between these two periods of state officeholding, he was elected to the Fourth U.S. Congress as a Republican (Jeffersonian). He was then chosen as a United States Senator, holding that office from 1799 to 1805. He was elected President *pro tempore* of the U.S. Senate in 1804. Franklin left the Senate briefly for politics back home, but he returned in 1806 and remained until 1813. After leaving Congress, Franklin was named a commissioner to deal with the Chickasaw Indians in 1817. He was governor of North Carolina in 1820–1821.

See also: Jeffersonian Republicans

Kathryn A. Malone

Donald Fraser (1924–)

Democratic reform leader of Congress in the 1970s. Donald Fraser is one of the more unnoticed yet influential members of the Democratic Party in the United States. He was first elected to Congress from Minnesota's Fifth District in 1962, and early in his career he chaired the Democratic Study Group in the House. An early critic of the Vietnam War, he still gave strong support to his fellow Minnesotan, Hubert Humphrey, in 1968. In the late 1960s, he was appointed a member of the Democratic Party commission headed by Harold Hughes of Iowa to examine rules and discrimination within the party, leading to the most significant event in Donald Fraser's career—his chairmanship of the Commission on Party Structure and Delegate Selection (CPSDS)—the McGovern-Fraser Commission.

Fraser became the reform-oriented chairman of the McGovern-Fraser Commission after George McGovern resigned to run for President in 1971. Moreover, his wife Arvonne was a charter member of the National Women's Political Caucus, and when the CPSDS was generating its historic reforms, she was deeply involved in the progressive activities of the women's caucus. Later, when enthusiasm for reform waned within the Democratic Party, Fraser remained a genuine supporter of CPSDS reforms in opposition to the "restorationists." Despite his support for the reforms and openness in the decision-making process, Fraser insisted that party regulars had an essential and undeniable role to play in the presidential selection process (and thus all delegates should *not* be selected in primaries).

Fraser's political career has had lows since his chairmanship of the CPSDS. He left his Fifth District congressional seat in 1978 to run for the U.S. Senate from Minnesota, and although endorsed by the party, he lost to Bob Short, a conservative anti-environmentalist, in the primary (Republican David Durenburger eventually won the seat). Later, Fraser won election as mayor of Minneapolis.

See also: Democratic Study Group, Hubert Humphrey, George McGovern, McGovern-Fraser Commission

David A. Bositis

REFERENCES

Baer, Denise L., and David A. Bositis. 1988. *Elite Cadres and Party Coalitions*. Westport, CT: Greenwood.

Crotty, William. 1983. *Party Reform*. New York: Longman.

Kirkpatrick, Jeane. 1978. *Dismantling the Parties*. Washington: American Enterprise Institute.

Price, David E. 1984. *Bringing Back the Parties*. Washington: Congressional Quarterly.

Shafer, Byron E. 1983. *The Quiet Revolution*. New York: Russell Sage.

Free Congress Political Action Committee

Formerly the Committee for the Survival of a Free Congress (CSFC), the Free Congress Political Action Committee (FCPAC) was established in 1974 (change in names occurred in 1985) to provide technical and financial support to conservative candidates for Congress. Its founder and PAC director is the well-known conservative activist Paul M. Weyrich. The Free Congress Research and Education Foundation is a tax exempt organization headed by Weyrich and associated with FCPAC. The Free Congress Foundation publishes *Political Report*, a newsletter that describes congressional races.

From its inception, CSFC/FCPAC has been among the leading "ideological" PACs in terms of funds raised and expended. It has been criticized by fellow conservatives for its high overhead costs and the relatively small percentage of total funds contributed to candidates, a problem shared by most nonconnected PACs.

Historically, the organization has been challenger-oriented, putting its emphasis on recruiting conservative candidates, training staff and candidates in campaign management, and providing technical campaign services. Unlike most other PACs, it has usually used its own field staff and in-kind contributions for these goals. In the past it has hosted weekly meetings (referred to as the "Kingston" meetings) of "New Right" leaders and conservative groups to coordinate support for selected candidates. FCPAC has shown a willingness to become involved in primary elections and, through its Committee for Effective State Government, in state legislative races. In many respects, the FCPAC supplies the same services in the same way to conservative candidates that the National Committee for an Effective Congress (NCEC) provides for liberal candidates.

See also: Political Action Committees

Clyde Brown

REFERENCES

Crawford, Alan. 1980. *Thunder on the Right*. New York: Pantheon.

Roberts, James C. 1980. *The Conservative Decade*. Westport, CT: Arlington House.

Free Soil Party

A pre-Civil War antislavery party built on the failure of the Liberty Party. Formally organized in 1848, the party began support for the Wilmot Proviso, which sought to limit the extension of slavery into new territories. The party arose because of a split in the New York state Democratic Party between the "hunkers" (those who "hunkered" for office regardless of principle) who turned a blind eye to slavery, and the "barnburners" (alluding to the Dutch farmer who burned his barn to get rid of the rats inside) who opposed slavery. The barnburners withdrew from the Democrats, joining with dissident "conscience" Whigs and former Liberty Party members.

The approach of the Free Soilers was more pragmatic than that of their predecessor party, and much of their political effort was aimed at applying political leverage on the major parties, rather than solely advancing free-soil principles. In fact, strong anti-Black sentiment existed within the party. Although the Wilmot Proviso sought to limit slavery, it also served as a convenient means for keeping Blacks in the South. At the same time, however, the party promoted racial reforms in northern states, fighting for

Blacks' right to vote, testify in court, attend school, and travel freely between the states.

About 20,000 delegates and spectators met in Buffalo, New York, in August 1848. In addition to being the only party to endorse the Wilmot Proviso, the Free Soilers also advocated cheap postage, reduced federal spending, tariff reform, free homesteading, and upgrading of rivers and harbors. These planks were added to broaden the party's appeal. Free Soilers did not, however, endorse the abolition of slavery, nor did they denounce the Fugitive Slave Act or the three-fifths clause in the Constitution. The party's pragmatic approach was seen in its endorsed candidate for President, former President Martin Van Buren. Van Buren had been known as "the Northern man with Southern principles," but he was strongly supported by his fellow New Yorkers. The vice presidential candidate was Charles Francis Adams, a dissident Whig and the son of one President and grandson of another; his antislavery credentials were also undistinguished. Despite this well-known ticket, the Free Soil showing was a disappointment. Van Buren and Adams received about 10 percent of the votes cast, with most of their support coming from New York and Massachusetts. Van Buren failed to carry any state, even though he did win counties scattered throughout the country. The party also elected twelve Congressmen and held the balance of power in the Ohio state legislature. Most important, Free Soilers succeeded in pushing the major parties into coming to terms with the free-soil issue. After the election, the party quickly withered, as most dissidents returned to the major parties, who enticed the renegades with patronage as well as concessions on the free-soil issue.

By 1852 the Free Soil Party consisted mostly of former Liberty men and Whigs. When they met again in 1852, the remaining supporters were more ideological and more openly critical of slavery. Under the name of Free Democrats, the party nominated former Liberty man John P. Hale for President, but he received only 5 percent of the vote. The final blow to the party's aspirations was the Compromise of 1850, which made concessions to both sides of the slavery dispute and was initially embraced as the end of the controversy.

See also: Charles Francis Adams, Barnburners, Conscience Whigs, Election of 1848 and 1852, Fugitive Slave Law, John P. Hale, Hunkers, Liberty Party, Slavery, Martin Van Buren, Wilmot Proviso

Robert J. Spitzer

REFERENCES

Blue, Frederick. 1973. *The Free Soilers.* Urbana: U. of Illinois Pr.

Rayback, Joseph G. 1970. *Free Soil: The Election of 1848.* Lexington: U. Pr. of Kentucky.

John C. Frémont (1813–1890)

First presidential candidate of the Republican Party. In 1856 the newly formed Republican Party nominated the popular and dashing John Charles Frémont as its presidential standard-bearer. This first Republican presidential nominee was born in Georgia and educated at Charleston College. By the time of his nomination, Frémont had developed a reputation as a soldier and explorer and was called the "Pathfinder" because of his several journeys to the Far West. During the campaign Republicans presented the election as a struggle between northern democracy and southern aristocracy. In a close race, James Buchanan, the Democratic Party candidate, defeated Frémont by half a million votes, although Frémont beat the American Party's Millard Fillmore by the same margin.

During the Civil War, President Abraham Lincoln gave Frémont the command of the Western Department, where he was not very successful. Lincoln, alarmed when Frémont established martial law in Missouri and freed the slaves, immediately revoked the emancipation because he feared that it would drive the Border States out of the Union. After issuing his abortive emancipation edict of 1861, Frémont became something of a hero to the abolitionists and radicals of the Republican Party. During the presidential election of 1864, some anti-Lincoln radicals and War Democrats convened in Cleveland, calling themselves the Radical Democratic Party, and nominated Frémont as their presidential candidate. But when no prominent Republicans endorsed him, Frémont withdrew his third-party candidacy, perhaps remembering his own margin over Fillmore eight years earlier.

After the Civil War, railroad speculation not only cost him his fortune but also left his reputation tarnished. He was saved from poverty by appointment by Rutherford Hayes as the territorial governor of Arizona (1878–1883).

See also: James Buchanan, Millard Fillmore, Formation of the Republican Party, Rutherford Hayes, Abraham Lincoln

Margaret Horsnell

REFERENCES

Nevins, Allan. 1928. *Frémont, The West's Greatest Adventurer*. New York: Harper.

———. 1955. *Frémont: Pathfinder of the West*. New York: Longmans, Green.

French Revolution and the First Party System

Almost without exception Americans welcomed the early stages of the French Revolution, and newspapers from Vermont to Georgia filled their pages with enthusiastic accounts of events in France. By the mid-1790s, however, the revolution had become far more controversial in America, and disagreement over events in France served as a basic foundation of the first party system. The increasing radicalism of revolutionary activities in France, particularly the executions of Louis XVI and Marie Antoinette, shocked and frightened those Americans who were starting to identify themselves with the emerging Federalist Party. Led by Alexander Hamilton and John Adams, these Americans supported the establishment of a strong, centralized American government, based on a clear social hierarchy, whose elite would preside over the government. The spread of French radicalism across Europe and even the Atlantic threatened this Federalist status quo. However, the opposing Democrats who rallied around Thomas Jefferson and James Madison interpreted events in France as a vindication of the radicalism of the American Revolution, and an indictment of what they interpreted as the counter-revolutionary policies of the Federalists.

As the first party system took shape during the 1790s, the French Revolution functioned as a crude but accurate political weather vane. While Hamilton's fiscal program had brought about the tentative formation of parties in the First Congress, the radical French Revolution politicized the entire American nation. President George Washington's proclamation of neutrality brought angry attacks from Democrats who thought American treaty obligations to France, now a sister republic struggling for her survival, were selfishly being ignored. The arrival of French ambassador Edmond Genêt occasioned a remarkable series of public receptions from Charleston to Philadelphia, at which tens of thousands of Americans gathered to express their support of the French people. Democrats throughout the nation formed clubs and societies, every one of which included in its constitution a clause upholding France and its revolution. For Democrats, support for France was proof of loyalty to the ideals of the American Revolution—liberty, equality, democracy, and republicanism. They interpreted opposition to the French Revolution as the counter-revolutionary efforts of aristocratic "monarchists" or "monocrats." Federalists, for whom the federal Constitution was the successful institutionalization of a politically and socially conservative reaction to the more radical ideology of the American Revolution, saw events in France as threats to the very fabric of their own society. Horrified Federalists accused deist or even atheist American "Jacobins" of joining subversive Democratic-Republican societies, groups that encouraged class antagonism and the destruction of legitimate political authority.

The French Revolution did not bring about the first American party system; however, by adding a new dimension to existing political discourse, it encouraged the emergence of political parties and partisan sympathies in America. An American's attitude toward France helped to define his or her politics and strengthened the emerging differences between Federalists and Democrats.

See also: John Adams, Federalist Party, Alexander Hamilton, Thomas Jefferson, James Madison, George Washington

Simon P. Newman

REFERENCES

Ammon, Harry. 1973. *The Genet Mission*. New York: Norton.

Combs, Jerald A. 1970. *The Jay Treaty: Political Battleground of the Founding Fathers*. Berkeley: U. of California Pr.

Hazen, Charles Downer. 1897. *Contemporary American Opinion of the French Revolution*. Baltimore: Johns Hopkins U. Pr.

Hyslop, Beatrice F. 1960. "The American Press and the French Revolution of 1789." 104 *Proceedings of the American Philosophical Society* 54–85.

Kaplan, Lawrence S. 1967. *Jefferson and France: An Essay on Politics and Political Ideas*. New Haven: Yale U. Pr.

Link, Eugene Perry. 1942. *Democratic-Republican Societies, 1790–1800*. New York: Columbia U. Pr.

Philip M. Freneau (1752–1832)

Political journalist of the early national period. In February 1791, Thomas Jefferson offered Philip M. Freneau, a Princeton University graduate and former Revolutionary War sea captain, by that time a poet and editor of the New York *Daily Advertiser*, a job as translating clerk for the Department of State. Although the job paid only $250 a year, Jefferson hoped that

Freneau's talents could be used far beyond translating foreign dispatches; he hoped that Freneau would use his editorial skills to establish a Democratic-Republican Party paper in the nation's capital. Both Jefferson and James Madison realized that they needed to go beyond Congress and the Cabinet in fostering public support for their policies. Freneau had attracted a wide audience a decade earlier by describing the brutality of his imprisonment by the British in his poem "The British Prison Ship."

Though he at first declined the position, Freneau was eventually persuaded by Madison to lend his pen to the Jeffersonians. On October 31, 1791, the first issue of the *National Gazette* was published. It was strongly pro-French; Freneau praised Thomas Paine and excoriated Edmund Burke. He was more inclined to radical views than either Jefferson or Madison, but by communicating the views of party leaders he gave a cohesiveness to the Democratic-Republican Party. His editorials were subscribed to by many county weeklies, and as a result he helped spread the party line throughout the country. By 1793 Jefferson had made his decision to leave the government, and Freneau had lost his taste for political competition. The *Aurora* under Benjamin Franklin Bache replaced the *National Gazette* as the party paper in Philadelphia, and Freneau retired to New Jersey and the somewhat impecunious life of a poet.

See also: Democratic-Republican Societies, Thomas Jefferson, Jeffersonian Republicans, James Madison

Daniel Dean Roland

REFERENCES

Chambers, William Nisbett. 1963. *Political Parties in a New Nation*. New York: Oxford U. Pr.

Cunningham, Noble. 1957. *The Jeffersonian Republicans: The Formation of Party Organization, 1789–1801*. Chapel Hill: U. of North Carolina Pr.

Ford, Paul Leicester. 1892–1899. *Thomas Jefferson, Writings*. 10 vols. New York: Putnam.

Hamilton, Stanislaus Murray. 1898–1903. *James Monroe, Writings*. 7 vols. New York: Putnam.

Hunt, Gaillard. 1898–1910. *James Madison, Writings*. 9 vols. New York: Putnam.

Leary, Lewis. 1941. *That Rascal Freneau*. New Brunswick, NJ: Rutgers U. Pr.

Marsh, Philip M. 1970. *Freneau's Published Prose: A Bibliography*. Metuchen, NJ: Scarecrow Press.

Miller, John C. 1960. *The Federalist Era*. New York: Harper.

Syrett, Harold. 1961–1987. *Papers of Alexander Hamilton*. 27 vols. New York: Columbia U. Pr.

Betty Friedan (1921–)

Feminist author and organizer. Betty Friedan was born Betty Naomi Goldstein in Peoria, Illinois, one year after women won the right to vote. She was to ignite the modern-day feminist movement with the publication of her 1963 bestseller *The Feminine Mystique*. During the late 1960s and 1970s she was a dominant figure in the feminist battle to change America's outlook on women's roles and its treatment of women in the workplace and at home. In her 1982 book *The Second Stage* Friedan laid out revisionist views on the goals of the women's movement, including a controversial suggestion that women's groups should devote greater attention to supporting family issues such as child care and parental leave.

"The choices we sought in the 1970s are not as simple as they once seemed," Friedan said, as the 1980s began. "We must now make our new position more livable . . . or else we are going to see a lot of tired, bitter, lonely, disillusioned women out there."

The daughter of immigrant Jewish parents, Friedan grew up an outsider in a homogeneous midwestern community. "I was that girl with all A's and I wanted boys worse than anything," she once said. After graduating from Smith College in 1942, Friedan found what she thought she wanted, a husband. Friedan married, moved to the suburbs, raised three children, and, in time, divorced. Friedan later wrote about her dissatisfaction with life as a suburban housewife: "Eight schizophrenic years of trying to be a kind of woman I wasn't." But her cogent analysis of the immense social pressures militating against women's freedom to lead more multidimensional lives did help spur a feminist revolution.

Along with writing and public speaking, Friedan was a prodigious organizer. As she observed in an interview in 1983, "You can just spend so long on consciousness-raising and then it's like looking at your navel." In 1966 Friedan founded NOW, the National Organization for Women, to press for "full equality for women in a fully equal partnership with men." The next year Friedan reinitiated the battle for the Equal Rights Amendment, which had been dropped in 1923; in 1969, she co-founded NARAL, the National Abortion Rights Action League, to support a woman's right to choose an abortion; in 1970 she started up the NOW Legal Defense and Education Fund, to raise and distribute money for legal defense of women's rights issues; in 1971 Friedan co-founded the National

Women's Political Caucus to support profeminist candidates.

As the 1990s approached, Friedan turned her attention to the issue of aging, but her commitment to feminism never wavers: "If someone says to me, 'I'm not a feminist but I want to be an astronaut,' or whatever, I have no patience."

See also: Equal Rights Amendment, National Women's Political Caucus

Melissa Ludtke

REFERENCES

Gardner, Marilyn. 1988. "Where Were You When the Mystique Was Shattered?" (January 11) *The Christian Science Monitor*, 1.

Suplee, Curt. 1983. "Betty Friedan: The Dream Coming True." (October 19) *The Washington Post*, B1.

Furth, Jane. 1988. "Her Cause and Effect" (February) *Life*, 97.

French, Marilyn. 1983. "The Emancipation of Betty Friedan" (December) *Esquire*, 510.

William P. Frye (1830–1911)

Maine Republican Congressman and Senator at the turn of the century. William Pierce Frye represented Maine in the U.S. Congress, both in the House and Senate, continuously from 1871 to 1911. He rose to top leadership positions in each chamber, and when he died he was President pro tempore of the U.S. Senate.

In his early political life Frye was known as a radical Republican, demanding full "reconstruction" of the South, protection of the civil rights of southern Blacks, and generous pensions for Union veterans. After his election to the U.S. House of Representatives, Frye advanced quickly within the hierarchy, serving on the Judiciary, Ways and Means, and Rules committees. In this latter role, he was instrumental in designing the recodification of House Rules in the Forty-sixth Congress (1880). Frye was selected for the Senate in 1881 to fill the unexpired term of James G. Blaine; at the time, it was reported that Frye had been a principal contender for election to the speakership.

Frye continued his national political career in the Senate, continuing his support for mainline Republican principles and quickly entering the inner circle of Republican Party leadership. He became chairman of the Senate Rules Committee in 1883 and matched his House service by leading the effort to recodify the Senate rules in the Forty-eighth Congress. His other committee memberships also indicated his authority within the Senate: Commerce (chair), Foreign Relations, and Appropriations committees.

He was elected President pro tempore of the Senate in 1896 and served in that position until his death in 1911. Frye was frequently in the chair during this tenure contrary to modern practice, and he used this thorough knowledge of Senate procedures to guide floor proceedings in the favor of "regular" Republicans. Frye actually resigned from this position four months before he died, beset by poor health and the rising progressive insurgency in the Senate. Yet contention was so great over selecting a successor that no permanent replacement was elected for the remainder of the Sixty-second Congress.

See also: James G. Blaine, Reconstruction

Charles Stewart III

Fugitive Slave Law

In terms of actual numbers, the slaves who successfully escaped to freedom in the North or in other nations were quite few: the best estimate is that no more than 1,000 slaves annually eluded recapture. To southerners, however, the "rendition" (return) of fugitive slaves took on a high symbolic value that increased as antislavery sentiment grew in the North.

The United States Constitution permitted legislation to systematize the return of runaway slaves who had reached the jurisdiction of nonslaveholding states. Congress enacted a vaguely worded fugitive slave law in 1793, but many northern states passed their own personal liberty laws that guaranteed accused fugitives the protection of due process. Southern displeasure with these laws led to the inclusion of a new and more stringent fugitive slave law as a part of the package of legislation popularly known as the Compromise of 1850.

President Millard Fillmore signed the new fugitive slave law on September 18, 1850. This measure authorized the appointment of special commissioners empowered to issue warrants and grant certificates for the return of slaves to their owners. A controversial provision of the law paid these federal commissioners a $10 fee if they remanded or sent back an accused fugitive rather than a $5 fee if they released him or her. Critics also noted that the law defined "satisfactory proof" of ownership as a copy of the testimony of the master before his or her home state court along with a description of the fugitive. The new law made anyone interfering with the apprehension of a fugitive liable to fine and imprisonment and empowered federal marshals to use as much manpower as necessary to return a slave to his owner. State governments and local officials were prohibited from attempting to block the recapture of runaways.

Northern abolitionists and free Blacks condemned the Fugitive Slave Law of 1850 as inherently unfair and as a symbol of the subservience of the federal government to the dictates of slaveholders. A majority of northerners, including some politicians, opposed the extension of slavery into western territories; however, they conceded the existence of the constitutional obligation of the free states to help enforce the new law.

A fear of reenslavement prompted an undetermined number of runaway slaves residing in the North in the 1850s to flee to Canada or to Great Britain to escape rendition. Most runaways, however, remained in the North, and efforts to enforce the new law created bitter controversy. On several occasions, mixed mobs of Blacks and white abolitionists managed to free arrested fugitives from federal authority. A well-publicized series of renditions of runaways, sometimes featuring the employment of federal troops to assist the legal authorities, created unprecedented sympathy in the North for the plight of the slaves.

The growing displeasure of many northerners with the federal government's slave-catching efforts led several state legislatures to revive or strengthen their personal liberty laws, in turn causing southerners to charge a breach of the Compromise of 1850. In the North, this issue assisted the newly formed Republican Party in winning control of several state governments and finally the White House in 1861. In the South, the dispute over enforcement of the Fugitive Slave Law strengthened forces calling for secession. The controversial Fugitive Slave Law finally was repealed by the Republican-dominated Congress in 1864 in the midst of the Civil War.

See also: Abolition Movement, Millard Fillmore, Slavery

John R. McKivigan

REFERENCES

Campbell, Stanley W. 1968. *The Slave Catchers: Enforcement of the Fugitive Slave Law, 1850–1860.* Chapel Hill: U. of North Carolina Pr.

Cover, Robert M. 1975. *Justice Accused: Antislavery and the Judicial Process.* New Haven: Yale U. Pr.

Thomas D. Morris. 1974. *Free Men All: The Personal Liberty Laws of the North, 1780–1861.* Baltimore: Johns Hopkins U. Pr.

J. William Fulbright (1905–)

Democratic Senator from Arkansas. Senator J. William Fulbright pursued two careers—one as a university faculty member and administrator and the second as a United States Senator. While these can be quite diverse career patterns, Senator Fulbright managed to combine them in a coherent fashion. His devotion to education in general and to strengthening international understanding in particular was at the center of his careers in both arenas.

Fulbright was born in Sumner, Missouri, and at an early age he moved with his family to Fayetteville, Arkansas, the home of the University of Arkansas. Fulbright graduated from that university in 1925 and then attended Oxford University as a Rhodes Scholar. After taking a law degree from George Washington University, Fulbright went to work at the Department of Justice in 1934, returning to his alma mater in 1936 as a professor of law. He was then named president of the University of Arkansas in 1939 at 34 years old, one of the youngest college presidents in the nation. Fulbright headed the university until 1941 when he was removed by Governor Homer Adkins in a political dispute triggered by criticism of the governor aired in the Fulbright family newspaper.

In 1942 Fulbright ran for and was elected to the House of Representatives where he served one term. During that term he authored a resolution that helped lead the United States out of isolationism and into the United Nations at the end of World War II. In 1944 Fulbright was elected to the U.S. Senate. Ironically, in the Democratic primary he beat the governor who had fired him, Homer Adkins. Fulbright had a distinguished career in the Senate, where he authored the Fulbright Act of 1946, establishing the faculty and student program for international educational exchanges that still bears his name. The Fulbright fellowships have become the largest and most prestigious academic exchange program of their kind in the world, facilitating the exchange of hundreds of students and faculty each year between the United States and other countries of the world. This exchange program was probably Fulbright's most enduring intellectual contribution during his service in the Senate.

Fulbright was a Democrat, usually associated with the more moderate to liberal wing of his party, an image especially reinforced by Fulbright's interest in the international arena. He was elected chair of the Senate Foreign Relations Committee in 1959, a position he held until his defeat for the Senate in 1974. Always known as an internationalist because of his interest in expanding his nation's relations with the rest of the world and in its active role in world affairs, intellectually, Fulbright was often identified with the school of "realism" as defined by Hans Morgenthau in political science circles and George Kennan in diplomatic circles. Fulbright believed in the pursuit of America's national interests—without much distraction by ideology and devoid of any romanticism in defining that national interest—and he was an early supporter of the policy of "containment" of communism. Nevertheless, later in his career Fulbright became skeptical of what he saw as the overemphasis on the employment of military power in American foreign and defense policy. As chair of the Senate Foreign Relations Committee, Fulbright became a leading critic of the war in Vietnam. This criticism led to a break with Lyndon Johnson over his escalation of the war and to Fulbright's alienation from some of his former friends in the Foreign Relations Committee; Senator Fulbright held well-publicized hearings on the conduct of the war in Vietnam. Those hearings were widely credited with having helped move American public opinion toward a position of opposition to the Vietnam War. In 1974 Senator Fulbright was defeated by Governor Dale Bumpers in the Democratic primary. Bumpers at that time was highly popular and considered to be an ally of Fulbright, and they did not differ materially on the issues.

Although Fulbright was a dependable Democrat on most issues, his partisanship never seemed to run deep. He became a critic of and nemesis to both Presidents Harry Truman and Lyndon Johnson. He was often seen as something of an idealist because of his international involvements; however, he could also be a very pragmatic politician. He took pride in looking out for the farmers of Arkansas, often stressing the importance of the export market for jobs in Arkansas. At the time of greatest racial tension in the South, Fulbright signed the "Southern Manifesto," a response to the 1954 Supreme Court decision on desegregation. It was frequently speculated that this act alone cost him an opportunity to become John Kennedy's Secretary of State in 1960; however, this was a position Fulbright publicly professed not to want at all, saying instead that he was quite happy in the Senate. At the time of his defeat in 1974,

Fulbright had served in the Senate for 30 years. He then became a lawyer with a large law firm in Washington, D.C., and continued to write and speak out on issues relevant to foreign policy.

See also: Isolationism in American Politics, Lyndon B. Johnson, John F. Kennedy, Harry S Truman

John S. Jackson III

REFERENCES

Coffin, Tristam. 1966. *Senator Fulbright: Portrait of a Public Philosopher*. New York: Dutton.

Fulbright, J. William. 1963. *Prospects for the West*. Cambridge, MA: Harvard U. Pr.

———. 1989. *The Price of Empire*. New York: Pantheon Books.

Meyer, Karl E., ed. 1963. *Fulbright of Arkansas*. Washington, DC: Robert B. Luce, Inc.

Fund for a Conservative Majority

Founded in 1972 by former members of Young Americans for Freedom, the Fund for a Conservative Majority (FCM) claims to be the first conservative political action committee. It raises money through direct-mail solicitation, makes contributions to candidates, and spends directly on behalf of candidates. In addition, it has engaged in some lobbying, including opposition to federal regulation of election activitie1s; it has also called for abolition of the Federal Election Commission. Also known as Young America Campaign, it is incorporated under Virginia laws and is based in Washington, D.C.

The organization seems to have reached its peak in the 1983–1984 election cycle, when it spent $5.4 million on behalf of the reelection of President Ronald Reagan. It also contributed $218,338 and $3,310 to Republican and Democratic congressional candidates, respectively.

FCM was a party to *Federal Election Commission v. National Conservative PAC, et al.* (470 U. S. 480 (1985)), in which the right of political action committees to spend without limit on behalf of President Reagan's candidacy was challenged. The Supreme Court ruled that the statute limiting political committee expenditures to $1,000 was unconstitutional.

Like other conservative organizations that have encountered complacency or burnout among their supporters, FCM seems to have entered a period of particular difficulty. In 1988 the organization filed for protection under the bankruptcy code, which permits it to remain in business while working its way out of debt.

See also: Federal Election Commission, Ronald Reagan, Young Americans for Freedom

Douglas I. Hodgkin

REFERENCES

Federal Election Commission v. National Conservative PAC, et al. 470 U. S. 480 (1985).

Zuckerman, Ed, ed. 1988. *Almanac of Federal PACs: 1988.* Washington, DC: Amward Publications.

Fundamentalism and Politics

A conservative religious movement born in the early twentieth century to combat theological liberalism and to convert individuals to Christ, fundamentalism also had a political dimension. Before World War I, fundamentalists remained aloof from politics, supporting prohibition, but pushing for few progressive reforms. During the 1920s, however, the movement became more political as fundamentalists fought to preserve "Christian civilization," a culture putatively based on biblical values. Although their predecessors—nineteenth-century evangelicals—had no firm political philosophy, they reacted somewhat haphazardly to perceived threats. Ministers emphasized the premillennial return of Christ yet focused on the temporal by becoming increasingly politicized. Political struggles, especially religious ones, turned into battles between good and evil. In any event, most fundamentalists merely reflected the conservatism of the era, and northern and midwestern fundamentalists tended to be Republican, while southerners were Democrats.

In the early 1920s conservative evangelicals fought the teaching of evolution in public schools as a threat to the authority of the Bible. A prominent Democratic politician and Presbyterian layman, William Jennings Bryan, led the anti-evolution crusade. Several state legislatures debated anti-evolution laws, but only a few southern states passed them, notably Tennessee. At the ensuing Scopes Trial there, involving the legality of teaching evolution to high school students, evangelicals suffered a humiliating defeat in the court of public opinion.

In their other major political crusade of the decade, fundamentalists opposed the 1928 presidential candidate Al Smith. As a "wet," Catholic, ethnic urbanite, Smith symbolized to conservative Protestants all that was degenerate in America. Most evangelical ministers supported Herbert Hoover—no easy choice for southern Democratic fundamentalists, in a region where one-party politics dominated electoral life. John Roach Straton, fundamentalist pastor of New York City, led the charge against Smith. In the end, however, religion probably played only a minor role in the outcome, since economic prosperity assured a Hoover victory.

In the 1930s fundamentalists unsuccessfully fought repeal of prohibition. They supported "Fighting Bob" Shuler of Los Angeles, the nominee of the Prohibition Party of California for the United States Senate, who lost by only 50,000 votes. Most conservative evangelicals avoided the political arena directly but criticized the New Deal as regimentarian and destructive of free enterprise. At the same time, many ministers viewed Mussolini and Hitler as possible anti-Christs.

Fundamentalists spoke out against the Bolshevik menace in the decades after World War I. Communism represented the ultimate atheistic threat, but fundamentalists also believed that communism's emergence fulfilled the prophecies of scripture concerning the premillennial return of Christ. Strong anticommunism marked the cold war politics of fundamentalists like Carl McIntire and Billy James Hargis. Both men wanted a more vigorous war against the Soviet enemy at home and in the world.

In the 1970s conservative Protestants re-emerged in politics, primarily in response to the liberal policies of the era—removal of prayer and Bible reading in schools, defeat in Vietnam, the feminist movement, and abortion. As in the 1920s they sensed serious threats to their values. In 1976 Jimmy Carter introduced "born again" into the American political lexicon (Carter was a born-again Christian), and with the support of southern white evangelicals he won the presidency. In 1979, disappointed by Carter's policies, fundamentalists working with conservative Catholics and Mormons organized the Moral Majority, led by Baptist minister Jerry Falwell. Religious conservatives played a key role in the defeat of the Equal Rights Amendment and were instrumental in the successful 1980 election of Ronald Reagan, who received 60 percent of the white born-again Christian vote.

In the 1980s charismatic Christians, those who practiced faith healing and spoke in "tongues," joined the political fray; their addition meant greater electoral potential for the Religious Right. Pat Robertson relied on this group as his political base in his 1988 bid for the Republican presidential nomination.

In the twentieth century, fundamentalists have used politics as a tool to advance their conservative agenda, just as liberal Protestants, Catholics, and Jews fought for specific policies. Conservative Protestants also learned that in a pluralist society democracy could work for them as well.

See also: William Jennings Bryan, Jimmy Carter, Herbert Hoover, Ku Klux Klan, Prohibition, Alfred E. Smith

Douglas Carl Abrams

REFERENCES

Jorstad, Erling. 1970. *The Politics of Doomsday.* New York: Abingdon.

Kater, John L., Jr. 1982. *Christians on the Right.* New York: Seabury.

Marsden, George M. 1980. *Fundamentalism and American Culture.* New York: Oxford U. Pr.

Fusion Party in New York City

For more than a century following the Civil War, elections in New York City were dominated by the Manhattan-based Democratic Party Organization, popularly known as Tammany Hall. So effective was the Hall's ability to mobilize voter support, and so strong was the antipathy felt by a large portion of the city electorate toward the Republican Party, that during this period the only strategy open to would-be challengers of Democratic control was the formation of an anti-Tammany coalition; good-government groups, local political parties, and (usually) the Republican Party would have to work together on a common slate of candidates for city offices. This strategy generated what came to be styled "Fusion" movements, with candidates backed by them known as "Fusion" candidates. Fusion mayoral candidates were successful in 1871 (William Havemeyer), 1895 (William Strong), 1901 (Seth Low), 1913 (John Mitchel), and, most notably, in 1933, 1937, and 1941, when Fiorello La Guardia led the Fusion cause. Other local election years in New York City featured less successful Fusion campaigns.

The term "fusion" was commonplace in American politics during the latter half of the nineteenth century, referring to the nomination of the same candidate by two or more political parties. Such candidacies became increasingly rare after 1890s, however, as one state after another outlawed multiple-party nominations. Only because New York State remained an exception to this trend were the forces for good government in New York City able to continue the fusion tactic, thereby allowing the label "Fusion" to acquire its present connotation of good government, nonpartisanship, and anti-Tammany. The party-column ballot format used in New York City further contributed to the success of the fusion tactic: each of the nominated parties was able to list the Fusion candidate in its own ballot column.

Before 1933 there was no actual Fusion party, and in the various elections that featured Fusion candidates, the only Fusion ballot column that could be said to belong to an established political party was the Republican column. The other columns that listed the Fusion candidates resulted from ballot petition efforts of citizen groups, such as the Citizens Union, or of ad hoc groups, such as those formed by dissident Democrats. Thus in the election of 1901 the name of the Fusion mayoral candidate (Low) appeared in the Republican column, in the Citizen's Union column, and in a column labeled "Greater New York Democracy."

The City Fusion Party was organized in 1933 by prominent good-government activists whose intention was to create an organization that would become a permanent force in city politics, he immediate aim of which was defeating Tammany in the 1933 mayoral election. The party organized branches in each borough and most assembly districts and in its first year was able to enroll a membership of nearly 50,000. La Guardia's initial victory in 1933 resulted from combining the 446,833 votes in the Republican column with 421,689 votes cast in the City Fusion Party column. Neither total by itself would have been sufficient to defeat his Tammany opponent. By 1937 the party had become an insignificant actor in city politics. Ignored by La Guardia and forced to compete with new good-government organizations and a new political party (the American Labor Party), the City Fusion Party contributed a mere 7 percent to La Guardia's vote total in the year's election. Through 1957 the party continued to enter the name of the anti-Tammany mayoral candidate in a City Fusion ballot column, but it remained an organization on paper only, without structural underpinnings.

See also: American Labor Party, Fiorello La Guardia, Tammany Hall

Howard Scarrow

REFERENCES

Garrett, Charles. 1961. *The La Guardia Years.* New Brunswick, NJ: Rutgers U. Pr.

Mann, Arthur. 1965. *La Guardia Comes to Power 1933.* Philadelphia: J. P. Lippincott.

Scarrow, Howard A. 1986. "Duverger's Law, Fusion, and the Decline of American 'Third' Parties." 39 *Western Political Quarterly* 634.

G

Guy G. Gabrielson (1891–1976)

Chairman of the Republican National Committee. Guy George Gabrielson chaired the Republican Party in the tense period (1949–1952) leading up to the Dwight Eisenhower–Robert Taft contest at the 1952 national convention. Gabrielson was born on an Iowa farm, attended the University of Iowa, and got a law degree from Harvard in 1917. During World War I, he was commissioned a second lieutenant in the air service. Settling in New Jersey after the war, he practiced there for a decade before extending his law practice to New York City in 1931.

Elected to the New Jersey Assembly, Gabrielson served from 1926 to 1930—in 1928 as its majority leader and in 1929 as speaker. By the 1940s he had become a member of the Republican National Committee (RNC). Following Thomas E. Dewey's defeat in the 1948 presidential election, supporters of Senator Robert A. Taft and former Governor Harold Stassen sought to retire National Chairman Hugh D. Scott, Jr., a Dewey associate. The RNC appointed a seven-member "peace committee" (including the neutral Gabrielson) to explore the prospects for a compromise. Although the efforts of the committee failed, Gabrielson was elevated to the executive committee of the RNC.

When Scott eventually resigned, the choice of his successor was expected to be a Taft-Dewey-Stassen free-for-all. Gabrielson campaigned for the office actively, and Senator Taft indicated that he was "acceptable." Dewey followers, however, favored Axel J. Beck of South Dakota. Gabrielson beat Beck 52 to 47, the vote predicting the outcome of the 1952 national convention.

Chairman Gabrielson promptly authorized the preparation of an organizational study to put GOP national headquarters on a "businesslike basis." With the approval of specific state and county party leaders, he put teams of professional organizers into the field as a "School for Politics." His midterm platform themes decried "socialism in government" and endorsed the investigative activities of Senator Joseph McCarthy. Republican gains in the 1950 elections were generally credited to Gabrielson.

Gabrielson survived charges that, even as national chairman, he sought favors for one of his business interests from the Reconstruction Finance Corporation. In his final year in the chairmanship, he tried to consolidate the House and Senate campaign committees that were consolidated with the national committee. Gabrielson favored Taft in the 1952 Eisenhower-Taft presidential contest, and he resigned as RNC chairman after Eisenhower's victory.

See also: Thomas E. Dewey, Dwight D. Eisenhower, Joseph McCarthy, Republican National Committee, Robert A. Taft

Ralph M. Goldman

REFERENCES

Goldman, Ralph M. 1990. *The National Party Chairmen and Committees: Factionalism at the Top.* Armonk, NY: M. E. Sharpe.

Gaffney v. Cummings
412 U.S. 735 (1973)

In this case, the Supreme Court upheld a state legislative districting plan for the state of Connecticut in which the maximum deviation between the sizes of districts was 7.8 percent.

The suit was brought under a theory that such inequity in voting populations was invidious discrimination under the equal protection clause of the Fourteenth Amendment.

Although the Court has held that smaller discrepancies are impermissible for federal congressional districting, it was consciously more deferential to the autonomy of the states in designing state districting plans. Thus, the Court held that the deviations in Connecticut's plan did not make out a prima facie case under the Fourteenth Amendment.

The plaintiff in *Gaffney* also alleged that the districting plan was unconstitutional because it had been drawn with an improper purpose in mind. Specifically, he alleged that the plan was designed to create a legislature whose composition fairly reflected the relative strength and weakness of the Republican and Democratic parties in the state of Connecticut. This allegation was not denied.

The Court, however, ruled that such political motivations did not necessarily make a districting plan unconstitutional. Writing for the majority, Byron White recognized, "The reality is that districting inevitably has and is intended to have substantial political consequences." Thus, apportionment is a political task, and in arguing that an apportionment plan is unconstitutional, it is insufficient merely to allege that political considerations were taken into account in determining the sizes and shapes of new districts. Something more must be alleged and proven if a redistricting plan is to be declared unconstitutional.

Keith Barnett

Gag Rule

From the 1790s until the 1820s, Congress annually received several petitions calling for an end to the slave trade or the gradual emancipation of all slaves. These petitions routinely were referred to committee with little discussion and then forgotten. In the early 1830s, however, the newly founded American Anti-Slavery Society made these petitions to Congress for the immediate abolition of slavery in the federal territories one of its major propaganda tools. Soon the volume of abolitionist petitions arriving in Congress threatened to bog down the regular flow of business; moreover, antislavery Congressmen also used the presentation of these petitions as occasions to make antislavery speeches. Their inflammatory rhetoric convinced southern militants of the need to act decisively to suppress the discussion of slavery in Congress.

In 1836 the House of Representatives passed a resolution introduced by Henry L. Pinckney of South Carolina barring the printing or reading of abolitionist petitions to Congress and requiring all such petitions to be tabled permanently without action. Northern Democrats joined southern Democrats and Whigs to pass the measure 117 to 68. Ironically, Pinckney's "gag rule" angered militant anti-abolitionists like John C. Calhoun of South Carolina, who argued that Congress should not even have received the petitions from abolitionists.

Passage of the gag rule disturbed many believers in free speech and helped sensitize them to the abolitionist complaints against the minority South's domination of the federal government. The American Anti-Slavery Society redoubled its drive to embarrass the South and sent Congress over 400,000 petitions in 1837 and 1838. Southern members of the U.S. Senate, led by Henry Clay who realized that the House's action had inadvertently aided the abolitionists, rejected passing a similar "gag rule" in the Senate.

Former President John Quincy Adams, who served in the House from 1831 to 1848, became the leading opponent of the gag rule in that chamber. Adams and a growing number of northern Whigs, including Joshua R. Giddings of Ohio, also tried to circumvent the gag by various parliamentary stratagems. In 1837 and 1842, outraged southern members attempted but failed to censure Adams for violation of House rules. When the House did censure Giddings for a similar offense in 1842, he resigned and won a triumphal reelection by his district. Such incidents attracted the very national attention to the issue of slavery that the gag rule had hoped to avoid.

To counter the maneuvers of antislavery members, the House in January 1840 adopted Standing Rule 21: antislavery petitions "shall not be received by this House, nor entertained in any way by it." Each subsequent year, Adams and Giddings made the debate over renewal of this rule a nationally publicized forum on free speech and slavery. The votes against the gag rule grew more numerous each session in the 1840s: it was rejected in December 1844 by 108 to 80; a majority of northern Democrats and four southern Whigs joined the unanimous northern Whigs in opposing it. The gag rule dispute was an early indication of the potential for slavery-related questions to agitate public opinion and disrupt the national political system.

See also: Abolition Movement, John Quincy Adams, John C. Calhoun, Joshua Giddings, Emancipation as a Political Issue, Slavery

John R. McKivigan

REFERENCES

Barnes, Gilbert Hobbs. 1933. *The Antislavery Impulse, 1833–1844.* New York: Appleton-Century-Crofts.

Freehling, William W. 1966. *Prelude to Civil War: The Nullification Controversy in South Carolina, 1816–1836.* New York: Harper & Row.

Nye, Russell B. 1963. *Fettered Freedom: Civil Liberties and the Slavery Controversy, 1830–1860.* Urbana: U. of Illinois Pr.

Richards, Leonard L. 1986. *The Life and Times of Congressman John Quincy Adams.* New York: Oxford U. Pr.

John Gaillard (1765–1826)

Early national period leader of the U.S. Senate from South Carolina. Born into one of South Carolina's wealthiest and most powerful families, John Gaillard and his brother were sent to London to study law at the Middle Temple as soon as the Revolutionary War ended in 1782. Gaillard himself never did practice law, preferring the life of a planter in St. Stephen's Parish after his marriage in 1792. He was elected to the South Carolina legislature in 1794, and then to the state senate, where he served from 1796 to 1804. Gaillard was a Jeffersonian Republican and a presidential elector in 1804. He was chosen to fill the unexpired term of South Carolina's Pierce Butler, taking his seat in the United States Senate in January 1805. He was elected in his own right the next year and remained in the Senate until his death 20 years later.

Gaillard was an ideologically consistent southern Republican, a partisan who supported Thomas Jefferson on every issue except the Samuel Chase impeachment, when he voted to acquit. He opposed the rechartering of the Bank of the United States, the establishment of the Second Bank of the United States, as well as federally financed internal improvements. He guarded the interests of slavery and supported war in 1812 and joined most of his colleagues in voting for the Tariff of 1816 in a burst of postwar nationalism. He steadfastly opposed all subsequent protective measures. Gaillard was first chosen President *pro tempore* of the Senate in 1814, and served in that post almost continuously until his death. He spent much influential time presiding because of the death in office of two Vice Presidents, George Clinton and Elbridge Gerry. Gaillard was one of the paradoxical South Carolina aristocrats who provided so much early leadership to the great republican experiment.

See also: Jeffersonian Republicans, Second Bank of the United States, Slavery

Kathryn A. Malone

Albert Gallatin (1761–1849)

Statesman, diplomat, and ethnologist. Albert Gallatin was an important yet neglected figure in the economic, political, and cultural history of the early Republic. Born in Switzerland, Gallatin immigrated to Massachusetts in 1780 and by 1784 had settled in the Pennsylvania back country. In 1793 he was elected to the U.S. Senate as a Republican, only to be unseated the following year by the Federalist majority on the grounds that he did not meet the citizenship requirement. Though opposed to Alexander Hamilton's federal excise tax of 1791, Gallatin steered a moderate course during the 1794 Whiskey Rebellion. In 1795 he was elected to the House, where he soon emerged as the leader of the Republican minority. A sharp and well-informed critic of Federalist financial policy, his efforts led to the establishment of the Standing Committee on Ways and Means.

With the victory of Thomas Jefferson in 1800, Gallatin emerged as the new administration's leading authority on public finance. Appointed Secretary of the Treasury, Gallatin served for 14 years—the longest tenure in American history. His proposals included an ambitious system of federally funded internal improvements and the extinction of the federal deficit. Unfortunately, these proposals fell victim after 1807 to the increasingly unstable international environment and were never implemented. Recently, Gallatin's initiatives have been the subject of close scrutiny by historians intent on reconstructing the basic political and economic assumptions of the Jeffersonians.

As a diplomat, Gallatin helped to draft the Treaty of Ghent with Great Britain ending the War of 1812, and he served as minister to France (1816–1823) and Great Britain (1826–1827). In 1824 Gallatin was nominated for the vice presidency on a ticket headed by William H. Crawford of Georgia. Called the "father of American ethnology," in his retirement he published a pioneering work on the Indian tribes of North America, and in 1842 he founded the American Ethnological Society.

See also: Alexander Hamilton, Thomas Jefferson

Richard R. John

REFERENCES

Nelson, John, Jr. 1987. *Liberty and Property: Political Economy and Policymaking in the New Nation, 1789–1812*. Baltimore: Johns Hopkins U. Pr.

Walters, Raymond, Jr. 1957. *Albert Gallatin: Jeffersonian Financier and Diplomat*. New York: Macmillan.

Watts, Steven. 1987. *The Republic Reborn: War and the Making of Liberal America, 1790–1820*. Baltimore: Johns Hopkins U. Pr.

George Gallup (1901–1984)

Leading chronicler of American public opinion. More than any other practitioner's, George Gallup's name is synonymous with public opinion polling; and more than anyone else, he is responsible for making it the important force in American politics and society that it is today. Gallup made his name through a combination of technical skill, business acumen, and risk taking. Born in Jefferson, Iowa, he graduated from Iowa State University in 1923 and remained there as an instructor in journalism, while pursuing a masters degree in psychology and a Ph.D. in journalism. He then went on to teach journalism at Drake and Northwestern universities.

In 1932 Gallup became director of research for the advertising firm of Young and Republican, an association that continued until 1947. In his spare time he worked to develop the Gallup Poll and to establish the American Institute of Public Opinion (AIPO). Although the first release from AIPO appeared on October 20, 1935, it was Gallup's performance in the 1936 presidential election that insured his position in polling history. Confident of the superiority of his quota sampling technique over the straw poll procedure of the *Literary Digest* poll, and cognizant of the upper-class bias of the *Digest's* sample, Gallup confidently predicted, even before the other poll was published, that the *Digest* would give Alfred Landon 56 percent. He went on to contend that this prediction would be totally incorrect and that Franklin Roosevelt would easily win. When both the *Digest* poll and the election results corroborated his predictions, Gallup's established methods of scientific polling emerged as the only legitimate technique.

Gallup's one major setback occurred in 1948 when he, along with most other pollsters, predicted a Thomas Dewey victory. But since the primary causes of this failure (quota sampling and the cessation of surveying too long before the election) were obvious, Gallup was able to use this failure to improve his own techniques.

His credibility gained with each subsequent correct prediction.

The Gallup Poll was instrumental in introducing questions that are now taken for granted, asking them over a long period of time. Presidential approval, the role of women, and the most important problem facing the country are only three examples that date from 1940 or before. His concern with the intensity of opinions was vitally important in attitude measurement. Gallup consistently defended the industry he had helped make, frequently stating his belief that public opinion polls provided an important channel for the citizen to communicate with decision-makers.

See also: Election of 1936

Ronald Rapoport

REFERENCES

Converse, Jean. 1987. *Survey Research in the United States*. Berkeley: U. of California Pr.

Gallup, George. 1972. *Sophisticated Poll Watcher's Guide*. Princeton: Princeton U. Pr.

———, and Saul F. Rae. 1940. *The Pulse of Democracy*. New York: Simon & Schuster.

John W. Gardner (1912–)

Founder of Common Cause. Born in Los Angeles, John William Gardner was trained as a psychologist at Stanford University (A.B. 1935) and at the University of California, Berkeley (Ph.D. 1938). Gardner taught briefly at Berkeley, Connecticut College, and Mount Holyoke College from 1936 to 1942. He served in the Marines in World War II as an intelligence analyst. From 1946 to 1965, he was a staff member of the Carnegie Corporation and Foundation and was its president from 1956 to 1965. Gardner was Secretary of the Department of Health, Education, and Welfare in the Johnson administration from 1965 to 1968. Despite his impressive service to well-established organizations, Gardner's main fame is as the architect, inventor, and founder of public service institutions both inside the government (White House Fellows) and outside [Common Cause (1970), Independent Sector (1980)]. He also energized the infant Urban Coalition as its chairman (1968–1970).

Gardner is a successful modern embodiment of the good-government impulses that inspired the progressive era of his California youth and gave the nation city managers, primary elections, the initiative and referendum, and other such—mainly antiparty—devices for curbing favoritism and instilling objectivity and high principles in the conduct of the public's business. Gardner's modern gloss on this heritage has been to seek to organize—within the context of a polity overwhelmingly responsive to interest groups—those groups that may wish to express interests in fairness, equity, and altruism in public life. Thus he has mobilized mostly middle-class constituencies for the purpose of effecting procedural reforms, such as improvements in the management of Congress and in financing of elections. Gardner believes in *Excellence* and *Self-Renewal*, the titles of two of his books, and he conducts his life in such a way as to make these and his other high-minded goals seem almost attainable by ordinary citizens.

See also: Common Cause, Lyndon B. Johnson

Nelson W. Polsby

REFERENCES

Gardner, John W. 1964. *Self-Renewal: The Individual and the Innovative Society*. New York: Harper & Row.

———. 1968. *No Easy Victories*. New York: Harper & Row.

———. 1970. *The Recovery of Confidence*. New York: Norton.

———. 1971. *Excellence: Can We Be Equal and Excellent Too?* New York: Harper & Row.

———. 1973. *In Common Cause*. New York: Norton.

———. 1978. *Morale*. New York: Norton.

McFarland, Andrew S. 1984. *Common Cause: Lobbying in the Public Interest*. Chatham, NJ: Chatham House.

James A. Garfield (1831–1881)

President of the United States, assassinated in 1881. James A. Garfield, born near Orange, Ohio, was two years old when his father died, leaving his mother to work the family's 30-acre farm. Garfield was the last President who was actually born in a log cabin. He left home when he was 16 years old and briefly took jobs as a sailor on the Great Lakes and a team driver on the Ohio Canal. At the age of 18 he was baptized in the Disciples of Christ, and his life took on a more serious purpose.

Enrolling in what is now Hiram College, he left after three years to enter Williams College in Massachusetts. After graduating from Williams, Garfield returned to Hiram as professor of ancient languages and literature. At the age of 26 he was named president of the college, and in 1858 he married one of his former students, Lucretia Rudolph.

Growing restless with the problems associated with running a small college, Garfield resigned to enter politics. He was a strong opponent of slavery, a supporter of the free-soil movement, and an early campaigner for the Republican Party. In 1859 he was elected to the Ohio Senate.

In 1861 Garfield was commissioned a lieutenant colonel and helped organize the 42nd Ohio Infantry. In 1862 he became the youngest brigadier general in the Union Army; in 1863 he was promoted to major general. In 1862 he was elected to the U.S. House of Representatives, although he remained on active military duty until December 1863. In the House he supported Radical Reconstruction and the impeachment of President Andrew Johnson.

Garfield served for 18 years in the House. In 1880 the Ohio legislature elected him to the United States Senate, but before he took his seat he was nominated for President. He attended the Republican National Convention in Chicago to manage the presidential candidacy of Secretary of Treasury John Sherman. The principal Republican candidates were Ulysses S. Grant, who was seeking to return to the White House after a four-year absence, and Senator James G. Blaine of Maine. The party was sharply divided between Blaine, who represented the Half-Breeds, and the Stalwarts, who supported Grant.

Garfield's actions at the convention indicated that he was more interested in advancing his own candidacy than Sherman's. When neither Grant nor Blaine were able to win the nomination early, the convention deadlocked. On the thirty-fourth ballot some Wisconsin delegates threw their support to Garfield, starting a landslide, and his nomination was made unanimous on the thirty-sixth ballot.

The Democrats nominated General Winfield Hancock and the Greenback movement selected General James B. Weaver. Garfield was able to unite the Stalwarts and Half-Breeds and eventually won by 39,000 votes out of 9.2 million votes cast. Garfield received 214 electoral votes to Hancock's 155. A shift of a few thousand votes in New York would have given the presidential election to Hancock.

Garfield served just four months in office. During that time his administration was paralyzed by fighting between the Half-Breeds and Stalwarts over appointments. Garfield, who usually sided with Secretary of State Blaine and the Half-Breeds, was finally able to break the power of Senator Roscoe Conkling of New York and the Stalwarts.

On July 2, 1881, Garfield entered a Washington railway station for a trip to Williams College. As he walked through the station, he was shot twice by Charles J. Guiteau, an itinerant author, lawyer, and minister. Guiteau, who was clearly insane, had given an incoherent speech for the Garfield-Arthur ticket during the campaign and believed he should be rewarded with an ambassadorship. Guiteau lobbied for the position with Blaine and other Republicans and once entered the President's office with a group of other office seekers, although it is not clear whether he talked with Garfield.

At first Garfield's doctors thought his death was imminent, but he survived for 81 days. Shortly before his death his doctors gave in to his wishes that he be moved from heat-plagued Washington to the New Jersey beach community of Elberon. He died in Elberon from infection brought on by unsanitary medical treatment.

See also: James G. Blaine, Election of 1880, Free Soil Party, Ulysses S. Grant, Greenback Party, Andrew Johnson, Reconstruction, John Sherman, Stalwarts (and Half-Breeds)

James C. Clark

REFERENCES

Clancy, Herbert J. 1958. *The Presidential Election of 1880*. Chicago: Loyola U. Pr.

Doenecke, Justus D. 1981. *The Presidencies of James A. Garfield & Chester A. Arthur*. Lawrence: U. Pr. of Kansas.

Peskin, Allan. 1978. *Garfield*. Kent, OH: Kent State U. Pr.

John Nance Garner (1868–1967)

Texas Democrat who served as Speaker of the House and as Vice President. John Nance Garner spent almost 40 years in Washington as a member of the House of Representatives (1903–1933) and as Vice President of the United States (1933–1940). During this time he was one of the leading figures in the Democratic Party, helping the Democrats to shape an effective opposition to the dominant Republican Party during the first three decades of the twentieth century. Eventually Garner saw the emergence of the Democrats as a governing party during the presidency of Franklin D. Roosevelt.

Garner's early political education in rural Texas was significant in shaping his early political career. From his family and community Garner acquired a strong commitment to the Democratic Party, which thoroughly dominated Texas politics at the end of the post-Civil War era.

Garner first became a member of the House of Representatives in 1903, when he was selected to represent the newly created Fifteenth Congressional District in Texas. As a member of the Texas state legislature, Garner sponsored the legislation that created this district, frankly admitting to his astonished colleagues that the bill he was asking them to pass was framed by him for the express purpose of creating a congressional district in which he could be elected to Congress. In this incident, as was to be the case throughout his long political career (he was reelected 15 times), Garner's straightforward manner won the day.

In Washington, Garner was the "apostle of party regularity." "I have always done what I thought best for my country," he supposedly said, "never varying unless I was advised that two-thirds of the Democrats were for a bill and then I voted for it." The Democratic Party to which Garner held such strong allegiance then was rooted in Jeffersonian and Jacksonian principles that celebrated states' rights and considered the national government as a political instrument favoring the privileged few. As a representative of the "new" Southwest, Garner was comfortable with the principles of his party, and during his legislative career he continuously strove to limit the role of the national government.

Garner's commitment to party loyalty was combined with a love of and talent for parliamentary maneuvering. Thus, he advanced steadily through the Democratic ranks, becoming Majority Whip and a top lieutenant to the Speaker during the Democratic Party's brief national dominance marked by Woodrow Wilson's election to the presidency in 1912. Garner's career in the House was capped by his election as Minority Leader in 1929 and Speaker in 1931, when the Great Depression enabled Democrats to gain control of the House for the first time in 12 years.

The conditions of economic collapse severely tested the fiscal conservativism of Speaker Garner, and, although he never abandoned his support of Jeffersonian principles, Garner sponsored a public works program in 1932 (vetoed later by President Herbert Hoover), an emergency relief measure that was one of only four major bills he introduced in his congressional career.

Garner was a leading candidate for the Democratic presidential nomination in 1932, an honor eventually won by New York governor Franklin Delano Roosevelt. Roosevelt's nomination on the fourth ballot at the Democratic convention was assured by Garner's support, and the Speaker was rewarded with the second spot on the ticket. The nomination of Garner for Vice President assuaged southern concerns about the election of a progressive northeastern governor to the White House, thus contributing significantly to FDR's landslide victory; after the 1932 election, the Vice President's old congressional friendships made him a valuable member of the administration during the early days of the Roosevelt presidency.

Yet the relationship between FDR and Garner, warm during the administration's first term, began to sour after FDR's reelection. The severity of the depression and party loyalty inclined Garner to stay with Roosevelt through 1937, but he and other conservative Democrats became increasingly unhappy with the New Deal, particularly its relief and labor policies.

Garner's greatest concern over the New Deal was that its consolidation of national power would undermine the constitutional balance of power in the United States. In the final analysis, Garner was an advocate of legislative power, and he abhorred the shift of responsibility from the Congress to the President and executive agencies during the 1930s. He viewed Roosevelt's 1937 court-packing plan and the 1938 purge campaign to rid the President's party of those who opposed the New Deal as examples of executive usurpation; and his final break with FDR was precipitated by the President's defiance of the two-term tradition in 1940. When Roosevelt became the first President in American history to seek election to a third term, Garner found himself standing alone as the only major elected officer in the nation trying to prevent this precedent-shattering development. The declaration by Garner of his own candidacy for the nation's highest office in early 1940 marked the first time since the development of the party system that a President and Vice President would be fighting each other for their party's nomination. FDR's victory crushed "Cactus Jack" Garner.

After the 1940 election, Garner retired to Uvalde, Texas, where he lived comfortably until his death at the age of 97.

See also: New Deal, Franklin D. Roosevelt, Speaker of the House

Sidney Milkis

REFERENCES

Leuchtenburg, William E. 1963. *Franklin D. Roosevelt and the New Deal*. New York: Harper & Row.

Patterson, James T. 1967. *Congressional Conservativism and the New Deal: The Growth of the Conservative Coalition in Congress, 1933–1939*. Lexington: U. Pr. of Kentucky.

Stokes, Thomas L. 1937. "Garner Turns on FDR." 144 (June 26) *Nation* 722.

Timmons, Bascom N. 1948. *Garner of Texas*. New York: Harper.

William Lloyd Garrison (1805–1879)

Social reformer, newspaperman, and pacifist. William Lloyd Garrison was the best known and most inflammatory of all American abolitionists. Born in Newburyport, Massachusetts, and brought up with little formal education, Garrison began his career as an apprentice printer under Nathanial White at the *National Philanthropist*. Garrison's most important forum, however, became the *Liberator*, which he edited continuously from its first publication on January 1, 1831, until 1865.

Although it addressed numerous social issues, including women's rights, prostitution, and intemperance, Garrison's *Liberator* emerged as the principal organ of the abolitionist movement. Garrison believed slavery to be such a devastating social evil that no compromise could be attempted; moral suasion alone must be used to persuade individual slaveholders to manumit their slaves immediately. In staking out this position, Garrison severed ties with those advocating gradual abolitionism and the colonization of ex-slaves.

Garrison participated in the first meeting of the American Anti-Slavery Society (AAS) in December 1833, drafted much of the Society's constitution, and later became its president in 1843. Garrison was a pacifist and yet was adamant in his moral conviction, a path that led him into political turmoil with other abolitionists and occasional brushes with anti-abolitionist mobs, even in his native Boston. The American Anti-Slavery Society split in 1840 over the issue of political participation. A majority formed the Liberty Party, which first nominated James Birney for President in 1840. Garrison insisted that political participation was a compromise with evil and would not join the Liberty Party. His radicalism placed him at the extremes of the antislavery movement, a movement that as the 1840s and 1850s progressed, increasingly influenced national party politics. Indeed, in the 1844 elections, Garrison became an active disunionist, advocating a complete break with the slave South. On Independence Day of 1854, Garrison carried out his best-known symbolic act of defiance: he publicly burned the U.S. Constitution, calling out "so perish all compromises with tyranny!"

Initially cool to the Civil War and to the administration of Abraham Lincoln, Garrison eventually and somewhat reluctantly came to support the Union cause after Lincoln's Emancipation Proclamation. In January 1865, he resigned from the American Anti-Slavery Society, asserting that its task was done; and in December he published the last issue of the *Liberator*. Illness prevented him from significant reform activity in the postwar years.

See also: Abolition Movement, Emancipation as a Political Issue, Liberty Party

John Walsh

REFERENCES

Kraditor, Aileen Sema. 1970. *Means and Ends in American Abolitionism: Garrison and his Critics on Strategy and Tactics, 1834–1850.* New York: Vintage Books.

Merrill, Walter M., ed. 1981. *The Letters of William Lloyd Garrison.* Cambridge, MA: Belknap.

David Garth (1930–)

Prominent political campaign consultant and advertising executive. David Garth heads Garth Associates, based in New York City, which employs a large professional staff offering expertise in all aspects of electioneering, including media, scheduling, polling, speech writing, fundraising, and staffing. Clients, generally liberals, have included presidential candidates Eugene McCarthy (1968), John Lindsay (1972), and John Anderson (1980); and dozens of candidates for Senator, governor, and mayor, including Pennsylvania's Republican Senators H. John Heinz III and Arlen Specter and Democratic Governor Hugh Carey and Mayor Ed Koch of New York.

Garth established his reputation with the successful 1965 mayoralty campaign of John V. Lindsay, whose then-innovative television commercials featured the candidate walking the streets of New York City. Placing candidates in casual settings and attire subsequently became standard political fare. According to critic Larry Sabato, the style of Garth's television spots was "noisy, rough-edged, brimming with information (because Garth thinks the audience absorbs more that way) with visual statistics streaming across the screen while the announcer adds still more. Each commercial requires several viewings for all the data to be taken in." Garth came to be known for the degree of control over the campaign that he demanded.

Garth also made his mark with the unprecedented stratagem of suggesting that his underdog candidates address their own weaknesses. Lindsay (1969) and Governor Brendan T. Byrne of New Jersey (1973) admitted to errors and came from behind to win their respective re-elections.

See also: John Anderson, Edward Koch, John V. Lindsay, Eugene McCarthy

Douglas I. Hodgkin

REFERENCES

Sabato, Larry J. 1981. *The Rise of Political Consultants: New Ways of Winning Elections.* New York: Basic Books.

Marcus Garvey (1887–1940)

Controversial African-American political organizer. Marcus Garvey, a Jamaican, founded and led the Universal Negro Improvement Association (UNIA), the largest mass organization of African-Americans in U.S. history. Garvey's personal success was undermined by his conviction for mail fraud in 1923, followed by deportation from the United States on his release from prison in 1927; still, many Pan-African nationalists continue to consider him the preeminent figure in their tradition.

The UNIA had over 1 million official members in the 1920s, with another 2 million or 3 million followers. The largest contingent was in the United States, but UNIA was also strong in the Caribbean and Latin America, and it maintained divisions in Canada, Europe, and Africa (where it functioned illegally) as well. It was simultaneously a political movement, a fraternal and sororal order, and a network of businesses, including restaurants, factories, and a steamship company, the Black Star Line.

Garvey and the UNIA advocated unity and self-reliance for Africans and the African diaspora. He is sometimes portrayed as a Back-to-Africa theorist, but his position can be described more accurately as race first. His emphasis was on achieving a strong independent Africa as a center of support for Black people everywhere. The Black Star Line, which would both improve and place Black people in control of commerce between Africa, the Caribbean, and Blacks in the United States, was central to this strategy. Thousands of Black people bought stock at five dollars a share, but the line's three ships were never profitable. Garvey's attempts to salvage its finances by selling more stock were the basis of his conviction, imprisonment, and deportation.

Electoral politics was of secondary importance to Garvey. However, the UNIA launched the Negro Political Union in 1924. The Union endorsed Calvin Coolidge in 1924 and Al Smith in 1928, and it worked hard in 1928 to elect Oscar DePriest (D-Ill.), the first Black member of the House of Representatives in the twentieth century.

See also: Calvin Coolidge, Alfred E. Smith

John C. Berg

REFERENCES

Clarke, John Henrik, ed., with Amy Jacques Garvey. 1974. *Marcus Garvey and the Vision of Africa.* New York: Vintage.

Cronon, E. David. 1969. *The Story of Marcus Garvey and the Universal Negro Improvement Association.* 2d ed. Madison: U. of Wisconsin Pr.

Garvey, Amy Jacques. 1970. *Garvey and Garveyism.* New York: Collier.

Garvey, Marcus. 1923. *The Philosophy and Opinions of Marcus Garvey.* Ed. Amy Jacques Garvey. 2 vols. New York: Universal Publishing House.

Hill, Robert A., ed. 1983–1985. *The Marcus Garvey and Universal Negro Improvement Association Papers.* 4 vols. Berkeley: U. of California Pr.

Martin, Tony. 1983. *Marcus Garvey, Hero: A First Biography.* Dover, MA: Majority Press.

———. 1983. *The Pan-African Connection: From Slavery to Garvey and Beyond.* Dover, MA: Majority Press.

Meier, August, Robert J. Cottrol, David G. Nielson, Robert E. Perdue, and Tony Martin. 1976. *Race First: The Ideological and Organization Struggles of Marcus Garvey and the Universal Negro Improvement Association.* Westport, CT: Greenwood.

Stein, Judith. 1986. *The World of Marcus Garvey: Race and Class in Modern Society.* Baton Rouge: Louisiana State U. Pr.

Gender Gap

The gender gap—a shorthand reference to the recent phenomenon of diverging political preferences of men and women—represents an anomaly in public opinion. Averaging only a 5 to 7 percent difference in presidential voting, it has never become a voting bloc for either party. Unlike the voting behavior of whites and Blacks, the gender gap does not provide any particular benefit for female candidates. Further, the magnitude of the gender gap is highly sensitive to factors unique to specific campaigns. In 1984 it ranged from a minor four percentage points in the New Jersey Senate race to an 11 percent gap in the North Carolina Senate race and a 14 percent gap in the Massachusetts Senate race. The gender gap is politically significant because women, who comprise 53 percent of the potential electorate, now turn out to vote at a rate comparable to or exceeding that of men.

The gender gap was discovered by pollsters in their analysis of the 1980 election: the CBS/ *New York Times* exit poll found women splitting their vote evenly, while men preferred Ronald Reagan to Jimmy Carter 54 percent to 46 percent. Reagan's job approval ratings consistently showed a gender gap among all social groups, with women approving of his job performance on average 9 percent to 10 percent less than men—a disparity three times the size of any previous gender difference in approval ratings of Presidents since Gallup began collecting data on presidential job approval.

In contrast to the 1950s when females were 3 percent to 5 percent more likely to vote Republican, women in the electorate now identify more strongly with the Democratic Party and take (on average) more liberal and less militaristic positions on issues of defense, environment, and social welfare. The gender gap differs at mass and elite levels. Among the mass public, men and women do not differ on such feminist issues as abortion or the Equal Rights Amendment, while women party elites are more supportive of women's role in politics and feminist issues than are males of the same party.

The malleability of the gender gap lends itself to differing interpretations. The Democratic Party is uncertain whether the gender gap represents a net benefit when balanced against the declining support of white males. Thus, the Democratic dilemma is whether to appeal to women with liberal positions that may alienate men or to try other types of appeals. In 1983 and 1984, a coalition of feminist political leaders working through the Women's Presidential Project achieved the nomination of Geraldine Ferraro as the Democratic vice presidential candidate by arguing that a female candidate would prove to be a net electoral benefit to the party. Their arguments proved nothing in 1984 in President Reagan's Republican landslide victory. The Republican Party has taken the public posture that the gender gap is based in misinformation that can be corrected through the course of a campaign. Yet Republican public officials like Senator Daniel Evans and Congressman Bill Green and consultants like Ed Rollins have argued that the gender gap is a real phenomenon based in the changing values of contemporary working women with young families that the Republican Party must acknowledge.

See also: Jimmy Carter, Equal Rights Amendment, Geraldine Ferraro, Ronald Reagan

Denise L. Baer

REFERENCES

Abzug, Bella, and Mim Kelber. 1984. *Gender Gap: Bella Abzug's Guide to Political Power for American Women.* Boston: Houghton Mifflin.

Baer, Denise L., and David A. Bositis. 1988. *Elite Cadres and Party Coalitions: Representing the Public in Party Politics.* Westport, CT: Greenwood.

Brown, Kirk. 1983. *The "Gender Gap": Differences Between Men and Women in Political Attitudes and Voting Behavior.* Report No. 83–633 GOV. Washington: Congressional Research Service.

Frankovic, Kathleen A. 1982. "Sex and Politics—New Alignments, Old Issues." 15 *P.S.* 439–48

Mueller, Carol, ed. 1988. *The Politics of the Gender Gap: The Social Construction of Political Influence.* Beverly Hills, CA: Sage.

Citizen Genêt (1763–1834)

Interventionist French minister to the U.S. during the George Washington administration. In 1793, France appointed Edmund Charles Genêt minister to the United States, thus rekindling the tension between the two countries. If the United States had accepted Genêt (called Citizen Genêt), it would have given approval to the revolutionary government in France. Thomas Jefferson was for recognition, but Genêt's behavior made acceptance difficult. Genêt—who hoped to use the U.S. as a base for attacking Louisiana, Florida, and Canada—insisted that the United States take literally the Treaty of 1778 and used American ports to commission privateers to capture British ships.

Genêt threatened to take his case to the people if the U.S. government did not support him, arousing some dissension within the Cabinet. Alexander Hamilton called for a direct and forceful demand for Genêt's recall; Jefferson hoped that Genêt might be made to leave under less damaging circumstances. Hamilton wrote several articles chastising Genêt and used public meetings to make Genêt's personal behavior as notorious as possible. Jefferson and James Madison tried to maintain a distinction between the new French republic and its obnoxious minister. Eventually, Genêt was allowed to remain in the United States but not as French minister.

Genêt's activities gave to these early political factions something tangible over which to fight. Both Jefferson and Hamilton began to think in terms of their party's interests when forming policy. The debate over Genêt imbued the American political system with more democracy as it honed the ideological lines of the two parties. In fact, Genêt's controversial behavior forced two rather undefined political groups to shape themselves into identifiable organizations.

See also: Alexander Hamilton, French Revolution and the First Party System, Thomas Jefferson

Daniel Dean Roland

REFERENCES

Ammon, Henry. 1973. *The Genêt Mission.* New York: Norton.

Cunningham, Noble. 1957. *The Jeffersonian Republicans: The Formation of Party Organization, 1789–1801.* Chapel Hill: U. of North Carolina Pr.

de Conde, Alexander. 1958. *Entangling Alliance: Politics and Diplomacy Under George Washington.* Durham, NC: Duke U. Pr.

Gentrification

The improvement of dilapidated neighborhoods by the immigration of young, upwardly mobile professionals ("Yuppies"), often reversing the urban decay caused by the "white flight" of the middle class to the suburbs. Some areas (e.g., around New York's Columbia University or near Cambridge's M.I.T.) are revitalized by the magnet of a major university; others, like Baltimore in the late 1970s, succeeded through a partnership of federal funds, municipal administration, and private initiative.

Political effects come from the improved tax base delivered by the corporations employing yuppies, tending to sustain the Democratic administrations despite the death of political machines; but some middle-class Republican voters also returned to the Democratic cities.

Simply building a massive commercial edifice, such as Detroit's Renaissance Center, in a decayed urban center often failed to effect the return of the middle class. Boston's more casual entertainment center at Quincy Market, however, served as a model to gentrifiers as far away as Covent Garden in London. Expensive condominiums on Boston's waterfront mark the arrival of upper-middle-class Republicans and the gradual departure of working-class Italian-Americans from the adjacent North End.

Baltimore combined rebuilding of inner harbor docklands for entertainment with "Urban Homesteading," whereby the city sold decrepit row houses to young professional couples for rehabilitation. One successful developer of "urban malls" in Boston and Baltimore and the South Street Seaport in Manhattan was a New Dealer, James Rouse, seeking in part to restore political and economic strength to Democratic inner cities.

Jeremy R. T. Lewis

REFERENCES

Lottman, Herbert R. 1976. *How Cities Are Saved*. New York: Universe Books.

Nelson, Kathryn P. 1988. *Gentrification and Distressed Cities: An Assessment of Trends in Intrametropolitan Migration*. Madison: U. of Wisconsin Pr.

Palen, J. John, and Bruce London. 1984. *Gentrification, Displacement, and Neighborhood Revitalization*. Albany: State U. of New York Pr.

Smith, Neil, and Peter Williams, eds. 1986. *Gentrification of the City*. Boston: Allen and Unwin.

Henry George (1839–1897)

Theorist of progressive tax policies. Born in Philadelphia, Henry George, after several voyages as a sailor and training in Philadelphia as a printer, finally settled in California. Here he witnessed the spectacular boom and consequent bust of the frontier economy. Appalled by the widening class lines evident in the labor conflicts of the 1870s, George called for a solution to the dilemma of progress and poverty by a single tax on the unearned increment of rising land values. Rejecting Marxian arguments, George argued that capital and labor are partners in productivity and that it is the exploitative *rentier* class that siphons off wealth and creates poverty in the midst of plenty. George, an ardent Democrat, was rewarded by appointment as state inspector of gas meters. He also ran as a delegate for the California constitutional convention and, although defeated, led the Democratic ticket. It was not, however, until his move to New York City in 1880 that he truly entered electoral politics when, after much cajoling, he agreed to run for mayor against the reform Democrat, Abraham Hewitt, and the Republican, Theodore Roosevelt. Despite an earlier animosity to strikes and third parties, George had become more sympathetic to the condition of the workers and accepted the nomination of the United Labor Party. George, nevertheless, saw his role in politics as restoring the old Jacksonian alliance of the producing classes. The 1886 election was hotly contested and can justifiably be viewed as an archetypal example of mass politics. Certainly all the established forces rallied to defeat him. Since this election occurred before New York's adoption of the Australian ballot, there may be merit in George's contention that he was "counted out." George finished a respectable second behind Hewitt, which—considering the lack of party machinery, money, and particularly poll watchers—was a significant achievement. George was also defeated in 1887 as a candidate for Secretary of State and died five days before the mayoral election of 1897, in which he was once more a candidate.

George's writings influenced many of the leading social reformers of the late nineteenth century not only in the United States but also in Great Britain. Radicals in England and land reformers in Scotland and Ireland invited George on speaking tours, and he earned further fame by his attack on the leading social philosopher of the time, Herbert Spencer.

See also: Australian Ballot, Theodore Roosevelt, Union Labor Party

Joseph A. Dowling

REFERENCES

Barker, Charles A. 1955. *Henry George*. New York: Oxford U. Pr.

Rose, Edward J. 1968. *Henry George*. New York: Twayne.

Thomas, John L. 1983. *Alternative America: Henry George, Edward Bellamy, Henry Demarest Lloyd, and the Adversary Tradition*. Cambridge: Belknap Pr.

Walter F. George (1878–1957)

Conservative Georgia Democratic Senator. Walter F. George served as his state's U.S. Senator from 1922 to 1957. When Democrats nominated Alfred E. Smith, a Catholic and an antiprohibitionist, for President in 1928, many southerners refused to support him. George, on the other hand, accepted the party's choice and campaigned for Smith in Georgia. In 1932 George initially opposed Franklin Roosevelt's nomination but later acquiesced and even voted for early New Deal legislation. However, he opposed the second New Deal in 1935 because of its liberal measures and led the attack against the administration's court-packing plan in 1937.

In 1938 Roosevelt planned to purge his party of New Deal opposition and naturally targeted George as a victim. In a speech in Barnesville, Georgia, the President asked voters to replace George with New Deal advocate Lawrence Camp. George, using demagoguery for the first time in his career, warned voters that Roosevelt's attempt to unseat him was the first step toward federal intervention into Georgia politics. This ploy worked, and George returned to the Senate.

George's political power in the Senate reached its zenith in 1955 and then dissipated. In this year, he was elected President *pro tempore* and appointed chairman of the Foreign Relations Committee. Yet the next year he had to withdraw his bid for reelection because he lacked financial support. In 1957 Dwight D. Eisenhower appointed him as an ambassador to NATO and as special foreign policies adviser; he served in these positions until his death later that year.

See also: Dwight D. Eisenhower, New Deal, Franklin Roosevelt, Alfred E. Smith

Henry J. Walker, Jr.

REFERENCES

Coleman, Kenneth, and Charles S. Gurr, eds. 1983. *The Wild Man from Sugar Creek: The Political Career of Eugene Talmadge.* Baton Rouge: Louisiana State U. Pr.

Donovan, Robert J. 1955. "Senator George—Ike's Favorite Democrat." 135 *Colliers* May 13:32.

Georgia County Unit Rule System

This system was a unique nominating process in Georgia. Following Reconstruction, the Democratic Party gave each county two unit votes at the state convention for each of its Democratic Representatives in the lower house of the legislature. Eventually, Democrats began using the primary election system but retained the county unit rule. In 1917 the Neill Primary Act required all parties holding primaries to use the county unit rule giving a county's unit votes to the candidate winning a plurality of popular votes in that county.

Although the population of urban counties generally increased in the twentieth century, their number of county unit votes remained fairly constant. This apportionment gave rural counties undue influence in the nominating process; and since the Democratic nominee automatically won the general election, this influence was vital. The abuses caused by the unfair influence of rural counties eventually led to the end of the county unit system. One abuse was exemplified by Eugene Talmadge's gubernatorial nominations in 1932 and 1946. Rural support gave him a majority of county unit votes in both years, but in neither race did he have a majority of popular votes. Despite a 1962 law giving larger counties more unit votes, the U.S. District Court ruled in that year that, as apportioned, Georgia's county unit system violated the Fourteenth Amendment's equal protection clause. This decision marked the end of the county unit system.

See also: Eugene Talmadge

Henry J. Walker, Jr.

REFERENCES

Anderson, William. 1985. *The Wild Man From Sugar Creek: The Political Career of Eugene Talmadge.* Baton Rouge: Louisiana State U. Pr.

Key, V. O. 1949. *Southern Politics in State and Nation.* New York: Knopf.

Sanders v. Gray. 1962. *Federal Supplement.* Vol 203. St. Paul, MN: West Publishing.

Saye, Albert B. 1970. *A Constitutional History of Georgia 1732–1968.* Athens: U. of Georgia Pr.

State of Georgia v. National Democratic Party

447 F.2d 1271 (D.C. Cir. 1971), *cert. denied,* 404 U.S. 858

Decided in 1971 by the United States Court of Appeals for the District of Columbia, this case was one of two unsuccessful challenges to the methods used by both the Democratic and Republican parties to distribute among the states the available number of delegates to the 1972 presidential nominating conventions. By rejecting both challenges, the court made it possible for national political parties to exercise considerable discretion in the apportionment of delegates to the states.

Following the tumultuous 1968 Democratic National Convention, the Democrats revised their formula for apportioning delegates. The new formula apportioned 46 percent of the delegates on the basis of each state's average Democratic voting strength in the prior three presidential elections and then apportioned 54 percent on the basis of the number of electors allocated to each state by the Electoral College system. This formula was criticized for discriminating both against states with large general populations and against states with small populations of citizens who voted for the Democratic candidate in presidential elections.

Georgia fell into the latter category and brought suit on the grounds that apportionment must be based primarily upon population—the "one-man, one-vote" principle. Under Georgia's theory, each delegate to his party's national convention must be representative of an equal segment of the national population. Georgia argued that any system other than one based on "one man, one vote" violated the equal protection clause of the Fourteenth Amendment.

The impact of an apportionment formula along the lines suggested by Georgia would have been to eliminate the effect of longstanding local disparities in party strength on the number of delegates a state party was entitled to send to the national convention. As a result, two states of similar population would have an equal voice in selecting the party's nominee, regardless of the likelihood of the nominee's success in each state in the general election.

In denying Georgia's challenge, the U.S. Court of Appeals stated that "population alone is an inappropriate test of representation in the framework of national politics where parties compete for membership." The court pointed out that the formula proposed by Georgia would lead to an overrepresentation from predominantly Democratic states. The one-man, one-vote principle of equal representation is inapplicable in the context of national convention delegates since the function of delegates is to participate in nominating the candidate for a single party—not the whole electorate.

The refusal of the court to impose a strict population-based apportionment formula on the Democratic Party—as well as its subsequent refusal in *Bode v. National Democratic Party*, 452 F.2d 1302 (D.C. Cir. 1971), to insist on a one-Democrat, one-vote formula—allowed the national political parties substantial latitude in delegate apportionment and paved the way for future apportionment skirmishes.

See also: Bode v. National Democratic Party

Jeffra Becknell

REFERENCES

Bogus, Carl T. 1972. "Delegate Apportionment to National Political Party Conventions." 23 *Syracuse U. Law Review* 919.

Richard A. Gephardt (1941–)

Missouri Democratic congressional leader and presidential hopeful. A Democratic Representative to Congress from the Third District of Missouri since 1976, Richard Gephardt's political career has been that of a leader looking for a position. Raised in St. Louis and educated at Northwestern University and the University of Michigan Law School, Gephardt presents the squeaky-clean image of the Eagle Scout he once was. But beneath that veneer is a savvy politician who is determined to play a leadership role on the American political stage.

After having served a brief apprenticeship in local St. Louis politics, Gephardt was elected to Congress at the age of 35. In his early years he was a protégé of Missouri's Richard Bolling, a longtime House leader who was then Democratic Caucus chairman. Bolling was instrumental in securing a seat for Gephardt on the prestigious Ways and Means Committee. The young Gephardt used that position to build alliances with influential members of his party. In 1985 he was the founder of the Democratic Leadership Conference, a group seeking to reposition the national Democratic Party in the center of the political spectrum. He ran for and was elected chair of the Democratic Caucus, following in the footsteps of his mentor, Bolling. Gephardt,

with a reputation for working hard to find solutions for long-term problems without ignoring short-term political realities, seemed destined for an influential congressional career.

However, in 1987 Gephardt changed course, announcing that he would seek the Democratic nomination for the presidency. Though Congressmen traditionally have had little luck in seeking national elective office, Gephardt's campaign surprised many. He was supported by a large number of his fellow Congressmen and, unlike others, his image survived the scrutiny of the national press corps. His campaign was closely linked to the centerpiece of his legislative agenda—a trade amendment that called for retaliation against countries that exported much more to the United States than they imported from us. After some success in the early primaries in 1988, Gephardt's campaign failed to find support in the South; his trade bill came under attack as protectionist; scrutiny of his record showed inconsistencies on some controversial issues such as abortion and antibusing measures. Nevertheless, 170 delegates at the 1988 national convention were interpreted as a good first effort for one who would likely reappear as a presidential candidate.

Gephardt withdrew from the 1988 presidential race in time to file to retain his seat in Congress. Most viewed Gephardt's congressional seat as the platform from which he would launch his next presidential bid. But fate—and the scandals that ended the congressional careers of Speaker Jim Wright and Majority Whip Tony Coelho (Calif.)—intervened. When it became clear that Wright and Coelho would give up leadership positions and that Majority Leader Tom Foley (Wash.) would become Speaker, Gephardt decided to reposition himself on the congressional leadership track. And again he met with success. Just as he used his position as Democratic Caucus chair as the base for his presidential campaign, he used the national reputation he had earned during his presidential campaign as an articulate and reputable spokesman for his party to aid his bid to become Majority Leader. The Democrats in Congress decided that Gephardt, the congressional insider who had sought to move beyond the legislature's halls, was just the type of leader they would need to combine with Speaker Foley as they sought to rectify their image so tarnished by the Wright and Coelho resignations; accordingly they elected Gephardt as Majority Leader in June 1989. It remains to be seen whether congressional leadership will be enough to satisfy this obviously ambitious politician or if another presidential bid is in the offing.

See also: Tony Coelho, Thomas Foley, Jim Wright

L. Sandy Maisel

Elbridge Gerry (1744–1814)

Massachusetts politician famed for designing political districts to suit his party's advantage. Few of his contemporaries had as distinguished a career as Elbridge Gerry: Harvard graduate, signer of the Declaration of Independence, member of the Continental Congress, delegate to the federal convention that wrote the Constitution, member of the U.S. House of Representatives, Vice President of the United States under James Madison, and governor of Massachusetts. Gerry is best remembered, however, for "gerrymandering," the process of drawing electoral boundaries for partisan advantage.

With Gerry as governor, the majority Jeffersonian-Republicans in Massachusetts passed a redistricting measure for the upcoming state senate elections in 1812. The new map diluted Federalist strength by creating a variety of oddly shaped districts. Upon seeing the map, a Federalist is said to have sketched in head, wings, and claws on one serpentine-like district, explaining, "That will do for a salamander." Another Federalist remarked, "Gerrymander!" Though the method was not new, the advantage to Gerry's party was extreme; in the Massachusetts elections in the spring of 1812, Federalist candidates received 51 percent of the vote but won only 11 of 40 Senate seats.

Beginning with *Baker v. Carr* in 1962 and following with *Wesberry v. Sanders* and *Reynolds v. Sims* (both in 1964), the U.S. Supreme Court ruled that legislative districts for the U.S. House and for both houses of state legislatures must be as nearly equal in size as possible ("one person, one vote"). Gerrymandering for partisan advantage, however, was not considered judiciable until *Davis v. Bandemer* in 1986.

See also: Baker v. Carr, Davis v. Brandemer, Federalist Party, Gerrymandering, Jeffersonian Republicans, James Madison, *Reynolds v. Sims, Wesberry v. Saunders*

Tom A. Kazee

REFERENCES

Bickel, Alexander M. 1965. *Politics and the Warren Court*. New York: Harper & Row.

Claude, Richard. 1970. *The Supreme Court and the Electoral Process*. Baltimore: Johns Hopkins U. Pr.

Hardy, Leroy, Alan Heslop, and Stuart Anderson, eds. 1981. *Reapportionment in the 1980s*. Claremont, CA: Rose Institute.

Gerrymandering

In 1812 the Massachusetts legislature passed a bill redrawing boundaries for state senate election districts. Governor Elbridge Gerry's party, seeking to maximize its representation in the senate, drew a map that concentrated opposition Federalist support in a few districts. Federalists easily captured those legislative seats, but most of the districts were won by Gerry's party, albeit by much smaller majorities. One "packed" Federalist district looked like a salamander to some observers; Gerry's opponents dubbed it a "gerrymander."

As in the original Massachusetts case, redistricting, which occurs whenever a state legislature votes to redraw the political map, represents an opportunity for the majority party to consolidate or increase its power in the state or in Congress. Such opportunities present themselves regularly, for redrawing district lines may be necessitated by demographic changes that create districts of unequal population or by changes that cause states to gain or lose U.S. House seats. In California, for example, the size of that state's congressional delegation increased by two seats after the 1980 census. Democratic state legislators turned the new district line–drawing job over to Phillip Burton, a member of the U.S. House. Burton's assurances that his map would benefit Democrats—"you're in your mother's arms," he said—proved sound; a 22-to-21 Democratic majority became 27 to 18 after the redistricting. Republican Congressman William M. Thomas complained that Burton "personally place[d] his thumb print on the state of California."

Gerrymanders may take various forms. Packing, or concentrating supporters of one party in a few districts, achieves the same goal as "cracking," or diffusing partisans across several districts. In each instance, the affected party wins a smaller percentage of seats in the electorate than is proportionate to their strength among the electorate.

Until 1986, the U.S. Supreme Court considered gerrymandering to be a nonjudiciable political question. Before 1962, in fact, the Court had avoided involvement in *all* apportionment cases. In *Colegrove v. Green* (1946), Justice Felix Frankfurter wrote, "It is hostile to a democratic system to involve the judiciary in the politics of the people. . . . Courts ought not to enter this political thicket." In 1962, however, the Court declared that malapportionment was judiciable (*Baker v. Carr*, 1962) and began to establish the "one-person, one-vote" standard when it ruled, in *Gray v. Sanders* (1963), that population inequalities for state electoral districts were unconstitutional. The Court extended this principle to U.S. House districts in *Wesberry v. Sanders* (1964) and, in the same year, declared in *Reynolds v. Sims* that one person, one vote applied to both houses of state legislatures. The passage of the Voting Rights Act in 1965 further constrained state legislatures. In the areas covered by the act—largely in the Deep South—legislatures were prohibited from drawing district lines that diluted minority voting strength. And even in those areas not covered, federal courts have emphasized the maximization of minority representation as a goal to be encouraged; underrepresentation of minorities is often sufficient reason for rejection of a redistricting plan.

Partisan gerrymandering has increased as a result of the Court's equal population mandate. Each decennial census reveals new population inequalities, and the Court has been unwilling to permit even small variations between districts. In *Kirkpatrick v. Preisler* (1969), the justices rejected a Missouri districting plan with a 3.1 percent district population variance, and more recent maps have been thrown out with even smaller variations between districts [e.g., *Karcher v. Daggett* (1983)].

Given this impetus, after 1980 state legislatures acted by approving obvious partisan gerrymanders—constitutional because they met the Court's population requirements—in a number of states, including Indiana, Illinois, New Jersey, and California. The Indiana plan was contested, leading the Supreme Court to find for the first time that partisan gerrymandering could be subject to constitutional challenge. In *Davis v. Brandemer* (1986), the Court accepted the Indiana redistricting plan, but as Justice Byron White wrote, "we decline to hold that such claims are never judiciable." An unconstitutional gerrymander, according to the six-to-three Court majority, must have the intent and effect of discriminating against an identifiable political group and must "consistently degrade a voter's or a group of voters' influence on the political process as a whole." Future plaintiffs may have a difficult time proving that a gerrymander is unconstitutional, but the judiciability of the issue may reduce the extent to which legislatures will redistrict in a blatant partisan fashion.

See also: Baker v. Carr, Davis v. Brandemer, Federalist Party, Elbridge Gerry, *Gray v. Sanders, Karcher v. Daggett, Kirkpatrick v. Preisler, Reynolds v. Sims,* Voting Rights of 1965 and Extensions, *Wesberry v. Sanders*

Tom A. Kazee

REFERENCES

Cain, Bruce. 1981. *The Puzzle of Reapportionment.* Berkeley: U. of California Pr.

Ehrenhalt, Alan. 1983. "Reapportionment and Redistricting." In Thomas E. Mann and Norman J. Ornstein, eds. *The American Elections of 1982.* Washington: American Enterprise Institute.

Griffith, Elmer. 1974. *The Birth and Rise of the Gerrymander.* New York: Arno Press.

Grofman, Bernard, et al. 1985. "Political Gerrymandering: *Badham v. Eu,* Political Science Goes to Court." 18 *P.S.* 537.

Hacker, Andrew. 1964. *Congressional Districting: The Issue of Equal Apportionment.* Washington: Brookings.

Hardy, Leroy, Alan Heslop, and Stuart Anderson, eds. 1981. *Reapportionment in the 1980s.* Claremont, CA: Rose Institute.

Jewell, Malcolm E. 1962. *The Politics of Reapportionment.* New York: Atherton Press.

Polsby, Nelson W., ed. 1971. *Reapportionment in the 1970s.* Berkeley: U. of California Pr.

Kenneth A. Gibson (1931–)

African-American mayor of Newark, New Jersey. Kenneth A. Gibson became the mayor of Newark, New Jersey, in 1970, among the first big-city African-American mayors. A graduate of the Newark College of Engineering, Gibson became an engineer in the Newark city government. At the same time, he was active in the civil rights movement.

In 1966 Gibson challenged Newark's incumbent Mayor Hugh Addonizio, finishing a surprisingly strong third among six candidates. The city was rocked one year later by violent racial disorders, and the city's 54 percent African-American majority made serious preparations to elect a Black mayor.

When Gibson ran again in 1970, he built a unified African-American base through ties to militant Black leaders while presenting himself as a technically skilled moderate reformer in the white community. His strategy was greatly aided by Addonizio's corruption, indictment, and trial during the campaign. Gibson was victorious with 56 percent of the vote and thereupon faced the task of running a city that, by 1970 census ratings, clearly had the lowest quality of life in America.

In his first six months, Gibson faced a massive budget crisis and a major teacher's strike. He became a national spokesman for troubled cities, widely quoted for his remark, "Wherever America is heading, Newark will get there first."

He was reelected in 1974, 1978, and 1982. Newark also became a symbol of the mixed blessings of African-American electoral success.

Following various legal entanglements and increasing conflict with members of the city council, Gibson was soundly defeated for reelection by Black councilman Sharpe James in 1986.

Raphael J. Sonenshein

REFERENCES

Cole, Leonard. 1976. *Blacks in Power: A Comparative Study of Black and White Elected Officials.* Princeton: Princeton U. Pr.

Louis, Arthur M. 1975. "The Worst American City." 250 (January) *Harpers* 67.

Sonenshein, Raphael J. 1971. "Mayor Kenneth Gibson's Newark." B.A. thesis, Princeton University.

Joshua Giddings (1795–1864)

Abolitionist politician from Ohio. Joshua R. Giddings was a central figure in the political antislavery movement and a key participant in the Whig, Free Soil, and Republican parties. Originally Pennsylvanians, his family settled in Ohio's Western Reserve when Giddings was a young boy. He began his legal practice in Jefferson, Ohio, in 1821.

Giddings's early political activities peaked in 1838 when he was elected to Congress as a Whig. In part motivated by the strong current of antislavery sentiment in the Western Reserve, he immediately became an outspoken friend of the slave. Closely allied with John Quincy Adams in the fight against the House gag rule against antislavery debates, he defied southerners in his efforts to get the House to oppose the coastwide slave trade in the *Creole* case. His reward was censure by the House, but Giddings was quickly vindicated when his constituents overwhelmingly reelected him. He joined with Adams and other antislavery Whigs and Democrats in opposing Texas annexation and supporting the Wilmot Proviso; Giddings gladly denounced President James Polk's role in provoking the Mexican War.

Despite his antislavery leanings, Giddings steadfastly refused to desert the Whigs and join the abolitionist Liberty Party. With the Whig nomination of slaveholder Zachary Taylor in 1848, however, he helped form the new Free Soil Party. Giddings remained an integral part of the free-soil movement until its absorption by the Republicans in 1854. With Salmon Chase and Charles Sumner he helped to author "The Appeal of the Independent Democrats" in bitter response to the Kansas-Nebraska Act. Believing the repeal of the antislavery limitations of the Missouri Compromise to be another aggressive victory of slave interests in Congress, he became an important leader in the Republican movement dedicated to the containment of slavery. He remained in Congress until 1859 and served as consul general in Canada during the Civil War.

See also: John Quincy Adams, Salmon Chase, Free Soil Party, Gag Rule, Kansas-Nebraska Act, Liberty Party, Mexican War, Missouri Compromise, James Polk, Charles Sumner, Zachary Taylor, Wilmot Proviso

Frederick J. Blue

REFERENCES

Blue, Frederick. 1987. *Salmon P. Chase: A Life in Politics.* Kent, OH: Kent State U. Pr.

Giddings, Joshua. 1864. *History of the Rebellion: Its Authors and Causes.* New York: Follett, Foster.

Julian, George W. 1892. *The Life of Joshua R. Giddings.* Chicago: A. C. McClurg.

Maizlish, Stephen E. 1983. *The Triumph of Sectionalism: The Transformation of Ohio Politics, 1844–1856.* Kent, OH: Kent State U. Pr.

Stewart, James B. 1970. *Joshua R. Giddings and the Tactics of Radical Politics.* Cleveland: Pr. of Case Western Reserve U.

Wilson, Henry. 1872. *History of the Rise and Fall of the Slave Power in America.* Vol. I. Boston: Houghton Mifflin.

William Branch Giles (1762–1830)

Prominent congressional opponent of Alexander Hamilton's policies. A prominent congressional Republican, William Branch Giles helped lead the early legislative opposition to Federalist Presidents George Washington and John Adams; he served as Republican Thomas Jefferson's floor whip and strategist; and he ended up opposing his own party's President, James Madison.

Born in Virginia and educated at Hampton-Sidney College and Princeton University, Giles was a lawyer by profession. Active in state politics, he was elected to Virginia's governorship, state legislature, and the state constitutional convention in 1829 and 1830. On the national level, he served in the U.S. House from 1790 to 1798 and again from 1801 to 1803, and he served in the U.S. Senate from 1804 to 1815.

As a House leader during the presidencies of Washington and Adams, Giles spearheaded the opposition by leading an investigation of the Treasury Department and fighting to defeat the Jay Treaty. Through these and other actions, Giles helped form Congress' Republican Party.

With the election of Jefferson, Giles functioned as the President's lieutenant first in the House and later in the Senate, sponsoring executive measures, advising the administration on congressional relations, and working to ensure Republican Party unity and success.

Although Giles supported Madison's candidacy, he came to oppose many of his executive initiatives, including plans for nominating Albert Gallatin as Secretary of State, legislation on military preparedness, and renewal of the charter of the Bank of the United States.

See also: John Adams, First Bank of the United States, Albert Gallatin, Jay Treaty, Thomas Jefferson, James Madison, George Washington

Elaine K. Swift

REFERENCES

Anderson, Dice Robin. 1965. *William Branch Giles: A Study in the Politics of Virginia and the Nation from 1790 to 1830.* Gloucester, MA: Peter Smith.

Giunta, Mary Antonia. 1980. "The Public Life of William Branch Giles, Republican, 1790–1815." Ph.D. dissertation, Catholic U., Washington, D.C.

Swift, Elaine K. 1989. "Reconstitutive Change in the United States Congress: The Transformation of the Senate, 1789–1841." Ph.D. dissertation, Harvard U.

Frederick H. Gillett (1851–1935)

Early-twentieth-century Republican Speaker of the House. Massachusetts Republican Frederick H. Gillett, Speaker of the House of Representatives from 1919 to 1925, served as Congressman from 1893 to 1925, and as U.S. Senator from 1925 to 1931. From an old New England family, he graduated from Amherst College and studied law at Harvard. After terms as assistant attorney general for Massachusetts and in the Massachusetts legislature, Gillett was elected to the U.S. House in 1892 against substantial Democratic opposition.

In subsequent elections, he was seriously challenged only in 1910, when many Republicans lost in the face of rising progressive opposition to the conservative Republican wing that Gillett supported. Not known as an orator, Gillett had success in the House chiefly in committee, particularly the Appropriations Committee on which he sat from 1902 until 1918. Concerned about fiscal economy, he urged the creation of a budget bureau achieved in the Budget Act of 1921.

In 1918 the Republican Party once again won majority status in Congress, and Gillett was elected Speaker of the House in 1919. As Speaker, Gillett vowed to be impartial and fair; unlike many of his predecessors, he maintained his pledge. His political opponents in both parties respected him, despite intraparty difficulties in 1923 and 1924 resulting from progressive and insurgent Republican opposition to the Warren Harding administration's political agenda.

Gillett nominated Calvin Coolidge for President in 1920, and in 1924 he capitulated to Coolidge and other Republicans by giving up his House seat and his position as Speaker to run for the Senate against the popular Democratic incumbent, David I. Walsh, whom he barely defeated. Gillett found his Senate position less satisfying than his service in the House, and at age 79 he chose not to stand for reelection, retiring in 1931.

See also: Calvin Coolidge, Warren G. Harding, Speaker of the House

Eugene S. Larson

REFERENCES

McCoy, Donald R. 1967. *Calvin Coolidge. The Quiet President.* New York: Macmillan.

Murray, Robert K. 1969. *The Harding Era.* Minneapolis: U. of Minnesota Pr.

Carter Glass (1858–1946)

Four-term Democratic Senator from Virginia. Born in Lynchburg, Virginia, Carter Glass is cited as one of the foremost banking experts ever to serve in Congress. He is credited with fathering the Federal Reserve Act (1913) and the Glass-Steagall Act that separated commercial and investment banking and created the Federal Deposit Insurance Corporation (1933). A major force within the Democratic Party, he was a delegate to every national convention from 1892 to 1940, and he also served on the Democratic National Committee from 1916 to 1928.

Glass was mostly self-educated, having left school at the age of 13. He became a successful businessman, working his way up from printer's devil to owner of the *Lynchburg Daily News* and the *Daily Advance.*

He served as a delegate to the state constitutional convention in 1901, in the state senate from 1899 until he resigned to take a seat in the U.S. House of Representatives vacated by the death of Peter J. Otey. His tenure in the House lasted from 1902 until 1918 when he resigned to serve as Secretary of the Treasury under Woodrow Wilson. Glass later returned to Congress when he accepted an appointment to the U.S. Senate in 1919 to fill the vacancy caused by the death of Thomas S. Martin. He was returned to the Senate by the voters of Virginia in 1924, 1930, 1936, and 1942.

He declined to serve as Secretary of the Treasury under Franklin D. Roosevelt, remaining, instead, in the Senate until his death. There he was a leader of southern, conservative Democrats, openly opposing much of the New Deal, including the National Recovery Act. In 1941 he was elected President *pro tempore* of the Senate, a post he held until 1945.

See also: Democratic National Committee, New Deal, Franklin Roosevelt, Woodrow Wilson

James V. Saturno

Gold Democrats

The Democratic National Convention of 1896 in Chicago was marked by numerous challenges to the credentials of delegates and even of whole delegations. The victory of William Jennings Bryan in obtaining the presidential nomination, and the delegates' acceptance of a platform that advocated the free coinage of silver and repudiated the "sound money" policies of the Grover Cleveland administration, was undercut when a number of delegates walked out of the convention. Bryan's nomination left the party's gold supporters out of power for the first time. Unable or unwilling to support Bryan's candidacy, they referred to the Chicago convention as a "grave departure from Democratic principles," and some of these dissidents decided to hold their own convention in Indianapolis in September.

Although none of the most prominent party regulars attended the rump convention, 884 activists attempted to form a party that would represent their more traditional views; they wrote a platform emphasizing their support of the Cleveland administration's more conservative monetary policies. Calling themselves the National Democrats, for President they nominated a political maverick, U.S. Senator and former Illinois governor John McAuley Palmer, and for Vice President, Simon Bolivar Buckner, a former governor of Kentucky and general in the Confederate Army.

With the tacit approval of President Cleveland, Palmer campaigned in most of the major cities east of the Mississippi River. The effect, however, was mainly to "build a bridge" to William McKinley and the Republicans. The campaign was chiefly anti-Bryan, and active support for the National Democrats was limited mostly to those voters who opposed both Bryan's free-silver stance and McKinley's protectionist ways.

In the 1896 election these "gold" Democrats could only muster 135,456 votes, less than 1 percent of the total votes cast. Palmer and Buckner received their largest support in New Hampshire where they got 4.1 percent of the vote.

Following the election, the issue of free-silver diminished in importance, and the National Democrats disappeared, most being reabsorbed into the Democratic Party.

See also: William Jennings Bryan, William McKinley

James V. Saturno

REFERENCES

Palmer, George Thomas. 1941. *A Conscientious Turncoat.* New Haven: Yale U. Pr.

Rosenstone, Steven J., Roy L. Behr, and Edward H. Lazarus. 1984. *Third Parties in America.* Princeton: Princeton U. Pr.

Bernard Goldfine (1891–1967)

Influence peddler. A wealthy New England textile manufacturer and real estate developer, Bernard Goldfine was the principal subject in an influence peddling scandal during Dwight Eisenhower's presidency. A Russian immigrant who came to the United States in 1899, Goldfine began his own business by buying and selling wool remnants at age 19, and with the sizable profits earned during World War I, he invested heavily in the textile industry. Goldfine substantially expanded his holdings during the Great Depression, eventually controlling six textile mills in New England and two development firms in Boston.

Largely to assist him in answering complaints filed against his businesses by various government regulatory agencies, Goldfine cultivated the friendship of politicians from both parties, including Congressman John McCormack of Massachusetts, Senators Norris Cotton and Styles Bridges of New Hampshire, and Governor Sherman Adams of New Hampshire. In June 1958 congressional investigations revealed that Goldfine had enlisted the help of Adams, then President Eisenhower's Chief of Staff, to answer Federal Trade Commission charges against his textile mills. Investigators also disclosed that Goldfine, in an apparent show of gratitude, had given Adams a $700 vicuna coat, a $2,400 oriental rug, and had also paid for many of Adams's hotel expenses throughout the 1950s. Adams resigned in disgrace, and for his role in the scandal, Goldfine eventually received a one-year suspended sentence for contempt of Congress.

The scandal was a major embarrassment for the Eisenhower administration, which had promised in 1952 to adhere to the highest ethical standards in order to counter what it charged was the influence peddling common in Harry Truman's administration. Goldfine's gaffe contributed, moreover, to the wholesale defeat of Republican candidates in the 1958 elections, generally regarded as one of the worst defeats ever suffered by an incumbent party in a midterm election.

See also: Dwight D. Eisenhower

John W. Malsberger

REFERENCES

Adams, Sherman. 1961. *Firsthand Report: The Story of the Eisenhower Administration.* New York: Harper.

Frier, David. 1970. *Conflict of Interest in the Eisenhower Administration.* Baltimore: Penguin.

Manchester, William. 1973. *The Glory and the Dream: A Narrative History of America 1932–1972.* Boston: Little, Brown.

Barry M. Goldwater (1909–)

Presidential candidate and leader of the conservative Republicans. Arizona Senator Barry Goldwater—the reluctant, personally modest champion of a grass-roots conservative movement—won the 1964 Republican presidential nomination. Yet he lost the election to Lyndon Johnson because he became known as a dangerous radical, eager to dismantle the New Deal structure at home and launch military adventures abroad. Goldwater's campaign reinforced this image: first party unity and then responsiveness to public opinion were sacrificed on the altar of a conservative purity expressed with blunt, colorful—and sometimes frightening—phrases.

Grandson of a frontier Jewish merchant (but raised as an Episcopalian), Goldwater graduated from the Staunton Military Academy and enrolled in the University of Arizona in 1928. He went to work in the family-owned department store upon the death of his father in 1929 and became its president in 1937. He served as a pilot in the U.S. Army Air Force from 1941 to 1945 and in the Arizona National Guard until 1952, when he was elected to the U.S. Senate after a term on the Phoenix City Council. He became a major general in the Air Force Reserve in the 1960s.

Barry Goldwater published 13 books between 1940 and 1979. The short volumes that made him a conservative champion were *The Conscience of a Conservative* (1960) and *Why Not Victory?* (1962). Goldwater believed that victory for the Republican Party would come only from presenting the voters "a choice, not an echo." Republican Party candidates should frankly describe the threat posed by big government to individualist values. Goldwater would have relished that debate against John Kennedy, but the assassination in Dallas made Lyndon Johnson his opponent.

The 1964 presidential nomination was essentially won when Goldwater's zealous supporters managed to gather national convention delegates through state party organizations. Goldwater clinched the nomination by narrowly winning the California primary—his only primary victory. Angered by charges of "extremism" made by his primary opponents, Goldwater disdained gestures toward unity at the national convention. As it turned out, only 22 percent of Republican voters favored Goldwater's nomination. As the minority candidate of a minority party, he carried only Arizona and four states in the Deep South, losing to Johnson in a historic landslide. Yet he laid foundations for southern Republicanism and for a less frightening conservative candidate in 1980—Ronald Reagan.

After his defeat, Barry Goldwater returned to Arizona, which again elected him to the U.S. Senate in 1968. In the Watergate crisis, Goldwater advised President Richard Nixon to resign. He became chairman of the Armed Services Committee, designating the 1986 reform of the Joint Chiefs of Staff as his most notable legislative accomplishment. Goldwater enjoyed his role as crusty "grandfather of the conservative movement," condemning the pretensions of religious organizations claiming a conservative mantle. He retired from the Senate in 1987.

See also: Election of 1964, Lyndon Johnson, John F. Kennedy, New Deal, Ronald Reagan, Watergate

Karl A. Lamb

REFERENCES

Goldwater, Barry. 1960. *The Conscience of a Conservative.* Shepardsville, KY: Victor Pub.

———. 1962. *Why Not Victory?* New York: McGraw-Hill.

Ladd, Everett Carll, Jr., with Charles D. Hadley. 1975. *Transformations of the American Party System.* New York: Norton.

White, Theodore H. *The Making of the President 1964.* New York: Atheneum.

Gomillion v. Lightfoot
364 U.S. 339 (1960)

This case declared that the drawing of political boundaries for the purpose of disenfranchising racial minorities is prohibited by the

Fifteenth Amendment. A 1957 Alabama statute changed the shape of the boundaries of the city of Tuskegee from a square to a 28-sided figure. The redrawing removed from the city all but four or five Black voters. It excluded no whites. C. G. Gomillion (and other Black residents of Tuskegee) brought an action in U.S. District Court for a declaratory judgment that the act was unconstitutional and for an injunction to restrain Mayor Phil M. Lightfoot and other officials from enforcing the act, claiming that enforcement of the act would constitute discrimination in violation of the due process and equal protection clauses of the Fourteenth Amendment and that it would deny them the right to vote as protected by the Fifteenth Amendment. The district court held that "This Court has no control over, no supervision over, and no power to change any boundaries of municipal corporations fixed by a duly convened and elected legislative body acting for the people of the State of Alabama." The U.S. Court of Appeals for the Fifth Circuit affirmed the judgment with one judge dissenting. The Supreme Court reversed. Though technically a reversal on an issue of jurisdiction, this decision had the effect of nullifying the act because the respondents never argued that the new boundaries served any countervailing municipal function. Their position had been that states had the power to "establish, destroy, or reorganize by contraction or expansion its political subdivisions."

Writing for the majority, Justice Felix Frankfurter held that the act violated the Fifteenth Amendment. Quoting *Lane v. Wilson*, he wrote, "The [Fifteenth] Amendment nullifies sophisticated as well as simple-minded modes of discrimination." Frankfurter distinguished *Gomillion* from *Colegrove v. Green* where he had argued that courts should refrain from entering the "political thicket" of vote dilution by malapportionment. In *Gomillion*, he characterized *Colegrove* as a case in which the Supreme Court refused to resolve a "political question" of malapportioned congressional districts that had resulted from population shifts and from the failure of a state legislature to act to remedy the situation. Frankfurter saw *Gomillion* as a situation in which voting was deprived by "affirmative legislative action . . . [that] singles out a readily isolated segment of a racial minority for special discriminatory treatment." Regardless of a state's primary responsibility for drawing political boundaries, it could not deny the rights protected by the Fifteenth Amendment.

Justice Charles Whittaker concurred in the judgment but thought that the decision should be rested on the equal protection clause of the Fourteenth Amendment rather than the Fifteenth Amendment. Justice William Douglas joined the opinion of the Court without comment except to note that he adhered to the dissents in *Colegrove v. Green* (328 U.S. 549) and *South v. Peters* (339 U.S. 276).

See also: Fifteenth Amendment

H. W. Perry, Jr.

Samuel Gompers (1850–1924)

Foremost labor leader of his era. Samuel Gompers was president of the American Federation of Labor (AFL) for 38 years. A devotee of European socialist literature in his youth, as AFL head he became an implacable foe of working-class radicalism. To the skilled, largely native-born, and Protestant members of the AFL, he offered significant material advantages and to the AFL generally a more respectable place within American capitalism. But Gompers's business unionism—"pure and simplism"—did little to assist unskilled workers.

Samuel Gompers was born in London to Dutch-Jewish parents, but in 1863 the Gompers family emigrated to New York City's East Side. Gompers received little formal education, a fact that led to his later distrust of radical intellectuals. As a journeyman cigarmaker in the 1870s, however, he studied the works of Marx, Engels, and Lassalle under the tutelage of Ferdinand Laurell, a Swedish Socialist.

Gompers joined the Cigarmakers International Union (CMIU) in the early 1870s and was active in the CMIU strike of 1877 called in support of the railway workers. This strike failed, leaving the CMIU shattered. Using the English "new Model" trade union as his base, Gompers reorganized the New York cigarmakers and in the process revolutionized American trade unionism. The new cigarmakers' union was a high-dues, top-down organization that bargained hard and offered welfare benefits to its membership but avoided political action.

In 1882 the Federation of Organized Trade and Labor Unions (FOTLU) was founded, with Gompers chairing the Committee on the Constitution. In 1886 the FOTLU was reorganized and renamed the American Federation of Labor; Gompers was elected its first leader. The new federation's policies bore Gompers's imprint: the AFL was a loose federation of autonomous craft unions. Gompers also disallowed dual unionism—the practice of organizing workers of the same industry into two or more unions.

The AFL policy on dual unionism led to struggles with rival union organizations. Initially, the AFL competed against the Knights of Labor, a class-collaborationist organization that emphasized the principle of social cooperation. In the 1890s, Daniel De Leon's Socialist Labor Party (SLP) attempted to infiltrate the AFL, a move repulsed by Gompers; in the same way he fended off a subsequent attempt by the Socialist Party of America (SPA). The most significant union rival to the AFL was the syndicalist Industrial Workers of the World (IWW), founded in 1905. Gompers refused to credit the IWW's enthusiasm for industrial unionism; the IWW, on the other hand, proved to be ineffectual at organizing unskilled workers.

Although outspoken against socialism, the Gompers-led AFL did not remain completely nonpolitical. Gompers believed that bosses and political opportunists controlled national politics, and he sought to place industrial relations outside the interference of government and the courts. However, the AFL did draw up a modestly progressive Bill of Grievances and began a policy of rewarding or punishing individual politicians depending on their union stance. The AFL devoted a great deal of energy to defeat Republican Congressman Charles Littlefield of Maine, a labor enemy. In the 1908 election, an informal alliance was forged between the AFL and the Democratic Party, whose partisans were most responsive to AFL policies.

Gompers's most explicitly political role came during World War I. Appointed by President Woodrow Wilson to the Council of National Defense, Gompers himself set up the War Committee on Labor, which rallied labor effort for the war and kept industrial relations peaceful. Gompers was among the harshest critics of pacifists, a posture that made labor respectable in xenophobic wartime America and lent credence to government persecutions of antiwar radicals. At the Versailles peace conference, President Wilson appointed Gompers to the Committee on International Labor Legislation.

A man of action, Gompers remained leader of the AFL until his death. During his tenure as president, the AFL grew from 100,000 to 3 million members, a testament to the appeal of Gompers's practical approach to trade unionism.

See also: Daniel De Leon, Socialism in American Politics, Woodrow Wilson

John Walsh

Good Neighbor League

An auxiliary group of the Democratic Party established during the 1936 election to secure support for Franklin D. Roosevelt's reelection of Black Americans, social workers, educators, religious leaders, Independents, former Republicans, and other voters who wished to support Roosevelt but not the Democratic Party. The League extolled such basic Christian principles as the superiority of human values to property values and the truism that a better life for one's self depends upon a better life for one's neighbor. The League directed its efforts to voter groups open to such idealistic appeals.

The League contributed significantly to Roosevelt's reelection effort. It raised over $133,000 for the campaign (a significant amount of money in the Great Depression) and claimed a membership of 30,000 in 20 states. The League aided the Democratic Party's recruitment of African-Americans through a separate Colored Committee, and it proved an effective propaganda machine by sponsoring major campaign rallies, conducting dinners and meetings, and publishing pamphlets that praised Roosevelt's leadership and defended his New Deal policies.

The Good Neighbor League was but one means that the Democratic Party used to recruit new voters into the Roosevelt coalition in 1936. However, it dramatized the importance of such organizations in raising funds and recruiting voters, and it served as a model for auxiliary activity for years to come. With the assistance of the Democratic National Committee, the League continued to operate until 1939, demonstrating that many of its members considered the commitment to Christian principles more than a political concern.

See also: New Deal, Franklin D. Roosevelt

Thomas T. Spencer

REFERENCES

Key, V. O., Jr. 1958. *Politics, Parties, and Pressure Groups.* New York: Crowell.

McCoy, Donald R. 1960. "The Good Neighbor League and the Presidential Campaign of 1936." 13 *Western Political Quarterly* 1011.

Spencer, Thomas T. 1976. "Democratic Auxiliary and Non-Party Groups in the Election of 1936." Ph.D. dissertation, U. of Notre Dame.

———. 1978. "The Good Neighbor League Colored Committee and the 1936 Democratic Presidential Campaign." 13 *The Journal of Negro History* 307.

Charles E. Goodell (1926–1987)

Anti-Vietnam War Republican Senator from New York. In 1968, Charles E. Goodell was appointed by Governor Nelson Rockefeller to the

Senate seat left vacant when Robert Kennedy was assassinated. In 1970 Conservative Party candidate James Buckley thwarted his bid for a full term.

A 1959 special election in southwestern New York sent Goodell to the House, where he joined Gerald Ford's "Young Turk" faction. When Ford became Minority Leader in 1965, he named Goodell to head a new GOP organ, the Committee on Planning and Research (later the Research Committee).

Goodell had a relatively liberal record for a House Republican. Although critical of the War on Poverty, he was central in developing the Manpower Development and Training Act of 1962 and supported civil rights legislation. At the 1968 Republican National Convention, he led a prescient but abortive effort to deny the vice presidential nomination to Spiro Agnew.

In the Senate, he opposed the Richard Nixon administration on the Vietnam War and voted against the Supreme Court nominations of G. Harrold Carswell and Clement Haynsworth. In 1970 Nixon's partisans returned the favor by opposing Goodell's election bid. Vice President Agnew called him a "radical liberal" and tacitly supported Conservative Party candidate James Buckley. After losing, Goodell returned to his law practice. In 1974 Gerald Ford, now President, named him to hear the Clemency Board for Vietnam draft evaders.

See also: Spiro Agnew, James Buckley, Gerald Ford, Robert Kennedy, Nelson Rockefeller

John J. Pitney, Jr.

REFERENCES

Berger, Jason. 1979. "Charles E. Goodell." In Eleanora W. Schoenebaum, ed. *Political Profiles: The Nixon/Ford Years.* New York: Facts on File.

Jones, Charles O. 1970. *The Minority Party in Congress.* Boston: Little, Brown.

Safire, William. 1975. *Before the Fall.* New York: Ballantine.

William Goodell (1792–1878)

Reform journalist and abolitionist. William Goodell was best known as an uncompromising proponent of the Liberty Party. Born in Coventry, New York, he gave up business to pursue his interest in temperance and abolitionism through speaking and writing. Most significant of the several newspapers he edited was the *Friend of Man,* published in Utica, New York.

By the 1830s, abolition became his major concern. At first opposed to political activities by abolitionists, he gradually evolved from

questioning of major party candidates to the reluctant conclusion that the third-party approach was the only effective way to achieve abolition. Prominent in the formation of the Liberty Party in 1840, he thus broke with the antipolitical William Lloyd Garrison.

Following James G. Birney's token campaign of 1840, Goodell, along with Gerrit Smith, urged the party to broaden its platform to include other reforms. Concomitant to that broadening Smith and Goodell also opposed a Liberty coalition with less radical antislavery Democrats and Whigs. In 1847 Goodell led the secession of a small faction angered over the party's refusal to label slavery unconstitutional everywhere. Rejecting the Free Soil Party as too moderate on slavery, Goodell helped to form the Liberty League that nominated Smith as its presidential candidate in 1848. In 1852 the Free Soilers again ignored the Liberty effort, resulting in the tiny party's nomination of Goodell for President. An advocate of racial equality in the North, Goodell was best known for his belief that slavery and the Constitution were incompatible. He developed this argument most fully in *Slavery and Anti-Slavery* (1852) and continued to write and speak against slavery until its abolition. Following the Civil War, he renewed his interest in temperance and was among the organizers of the National Prohibition Party.

See also: Abolition Movement, James G. Birney, Election of 1852, William Lloyd Garrison, Liberty Party, Gerrit Smith, Third Parties in American Parties

Frederick J. Blue

REFERENCES

Filler, Louis. 1960. *The Crusade Against Slavery, 1830–1860.* New York: Harper & Row.

Goodell, William. 1952. *Slavery and Anti-Slavery.* New York: Harned.

Sewell, Richard H. 1976. *Ballots for Freedom: Antislavery Politics in the United States, 1837–1860.* New York: Oxford U. Pr.

Sorin, Gerald. 1971. *The New York Abolitionists: A Case Study of Political Radicalism.* Westport, CT: Greenwood.

Wilson, Henry. 1872. *A History of the Rise and Fall of the Slave Power in America.* Vol. I. Boston: Houghton Mifflin.

Arthur P. Gorman (1839–1906)

Undisputed leader of "Old Guard" conservative Maryland Democrats. In partnership with I. Freeman Rasin, boss of Baltimore's Democratic machine, Arthur Pue Gorman dominated Maryland politics for three decades and was four times sent to the United States Senate by the Maryland legislature.

Born in Howard County, Maryland, Gorman received no formal schooling beyond the age of 11, when he was appointed a page in the U.S. Senate. After 16 years on the Senate staff, he became a Maryland customs collector in 1866. Following election to the state legislature in 1869, Gorman served as president of the Chesapeake and Ohio Canal from 1872 to 1882. He operated the canal as an adjunct to the Democratic Party, but his astute management insured successful operation despite its economic obsolescence.

Elected to the U.S. Senate in 1880, Gorman became the manager of Grover Cleveland's first presidential campaign. He hired the stenographer who recorded the fatal "Rum, Romanism, and Rebellion" remark by a supporter of Cleveland's opponent, James G. Blaine.

Ever the party stalwart, Gorman even supported William Jennings Bryan. Defeated for a fourth term in 1897, he was returned to the Senate in 1902. As Senate Democratic leader, Gorman attacked Theodore Roosevelt's support of the rebellion in Panama. Gorman supported the idea of a canal but deplored the methods used. Success might have won Gorman the Democratic presidential nomination, but the American people supported Roosevelt's actions.

See also: James G. Blaine, William Jennings Bryan, Grover Cleveland, Theodore Roosevelt, Stalwarts (and Half-Breeds)

Karl A. Lamb

REFERENCES

Kent, Frank R. 1968. *The Story of Maryland Politics.* Hatboro, PA: Tradition Press. Orig. pub. 1911.

Lambert, John R., Jr. 1953. *Arthur Pue Gorman.* Baton Rouge: Louisiana State U. Pr.

———. 1963. "The Biographical Writings of Senator Arthur Pue Gorman." 58 *Maryland Historical Magazine* 93.

Harold F. Gosnell (1896–)

One of the pioneer figures in the study of American political parties and elections. Harold F. Gosnell was the complete scientist, both methodologically and statistically sophisticated and yet very close to his subject of study—a scientist in the field rather than a specialist on a bureaucratized scientific team. Harold Gosnell was doing field experiments and empirical studies of party organizations long before the advent of the behavioral era in political science. He was performing factorial and correlational analyses in the 1930s when "political science"

was mostly the study of government, constitution, and political philosophy.

Gosnell's early work includes the first use of experimentation in political science. His early interest in Chicago politics led him to study those factors that influence voter turnout; his research motif was a field experiment in which an experimental group was manipulated (via a mailed postcard) with information pertaining to registration rules and locations; his conclusion was that the provision of such information would substantially increase turnout rates. Gosnell was not one to study only the mass public; he also engaged in empirical studies of party elites. Similar to earlier party scholars like Robert Michels, he closely observed the workings of a political party—in Gosnell's case the Chicago Democratic machine in the 1930s. His observations clearly illustrated the complex operations of a political machine. He included both tangible (i.e., patronage) as well as personal and social elements in his examination of the workings of machine politics.

Harold Gosnell was years ahead of his scholarly cohorts in his methods. His empirical and methodological approaches later came to be the norm in political science; his work anticipated some of the more modern subjects relating to parties and elections—in particular the study of the media and campaigns. In the 1930s Gosnell studied the influence of the press on local elections (in Chicago), and in the early 1950s he wrote perceptively on Franklin D. Roosevelt and his campaigns.

David A. Bositis

REFERENCES

Gosnell, Harold. 1927. *Getting Out the Vote: An Experiment in the Stimulation of Voting.* Chicago: U. of Chicago Pr.

———. 1937. *Machine Politics: Chicago Model.* Chicago: U. of Chicago Pr.

———. 1952. *Champion Campaigner: Franklin D. Roosevelt.* New York: Macmillan.

———, and N. Pearson. 1939. "The Study of Voting Behavior by Correlational Techniques." *American Sociological Review.*

———, and M. J. Schmidt. 1936. "Factorial Analysis of the Relation of the Press to Voting in Chicago." 7 *Journal of Social Psychology* 375.

Gospel of Wealth

The most articulate justification for the amassing of huge fortunes in the late 1800s and for governmental restraint in the regulation of big business was the Gospel of Wealth. The term is derived from an article written by Andrew

Carnegie in 1889; there he argued that wealth naturally flows into the hands of great entrepreneurs who have demonstrated, through the rigors of intense competition, that they were the "fittest" members of society. The accumulated wealth of these individuals should not, Carnegie insisted, be viewed as their personal possessions, for it is in fact the wealth of society. The entrepreneur is the trustee of that wealth. Having demonstrated their superiority over their fellow man, the wealthy should dispose of their fortunes for the benefit of mankind during their lifetimes, using the insight exhibited during their successful industrial careers. Carnegie's gloss made more palatable the Social Darwinist, laissez faire approach to business embraced by both Republicans and Democrats from 1865 to 1892.

David B. Raymond

REFERENCES

Carnegie, Andrew. 1962. "Wealth." In Edward C. Kirkland, ed. *The Gospel of Wealth and Other Timely Essays*. Cambridge: Belknap Pr.

Hofstadter, Richard. 1944. *Social Darwinism in American Thought*. Philadelphia: U. of Pennsylvania Pr.

William Philip (Phil) Gramm (1942–)

Conservative Republican Senator from Texas. Phil Gramm is known chiefly for three pieces of legislature bearing his name. The first two came in 1981 when he was a Democratic member of the House of Representatives from the Sixth Congressional District of Texas. Gramm joined with Ohio Republican Delbert Latta to sponsor a bill favored by the new Ronald Reagan administration that sharply reduced spending on nondefense matters, and in a second bill (also with Latta) he used a device (called "Reconciliation") to require committees of Congress to scale back budgetary authorizations to meet spending ceilings.

That a relatively junior member of the House could exert such influence was due to the intervention of then–Majority Leader Jim Wright of Texas, who helped Gramm become a member of the House Budget Committee from which the legislation came. Gramm's cooperation with the Reagan administration went further than that of any other southern conservative Democrat (known as "boll weevils") and led to Gramm's great unpopularity among House Democrats. At the next opportunity (January 1983) the House Democratic Steering and Policy Committee voted to remove Gramm from the Budget Committee. He resigned from Congress, switched to the Republican Party, and won re-election as a Republican to the same seat. In 1984 he was elected as a Republican to the U.S. Senate from Texas; he was reelected in 1990.

His third legislative innovation was the cosponsoring in the Senate of a bill—the Gramm-Rudman-Hollings bill—requiring all spending to meet deficit-reducing targets by means of automatic formulas applied across the board.

Gramm was born in Fort Benning, Georgia, to a career military family. He was a professional economist, holding a Ph.D. from the University of Georgia; before entering Congress in 1978, he spent his entire career on the economics faculty at Texas A & M University. He married Wendy Lee, a budget analyst, in 1970.

See also: Ronald Reagan, Jim Wright

Nelson W. Polsby

Grand Army of the Republic

Organized in Illinois in 1866 ostensibly as a veterans' association to assist Union veterans and their widows and orphans, the Grand Army of the Republic (GAR) was from its inception a political interest group lobbying for veterans' benefits and pensions. In 1868 detachments of the organization prepared to mobilize in defense of Congress during the impeachment crisis; after nearly fading into insignificance during the administration of Ulysses S. Grant, the organization found new life in the 1870s and became an important arm of the Republican Party, despite its pretensions of nonpartisanship. It played an important part in rallying support to the candidacy of Rutherford B. Hayes in 1876, pushed for the nomination of Grant in 1880, and supported longtime leader John A. Logan in 1884, becoming a factor in Logan's nomination for the vice presidency.

The GAR seemed equally devoted to waving the bloody shirt and to securing benefits and offices for its members. It worked hard to win passage of pension and relief legislation. Unsuccessful in winning significant concessions from Grant, the GAR achieved more success in its subsequent lobbying efforts through the 1880s. In 1887, after vetoing several veterans' pension bills, President Grover Cleveland ordered the return of captured Confederate battle flags. The proposal initially met with widespread opposition in the GAR, capped by the emotional response of its commander, Lucius Fairchild, who demanded divine retribution for such a crime. Cleveland's defeat in 1888 was the last triumph of the organization. In 1890, as a reward for its contributions to the Republican electoral triumph, Congress passed and Benjamin Harrison signed a major veterans' disability pension bill.

See also: Bloody Shirt, Grover Cleveland, Benjamin Harrison, Rutherford Hayes

Brooks Donohue Simpson

REFERENCES

Buck, Paul H. 1938. *The Road to Reunion, 1865–1900.* Boston: Little, Brown.

Dearing, Mary R. 1952. *Veterans in Politics: The Story of the G. A. R.* Baton Rouge: Louisiana State U. Pr.

Ross, Sam. 1964. *The Empty Sleeve: A Biography of Lucius Fairchild.* Madison: State Historical Society of Wisconsin.

Grand State Farmers' Alliance

The forerunner of the National Farmers' Alliance and Industrial Union (NFAIU). Begun in Lampasas, Texas, in 1877, the Grand State Farmers' Alliance (GSFA) soon spread to a three-county area, primarily as an organization of mutual protection against cattle and horse thieves. It faded from existence in 1880 after abortive involvements with the Greenback Party in the 1878 and 1880 local elections.

In the spring of 1879, the Alliance idea spread to nearby Parker, Texas, and found a ready audience among farmers angry at economic and class discrimination. Soon other organizers fanned out across Texas, and the second Grand State Farmers' Alliance was formed in December 1880.

By 1883 the GSFA had over 140 suballiances, but many soon began dropping away from lack of interest. A dynamic traveling lecturer, S. O. Daws, helped keep these groups involved as the GSFA increasingly moved to grapple with the wider problems of agriculture in a rapidly changing economy.

By April 1886, Daws and other lecturers had built the GSFA to 1,650 suballiances in Texas. The order now began to expand beyond the state's borders and also became involved in politics. A split over this political involvement developed, but a compromise resulted in the naming of Charles McCune as president; subsequently the GSFA merged with the Farmers Union of Louisiana (FUL) to form the National Farmers' Alliance and Cooperative Union (NFACU). McCune established a state cooperative exchange in Texas, but lack of capital doomed this enterprise. Meanwhile, Macune continued his organizing and merging activity, and in December 1889, the National Farmers' Alliance and Industrial Union (NFAIU) was born.

The issue of politics had caused controversy since the first days of the GSFA, and the 1889 St. Louis meeting of the NFAIU saw the issue come to a head for the national group. The major issue became a "subtreasury plan" introduced by Macune, calling for the establishment of government facilities for the storage for nonperishable farm commodities on which farmers could be granted loans. This idea failed to gain legislative support, but it turned out to be a forerunner of the New Deal Commodity Credit Corporation of 1933.

The major political controversy within the NFAIU was whether to support a third party or to work within the existing party structure. When the NFAIU support of the People's Party candidate in the 1892 presidential election failed, the organization rapidly fell apart. At its peak in 1890, the National Farmer's Alliance and Industrial Union had some 1.5 million members in over 40 states. The small Grand State Farmers' Alliance had grown into the National Farmers' Alliance and Industrial Union, but both organizations were the victims of political failure. Still, they were at the heart of the farmers' protest movement that shook the United States in the late nineteenth century.

See also: Greenback Party, National Farmers' Alliance and Industrial Union, New Deal, People's Party

John F. Marszalek

REFERENCES

Dyson, Lowell K. 1986. "National Farmers' Alliance and Industrial Union." In *The Greenwood Encyclopedia of American Institutions.* Westport, CT: Greenwood.

Goodwyn, Lawrence. 1976. *Democratic Promise: The Populist Moment in America.* New York: Oxford U. Pr.

McMath, Robert C., Jr. 1975. *Populist Vanguard: A History of the Southern Farmers' Alliance.* Chapel Hill: U. of North Carolina Pr.

Francis Granger (1792–1868)

Antebellum Whig Party leader. Although he was a Connecticut native, Francis Granger's adult years and political career were associated with New York. A handsome and personable man, he was a contemporary of William H. Seward and Thurlow Weed and, for many years, a member of their political circle.

Granger entered the New York Assembly in 1825 and achieved prominence during the Antimasonic upheavals of that day. He was the National Republicans' candidate for lieutenant governor in 1828 and was nominated by both the Antimasons and the National Republicans for governor in 1830 and 1832. On each occasion, he was defeated.

From the party realignments of the 1830s, Granger emerged a Whig. He was elected to Congress in 1834 and reelected in 1838 and 1840. With the Whig victory in the presidential election of 1840, however, Granger accepted the position of Postmaster General in the William Henry Harrison Cabinet. When, after Harrison's death, John Tyler broke with the Whig leadership, Granger resigned in protest but was returned to Congress, retiring in 1843.

In the fractious Whig Party of the 1840s, Granger was a conservative in contrast to Seward and Weed, his former allies. He supported the Compromise of 1850 and Seward's rival, Millard Fillmore. As chair of the Whig New York state convention of 1850, he led a conservative walkout in protest of resolutions praising Seward, and Granger's white mane gave to his followers the sobriquet Silver Grays. Granger was, subsequently, a member of the Washington Peace Conference of 1861, an assembly of distinguished politicians who attempted to resolve the secession crisis, but contributed little to that failed enterprise.

In the turbulent politics of his lifetime, Granger was neither as nimble nor as shrewd as Seward and Weed and, consequently, his achievements were more modest.

See also: Antimasons, Millard Fillmore, William Henry Harrison, William H. Seward, John Tyler, Thurlow Weed

John F. Coleman

REFERENCES

Van Deusen, Glyndon G. 1967. *William Henry Seward.* New York: Oxford U. Pr.

Granger Movement

The term "Granger movement" traditionally has been used to designate the political manifestation of an upsurge of agrarian discontent, particularly in the upper Midwest, in the decade after the Civil War. The principal, but not the only, farmers' organization in the period was the Patrons of Husbandry. Its arrangement into national, state, and subordinate granges (a "grange" is simply a farm in all of its symbolic meanings) led to the application of the name "Granger" not only to that particular group but also to the agricultural movement as a whole.

The Patrons of Husbandry was founded in Washington, D.C., in 1867 by Oliver H. Kelley who, as a clerk for the Bureau of Agriculture, had studied primitive farming methods and conditions in the South soon after the war. Kelley's aim was to bring farmers together in a fraternal social setting where they could discuss their common difficulties and educate themselves in modern ways of improving their operations. Growth of the Patrons was initially slow, primarily limited to Kelley's home state of Minnesota, but farmers' perceived grievances in the early 1870s stimulated the recruitment drive. Consequently, by mid-decade, the organization claimed 800,000 members enlisted in 20,000 granges, mostly in the upper Mississippi River valley.

The Patrons was avowedly nonpolitical in purpose, and the National Grange specifically forbade local granges from acting like political parties, including making nominations for office or even discussing candidates or issues in their meetings. Yet many of the farmers who enlisted in the Grange looked to political action for solutions to their common problems. Many who joined the Grange also participated in protest political movements, the most formal of which were the Independent and Anti-Monopoly parties of the Midwest, which reached their height in 1873 and 1874 and then quickly declined or were swallowed by the Greenback Party. Probably the greatest impact of these third parties was to upset the election calculations and strategies of major-party leaders in the states where Granger numbers were largest. They generally achieved their greatest influence through fusion with one of the major parties—most often the Democrats.

The agrarian discontent that persisted through several decades following the Civil War grew out of the profound changes affecting American agriculture in the nineteenth century. Whereas farmers had typically exchanged their products in a local or regional market where they believed they met buyers on an equal level, improvements in transportation (especially railroads) now made them dependent on a vast national market over which they felt that they exercised little control. With the decline in agricultural prices in the decade after the war, when farmers could no longer pay the high costs of transportation and elevator storage, they looked to a political solution through state regulation of railroad rates and grain elevator companies.

Historians traditionally refer to the state regulatory legislation passed in the 1870s as Granger laws, but in the last few decades research indicates that the farmers' influence was generally overstated. Farmers from areas without railroads refrained from supporting laws that would discourage their development, and the drive for regulation was initiated by merchants, grain dealers, and other businessmen.

See also: Agrarianism, Greenback Party, Railroads

Charles W. Calhoun

REFERENCES

Buck, Solon J. 1913. *The Granger Movement: A Study of Agricultural Organization and Its Political, Economic and Social Manifestations, 1870–1880.* Cambridge: Harvard U. Pr.

Kleppner, Paul. 1979. *The Third Electoral System, 1853–1892: Parties, Voters, and Political Cultures.* Chapel Hill: U. of North Carolina Pr.

Miller, George H. 1971. *Railroads and the Granger Laws.* Madison: U. of Wisconsin Pr.

Ulysses S. Grant (1822–1885)

Civil War general and postwar President. One of the least understood and most underestimated political figures in American history, Ulysses Simpson Grant played a prominent role in the politics of war and Reconstruction in the mid-nineteenth century. Often perceived by contemporaries and some later historians as a bumbling and naive politician, Grant actually demonstrated considerable political awareness and skill both as military commander and President. As a field commander during the American Civil War, Grant understood the political ramifications of military decisions. His initial support of a limited war strategy, designed to enhance rapid reconciliation between North and South, soon faded in the face of determined Confederate resistance to his offensives along the Mississippi and Tennessee rivers. Thereafter Grant favored a "total war" approach, designed to destroy the enemy's material and morale. One component of this strategy was the emancipation of Black slaves and their enlistment in the Union Army—measures Grant supported.

Grant was also aware of the political consequences of the outcome of military operations. In early 1863 he refused to abandon his Vicksburg offensive, concerned with the impact of such a setback on Northern morale; appointed general-in-chief by President Abraham Lincoln in 1864, his grand strategy of coordinated offensives was designed in part to force a favorable military decision before the fall presidential contest to enhance Lincoln's chances of reelection. In 1865 Grant sought to win peace either by negotiation or by combat, and the terms he offered General Robert E. Lee when Lee surrendered at Appomattox in Virginia were designed to forestall guerrilla warfare and postwar reprisals by United States authorities.

After Appomattox, Grant hoped for a rapid return to peace, involving magnanimity toward the defeated and justice for the freedmen. Believing it had been the inability of politicians to reconcile their differences that led to the outbreak of hostilities in 1861, he dreaded the impact of partisan squabbling and vindictiveness upon the process of readjustment. The actions of President Andrew Johnson alarmed him; despite his best efforts to work with the new chief executive in the interests of national harmony, Grant grew increasingly concerned that Johnson seemed only too willing to welcome white southerners back into the Union while overlooking evidence of southern hostility and violence toward Blacks, white Unionists, and army personnel. Grant's support of a continued military presence in the South, the Fourteenth Amendment, and eventually (after some initial reluctance) Black suffrage marked his growing divergence from administration policies in 1866—a process culminating in the general's participation in the framing of the Military Reconstruction Acts in 1867. Although in August 1867 he accepted Johnson's offer of the War Department portfolio on an *ad interim* basis, his compliance with the Senate's action in restoring Edwin M. Stanton to the post the following January resulted in an ugly controversy with Johnson.

Grant's open break with Johnson secured his nomination as the Republican presidential candidate in 1868. He reluctantly accepted the nomination, convinced that the only alternatives were a Democratic victory or continued political bickering, and he triumphed over Horatio Seymour in the fall election. His first 15 months as President provided him with an education on American politics. His initial Cabinet appointments upset many party regulars; his desire to annex Santo Domingo stirred several prominent Republicans—notably Charles Sumner and Carl Schurz—into open opposition, as they attacked the President's highhandedness at home and abroad as "Caesarism." Historians see some truth in these charges, for once Grant had learned the rules of the political game, he formed a powerful coterie of Senate supporters, wielded patronage skillfully to build support, and punished his enemies (as when he engineered the removal of Sumner from his committee chairmanship). At the same time he pursued a tougher policy toward intransigent southerners, directing the arrest and trial of white terrorists in several southern states; Congress enhanced his power to do so under the Enforcement Acts of 1870 and 1871. Other than his failure to annex Santo Domingo, his foreign policy, under the able supervision of Secretary of State Hamilton Fish, scored several signal triumphs, most notably in resolving several serious points of dispute with England.

By the end of Grant's first term his vigorous exercise of executive powers aroused significant opposition within his own party. These Liberal Republicans, as they soon called themselves, had diverse views on civil service reform, tariffs, Reconstruction, and other issues, but they were united in their desire to depose the incumbent—"Anything to beat Grant!" The President skillfully stripped the opposition of many of its planks by calling for the establishment of the first Civil Service Commission (1871) and approving reduced tariff rates. Renominated in 1872 by Republican convention at Philadelphia, Grant won easily over newspaper editor and erstwhile politico Horace Greeley, the Liberal Republican and Democratic nominee.

Grant's second term was marked by economic depression, frustrations in southern policy, and scandal. A panic in the fall of 1873 evolved into a long-term depression, helping Democrats to regain majority control of the House of Representatives in 1874 and forcing Republicans to reconsider their support of an increasingly unpopular Reconstruction policy. Grant's efforts to exonerate southern Republican regimes against charges of violence and fraud were the target of scorn and derision, until he admitted in 1875 that the public was tired of Reconstruction and that to continue to intervene in the South was to court political disaster in the North. While revelations of scandal first touched Congress in Credit Mobilier, evidence of corruption soon came to haunt the administration, exposing Cabinet officers, diplomats, and even members of the President's staff. Grant's private secretary, Orville Babcock, was indicted for assisting the "Whiskey Ring" to defraud the government; Secretary of War William W. Belknap resigned when it was revealed that his wives had accepted kickbacks for their involvement in Army post tradership appointments. The Democratic-controlled House of Representatives launched a series of investigations designed to provide fodder for the forthcoming campaign. Whatever notions Grant had of a third term were dashed by these incidents, as Rutherford B. Hayes took the nomination. In the disputed election that followed, Grant played a key role in maintaining order while ensuring the peaceful adjudication of the controversy.

Leaving the White House in 1877, Grant embarked upon an around-the-world tour. Before long several Republican leaders, denoted as Stalwarts (they were disgruntled with the Hayes administration and worried by Democratic triumphs in the midterm election), began to tout Grant as a possible presidential nominee in 1880. Although not ambitious for a third term, Grant succumbed to his supporters' urgings, only to be defeated at the 1880 Chicago convention when the anti-Grant forces, known as the Half-Breeds, finally united on James A. Garfield as the standard-bearer. A disappointed Grant nevertheless took the stump for Garfield in a rare display of public speaking; after the election, however, he became increasingly angered by the efforts of Garfield and Secretary of State James G. Blaine to oust Stalwarts from important positions. Grant, disillusioned by the conduct of affairs under Garfield and Chester A. Arthur, lost interest in politics in his final years.

Grant's presidency can perhaps be best understood as a time of transition for both the Republican Party and the nation at large. As the nation shifted from the war and its aftermath to questions of industrial growth and political reform, the original antislavery coalition that composed the Republican Party gave way to a tighter, more professional and pragmatic political organization devoted to economic development. Recent historians, have questioned the prevailing stereotype of Grant as a failure in the White House, although a compelling alternative has yet to emerge.

See also: James G. Blaine, Election of 1868, and 1880, James A. Garfield, Rutherford B. Hayes, Andrew Johnson, Reconstruction, Stalwarts (and Half-Breeds), Charles Sumner, Union Party

Brooks Donohue Simpson

REFERENCES

Carpenter, John A. 1970. *Ulysses S. Grant.* New York: Twayne.

Gillette, William. 1979. *Retreat from Reconstruction, 1869–1879.* Baton Rouge: Louisiana State U. Pr.

Hesseltine, William B. 1935. *Ulysses S. Grant: Politician.* New York: Dodd, Mead.

McFeely, William S. 1981. *Grant: A Biography.* New York: Norton.

Simon, John Y., ed. 1967–1988. *The Papers of Ulysses S. Grant.* 16 vols. Carbondale: Southern Illinois U. Pr.

Simpson, Brooks D. 1987. "Butcher? Racist? An Examination of William S. McFeely's *Grant: A Biography*." 33 *Civil War History* 63.

Ella T. Grasso (1919–1981)

First female governor of Connecticut. Ella T. Grasso, two-term Democratic governor of Connecticut (1974–1980), was the first woman in America to be elected state chief executive without having succeeded her husband. During 28 years as a public figure, she was the political protégé of state and national Democratic Party chairman John M. Bailey and never lost an election.

Born of immigrant parents, James and Maria Tambussi, Grasso began her political career after graduating with honors in economics from Mount Holyoke College, marrying, and mothering two children. Elected to the Connecticut House of Representatives in 1952, where she served two terms, she chaired the Democratic State Committee for 12 years (1956–1968). While heading the platform committee, Grasso completed three terms as secretary of the state (1958–1970) and was a member of the Democratic National Committee in 1960, 1964, and 1968, chairing the resolutions committee. As a delegate from the Sixth Congressional District, she was Democratic floor leader of the 1965 Connecticut Constitutional Convention and chaired the commission that drafted the new constitution required by U.S. Supreme Court reapportionment decisions. Building on expanding congressional district and statewide recognition, Grasso was elected for two terms to the U.S. House of Representatives (1970–1974).

Although she appeared on the cover of *Newsweek* (Nov. 1, 1974) and was considered for selection as a U.S. vice presidential nominee in 1976, she was a symbolic rather than doctrinaire feminist leader. She was opposed to legalized abortion and did not actively support affirmative action. Although she supported the Equal Rights Amendment, she did not campaign for it. For her public service, she was honored by The Ella T. Grasso Turnpike in her hometown of Windsor Locks, Connecticut; a painting by artist Peter Tria on display at Mt. Holyoke College; the Medal of Freedom, the nation's highest civilian award, presented by President Ronald Reagan in 1981; and by a seven-foot statue by Frank C. Gaylord that occupies a niche over the southwest entrance to the Connecticut Capitol, her office as governor.

See also: John M. Bailey

Clyde D. McKee, Jr.

REFERENCES

Bysiewicz, Susan. 1984. *Ella: A Biography of Governor Ella Grasso*. Old Saybrook, CT: Peregrine Press.

Lieberman, Joseph I. 1966. *The Power Broker*. Boston: Houghton Mifflin.

George Gray (1840–1925)

Democratic leader in the turn-of-the-century Senate. George Gray, United States Senator and jurist, was born in New Castle, Delaware, and attended what is now Princeton University, graduating in 1859. After the private study of law and a year at Harvard Law School, he was admitted to the Delaware bar in 1863. Drawn into politics, Gray held several public offices and achieved statewide prominence. In 1885 he was elected to the uncompleted term of United States Senator Thomas F. Bayard, who had resigned. Twice reelected, he served for a total of 14 years.

A Democrat, Gray was highly respected by his Senate colleagues and was influential in the Democratic inner circle in the Senate. Although he declined a Cabinet post in Grover Cleveland's second administration, he was one of Cleveland's most reliable Senate supporters. A delegate to every Democratic National Convention from 1876 to 1896 save one (1888), he broke with William Jennings Bryan in 1896 on the free-silver issue and was defeated for reelection to the Senate in 1889. He departed with a well-earned reputation for honesty and fairness.

In March 1899 President William McKinley appointed Gray to the U.S. Third Circuit Court of Appeals where he served until his retirement in 1914. Additionally, he was a longtime member of the Permanent Court of Arbitration at The Hague by virtue of successive appointments by Presidents McKinley, Theodore Roosevelt, William Taft, and Woodrow Wilson. He was also a member of the commission that arranged terms at the conclusion of the Spanish-American War and of commissions that mediated American differences with Canada, Mexico, Great Britain, and the Dominican Republic. He also chaired the commission that successfully arbitrated the coal strike of 1902, his most visible public service. Gray died in Wilmington, Delaware, at age 85.

See also: William Jennings Bryan, Grover Cleveland, Theodore Roosevelt, Woodrow Wilson

John F. Coleman

William H. Gray III (1941–)

African-American leader of the Democrats in the U.S. Congress. William H. Gray III is an African-American minister from Philadelphia who was just beginning his sixth term in the House of Representatives when he was chosen in June 1989 by the Democratic Caucus for the third-ranking position within the party—Majority Whip. Gray thus became the highest-ranking Black official in the history of the Congress. He remained on a fast track as an up-and-coming national leader, an establishment alternative to Jesse Jackson among Black politicians.

Bill Gray's family moved north from his birthplace of Baton Rouge, Louisiana; he was educated at Franklin and Marshall College in Pennsylvania and at Drew and Princeton Theological seminaries. Gray's entrance to politics followed a route familiar to many Black politicians—from the pulpit of one of his community's largest churches. Gray unsuccessfully sought the Democratic Party nomination for Congress in 1976; in 1978 he won not only the nomination but also the election. Since that time, his rise to leadership positions has been fast and steady.

As a freshman Representative, Gray won seats on the Budget Committee and the Steering and Policy Committee, largely because of the intervention of fellow Pennsylvanian John Murtha. Two years later, he was appointed to the Appropriations Committee, another powerful position. Gray made it clear that he wanted his role in Congress to extend beyond what many thought would be his natural bases of support, the Congressional Black Caucus and other urban liberal organizations. By 1985 he had convinced a broad coalition of Democrats that he could attract support from colleagues throughout the ideological spectrum and that he understood the need to cut waste from the nation's budget. He was chosen as chairman of the House Budget Committee and thus the leader of the effort to form a united Democratic opposition to President Ronald Reagan's fiscal policies. In that role he successfully brought diverse coalitions of Democrats together on each of the four budget resolutions he saw through the House.

Chairmen the Budget Committee in the House of Representatives can serve for only four years. In 1987, seeing that his term would expire after the One Hundredth Congress, Gray announced that he would run to be chairman of the Democratic Caucus, a position being vacated by Richard Gephardt, then a candidate for the party's presidential nomination. Gray, by then the leading African-American Democrat in the House, was immediately the front-runner for Caucus chairman. Even though he had alienated some natural allies among liberals and members of the Black Caucus because of some

of the agreements he had made as Budget Committee chairman, he built a broad coalition, enhanced by well-placed contributions to Democrats running for the House, and easily was elected in December 1988 when the Caucus met to select the leadership team for the next Congress.

In early 1989, when Jim Wright (Tex.) and Tony Coelho (Calif.) were forced to give up Democratic leadership positions and their seats in the House because of scandals involving their personal finances, Gray announced his candidacy for Majority Whip. But this election would prove to be more difficult than his previous ones. Less than a month before the Caucus met to select new leaders, press reports noted that Gray had been interviewed by the Justice Department in connection with an ongoing investigation involving his office. Gray admitted that he had been interviewed but denied that he was under investigation. In an era of increased concern over congressional ethics, many wondered if Gray's candidacy could survive. However, many in his party came to his defense and argued that it was unfair to impute wrongdoing based only on press allegations. Gray was elected; the Justice Department eventually announced that he had never been the subject of a potential indictment.

William Gray now stands as an important figure in congressional partisan politics. He has gone further within the House hierarchy than has any other African-American Representative. He might well be the first Black Majority Leader, Speaker, or even presidential nominee. Gray is a child of the pulpit and of the television screen; he is a clergyman and a natural politician; he has maintained his ties to his geographic and demographic constituencies, but he has built a reputation as a coalition builder—one willing to compromise and to forge compromises among others in order to achieve success. His path to leadership among America's Black politicians has not been as visible as that of Jesse Jackson but neither has it been as confrontational. Critics still disagree over which path leads to greater eventual success and impact.

See also: Tony Coelho, Congressional Black Caucus, Richard Gephardt, Jesse Jackson, Jim Wright

L. Sandy Maisel

Gray v. Sanders
372 U.S. 368 (1963)

This Supreme Court case involved an apportionment problem in Georgia, a state that used a county unit system for tabulating votes in statewide elections. The candidate with the highest number of popular votes in a county was considered to have carried the county, and thus received all of the county's unit votes. Not all counties had the same number of votes, but the largest counties were only marginally more influential than the smallest. For example, Georgia's largest county, Fulton, had a 1960 population of 556,326, equivalent to 14.11 percent of the residents of the state. However, under the county unit system, it possessed only 1.46 percent of the unit votes. Georgia's smallest county, Echols, had a 1960 population of 1,876, only 0.05 percent of the state's population. Echols had 0.48 percent of the unit votes. One person in Echols County had an electoral influence equivalent to that of 99 residents of Fulton County.

The Georgia state legislature amended the statute regulating the county unit system after Gray brought this suit, but the Georgia Federal District Court ruled that the revisions maintained the same vices because the vote of each citizen still counted for less and less as the population of the county increased. The court did not reject the use of a county unit system outright, but it did demand equitable changes. The district court drew an analogy to the Electoral College, arguing that if no county were more disadvantaged than any state had been in national elections, then a county unit system would be acceptable.

The Supreme Court, in an opinion by Justice William Douglas, disagreed. The Court considered the Electoral College analogy inapposite because the federal system resulted from political compromise and was thus far from an ideal electoral structure. The Court found no constitutional or historical support for a state's reliance on similarities to the Electoral College as justification of its own apportionment plans.

The Supreme Court asserted that geographic discrimination could be as invidious as any other form of discrimination, insisting that "The idea that every voter is equal to every other voter in his state when he casts his ballot in favor of one of several competing candidates underlies many of our decisions." The Court discussed permissible and impermissible voting restrictions, concluding that once the class of voters has been chosen and their qualifications specified, there is "no Constitutional way by which equality of voting power may be evaded." The Court asserted that the basic democratic principal of "one person, one vote" had been violated by Georgia's county unit system.

Justice John Marshall Harlan dissented, arguing that the "one person, one vote" principle had never been the absolutely accepted political philosophy in the United States that the Court's majority seemed to think it was. Justice Harlan believed that no violation of the equal protection clause could be found in the mere circumstance that the Georgia county unit system resulted in disproportionate vote weighting.

See also: Electoral College System

Scott Cameron

Horace Greeley (1811–1872)

Journalist and reformer. Horace Greeley was the unsuccessful presidential candidate of the Democratic and Liberal Republican parties in 1872. Born in Amherst, New Hampshire, Greeley was apprenticed to a printer at the age of 19. In 1831 he moved to New York City where he worked his way up from printer to reporter to editor on the staff of various newspapers and periodicals.

A decade later, Greeley borrowed the capital to launch his famous newspaper, the *New York Tribune*. By the 1850s the weekly edition of the *Tribune* had an unprecedented national subscription exceeding 100,000. During the antebellum years, Greeley's editorial pen championed an assortment of reforms ranging from Fourierism and spiritualism to the establishment of an international copyright and the abolition of capital punishment. Originally a Whig, Greeley's antislavery views led him into the new Republican Party in the mid-1850s. During the Civil War, his desire for peace alternated with his advocacy of emancipation as a war goal. After Appomattox, Greeley sided with Radical Republicans in favoring the passage of the Fourteenth and Fifteenth amendments and the impeachment of Andrew Johnson. He broke with President Ulysses S. Grant, however, over the issues of corruption in the federal government and the annexation of Santo Domingo. The newly formed Liberal Republican Party nominated Greeley for President in May 1872 (B. Gratz Brown of Missouri was his running mate).

In July the Democrats also adopted this ticket to run against Grant. In a bitterly fought campaign, Greeley advocated sectional reconciliation even while Republicans ridiculed his erratic political course and Democrats could not forget his previous antislavery record. Although

Greeley traveled extensively, he carried only six states, all in the South.

See also: Election of 1872, Fifteenth Amendment, Ulysses S. Grant, Andrew Johnson

John R. McKivigan

REFERENCES

Fahrney, Ray. 1936. *Horace Greeley and the Tribune in the Civil War.* Cedar Rapids, IA: Torch Press.

Hale, William Harlan. 1950. *Horace Greeley: Voice of the People.* New York: Harper & Brothers.

Iseley, Jeter Allen. 1947. *Horace Greeley and the Republican Party, 1853–1861: A Study of the New York Tribune.* Princeton: Princeton U. Pr.

Van Deusen, Glyndon G. 1953. *Horace Greeley: Nineteenth Century Crusader.* Philadelphia: U. of Pennsylvania Pr.

Edith S. Green (1910–1987)

Influential Democratic Congresswoman from Oregon. Edith Green was a strong advocate of federal aid to education and women's rights throughout her 23-year congressional career, and she was an early opponent of U.S. involvement in Vietnam.

Green began her professional career as an elementary teacher. She became interested in politics through her involvement with the Oregon Education Association. After an unsuccessful race for Oregon secretary of state in 1952, she won election to Congress in 1954. She remained there until her retirement in 1974.

Edith Green repeatedly demonstrated that she was not afraid to take politically unpopular stands. She joined with other House liberals to form the Democratic Study Group in 1959. Although she was in general agreement with the goals of organized labor, the strength of unions in her district was not enough to force her compliance on all policy questions. After retiring from the House, she co-chaired the National Democrats for Gerald Ford in the 1976 presidential campaign and appeared in television commercials with the former Republican Congressman.

John A. Clark

Theodore F. Green (1868–1966)

Longtime Rhode Island Democratic politician. A Yankee aristocrat, Theodore Francis Green revolutionized Rhode Island politics. Born and reared in late-nineteenth-century Republican-dominated Rhode Island, he graduated from Brown University in 1887 and earned a law degree from Harvard in 1890.

A life-long Democrat, Green entered politics in 1907, winning a seat in the Rhode Island legislature. But his experience as a legislator proved frustrating, since both houses were ruled by autocratic Republican bosses. In 1912 Green won the Democratic nomination for governor, losing narrowly to the Republican candidate. Six years later he tried unsuccessfully for a seat in the U.S. House of Representatives.

After losing his bid for a congressional seat, Green began a 12-year exile from politics. He returned to the political stage in 1930, once again as the Democratic candidate for Rhode Island's governor. He lost again, but won the post two years later. By then Rhode Island was experiencing a political realignment. Democrat Alfred E. Smith, a Roman Catholic, had won this heavily Catholic state in 1928, and Franklin D. Roosevelt carried "Little Rhody" into the Democratic column in 1932. Still, the legislature remained in Republican hands, and Green was stymied during his first term.

Green won reelection in 1934, and on January 2, 1935—the day of his second inauguration—he began the "Green Revolution." The revolution had its origins in 1901 when Republican Party boss Charles R. Brayton, fearing that an influx of immigrants would allow the Democrats to win the governorship, maneuvered the GOP legislature into passing a statute that stripped the governor of all appointive power, vesting it in the Republican-dominated state senate. Under this law, if the senate did not confirm gubernatorial appointments within three days, it could designate its own choices. Thus, during Green's first term, Rhode Island found itself in the unusual position of having a Democratic governor and Republicans in nearly all other administrative and judicial positions.

The emerging Democratic majority during Franklin Roosevelt's first presidential term provided Green with an opportunity. In 1934, for the first time in many years, control of the state house of representatives passed into Democratic hands. Republicans, however, appeared to have a two-seat majority in the state senate. When this body convened on January 1, 1935, the Democratic lieutenant governor and presiding officer of the senate, Robert E. Quinn, refused to seat two narrowly elected GOP Senators. A committee consisting of two Democrats and one Republican was appointed to recount the ballots and, predictably, two Democrats were certified as the winners.

With the Democratic majority in the senate, effective control of the state government passed for the first time into Democratic hands. The

Brayton law was repealed. The legislature passed a law vacating the state supreme court, and five new judges were appointed: three Democrats and two Republicans. The Finance Commission was dismissed, one high sheriff was turned out of office, the Public Safety Board was abolished, and eighty state commissions were reorganized into eleven departments.

Having completed their coup, the legislature passed several New Deal reforms: 48-hour work-week for women and minors, mandatory school attendance for children under 16, liberalization of workmen's compensation, and extension of a mother's aid program to include foreign-born mothers. The 1936 Rhode Island Democratic platform boasted, "Never in the history of the state was so much legislation beneficial to labor enacted as was placed on the statue books of the state during the legislative sessions of 1935 and 1936," adding, "For generations the Democratic Party in this state was only able to make promises to the people of what it would accomplish if entrusted with power, and on this occasion the party is able to report on the accomplishments made."

Green was elected to the United States Senate in 1936, and was returned three more times before retiring in 1961 at 93 years old—the oldest man ever to sit in the United States Congress. An ardent supporter of Franklin D. Roosevelt and Harry Truman, Green served as chairman of the Senate Foreign Relations Committee from 1957 to 1959. By then, how-ever, he was no longer vigorous, and the num-ber two Democrat on the committee, J. William Fulbright, was really in charge. The "iron law of seniority" kept Fulbright from challenging Green for the committee chairmanship.

See also: Bosses, William J. Fulbright, New Deal, Franklin Roosevelt, Alfred E. Smith, Harry S Truman

John K. White

REFERENCES

Gabriel, Richard A. 1969. *The Political Machine in Rhode Island.* Kingston: U. of Rhode Island Pr.

Goodman, Jay S. 1967. *The Democrats and Labor in Rhode Island: Changes in the Old Alliance.* Providence: Brown U. Pr.

Lockard, Duane. 1959. *New England State Politics.* Princeton: Princeton U. Pr.

White, John Kenneth. 1983. *The Fractured Electorate.* Hanover, NH: U. Pr. of New England.

William J. Green, Sr. (1910–1963)

Leader of the mid-twentieth-century Phila-delphia Democratic machine. William "Bill" Green served as a Congressman in the U.S. House of Representatives from the Fifth Congressional District in Pennsylvania and chairman of the Democratic Party in Philadelphia. During the Great Depression his father, a Republican, took him to John F. Breen, a Democratic ward leader in Philadelphia, to get work. Breen made him a committeeman, and Green eventually became a hard-working Democratic loyalist. In 1936 Green ran for a seat of the city council and lost. After holding several positions in state government, he ran for the House of Representatives in 1944, and though drafted into the Army during the campaign, Green was elected and given a con-venience of government discharge to assume office. He lost his reelection bid in 1946 to Republican George Sarbacher, only to regain the seat in 1948.

In 1953 Green was elected chairman of Philadelphia's Democratic Party, replacing James Finnegan. Green occasionally experienced strained relations with Democratic reformers like Joseph Clark and Richardson Dilworth, but he considered himself a chairman of the board, someone who could unite feuding factions within the party. He ran the Democratic Party meetings democratically, thus ensuring the loyalty of the ward leaders. Green also worked to get Pennsylvania's first Black Congressman, Robert N. C. Nix, elected from Philadelphia in 1958. In the 1960 presidential election, Green supported John Kennedy, and through the ef-forts of his organization, Green delivered a 331,000-vote margin for Kennedy in Philadel-phia—a plurality that enabled Kennedy to carry Pennsylvania. On Green's death, his son, Wil-liam J. Green, Jr., was elected to his vacant seat in the House and later served as mayor of Philadelphia from 1980 to 1983.

See also: John F. Kennedy

Thomas J. Baldino

REFERENCES

Petshcek, Kirk R. 1973. *The Challenge of Urban Reform.* Philadelphia: Temple U. Pr.

Greenback Party

A single-issue minor party formed by oppo-nents to the Ulysses Grant administration's at-tempts to contract the money supply after the Civil War by withdrawing paper currency ("greenbacks"). The party was part of a broad, diverse political and social movement incorpo-rating Greenback clubs, the Granger movement, rising labor unionism, and a significant wing of the Democratic Party. Fanned by the panic of 1873, midwestern farmers and their sympathizers drew initially on the Grangers' Independent Party structure, convening their first national meeting in Indianapolis in November 1874. Representatives from seven states attended. The first full national convention was held the following year in Cleveland. Although officially called the Independent Party at that point, the organization continued to be known as the Greenback Party.

Representatives from 18 states met in 1876 to nominate the party's presidential candidate, Peter Cooper. A victim of poor organization and inadequate funds, Cooper polled less than 1 percent of the vote. Much of the party's thunder was stolen by the sympathetic wing of the Democratic Party, which was the primary beneficiary of greenback discontent. Although demoralized, the Greenbacks revived the following year when local Greenback candidates polled up to 15 percent in important races around the country. The party's strongest showing occurred in 1878. Its midterm convention attracted delegates from 28 states, and Greenbackers also promoted labor-inspired proposals to limit the work day, create a government labor bureau, and restrict Chinese immigration. That year, the party elected 15 Representatives to Congress, and its candidates won almost a million votes nationwide.

The party split in 1880 over the question of whether to fuse with major party elements or maintain autonomy. The anti-fusionist "radicals" sought to preempt the fusionists by calling their own convention early in 1880. When the faction's presidential nominee declined, the convention adjourned, agreeing to reconvene at the very time and place of the full convention. When the full party met, the radicals won the day with the nomination of General James B. Weaver for President. Weaver made history by becoming the first presidential candidate to aggressively stump for support. Despite logging 20,000 campaign miles, he polled only about 3 percent of the vote. Party disintegration set in after 1880. The intra-organization struggle intensified, but most pragmatic members drifted toward the Democratic Party, which did exceptionally well in the 1882 elections. The Greenback Party met for the last time in 1884, nominating the presidential candidate of the Anti-Monopoly Party, General Benjamin F. Butler. Despite hard campaigning, Butler did only about half as well as Weaver. The fortunes of the Greenback Party and movement rose and fell commensurately with the state of the economy. Still, the call for paper currency as a solution to economic woes persisted for many years. Even though it was an economic issue, Greenback politics was also heavily laden with moral fervor, very like the slavery or abortion issues, which also generated minor parties.

See also: Peter Cooper, Granger Movement, James B. Weaver

Robert J. Spitzer

REFERENCES

Buck, Solon. 1920. *The Agrarian Crusade, A Chronicle of the Farmer in Politics.* New Haven, CT: Yale U. Pr.

Unger, Irwin. 1964. *The Greenback Era: A Social and Political History of American Finance, 1865–1879.* Princeton: Princeton U. Pr.

Andrew Gregg (1755–1835)

Pennsylvania Republican leader of the early national period. Andrew Gregg was an upstate Pennsylvania Republican who served an extraordinary eight terms in Congress, as well as one term in the United States Senate, between 1791 and 1813. Gregg was born in Carlisle, Pennsylvania, and attended school there and, later, in Newark, Delaware. While in Delaware, during the Revolutionary War, he served in the militia, although he apparently never got into combat. He was first employed as a tutor at the University of Pennsylvania in Philadelphia from 1779 to 1783. That year he left Philadelphia and moved to Middletown in Dauphin County, Pennsylvania, close to Harrisburg, and became a shopkeeper. He began his third career as a farmer when he moved to Center County in 1789.

Gregg made sufficient mark in his new home to be elected to Congress from that district a mere two years later, and the first impression was obviously a lasting one because he was reelected seven times and only left the House upon election to the United States Senate. He served one term in the Senate, from 1807 through 1813, and was of sufficient stature among the Jeffersonians to serve as President *pro tempore* in 1809. Gregg was a Jeffersonian agrarian who protected the interests of his constituents jealously, thus ensuring his good standing among leaders of the Republican Party.

After leaving the Senate in 1813 he moved to Bellefonte, Pennsylvania, and became a banker. He got embroiled in intraparty politics within Pennsylvania, a battle that cost him a bid for the governorship in 1823, even though he had been serving as secretary of state during the previous four years.

See also: Jeffersonian Republicans

Kathryn A. Malone

Walter Q. Gresham (1832–1895)

Principal contender for the Republican presidential nomination in the 1880s. In 1892 many Populists favored Walter Quintin Gresham's nomination, but he declined and threw his support to Democrat Grover Cleveland, who later appointed him Secretary of State.

Gresham had moved from the Whigs to the Know-Nothings to the Republican Party in the mid-1850s. He served in the Indiana legislature in 1861 and was a general in the Union Army. After two losses for Congress, he became federal district judge for Indiana in 1869. Off and on he considered running for governor or Senator and in 1883 became Postmaster General under President Chester Arthur. In the 1884 presidential race, Gresham emerged as a possible dark horse, but when Arthur's managers would not join with the so-called Independents in support of Gresham, James G. Blaine won the nomination.

Gresham returned to the bench as federal circuit judge and issued several decisions that won him a following among labor and farmers. With his strength in the Midwest, he attracted considerable support for the 1888 nomination but lost his home state to his arch rival Benjamin Harrison, who went on to win nomination and the election. Increasingly disenchanted with the Republicans over the tariff issue, Gresham flirted with the Populists but finally declined to be considered for nomination in 1892. He publicly backed Cleveland, who made substantial gains in the Midwest and unseated Harrison. As Cleveland's Secretary of State, Gresham pursued conservative, anti-expansionist policies, the unpopularity of which helped undermine the appeal of the Democrats, who lost disastrously in the elections of 1894 and 1896.

See also: Grover Cleveland, Benjamin Harrison, Know-Nothings, Populist (People's) Party

Charles W. Calhoun

REFERENCES

Calhoun, Charles W. 1981. "Republican Jeremiah: Walter Q. Gresham and the Third American Party System." In Robert G. Barrows, ed. *Their Infinite Variety: Essays on Indiana Politicians.* Indianapolis: Indiana Historical Bureau.

———. 1988. *Gilded Age Cato: The Life of Walter Q. Gresham.* Lexington: U. Pr. of Kentucky.

Gresham, Matilda. 1919. *Life of Walter Quintin Gresham, 1832–1895.* Chicago: Rand, McNally.

Tyner, Martha Alice. 1933. "Walter Q. Gresham." 29 *Indiana Magazine of History* 297.

Robert P. Griffin (1923–)

Republican Senator from Michigan. Robert Paul Griffin was Minority Whip of the United States Senate from 1969 to 1977. An attorney, Griffin won a 1956 Michigan election to the U.S. House of Representatives, where he co-sponsored the Landrum-Griffin labor act in 1959. In 1966, Governor George Romney of Michigan appointed him to the U.S. Senate seat vacated by the death of Patrick McNamara (D). Later that year, he defeated former Governor G. Mennen Williams for election to a full term. In 1968 he led the Senate opposition to President Lyndon Johnson's nomination of Abe Fortas as Chief Justice of the Supreme Court.

In the fall of 1969 he was elected Senate Minority Whip. Although he generally worked the party line, he opposed President Richard Nixon several times: in 1969 he led a Senate delegation asking Nixon to withdraw the Supreme Court nomination of Clement Haynsworth; in August 1974 he called on Nixon to resign because of Watergate. He was close to President Gerald Ford, another former Michigan Congressman.

In 1976 Griffin sought to succeed the retiring Hugh Scott as Minority Leader, but Howard Baker of Tennessee beat him by a 19-to-18 vote. Republicans thought that Griffin made a poorer media impression than Baker, who had starred during the Senate Watergate hearings. Griffin lost the 1978 general election to Democrat Carl Levin.

See also: Gerald Ford, Richard Nixon, Watergate

John J. Pitney, Jr.

REFERENCES

Asbell, Bernard. 1981. *The Senate Nobody Knows.* Baltimore: Johns Hopkins U. Pr.

Martha W. Griffiths (1912–)

Congressional advocate of women's rights. Before entering public service, Martha Wright Griffiths worked as an attorney, a judge, and a contract negotiator in Michigan. In 1948 she was elected to serve in the Michigan House of Representatives, continuing until 1952. On her second bid for a seat in the U.S. House of Representatives, Griffiths earned the privilege of representing the Seventeenth Congressional District of Michigan in Congress.

Griffiths served in the House from 1955 until 1975. During her 20-year career, Griffiths was an active spokesperson for women's issues. She successfully lobbied for the inclusion of an anti-sex discrimination provision in the 1964 Civil Rights Act. In addition, she sought the passage of the Equal Rights Amendment and was a founding member of the National Organization for Women. Griffiths also helped to effect changes to eliminate discrimination based on sex in the Social Security system. Besides her activism for equal opportunity for women, she also worked for the implementation of a national health insurance bill, a measure that she characteristically attempted to sell by labeling it cost effective for the nation. While in the House, Griffiths became the first female member of both the Ways and Means Committee and the Joint Economic Committee

In 1982, at the age of 70, Griffiths was persuaded to emerge from a 7-year retirement to be elected lieutenant governor of Michigan. Two years later, Griffiths was mentioned as a possible vice presidential candidate on the Democratic ticket. While Griffiths was not chosen to be on the national ticket in 1984, she was reelected in 1986 to serve a second term as lieutenant governor of Michigan.

See also: Civil Rights Legislation and Southern Politics, Equal Rights Amendment

Reagan Robbins

REFERENCES

Chamberlin, Hope. 1973. *A Minority of Members: Women in the U.S. Congress.* New York: Praeger.

The Grimké Sisters
Angelina Grimké (1805–1879)
Sarah Moore Grimké (1792–1873)

Abolitionist members of a wealthy and aristocratic South Carolina slave-owning family, Angelina and Sarah Grimké exiled themselves from the antebellum South to become active participants in the abolitionist and women's rights movements as well as a host of other reform causes. Both sisters questioned the moral legitimacy of slavery, and by 1835 they had become Quakers and had moved to Philadelphia. In that year Angelina wrote to William Lloyd Garrison encouraging him in his antislavery activities. Subsequently, Garrison published Angelina's letter in the *Liberator,* and a year later both sisters were playing active roles in the antislavery movement by writing abolitionist pamphlets that opposed the gradual emancipation of slaves (they favored immediate emancipation) and urged southern women to speak out against the institution of slavery.

At first the Grimké sisters presented their views only to small groups of women, but eventually, because of the eloquence, their lectures began to attract large, mixed audiences. The Grimkés' rhetoric stimulated great interest in the antislavery movement; however, they also encountered the prevailing prejudice against women speaking in public. Angelina and Sarah Grimké understood that the oppression of women was related to the oppression of slaves; they consistently cited the incongruity of working against one while ignoring the other. By their writings and lectures, the Grimké sisters did much to link the women's rights movement and the antislavery crusade.

In 1838 Angelina married Theodore Weld, an influential and dedicated abolitionist. Both sisters died in Hyde Park, Massachusetts, Sarah at 81 years old and Angelina at 74.

See also: Abolition Movement, Emancipation as a Political Issue, William Lloyd Garrison

Margaret Horsnell

REFERENCES

Barnes, Gilbert H., and Dwight L. Dumond, eds. 1934. *Letters of Theodore Dwight Weld, Angelina Grimké Weld, and Sarah Grimké, 1822–1844.* 2 vols. Gloucester, MA: Peter Smith.

Lerner, Gerda. 1967. *The Grimké Sisters from South Carolina: Rebels Against Slavery.* Boston: Houghton Mifflin.

Perry, Lewis, and Michael Fellman, eds. 1979. *Antislavery Reconsidered: New Perspectives on the Abolitionists.* Baton Rouge: Louisiana State U. Pr.

Galusha A. Grow (1822–1907)

Antebellum Republican advocate of homestead legislation. Born in Connecticut, Galusha Aaron Grow was reared in northeastern Pennsylvania. After practicing law briefly as a partner of David Wilmot, he was elected to Wilmot's seat in Congress in 1850 as that body's youngest member. As an antislavery Democrat, Grow joined the new Republican Party at the time of its formation in 1854. An aggressive opponent of proslavery elements in Congress, in 1859 he was involved in a fist fight on the floor of the House with a southern Congressman over the Kansas issue of slavery expansion.

Grow worked hardest in Congress on behalf of free government land grants to actual settlers. He was among several to introduce homestead bills in 1853. Grow's support of land reform came from his early Pennsylvania experiences when he had witnessed the negative impact of land speculation. He was also influenced by Horace Greeley and other land reformers including George H. Evans. With sectionalism reaching a climax in 1860, homesteading had become an issue of northern support and southern opposition. After several Grow-backed bills passed the House, President James Buchanan vetoed a modified homestead proposal in 1860. Only after the secession of 11 southern states did a measure closely resembling Grow's original bill granting 160 acres of the federal domain to settlers become law in 1862.

That same year saw a long pause in Grow's congressional career, when a Pennsylvania gerrymander cost him reelection. Although remaining active in Republican politics, he turned in succeeding years to a variety of business enterprises. After a 30-year absence, he returned to the House in 1893, serving 4 terms and again championing the further extension of the homestead principle.

See also: James Buchanan, David Wilmot

Frederick J. Blue

REFERENCES

DuBois, James T., and Gertrude S. Mathews. 1917. *Galusha Grow, Father of the Homestead Law.* Boston: Houghton Mifflin.

Ilisevich, Robert D. 1988. *Galusha Grow: The People's Candidate.* Pittsburgh: U. of Pittsburgh Pr.

Nevins, Allan. 1950. *The Emergence of Lincoln.* 2 vols. New York. Scribner's.

Robbins, Roy M. 1976. *Our Landed Heritage: The Public Domain, 1776–1970.* 2nd ed. Lincoln: U. of Nebraska Pr.

Stephenson, George M. 1917. *The Political History of the Public Lands from 1840 to 1860, from Preemption to Homestead.* New York: Russell & Russell.

Gubernatorial Nominations

In almost all 50 states the Democratic and Republican candidates for governor are nominated by the voters in direct primary elections.

Primary elections were first used late in the nineteenth century in southern states, where the one-party system was strongest. The first primaries were established by party rules, and subsequently they were mandated by law in most southern states. In the South, one purpose was to strengthen Democratic control and another was to exclude participation by African-Americans in the selection process.

Outside the South, primary elections were adopted in the early twentieth century as part of the Progressive movement. After Wisconsin adopted the first relatively comprehensive state primary law in 1903, other states followed in quick succession; by 1917 only a few states, mostly in the Northeast, were holdouts. By 1955

no state relied entirely on the convention system to nominate its governor, although parties are still permitted to choose between primaries or conventions in several southern states. Both parties in Virginia still occasionally use conventions, and in several other southern states the Republican Party used conventions until relatively recently.

Qualifications for Voting

One of the fundamental differences among state primaries is the qualifications for voting. The basic distinction is between closed primaries (limited to members registered with a party), and open primaries (open to anyone qualified to vote in the general election). In open primary states, voters can more easily shift back and forth from one party primary to the other.

As of 1987, sixteen states were using completely closed primaries (in which voters must be registered with a party in advance of the primary): Delaware, Maryland, New York, Pennsylvania, Nebraska, South Dakota, Kentucky, Oklahoma, West Virginia, Florida, North Carolina, Arizona, California, Nevada, New Mexico, and Oregon. Eleven other closed primary states permitted some flexibility to certain voters, particularly those who had previously been Independents: Massachusetts, New Hampshire, Connecticut, Maine, New Jersey, Rhode Island, Iowa, Kansas, Ohio, Colorado, and Wyoming.

Eleven open primary states asked voters to publicly announce a party preference: Illinois, Indiana, Missouri, Alabama, Arkansas, Georgia, Mississippi, South Carolina, Tennessee, Texas, and Virginia. Nine other open primary states allowed the voter to keep his or her choice completely private: Vermont, Michigan, Minnesota, North Dakota, Wisconsin, Hawaii, Idaho, Montana, and Utah. Alaska and Washington had "blanket primaries" (voters could vote for candidates in different parties for various offices in the same election). Louisiana had a completely nonpartisan primary (open to candidates from all parties) for governor and other major offices.

In ten of the traditional southern states (all except Tennessee) and in Oklahoma as well, if no candidate gets a majority in the first primary vote, a runoff primary is held between the top two candidates. This runoff has been used in southern states because the Democratic primary in the past usually has been the decisive election, in the absence of strong Republican opposition, and thus has attracted a large number of candidates. Although gubernatorial general elections are now more closely contested, southern states continue to use runoff primaries.

Candidate Nominations and Endorsements

Direct primary election systems give the voters, rather than party organizations, the right to select the nominees of each party. In a number of states, however, party organizations seek to influence the outcome of gubernatorial primaries by endorsing candidates before the primary elections. These party endorsements may result from state law or from party rules. State law allows state political parties to endorse candidates in Connecticut, Rhode Island, New York, Delaware, Colorado, North Dakota, New Mexico, and Utah. The rules of one or both parties provide for public endorsements in convention by parties for candidates in gubernatorial races in Massachusetts, Minnesota, and Wisconsin; and endorsements are made behind the scenes by state parties in several other states, including Illinois.

In those states where the law provides for preprimary endorsements, the endorsed candidates gain some formal advantage in the balloting. They may gain automatic access to the ballot, while other candidates have to get petitions signed, or they may be listed first on the ballot. In two states (Utah and Connecticut) getting on the ballot is impossible without gaining a minimum number of votes (but not necessarily a majority) at a party-endorsing convention.

One of the major consequences of party endorsements is the mobilization of support among party activists for the endorsee—true both for state parties that have legal authority to make endorsements and for those that do so under party rules. Party activists are more likely to work for and contribute funds to those candidates who have been endorsed by the party organization. No convincing evidence shows that a significant number of primary voters are aware of or are influenced by endorsements.

In some states allowing either legal or informal endorsements, the nonendorsed candidates frequently drop out of the race before the primary election; good examples are Connecticut, Rhode Island, and Delaware. In the years since 1960, more than half of the candidates receiving legal endorsement and one-fourth of those getting informal endorsements have been unopposed in primaries; about three-fourths of those

who were endorsed but had opposition (in both types of states) won the primary election.

Levels of Primary Competition

Voters can determine the party nominees only in a contested nominations. In the period from 1960 through 1986, more than one candidate sought office in three-fourths of the gubernatorial primaries. Primaries were more likely to be competitive when the party did not have an incumbent running, and the Democratic primary was more competitive than the Republican (largely because most southern Democratic primaries were contested). During these years Democratic gubernatorial primaries were contested 65 percent of the time when an incumbent was running and 86 percent when he was not; Republicans held contested primaries 56 percent of the time with and 74 percent of the time without incumbents. Competition was less likely in both party primaries when the party organization endorsed a candidate.

Primary competition is more frequent in the South and West than in the Midwest and Northeast. Within each state, competition is also more likely in the primary of the party with the greater electoral strength. This contrast was particularly evident in the South between 1960 and 1986, when almost 95 percent of the Democratic gubernatorial primaries were contested, compared to less than two-thirds of the Republican primaries. During this period, the proportion of contested southern gubernatorial primaries grew from less than one-fourth in the early 1960s to over three-fourths in the late 1970s and the 1980s.

Voter Participation in Gubernatorial Primaries

Those who are likely to vote in general elections are also more likely to vote in primaries (the better educated, those with higher status occupations, those who are older, and those with more interest in politics and a high sense of civic duty). Primary voters also have several special characteristics. A strong sense of identification with a party affects turnout in primaries more than it does in general elections. Persons who consider themselves to be independents may have less interest in primaries, and in closed primary states, they may be less willing to register with a party in order to vote in the primary. We have no consistent evidence as well that those who are liberal or conservative are more likely to vote in a party's primary than those who are moderate.

Gubernatorial primary voting is motivated not only by the voter's personal characteristics but also by certain political variables and by the characteristics of the states. This complexity leads to substantial variations among the states in the level of turnout when both gubernatorial primaries are contested. In the 1951–1982 period, primary turnout (as a percentage of voting-age population) was over 40 percent in eight states and under 25 percent in fifteen states. Turnout has been considerably higher in the West and South than it has been in the Northeast and Midwest. Many western states also have above-average voter turnout in general elections.

In states in which one party usually wins the gubernatorial elections, voting turnout is much higher in the primary of that party. Voters obviously are more inclined to participate in choosing the candidates who are likely to win the general elections. Turnout is also higher when a primary is closely contested, and it is always higher in the primary of the party that has traditionally had closer competition. In other words, voters get into the habit of voting for the party that has close primaries.

In the South, where the Democratic Party has usually won gubernatorial races and where the Democratic gubernatorial primary is usually much more competitive, turnout is much higher in the Democratic than in the Republican primary, even in years when the Republican primary is competitive. At one time in most southern states, turnout was higher in the Democratic primary for governor than in general elections. In recent years, however, Democratic gubernatorial primary turnout has declined in most of the states where Republican competition has been growing.

The turnout in and the outcome of gubernatorial primaries can be affected by local primaries, particularly if local primaries are held in the same years as gubernatorial races. Voters may choose to register with the party that is stronger in their county rather than the one that is stronger statewide. The size of turnout for gubernatorial primary races may also be affected by the closeness of local contests. As a consequence, a disproportionate share of the vote in a party's gubernatorial primary may be cast by voters in counties where that party is traditionally strong. On occasion, the result may be the nomination of a candidate with more appeal in the areas of traditional party strength than in the more competitive parts of the state where the party needs to win. This configura-

tion can be a particularly serious problem for the minority party in a state.

Who votes in what primary? National surveys have shown that a very high proportion (over 90 percent) of those who identify with a party vote in that party's primary. Exceptions are likely to occur among those who identify with a badly outnumbered minority party without primary competition or among voters in open primary states. Those who call themselves independents are more likely to vote with the dominant party in a state.

In open primary states, little is known about the proportion of voters who shift back and forth frequently from one party primary to another over a period of years. Aggregate data in some states, showing variations in party primary turnout, suggest that considerable shifting occurs. But surveys of voters in gubernatorial primaries in open primary states are rare and inconclusive.

Explaining Gubernatorial Primary Outcomes

The most obvious way of explaining the outcome of gubernatorial primaries is to say that when the incumbent runs, he or she nearly always wins. In the elections from 1982 through 1988, 58 incumbents ran for renomination; 32 of them had an opponent in the primary; only 2 lost. One of those defeated, Governor Edward King of Massachusetts in 1982, lost to former Governor Michael Dukakis (whom King had defeated in the primary four years earlier). The other, Governor Bill Sheffield of Alaska in 1986, had been nominated four years earlier by the narrowest of margins.

Incumbents in a gubernatorial primary have most of the advantages enjoyed by incumbents in other elective offices. The governor is nearly always much better known than any challenger and is usually perceived as being more experienced. An incumbent governor has hundreds of opportunities during a term to make personal appearances and to be seen on television. These opportunities can be used to build a favorable image. The incumbent has a great advantage over challengers in raising money because he or she holds office and is usually expected to be renominated.

Anyone who challenges the incumbent governor in the primary faces major obstacles. Because the odds are usually perceived as great, recruiting workers and raising money is difficult. Unless an incumbent governor has been very controversial or has suffered from serious scandals, the incumbent is unlikely to be challenged by politically strong, experienced candidates. Even in the South, where primary competition is usually greater, few serious challenges to governors have occurred in recent years. Governors are often vulnerable to attack on issues, particularly if they have found it necessary to raise taxes. While this vulnerability is a potential problem in the primary, a sitting governor is much more likely to come under attack in the general election than in the primary.

Because modern media campaigns are expensive, the candidate who can raise the most money has an obvious advantage in a primary campaign. This fact does not necessarily mean that the outcome is determined by differences in spending. The incumbent, who normally is able to raise more money, will normally win the primary election if spending levels are even because of the many other advantages that he or she enjoys.

An analysis of spending in nearly all of the contested gubernatorial primaries in 1982 shows that in 37 of the 50 races the winner spent more than the loser. All of the incumbents spent more money than any of their challengers (and all but one of them won). In lopsided primary races, the winner usually spent an even larger percentage than the share of the vote that he or she won. In 1982, however, there were several examples of winning candidates (in races without incumbents) who were outspent by losers. These include Mario Cuomo of New York and George Deukmejian of California.

If no incumbent is running in a primary, and the race is between two or more candidates who have already achieved substantial name recognition through holding public office, the amount of money spent is less likely to be important than the issues raised and the political skills exhibited by the candidates. A candidate who is relatively unknown or who is a political newcomer must gain name recognition and develop an image—acknowledgment that is possible in a governor's race in a medium-sized or large state only through heavy reliance on expensive television advertising. In cases like this, an obscure candidate who is well financed may gain an advantage over candidates with more political experience.

In the 1978 Texas Republican gubernatorial primary, for example, Bill Clements, a millionaire businessman who had never before run for office, defeated Ray Hutchison, a party chairman and a former state legislator, by outspending him by a huge margin. The winner of the 1982 New York Republican primary for governor was Lew Lehrman, the owner of a large chain of discount drug stores, who had been a full-time resident of New York for only five years. He won the party organization's endorsement after spending $3 million and won the the primary election after spending another $4 million.

The two examples illustrate not only the importance of campaign funds in a primary campaign but also the possible increasing success of political outsiders. The traditional route to the governorship has been through other elective offices, usually legislators, mayors, or attorneys general. But candidates from outside the political system—often wealthy business persons—can be competitive if they have enough financing and hire skillful advisers and media experts. Some of them already have gained fame as well as fortune in private life. An example is John Y. Brown, who won the 1979 Democratic gubernatorial primary in Kentucky and who had previously become well known as owner of both Kentucky Fried Chicken and a professional basketball franchise in the state.

When statewide political campaigns involve candidates who do not have an established record in politics, voters are more heavily dependent on political advertising and media coverage of the campaign. This media dependence is particularly true in primary elections because voters cannot use party identification as a voting cue. Under these conditions, voters are likely to be volatile and may make up their minds late in the campaign. These late trends in voter preferences can be documented by tracking polls conducted daily in the closing weeks of a campaign. One example is the Kentucky Democratic gubernatorial primary in 1987, which involved four experienced political leaders (including two ex-governors) and one well-financed businessman. The businessman, Wallace Wilkinson, made skillful use of television, promised voters a lottery instead of higher taxes, and won the election by 9 percentage points. Polls showed that he trailed another candidate by 14 points only 2 weeks before the primary, picking up those 14 points in the last week of the campaign. Similarly, the winner of the 1987 nonpartisan gubernatorial primary in Louisiana doubled his strength in the last 5 weeks of the race.

The Impact of Primaries on General Elections

The purpose of a primary election is to choose the party's strongest candidate to run in the general election—a result not always achieved. Because voter turnout is low or because voters from some parts of the state are underrepresented, primary winners may be candidates who are less able than some others to appeal to the broader range of voters in the general election. In order to win support in the primary from party activists and organized interests, a candidate may have to make promises that will turn out to be liabilities in the general election. These problems faced by candidates in gubernatorial primaries are similar to those that are often debated by critics of the presidential primary system.

Moreover, a primary race may be so divisive that the winning candidates will be unable to mobilize political activists and voters behind their candidacies. Measuring divisiveness exactly in a primary is difficult. Primary elections are most likely to be close in races in which no incumbent is running and in political parties that usually dominate state politics. Consequently, those who win close primaries are not necessarily vulnerable to defeat in the general elections, as various studies have shown. Primaries are often described as divisive when they are characterized by bitterness, but no accurate way of measuring "bitterness" in a primary race has been devised.

Some evidence from voter surveys shows that a substantial number of voters who support the losing candidate in a primary will vote for the candidate of the other party in the general election. This shift may occur if sharp ideological divisions or factional rivalries divide the party or if the primary campaign has been particularly acrimonious. But certain types of voters are more likely to defect after the primary, particularly those whose party loyalties are not strong. In southern states, many of those who vote in Democratic primaries have Republican loyalties and will vote for a credible Republican candidate if one is on the ballot.

See also: Blanket Primaries, Closed Primary, Michael Dukakis, Open Primary

Malcolm E. Jewell

REFERENCES

Black, Merle, and Earl Black. 1982. "The Growth of Contested Republican Primaries in the American South." In Laurence W. Moreland, Tod A. Baker, and Robert P. Steed, eds. *Contemporary Southern Political Attitudes and Behavior*. New York: Praeger.

Carr, Craig L., and Gary L. Scott. 1984. "The Logic of State Primary Classification Systems." 12 *American Politics Quarterly* 465.

Finkel, Steven E., and Howard A. Scarrow. 1985. "Party Identification and Party Enrollment: The Difference and the Consequence." 47 *Journal of Politics* 620.

Jewell, Malcolm E. 1984. *Parties and Primaries: Nominating State Governors*. New York: Praeger.

———, and David M. Olson. 1988. *Political Parties and Elections in American States*. 3d ed. Chicago: Dorsey Press.

Key, V. O., Jr. 1956. *American State Politics: An Introduction*. New York: Knopf.

Pierson, James E., and T. Smith. 1975. "Primary Divisiveness and General Election Success: A Reexamination." 37 *Journal of Politics* 555.

Charles Guggenheim (1924–)

Media consultant for Democratic candidates. A highly respected, award-winning documentary filmmaker, Charles Guggenheim used his talent to help elect such leading Democratic politicians as Senators Robert Kennedy (N.Y., 1965), Edward Kennedy (Mass., 1963), and George McGovern (S.D., 1962) in the 1960s and 1970s. He played roles of varying influences in the presidential campaigns of Adlai Stevenson (1956), Robert Kennedy and Hubert Humphrey (1968), George McGovern (1972), Edward Kennedy (1980), and Ernest Hollings (1984).

Guggenheim often used the cinema verité style in which the candidate is filmed without using a scripted performance, and the most relevant and interesting footage is culled and used in spot commercials and longer documentary films.

As McGovern's presidential campaign manager, Gary Hart noted that Guggenheim would frequently show the candidate "talking and relating to small groups of citizens about particular problems they faced." Sometimes the candidate would be featured responding to heated criticism of his record.

Guggenheim's advertising generally focused on presenting his client's story, usually avoiding mention of the opponent's shortcomings. Indeed, Guggenheim's dislike of negative advertising probably hurt his reputation as a media consultant. One notable exception to Guggenheim's refusal to employ negative advertising occurred in 1966 when actor-turned-politician Ronald Reagan (R) was elected governor of California. Guggenheim's advertising on behalf of incumbent Edmund G. "Pat" Brown (D) urged voters to elect "a *real* governor, not an acting one."

Another noteworthy Guggenheim effort occurred when his client, wealthy Pennsylvania businessman Milton Shapp, upset the organization-backed candidate for governor. Guggenheim's film for Shapp was appropriately called "The Man Against the Machine" and, in retrospect, symbolizes the coming power of the new-style media consultant over the old-style political boss.

See also: Hubert Humphrey, Edward M. Kennedy, Robert F. Kennedy, George McGovern

Steve Lilienthal

REFERENCES

Diamond, Edwin, and Stephen Bates. 1988. *The Spot: The Rise of Political Advertising on Television.* 2nd ed. Cambridge: MIT Pr.

Hart, Gary Warren. 1973. *Right from the Start: A Chronicle of the McGovern Campaign.* New York: Times Books.

H

Herbert S. Hadley (1872–1927)

Progressive era Missouri Republican leader. During the Progressive era, Republican Herbert Spencer Hadley served as Missouri's attorney general, then governor, and later as a leading supporter of Theodore Roosevelt at the Republican National Convention of 1912. Born to Quaker parents in Kansas, Hadley received his undergraduate degree from the University of Kansas and his law degree from Northwestern University. He served as first assistant city counselor of Kansas City in 1898 and two years later won election as prosecuting attorney of Jackson County; subsequently he won a term as state attorney general (1905–1909). His prosecution of Standard Oil, International Harvester, and railroads and insurance companies established his progressive credentials and laid the foundation for his successful bid for governor.

His record and serious division within the Democratic Party allowed Hadley to become the first Republican governor of Missouri in over 30 years. A Democratic legislature, however, blocked many of his initiatives, including creation of a statewide public utilities commission, taxation of the capital stock of corporations, and establishment of a state board of control. Hadley was more successful in winning support for limiting the hours women could work and outlawing railroad passenger rate discrimination.

Although he enjoyed cordial relations with both President William H. Taft and Theodore Roosevelt, Hadley joined six other Republican governors in 1912 in publicly asking Roosevelt to become a candidate for President. He accepted, and Hadley served as Roosevelt's floor leader at the convention. When Taft won renomination, Hadley declined to follow Roosevelt into a new party. He ended his career as chancellor at Washington University in St. Louis.

See also: Railroads, Theodore Roosevelt, William Howard Taft

Nicholas C. Burckel

REFERENCES

Hahn, Harlan. 1965. "The Republican Party Convention of 1912 and the Role of Herbert S. Hadley in National Politics." 59 *Missouri Historical Review* 407.

Worner, Lloyd Edson. 1946. "The Public Career of Herbert Spencer Hadley." Ph.D. dissertation, U. of Missouri.

Hadley v. Junior College District of Kansas City
397 U.S. 50 (1970)

"This case," in the words of the Supreme Court, "involves the extent to which the Fourteenth Amendment and the 'one man, one vote' principle apply in the election of local government officials." In 1970 the Supreme Court ruled that whenever local governments choose popularly to elect officeholders who will exercise general governmental powers, the equal protection clause of the Fourteenth Amendment requires that each voter's vote be given the same weight. Additionally, when officials are elected from separate districts, the apportionment plan must not discriminate—that is, "equal numbers of voters can vote for equal numbers of officials."

Under Missouri state law the consolidated Junior College District of Kansas City elected a governing board of six trustees with the trustees to be apportioned to the districts on the basis of school-age population. The apportionment plan resulted in 50 percent of the trustees being elected from the Kansas City school district, which contained about 60 percent of the school-age population. Residents of the Kansas City subdistrict complained that their votes were being diluted unconstitutionally. The Missouri Supreme Court upheld the state law on the grounds that the trustees did not perform general governmental functions and therefore the "one man, one vote" principle did not apply. The U.S. Supreme Court reversed and remanded the case on the grounds that the trustees did indeed exercise general governmental powers in managing the junior college, that "one man, one vote" was applicable since government officials were being elected by popular vote, and that the apportionment plan was not acceptable since it automatically discriminated against certain districts.

This decision continued a series of decisions beginning with *Baker v. Carr*, 369 U.S. 186 (1962), which constitutionally guaranteed that each voter's vote would, to the extent practical, be given equal weight. As was the case with congressional districts (*Westberry v. Sanders*, 376 U.S. 1), state legislative districts (*Reynolds v. Sims*, 377 U.S. 533), and local electoral districts such as counties (*Avery v. Midland County*, 390 U.S. 474) and municipalities (lower federal courts), the "one man, one vote" principle generally applies to local governmental units performing general governmental powers. The significance of *Hadley* is that it extended the equal vote weight requirement to another set of elected offices and thereby further expanded the constitutional right of each citizen to equal voting power.

In some instances the "one man, one vote" rule still does not automatically apply: governmental units that perform only specific functions, and governmental bodies filled by appointment rather than election need not necessarily comply with the "one man, one vote" principle. Likewise, the *Hadley* decision did not demand mathematical precision in the apportionment of seats, but it did find objectionable an apportionment plan based on rules that consistently discriminated against certain districts.

See also: Baker v. Carr

Clyde Brown

Frank Hague (1876–1956)

Boss of the Jersey City Democratic political machine. Frank Hague, mayor of Jersey City, long-term Democratic national committeeman,

and power in New Jersey politics, was a big-city boss in the classic nineteenth-century mold. The fourth child of eight born to Irish immigrants, Hague was raised in a characteristically tough urban neighborhood. He rose through the political ranks from sheriff's office to street and water commissioner to the mayoralty of Jersey City in 1917.

Hague had been barred from the national convention in 1916, but he was elected to the national committee in 1920. During the 1920s he was close to New Yorker Al Smith. Part of the Stop Roosevelt movement in 1932, he was eventually forced to make peace with Franklin Roosevelt and his lieutenant, Jim Farley (much as Tammany boss Carmine DeSapio was forced to come to terms with John Kennedy and his lieutenants in 1960).

During Hague's career his machine in Jersey City experienced many of the usual ailments of machine politics (e.g., investigations for fraud, patronage abuse, election day machinations, and eventually the rise of an active reform faction in opposition to the Hague forces). During the later stages of his career, Hague became a typical "rentier" type, opposed to all change and calling reformers, including labor organizers, "Communists" and "Reds." His political hubris was reflected in his famous statement, "I am the law" in Jersey City. He remained a member of the Democratic National Committee until his death.

See also: Bosses, Carmine DeSapio, James Farley, John F. Kennedy, Franklin D. Roosevelt, Al Smith

David A. Bositis

REFERENCES

McKean, David D. 1967. *The Boss: The Hague Machine in Action.* New York: Russell & Russell.

John P. Hale (1806–1873)

Presidential candidate of antislavery "third" parties. John Parker Hale, Congressman and U.S. Senator from New Hampshire, was the presidential nominee of the Liberty Party in 1848 and of the Free Soil (Free Democratic) Party in 1852. Born in Rochester, New Hampshire, he graduated from Bowdoin College in 1827 and took up his father's profession—the law. New Hampshire first elected him to Congress in 1842 but his opposition to the annexation of Texas as a slave state cost him the renomination of the regular Democratic Party in 1844. He then helped to organize a coalition of antislavery Whigs and Independent Democrats that gained control of the New Hampshire legislature in 1846 and elected him to the U.S. Senate.

Although a cautious and legalistic opponent of the extension of slavery, Hale gained nationwide notoriety as the sole antislavery champion in the upper chamber during his first two years there. Hale reluctantly accepted the nomination of the Liberty Party for President but volunteered to step aside if a broader antiextension coalition emerged. When the Free Soil Party was founded in August 1848, it chose ex-President Martin Van Buren over Hale as its candidate. Four years later, the same party, redubbed the Free Democrats, selected Hale for President along with Congressman George W. Julian of Indiana for Vice President. Both men campaigned strenuously, but the ticket received only 150,000 votes or 5 percent of the nationwide total. Not reelected in 1853, Hale was returned to the Senate three years later when another antislavery coalition gained control of the New Hampshire legislature. He became a leader of the fledgling Republican Party in the Senate and chaired the important Committee on Naval Affairs during the Civil War. Hale served as U.S. minister to Spain (1865–1869) but was recalled after publicized charges of corruption.

See also: Free Soil Party, Liberty Party, Martin Van Buren

John R. McKivigan

REFERENCES

Blue, Frederick J. 1973. *The Free Soilers: Third Party Politics, 1848–54.* Urbana: U. of Illinois Pr.

Foner, Eric. 1970. *Free Soil, Free Labor, Free Men: The Ideology of the Republican Party before the Civil War.* New York: Oxford U. Pr.

Sewell, Richard H. 1965. *John P. Hale and the Politics of Abolition.* Cambridge: Harvard U. Pr.

Half-Breeds

See Stalwarts.

Gus Hall (1910–)

Four-time presidential candidate of the Communist Party. Gus Hall has been the party's general secretary for more than 30 years.

Hall was born Arvo Justa Halberg in Minnesota in 1910; like many Communists of his time, he changed his name when he became politically active. He joined the Young Communist League in 1926 and traveled in Europe from 1929 to 1933, studying at the Lenin Institute in Moscow for the last three years of his stay.

Hall became a steelworker and helped to organize the United Steelworkers of America and the Congress of Industrial Organizations. He joined the Communist Party in 1934 and became a full-time party organizer in the mills of Youngstown, Ohio, in 1938. He became party secretary for Cleveland in 1941 and again in 1946 after four years of service in the United States Navy.

Hall was one of 11 national CPUSA leaders indicted in 1948 under the Smith Act for conspiring to "teach and advocate the overthrow and destruction of the Government of the United States by force and violence." Following a trial in which the prosecution read aloud portions of *The Communist Manifesto* as evidence of subversion, Hall was sent to prison in 1951 remaining there until 1957.

On his release from prison Hall joined the intense intraparty struggles of the late 1950s on the side of the victorious orthodox faction, which supported the Soviet invasion of Hungary and downplayed the significance of Khrushchev's anti-Stalinism campaign. During the next two years he gained influence at the expense of centrist Eugene Dennis and was formally named general secretary upon Dennis's death in 1959.

Hall took over a floundering party. His leadership has been marked by orthodoxy, formula-laden rhetoric, and the CPUSA's continuing isolation. Conversely, Hall also brought organizational stability, a return to legal and open operation, and a modest revival of the party press.

See also: Communist Party of the United States, Eugene Dennis

John C. Berg

REFERENCES

Brandt, Joseph, assisted by Sylvia Opper Brandt. 1981. *Gus Hall Bibliography: The Communist Party, USA: Philosophy, History, Program, Activities.* New York: New Outlook Publishers.

Foster, William Z. 1952. *History of the Communist Party of the United States.* New York: International Publishers.

Hall, Gus. 1987. *Working Class USA: the Power and the Movement.* New York: International Publishers.

———. 1985. *Fighting Racism: Selected Writings.* New York: International Publishers.

———. 1980. *Basics: for Peace, Democracy, & Social Progress.* New York: International Publishers.

Howe, Irving, and Lewis Coser. 1962. *The American Communist Party: A Critical History.* 2nd ed. New York: Praeger.

Leonard W. Hall (1900–1979)

Republican National Chairman during President Dwight D. Eisenhower's first term. Leonard Wood Hall was born to Republicanism in Nassau County, New York. Hall received his law degree from Georgetown University at age 19 and immediately plunged into Nassau County Republican politics. Two years later he began practice as a lawyer in New York City. Republican Hall served three terms in the New York Assembly and then agreed to run for sheriff in 1928 as a compromise candidate. After a term as sheriff, Hall returned to the assembly for terms from 1934 to 1938.

In 1938 Hall was elected to the United States House of Representatives, where he served until 1952, devoting himself chiefly to the revitalization of the Republican congressional campaign committee. A supporter of Thomas E. Dewey for the presidential nomination, he served as the manager of Dewey's speakers bureau in 1944.

After 1944 Hall lined up Dewey support for the 1948 presidential race. In March 1947 he was chosen as chairman of the congressional campaign committee, a position he held until he became national chairman in 1953. In the aftermath of the Dewey defeat in 1948, Hall was vociferously critical of both Dewey and his campaign manager, Herbert Brownell, Jr., which led to an estrangement.

Wishing to return to his home state political base, Hall retired from the House of Representatives in 1952 to run successfully for Nassau County surrogate in New York. After his presidential nomination, some 47 Congressmen and others petitioned Eisenhower to choose Hall as his Republican national chairman—the appointment to be eased by a reconciliation with Dewey and an approving comment from Senator Robert A. Taft. Resigning as surrogate, Hall was elected national chairman and served through a difficult term. Republican control of the presidency for the first time in 20 years brought with it a massive patronage problem, including some 15,000 presidential appointments. In 1954 Hall had to deal with the eventual censure of Senator Joseph McCarthy. In 1955 and 1956, he kept alive Eisenhower's availability for a second term despite the President's illnesses.

Reelected national chairman in 1956, Hall managed the successful Eisenhower campaign, resigning in 1957 to run for governor of New York. However, the state party leaders gave the nomination instead to Nelson Rockefeller. Hall supported Vice President Richard M. Nixon for the presidential nomination in 1960, although in 1964 and 1968 he backed the candidacy of Rockefeller.

See also: Thomas Dewey, Dwight D. Eisenhower, Election of 1948, Joseph McCarthy, Richard Nixon, Republican National Committee, Nelson Rockefeller, Robert Taft

Ralph M. Goldman

REFERENCES

Bone, Hugh A. 1958. *Party Committees and National Politics*. Seattle: U. of Washington Press.
Goldman, Ralph M. 1990. *The National Party Chairmen and Committees: Factionalism at the Top.* Armonk, NY: M. E. Sharpe.

Charles A. Halleck (1900–1986)

Conservative Indiana Republican leader of the House of Representatives. Charles Abraham Halleck entered Congress after winning a vacant seat in a special election. He built a base of support as chair of the Republican Congressional Campaign Committee from 1943 to 1947. Halleck served as Majority Leader when the Republicans controlled the House from 1947 to 1949 and from 1953 to 1955. From 1955 to 1959 he acted as the unofficial deputy Minority Leader under Joseph Martin. He challenged Martin for the minority leadership following the 1958 elections and won on the second ballot.

During his tenure as Minority Leader, Halleck concentrated on increasing the party unity of House Republicans. They joined with conservative Democrats to pass the programs of the Dwight Eisenhower administration and to stymie many of the legislative goals of Presidents John Kennedy and Lyndon Johnson. Halleck teamed with Senate Republican leader Everett M. Dirksen on weekly press conferences ("The Ev and Charlie Show") that presented alternatives to Democratic proposals.

Halleck was challenged and defeated by Gerald Ford for the leadership position in 1965. As was the case in his earlier victory over Martin, this defeat followed an election in which the Republican delegation lost a large number of seats. Liberal Republicans were frustrated over Halleck's emphasis on party unity at all costs, and conservatives were angered at his role in moving civil rights legislation through Congress. While Ford was ideologically similar to Halleck, he promised a more positive and open leadership style.

See also: Everett Dirksen, Gerald Ford, Lyndon Johnson, John F. Kennedy

John A. Clark

REFERENCES

Peabody, Robert L. 1966. *The Ford-Halleck Minority Leadership Contest.* New York: McGraw-Hill.

Benjamin F. Hallett (1797–1862)

First national committee chairman of the Democratic Party (1848–1852). Benjamin Franklin Hallett was chosen for this position at the national convention that nominated Lewis Cass for President. New England Democratic leaders were supporting Levi Woodbury of New Hampshire for the nomination. Hallett, chairman of the Massachusetts Democratic State Committee and spokesman for most of the New England delegations, at a critical moment led the New England delegations from Woodbury to Cass.

Indiana Senator J. D. Bright moved for the creation of the first comprehensive Democratic national committee, every state to be represented by a member appointed by his state's delegation. Senator Bright's motion included a requirement that the national committee assume a major responsibility for the conduct of the presidential campaign. Hallett was chosen national committee chairman.

Hallett was probably appointed by the permanent chairman of the national convention, Andrew Stevenson, in consultation with Senator Bright and the Cass managers. He had, after all, led the decisive New England shift from Woodbury to Cass. He was chairman of the platform committee whose northern majority wrote a plank on abolition that was conciliatory to the South. Perhaps most influential were Hallett's long years of experience in party management and his ability to produce campaign propaganda.

An 1816 graduate of Brown University, Hallett was a polemical and controversial journalist in New England in the 1820s and 1830s. He edited the publications of the Antimasonic Party. When Antimasonry waned, Hallett was instrumental in leading his state party into Andrew Jackson's Democratic-Republican organization, particularly in support of the fight against the national bank. Hallett's radicalism mellowed during the next decade. By 1844 he was one of the principal leaders of the Tyler-Calhoun faction in the Massachusetts Democratic Party, bent upon conciliating the emerging North-South split over slavery. When, in 1847, the pro-South "doughface" Tyler-Calhoun faction defeated the strictly abolitionist Van Burenites, Hallett be- came chairman of the Massachusetts central committee.

During his entire tenure as national chairman, Hallett mediated the factional bitterness over the slavery issue. Even at the end of his tenure in 1952, he led the difficult work of the national convention's platform committee, and did so again in 1856.

President Franklin Pierce appointed Hallett as a United States district attorney in 1853. At the divisive Democratic National Convention of 1860, he supported the candidacy of a southerner, Vice President John C. Breckinridge.

See also: Antimasons, John C. Breckinridge, Lewis Cass, Democratic National Committee, Franklin Pierce

Ralph M. Goldman

REFERENCES

Bean, W. G. 1922. "Transformation of Political Parties in Massachusetts, 1850–1860." Ph.D. dissertation, Harvard U.

Goldman, Ralph M. 1990. *The National Party Chairmen and Committees: Factionalism at the Top.* Armonk, NY: M. E. Sharpe.

Fannie Lou Hamer (1917–1977)

Central figure of the civil rights movement. Fannie Lou Hamer was a founder of the Mississippi Freedom Democrat Party (MFDP), a group whose immediate goals included Black voter registration and racial justice in political representation. As MFDP's representatives at the 1964 Democratic National Convention in Atlantic City, New Jersey, Hamer and her colleagues led a challenge to the all-white regular Mississippi delegation. MFDP sought to unseat the delegation on the grounds that African-Americans were excluded from the state Democratic Party. In response to their action, the Credentials Committee proposed a compromise that would seat the regular delegation plus two Freedom Democrats as delegates at large. Although rejected, this proposal was viewed as a victory for civil rights. Subsequently, MFDP unsuccessfully sought to remove the Mississippi members from Congress on the grounds that they were chosen through a discriminatory voting procedure. More successful grass-roots efforts culminated in 1964, when MFDP fielded three Black congressional candidates. Among these candidates, Fannie Lou Hamer made a strong showing, garnering 33,009 votes.

MFDP played a highly visible role in the civil rights movement that unfolded in three distinct but overlapping phases. In the early and mid-1960s, the strategy of nonviolent direct action supplemented the existing tradition of NAACP legal work. Both were supplanted in part by the Black Power movement of the late 1960s. The MFDP Mississippi voter registration drive from 1962 to 1964 was an important and successful instance of nonviolent direct action.

Voter registration was crucial to Hamer's work with MFDP and later as a field secretary of the Student Nonviolent Coordinating Committee (SNCC). An MFDP party statement of the time reported that "94 percent of Mississippi's Negroes of voting age are not registered." The attempt to register Blacks to vote and run for office in Mississippi met with violent opposition. Hamer's personal experience proves an example.

Fannie Lou Hamer was born one of twenty children of a Mississippi sharecropping family. She began picking cotton at age six, and in 1962 she was forced to continue in plantation work, when she lost her job after registering to vote. In 1963 she was severely beaten and jailed after attempting to integrate a restaurant. Her home was bombed in 1971 as a result of her activities. After her work for MFDP, Hamer devoted herself to organizing economic cooperatives with neighbors in Sunflower County.

See also: Mississippi Freedom Democrat Party, Student Nonviolent Coordinating Committee

Victoria A. A. Kamsler

REFERENCES

Evans, Sara. 1979. *Personal Politics: The Roots of Women's Liberation in the Civil Rights Movement and the New Left.* New York: Knopf.

Lerner, Gerda, ed. 1972. *Black Women in White America: A Documentary History.* New York: Vintage.

Meier, August, and Elliot Rudwick, eds. 1970. *Black Protest in the Sixties.* Chicago: Quadrangle.

Alexander Hamilton (1757–1804)

Advocate for the Constitution and leader of the Federalist Party. Alexander Hamilton was born in the British West Indies, and after education at King's College (now Columbia University) and military service in the American Revolution, he gained legislative experience in the Continental Congress and in the New York legislature. At the Constitutional Convention (1787) and in essays that he anonymously contributed with James Madison and John Jay to *The Federalist* (1788), he advocated strengthening the central government's executive power.

Hamilton became the leader of the Federalist Party. As Secretary of the Treasury in George Washington's administration (1789–1795), he proposed that the federal government assume the debt accumulated during the Revolutionary War by the Confederation and state governments, establish the Bank of the United States, and provide tariff protection for developing industries. He argued that the Constitution's general welfare clause granted implied powers to the federal government for encouraging investment in the nation's commercial and industrial development.

Hamilton initiated new methods of partisan organization, to which several of his Republican opponents reacted fervently. He provided financial support and wrote anonymous articles for *The Gazette of the United States*, a Federalist Party organ. He organized public meetings to agitate and petition Congress on public issues such as Washington's Neutrality Proclamation (1793) and the Jay Treaty (1795). These actions were in response to the French Revolution, which polarized American politics. While both parties advocated a de facto neutrality, Republicans under the leadership of James Madison and Thomas Jefferson sympathized with the French. Hamilton's Federalists favored a pro-British foreign policy and hoped to establish institutions based on British models.

Hamilton was more effective in establishing than in sustaining the Federalist Party. After resigning as Secretary of the Treasury, he returned to his New York law practice. He never sought the presidency but remained an active partisan. He had urged Washington to stand for reelection in 1792. In 1796 he tried to secure the election of Thomas Pinckney, John Adams's running mate, to the presidency (electors did not vote separately for vice presidential candidates until the Twelfth Amendment took effect in 1804). During the Quasi-War with France in the late 1790s, Hamilton served as inspector general and second in command of the provisional army under Washington. In 1799 President Adams sent commissioners to negotiate all outstanding differences with France. This diplomatic initiative split the Federalists between the Adams moderates and Hamilton's prowar ultra-Federalists.

In 1800 Hamilton again attempted to arrange the election of Adams's running mate—this time Charles Cotesworth Pinckney (brother of Thomas Pinckney)—as President. He rashly wrote and circulated a letter (the Republicans published it widely) denouncing Adams as unfit for the presidency. When the electoral vote tied between Republicans Jefferson and Aaron Burr, and the election went to the House of Representatives,

Hamilton urged Federalist Congressmen to support Jefferson as the lesser of evils. Hamilton also helped to defeat Burr's candidacy in the 1804 New York gubernatorial election. This incident resulted in the duel in which Burr fatally wounded Hamilton. The Federalist Party did not long survive Hamilton. His lasting legacy lies in his vision of a government energetic in advancing the nation's economic development.

See also: John Adams, Aaron Burr, Jay Treaty, Thomas Jefferson, James Madison, Twelfth Amendment, George Washington

Thomas A. Mason

REFERENCES

Cooke, Jacob E. 1982. *Alexander Hamilton.* New York: Scribner's.

Mitchell, Broadus. 1957–1962. *Alexander Hamilton.* 2 vols. New York: Macmillan.

Syrett, Harold C., and Jacob E. Cooke, eds. 1961–1987. *The Papers of Alexander Hamilton.* 27 vols. New York: Columbia U. Pr.

John D. M. Hamilton (1892–1973)

Republican National Committee chairman in the 1930s. John D. M. Hamilton managed Alfred Landon's 1936 presidential campaign and as Republican national chairman (1937–1940), he restored the party's organization and guided its comeback in the 1938 congressional elections.

Hamilton was active in the conservative faction of the Kansas Republican Party. Elected to the legislature in 1924, he served as speaker of the Kansas House of Representatives from 1926 to 1928 and unsuccessfully sought the gubernatorial nomination in 1928. Appointed general counsel of the Republican National Committee in 1934, Hamilton resigned to manage Landon's campaign, traveling extensively to raise campaign funds and renew moribund local organizations. His dynamic but quite conservative speeches contrasted with Landon's moderate positions and were eventually curtailed.

Following Landon's defeat, Hamilton was appointed the first full-time, salaried chairman of the Republican National Committee, promising to establish the first permanent GOP headquarters. Hamilton supplied research services to Republicans in Congress, formed national Republican women's and young people's clubs, and organized undercover opposition to President Franklin Roosevelt's proposal to "pack" the Supreme Court (as a party, Republicans did not oppose court packing for fear they would unite the Democrats). Congressional gains in 1938 quite probably saved the Republican Party from extinction.

Replaced as chairman by the 1940 Republican nominee, Wendell Willkie, Hamilton joined a leading Philadelphia law firm. In 1952 he managed the eastern states' campaign of Robert A. Taft for the Republican presidential nomination.

See also: Alfred Landon, Republican National Committee, Robert A. Taft, Wendell Willkie

Karl A. Lamb

REFERENCES

Lamb, Karl A. 1960. "John Hamilton and the Revitalization of the Republican Party, 1936–1940." 45 *Papers of the Michigan Academy of Science, Arts, and Letters* 233.

———. 1961. "The Opposition Party as Secret Agent: Republicans and the Court Fight, 1937." 46 *Papers of the Michigan Academy of Science, Arts, and Letters* 539.

Hannibal Hamlin (1809–1891)

Abraham Lincoln's first Vice President. A leading nineteenth-century Maine politician, Hannibal Hamlin achieved his greatest fame as Vice President during the first administration of Abraham Lincoln (1861–1865). Born in Paris, Maine, Hamlin lacked the financial resources to attend college and worked briefly at surveying, printing, and teaching before becoming a lawyer. He practiced law in Hampden but devoted most of his attention to advancing his career in the Democratic Party. After serving in the state legislature, he won election to the U.S. House of Representatives (1843–1847) and the U.S. Senate (1848–1861). Hamlin first voiced antislavery sentiments during the Mexican War and ultimately left the Democrats for the Republican Party in 1856.

Maine Republicans elected him governor in 1856, but he held the office for only a few weeks before returning to the Senate. After nominating ex-Whig Lincoln for President, the 1860 Republican convention took two ballots to select ex-Democrat Hamlin as the ideological as well as geographical balance for their ticket. During his term he presided over the Senate, supporting efforts for emancipation but playing a minor role in Lincoln's administration. In the 1864 campaign, Lincoln sought to broaden his sectional appeal and privately directed the move by convention delegates to replace Hamlin with Tennessee Unionist Andrew Johnson on the ticket.

After briefly serving as collector of the port of Boston (1865–1866), Hamlin headed a Maine railroad company. He returned to politics and won two more terms in the Senate (1869–1881), where he sided with Radical Republicans in the debates over Reconstruction. Hamlin completed his long career in public service as U.S. ambassador to Spain (1881–1882).

See also: Andrew Johnson, Abraham Lincoln, Mexican War, Reconstruction, Union Party

John R. McKivigan

REFERENCES

Hamlin, Charles Eugene. 1899. *The Life and Times of Hannibal Hamlin.* Cambridge, MA: Riverside Press.

Hunt, H. Draper. 1969. *Hannibal Hamlin of Maine: Lincoln's First Vice-President.* Syracuse: Syracuse U. Pr.

Wade Hampton (1818–1902)

Powerful South Carolina political leader. Wade Hampton served as a Confederate general, governor, and United States Senator from South Carolina. He inherited the huge cotton-planting empire built by his grandfather and father (both of whom were also called Wade). In 1852 Hampton was elected to his state's house of representatives by the voters of Richland County. After three terms in the house (1852–1858), he was promoted to the state senate. Opposed to secession in 1860, he went with his state in 1861, resigning his senate seat and raising "Hampton's Legion" to fight for the Confederacy. By the time the war was over he had been wounded three times and had risen to the rank of lieutenant general, commanding the cavalry corps of the Army of Northern Virginia.

In 1876 the Democratic Party nominated Hampton for governor of South Carolina. This election was critical as the outcome would mean either a continuation of Republican rule in the state or "redemption" from it. In a campaign marked by widespread fraud and intimidation, Hampton was declared the winner by a narrow margin. The Republican administration refused to yield, and Hampton took office only after Rutherford B. Hayes removed federal troops from the state. Hampton won a second term in 1878 and was elected to the United States Senate the following year. In 1890 the populist agrarian wing of South Carolina's Democratic Party rose to power under the leadership of Benjamin R. Tillman, and the planter-aristocrat Hampton was defeated for reelection. Grover Cleveland appointed him United States railroad commissioner in 1893, a position he held until 1897.

See also: Grover Cleveland, Rutherford B. Hayes, Railroads, Secession, Benjamin Tillman

Gregg Cantrell

REFERENCES

Cooper, William J., Jr. 1968. *The Conservative Regime: South Carolina, 1877–1890.* Baltimore: Johns Hopkins U. Pr.

Jarrell, Hampton M. 1950. *Wade Hampton and the Negro: The Road Not Taken.* Columbia: U. of South Carolina Pr.

Wellman, Manly Wade. 1949. *Giant in Gray: A Biography of Wade Hampton of South Carolina.* New York: Scribner's.

Wells, Edward L. 1907. *Hampton and Reconstruction.* Columbia, SC: State Company.

Williams, Alfred B. 1935. *Hampton and His Red Shirts: South Carolina's Deliverance in 1876.* Charleston, SC: Walker, Evans & Cogswell.

Winfield S. Hancock (1824–1886)

A Civil War hero and the unsuccessful Democratic presidential candidate in 1880. Winfield Scott Hancock was the son of a lawyer from Norristown, Pennsylvania, and a graduate of the U.S. Military Academy in 1844. Hancock fought with distinction in the Mexican War under the very general for whom he had been named, Winfield Scott. Hancock served in numerous routine peacetime military assignments on the frontier until the beginning of the Civil War in which he steadily rose in rank, eventually commanding the Second Corps of the Union Army of the Potomac. Hancock became a national hero in 1863 at the Battle of Gettysburg where he had skillfully fended off several Confederate assaults, including the famous Pickett's Charge.

After the war, Hancock presided over the military occupation of Texas and Louisiana where he generated considerable controversy by embracing the lenient Reconstruction program of President Andrew Johnson. Hancock's actions, however, outraged militant northern Republicans who persuaded Ulysses S. Grant, as general in chief, to overrule many of his policies. The controversy soon led Grant to transfer Hancock to a frontier command and encouraged Democratic politicians to consider Hancock as possible presidential material. He received significant support at the party's national conventions of 1868 and 1876. In 1880 Hancock finally received the Democrats' nomination on the first ballot when no other veteran party leader attracted broad-based support. That year the Republicans nominated Ohio's governor James A. Garfield, also a former general in the Union Army. Hancock's poorly articulated pronouncements on the tariff question allowed the Republicans to portray him as politically inexperienced. Coupled with charges that ex-Confederates would control a Hancock administration, this accusation gave the Republicans a narrow victory. Hancock remained in the active army until his death.

See also: Election of 1880, James Garfield, Ulysses S. Grant, Andrew Johnson, Reconstruction

John R. McKivigan

REFERENCES

Dawson, Joseph G., III. 1982. *Army Generals and Reconstruction: Louisiana, 1862–1877*. Baton Rouge: Louisiana State U. Pr.

Tucker, Glenn. 1960. *Hancock the Superb*. Indianapolis: Bobbs-Merrill.

Warner, Ezra J. 1964. *Generals in Blue: Lives of the Union Commanders*. Baton Rouge: Louisiana State U. Pr.

Marcus A. (Mark) Hanna (1837–1904)

Ohio Republican kingmaker. Marcus Alonzo Hanna, an Ohio industrialist and U.S. Senator, rose to political prominence as mentor to William McKinley, whom he guided to two terms as governor and then to the presidency in 1896. Hanna started out as a grocery clerk in the family business, but became a millionaire in Great Lakes shipping, banking, and street railroads. Hanna was at first a leader of the Republican Party in Cuyahoga County, Ohio, and finally the virtual political boss of the United States. He served as delegate to the Republican national conventions in 1884, 1888 (as chairman of the Ohio delegation and manager for John Sherman's unsuccessful quest for the nomination), and 1896, when he engineered McKinley's nomination on the first ballot.

Proud of his work in the National Civic Federation, which sought to promote harmony between capital and labor, Mark Hanna favored tariff protection of American industry and a sound, gold-based currency. Shrewd, intelligent, and conservative but not reactionary, Hanna supported the recognition of trade unions and collective bargaining, as did McKinley. He saw government assistance to business as a means to improve society.

Hanna was an astute chairman of the Republican National Committee from 1896 to 1904. Hanna was first appointed to the Senate by Ohio's governor and then the Ohio legislature elected him to a full term in January 1898 in a close contest, with charges of bribery on both sides. He was overwhelmingly reelected in 1904 as a man who had grown in political responsibility as well as power. Yet he was regularly depicted by newspaper cartoonists as a brute with dollar signs on his clothing—a monster of special interest.

Hanna had run McKinley's 1896 campaign

positively by emphasizing the return of prosperity with slogans such as "McKinley and the Full Dinner Pail" and negatively with the motto "Stop Bryan, Save America." Hanna funded McKinley's carefully programmed front-porch campaign with solicited donations from business and financial interests worth an unprecedented $3.5 million.

In the Senate, Hanna opposed the war with Spain as unsettling to the economy but was, as was McKinley, drawn into its support. He revealed unease at the succession to the presidency of Theodore Roosevelt, whose selection as Vice President he had only supported at the last moment. Although Hanna disavowed personal interest in the presidency himself, conservative eastern Republican opponents of Roosevelt mentioned him in this regard, thus exacerbating the strain between the two. A reconciliation was scheduled when Hanna's death from typhoid fever in February 1904 effectively ended the agitation within Republican ranks against Roosevelt's nomination.

See also: Bosses, William McKinley, Republican National Committee, Theodore Roosevelt

Frederick J. Augustyn, Jr.

REFERENCES

Beer, Thomas. 1973. *Hanna*. New York: Octagon Books.

Croly, Herbert. 1912. *Marcus Alonzo Hanna: His Life and Work*. New York: Macmillan.

Goldman, Ralph M. 1990. *The National Party Chairmen and Committees: Factionalism at the Top*. Armonk, NY: M. E. Sharpe.

Stern, Clarence Ames. 1968. *Resurgent Republicanism: The Handiwork of Hanna*. Ann Arbor, MI: Edward Bros.

Robert E. Hannegan (1903–1949)

Democratic National Committee chairman from 1944 to 1947. Robert Emmet Hannegan was born and raised in St. Louis and graduated with honors from St. Louis University Law School in 1925. He began his political career in 1933 with an appointment to the St. Louis Democratic City Central Committee. Rising quickly in local and state Democratic circles, he allied himself with Senator Harry Truman and was credited with helping Truman win reelection to the Senate by a marrow margin in 1940. Truman rewarded Hannegan with an appointment as collector of internal revenue in the Eastern District of Missouri in 1942, and in 1944 he secured Hannegan's selection as chairman of the Democratic National Committee.

As chairman of the Democratic Party, Hannegan maneuvered Truman's 1944 nomination as Vice President over Henry Wallace and William O. Douglas in a move that is still a source of historical debate. When Truman assumed the presidency in April 1945 at the death of Franklin Roosevelt, his first appointment was Hannegan as Postmaster General.

Hannegan's hard-nosed political deals on the state and national levels made him a controversial and often criticized figure, but at the same time he was credited with maintaining high standards in both the Internal Revenue Service and the Post Office Department. Health problems forced his resignation as party chairman and Postmaster General in November 1947. He retired from politics, purchased a share of the St. Louis Cardinals baseball team, and devoted full time to his business interests.

See also: Democratic National Committee, Harry S Truman, Henry Wallace

Thomas T. Spencer

REFERENCES

Goldman, Ralph M. 1990. *The National Party Chairmen and Committees: Factionalism at the Top.* Armonk, NY: M. E. Sharpe.

Jarman, Rufus. 1946. "Truman's Political Quarterback." 218 (March 7) *Saturday Evening Post* 18.

Rodell, Fred. 1946. "Robert E. Hannegan." 63 (August) *American Mercury* 133.

William Jefferson Hardin (1830?–1890?)

African-American territorial legislator from Wyoming. A Republican African-American who served in the Wyoming Territory House of Representatives from 1879 to 1884, William Jefferson Hardin was one of only two Black members of state or territorial legislative bodies outside the South during his tenure of office. Hardin, a dynamic speaker, often presided over the house when the speaker was absent. During his second two-year term, he served as a committee chairman.

Hardin was born free in Kentucky around 1830. He claimed that his father, who was white, was the brother of Kentucky Congressman Ben Hardin. He settled in Denver, Colorado, in 1863, where he operated a barber shop, became a leading spokesman for the city's large Black community, and supported the Republican Party. He worked briefly in the local branch of the U.S. Mint before moving north to Cheyenne in 1873.

Hardin soon became a popular figure in the Wyoming capital, where he was often asked to be a guest speaker at public functions. In 1879, when the Republican county convention nomi-

nated him for a seat in the territorial legislature, the Democrats enthusiastically endorsed his candidacy. As a legislator, Hardin supported the passage of a married woman's property act and the repeal of Wyoming's ban on interracial marriages.

Hardin left Cheyenne around 1884. He did not, as some accounts state, serve as mayor of small towns in Colorado and Utah. Reports that he died in Colorado around 1890 cannot be substantiated.

See also: Speaker of the House

Roger D. Hardaway

REFERENCES

Berwanger, Eugene H. 1975. "William J. Hardin: Colorado Spokesman for Racial Justice, 1863–1873." 52 *The Colorado Magazine* 52.

————. 1979. "Hardin and Langston: Western Black Spokesmen of the Reconstruction Era." 44 *Journal of Negro History* 101.

Hardaway, Roger D. 1991. "William Jefferson Hardin: Wyoming's Nineteenth-Century Black Politician." 63 *Annals of Wyoming* 1.

Warren G. Harding (1865–1923)

Scandal-burdened President of the U.S. in the 1920s. Disenchantment with domestic and overseas Wilsonian activism helped elect dark horse U.S. presidential candidate Warren Gamaliel Harding by a landslide in 1920. A journeyman politician, Harding ascended to the White House more on the basis of durability than charisma or intellect. He first made his political reputation in Marion, Ohio, where he edited and published a newspaper. He sat for two terms in the state senate, then served as the Republican lieutenant governor from 1903 to 1904. Harding had a conservative but flexible probusiness philosophy. His steadfast party regularity and a knack for mediation and harmonizing enabled him to survive the constant factional warfare of Ohio's GOP. Moreover, Harding often clouded his stand on controversial issues until a popular consensus emerged. If he collected no fervent disciples, he made few permanent enemies.

A good orator, Harding gained wider prominence when he nominated William Howard Taft for President at the 1912 Republican convention. Two years later he won election to the U.S. Senate. He was a mediocre but not inept legislator, with party loyalty and strong nationalism his most distinguishing characteristics. Yet the affable Harding was popular in the Senate and was among the Republican Old Guard. In 1916 he delivered the keynote address at the GOP national convention.

When a leadership vacuum developed in the party, Harding became a presidential contender in 1920. Because he neither hungered for nor shied from the nomination, he allowed Ohio admirers, led by Harry C. Daugherty, to form a campaign organization. Once Harding made a firm decision to run, he began to cultivate an incipient national base of support, but unimpressive showings in the Ohio and Indiana primaries seemed to dim his nomination prospects. For all that, none of the favored candidates broke from the field at the leaderless, divided Republican convention of 1920. Harding's speaking ability, geniality, moderate conservatism, and nationalism combined with the promise of Ohio's electoral votes to make him an acceptable compromise candidate to the Old Guard, to isolationist western progressives, and to the internationalists. Moreover, Republicans judged correctly that Americans, disillusioned with the Versailles Treaty and frightened by postwar racial and class strife, would find attractive the small-town ethic personified by the handsome Ohioan ("He looks like a President").

Harding, Daugherty, and GOP national chairman Will H. Hays ran a masterful front porch campaign that emphasized style and image over substance. Harding called for high tariffs, immigration restriction, fiscal retrenchment, "America first," and diminished presidential authority. He obfuscated his position on the burning League of Nations issue and thereby held the Republican Party together. Above all, Harding campaigned for "normalcy" and restoration of tranquillity. He defeated Democrat opponent James M. Cox by nearly 2 to 1 in the popular voting and almost 4 to 1 in the electoral count. Harding's margin of victory demonstrated that he suited the postwar, post-Woodrow Wilson mood of the country. The scandals that subsequently rocked his administration did not slow the 12 years of Republican ascendancy in national politics launched by his election. After his death, his successors, Calvin Coolidge and Herbert Hoover, carried on the Harding policies of business support, fiscal conservatism, and independent internationalism.

See also: Calvin Coolidge, William Hays, Herbert Hoover, League of Nations, William Howard Taft, Teapot Dome

Jeffery C. Livingston

REFERENCES

Bagby, Wesley M. 1962. *The Road to Normalcy: The Presidential Campaign and Election of 1920*. Baltimore: Johns Hopkins U. Pr.

Downes, Randolph C. 1970. *The Rise of Warren Gamaliel Harding, 1865–1920*. Columbus: Ohio State U. Pr.

McCoy, Donald R. 1971. "Election of 1920." In Arthur M. Schlesinger, Jr., and Fred L. Israel, eds. *History of American Presidential Elections, 1789–1968*. New York: Chelsea House.

Murray, Robert K. 1969. *The Harding Era: Warren G. Harding and His Administration*. Minneapolis: U. of Minnesota Pr.

Russell, Francis. 1968. *The Shadow of Blooming Grove: Warren G. Harding in His Times*. New York: McGraw-Hill.

Sinclair, Andrew. 1965. *The Available Man: The Life Behind the Masks of Warren Gamaliel Harding*. New York: Macmillan.

Harper v. Virginia State Board of Elections
383 U.S. 663 (1966)

This case invalidated the imposition of poll taxes as a prerequisite to voting in state and local elections. Two years before the Supreme Court's ruling in *Harper*, the states ratified the Twenty-fourth Amendment prohibiting the use of any poll tax as a prerequisite to voting in federal elections. Despite this national prohibition, the Virginia Constitution continued to require potential voters in state and local elections to pay a $1.50 poll tax before voting. Harper challenged the constitutionality of the Virginia tax. Before *Harper*, the Court had handed down several inconsistent rulings on the authority of the states to restrict access to the ballot box. In 1938 in *Breedlove v. Suttles*, 302 U.S. 277, the Court held that poll taxes were permissible as a prerequisite to voting. Nonetheless, in 1964, in *Reynolds v. Sims*, 377 U.S. 533, the Court found that suffrage is a fundamental right upon which other basic civil rights depend. *Harper* resolved the inconsistencies by overruling *Breedlove*.

The *Harper* Court determined that distinguishing qualified voters based upon wealth constituted discrimination in violation of the equal protection clause of the Fourteenth Amendment. The *Harper* Court found that even though the poll tax appeared to be evenhanded, its effect was discriminatory. The tax imposed a standard for voter qualification that disqualified many Blacks from voting because Blacks were traditionally economically deprived and hence less able to pay the tax.

The *Harper* Court held that while states may set certain standards for voter qualification, those standards must bear some reasonable relationship to the intelligent use of the ballot. The Court said that wealth bears no such relationship, is arbitrary and capricious, and is therefore in violation of the equal protection clause, insofar as it is a standard for distinguishing qualified voters.

Harper demonstrated the high priority that the Court places on the fundamental right to vote. States could no longer withhold the electoral franchise from African-Americans or any group under the pretense of an evenhanded test to determine voter qualification. Any test established to distinguish qualified voters must contain standards that bear a reasonable relationship to the responsible exercise of the right to vote. The equal protection clause invalidates legislation establishing tests, which, although apparently fair on their face, would result in unfair treatment, such as the denial of voting rights owing to an inability to pay poll taxes. *Harper* is a reflection not only of the Supreme Court's intolerance of racial discrimination in general but also of the priority the Court has established regarding the fundamental right of suffrage.

See also: Poll Tax, *Reynolds v. Sims*, Twenty-fourth Amendment

Morton A. Brody

Fred R. Harris (1930–)

Democratic Senator and presidential hopeful from Oklahoma. Fred R. Harris sought the Democratic nomination for President in 1976. Harris, a former Senator from Oklahoma running as a populist, asserted, "The fundamental problem [in America] is that too few people have all the money and power, and everybody else has very little of either." To rectify this inequality, Harris advocated a complete tax overhaul and the breaking up of all monopolistic industries. Running a grass-roots campaign out of his camper and collecting funds in old ice cream cartons, Harris sought to create a new populist coalition of young liberals, minorities, and blue-collar workers. Instead, Harris was perceived as being too radical. He came in third in the Iowa caucus and never placed better than third in any other primary. Harris's withdrawal from the race on April 8, 1976, concluded his second failed attempt at the presidency. In 1971 he had campaigned for six weeks before running out of money.

Harris began his career as an establishment Democrat. The son of a poor farmer, Harris graduated first in his class at the University of Oklahoma Law School and won election to the Oklahoma State Senate at the age of 26. In 1966 he was elected to the U.S. Senate. He served as co-chairman of Hubert Humphrey's 1968 presidential nomination campaign and became Democratic national chair the following year. His politics were radicalized by his work on the 1967 Presidential Commission on Urban Violence. The commission, established after the urban riots of the 1960s, reached the controversial conclusion that violence in American cities was caused by white racism and Black despair. Harris's increasingly liberal stands precluded any reelection bid for the Senate from conservative Oklahoma. Thus, he left the Senate to run for the White House. In recent years, Harris has written several books as a professor at the University of New Mexico.

See also: Democratic National Committee, Elections of 1968 and 1976, Hubert Humphrey

Barbara Norrander

REFERENCES

Witcover, Jules. 1977. *Marathon: The Pursuit of the Presidency, 1972–1976.* New York: Signet.

Benjamin Harrison (1833–1901)

Republican President during the Gilded Age. Benjamin Harrison, an Indianapolis lawyer and politician, was President of the United States from 1889 to 1893. A skillful and powerful leader, he dominated the Indiana political scene for a score of years both in office (as Senator and as President) and out. The factionalized Indiana Republican Party was in thrall to the austere figure of Benjamin Harrison for several decades after the Civil War, even though his reserved manners and aristocratic bearing antagonized some of the party faithful.

Harrison was born in North Bend, Ohio, the son of a Whig Congressman and grandson of a Whig President. He grew up along the banks of the Ohio River, attending a log cabin school and then the local Farmer's College before entering Miami University in Oxford, Ohio. Admitted to the Ohio bar in 1853, Harrison began his career in Indianapolis, where he advanced quickly in his profession while also establishing himself as a loyal and hard-working member of the new Republican Party.

In 1860 he was elected Indiana Supreme Court reporter, a potentially rewarding position, and his career flourished along with that of Civil War governor and then-Senator Oliver P. Morton. With Governor Morton's assistance Harrison organized (and became colonel of) Company A, 70th Indiana Infantry Regiment; a diligent soldier, he participated in General William Tecumseh Sherman's campaign through

Georgia and was breveted general in 1865. Following the war, Harrison reestablished his legal practice and continued to rise in the Republican Party. He replaced his party's discredited nominee for governor in 1876, only to lose the election to the popular James D. "Blue Jeans" Williams, but Harrison's willingness to serve the GOP in time of crisis helped give him a seat in the United States Senate following a Republican sweep of Indiana in 1880. This single term was important for Harrison, both for learning national politics and for broadening his personal and political cohort.

The Harrison presidency, as indeed Gilded Age politics in general, underwent major reassessment at the centennial of his inauguration. Far from being a leader without purpose or principles in an era without significant issues, Harrison and his colleagues confronted a new dynamic and new problems in the 1890s. Under Harrison's quiet guidance, new initiatives in both domestic affairs (westward expansion, industrial regulation, immigration policy) and foreign policy, including tariff policy, were undertaken. In 1889 and 1890, six new states (representing nineteen potential Republican electoral votes) entered the Union, the first Pan-American conference convened in Washington, the McKinley Tariff and the Sherman Antitrust Act were signed into law by Harrison, and potential crises in foreign affairs (involving Samoa, Italy, and Chile) were resolved peacefully. Indeed, despite some indications of an aggressive expansionist sentiment in the Harrison administration, the President's activities following his years in office—particularly his opposition to the imperialism of the Treaty of Paris, 1898—are a truer indication of his own views. In retrospect, Harrison's most conspicuous failure was his impolitic use of the patronage, the most likely explanation both for the Republican losses in the off-year election of 1890 and for Harrison's failure to be reelected in 1892. Undismayed at this outcome, Harrison returned to Indianapolis and an extensive law practice.

See also: Oliver Morton, Sherman Antitrust Act

Ralph D. Gray

REFERENCES

Calhoun, Charles W. 1988. *Gilded Age Cato: The Life of Walter Q. Gresham.* Lexington: U. Pr. of Kentucky.
Kinzer, Donald L. 1977. "Benjamin Harrison and the Politics of Availability." In Ralph D. Gray, ed. *Gentlemen from Indiana: National Party Candidates, 1836–1940.* Indianapolis: Indiana Historical Bureau.
Phillips, Clifton J. 1968. *Indiana in Transition: The Emergence of an Industrial Commonwealth, 1880–1920.*
Indianapolis: Indiana Historical Bureau and Indiana Historical Society.
Socolofsky, Homer E., and Allan B. Spetter. 1987. *The Presidency of Benjamin Harrison.* Lawrence: U. Pr. of Kansas.

Byron Patton (Pat) Harrison (1881–1941)

Legislator from Mississippi for three decades. Mississippi Democrat "Pat" Harrison served as Congressman from 1911 to 1919 and as Senator from 1919 to 1941, chairing the Senate Finance Committee during the New Deal. Born in Mississippi and distantly related to Presidents William Henry Harrison and Benjamin Harrison, he attended Louisiana State University, briefly taught school, and began his law practice in 1902. In 1910 he won the first of four consecutive terms in the House of Representatives, loyally supporting Woodrow Wilson, particularly on foreign policy issues.

In 1918 Harrison ran for the Senate against James K. Vardaman, the anti-administration Democratic incumbent. When President Wilson repudiated Vardaman, Harrison won easily, as he did against little opposition in 1924 and 1930. He was a noted partisan orator, rising to party leadership in the 1920s. In 1924 Harrison was both the temporary chairman and the keynote speaker at the Democratic convention, and in 1928, although a southerner, he loyally campaigned for Al Smith.

Harrison early but cautiously backed Franklin D. Roosevelt in 1932. Though generally conservative, as chairman of the Senate Finance Committee, he supported the many bills designed to alleviate the Great Depression. A gifted conciliator and parliamentarian with friends in both parties, he was reelected in 1936 by a two-to-one margin. Harrison's support for Roosevelt waned with the country's apparent economic recovery during Roosevelt's second term. Concomitantly, FDR played a key role in Harrison's defeat when he ran for Senate Majority Leader in 1937.

Though more independent afterward, Harrison refused to condemn the New Deal, and he contributed to Roosevelt's foreign policy as another war developed. He was elected Senate President *pro tempore* in 1940 but died only a few months later.

See also: New Deal, Franklin Roosevelt, Al Smith, Woodrow Wilson

Eugene S. Larson

REFERENCES

Burner, David. 1968. *The Politics of Provincialism.* New York: Knopf.

Patterson, James T. 1967. *Congressional Conservatism and the New Deal.* Lexington: U. Pr. of Kentucky.

Swain, Martha H. 1978. *Pat Harrison: The New Deal Years.* Jackson: U. Pr. of Mississippi.

William Henry Harrison (1773–1841)

Whig President for a month. William Henry Harrison, a brilliant and effective military and political leader in the Old Northwest from the 1790s through the War of 1812, capped a return to national affairs with his election to the presidency in 1840. The first of only two Whigs to be elected to the office (both of whom died there), Harrison did not survive pneumonia that he contracted on his inauguration day and died some 30 days later.

Harrison belonged to a distinguished Virginia family, his father Benjamin having signed the Declaration of Independence and served as governor of the state. The younger Harrison was born at Berkeley, the family estate in Charles City County, and at one time planned a medical career to please his father. At his father's death, however, Harrison abandoned medicine for the military and soon found himself on the northwestern frontier as an aide to General Anthony Wayne, where he participated in the Battle of Fallen Timbers (1794) and in the negotiations of the Treaty of Greenville (1795).

In 1798 Harrison was selected (over Northwest Territory governor Arthur St. Clair's son) as the territorial delegate to Congress, where he sponsored (but, as delegate, could not vote for) two significant pieces of legislation—the Harrison Land Act and the act creating the Indiana Territory, both adopted in 1800. Appointed governor of the new territory, an office he retained for 12 years, Harrison proved to be an able and resourceful negotiator of Indian treaties (12 in all) as well as an effective territorial administrator and politician. The proslavery, aristocratic nature of the "Harrison group" in Indiana, however, alienated many in the territory, who coalesced under the more Democratic leadership of Jonathan Jennings. In 1811, after direct negotiations with Tenskwatawa, the Shawnee prophet, and his brother, Tecumseh, had failed, Harrison and a unit of regular and militia troops prevailed over Indian forces led (in Tecumseh's absence) by Tenskwatawa. Harrison's victory at the Battle of Tippecanoe, fought on November 7, 1811, was instrumental in leading to the War of 1812, a contest in which Major General Harrison commanded the Army of the Northwest and defeated a combined British-Indian army at the Battle of the Thames in Canada in October 1813.

Following the war, Harrison returned to Ohio and reentered politics, serving successively as a Congressman, a state legislator, a United States Senator, and (briefly) as minister to Colombia. Recalled in 1829, he faced several personal misfortunes, but his well-publicized visits to anniversary celebrations of the battles of Tippecanoe and the Thames in the 1830s rekindled interest in Harrison as a national political figure. Nominated by a number of Whig state conventions in 1836, Harrison was one of four candidates for the presidency put forward by the new political party (an anti-Jackson coalition organized in 1834). Although Democrat Martin Van Buren was elected in 1836 over the combined Whig opposition of Harrison, W. P. Morgan, Daniel Webster, and Hugh Lawson White, the man from the Old Northwest proved the most popular of the Whig candidates and easily became the only Whig nominee in 1840. He was joined on the ticket by John Tyler, a dissident Democrat from Virginia, and "Tippecanoe and Tyler Too" were marched and paraded to victory over a discredited President Van Buren. The Whigs neglected to adopt a platform; instead, in ways that forever changed the nature of presidential campaigns, they ballyhooed their candidates into office, making effective use of songs, banners, parades, and symbols—especially a log cabin and a hard cider jug, thereby creating an inappropriate but nevertheless powerful myth about Harrison's humble origins.

See also: John Tyler, Martin Van Buren, Daniel Webster

Ralph D. Gray

REFERENCES

Barnhart, John D., and Dorothy L. Riker. 1971. *Indiana to 1816: The Colonial Period.* Indianapolis: Indiana Historical Bureau and Indiana Historical Society.

Buley, R. Carlyle. 1950. *The Old Northwest: Pioneer Period, 1815–1840.* Bloomington: Indiana U. Pr.

Cleaves, Freeman. 1939. *Old Tippecanoe: William Henry Harrison and His Time.* New York: Scribner's.

Goebel, Dorothy Burne. 1926. *William Henry Harrison: A Political Biography.* Indianapolis: Indiana Historical Bureau.

Gunderson, Robert Gray. 1957. *The Log Cabin Campaign.* Lexington: U. Pr. of Kentucky.

Peterson, Norma Lois. 1989. *The Presidencies of William Henry Harrison and John Tyler.* Lawrence: U. Pr. of Kansas.

William F. Harrity (1850–1912)

Pennsylvania politician and Democratic National Committee chairman. William Francis Harrity, who had been working closely with former President Grover Cleveland's political advisers at the 1892 Democratic National Convention, was elected Democratic National Committee chairman (1892–1896). A lawyer and trust company president by profession, Harrity spent a substantial portion of his career in party and public offices. He was chairman of the Democratic city committee of Philadelphia and a member of the executive committee of the Democratic state central committee. His efforts in the Cleveland campaign of 1884 won him the postmastership of Philadelphia.

When one of Pennsylvania's few Democratic governors, Robert E. Pattison, was reelected to that office in 1890, he chose Harrity as his secretary of the commonwealth. In cooperation with Congressman William L. Scott, a Grover Cleveland spokesman in Congress and the Democratic National Committee, Harrity built state support for Cleveland's renomination in 1892. Scott's unexpected death created a void in the Cleveland leadership, particularly on the national committee.

During his fatal illness, Scott arranged for Harrity to hold his proxy on the national committee. When Cleveland's supporters in Pennsylvania proposed Harrity as Scott's successor, they also intended that he replace Calvin S. Brice as national committee chairman. After several parliamentary skirmishes with the anti-Cleveland faction in Pennsylvania, Harrity was elected by the state central committee as national committeeman. By 1896 Harrity was forced off the national committee by the silverite supporters of William Jennings Bryan. In that election, he joined the Gold Democrats in their defection from the Democratic Party.

See also: William Jennings Bryan, Grover Cleveland, Democratic National Committee, Gold Democrats

Ralph M. Goldman

REFERENCES

Correspondence in Grover Cleveland Papers, Library of Congress.

Correspondence in William C. Whitney Papers, Library of Congress.

Goldman, Ralph M. 1990. *The National Party Chairmen and Committees: Factionalism at the Top.* Armonk, NY: M. E. Sharpe.

Hatch Acts of 1939 and 1940

One of the consequences of the New Deal was a tremendous increase in the size of the federal labor force, and a concomitant concern among those opposed to the Franklin Roosevelt administration was that this new army of federal government employees would become enlistees in the Democratic Party. The Hatch Act of 1939, also known as the Clean Politics Act, and the Hatch Act Amendments of 1940, were responses to these fears. The 1939 act, named for its sponsor Senator Carl A. Hatch (D-N.M.), prohibited political activity by those federal workers whose activity had not previously been constrained by the Pendleton Act of 1883; another provision of the Hatch Act prohibited political solicitation from federal employees, thus removing a source of revenue that had filled the coffers of several state and local political organizations. These constraints gave rise to the neologistic verb "to be hatched," meaning that an employee is covered by the restrictions of this legislation.

In 1940 Hatch introduced a series of amendments to the 1939 act. The goal of these amendments was to restrict the amount of money given to political candidates and the amount spent on campaigns. Individuals were restricted to contributions of $5,000 per year to a national committee or campaign for federal office; a total limit of $3 million per year was placed on the total contributions and expenditures of any political committee active in two or more states. While the second act went through the Senate with some ease, in the House an amendment was added that exempted state and local political committees from the $5,000 limit. Shortly after President Roosevelt signed the bill, the Republican National Committee advised contributors that contributions over $5,000 could still be sent to state and local committees.

The limitations of the second Hatch Act were repealed by the Federal Election Campaign Act. However, during their 30 years of existence they had little impact. While the goals of these acts were laudable, enforcement was lax and political committee after political committee found ways to avoid the restrictions intended.

See also: Civil Service Act of 1883, Federal Election Campaign Act, Political Action Committees, Franklin Roosevelt

L. Sandy Maisel

REFERENCES

Alexander, Herbert E. 1984. *Financing Politics: Money, Elections, and Political Reform.* 3rd ed. Washington: Congressional Quarterly.

Mutch, Robert E. 1988. *Campaigns, Congress, and Courts: The Making of Federal Campaign Finance Law.* Westport, CT: Praeger.

Richard G. Hatcher (1933–)

African-American mayor of Gary, Indiana. Richard Gordon Hatcher made history as one of the nation's first African-American mayors. His career reflected the conflict between Black political empowerment and local Democratic Party organizations.

Initially elected to the city council with Democratic Party support, Hatcher challenged the United States Steel Corporation, the Lake County Democratic machine, organized crime, and the local media. Hatcher sought and won the Democratic mayoral nomination in 1967. When he refused the party leaders' cash offer to cooperate, they switched to the Republican candidate. The polarized city seemed on the verge of violence. After Hatcher appealed to national Democrats, the Department of Justice halted election abuses by the machine, and Indiana's governor called out the National Guard. Hatcher narrowly won the general election, receiving over 90 percent of the Black vote and about 17 percent of the white vote, mostly from liberals.

As mayor, Hatcher faced a hostile party and city council. He drew on substantial federal aid, which in his first year exceeded the city's annual budget. Hatcher aggressively opposed machine rule and closed down organized criminal activities. His strong political organization and approval of his performance by the African-American community gave him a durable base.

By 1971 Hatcher had proven that he would last, and Gary's Democratic Party endorsed him. He was reelected four times and then in 1987 lost the Democratic Party nomination to a former Black ally, Thomas Barnes. After leaving office, Hatcher played a major role in Jesse Jackson's 1988 presidential campaign, leading the effort to define a new African-American political agenda.

Raphael J. Sonenshein

REFERENCES

Greer, Edward. 1971. "The 'Liberation' of Gary, Indiana." 8 *Trans-Action* 30.

Hadden, Jeffrey K., Louis H. Masotti, and Victor Thiessen. 1968. "The Making of the Negro Mayors 1967." 5 *Trans-Action* 21.

Keller, Edmond J. 1979. "Electoral Politics in Gary: Mayoral Performance, Organization, and the Political Economy of the Black Vote." 15 *Urban Affairs Quarterly* 43.

Levine, Charles H. 1974. *Racial Conflict and the American Mayor: Power, Polarization, and Performance.* Lexington, MA: Lexington Books.

Pettigrew, Thomas. 1971. "When a Black Candidate Runs for Mayor: Race and Voting Behavior." In Harlan Hahn, ed. *People and Politics in Urban Society.* Beverly Hills, CA: Sage.

Mark O. Hatfield (1922–)

Moderate Republican Senator from Oregon. In the early 1960s, Mark Odum Hatfield was among the rising stars in the Republican Party. His career in politics began with service in the Oregon state legislature from 1950 to 1956. Hatfield went on to be Oregon's secretary of state, a post he was elected to in 1956 and held until 1959, when he was elected as Oregon's youngest-ever governor. In that office, his primary interests included the economic enhancement of his state and the causes he had fought for in the state legislature: human rights, education, improved labor relations, and the preservation of the environment.

Hatfield's popularity in the national Republican Party was demonstrated when he was chosen to nominate Vice President Richard Nixon for President at the Republican National Convention in 1960. In addition, four years later Hatfield was picked to give the keynote address at the Republican National Convention.

The key issue in Hatfield's 1966 race for the Senate was America's involvement in the Vietnam War, a conflict he openly declared to be a civil war. His continued opposition to U.S. involvement in Vietnam, especially to the "indiscriminate" bombing of targets there, caused him to lose the high regard of national Republican leaders.

Hatfield's philosophy on international questions stems, in part, from his service in the Navy during World War II—service that allowed him to see first-hand the grisly aftermath of the atom bomb in Japan. While he entered the Navy an isolationist, he clearly left with a much-expanded view of American responsibilities abroad.

During his more than 20 years in the United States Senate, Hatfield, still officially a Republican, was fiercely independent. Among his legislative initiatives was the Hatfield-McGovern Amendment, which sought to set a deadline for the withdrawal of American troops in Indochina. He also regularly opposed military assistance to foreign nations and military appropriations for weapons systems. Furthermore, Hatfield repeatedly (and unsuccessfully) introduced the World Peace Tax Fund bill allowing conscientious objectors to earmark their tax dollars for nonmilitary programs. Hatfield's advocacy of peace and individual liberty was also apparent in his initiative to abolish the peacetime draft.

During his 1984 bid for a fourth Senate term, Hatfield's wife earned media attention for accepting money from a Greek entrepreneur whose $10 billion oil pipeline project had been supported by Senator Hatfield. While the Hatfields contended that the money was for Mrs. Hatfield's services as a real estate agent, they decided to donate the $55,000 total to charity to avoid the appearance of impropriety. After the Senate Ethics Committee investigated the circumstances and found insufficient grounds to pursue the matter, Hatfield defeated his Democratic challenger.

See also: Election of 1968, Isolationism in American Politics, Richard Nixon, Vietnam War as a Political Issue

Reagan Robbins

REFERENCES

Lichtenstein, Nelson, ed. 1976. *Political Profiles: The Johnson Years*. New York: Facts on File.

Schoenebaum, Eleanora W., ed. 1979. *Political Profiles: The Nixon/Ford Years*. New York: Facts on File.

Carl T. Hayden (1877–1972)

Longtime Democratic Senator from Arizona. Carl Trumbull Hayden, who served as Arizona's Senator from 1927 to 1969, was instrumental in securing passage of some of the most important irrigation and transportation legislation of the twentieth century. Born in his ancestor's town, Hayden's Ferry, Arizona (now Tempe), the young Carl Hayden, after graduating from Stanford University in 1900, returned to pursue various business interests. His long political career began with election to the Tempe Town Council in 1902. Following terms as county treasurer and county sheriff, Hayden was elected to the U.S. House of Representatives when Arizona became a state in 1912. During his tenure in the House, the Arizona Democrat began a lifelong campaign for conservation when he fought for legislation establishing the Grand Canyon National Park.

Hayden was elected to the Senate in 1926 and remained there for 42 years, serving as President *pro tempore* from 1957 to 1969. His long Senate career revealed three consistent trends. The Arizona Democrat rarely spoke in Senate debate, preferring to wield his influence in the cloakrooms. Yet he became one of its most powerful members, serving for many years as chairman of the Appropriations Committee. Moreover, throughout his Senate years, Hayden was a liberal Democrat, generally supporting the Democrats' social welfare legislation as well as its foreign policy. Most importantly, however, Hayden's legislative career was dedicated to promoting the interests of western states, including mining, water, reclamation, and transportation. Hayden was instrumental, for example, in framing the landmark 1956 Interstate Highway Act. During the 1950s he also was a vigorous champion of a massive federal irrigation measure, the Central Arizona Project, designed to divert water from the Colorado River to his arid state. This goal was finally realized in 1968 with the creation of the Colorado River Project. Thus, when he retired in 1969, after serving in the Senate longer than anyone in the upper chamber's annals, Hayden indeed left a mark on modern legislative history.

John W. Malsberger

REFERENCES

Colley, Charles C. 1977. "Carl Hayden–Phoenician." 18 *Journal of Arizona History* 247.

Rutherford B. Hayes (1822–1893)

Nineteenth President of the United States. Rutherford Birchard Hayes, an Ohio Republican, became President of the United States following the most controversial election in American history. Once in office, he ended Reconstruction in the South and restored public confidence in government.

Hayes's political career was wrought with close elections. The Cincinnati City Council elected him to an unexpired term as city solicitor in 1858: he won on the thirteenth ballot by a single vote. Hayes served in the Union Army during the Civil War and was elected to Congress while still in uniform. Reelected in 1866, he resigned when he received the Republican nomination for governor in 1867. He won the election by less than 1 percent of the total vote and was reelected two years later with only a slightly greater margin. After an unsuccessful run for Congress, Hayes retired to private life, only to be returned to the governorship in 1875 by less than 6,000 votes.

The 1876 Republican National Convention was held in Cincinnati, Hayes's political base. While not a front-runner, his repeated success in Ohio made Hayes a candidate worth consideration. Not the favorite of any of the party's factions, he was nonetheless acceptable to most delegates. After placing fifth among six candidates on the first ballot, Hayes clinched the nomination on the seventh ballot. William

Wheeler of New York was nominated for Vice President.

The Democratic Party selected New York governor Samuel J. Tilden, a political reformer, to oppose Hayes. Hayes had also called for reform, distancing himself from President Ulysses S. Grant's corrupt administration and effectively neutralizing the issue. By promising to serve only one term, Hayes vowed not to use the civil service as a tool for reelection.

Election returns gave Tilden 184 electoral college votes to Hayes's 165, with 20 votes from Oregon, Florida, South Carolina, and Louisiana in dispute. Tilden needed a single elector to gain victory. The partisan election boards in the latter three contested states threw out enough ballots on the grounds of fraud to make Hayes the winner. Rampant fraud occurred on both sides, however; in South Carolina, more votes were cast than there were eligible voters. With no laws to deal with disputed elections, the Republican Senate and the Democratic House agreed on a bipartisan commission to decide the election. Seven members of each party were to be joined by a political independent from the Supreme Court. When the independent member was elected to the Senate, he was replaced on the commission by a moderate Republican justice. The commission's votes followed straight partisan lines, and Hayes was declared the winner by an electoral count of 185 to 184.

As President, Hayes acted quickly to remove federal troops from the South. Some historians suggest that ending Reconstruction was part of a deal to ensure Hayes's electoral victory. Others argue that he was attempting to forge a coalition of northern Republicans and former Whigs in the South, but his efforts failed. Hayes also took steps toward ending patronage in the civil service system.

See also: Ulysses S. Grant, Reconstruction, Samuel Tilden

John A. Clark

REFERENCES

Davison, Kenneth E. 1972. *The Presidency of Rutherford B. Hayes.* Westport, CT: Greenwood.

Hoogenboom, Ari. 1988. *The Presidency of Rutherford B. Hayes.* Lawrence: U. of Kansas Pr.

Polakoff, Keith Ian. 1973. *The Politics of Inertia: The Election of 1876 and the End of Reconstruction.* Baton Rouge: Louisiana State U. Pr.

William H. Hays (1879–1954)

Republican politician and film arbiter. William Harrison Hays was national chairman of the Republican Party and Postmaster General under President Warren G. Harding. He eventually was lured away from party affairs in 1922 to be president of the motion picture industry's influential "Hays Office."

Hays's father was a prominent Indiana corporation lawyer, active in county and state Republican politics. Will graduated from Wabash College in 1900 and also took a master's degree there in 1904, writing a dissertation on the "Negro problem." Admitted to the Indiana bar at 21, he became a partner in his father's law firm (representing railroad and mining interests) and ran unsuccessfully as his party's nominee for prosecuting attorney.

A small man (5 ft. 4 in., 120 lbs.), Hays had inexhaustible energy. Consistently active, he rapidly moved up the ladder in Indiana politics. When the William Taft–Theodore Roosevelt conflict split the Indiana Republican organization in 1912, Hays was offered the state party chairmanship, but declined in favor of the vice chairmanship. After Taft became the regular party nominee, Hays worked vigorously for Taft's reelection. And after Taft's defeat, Hays went out of his way to cajole Progressive leaders back into the state's Republican Party. In 1914 he accepted the state chairmanship.

His organizational achievements in the 1916 Indiana campaign, which carried the state for the GOP, brought Hays to national attention. Reputed to know "more people by their first names than any other man in Indiana," Hays developed an impressively successful state political machine.

Success in Indiana vaulted Hays to the national chairmanship of the Republican Party in 1918. Hays immediately brought new life to the party's national headquarters: he traveled incessantly, established a permanent headquarters facility in Washington, and set up a party newspaper. Hays employed professional fundraisers and set a $1,000 limit on contributions that would be accepted by the national committee, both important innovations. His leadership in the 1918 midterm campaign resulted in a historic defeat for the Woodrow Wilson administration. By 1920, Republican leaders were in complete agreement that Hays should continue as chairman after the national convention and some spoke of him as a prospective presidential candidate.

Hays was reelected national chairman in 1920, resigning in 1921 to become President Harding's Postmaster General. In 1922 he became president of the Motion Picture Producers and Distributors of America, a position he held until 1945.

See also: Warren G. Harding, Woodrow Wilson

Ralph M. Goldman

REFERENCES

Goldman, Ralph M. 1990. *The National Party Chairmen and Committees: Factionalism at the Top.* Armonk, NY: M. E. Sharpe.

Greenlee, Howard S. 1950. "The Republican Party in Division and Reunion." Ph.D. dissertation, U. of Chicago.

Hays, Will. 1955. *Memoirs.* Garden City, NY: Doubleday.

Routt, Garland C. 1937. "Will Hays: A Study in Political Leadership and Management." M.A. thesis, U. of Chicago.

Alexander Heard (1917–)

Expert on campaign finance and elections. Alexander Heard enjoyed two distinguished careers—one as a scholar and the other as an academic administrator. In his early professional life, Heard made several important scholarly contributions. He was V. O. Key's research assistant on the monumental project that became Key's *Southern Politics in State and Nation* (1949). As Key's aide, Heard, along with Donald Strong, conducted many of the interviews with southern politicians and political elites, which served as part of the empirical foundation for this seminal work. The book was re-released by the University of Tennessee Press with a new introduction by Heard in 1984.

In 1950 Heard compiled and edited (with Donald Strong) *Southern Primaries and Elections*, and in 1952 he published *A Two-Party South?* These books, along with Key's work, helped to set the research agenda for a generation of political scientists interested in southern politics in particular and electoral politics in general. Heard's major scholarly contribution was made in *The Costs of Democracy* (1960). His was the first empirical research in the post–World War II era of political science to focus on campaign finance. Heard's book became the benchmark for a whole generation; his work helped launch the modern era of research on this increasingly important subject. Heard was also named by President John Kennedy in 1961 to chair the President's Commission on Campaign Costs.

From 1958 through 1963, Heard was dean of the Graduate School at the University of North Carolina at Chapel Hill. From that position he served as chancellor of Vanderbilt University from 1963 to 1985.

After retiring from his active administrative duties, Heard returned to research. In 1985, funded by the Russell Sage Foundation, he launched a study of the presidential nominations process. The project focused on the presidential nominations process with contributions written especially for the study by the leading scholars in this field. Heard's work on presidential elections was a natural outgrowth of his earlier interest in campaign finance and his work on southern primaries and the growth of the two-party South. In 1988 the American Political Science Association awarded *The Costs of Democracy* the Leon Epstein Outstanding Book Award for the field of political organizations and parties.

See also: Campaign Finance and the Constitution, V. O. Key, Southern Politics

John S. Jackson III

REFERENCES

Heard, Alexander. 1952. *A Two-Party South?* Chapel Hill: U. of North Carolina Pr.

———. 1960. *The Costs of Democracy.* Chapel Hill: U. of North Carolina Pr.

———, and Michael Nelson, eds. 1987. *Presidential Selection.* Durham: Duke U. Pr.

———, and Donald Strong. 1950. *Southern Primaries and Elections, 1920–1949.* University: U. of Alabama Pr.

Key, V. O., Jr. 1949. *Southern Politics in State and Nation.* New York: Knopf.

William Randolph Hearst (1863–1951)

Journalistic mogul and would-be Democratic politician. Born in San Francisco to wealthy parents, William Randolph Hearst moved to New York City in 1895 and began to forge what would become the nation's greatest newspaper empire. In his distortion and sensationalism of the news, Hearst became a leading practitioner of "yellow journalism." Craving both the presidency and immense wealth, he obtained only the latter, for the prize he so covetously treasured—the White House—always eluded him.

In his early days, Hearst portrayed himself as a champion of progressive reform, at the same time, paradoxically, aligning himself with the powerful Tammany Hall machine of New York. Supported by the political bosses, he served two successive terms from 1903 to 1907 as a Democratic Congressman from New York City. In 1904 he waged a strong but fruitless effort to wrest the Democratic presidential nomination from Alton B. Parker.

With his eye on the 1908 nomination, Hearst next ran for mayor of New York City in 1905.

Abandoning the bosses to run independently, he narrowly lost to Democrat George B. McClellan (224,925 to 228,397). Undaunted, Hearst temporarily mended his political fences with Tammany but suffered yet another heart-breaking defeat in the 1906 gubernatorial contest—losing to Republican Charles Evans Hughes by a scant 58,000 votes out of 1.5 million cast.

These setbacks, along with accusations of demagoguery and an inability to placate party potentates, effectively shattered Hearst's quest for high office. Still, through control of his vast communications network, he continued to wield a strong, albeit conservative, influence in American politics until his death.

See also: Charles Evans Hughes, Tammany Hall

Karl G. Valois

REFERENCES

Carlson, Oliver, and Ernest S. Bates. 1936. *Hearst, Lord of San Simeon*. New York: Viking.

Coblentz, Edmond D., ed. 1952. *William Randolph Hearst: A Portrait in His Own Words*. New York: Simon & Schuster.

Swanberg, W. A. 1961. *Citizen Hearst: A Biography of William Randolph Hearst*. New York: Scribner's.

Tebbel, John. 1952. *The Life and Good Times of William Randolph Hearst*. New York: Dutton.

Winkler, John Kennedy. 1955. *William Randolph Hearst: A New Appraisal*. New York: Hastings House.

Jesse A. Helms (1921–)

Controversial Republican Senator from North Carolina. Jesse Alexander Helms was educated at Wingate College and Wake Forest University, before working as an editor of the *Raleigh Times* and serving in World War II. Helms returned to work in the media, this time as a television news program director from 1948 to 1951. From 1951 to 1953, he served as administrative assistant to Senators Willis Smith and Alton Lennon, both Democrats from North Carolina. From 1953 to 1960 he was executive director of the North Carolina Bankers Association and from 1960 to 1972 the executive vice president of Capitol Broadcasting Company in Raleigh.

Originally a Democrat, Helms switched parties in 1970, and in 1972 he defeated Nick Galifiankis, a popular and heavily favored Democratic member of the U.S. House, to become the first Republican Senator elected from North Carolina in the twentieth century. In the Senate, Helms, a staunch anti-Communist, became a champion of such conservative social causes as school prayer and right to life.

In line with his increased national visibility, Helms has received considerable financial support from conservative political action committees (PACs). He organized the National Congressional Club, which funds conservative candidates for Congress. In the 1984 Senate race, Helms defeated popular Governor James Hunt; the election was not only bitterly contested, but it was also the most expensive Senate contest in history. Helms served as ranking member and chairman of the Agriculture, Nutrition, and Forestry Committee. But in a surprising move in 1987, he relinquished this position to become the ranking minority member of the Foreign Relations Committee. In 1990 Helms defeated Harvey Gantt, an African-American who was the former mayor of Charlotte, in another extremely expensive and bitterly negative campaign for the Senate—a campaign marked by racist posturing and innuendo in its final weeks. Not surprisingly, Helms continues to be considered a leading figure for the Far Right in national politics.

See also: James Hunt, Political Action Committees

Thomas J. Baldino

REFERENCES

Furgurson, Ernest B. 1986. *Hard Right: The Rise of Jesse Helms*. New York: Norton.

Snider, William D. 1985. *Helms and Hunt: The North Carolina Senate Race, 1984*. Chapel Hill: U. of North Carolina Pr.

David B. Henderson (1840–1906)

Iowa Republican Speaker of the U.S. House. David Brenner Henderson was a ten-term Iowa Republican Congressman who served as Speaker of the House from 1899 to 1903 when he declined to seek reelection. Born in Scotland, Henderson moved as a child with his parents to the United States, eventually settling in northeastern Iowa. He left college to join the Union Army; a war injury required partial amputation of his leg. After the war Henderson began practicing law and held minor federal offices until 1882 when he won election to the House of Representatives from Iowa.

Politically, Henderson was a "stand-pat" Republican who worked for Civil War veterans' pensions, supported protective tariff legislation and the gold standard, and sponsored the first important bankruptcy bill in Congress. Before his election as Speaker he served on several powerful committees, including Appropriations, Judiciary, and Rules. His tariff and gold-standard positions put him at odds with progressive Iowa Republicans. That growing opposition and his own declining health from war injuries combined to convince him not to seek reelection in 1903. During a period of strong leadership by Speakers of the House, Henderson was neither as powerful nor as effective as his predecessor (Thomas B. Reed) or his successor (Joseph G. Cannon).

See also: Joseph Cannon, Thomas B. Reed, Speaker of the House

Nicholas C. Burckel

REFERENCES

Hoing, William L. 1957. "David B. Henderson: Speaker of the House." 55 *Iowa Journal of History* 1.

Smith, William Henry. 1971. *Speakers of the House of Representatives of the United States.* New York: AMS Press.

Thomas A. Hendricks (1819–1885)

Leading Democratic Indiana politician for more than three decades. Thomas Andrews Hendricks served successively in the United States House of Representatives, in the U.S. Senate, as Indiana's governor, and as Vice President under Grover Cleveland. A lifelong Democrat, Hendricks began his political career in the Indiana General Assembly in 1848 and was a member of the second Indiana Constitutional Convention of 1850–1851. Popular and well spoken, Hendricks made the first of his three campaigns for the governor's seat in 1860, but the state and then the nation turned Republican in that year. Hendricks was, nevertheless, elected to the United States Senate in 1863.

It was Hendricks's fate to serve in a Republican-dominated Senate, where he was one of the twelve Democrats (eventually joined by seven Republicans) to oppose President Andrew Johnson's impeachment and where he resisted other measures of the Radical Republicans, including the three "Civil War" amendments to the Constitution. "The Union as it was, the Constitution as it is" was the rallying cry of Hendricks and his few fellow Democrats.

In 1868 Senator Hendricks again ran for governor (knowing the Republican-controlled legislature would not return him to the Senate), but he failed in the election by fewer than a thousand votes. In 1872, however, he was elected to the office, thus becoming the first Democrat from a northern state after the Civil War to be so honored. While still governor, Hendricks was chosen to run with presidential candidate Samuel J. Tilden on the national Democratic ticket in 1876, the year of the famous "disputed election" and an eventual Republican victory. Hendricks went on to become Grover Cleveland's successful running mate in 1884.

Installed as Vice President in March 1885, Hendricks died the following November.

Hendricks's political career exemplifies the "swing state" nature of Indiana politics during the latter half of the nineteenth century as well as the state's relative importance in the electoral process at that time. In six of seven elections immediately after the Civil War, a Hoosier (usually teamed with a New Yorker) ran for either President or Vice President. Three of the men—Schuyler Colfax, Hendricks, and Benjamin Harrison—were elected.

See also: Grover Cleveland, Schuyler Colfax, Benjamin Harrison, Andrew Johnson, Radical Republicans, Samuel Tilden

Ralph D. Gray

REFERENCES

Gray, Ralph D. 1977. "Thomas A. Hendricks: Spokesman for the Democracy." In Ralph D. Gray, ed. *Gentlemen from Indiana: National Party Candidates, 1836–1940.* Indianapolis: Indiana Historical Society.

Holcombe, John W., and Hubert M. Skinner. 1886. *Life and Public Service of Thomas A. Hendricks, with Selected Speeches and Writings.* Indianapolis: Carlon and Hollenbeck.

Memorial Addresses on the Life and Character of Thomas A. Hendricks. Senate Miscellaneous Document No. 120, 49th Congress, 1st session.

Thornbrough, Emma Lou. 1965. *Indiana in the Civil War Era, 1850–1880.* Indianapolis: Indiana Historical Bureau and Indiana Historical Society.

Aaron Henry (1922–)

Leader of the civil rights movement from Mississippi. Aaron Henry, an African-American pharmacist from Clarksdale, Mississippi, was one of the key leaders of the civil rights movement in his state in the turbulent 1960s, serving as president of the Mississippi NAACP. He committed himself to voter registration efforts as a way of freeing many whites as well as Blacks and was chosen to run for governor on the Freedom Ballot in 1963 in a mock election.

Henry was one of the founders of the primarily Black Mississippi Freedom Democratic Party (MFDP) in 1964, which set up a parallel process to select delegates to attend the national Democratic convention and challenge the regular Democratic Party delegation. As a political realist who sought a mainstream political coalition of Blacks and whites that would ultimately take over the regular Democratic organization, he unsuccessfully urged the MFDP national delegation to accept the Credentials Committee compromise over the seating of the two delegations.

After radical Blacks gained control of the MFDP, Henry became chair of a new biracial coalition loyal to the principles of the national Democratic Party, called the Loyalist Democratic Party, which successfully gained control of the Young Democrats charter. Henry became the chief fundraiser and builder of the Loyalist Party. Henry chaired the Loyalist delegations to the 1968 and 1972 Democratic national conventions, both of which unseated the regular Democratic delegations. Out of gratitude to the Credentials Committee in 1972, Henry sided with the committee and political "professionals" on retroactively abolishing the winner-take-all system in California, causing many Mississippi supporters of California winner George McGovern to reject his position on this issue.

Henry was an early supporter of unification between the Loyalists and regular Democrats, urging a fifty-fifty split of convention delegates and places on the party executive committee. Unification began with the state delegation to the 1974 midterm Democratic Conference, co-chaired by Henry and moderate governor William Waller. Unification was accomplished by 1976, and the Mississippi delegation to the Democratic National Convention was co-chaired by Henry and a regular Democrat. Aaron Henry cautioned African-Americans against supporting Black independent candidates instead of white Democratic Party nominees, fearing that Blacks would lose the substantial position they had gained in the contemporary Democratic Party. Retaining his NAACP presidency, Henry was elected to the Mississippi House of Representatives in 1979.

See also: George McGovern, National Association for the Advancement of Colored People

Stephen D. Shaffer

REFERENCES

Bass, Jack, and Walter DeVries. 1977. *The Transformation of Southern Politics*. New York: New American Library.

Holtzclaw, Robert. 1984. *Black Magnolias: A Brief History of the Afro-Mississippian, 1865–1980*. Shaker Heights, OH: Keeble Press.

Lamis, Alexander. 1984. *The Two-Party South*. New York: Oxford U. Pr.

Patrick Henry (1736–1799)

Most celebrated political orator of Virginia's revolutionary generation. Patrick Henry used his rhetorical skills ("Give me liberty or give me death!") to influence public opinion during the turbulent years between the Stamp Act Crisis (1765) and the adoption of the Constitution (1788). The notoriety he gained as a young defense lawyer in the Parson's Cause (1763) helped assure his first election to the House of Burgesses, and his persuasive powers with the freeholders brought him 20 more electoral victories over a 35-year period. Ten days after his first election, he convinced his fellow Burgesses to pass the Stamp Act Resolves (1765), challenging Parliament's right to tax the colonies. In 1774 he again encouraged the passage of resolutions denouncing a new set of punitive laws imposed on Boston.

Although Patrick Henry dealt with patriots outside his home colony/state, his orientation was always provincial. Consequently, his actions throughout the Revolutionary era were guided first and foremost by what he thought was best for Virginia. He argued for proportional representation in the First Continental Congress because that would favor Virginia, and he thought in terms of a "Virginia Declaration of Independence" rather than the document finally written by Thomas Jefferson. Like George Mason, he opposed the new federal Constitution in 1788 both because it lacked a bill of rights and because the proposed legislative districts, he believed, would be much too large to be workable.

John G. Kolp

REFERENCES

Beeman, Richard R. 1974. *Patrick Henry: A Biography*. New York: McGraw-Hill.

Mayer, Henry. 1986. *A Son of Thunder: Patrick Henry and the American Republic*. New York: Franklin Watts.

Morgan, Edmund S. 1988. *Inventing the People: The Rise of Popular Sovereignty in England and America*. New York: Norton.

Sydnor, Charles S. 1952. *Gentlemen Freeholders*. Chapel Hill: U. of North Carolina Pr.

Abram S. Hewitt (1822–1903)

A Democratic National Committee chairman during the Rutherford Hayes–Samuel Tilden disputed election. In a rags-to-riches career, Abram Stevens Hewitt was reared in poverty. In New York City, Hewitt entered the Grammar School of Columbia College as a free student and, later, at Columbia College, earned his way, in part, by tutoring.

At 22, suffering from eye strain, Hewitt gave up the legal studies on which he had already entered to become a partner in the management of an iron mill. By 1847 Cooper & Hewitt was the firm name.

Hewitt cast his first vote for the Whig national ticket in 1848. However, inclination and personal friendships soon brought him into the Democratic Party. Hewitt's New York residence was just across Gramercy Park from Samuel Tilden. In 1871 Hewitt joined Tilden and Edward Cooper in their efforts to reform the Tammany Hall Democratic machine. Thereafter, Hewitt continued to be closely identified with civic reform in New York City.

When Samuel Tilden ran for governor of New York in 1874, Hewitt put time, money, and oratory into the campaign. Tilden urged Hewitt to run for Congress so that he could have a close friend in Washington while he made his own way as a reform governor in Albany. Both men were elected. In Washington, Congressman Hewitt served as Tilden's advance scout in national party affairs.

Although Tilden won 250,000 more popular votes than Rutherford B. Hayes in 1876, the result in the Electoral College was 184 for Tilden and 165 for Hayes, with 20 votes in dispute. As Democratic national chairman, Hewitt was at the center of congressional negotiations on the disputed election. The Special Election Commission gave the disputed returns, hence, the election, to Hayes. Hewitt, blamed for the defeat, resigned from the chairmanship.

Hewitt continued to be active in Democratic politics as New York's national committeeman for another seven years and as U.S. Congressman for four terms. He was elected mayor of New York City in 1887 and was often mentioned for the presidency. In 1896, he joined the Gold Democratic bolt that contributed to the William Jennings Bryan's defeat.

See also: William Jennings Bryan, Democratic National Committee, Gold Democrats, Rutherford Hayes, Tammany Hall, Samuel Tilden

Ralph M. Goldman

REFERENCES

Goldman, Ralph M. 1990. *The National Party Chairmen and Committees: Factionalism at the Top.* Armonk, NY: M. E. Sharpe.

Nevins, Allan. 1935. *Abram S. Hewitt.* New York: Harper & Bros.

———. 1937. *Selected Writings of Abram S. Hewitt.* New York: Columbia U. Pr.

David B. Hill (1843–1910)

Classic leader of the Gilded Age Democrats. David Bennett Hill was born in Havana, New York, studied law in Elmira, and was admitted to the bar in 1864. Well positioned, as an able upstate Democrat, to exploit the rivalries between New York City and upstate factions, Hill wielded considerable influence. He served in every state party convention from 1865 to 1881 and presided over those in 1877 and 1881. Elected to the New York Assembly in 1871, his talents were noted by Samuel J. Tilden, and he was elected Speaker in 1872 and actively promoted Tilden's political ambitions. In 1882 he was elected mayor of Elmira but resigned upon his election as lieutenant governor on a ticket with Grover Cleveland. Succeeding Cleveland upon the latter's elevation to the White House in 1885, Hill served two additional terms as a moderate reform governor. He reduced the hours of state employees, abolished contract labor in the prisons, and established forest preserves, while preserving a strong party organization based on patronage.

In 1881 Hill was elected to the U.S. Senate and used this position to challenge Cleveland for the presidential nomination in 1892. Although agrarian discontent abounded, Hill was too conventional in his policies to win over enough dissidents, and he had frightened some regulars with questionable preconvention tactics. (A quickly-held "snap" convention awarded New York's delegates to Hill.) He generally supported Cleveland in the latter's troubled second term, but the shift of the Democrats to William Jennings Bryan in 1896 left Hill politically isolated. He ran unsuccessfully for governor in 1894 and permanently retired from the Senate in 1897.

See also: William Jennings Bryan, Grover Cleveland, Speaker of the House, Samuel Tilden

Phyllis F. Field

REFERENCES

Bass, Herbert J. 1961. *"I Am a Democrat": The Political Career of David Bennett Hill.* Syracuse: Syracuse U. Pr.

John F. Hill (1855–1912)

Republican National Committee chairman during the Taft administration. Although educated as a physician, in 1879 John Fremont Hill began instead to publish periodical journals. Ten years later, he was elected to the house of representatives in Maine, and in 1892 moved on to the state senate. He served as a member of the Maine Executive Council in 1898 and 1899, winning election as governor for the two terms beginning in 1901 and 1903.

An intimate friend of Boston-bred Frank H. Hitchcock, the Republican national chairman in 1908 and 1909, Hill became an important factor in mobilizing northeastern support during William Howard Taft's prenomination campaign, leading to Hill's election to the national committee. On the eve of President Taft's 1909 inauguration, Chairman Hitchcock appointed Hill vice chairman of the national committee, a position usually filled by election and thus a significant point of contention in 1911 and 1912.

Hill's selection as vice chairman was intended to keep the national committee in friendly hands after Hitchcock's resignation. Hill automatically became acting chairman, and served in this position until 1911, when the national committee formally elected him chairman. At the same time, as the result of an agreement between Hitchcock and Hill, Victor Rosewater of Nebraska was appointed vice chairman by the executive committee, again a breach of procedure. Hill fell ill and died the following March, and Rosewater became acting chairman until the beginning of the 1912 national convention.

See also: Republican National Committee, William Howard Taft

Ralph M. Goldman

REFERENCES

Goldman, Ralph M. 1990. *The National Party Chairmen and Committees: Factionalism at the Top.* Armonk, NY: M. E. Sharpe.

Rosewater, Victor. 1932. *Backstage in 1912.* Philadelphia: Dorrance.

Charles D. Hilles (1867–1949)

Republican National Committee chairman after the Bull Moose revolt. Charles Dewey Hilles, secretary to President William Howard Taft, became national committee chairman of the Republican Party (1912–1916) at the time of the bolt of the Theodore Roosevelt Progressives.

Born in Ohio, Hilles went to Oxford Academy in Maryland and devoted over 20 years to youth welfare work; 15 of those years were spent as an officer and eventually president of the Boys' Industrial School at Lancaster, Ohio. In 1902 Hilles was hired as superintendent of the New York Juvenile Asylum at Dobbs Ferry, but he maintained his Republican connections in Ohio, helping in the Taft campaign in 1908. He also became well known among Republican leaders in New York. His work for the party led to his appointment as assistant secretary of the treasury in 1909. Thenceforth, Hilles was frequently mentioned for Republican state chairman in New York.

As 1912 approached, former President Roosevelt, disenchanted with the conservatism of his former protégé, prepared to challenge Taft's renomination. Anticipating a difficult

national convention, Taft appointed Hilles as his private secretary and put him in charge of preconvention operations. Defeated for the presidential nomination by a narrow margin in the Republican National Convention, Roosevelt helped launch the Progressive Party and became its nominee, thus assuring Taft's defeat in the election. At Taft's request, Hilles reluctantly accepted the Republican national chairmanship out of affection for the President. No one else cared to manage a campaign bound for certain defeat.

After the election, Chairman Hilles succeeded in having the convention apportionment rules changed, thereby reducing southern over-representation. He refused to support Charles E. Hughes for the nomination in 1916 because Hughes would be unlikely to reward the party's workers. Hilles continued as a member of the national committee until 1946, pursuing his livelihood as an insurance company executive.

See also: Republican National Committee, Theodore Roosevelt, William Howard Taft

Ralph M. Goldman

REFERENCES

Goldman, Ralph M. 1990. *The National Party Chairmen and Committees: Factionalism at the Top.* Armonk, NY: M. E. Sharpe.

Nicholas Murray Butler Papers, Columbia University, New York City.

Pringle, Henry F. 1939. *The Life and Times of William Howard Taft.* New York: Farrar and Rinehart.

Rosewater, Victor. 1932. *Backstage in 1912.* Philadelphia: Dorrance.

James Hillhouse (1754–1832)

Federalist legislator from New England. A Representative and Senator from Connecticut, James Hillhouse's political career accurately reflected the strong Federalist tendencies of his region. Hillhouse was born in Montville, Connecticut, but was educated in New Haven after being adopted by his uncle; he graduated from Yale in 1773. He studied law and subsequently inherited his uncle's lucrative New Haven practice. Hillhouse saw military service locally during the Revolutionary War, then began his political career in the state house of representatives from 1780 to 1785. He was a member of the upper house, the Council in 1790. Although he was chosen as a Connecticut delegate to the Continental Congress in 1786, 1787, and 1788, he never attended. He was elected a Federalist Representative to the Second, Third, and Fourth Congresses, serving from 1791 until his resignation in 1796 to take the Senate seat surrendered by Oliver Ellsworth. Hillhouse remained in the U.S. Senate until June 1810 when he resigned to become commissioner of the School Fund in Connecticut. Hillhouse dedicated himself to the School Fund with great success until his resignation in 1825 leaving the Connecticut public schools in sound financial and educational shape. Throughout his time he also served as the treasurer of Yale College, a post that he held for 50 years (1782–1832).

Hillhouse was a Federalist from his early days, but when the Republicans took over the government he underwent the curious transformation that so often affects the "ins" when they become "outs." In Hillhouse's case, the transformation was confirmed when this stout supporter of the executive prerogatives of George Washington and John Adams offered a series of seven constitutional amendments in 1808 designed to curb the power of the President. They included a call for annual election of United States Representatives, three-year terms in the Senate, the abolition of the vice presidency, a one-year term for the President who was to be chosen by lot from among the Senators, the confirmation of executive appointments by the House as well as the Senate, and the ratification by both houses of all removals from office. His proposals were an appropriate prelude to his participation in the 1816 Hartford Convention, the graphic statement that the New England Federalists recognized their own permanent minority status within the Republic.

See also: John Adams, Federalist Party, George Washington

Kathryn A. Malone

Sidney Hillman (1887–1946)

Labor organizer and progressive political reformer. Sidney Hillman became the single most important labor leader in Franklin D. Roosevelt's New Deal coalition. Born in Zagare, Lithuania, Hillman immigrated to Chicago in 1907, first becoming involved in the American union movement during a United Garment Workers Union of America (UGW) strike against clothiers Hart, Schaffner, and Marx four years later. Hillman split with the UGW in 1914 and moved to New York, where he became president of the Amalgamated Clothing Workers of America (ACWA).

The ACWA grew tremendously from 1916 to 1919, and Hillman, influenced by Progressives Florence Kelly, Felix Frankfurter, and Louis Brandeis, and such advocates of scientific management as William Leiserson and Meyer Jacobstein, sought to shape the enlarged ACWA into a model of "new Unionism." The ACWA called for greater shop-floor worker participation in decision-making and an institutional means of resolving labor-management grievances. Hillman created a tighter internal hierarchy within the ACWA itself, offered his members subsidized housing, and formed a cooperative labor bank. Under his leadership, the ethnically diverse ACWA became a coherent example of progressive unionism.

Along with a coalition of other Progressives and Socialists, Hillman endorsed Robert La Follette for President in 1924. Hillman's real era of political influence, however, came in the 1930s and 1940s. A founder and the first vice president of the Congress of Industrial Organizations (CIO), Hillman with John L. Lewis created Labor's Non-Partisan League (LNPL), which in practice gradually drifted into the Democratic Party's camp. The LNPL supported Roosevelt in 1936. In 1940, however, Hillman and Lewis split over politics, with Lewis abandoning Roosevelt and the Democratic Party.

Hillman held numerous posts within the Roosevelt administration, beginning with his appointment to the National Recovery Administration's Labor Relations Board. During the war he played a key role in quieting labor unrest as associate director in the Office of Production Management. More importantly, Hillman was a personal confidante of President Roosevelt; his influence was most keenly felt in 1944 when he orchestrated the removal of Henry Wallace from the 1944 Democratic presidential ticket.

Still Hillman's political influence had limits. In 1944 he founded the CIO's political action committee, whose "People's Program" called for full employment and a wide range of federally sponsored social policies. The Democratic Party did not embrace the People's Program. Indeed, the Republicans successfully attacked Roosevelt in the 1944 election for too closely adhering to Hillman's ideas.

See also: Robert La Follette, New Deal, Franklin D. Roosevelt, Henry Wallace

John Walsh

REFERENCES

Josephson, Matthew. 1952. *Sidney Hillman: Statesman of American Labor.* Garden City, NY: Doubleday.

Morris Hillquit (1869–1933)

Socialist politician, theorist, lawyer, and writer. Morris Hillquit was born in Russia of Jewish parents and immigrated to New York City's East Side in 1881. Active early in New York radical circles, Hillquit worked as a clerk for the Socialist Labor Party (SLP) while attending law school at the City University of New York; he got his degree in 1893.

Quickly establishing himself as a leading Socialist tactician, by the late 1890s Hillquit stood second only to Daniel De Leon in the SLP. He broke with De Leon in 1899 over De Leon's policy of forming Socialist unions to rival the American Federation of Labor (AFL). Taking a minority of SLP members with him, Hillquit joined with Eugene Debs and Victor Berger to form the Socialist Party of America (SPA) in 1901.

Hillquit became a major force in the SPA. Sitting on its executive committee, he guided SPA toward a moderate, nonrevolutionary path. He favored working with the AFL, a position that angered the syndicalist Industrial Workers of the World, whose fire-breathing leader, William Haywood, was expelled by the SPA in 1913. Hillquit also believed that the SPA should be active in both national and municipal politics. Many times an unsuccessful candidate for Congress and once defeated for mayor of New York City, Hillquit nonetheless was pivotal in organizing party politics in New York.

In 1917 Hillquit drafted the majority report of the SPA opposing American entry into Word War I. Although he himself was not indicated, several other Socialists, including Eugene Debs and Victor Berger, were convicted of sedition for their antiwar stance.

As the SPA fell apart in the postwar era, Hillquit sought to form still another labor party to support Progressive Robert La Follette. When other Socialists failed to support La Follette, the new labor party never materialized.

See also: Eugene V. Debs, Daniel De Leon, Robert La Follette, Socialist Labor Party, Socialism in American Politics

John Walsh

REFERENCES

Pratt, Norma Fain. 1979. *Morris Hillquit: A Political History of an American Jewish Socialist.* Westport, CT: Greenwood.

Alger Hiss (1904–)

Victim of McCarthyism. Raised in Baltimore and graduated from Johns Hopkins University, Alger Hiss was a protégé of Felix Frankfurter at Harvard Law School and became a law clerk for Justice Oliver Wendell Holmes in 1929. After several years with prestigious law firms, in 1933 Hiss became one of the many talented young lawyers migrating to Washington to staff various New Deal agencies. He became a prototype of the liberal New Deal idealists of the 1930s.

In 1936 Hiss joined the State Department and rose swiftly through its bureaucracy. He was a part of the State Department delegation accompanying President Franklin Roosevelt to the Yalta conference in 1945 and served as temporary secretary general at the United Nation's founding conference. In 1946 doubts about Hiss's loyalty developed, and his promotions ceased. In 1947 Hiss resigned to become president of the Carnegie Endowment.

In 1948, Whittaker Chambers, a *Time* magazine editor and former Communist, testified before the House Un-American Activities Committee (HUAC) that he had known Hiss as a Communist. Hiss denied the charge and sued Chambers. Chambers, however, produced documents implicating Hiss in Soviet espionage, and a grand jury indicted Hiss for perjury. Hiss's first trial produced a hung jury, but the second convicted and imprisoned him from 1951 until 1954.

The Hiss-Chambers case gave a major boost both to the career of Congressman Richard Nixon (R-Calif.), the HUAC member who had pushed hardest to pursue the affair, as well as to the growth of public and political concern with domestic communism in the late 1940s and 1950s. The case was a cause célèbre from the day of Chambers's testimony, and emotions about the affair remained strong into the 1990s.

See also: House Un-American Activities Committee, New Deal, Richard Nixon, Franklin Roosevelt, United Nations

John E. Haynes

REFERENCES

Chambers, Whittaker. 1952. *Witness.* New York: Random House.

Cooke, Alistair. 1950. *Generation on Trial.* New York: Knopf.

Hiss, Alger. 1957. *In the Court of Public Opinion.* New York: Knopf.

———. 1988. *Recollections of a Life.* New York: Seaver/Henry Holt.

Levitt, Morton, and Michael Levitt. 1979. *A Tissue of Lies: Nixon vs. Hiss.* New York: McGraw-Hill.

Smith, John Chabot. 1976. *Alger Hiss: The True Story.* New York: Holt, Rinehart & Winston.

Weinstein, Allen. 1978. *Perjury: The Hiss-Chambers Case.* New York: Knopf.

Frank H. Hitchcock (1867–1935)

National chairman of the Republican Party under Taft. President William Howard Taft's Postmaster General, Frank Harris Hitchcock was the son of an Ohio Congregationalist clergyman, went to Harvard in 1887, was active in the Young Republican movement, and was elected precinct committeeman.

While a junior civil servant in the Agriculture Department in Washington, Hitchcock studied law at Columbian (later George Washington) University, graduating in 1895. He was friendly with another part-time student, George B. Cortelyou, secretary to President Grover Cleveland.

When Cortelyou became secretary of the new Department of Commerce and Labor in 1903, he invited Hitchcock to become the department's chief clerk. During Cortelyou's tenure as Republican national chairman and manager of Theodore Roosevelt's election campaign, he appointed Hitchcock as assistant secretary of the national committee. In 1905, Hitchcock followed Cortelyou into the Post Office Department as First Assistant Postmaster General. In 1907 Theodore Roosevelt appointed Cortelyou Secretary of the Treasury, thus giving Hitchcock a freer hand in distributing patronage to those—particularly in the South—who were most likely to be Roosevelt loyalists at the 1908 national convention. On January 19, 1908, Hitchcock resigned from the Post Office Department in order to be full-time manager of the Taft preconvention campaign.

Elected to the chairmanship, Hitchcock ran a tightly controlled and successful campaign for Taft. He was rewarded with the postmaster generalship in 1909. Some of his innovations in the post office earned him the title "Father of the United States airmail."

Hitchcock served as Postmaster General until 1913, after which he practiced law, published a newspaper in Arizona, and operated a mining company. He remained active in GOP affairs, as Arizona's national committeeman until 1932, and as manager of Charles E. Hughes's preconvention campaign in 1916.

See also: Grover Cleveland, Charles Evans Hughes, Theodore Roosevelt, Young Republicans

Ralph M. Goldman

REFERENCES

Goldman, Ralph M. 1990. *The National Party Chairmen and Committees: Factionalism at the Top.* Armonk, NY: M. E. Sharpe.

George F. Hoar (1826–1904)

Leading Republican Senator in the late nineteenth century. George Frisbie Hoar castigated William McKinley's annexation policy but nonetheless fought for and helped secure the President's reelection in 1900. Initially a Free Soiler, Hoar joined the Republican Party upon its formation. In 1869 he was elected from Massachusetts to the U.S. House of Representatives. Eight years later he entered the Senate, remaining there until his death.

A member of the Electoral Commission of 1877, Hoar cast a partisan vote to give disputed electoral votes to the victorious Rutherford B. Hayes but sincerely believed that doing so reflected the will of the majority of voters in the contested states. Hoar chaired the Republican convention in 1880 and at crucial points rendered platform decisions that permitted the dark-horse nomination of James A. Garfield. After the 1880s witnessed the increasing suppression of the Black vote in the South, Hoar led the unsuccessful Republican effort to enact a federal elections law in 1890.

As a U.S. Senator, Hoar played a leading part in formulating Republican doctrines of reliable currency, tariff protection, and overseas market expansion. But during the Spanish-American War he drew the line at territorial imperialism and was the leading Senate critic of the McKinley administration's plan to annex the Philippines. Denouncing annexation on constitutional, moral, and strategic grounds, he was one of only two Republicans to vote against the Treaty of Paris. Still, a committed Republican who chose to fight imperialism from within the Republican Party, Hoar endorsed McKinley's 1900 reelection and triumphantly won a fifth Senate term himself the next year.

See also: Free Soil Party, James A. Garfield, Rutherford B. Hayes, William McKinley

Charles W. Calhoun

REFERENCES

Beisner, Robert L. 1968. *Twelve Against Empire: The Anti-Imperialists of 1898–1900.* New York: McGraw-Hill.

Hoar, George F. 1903. *Autobiography of Seventy Years.* 2 vols. New York: Scribner's.

Tompkins, E. Berkeley. 1970. *Anti-Imperialism in the United States: The Great Debate, 1890–1920.* Philadelphia: U. of Pennsylvania Pr.

Welch, Richard E., Jr. 1971. *George Frisbie Hoar and the Half-Breed Republicans.* Cambridge: Harvard U. Pr.

Homestead Act

On May 20, 1862, Abraham Lincoln signed the Homestead Act into law. This act enabled heads of households or males or females 21 years of age or older, who were citizens or who had filed a declaration to become citizens, to claim 160 acres of surveyed land in the public domain. The settler gained title to this land at no cost after living on that tract and improving it for five years, although the local land office required a modest filing and commission fee. The settler, however, could commute, that is, purchase his land for $1.25 per acre and receive full title to it before the end of his residency obligation (as soon as six months).

By the 1840s, Congress had frequently received demands for free land from farmers and speculators. In 1848 and 1852 the Free Soil Party and the Free Soil Democrats, respectively, supported a free land policy. During the early 1850s, however, many northerners opposed a homestead bill on constitutional grounds because Congress was not supposed to have the authority to transfer the public domain to private possession in this manner. Others contended that a free land policy would drain the labor force from eastern cities, encourage immigration, and decrease the value of railroad land grants. By the mid-1850s, supporters of homestead legislation had alienated southern Democrats, who believed the northerners were attempting to lure abolitionists into the West in order to block the expansion of slavery into the territories. Despite these regional objections to a homestead act, westerners continued to agitate for free public lands, and state legislatures passed resolutions supporting those demands while western Congressmen championed a free land policy in Washington.

In 1860 the Republican Party supported a plank favoring a homestead act, and public land policy became a minor issue during the campaign because President James Buchanan had vetoed such an act earlier that year. Buchanan did not believe that Congress had the constitutional authority to alienate public lands in this fashion, because a free public land policy, in part, would encourage speculation, discriminate against those settlers who had paid for their lands, and reduce federal revenue. The Senate had failed to override his veto.

In 1861, after southern opponents had seceded from the Union and with Abraham Lincoln in the White House, passage and approval of a homestead bill became certain. On February 28, the House passed the Homestead Bill, and the Senate approved it on May 6. Lincoln signed the bill 14 days later.

Between 1862 and 1900 some 400,000 families applied for free homesteads under this act, but homesteading was not really "free." Land office fees, materials for the requisite dwelling, tools and seed, and capital to furnish necessities before the crops came in excluded the truly impoverished. Moreover, two-thirds of all homesteaders before 1890 failed at the venture.

See also: Abolition Movement, James Buchanan, Free Soil Party, Abraham Lincoln

R. Douglas Hurt

REFERENCES

Gates, Paul Wallace. 1968. *History of Public Land Law Development.* Washington: U.S. Government Printing Office.

———. 1968. "The Homestead Law in an Incongruous Land System." In Vernon Carstensen, ed. *The Public Lands: Studies in the History of the Public Domain.* Madison: U. of Wisconsin Pr.

Hibbard, Benjamin Horace. 1965. *A History of the Public Land Policies.* Madison: U. of Wisconsin Pr.

Opie, John. 1987. *The Law of the Land: Two Hundred Years of American Farmland Policy.* Lincoln: U. of Nebraska Pr.

Shannon, Fred A. 1968. "The Homestead Act and the Labor Surplus." In Vernon Carstensen, ed. *The Public Lands: Studies in the History of the Public Domain.* Madison: U. of Wisconsin Pr.

Herbert C. Hoover (1874–1964)

Thirty-first President of the United States. Born in West Branch, Iowa, Herbert Clark Hoover was the son of a blacksmith and schoolteacher. His father died of typhoid fever when Hoover was six; two years later his mother died of pneumonia. Hoover and his siblings were sent to live with relatives—young Herbert with an uncle in Oregon. He got his first job at the age of ten as an office boy.

Hoover saved enough money to enroll in Stanford University in 1891, graduating as a mining engineer in 1895. His first job was pushing a mine cart in the Reward Mine of Nevada for two dollars per day. In 1897 he left for Australia and worked as a mine manager, becoming at age 27 a company partner. In 1899 he married Lou Henry, a college sweetheart. Together they had two sons, Herbert Clark and Allan.

As a mining engineer, Hoover traveled the globe. From 1901 to 1908 he visited 46 countries including Egypt, China, and Australia. But it was during World War I that Hoover received international recognition. When war broke out in Europe, the American consul general in London asked for assistance in getting stranded tourists home. (At the time, Hoover was in London on business.) Hoover returned 120,000 Americans to the United States. After the Armistice, Hoover was named director general for European Relief and Rehabilitation by President Woodrow Wilson. Hoover shipped more than 23 million tons of food to 23 countries with a population of approximately 300 million people. A popular slogan at the time was "to Hooverize," meaning to save food.

Hoover's success earned him worldwide acclaim. In 1921 President Warren G. Harding named Hoover Secretary of Commerce, and he was kept in the post by Harding's successor, Calvin Coolidge. When Coolidge made his famous declaration, "I do not choose to run for President in 1928," Hoover became the odds on favorite for the Republican presidential nomination, subsequently defeating Democrat Alfred E. Smith by 6,375,477 votes, accumulating 444 electors to Smith's 87. Smith's Roman Catholicism was an issue during the campaign, but Hoover never referred to it. Instead, the economic boom associated with the "Roaring Twenties" was still strong, prompting Hoover's slogan of "a chicken in every pot and a car in every garage." This seemingly healthy economy was enough to insure Hoover's election.

But in October 1929 the boom came to an end with the stock market crash. Hoover was slow to recognize its magnitude. In 1930 he signed the Smoot-Hawley Tariff Act, a measure that closed the U.S. market to European manufacturers, thereby making things worse for American agriculture. He later established the Reconstruction Finance Corporation, a government agency that lent money to railroads, banks, agricultural agencies, and state and local governments in an attempt to restart the national economic engines.

But these measures were too little, too late. A President who had once been hailed as a "Great Humanitarian" now was associated with abject poverty. "Hoovervilles," pathetic temporary dwellings made of cardboard and tar paper became home to the unemployed. More than 11,000 unemployed veterans from World War I marched on Washington in 1932 demanding federal assistance. In a clash with police, two of the "Bonus Marchers" died, and the President had to summon the Army to clear the streets.

Hoover suffered a resounding defeat in the 1932 presidential election, as Democratic candidate Franklin D. Roosevelt amassed 22 million votes to Hoover's 15 million. Roosevelt also won 472 electors to Hoover's 59. On the eve of the election Hoover reportedly told his secretary, "I'll tell you what our trouble is—we are opposed by six million unemployed, ten thousand bonus marchers, and ten cent corn." Hoover's loss was the worst suffered by an incumbent President since William Howard Taft's third place finish in 1912. A presidency that had begun with so much promise ended in bitterness.

Hoover returned to private life, only entering public service once more when asked by President Harry Truman in 1947 to chair the Commission on the Organization of the Executive Branch of the Government. By 1949 the Hoover Commission had made 275 recommendations to streamline the Executive Branch, of which 200 were enacted. In 1953 a second Hoover Commission was created by President Dwight D. Eisenhower.

In the years after his presidency, Hoover wrote 30 books and maintained an active correspondence. He adhered to his philosophy of laissez faire, once remarking that in the last two centuries " a God-fearing people under the right-wing systems of freedoms have built up quite a plant and equipment on this continent. Possibly another ideology could do it better in the next two hundred years. But I suggest we had better continue to suffer the evil of the right-wing freedoms than to die of nostalgia."

See also: Calvin Coolidge, Dwight D. Eisenhower, Warren G. Harding, Franklin Roosevelt, Alfred E. Smith, William Howard Taft, Harry S Truman, Woodrow Wilson

John K. White

REFERENCES
Best, Cary Dean. 1975. *The Politics of American Individualism: Herbert Hoover in Transition, 1918–1921.* Westport, CT: Greenwood.

Hoover, Herbert. 1922. *American Individualism.* Garden City, NY: Doubleday.

———. 1934. *The Challenge to Liberty.* New York: Scribner's.

———. 1938. *Addresses upon the American Road.* New York: Scribner's.

———. 1951. *Memoirs, Volume One: Years of Adventure, 1874–1920.* New York: Macmillan.

———. 1951. *Memoirs, Volume Two: The Great Depression, 1929–1941.* New York: Macmillan.

———. 1958. *The Ordeal of Woodrow Wilson.* New York: McGraw-Hill.

———. *An American Epic.* Chicago: Regnery.

Lorant, Stefan. 1951. *The Presidency.* New York: Macmillan.

Nash, George H. 1983. *The Life of Herbert Hoover.* New York: Norton.

Wilson, Joan Hoff. 1975. *Herbert Hoover: Forgotten Progressive.* Boston: Little, Brown.

Harry L. Hopkins (1890–1946)

Adviser to Franklin D. Roosevelt. Harry Lloyd Hopkins was one of Roosevelt's closest associates and most important lieutenants during the Great Depression and World War II. Born in Sioux City, Iowa, and educated at Grinnell College, Hopkins left small-town Iowa for New York City in 1912 and a career as a social worker. As governor of New York, Roosevelt appointed Hopkins to head the state's Temporary Emergency Relief Administration in 1931, and then as President, FDR brought Hopkins to Washington where—from 1933 to 1938—he directed the New Deal's Federal Emergency Relief Administration, Civil Works Administration, and Works Progress Administration. Hopkins energetically administered these controversial, sometimes inefficient, and enormously helpful relief programs with imagination, humanity, and probity; he also had a practical eye to their political dimensions and impact. After stomach cancer and a severe digestive disorder caused Hopkins to resign as relief administrator, FDR appointed him Secretary of Commerce in 1938, a post he held until 1940.

At the Democratic National Convention of 1940, Hopkins helped arrange both the third-term "draft" of Roosevelt and the rather unpopular vice presidential nomination of FDR's choice, Henry A. Wallace. Despite the ill health that dogged him for the rest of his life, Hopkins became closer and more important to Roosevelt during World War II, when he frequently lived in the White House and served as an all-purpose presidential adviser and emissary. He played a particularly important role in Roosevelt's negotiations with Winston Churchill and Joseph Stalin. After Roosevelt's death, Hopkins assisted President Harry S Truman in dealing with the Soviet Union and in ensuring the successful creation of the United Nations. He left government in mid-1945, his health ruined, and died soon thereafter.

See also: Franklin Roosevelt, Harry S Truman, United Nations, Henry Wallace

John W. Jeffries

REFERENCES

Charles, Searle F. 1963. *Minister of Relief: Harry Hopkins and the Depression.* Syracuse: Syracuse U. Pr.

McJimsey, George. 1987. *Harry Hopkins: Ally of the Poor and Defender of Democracy.* Cambridge: Harvard U. Pr.

Sherwood, Robert E. 1948. *Roosevelt and Hopkins: An Intimate History.* New York: Harper.

Henry H. Horner (1878–1940)

Two-term Democratic governor of Illinois during the Great Depression. Henry H. Horner gained national prominence because of his battles with the powerful Democratic machine in Chicago. Once a loyal member of that organization, he became estranged from the machine's leader, Mayor Edward Kelly, more for reasons of power than principle (although where principle applied, Horner had a distinct advantage).

Horner was both a political idealist and yet a realist, roles that enabled him to participate in the rough and tumble, turn-of-the-century politics in the notorious First Ward of Chicago, yet maintain his integrity as probate judge. A great admirer of Abraham Lincoln, he had some of the Lincoln mystique rub off on him. Carl Sandburg characterized Horner as collaborating with those who were purchasable without becoming purchasable himself.

Unmarried and lonely, Illinois' first Jewish governor focused entirely on his work. Periodic crises in welfare funding compounded the myriad other Depression-related problems confronting him. Horner needed the cooperation of Chicago Democrats in the legislature; however, to maintain a position of leadership, he had to accommodate the wishes of downstate Democrats who blanched at the enormous costs of relief in Chicago.

Mayor Kelly shouldered Governor Horner aside as the Democratic favorite of President Franklin D. Roosevelt, but lost an attempt to replace Horner in the 1936 primary. Horner campaigned as the reformer versus the machine and won an astounding victory.

Horner virtually worked himself to death during his second term. Stricken with a cerebral thrombosis in 1938, he refused to turn his office over to the lieutenant governor, who he feared would exploit the state. Horner died 91 days short of finishing his term.

See also: Anton Cermak, Edward Kelly, New Deal, Franklin Roosevelt

Gene D. L. Jones

REFERENCES

Gottfried, Alex. 1962. *Boss Cermak of Chicago: A Study of Political Leadership.* Seattle: U. of Washington Pr.

Jones, Gene D. L. 1974. "The Origins of the Alliance Between the New Deal and the Chicago Machine." 67 *Journal of the Illinois State Historical Society* 253.

Littlewood, Thomas B. 1969. *Horner of Illinois.* Evanston, IL: Northwestern U. Pr.

Edward M. House (1858–1938)

Adviser to President Woodrow Wilson. The son of a wealthy Texas businessman, Edward Mandell House was drawn into Texas politics through his friendship with Governor James Stephen Hogg, who in 1892 faced a formidable challenge for renomination and reelection from conservative Democrats and Populists. House directed Hogg's campaign, creating a network of local, influential Democratic leaders, manipulating the electoral machinery, and bargaining for the votes of African- and Mexican-Americans. Hogg triumphed in a bitter, three-way race and rewarded House with the title of Colonel.

Concerned more with the process of politics than with the substance, House proceeded to build his own faction—"our crowd," as he called it—that became a powerful force in Texas politics. He was an ambitious political operator, skilled in organizing and inspiring others. House worked largely behind the scenes, developing ties of loyalty and affection with his close associates and using patronage to rally party workers behind his candidates. From 1894 to 1906, House's protégés served as governor of Texas.

By the turn of the century House tired of Texas and sought a larger role in national affairs. A conservative, sound-money Democrat, he disliked the platform of William Jennings Bryan and in 1904 supported Alton B. Parker for the presidential nomination. Discouraged by the prospects of the Democratic Party after Parker's defeat in 1904 and Bryan's in 1908, House continued his search for a Democratic presidential candidate amenable to his advice. In 1911 he met Woodrow Wilson, gradually forming a close friendship that would last until 1919. While House was on the periphery of Wilson's campaign for the Democratic nomination and the presidency, after his election he played a key role in patronage decisions, eventually placing five friends in the Cabinet. House displayed an unusual gift for intrigue and catered to many of Wilson's personal needs. He was soon the President's most trusted confidant.

Between 1908 and 1912, House had been caught up in the progressive ferment sweeping the country, expressing his conversion to reform in a utopian novel, *Philip Dru: Administrator,* published in 1912. As Wilson pushed his New Freedom agenda through the Congress, Colonel House served as a high-level political intermediary, quieting Democratic factional squabbles and helping to fuse the needs of many special interest groups into a coherent moderate legislative program. He collaborated with Wilson in moving the Democratic Party away from its traditional advocacy of states' rights and limited government toward an extension of federal authority over the nation.

With the outbreak of World War I, House concentrated on diplomacy and quickly became Wilson's closest foreign policy adviser. Before American intervention in April 1917, House traveled to Europe twice on special diplomatic missions, becoming so absorbed in international events that he played only a modest role in the 1916 campaign. He served as Wilson's special emissary during the armistice negotiations in October and early November 1918. A member of the American Commission to Negotiate Peace at the Paris Peace Conference, House lost touch with the direction of the President's thought and seriously strained his friendship. For the remainder of Wilson's presidency, House found himself on the sidelines.

During the 1920s, House made frequent trips to Europe and energetically supported American membership in the League of Nations and the World Court. He also sought to mediate the bitter quarrels within the Democratic Party and to strengthen the party's organization. In 1932 he supported Franklin D. Roosevelt for the nomination and, with Roosevelt's election, sought to reestablish his role as a presidential confidant. While House influenced some diplomatic appointments, he was excluded from FDR's inner circle and became increasingly unsympathetic with the New Deal. His long, unique career as a confidential adviser ended in frustration.

See also: Woodrow Wilson

Charles E. Neu

REFERENCES

Floto, Inga. 1980. *Colonel House in Paris: A Study of American Policy at the Paris Peace Conference 1919.* Princeton, NJ: Princeton U. Pr.

House, Edward M. 1912. *Philip Dru: Administrator.* New York: B.W. Huebsch

Richardson, Rupert N. 1964. *Colonel Edward M. House: The Texas Years. 1858–1912.* Abilene, TX: Harelin-Simmons U. Pr.

Seymour, Charles. 1926–1928. *The Intimate Papers of Colonel House,* 4 vols. Boston: Houghton Mifflin.

Smith, Arthur D. H. 1940. *Mr. House of Texas*. New York: Funk and Wagnalls.

Weinstein, Edwin A. 1981. *Woodrow Wilson: A Medical and Psychological Biography*. Princeton, NJ: Princeton U. Pr.

House Democratic Steering and Policy Committee

This committee represents an effort to strengthen the party organization in Congress. Designed to advise the Speaker and other Democratic leaders, it serves as an extension of the leadership's authority and information network. The roots of the Steering and Policy Committee can be traced back to 1933. In that year House Democrats created a Steering Committee to shape policy. It had virtually no impact on decision-making, however, and was dissolved in 1956. The Steering Committee was revived in 1962 at the behest of party liberals, but it seldom met.

The modern Steering and Policy Committee developed out of the congressional reform movement of the 1970s. The Steering and Policy Committee was resurrected by the Democratic Caucus in 1973 to strengthen party leaders in relation to committee chairmen. The Speaker serves as chairman of the committee, while the Majority Leader, the caucus chair, and the Whip represent the leadership on the committee, as do eight other members appointed by the Speaker. Twelve members are elected to represent geographic regions. The committee was expanded from 24 to 31 members before the Ninety-seventh Congress (1981–1983), as the caucus secretary, chief deputy whip, campaign committee chair, and chairmen of the Appropriations, Budget, Ways and Means and Rules committees were added.

The Steering and Policy Committee became the Democrats' "committee on committees" at the start of the Ninety-fourth Congress (1975–1977). The task of making committee assignments and nominating committee chairs had formerly belonged to the Democratic members of the Ways and Means Committee, a group largely immune to leadership pressure. Control over committee assignments gives the leadership a potential weapon through which to enforce party discipline, but it is rarely used in this manner.

See also: Speaker of the House

John A. Clark

House Republican Policy Committee

This committee is an arm of the leadership and an advisory body for the membership of the GOP. It considers policy alternatives and encourages consensus among Republican members. It also approves the committee assignment recommendations of the Republican committee on committees.

The Republican Policy Committee was created in 1949 with Republican leader Joseph W. Martin, Jr., as chairman. It was largely inactive until 1959, when Charles Halleck replaced Martin as floor leader. The chairmanship became a separate position in that year, elected by the Republican Conference (made up of all Republican Congressmen). The committee was an important instrument of Halleck's collegial leadership style between 1959 and 1965. The Republican Conference began taking policy positions in 1965 after Gerald Ford defeated Halleck to become floor leader. Ford, who had been chairman of the conference, deemphasized the role of the Policy Committee as the party's voice. Today it is used as a means of narrowing the alternatives and fine tuning the proposals to be presented to the conference.

The Policy Committee is composed of 31 members. The chairman is ranked fourth among Republican leaders behind the floor leader, Whip, and conference chair. These and four other leaders serve on the committee by virtue of their leadership positions, as do the ranking members of the Rules, Ways and Means, Appropriations, and Budget committees. Eight regional representatives and two from each of the two most recent election-year classes are elected by their respective constituencies. The floor leader appoints the remaining seven members.

See also: Gerald Ford, Charles Halleck

John A. Clark

REFERENCES

Jones, Charles O. 1964. *Party and Policy-Making: The House Republican Policy Committee*. New Brunswick, NJ: Rutgers U. Pr.

House Un-American Activities Committee

A committee formed in 1938 as the U.S. House of Representatives Special Committee on Un-American Activities. The committee investigated the German-American Bund, native fascist organizations, and the Communist Party of the United States of America (CPUSA). It received its greatest notoriety for investigations of Communists in New Deal agencies and popular front political organizations.

In 1945 the committee became a permanent House standing committee. During the early years of the cold war, HUAC helped to spark and benefited from popular concern with the activities of American Communists and their ties to Soviet foreign policy. In 1946 HUAC gained attention through the testimony of Louis Budenz, a former senior official of CPUSA who had become a passionate anti-Communist. Budenz described the CPUSA as largely a front for a Soviet conspiracy to infiltrate and subvert American institutions.

In 1947, HUAC attracted considerable public interest by investigating Communist influence in the Hollywood film industry. Ten filmwriters, most of whom were indeed Communists, refused to testify but declined to invoke their rights under the Fifth Amendment; the "Hollywood Ten" were convicted of contempt of Congress. In 1948 HUAC took up the case of Elizabeth Bentley, a former Communist who discussed her years as a Soviet spy and contacts with secret Communists in the government. The Bentley case led to the testimony of Whittaker Chambers and his implication in espionage of such government officials as Harry Dexter White, a leading international monetary expert, and Alger Hiss, a senior diplomat.

The chief legislation written by HUAC was the draconian Internal Security Act of 1950, a measure that passed over President Harry Truman's veto. Its key provisions were later judged unconstitutional by the U.S. Supreme Court. In the 1950s HUAC investigated Communist influence in education, in Protestant churches, and in labor unions. Particularly after the near disintegration of the CPUSA in the late 1950s, public concern about domestic communism receded, and concomitantly interest in HUAC's hearings declined. In the 1960s HUAC investigations of the Ku Klux Klan resulted in the conviction of several Klan officials for refusal to provide subpoenaed records. HUAC hearings on Communist influence in the anti-Vietnam War movement of the late 1960s produced widespread defiance by witnesses and disruption by antiwar activists.

Although HUAC hearings produced a great deal of information about Communist activities, the manner in which several of the Congressmen who dominated HUAC conducted themselves gave HUAC a reputation for partisanship, ignorance, and viciousness. Congressman Martin Dies (D-Tex.), who led HUAC during its early years, seemed to be as interested in discrediting

President Franklin Roosevelt's New Deal by linking it to CPUSA as he was in exposing Communist activities. From 1945 to 1947, Congressman John Rankin (D-Miss.), an ardent racist and anti-Semite, dominated HUAC with his view that the New Deal was a Jewish-Communist conspiracy. Congressman J. Parnell Thomas (R-N.J.), HUAC chairman in 1947 and 1948, was convicted of payroll padding.

In the 1960s and 1970s, HUAC became the target of an increasingly vocal campaign for its abolition. Many liberals denounced HUAC as an instrument of political oppression that harassed or abused the political rights of dissenters. The House did abolish the committee in 1975.

See also: Whittaker Chambers, Communism as a Political Issue, Communist Party of the United States, Alger Hiss, Ku Klux Klan, New Deal, Harry S Truman

John E. Haynes

REFERENCES

Beck, Carl. 1959. *Contempt of Congress: Prosecutions Initiated by the Committee on Un-American Activities, 1951–1957.* New Orleans, LA: Hauser Press.

Bentley, Eric, ed. 1971. *Thirty Years of Treason: Excerpts from Hearings Before the House Committee on Un-American Activities, 1938–1968.* New York: Viking.

Buckley, William F., Jr., and the editors of *National Review.* 1962. *The Committee and Its Critics: A Calm Review of the House Committee on Un-American Activities.* New York: Putnam's.

Carr, Robert K. 1952. *The House Committee on Un-American Activities, 1945–1950.* Ithaca: Cornell U. Pr.

Goodman, Walter. 1968. *The Committee: The Extraordinary Career of the House Committee on Un-American Activities.* New York: Farrar, Straus and Giroux.

Ogden, August Raymond. 1945. *The Dies Committee: A Study of the Special House Committee for the Investigation of Un-American Activities, 1938–1944.* Washington: Catholic U. of America Pr.

Samuel Houston (1793–1863)

Powerful Texas political leader. After a brief military career, "Sam" Houston served two terms in Congress from Tennessee (1823–1827) and was then twice elected governor (1827–1829), resigning because of a family scandal. In 1832, he went to Texas where he took a prominent part in Texas' brief independence and later annexation to the United States. As a Congressman, as president of the Texas republic (1836–1844), and then as a United States Senator (1848–1859), Houston dominated Texas politics and made its parties largely pro- or anti-Houston factions. In Washington he was a devoted disciple of Jacksonian democracy, territorial expansion, and the Union. He supported the national Democratic Party until 1854 when he broke with its leaders over the Kansas-Nebraska Act. His opposition to the bill won acclaim in the North but undermined his support in Texas. As an ambitious and colorful southern Unionist, Houston was widely mentioned as a presidential candidate in every election from 1848 to 1860. After 1855 he turned to the Know-Nothings and Constitutional Unionists as the best hope for southern moderates and received a sizable number of votes in these parties' national conventions in 1856 and 1860. In 1860 Houston launched a brief independent "people's" candidacy based on preservation of the Union, repudiation of the old parties, and schemes to conquer Mexico. In 1859 he lost his U.S. Senate seat but won election as governor of Texas as a Unionist. By 1861 the tide of secession sentiment overwhelmed Houston's stubborn attempt to prevent or delay Texas secession. Unwilling either to take the oath of allegiance to the Confederacy or to accept military help from the Abraham Lincoln administration, Houston ended his career when he was deposed as governor by the legislature.

See also: Constitutional Union Party, Jacksonian Democracy, Kansas-Nebraska Act, Know-Nothings, Abraham Lincoln, Secession

Harold B. Raymond

REFERENCES

Friend, Llerena. 1954. *Sam Houston, the Great Designer.* Austin: U. of Texas Pr.

Marquis, James. 1929. *The Raven: A Biography of Sam Houston.* New York: Blue Ribbon Books.

Merk, Frederick, with Lois B. Merk. 1972. *Slavery and the Annexation of Texas.* New York: Knopf.

Richardson, Rupert N. 1943. *Texas, the Lone Star State.* New York: Prentice-Hall.

Siegel, Stanley. 1956. *A Political History of the Texas Republic, 1836-45.* Austin: U. of Texas Pr.

John E. Howard (1752-1827)

Distinguished Revolutionary War hero and Federalist political leader from Maryland. John Eager Howard was born near Baltimore and educated privately. He emerged as one of the genuine heroes of the Revolutionary War, rising to the rank of colonel and being decorated for bravery at Cowpens. He served as a Maryland delegate to the Continental Congress from 1784 to 1788, and then as governor of Maryland from 1789 to 1791. Howard was next elected to the United States Senate to fill a vacancy created by the resignation of Richard Potts. He was reelected in 1794 and remained in the Senate until 1803. Howard was a strong Federalist; he was thus offered the post of Secretary of War by President George Washington in 1795. His political orientation and military reputation were further attested to by his nomination as a brigadier general in 1798 when preparations for a threatened war with France were undertaken by John Adams's administration.

Although a Federalist leader, Howard supported the War of 1812, during which he was involved in the defense of Baltimore and raised a corps of veterans who never saw active service. Howard was a wealthy and powerful man with valid claims to the enormous reputation he enjoyed as one of the aristocratic leaders of the new Republic.

See also: Federalist Party, George Washington

Kathryn A. Malone

Charles Evans Hughes (1862-1948)

Statesman, jurist, and political leader for three decades. Charles Evans Hughes, one of the most distinguished lawyers of his generation, brought a tone of moderate progressivism to the several high political offices he held between 1907 and 1941. A graduate of Brown University and the Columbia Law School, he first won public applause for his work as legal counsel for state investigations into malpractice among New York City utilities and insurance companies. Elected Republican governor of New York in 1906, Hughes pursued a somewhat austere program of regulatory reform during his two terms. After brief service as a U.S. Supreme Court justice (1910-1916), he was the Republican presidential nominee in 1916 but failed to mobilize a national Republican majority against Woodrow Wilson.

Appointed Secretary of State by Warren Harding in 1921, Hughes strove to stabilize the shaky peace that followed World War I through international naval arms limitation agreements and by arranging financial relief for postwar Germany through the Dawes Plan in 1924. In 1925 he returned to his lucrative Wall Street law practice. Herbert Hoover named Hughes Chief Justice of the U.S. Supreme Court in 1930, just as the country entered the Great Depression. His ability to guide the politically divided Court through the constitutional crisis created by the New Deal's innovative response to hard times was Hughes's major political achievement. He presided over a judicial revolution that eased the Court's watchdog stance on the limits of public regulatory authority at both the state and federal levels and thus helped to protect the Court against Franklin Roosevelt's court-packing plan of 1937.

See also: Warren G. Harding, Herbert Hoover, Woodrow Wilson

Geoffrey Blodgett

REFERENCES

Danelski, David, and Joseph Tulchin, eds. 1973. *The Autobiographical Notes of Charles Evans Hughes.* Cambridge: Harvard U. Pr.

Glad, Betty. 1966. *Charles Evans Hughes and the Illusions of Innocence.* Urbana: U. of Illinois Pr.

Hendel, Samuel. 1951. *Charles Evans Hughes and the Supreme Court.* New York: King's Crown Press.

Pusey, Merlo. 1951. *Charles Evans Hughes.* New York: Macmillan.

Wesser, Robert. 1967. *Charles Evans Hughes: Politics and Reform in New York.* Ithaca: Cornell U. Pr.

Emmet John Hughes (1920–1982)

Journalist, author, and political adviser. Emmet John Hughes was influential in Republican Party politics during the 1950s and 1960s. Following graduation from Princeton University in 1941, when his mentor, Carlton J. H. Hayes, was appointed U.S. ambassador to Spain, Hughes went along to serve as press attaché. Through his embassy duties, Hughes became acquainted with the Paris bureau chief for *Time* who in 1946 offered him a job with the magazine's Rome office. He advanced rapidly through the ranks of Henry Luce's publishing empire, and in 1952 when the GOP turned to *Time*'s publisher for speechwriters, Hughes was assigned to Dwight Eisenhower's campaign.

Although Hughes had been a liberal Democrat in the 1940s, he chose to help elect a Republican President in 1952 as a way of reviving the two-party system and because the rise of McCarthyism convinced him that a fresh reappraisal of American foreign policy could come only from the GOP. Hughes wrote Eisenhower's "I shall go to Korea" speech, which played a major role in the GOP's 1952 victory. He remained on the White House staff and wrote many more of Eisenhower's speeches, including his first inaugural address. Hughes resigned in September 1953, disenchanted with the conservative policies of two key members of the administration, John Foster Dulles and Richard Nixon, and also by the unwillingness of Eisenhower to disapprove publicly of McCarthy's tactics. Thereafter, Hughes resumed his journalistic career with the Luce organization, returning intermittently to politics to help in Eisenhower's 1956 reelection campaign and to serve as the chief strategist for Nelson Rockefeller's 1968 campaign for the GOP presidential nomination. Hughes wrote a number of books, including *The Ordeal of Power* and *The Living Presidency*, in which his beliefs in a strong chief executive were developed. For the last 12 years of his life Hughes was a professor of political science at Rutgers University.

See also: Dwight D. Eisenhower, McCarthyism, Richard Nixon, Nelson Rockefeller

John W. Malsberger

Harold E. Hughes (1922–)

Iowa reform politician. A modern-day populist, Harold Everett Hughes served as governor of Iowa, as a U.S. Senator from that state, and as a member of several commissions of the Democratic Party. After service in World War II, Hughes was an independent truck driver and founded the Iowa Better Trucking Bureau. From 1958 to 1962 Hughes was Iowa's Commerce Department commissioner. In 1962 he ran for governor of Iowa as a Democrat, defeating the Republican Norman Erbe. During his years as governor (1963–1969), Hughes was instrumental in rebuilding Iowa's Democratic Party. In 1968 Hughes launched a campaign for the U.S. Senate based on his opposition to the Vietnam War, and he narrowly defeated Republican David M. Stanley. His reputation as a reformer brought him in 1968 to the attention of aides to presidential candidate Eugene McCarthy, who were attempting to revise the party's selection process. Hughes was asked to chair the Commission on the Democratic Selection of Presidential Nominees. With only one formal meeting on August 13, 1968, it issued recommendations, published as *The Democratic Choice*, which called for changing the manner in which the size of a state's delegation was determined and instituting racial and gender quotas for state delegations. Hughes introduced these recommendations at the convention, but most were defeated. Later, the Commission on Party Structure and Delegate Selection was formed with George McGovern as chair and Hughes as vice chair, and it worked from 1968 to 1972 on the same problem. In 1972 Hughes explored the possibility of mounting a presidential campaign but decided against it. Known as something of a loner in the Senate, Hughes was a liberal voice on the Armed Services Committee. Hughes retired from the Senate in 1975.

See also: Joseph McCarthy, George McGovern, Populist (People's) Party, Vietnam as a Political Issue
Thomas J. Baldino

REFERENCES

Hughes, Harold E., and Dick Schneider. 1979. *The Man from Ida Grove.* Lincoln, VA: Chosen Books.

Shafer, Byron E. 1983. *The Quiet Revolution: The Struggle for the Democratic Party and the Shaping of Post-Reform Politics*. New York: Russell Sage.

Cordell Hull (1871–1955)

Democratic statesman and politician from Tennessee. Cordell Hull's distinguished career as a U.S. Congressman, a U.S. Senator, and as Franklin Roosevelt's Secretary of State also included a term as national committee chairman of the Democratic Party (1921–1924). His father was a Tennessee farmer, merchant, lumberman, and banker who accumulated a modest fortune. Hull graduated from the law program at Cumberland University in Tennessee.

Barely 21 years old, he was elected to the Tennessee House of Representatives, where he served for 4 years. After active service in the Spanish-American War, he returned to Tennessee to practice law, and in 1903 he became judge of Tennessee's Fifth Judicial Circuit. Three years later he was elected to Congress where he specialized in economic and monetary problems. Hull was active in the revolt against Speaker Joseph Cannon in 1911, and this won him a place on the House Ways and Means Committee, where he was instrumental in the formulation of the economic policies of Woodrow Wilson's administration.

Hull came on to the Democratic National Committee in 1919. His experience as chairman of the congressional campaign committee and his popularity among his colleagues in Congress led immediately to his appointment to the executive committee. When Hull was defeated for reelection to Congress in 1920, President Wilson offered to nominate him to be chief justice of the court of customs. Hull declined, preferring to return to Tennessee to mend political fences for another run for Congress.

After he became Democratic national chairman, Hull's tenure was a busy one, conscientiously performed. He had to liquidate a substantial party debt, rebuild a skeleton national headquarters, assume major responsibility for the 1922 midterm congressional election campaign, deal with controversial proposals for a midterm national convention, and make the most of the scandals of the Warren Harding administration. Returned to the House in 1923, he also took time to meet regularly with the party's two elder statesmen—Woodrow Wilson and William Jennings Bryan.

Hull continued in the House of Representatives until he was elected to the Senate in 1932.

He played a major role in bringing the southern leadership behind Franklin D. Roosevelt's candidacy for President in 1932. Although he opposed Roosevelt's third term bid, Hull served as his Secretary of State from 1933 through the trying years of World War II until November 1944. In February 1945 he was the leading United States delegate to the founding United Nations Conference in San Francisco. In that same year he was awarded the Nobel Peace Prize.

See also: Franklin Roosevelt, United Nations, Woodrow Wilson

Ralph M. Goldman

REFERENCES

Goldman, Ralph M. 1990. *The National Party Chairmen and Committees: Factionalism at the Top*. Armonk, NY: M. E. Sharpe.

Hinton, Harold B. 1942. *Cordell Hull*. Garden City, NY: Doubleday.

Hull, Cordell. 1948. *The Memoirs of Cordell Hull*. New York: Macmillan.

Hubert H. Humphrey (1911–1978)

"The Happy Warrior." Hubert Horatio Humphrey played a central role in the Democratic Party and in national politics for 30 years. As party reformer, mayor of Minneapolis, United States Senator, Vice President, and presidential candidate, he was one of the most fiery of Democratic liberals. Throughout his career Humphrey was a leading Democratic spokesperson for the causes with which he so closely identified: human rights, arms control and disarmament, and a redirection of national priorities toward social and economic reform.

Hubert Humphrey was born in South Dakota, the son of a druggist who served in the state legislature as one of the state's few Wilsonian Democrats. His father's political idealism and the experience of living on the Great Plains during the Great Depression helped shape Humphrey's political philosophy. As a student at the University of Minnesota, and later a teacher at that university and at Macalester College, Humphrey became an ardent supporter of Franklin D. Roosevelt. In fact, he left teaching to serve as the director of the War Production Board and assistant director of the War Manpower Commission for Minnesota.

In 1943 Humphrey ran unsuccessfully for mayor of Minneapolis. During 1944, while directing the Roosevelt reelection effort in Minnesota, Humphrey and his political allies (Eugene McCarthy, Orville Freeman, Don Fraser, and John Blatnik) initiated the merger and reform of the Minnesota Democratic and Farmer-Labor parties into the unified Democratic-Farmer-Labor Party, a condition that emerged as the bulwark of Humphrey's future strength in a state previously dominated by Republicans.

Humphrey's 1945 campaign for mayor of Minneapolis was successful; he was reelected in 1947 with the largest plurality in the city's history. In 1948 he burst on the national scene with an impassioned speech supporting a strong civil rights plank in the Democratic Party platform. His speech drove Strom Thurmond and the southern anti-civil rights Dixiecrats out of the party but led many others to commit themselves to President Harry Truman's reelection.

In November 1948 Hubert Humphrey became the first Democrat ever elected to the Senate from Minnesota by that state's voters. During his early years in the Senate, he was burdened with the reputation as a brash, abrasive, overglib, "do-good" liberal—a maverick in an institution dominated by an "inner club." His legislative agenda constantly called for a greater federal role in helping the poor. He introduced a bill calling for medical care for the elderly 16 years before Medicare eventually passed. He worked for increased spending for federal welfare, expansion of unemployment and Social Security benefits, promotion of civil rights, and increases in aid to education. His Senate experience increased his concern for foreign affairs and for aiding those in other countries. Humphrey eventually learned to accommodate to the ways of the Senate while remaining committed to his own policy positions. By the mid-1950s he was no longer a maverick but an accepted part of the Senate establishment; he was, in fact, Lyndon Johnson's liaison to labor, intellectuals, and northern liberals.

In 1960 Humphrey announced his candidacy for the presidency. While he had the support of many leaders of the liberal establishment, he dropped out of the race after losing critical primaries to John F. Kennedy in Wisconsin and in West Virginia. He returned to Minnesota to be reelected to the Senate. When Lyndon Johnson left the Senate to become Kennedy's Vice President, and Mike Mansfield succeeded him as Majority Leader, Humphrey was elected Majority Whip, the second ranking position in the party.

Following Kennedy's assassination and Johnson's succession to the presidency, many Democrats thought they knew who the President would choose as his running mate in 1964. Johnson somewhat surprisingly chose Humphrey, who would appeal to the North and to liberals; the Johnson-Humphrey ticket won in a landslide. As Vice President, Humphrey proved to be extremely loyal, moving from the left to the center and refusing to join those who criticized Johnson's policy in Vietnam.

After Johnson removed himself from consideration for reelection in 1968, Humphrey declared his own candidacy. Although he successfully gained the party nomination, defeating his longtime friends and allies Eugene McCarthy and George McGovern (who stood in as the candidate for those who had favored the slain Robert F. Kennedy), the turmoil at the Democratic National Convention in Chicago and Humphrey's reluctance and inability to separate himself from the President he had served divided the party and handicapped his campaign. He and his running mate, Edmund S. Muskie (Maine) eventually lost a close race to Richard M. Nixon and Spiro Agnew by less than 1 percent of the popular vote. The third-party candidacy of conservative Alabama governor George Wallace drew approximately 14 percent of the vote and 46 electoral votes.

After this defeat Humphrey returned to the Senate. In 1972 he sought his party's presidential nomination again. He narrowly lost the California primary to George McGovern, but that victory assured McGovern a majority at the convention. In 1976 Humphrey toyed with the idea of seeking the presidency one more time but finally decided to stay out of the race when victory seemed more and more remote.

Hubert Humphrey was consistently frustrated in his goal to be elected President. As Vice President, he was too often ignored by Lyndon Johnson. But he left his mark on American politics as one of the significant contributors to the post-FDR era. He was the "happy warrior" of that era, the pragmatic liberal who never forgot his populist roots.

See also: Spiro Agnew, Democratic Farmer-Labor Party of Minnesota, Elections of 1964 and 1968, Lyndon B. Johnson, John F. Kennedy, Eugene McCarthy, George McGovern, Richard Nixon

James A. Thurber

REFERENCES

Berman, Edgar. 1979. *Hubert: The Triumph and Tragedy of the Humphrey I Knew.* New York: Putnam's.

Griffith, Winthrop. 1965. *Humphrey, A Candid Biography.* New York: Morrow.

Humphrey, Hubert H. 1970. *The Political Philosophy of the New Deal.* Baton Rouge: Louisiana State U. Pr.

———, with Norman Sherman. 1976. *The Education of a Public Man. My Life and Politics*. Garden City, NY: Doubleday.

Solberg, Carl. 1984. *Hubert Humphrey: A Biography*. New York: Norton.

Hunkers

One of the warring factions of the New York Democratic Party in the 1840s. Remaining loyal to the James Polk administration when their rivals, the Barnburners, bolted, the Hunkers were willing to accede to the demands of southern Democrats on slave-related issues in order to preserve national party unity.

The origin of New York's Democratic factionalism was a complex combination of local and sectional issues. The name Hunker can be traced back to the late 1820s when critics charged that William L. Marcy, a leading New York Jacksonian Democrat, "hunkered" after patronage during Andrew Jackson's presidency. Coining the phrase "to the victor belongs the spoils," Marcy and his partisans were accused of seeking an overlarge "hunk" of Jacksonian appointments in return for their support.

New York Democrats became seriously divided in 1844 when Martin Van Buren sought the party's presidential nomination. Denied the choice because of his antislavery leanings, Van Buren and his supporters nonetheless campaigned loyally and helped to secure James K. Polk's narrow victory over Henry Clay. When the new President denied the Van Burenites patronage and instead granted it to their rivals (especially Marcy's appointment as Secretary of War), bitterness increased. Determined to press for the containment of slavery within existing boundaries, the Van Burenites sought enactment of the Wilmot Proviso to prevent slavery's expansion into territories acquired during the Mexican War.

In contrast, the Marcy faction remained loyal to the Polk administration's opposition to the Proviso. The issue reached a climax when Van Burenite governor Silas Wright was denied reelection in 1846 when the Hunkers withheld their support. The following fall at the Democratic state convention in Syracuse, the Hunkers seized control, naming a state ticket excluding their rivals and adopting a platform endorsing Polk and ignoring the Proviso. The infuriated Van Burenites boycotted the election, allowing the Hunker ticket to be routed by the Whigs. By now the Van Burenites appeared ready to secede from the party to get their way and were being labelled Barnburners (after a Dutch farmer who supposedly burned down his barn to get rid of the rats). The Barnburners accepted the name with pride, identifying it with antislavery principle and claiming that their hated rivals, the Hunkers, were always willing to sacrifice principle to southern demands in order to maintain their power and office.

In 1848 each of the rival New York groups sought recognition at the national party convention in May. Seeking party harmony, convention leaders tried to compromise the differences by admitting both factions provided that each would endorse the Democrats' nominee, Lewis Cass. With the Proviso rejected and a hated Hunker ally Cass chosen, the Barnburners instead withdrew to become part of the new Free Soil Party.

More extreme Hunkers like Senator Daniel S. Dickson were then delighted and recommended that President Polk remove Barnburners from federal office as an act of Democratic Party discipline. The Barnburner revolt, however, cost the Democrats the state's electoral votes with the Whigs also winning 31 of 34 seats in the New York congressional delegation and totally dominating the state legislature.

The results of Democratic division were now all too obvious, and both factions sought reunion in 1849. It was the Hunkers who secured it on their own terms: meetings of the two groups led to a Hunker offer to divide the state ticket provided the Barnburners give up their support for the Wilmot Proviso. With that agreed to, a semblance of party unity was restored, and separate Hunker and Barnburner factions gradually disappeared.

See also: Barnburners, Henry Clay, Free Soil Party, Andrew Jackson, Jacksonian Democrat, James Polk, Wilmot Proviso

Frederick J. Blue

REFERENCES

Blue, Frederick J. 1973. *The Free Soilers: Third-Party Politics*. Urbana: U. of Illinois Pr.

Donovan, Herbert. 1925. *The Barnburners: A Study of the Internal Movements in the Political History of New York and of Resulting Changes in Political Affiliations*. New York: New York U. Pr.

Morrison, Chaplain W. 1967. *Democratic Politics and Sectionalism: The Wilmot Proviso Controversy*. Chapel Hill: U. of North Carolina Pr.

Sellers, Charles G. 1966. *James K. Polk, Continentalist, 1843–1846*. Princeton: Princeton U. Pr.

Spencer, Ivor D. 1959. *The Victor and Spoils: A Life of William L. Marcy*. Providence: Brown U. Pr.

James B. Hunt, Jr. (1937–)

Moderate governor of North Carolina. A Democrat known foremost for being a moderate, sometimes even liberal, governor of North Carolina, James Baxter Hunt, Jr., chaired one of the Democrat's periodic reform commissions and battled Jesse Helms in 1984 for North Carolina's Senate seat in the most expensive Senate campaign up to that date.

Hunt was the Democratic governor of North Carolina from 1977 to 1984. He combined advocacy of liberal positions—such as supporting civil rights and backing higher spending on education—with enthusiasms for conservative positions, such as recommending capital punishment. Before being elected governor, Hunt was the lieutenant governor (1973–1977), a post from which he ran the state senate and built his own personal political organization.

Hunt chaired the fourth Democratic reform commission, which has come to be known as the Hunt Commission. These commissions (McGovern-Fraser, Mikulski, Winograd, Hunt, and Fairness) set delegate selection rules for Democratic national conventions. The Hunt Commission, establishing rules for the 1984 convention, made three major changes: (1) it repealed the provision that all delegates must be bound to the candidate under whose name they were chosen, (2) it relaxed rules requiring proportional representation, and (3) it increased the number of delegate slots reserved for elected and party officials.

In 1984 Hunt challenged Jesse Helms for the U.S. Senate seat from North Carolina. Helms, the incumbent Senator and a leader of the New Right, was known as one of the most conservative and flamboyant U.S. Senators. The race was characterized by numerous charges and huge expenditure. Helms spent over $16 million, Hunt over $9 million. Final vote totals were close, with Hunt receiving 1,070,488 votes, or 48 percent.

See also: Jesse Helms, McGovern-Fraser Commission, Winograd Commission

Barbara Norrander

REFERENCES

Crotty, William. 1983. *Party Reform.* New York: Longman.

Robert M. T. Hunter (1809–1887)

Antebellum states' rights leader from Virginia. A sectional politician, Robert Mercer Taliaferro Hunter was the son of a planter in Essex County, Virginia. He graduated from the University of Virginia (1828), where he studied law and was admitted to the bar in 1830. An admirer of John C. Calhoun, Hunter came to put states' rights particularism above party allegiance. He served as an independent in the Virginia General Assembly (1834–1837) and was elected to Congress as a states' rights Whig in 1837 (Speaker 1839–1841). His faction ("the Chivalry") ultimately aligned with the Democrats, and Hunter was defeated for reelection in 1843. He regained his seat in 1845, then was elected to the U.S. Senate in 1847 in the charged sectional atmosphere that followed the introduction of the Wilmot Proviso. Throughout the 1850s he defended southern interests and he was his state's presidential candidate at the Democratic convention in 1860.

Although he served on the Committee of Thirteen seeking a sectional compromise, he ultimately resigned his Senate seat before Virginia's secession. He served the Confederacy in its Provisional Congress, as Secretary of State from July 25, 1861, to February 18, 1862, and as Senator. He was a delegate to the unsuccessful Hampton Roads Conference, which sought a negotiated peace in January 1865. Determined to resist, he still opposed such extraordinary measures as freeing or arming slaves to fight for the South. Preferring military rule to sharing power with Blacks, he helped organize the conservative opposition to Reconstruction in 1867. Although he ultimately modified his states' rights stand to accommodate state assistance to economic enterprises, his identification as an "old fogey" cost him the caucus nomination for Senator in 1874. He did serve as Virginia state treasurer (1874–1880) and at his death was collector of the port of Rappahannock.

See also: John C. Calhoun, Reconstruction, Secession, Wilmot Proviso

Phyllis F. Field

REFERENCES

Ambler, Charles H., ed. 1918. *Correspondence of Robert M. T. Hunter, 1826–1876.* Washington: U.S. Government Printing Office.

Hitchcock, William S. 1973. "Southern Moderates and Secession: Senator Robert M. T. Hunter's Call for Union." 59 *Journal of American History* 871.

Simms, Henry Harrison. 1935. *The Life of Robert M. T. Hunter: A Study in Sectionalism and Secession.* Richmond, VA: William Byrd Press.

Claudius H. Huston (1876–1952)

Republican National Committee chairman from 1929 to 1930. Claudius Hart Huston was born in Indiana and educated at Valparaiso

University and the Chattanooga Normal University. He eventually became chairman of the Transcontinental Oil Company and a director in many other companies. For his civic efforts on behalf of business, he was elected president of the Chattanooga Manufacturers Association and the Chattanooga Chamber of Commerce.

During 1920 Huston became chairman of the campaign and advisory committees of the Tennessee Republican state committee and raised considerable money in that year's campaign. At all times a behind-the-scenes political operator, Huston's success as a fundraiser was so striking that he became well known throughout the national party. He was among those mentioned for Secretary of Commerce in President Warren Harding's Cabinet, but that post went to Herbert Hoover. Instead, Huston was appointed assistant secretary of commerce, a position he held from 1921 to 1923. During this period he also served as chairman of the national committee's ways and means committee.

In 1923 Huston returned to his business interests, particularly at Transcontinental Oil, but remained a devoted political supporter and adviser to Hoover. When Hubert Work resigned from the national chairmanship, Huston was elected to the position—an important recognition of the growing importance of the changing South. However, Huston very soon had to deal with public charges that he had used lobby funds for personal speculation. Although he persisted in his denials of wrongdoing, he did resign from the chairmanship in August 1930.

See also: Herbert Hoover, Republican National Committee

Ralph M. Goldman

REFERENCES

Goldman, Ralph M. 1990. *The National Party Chairmen and Committees: Factionalism at the Top.* Armonk, NY: M. E. Sharpe.

I

Ideology

The term "ideology" is often used by political scientists to represent broad intellectual frameworks like communism, Marxism, fascism, Nazism, social democracy, and classical liberalism. Within the United States, however, ideology most often refers specifically to differences between liberals and conservatives. American research on ideology has centered on its influence of voters, parties, and elections.

What are liberals and conservatives? The meanings given to ideological labels vary over time. They reflect a rolling total of previous and current usages; consequently, experts never completely agree about, nor can they even give a precise definition of, the terms "liberal" and "conservative." From the 1930s through the 1950s, "liberal" largely stood for the popular activist economic policies of the Roosevelt administration. From the 1960s on, liberalism has also come to be identified with a set of positions of "social" policies—some of them unpopular with the majority of voters. Liberalism now involves support for civil rights policies, affirmative action, and the ERA as well as protection of the domestic welfare policies of the New Deal and Great Society. Conservatism once stood for big business and against an expanded role of government but now also includes support for the military, lower taxes, and the protection of "traditional" or "family" values (including prayer in the schools, suppression of pornography, and opposition to abortion). Few citizens are liberal or conservative across all issues. However, the liberal and conservative labels are attached to the opposing sides of most major political conflicts.

Ideology in the Electorate

Using a broad and traditional definition of ideology, political scientists have tested the hypothesis that voters tend to formulate issue preferences from ideological stances, and that they use these preferences to come to an ideologically informed choice in the voting booth. These tests reveal, however, that the "ideological" hypothesis is not convincing. Employing less-restrictive definitions of ideological thinking—such as whether people describe politics in general liberal-conservative terms or whether voters can even explain what the terms mean—researchers have found that ideologues make up, on a small minority, less than 10 percent of the American electorate. Their analyses show that few Americans use ideology as an intellectual organizing framework.

Even though few Americans have the sort of highly rationalized ideologies described in the traditional definitions, when asked, most people will say that they are either liberal, moderate, or conservative. If given a way out, about a third will say that they never think of themselves in these terms. Of those who accept ideological labels, the most popular choice is "moderate" or "middle-of-the-road." Of those who take a stand, conservatives outnumber liberals by a healthy margin, often approaching two to one in surveys in the 1980s. This conservative bent among Americans has grown over the years—although not as much as many media commentators have suggested during the Reagan years. The net shift from liberals to conservatives over the last 20 years has been less than 10 percent. The balance of ideological adherents changes quite slowly.

Ideology for most citizens combines a mixture of stances on policy issues, affective feelings toward groups in society, and assessments of political figures. Thus, to be a liberal entails having more "liberal" positions on issues, feeling more positively about groups like labor, feminists, Black leaders, and the poor. Liberalism also is associated with support for politicians like Senator Edward Kennedy, former Vice President Walter Mondale, and the 1988 Democratic presidential nominee, Michael Dukakis. Conservatives tend to take the appropriate stands on issues but also tend to feel relatively positive toward business, the military, whites, and the middle class. Conservatives gave overwhelming support to Ronald Reagan during his presidency, and subsequently to George Bush in the 1988 election. Thus, for the average voter, ideology is not as much a set of principles as a thread connecting issues, groups, and political personalities.

Reliance on ideology in political behavior varies a great deal, among voters, across time, and in types of elections. The well educated and those most interested in politics are the most likely to rely on ideology in evaluating candidates and policies. Voters less involved in politics and with fewer years of formal education are more likely to rely on party or general judgments of personality or character. Over the last 30 years the importance of ideology has increased. The Barry Goldwater (1964), George McGovern (1972), and Reagan (1980, 1984) candidacies especially contributed to the definition of political choices in ideological terms.

Voters respond to the choices that are offered and largely in the terms in which they are offered. For this reason ideology plays a smaller role in subpresidential elections, which are influenced relatively more by party attachments and, especially in House elections, incumbents' advantages in visibility and service to their constituencies. Although ideological differences and issues are seldom the determining factor in congressional elections, they do influence enough votes to keep incumbents attentive to their constituents.

The apparent role of ideology in politics changes as we move from looking at individual voters to looking at electorates. Many of the idiosyncrasies and random misperceptions that exist at the individual level largely cancel out at the level of the electorate. Interestingly, the behavior of large groups of voters or electorates are ideologically coherent and orderly—despite the fact that surveys reveal that substantial portions of the public are poorly informed and not ideologically motivated in their political thinking.

Party Activists

Most people in the United States identify with one of the political parties, but at the same time, most are not active members. Those who are—the canvassers, contributors, party officials, and especially those who participate in party conventions to select nominees—make up only a fraction of the population. However, this elite group is highly ideological, and their intense involvement in issues and candidates does a great deal to shape the sorts of choices offered to voters. They are influential because most candidates must first be nominated in primaries, and to win, they need the support of the ideologically motivated activists in their parties.

Major ideological positions differentiate the two parties' activist supporters. Democratic Party elites are overwhelmingly liberal while Republican Party elites are even more cohesively conservative. This ideological gulf between Democratic and Republican party elites has grown over the last two decades. The Democratic Party has lost some of its conservatives, while the Republican Party has become cohesively conservative. Democrats continue to be more heterogeneous, largely owing to the continuing representation among them of moderates and conservatives from the southern and Border states.

Within each of the parties are evolving candidate-based coalitions that are largely ideological. Jesse Jackson's supporters in 1988 were more liberal than the Dukakis delegates, while in earlier years, Reagan supporters provided a very strong conservative contrast to Gerald Ford's supporters (1976) or George Bush's partisans (1980) in the Republican primaries and convention. Thus, both within the parties and especially between them, ideological preferences are important in party elites' support of candidates. This development contrasts to earlier decades when jobs and patronage were more important incentives in the formation of party coalitions.

To this point the discussion has centered on ideological commitment among members of the major political parties. This emphasis is appropriate because a vast majority of Americans identify with one or the other of the major parties. However, ideology plays a more central role in minor party politics. The names of some of the well-known minor party reflect their ideological stance (e.g., the Communist Party, the Socialist Workers Party, the Libertarian Party). And at other times, during the Progressive era as an obvious example, these parties have played more significant roles in determining the direction of American politics. Third parties have often been the home of the ideologically committed; their role in the American system has often been to raise the level of ideological debate and should not be underestimated simply because of their lack of electoral success.

Elected Officials

Democrats outnumber Republicans in the electorate, but self-identified conservatives outnumber liberals. Republican presidential candidates have profited from this conservatism as the salience of party has declined and the role of ideology has increased in presidential elections since the 1960s. In 1980 Ronald Reagan ran on a conservative platform, and although issues were not the main reason for his election, he was able to parlay that "mandate" into major changes in U.S. national policy. Thus, ideology is important both for how voters make decisions and for how politicians interpret those decisions as they make public policy.

The ideological differences seen among party activists and, recently, between presidential candidates are reflected in Congress and the state legislatures, whether ideology is measured by interviews with legislators, by their roll-call voting, or by ratings by concerned interest groups. In general the ideological differences between the parties are smallest in the southern states because of the relative moderation and conservatism of southern Democrats.

Ideological differences among elected officials are important for policy change. If both parties appealed equally to the average voter, then there would be little difference between the two parties. Electing Democrats or Republicans would have little impact on directions of public policy—at least not in predictable liberal-conservative terms. However, the intense ideological values of party activists work to separate the nominees of the parties and thereby provide differences in the policy packages the parties and candidates stand for. Accordingly, electing Democrats to Congress or the state legislatures will generally result in more liberal legislators, and electing Republicans will generally result in more conservative representatives. In this way

ideology provides a coherence over issues to the two political parties and offers the public means for at least some control of the general directions of policy in the country, even though ideology is not a particularly powerful organizing principle for the average individual voter.

See also: George Bush, Communist Party of the United States, Michael Dukakis, Equal Rights Amendment, Barry Goldwater, Jesse Jackson, Edward M. Kennedy, George McGovern, Walter Mondale, New Deal, Third Parties in American Elections

Gerald Wright

REFERENCES

Converse, Philip E. 1964. "The Nature of Belief Systems in Mass Publics." In David E. Apter, ed. *Ideology and Discontent*. New York: Free Press.

Erikson, Robert S., and Gerald C. Wright. 1989. "Voters, Candidates, and Issues in Congressional Elections." In Lawrence C. Dodd and Bruce I. Oppenheimer, eds. *Congress Reconsidered*. 4th ed. Washington: Congressional Quarterly.

Flanigan, William H., and Nancy H. Zingale. 1983. *Political Behavior of the American Electorate*. 5th ed. Boston: Allyn and Bacon.

Kinder, Donald R. 1983. "Diversity and Complexity in American Public Opinion." In Ada W. Finifter, ed. *Political Science: The State of the Discipline*. Washington: American Political Science Association.

Kirkpatrick, Jeane. 1976. *The New Presidential Elite: Men and Women in National Politics*. New York: Russell Sage.

Miller, Warren E. and M. Kent Jennings. 1986. *Parties in Transition: A Longitudinal Study of Party Elites and Party Supporters*. New York: Russell Sage.

Miller, Warren E., and Treasa E. Levitin. 1976. *Leadership and Change*. Cambridge, MA: Winthrop.

Niemi, Richard G., and Herbert F. Weisberg. 1984. "Do Voters Think Ideologically?" In Richard Niemi and Herbert Weisberg, eds. *Controversies in Voting Behavior*. 2nd ed. Washington: Congressional Quarterly.

Illinois State Board of Elections v. Socialist Workers Party
440 U. S. 173 (1978)

This case uses the equal protection clause of the Fourteenth Amendment to ease petition requirements for access to the ballot. It extends *Williams v. Rhodes* [393 U. S. 23 (1968)] in which certain ballot access restrictions were determined to burden the fundamental rights of individuals to political association as protected in the First Amendment and of voters to cast their votes effectively without regard to political persuasion. Here the issue concerned a discrepancy between statewide offices and local offices regarding the number of signatures required for independent candidates and new political parties.

The Illinois Election Code required independent candidates and new parties seeking to appear on the ballot for statewide elections to obtain signatures of 25,000 qualified voters. However, in elections for offices of political subdivisions, the requirement was 5 percent of the votes cast at the previous election. Upon the death of Mayor Richard J. Daley in 1977, the Chicago City Council ordered a special election. The Chicago Board of Election commissioners and the State Board of Elections ultimately determined that independent candidates and new parties needed to collect 35,947 valid signatures.

The larger number of signatures for Chicago elections had not been previously considered anomalous when statewide petitioners had had the more burdensome task of collecting at least 200 signatures in each of 50 counties to constitute the 25,000. The geographic distribution, however, had been invalidated in *Moore v. Ogilvie*, 394 U.S. 814 (1969).

Because they had received less than 5 percent of the vote in the previous election for mayor, the Socialist Workers Party and the United States Labor Party were new political parties. In addition, Gerald Rose was an independent candidate. They and certain voters challenged the number of signatures and the short time for collecting them.

The Court noted that a compelling state interest was necessary to justify a classification that impinged on rights of ballot access. The Court had previously recognized that there is a legitimate interest in restricting the number of candidates on the ballot. However, the means chosen must be the least restrictive to achieve that end. It seemed clear to the Court that the 25,000-signature requirement for statewide offices was the maximum that might be required for a local office. Moreover, the state had given no reason for the more stringent requirement for Chicago. Therefore, the 5 percent requirement as it applied to Chicago was unconstitutional, and no more than 25,000 signatures could be required.

See also: Richard Daley, Socialist Workers Party, *Williams v. Rhodes*

Douglas I. Hodgkin

REFERENCES

Young, Rowland L. 1979. "Illinois Voter Signature Act Is Held Unconstitutional." 65 *American Bar Association Journal* 613.

Independent Party of New York City

John Lindsay was first elected mayor of New York City in 1965 as the candidate of the Republican Party as well as the candidate of two additional minor parties. Like Fiorello La Guardia and other Republicans before him, Lindsay knew that a Republican could defeat a Democrat in New York City only if he was part of a "fusion" effort. The two minor parties in 1965 were the Liberal Party (one of the [then] three officially recognized parties in the state) and the other was a party more accurately described as simply a column on the ballot, secured by the circulation of petitions and labeled "Independent Citizens." Thanks to the combined votes recorded under the three party labels, Lindsay won the 1965 contest against his Democratic opponent.

In his quest for reelection four years later, Lindsay was deprived of his own party's nomination, losing the Republican primary to the more conservative John Marchi. That defeat left Lindsay with only the Liberal Party nomination. To attract additional support, Lindsay announced the formation of a new party styled "The Independent Party of New York City," citing as sponsors an impressive list of names from the ranks of both Republicans and Democrats. Opening storefront headquarters throughout the city, party workers insisted that Lindsay was an independent, nonpartisan candidate. The strategy was successful; Lindsay won the November election, defeating both his Republican and Democratic opponents. The 130,000 votes that he polled on the Independent Party column provided his margin of victory. Like the Independent Citizens in 1965, the Independent Party was never heard from again.

See also: Fiorello La Guardia, Liberal Party, John Lindsay

Howard A. Scarrow

Indiana Ballot

In response to growing electoral fraud and corruption during the late nineteenth century, a number of election and ballot reforms were introduced by the states. These reforms included the widespread adoption of the Indiana (party column) and the Australian (secret) ballots. In 1889 Indiana adopted the Australian ballot (one of the first states to do so), and the state legislature also mandated the practice of listing the names of candidates for the various offices in columns according to party affiliation, with a party emblem, the party name, and a circle (or square) for straight-ticket voting appearing at the top of each column. This type of ballot was designated the Indiana ballot to distinguish it from the traditional Massachusetts ballot, which listed candidates by office rather than party, thus discouraging straight-ticket voting.

The Indiana ballot was quickly adopted by most of the states as was the Australian ballot (35 of the 44 states in 1892 used some form of secret ballot). Under the new system, the state rather than the political parties furnished ballots uniform in size, color, and quality (of sufficient thickness, for example, to prevent inkmarks from showing through) to qualified voters, who marked them in secret.

Of course, many objected to the Indiana ballot. In addition to being long and unwieldy, such a ballot (even when marked in secret, as in a voting booth) permits a bystander to know whether or not a straight-ticket has been voted, makes independent voting difficult and write-in voting perhaps impossible, and has the effect of encouraging party-line voting. Attempts at additional ballot reforms during the Progressive era, however, went largely unrealized, and little has been done in the decades since to improve the situation. In the 1980s only 17 of the 50 states and the District of Columbia (one more than in 1917) used the office-group as opposed to the party-column ballot, with the remaining 33 states using the party-column ballot, 22 of which also permit straight-ticket voting.

See also: Australian Ballot

Ralph D. Gray

REFERENCES

Dunn, Jacob P. 1889. *A Manual of the Election Laws of Indiana*. Indianapolis: State of Indiana.

Evans, Eldon. 1917. *A History of the Australian Ballot System in the United States*. Chicago: U. of Chicago Pr.

La Follette, Robert. 1929. "The Adoption of the Australian Ballot in Indiana." 24 *Indiana Magazine of History* 108.

Indiana's 2% Club

The system by which patronage employees in Indiana return 2 percent of their salaries to state and local parties is commonly known as the "2% club." Beginning in 1933, the system applied only to state employees; eventually the program expanded to include county and city employees as well. Although less pervasive than it once was, the 2% club still exists today.

The 2% club has provided a systematic source of revenue for both the Democratic and Republican parties in Indiana. While the program originated under a Democratic gubernatorial administration, Indiana Republicans are now the greater beneficiary by virtue of their relative success in state politics over the past 20 years. Estimates vary, but they place annual contributions to the state Republican Party between $100,000 and $400,000.

A variety of mechanisms have been used to implement the 2% "kickback." Under its original tenets, the parties sent representatives to collect contributions. At one point in the early 1890s, a check-off system was used. While the parties have insisted that the contributions have been and continue to be purely voluntary, others emphasize that they are, realistically, compulsory. From the latter perspective the contribution is perceived as being either a condition of employment (prohibited by federal law) or a prerequisite for advancement.

In any case, Indiana's 2% club, as well as comparable enterprises in other states, provides a systematic and largely predictable source of revenue for political parties. The parties themselves contend that this broad-based financing system is desirable because it approaches a truly public financing system. At the same time, opponents' objections point to the perceived mandatory character of the 2 percent contribution, and they question its constitutional basis.

Barbara Trish

REFERENCES

Broder, David S. 1972. "Old-Style Politics: Patronage Rules in Indiana County." *Washington Post*, June 15.

Laing, Jonathan R. 1971. "'The 2% Club': Kicking Back Pay Is Way of Life in Indiana for Employees of State." *Wall Street Journal*, April 8.

Industrial Communist Party

One of the most obscure and ephemeral of the various leftist parties formed in the United States in the aftermath of World War I, the Industrial Communist Party (ICP) left behind almost no traces in the historical record, and if it had not been coincidentally organized in the home city of an early historian of American communism, then it might be completely forgotten today. The ICP is of interest, however, both because its experience illustrates the fragmented nature of the American Left during these years and because of its very unusual intellectual basis.

The party was organized in Terre Haute, Indiana, in November 1919 during the "Red Scare" when the nation's Communist parties were going underground in the face of government repression. Those who formed the Industrial Communist Party chose not to become a secret society but rather to create an organization that, by eschewing all talk of armed rebellion and the dictatorship of the proletariat, would be able to operate in the open. They did, nevertheless, profess allegiance to the Third International. The group soon was renamed the Proletarian Socialist Party (not to be confused with the longer-lived Proletarian Party formed by Michigan Socialists in 1919). The ICP cited as its "legal basis" the second paragraph of the Declaration of Independence ("We hold these Truths to be self-evident, that all Men are created equal . . ."). Its political economy was unique. Society was, according to the Industrial Communists, built upon six basic industries: agriculture, transportation, mining, manufacturing, construction, and education. Any working-class party that aimed to win power in the United States had of necessity to be organized along the same lines as the larger society, so every Industrial Communist branch had to be composed of members who worked in these six industries. National conventions were to be similarly representative. This structure, it was argued, insured that "when it [the party] goes into power we will have Industrial Communism."

The party invited members of the nation's Socialist and Communist organizations to join it, and it published a few issues of a paper, *The Industrial Communist*. In June 1920 its headquarters were moved to Chicago, and later that summer it issued an unheeded call for Socialist and Communist parties to meet in a unity convention. The only significant historical source estimates the party's peak membership at no more than 100 or 200. The group soon abandoned political action and reorganized as the Rummagers' League, an educational society. Members announced their intention to "rummage the field of history and science so as to develop the keenest intellect possible. Special consideration [is] given to present-day problems. . . . The main point of view is the highest possible working-class education." The Rummagers' League published several numbers of a paper entitled *The Rummager* and established study groups in some disciplines. Again ineffectual, the Rummagers quietly disappeared from the scene in the 1920s.

See also: Communism as a Political Issue, Red Scare, Socialist Party of America

Gary L. Bailey

REFERENCES

Oneal, James. 1924. "Changing Fortunes of American Socialism." 20 *Current History* 92.

————. 1927. *American Communism: A Critical Analysis of Its Origins, Development and Programs*. New York: Rand Book Store.

Industrial Workers of the World

At a convention held in Chicago in June 1905 attended by western miners, migratory farmworkers, Pacific Northwest lumberjacks, dockers, and unorganized workers from the East Coast, the Industrial Workers of the World (IWW or "Wobblies") was founded. The delegates espoused industrial unionism (organizing the skilled and the unskilled), in contrast to the craft unionism of the American Federation of Labor (AFL), and refused to recognize any common ground between labor and capital. Organizers sought to overthrow the capitalist wage system and replace it with an industrial syndicate, or "one big union." Representatives of the Socialist Party, including Eugene V. Debs and Daniel De Leon, were present in 1905 as well as representatives of the Western Federation of Miners, led by William "Big Bill" Haywood. The Socialists quickly withdrew from the IWW, preferring to introduce changes peaceably through the electoral process rather than by direct economic action. In addition to strikes, which the AFL also used, the IWW openly called for sabotage, a tactic the AFL disavowed. The Western Federation of Miners also disaffiliated, although their leader Haywood remained with the Wobblies.

In 1912 the IWW won a textile strike in Lawrence, Massachusetts, and succeeded in organizing the workers. Lawrence was the high point of their power. In 1913 they suffered defeat in a silk industry strike in Paterson, New Jersey, and in a rubber industry strike in Akron, Ohio.

In 1906 Haywood and others were charged with the assassination of former Idaho governor Frank R. Steunenberg. Defense attorney Clarence Darrow, however, secured their acquittal. In 1918 the Justice Department sent most of the IWW leadership to prison for opposing U.S. participation in the war. Haywood skipped bail while being prosecuted and fled to the Soviet Union, where he died. By 1924 the IWW had almost completely dissolved, although remnants of the Wobblies remain today, headquartered in Chicago. Membership had always been small, never numbering more that 15,000.

See also: Eugene V. Debs, Daniel De Leon, Socialist Party of America

Frederick J. Augustyn, Jr.

REFERENCES

Brissenden, Paul Frederick. 1971. *The Launching of the Industrial Workers of the World.* New York: Haskell House.

Dubofsky, Melvyn. 1969. *We Shall Be All: A History of the Industrial Workers of the World.* Chicago: Quadrangle Books.

Informal Party Caucuses in Congress

Informal party caucuses are voluntary associations of members of Congress, without recognition in chamber rules or line-item appropriations, which seek to play a role in the policy process. Informal party caucuses are formed to represent the perspective and to articulate and advance the views of groups of members within the congressional parties. Members of these intraparty factions share a similar ideology.

Party caucuses are one type of informal congressional caucus. Other types are based on members' shared issue concerns (e.g., the Arms Control and Foreign Policy Caucus) or on shared constituency characteristics, such as a national constituency (e.g., the Congressional Black Caucus or the Congressional Caucus on Women's Issues), a regional constituency (e.g., the Northeast-Midwest Congressional Coalition), a state/district constituency (e.g., the Rural Caucus or the family farm task forces), or a state/district industry (e.g., the Automotive Caucus, the Steel caucuses, or the Textile Caucus). Caucuses are termed "informal" because they operate outside the formal structure of the Senate and the House. Caucuses, however, have typical organizational attributes, with membership lists, leaders, staff, and on occasion, offices separate from the members' personal offices.

Caucuses help members achieve individual goals of reelection, representation, and policymaking; caucuses also serve collective institutional goals of representation, legislation, and oversight. More than 100 caucuses were active during the One Hundredth Congress (1987–1988), although only four caucuses of any type existed in the Eighty-sixth Congress (1959–1960). Two party caucuses, the Democratic Study Group and the House Republican Wednesday Group, were among the first caucuses established in the contemporary era.

During the One Hundredth Congress, 19 informal party caucuses were active. House party caucuses included the moderate-to-liberal Democratic Study Group, the Budget Study Group, and the Conservative Democratic Forum. The moderate-to-liberal House Wednes-

day Group, the more-conservative Republican Study Committee, and the Conservative Opportunity Society were among the active Republican groups. There are fewer party caucuses in the Senate: the Wednesday Group of moderate-to-liberal Republican Senators and the conservative (Republican) Steering Committee were the only groups active during the One Hundredth Congress. Class clubs, which tend to be ideologically more diverse than the other party caucuses, are established in the House by freshmen members of each party (e.g., the One Hundred First New Members Caucus and the One Hundred First Republican Club). Party caucuses differ from all other types of caucuses in two ways: they are partisan and they operate only within one chamber.

Party caucuses work within the congressional party and with party leaders to affect issue agendas, caucus rules and procedures, and policy outcomes. In the late 1960s and the 1970s, the Democratic Study Group worked within the House Democratic Caucus to achieve reforms that distributed resources more equitably, increased accountability of the party's committee leaders, and dispersed decision-making power. The Budget Study Group, which began as a task force of the Ninety-Eighth New Members Caucus, expanded to include party leaders and now serves as a party forum for informal discussion and study of budget matters. The United Democrats of Congress (UDC) sought to influence congressional party leaders regarding the floor schedule, arguing that votes that would be controversial, votes on which UDC members might oppose a majority of their party colleagues, should not be scheduled for a floor vote if the Senate would not also agree to act. In recent Congresses, the Conservative Democratic Forum has sought and achieved "parity" in committee assignments for its members from party leaders.

Informal party caucuses seek to affect policy outcomes. The Democratic Study Group proposed rules changes in order to achieve liberal legislation that had been kept from a vote by independent committee chairmen who were not accountable to the Democratic Caucus. The Conservative Democratic Forum sought favorable committee assignments so as to position members to affect formulation of legislation. The Republican Steering Committee regularly places issues on the agenda of the House Republican Conference. The Conservative Opportunity Society plays a major role in planning party conferences to develop a "Republican agenda."

Although party caucuses form in order to influence party leaders and affect policy outcomes, party leaders use caucuses to stay in touch with party factions and to communicate with groups of members. And as party leadership, especially in the House, has expanded leadership deliberations to more members, caucus leaders serve as intermediaries between leaders of the congressional party and caucus members.

Caucuses of the same party as the President have a special entrée to executive branch and White House personnel, and through informal briefings and meetings, as well as formal written documents, influence administrative thinking and action. Cabinet members, White House staff, and on occasion the President, meet in off-the-record sessions with members of party caucuses. After informal meetings of the (Senate) Republican Steering Committee with President Reagan, for example, issues of concern to the Senators appeared on administrative agendas. Also during the Reagan presidency, the Gypsy Moths (Northeast-Midwest Republicans) held meetings with Office of Management and Budget Director David Stockman on both budget and tax issues to assure proposals that would be acceptable to the diverse interests of House Republicans.

Party caucuses also work at the national party level, seeking to affect delegate selection rules and the party platform. Members of Congress want to see elected officials serving as delegates and want to have party platforms on which diverse congressional candidates can campaign. The United Democrats of Congress opened a caucus office at recent Democratic presidential-nominating conventions to pursue these goals.

Party caucuses thus serve as organizations to advance the views of a particular intraparty group of members of Congress and to represent different groups in the congressional parties. Members of party caucuses have a unique opportunity to influence policy at all stages of the legislative process, and to affect both agendas and outcomes within Congress, within the executive branch, and within the national parties. Because party caucuses help members of Congress to achieve personal and collective goals, they have become important subunits within in the congressional parties.

See also: Democratic Study Group

Susan Webb Hammond

REFERENCES

Dilger, Robert Jay. 1982. *The Sunbelt/Snowbelt Controversy: The War Over Federal Funds.* New York: New York U. Pr.

Ferber, Mark F. 1971. "The Formation of the Democratic Study Group." In Nelson W. Polsby, ed. *Congressional Behavior.* New York: Random House.

Feulner, Edwin J., Jr. 1983. *Conservatives Stalk the House: The Republican Study Committee.* Ottawa, IL: Green Hill Publishers.

Hammond, Susan Webb. 1989. "Congressional Caucuses in the Policy Process." In Lawrence C. Dodd and Bruce I. Oppenheimer, eds. *Congress Reconsidered,* 4th ed. Washington: Congressional Quarterly.

———, Daniel P. Mulholland, and Arthur G. Stevens, Jr. 1983. "Congressional Caucuses: Legislators as Lobbyists." In Allan J. Cigler and Burdett A. Loomis, eds. *Interest Group Politics.* Washington: Congressional Quarterly.

Loomis, Burdett A. 1981. "Congressional Caucuses and the Politics of Representation." In Lawrence C. Dodd and Bruce I. Oppenheimer, eds. *Congress Reconsidered,* 2d ed. Washington: Congressional Quarterly.

Stevens, Arthur G., Jr., Arthur H. Miller, and Thomas E. Mann. 1974. "Mobilization of Liberal Strength in the House, 1955-1970." 68 *American Political Science Review* 667.

Inter-University Consortium for Political and Social Research

Much as a library exists to facilitate the dissemination of knowledge in the form of books and periodicals, the Inter-University Consortium for Political and Social Research (ICPSR), founded in 1962 under the leadership of Professor Warren E. Miller of the University of Michigan, exists to make knowledge in the form of quantitative data public and accessible to scholars and other close observers of social phenomena. In particular, the ICPSR collects and distributes data of interest to political and social researchers in a form readily accessible by computer. In support of its commitment to furthering systematic social research, the consortium also conducts an active program of education in the methods of quantitative social science, at the same time supporting the development of computer applications in social and political research. The consortium is supported primarily by its membership, chiefly in universities and other research organizations worldwide.

The ICPSR archive includes over 25,000 data files on a wide variety of social questions ranging from surveys of national electorates in the United States, Europe, and Japan to studies of legislatures and other political institutions in the U.S. and abroad, to data on social and economic indicators on the countries of the world. The data files have often been generated by individual researchers who release their data to the consortium, but files may also be made up of large sets of governmental data such as census returns, congressional roll-call records, and aggregate election totals. After formatting the data to make them generally accessible, the consortium "archives" the data along with appropriate documentation so that the files can be used by others not involved in the original data collection project. Those who request the data are then free to carry out their own analysis.

The ICPSR also runs a summer program in quantitative methods for social scientists. Leading social scientists teach a wide variety of courses and workshops ranging from those designed to introduce quantitative methods to the uninitiated, to highly sophisticated techniques. Every summer hundreds of scholars come to Ann Arbor to study methods, to begin an active research career, or to catch up with the latest computer and statistical techniques. By offering a rich diversity of summer courses, the consortium supplements the graduate education offered by universities throughout the world. By bringing together scholars concerned with advancing their methodological skills, the ICPSR helps to create the networks necessary to foster an environment supportive of the increasingly complex nature of social-scientific research.

At the time of its founding, the idea of a worldwide data resource of the scope of the ICPSR was visionary and, some would have said, farfetched. For Warren Miller and his colleagues, the idea was the natural result of a collaborative and enterprising spirit brought to bear on significant questions in social research. That spirit has not only directly increased research resources for hundreds of scholars and their students, but it also has virtually revolutionized the norms of social science as far as collaboration, cooperation, and sharing of data are concerned. The concept of the consortium has spawned similar institutions abroad, notably the European Consortium for Political Research; it has dramatically enhanced the standards of scholarship in the social sciences and has promoted shared resources of incalculable worth.

Walter J. Stone

Isolationism in American Politics

Throughout the nineteenth century isolationism was the norm in American foreign policy and politics. The advice of Founding Fathers George Washington and Thomas Jefferson to refrain from entangling alliances, to stay out of other nation's wars, and to abstain from international politics was strengthened by commitments to neutrality and to James Monroe, a policy that declared the New World off limits to European states in return for noninterference by the United States in European affairs.

Isolationism guided U.S. policymakers and diplomats down to President Woodrow Wilson's irrevocable German submarine warfare. Wilson deceptively pursued neutrality but sought a pretext to fight against a German nation that he hated. His 1916 pledge to stay out of the war measurably helped him win reelection, but shortly afterward he asked a divided Congress to declare war. Belatedly reacting to Wilson's policies, the isolationists insured nonparticipation in world affairs during the post-World War I years by twice defeating the Treaty of Versailles, which included membership in the League of Nations. Isolationists dominated interwar foreign policy and helped dissuade Presidents and policymakers from interventionist policies. Americans believed that World War I had made the world safe for dictatorship, not democracy; the rest of the world was a fertile environment for injustice and conflict.

Isolationists were so successful in the 1930s that President Franklin Roosevelt conceded that he too favored isolationism and would keep the United States out of war. Thus he encouraged the Nye Committee's investigation into the armaments industry and excess profits in World War I and signed the 1935 Neutrality Law. Congressional noninterventionists enacted the 1935–1937 Isolationist-Neutrality Acts, designed to keep the United States out of another world war by impeding presidential discretion. Isolationists thus ignored the reality of the impending crises in Europe and the Far East. Initially the threat of another European war increased the popularity of the isolationists, but FDR chipped away at the noninvolvement position, which was further weakened by legislative changes successfully won by the President in 1939–1941 neutrality revisions. Roosevelt, like Wilson, declared one policy and pursued another. He said he wanted to avoid war, but in reality he desperately sought to intervene to stop Adolf Hitler. He claimed that aid to the Allies would enable him to keep his election promise of 1940 to stay out of the war, but he edged the United States toward belligerency. The debate over involvement or isolation ended when the Japanese attacked American naval installations at Pearl Harbor, and Germany declared war against the United States. World War II ended isolationism as a political issue except for a few brief rhetorical flourishes.

The isolationists creditably wanted to stay out of war and wanted to insure that the United States would enter a war only through proper constitutional processes, but they failed to understand that a great economic and military power cannot isolate itself from world politics and that Germany and Japan threatened vital American interests. Roosevelt deceived the people and proved unwilling to wager a portion of his huge political capital to convince Americans that the United States had to enter the war to protect its own long-term interests.

See also: Thomas Jefferson, League of Nations, James Monroe, Franklin Roosevelt, George Washington, Woodrow Wilson

C. David Tompkins

REFERENCES

Adler, Selig. 1957. *The Isolationist Impulse.* New York: Abelard-Schuman.

Cole, Wayne S. 1983. *Roosevelt and the Isolationists, 1932–1945.* Lincoln: U. of Nebraska Pr.

Doenecke, Justus D. 1972. *The Literature of Isolationism.* Colorado Springs: R. Myles.

———. 1979. *Not to the Swift: The Old Isolationists in the Cold War Era.* Lewisburg, PA: Bucknell U. Pr.

Jonas, Manfred. 1966. *Isolationism in America, 1935–41.* Ithaca: Cornell U. Pr.

Leopold, Richard. 1962. *The Growth of American Foreign Policy.* New York: Knopf.

Ralph Izard (1742–1804)

Early national period U.S. Senator from South Carolina. Ralph Izard was one of the Revolutionary Americans who could make a valid claim to aristocratic standing. He was born into a wealthy and powerful family, near Charleston, South Carolina. After studying in England and graduating from Christ College, Cambridge, Izard came back to the United States, married and returned to London in 1771, where he had intended to take up permanent residence. He participated in the prerevolutionary maneuvers undertaken by Americans in London trying to prevent the cataclysm from separating England from its American colony. Eventually he conceded to reality and moved to Paris in 1776. Even though he was appointed United States commissioner to the Court of Tuscany in 1776, he was never received by that government. Nevertheless, he remained in France, quarreling with Benjamin Franklin about salaries and prerogatives, until he was recalled in 1779. In spite of his spats with Franklin, Izard was devoted to the American cause, a loyalty that he demonstrated by pledging his extensive South Carolina estates as security to finance the building of warships for the United States in Europe. When he returned to the United States in 1780, Izard approached George Washington directly to advise that General Nathanael Greene be sent south to command military operations in that newly critical area, thus making another major contribution to the war effort.

Izard was a delegate to the Continental Congress in 1783 and 1784, then was elected to the first Congress as a Senator from South Carolina. He remained in that office until 1795, and served as President *pro tempore* of the Senate from May 1794 to February 1795. Izard retired from public life at the end of his Senate term, suffering a debilitating stroke three years later. Izard, an aristocrat in terms of wealth, power, and inclination, was a firm friend and supporter of Washington, and one of those remarkably undemocratic advocates of republicanism who shaped the American Revolution.

See also: George Washington

Kathryn A. Malone

J

Andrew Jackson (1767–1845)

First "people's President." Andrew Jackson, who has always been rated among the ten best American Presidents by historians, dramatically changed the nature of presidential power during his presidency from 1829 to 1837. The Jackson presidency differed in many respects from the pattern that had been constructed by his Virginia and Massachusetts predecessors. A westerner and therefore not a member of the small group of elite public men who had dominated national politics until the 1820s, Jackson "revolutionized" the presidency by challenging Congress for control of the federal government. Unlike any chief executive who had preceded him, Jackson appealed to the people as their "direct representative" to sustain his actions as President. He also ended the tradition of a strong, independent Cabinet by insisting that he was ultimately responsible for the policy of the executive branch.

Jackson's victory over the British in New Orleans at the end of the War of 1812 was a spectacular one in which over 2,000 British troops were killed, while fewer than 20 Americans lost their lives. Coming at the end of a divisive, unpopular, and often unsuccessful war, Jackson's victory brought him great public acclaim.

As one of five presidential candidates in 1824, Jackson won a plurality of the popular votes but failed to get a majority of electoral votes. The election was then decided in the House of Representatives where Jackson was defeated by John Quincy Adams of Massachusetts.

Running again in 1828, Jackson easily defeated Adams, sweeping the South and West.

The election of 1828 represented a major increase in the turnout of popular vote in presidential elections with 56.3 percent of the eligible voters going to the polls in contrast to only 26.5 percent in 1824. By 1840 popular turnout had increased to 78 percent.

Jackson boldly asserted presidential power during his two terms, vetoing twelve measures passed by the Congress in sharp contrast to his predecessors who, between the six of them, had cast a total of only ten vetoes. The two major issues during Jackson's presidency were his successful challenge of South Carolina's nullification of federal law and, most important, his destruction of the Second Bank of the United States (BUS).

Chartered in 1816 for 20 years, the BUS was the largest and most influential bank in America. Vetoing a recharter bill in 1832, Jackson feared that the BUS might use its power in its remaining four years to win enough congressional support to override his veto. Therefore in 1833, in a direct confrontation with Congress who had resolved that the federal funds were safe in the BUS, Jackson ordered the funds removed and fired the head of the BUS, Nicholas Biddle, who refused to do his bidding.

The Senate passed a resolution censuring Jackson's actions and charging him with executive usurpation. For almost the entire congressional session between December 1833 and June 1834, the Senate debated Jackson's actions. His detractors accused him of dramatically and illegally expanding the scope of executive power, while his defenders argued that the President must have the authority to manage and supervise public funds as well as to remove any subordinate from office. President Jackson, outraged by the vote of censure, took his case to the voters, claiming that he was "the direct representative of the American people." The issue ended in a standoff with the Senate refusing to withdraw censure and Jackson refusing to restore public funds to the BUS.

See also: John Quincy Adams, Elections of 1824 and 1828, Jacksonian Democracy, Jacksonian Party System, Nullification, Second Bank of the United States

James R. Sharp

REFERENCES

Benson, Lee. 1961. *The Concept of Jacksonian Democracy: New York as a Test Case.* Princeton: Princeton U. Pr.

Pessen, Edward. 1978. *Jacksonian America: Society, Personality, and Politics.* Homewood, IL: Dorsey.

Pious, Richard M. 1979. *The American Presidency.* New York: Basic Books.

Remini, Robert V. 1963. *The Election of Andrew Jackson.* Philadelphia: Lippincott.

Schlesinger, Arthur M., Jr. 1945. *The Age of Jackson.* Boston: Little, Brown.

Sharp, James Roger. 1970. *The Jacksonians Versus the Banks: Politics in the States After the Panic of 1837.* New York: Columbia U. Pr.

Henry M. Jackson (1912–1983)

"The Senator from Boeing." Henry M. "Scoop" Jackson, a Democrat from the state of Washington, served in Congress from 1941 until his death. Liberal on social issues but conservative on defense and the military, Jackson's views on policy remained remarkably consistent in his 12 years in the House and 30 years in the Senate. He was a staunch supporter of organized labor, civil rights, military preparedness, the survival of Israel, and freedom for Soviet Jewry.

Jackson was first elected to the House of Representatives when he was only 28 years old. Moving to the Senate in 1953, he was assigned to serve on Joseph McCarthy's Permanent Investigations Subcommittee of the Government Operations Committee. An opponent of the flamboyant McCarthy and his witch-hunting tactics, Jackson was active in the televised hearings that exposed the Wisconsin Senator as a demagogue. Jackson was awarded a seat on the Armed Services Committee for his role in McCarthy's censure.

Because of his advocacy for his state's largest employer, Jackson, who used his visibility in the Senate to become one of the nation's leading spokesmen on defense issues, became known as the "Senator from Boeing." As chairman of the National Security Policy Subcommittee of the Government Operations Committee in the 1960s, he conducted wide-ranging hearings on national security organization. His hawkish reputation was enhanced by his support for American involvement in Vietnam. He became ranking minority member of the Senate Armed Services Committee in 1983.

Jackson entered the race for the Democratic presidential nomination in 1972 and 1976. Although both campaigns failed, he won the New York and Massachusetts primaries in 1976.

See also: Joseph McCarthy

John A. Clark

Jesse L. Jackson (1941–)

Minister, civil rights leader, and contender for the Democratic presidential nomination. Jesse Louis Jackson became the most influential spokesman for African-Americans during the 1980s. Jackson early chafed at both the segregationist patterns in his native Greenville, South Carolina, and the gossip among Black neighbors about his illegitimate origins. As a man of intense drive, academic ability, and athletic prowess, he gained administration to the University of Illinois; but he left on learning that he would never be allowed to play quarterback because of his race. Instead the six foot three inch Jackson became a star quarterback as well as a track and baseball competitor at North Carolina A&T College, a historically Black college in Greensboro.

As a college senior in 1963, Jackson became active in the civil rights movement, leading fellow students in downtown protests that desegregated Greensboro's restaurants and theaters. Three years later, Martin Luther King, Jr., chose Jackson (then enrolled in a Chicago seminary) to organize a local branch of "Operation Breadbasket," a program that King had begun in Atlanta to induce white merchants to provide more jobs and business opportunities to African-Americans. Jackson's success in extracting concessions from white corporations (through the use of boycotts and moral pressure) led him to expand "Operation Breadbasket" to other cities in campaigns that he coordinated between 1967 to 1971.

By 1968 Jackson had become a key aide to Dr. King's Southern Christian Leadership Conference. He traveled to Memphis for a series of rallies to support a strike by the city's mostly Black sanitation workers, which proved to be King's last campaign. Eloquent and charismatic,

Jackson nonetheless alienated many on King's staff by his ambition. This breach widened after King's assassination in April 1968, when Jackson falsely claimed to have cradled the dying King, a myth he reinforced by wearing a bloody shirt for television cameras. Shunted aside by King's organization, Jackson in 1971 transformed the Chicago-based "Operation Breadbasket" into his own institute, called People United to Save Humanity (later changed to People United to Serve Humanity). While continuing to press white corporations to employ and otherwise aid ghetto residents, Jackson spent much of his time exhorting Black youths to avoid drugs, stay in school, and succeed through superior discipline and hard work.

During the 1970s Jackson's impact as a civil rights leader and evangelist for educational excellence propelled him to national fame, yet his condemnations of American society as racist, militaristic, and class-biased kept him on the fringes of political life. In 1979 Jackson visited the Middle East as part of an effort to assert a greater, more independent voice for Blacks in foreign affairs. He embraced Yassir Arafat of the Palestine Liberation Organization (widely viewed by Americans as a terrorist leader) and called for the creation of a Palestinian state. Although Jackson's activities enhanced his prominence as a maverick moralist, they also sharpened his widespread public image as a dangerous radical.

During the 1980s, as President Ronald Reagan cut federal aid to minorities and the poor, Jackson began to temper his message in hopes of forming a revitalized coalition for reform within the Democratic Party. Jackson campaigned in the 1984 Democratic presidential primaries, drawing large crowds and intense media coverage with his mixture of evangelical fervor, nimble wit, and self-conscious identification with minority hopes. He spoke of a "Rainbow Coalition" that would transcend racial lines, though his campaign focused chiefly on mobilizing African-American voter registration and support with the aid of Black churches. This strategy enabled Jackson to win nomination contests in South Carolina, Louisiana, and Washington, D.C., and to finish a surprising third in delegates at the Democratic National Convention (behind Walter Mondale and Gary Hart). Partly offsetting this achievement was his failure to win even 5 percent of the white primary vote, whether because of his race, radical past, lack of previous service in elective office, or suspect character. (Jews in particular recoiled at

his ties with the Black Muslim leader Louis Farrakhan, who had branded Judaism a "gutter religion.") Despite these weaknesses, Jackson's campaign legitimized "Black Power" to the American people in a way that African-American activists in the 1960s (such as Stokely Carmichael) had vainly tried to do from outside the political mainstream.

In 1988 Jackson hewed closer to the political center and reached well beyond his core supporters in a second bid for the Democratic presidential nomination. The by then seasoned candidate trimmed his radical rhetoric, conciliated many who had thought him opportunistic and divisive, and emphasized broadly appealing liberal themes of economic opportunity for all citizens. Jackson's approach, which this time won him second place (to Massachusetts governor Michael Dukakis) among seven competitors, reflected and fostered a new openness toward Blacks in the Democratic Party. An especially prominent landmark of changing political conditions was Jackson's primary victory in Michigan with 54 percent of the vote, just 20 years after that state's Democratic primary had gone to Alabama segregationist George Wallace. In 1990 Jackson was elected the first "shadow U.S. Senator" from the District of Columbia. Without a vote or speaking privileges on the floor of the Senate, Jackson was charged with the task of lobbying for statehood for the nation's capital.

Jackson's political success has remained in key aspects largely personal, for it has not appreciably changed his party's stands on key issues, nor has it dispelled racism as a factor in presidential politics. Still, Jackson's candidacies have imbued Blacks with pride and helped to keep issues of racial justice in view during an era of languishing enforcement of minority rights.

See also: Stokely Carmichael, Civil Rights Legislation and Southern Politics, Evangelicals, Martin Luther King, Jr., George Wallace

Robert S. Weisbrot

REFERENCES

Barker, Lucius J., and Ronald W. Walters, ed. 1989. *Jesse Jackson's 1984 Presidential Campaign: Challenge and Change in American Politics.* Urbana: U. of Illinois Pr.

Colton, Elizabeth O. 1989. *The Jackson Phenomenon: The Man, the Power, the Message.* Garden City, NY: Doubleday.

Reed, Adolph L., Jr. 1986. *The Jesse Jackson Phenomenon: The Crisis of Purpose in Afro-American Politics.* New Haven: Yale U. Pr.

Reynolds, Barbara A. 1985. *Jesse Jackson: America's David.* Washington: JFJ Associates.

Jacksonian Democracy

A label often applied by American historians to the period roughly from 1825 to 1850. One rather straightforward and limited definition of Jacksonian democracy simply links Andrew Jackson with the name of his Democratic Party, which became known as "the American democracy."

The other and more controversial meaning implies a direct relationship between the election of Jackson in 1828, the rise of the Democratic Party, and the democratization of American life during the second quarter of the nineteenth century. This second interpretation raises two questions: did a democratization of American life take place during this period, and if it did, what is the relationship between this democratization and Andrew Jackson and his party?

On these questions historians have varied and conflicting views. Some, for example, would argue that inegalitarianism, rather than egalitarianism, was a dominant condition throughout the period, and others point out that the Jacksonians had an abysmal record on social legislation concerning women, prison reform, and education. In addition, Jackson's brutal policy, removing the Indians to areas west of the Mississippi River, and the Democratic Party's complicity and active support in protecting slavery are ample evidence of the insensitivity to the human rights of nonwhite Americans on the part of Jackson and his party.

Nevertheless, egalitarianism was one of the characteristics that helped define the nature and character of Jackson's administration. In his first annual message, for example, he endorsed the principle of rotation in office, calling for a law that would limit political appointments to four years. But it was the banking issue that became the crucible of Jacksonian democracy. At the heart of Jackson's message vetoing the bill to recharter the Bank of the United States in 1832 was an egalitarian theme: "It is to be regretted," Jackson thundered, "that the rich and powerful too often bend the act of government to their selfish purposes." Government, he concluded must "confine itself to equal protection," and the bank bill violated this principle because it extended special privileges to a small, select group of men.

Was there a democratization of American life during that Jacksonian period, and, if there was, was there any relationship between this democratization and the Jacksonians? Despite some evidence to the contrary, most Americans of the

1830s, it appears, believed in the virtues of a democratic, egalitarian society, which, among other things, should seek to extend to its members equal protection before the law as well as equal opportunity to gain wealth and status, a value that shaped the way that men treated one another. The Jacksonians were generally more closely identified with this democratic spirit than were their opponents. And, notwithstanding the fact that elites controlled both parties and that the Democrats avoided or even contradicted themselves on some issues, many Americans looked to the Jacksonians for leadership in dealing with the unsettling forces of industrialization and the expansion of the market economy and in challenging—in the name of egalitarianism—privilege and unresponsive power.

See also: First Bank of the United States, Andrew Jackson

James R. Sharp

REFERENCES

Benson, Lee. 1961. *The Concept of Jacksonian Democracy: New York as a Test Case.* Princeton: Princeton U. Pr.

Pessen, Edward. 1978. *Jacksonian America: Society, Personality, and Politics.* Rev. ed. Homewood, IL: Dorsey.

Schlesinger, Arthur M., Jr. 1945. *The Age of Jackson.* Boston: Little, Brown.

Sharp, James Roger. 1970. *The Jacksonians Versus the Banks: Politics in the States After the Panic of 1837.* New York: Columbia U. Pr.

Jacksonian Party System

The idea of a Jacksonian party system like that of "the Age of Jackson" is rather abstract. Andrew Jackson was, of course, the hero of New Orleans and a well-known Indian fighter. Although he was clearly the most popular of the four candidates in 1824, the House of Representatives chose John Quincy Adams to be President. Four years later, however, Jackson defeated Adams and began an eight-year reign that divided the country on major issues such as Indian policy, money and banking, internal improvements, the tariff, land policy, and the federal government's response to the abolitionists. The opposition to Jackson on these matters gave rise to the Whig Party that would contend with the Democrats over these same issues until the 1850s. This "Great Man approach," however, does little to show the organizational development of the American political system during these years. Parties and elections in the United States between 1824 and 1852 may also be looked upon in terms of the invention of modern parties through the evolution of the second party system.

Probably the best way to begin is with a narrative of generally accepted facts before attempting a general interpretation. Most historians have focused on presidential elections. In 1824 the four main candidates were all closely connected with James Monroe's administration. The poorly attended congressional caucus—led by Martin Van Buren—threw its support to the Secretary of the Treasury, William H. Crawford. Various state legislatures nominated the Secretary of State, John Quincy Adams; the Speaker of the House, Henry Clay; and Jackson, who was a Senator from Tennessee at the time. After failing to obtain the necessary support in the Middle States, the former Secretary of War, John C. Calhoun, was nominated by Pennsylvania as the sole candidate for Vice President. When none of the four presidential candidates received a majority in the Electoral College, the election devolved upon the House, which chose Adams, despite Jackson's plurality of both popular and electoral votes.

Jackson felt cheated by a "corrupt bargain" after the newly elected President chose Clay, who had thrown his support to Adams in the House, to be Secretary of State—the traditional stepping stone to the presidency. Jackson vowed to defeat Adams in 1828 and in the course of the intervening years gained the support of Van Buren and those who had supported Crawford. With an improved organization and united support of the congressional "opposition" to the Adams administration, Jackson won the election with 56 percent of the popular vote and more than twice the electoral vote of Adams. Calhoun was reelected to the vice presidency over Richard Rush who was running with Adams.

Four years later Jackson, running with Van Buren, defeated Clay and John Sergeant. This election also included the first real "third party" in a presidential election and the introduction of the national nominating convention at which the "Democratic Antimasons" chose William Wirt and Amos Ellmaker as their candidates. Actually, Clay and Sergeant were anointed by a convention of "National Republicans." Finally, the "Republican Delegates of the states of the Union," met in Baltimore to nominate a vice presidential candidate, in this case Van Buren, to run with Jackson. Calhoun had broken with Jackson and eventually resigned the vice presi-dency to return to the Senate and defend Nullification.

While Jackson received only slightly fewer popular votes than he had in 1828, the returns were complicated by the participation of the Antimasons. Eight states saw three different tickets in the field, and in others deals were made between Clay and the Antimasons. In the Electoral College Jackson won by a much larger margin over Clay than he had over Adams. South Carolina cast its votes for Virginia governor John Floyd and Henry Lee of Massachusetts. Pennsylvania's electors voted for Jackson but rejected Van Buren in favor of a favorite son.

Such party confusion multiplied during by the election of 1836. In preparation for the election, the "Democratic Republicans" met in a rather irregularly attended convention in 1835 to support the elevation of Van Buren and to choose a running mate. Against the wishes of Virginia, they selected Jackson's favorite, Richard Mentor Johnson of Kentucky, equally famous for possibly killing the Indian chief Tecumseh and for having a mulatto mistress. From 1834 on, the diverse opponents of "King Andrew" began to refer to themselves as "Whigs." In 1836 this coalition called no convention, set no platform, and organized no national party. Traditional methods of nomination produced three opposition candidates who together received 49 percent of the popular vote. The name Whig was not universally used by the opposition and one candidate, Hugh Lawson White, even denied being a Whig. The Electoral College saw further confusion. South Carolina exercised her right of eccentricity. Virginia's Van Buren electors refused to support Johnson. In all, five presidential candidates and eight tickets received electoral votes. For the only time in American history, the Senate was asked to choose the Vice President and, by a vote of 33 to 16, picked Johnson who had a clear plurality among the electors.

Although famous for log cabins and hard cider, buncombe and ballyhoo, the election of 1840 ushered in a new period in the organization of presidential politics as well as a new style of campaigning. Both major parties held conventions. Whigs meeting in Harrisburg in 1839 overlooked their party's best-known figure, Henry Clay. Instead they chose William Henry Harrison of Ohio and the Virginian John Tyler. Harrison had been the leading opposition candidate in 1836, and Tyler had received 47 electoral votes for the vice presidency that year.

Although the Whigs nominated a balanced ticket, they foreswore writing a platform. When the Democrats met the following year, they renominated Van Buren and drew up what most historians consider to be the first modern platform designed to propound the principles of limited government and to allay southern fears about a northern candidate. The Democrats, however, did not pick a vice presidential candidate. Opposition to Johnson led them to leave the choice up to each state's electors. Harrison swept the famous log cabin campaign, polling nearly four times more electoral votes than Van Buren, although he only took 53 percent of the popular vote.

After that date, presidential and vice presidential nominations were usually contested within party conventions, and generally uniform partisan support was given to the chosen candidates. Conventions also adopted the practice of drawing up platforms formally expressing the party's basic principles, a feature clearly evident in the election of 1844. In convention, "the American Democracy" rejected their front-runner, Van Buren, in favor of a dark horse, James K. Polk, and drew up a platform that included, along with traditional party principles, the famous demand for "the reoccupation of Oregon and the re-annexation of Texas." The Whig convention nominated Clay and New Jersey minister and Congressman, Theodore Frelinghuysen, on a rather brief quasi-platform reiterating the principles associated with their candidate. By far the longest platform in 1844 was that of the Liberty Party. This third party had grown out of the abolitionist movement of the 1830s and had made a modest effort in the election of 1840; it also met in convention to pick as candidates a former Alabama slaveholder, James G. Birney, and Thomas Morris of Ohio. Although they won only slightly over 2 percent of the popular vote, the Liberty Party decisively affected the election by drawing enough votes away from Clay in New York to give the state and the election to Polk. Not one elector in the Electoral College deviated from supporting his party's ticket.

This pattern was repeated in both 1848 and 1852, and so for the most part were the other changes just mentioned. At the same time, national committees began to play a role. By 1848 the Mexican War and the Wilmot Proviso (outlawing slavery in any acquired territory) had split both parties but most particularly, the Democrats. To reunify the party, the Democratic convention produced a moderate and balanced ticket of northerner Lewis Cass and southerner William O. Butler and a platform steering away from the Proviso in the direction of popular sovereignty. The Whigs, meeting in Baltimore, followed a different strategy, putting forward Mexican War hero Zachary Taylor, a slaveholder from Louisiana, and New York moderate Millard Fillmore. They chose not to write a platform given the fact that their candidate Taylor had never voted in a national election, although he assured party leaders that he was a Whig "in principle." The Proviso controversy involved a crucial split in the Democratic Party that was not patched over by the convention. A significant number of Democrats—mostly New York Van Burenites who were called "Barnburners"—joined with Whig dissidents and former supporters of the Liberty Party to form the Free Soil Party. At their New York City convention, the Free Soilers named a ticket of ex-President Van Buren and Charles Francis Adams, John Quincy's son, and drew up a platform that reflected their motto "Free Soil, Free Speech, Free Labor, and Free Men." While Van Buren's 10 percent of the popular vote won the Free Soil ticket no electoral votes, it eased Taylor's victory.

Most of the administrations of Taylor (who died in 1850) and Fillmore were taken up with the debates that led to the Compromise of 1850 and the subsequent struggle between Unionists and radicals in the southern states. Both Democrats and Whigs attempted to silence agitation over the slavery question and to bring about both national and party unity. After 49 ballots, the Democratic convention in 1852 settled on Franklin Pierce—the "Young Hickory of the Granite Hills"—for President and William R. King of Alabama as his running mate on a platform affirming the Compromise of 1850. The Whigs once again looked to a Mexican War hero, General Winfield Scott, as their presidential candidate. William A. Graham of North Carolina was their vice presidential candidate. The Whigs' somewhat unusual platform tilted in the direction of states' rights and in extremely convoluted language supported the Compromise and opposed agitation of the slavery question in the interest of "the nationality of the Whig Party and of the Union." The remnant of the Free Soil Party minus the New York Barnburners met in Pittsburgh to nominate John P. Hale, who had stepped aside in favor of Van Buren four years earlier, and George W. Jullian, both northerners. The platform of the "Free Democracy" differed radically from those of the major parties in that it repudiated the Compromise of 1850 and called slavery "a sin against God and a crime against man." This platform was also much more comprehensive in the discussion of policies unrelated to slavery. Hale was able to gain only a bit over 5 percent of the popular vote, and the Free Democrats seem to have had little impact on Pierce's overwhelming victory. While the popular vote was much closer, Pierce and King received 254 votes in the Electoral College in contrast to 42 cast for Scott and Graham. The presidential election of 1852 would be the last to feature a contest between Democrats and Whigs.

The presidential elections from 1824 to 1852 fall into two groups, each of which represents a distinctly different phase of party development. The correlation among the areas that showed support for Jackson in the first three of these elections—Phase I (1824–1832)—was relatively high, but bore little relation to the areas of Van Buren's strength in 1836. That election began a new and relatively stable era—Phase II (1840–1852)—in which the distributions of Democratic strength from one election to the next were highly intercorrelated.

The election of 1836 was a transitional one that reflected some of the characteristics of both phases. Turnout in the last two elections of Phase I and in 1836 was moderately high (approximately 55 percent of those eligible), but it lagged below that for state elections. Phase II initiated a 50-year period of high and consistent popular interest in American presidential elections. Accompanying the jump in turnout (to 78 percent of those eligible in 1840) was a shift in the sectional patterns of party support. The elections of Phase I were distinctly sectional; the candidates obviously appealed to different parts of the country. New England went radically one way in each of these elections while the slave South leaned in the opposite direction. The second party system evolved with each successive presidential election, spreading from the Middle States where it appeared in 1828, to New England in 1832, and penetrating the South finally in 1836.

But historians following Frederick Jackson Turner have generally overemphasized the political importance of "sections" in the 1820s and 1830s. States were the most important entities, and most evidence of sectionalism—with the exception to slavery—represented only short-term shared interests of sets of contiguous states. In the first place most states gave their vote heavily to one candidate, with little intrastate competition. Where competition did exist, it did not reflect the development of two national parties. In 1832 the voters of four states split their votes among three candidates. Voters in only six states in that election decided real two-ticket contests, but the same tickets did not battle in each of these states. Four years later, the number of two-ticket contests doubled, and the confusion of tickets increased.

A new phase characterized by high turnout and two-party competition in all of the states (except South Carolina) appeared in 1840: the nature of the presidential contest changed from one rooted in cohesive state interests to one structured by national parties that penetrated into the states. This change came in two distinct steps: competition appeared in most states between 1832 and 1836; participation increased between 1836 and 1840. While the latter was undoubtedly influenced by the economic miseries attending the panic of 1837, shifts in the partisan allegiances of social classes had little to do with these changes.

Between 1824 and 1832 the vote for Jackson fluctuated widely from state to state—in fact, he received no votes in New Hampshire in 1824 and all of those cast in Mississippi in 1832. A similar wide range characterized Van Buren's vote in 1836; after 1840 the difference between the states giving the highest and lowest Democratic vote seldom exceeded 10 percent, and generally it was within a 5 percent range. Similarly, the Adams vote in 1828 correlated only moderately with both the Adams vote in 1824 and the Clay vote in 1832, and the later was not correlated with the vote for any of the candidates in 1836. In contrast, relatively high correlations existed between elections for both parties from 1840 to 1852.

If one moves from the nation with the states as the units of analysis to the states with the counties as the unit of analysis, then the difference between the two phases becomes even clearer. While a variety of patterns existed in both phases, what stands out is the diversity of these patterns in the first phase and their basic similarity in the second phase. The seeming stability of the presidential elections in Phase I masks intrastate volatility through 1836. Only after the late 1830s did American parties exhibit the stability that historians invariably have associated with them. In terms of the development of the second party system, Phase I was characterized by a diversity of responses in turnout and distribution of the vote within the states, while Phase II witnessed a uniformity of voter behavior throughout the country. Phase II did not owe to sectional responses but rather to the growth of party development within each state. Not only did New Jersey differ from Pennsylvania in Phase I, but both also differed from New York. Missouri and Alabama followed fairly similar patterns in the presidential elections of Phase I, but each differed from the neighboring states of Illinois and Mississippi. Virginia differed from North Carolina.

Although state gubernatorial and legislative elections did not occur at the same time as presidential elections, they also reflect two phases of development that roughly coincide with those discussed above. State politics in Phase I was for the most part a factional and personal politics that was dominated by intrastate regional conflict. Elections and legislatures were dominated by cliques such as the Albany Regency in New York (although Tammany Hall controlled New York City), the Richmond Junto in Virginia, and the Nashville Junto in Tennessee. Pennsylvania politics pitted the "Family party" against the "Amalgamation party." Georgia was run by the "Royal party." In Arkansas, opponents charged that the territory was in the hands of a clique colorfully designated "Ambrose Seivers' Hungry Kin." Similar groups often emerged to oppose the establishment, usually in the name of republicanism. In 1824 the People's Party was organized in New York to demand popular election of presidential electors. In Kentucky the New Court "party" favored relief of debtors. In New York City the Workingmen's Party was formed to oppose Tammany, and it served as a model for sporadic workingmen's parties in other cities and towns. The most successful of such groups was the Antimasons. In many states dubious organization generated gubernatorial elections that were contested by three or more candidates. By the late 1820s the convention system provided some formal organization for state parties in the Middle States where the idea of conventions had first taken root. In New England, conventions coexisted with other forms of nomination beginning in the early 1830s, but not until the end of that decade did the system penetrate most southern and western states. Although the patterns of state party development differed from

state to state, most state parties exhibited remarkably similar characteristics by 1840.

Historians have assumed a close relationship between state and federal elections. Local leaders sided with one candidate or the other, and it is well known that the Jacksonian candidacy in 1828 depended heavily on the alliance of the Albany Regency and the Richmond Junto. Generally, however, state and federal elections in Phase I were not closely correlated because of multiple candidacies in state elections and a general lack of continuity of organization from one election to the next. Several states at this time practiced what has been called "dual" politics, in which separate organizations contested state and federal elections. Gradually this situation gave way to a more stable relationship in Phase II. After the mid-1830s voters began to respond to candidates at both levels in a partisan fashion. Emerging was a sense of party identification that transcended the popularity of an individual; voters went to the polls with the conviction that they were either Democrats or Whigs.

The effect of partisanship in Congress fits roughly with the two phases found in the response of the electorate. While the party association of many congressional leaders was clear, the partisan affiliation of many Congressmen is difficult to ascertain until at least the middle of Jackson's second term. From Monroe's presidency until the last two years of Jackson's (Phase I), patterns of voting behavior in Congress reflected high cohesion within state delegations, and given the kinds of issues under consideration—Indian removal, internal improvements, public lands, the Bank of the United States, and the tariff—one can readily understand why. Historians have had less difficulty comprehending this pattern or understanding why the Turnerians confused it with sectionalism than they have had explaining why they have come to favor a pattern structured by party. While Jackson, for example, wished to alter traditional policies in several areas, "Jacksonian" Congresses did not always go along. All in all we have little evidence to suggest that party structured the roll-call behavior of Congressmen. After 1835 and throughout Phase II, party cohesion and competitiveness were generally high, although some fluctuation and slightly different patterns marked relations between the Democrats and the Whigs. Such partisanship reflected developing party institutions. In the late 1820s New Jersey, Delaware, and Ohio initiated the nomination of congressional candidates by party conventions, and the procedure gradually spread during the next decade. With the Twenty-fourth Congress in 1835, contests for the speakership of the House generally became two-party affairs. After that date only the elections of 1839 and 1849 (ones with sectional overtones) disrupt the pattern of well-managed party control. Finally, in 1846 the Senate made party organizations responsible for committee assignments. With these changes an altered conception of representation and a new legislative style emerged; independence gave way to party discipline. In dealing with one another, these "new" politicians demonstrated a flexibility in compromising on issues and a keen respect for manipulation of parliamentary procedures. In the mid-1840s, the Democrats annexed Texas, lowered the tariff, reinstituted the Independent Treasury, and prosecuted the Mexican War. These were party measures, and roll calls showed high Democratic cohesiveness and sharp conflict with an equally unified Whig opposition. Party unity and competitiveness were at their height in Congress in the mid-1840s. Even after 1849, when sectionalism increasingly intruded into congressional business, partisanship remained extremely important.

Generalizing about state legislative behavior is more difficult during these years, since relatively little systematic work has been done. While some locally popular candidates continued to run unopposed, the majority after the middle 1830s ran as major party candidates in fairly competitive elections. The scattered available roll calls tend to conform to the idea that, during Phase I, party as such had little effect upon any state legislation except appointments. Gradually, in Phase II partisan perspectives came to dominate in several areas (most particularly money and banking) before declining in relative importance at the end of the 1840s. At their height party cohesion and party dissimilarity in state legislatures were not equal to the levels in Congress. The difference between Phase I and Phase II can also be seen in constitutional conventions. The state constitutional conventions that created the western states in the 1810s and those up to that in Virginia in 1829 and 1830 were dominated by intrastate sectionalism. While sectionalism was never entirely absent and there was a good deal of antiparty rhetoric especially among the Whigs, partisanship dominated the Pennsylvania convention that met in 1837 and those of the other states that

followed it in the 1840s and early 1850s. From the mid-1840s on, the *Democratic Review* laid out a nationwide program of reform that included an elective judiciary, biennial sessions of limited duration, limitations on spending, a strong veto, and opposition to banks that formed a basic part of the agenda in most of the conventions. During Phase II, especially in the mid-1840s, partisan conflict in state legislatures and constitutional conventions took on remarkably similar outlines from state to state.

In each state the Democrats and the Whigs assumed positions shared by their fellow partisans throughout the country. The behavior of the voters, however, reflected the unique social and economic situations within each of the states. The social basis of party politics in the South differed from that in the North. Yet, in distinct contrast to traditional views, recent voting studies from all parts of the country suggest that the relative wealth of citizens had little to do with their party preference.

In the North some occupational and status difference occurs between Whigs and Democrats; a strong Whiggish bias marked the wealthy in northern cities. But the major distinctions between the rank and file of Whig and Democratic voters grew from their relation to certain ethnoreligious communities. For the most part recent studies counsel caution on such traditional conceptions as an "immigrant vote"; historians now reject as reductionist a stance that views denominational affiliation as an indicator of economic class only. Immigrants divided their vote in New York and Pennsylvania. In these states the "invisible immigrants"—the English, Scots, and Welsh—were Whigs. While the Irish and the German newcomers better fit the traditional picture of strong Democratic support, both groups were split by religious differences. The political behavior of Irish Catholics who were Democrats, virtually to the man, stood in sharp contrast to that of the Irish Protestants who were predominantly Whigs. Among Germans the minority sects, such as the Brethren and the Moravians, bitterly opposed the majority who were Lutheran, German Reformed, or Catholic. Such denominational differences continued to affect members of these ethnic groups even though they had lived in the United States for several generations. For all that, political behavior was also related to doctrinal disputes within denominations, a split that reflected differences in religious style. Most northern Presbyterians tended to be Whigs, but in the Middle States the Old School "party" leaned toward the Democrats. In Illinois, Baptists favoring home missions tended to be Whigs, while those who opposed home missions supported Jackson and his followers. Often these differences in religious style were only aspects of other forms of group hostility. In the lower Midwest, settlers from the upland South almost invariably clashed with the Yankees who moved into the area in the 1820s and 1830s. Generally these group conflicts had economic overtones as well, but the shared values and group perspectives of certain ethnocultural communities enabled their members to comprehend the meaning of political action in personally relevant terms. Even partisan response to economic issues must be understood in relation to the economic orientation consonant with the group's values.

In the South wealth seems to have had only a minor relation to political preference. The allegiance to the Democrats of the Germans in Virginia, the Catholics and foreign-born in Louisiana, the handful of Episcopalians and Presbyterians in Georgia and Arkansas, as well as the contrasting roles of the Germans and native-born Presbyterians in Missouri all point to the relevance of ethnic and religious differences in these states. But the dominance of Anglo-Protestants, particularly Methodists and Baptists, in most of the South, and the compartmentalized nature of religious outlooks in that section have frustrated historians' attempts at developing an ethnoreligious synthesis. Studies of Mississippi, Alabama Georgia, Tennessee, North Carolina, and Virginia have connected Whig sentiments with those flourishing economic areas that had a commercial orientation toward the outside world. For example, southern cities and towns had a distinct Whiggish cast. Whigs often predominated in nonagricultural occupations, while those isolated completely from market forces were more likely to be Democrats. Yet leaders of both parties who were drawn from the social and economic elite retained a personal following that involved a combination of deference and the response of leaders to local needs. County studies emphasizing the importance of kin relationships— "friends and neighbors politics"—and the continuing impact throughout the South of intrastate regionalism suggest that certain aspects of Phase I were simply extended and redefined during Phase II to relate to national issues and the relevant market perspectives shared with their northern counterparts.

Hindsight enables historians to see that the presidential election of 1852 represented the last hurrah of the Whigs and that the second party system was in shambles by the end of 1854. Turnout had declined and competition was becoming less marked, especially in the Gulf States. Antisouthernism seemed to be on the rise in the North. At least one historian has equated the growth of the second party system to the spread of favorable attitudes toward party conflict and its decline to the widespread belief that the Whigs and Democrats presented an echo rather than a choice. Yet, on most grounds, the Whigs and the second party system seemed to remain viable, even after the defeat in 1852. The Whigs had received more votes than ever before and a larger percentage of the vote in the North. The party was still strong in Congress, the upper South, and in the North; it was more than a respectable minority. Shrewd politicians such as William Seward and Abraham Lincoln were not about to desert the ship, although both would soon become leaders of the Republican Party and the latter its first President.

Although some historians of the Jacksonian party system have understood the mid-1820s in terms of partisan realignment and 1828 as a critical election, others have pointed to some of the problems involved in applying twentieth-century concepts to the early nineteenth century. If the term *party* is applied loosely, however, it can be used to describe what was happening. The election of 1828 featured two candidates with a certain amount of new organizational support and a significant increase in voter interest. Although traditional party conflict, as it existed in the days of the Federalists and the Republicans, had been dormant for over a decade, former partisans split their allegiance between the two candidates. The followers of Jackson formed the core of what would become the Democratic Party while the supporters of Adams would become the nucleus of the Whig Party. Jackson's presidency, moreover, did bring major changes in several areas of public policy that lasted until the Civil War. Yet the system went through two stages of development and, in Phase I, was hardly a "system" at all. Partisanship barely extended beyond presidential elections into Congress and had minimal impact on state government. During Phase II modern parties emerged and penetrated into the electoral and legislative politics of the states. While Jackson was no longer on the scene, he remained a symbolic presence.

See also: Election of 1824, 1828, 1844, and 1852, Andrew Jackson, Stages of Party Development, Martin Van Buren

William G. Shade

REFERENCES

Alexander, Thomas P. 1967. *Sectional Stress and Party Strength: A Study of Roll-Call Voting Patterns in the House of Representatives.* Nashville: Vanderbilt U. Pr.

Benson, Lee. 1961. *The Concept of Jacksonian Democracy: New York, a Test Case.* Princeton: Princeton U. Pr.

Chase, James S. 1973. *Emergence of the Presidential Nominating Convention, 1789–1832.* Urbana: U. of Illinois Pr.

Formisano, Ronald P. 1971. *The Rise of Mass Political Parties: Michigan, 1827–1861.* Princeton: Princeton U. Pr.

———. 1983. *The Transformation of American Political Culture: Massachusetts Parties, 1790s–1840s.* New York: Oxford U. Pr.

Levine, Peter. 1977. *Behavior of State Legislative Parties in the Jacksonian Era: New Jersey, 1829–1844.* Rutherford, NJ: Fairleigh Dickinson U. Pr.

McCormick, Richard P. 1966. *The Second American Party System: Party Formation in the Jacksonian Era.* Chapel Hill: U. of North Carolina Pr.

Remini, Robert. 1963. *The Election of Andrew Jackson.* Philadelphia: Lippincott.

Schlesinger, Arthur M., Jr., ed. 1973. *History of U.S. Political Parties.* 4 vols. New York: Chelsea House.

———, and Fred L. Israel, eds. 1971. *History of American Presidential Elections.* 3 vols. New York: Chelsea House.

Shade, William G. 1972. *Banks or No Banks: The Money Issue in Western Politics, 1832–1865.* Detroit: Wayne State U. Pr.

Sharp, James Roger. 1970. *The Jacksonians Versus the Banks: Politics in the States After the Panic of 1837.* New York: Columbia U. Pr.

Thornton, Mills, III. 1978. *Politics and Power in a Slave Society: Alabama, 1800–1860.* Baton Rouge: Louisiana State U. Pr.

Watson, Harry L. 1981. *Jacksonian Politics and Community Conflict: The Emergence of the Second American Party System in Cumberland County, North Carolina.* Baton Rouge: Louisiana State U. Pr.

Jay Treaty

In the summer of 1794, John Jay was sent to Great Britain to negotiate a treaty that would settle outstanding disputes arising from the American Revolution. The British still occupied posts on the western frontier and continued to seize American seamen. The United States, on the other hand, still owed debts to British citizens and wished to improve trade relations. The terms of the treaty turned out to have dramatic effects on party formation and public opinion in the United States. Though Jay obtained no commercial privileges other than restricted trade with the West Indies, he gave up the right to regulate British imports for ten years. In addition, the treaty did not maintain the honor of the federal courts regarding debts to British subjects, gave no recognition to American-backed principles of maritime law, guaranteed no protection from impressment of U.S. sailors, and (though the British promised to abandon the western forts) did not prohibit British interference with the Indians. Nevertheless, Jay had made perhaps the best deal that could have been made at the time, and he did keep the United States out of war.

Washington so disliked the treaty that he waited six months before submitting it to the Senate for ratification, where it passed in 1795 by a 20-to-10 margin—the bare two-thirds required. The real contest began when Republicans in the House attempted to block appropriations to put the treaty into effect. The constitutional principle that the lower house had concurring power with the Senate in regard to treaties by withholding appropriations was the focus of their opposition. They argued that American independence had to be economic as well as political and that America stood at the crossroads of aligning with either aristocratic Britain or republican France.

When the treaty came before the House in 1796, Congressmen voted 62–37 to ask Washington for additional documents to explain the negotiation. He adamantly refused. After bitter debate, the appropriations passed, 51–48. Forty-five Republicans and 3 Federalists voted against and 44 Federalists and 7 Republicans voted for. Unsurprisingly, 7 Republicans voting for the treaty were from the Middle Atlantic States that would commercially benefit most from the treaty.

The Jay Treaty was a significant chapter in the foreign policy of the infant Republic. The chief political effect of the treaty was to align the infant parties along much clearer lines; it helped to transform the Republican faction into a Republican Party as the coordination among federal-state-local partisans as well as executive-legislative relations firmly established. The treaty was also important in helping the Republicans organize popular support. James Madison, especially, paid close attention to party tactics, and party strategy became an important consideration in congressional decisions. Unfortunately for him, party discipline among the Republicans was not quite advanced enough to insure defeat of the treaty. For the Federalist Party, the treaty proved disastrous in the South because the planter class was dissatisfied. Not insignificantly, the quarrel over the treaty also convinced Jefferson that he should run for President in order to move the nation in the right direction.

See also: Federalist Party, George Washington

Daniel Dean Roland

REFERENCES

Bemis, Samuel Flagg. 1923. *Jay's Treaty, A Study in Commerce and Diplomacy*. New York: Macmillan.

Charles, Joseph. 1956. *The Origins of the American Party System*. Williamsburg, VA: Institute of Early American History and Culture.

Cunningham, Noble. 1957. *The Jeffersonian Republicans: The Formation of Party Organization*. Chapel Hill: U. of North Carolina Pr.

Monaghan, Frank. 1935. *John Jay*. New York: Bobbs Merrill.

Thomas Jefferson (1743–1826)

Philosopher, statesman, diplomat, public servant, and the nation's most brilliant President. Thomas Jefferson, the third President of the United States, who served from 1801 to 1809, had a busy public career that spanned one of the most creative periods in the history of the nation. The Virginia statesman played a key role in shaping the new Republic and in preserving the Union and the Constitution in the face of major foreign and domestic challenges.

Chief author of the Declaration of Independence, member of the Continental Congress, Revolutionary War governor of Virginia, and minister to France, Jefferson was appointed Secretary of State in the Cabinet of President George Washington in the first government under the new Constitution. Although Jefferson had been out of the country while the Constitution had been drafted, debated, and ratified, he cautiously supported the new frame of government. At the same time, however, he was critical of the lack of a bill of rights in the original document and worried about the power of the presidency.

Contrary to the widely accepted civic humanist belief that selfless citizens would come together and legislate for the public good, there were bitter divisions within the Washington administration and between that administration and Congress in defining the national public good. Jefferson, much to his dismay, found himself allied with fellow-Virginian James Madison in the leadership of a developing southern-based opposition to a number of Washington administration policies. Specifically Jefferson and the incipient opposition objected to Secretary of the Treasury Alexander Hamilton's financial plan for funding the national debt, assuming the state debts, and creating a national bank. Jefferson charged that the bank was unconstitutional, that it shifted power from the states to the national government, and that it favored the more commercial northern states over the more agrarian southern ones. An equally bitter division arose over Washington's neutrality policy, one that, Jefferson and his friends believed, abandoned revolutionary France, a faithful ally during the American Revolution.

These divisions formed the basis for the subsequent development in the 1790s of the two proto-parties, the Federalists and the Republicans. And after supposedly retiring from public life in 1793, Jefferson reluctantly allowed himself to stand as the Republican candidate for President in 1796. Losing the election to his old revolutionary colleague, Federalist John Adams, Jefferson spent the next four years as Vice President (having received the second highest number of electoral votes) and as the leader of the Republican opposition.

Jefferson and the Republicans defeated Adams and the Federalists in 1800. Serving two terms, Jefferson was a strong executive who exercised considerable influence in Congress despite the absence of strong party loyalties there. Economy in government, strict construction of the Constitution, and limitations on federal authority were the themes of his administration. Jefferson's greatest success, one that compromised his strict constructionist principles, was the purchase of the Louisiana Territory from France in 1803, freeing the United States from a potentially troublesome and powerful neighbor and opening up an immense new territory for settlement. Less successful were his attempts to isolate the United States from the war between France and Great Britain with his Non-Importation and Embargo policies.

Finally retiring from public life in 1809, he died on the fiftieth anniversary of the Declaration of Independence.

See also: John Adams, Alexander Hamilton, Jeffersonian Republicans, James Madison, First Bank of the United States, George Washington

James R. Sharp

REFERENCES

Cunningham, Noble E., Jr. 1978. *The Process of Government Under Jefferson*. Princeton: Princeton U. Pr.

Ellis, Richard E. 1971. *The Jeffersonian Crisis: Courts and Politics in the Young Republic*. New York: Oxford U. Pr.

Koch, Adrienne. 1969. *Jefferson and Madison: The Great Collaboration*. New York: Oxford U. Pr.

Malone, Dumas. 1948. *Jefferson and His Time*. Boston: Little, Brown.

Peterson, Merrill D. 1962. *The Jefferson Image in the American Mind*. New York: Oxford U. Pr.

———. 1970. *Thomas Jefferson and the New Nation: A Biography*. New York: Oxford U. Pr.

Young, James Sterling. 1966. *The Washington Community, 1800–1828*. New York: Harcourt, Brace, & World.

Jeffersonian Republicans

The modern Democratic Party traces its origins to the Jeffersonian Republican Party (also called the Democratic-Republicans) that emerged at the end of the eighteenth century. This party began as a legislative faction that eventually coalesced around Thomas Jefferson by the end of the First Congress. While its members had no formal party identification, much less any organizational structure, this "republican interest" shared several political principles. They were deeply suspicious of Alexander Hamilton and his fiscal programs, worried about monarchical tendencies in the new government, and generally protective of the rights of local government (which they thought indispensable to the protection of personal liberty).

At first Jefferson sought to distance himself somewhat from the Republican faction. He was, after all, Secretary of State of the very administration that the faction suspected of antirepublican sentiments. But Jefferson thought it important to compete against Hamilton for the soul of that administration. By 1793, however, Jefferson recognized that George Washington and his administration were now irrevocably aligned with the Federalists. He resigned and immediately became the symbolic leader of the opposition.

The organizational heart of the Republican faction was James Madison. Like most prominent Americans of that generation, he had been a fervent antiparty man. But Madison set about to mobilize public opinion against the Federalists, principally by subsidizing newspapers and pamphlets and by coordinating Republican electoral efforts locally as well as nationally. Democratic societies, dedicated to advancing republicanism in America and the revolution in France, began to spring up in many communities. Though not formally connected to the Jeffersonian Republicans (as the Federalists claimed) they proved to be a fertile recruiting ground for the party.

By 1796 party leaders convinced Jefferson to try for the presidency. The election was close. Only three electoral votes separated Adams from Jefferson; conflicts within the Federalist camp had divided many of their electors. Thus, unexpectedly, Jefferson (as the winner of the second-highest total of electoral votes) became Vice President.

In 1800 Adams and Jefferson again squared off for the Presidency, and the election was again close. The outcome was in doubt until the last slate of electors chosen (South Carolina) broke the tie between the two parties and gave the election to the Republicans. The election was notable in several respects. It was the first election in which the presidency was transferred to a party that previously had been the opposition. It was the first realigning election in which a new party supplanted the old party at nearly every level of government. It was the first presidential election in which electors no longer acted as free agents. All but one elector voted for both of his party's nationally recognized candidates. Finally, there was an unintended consequence of this newfound party solidarity. Because each elector cast two votes for President, Jefferson and Aaron Burr (the party's Vice President–designate) obtained the same number of electoral votes. The election was thrown into the House of Representatives where Hamilton finally convinced his Federalist supporters (who controlled the deciding state delegations) to elect Jefferson rather than the faithless Burr.

The party continued its appeals to the electorate until by 1816 it was the only effective party in American politics. But in 1824, growing resentment of southern domination led to its fractionalization. When Andrew Jackson was elected President in 1832, he signaled the death of the Jeffersonian Republicans and the birth of its offspring, the Democratic Party.

See also: Aaron Burr, Democratic-Republican Societies, Election of 1796, 1800, and 1824, Federalists, Thomas Jefferson, James Madison

Glenn A. Phelps

REFERENCES

Banning, Lance. 1978. *The Jeffersonian Persuasion: Evolution of a Party Ideology*. Ithaca: Cornell U. Pr.

Cunningham, Noble E., Jr. 1957. *The Jeffersonian Republicans: The Formation of Party Organization, 1789–1801*. Chapel Hill: U. of North Carolina Pr.

Formisano, Ronald P. 1983. *The Transformation of Political Culture: Massachusetts Parties, 1790s–1840s*. New York: Oxford U. Pr.

Schlesinger, Arthur M., Jr., and Fred L. Israel, eds. 1985. *History of American Presidential Elections, 1789–1968*. Vol. 1. New York: Chelsea House.

Jenness v. Fortson

403 U.S. 431 (1971)

In this case, the Supreme Court unanimously rejected a challenge to Georgia's election laws that denied independent and nonparty candidates access to the ballot at the general election unless they filed a nominating petition. The petition, which had to be signed by at least 5 percent of those eligible to vote in the previous election, was apparently designed to restrict ballot access to those candidates who could demonstrate that they had some degree of political support within the state.

Georgia law recognizes "political parties" and "political bodies." A "political party" is any political organization whose candidate received 20 percent or more of the vote at the most recent gubernatorial or presidential election. Any other political organization is a "political body." Political parties conduct primary elections, and only the name of the candidate who wins the primary election is printed on the ballot at the general election. A nominee of a "political body" or an independent candidate may have his or her name printed on the ballot at the general election by filing a nominating petition.

These provisions were challenged by a group of prospective candidates and registered voters who argued that this requirement of demonstrated support abridged the rights of free speech and association guaranteed to a candidate and his supporters by the First and Fourteenth amendments and violated the equal protection clause of the Fourteenth Amendment. A three-judge district court upheld the constitutionality of the nominating-petition requirement. The court did, however, enter an injunction with respect to the requirement that a candidate for public office pay a filing fee equal to 5 percent of the annual salary of the office he is seeking. No appeal was sought on the issue of the validity of the fee requirement.

The Supreme Court affirmed the judgment of the district court. Justice Potter Stewart, speaking for the Court, compared Georgia's election laws to the Ohio provisions held unconstitutional in *Williams v. Rhodes*, and found the two statutory schemes "vastly different." Unlike Ohio, Georgia did not require every candidate to be the nominee of a political party, did not fix an unreasonably early filing deadline for a candidate not endorsed by established parties, nor did it impose upon a small or new party the requirement of establishing elaborate primary election machinery. In short, Georgia's

election laws did not "operate to freeze the political status quo," and therefore, did not abridge the rights of free speech and association secured by the First and Fourteenth amendments.

With respect to the issue of equal protection, the Court said that gathering the signatures of 5 percent of the total eligible electorate is not inherently more burdensome than winning the votes of a majority in a party primary. The Court also pointed out that "there are obvious differences in kind between the needs and potentials of a political party with historically established broad support . . . and a new or small political organization." In providing different routes to the printed ballot, Georgia law was deemed properly to recognize these differences.

Justice Stewart concluded his opinion in *Jenness v. Fortson* by noting that Georgia's interest in avoiding "confusion, deception, even frustration of the democratic process at the general election" was sufficient to justify the demonstrated support requirement. The Court did not address the issue of whether a petition requirement of less than 5 percent would have satisfied the state's interest.

See also: Williams v. Rhodes

Robin Bye Wolpert

REFERENCES

Tribe, Laurence. 1988. *American Constitutional Law.* 2nd ed. New York: Foundation Press.
Williams v. Rhodes, 393 U.S. 23 (1968).

Marshall Jewell (1825–1883)

Republican national chairman from Connecticut. Marshall Jewell was a governor of Connecticut, Postmaster General under President Ulysses S. Grant, and chairman of the Republican National Committee (1880–1883). Jewell first entered Connecticut politics in an unsuccessful race for the United States Senate; he next won election as governor in 1869 and was reelected in 1871. Jewell helped carry his closely contested state for Grant in 1868 and again in 1872; his reward in 1873 was an appointment as minister to Russia.

Jewell next became Grant's Postmaster General, a position whose patronage gave him substantial connections with GOP leaders throughout the nation and familiarity with the party's problems in the South. When he failed to receive a position in President Rutherford B. Hayes's Cabinet, Jewell went into semiretirement from politics. He absented himself from the 1880 national convention because of his former service in Grant's Cabinet and his declared opposition to a third term for Grant. Jewell himself received a substantial number of votes in the vice presidential balloting.

At the national committee, the pro-Grant coalition of state bosses did what they could to reelect Don Cameron of Pennsylvania as chairman. The presidential nominee, James A. Garfield, hoping to avoid alienating the coalition of bosses, asked the much-esteemed Jewell to take the chairmanship. He agreed, but indicated that he would not take a very active management role. He, in fact, later lost control of the campaign to the bosses.

See also: James Donald Cameron, James Garfield, Ulysses S. Grant, Rutherford B. Hayes, Republican National Committee

Ralph M. Goldman

REFERENCES

Goldman, Ralph M. 1990. *The National Party Chairmen and Committees: Factionalism at the Top.* Armonk, NY: M. E. Sharpe.
William E. Chandler Papers, Library of Congress.
William E. Chandler Papers, New Hampshire Historical Society, Manchester, New Hampshire.

Jim Crow Laws

Various statutes designed to establish a racially segregated society that would ensure an inferior status for Blacks by prescribing the "acceptable" place for the African-American in American society, the Jim Crow laws segregated the races in the workplace, in places of residence, and even in recreation. Such laws included zoning ordinances, curfew laws, ordinances for segregation of public places and schools, legal definitions of how much Black blood constituted a "Negro," laws forbidding interracial marriages, vagrancy laws, and voting restrictions. Such discriminatory laws also maintained white supremacy in southern Democratic parties and helped preserve Democratic Party dominance of the South.

Reconstruction governments had been shaky coalitions of African-Americans and sympathetic whites who suffered from the absence of finance capital in the postwar South. Such coalition governments soon lost power to conservative southerners—the Redeemers—who sought to rebuild the South and to deprive Blacks of their rights. The disputed 1876 presidential election marked the beginning of the Jim Crow era, as northern Republicans compromised with southern conservatives to elect as President Republican Rutherford B. Hayes, who had agreed to withdraw federal troops from the South.

Henceforth, both national parties refrained from championing the cause of Blacks in the South. Southern African-Americans were left to the mercy of conservative white Redeemers, who enacted discriminatory Jim Crow and voting laws.

Elements promoting Jim Crow laws included the long-established norms and mores in the South, the withdrawal of federal troops, and the lack of northern interest in continuing assistance to Blacks. Most northerners had become more interested in business ventures, in settling the West, and in seeking national unity after a bloody civil war than in the plight of the freed slave. Discrimination had also become a worldwide development, as other western imperial and colonial powers practiced the segregation of colonial races. Finally, African-Americans were at a disadvantage economically in their competition with the white population.

Several legal cases opened the way for the widespread enactment of Jim Crow laws. In a series of civil rights cases in 1883, the Supreme Court ruled that the Fourteenth Amendment could not be used to restrict individuals from acts of racial discrimination and segregation. In the 1890 *Louisville, New Orleans, and Texas Railroad v. Mississippi* case, the Court opened the way for segregation on railroads. In the landmark *Plessy v. Ferguson* case of 1896, the Court established the "separate but equal" rule, holding that racial segregation was permissible as long as facilities for both races are equal. *Plessy* was henceforth used by the South to justify and defend its racial segregation laws.

Racial discrimination was open and direct in the South, but it also existed in the North in a more informal and indirect way. After the turn of the century, Jim Crow laws expanded from the railroads, to which they had previously largely been confined, to other areas of society. While Jim Crow laws applied chiefly to Blacks, they also could apply to other nonwhite groups. Their primary effect was to stratify society along racial lines and widen the economic, social, and political gap between the races.

Attempts to end the Jim Crow laws by executive order were not as effective as judicial and legislative efforts. Ultimately, the Supreme Court ruled in the *Brown v. Board of Education* (1954) decision that separation was inherently unequal, reversing *Plessy v. Ferguson.* Legislative actions culminated in the 1964 Civil Rights Act forbidding discrimination and the 1965 Voting Rights Act guaranteeing minorities the right to vote.

See also: Civil Rights Legislation and Southern Politics, Election of 1876, Voting Rights Act of 1965 and Extensions

Grady L. Johnston

Andrew Johnson (1808–1875)

Only President to be impeached. Andrew Johnson openly boasted that he had served at every level of government, from town alderman to President. A native of North Carolina, he moved to Tennessee in 1826, opening a tailor shop in Greeneville. Elected alderman in 1828 and mayor in 1830, he advanced to state politics, serving two terms as a representative (1835–1837, 1839–1841) and another in the state senate (1841–1843). In 1842 he was elected to the first of five terms as a United States Representative; eleven years later he was elevated to the governor's chair for two terms. Chosen United States Senator by the state legislature in 1857, he began to entertain notions of running for President on the Democratic ticket in 1860, only to be passed over by the nominating conventions. During all these years Johnson's politics seem to have been characterized by a devotion to the common farmer and artisan, an unrelenting attack upon aristocracy, and an irritating inability to compromise with his opponents. His efforts to pass a federal homestead bill and his success as governor in establishing public education proved his most noteworthy accomplishments; more memorable to many was his stump oratory, which at times verged on demagoguery. He was never afraid to stand up for his principles, demonstrating physical as well as political bravery on several occasions in facing down assassination threats.

The Tennesseean's courage was most evident during the secession crisis and the outbreak of sectional hostilities in 1860 and 1861. The only southern Senator from a seceded state to remain in Washington, Johnson risked his life campaigning against secession in East Tennessee, enduring charges that he had betrayed his section. At the same time he cosponsored resolutions in Congress explicitly declaring that the aim of the war was limited to reunion and repudiating any desire for emancipation. In the wake of Union military victories in western Tennessee in early 1862, President Abraham Lincoln appointed Johnson military governor of the state, and for the next three years he grappled firsthand with the problems of wartime reconstruction. Eventually he accepted emancipation as a war measure; although he supported this step primarily as a blow against the slaveholding aristocracy, several of his addresses, notably one in which he declared that he was willing to serve as the Moses of the emancipated Blacks, led at least some people to believe that he had recanted his earlier racism. Johnson was rewarded for his troubles in 1864 when Lincoln chose him as his running mate. The resulting Republican triumph moved Johnson into the nation's second-highest office; John Wilkes Booth's bullet finished the process of Johnson's political advancement by elevating him to the presidency.

As the seventeenth President of the United States, Johnson's chief responsibility was to oversee Reconstruction, a process that involved determining the status of the Black freedmen as well as outlining a process of reunion and reintegration of the rebellious southern states. The President's early statements condemning treason and traitors, encouraging to many Republicans, soon gave way to a far more lenient approach, undertaken without the sanction of Congress. While the Tennesseean's anti-aristocratic leanings were revealed in his pardon policy—calling upon wealthy southerners as well as military and civil leaders to make personal application for pardon—his refusal to consider the possibility of property confiscation or the federal imposition of Black enfranchisement aggravated the many Republicans who looked to Reconstruction as an opportunity to revolutionize southern society. In addition, President Johnson's seeming indifference to reports of racial violence against African-Americans and a resurgent rebel spirit caused many moderate Republicans to wonder whether the chief executive himself was bent on frittering away the fruits of Union victory. These impressions were reinforced when Johnson vetoed legislation to protect the freedmen and grant them civil equality; Congress overrode his veto of the Civil Rights Act and eventually prolonged the life of the Freedman's Bureau to assist Blacks in the transition from slavery to freedom.

While Johnson had accepted the second spot on the Republican ticket in 1864, he never really considered himself a Republican. His refusal to reach a compromise with congressional Republicans over the proper course to pursue toward the South was highlighted by some intemperate speeches in which he characterized several Republican leaders as traitors. Instead, he sought to form a new political movement composed of moderate Democrats, conservative Republicans, and repentant white southerners, devoted to restoring the Union and limiting the impact of the war on the South beyond emancipation. This coalition, christened the National Union Movement, proved to be little more than a stalking-horse for Johnson's attempts to gain support for the election of a Congress favorable to his policies—an achievement that might eventually lead to an electorate willing to reelect him in 1868. In August and September 1866, the President took to the field to stump for his policy, which by now encompassed opposition to all Republican Reconstruction measures, including the proposed Fourteenth Amendment. This campaign trip, which he called the "Swing Around the Circle," proved a disastrous embarrassment. Johnson relived the days when he stumped East Tennessee exchanging barbs with rowdy crowds, behavior that was not only unpresidential but shameful; a disgusted Ulysses S. Grant termed the entire enterprise "a National disgrace." The fall off-year elections resulted in an overwhelming Republican triumph that secured veto-proof majorities in both houses of Congress.

Undeterred by defeat, Johnson continued to obstruct Reconstruction at every opportunity. When his vetoes of Reconstruction legislation in 1867 were overridden, he construed the resulting legislation so narrowly as to defeat its aims. As a result, subsequent legislation attempted to tie his hands. Most important in this regard was the passage of the Tenure of Office Act, a law that required Senate approval for the removal of any officeholder who had been appointed with the Senate's consent. In August 1867, Johnson, appearing to act in compliance with this legislation, suspended Secretary of War Edwin M. Stanton, primarily in retaliation for Stanton's zealous support of Reconstruction; Grant was named to the post on an *ad interim* basis. Republican setbacks in the elections of 1867 and the collapse of several efforts at impeachment encouraged the President so much that he chose to resist the Senate's attempt to reinstate Stanton, an action that brought him in to open conflict with Grant, who refused to participate in the plot. A second attempt by Johnson to remove Stanton in outright defiance of the Tenure of Office Act resulted in the passage of articles of impeachment by the House of Representatives on February 24, 1868. The misgivings of Republican moderates about whether Johnson's actions considered impeachable offenses, concern about the economic

policies endorsed by President *pro tempore* Benjamin F. Wade (who would have succeeded to the presidency upon conviction), and some uncharacteristically moderate behavior on Johnson's part saved the President from conviction, although acquittal was by the slimmest of margins, a single vote. Whatever notions Johnson entertained of securing the Democratic nomination for President were quickly squashed, leaving him to watch in frustration as Grant won the ensuing election. Johnson left the White House vowing to return to Washington; he achieved his goal in 1875 when the Tennessee legislature named him United States Senator once more, although he died later that year.

While many historians once applauded Johnson for his adherence to constitutional forms, recent scholars have condemned him for his racism, his inability to compromise, and his encouragement of postwar southern intransigence. While Johnson's behavior resulted in the passage of amendments and legislation that pushed Reconstruction beyond its original bounds, his obstructionism, by diverting Republican attention from the South, was essential to the final frustration of Reconstruction policy in its efforts to achieve racial equality and justice for generations to come. The failure of Republicans to win a conviction in the impeachment crisis demonstrated that the impeachment process works better as an implicit threat than as an explicit sanction.

See also: Ulysses S. Grant, Homestead Act, Abraham Lincoln, Race and Racial Politics, Reconstruction, Secession, Edwin Stanton, Benjamin Wade

Brooks Donohue Simpson

REFERENCES

Beale, Howard K. 1930. *The Critical Year: A Study of Andrew Johnson and Reconstruction.* New York: Harcourt, Brace.

Benedict, Michael Les. 1973. *The Impeachment and Trial of Andrew Johnson.* New York: Norton.

Bergeron, Paul, et al., eds. 1967–1989. *The Papers of Andrew Johnson.* 8 vols. to date. Knoxville: U. of Tennessee Pr.

Castel, Albert. 1979. *The Presidency of Andrew Johnson.* Lawrence: U. Pr. of Kansas.

McKitrick, Eric L. 1960. *Andrew Johnson and Reconstruction.* Chicago: U. of Chicago Pr.

Sefton, James E. 1980. *Andrew Johnson and the Uses of Constitutional Power.* Boston: Little, Brown.

Simpson, Brooks D., et al., eds. 1987. *Advice After Appomattox: Letters to Andrew Johnson, 1865–1866.* Knoxville: U. of Tennessee Pr.

Trefousse, Hans L. 1975. *Impeachment of a President: Andrew Johnson, the Blacks, and Reconstruction.* Knoxville: U. of Tennessee Pr.

Hiram W. Johnson (1886–1945)

Republican governor and United States Senator from California. Republican Hiram Warren Johnson was an ardent Progressive reformer and a fierce isolationist. The son of a Sacramento corporate lawyer and state legislator, Johnson was a successful trial lawyer before he was drawn into local reform politics in the early 1900s. He gained national prominence in 1906 when, as assistant district attorney in San Francisco, he helped prosecute members of Abraham Ruef's political machine. Johnson's battle against political corruption helped elect him as a Progressive Republican governor of California in 1910, and during his tenure, a vast array of reforms was adopted, ranging from the initiative and the recall, to restriction of child labor and creation of a public utilities commission.

As a Progressive governor, Johnson was quick to align himself with the reform element in the GOP, and in 1912 he helped found the Progressive Party. After an unsuccessful campaign as Theodore Roosevelt's running mate in the 1912 presidential election, Johnson continued his battle for Progressive reform by winning election to the U.S. Senate in 1916, a seat he retained until his death. During his Senate years, he followed an independent course, criticizing the conservative domestic policies of the Republican Presidents in the 1920s and breaking publicly with the GOP in 1932 to support Franklin Roosevelt. Although he supported much of the early New Deal, its deficit spending and imperial presidency gradually alienated Johnson. By the late 1930s, he had become a frequent member of the Senate's conservative coalition.

In the Senate Johnson was perhaps best known for his fierce and consistent isolationism. Despite his early cautious support for Woodrow Wilson's war policies, Johnson eventually became one of the "irreconcilables" who helped prevent American participation in the League of Nations. After World War I, Johnson continued to struggle against American internationalism, casting votes against the World Court, the London Naval Treaty, Roosevelt's reciprocal trade, the Lend-Lease Act, and the United Nations. Thus, as an unyielding isolationist and an opponent of the New Deal's centralizing tendencies, Johnson ended his career pushed aside by the mainstream, a Progressive turned conservative but always an outsider.

See also: Isolationism in American Politics, League of Nations, New Deal, Progressive Party, Franklin D. Roosevelt, Theodore Roosevelt, United Nations, Woodrow Wilson

John W. Malsberger

REFERENCES

Feinmen, Ronald L. 1981. *Twilight of Progressivism: The Western Republican Senators and the New Deal.* Baltimore: Johns Hopkins U. Pr.

Fitzpatrick, John James, III. 1975. "Senator Hiram W. Johnson: A Life History, 1866–1945." Ph.D. dissertation, U. of California, Berkeley.

Mowry, George E. 1951. *The California Progressives.* Berkeley: U. of California Pr.

Lyndon B. Johnson (1908–1973)

Thirty-sixth President of the United States. Lyndon Baines Johnson was born in Stonewall, near Austin, Texas, the son of Rebecca Baines Johnson and Sam Ealy Johnson, a farmer and Texas state legislator. He graduated in 1930 from Southwest State Teacher's College at San Marcos and taught public speaking for a year at Sam Houston High School in Houston. In 1932 he became a staff assistant to the newly elected U.S. Representative Richard Kleberg of the Fourteenth District of Texas. In Washington, Johnson attended Georgetown Law School on a part-time basis but failed to secure a law degree. He was instrumental in founding an organization of House staff members and was elected "speaker" of that body. In late 1934, he married Claudia Alta (Lady Bird) Taylor.

In 1935, at the age of 27, Johnson returned to Texas as state administrator of the National Youth Administration, a New Deal agency; this was a presidential appointment that Johnson obtained through the intercession of Texas Congressman Sam Rayburn, who had been a friend of Johnson's father in the state legislature. This job permitted Johnson to begin to build a political base in his home state. In 1937 he ran for Congress in a special election as a New Deal Democrat and was elected to serve the Tenth District of Texas (Austin and environs). He was reelected to the Seventy-sixth and the four succeeding Congresses, serving from 1937 to 1949. In 1941 he ran unsuccessfully for the Senate and served briefly in the Navy from 1941 to 1942. In 1948 he was elected to the U.S. Senate after a primary runoff election (marred by probable fraud) that he won by 87 votes. Thereafter he was known to his political enemies as "Landslide Lyndon."

Always an apt protégé, Johnson rose fast in the Senate under the wing of Richard Russell of Georgia. He became the Democratic Whip in 1951 and succeeded in the Minority Leadership in 1953 after the electoral defeat of the Democratic leader, Ernest McFarland of Arizona. In 1955 the Democrats became the majority party in the Senate, and Johnson therefore became Majority Leader.

At this stage in his career Johnson's ferociously devoted work habits became the focus of national attention owing in part to favorable publicity generated by Johnson's fellow-Texan, William S. White, Senate correspondent of the *New York Times*. Johnson's domineering, lapel-grabbing, fast-taking "treatment" of his colleagues, backed up by careful intelligence work and the skillful management of the occasional perquisites and favors at the Majority Leader's disposal were given credit for numerous small Democratic legislative successes in an era when the presidency was in the hands of the Republican Dwight Eisenhower. In a major institutional innovation, Johnson changed the Democratic committee assignment process in the Senate so as to give each Democratic Senator, no matter how junior, at least one important committee.

In 1960 he ran for President and was beaten for the nomination by John Kennedy, who unexpectedly picked Johnson as his running mate. Johnson's campaigning in the South is widely credited with overcoming Kennedy's electoral liabilities there and with helping the ticket eke out a narrow victory. As Vice President, Johnson was restless and unhappy. His erstwhile colleagues sharply rebuffed his attempt as Vice President to take over the Senate Democratic caucus, and the Kennedy staff accorded him far less deference than he was accustomed to receiving.

Kennedy's assassination in November 1963 thus released a great deal of Johnson's pent-up energy, which he devoted in the first instance to enacting Kennedy's ambitious projected program of legislation, notably reciprocal trade, a tax cut, and, after the election of 1964—in which Johnson won over Barry Goldwater in a large landslide—civil rights and Medicare. The 1964 election also brought a bumper crop of Democrats to Congress providing Johnson with the opportunity, which he seized, in effect to complete the enactment of the New Deal.

Johnson's assiduous prosecution of the war in Vietnam, however, proved to be extremely unpopular, especially within a Democratic Party that increasingly turned against him. Johnson's own overbearing style, secretiveness, and disinclination to share the limelight meant that he personally would receive the blame for policies that were pursued largely on the advice of the foreign policy team that he inherited from John Kennedy. It was his decision to risk inflation and budget deficits by refusing to fight the Vietnam War on a pay-as-you-go basis and concealing the costs of the war. In late March of 1968, after early soundings suggested that he would have to fight for renomination as presidential candidate of his own party, Johnson decided not to run for reelection.

Johnson's was a large and energetic presence. He greatly enlarged several of the political offices he held, but he frequently also provoked reactions so strong as to jeopardize the gains he sought to make. Thus there was a sizable backlash against various of his Great Society legislative measures. The office of the Senate Majority Leader was placed in the hands of far less self-aggrandizing successors, and much legislation was enacted to restrict the ability of Presidents to commit troops without explicit congressional approval.

In later years several of those who worked for Johnson testified to his monumental selfishness, his extreme personal greed, his boorish manners bordering on occasional sadism, and his excessive demands for loyalty to him that he repaid with disloyalty toward others. These personal qualities hampered the satisfaction that many of his coworkers took in their legislative achievements, and in time made his administration vulnerable to the attacks of its enemies. Johnson retired to his Texas ranch in 1969.

See also: Dwight D. Eisenhower, Election of 1964, Barry Goldwater, John F. Kennedy, New Deal, Sam Rayburn, Vietnam War as a Political Issue

Nelson W. Polsby

REFERENCES

Anderson, James E., and Jared Hazelton. 1986. *Managing Macroeconomic Policy: The Johnson Presidency.* Austin: U. of Texas Press.

Baker, Bobby. 1978. *Wheeling and Dealing: Confessions of a Capitol Hill Operator.* New York: Norton.

Caro, Robert. 1982. *The Years of Lyndon B. Johnson: The Path to Power.* New York: Knopf.

———. 1990. *The Years of Lyndon B. Johnson: The Means of Ascent.* New York: Knopf.

Evans, Rowland, and Robert Novak. 1966. *Lyndon B. Johnson: The Exercise of Power, A Political Biography.* New York: New American Library.

Goldman, Eric. 1969. *The Tragedy of Lyndon B. Johnson.* New York: Knopf.

Gulley, Bill. 1980. *Breaking Cover.* New York: Simon & Schuster.

Huitt, Ralph K., and Robert L. Peabody. 1969. *Congress: Two Decades of Analysis.* New York: Harper & Row.

McPherson, Harry. 1972. *A Political Education*. Boston: Little, Brown.

Reedy, George. 1982. *Lyndon B. Johnson: A Memoir*. Kansas City: Andrews and McMeel.

Richard Mentor Johnson (1780–1850)

Only Vice President elected by the Senate. Richard Mentor Johnson served as the ninth Vice President of the United States (1837–1841). Johnson was the first native Kentuckian elected to that state's legislature, to the U.S. Congress, and to the vice presidency. In 1804 Johnson began his political career when he won election as the youngest member of the Kentucky state legislature. Two years later, barely the minimal age, he was elected to the U.S. House of Representatives. Over the next 33 years he served in Congress as either a Representative or a Senator from Kentucky.

Before the War of 1812, Johnson aligned himself with the expansionist War Hawks, who strongly advocated hostilities against England and, from his seat on the Military Affairs Committee, he urged Congress to prepare for war. When the conflict finally came, he took leave of his legislative duties to organize and command a volunteer regiment of Kentucky riflemen. Colonel Johnson was seriously wounded while leading his troops in the Battle of the Thames on the Canadian border. The claim that he had personally slain the infamous Indian chief and British ally Tecumseh in that battle made him a military hero and furthered his political fortunes.

In Congress, Johnson became a staunch Democrat and a loyal supporter and confidant of Andrew Jackson. When the question of whether General Jackson had exceeded his authority during the Seminole War of 1818 came before the House, Johnson was the only member of the Military Affairs Committee to speak in defense of Jackson's indiscretion in invading Spanish Florida. When Jackson became President, Johnson signed the report condemning the Bank of the United States. He also supported the President in his tariff policies and opposition to internal improvements. As a Senator, Johnson added to his national reputation as the author of the bill abolishing imprisonment for debt. In addition, Jackson used Johnson as his personal agent on various occasions, notably during the Eaton Affair, when he tried to force his Cabinet to welcome at official social functions Peggy O'Neill, the ostracized bride of Secretary of War John H. Eaton.

When Jackson decided not to run for reelection, he selected Johnson as the vice presidential candidate on the 1836 Democratic ticket headed by Martin Van Buren. The political hoopla and rhetoric characteristic of this period led politicians to appeal to increased voter interest and popular participation in the political process, accordingly, Johnson campaigned on the slogan, "Rumpsey, dumpsey, rumpsey, dumpsey, Colonel Johnson killed Tecumseh!" Van Buren won the presidency handily, but Johnson fell short of receiving the required majority of the Electoral College. Although Johnson never married, he alienated some segments of political support— particularly the deep southern element—by maintaining a mulatto slave woman (inherited from his father) as his mistress. He was ultimately chosen Vice President by the Senate in 1837, as provided for by the Twelfth Amendment to the Constitution—the only time the procedure has been employed.

See also: John Henry Eaton, Electoral College, First Bank of the United States, Andrew Jackson, Twelfth Amendment, Martin Van Buren

Hal T. Shelton

REFERENCES

Barzman, Sol. 1874. *Madmen and Geniuses: The Vice President of the United States*. Chicago: Follett.

Emmons, William. 1833. *Authentic Biography of Colonel Richard M. Johnson of Kentucky*. New York: H. Mason.

Lindop, Edmund. 1987. *By a Single Vote: One-Vote Decisions That Changed History*. Harrisburg, PA: Stackpole Books.

Meyer, Leland Winfield. 1932. *The Life and Times of Colonel Richard M. Johnson of Kentucky*. New York: Columbia U. Pr.

Young, Klyde, and Lamar Middleton. 1948. *Heirs Apparent: The Vice Presidents of the United States*. New York: Prentice-Hall.

Benjamin F. Jones (1824–1903)

Chairman of the Republican National Committee from 1884 to 1888. When he was announced as James G. Blaine's choice to chair the Republican National Committee, Benjamin Franklin Jones declared, by way of explanation, that the nominee and he had been personal friends for over 30 years. Jones was also senior partner in one of the major steel mills in the country.

Jones was born in Washington County, Pennsylvania, also Blaine's birthplace and boyhood home. He went to work for a canal boat company, then went into iron manufacture and became the first to produce cold rolled iron.

Initially a Democrat, he became a Republican when the Civil War began. His main political experience before 1884 was his work with the American Iron and Steel Association, of which he was president from 1885 to 1903. He was also active in the the protective tariff cause.

Although not a delegate, Jones attended the 1884 national convention, actively promoted the Blaine candidacy, and became Pennsylvania's national committeeman during the proceedings. The Republican press received his selection with favor, characterizing him as "a business man of the highest character and of the soundest judgment. . . ." He also was a major source of funds during the campaign.

Blaine's defeat in the election provoked unprecedentedly harsh public reactions from Chairman Jones, who lashed out against Republican tariff reductionists in local elections and charged President Chester A. Arthur with failing to support the Blaine ticket. Thereafter, Jones retreated to his business and to the presidency of the American Iron and Steel Association.

See also: Chester A. Arthur, James G. Blaine, Republican National Committee

Ralph M. Goldman

REFERENCES

Goldman, Ralph M. 1980."Benjamin Franklin Jones." 3 *American Historical Magazine* 30.

———. 1990. *The National Party Chairmen and Committees: Factionalism at the Top.* Armonk, NY: M. E. Sharpe.

James K. Jones (1839–1908)

"The Plumed Knight of Arkansas." Senator James Kimbrough Jones was a principal leader of the silverite faction of the Democratic Party when he served as chair of the national committee (1896–1904) at the request of presidential nominee William Jennings Bryan.

At the 1896 national convention, Jones was the principal manager of the platform fight for the unlimited and inflationary coinage of silver. He asked the popular 36-year-old Bryan, the only silverite leader who had not yet spoken on the issue, to arrange the silverite side of the convention floor debate. When Bryan closed the debate with his famous "Cross of Gold" speech, the "Boy Orator" had locked up the nomination for the presidency. In appreciation of Jones's role and out of respect for the older silverite leadership, Bryan requested that Jones be elected Democratic national chairman.

Born into a plantation-owning family, Jones, a lawyer, rose rapidly in state politics during the Reconstruction era and won his first term in the House of Representatives in 1880. In 1884 he managed the speakership fight of a tariff-reductionist candidate, John G. Carlisle. When Carlisle won, Jones was appointed to the powerful Ways and Means Committee where he became spokesman for the reductionists.

In 1885 Jones was elected to the United States Senate by the Arkansas legislature. During his first term, he led the Grover Cleveland administration forces on behalf of tariff reduction. In his second term, which began in 1891, Jones became increasingly involved in the leadership of the free-silver cause. He was soon considered an expert on financial legislation and one of the few silverite leaders on friendly terms with the pro-gold standard Cleveland administration. His enthusiasm earned him the title of "The Plumed Knight of Arkansas."

The fall election campaign in 1896 found Jones struggling to coordinate the efforts of the several silverite parties: Democrats, Populists, National Silverites, and Silver Republicans; the task was more than he or anyone else could handle. Worse still, Jones had no talent for the detailed management of a national headquarters. Meanwhile, Bryan carried on his own campaign arrangements independently.

Although relations between the two men were always relatively cool and formal, when renominated in 1900, Bryan again asked Senator Jones to serve as national chairman. The election of 1900 was a second defeat for both.

See also: William Jennings Bryan, John G. Carlisle, Election of 1896, Reconstruction

Ralph M. Goldman

REFERENCES

Newberry, Farrar. 1913. *James K. Jones: The Plumed Knight of Arkansas.* Siftings-Herald Printing.

John W. Jones (1791–1848)

Embattled Speaker of the House in the 1840s. John Winston Jones entered public service in 1818 by receiving appointment as prosecuting attorney for the Fifth Virginia Judicial Circuit, continuing in this office for 17 years. He also served as a delegate of the state constitutional convention from 1829 to 1830. He won election to the U.S. House of Representatives as a Democrat in 1834 and gained reelection to four succeeding Congresses. While in Congress, he presided as chairman of the Ways and Means Committee (1841–1843). During his last term

(1843–1845), Jones was elected Speaker of the House even though his seat in Congress was then being contested (he had been returned to office with a majority of 33 votes). The closeness of the final count during a heavy poll and the probability of illegal ballots in an exciting political campaign cast doubts on the veracity of Jones's election.

Under these circumstances, Jones requested that he be relieved of his traditional duty as Speaker in selecting the Committee on Elections, and this appointment was delegated to a Speaker *pro tempore*. The precedent thus established has always been followed in choosing committees in which the Speaker may have a conflict of interest. National Republican John Quincy Adams refused to vote for the conventional thanks offered to the Democratic Speaker by the House at the end of a session. In his memoirs, Adams explained, "The testimony to his [Jones's] impartiality was too broad a lie for me to swallow." Declining to stand for reelection in 1844, Jones later served several more terms in the Virginia legislature (1846–1847).

See also: Speaker of the House

Hal T. Shelton

REFERENCES

Alexander, DeAlva Stanwood. 1916. *History and Procedure of the House of Representatives*. Boston: Houghton Mifflin.

Follett, M. P. 1896. *The Speaker of the House of Representatives*. New York: Longmans, Green.

Fuller, Hubert Bruce. 1909. *The Speaker of the House*. Boston: Little, Brown.

Smith, William Henry. 1928. *Speakers of the House of Representatives of the United States*. New York: AMS Press.

K

Kansas-Nebraska Act

Introduced in January 1854 by Senator Steven Douglas, this bill provided for the organization of two territories in which the "popular sovereignty" of the settlers would decide the acceptance or exclusion of slavery. Douglas was primarily interested in railway development and creating a new, dramatic issue for the faction-ridden Democratic Party. He soon discovered that he could not get any territorial bill passed without the support of a powerful clique of southern Senators who insisted on a specific repeal of the Missouri Compromise, which in 1820 had banned slavery in territories north of 36°30'. Douglas realized that repeal would raise "one hell of a storm" but was contemptuous of the free-soil agitation.

The bill aroused northern opinion previously indifferent to the antislavery movement. It was regarded as a violation of a sectional compact that had been generally accepted since 1820 and a departure from the supposedly "final" settlement of the slavery issue in 1850. A militant "slave power" seemed determined to force slavery on the western territories and impose a new declaration of national purpose: slavery was to be a perpetual, acceptable, and expanding part of American society.

Party discipline, administrative patronage, and Douglas's dynamic leadership combined to pass the Kansas-Nebraska Act in May 1854. The controversy it aroused, however, had a devastating effect on an American party system already severely strained by sectional and ethnic tensions. The weaker and less-disciplined Whigs split along sectional lines. Northern Whig Congressmen all voted against the bill, and many Whig voters moved into the new Republican or American parties. Southern Whigs supported the bill and then joined the Democratic or various proslavery opposition groups.

Unlike the Whigs, the Democratic Party did not disintegrate, but the Nebraska controversy dealt its northern wing a crippling blow. Northern Democratic Congressman divided 45 to 45 on the bill, and in the election of 1854 the party lost 66 of its 91 seats in the free states and an estimated 25 percent of its supporters. Many of these voters later returned to the party, but it lost control of all but one or two northern states. In Congress, southern Democrats outnumbered northern by more than two to one, thus giving the party a proslavery orientation. In the North, Democrats could survive only by an increasing show of independence from "the slave power," and by 1860 this led to a disastrous split—two different Democratic presidential tickets and an eventual Republican victory.

The anti-Nebraska agitation served as a catalyst that not only pulled voters from their traditional party allegiances but also created new parties out of a suddenly volatile electorate that often saw free soil and nativistic attitudes combined in the same voters. The nativistic American or Know-Nothing Party had a brief, spectacular rise, but the Republicans as an anti-Nebraska free-soil party had a more enduring success. When the Kansas territory turned into an arena for sectional conflict, the Republicans were able to exploit the issue of "bleeding Kansas" to establish their position as the dominant party in the free states.

Douglas's Kansas-Nebraska bill produced no railway, no new slave states, and no consolidation of the Democratic Party. It did destroy the bisectional second party system and with it the last and most vital bond of union.

See also: Know-Nothings, Missouri Compromise, Slavery

Harold B. Raymond

REFERENCES

Fehrenbacher, Don. 1962. *Prelude to Greatness: Lincoln in the 1850s.* Palo Alto: Stanford U. Pr.

Foner, Eric. 1970. *Free Soil, Free Labor, Free Men: The Ideology of the Republican Party Before the Civil War.* New York: Oxford U. Pr.

Gienapp, William. 1987. *The Origins of the Republican Party 1852–1856.* New York: Oxford U. Pr.

Hodder, Frank. "The Railway Background of the Kansas-Nebraska Act." 12 *Mississippi Historical Review* 3.

Holt, Michael. 1978. *The Political Crisis of the 1850s.* New York: Wiley.

Jaffa, Henry. 1959. *The Crisis of the House Divided: An Interpretation of the Issues in the Lincoln, Douglas Debates.* Chicago: U. of Chicago Pr.

Malin, James. 1953. *The Nebraska Question.* Lawrence: U. Pr. of Kansas.

Nevins, Alan. 1947–1971. *The Ordeal of the Union.* Vol. II. New York: Scribner's.

Nichols, Alice. 1954. *Bleeding Kansas.* New York: Oxford U. Pr.

Potter, David. 1976. *The Impending Crisis 1848–1861.* New York: Harper & Row.

Rawley, James. 1954. *Race and Politics: Bleeding Kansas and the Coming of the Civil War.* Philadelphia: Lippincott.

Karcher v. Daggett
455 U.S. 1033 (1982)

This 1982 Supreme Court case involved a dispute over the apportionment of New Jersey's congressional districts. On the average, each New Jersey congressional district differed from the ideal figure by 0.1384 percent or about 726 people. The largest of the districts had 527,472 people; the smallest, 523,798. This disparity of 3,674 people produced a deviation of 0.6984 percent from the average district. The New Jersey Federal District Court held that the representation system was unconstitutional because population deviations among districts, although small, were not the result of a good-faith effort to achieve population equality.

The Supreme Court, in an opinion by Justice William Brennan, affirmed the decision of the district court. Although precise mathematic equality of district size was not required, the court held that a "nearly as practicable" standard

applied and that the state must still show that a good-faith effort had been made to achieve precise mathematic equality.

The Supreme Court held that parties challenging apportionment legislation bore the initial burden of proof; if they failed to show that the differences in district size could have been avoided, the apportionment plan already in place had to be allowed to stand. However, if it could be shown that the population differences did not result from a good-faith effort to achieve equality, then the state would bear the burden of proving that each significant variance between districts was necessary to achieve some legitimate goal. The court also noted that numerical quality was more important in congressional districts than state legislative districts where local interests might be relevant to apportionment.

The Supreme Court rejected the state's argument that the differences between districts were *de minimus* (inconsequential). The Court asserted that the state had not been able to justify the differences that *did* exist and that the system was unconstitutionally burdensome on residents of districts with larger population bases. The Court required New Jersey to show with some specificity that a particular objective required the specific deviations evident in its districting plan. New Jersey had been unable to rely on anything more than general assertions to justify its plan. Because this vagueness was insufficient, the Court held that the districting plan was unconstitutional.

Justice John Paul Stevens wrote a concurring opinion emphasizing that the equal protection clause protected against vote dilution in instances not limited to racial discrimination. He also asserted that New Jersey's system was clearly the result of partisan gerrymandering. He believed that the Court should have spoken more forcefully against such gerrymandering.

Justice Byron White wrote a dissenting opinion, which was joined by Chief Justice Warren Burger, Justice Lewis Powell, and Justice William Rehnquist. They expressed disbelief that the court would strike down a districting plan with an average and maximum population variance of under 1 percent. The minority argued that the variance in the New Jersey plan was statistically insignificant and that the majority placed an unrealistic overemphasis on the importance of raw population figures.

See also: Gerrymandering, *Kirkpatrick v. Preisler, Wesberry v. Saunders*

Scott Cameron

Estes Kefauver (1903–1963)

Crusading U.S. Senator from Tennessee. Born in Madisonville, Tennessee, during his political career Carey Estes Kefauver became a political outsider, a foe of the Crump Democratic machine in Memphis, and a liberal. Elected to the Senate in 1948 after ten years in the U.S. House, he achieved national recognition by chairing a committee on organized crime. The committee highlighted the link between organized crime and big-city Democratic political machines, angering Democratic party regulars. Kefauver also alienated the South by opposing political practices that perpetuated segregation—practices as common as the poll tax and the filibuster.

In 1952 Kefauver defeated President Harry Truman in the New Hampshire presidential primary thanks to a tireless handshaking campaign and a television-created image; Truman subsequently withdrew from the race while continuing to oppose Kefauver. The Tennessee Senator's public popularity, funding, and campaign support increased, and he won 12 of the 13 primaries that he entered (unopposed in most). Despite being the first choice of Democratic Party identifiers nationally and leading the first two convention ballots, Kefauver lost the nomination on the third ballot to Governor Adlai Stevenson II of Illinois. Kefauver was hurt by opposition from party regulars, Truman, and the South; the strategy of publicity seeking in nonbinding preference primaries rather than contesting delegate races; lack of a large corps of dedicated and energetic amateur supporters who were motivated and organized enough to capture control of the caucus convention machinery in nonprimary states.

In 1956 Stevenson was initially favored over Kefauver by the party rank and file as well as by party leaders. Despite the opposition of Democratic officials in Minnesota, Kefauver's folksy handshaking campaign and attacks on Democratic "boss" politics led to a victory over Stevenson in that state's primary, and the gap in rank-and-file support greatly narrowed. When Stevenson came back with victories in the Oregon, Florida, and California primaries, Kefauver withdrew from the race. When presidential nominee Stevenson threw the vice presidential decision open to the convention, Kefauver defeated Roman Catholic Massachusetts Senator John Kennedy on the second ballot. After the 1956 defeat, Kefauver's remaining national popular support drifted away, and he became a Senate workhorse fighting for consumer protection.

See also: John F. Kennedy, Adlai E. Stevenson II, Harry S Truman

Stephen D. Shaffer

REFERENCES

Anderson, Jack, and Fred Blumenthal. 1956. *The Kefauver Story.* New York: Dial.

Fontenay, Charles. 1980. *Estes Kefauver: A Biography.* Knoxville: U. of Tennessee Pr.

Gorman, Joseph B. 1971. *Kefauver: A Political Biography.* New York: Oxford U. Pr.

Keech, William, and Donald R. Matthews. 1977. *The Party's Choice.* Washington: Brookings.

J. W. Keifer (1836–1932)

Post-Reconstruction Speaker of the House. During his one term as Speaker of the House of Representatives, Joseph Warren Keifer earned more enemies than friends for his attempts to impose order and partisan control over the business of the lower chamber. An Ohio native, he practiced law until the Civil War; he was commissioned major in the 3rd Ohio Infantry, and at the outset of the war, he soon became a colonel in command of the 110th Ohio Infantry, serving in the Virginia theater of operations. Wounded at the Battle of the Wilderness (May 1864), he returned to service in the Shenandoah Valley campaigns and was present at Appomattox. Brevetted major general of volunteers for war service, Keifer entered Ohio politics as a Republican, serving in the state senate (1868–1869).

Elected to the U.S. House of Representatives in 1876, he served four terms, rising to the speakership for the Forty-seventh Congress (1881–1883). As Speaker, Keifer sought to increase the powers of his position to impose cloture upon filibustering efforts; he also won a degree of notoriety for his notoriously overt partisanship in making committee appointments. Such action foreshadowed the speakership of Thomas B. Reed at the end of the decade; indeed, Reed was rumored to be the power behind the throne even during Keifer's term. Serving three more terms in the House from 1905 to 1911, Keifer revived old sectional division when he called for the reduction of southern representation in Congress according to the terms of the Fourteenth Amendment as a result of Black disfranchisement.

See also: Thomas Reed, Speaker of the House

Brooks Donohue Simpson

Sidney S. Kellam (1903–1986)

Machine politician from eastern Virginia. Born into a large family in rural Princess Anne, Virginia, Sidney Severn Kellam was the son of Abel E. Kellam, a clerk of the Virginia Circuit Court for 20 years. At 15 years old, Kellam left school and took on a series of jobs, before winning election as county treasurer for Princess Anne in 1931, a post he held until 1950. In 1950 Kellam became the director of Virginia's Department of Conservation and Development, resigning in 1953. Meanwhile, Kellam aligned himself with conservative U.S. Senator Harry S. Byrd, Sr., and played an instrumental part in helping to churn out large pluralities for both Byrd and the Byrd organization's other candidates throughout the state in the 1940s, 1950s, and early 1960s.

By 1964, Kellam was one of the most powerful Democrats in Virginia—second only to Byrd. He successfully spearheaded the effort to merge Princess Anne County with the town of Virginia Beach in 1962. In 1964 he almost singlehandedly managed President Lyndon B. Johnson's presidential campaign in Virginia and won high praise from the state's political circles after Johnson carried Virginia in the election. Although long rumored as a possible candidate for governor or U.S. Senator in the late 1960s and early 1970s, Kellam stayed in the background, backing a series of successful conservative Democratic candidates for statewide offices.

See also: Harry F. Byrd, Sr., Election of 1964, Lyndon B. Johnson

Garry Boulard

REFERENCES

Blackford, Frank R. 1965. "A Democrat's Democrat: Sidney Severn Kellam." 12 *Virginia Record* 36.
Wilkinson, Harvey J., III. 1969. *Harry Byrd and the Changing Face of Virginia Politics, 1945–1966.* Charlottesville: U. Pr. of Virginia.

Edward J. Kelly (1876–1950)

Boss of the Chicago Democratic political machine. Following the assassination of Mayor Anton Cermak in 1933, the Chicago City Council appointed Edward J. Kelly to fill the unexpired term. Kelly won reelection three times, his mayoralty spanning the years of the Great Depression and World War II. One of the most effective of the Democratic big-city bosses during an era when giants in that category reigned, Kelly built upon the base that Cermak had established and ruled over a machine of enormous power and influence.

Critical relief issues during the Depression provided Kelly an early opportunity to support New Deal policies. This support was a first step in restoring good relations with President Franklin D. Roosevelt, a Democrat who Chicago machine leaders had opposed for nomination. Eventually Kelly achieved so strong an alliance with the President that Chicago became the linchpin of FDR's urban strategy.

Kelly was born and raised in an Irish community on Chicago's southwest side, the same neighborhood that would spawn his eventual successor as machine boss, Richard J. Daley. Employed at age 18 by the Sanitary District as an ax man, he moved steadily through the ranks to become chief engineer. Later he combined that position with the presidency of the South Park Board. Both offices were rich with patronage and contracts.

As chief engineer, Kelly formed a close relationship with Patrick A. Nash, a leader in the local Democratic Party and a favored plumbing contractor for the Sanitary District. Nash was responsible for Kelly's emergency appointment as mayor. In tandem, the two consolidated the local organization—Kelly as the visible leader, Nash content to moderate intraparty strife behind the scenes.

A widely held notion persists that boodle and vote stealing best account for the Chicago Democratic machine's success at the polls. To be sure, Kelly was tolerant of graft within the ranks. He was himself indicted, albeit acquitted, for contract improprieties while serving as chief engineer of the Sanitary District. Moreover, charges of voting irregularities and misuse of public funds surfaced throughout his tenure, and he had to pay an IRS settlement for tax shortfalls during the 1920s.

More significant, however, to the continuing success of the machine were the rational goals of its leaders, the fraternal loyalty within the ranks, broker services for businessmen and bankers, and a centralized control over the rewards of office. As carefully balanced tickets maximized ethnic voting blocs, the Chicago machine imposed an informal cohesion upon a decentralized and chaotic formal structure of government. Kelly's capsule description of machine leadership applied: "You gotta be boss!"

Kelly lured many Black leaders over from the Republican Party. In this recruitment he was eventually aided by New Deal programs for which Kelly was not loath to take credit. Black power within the machine hierarchy was, however, carefully circumscribed.

Kelly recognized as early as 1934 the advantage of having Roosevelt's name at the head of the ticket. He became a drum major for the President's reelection in 1936 and led the charge for Roosevelt's third-term nomination in 1940. Over the years Kelly had easier access to the White House than any of the other urban bosses. Rather than undercutting urban machines, as one thesis holds, New Deal programs shored up the Chicago organization. By 1940 Kelly had reached the pinnacle of his power. With the death of Nash in 1943, factional opposition to Kelly grew, and by 1947 he was persuaded not to seek renomination.

See also: Bosses, Anton Cermak, Richard Daley, Henry Horner, New Deal, Franklin Roosevelt

Gene D. L. Jones

REFERENCES

Biles, Roger. 1984. *Big City Boss in Depression and War: Mayor Edward J. Kelley of Chicago.* DeKalb: Northern Illinois U. Pr.

Gosnell, Harold F. 1937. *Machine Politics, Chicago Model.* Chicago: U. of Chicago Pr.

Jones, Gene D. L. 1974. "The Origin of the Alliance Between the New Deal and the Chicago Machine." 67 *Journal of the Illinois State Historical Society* 253.

Littlewood, Thomas B. 1969. *Horner of Illinois.* Evanston, IL: Northwestern U. Pr.

John Kelly (1822–1885)

Tammany Hall machine politician. As the leader of New York City's Tammany Hall from 1872 to 1885, "Honest John" Kelly played a major role in transforming Tammany into a centralized political machine. Kelly served as an alderman, a Congressman, and a sheriff between 1854 and 1867, and after the overthrow of the Tweed Ring, he led Tammany. The rampant corruption of the Tweed era threatened to discredit the Democrats, and in an effort to salvage the party's organization, Kelly imposed discipline upon Democratic ward politicians and public officials. Toward this end, he centralized control over the distribution of patronage and purged the organization of politicians who refused to follow his lead.

Kelly's efforts to centralize control over Tammany threatened the influence of other Democratic leaders, and in the late 1870s and early 1880s, a number of dissident ward politicians and party notables established Democratic organizations that competed with Tammany. Patronage provided by Democratic governors hostile to Tammany helped to sustain these competing factions. So long as ward politicians had the option of joining other Democratic factions, Tammany's leader faced difficulties imposing discipline upon his nominal subordinates.

At the time of Kelly's death, Tammany was better organized and more highly centralized than it had been under his predecessors, but other Democratic factions still challenged its position. In the 1890s, however, under Kelly's successor, Richard Croker, Tammany overwhelmed its major rivals. Finally, Kelly's efforts to construct a dominant political machine in New York City came to fruition.

See also: Bosses, Tammany Hall

Martin Shefter

REFERENCES

Genen, Arthur. 1971. "John Kelly: New York's First Irish Boss." Ph.D. dissertation, New York University.

Hammack, David. 1982. *Power and Society: Greater New York at the Turn of the Century.* New York: Russell Sage Foundation.

Mandelbaum, Seymour. 1965. *Boss Tweed's New York.* New York: Wiley.

Shefter, Martin. 1976. "The Emergence of the Political Machine: An Alternative View." In Willis Hawley and Michael Lipsky, eds. *Theoretical Perspectives on Urban Politics.* Englewood Cliffs, NJ: Prentice-Hall.

Jack F. Kemp (1935–)

Conservative Republican political leader in the late twentieth century. In the late 1970s, Republican New York Congressman Jack F. Kemp pioneered "supply-side economics," a philosophy emphasizing economic growth and opportunity. Arguing that lower taxes would spur savings and investment, Kemp sponsored (with Senator William Roth, R-Del.) the Kemp-Roth bill to slash personal income tax rates by 30 percent. As part of President Ronald Reagan's economic program, a version of this proposal became law in 1981. Kemp also helped pass the 1986 tax-reform act, which cut the top marginal income tax rate to 28 percent. Despite these accomplishments, Kemp lost the 1988 Republican presidential nomination.

After graduating from Occidental College in 1957, Kemp starred as a professional football quarterback for the San Diego Chargers and was spotted as a potential GOP candidate by Herb Klein, a Nixon aide then serving as editor of the *San Diego Union.* Klein encouraged him to write newspaper columns, an outlet that he continued even after he was sold to the Buffalo Bills in 1962.

In 1970 Erie County (N.Y.) Republicans chose Kemp to run for an open U.S. House seat. He won narrowly but widened his margins in later elections. Contrary to popular belief, he represented Buffalo's suburbs but not the city itself.

"I came in as a balance-the-budget, root-canal austere Republican," he said. In the mid-1970s, conservative writers Irving Kristol and Jude Wanniski convinced Kemp that the optimism of supply-side economics would furnish him and his party with greater appeal. He built a following among his colleagues and won the chairmanship of the House Republican Conference in 1980.

After the 1981 tax cut Kemp fought subsequent tax increases. He also blocked efforts to trim Social Security benefits. He backed a modified gold standard, enterprise zones, and the Strategic Defense Initiative. His support of the Ways and Means Committee tax reform bill antagonized the many House Republicans who opposed the plan. Kemp, overly pragmatic, thought the issue would help him win the White House.

It did not. Bored with tax reform, voters found the rest of his message contradictory. On the one hand, he tried to woo hard-line conservatives by taking strong stands on defense and abortion. On the other hand, he said, "[T]he conservative ideology, the conservative philosophy for a party [must] be jettisoned for either a new word or new phrases that give a better appeal to blacks and blue-collar workers and inner-city minorities." Conservatives disliked such statements, as well as his opposition to the Gramm-Rudman deficit bill and a balanced-budget constitutional amendment. Seeking at once to champion the Right and to broaden the GOP's base in his 1988 campaign, Kemp did neither.

After failing to win a single primary or caucus, he withdrew in favor of George Bush early in 1988. When he did not seek reelection to the House, Bush appointed him Secretary of the Department of Housing and Urban Development.

See also: George Bush, Ronald Reagan

John J. Pitney, Jr.

REFERENCES

Kemp, Jack S. 1984. *The American Idea: Ending Limits to Growth.* Washington: American Studies Center.

———. 1986. *The Rise of the Counter-Establishment.* New York: Times Books.

Rowe, Jonathan. 1985. "What the Democrats Can Learn from Jack Kemp." 16 (January) *Washington Monthly* 28.

Edward M. Kennedy (1932–)

Liberal Democratic Senator and presidential aspirant from Massachusetts. From a famous political family in Massachusetts, Edward Moore Kennedy was born in Boston and was elected to the Senate in 1962 at the age of 30. Legislative experts rate him as one of the best members in that body largely because of his hard work and ability to cooperate with those of opposing political philosophies. Despite several personal and political setbacks, his endurance in office ranks him among those who have served longest in the Senate as well as one of the most admired individuals in the United States, according to a Gallup poll. These achievements enhance his role in Congress as a "presidential Senator" and as a significant force within the Democratic Party.

Edward ("Ted") Kennedy was the youngest of the nine children in the Joseph P. and Rose Fitzgerald Kennedy family. After attending more than ten elementary and secondary schools, he entered Harvard University, only to be suspended after a friend took a Spanish examination for him. From 1951 to 1953, he served in the U.S. Army. Readmitted to Harvard, he graduated with honors in 1956. Three years later, he earned a law degree from the University of Virginia.

Even as a law student he managed his brother John Kennedy's campaign for reelection to the U.S. Senate. In 1960 he served as JFK's floor leader at the Democratic National Convention in Los Angeles and then managed the presidential campaign in the West.

In 1962 Edward was elected to his brother John's old Senate seat with 55 percent of the vote. He was reelected in 1964 to a full term by the greatest plurality (74 percent) in Massachusetts history. During his long career, his legislative skills have won him a significant role in the Congress. Senate Democrats elected him the youngest Majority Whip in history in 1969. But the assassination of his brother Robert, a failing marriage, and political pressure took their toll as did his car accident on Chappaquiddick Island in 1969 that resulted in the drowning of Mary Jo Kopechne, in which he pleaded guilty to leaving the scene of the accident. Robert Byrd defeated him for the Majority Whip position in 1971. Despite a close relationship with their three children (Kara; Edward, Jr.; and Patrick), Kennedy's twenty-four-year marriage to Joan Bennett ended in divorce in 1983.

Kennedy's reelection campaigns during the past 20 years have achieved success with relative ease: 1970 (63 percent), 1976 (69 percent), 1982 (61 percent), and 1988 (65 percent). He chaired the Judiciary Committee in 1979, and since 1986, the Labor and Human Resources Committee. As a proponent of a national health insurance program, civil rights at home, and human rights abroad, he is a leader of the liberal wing of the Democratic Party.

Edward ran for the Democratic nomination for President in 1980 in a campaign directed against Jimmy Carter's economic policies. Although this effort failed, Edward's charisma, legislative skills, and rhetorical prowess continue to make him a major force in the U.S. Senate and in the Democratic Party.

See also: Robert Byrd, Jimmy Carter, Elections of 1968 and 1980, John F. Kennedy, Joseph P. Kennedy, Robert F. Kennedy

William David Pederson

REFERENCES

Burns, James MacGregor. 1976. *Edward Kennedy and the Camelot Legacy*. New York: Norton.

Pederson, William D. 1987. "Edward Moore Kennedy." In Bernard K. Duffy and Halford R. Ryan, eds. *American Orators of the Twentieth Century*. Westport, CT: Greenwood.

———. 1989. "'Presidential Senator' Ted Kennedy and a Character Test." In William D. Pederson, ed. *The "Barberian" Presidency*. New York: Peter Lang.

Randolf, Eleanor. 1982. "The Best and the Worst of the U.S. Senate." 13 (January) *Washington Monthly* 30.

John F. Kennedy (1917–1963)

Thirty-fifth President of the United States. John Fitzgerald Kennedy, born in Brookline, Massachusetts, became President of the United States by following a game plan originally mapped out by his father, Joseph Kennedy, for his older brother Joseph, Jr., who had been killed in World War II. Some biographical material on Kennedy suffers from the hagiography arising from the tragedy of his assassination on November 22, 1963, in Dallas, Texas—one of the most vivid and shattering events of the late twentieth century—and from deliberate and generally successful efforts and disinformation practiced by the Kennedy family for two generations. Thus it is difficult to determine, for example, simple facts about Kennedy's health, his education, or his war record, or to sort out precisely what share Kennedy took in the actual writing of the book *Profiles in Courage*, for which he received the Pulitzer Prize in biography in 1957 as its ostensible author.

Kennedy was born into the family of one of America's richest and most politically active men, the second of four sons, all of whom were groomed for political careers. While his sisters were reared in lace-curtain Irish gentility and sent to Catholic schools, John Kennedy went to Choate, (briefly) to Princeton, where he dropped out with health problems, and to Harvard (B.A., 1940), also his father's and his brothers' alma mater.

After Harvard he briefly went to Stanford Business School, dabbled in journalism, and then entered the U.S. Navy where he was assigned to intelligence work in Washington. He was rescued by his father's connections from what could have become a scandalous liaison and sent to the South Pacific theater and to duty on board a PT boat, which was rammed by a slow-moving Japanese destroyer. The story of the rescue of Kennedy's crew was written for the *New Yorker* by John Hersey; the *Reader's Digest* version was distributed widely and made him a war hero on his return to civilian life.

Although the Kennedy family had long since abandoned Boston, a safe Democratic Boston congressional district was found for Kennedy, and he entered Congress after the election of 1946, moving to the Senate in the election of 1952 when he beat the incumbent, Henry Cabot Lodge, even though Lodge was a leading supporter of Dwight Eisenhower, the popular World War II general who headed the Republican ticket.

Kennedy's service in the Senate was not marked by notable accomplishments. He divided his efforts between an active social life, punctuated by his marriage in 1953 to the former Jacqueline Bouvier; service on the Government Operations, Foreign Relations, and Labor Committees; and planning for a run at the presidency, especially after 1956. In that year Adlai Stevenson, the Democratic presidential nominee, threw open to the national nominating convention the choice of a vice presidential candidate, and Kennedy lost narrowly to Estes Kefauver. The most dramatic Senate episode of the early 1950s—the censure of the Red-baiting Joseph McCarthy—found Kennedy on the sidelines, hospitalized with a bad back and allegedly writing *Profiles in Courage*. Kennedy's health problems were genuine, but his absence was uncommonly convenient, given his wishes to alienate neither liberal Democrats whose support would be needed for a presidential run nor conservatives like his father who supported McCarthy.

In 1960 he ran successfully in the early primaries so as to convince the predominantly

Irish Catholic grandees of the Democratic Party, who controlled the delegates from the urban machines, that an Irish Catholic presidential candidate could indeed win the election. Kennedy gained the nomination in a divided field and then beat Richard Nixon by the smallest margin recorded in any presidential election in the twentieth century.

As President, he proved extraordinarily successful in keeping Washington journalists happy; many of them enjoyed his confidence and they all were entertained by his quick, inquisitive mind and his sharp sense of humor. In foreign relations his administration endured failure at the Cuban Bay of Pigs invasion and nuclear confrontation at the Cuban Missile Crisis; standoffishness from French president Charles de Gaulle; and the contemptuous hostility of Soviet leader Nikita Khrushchev, who inspired the building of the Berlin Wall on Kennedy's watch. Domestically he met the overwhelming challenge of civil rights with caution and extreme deference to southern congressional committee chairmen. Many promising beginnings in defense, in tax trade policy, in foreign affairs (Peace Corps, Food for Peace, Alliance for Progress), and in the management of Congress were cut short by his tragic assassination.

See also: Dwight D. Eisenhower, Election of 1960, Estes Kefauver, Edward M. Kennedy, Joseph P. Kennedy, Robert F. Kennedy, Richard M. Nixon

Nelson W. Polsby

REFERENCES

Blair, Joan, and Clay Blair. 1976. *In Search of JFK*. New York: Berkeley.

Bradlee, Benjamin. 1975. *Conversations with Kennedy*. New York: Norton.

Parmet, Herbert. 1980. *Jack: The Struggles of John F. Kennedy*. New York: Dial.

———. 1983. *J.F.K.: The Presidency of John F. Kennedy*. New York: Dial.

Schlesinger, Arthur M., Jr. 1965. *A Thousand Days: John F. Kennedy in the White House*. Boston: Houghton Mifflin.

Sorensen, Theodore. 1965. *Kennedy*. New York: Harper & Row.

White, Theodore H. 1961. *The Making of the President, 1960*. New York: Atheneum.

Joseph P. Kennedy (1888–1969)

Scion of powerful Massachusetts political clan. Millionaire businessman and financier, important political ally of Franklin D. Roosevelt in the 1930s, and member of the Roosevelt administration, Joseph P. Kennedy despite his own exceptional career is probably best known as the father of President John F. Kennedy and of Senators Robert F. Kennedy and Edward M. Kennedy. Born in Boston to a second-generation Irish saloonkeeper and politician, Kennedy graduated from Harvard and married Rose Fitzgerald, the daughter of the magnetic Boston politician John F. ("Honey Fitz") Fitzgerald. He made himself a millionaire many times over with his shrewd dealings in a variety of financial and business enterprises.

Kennedy actively supported Franklin D. Roosevelt's campaigns for nomination and election in 1932, and he was rewarded with a job as the effective first chairman of the new Securities and Exchange Commission in 1934. Though he left government to reenter business in 1935, Kennedy continued to serve as an emissary from Roosevelt to businessmen and to Catholics and vigorously supported FDR's 1936 reelection. In 1938 FDR made Kennedy the first Irish Catholic to serve as the U.S. ambassador to Great Britain. Kennedy grew increasingly disturbed, both publicly and privately, at Roosevelt's opposition to the Axis, though he did endorse FDR's third-term candidacy in 1940. Nonetheless, Kennedy resigned his ambassadorship just after the election, and he never resumed his close relationship with Roosevelt. He also failed to overcome suspicions that he had been an isolationist and perhaps even an anti-Semitic German sympathizer.

After World War II, Kennedy, fiercely ambitious not only for himself but also for his family, turned his attention to his business ventures and to his sons' political careers. He played a particularly important behind-the-scenes role in financing and in other ways facilitating John F. Kennedy's quest for the presidency in 1960.

See also: Elections of 1932, 1936, 1940, and 1960; John F. Fitzgerald; Edward M. Kennedy; John F. Kennedy; Robert F. Kennedy; Franklin D. Roosevelt

John W. Jeffries

REFERENCES

Beschloss, Michael R. 1980. *Kennedy and Roosevelt: The Uneasy Alliance*. New York: Norton.

Goodwin, Doris Kearns. 1987. *The Fitzgeralds and the Kennedys*. New York: Simon & Schuster.

Koskoff, David E. 1974. *Joseph P. Kennedy: A Life and Times*. Englewood Cliffs, NJ: Prentice-Hall.

Whalen, Richard J. 1964. *The Founding Father: The Story of Joseph P. Kennedy*. New York: New American Library.

Robert F. Kennedy (1925–1968)

Attorney General, U.S. Senator, and assassinated presidential candidate. Robert Francis

Kennedy's political career is inextricably linked to the changes and turbulence that beset the American party system during 1960. His assassination shortly after he won the 1968 California Democratic primary was the fourth shooting of a major American political figure in five years and, for many, symbolized the frequently violent nature of politics in the Vietnam era.

Robert was the seventh of nine children born into the wealthy and politically influential Kennedy family. After serving in the Navy during World War II, he graduated from Harvard University in 1948 and from the Virginia Law School in 1951. His political baptism occurred when he successfully managed his brother John Kennedy's 1952 Senate election in Massachusetts. Thereafter Kennedy served as chief Democratic counsel for the Senate Permanent Subcommittee on Investigations and then, in 1957, as chief counsel for the Senate Rackets Committee, achieving national prominence for his investigations of Teamsters leaders Jimmy Hoffa and David Beck.

In 1960 Kennedy managed his brother's successful bid for the presidency and in 1961 was named Attorney General. Robert Kennedy's major achievement while heading the Justice Department was to increase federal support for politically controversial civil rights movements. Perhaps more importantly, Robert also served as his brother's trusted confidant.

When Lyndon Johnson succeeded John Kennedy after the latter's assassination, Robert's impact as Attorney General lessened. Neither man liked the other, and for the next four years the Johnson-Kennedy rivalry gradually became the focal point for Democratic politics. Subsequently, Robert announced that he would seek Republican Senator Kenneth B. Keating's Senate seat in New York. Ironically, Johnson's landslide 1964 presidential election helped Kennedy win the Senate contest by 719,000 votes.

Partly shedding his "Ruthless Bobby" image, Kennedy consistently compiled a liberal voting record in the Senate, particularly on minority affairs. Despite his increasingly dovish views toward the Vietnam War and his personal antagonism toward the President, Kennedy at first publicly expressed support for Johnson's reelection in 1968. However, as his doubts about Johnson's handling of the war and urban problems increased, Kennedy began serious consideration of a race for the Democratic presidential nomination in 1968.

The 1968 North Vietnamese Tet Offensive, which seemed to discredit Johnson's claim of U.S. success in Vietnam, coupled with Senator Eugene J. McCarthy's strong showing in the New Hampshire Democratic primary convinced Kennedy that the time was right for his candidacy. In 1968, he formally announced that he was seeking the Democratic nomination for the presidency, and President Johnson decided that he would not seek reelection.

Kennedy drew support from a coalition of blue-collar workers, minorities, and young professionals. His campaign strategy was to demonstrate his political viability by winning the remaining Democratic primaries.

In May he easily won the Indiana primary and one week later took the Nebraska primary with 52 percent of the popular vote; McCarthy, however, rebounded to beat Kennedy in Oregon. That set up the crucial confrontation with McCarthy in the California primary, which Kennedy won with 46 percent of the vote to McCarthy's 42 percent.

Leaving a victory rally shortly after midnight on June 5, Kennedy was shot by Sirhan B. Sirhan, a disaffected Jordanian, and died the following day. President Johnson declared a national day of mourning. Kennedy's body was carried by train from New York to Washington and was met by thousands of mourners who paid their final respects.

See also: Elections of 1960 and 1968; Lyndon B. Johnson; Edward M. Kennedy; John F. Kennedy; Joseph P. Kennedy; Eugene McCarthy; Vietnam War as a Political Issue

Matthew J. Dickinson

REFERENCES

Kennedy, Robert F. 1971. *Thirteen Days: A Memoir of the Cuban Missile Crisis.* New York: Norton.

Schlesinger, Arthur M., Jr. 1978. *Robert Kennedy and His Times.* Boston: Houghton Mifflin.

White, Theodore. 1968. *The Making of the President 1968.* New York: Atheneum.

Kentucky Resolutions

Two sets of resolutions that were passed in 1798 and 1799 in reaction to the Alien and Sedition Acts of the Federalist-controlled Congress of 1798. The alien acts empowered the President to deport "dangerous" aliens and, in event of war, to apprehend and remove subjects of the hostile government. The sedition act made it unlawful to combine or conspire against any lawful measure, or to prevent any United States officer from performing his duties, or to aid "any insurrection, riot, unlawful assembly, or combination." This act called for the punishment of any person writing, speaking, or publishing "any false, scandalous and malicious writing" against the President, Congress, or United States government. Thomas Jefferson, leader of the Republican Party and Vice President under John Adams, viewed both acts as "palpably in the teeth of the Constitution"; in particular, he believed that the sedition act was a blatant attempt to silence the "whig press" and the Republican Party. Jefferson drafted the first set and urged passage of the second set of Kentucky Resolutions, but for political reasons, including his fear of actually being tried under the Sedition Act, he kept his involvement secret for nearly 25 years.

Although Jefferson intended the resolutions for North Carolina, others introduced them in Kentucky. The first sentence affirmed the "compact theory" of the Constitution: Since the states created the "General Government" with limited powers, "whensoever the General Government assumes undelegated powers, its acts are unauthoritative, void, and of no force." The resolutions also argued that each party to the compact "has an equal right to judge for itself, as well of infractions as of the mode and measure of redress." In spite of this volatile beginning, the resolution concluded calmly, calling for other states to assist Kentucky in repealing the acts. Jefferson's more radical first draft, in contrast, invited the states to "concur in declaring these acts void" and to "take measures of [their] own for providing that neither of these acts, nor any others of the General Government not plainly and intentionally authorized by the Constitution, shall be exercises within their respective territories." When news of the negative reaction to the resolutions was received, Jefferson urged Kentucky to reaffirm its position. In a 1799 letter to James Madison, Jefferson clearly indicated that he considered the Alien and Sedition Acts so noxious that he was willing "to sever ourselves from that union we so much value, rather than give up the rights of self-government." Although Jefferson was not the author of the second set of resolutions, they did revive use of the word "nullification" from his draft of the 1798 resolutions. On the other hand, Kentucky never pursued its claim of nullification as a rightful remedy.

The effects of the resolutions were twofold: they united the Republicans into a party determined to restore the "General Government" to its proper role, and they served as a rationale for the advocates of states' rights in the debates leading up to the Civil War.

See also: John Adams, Alien and Sedition Acts, Federalist Party, Thomas Jefferson, James Madison, Nullification

Richard K. Matthews

REFERENCES

Banning, Lance. 1978. *The Jeffersonian Persuasion.* Ithaca: Cornell U. Pr.

Cunningham, Noble. 1987. *In Pursuit of Reason.* Baton Rouge: Louisiana State U. Pr.

Koch, Adrienne. 1950. *Jefferson & Madison.* New York: Oxford U. Pr.

Malone, Dumas. 1962. *Jefferson and the Ordeal of Liberty.* Boston: Little, Brown.

John W. Kern (1849–1917)

Democratic Senate leader in the Wilson administration. John Worth Kern capped a long and often unsuccessful career in Indiana politics with a single term in the U.S. Senate from 1911 to 1917. But what a term! Between 1910 and 1920 both the House and Senate restructured their party leadership, and Kern is generally recognized as being the institutional founder of the role of majority floor leader in the Senate. His skillful handling of Woodrow Wilson's numerous proposals during that President's first term puts Kern among the most successful Senate floor leaders of the twentieth century.

Kern had earned the respect of Democratic Party regulars as an unsuccessful candidate for governor in 1900 and 1904 and as the party nominee for Vice President on the 1908 William Jennings Bryan ticket. Although Democrats captured the Indiana legislature in 1908, that body met in secret and passed over Kern for the state senate. Two years later state law required the parties to nominate candidates for the U.S. Senate, and Kern was confirmed by the legislature to replace Republican Albert Beveridge. Friendly to labor, on close terms with Bryan, and respected by younger progressive Democrats, Kern rapidly established himself in the Senate, where he served on the Finance Committee.

After Wilson's election in 1912 the Senate Democratic majority, including an influx of progressive young Democrats, voted to make Kern the party leader, replacing the conservative Virginian, Thomas S. Martin. Kern worked out committee assignments that generally respected committee seniority, but moved progressive Democrats onto key committees; committee rules were also made more democratic. While doing his utmost for Wilson's extensive legislative program, Kern sought to maintain good working relations with every Democratic Senator and to be an "honest broker" between the Democratic majority and the White House. Narrowly defeated for reelection in 1916, Kern left an institutional role that the Senate has subsequently found indispensable.

See also: Thomas Martin, Woodrow Wilson

H. Douglas Price

REFERENCES

Bowers, Claude G. 1918. *The Life of John Worth Kern.* Indianapolis: Hallenbeck Press.

Haughton, Virginia F. 1973. "John Worth Kern and Wilson's New Freedom: A Study of a Senate Majority Leader." Ph.D. dissertation, U. of Kentucky.

Michael C. Kerr (1826–1876)

Indiana "hard money" Congressman. Election as Speaker of the U.S. House of Representatives during the Forty-fourth Congress (1875–1876) both capped and virtually concluded the political career of Indiana Democrat Michael Crawford Kerr. Already in poor health when the congressional session began, Kerr was forced to seek relief at a mountain spa before his term was over. He died in Rockbridge County, Virginia.

Born in Titusville, Pennsylvania, Kerr graduated from Erie Academy in 1845 and completed his law studies at the University of Louisville in 1851. He crossed the Ohio River the next year, establishing his practice in New Albany, Indiana. His political career began in 1854 with election as city attorney. During the following decade he served as Floyd County prosecuting attorney (1855); as a member of the Indiana House of Representatives (1857); and as reporter of the Indiana Supreme Court (1862–1865). First elected to the U.S. House of Representative in 1864, he served in four successive Congresses (1865–1873) before suffering a narrow defeat in an at-large election in 1872.

Kerr's final campaign, and his subsequent election as Speaker, were closely tied to the money question. A "hard money" advocate, Kerr disapproved of the inflationist plank adopted by the Democratic state convention in 1874 and ran in his own district on a sound money platform. Although inflationist Democrats scored huge successes all across the state, Kerr (with the help of Republican crossovers) eked out a close win. Indiana historian William Carleton believed that "[t]his notable victory of a conservative who successfully defied his inflationist party in the inflationist district of an inflationist state made Kerr nationally famous and very popular with conservatives." Kerr's

notoriety, coupled with his congressional experience, doubtless influenced his selection as Speaker.

See also: Speaker of the House

Robert G. Barrows

REFERENCES

Carleton, William G. 1946. "The Money Question in Indiana Politics, 1865–1890." 42 *Indiana Magazine of History* 107.

Dunn, Jacob Piatt. 1919. *Indiana and Indianans.* 5 vols. Chicago: American Historical Society.

Woollen, William Wesley. 1883. *Biographical and Historical Sketches of Early Indiana.* Indianapolis: Hammond.

Robert S. Kerr (1896–1963)

Oilman and powerful Democratic politician from Oklahoma. In the rotunda of the Oklahoma State Capitol are four portraits of Oklahomans who are not only famous worldwide but who also have had a deep, long-lasting influence on the nation as a whole. One of the four is of Robert Samuel Kerr. Born in Pecan Grove Valley in what was to become the state of Oklahoma, Kerr became one of the most powerful men on the Oklahoma and national scene. He attended East Central Norman School and Oklahoma Baptist University. Despite his natural inclination, he followed the advice of his father and joined the debating team rather than the football team while attending law school at the University of Oklahoma. His skill in debating was to later make him a respected and feared opponent of the floor of the U.S. Senate and on the election trail.

During World War I, he served as a major in the National Guard and in 1925 was elected state commander of the American Legion; he later used veterans as a key component of coalitions that would elect and reelect him to public office. However, the Democratic Party really served as the base of his political power. Starting in 1919 he served the Democratic Party in many positions and capacities and was thus nearly always supported by party regulars in elections. He was national committeeman from Oklahoma in 1940 and keynote speaker for the 1944 Democratic National Convention. In 1948 he was considered as a running mate for Harry Truman, and in 1952 he was a candidate running for the Democratic nomination for President of the United States. However, Kerr was unable to translate his considerable influence in Congress into national popularity and primary election victories. Throughout most of his political career he was considered the titular head of the Democratic Party in Oklahoma although he did not entirely dominate it.

When he was elected in 1942, he became the first native-born Oklahoma governor. At the end of his term, he became the first Oklahoma governor to get to the U.S. Senate, elected by basically the same coalition that was to support him throughout his electoral career: party regulars, New Dealers, Baptists, veterans, Blacks, and small-business owners. Businessman, oilman (a founder of Kerr-McGee Oil Industries), lawyer, and rancher, he successfully blended urban and rural interests into a coalition that was never defeated at the polls in Oklahoma.

It was as a U.S. Senator that Robert S. Kerr reached the pinnacle of his political power. He was one of the first modern southern politicians who saw the federal government as a source of economic development for his state rather than as a threat. His service on congressional committees and subcommittees, moreover, left no doubt that the well-being of Oklahoma was his primary concern. By the 1960s he was considered the "Uncrowned King of the Senate" and was responsible for carrying much of the New Frontier's legislative program through Congress. Future generations may well remember him for his key role in the American space effort as well as for his efforts at conservation and development of natural resources. However, it was as a vote-getter and party loyalist that he earned his true place in America's political history.

See also: Harry S Truman

Thomas H. Clapper

REFERENCES

Benson, Oliver, et al. 1964. *Oklahoma Votes: 1907–1962.* Norman, OK: Bureau of Government Research.

Jones, Stephen. 1974. *Oklahoma Politics in State and Nation.* Enid, OK: Haymaker Press.

Kirkpatrick, Samuel A., David R. Morgan, and Thomas G. Kielhorn. 1977. *The Oklahoma Voter: Politics, Elections and Parties in the Sooner State.* Norman: U. of Oklahoma Pr.

Morgan, Anne Hodges. 1977. *Robert S. Kerr: The Senate Years.* Norman: U. of Oklahoma Pr.

Scales, James R., and Danny Goble. 1982. *Oklahoma Politics: A History.* Norman: U. of Oklahoma Pr.

V. O. Key, Jr. (1908–1963)

Preeminent scholar of political parties. Vladimer Orlando Key, Jr., was born in Texas and spent his undergraduate years at the University of Texas at Austin, subsequently entering the University of Chicago as a graduate student in political science. With Charles Merriam as his adviser at Chicago, he completed his dissertation, *The Techniques of Political Graft,* and earned his Ph.D. in 1934. He then served on the faculties of Johns Hopkins, Yale, and Harvard universities. V. O. Key is generally regarded as one of the leaders of the postwar "behavioral revolution" in American political science. His work has been selected as the focus of the first volume in the American Political Science Association's monograph series on the intellectual issues and history of political science. As Milton C. Cummings, Jr., wrote there, Key's scholarship emphasized the importance of linking empirical inquiry to larger theoretical questions, the "imaginative" use of methodology, and the need for rigorous scholarship to contemplate issues of relevance to society at large. The author of nine books and numerous articles, Key developed an extensive research program dealing with a variety of aspects of American national and state politics. He is credited with major contributions to the study of political parties, regional politics, voting and elections, and public opinion.

While his intellectual legacy is apparent in many areas, Key is perhaps best known today for his 1955 article, "A Theory of Critical Elections." There he developed the concept of partisan realignment to explain abrupt and lasting changes in the political party system, changes triggered by "critical" elections. While he later considered the possibility that realignments represented the cumulative effect of a more gradual set of changes in the partisan landscape, his identification of critical elections and their impact on the party system was the central inspiration behind later attempts to classify different types of elections and to understand the impact of partisan realignments on both electorate and government.

Key's work on realignment reflected his enduring interest in the relationship in American democracy between those who govern and those who are governed. This interest found expression in a number of his other major works. *Politics, Parties, and Pressure Groups,* the first edition published in 1942 and a fifth and final edition in 1964, was a survey of the American political system at the national level that not only cast existing scholarship in perspective but also provided important new insights into the political process. His *Southern Politics* (1949), a study regarded by some as his masterpiece, explored the causes and consequences of the dominance of the Democratic Party in the South for the electorate as well as for state and federal governments. It was followed by *American State Politics* (1956), a book that examined states outside the South with particular attention to the impact of Progressive era reforms on two-party politics. In *Public Opinion and American Democracy* (1961), Key was especially concerned with the influence of elites on public opinion and, in turn, the influence of public opinion on those with the power to govern. Finally, in *The Responsible Electorate*, published posthumously in 1966, Key analyzed the role of the mass electorate in American democracy and developed the "theory of reward and punishment" in which voters rewarded (with their votes) officeholders whose performance they approved and punished (by voting for the opposition) those whose performance they deemed unsatisfactory.

See also: Political Realignment entries

Melissa P. Collie

REFERENCES

Cummings, Milton C., Jr. 1988. *V. O. Key, Jr., and the Study of American Politics*. Washington: American Political Science Association.

Key, V. O. 1936. *The Techniques of Political Graft in the United States*. Chicago: U. of Chicago Libraries.

———. 1942. *Politics, Parties, and Pressure Groups*. New York: Crowell.

———. 1949. *Southern Politics*. New York: Knopf.

———. 1955. "A Theory of Critical Elections." 17 *Journal of Politics* 3.

———. 1956. *American State Politics*. New York: Knopf.

———. 1959. "Secular Realignment and the Party System." 21 *Journal of Politics* 198.

———. 1961. *Public Opinion and American Democracy*. New York: Knopf.

———. 1966. *The Responsible Electorate*. Cambridge: Harvard U. Pr.

Martin Luther King, Jr. (1929–1968)

Civil rights leader. Dr. Martin Luther King, Jr., was the preeminent spokesman for the African-American protests that transformed American race relations during the 1960s. Born into a middle-class Baptist minister's family in Atlanta, King was early attracted to the sheltered life of a pastorate or a professorship. After earning a B.A. (1948) at Morehouse, Atlanta's prestigious Black college, and a B.D. three years later at Crozer Seminary in Pennsylvania, he continued his religious studies at Boston University. In 1954, a year before receiving his doctorate, King became minister to the Dexter Avenue Baptist Church in Montgomery, Alabama.

In December 1955 Montgomery's Black residents unanimously chose King to direct a boycott against the city buses after the arrest of Rosa Parks, who had refused to yield her seat to a white man. King at that time was scarcely a leading activist: he had declined to run for president of his local NAACP branch the previous year, preferring to spend more time with his family, congregation, and books. Once selected, though, King began to draw national attention and considerable aid from northern liberals with his eloquent depictions of the boycott as a moral crusade, not against whites but against injustice. His message fused Christian ideals of universal love with Mohandas Gandhi's belief in nonviolent civil disobedience to unjust laws. The triumph of the boycott in December 1956, after the NAACP won a Supreme Court ruling that voided Montgomery's bus segregation law, propelled the 27-year-old King to the forefront of civil rights leadership.

In January 1957 northern volunteers helped King organize the Southern Christian Leadership Conference, a network of African-American ministers dedicated to nonviolent struggle for equal citizenship rights. King exerted his greatest influence on this struggle during the 1960s as a charismatic presence who focused attention and support on protests that were already gathering momentum. His arrest in October 1960 at a protest against segregation in Atlanta was one of thousands made that year against civil rights demonstrators, but it commended such national publicity that John F. Kennedy, the Democratic presidential candidate, privately intervened to secure King's release. The resulting increase in Black electoral support helped provide Kennedy his razor-thin margin of victory, and this in turn encouraged African-Americans to mount further nonviolent protests across the South.

In 1963 King directed demonstrations in Birmingham, Alabama, that police countered with beatings and attack dogs. The nightly televised scenes of brutality against men, women, and children stirred national outrage against racism. As scores of other protests in the South added to the pressure for federal action, President Kennedy proposed a comprehensive civil rights bill in June 1963. To promote its passage, civil rights leaders sponsored an interracial march on Washington on August 28, 1963, at which King proclaimed his "dream that one day this nation will rise up and live out the true meaning of its creed" that all people were created equal. In affirming his faith both in nonviolence and in the coming redemption of American society,

King projected with matchless eloquence the hopes of civil rights activists with the support of liberal whites to transform race relations.

The reform coalition strategy pursued by King appeared vindicated in July 1964 when President Lyndon Johnson signed an omnibus Civil Rights Act. The new law barred discrimination in public accommodations, employment, and voting; and it prohibited federal aid to segregated institutions. Early in 1965 Dr. King led a campaign for voting rights in Selma, Alabama, that again stirred national awareness of racism through media coverage of police violence against peaceful Black marchers. With President Johnson's emphatic support, Congress easily overcame a southern filibuster and, in August 1965, passed a Voting Rights Act that strengthened federal safeguards for African-Americans seeking the ballot.

During the late 1960s the persistence of prejudice, poverty, and ghetto slums led King to brand liberal policies as wholly inadequate. The Watts riot of August 1965 (which left 34 dead) and the failure of King's efforts the following year to end racist housing patterns in Chicago sharpened his criticisms of capitalism for permitting "a vast gulf between superfluous wealth and abject poverty." In April 1967, as America's involvement in Vietnam eclipsed federal antipoverty spending, King irreparably alienated President Lyndon Johnson by deploring "the greatest purveyor of violence in the world today—my own country." Despite harassment by the FBI and desertion by many white liberals, he began mapping campaigns of civil disobedience in northern cities. He also planned a Poor People's March in the capital to dramatize his demand for immediate abolition of poverty through a guaranteed annual income. By 1968, when an assassin took his life in Memphis, Tennessee, King had moved far beyond his earlier calls for Black citizenship rights to work for a "radical restructuring" of American society.

Although King had appeared in his last years to be losing his hold on the nation's shrinking political center, he remained committed to interracial coalition and peaceful democratic change. Since the 1960s, the dissolution of legal caste lines in the South, the rise of southern Black voter registration (to 64 percent in 1988), the withering of openly racist political discourse, and the bipartisan support for preserving key civil rights laws have attested to the strength of the movement that King championed as a strategist and moral symbol. In 1983 Congress honored King's memory by declaring his birthdate (January 15) a national holiday.

See also: Civil Rights Legislation and Southern Politics, Lyndon B. Johnson, John F. Kennedy, NAACP, Voting Rights Act of 1965 and Extensions

Robert S. Weisbrot

REFERENCES

Branch, Taylor. 1988. *Parting the Waters: America in the King Years, 1954–1963.* New York: Simon & Schuster.

Garrow, David J. 1986. *Bearing the Cross: Martin Luther King, Jr. and the Southern Christian Leadership Conference.* New York: Morrow.

Lewis, David L. 1978. *King: A Biography.* 2d ed. Urbana: U. of Illinois Pr.

Oates, Stephen B. 1982. *Let the Trumpet Sound: The Life of Martin Luther King, Jr.* New York: Harper & Row.

Preston King (1806–1865)

One of the founders of the Republican Party. Preston King served four terms in the New York State Assembly as a dedicated Jacksonian Democrat and follower of Martin Van Buren. Involvement in the Canadian revolt of 1837 and 1838 may have caused a temporary mental breakdown, but he soon returned to politics and served in the U.S. House of Representatives beginning in 1843. King was sincerely antislavery by conviction and resented the James Polk administration's support of the prosouthern "hunker" faction over Van Buren's "barnburner" Democrats in New York. He therefore cooperated with David Wilmot in presenting his proviso restricting slavery expansion in 1846, and when Wilmot avoided pushing the issue, King brought it before Congress a second time. In 1848 he supported Van Buren's Free Soil candidacy, and in 1850 he was elected to Congress as a Free Soiler. After a brief return to the Democrats in 1852, King broke with them permanently over the Kansas-Nebraska Act.

He became one of the founders of the Republican Party, promoted Frémont's nomination, and was himself considered for the vice presidential nomination. In 1857 he was elected to the United States Senate where he was rated as one of the more radical Republicans. In 1860 he served as chairman of the party's congressional campaign committee and undertook extensive election management. King was dedicated, idealistic, and personally popular with his associates, but even he was unable to survive the factional feuds of New York Republican politics. In 1863 he lost his Senate seat to Governor John Morgan. Afterward he became an adviser to Andrew Johnson, and in 1865 Thurlow

Weed persuaded Johnson to appoint King collector of customs for New York. Unsuited to the pressures of this busy office and harassed by patronage seekers, King suffered a return of his mental illness and committed suicide.

See also: Barnburners, Election of 1848, Free Soil Party, Hunkers, Andrew Johnson, Kansas-Nebraska Act, Martin Van Buren

Harold B. Raymond

REFERENCES

Blue, Frederick. 1973. *The Free Soiler: Third Party Politics 1848–1854*. Urbana: U. of Illinois Pr.

Bogue, Allan. 1981. *The Earnest Men*. Ithaca: Cornell U. Pr.

Donavan, Herbert D. A. 1925. *The Barn Burners*. New Haven: Yale U. Pr.

Gienapp, William E. 1987. *The Origins of the Republican Party 1852–1856*. New York: Oxford U. Pr.

Muller, Ernest Paul. 1957. *Preston King: A Political Biography*. New York: Columbia U. Pr.

William R. D. King (1786–1853)

Congressman, United States Senator, minister to France, and in 1852 Vice President of the United States. William Rufus de Vane King was born in Sampson County, North Carolina, was educated at the University of North Carolina, read law, and in 1806 was admitted to the bar. He was elected to Congress in 1810 where he remained for six years as an ardent supporter of war with England.

In 1816 King left the Congress for diplomatic service. Upon his return two years later, he relocated to Alabama. When Alabama achieved statehood in 1819, King was elected to the U.S. Senate and served until 1844. In that year, President John Tyler appointed him minister to France (1844–1846). In 1848 he regained his Senate seat and was, for a time, President *pro tempore* as he had also been during his earlier service there.

In the turbulent sectional politics of the period, King pursued a moderate course. When he supported the Compromise of 1850, he was drawn into the political orbit of James Buchanan. At the Democratic convention of 1852, he vigorously supported Buchanan's bid for the nomination, and when Franklin Pierce gained the nod on the forty-ninth ballot, King was placed second on the ticket as a gesture to the Buchanan forces. The Democrats won the election handily, but King, in the advanced stages of tuberculosis, had gone to Cuba for his health. By special act of Congress, he was sworn in as Vice President in Cuba on March 4, 1853.

Anxious to be home, he returned to Alabama where he died in April.

King's career was notable less for its achievement than for its longevity. In that respect, he was typical of a generation of politicians of whom James Buchanan is, perhaps, most representative.

See also: James Buchanan, Election of 1852, Franklin Pierce, John Tyler

John F. Coleman

Paul Grattan Kirk, Jr. (1938–)

Chairman of the Democratic National Committee. Paul Grattan Kirk, Jr., was born in Newton, Massachusetts, the son of a lawyer, who later became a Justice of the Massachusetts Supreme Court. Educated at Harvard (B.A. 1960, LL.B. 1964), he practiced law privately with Massachusetts firms and as an assistant district attorney. He was an aide to Senator Edward Kennedy and, in 1980, the national director of the Kennedy for President Committee.

When he became Democratic National Committee chairman in 1985, Kirk was generally perceived to be little more than a Kennedy satellite. He rapidly established an independent identity, however, by acting promptly to undo a number of the more egregious mistakes made by his predecessors. He disestablished those special interest caucuses that had brought the severe fragmentation of the Democratic Party into the organization of the national committee itself. He secured the abandonment of the useless and divisive midterm national convention, and he made a long overdue peace with the Wisconsin state party, whose open presidential primary had caused the national party to instigate a lawsuit that had to be settled (in favor of the national committee) in the U.S. Supreme Court. His management of party affairs coincided with and encouraged retreat from the self-destructiveness that had plagued the Democratic Party from 1968 through 1988.

See also: Democratic National Committee, Edward Kennedy

Nelson W. Polsby

Jeane J. Kirkpatrick (1926–)

First woman to serve as the United States ambassador to the United Nations. Jeane Jordan Kirkpatrick has the unique distinction of serving as a policymaker in both the Democratic and Republican parties. Kirkpatrick began her career as a political scientist, receiving her M.A. (1950) and Ph.D. (1967) from Columbia University. In

1955 she married Evron M. Kirkpatrick, a political scientist and executive director of the American Political Science Association from 1954 to 1981. Her career spans both academic and nonacademic roles. Kirkpatrick joined the faculty at Trinity University in 1961, moving to Georgetown University in 1967. She became the Thomas and Dorothy Leavey University Professor of the Foundations of American Freedom at Georgetown and serves as Senior Fellow and Counselor to the President for Foreign Policy Studies at the American Enterprise Institute (where she has been a resident scholar since 1977). Earlier Kirkpatrick had been employed as a Defense Department research analyst (1951–1953) and has served as consultant intermittently from 1955 to 1972 for the departments of State, Defense, and Health, Education, and Welfare; and for the American Council of Learned Societies.

While Kirkpatrick's primary scholarly interests lie in comparative and international politics, her published books also reflect her interest in the roles adopted by women in elite politics (*Political Woman*, 1974) and her active opposition to Democratic Party reforms. Her third book, *The New Presidential Elite* (1976), was an empirical analysis of the attitudes and roles of Democratic and Republican convention delegates to the 1972 conventions. Here she concludes that the effect of party reforms has been to open up the parties to new "symbol" specialists, resulting in a "new presidential elite." She formalized this critique of Democratic reforms in *Dismantling the Parties* (1979) in stating her opposition to quotas as allowing parties to be penetrated by those without "seasoned and reliable ties."

Jeane Kirkpatrick, who describes herself as a "welfare-state conservative" was associated with the Humphrey-Jackson wing of the Democratic Party. Kirkpatrick was a longtime political associate and personal friend of Hubert H. Humphrey; she and her husband served as polling analysts for Humphrey in 1968 and 1972. In 1976 she was Senator Henry M. Jackson's representative to the Democratic platform committee. She was the vice chairman of the Democratic National Commission of Vice-Presidential Selection (1973). Kirkpatrick served on the original Winograd Commission (1975–1976), which was appointed by national chair Robert Strauss prior to formal authorization by the 1976 convention. She has served as a member of the board of directors and executive committee of the Coalition for a Democratic Majority, an organization of prominent party reform critics.

After switching parties, Kirkpatrick was a keynote speaker at the 1984 Republican National Convention, receiving acclaim for her attack on Democrats "who always blame America first." Kirkpatrick, however, remains closer to the Democrats on some social issues. She favors the Equal Rights Amendment and was critical of the Ronald Reagan administration's treatment of women. Nevertheless, she is strongly supported by Republican conservatives. Phyllis Schlafly and the Eagle Forum honored Jeane Kirkpatrick at the 1988 Republican convention for her strong stands on "American defense and security in a dangerous world."

See also: Eagle Forum, Equal Rights Amendment, Hubert Humphrey, Henry M. Jackson, Phyllis Schafly, United Nations, Winograd Commission

Denise L. Baer

REFERENCES

Kirkpatrick, Jeane J. 1974. *Political Woman*. New York: Basic Books.

———. 1976. *The New Presidential Elite*. New York: Russell Sage.

———. 1979. *Dismantling the Parties: Reflections on Party Reform and Party Decomposition*. Washington: American Enterprise Institute.

Kirkpatrick v. Preisler
394 U.S. 526 (1969)

The decision in this case is part of the Supreme Court's attempts to prevent gerrymandering by giving meaning to the requirement of the 1964 *Wesberry v. Sanders* decision: "as nearly as is practicable one man's vote in a congressional election is to be worth as much as another's." In *Kirkpatrick* and other cases, the Court has struggled to determine how much population variance is tolerable in the drawing of electoral districts. Specifically, in this case, the Court rejected a 1967 Missouri reapportionment plan for congressional districts that deviated no more than 3.13 percent from population equity as not meeting the "one man, one vote" standard.

The Court does not expect exact mathematical precision in the drawing of congressional districts, but it did establish in this case that the state must make a "good faith" effort to achieve mathematical precision and that it must justify to the Court's satisfaction any variances from population equality. The Court rejected Missouri's argument that the small differences in population between congressional districts should be considered *de minimis* (insignificant) by ruling that no variance from strict population equality is constitutionally permissible unless it proves unavoidable even after a "good faith" effort to achieve mathematical equality. If population variances exist despite a "good faith" effort, then the state must justify the variances however small in terms of other legitimate state objectives, such as maintaining political subdivisions or the compactness of districts. The Court ruled that Missouri did not make a "good faith" effort and did not justify population differences between districts.

The case is significant because the Court rejected a plan that would have been accepted without question only a few years before, thereby further strengthening the "one man, one vote" principle. As the Court would reiterate in *Karcher v. Daggett* (1983), if a congressional district plan can be made more equitable in terms of population equality, then it should be. Otherwise, the state must provide an acceptable rationale for deviating from the "one man, one vote" rule.

See also: Gerrymandering, *Karcher v. Daggett, Wesberry v. Sanders*

Clyde Brown

REFERENCES

Baker, Gordon E. 1968. "New District Criteria." 57 *National Civic Review* 291.

Keefe, William J., and Morris S. Ogul. 1985. *The American Legislative Process: Congress and the States.* Englewood Cliffs, NJ: Prentice-Hall.

Knights of Labor

Part trade union, part political party, and part cooperative reform society, the Knights of Labor emerged as the largest American popular movement of the late nineteenth century. At its peak in 1887, it enrolled some 700,000 members. The Knights of Labor sought to unite all workers—defined broadly to mean all skilled and unskilled workers except lawyers, doctors, bankers, and saloonkeepers—and to create a cooperative alternative to competitive capitalism. The Knights did not seek to overturn the existing social and economic order; rather the group desired to reshape capitalism along somewhat vaguely defined ethical grounds, grounds that would protect the dignity of the American worker and maintain a sense of community.

Founded in Philadelphia in 1869 as a secret society of garment workers, the Knights quietly grew in Pennsylvania and other northeastern states throughout the 1870s, incorporating miners, machinists, shoemakers, and carpenters. In 1878 the Knights reformed into a national association, their deliberations opened to the public with Terence Powderly of Scranton, Pennsylvania, as its grand master. The Knights' moment of national prominence occurred in 1885 and 1886, when the party successfully organized strikes against Jay Gould's railroad interests. Although they continued to be active in municipal politics and in organizing producer and consumer cooperatives throughout the 1890s, the Knights could not match their mid-1880s success and fell from popularity as rapidly as they had gained it. The economic panic of 1893, a concerted campaign of resistance against the Knights by corporations, a lack of clarity about how the goal of a cooperative commonwealth was to be realized, and uncertainty among leaders of the Knights over the tactic of the strike, all contributed to the decline of the Knights of Labor.

See also: Railroads

John Walsh

Know-Nothings

A group of anti-immigrant, anti-Catholic Americans who emerged after the 1830s in response to the waves of immigration occurring during that period, the "Know-Nothings" originated in the lodges of the Supreme Order of the Star Spangled Banner. In 1854 they changed their name to the American Party, successfully fielding candidates in Massachusetts, New York, Maryland, Kentucky, and California.

Founded on the principle that "Americans should rule America . . . foreigners have no right to dictate our laws, and therefore have no just ground to complain if Americans see proper to exclude them from offices of trust," the Know-Nothings experienced their greatest success in Massachusetts where immigrants were pouring into the state at the rate of 100,000 a year. In 1854 the Know-Nothings won all but 3 of more than 350 seats in the Massachusetts House of Representatives, all of the state senate seats, all of the congressional seats, and all of the statewide offices including the governorship.

Their platforms included a demand that aliens live in the United States for 21 years before being allowed to vote; that immigrants never be allowed to hold public office and that their children should have no rights unless they were educated in the public schools. Know-Nothings believed that only native-born Protestants had the right to hold political office. They particularly opposed the Roman Catholic Church and the order of Jesuits, claiming that they owed allegiance to a foreign power—the Pope.

Appearing on the scene at a time of significant party instability and political corruption in the United States, the Know-Nothings capitalized on already existing anti-immigrant, anti-Catholic bias. Originally supported by the Whigs, the Know-Nothings themselves eventually disappeared as a party—most of them apparently being absorbed into the Republican Party after the Civil War.

See also: Ku Klux Klan

Elinor C. Hartshorn

REFERENCES

"An American," pseudonym, A. B. Ely. 1855. *The Sons of Sires: A History of the Rise, Progress and Destiny of the American Party.* Philadelphia: Lippincott.

Haynes, G. H. 1897. "A Know-Nothing Legislature." *Annual Report of the American Historical Association* for the year 1896. Washington: American Historical Association.

Massachusetts. 1853. *Constitutional Convention of 1853. Official Report of the Debates and Proceedings in the State Convention Assembled May 4, 1853, to Revise and Amend the Constitution of the Commonwealth of Massachusetts.* Boston: Commonwealth of Massachusetts.

William F. Knowland (1908–1974)

Republican Senate leader from California. William F. Knowland served as U.S. Senate Majority Leader from 1953 to 1955 and as Minority Leader from 1955 to 1959. He was the son of a six-term Congressman and owner of the *Oakland Tribune.* After serving in the California State Legislature, he joined the Army in World War II. In 1945 Governor Earl Warren appointed him to fill the Senate seat vacated by the death of Republican Hiram Johnson.

In 1953 he became chairman of the Senate Republican Policy Committee. Later that year, his GOP colleagues chose him as Majority Leader, following the wishes of his predecessor, the late Robert A. Taft. When the Republicans lost the Senate majority in 1954, Knowland spent the next four years as Minority Leader.

Knowland helped lead the "China Lobby," a loose group of lawmakers and citizens dedicated to supporting Chiang Kai-shek's Nationalist Chinese. Even though he was Senate Republican leader, he chided President Dwight Eisenhower for failing to take a stronger stand against communism in China, Korea, and Vietnam. He also strongly supported Senator Joseph McCarthy, the chief Red-baiter of the 1950s.

In 1958, eying the White House, Knowland ran for governor of California after persuading incumbent Republican Goodwin Knight to seek his Senate seat. In a Democratic year, both lost. Knowland went back to the newspaper business and reportedly killed himself in 1974.

See also: Dwight D. Eisenhower, Joseph McCarthy, Robert A. Taft

John J. Pitney, Jr.

REFERENCES

Ambrose, Stephen E. 1985. *Eisenhower the President.* New York: Touchstone.

———. 1987. *Nixon: The Education of a Politician 1913–1962.* New York: Simon & Schuster.

Matthews, Donald R. 1960. *U.S. Senators and Their World.* New York: Vintage.

White, William S. 1957. *Citadel: The Story of the U.S. Senate.* New York: Harper.

William Franklin (Frank) Knox (1874–1944)

Republican Party leader and journalist. Born in Boston, Massachusetts, but raised in Grand Rapids, Michigan, William Franklin Knox left high school after his junior year but later attended Alma College (Mich.), where he became known as Frank. He volunteered and served in the Spanish-American War as one of Theodore Roosevelt's Rough Riders. Upon returning, he began his long career in journalism by working successively as a reporter, editor, and circulation manager before purchasing his first newspaper in 1902. Knox used his newspapers to advocate what he saw as progressive policies. He also became directly involved with politics on occasion, managing the unsuccessful gubernatorial campaign of Chase Osborn in 1910, and becoming chairman of the Republican State Central Committee in that same year. In 1912 he played a major role in Theodore Roosevelt's presidential bid, both before and after the formation of the Progressive Party.

He suddenly shifted his base to New Hampshire in 1912, and became a dominant force in journalism and politics there. After volunteering for service in France during World War I, Knox returned to become chairman of the New Hampshire delegation at the 1920 Republican National Convention and leader of Leonard Wood's unsuccessful bid for the presidential nomination. His own political ambitions were stunted, however, when he was defeated in the 1924 New Hampshire Republican gubernatorial primary.

A vocal critic of the New Deal, he was unsuccessfully considered for the Republican presidential nomination in 1936. In June 1940, on the eve of World War II, he sacrificed his position as a leader of the Republican Party to accept the position of Secretary of the Navy in Franklin D. Roosevelt's bipartisan Cabinet. Traveling extensively to inspect the fleet and far-flung naval bases, he served in Washington until his death.

See also: Progressive Party, Franklin D. Roosevelt, Theodore Roosevelt

James V. Saturno

Edward I. Koch (1924–)

Flamboyant mayor of New York City. Edward Irving Koch was born to poor Polish Jews in the Bronx, fought in the infantry in World War II, and studied at City College and New York University Law School. He served as a feisty and outspoken U.S. Congressman and then as Mayor of New York City for three terms, capturing the support of both the machine and reform factions.

Koch began his political career by joining the Village Independent Democrats and the Tammany machine of Carmine DeSapio; he became district leader, then a civil rights lawyer in the early 1960s, and finally a city councillor in 1966. He reduced drug dealing in Washington Square, pleasing many Italian-Americans in Greenwich Village. In 1968 he was elected to Congress from the Silk Stocking District, voting for weapons cuts, Israel, school busing, federal aid for abortions, public broadcasting, public transport, consumer protection, tax relief for single adults, the Cooper-Church Amendment to end the bombing of Cambodia, and the Privacy Act of 1974.

Koch first ran for mayor in 1973, withdrawing because he lacked funds. During the fiscal crisis of 1975, he obtained federal loan guarantees over President Gerald Ford's objections. In 1977 he became mayor aided by television commercials written by David Garth, arguing against criminal corruption, callous charisma, and clubhouse clout, and for creative competence. He protected Jewish and Catholic taxpayers but disappointed Blacks and Hispanics. In 1982, he lost the governorship to Mario Cuomo, never campaigning comfortably in upstate New York. Koch required merit selection in central offices, but elsewhere he allowed patronage, and by 1987 Bronx and Queens leaders were being indicted for corruption. He eventually lost in his quest for a fourth term as mayor

in 1989 to the Democratic primary winner, African-American David Dinkins.

See also: Carmine DeSapio, Gerald Ford, David Garth

Jeremy R. T. Lewis

REFERENCES

Browne, Arthur, Dan Collins, and Michael Goodwin. 1985. *I, Koch: A Decidedly Unauthorized Biography of the Mayor of New York, Edward I. Koch.* New York: Dodd, Mead.

Koch, Edward I., and William Rauch. 1984. *Mayor.* New York: Warner.

———, and———. 1985. *Politics.* New York: Warner.

Ku Klux Klan

A perennial debate in the study of American politics is whether a fundamental social consensus has undergirded American politics or whether deep social conflict has dominated the American political system. Although it does not resolve the debate, the history of the Ku Klux Klan bears directly on it.

Understanding the relevance of the Klan's history to this debate demands abandonment of a common view of the Klan—namely, that the KKK is an ancient, dramatic fixture of violent white supremacist politics in the South. A more accurate view of the Klan would emphasize that there has not been one Klan, but three Klans, each with a separate history and its own political aims; secondly, each of the Klans emerged during periods of intense national conflict over who legitimately belonged in the American electorate and in American society. The history of the Klan thus suggests that violence and coercion have been significant elements in the development of American electoral politics.

The first Klan, a group that formed in 1865 and flourished until a Republican-controlled federal government suppressed it shortly before the 1872 presidential election, was modeled in part on informal, antebellum slave patrols and was often staffed by Confederate Army veterans. It arose in the context both of the rapid expansion of the southern electorate to include millions of freedmen and of the Republican Party's efforts to institute a southern organization. The first Klan was, in effect, the paramilitary arm of the Democratic Party in the South; its purpose was to intimidate talented Black and white Republican leaders and to weaken or eliminate local institutions (e.g., churches, newspapers, and schools) that supported Reconstruction and the new two-party system in the South. In part because those southern state militias controlled by Republican governors were weak and ineffective and in part because the number of federal Army units stationed in the South was dwindling, the Klan succeeded in badly weakening local and state Republican organizations. By the time the federal government got around to prosecuting the KKK in 1871 and 1872, irreparable damage had been done to fragile Republican organizations, helping to set the stage for the redemption of the South by conservative Democrats.

The second Klan (1915–1925) was a vast social movement, like the earlier nativist Know-Nothings. It was only partly white supremacist, for the KKK was also avowedly nationalist. The first Klan venerated the Confederate flag; the second Klan venerated the Stars and Stripes. White supremacism was not even its main theme: KKK politics were primarily antiradical, anti-immigrant, anti-Catholic, and anti-Semitic. Emphasizing patriotic symbols, the Klan's purpose was to popularize a fundamentalist social vision of a supposedly purified America.

In the early 1920s the second Klan attached itself to state and local Republican parties in the North and West and to the Democratic Party in the South. The Klan's influence over state and local politics in several jurisdictions—Alabama, Oregon, Texas, Colorado, Georgia, Florida, Indiana, Ohio—was extraordinarily great, and KKK votes often made the difference in senatorial and congressional contests. In Oklahoma in 1923 and 1924, the Klan fought and won a local civil war against a farmer-labor faction in the Oklahoma Democratic Party.

The scope of the second Klan's influence in the early 1920s was related to the resurgence of Protestant evangelical fundamentalism, to Prohibitionism, to fears of aliens and radicals that lingered from the Red Scare of 1919, and (in certain parts of the South) to the survival of a racist version of populism. But by 1925 a national backlash, fueled in part by outrage over much-publicized corruption within the Klan's national administrative arm, left the second Klan disorganized and weak.

The third Klan, still alive in the 1990s, is a small, although still dangerous, hate group that emerged during the "second Reconstruction" of the South in the 1950s and 1960s. Like its two predecessors, it emerged in the context of national conflict over who belonged in the American electorate and society. The civil rights revolution brought millions of African-Americans into active politics in the South. But unlike its two predecessors, the third Klan quickly be-

came illegitimate among southerners and the object of constant federal surveillance. Indeed, at one point in the 1960s about one-fifth of all KKK members may have been FBI informers.

In the early 1990s, ex-Klansmen have gained some electoral support in the South running as Republicans. But the Klan is still weak. Its relative weakness strongly suggests that American politics has in certain respects become much more consensual and tolerant. Interestingly, however, the first Klan created a model for linking coercive tactics to electoral politics, a paradigm that was adapted to new purposes in later periods, once successfully, once unsuccessfully. Whether that model will ever be successful again is problematic, but the Klan's unusual history can still inspire a debate over the limits of tolerance in American electoral politics.

See also: Know-Nothings, Reconstruction, Red Scare
Richard M. Valelly

REFERENCES

Goldstein, Robert J. 1978. *Political Repression in Modern America.* Cambridge, MA: Schenkman.

Higham, John. 1981. *Strangers in the Land: Patterns of American Nativism, 1860–1925.* New York: Atheneum.

Trelease, Allen W. 1971. *White Terror: The Ku Klux Klan Conspiracy and Southern Reconstruction.* New York: Harper & Row.

Thomas H. Kuchel (1910–)

Republican Senate leader from California. Thomas H. Kuchel (pronounced *Kee*-kul) of California was Senate Republican whip from 1959 to 1969; his rise and fall mirrored the fate of the liberal wing that he championed. After serving in the California State Legislature and the U.S. Navy, Kuchel was appointed the state's controller in 1946 by Governor Earl Warren. He won election to a full term later that year. After Richard Nixon's election as Vice President in 1952, Warren named Kuchel to replace Nixon in the U.S. Senate.

Kuchel's liberalism helped his 1956 bid for election in his own right, when he gained many Democratic votes. In 1959 it boosted him further. When GOP Senators chose conservative Everett Dirksen of Illinois as party leader, they sought balance by naming Kuchel party whip. In 1962, an otherwise disappointing year for Republicans, Kuchel kept his seat by 728,000 votes, becoming California's top Republican.

In the 1960s he clashed with the rising conservative wing of the GOP, both on Capitol Hill and in California. In 1964 he served as Republican floor manager for the civil rights bill that Barry Goldwater, that year's GOP presidential candidate, opposed. In 1966 he did not support California Republican gubernatorial nominee Ronald Reagan. In 1968 conservative Max Rafferty bested Kuchel for the GOP Senate nomination. Rafferty eventually lost to Democrat Alan Cranston, who proved to be far more liberal than Kuchel.

See also: Civil Rights Legislation and Southern Politics, Richard M. Nixon, Ronald Reagan

John J. Pitney, Jr.

REFERENCES

Oleszek, Walter J. 1985. *Majority and Minority Whips of the Senate.* Senate Document 98–45. Washington: U.S. Government Printing Office.

Kusper v. Pontikes
414 U.S. 51 (1973)

In this case, the Supreme Court struck down an Illinois statute that prohibited a voter from participating in the primary election of a political party if he had voted in the primary of another party within the preceding 23 months.

The constitutionality of the 23-month rule was challenged by Harriet Pontikes, a qualified Chicago voter, who was barred from voting in the March 1972 Democratic primary election because she had voted in the Republican primary in February 1971. In her suit, Pontikes argued that Illinois' election law, by denying her the opportunity to vote in the Democratic primary, deprived her of her rights under the First and Fourteenth amendments to associate with the political party of her choice. A three-judge federal district court had held the 23-month rule unconstitutional. The Supreme Court, in a 7-to-2 decision, affirmed the judgment of the district court.

In his majority opinion, Justice Potter Stewart wrote that the Illinois statute "locked" voters into their preexisting party affiliation by forcing them to forgo participation in any primary elections for almost two years until their party registration became effective. The Court held this to be an unconstitutional infringement on the right of free political association. "By preventing the appellee from participating at all in Democratic primary elections during the statutory period, the Illinois statute deprived her of

any voice in choosing the party's candidates, and thus substantially abridged her ability to associate effectively with the party of her choice."

Although the Court's previous decision in *Rosario v. Rockefeller* recognized that a time limit on party registration was a proper means of supporting the state's legitimate interest in preventing party raiding, the Court in *Pontikes* held that Illinois' interest in preventing raiding did not justify the 23-month rule. In *Rosario*, the Court had upheld a New York statute that prevented a change in party affiliation during the 8- to 11-month period between the registration deadline and the next party primary.

The Court found a significant difference between this statute and the Illinois election law. Unlike New York, which "merely imposed a time deadline on [party] enrollment," Illinois absolutely denied the appellee the right to vote. The disenfranchisement of the petitioners in *Rosario*, wrote Justice Stewart, was caused by their own failure to take steps to enroll in a party before the state's registration deadline. Illinois, on the other hand, absolutely precluded Pontikes from participating in the 1972 Democratic primary and "there was no action Mrs. Pontikes could have taken to make herself eligible to vote."

In his dissent, Justice Harry Blackmun argued that because the state had a legitimate interest in preventing party raiding, the Illinois statute was reasonably related to that goal. He noted that "this very limited statutory restriction on the appellee's exercise of her franchise is triggered solely by her personal and voluntary decision" to switch parties. Because party switchers "clearly are the group most amenable to organized raiding," the 23-month rule was properly tailored to the threat of raiding.

See also: Rosario v. Rockefeller

Robin Bye Wolpert

REFERENCES

Lewy, Glen S. 1973. "The Right to Vote and Restrictions on Crossover Primaries." 40 *University of Chicago Law Review* 636.

Taslitz, Neal. 1974. "*Rosario v. Rockefeller* and *Kusper v. Pontikes*: Voters and Other Strangers." 23 *De Paul University Law Review* 838.

Tribe, Laurence. 1988. *American Constitutional Law.* 2nd ed. New York: Foundation Press.

L

Philip F. La Follette (1897–1965)

Leader of the Wisconsin Progressive Party. Philip Fox La Follette followed his father, Robert M. La Follette, into Wisconsin politics in 1924 when he was elected district attorney. When their father died in 1925, Philip's brother, Robert, Jr., became U.S. Senator, and Philip remained in Wisconsin to become principal organizer of the Progressive movement, at that time a faction of the state Republican Party. He was elected governor as a Republican in 1930, but was defeated in the primary in 1932, when many Progressives voted Democratic in Wisconsin's open primary. Reluctant at first, La Follette agreed in 1934 to head the new Wisconsin Progressive Party and was again elected governor. However, only after his reelection in 1936, when he carried a Progressive legislative majority, was he able to enact Progressive programs, including labor relations, relief, and public power authority acts.

La Follette wanted, from the start, to build a national Progressive movement, but his close ties to Franklin Roosevelt made him cautious. When the economy worsened again in 1937, La Follette turned to criticizing the administration and the growth of government, and in April 1938, he suddenly announced the formation of the National Progressives of America (NPA). La Follette criticized the New Deal and appeared to be moving in a more conservative direction; most liberals rejected this new La Follette. Even his brother, who publicly defended the NPA, kept his distance. The NPA failed, La Follette lost his reelection bid, and the Wisconsin Progressive Party began to decline.

Out of the office in the late 1930s, La Follette helped found the right-wing America First Committee. Later he boosted General Douglas MacArthur's conservative presidential bids, but he never actively returned to politics.

See also: Douglas MacArthur, New Deal

Mary T. Curtin

REFERENCES

La Follette, Philip Fox. 1970. *Adventure in Politics: The Memoirs of Philip La Follette.* New York: Holt, Rinehart, and Winston.

Miller, John E. 1982. *Governor Philip F. La Follette, the Wisconsin Progressives, and the New Deal.* Columbia: U. of Missouri Pr.

Robert M. La Follette (1855–1925)

Leader of the Wisconsin and national Progressive movements. Significant in American party development because of his early sponsorship of the mandatory statewide direct primary, Robert Marion La Follette led the Progressive movement first in Wisconsin and then in national politics during most of the first quarter of the twentieth century. Under the Republican label, he was a United States Representative (1885–1891), governor of Wisconsin (1901–1906), and a United States Senator (1906–1925). In 1912 he campaigned for the Republican presidential nomination, and in 1924 he ran for President as a third-party Progressive, carrying only Wisconsin though polling nearly 17 percent of the national popular vote. In the Senate, La Follette promoted labor legislation and business regulation. He opposed American involvement in World War I, a highly unpopular stance at the time.

Despite his substantial role in national affairs, La Follette's most striking accomplishments were in Wisconsin. Laws that he and other Progressives enacted in the fields of taxation, public utilities, and primary elections influenced legislation elsewhere, and his impact in Wisconsin was remarkably durable. La Follette himself remained the state's dominant political force for almost two decades after he left the governorship for the Senate, and the political legacy was maintained by two sons—Robert, Jr. (U.S. Senator, 1925–1947) and Philip (governor, 1931–1933 and 1935–1939)—and by a grandson—Bronson (state attorney general, 1965–1969 and 1975–1987). Many other Wisconsin politicians, Democrats and Republicans, have invoked the La Follette tradition, especially to defend the state's primary law. Among early twentieth-century governors, he was one of the first to develop a large personal following not only to win nomination and election but also to support strong executive leadership in behalf of a legislative program. La Follette helped to elect legislators of his Progressive persuasion, building an effective majority within the dominant Republican Party. His organization was often successful in contests against stalwart, or conservative, Republicans for control of the party label.

La Follette had challenged the established Republican leadership when he first sought the gubernatorial nomination through the old caucus-convention system. Losing in 1896 and 1898 to what La Follette perceived to be a corrupt machine, he became committed to the direct primary as the democratic means for voters to choose party nominees. His commitment, expressed in speeches in Wisconsin and elsewhere, was no less tenacious after he won the Republican convention's gubernatorial nomination in 1900. Urging the legislature to enact a direct primary law became a high priority of his subsequent governorship. Though party primaries of various sorts had been tried in the United States, La Follette's proposal was innovative in its required use of official election machinery along with its statewide application. Enacted in 1903 and put into effect in 1906, the Wisconsin primary law is thus usually regarded as groundbreaking legislation. Almost all states eventually adopted primary laws of a broadly similar kind, but only a minority followed the completely open form that Wisconsin exemplified in presidential primaries as well as in state and congressional primaries. Wisconsin's open primary, in which voters choose party nominees without prior party enrollment or even party declaration at the polls, was not the form originally proposed by La Follette. He eventually embraced it, however, as part of the legislation he wanted, and he may even have liked the open feature at least as well as his first suggestion that voters declare their party in order to vote in its primary. At any rate, La Follette is as much identified with the open primary as he is with direct primary more generally.

See also: Robert M. La Follette, Jr.

Leon D. Epstein

REFERENCES

La Follette, Belle C., and Fola La Follette. 1953. *Robert M. La Follette*. New York: Macmillan.

Robert M. La Follette, Jr. (1895–1953)

Progressive Republican Senator from Wisconsin. Robert Marion La Follette, Jr., was elected to the U.S. Senate upon his father's death in 1925. He had worked as his father's secretary for six years and once elected plunged into battles against the entry of the United States into the World Court and for farm price supports. He soon established himself as more than caretaker of his father's legacy. La Follette urged unemployment relief and public works spending and, after Franklin Roosevelt's election, was important in the passage of New Deal legislation. In the 1930s he held much-publicized hearings on labor's civil rights.

La Follette never liked the campaigning and organizing essential to politics and never initiated efforts to create a third party, neither in Wisconsin nor nationally. However, he was consistently seen as the Progressives' leader, and his participation was essential in efforts to rebuild the movement. He vetoed his brother Philip's idea of a new state party in 1931. But he accepted support from the Wisconsin Progressive Party in 1934, leading a sweep of state offices that year. La Follette convinced Progressives not to run a national campaign in 1936 because he supported Roosevelt and feared splitting the liberal vote. He was unhappy when his brother Phil created the short-lived National Progressives of America in 1938, but he publicly defended his sibling. By that time La Follette was disillusioned with FDR over his handling of the 1937 recession and, especially, over foreign policy, but many voters disagreed with him. He was reelected in 1940 with only 45 percent of the vote. By 1946 the Wisconsin Progressive Party had folded. In that year La Follette was upset in the Republican primary by Joseph McCarthy, an obscure right-wing district judge. Although La Follette was held in high esteem by Senate colleagues, he had lost touch with voters.

La Follette never found satisfaction outside the Senate and became plagued with ill health. Eventually he committed suicide.

Mary T. Curtin

REFERENCES

Johnson, Roger T. 1970. *Robert M. La Follette, Jr., and the Decline of the Progressive Party in Wisconsin.* Hamden, CT: Archon Books.

Maney, Patrick J. 1978. *"Young Bob": A Biography of Robert M. La Follette, Jr., 1895–1953.* Columbia: U. of Missouri Pr.

Fiorello H. La Guardia (1882–1947)

"The Little Flower." Fiorello Henry La Guardia, a maverick liberal Republican, achieved his greatest prominence as mayor of New York City in the New Deal era. The child of an Italian father and Jewish mother, the idealistic, ambitious "Little Flower" aligned with the Republican Party when he entered politics, partly because he opposed Tammany Hall, partly because the local GOP offered better prospects for Italian-Americans than did the Irish-dominated Democrats. La Guardia was elected to Congress in 1916 and 1918 and to the presidency of the New York Board of Aldermen in 1919, before emerging as a national figure in the 1920s. Serving five consecutive terms as a Congressman from New York City beginning with the 1922 election, the colorful La Guardia won a reputation for a fierce, independent liberalism that saw him align in 1924 with the Progressive Party and champion liberal measures throughout the decade.

After a reelection defeat in 1932, La Guardia won the mayoralty of New York on an anti-Tammany fusion ticket in 1933. He went on to become the first modern New York mayor to serve three consecutive terms and the first anti-Tammany reform mayor to succeed himself. Overseeing important administrative and social reforms in New York, La Guardia benefited from New Deal funds and programs and supported Franklin D. Roosevelt. In local politics, La Guardia helped weaken Tammany Hall and allied with New York's new American Labor Party, but he left behind no ongoing reform organization when he retired from New York politics in 1945.

See also: American Labor Party, New Deal, Progressive Party, Franklin D. Roosevelt, Tammany Hall

John W. Jeffries

REFERENCES

Heckscher, August. 1978. *When La Guardia Was Mayor: New York's Legendary Years.* New York: Norton.

Kessner, Thomas. 1989. *Fiorello H. La Guardia and the Making of Modern New York.* New York: McGraw-Hill.

Mann, Arthur. 1959. *La Guardia: A Fighter Against His Times: 1882–1933.* Philadelphia: Lippincott.

———. 1965. *La Guardia Comes to Power: 1933.* Philadelphia: Lippincott.

Melvin R. Laird (1922–)

Republican congressional leader from Wisconsin. Melvin R. Laird, a Republican from Wisconsin, served first in Congress and then as a Cabinet officer in the Richard Nixon administration. As a member of the House Armed Services Committee, he developed a reputation for pragmatism and for expertise on defense policy.

Laird received the Purple Heart and other decorations for his service in the Navy during World War II. He was elected to Congress in 1952 after six years in the Wisconsin state senate. An active partisan, he served as chairman of the platform committee at the 1964 Republican National Convention. Laird helped to shape a conservative platform that was acceptable to both the Barry Goldwater delegation and to more moderate delegates. He succeeded Gerald Ford as Republican Conference chair in the House in 1965. He remained his party's third-ranking leader for four years.

In 1969 Laird left Congress to become Secretary of Defense under Richard Nixon. He resigned that post in 1973, but joined Nixon's White House staff as chief domestic adviser only a few months later. Although he was not a member of Gerald Ford's administration, Laird acted as an informal adviser to Ford after he became President in 1974.

See also: Gerald Ford, Richard Nixon

John A. Clark

Alfred M. Landon (1887–1987)

Republican presidential candidate in 1936. Alfred Mossman Landon served two terms as governor of Kansas and became the Republican presidential nominee to oppose President Franklin D. Roosevelt. Born in Pennsylvania, Landon moved to Kansas as a teenager. He supported the Bull Moose candidacy of Theodore Roosevelt in 1912 and achieved early success in student politics at the University of Kansas, where he earned a law degree (however, he never practiced). Initially a banker, Landon achieved substantial wealth as an independent oil producer.

In 1932 Landon defeated an incumbent Democrat and was the only Republican governor to be reelected in 1934. Potential Republican presidential candidates in 1936 included Senator William Borah of Idaho, the aging Progressive champion; Chicago newspaper publisher Colonel Frank Knox; and former President Herbert Hoover. Landon was nominated on the first ballot in Cleveland, with Knox as his running mate.

Clearly an underdog presidential candidate, Landon hoped his midwestern voice would be a welcome contrast to FDR's patrician tones, but he was no match for Roosevelt's effective radio presence. He began the campaign accepting the goals of New Deal programs but promised better administration. Pressured by his conservative contributors, Landon was by campaign's end shrilly denouncing FDR. He carried only Maine and Vermont, winning just eight electoral votes. Five million new voters protected their New Deal gains.

Landon accepted his defeat philosophically. He was eventually to see his daughter, Nancy Landon Kassebaum, elected to the U.S. Senate from Kansas in 1978. On September 9, 1987, he became the first presidential nominee to reach the age of 100.

See also: William Borah, Election of 1936, Herbert Hoover, New Deal, Franklin D. Roosevelt

Karl A. Lamb

REFERENCES

Lubell, Samuel. 1956. *The Future of American Politics.* Rev. ed. Garden City, NY: Anchor Books.

Schlesinger, Arthur M., Jr. 1960. *The Age of Roosevelt: The Politics of Upheaval.* Boston: Houghton Mifflin.

William L. Langer (1886–1959)

Leader of the Nonpartisan League of North Dakota. "Wild Bill" Langer began his political career as State's attorney for Morton County, North Dakota, in 1914. In 1916 he was elected to the office of attorney general in a Nonpartisan League (NPL) sweep of the state. Although he agreed with the NPL's program, he soon broke with party leaders, whom he thought corrupt and socialistic. After an unsuccessful bid for governor in 1920, he returned to private law practice.

Langer reemerged in the 1930s as leader of a resurgent NPL. As before, the organization was not a third party; rather the NPL took over the Republican Party. Langer was elected governor in 1932. His controversial actions, including a moratorium on farm mortgages and an embargo on shipping wheat out of the state, again made the NPL the dominant political force in the state. He was removed from office in 1934 for soliciting funds from federal employees but was reelected in 1936. North Dakotans found him remarkably effective.

Langer was elected to the U.S. Senate in 1940 and seated only after an investigation into charges of corruption. Although he caucused with the Republicans, he often voted with the Democrats, defying easy categorization as a radical or reactionary throughout his tenure. Langer remained dedicated to farm issues but became better known for his isolationist foreign policy. He was an ardent anti-Communist, but he defended civil liberties just as ardently.

In 1956 Langer split with the NPL—by then no longer a real political force in North Dakota—over its decision to move to the Democratic Party. He was reelected in 1958 without NPL endorsement, but died a year later, one of the last of an era of midwestern insurgents.

See also: Isolationism in American Politics

Mary T. Curtin

REFERENCES

Geelan, Agnes. 1975. *The Dakota Maverick. The Political Life of William Langer, Also Known as Wild Bill Langer.* Fargo, ND: Geelan.

Morlan, Robert L. 1955. *Political Prairie Fire: The Nonpartisan League, 1915–1922.* St. Paul: Minnesota Historical Society Press.

Smith, Glenn H. 1979. *Langer of North Dakota: A Study in Isolationism, 1940–1959.* New York: Garland.

John M. Langston (1829–1897)

Lawyer, educator, and Republican politician after the Civil War. John Mercer Langston was a prominent figure in the interracial politics of the post–Civil War era. He was born in Virginia, the son of a white plantation owner; his mother, a former slave, was part African and part Native American in descent. Orphaned at age 5, Langston was sent to Ohio for his education, graduating from Oberlin College in 1849. After training in the law, he began practice in 1854 and soon became a leader in Oberlin's interracial community, holding several important local offices. His eloquence in behalf of abolition and Black suffrage gained him widening regional renown as the Civil War approached.

After the war he worked as an inspector general for the Freedmen's Bureau. In 1869 he joined the new Howard University in Washington, where he served as dean of the law department and then as vice president of the university. In 1877 Republican President Rutherford B. Hayes appointed him minister to Haiti, a post he held till the Democrats returned to power in 1885. He then became president of Virginia Normal and Collegiate Institute in Petersburg, Virginia. In 1888 he won the Republican nomination for Congress in Virginia's Fourth Congressional District. Though defeated in the ballot count on election day, he successfully contested the outcome and was seated by vote of the House of Representatives in September 1890. After one abbreviated term, he failed to be reelected. Thereafter he turned to the writing of his memoirs, recording with ample pride his long service on the country's racial frontier.

See also: Abolition Movement, Rutherford B. Hayes, Suffrage

Geoffrey Blodgett

REFERENCES

Cheek, William Francis, and Aimee Lee Cheek. 1989. *John Mercer Langston and the Fight for Freedom, 1829–65.* Urbana: U. of Illinois Pr.

Langston, John Mercer. 1894. *From the Virginia Plantation to the National Capitol.* Hartford, CT: American Publishing.

Lyndon LaRouche (1923–)

Perennial extremist presidential candidate. Lyndon LaRouche, a quadrennial third-party candidate for President, first came into national prominence in 1976 when he attempted to challenge Republican President Gerald Ford and Democratic nominee Jimmy Carter for the presidency. Often described as a "right-wing extremist" within the Democratic Party, LaRouche actually began his political career as a left-wing activist.

As leader of the National Democratic Policy Committee (NDPC), LaRouche has worked since 1980 to build a wide base of electoral support for himself at the presidential level as well as for his followers seeking office at the congressional and state level. In 1984 his followers were moderately successful in congressional races, particularly in the Midwest where his organization has been strongest. Two "LaRouchians" won the Democratic Party nomination for Congress in Ohio, and other LaRouche followers ran well across the country in House and Senate races in states as diverse as North Carolina, Oregon, California, Pennsylvania, Michigan, and Georgia.

In 1986 LaRouche gained national attention when two more of his followers successfully infiltrated regular party ranks in Illinois and seized the Democratic nomination in that state for the offices of lieutenant governor and secretary of state. While none of LaRouche's supporters has yet won high office, the NDPC claims to hold hundreds of offices in government in states throughout the country.

Known most for his flamboyant personality and extremist statements, LaRouche has charged in the past that Democratic presidential candidate Walter Mondale was a Soviet agent, that Queen Elizabeth II controlled the world drug trade, and that the Holocaust was a hoax. LaRouche has advocated strict quarantine for AIDS patients, the nationalization of the U.S. steel industry, and an expansion of the use of nuclear power, indicating no real ideological consistency in policy positions.

Most recently, Lyndon LaRouche came to national attention when his supporters spread rumors that 1988 Democratic presidential nominee Michael Dukakis had a history of mental illness. LaRouche was convicted of credit card fraud and jailed in 1989; from prison he continued to run for political office.

See also: Jimmy Carter, Michael Dukakis, Gerald Ford, Walter Mondale

Michael Heel

REFERENCES

King, Dennis, and Ronald Radosh. 1984. "The LaRouche Connection." *The New Republic,* November 19.

Levin, Bob, and William Lowther. 1987. "Indicted Candidate." 28 *Maclean's* 18.

David Lawrence (1889–1966)

Pittsburgh Democratic boss. David Lawrence, a prominent Pennsylvania political figure and Democratic Party leader, worked his way up through the organizational ranks of the Democratic Party to become one of the most powerful leaders in Pennsylvania. He also had a significant impact on national politics.

Born in Pittsburgh, Lawrence became active in party politics at the age of 14 when he dropped out of school to become an office boy for William J. Brennan, the local Democratic leader. Lawrence served in a variety of official party positions, including the chairmanship of the Pennsylvania Democratic State Committee, before his election as mayor of Pittsburgh in 1945. In the mayoral seat that he held for four terms, Lawrence, working with the Allegheny Conference on Community Development and Republican business leaders, engineered the Pittsburgh renaissance of the 1950s.

Although Lawrence was once indicted (but later acquitted) on charges of graft and corruption, his administration is generally remembered as scandal free. And in 1958 Pittsburgh was chosen by *Fortune* magazine as one of the eight best-governed cities in the nation.

In 1959 Lawrence was elected as Pennsylvania's first Roman Catholic governor. Repeatedly declining the party's invitation to run that year, the 69-year-old Lawrence eventually agreed and waged a rigorous campaign against his opponent, Arthur T. McGonigle. Although Lawrence was favored to win by a landslide, he won in a close contest; analysts believe that anti-Catholicism led to his small margin of victory.

Lawrence's impact on the Democratic Party was widespread. Dominating the Pittsburgh organization on his own, he and William Green, Jr., of Philadelphia shared control of the Pennsylvania Democrats. But Lawrence was also a prominent national party leader. He served on the Democratic National Committee beginning in 1940 and is credited with such acts of national significance as delivering the state of Pennsylvania—a traditional Republican stronghold—to Franklin Roosevelt in 1932 and to John Kennedy in 1960. Lawrence is also responsible for securing vice presidential nomination in 1944 for his close ally Harry Truman, thereby denying it to the more liberal incumbent, Henry A. Wallace.

In addition to his Democratic Party and elected positions, Lawrence became chairman of the President's Committee on Equal Opportunity in Housing at the conclusion of his gubernatorial term, holding that position until his death.

See also: Democratic National Committee, Elections of 1932 and 1960, William Green, Henry Wallace

Barbara Trish

REFERENCES

McGeary, M. Nelson. 1972. *Pennsylvania Government in Action: Governor Leader's Administration*. State College, PA: Pennsylvania Valley Publishers.

Peirce, Neal R. 1972. *The Megastates of America*. New York: Norton.

Stevens, Sylvester K. 1964. *Pennsylvania: Birthplace of a Nation*. New York: Random House.

League of Nations

Founded in the wake of World War I as an organization to promote international coop-

eration and security, and headquartered in Geneva, Switzerland, the League of Nations in structure closely resembled its successor, the United Nations. The League featured a secretariat, an assembly made up of representatives from all members, and a council whose membership consisted of permanent representatives from Great Britain, France, Italy, and Japan, along with Germany and the Soviet Union after their admittance, as well as rotating membership that varied from 4 to 11 nations during the life of the League. The League's covenant also provided for a Permanent Court of International Justice.

The League's founding document was a covenant adopted by the Paris peace conference in April 1919 and included in the peace treaties ending World War I. The League formally came into being in January 1920 with 42 member nations, and by the time of its official demise in April 1946, 63 nations had been members at some time during the League's sometimes stormy existence.

Although the League emerged from many cherished ideals, the catalyst for its founding came from groups within the Allied nations who advocated a postwar organization to keep the peace. These were summed up for Americans by Woodrow Wilson in his "Fourteen Points," first enunciated in a speech he gave in January 1918.

The League's status suffered a serious blow even before it began operation when the United States Senate refused to ratify the Treaty of Versailles, thus preventing America's entry into the League. Having been instrumental in the drafting of the League covenant, Woodrow Wilson regarded the League as perhaps his greatest cause, and he worked strenuously to convince the public and the Senate of the truth of that cause. Opposed by a group of Senators collectively referred to as the Irreconcilables, the treaty was defeated on three separate votes in November 1919 and again in March 1920. The effort to keep alive the possibility for the entry of the United States into the League effectively ended when many of its supporters in the Democratic Party were resoundingly defeated in the election of 1920.

The 1920s, however, were generally a period of growth for the League. Many of the nations that had been either neutral or enemies during the war were admitted. The League achieved success in arbitrating several boundary disputes and in redistributing the colonial holdings of

Germany and Turkey as trusts in the form of mandates. An area of particular success was public health: the League's various health efforts included major roles in collecting information on drug use and disease and in combating epidemics.

In the 1930s the League's significant role in international affairs was eroded. Attempts to promote disarmament, begun so earnestly in the 1920s, ended in signal failure. More importantly, the League's position as arbitrator of international disputes was limited by its inability to cope with the beginnings of the expansion of the Axis powers. Efforts to impose sanctions against Japan, Germany, Italy and several other nations were largely fruitless, and the League played only a minor role in the events leading to the outbreak of World War II.

See also: Election of 1920, Woodrow Wilson

James V. Saturno

REFERENCES

Bendiner, Elmer. 1975. *A Time for Angels*. New York: Knopf.

Flemming, Denna Frank. 1968. *The United States and the League of Nations, 1918–1920*. New York: Russell and Russell.

Northedge, F. S. 1986. *The League of Nations: Its Life and Times, 1920–1946*. New York: Holmes and Meier.

Stone, Ralph A. 1967. *Wilson and the League of Nations*. New York: Holt, Rinehart, and Winston.

———. 1970. *The Irreconcilables*. Lexington: U. Pr. of Kentucky.

League of Women Voters

At the urging of Carrie Chapman Catt, president of the National American Woman Suffrage Association (NAWSA), the League of Women Voters was established in 1919. Once the Nineteenth Amendment was ratified in 1920, the League became an independent organization and official successor to NAWSA.

Politicians' fears that the League would engender a women's bloc vote or a separate political party were unfounded. Members chose to create a nonpartisan organization that would educate women to work effectively within parties and to support reform programs where needed. To this end, the League advocated a method similar to the one used by social reformers in the early twentieth century. Before a stand was taken, the League prepared an thorough study and conducted a unreserved discussion of an issue. It then used this as a basis to mobilize public opinion and lobby the government.

This approach enabled the League to attract a large membership regardless of political affiliation, so that by 1930 it had 100,000 dues-paying members. The organization did its utmost to be representative of its members, and any issue that could not achieve a consensus was avoided. The League was organized on hierarchical lines with power clearly divided among the national, state, and local divisions. The latter were free to determine their own priorities using the League's methodology, but locals were expected to support the national program.

In the early years, the League actively advocated disarmament, government reform, and special labor laws designed to protect working women. When the Equal Rights Amendment (ERA) was proposed by the National Woman's Party and introduced in the 1923 Congress, the League vigorously condemned it. League members feared that under the ERA, equality would be interpreted as identical treatment, with women losing needed protections. The League held that since women were different from men, they could not and should not be treated in the same manner. Members argued that special labor laws brought equity to the workplace, claiming these laws were able to bridge the differences between the sexes by protecting the weaker woman worker. To achieve equality, the League advocated individual laws rather than the blanket legislation offered by the amendment. When other women's groups concurred, this clash over the ERA so split the post-1920 women's movement that unity on any other issue was impossible. The League continued to oppose the amendment until 1959, long after other groups had done so.

Throughout the years, the League's membership has remained sizable, drawn primarily from the upper and middle classes. Local chapters were often involved with such concerns as planning and zoning, recreation and ecology while state Leagues focused on election reforms or state constitutional revisions. The national continued to support equal opportunity legislation, direct election of the President, and welfare reform, and to serve as the sponsor for candidate debates. On the whole, the League offered women who were concerned with political issues a nonpartisan forum for expression.

See also: Carrie Chapman Catt, Equal Rights Amendment, National American Woman Suffrage Association, National Women's Party, Nineteenth Amendment

Joy A. Scimé

REFERENCES

Chafe, William H. 1972. *The American Woman: Her Changing Social, Economic, and Political Role, 1920–1970.* New York: Oxford U. Pr.

Lemons, J. Stanley. 1973. *The Woman Citizen.* Urbana: U. of Illinois Pr.

O'Neill, William. 1969. *Everyone Was Brave: The Rise and Fall of Feminism in America.* Chicago: Quadrangle.

Scimé, Joy A. 1987. "Government Policy, Working Women and Feminism in the Great Depression: Section 213 of the 1932 Economy Act." Ph.D. dissertation, State U. of New York at Buffalo.

Sealander, Judith. 1983. *As Minority Becomes Majority.* Westport, CT: Greenwood.

Richard C. Lee (1916–)

Democratic reform mayor of New Haven, Connecticut. Born to Catholic parents, Richard C. Lee was reared in New Haven and attended its public schools. From 1935 to 1940, he worked as a staff writer for the *New Haven Journal-Courier.* He later served for a decade as director of Yale University's Public Relations Department.

Lee became involved in Democratic Party politics at an early age. In 1938 he was elected to the New Haven Board of Aldermen. Seven years later he was named the board's minority leader. He made his first bid for mayor of New Haven in 1949, losing by a narrow margin. Two years later he tried again, this time losing by a mere two votes.

In 1954 Lee finally won the job he had so long coveted. Immediately, he established a Citizen's Action Commission to study prospects for economic development. After the commission filed its report, Lee hired Edward Logue for development administrator. By 1958 New Haven had spent more on redevelopment than any other city in New England. Lee's talent for public relations helped to attract media attention to his redevelopment program, articles appearing in *Harper's* and *The Saturday Evening Post.* Economic revitalization became the hallmark of the Lee administration, and the professional administrator became a standard feature of the redevelopment process.

Redevelopment also proved popular with the voters. Lee overwhelmingly won reelection, serving as New Haven's mayor for 16 years. Robert Dahl (1961) writes that he was an incessant worrier:

> Possibly as much by temperament as by his experience of an electoral defeat that could be regarded only as sheer chance, he was prone to worry about dangers of unexpected and uncontrolled events. For many years he suffered

badly from ulcers, which sometimes sent him to the hospital at critical moments. He was a worrier, who spent much of his time laying plans to ward off incipient dangers.

John K. White

REFERENCES

Dahl, Robert A. 1961. *Who Governs: Democracy and Power in an American City.* New Haven: Yale U. Pr.

Lockard, Duane. 1959. *New England State Politics.* Princeton: Princeton U. Pr.

Legislative Districting

America never knew the rotten boroughs that John Locke called "gross absurdities" and that he condemned as being incompatible with the right of equal representation. Rotten boroughs were, Locke wrote in 1912, towns "of which there remain[ed] not so much as the ruins, where scarce so much housing as a sheepcote, or more inhabitants than a shepherd [were] to be found, [but that sent] as many representatives to the grand assembly of law-makers, as a whole country numerous in people, and powerful in riches."

The United States did inherit from Britain the so-called Westminster system, in which legislators are elected, usually one apiece from geographically defined districts, with the candidate receiving the most votes declared the winner. Perhaps the system was inevitable in an earlier time with neither full-fledged political parties nor modern devices of transportation and communication. In any event, the system has been permanently embedded in American political thought and practice.

Fear of Gerrymandering

Americans soon learned that drawing district lines had electoral consequences. Attention to this fact did not originate with Elbridge Gerry, signer of the Declaration of Independence and later governor of Massachusetts. But a cartoon in an opposition newspaper lampooning a district, allegedly shaped like a salamander, that had been created by Gerry's allies, gave the word "gerrymander" to the English language, thus helping to create an American tradition of distrust of both legislative districting and those who engage in it.

The word "gerrymander" has no universally accepted definition, but it is generally a pejorative way of referring to partisan legislative districting. The term's origin suggests a reference to districts with peculiar shapes, still no doubt what the term brings to mind for many people.

What excites reform sentiment is the prospect of electoral distortion resulting from manipulative line-drawing, and although such manipulation may be correlated with peculiar shapes, it need not be. The line drawer may be able to accomplish his or her objectives just as well with evenly drawn districts, while odd shapes may result from such "natural" considerations as the meandering paths of rivers or even of state boundaries.

Since odd shapes may be good and regular shapes bad, reformers have looked for more sophisticated definitions of gerrymandering. They have tended to split over whether what makes a districting plan bad is its actual consequences or the intent with which it was drawn. Each approach has its difficulties. A definition of gerrymander based on the consequences of a districting plan must provide some criterion that distinguishes good consequences from bad. A definition based on the intent of the author of the plan must be able to separate good motives from bad. All this is not easy, since most observers recognize that eliminating all traces of self-interest from the districting process is impossible. No consensus has emerged on criteria for normative evaluation of either consequences or intent in legislative districting.

Although most of the controversy over redistricting has centered on the plans themselves or on the criteria according to which they should be judged, some reformers have targeted instead the procedures by which the plans are adopted. Their proposals may have included a requirement for public hearings and open processes within the state legislature; still others ask for a supermajority that, as a practical matter, would require bipartisan assent to a redistricting bill.

More drastically, some reformers have proposed to prevent gerrymandering and to insulate line-drawing from political pressures by creating nonpartisan commissions to draw district boundaries in lieu of the state legislatures. Commissions have been established in nearly a third of the states, but they have turned out to be nonpartisan neither in design nor in performance. Reform proposals for commissions continue to encounter skepticism over whether a nonpolitical approach to districting is a coherent objective as well as the objection that the approach has the vice of its virtues, in that it removes a significant and constitutive public decision from democratic control.

Population Equality

During the middle third of the twentieth century, controversy centered on the question of unequally populated districts. The steady shift of population from rural to urban and then to suburban communities meant not only that the population within old district boundaries had become increasingly unequal but also that the resulting inequality tended systematically to favor certain interests, principally those supported by legislators from rural areas.

In some states, inequality was perpetuated by constitutional provisions requiring state legislative districts to be drawn along county lines. One such provision resulted in a 90 to 1 population ratio between the most- and least-populated state senate districts in California in the early 1960s. Even in states whose constitutions required periodic redistricting to equalize populations, state legislatures often failed to act. In the 1960s, many state legislative chambers were elected from the same districts that had been drawn in 1900.

Occasional redrawing of congressional districts became compulsory because many states gained or lost House seats after each census. Nevertheless, farmer-dominated state legislatures often favored the rural areas or the incumbent Congressmen, who were disproportionately from rural areas. Population disparities did not approach those that existed in the state legislatures, but some ratios were as high as three to one in the population of congressional districts within a single state. Congress had the power to demand equal population in congressional districts, but the incumbent members of the U.S. House had little incentive to do so.

Lopsided population disparities in legislative districting aroused opposition on ideological grounds, since the disparities were as much in tension with democratic principles as in Locke's day, and on more practical grounds among those favoring urban and suburban interests, or among those (usually Democrats) whose partisan interests were adversely affected by the prevailing rural dominance in a particular state.

But it was not easy to mobilize opposition effectively. For one thing, urban and suburban interests were not necessarily united with each other and, even within the cities, interests at odds with majority urban sentiment often supported the districting status quo, frequently forming coalitions with the prevalent rural legislators. What made accomplishment of the reformers' objectives through the conventional legislative process especially difficult was the need to persuade rural legislators to vote not only against the interests of their overrepresented constituents but also against their own personal interests in retaining their districts for reelection. Not surprisingly, reformers often turned instead to the courts.

At first, they seem to have turned into a blind alley. The most important early case to reach the Supreme Court, *Colegrove v. Green* (1946), was a challenge to unequally populated congressional districts in Illinois. The majority of the Court at that time, still reacting against the excesses that had led to the Court controversy in Franklin Roosevelt's second term, was generally inclined against the activist exercise of judicial review. Justice Felix Frankfurter, the leading spokesman for this group, wrote an opinion concluding that legislative districting was a "political question," and therefore not "justiciable." Invocation of the "political question" doctrine, then more than a century old but still vaguely defined, meant that the federal courts would not even consider whether the practice in question violated the Constitution.

Only seven justices participated in *Colegrove*, only four of the seven voted to dismiss the constitutional claim, and only three of these four joined in Frankfurter's opinion finding the claim nonjusticiable. Nevertheless, through the 1950s, the Court dismissed numerous challenges to districting plans or related practices on *Colegrove*'s authority, usually without even conducting a hearing or issuing an opinion.

By the early 1960s, midway through Earl Warren's term as Chief Justice, continued population shifts and legislative inaction had further aggravated the districting problem, while the Court's New Deal aversion to judicial activism had faded. In *Baker v. Carr* (1962), Tennessee voters claimed that they were deprived of equal protection of the laws by state legislative districts that had not been changed since 1900. Over an eloquent dissent by Frankfurter, the Court ruled that the claim was justiciable.

Justice William Brennan, writing for the Court, correctly observed that despite its name, the "political question" doctrine had never prevented the Court from deciding a case simply because its subject matter involved politics. Rather, the doctrine was a technical one that had been invoked in varying circumstances when the Court had deemed its own intervention improper or inadvisable. Brennan's opinion imposed systematic bounds on the doctrine and

now stands as the leading statement of the Court's definition of justiciability.

Baker's more immediate effect was to provoke a mass of redistricting litigation. Three cases decided by the Supreme Court in the next two years set the pattern. In *Gray v. Sanders* (1963), the Court struck down a Georgia gubernatorial election system, resembling the electoral college, on the grounds that votes in some counties were weighted more heavily than in others. In *Wesberry v. Sanders* (1964), the Court ruled that congressional districts must be equally populated. *Wesberry* was decided under Article I, Section 2 of the Constitution, governing election of the House of Representatives and therefore was not directly applicable to state and local elections. The climax came in *Reynolds v. Sims* (1964), in a challenge to Alabama state legislative districts, when the Court ruled that the equal protection clause of the Fourteenth Amendment imposed a standard of "one person, one vote."

Reynolds provoked a torrent of opposition, and serious efforts, led by Senator Everett Dirksen (R-Ill.), were made to amend the Constitution to permit at least one chamber of a two-house state legislature to be districted on the basis of municipal subdivisions without regard to population. To observers at the time, the Court seemed to be faced with a potentially drawn-out struggle comparable to the one that followed upon the 1954 school desegregation decision.

With the benefit of hindsight, protracted "massive resistance" to the redistricting decisions proved never to be a possibility. Redistricting has nothing like the emotional impact of race relations, and to the extent that the American people cared, they responded favorably to the "one person, one vote" slogan. By far the strongest resistance came from elected officials, and what the resisters failed to foresee was that, after the first election in each state conducted in *equally* populated districts, the newly elected officials had the same vested interest in supporting the Court as the old officials had had in resisting it. The torrent turned out to be a summer storm.

Reynolds v. Sims left open several questions regarding the meaning, scope, and rigor of the "one person, one vote" rule:

1. *Reynolds* was vague on whether equalization applied to the total population of districts, the number of actual voters, or some other figure, such as the number of eligible

voters or of citizens. The question has both practical and theoretical significance. The percentage of the population composed of resident aliens, children, and eligible non-voters tends to be larger than average among racial and ethnic minority groups. Thus, the more inclusive the group that is counted for purposes of "one person, one vote," the better for these minority groups and also for the Democratic Party, most often the recipient of their votes.

More theoretically, one who conceives of elections as the aggregation of individual choices, separately determined, might favor a rule of equal numbers of voters, because counting nonvoters would result in some actual votes being weighed more heavily than others. One with a greater group- or interest-oriented conception of elections would be more likely to favor a rule of equal population. In this conception, those who vote represent the interests of their ineligible and nonvoting neighbors in a manner somewhat akin to the Burkean theory of virtual representation.

In *Burns v. Richardson* (1966), the Supreme Court upheld redistricting based on numbers of registered voters, but it indicated a preference for equal population, which has become by far the most widely used measure.

2. *Reynolds* did not consider districting below the state level. In *Avery v. Midland County* (1968), the Warren Court decided that the "one person, one vote" rule applied to government bodies elected locally. The more conservative Warren Burger Court later created an exception for certain single-purpose districts in *Salyer Land Co. v. Tulare Lake Basin Water Storage District* (1973) and in *Ball v. James* (1981).

3. Several states have made regular or occasional use of districts that elect two or more representatives at large, but the validity of such districts was placed in doubt by *Reynolds v. Sims*. In *Fortson v. Dorsey* (1965) the Court declined to rule that multimember districts are automatically unconstitutional, as long as the requirement of population equality is satisfied. A district electing two members must contain twice the population of a single-member district. However, the Court (in *White v. Regester*, 1973) has been willing to review plans that do satisfy the population re-

quirement on the suspicion that multimember districts are being used to submerge groups that would otherwise be able to elect their own representatives.

4. Probably the most often contested issue has been how close to exact equality the districts must be so as to conform to the "one person, one vote" rule. In *Kirkpatrick v. Preisler* (1969), a challenge to Missouri congressional districts, the Court ruled that no avoidable deviation from mathematical equality would be permitted. In the 1970s, the more conservative Court continued to apply this doctrine to congressional districts, *White v. Weiser* (1973), but the Burger Court was more permissive in cases challenging state and local districts. Deviations from equality as high as 10 percent are permitted as a general rule, *Gaffney v. Cummings* (1973), and larger deviations, at least as high as 16 percent, were allowed to pass muster if necessary in order to conform state legislative districts to municipal boundaries in *Mahan v. Howell* (1973).

The Court's explanation for the disparity has been that the requirements of Article I, Section 2, governing congressional redistricting, are more stringent than those of the equal protection clause, which governs state and local districting. Given the degree of creativity that was required to discover the "one person, one vote" rule in either of these clauses in the first place, the Court's claim to have discovered in addition any detailed and differentiated guidance to the rule's application may be regarded with skepticism. But the Court continues to adhere rigorously to the distinction. On a single day in 1983, the justices struck down a New Jersey congressional plan whose maximum deviation from equality was 0.69 percent, *Karcher v. Daggett*, while upholding, in a case that has limited applicability because of its peculiar background, a Wyoming state legislative plan whose maximum deviation exceeded 90 percent (*Brown v. Thomson*). What hath Locke wrought?

Aside from making or breaking the careers of a number of individual politicians, the overall effects of the "one person, one vote" rule on American policy and politics are problematic. Some who hoped for a major increase in the influence of urban voters may have had their hopes frustrated by the fact that suburbs were benefited at least as much by the redistricting decisions as were cities. Furthermore, malapportionment was not the only aspect of the American system giving special weight to rural areas; others include the seniority system in Congress and the fixed apportionment of two Senators to each state. At the same time, the fears of those who anticipated a breakdown of the Madisonian system have not been realized. Whatever its effects, "one person-one vote" now seems a settled part of the American consensus on democratic procedures.

Group Claims and Districting Criteria

In his 1964 opinion for the Court in *Reynolds v. Sims*, Chief Justice Warren was explicit that the right to an equally weighted vote was "individual and personal in nature." Enforcement of that right might have broad institutional consequences, but these were incidental to the Court's goal of protecting individuals against discrimination.

The Chief Justice's theoretical framework was in sharp contrast to that of Justice Potter Stewart, who concurred in the result in *Reynolds* but dissented from one of the other districting cases decided the same day, *Lucas v. Forty-fourth Colorado General Assembly* (1964). Stewart, who considered representative government to be "a process of accommodating group interests," maintained that districting should "insure effective representation . . . of the various groups and interests making up the electorate."

Significant differences flow from these competing theoretical approaches. Warren's formal conception of individual voting rights led him and the majority on the Court to insist on a more rigorous population equality requirement than Stewart favored. In other respects, however, the Warren approach called for less drastic judicial intervention into districting than the Stewart approach. For Warren, a case turned primarily on the relatively simple facts of distribution of population. Stewart, who sought substantive fairness for groups rather than formal equality for individuals, had to look beyond the numbers and consider the actual nature of political cleavages and coalitions as well as the effects on these maneuverings of the districting plan under challenge. Finally, Stewart's approach, but not Warren's, would be receptive to claims brought in the name of groups of voters contending that a districting plan conforming

to the "one person, one vote" rule improperly dilutes the group's political effectiveness.

In *Reynolds* and *Lucas*, over Stewart's objection, the formal individual right to an equally weighted vote was enshrined. However, this canonization in itself did not negate the possibility that the kind of group right Stewart sought to protect would *also* be recognized. The two kinds of rights have different thrusts but are not inconsistent. The controversy over the Stewart approach has continued on and off in the Court to the present day, resulting in uneasy compromises. Now the possibility of constitutional protection for group rights is recognized, but the nature of the rights remains shadowy and their vindication in actual litigation difficult.

Soon after *Reynolds*, the Stewart approach received its first recognition in *Fortson v. Dorsey* (1965). Here the Court said that multimember districts might be struck down if they "minimize or cancel out the voting strength of racial of political elements of the voting population." The Court has repeated this formulation on many occasions since, and it is the *racial* half of it that has borne the most fruit. The Court long has accorded racial and ethnic minorities special status under the equal protection clause, largely in recognition of the historical background of the adoption of the Fourteenth Amendment following the Civil War. Nevertheless, and despite some successes, even racial groups have difficulty asserting successful constitutional claims against redistricting plans. Congress, in the amended Section 2 of the Voting Rights Act, has found it necessary to grant them additional protection.

Meanwhile, the political half of the *Fortson* formulation lay dormant for two decades, despite the efforts of numerous social scientists to work out the basis for judicial attack on partisan gerrymandering by either of the major parties. Reformers have proposed a variety of criteria by which, they contend, redistricting plans should be judged. The criteria have been categorized broadly as "formal" if they are based on the characteristics of the districts themselves, and as "result-oriented" if they look instead to the actual or expected electoral consequences of the plan considered as a whole.

Formal criteria call for districts that are compact in shape, or that have boundaries coinciding with local governments, or that constitute "communities of interest." These criteria draw their appeal from the original association of gerrymandering with odd-shaped districts.

Nevertheless, they bear no direct relation to the concern of fairness to political groups, since that concern relates to the dynamics and outcomes of elections, immaterial to the formal criteria.

Some theorists suggest that formal criteria, especially if they are strictly applied, will prevent manipulation and distortion through districting. But reducing the options available to the district-line drawer does not inhibit "manipulation" any more than it inhibits accomplishment of benign goals, even if we assume that some discernible difference exists between the two. Nor do we have any reason to expect that formal criteria will operate neutrally among political parties and other groups. Since the case for the formal criteria aside from their possible prophylactic effect is relatively weak, many reformers have turned instead to result-oriented criteria.

These are even more varied than the formal criteria and include the following:

1. Districts should be drawn so as to assure a large number of competitive elections.
2. Incumbents should be protected or (more likely from most reformist perspectives) should not be protected.
3. The "swing ratio" should be such that within a broad range a modest increase in a party's share of the statewide vote will yield a modest increase in its share of legislative seats.
4. The partisan division of seats in the legislature should be proportional to the statewide party vote.
5. The partisan division of seats should be "symmetric," meaning that a majority party may receive a disproportionate number of seats, so long as the opposing party would have received the same number of seats if it had received the same majority percentage of the votes.

Each of the result-oriented criteria is subject to both methodological and theoretical objections. The swing ratio and symmetry criteria require comparison of an actual (or projected) election result with a hypothetical result involving a different statewide partisan vote division, and we have no easily defended basis for selecting geographical distribution of the partisan vote in the hypothetical case. A plan designed for proportional results is likely to yield sharply disproportional results if the partisan split is significantly different from what was anticipated. Districts designed as competitive may cease to be competitive once an incumbent is seated.

A broader concern is that each of the criteria looking to a statewide party vote does so artificially, since under the American system, voters choose among specific candidates within their districts, and their votes are not cast as part of a statewide partisan total. Voters might favor their local Democratic candidate based on individual characteristics, but they might also favor Republican control of the legislature.

Finally, some of the criteria may conflict with others. For example, a modest statewide partisan shift may cause a plan with numerous competitive districts to yield sharply disproportional results. Reformers often seek to avoid these difficulties by asserting that only the most flagrantly partisan gerrymanders should be regarded as unconstitutional and that such plans are likely to come out poorly under most of the criteria.

Other than the often repeated verbal formula of *Fortson v. Dorsey* regarding minimization or canceling out of the voting strength of racial or political groups, the first sign that the Supreme Court might entertain the constitutionalization of partisan gerrymandering came in *Karcher v. Daggett* (1983). The majority decided this case on the basis of the "one person, one vote" rule, but two justices, John Stevens and Lewis Powell, separately stated their belief that even a plan complying with the equal population requirement might violate the equal protection clause if it treated partisan groups unfairly.

Following the Stevens-Powell lead, a lower federal court in Indiana ruled that a state legislative plan adopted by a Republican-controlled state government discriminated unconstitutionally against Democratic voters. The state appealed this decision to the Supreme Court, while waiting in the wings was a federal court challenge to the California congressional plan enacted by a Democratic-controlled legislature, probably the most controversial districting plan of the 1980s. In an unusually striking case of weird political bedfellows, the Republican National Committee supported the Indiana Democrats in the Supreme Court, while the Democratic members of the House from California urged the Court to uphold the Indiana Republican plan.

The Supreme Court's long-awaited decision in *Davis v. Brandemer* (1986) appeared to contain something for everyone. The one point on which the Court spoke clearly was their decision, by a six-to-three majority, that the gerrymandering claim under the equal protection clause was justiciable. This decision would not have been remarkable, given *Baker v. Carr*, except that the opponents of judicial intervention chose to cast their argument in terms of justiciability rather than simply to assert that the equal protection clause does not prohibit partisan gerrymandering. Having declared that the courthouse door was open to the plaintiffs, the Court then went on to overrule the lower court decision striking down the Indiana plan. This decision was reached by a seven-to-two majority that included the three justices who believed the controversy was not justiciable. Not surprisingly, given the views they expressed in *Karcher v. Daggett*, Justices Powell and Stevens would have affirmed the striking down of the Indiana plan.

Justice Byron White wrote for the four-judge plurality who regarded the challenge to the Indiana plan as justiciable but insufficient on the merits. That his opinion was less than a model of limpidity is suggested by the fact that it has received at least the following interpretations:

1. The plurality opinion is so confused or self-contradictory that is gives *no* useful guidance to federal judges who must decide future gerrymandering controversies.
2. Plaintiffs can prevail by showing significantly disproportional results under the challenged districting plan but only if such results occur in at least two elections conducted under the plan.
3. Despite Justice White's disclaimers, the plurality opinion either requires proportional results or will lead inexorably to the Court's imposing such a requirement.
4. A partisan gerrymander is unconstitutional under the plurality opinion if it is intentional, severe, and nontransient in its effects.
5. The gerrymandering claim recognized by the plurality is available only to outsider political groups who suffer discrimination comparable to that which has afflicted racial minorities; therefore, the claim is unlikely to be applicable to disputes between the two major parties.

Some impetus was given to the last of these interpretations when it was adopted by a California federal court in rejecting the challenge to the congressional districting plan in that state. The Supreme Court's summary affirmance of the lower court's action (*Badham v. Eu*, 1989)

validated the result, but it does not necessarily commit the Supreme Court to the lower court's reasoning.

As the 1980s drew to a close, each of the national parties was mobilizing legal teams in anticipation of another round of pathbreaking redistricting litigation in the 1990s. However, aside from questions of racial discrimination, some observers believe few (if any) cases with much significance beyond the specific districting plans in question will occur.

New justices may take a different approach, but for the time being the Supreme Court seems unreceptive to partisan gerrymandering claims from the major parties. Gerrymandering disputes are likely to be litigated in the name of population equality, as *Karcher v. Daggett* leaves open the possibility that the most minute population inequalities may leave a congressional plan vulnerable to attack from proponents of another plan with even smaller population inequality and greatly differing political consequences.

The American political system is intensely competitive. Fewer states are dominated by a single party than was the case when the "one person, one vote" rule was originally imposed. Under these circumstances, redistricting will be an inevitable source of controversy in many states in the 1990s and beyond. The judiciary will continue to be one battleground in the struggle, but political scientists predict fewer blockbuster decisions with nationwide impact than in the past few decades.

The principal battlegrounds will be political. Efforts will continue to revise the procedures for redistricting, and in states that permit it, the initiative process will sometimes be used toward this end. In years ending in "1," redistricting will tend to have a pervasive impact on state legislative politics. Not least, at a time when many observers lament a perceived decline in partisan politics, the desire to control redistricting will continue to provide a significant focus for party loyalty.

See also: Baker v. Carr, Brown v. Thomason, Colegrove v. Green, Davis v. Brandemer, Everett Dirksen, Gerrymandering, *Kirkpatrick v. Preisler, Mahan v. Howell*, New Deal, Republican National Committee, Voting Rights Act of 1965 and Extensions, Earl Warren

Daniel Hays Lowenstein

REFERENCES

Backstrom, Charles, Leonard Robins, and Scott Eller. 1978. "Issues in Gerrymandering: An Exploratory Measure of Partisan Gerrymandering Applied to Minnesota." 62 *Minnesota Law Review* 1121.

Bickel, Alexander M. 1978. *The Supreme Court and the Idea of Progress*. New Haven: Yale U. Pr.

Bicker, William E. 1971. "The Effects of Malapportionment in the States—A Mistrial." In Nelson W. Polsby, ed. *Reapportionment in the 1970s*. Berkeley: U. of California Pr.

Cain, Bruce E. 1984. *The Reapportionment Puzzle*. Berkeley: U. of California Pr.

Dixon, Robert G. 1968. *Democratic Representation: Reapportionment in Law and Politics*. New York: Oxford U. Pr.

Grofman, Bernard. 1985. "Criteria for Districting: A Social Science Perspective." 33 *UCLA Law Review* 77.

———. 1990. "Toward a Coherent Theory of Gerrymandering: *Brandemer* and *Thornburg*." In Bernard Grofman, ed. *Political Gerrymandering and the Courts*. New York: Agathon.

———, ed. 1990. *Political Gerrymandering and the Courts*. New York: Agathon.

Locke, John. 1812. *Two Treatises of Government*, in *The Works of John Locke*. Vol. 5. London: W. Otridge and Son.

Lowenstein, Daniel H., and Jonathan Steinberg. 1985. "The Quest for Legislative Districting in the Public Interest: Elusive or Illusory?" 33 *UCLA Law Review* 1.

———. 1990. "Brandemer's Gap: Gerrymandering and Equal Protection." In Bernard Grofman, ed. *Political Gerrymandering and the Courts*. New York: Agathon.

Note. 1986. "The Supreme Court, 1985 Term." 100 *Harvard Law Review* 153.

Polsby, Nelson W., ed. 1971. *Reapportionment in the 1970s*. Berkeley: U. of California Pr.

Schuck, Peter H. 1987. "The Thickest Thicket: Partisan Gerrymandering and Judicial Regulation of Politics." 87 *Columbia Law Review* 1325.

Tribe, Laurence H. 1988. *American Constitutional Law*. Mineola, NY: Foundation Press.

CASES CITED

Badham v. Eu, 488 U.S. 1024, 109 S.Ct. 829 (1989).

Baker v. Carr, 369 U.S. 186 (1962).

Ball v. James, 451 U.S. 355 (1981).

Brown v. Thomson, 462 U.S. 835 (1983).

Burns v. Richardson, 384 U.S. 73 (1966).

Colegrove v. Green, 328 U.S. 549 (1946).

Davis v. Brandemer, 478 U.S. 109, 106 S.Ct. 2797 (1986).

Fortson v. Dorsey, 379 U.S. 433 (1965).

Gaffney v. Cummings, 412 U.S. 735 (1973).

Gray v. Sanders, 372 U.S. 368 (1963).

Karcher v. Daggett, 462 U.S. 725 (1983).

Kirkpatrick v. Preisler, 394 U.S. 526 (1969).

Lucas v. Forty-fourth Colorado General Assembly, 377 U.S. 713 (1964).

Mahan v. Howell, 410 U.S. 315 (1973).

Reynolds v. Sims, 377 U.S. 533 (1964).

Salyer L. v. Tulare Lake Basin Water Storage District, 410 U.S. 719 (1973).

Wesberry v. Sanders, 376 U.S. 1 (1964).

White v. Regester, 412 U.S. 755 (1973).

White v. Weiser, 412 U.S. 783 (1973).

Legislative Government in the United States Congress, 1800–1900

Conceptual Theories

Most efforts to build or to apply theories of legislative behavior and institutional process in the United States Congress focus on the years since 1950. Older institutional studies are useful primarily for their descriptive content. In recent years increased interest in diachronic (changes over time) analysis has been evident, and scholars have suggested a variety of theoretical approaches and analytic techniques. Particularly they have explored the usefulness of modernization theory. In 1968 Nelson W. Polsby hypothesized that the differentiation of the institution from its environment, the degree of internal complexity in the legislative process, and the tendency to move from particularistic and discretionary practices to universalistic and automatic decision-making were measures of institutionalization. His time series suggested that significant changes in these respects occurred during the late nineteenth and early twentieth centuries. A major breakthrough, Polsby's article was admittedly oversimplified. It did not treat the environmental factors that are increasingly viewed as the generative forces in congressional operations and performance, particularly the party system. Scholars interested in developing conceptual frameworks for understanding congressional government during the nineteenth century now posit a constituency-driven congressional system, draw upon organization analysis (subject to the constraints on its application implied in a system of separated powers, geographic constituencies, and plurality electoral processes), and turn to rational choice theory in explanations of individual behavior. As yet such theory-based treatments of the nineteenth-century Congress are too few to serve as the foundation for a comprehensive discussion of legislative government there.

Periodization

We can identify successive eras of congressional development, although the exact points in time at which boundary lines should be drawn are arguable. A period of initial development extends into the late 1820s or early 1830s. These years were characterized by an expanding agrarian-mercantile economy, efforts to legitimize a national identity abroad, a diminution of habits of deference in politics, and the growth and decay of the first national party structure. Era 2, subsuming some fifty years, coincided with significant transformation toward an industrial economy, intense sectional or center-periphery conflict, and unbridled two-party patronage politics. In Era 3 the Union and the federal government stood reaffirmed, finance capitalism emerged, Congress enunciated formulas of industrial control, and changes appeared in the Congress that have been defined as institutionalization. Era 1 began in the late eighteenth century and Era 3 continued into the twentieth century. Although such periodization is useful, it can also be argued that the Civil War marks a significant break point in congressional development.

The Lawmakers

United States Representatives and Senators have typically been members of the country's elites. Some 40 percent of the Representatives entering during the 1790s had attended college. By the end of the next century more than 60 percent fell in that group, although David Crockett's frontier education clearly shocked de Tocqueville. Occupationally, legislators have been predominantly lawyers; some 40 percent during the first 20 years and more than 60 percent after 1830. Agriculturists represented more than 15 percent of the members in the first decade of the nineteenth century, but only 5 percent to 10 percent after 1830. Southern planters predominated in the group until the postbellum period. Ten percent to 15 percent of the Representatives had business backgrounds until the 1850s; that figure remained at a bit above 20 percent for the most part after 1860, northerners always predominating in this category. Other professionals always fell in the 5 percent to 10 percent range, and a small fringe of miscellaneous or unknown backgrounds appear consistently in the data. Military service, usually at the commissioned rank, has always been common, although veterans were only a majority during the 1790s. Individuals related to other Congressmen—earlier, current, or later—made up a third of the House during the 1790s, almost 20 percent during the 1840s, and some 12 percent during the 1880s and 1890s. Southern Representatives included larger proportions of veterans and had more congressional relatives.

During the early national period more than 70 percent of the Representatives had experience in state office. The proportion was still above 50 percent during the 1890s. Some 30 percent of early national Congressmen had held local-level office, the figure increasing to about one-half by 1900. Of the Representatives, some 8 percent to 15 percent had occupied federal or judicial posts. But during the nineteenth century, fewer than half of the Representatives had served at more than one level of service; experience in three was uncommon. Occasionally, local conditions or fortuitous occurrences enabled men with little political experience to win election.

The median length of public service among the cohort of Congressmen entering the House during the 1801–1810 period was four years—identical to that of the entrants of the 1890s. Between these dates, however, the median term fell to two years among the entering cohorts of the 1850s and 1860s—the contraction attributable, it is believed, to the fierce party competition of the antebellum years, the practice of rotation among officeholders in various regions, and the disruptive impact of the Civil War. Although some Representatives extended their service in Washington by moving to the Senate, the number of truly seasoned Representatives in the House was always small during the nineteenth century. A marked trend toward longer service became apparent only when the entering cohort of the 1890s marked the emergence of a growing number of one-party districts. Through the Seventh Congress (1801–1803) to the Fifty-fifth (1897–1899) a majority of the Representatives in thirty-three Congresses had not held seats in the previous House. Thus the membership of the House of Representatives was composed during the nineteenth century of a shifting mix of short-term Representatives with a relatively small core of longer-serving veterans. If the House was to be an effective legislative body, then it had to develop a structure of detailed rules and an institutional framework within which inexperienced legislators could work productively. As one author wrote, "this large, unwieldy, changing body holds its own with the smaller, longer-lived, more experienced Senate and Executive by centralizing its power remarkably in its older members—in the Speaker and the committee chairmen."

Early National Period

An apportionment of 106 seats was in effect in the House of Representatives when the members of the Seventh Congress assembled in December 1801, and the supporters of Thomas Jefferson assumed control of the federal government. Their basic charter of powers, rights, privileges—and to some degree, practice—lay in Article 1 of the Constitution. Although providing the time and frequency of meetings and restricting the length of adjournments within sessions, that document specified as to organization only that the "Representatives shall choose their speaker and other officers," be judge of "the elections, returns and qualifications" of their colleagues, accept a majority of members as a quorum, determine the rules of proceedings, punish members for disorderly conduct, and expel members, provided that a two-thirds majority assented. The Speaker could look for guidance to British and colonial parliamentary practice, a growing body of House rules and precedents, and the remembered example of four predecessors. Congress by Congress the Representatives also chose a clerk, a sergeant-at-arms, and a doorkeeper. These plus a few minor clerks and pages constituted the staff cadre of the Jeffersonian House.

A Standing Committee on Elections appeared in 1789 and Claims, Commerce, and Revisal and Unfinished Business committees followed in the 1790s. As the initial practice of using large numbers of ad hoc select committees proved unsatisfactory in areas of continuing interest, six more standing committees appeared between 1800 and 1810, including Ways and Means in 1802. But select committees were still used.

Committees, both standing and select, might be assigned portions of the President's message for consideration and for the possible reporting of bills. In this era the typical method of initiating legislative activity was a resolution from a member that initiated committee activity and bill drafting. Measures of particular interest to executive departments were drafted there and brought into the House by appropriate committees or friends of the administration.

What were the sources of authority to which Representatives looked in this era? The isolation of the early national lawmakers in the raw village of Washington has been exaggerated. They arrived with a deep understanding of their constituents' desires and needs, generally assumed that they were the delegates of their districts, received letters from their constituents, and presented and nurtured the petitions or requests of interests or groups at home. Discussion or caucusing within state delegations clarified understanding and provided moral reinforcement. They might expect to be requested (if Representatives) and instructed (if Senators) by their state legislatures to take particular positions on legislation.

Then as later, the Representative prospered in his designs if he stood well with sources of authority in the House. Preeminent among them was the Speaker. Although those of the 1790s have sometimes been dismissed as mere moderators of debate, they recognized party preference at an early date in exercising the power to make the committee appointments that the House bestowed upon the office in 1790. Nathaniel Macon (1801–1807) followed suit, although considerations of state and regional balance, native ability, and prior experience at the state or federal level were all involved. The originator of the seed resolution was generally considered to be the appropriate choice for chairman of a select committee. Jeffersonian Speakers were not, however, aggressive in using the appointive power, giving strict heed to President Jefferson's wishes. The Representatives' rejection in 1806 of a proposal to elect committee members by ballot was fateful in the institutional development of the House.

The Federalist and Democratic-Republican parties of the early national years lacked the national conventions, platforms, and organizational forms of later eras, but their members subscribed to common ideologies and legislative agendas. Party was a meaningful distinction under Jefferson, and he sought more actively than either of his predecessors to organize support for his policies in the Congress. During the Seventh and Eighth Congresses (1801–1805), Jefferson was notably successful; less success marked his second term because of disagreement over foreign policy issues.

Although William B. Giles initially exerted major influence on the floor, John Randolph, the chairman of Ways and Means, emerged as leader of the administration party in the House. But Randolph opposed the administration's request for funds with which to purchase West Florida. The incident highlighted congressional concern with enunciating standards for executive request, administration, and report of finances—a concern that continued through the initial era of institutional structuring. Randolph and a little band of Old Republicans were banished from party councils. But, given the importance of the fiscal measures under the control of Ways and Means, the logic of its chairman serving as floor leader remained. The arrangement held (with varying degrees of commitment to administrative policy on the part of its chairman) until the Appropriations Committee was created during the Thirty-eighth Congress (1865). Randolph's bitter harangues, criticizing the majority position in 1811, inspired his colleagues to accept a rule authorizing one-fifth of the members present to demand the previous question—a major step in developing the House's most effective device for limiting debate.

During the last generation scholars have conducted systematic scaling analyses of the roll calls in many of the nineteenth-century Congresses. The research shows that a Congressman's voting could usually be categorized as reflecting the influence of party, section, individual constituency, or personal idiosyncrasy. Party voting was usually dominant, but sectional deviation was intermittently important, and other types of deviation were of minor importance, although occasionally of prophetic or symbolic significance. The student of the nineteenth-century Congress must show how party agendas were translated into policy and law and the ways in which the institutional structure of the Congress was adapted to facilitate these processes.

During his presidency, Thomas Jefferson provided much of the vital force in these matters but by the early 1820s a state of highly factionalized nonpartisanship had been attained. Although the party caucus emerged during this era as a means of designating presidential candidates and focusing policy objectives, it was not a well-drilled force in the planning of legislative strategy and mobilization of voting majorities. But informally at least, party and subparty groups, including state delegations, caucused for these purposes. Although the boardinghouse or hotel mess facilitated communication among its residents up to and beyond the Civil War, such groups were almost invariably composed of kindred party spirits with a common regional affiliation. Shared party and regional values and objectives brought the messmates together and served as referents in subsequent behavior.

The unsettled authority structure in the House during the Jefferson years underwent significant change during the James Madison and James Monroe administrations. Henry Clay strongly influenced legislative proceedings and practice. A brilliant speaker of the Kentucky legislative assembly and twice briefly United States Senator, Henry Clay arrived in the Twelfth Congress as part of a cohort of aggressive young Democratic-Republicans who favored a more aggressive foreign policy toward the belligerents of the Napoleonic Wars than that of previous years. Elected Speaker, Clay asserted the dominance of the legislative branch; he and his colleagues forced Madison to lead the country into the War of 1812. Clay was reelected Speaker five more times before becoming Secretary of State, interrupting his service to be a peace commissioner subsequent to the War of 1812 and by resignation in 1820. Clay greatly increased the parliamentary power of the Speaker, strengthened the informal or personal influence wielded by that officer, and asserted his claim to be a major legislative leader. During his years, Congress assumed the initiative in developing the legislative agenda, and Clay controlled the legislative majorities more successfully than any other congressional leader to that time. The 1812 war agenda, the elements of the American system, the Missouri Compromise legislation, and policies supportive of the emergent republics of Latin America bore his stamp. Unlike earlier leaders, he participated actively in the shaping of legislation in the Committee of the Whole; he asserted his right to vote on measures, irrespective of whether that vote would change the outcome; and his tactical and partisan use of the House rules of procedure far surpassed that of his predecessors.

During the Clay years, the structure of standing committees took shape. Between 1813 and 1825, 17 more joined the 10 thus far created. Five of these were charged with reviewing the expenditures in executive departments, thus institutionalizing the supervisory authority that had been a source of contention. Although Clay found Monroe to be much less compliant than Madison, the precedents for a vigorous exercise of power by the Speaker and independent agenda formulation and realization in the Congress were now established. Clay is ranked among the greatest of innovative Speakers; his leadership style combined forensic skills, personal charm, imagination, and a talent for compromise. None of his antebellum successors matched him and none served for a comparable period of time.

Era of Major Sectional Stress

Although politicians labored throughout the period 1800–1860 to create national political parties, differing regional economies, institutions (notably slavery), and changing cultural values imparted sectional tilts to the party cohorts and leadership structures in the Congress. In the period of Federalist dominance, the 1790s, all 4 Speakers were from northern states; during the next 60 years 13 of 19 Speakers came from southern constituencies. Eight of 10 presiding officers selected between 1860 and 1900 came from northern states. Between 1800 and 1860 northerners presided over the House in approximately one year in four. That ratio was exactly reversed during the next 40 years. The same regional disparity marked the selection of the chairmen of the Ways and Means Committee in antebellum America. Although 8 northerners and 14 southerners held the office, southerners actually chaired this committee for 44 years, northerners for 16.

Some have suggested that the chairmanship of Ways and Means was a common stepping stone to the speakership. Yet for only 4 of the 45 men who were chairmen of either the Ways and Means or the Appropriations (subsequent to 1865) committees during the nineteenth century was this true: Langdon Cheves (1812), James K. Polk (1833), Samuel J. Randall (1875), and Joseph C. Cannon, who did not become Speaker until 1903. No Speaker of the nineteenth century matched Clay's record of six elections and ten years of service. The unremarkable Virginian, Andrew Stevenson, came closest, serving for seven years (1827–1834), while the second American party system emerged. The modal service among other Speakers before the Civil War was but one term. Although none thereafter equaled John Randolph's six years of service as chairman of Ways and Means, double terms in that post were common. But frequent turnover in the two most important offices was the rule, and although some incumbents moved to the Senate or accepted diplomatic posts, the usual explanation of turnover between 1830 and 1860 was the defeat of the incumbent's party.

Speakers in this era varied greatly in the vigor and skill with which they selected committees for partisan ends. It remained unclear as to whether the Speaker was to make common cause with his leading party colleagues in the House or to take his cues mainly from the executive branch. Factional allegiances, splinter group activity, recurrent realignment, and ineffective party discipline usually made authority structures ineffective during the the 20 years before the Civil War. Although party caucuses sought to solidify support behind particular candidates for the position of Speaker, 11 multiple-ballot Speaker elections took place during the period 1809–1861; those of 1839, 1849, 1855, and 1859 required 11, 63, 133, and 44 ballots. Once elected, Speakers differed in the degree to which they reconciled partisan commitments with fair treatment of all members. Some invited opposition members to preside over sittings of the Committee of the Whole and occasionally asked distinguished members of the opposition to chair committees. However, Speakers began to list all majority party members on committees before any minority party members—a change from the practice in the early national period when the names of members of the majority and minority parties were alternated.

His biographer maintains that James K. Polk was the "first speaker to be regarded frankly as a party leader, responsible for pushing a party program through the House." Presiding over the Twenty-fourth and Twenty-fifth Houses (1835–1839) Polk "passed through severer trials than any previous speaker" as militant Whigs challenged his rulings and even called him *"a tool of tools."* The presentation of abolitionist petitions demanding the extirpation of slavery in the District of Columbia provoked fierce debate, and Polk concluded that the House could refuse to receive a petition. A select committee based its report on this foundation, proposing the famous gag rule: petitions and other papers relating to slavery or its abolition "shall, without ever being printed or referred, be laid upon the table, and that no further action . . . be had thereon." Against this position the ex-President, now-Congressman John Quincy Adams, marshalled all his eloquence and parliamentary knowledge. Fierce challenges to the Speaker's rulings and floor behavior, intemperate to the point of fisticuffs, canings or subsequent invitations to the dueling ground occurred sporadically during this period.

While the southern wing of the Democracy controlled the Congress during 1854, the adoption of the Kansas-Nebraska Act appeared to surrender Kansas Territory to the incursions of slavery. Bleeding Kansas revitalized the slavery controversy and catalyzed party realignment. So mixed in their allegiances were the Representatives of the Thirty-sixth House (1859–1861) among Republicans, Whigs, American or Know-

Nothing Party adherents, and various Democratic factions that protracted balloting resulted in the selection of a first-term member as Speaker. A fair-minded Whig, William Pennington, had little impact upon the office except that he was the first Speaker to serve on the Rules Committee, at that point a select committee.

Governance within the House of Representatives changed little in terms of structure or major precedent during the years between the election of Polk to the speakership and the outbreak of the Civil War. Party voting was strong, but sectional issues related to southern expansion and the place of slavery in the Union recurrently shocked the system. Sectional and ideological commitments worked against the institutional development that might have accompanied longer-serving Speakers and a more stable alignment of opposing parties. The standing committee structure changed little; between 1837 and 1860 only the Standing Committee on Engraving was established with Expenditures in the Interior Department added in the latter year.

Many of the items of the issue agenda in the 30 years before the Civil War were developmental in nature. Should the federal government subsidize internal improvements, impose protective tariffs, provide strong central banking, and use federal lands for purposes other than fostering a class of virtuous freehold farmers? On these issues Whigs and Democrats differed, the former being most developmentally inclined. Representatives tried to shape national party policy in ways most favorable to their constituencies; they were also most apt to break party lines on issues of regional significance. The moral questions related to the institution of slavery increasingly complicated the developmental agendas; Congressmen evaluated legislative measures in terms of their impact upon slavery. The Speakers' selections of members for the committees on Territories, the District of Columbia, Public Lands, and the Judiciary were viewed as vital in efforts to protect, limit, or to destroy that institution.

Although party caucuses were used during this period and sometimes to good effect, their power to aggregate, plan, and enforce party strategy does not appear to have grown perceptibly. After Jackson, and excepting only James K. Polk (1845–1849), a succession of weak Presidents provided little legislative leadership, in part because party control was common to the executive branch and both houses in only

four of the ten Congresses between 1841 and 1861. During the Civil War, the Republican party controlled the House, Senate, and presidency and the magnitude of the crisis opened opportunities for the executive branch to provide leadership that might establish new patterns of governance.

Unhampered by Representatives from 11 southern states, the Republican majorities in House and Senate compiled one of the most impressive legislative records in congressional history during the Thirty-seventh Congress. A strongly protective tariff, the Homestead Law of 1862, provision of a national banking system, incorporation of a Pacific Railroad, and the Land Grant College Act were notable legislative achievements among others. However, Republicans had strong differences of opinion over the methods by which slavery was to be ended, the war prosecuted, and the Union reconstructed. The moderate Abraham Lincoln encountered strong opposition from radical elements of his party in the Congress.

National mobilization of material and human resources greatly increased congressional work loads; the numbers of resolutions and bills considered rose sharply. Both select and standing committees exercised investigative or oversight functions to a greater degree than during the previous decade. The unprecedented Joint Committee on the Conduct of the War vigorously investigated unsuccessful campaigns, military defeats, and atrocities. The House immediately (with the Senate ultimately following suit) elected to use a quorum based on the Representatives of states present, rather than the total in the Union. The houses adopted Joint Rule 22, allowing immediate and secret consideration of matters relating to the suppression of the rebellion on the request of the President. But the President never asked that the procedure be used. The Speakers of the Civil War—Galusha A. Grow and Schuyler Colfax—have been characterized as figureheads in style of leadership and conservative in their use of the powers of their office. Neither worked vigorously to advance the policies of the executive branch nor, with minor exceptions, to expedite particular legislative programs. Grow, a Pennsylvanian, was criticized for favoritism to the Middle States in making committee assignments and was defeated for reelection to the House because of a Democratic resurgence in his state. His successor, Colfax, twice won reelection before becoming Vice President, but he was suspected at the White House of being allied with the President's radical opponents.

Grow appointed his fellow Pennsylvanian, Thaddeus Stevens, as chairman of Ways and Means. Elderly and irascible, this radical Republican has been described as one of the great House floor leaders. During his tenure the House successfully developed the fiscal and monetary policies that allowed successful prosecution of the war. Stevens also actively supported radical policies in relation to war and reconstruction. Still, his motions on the floor were often defeated, and there were said to be considerable differences of opinion within his committee. He forthrightly espoused the prerogatives of the Congress relative to the executive branch and caustically denounced the President and Cabinet in caucus. The conflict between the executive and legislative branches to which Stevens contributed under Lincoln culminated when he became chairman of the House managers seeking impeachment of Lincoln's successor, Andrew Johnson. At his death in 1868, Stevens had served seven years as floor leader, longer than any predecessor.

Speaker Grow named chairmen of 37 nine-, five-, and three-man standing committees. Twenty-one members had not served on their committee during the previous Congress. The mean prior congressional service of the chairmen of Grow's large committees was 3.2 years and that of the smaller only 1.7 years. Just under 15 percent of the committee members of the next Congress, the Thirty-eighth, had served on the same committee in the preceding house. Such records of service were not wartime phenomena but symptomatic of the era. Like most senior leaders before them, Grow and Stevens had considerable congressional experience—ten and six years respectively—but the ranks of such veterans were always thin.

The Republicans enjoyed a substantial majority in the House during the Thirty-seventh Congress and a reduced but effective predominance in the Thirty-eighth. The radical Republicans rejected Lincoln's leadership on matters relating to slavery and southern reconstruction, but the presence of more moderate Republicans and Border State members provided the potential for the defeat of radical proposals. On southern issues, legislation failed to satisfy either the various congressional factions or the President. In both houses the party caucus developed legislative strategy and party positions on pending legislation. For all that, caucusing was not completely successful, although apparently more effective in the Senate than in the House. Senators carried caucus activity to the point of agreeing to request a reorganization of the Cabinet, but Lincoln astutely foiled them. House Republicans discussed the same subject in caucus, only to hear the chairman of a caucus committee charged with devising ways of instilling vigor into the administration ask to be excused from a hopeless task. Attendance at the caucuses was often sparse, and Stevens once declared that he would not be bound by majority opinion within any caucus.

Governmental power in Washington was quite diffused during the Civil War years. Immediately thereafter, however, the impeachment of Andrew Johnson suggested that Thaddeus Stevens and other radical Republican congressional leaders exercised unparalleled influence. On the other hand, impeachment failed, and the Democratic Party regained strength in the House until it won control in the Forty-fourth Congress. Slower paced institutionalizing processes would have more impact upon House governance than the coup directed at the Johnson administration.

Era of National Consolidation and Institutionalizing Processes

The federal census takers of 1860 counted some 31 million Americans; their successors of 1900 recorded the presence of almost 76 million. During this period great areas of western America passed through the territorial stages of government; the 33 states of 1850 had become 45 by 1900. The average number of bills per Congress during the first decade of the nineteenth century had been some 200; the figure was pressing 2,000 by the 1860s; it stood at more than 15,000 during the 1890s. James A. Garfield (1877) noted a great increase in the congressional business in the postbellum years, most of which he attributed to the Civil War. Much of the increase, as in the case of veteran's affairs, was indeed directly attributable to that conflict. But the rise also stemmed from positions endorsed by the Republican Party during the war relating to banking and monetary policy, railroads, the tariff, and land policy. The unbridled patronage of the 1850s and 1860s, moreover, spurred interest in civil service reform.

Increasing size, greater and more complex workloads, and the greater subdivision of functions suggested the need for the exercise of greater authority by some agency. Ultimately control derived from both the national party infrastructure and from party leaders in the Congress. The discipline displayed within the political parties of the late nineteenth century was unmatched in either earlier or later eras. Party leaders likened electoral contests to military campaigns and party workers to loyal soldiers. Given the prominent place of the Grand Army of the Republic and the empty sleeve in postbellum politics, the analogy was an obvious one. House leaders thought in the same terms, and members cooperated. Perhaps true as well, the issue agendas after the early years of Reconstruction were less value-laden and stressful than was true in antebellum America.

Although some alternation of party control took place in the House, a good deal of continuity remained. Beginning with the Thirty-sixth Congress, the Republican or Union Party controlled eight successive Houses. Starting with the Forty-fourth, the rejuvenated Democrats held a majority in eight of the next ten Houses; then with the convening of the Fifty-fourth, the Republicans gained the ascendancy for the next eight. Considerable continuity in party control thus enhanced the possibility that individual leaders might try to simplify the exercise of authority and reduce the uncertainties of members by introducing impersonal criteria in decision-making and standardizing legislative routines. Change in length of service on the part of the House leaders, however, was modest. After Clay's first election and prior to 1861, Speakers on the average had served 6.3 prior years in Congress and occupied the office some 2.7 years. From Grow through David B. Henderson (1899–1903), mean previous experience was nine years and the Speaker's mean term was 4.2 years. The day when House veterans with more than 20 years of prior service grasped the Speaker's gavel began with Joseph G. Cannon in 1903; the next six Speakers as well had served for more than 20 years.

Although the era of the wily veteran as Speaker did not come until the twentieth century, late-nineteenth-century officers were impressive. Scholars of those years compared the Speaker to the prime minister in the British system of legislative government. Michael C. Kerr (1874–1875) died shortly after taking office and J. Warren Keifer (1881–1883) is regarded as retrogressive. But five of the seven Speakers (1869–1899) are considered to have been innovative in their use of powers and effective in their leadership. James G. Blaine, Samuel J.

Randall, John G. Carlisle, Thomas B. Reed, and Charles F. Crisp raised the power of the speakership to its highest level in American political history.

All five men used the office to further the objectives of their party. The first, James G. Blaine, was a highly skilled parliamentarian who used the right of recognition to control business, reviewed and suggested changes in bill content, and framed resolutions for introduction on the floor. His committee selections reflected the legislative directions of which he approved. Ambitious for the presidency, Blaine sought, as Speaker, to bolster his personal popularity and, as a result, was less arbitrary in his behavior than some of his successors.

Samuel J. Randall (1876–1881) was the first of three strong Democratic Speakers during the late nineteenth century and the "first Speaker who aimed directly at power through alteration of the rules." During the Hayes-Tilden election controversy, he ruled that obstructive motions need not be recognized. John G. Carlisle (1883–1889) assumed that the Speaker should develop his own legislative program and use the powers of his office to get it accomplished. He also realized the potential of the House Rules Committee to serve as a de facto steering committee. Accordingly, he named the chairmen of the Appropriations Committee and of Ways and Means to serve with him as its majority members.

Despite his extraordinary action in controlling dilatory motions, Randall was unwilling to place meaningful curbs on such activity within the House rules. In 1880 he headed a talented Rules Committee that conducted a complete review of the rules, but Randall vetoed suggestions that would have impeded the minority's power to obstruct. Still a possibility was the opportunity to make repetitive dilatory procedural motions, resulting in successive time-consuming roll calls. Nor was Randall willing to change the definition of the quorum as a majority of all members of the House. This interpretation allowed members to refuse to answer their names even though present, thus allowing issues to be lost for lack of a quorum when party majorities were narrow (as was frequently the case during the late 1870s and the 1880s). Randall defended these positions forcefully as a member of the Rules Committee during Carlisle's service as Speaker.

Carlisle's attitude on such matters was similar to Randall's. In thus endorsing potentially obstructive practices the two men mirrored the

Democrats' negative legislative agenda of the time, emphasizing frugality in government and opposition to the use of the tariff to foster industrial development. The two were also very solicitous of the desires of southern members that federal powers should be curtailed and state prerogatives protected. Serving as a minority Representative on the Rules Committee in these years, Thomas B. Reed unsuccessfully offered proposals to expedite business. Critics complained by 1885 that only three types of general measures could win approval—minor bills for which unanimous consent could be obtained to consider them out of calendar order, legislation so important that a two-thirds majority voted to suspend the rules, and measures that the Appropriations Committee allowed as riders to appropriation bills.

When the Republicans returned to power in the House in 1889, Reed became Speaker. His impact upon the office was the greatest since Henry Clay's. Determined to remedy the legislative impotence of the House of Representatives and to allow the Republicans to compile a significant legislative record despite a thin majority, Reed moved on two fronts. Before the Speaker's Rules Committee reported, he counted House members who were present but not voting in order to achieve a quorum. The report of the Rules Committee of the Fifty-first Congress in 1890 constituted his second line of attack.

The "Reed Rules" involved changes in 18 of the 47 House rules of the previous Congress. The basic changes involved four categories of practice. Reed sought to eliminate dilatory behavior by eliminating the provision providing that privileged motions to fix the day of adjournment, to adjourn, and to take a recess should always be in order. A blanket clause provided that "No dilatory motion shall be entertained by the Speaker." Secondly, those present but not voting were to be counted in the determination of quorums. The quorum for decision-making in the Committee of the Whole was reduced to 100, and that new body was now allowed to close debate on sections or paragraphs of bills under discussion. The fourth category of innovative changes in the Reed Rules simplified the processes by which bills, memorials, and resolutions were placed in legislature train. Substituting action by the Speaker for the Monday call of the states and territories, the Speaker now referred a wide variety of material to appropriate committees without debate. The handling of "unfinished business" was acceler-

ated. A 60-minute period (extendable if required) was introduced after the handling of unfinished business, a period allowing committees to supervise consideration of "bills of a public character which do not appropriate money." Now committee reports would be delivered to the clerk of the House for printing and calendar entry, rather than formally being reported to the House.

Amid the Democratic denunciation that greeted the report of the Reed Rules, William S. Holman predicted that the "Speaker, instead of being as for the past one hundred years, the servant of the House, shall be its master; that the Speaker and the chairmen of committees shall be a petty oligarchy, with absolute control of the business of the House." When the Democrats regained control of the House in the next election, the Speaker, Charles F. Crisp, abandoned the Reed Rules. But he strengthened his powers of control by ruling that reports from the Rules Committee that he headed should be free of consideration. When the Fifty-third Congress assembled with a reduced Democratic majority, Crisp returned to the Reed Rules in somewhat revised form. After Reed assumed the Speaker's chair in the Fifty-fourth and Fifty-fifth Houses, he enforced a discipline on colleagues and proceedings unmatched in previous Congresses. But even Reed admitted that the powers of the President exceeded those of the Speaker, and he retired to the private practice of the law after becoming disenchanted with William McKinley's foreign policy. In general, the behavior of the House leaders of the late nineteenth century reflected the fact that the power of the House remained high in relation to the executive branch. But as the monetary stakes of lobbying increased beyond that of previous eras, the authority and esteem of the House was threatened from another quarter. Opponents accused both Blaine and Randall of succumbing to the enticements of lobbyists.

The committee system also developed considerably during the postbellum years. The process of enlarging the standing committee roster began during the Thirty-eighth Congress (1863–1865), reflecting the strains that the war placed upon old structures and also the Republican developmental agenda that reflected the structural changes occurring within the national economy. The decisions of 1865 to place the appropriations business of the Committee of Ways and Means in the hands of a new Committee on Appropriations and to create a committee on Banking and Currency were in part of the first type. The new committees on Coinage, Weights, and Measures (1864), Pacific Railroads (1865), and Mines and Mining (1865, but in the Thirty-ninth Congress), reflected the changing nature of the American economy. Pressing toward 40 by 1860, the number of standing committees had neared 60 by the turn of the century.

Certain standing committees dealt with private legislation. Others supervised executive expenditures. Some dealt with the specific processes of lawmaking. Still others framed public legislation—this sphere subdivided by a historian of the late nineteenth century into finance, industry, public property, war, law, social affairs, and international relations. The size of membership and the relative importance of the committees in House affairs varied. Three, five, or nine members was the practice during the Civil War; by 1900 as many as 17 served on some. Charged with raising and dispensing revenues, and authorized to report at will, Ways and Means was the most powerful of all House committees until the end of the Civil War. Its chairman ruled the floor, with the cooperation of the Speaker. Even by the time of the war, the committees charged with oversight of executive expenditures were moribund, the committee clerk primarily a secretary to the chairman. Despite some revitalization of these oversight committees during the Civil War, and the organization of an additional one later, their status as "slumbering watchdogs" was well recognized.

The committee power structure in the House changed significantly when the Appropriations Committee appeared in 1865. That committee's duties included the preparation and submission of the various appropriations bills; when the former chairman of Ways and Means, Thaddeus Stevens, became chairman, floor leadership moved with him. It is unclear that the Ways and Means Committee was thereafter always regarded as subordinate to Appropriations, but the vital source of power—control of the expenditures—now rested in that group. All other committees were dependent upon Appropriations, and the expanding practice of allowing substantive riders from other committees to be attached to appropriations bills enhanced its power. A decade later the position of the Appropriations Committee was strengthened still more when the House accepted an amendment of Congressman Charles S. Holman. Endorsed

by the members of the Appropriations Committee, this rule stated that additions to appropriations bills must be "germane to the subject matter of the bill" and "shall retrench expenditures."

In 1877 a forceful chairman of the Commerce Committee played upon the avarice of his fellow Representatives by winning a suspension of the rules under which the House acted upon his committee's bill appropriating funds for rivers and harbors improvement, repeating this coup in the following years. In 1880 the Commerce and Agriculture committees won the right to bring their appropriation bills directly to the floor. The Rules Committee of 1885 proposed that the committees on foreign, military, naval, and Indian affairs, as well as post offices and post roads, should be given the right to report appropriations measures and the Appropriations Committee thereafter retained charge of but six such bills. (The responsibilities for appropriations remained decentralized until 1920.) In part this decentralization reflected efforts to speed up House business, and in part it was an outgrowth of a contest for power between the chairman of Appropriations, Samuel J. Randall and rivals, some of whom opposed his Pennsylvania-tinged views on tariff legislation. The liberalized procedures also mirrored constituency pressures and a general sense that the prosperity and growth of the country could support higher levels of expenditure than members of the Appropriations Committee favored.

Although several notable joint select committees labored during the Civil War and Reconstruction years, the number of select committees in a Congress had become insignificant by the end of the 1870s. Conversely the use of subcommittees of standing committees greatly increased, their chairmen serving typically as floor managers for business emanating from them. Although well-endowed chairmen sometimes performed the functions of party Whip during the nineteenth century, that officer did not formally emerge until 1899.

The Senate as Contrast

This article has focused on the House because the House was the locus of many of the political struggles and much of the partisan and institutional development in the nineteenth century. But contrasts with the Senate are instructive. Lacking power under the Constitution to initiate appropriations bills, the Senate was initially believed to be a less-important body than the

House, despite its advisory powers relative to treaties and presidential nominees. Meeting at first behind closed doors, Senators attracted less public attention than did Representatives. But when major congressional figures of the early national period—particularly Clay, Webster, and Calhoun—moved into the Senate, it became the great national forum where the most eminent sectional and party leaders elaborated the problems of the era of sectional stress. And the Senator looked forward to longer service than the Representative. In the early 1830s, de Tocqueville found the quality of the men and proceedings in the Senate impressive in contrast to the House.

Institutional differences in both performance and function were apparent in the two houses during the nineteenth century. Neither the presiding Vice Presidents, nor the Presidents *pro tempore* elected to serve in their absence, wielded power comparable to that of the Speakers. As with the Representatives, the Senators initially placed most of the detail of legislative activity in the hands of special committees. They moved more slowly from this practice than did the Representatives, but by 1816 four standing committees had emerged and a substantial number of others were added in that year. Committee assignment did not become the continuing prerogative of the presiding officer. Until 1823 Senators elected their committee members by ballot, and for the next 23 years they experimented with various methods, in most of which the presiding officer named some or all of the committee. But in 1846 Senators adopted the practice of having a spokesman of the majority party present a list previously approved by the party caucus. Some years later the minority party was allowed to designate its Representatives for the minority slots on committees, although this practice was not followed during the Civil War. These lists came to be prepared by a party caucus committee on committees.

Although the chairman of the Senate Finance Committee had emerged by the time of the Civil War as the most powerful figure in Senate legislative proceedings, he was much less so than the chairman of Ways and Means. Nor at that time had the chairman of the caucus emerged as a preeminent leader in the Senate. The Republican Senators used a caucus steering committee during the Civil War, but it put few restrictions on self-willed Solons.

Senate rules were fewer and less complex than those in the House. Whereas Representatives developed restraints on debate—the previous question and the hour rule—and three calendars and two Committees of the Whole for the classification of business, Senate curbs on debate remained minimal and procedures for the handling of the various types of business and obtaining votes were much simpler.

By 1900 the United States had 90 Senators who faced problems of national growth and increased workload after the Civil War similar to those in the House. As a result significant consolidation of power in the hands of the party caucus chairman and steering committees occurred after 1880, culminating in William B. Allison's service as Republican caucus chairman. Beginning in 1897 Allison served both as chairman of the Republican caucus and of that group's committee on the order of business (steering committee) and sat unofficially on the caucus committee on committees. Allison and his trusted colleagues controlled these caucus committees completely and through them selected the membership of the Senate committees and managed floor business. Allison himself served as chairman of the Senate Appropriations Committee.

Allan G. Bogue

REFERENCES

Alexander, DeAlva S. 1916. *History and Procedure of the House of Representatives*. Boston: Houghton Mifflin.

Benton, Thomas H. 1968. *Thirty Years View: or, A History of the Workings of the American Government for Thirty Years, from 1820 to 1850*. 2 vols. Westport, CT: Greenwood. Orig. pub. 1854–1856.

Blaine, James G. 1884. *Twenty Years of Congress*. 2 vols. Norwich, CT: Henry Bill Publishing.

Bogue, Allan G. 1989. *The Congressman's Civil War*. New York: Cambridge U. Pr.

———, Jerome M. Clubb, Caroll R. McKibbin, and Santa A. Traugott. "Members of the House of Representatives and the Processes of Modernization, 1789–1960." 63 *Journal of American History* 275.

Brady, David W. 1988. *Critical Elections and Congressional Policy Making*. Stanford, CA: Stanford U. Pr.

———, and Joseph Cooper. 1981. "Toward a Diachronic Analysis of Congress." 75 *American Political Science Review* 988.

Cooper, Joseph. 1971. *The Origins of the Standing Committees and the Development of the Modern House*. Houston: Rice U. Pr.

Cunningham, Noble E., Jr. 1963. *The Jeffersonian Republicans in Power, 1801–1809*. Chapel Hill: U. of North Carolina Pr.

———. 1978. *The Process of Government Under Jefferson*. Princeton: Princeton U. Pr.

Dodd, Lawrence G. 1981. "Congress, the Constitution, and the Crisis of Legitimation." In Lawrence C. Dodd and Bruce I. Oppenheimer, eds. *Congress Reconsidered*. Washington: Congressional Quarterly.

———. 1985. "A Theory of Congressional Cycles: Solving the Puzzle of Change." *Working Papers in Political Science No. P–85–3*. Stanford, CA: Hoover Institution.

Fiorina, Morris P., David W. Rohde, and Peter Wissel. 1975. "Historical Change in House Turnover." In Norman J. Ornstein, ed. *Congress in Change*. New York: Praeger.

Follett, Mary P. 1902. *The Speaker of the House of Representatives*. New York: Longmans, Green.

Galloway, George B. 1976. *History of the House of Representatives*. Revised by Sidney Wise. New York: Crowell.

Garfield, James A. 1877. "A Century of Congress." 40 *Atlantic Monthly* 49.

Haynes, George H. 1938. *The Senate of the United States: Its History and Practice*. 2 vols. New York: Houghton Mifflin.

McConachie, Lauros G. 1898. *Congressional Committees: A Study of the Origins and Development of Our National and Local Legislative Methods*. New York: Crowell.

Polsby, Nelson W. 1968. "The Institutionalization of the U.S. House of Representatives." 62 *American Political Science Review* 144.

Price, H. Douglas. 1975. "Congress and the Evolution of Legislative Professionalism." In Norman J. Ornstein, ed. *Congress in Change*. New York: Praeger.

Robinson, William A. 1930. *Thomas B. Reed: Parliamentarian*. New York: Dodd, Mead.

Rothman, David J. 1966. *Politics and Power: The United States Senate, 1869–1901*. Cambridge: Harvard U. Pr.

Silbey, Joel H. 1981. "Congressional and State Legislative Roll Call Studies by U.S. Historians." 6 *Legislative Studies Quarterly* 597.

Thompson, Margaret S. 1985. *The 'Spider Webb': Congress and Lobbying in the Age of Grant*. Ithaca: Cornell U. Pr.

Herbert H. Lehman (1878–1963)

Liberal New York politician. As Franklin D. Roosevelt's lieutenant governor and then successor as governor, Herbert Henry Lehman significantly contributed to the popular appeal and electoral success of New Deal liberalism in New York. Born in New York City, Lehman graduated from Williams College in 1899. After working in his family's investment firm, he served briefly in the office of Assistant Secretary of the Navy Franklin D. Roosevelt during World War I.

Lehman became active in Democratic politics during the 1920s and managed Al Smith's gubernatorial campaign in 1926. As Franklin D. Roosevelt's running mate, Lehman was elected governor in 1932 and served in this office for ten years. Because of his close relationship with Roosevelt and the similarity of his state policies with the President's, his legislative program was referred to as the "Little New Deal."

In 1942 Lehman was appointed director of the Office of Foreign Relief and Rehabilitation by Roosevelt. In 1946 he ran for the Senate but lost. In 1949 Lehman was elected to fill an unexpired Senate term; he was elected to a full six-year Senate term in 1950. As a Senator, he was a prominent critic and opponent of the Red-baiting Senator Joseph R. McCarthy. Following his retirement from the Senate in 1957, he became active in reform efforts to destroy the power of Tammany Hall in New York City politics. Known as a generous philanthropist as well as a progressive politician, Lehman died one day before he was scheduled to receive the Medal of Freedom.

See also: Joseph McCarthy, Franklin D. Roosevelt, Al Smith, Tammany Hall

Sean J. Savage

REFERENCES

Bellush, Jewell. 1959. "Selected Case Studies of the Legislative Leadership of Governor Herbert H. Lehman." Ph.D. dissertation, Columbia University.

Ingalls, Robert P. 1975. *Herbert Lehman and New York's Little New Deal*. New York: New York U. Pr.

Lehman, Herbert H. 1934–1946. *Public Papers*. 9 vols. Albany: J. B. Lyon.

Nevins, Allan. 1963. *Herbert Lehman and His Era*. New York: Scribner's.

Curtis E. LeMay (1906–)

Saber-rattling running mate of George Wallace in 1968. A United States Air Force commander who developed effective methods of strategic bombing during World War II, Curtis Emerson LeMay was also the 1968 vice presidential candidate for the American Independent Party ticket led by Alabama governor George C. Wallace.

LeMay was born in Columbus, Ohio, his father a general laborer and his mother an elementary schoolteacher. During LeMay's boyhood, his family, which eventually included two brothers and two sisters, lived in Montana, California, and Pennsylvania before returning to Columbus where LeMay graduated from public high school and attended Ohio State University on an ROTC scholarship from 1924 to 1928. Although he failed to graduate from college, LeMay was awarded an ROTC reserve commission and joined the U.S. Army Air Corps in late 1928. LeMay then rose through the ranks, becoming a bombardment group leader in 1942 and the commander of a series of B-20 attacks in

1944 over Japanese installations in China and India. In 1945 LeMay led the 21st Bomber Command in the Mariana Islands and began low-level bombings of Tokyo and other Japanese cities. In 1948 LeMay became leader of the U.S. Strategic Air Command and was named command general in 1951. In 1957 LeMay was named vice chief of staff, and in 1961 he became chief of staff of the U.S. Air Force. In the 1960s LeMay was frequently at odds with the defense goals of the John Kennedy and Lyndon Johnson administrations. After his retirement in 1965, LeMay's only public notice came as Wallace's vice presidential nominee, a role that earned LeMay the scorn of the liberals when he suggested that nuclear weapons might be used in the Vietnam War.

See also: American Independent Party, Vietnam War as a Political Issue, George C. Wallace

Garry Boulard

REFERENCES

Chester, Lewis, Godfrey Hodgson, and Bruce Page. 1969. *An American Melodrama: The Presidential Campaign of 1968.* New York: Viking.

Coffey, Thomas M. 1986. *Iron Eagle—The Turbulent Life of General Curtis LeMay.* New York: Crown.

William Lemke (1878–1950)

Radical critic of Franklin D. Roosevelt. Union Party presidential candidate in 1936, Bill Lemke was raised in North Dakota. He received a law degree from Yale University in 1905. His interest in radical agrarian politics led him to join the North Dakota Non-Partisan League in 1916. In 1932, he was elected to the U.S. House of Representatives.

As a member of Congress, Lemke championed the cause of farm relief, in 1935 co-authoring the Frazier-Lemke Farm Mortgage Act. Originally a supporter of President Franklin Roosevelt, he broke with him over FDR's opposition to many of his proposed farm relief measures. In 1936 Lemke agreed to head the Union Party, a third-party movement that united various "radical" opponents of the New Deal, including Father Charles Coughlin, Dr. Francis Townsend, and the Reverend Gerald L. K. Smith.

Opponents portrayed Lemke as a country hick, owing in part to his disheveled appearance, but he reminded voters that "My coat may be wrinkled, but my record is not." Nicknamed "Liberty Bell" by his friends, detractors noted that the Liberty Bell was cracked and intimated that so too was Lemke. He conducted a colorful and energetic campaign and was the first presidential candidate to use the airplane extensively. His criticism of New Deal policies fell upon deaf ears, however, and he was soundly defeated in Roosevelt's landslide reelection. Following the election, Lemke returned to Congress where North Dakotans consistently reelected him to fight for his farm policies until his death.

See also: Election of 1936, New Deal, Franklin D. Roosevelt, Francis Townsend, Union Party

Thomas T. Spencer

REFERENCES

Bennett, David H. 1969. *Demagogues in the Depression.* New Brunswick, NJ: Rutgers U. Pr.

Blackorby, Edward. 1963. *Prairie Rebel: The Public Life of William Lemke.* Lincoln: U. of Nebraska Pr.

Powell, David O. 1962. "The Union Party of 1936." Ph.D. dissertation, Ohio State University.

John L. Lewis (1880–1969)

Labor leader extraordinaire. John Llewellyn Lewis was an aggressive, theatrical, defiant, and larger-than-life figure whose political vision for organized labor was a combination of rugged individualism, liberalism, and left-wing populism. Born in a southern Iowa coal-mining community, Lewis left school after the eighth grade to enter the mines. Although a Republican for most of his life, Lewis began his public life as a Wilsonian Democrat before and during World War I, campaigning for Woodrow Wilson in 1912 as an American Federation of Labor (AFL) organizer in the Southwest. Perhaps the Republican he was most like was Herbert Hoover, who also began as an ally of Wilson's. Lewis shared Hoover's dream of cooperative capitalism, a state favorably inclined toward labor. This utopian nation would restrain competition and encourage capital and labor to collaborate on economic goals that both shared.

Lewis, as president of the United Mine Workers (UMW) from 1920 to 1960, endorsed the Republicans Warren Harding, Calvin Coolidge, and Hoover during the four presidential elections during his own union presidency. Lewis's leadership of the UMW as acting president in 1919 in a strike against the federal government made him less sanguine about politicians and more willing to deal with corporate executives in the 1920s. In the 1919 strike, the government preferred to address concerns over inflation rather than labor demands. Lewis became the best-known labor Republican of the 1920s although he was disappointed with Coolidge and Hoover after 1924 for not promoting collective bargaining. Lewis countered calls in the UMW in the 1920s for the formation of a labor party and for the nationalization of the mines; later he expelled disruptive left-wing elements. Lewis always preferred to play Democrats off Republicans rather than to take a chance on a third party.

With the advent of the New Deal, Lewis used the National Industrial Recovery Act of 1933, whose Section 7(a) on a worker's right to bargain collectively he helped write, to increase the membership of the UMW. In December 1935 he helped establish the Committee for Industrial Organization (CIO) within the AFL. This collection of industrial unions was expelled at the end of 1937, becoming the AFL's rival Congress of Industrial Organizations. In 1936 FDR and Lewis had the same enemies—Wall Street and reactionaries—and they employed the same images on the radio. Lewis got both the UMW and the CIO, of which he was president, to endorse Roosevelt through the CIO's Non-Partisan League, which he set up. The UMW donated $600,000 to FDR's campaign, and Lewis appeared jointly with the President in industrial towns.

By reminding power brokers of their debts to him, especially politicians like Governor Frank Murphy of Michigan and FDR, Lewis greatly assisted the automobile strikers in 1937; neither federal nor state government forces were used against them in Michigan. But defeats in the steel strikes in Ohio and Pennsylvania because of political animosity and FDR's declaration of "a plague on both your houses" (labor and capital) in view of the popular backlash against the CIO, embittered Lewis. He turned against FDR in 1940 because of the administration's disinclination to press for further domestic reforms and because of its interventionist foreign policy. Lewis backed the Republican Wendell Willkie, also an internationalist but one who other isolationists like Lewis supported. Lewis followed through on his threat to resign as president of the CIO if Willkie lost; he was succeeded by his colleague Philip Murray. After 1940 Lewis was never strongly identified with either political party. Murray brought the CIO closer to the Democratic Party, prompting Lewis and the UMW to leave in 1942.

Although he acceded to the no-strike pledge during the war, Lewis led labor actions against government-imposed wage levels in 1943. FDR used federal troops at one point to keep the mines open, although the government reneged and granted the UMW a 35-hour workweek and safety improvements. President Harry Truman in April 1946 seized the mines when another strike ensued, yet the miners again won concessions. At any rate, Truman's showdown with Lewis added immeasurably to his reputation as a man just beginning to move out of FDR's shadow. The UMW briefly reaffiliated with the AFL (1946–1947) in opposition to Truman's reconversion policies.

After a 1950 strike again resulted in a government seizure of the mines, Lewis returned to his theme of the 1920s: a partnership between owners and miners. He sought less government involvement in labor-management relations, reflecting his basic suspicion of a powerful state. Lewis called for the repeal of the Wagner Act as well as the Taft-Hartley Act whose required non-Communist oaths for union officials offended his sense of civil liberty. But as coal became a less important commodity in the 1950s, Lewis's prominence waned.

See also: Calvin Coolidge, Warren G. Harding, Herbert Hoover, Isolationism in American Politics, Harry S Truman, Wendell Willkie

Frederick J. Augustyn, Jr.

REFERENCES

Dubofsky, Melvyn, and Warren Van Tine. 1977. *John L. Lewis: A Biography*. New York: Quadrangle.

———, and ———, eds. 1987. *Labor Leaders in America*. Urbana: U. of Illinois Pr.

Fink, Gary M., ed. 1984. *Biographical Dictionary of American Labor*. Westport, CT: Greenwood.

John R. Lewis (1940–)

Freedom Rider elected to the U.S. House from Georgia. John R. Lewis, a liberal Black Democrat, was elected to Congress from Georgia's Fifth District in 1986 after spending nearly 30 years as a prominent civil rights activist and organizer. Born in Dunn's Chapel, a rural village near Troy, Alabama, Lewis was one of ten children of a tenant farmer father and a mother who took in laundry to make ends meet. Lewis began his career in civil rights at the age of 19 by organizing one of the first lunch counter sit-ins by Blacks while he was a student at the American Baptist Seminary in Nashville.

By 1961, when Lewis graduated from college, he had become inspired by the nonviolent civil rights crusade of Martin Luther King, Jr. During that same year, Lewis was one of the leaders of the Freedom Riders and was severely beaten by racists in South Carolina and Alabama for his efforts in behalf of civil rights. In 1963 Lewis became the leader of the Student Nonviolent

Coordinating Committee and helped to coordinate the Mississippi Freedom Project the following year. Between 1964 and 1968, Lewis helped organize King's campaigns for civil and voting rights and economic equality.

After King's death, Lewis became the Voter Education Project's executive director (1970–1976), and in 1977 he was associate director of ACTION in President Jimmy Carter's administration. Lewis ran unsuccessfully for Congress in 1977, but he won a seat on the Atlanta City Council in 1981. In 1986 Lewis defeated Georgia state senator Julian Bond in the Georgia Democratic primary for Congress. He won the general election with more than 75 percent of the vote.

See also: Julian Bond, Jimmy Carter, Martin Luther King, Jr., Mississippi Freedom Democratic Party, Student Nonviolent Coordinating Committee

Garry Boulard

REFERENCES

King, Mary. 1987. *Freedom Song—A Personal Story of the 1960s Civil Rights Movement.* New York: Morrow.

Oates, Stephen B. 1982. *Let the Trumpet Sound—The Life of Martin Luther King, Jr.* New York: Harper & Row.

Liberal Party of New York

An offshoot of the New York–based American Labor Party (ALP), the Liberal Party was formed by a group of one-time ALP leaders who abandoned that party to more radical elements after a long struggle for control. Led by Alex Rose of the Millinery Workers and David Dubinsky of the International Ladies Garment Workers Union, the Liberal Party established itself in 1946, relying on support from garment and other union workers and from Jewish voters centered in New York City. The ALP eclipsed in 1954, while the Liberal Party survived as a more liberal voice in New York politics by advocating such programs as full employment, consumer rights, rent control, progressive taxation, equal rights, legislative and judicial reform, and expanded social welfare programs. It has also served as a counterbalance to the New York Conservative Party, formed in 1962.

The Liberal Party has survived by endorsing major party candidates for office in exchange for concessions and support, and alternately by running its own candidates for office as a means of drawing votes away from a major party. In 1954, for example, Liberal Party leaders pressured Democratic Party leaders to nominate Averill Harriman for governor instead of the then-frontrunner Franklin D. Roosevelt, Jr. Harriman was nominated and then won election with the added votes provided him on the Liberal line (such multiple endorsements are allowed by New York's cross-endorsement rule).

In 1966 the Liberals ran Roosevelt for governor instead of endorsing the Democratic nominee, Frank O'Connor. The move was designed to punish the Democrats for their failure to consult with the Liberals on their choice for governor. The Democratic-Liberal vote was split, allowing Republican governor Nelson Rockefeller to be reelected.

Liberal Party strength reached a high point in the 1960s when incumbent New York City (then Republican) mayor John Lindsay was denied his own party's renomination but was reelected mayor on the Liberal line alone, defeating more conservative Republican and Democratic candidates. Liberal Party ranks grew, and its leaders won influence and patronage.

The party's fortunes began to decline in the 1970s, first when master strategist Alex Rose died in 1977 and then when the Liberal Party was relegated to fifth place on the New York ballot by the new Right to Life Party. In the 1980s, factionalism within the party increased; the Liberals became almost an appendage of the Democratic Party. Liberals have continued to exert periodic influence, however, as when they endorsed underdog Mario Cuomo for governor instead of front-runner Ed Koch in 1982, helping Cuomo stage an upset victory in the Democratic primary that paved the way for his election.

The Liberal Party has shared an ideological affinity with the New York state Democratic Party, but it has also endorsed moderate Republicans, including former Senators Jacob Javits and Charles Goodell. In recent years, however, Liberal endorsements of Republicans have been few and far between. Some argue that the party continues to serve as a liberal conscience in state politics. Other voices in state politics, such as the *New York Times*, have called for the Liberals to disband.

See also: American Labor Party, Charles Goodell, Nelson Rockefeller

Robert J. Spitzer

REFERENCES

Behn, Dick. 1977. "Liberals and Conservatives: The Importance of New York's Two 'Third' Parties." 3 *Empire State Report* 164.

Karen, Robert. 1975. "The Politics of Pressure." 20 *The Nation* 235.

Spitzer, Robert J. 1987. *The Right to Life Movement and Third Party Politics.* Westport, CT: Greenwood.

Liberal Republican Party

The short-lived Liberal Republican Party of the early 1870s was evidence of large-scale dissatisfaction within the Republican Party over the program of Reconstruction in the South and the pervasive corruption of Ulysses Grant's administration. Initial electoral coalitions of Republican defectors and Democrats emerged in Border States such as Missouri in 1870. The two groups united on platforms favoring amnesty for former Confederates barred from the political process. Supporters claimed that amnesty would bring peace to the region by encouraging discontented whites to return to the political system.

In the North, the Liberal Republican movement coalesced around opposition to Grant. In addition to their disapproval of current Reconstruction policies, Liberals generally advocated free trade, civil service reform, and an end to Grant's imperialistic foreign policy. The Liberal Republicans had little grass-roots organization, relying heavily on the support of several of the nation's leading newspaper editors. Inconsistent procedures for picking delegates to the new party's first national convention in May 1872 resulted in a heterogeneous assemblage, representing reformers of all stripes, out-of-favor Republican office seekers, and southern white opponents of Reconstruction regimes. This incoherence caused the delegates to cast six indecisive ballots before passing over more experienced politicians such as Charles Francis Adams, David Davis, or Lyman Trurnbull to nominate the longtime editor of the New York *Tribune*, Horace Greeley. The party then chose a leading Greeley backer, Missouri governor B. Gratz Brown, as its vice presidential nominee.

The nomination of Greeley by the Liberal Republicans proved difficult for many potential supporters to swallow. Greeley was incorrectly thought to be among the most radical of Republicans and correctly thought to be an opponent of civil service reform and free trade. After efforts to convince Greeley to decline the nomination, some Liberals were forced reluctantly to endorse Grant. Most Democratic leaders, however, rallied behind Greeley's candidacy as better than four more years of Grant. The Democratic National Convention in July seconded Greeley's nomination and adopted the Liberals' platform word for word.

Republicans used the discomfiture over Greeley to put the Liberal Republican–Democratic coalition on the defensive during the ensuing campaign. Grant and the Republican-controlled Congress cut the tariff, granted amnesty to most ex-Confederates, and promised reform of the patronage system. The Republicans renominated former Union Army commander Grant and made personality a major issue of the election by ridiculing Greeley's erratic career as a reformer as editor of the *Tribune*.

The Liberal response was weak. Greeley's campaign never developed an effective national organization. The expected swell of recruits from anti-Grant Republican ranks failed to materialize, and many southern Democrats refused to endorse the northerner Greeley's candidacy. Worried by Republican victories in the state election in September, Greeley campaigned hard, delivering almost 200 speeches mainly advocating sectional reconciliation. Sometimes he went too far, as in a Pittsburgh speech during which he recognized the legality of secession. By trying to ingratiate himself with the South, Greeley alienated many northerners who still harbored strong resentments from the recently ended war.

The election results were heavily one-sided; Greeley lost all but six southern states. His disastrous campaign strategy had drawn away few Republicans and persuaded many Democrats to stay home on election day. The Liberal Republican movement never recovered from this defeat and disappeared. While failing to curb either the corruption or the protectionism of the Grant era, the Liberals' greatest impact was to influence the Republican Party to move in the direction of national reconciliation at the expense of the freedmen and southern Reconstruction.

See also: Charles Francis Adams, Ulysses S. Grant, Horace Greeley, Reconstruction, Secession

John R. McKivigan

REFERENCES

Gillette, William. 1979. *Retreat from Reconstruction, 1869–1879*. Baton Rouge: Louisiana State U. Pr.

Lunde, Erik S. 1981. *Horace Greeley*. Boston: Twayne.

Sproat, John G. 1968. *"The Best Men": Liberal Reformers in the Gilded Age*. New York: Oxford U. Pr.

Libertarian Party

The most successful minor political party in the United States since 1976, in the last four presidential elections through 1988, Libertarian Party candidates have received more votes than those affiliated with any other third party. (Independent candidates Eugene McCarthy in 1976 and John Anderson in 1980 surpassed the Libertarian Party totals, but neither ran under a party label.) Nevertheless, the party, which has enjoyed a few isolated victories in local races, received fewer than 1 percent of the popular votes in the 1988 presidential contest.

The Libertarian Party fielded its first presidential candidate in 1972. Its best effort was in the 1980 election when nearly 1 million voters cast ballots for California attorney Ed Clark. In contrast, former Republican Congressman Ron Paul of Texas, the Libertarian standard-bearer in 1988, received only half as many votes but still managed to edge out all other minor party candidates in the race.

Like other third parties, the Libertarians have failed to attract much support because of the strong two-party tradition in the United States. Libertarian candidates are never invited to participate in presidential debates, they have difficulty attracting news coverage, and they are underfinanced. Moreover, the political philosophy of the Libertarian Party is such that few people are attracted to it.

The cornerstone of Libertarian doctrine is that individuals should be free to live their lives as they choose with a minimum of governmental control. Thus, the party opposes all laws and programs that tend to restrict in any way basic civil rights. Libertarians, therefore, oppose all forms of discrimination and censorship. They support the right of a woman to choose to have an abortion, and they oppose such governmental intervention in people's lives as involuntary commitment to mental institutions, compulsory school attendance, mandatory jury service, and the military draft.

While the Libertarian Party's social programs are generally viewed as being on the liberal end of the political spectrum, the economic measures it advocates are conservative. For example, the party supports a constitutional amendment requiring a balanced budget, it advocates drastically reduced governmental spending, and it will accept only minimal taxation. Government programs and agencies that would be cut to accomplish these economic goals include Social Security, the postal service, the Federal Bureau of Investigation, the Central Intelligence Agency, the Federal Election Commission, the Internal Revenue Service, all welfare programs, federal aid to education, farm subsidies, and U.S. participation in the United Nations.

Other tenets of Libertarian philosophy include opposition to all gun control laws, the right of employers to refuse to recognize unions, the abolition of minimum wage laws, the

withdrawal of U.S. military troops from foreign countries, the termination of all U.S. foreign aid, independence for U.S. territories, and the right of individuals to homestead in outer space.

Currently, the Libertarian Party is apparently well organized and financially viable. However, its unique mix of liberal and conservative doctrine virtually assures that it will never become more than a minor party on the U.S. political scene.

See also: Election of 1980, Federal Election Commission, Eugene McCarthy, Third Parties in American Elections

Roger D. Hardaway

REFERENCES

Goodman, Walter. 1984. "Libertarian Asking Less Government." *New York Times.* Sept. 28, 1984, A22.

Judis, John. 1980. "Libertarians: Where the Left Meets the Right." 44 *The Progressive* 9, 36.

Libertarian Party News, Vol. 3. No. 5 (September-October 1988).

Nelson, Michael. 1980. "The New Libertarians: Stripping Government of Its Power." 7 *Saturday Review* (March), 21.

Polsgrove, Carol. 1978. "In Pursuit of 'Liberty.'" 42 *The Progressive* 1 (January) 38.

Wise, Steve. 1988. "Libertarian Presidential Candidate Would Like to Gut the Government." *Grand Forks [ND] Herald.* June 9, 1988, 1.

Liberty Party

The first American political party formed on the basis of opposition to slavery, the single-issue Liberty Party was forged from elements of various antislavery societies in the 1830s and was concentrated in New York, Ohio, New Hampshire, Pennsylvania, New Jersey, and Michigan. Its first convention, held in New York in 1839, nominated James Birney of New York and Francis Lemoyne of Pennsylvania for President and Vice President, respectively. The party's platform called for an end to slavery in the District of Columbia and other federal territories and an end to interstate slave trade. Although these planks might seem modest in retrospect, they represented the cutting edge of a part of the antislavery movement that was attempting to remain within "the system." The Liberty Party consequently incurred the wrath of many in the antislavery movement, including the doctrinaire abolitionist leader William Lloyd Garrison, who disdained what he viewed as corrupt party politics.

Religious convictions and church support were instrumental to the party's base. For example, many who attended the 1840 convention were ministers and clergy members of many denominations. Other party members and leaders included disaffected Whigs and Democrats. These political pragmatists struggled throughout the brief life of the Liberty Party to emphasize economic (as opposed to moral) arguments against slavery (e.g., the claim that slavery was detrimental to white workers) as a means of broadening the party's base and issue concerns. These coalitionists never succeeded in overcoming the single-issue devotion of the diehards.

Despite the rising antislavery tide, presidential nominee Birney polled a paltry 7,000 votes in 1840, the total depressed by poor organization and the fact that Birney spent the campaign in England. Most antislavery voters were persuaded to support the less odious Whig candidate, William Henry Harrison. Unfortunately, Harrison's death gave the country a new President, John Tyler, a Virginia slaveholder. Furthermore, both major parties turned out to be singularly unresponsive to the slavery issue.

The Liberty Party's best showing was in the 1842 Massachusetts gubernatorial race, when Samuel Sewall polled 5.4 percent on the Liberty line, forcing the contest into the state legislature. The Liberty Party held the balance of power in many Massachusetts elections in 1843 and 1844.

The election of 1844 yielded somewhat better national results. Presidential candidate Birney polled 62,000 votes (about 2.3 percent of votes cast). The most notable impact of Birney's race was the de facto delivery of New York, and therefore the election, to Democrat James K. Polk, as most antislavery voters preferred Whig Henry Clay. Party fortunes ebbed after 1844 because of the disappointing showing that year, escalating concern over other issues, and a shift in antislavery politics owing to the Wilmot Proviso, an act attempting to bar the extension of slavery into territories acquired from Mexico. This means of limiting slavery encouraged the rise of the Liberty Party's more pragmatic and successful successor, the Free Soil Party. Despite the Liberty Party's poor electoral showing, it was successful far beyond its numbers in spreading and legitimizing antislavery sentiment through its publications, lecturing activities, and conventions.

See also: James Birney, Henry Clay, Election of 1840 and 1844, Free Soil Party, William Lloyd Garrison, James K. Polk, John Tyler

Robert J. Spitzer

REFERENCES

Hesseltine, William B. 1962. *Third Party Movements in the United States.* New York: Van Nostrand.

Nash, Howard P. 1959. *Third Parties in American Politics.* Washington: Public Affairs Press.

Sewell, Richard H. 1976. *Ballots for Freedom.* New York: Oxford U. Pr.

Abraham Lincoln (1809–1865)

The Great Emancipator. More than a century after his death, the legacy of Abraham Lincoln lives on in American politics. His unprecedented expansion of presidential power demonstrated how powerful a chief executive could become in a time of crisis. He was a prime mover in the formative years of the Republican Party and was the party's first successful presidential candidate. And as an American political icon, Lincoln is unparalleled; the centrality of the presidency in American political culture in part owes to the legendary nature of Lincoln's life and death.

Lincoln was born near Hodgenville, Kentucky, and first ran for public office in 1832. He lost that race, a contest for a seat in the Illinois state legislature, but won in his second effort two years later. Lincoln served for eight years and in 1846 won a seat in the U.S. House of Representatives. In Washington, he supported the Wilmot Proviso, an attempt to outlaw slavery in territories acquired from Mexico, and he joined Whigs in criticizing President James K. Polk's military intervention in Mexico. Whig strength nationally was declining, however, and Lincoln's opposition to the Mexican War was unpopular. Accordingly, he returned to Illinois after a single term.

Lincoln reentered politics in 1854 after Democratic Senator Stephen A. Douglas of Illinois engineered the Kansas-Nebraska Act, which provided for "popular sovereignty" on the question of slavery in the new territories. Lincoln condemned the law, for it repealed the 1820 Missouri Compromise prohibiting slavery in territories north of Missouri's southern boundary. During this time the Whig Party breathed its last, and the Democrats struggled to contain growing divisions between northern and southern factions. With the emergence in 1854 of the Republican Party, which Lincoln joined two years later, it was clear that the slavery question had initiated a fundamental realignment of the American party system.

Lincoln campaigned for Republican presidential candidate John C. Frémont in 1856, and in 1858 he ran for Stephen A. Douglas's Senate seat. Although Douglas narrowly defeated Lincoln, their series of campaign debates thrust Lincoln into the national spotlight. Two years later, after a successful speaking tour of New York and New England, Lincoln emerged as a leading contender for the 1860 Republican presidential nomination. Lincoln argued that slavery was wrong—in the debates with Douglas he called slavery a "moral, social and political evil"—but he was no abolitionist; indeed, Lincoln was viewed as more conservative than Senators William H. Seward of New York and Salmon P. Chase of Ohio, his major competitors for the nomination. At their Chicago convention, the Republicans, looking to Lincoln to unite their various factions, nominated him on the third ballot.

Republican fortunes in the 1860 election were greatly helped by the internal forces tearing at the Democratic Party. The Democrats' first effort to nominate a presidential candidate, in Charleston, South Carolina, ended in a walkout by delegates from nine southern states. The remaining delegates, in session for ten days and unable to nominate a candidate after fifty-seven roll-call votes, agreed to reconvene in Baltimore six weeks later. That Baltimore meeting produced a new walkout, again by southern delegates, who disputed a plan to seat those who bolted the Charleston convention. Stephen A. Douglas then won the nomination, and the Democrats adopted a platform calling for the Supreme Court to resolve the slavery question.

Other party fragments coalesced to select their own presidential candidates. Disgruntled southern Democrats chose John C. Breckinridge of Kentucky and, in their platform, affirmed that the personal and property rights of settlers in territories (including slaveholders) should be free from governmental intervention. Remnants of the nativist Know-Nothing (American) Party and conservative Whigs joined these southerners in forming the Constitutional Union Party. The new group, denouncing the sectionalism of the major parties, nominated Senator John Bell of Tennessee.

In the November election, Lincoln, though not on the ballot in nine southern states, virtually swept the free states. Douglas won only Missouri and part of New Jersey; Bell carried Tennessee, Kentucky, and Virginia; and Breckinridge carried the rest of the South. The electoral vote and popular vote percentages went this way: Lincoln, 180 and 39.8 percent; Douglas, 12 and 29.5 percent; Breckinridge, 72 and 18.1 percent; and Bell, 39 and 12.6 percent.

By the time Lincoln took office in March 1861, the rebellious Confederacy had begun to form. Within a month of his inauguration, the first shots were fired on Fort Sumter, and within 18 months, major battles had been fought at Bull Run (twice), at Shiloh, on the James River peninsula, and at Antietam. Lincoln used a succession of generals to command Union forces, but Confederate resistance, ably led by Robert E. Lee and Thomas "Stonewall" Jackson, frustrated Union efforts to bring the war to a quick end. After Gettysburg, in which a Confederate invasion of the North failed in a bloody, three-day battle in Pennsylvania, the war's ultimate outcome, if not its duration, became clear.

The blueprint for ending the war became clear when General Ulysses S. Grant, who split the Confederacy with his capture of Vicksburg and the Mississippi River, moved to command Union operations in the eastern theater. Grant began a dogged and costly pursuit of Lee in Virginia, and General William T. Sherman embarked on a march from Tennessee toward Atlanta. Unfortunately for Lincoln, both drives stalled: Grant in a protracted siege at Petersburg, Virginia; and Sherman in a siege at Atlanta.

Lincoln's prospects for reelection in 1864 seemed dim. The war effort was stalled, and Lincoln was being vilified for his expansion of presidential power. He had blockaded southern ports, expanded the army beyond statutory limits, suspended the writ of habeas corpus, and ordered the expenditure of federal funds without congressional appropriation. A conscription law led to riots in New York City, and so-called "Copperheads" (antiwar Democrats) agitated for a cessation of hostilities. Radical Republicans in Congress claimed that Lincoln's emancipation of the slaves did not go far enough, since only slaves in rebel territories were affected. Moreover, they used the Congressional Committee on the Conduct of the War to criticize his military leadership.

Describing the 1864 election, historian Bruce Catton writes, "perhaps the strangest thing about this strangest of all elections was that it never occurred to anyone not to have it." Voters—not politicians or generals—were to decide if the war should continue, and the party platforms, at least, made their choices clear. The Republicans, now called the Union Party, renominated a chief executive committed to carrying on the war until the nation was reunited. The Democrats nominated General George B. McClellan and then presented him with a platform calling for a quick, negotiated peace with the South. McClellan, however, was "a war Democrat running on a peace platform," and he agreed with Lincoln that peace was impossible without complete reunification. For the Democrats, the problems created by the inconsistency between candidate and platform were minimal compared with the surge that Lincoln received from developments in the war. In August 1864, Admiral David Farragut won the Battle of Mobile Bay, and on September 1, Sherman wired Lincoln that "Atlanta is ours, and fairly won." Finally, in the Shenandoah Valley—long a refuge for southern armies menacing Washington—General Philip Sheridan won a series of convincing victories.

Union successes on the battlefield were reflected in November's voting, as Lincoln and his vice presidential running mate Andrew Johnson won 55 percent of the popular vote and 212 electoral votes to McClellan's 21. On April 9, 1865, barely more than a month after Lincoln's second inauguration, Lee surrendered to Grant at Appomattox Court House in Virginia; the Civil War, save a few minor skirmishes, had ended. For Lincoln, the next struggle was to be reconstruction of the nation: under what conditions would the rebel states be allowed to reenter the Union? The first words of his inaugural address on March 4 offer a clue to his thinking, as he spoke of healing the nation's wounds "with malice toward none; with charity for all." The problem of reunification, however, was to be left to Lincoln's successors. While watching *Our American Cousin* in Washington's Ford Theater, Lincoln was shot by John Wilkes Booth, a well-known actor and southern sympathizer. Lincoln died the next day, April 15, 1865.

See also: Abolition Movement, John Breckinridge, Salmon Chase, Constitutional Union Party, Copperheads, Stephen Douglas, Election of 1860, John C. Frémont, Ulysses S. Grant, Andrew Johnson, Kansas-Nebraska Act, Know-Nothings, Missouri Compromise, Slavery, Wilmot Proviso

Tom A. Kazee

REFERENCES

Angle, Paul M. 1981. *The Lincoln Reader.* Westport, CT: Greenwood.

Bailey, Thomas A. 1966. *Presidential Greatness: The Image and the Man from George Washington to the Present.* New York: Appleton-Century.

Catton, Bruce. 1965. *Never Call Retreat.* Garden City, NY: Doubleday.

Current, Richard N. 1980. *The Lincoln Nobody Knows.* Westport, CT: Greenwood.

Donald, David. 1961. *Lincoln Reconsidered.* New York: Vintage.

Handlin, Oscar, and Lilian Handlin. 1980. *Abraham Lincoln and the Union.* Boston: Little, Brown.

Johnson, Ludwell H. 1978. *Division and Reunion: America 1848–1877.* New York: Wiley.

Pole, J. R. 1964. *Abraham Lincoln.* New York: Oxford U. Pr.

Sundquist, James L. 1983. *Dynamics of the Party System: Alignment and Realignment of Political Parties in the United States.* Washington: Brookings.

John V. Lindsay (1921–)

Reform mayor of New York City. A former two-term mayor of New York City and an unsuccessful presidential candidate in 1972, John Vliet Lindsay followed in the state tradition of liberal Republicanism. Born the son of an investment banker, Lindsay graduated from Yale University and entered the Navy in 1943. At the conclusion of World War II, he got a law degree at Yale in 1948 and soon became active in Republican Party politics, co-founding the Youth for Eisenhower movement and serving as president of the New York Young Republican Club. In 1955 he went to work for the Justice Department, taking an active hand in drafting legislation, including the Civil Rights Act of 1957.

In 1958 Lindsay ran for Congress from New York's Seventeenth District, the only Republican stronghold in Manhattan. Known as the "Silk Stocking District," the locale incorporates wealthy residential, theatrical, and business areas, which was the constituency that Lindsay represented until 1965. While in Congress, he served on the Judiciary Committee, where he was a strong advocate of civil rights and other liberal measures.

In 1965 Lindsay ran for and was elected mayor of New York on the Republican and Liberal party lines (made possible by New York's cross-endorsement rule), receiving a decisive boost from the Liberal Party endorsement. Although a popular leader at the start of his term, Lindsay and his administration soon ran afoul of recurrent city problems including strikes by sanitation workers, schoolteachers, and transit workers. Generalized social turbulence in the 1960s peaked during Lindsay's mayoralty, and riots and other social disorders continued to plague the city and the Lindsay administration. In 1969 Lindsay sought renomination but was defeated in the Republican primary by a conservative state senator, John Marchi. Running solely on the Liberal and Independent lines, Lindsay was reelected with a plurality of the vote over Marchi and a conservative Democratic challenger.

Lindsay's reelection clearly owed to the Liberal Party endorsement and overwhelming support from the Black community. After the election, critics claimed that no Liberal Party activist seeking a municipal job went without work in New York City.

In 1972 Lindsay launched a presidential bid as a Democrat. Tall, handsome, and suave, Lindsay was considered by many to be the ideal presidential candidate of the television age, even a possible heir to John Kennedy's legacy within the Democratic Party. Several former Kennedy operatives, including advance man Jerry Bruno, joined the campaign. But Lindsay was unable to distinguish himself in a crowded field, and political troubles from New York City dogged his tracks. The campaign foundered, and Lindsay returned to New York to complete his term. He declined to seek a third term and returned to the practice of law. Still, John Lindsay remained a presence in New York political and social circles for years after his active political career came to an end.

See also: Election of 1972

Robert J. Spitzer

REFERENCES

Bruno, Jerry, and Jeff Greenfield. 1971. *The Advance Man.* New York: Bantam.

Walter Lippmann (1889–1974)

Undisputed dean of American journalism. Walter Lippmann broadly influenced American policy with his award-winning writings on national and international issues. In addition to his work for major periodicals, such as *New Republic, New York World, New York Herald-Tribune,* and *Newsweek,* he was the author of some two dozen books including *Drift and Mastery* (1914), *Public Opinion* (1922), *The Good Society* (1937), *U.S. Foreign Policy* (1943), and *The Communist World and Ours* (1959). His views on myriad political subjects were sought out, and he, in turn, enjoyed unparalleled access to world leaders, advising every American President from Calvin Coolidge to Richard Nixon, with the exception of FDR, whom he actively opposed.

Born in New York City, Lippmann was the only child of well-to-do secular Jewish parents who introduced him to culture and learning at a young age. Following his graduation from Harvard University in 1910, he began a varied career that included service as a captain with Army Intelligence during World War I, as well as his more familiar role as critic and author. Lippmann was disillusioned by the give and take of politics, however, as demonstrated by his short tenure in such positions as executive secretary for George R. Lunn, the Socialist mayor of Schenectady, New York, in 1912 and as a member of Colonel Edward House's staff at the peace negotiations following World War I.

Gradually moving away from the Fabian Socialism he supported in his youth, by the early 1930s Lippmann had gained a reputation as a detached observer, whose calm appraisals were generally nonpartisan. Although Lippmann was sometimes criticized for his shifting positions on a number of issues, he maintained his reputation for scholarship throughout his career.

See also: Edward House, Franklin D. Roosevelt

James V. Saturno

REFERENCES

Adams, Larry L. 1977. *Walter Lippmann.* Boston: Twayne.

Blum, D. Steven. 1984. *Walter Lippmann, Cosmopolitanism in the Century of Total War.* Ithaca: Cornell U. Pr.

Steel, Ronald. 1980. *Walter Lippmann and the American Century.* Boston: Little, Brown.

Literacy Tests

Receiving greatest notoriety from their use in the South between 1890 and 1964, literacy tests served as a means of preventing African-Americans from voting. Such discriminatory voting devices especially arose during the Populist era as higher-income white "Bourbons" sought to retain their political power and Democratic Party dominance in the face of possible Black and lower-income white coalitions. Some political leaders argued that literacy tests would guarantee a government of the wise and wealthy who would govern for the benefit of all citizens. Others urged it as a "good government" reform—if African-Americans were "legally" disenfranchised, then whites would no longer have to rely on illegal tactics of voter fraud and intimidation to prevent Black voting or political victories. Those state conventions enacting such voting controls typically excluded Blacks and did not submit the new constitutions to popular votes for ratification. At the turn of the century some nonsouthern states also made the ability to read English a requirement for voting as a way of providing wise government and striking against political bosses who allegedly exploited (mobilized) the immigrant and Black vote.

Many whites of lower socioeconomic status opposed literacy tests, fearing that they themselves would also be disenfranchised. Mississippi originated the idea of the "understanding and interpretation" alternatives to literacy, a strategy that spread to other southern states: illiterate voters could vote if they could understand and orally interpret any section of the state constitution. Many political leaders assured whites that since local registrars were white, they would generally be deemed literate. This voting device would be more strictly employed to disenfranchise Blacks. Alternatives to the "understanding and interpretation" tests used in some southern states included demonstrating "good character," understanding good citizenship, or owning property. As twentieth-century education made more Blacks literate, several southern states eliminated alternatives to literacy and implemented supplemental requirements. By the 1940s, for example, Alabama and Louisiana required that voters meet literacy, interpretation, good character, and good citizenship requirements. Even as late as the 1960s, the Alabama literacy test included 68 specific and sometimes obscure questions.

These voting devices were regarded as discriminatory against African-Americans for a number of reasons. Blacks were not only more likely than whites to be illiterate, but being born into slavery made it difficult to answer age and residency questions on application forms, while registrars usually helped only whites. Some registrars gave Blacks a blank sheet of paper, requiring them to write down all information required for application without telling them the questions. Often, whites were not required to complete literacy and interpretation tests, while African-Americans were asked a number of complex and obscure questions. Discrimination was especially prominent in rural areas with a high percentage of Blacks.

These and other voting devices like the poll tax were very effective in disenfranchising Blacks in the South. By the early 1900s, far less than 20 percent of eligible southern African-Americans were registered, and even as late as 1960 only 29 percent of Black adults were registered. The federal 1965 Voting Rights Act outlawed literacy tests, and by 1970, 66 percent of adult southern Blacks were registered to vote. As a direct consequence, the number of Black elected officials in the South soared in the last third of the twentieth century.

See also: Poll Tax, Voting Rights Act of 1965 and Extensions

Stephen D. Shaffer

REFERENCES

Ball, Howard, Dale Krane, and Thomas P. Lauth. 1982. *Compromised Compliance: Implementation of the 1965 Voting Rights Act.* Westport, CT: Greenwood.

Key, V. O. 1949. *Southern Politics in State and Nation.* New York: Random House.

Kousser, J. Morgan. 1974. *The Shaping of Southern Politics: Suffrage Restriction and the Establishment of the One-Party South, 1880–1910.* New Haven: Yale U. Pr.

Matthews, Donald R., and James W. Prothro. 1966. *Negroes and the New Southern Politics.* New York: Harcourt, Brace, and World.

Woodward, C. Vann. 1951. *Origins of the New South, 1877–1913.* Louisiana: Louisiana State U. Pr.

Henry Demarest Lloyd (1847–1903)

Journalist, author, and reformer. Henry Demarest Lloyd was an early opponent of monopolies and an organizer and spokesman for the failed Populist (People's) Party in 1896. He was born in New York City, educated at Columbia College, and accepted by the New York bar. However, Lloyd decided to pursue reform journalism instead. His first reform was a success, but the electoral campaign to defeat New York's Boss Tweed and Tammany Hall in 1871 was also his last political victory. Participation in the ill-fated 1872 Liberal Republican Party convention soured him forever on traditional politics. Lloyd worked for the *Chicago Tribune* from 1872 until 1885, contributing reviews, editorials, and articles to one of the most-respected newspapers of the day. He was able to retire from his position in 1885, and he devoted the remainder of his life to writing and agitating for social reforms.

Lloyd's best-remembered endeavor was his 1894 *Wealth Against Commonwealth*, a blistering attack on the Standard Oil Company that helped tilt governmental policies against monopolies. He supported the People's Party in 1896, endorsing a platform that included land, transportation and financial reforms. When the Populists were persuaded to merge with the Democrats in part by William Jennings Bryan's stirring "Cross of Gold" speech, Lloyd correctly predicted that the merger would lead to the downfall of populism. He became interested himself chiefly in producers' cooperatives and Fabian Socialism during the latter years of his life. Lloyd died unexpectedly while leading a fight to establish a publicly owned streetcar utility in Chicago.

See also: William Jennings Bryan, Liberal Republican Party, People's Party, Tammany Hall

Richard Digby-Junger

REFERENCES

Destler, Chester M. 1963. *Henry Demarest Lloyd and the Empire of Reform.* Philadelphia: U. of Pennsylvania Pr.

Jernigan, E. Jay. 1976. *Henry Demarest Lloyd.* Boston: Twayne.

Lloyd, Caroline A. 1912. *Henry Demarest Lloyd, 1847–1903: A Biography.* New York: Putnam's.

Lloyd, Henry D. 1896. "The Populists at St. Louis." 14 *Review of Reviews* 296.

Henry Cabot Lodge (1850–1924)

Successful Senate opponent of America's entry into the League of Nations. A member of the House of Representatives and United States Senator from Massachusetts, Henry Cabot Lodge was born to wealthy Boston parents, educated privately, and graduated from Harvard in 1871. He got his law degree from Harvard in 1874. In the meanwhile Lodge developed an interest in medieval history, and under the direction of Harvard's Henry Adams, he completed a Ph.D. in history there in 1876.

Lodge served as assistant editor of the *North American Review*, taught American history at Harvard, and wrote history and biography.

Lodge entered politics in 1879 when he served two terms as a Republican in the Massachusetts state legislature. He was elected to the U.S. House of Representatives in 1886, remaining in the House until 1893 when he was elected to the U.S. Senate. Lodge served in the Senate without interruption until his death.

As a Congressman, Lodge was an able and aggressive partisan Republican whose position on major domestic issues differed little from other northeastern Republicans. he staunchly opposed the reforms sponsored by Democrats and western Republicans during the Progressive era, but his main concern throughout his long career in the Senate was foreign affairs. Soon after he entered the Senate, he was put on the Foreign Relations Committee, where for over 20 years he proved to be one of the dominant personalities in the formulation of U.S. foreign policy.

Lodge and Theodore Roosevelt, his close friend, advocated a departure from the traditional isolationism that had characterized U.S. foreign affairs in the nineteenth century. Lodge advocated an aggressive, nationalistic foreign policy requiring that the United States participate actively in world affairs. He favored the construction of a large American navy and a dominant, imperialistic role for the United States in Latin America. As early as the 1890s he had frequent recourse to the Monroe Doctrine to justify American supremacy in Latin America; he was altogether willing to support the use of force if necessary to enforce American superiority in the Western Hemisphere. During Theodore Roosevelt's administration, Lodge was frequently consulted on foreign policy matters, but he played a much more negative role after Roosevelt left the presidency.

After Woodrow Wilson became President in 1913, Lodge emerged as one of the President's most vocal and partisan critics. He denounced Wilson's efforts to cope with the Mexican revolution as weak and ineffectual, and he condemned Wilson's efforts to preserve American neutrality in the early years of World War I. Lodge wholeheartedly supported the cause of Great Britain and France, and after the United States declared war on Germany in 1917, Lodge led the Republican assault against Wilson's conduct of the war. He believed that the interests of the country were best served by the unconditional surrender of Germany, and he was wholly convinced that Wilson's "weak" peace program would permit a future resurgence of German militarism. As chair of the Foreign Relations Committee in 1919 and 1920, Lodge was one of those most responsible for the Senate's refusal to ratify the Treaty of Versailles.

See also: Henry Adams, Isolationism in American Politics, Theodore Roosevelt, Woodrow Wilson

Howard W. Allen

REFERENCES

Garraty, John A. 1953. *Henry Cabot Lodge: A Biography.* New York: Knopf.

Henry Cabot Lodge, Jr. (1902–1985)

Republican moderate, Massachusetts U.S. Senator, journalist, and diplomat. Henry Cabot Lodge, Jr., was the grandson of Woodrow Wilson's nemesis, the elder Henry Cabot Lodge, who raised him after the early death of his father. Lodge was an almost perfect personification of the New England patrician ideal of devotion to public service. Originally named Henry Cabot Lodge, Jr., he dropped the "Jr." in 1956 and was called "Cabot" by family and friends.

Lodge graduated from Harvard in 1924 after earlier schooling in France, where he became fluent in the language. He became a journalist, heeding his grandfather's advice that journalism would be the best preparation for a public career. Lodge covered the Republican conventions of

1924, 1928, and 1932 for the *New York Herald-Tribune* after an earlier stint with the *Boston Transcript*. In 1933 he was elected to the lower chamber of the Massachusetts General Court (the House of Delegates) and was reelected in 1934. There he helped pass legislation that liberalized the state's workmen's compensation law. In 1936 he defeated the Boston-Irish spellbinding governor, James Michael Curley, for the U.S. Senate by 135,000 votes—the only Republican in the nation to win a Senate seat in that Democratic landslide year. As one of only 17 Republican Senators, Lodge immediately associated with Republican leader Charles McNary. As a freshman, Lodge generally backed Franklin D. Roosevelt's domestic programs. But he was an isolationist in foreign affairs, even more so than his grandfather had been. A turning point for him was his support of the Lend-Lease agreement. A member of the reserves since 1924, Lodge served with the U.S. Army in 1941 and 1942. When Secretary of War Henry Stimson refused his request for further duty, Lodge resigned from the Senate in 1944—the first member to resign to go to war since the Civil War.

Lodge was elected to the Senate from Massachusetts in 1946 as a much-decorated veteran. A member of the Senate Foreign Relations Committee, he became a leader of the liberal internationalist wing of the Republican Party. In this term, he voted for Greek-Turkish aid and the NATO treaty. He also co-sponsored the Lodge-Gassett constitutional amendment to abolish the Electoral College, a somewhat radical bill that easily passed the Senate in 1950 but was defeated in the House. The Lodge-Brown bill of 1947, creating the Hoover Commission for the purpose of reorganizing the executive branch, did pass.

A leader of the "modern Republican" movement even before that phrase was coined, Lodge helped write the 1948 Republican platform that called for federal aid to housing, more old-age insurance, and civil rights legislation. Lodge's was the platform that Harry Truman tactically called the Republican Congress into special session to enact, knowing that it did not reflect the usual party line. Lodge initiated and directed Dwight Eisenhower's presidential campaign in 1952, inducing him to enter primaries while still serving with NATO in Europe. Lodge was his campaign surrogate until Eisenhower returned in June. Lodge gained the enmity of the Robert Taft forces by securing Eisenhower's nomination on the first ballot after a bitter credentials fight to seat the Texas, Georgia, and Louisiana delegations. This partisanship, together with his own excessive attention to managing Eisenhower's presidential campaign, resulted in his own defeat for reelection by 70,000 votes by John F. Kennedy, even as Eisenhower carried Massachusetts and the nation.

Lodge presided over the transition team after the election. He became the longest serving U.S. ambassador to the United Nations (1953–1960), receiving both Cabinet rank and a position on the National Security Council. As a high-profile ambassador, Lodge really did formulate foreign policy rather than just enunciate it. He also counseled Eisenhower on domestic politics and public opinion.

In 1960 Richard Nixon selected Lodge as his running mate over Senator Thruston Morton. As the most popular of the four nominees for national office that year, the blunt Lodge probably undermined Nixon's overtures to the South with his unauthorized pledge in a Harlem speech that the Republican administration would put an African-American in the Cabinet. Some GOP leaders also criticized Lodge's restrained campaigning style as detrimental to the ticket.

In June 1963 Lodge was President Kennedy's appointee as ambassador to South Vietnam, probably the most difficult and sensitive foreign post existing at the time, to show bipartisan support for beleaguered American interests there. His acceptance of this position came on the heels of his own son's loss in Massachusetts to Edward Kennedy in the 1962 contest for the U.S. Senate seat that John Kennedy and Lodge had both held.

In March 1964 Lodge won the New Hampshire Republican presidential primary on a write-in with 35 percent of the vote in a crowded field. But the campaign, which he did not promote, ended in Oregon in May when Lodge did not return from South Vietnam. He resigned in June to do for another what he had not done for himself. He backed William Scranton for president, pleading with the Republican platform committee in vain to change conservative Barry Goldwater–endorsed planks. Devoting himself afterward to helping Republican state candidates in Massachusetts, Lodge assisted in the return of John Volpe as governor and the election of Edward Brooke as Massachusetts's first Black attorney general.

With the end of his active involvement in political campaigns, Lodge returned to diplomacy as ambassador to South Vietnam (1965–1967), ambassador at large (1967–1968), ambassador to West Germany (1968–1969), U.S. representative to the Paris peace talks in 1969, and special envoy to the Vatican (1970–1977).

See also: Dwight D. Eisenhower, Election of 1960, Hoover Commission, Edward M. Kennedy, John F. Kennedy, Richard M. Nixon, Harry S Truman, United Nations, Woodrow Wilson

Frederick J. Augustyn, Jr.

REFERENCES

Lodge, Henry Cabot. 1973. *The Storm Has Many Eyes: A Personal Narrative.* New York: Norton.

———. 1976. *As It Was: An Inside View of Politics and Power in the '50s and '60s.* New York: Norton.

Miller, William J. 1967. *Henry Cabot Lodge: A Biography.* New York: Heinemann.

Southwick, Leslie H. 1984. *Presidential Also-Rans and Running Mates, 1788–1980.* Jefferson, NC: McFarland.

Lodge Force Bill

See Federal Election Bill of 1890

William Loeb (1905–1981)

Controversial newspaper publisher who dominated New Hampshire. For 35 years, from 1946 until his death, William Loeb was the publisher and guiding force behind the arch-conservative, and often blisteringly offensive, *Manchester Union-Leader*, the preeminent newspaper in the state of New Hampshire. Loeb's brand of journalism—featuring colorful, hard-hitting, and irreverent front-page editorials and a breakdown in the distinction between the editorial and news coverage policies of the paper—made him an influential figure in state politics, in which he withheld support from any candidate who refused to take a Loeb-invented "pledge," which Loeb invented, not to support a sales or an income tax in New Hampshire. He also carried some weight in national politics because of New Hampshire's first-in-the-nation presidential primary.

Loeb's journalistic repertoire included relentless attack and ridicule of the major figures of the day. Presidential candidates whom he opposed were exposed to special treatment. Eisenhower became "Dopey Dwight"; Johnson, "Snake Oil Lyndon"; Nixon, "Tricky Dicky"; Ford, "Gerry the Jerk"; and Carter, "the little pip-squeak who calls himself our President." Personal attacks on Jane Muskie, reprinted in the *Union-Leader*, led to the famous speech in front of the paper's offices in 1972 in which Senator Edmund Muskie "cried" while defending his wife's honor, one of the first steps in his fall from front-runner status for the Democratic presidential nomination. In 1980 relentless attacks on George Bush by Loeb and the *Union-Leader* were instrumental in helping Ronald Reagan to regain the momentum that he had lost in the Iowa caucus during that year's Republican nominating campaign.

The overall influence of the *Union-Leader* has declined since Loeb's death, largely because of population shifts within New Hampshire and the subsequent influence of the Boston media market on the state's politics. But Loeb and his newspaper's suzerainty over the state's politics remains a quintessential example of the potential of a politically committed media monopoly to influence the democratic process.

See also: George Bush, Jimmy Carter, Dwight D. Eisenhower, Elections of 1972 and 1980, Gerald Ford, Lyndon B. Johnson, Edmund Muskie, Richard M. Nixon, Presidential Nominating Politics, Ronald Reagan

Robert E. Craig

REFERENCES

Cash, Kevin. 1975. *Who the Hell Is William Loeb?* Manchester, NH: Amoskeag Press.

Mayer, Andrew, John Mayer, Jim Becker, and D. B. Johnson. 1979. *Protect the President! and Other Outrageous Editorials from the Ultra-Right Newspaper Publisher.* Meredith, NH: Intervale Publishing.

Orren, Gary P., and Nelson W. Polsby. 1987. *Media and Momentum: The New Hampshire Primary and Nominating Politics.* Chatham, NJ: Chatham House.

John A. Logan (1826–1887)

Civil War period Illinois politician. As a youthful Illinois legislator, John Alexander Logan's first political act was to push through to enactment a law prohibiting the immigration of African-Americans into the state. That made him an instant hero in his conservative home district, Egypt, lying between the Ohio and Mississippi rivers. In 1858 Egypt sent Logan to Congress, the stout supporter of Stephen A. Douglas and enemy of any who, like Abraham Lincoln, opposed the Kansas-Nebraska Act allowing slavery in the territories.

Lincoln's 1860 election and southern secession left Egypt and Logan in the lurch. Months of hesitation followed before Logan recovered his political balance, raised a regiment, and as a colonel under fellow Illinoisian, Ulysses S. Grant, went to war. His military career culminated with command of the Army of Tennessee, service that made his sobriquet, "Black Jack," a legend in both the North and South. He emerged from the siege of Vicksburg as one of Grant's favorite generals. Under William Tecumseh Sherman he commanded the 15th Corps, taking the brunt of Confederate General Hood's furious attacks during the Battle of Atlanta. South Carolinians still think of Logan and his Corps as the incendiaries of Columbia during the war's final months.

Logan returned to Illinois politics waving the "bloody shirt," reminding Egypt's voters of his personal heroism and the "treason" of the party of his Democratic opponents. He was reelected to Congress in 1867, and he served there as a Senator from 1871 until his death. It helped him fashion one of the enduring Republican political machines of the Gilded Age. To organize Union veterans into a political force, he helped create of the Grand Army of the Republic (GAR). For patronage, he relied heavily on President Grant. As an apt machine politician, he resisted civil service reform. As a "Stalwart," he supported Grant in 1880 for a third term. Republican reformers ("Mugwumps") and moderates ("Half-breeds") successfully blocked Grant, but they could never break Logan's grip on Illinois. That grip put him on the national ticket with moderate James G. Blaine in 1884. Logan was preparing to run for the presidency when he died. His death brought down the final curtain on the politics of party building around the issues, the emotions, the folklore, and the personal relationships that grew out of the Civil War.

See also: James G. Blaine, Bloody Shirt, Stephen Douglas, Ulysses S. Grant, Andrew Johnson, Kansas-Nebraska Act, Abraham Lincoln, Mugwumps, Stalwarts (and Half-breeds)

Charles W. Bassett

REFERENCES

Bonadio, Felice A. 1970. *North of Reconstruction: Ohio Politics, 1865–1870.* New York: New York U. Pr.

Jones, James Pickett. 1967. *"Black Jack": John A. Logan and Southern Illinois in the Civil War Era.* Tallahassee: Florida State U. Pr.

———. 1982. *John A. Logan: Stalwart Republican from Illinois.* Tallahassee: Florida State U. Pr.

Marcus, Robert D. 1971. *Grand Old Party: Political Structure in the Gilded Age, 1880–1896.* New York: Oxford U. Pr.

Mohr, James C. 1973. *The Radical Republicans and Reform in New York During Reconstruction.* Ithaca: Cornell U. Pr.

———, ed. 1976. *Radical Republicans in the North: State Politics During Reconstruction.* Baltimore: Johns Hopkins U. Pr.

Woodward, C. Vann. 1951. *Reunion and Reaction: The Compromise of 1877 and the End of Reconstruction.* Boston: Little, Brown.

Martin Lomasney (1859–1933)

Boston ward heeler. Martin Lomasney ruled downtown Boston's West End for almost half a century and in his personal reputation took on legendary proportions as perhaps the strongest ward boss in America. Born in Boston, the son of an Irish immigrant who had fled the famine, Lomasney was orphaned as a boy, quit school at ten to find a job and join a gang, and came of age as a street-hardened working-class tough. Ward-heeling in the West End landed him city work as a lamplighter and grudging respect from Irish Democratic neighbors. He seized leadership of his ward in 1885 when he organized the Hendricks Club (named for Grover Cleveland's Vice President, a favorite among Irish immigrants) and then took charge of the local caucus. True to his working-class origins, he called himself a "six o'clock Democrat," admired Ben Butler, and mistrusted efforts to ally the Boston Irish with Yankee Mugwump "highbrows" to promote civic reform.

Lomasney's political purposes were more local. "I think that there's got to be in every ward somebody that any bloke can come to—no matter what he's done—and get help," he later told Lincoln Steffens. "Help, you understand; none of your law and your justice, but help." The depression of the 1890s greatly enhanced the power of politicians with these priorities. Elected an alderman in 1892, Lomasney later served his constituents for several terms in the state legislature, becoming Democratic floor leader in the Massachusetts House after 1910. His voting record revealed him as a pro-labor bread-and-butter liberal who opposed executive authority and public meddling in private lives. Devilishly skilled in the infighting of citywide factional politics, throwing his strength unpredictably over the years, Lomasney won few close friends, but a durable host of devoted admirers.

See also: Bosses, Grover Cleveland, Mugwumps

Geoffrey Blodgett

REFERENCES

Ainley, Leslie. 1949. *Boston Mahatma: The Public Career of Martin Lomasney.* Boston: Bruce Humphreys.

Blodgett, Geoffrey. 1966. *The Gentle Reformers: Massachusetts Democrats in the Cleveland Era.* Cambridge: Harvard U. Pr.

Buenker, John D. 1973. *Urban Liberalism and Progressive Reform.* New York: Scribner's.

Steffens, Lincoln. 1931. *The Autobiography of Lincoln Steffens*. New York: Harcourt Brace.

Van Nostrand, A. D. 1948. "The Lomasney Legend." 21 *New England Quarterly* 435.

Earl K. Long (1895–1960)

Keeper of the Long machine's flame. Earl Kemp Long significantly contributed to the power and longevity of the most successful, enduring political dynasty in Louisiana. Earl was the younger brother of Huey Long, a governor and later Senator of Louisiana who became nationally famous during the early 1930s for his "Share the Wealth" proposal and leftist criticism of the New Deal. Born in 1895 in Winfield, Louisiana, Earl attended Loyola University in New Orleans and passed his bar exam as a special student. He was appointed to his first public office, as inheritance tax collector for the parish of Orleans, in 1928 and held it until 1932.

In 1936 Long was elected lieutenant governor and served in this office until 1939 when he succeeded Governor Richard Leche, who resigned in the wake of well-publicized scandals involving Leche and other top state officials. Long ran for governor in his own right, narrowly loosing the 1940 Democratic gubernatorial primary to the anti-Long reform candidate, Sam Houston Jones. He came back to defeat Jones in the 1948 Democratic primary and served as governor until 1952.

Long was again elected governor in 1956, serving until 1960. Despite his womanizing, drinking, and brief but widely publicized committal to mental hospitals in Texas and Louisiana in 1959, Long easily won the Democratic primary for the Eighth Congressional District of Louisiana in 1960. He died of a heart attack in September 1960, one week after his victory in the runoff primary.

See also: Huey Long, New Deal

Sean J. Savage

REFERENCES

Bass, Jack, and Walter De Vries. 1976. *The Transformation of Southern Politics*. New York: Basic Books.

Key, V. O., Jr. 1984. *Southern Politics in State and Nation*. Knoxville: U. of Tennessee Pr.

Liebling, A. J. 1970. *The Earl of Louisiana*. Baton Rouge: Louisiana State U. Pr.

Opotowsky, Stan. 1960. *The Longs of Louisiana*. New York: Dutton.

Sindler, Allan P. 1980. *Huey Long's Louisiana: State Politics, 1920–1952*. Westport, CT: Greenwood.

Huey Long (1893–1935)

"Kingfish" of Louisiana politics. Hugh Pierce ("Huey") Long, Jr., Louisiana governor (1928– 1932) and U.S. Senator (1932–1935), posed probably the most serious political challenge to President Franklin D. Roosevelt in the mid-1930s. Though he has been called an American fascist and often acted the part of a rural buffoon, Huey Long was neither; rather, he was an extraordinarily bright and able man, fueled by both personal ambition and social concern and flawed by his self-aggrandizing and corrupt use of power. A product of the populistic piney woods and hill country of northern Louisiana, Long, a largely self-educated lawyer, came to public prominence in the 1920s as chairman of the Louisiana Public Service Commission. After first being defeated for governor in 1924, Long came back to win the governorship in 1928 by rallying Louisiana's rural areas and common folk against the planter class, the big corporations (especially oil), and the Old Regular machine of New Orleans. As governor, Long implemented impressive programs for public roads, buildings, education, and health and brought some tax reform as well. A force for dramatic change and no racial demagogue, Long nonetheless provided little significant social reform for Louisiana. He ruthlessly turned the state into a virtual dictatorship, after escaping conviction following his impeachment for bribery and misconduct in 1929.

But the "Kingfish" of Louisiana had larger national ambitions. After arranging a satisfactory succession to his governorship and continued control of state politics, in 1932 Long assumed the U.S. Senate seat to which he had been elected in 1930. He fiercely criticized Herbert Hoover's administration, advocated redistribution of wealth as the solution to the Great Depression, and provided important early support for Roosevelt's nomination. Long soon fell out with FDR, however, partly because the New Deal seemed too conservative to Long and partly because Roosevelt (who denied him federal patronage) plainly stood in the way of Long's desire for national power. In January 1934 Long organized the Share Our Wealth Society. His "Share Our Wealth" plan called for the liquidation of large personal fortunes and a redistribution of wealth that would, among other things, provide each American family with a homestead allowance of $5,000, an annual income of $2,500, a car, and a radio. Long and his program attracted considerable support outside the South and the countryside, his millions of followers evidently coming largely from the struggling lower middle class. A poll conducted for the

Democratic National Committee indicated that Long might poll as much as 10 percent of the presidential vote on a third-party ticket in 1936. In August 1935 Long declared for the presidency; in September he was assassinated by Dr. Carl A. Weiss in Baton Rouge.

Huey Long's impact proved ephemeral nationally but far more lasting in Louisiana. He perhaps helped speed the passage of parts of FDR's "Second New Deal" of 1935 and certainly (and probably excessively) worried Democratic Party leaders; for all that, after his death the Share Our Wealth movement collapsed and few of his supporters followed Long lieutenant Gerald L. K. Smith into the ill-fated Union Party of 1936. In Louisiana, economic issues and Long's legacy remained central to politics, as did the Long machine, which soon came to terms with the Roosevelt administration and with local conservative interests in order to perpetuate its power.

See also: Democratic National Committee, Election of 1936, Franklin D. Roosevelt, Union Party

John W. Jeffries

REFERENCES

Brinkley, Alan. 1982. *Voices of Protest: Huey Long, Father Coughlin, and the Great Depression.* New York: Knopf.

Sindler, Allan P. 1956. *Huey Long's Louisiana: State Politics, 1920–1952.* Baltimore: Johns Hopkins U. Pr.

Williams, T. Harry. 1969. *Huey Long.* New York: Knopf.

Russell B. Long (1918–)

Democratic Senator from Louisiana. Russell Billiu Long, a Democratic Senator from Louisiana from 1948 to 1986, made his major legislative marks as a member of the Senate's powerful Finance Committee. He served as its chairman from 1966 to 1980 and as its ranking minority member from 1981 to 1986. A skillful, combative debater like his father, Louisiana's legendary Huey Long, Russell played a major role in tax, health care, trade, and energy policy throughout his long and productive legislative career. A self-styled "economic populist," who professed to look after the "little people," Long seldom missed an opportunity to further the economic interests of his state—oil and gas production, sulphur mining, sugar cane–refining, lumbering and fishing, rice and cotton farming. Likable and ebullient, Long was quick to tap into the friendship, camaraderie, and goodwill that characterizes most American legislative bodies. He was especially adept at negotiating quid pro quos and crafting legislative compromises.

In 1965 Long successfully ran for Senate Majority Whip, only to lose four years later to a late challenge from Massachusetts Senator Edward Kennedy. In 1971 Kennedy would lose, in turn, to Robert Byrd of West Virginia, whose candidacy Long vigorously supported.

Although he was to occupy positions of great power and influence in the U.S. Senate for most of his career, Long's career was controversial, torn between advocacy of his father's more populist inspirations and his support of corporate interests in the Louisiana mold. "What is a loophole?" he once asked. "That is something that benefits the other guy. If it benefits you, it is tax reform." Russell Long retired from the Senate in 1985.

See also: Robert Byrd, Edward M. Kennedy, Huey Long

Robert L. Peabody

REFERENCES

Hess, Stephen. 1966. *America's Political Dynasties: From Adams to Kennedy.* Garden City, NY: Doubleday.

Peabody, Robert L. 1976. *Leadership in Congress: Stability, Succession and Change.* Boston, Little, Brown.

Long Ballot

A lengthy ballot containing an extraordinary number of elective offices and issues to be voted upon. Long ballots are most prevalent in state and local elections in which numerous executive and judicial offices must be filled in addition to legislative seats. The long ballot is a carry-over from the Jacksonian Democratic era of the late 1820s and 1830s. During this period, the number of elective offices was generally expanded on the premise that democracy would be strengthened if citizens had direct electoral control over all the officials who governed them.

The long ballot in some instances has had a negative impact on voter participation, particularly in contests and issues near the end of the ballot. Roll-off (alternately, drop-off or fall-off) occurs when fewer votes are cast for contests and/or issues placed further down a lengthy ballot. Roll-off can occur for a number of reasons: (1) the race itself is uninteresting; (2) the voter feels informed only about the salient, high-visibility contests near the top of the ballot; (3) referenda issues are confusing either in content or wording; or (4) the physical layout of the ballot itself is confusing.

Nevertheless, long ballots have been found to enhance the strength of political parties and political machines. Where an election features too many candidates, contests, and issues with which voters can become familiar, they tend to use party as their primary voting cue. Long ballots also enhance the power of incumbency, particularly in nonpartisan elections. Not being familiar with the qualifications of all the candidates running for a multitude of offices, voters are more likely to use name recognition as a primary voting cue.

Roll-off has been found to be most acute in initiative and referendum voting. Typically some 20 percent to 25 percent of the voters abstain from voting on initiative or referendum propositions. However, if the issue is highly newsworthy or controversial, roll-off may be minimal. Blacks, older voters, and less-educated voters have shown themselves to be less likely to vote for propositions at the end of the ballot.

Political parties can influence voting patterns on initiative and referendum issues. "For the most part voting on the propositions is a strikingly idiosyncratic process, although campaigning, especially if it is by political parties, does seem to structure opinion on these few propositions on which it is conducted." America has seen a slight trend toward short ballots since they were first advocated by progressive reformers at the end of the nineteenth century. But state and local governments still tend to use much longer ballots than does the national government.

See also: Drop-Off

Susan A. MacManus

REFERENCES

Bain, Henry M., and Donald S. Hecock. 1957. *Ballot Position and Voters Choice*. Detroit: Wayne State U. Pr.

Butler, David, and Austin Ranney, eds. 1978. *Referendums: A Comparative Study of Practice and Theory*. Washington: American Enterprise Institute for Public Policy Research.

Clubb, Jerome M., and Michael W. Traugott. 1972. "National Patterns of Referenda Voting in the 1968 Election." In Harlan Hahn, ed. *People and Politics in Urban Society*. Beverly Hills, CA: Sage.

Darcy, R. 1986. "Position Effect with Party Column Ballots." 39 *Western Political Quarterly* 648.

———, and Anne Larason Schneider. 1987. "Confusing Ballots: Roll-off and the Black Vote." Paper presented at the annual meeting of the American Political Science Association, Chicago.

Magleby, David B. 1984. *Direct Legislation: Voting on Ballot Propositions in the United States*. Baltimore: Johns Hopkins U. Pr.

Mueller, John E. 1969. "Voting on the Propositions: Ballot Patterns and Historical Trends in California." 63 *American Political Science Review* 1197.

James B. Longley (1925–1980)

Independent governor of Maine. James B. Longley was elected governor of Maine as an Independent in 1974, defeating well-established Democratic and Republican candidates. Born, raised, and educated in Maine, Longley rose from a humble background to become a millionaire insurance executive while still in his early forties. In 1972 Kenneth Curtis, the Democratic governor of Maine, drew on Longley's reputation in business and his political independence, asking him to chair a group looking into more efficient management of the costs of state government. Longley used the Maine Management and Cost Survey as a pulpit from which to launch his own political career.

In 1974 Longley announced his candidacy for governor on a platform of cutting the cost of state government. Neither state Attorney General James Erwin, the Republican candidate, nor George Mitchell, the Democratic candidate, took Longley's candidacy as seriously as did the people of the state. Over the last weekend before the vote, Longley ran an advertisement aimed at giving his candidacy credibility: "Governor Longley: Think About It!" The appeal worked, and Longley was elected by approximately 40 percent of the frugal Maine voters in the three-way race.

Longley attracted national attention with his unique style and his efforts to apply business decision-making methods to state government problems. Highly energetic, he was a popular governor within Maine. He attracted considerable media attention for his efforts to reduce the size and costs of state government through substantial reductions in education, transportation, and social programs. Positioning himself in an adversarial relationship with both parties in the state legislature, he vetoed a record 109 bills during his single term; more than half of those vetoes were overridden.

Jim Longley billed himself as a citizen-politician, fighting the vested interests. Though tempted to remain in office, he fulfilled a pledge he made during the 1974 campaign to serve only one term. His short career was significant not only in demonstrating the potential for Independent or third-party candidacies but also for showing how difficult it could be really to govern effectively without support of one or the other of the major parties. Longley's fiscal conservatism and mastery of mass media were precursors of successful presidential politics in the years following his retirement.

See also: Kenneth Curtis, George Mitchell

Kenneth P. Hayes

Nicholas Longworth (1869–1931)

Republican Speaker of the pre-Depression House of Representatives. Nicholas Longworth was a longtime member of the U.S. House of Representatives, serving as Speaker from 1925 to 1931. Longworth was born into one of the wealthiest families in Cincinnati, Ohio. Longworth graduated from Harvard University in 1891 and from the Cincinnati Law School in 1894, entering law and politics in Cincinnati under the leadership of "Boss" George B. Cox's Republican political organization. In 1899 he was elected to the Ohio House of Representatives and in 1901 to the Ohio Senate.

In 1903 Longworth was elected as a Republican to the U.S. House of Representatives where he early identified himself as a dependable conservative Republican who always backed the party leadership during a period of insurgency and progressivism. In the bitter presidential election of 1912, the dependable Longworth supported GOP incumbent William H. Taft (even though he was the son-in-law of Taft's opponent Theodore Roosevelt); he was rewarded by the loss of his seat in the House. Two years later, however, he was reelected, and by 1920 he had become identified as one of the most effective and most popular Republicans in the House of Representatives. He served as Republican floor leader form 1923 to 1925 when he was elected Speaker, a position he held until the Democrats captured control of the House in 1931.

Despite his reputation as a bon vivant, Longworth was a serious legislator who revered the House of Representatives. Longworth's conservatism fit comfortably into the 1920s and the administrations of Warren Harding, Calvin Coolidge, and Herbert Hoover, and in these years he made his major mark on history. Longworth restored some of the power and prestige to the Speaker's position that had been lost after the 1910 reform of the House rules and during Woodrow Wilson's administration when the President often overshadowed the Speaker. In the administrations of the inactive Presidents in the 1920s, Longworth as Speaker became an important force in national politics. Such leadership in the Speaker's chair had not been seen since Joseph G. Cannon's tenure as Speaker, but unlike Cannon, Longworth did his job with good fellowship and congeniality. He accommodated, compromised, and charmed members on both sides of the aisle to conduct the House's business. He was especially close to John Nance Garner, a Democrat from Texas and Minority Leader from 1929 to 1931. The two of them conducted a regular informal meeting— "the Board of Education"—in which many of the controversies of the House were resolved in a friendly, bipartisan atmosphere. Some authorities rank Nicholas Longworth as one of the most able Speakers of the House of Representatives in the twentieth century.

See also: Joseph Cannon, Election of 1912, John Nance Garner, Theodore Roosevelt, Speaker of the House

Howard W. Allen

REFERENCES

de Chambrun, Clara Longworth. 1933. *The Making of Nicholas Longworth: Annals of an American Family.* New York: Ray Long & Richard R. Smith.

MacNeil, Neil. 1973. *Forge of Democracy: The House of Representatives.* New York: David McKay.

Ripley, Randall B. 1967. *Party Leaders in the House of Representatives.* Washington: Brookings.

Loophole Primaries

Winner-take-all primaries have been banned by the Democratic Party since the early 1970s. Loophole primaries produce results equivalent to winner-take-all primaries, while technically not using winner-take-all rules. In other words, loophole primaries are those in which a candidate who does not receive 100 percent of the vote can still receive 100 percent of a state's convention delegates.

Loophole primaries involve the direct election of national party convention delegates. Names of individuals seeking to be convention delegates are listed on the primary ballot along with an indication of which presidential candidate they support. Delegates are elected by congressional districts with several delegates selected from each district. Simple plurality election rules are used so as to assure that those individuals receiving the most votes are chosen.

In voting for convention delegates, primary voters tend to vote only for those delegates who are supporting one candidate. A CBS News/New York Times exit poll of voters in the 1984 California Democratic primary found that 87 percent voted for delegates supporting a single candidate. With voters casting ballots for delegates supporting one particular candidate, the presidential candidate with the most supporters in a congressional district will see all of his or her delegates elected. The results, then, appear as if winner-take-all rules had been used.

Loophole primary rules are most often used by more populous states. State party leaders feel that loophole primaries will give their states more clout in the nomination process, specifically because they can deliver a large bloc of delegates supporting a single candidate. Loophole primaries also are favored by front-runner candidates because they can acquire many delegates by winning a single primary.

See also: Delegates to State Nominating Conventions, Exit Polling

Barbara Norrander

REFERENCES

Lengle, James I. 1987. "Democratic Party Reforms." 4 *Journal of Law and Politics* 233.

William Lorimer (1861–1933)

Illinois Republican Party boss. Born in Manchester, England, William Lorimer immigrated with his family to the United States in 1865, moving to Chicago in 1870. As the son of a Presbyterian minister, he never drank, smoked, nor attended the theater. Starting in the 1880s, he developed a strong Republican organization among the traditionally Democratic Irish, Bohemian, and Russian Jewish immigrants on Chicago's West Side through the use of patronage and favors. He also formed alliances with Democratic machine politicians. Lorimer brought together and led several factions within the Republican Party, giving him great power in the GOP in Cook County and more widely in Illinois. From 1894 to 1905, he helped determine the nomination and election of two governors, two U.S. Senators, and numerous city, county, and state officials. From 1894 to 1900, and then from 1902 to 1909, Lorimer represented the Illinois Second District in the House of Representatives, where he was best known for his devotion to local Chicago interests.

William Lorimer was a "political entrepreneur" who regarded politics as a business and who used his power for personal as well as party gain. His organization had strong ties with leading Chicago entrepreneurs like traction magnate Charles Tyson Yerkes, electrical utility builder Samuel Insull, and banker John R. Walsh. Lorimer himself owned several construction companies that won city and county contracts as well as a bank that was loaded with public deposits.

In 1909 a coalition of 55 Republicans and 53 Democrats in the Illinois General Assembly elected Lorimer to the United States Senate. A year later, however, one Democratic state legislator confessed to receiving money for his vote. A U.S. Senate subcommittee investigating the bribery charge concluded that Lorimer's election was not corrupt, a judgment sustained by the entire Senate. In 1912, however, newly elected Republican and Democratic progressives reopened the investigation into the case. Although a majority of the investigating Dillingham Committee held that the doctrine of *res judicata* applied and that Lorimer's election was valid, the full Senate voted 55 to 28 to oust him from the chamber. The Lorimer case undoubtedly played a role in the ratification in 1913 of the Seventeenth Amendment to the Constitution providing for the direct election of U.S. Senators. After his expulsion, Lorimer spent the rest of his life in politics and in business, but he never regained his former power.

Joel A. Tarr

REFERENCES

Hutchinson, William T. 1957. *Lowden of Illinois.* Chicago: U. of Chicago Pr.

Tarr, Joel A. 1971. *A Study in Boss Politics: William Lorimer of Chicago.* Urbana: U. of Illinois Pr.

Louisiana's Nonpartisan Primary

Established in 1975, this type of primary election lists all candidates for an office together on the ballot without regard for party affiliation. In Louisiana's nonpartisan primary, if no candidate wins a majority of votes, then a runoff between the top two is held, regardless of party affiliation or lack thereof. However, since party labels are listed beside each candidate's name, the system is not strictly nonpartisan.

Since Louisiana Democrats had previously held both a primary and a runoff primary before the general election, the new nonpartisan system essentially reduced the number of elections from three to two. Proponents argued that fewer elections would reduce election administration and campaign costs; on the other hand, evidence indicates little diminution in administration because more runoffs have occurred. Campaign expenditures have increased, with most of the money spent on the open primary where candidates hope to win in that initial contest.

The minority Republican Party suffers somewhat because it usually cannot count on Democratic primary divisiveness carrying over to the general election. Indeed, in 1990, two Democrats and no Republicans made it into the runoff in the Second Congressional District. Moreover, incumbents seem to have an advantage. When several strong Democratic candidates divide the normally Democratic votes against a single Republican, however, that Republican may make the runoff and possibly defeat a Democrat who otherwise would have been eliminated in a Democratic runoff primary.

The nonpartisan reform generally undercuts political parties, since it eliminates the party role in making nominations, thereby encouraging voters to view contests as simply a choice among several candidates. Furthermore, to accommodate this change, the ballot had to be restructured from a party column to an office block format, further enhancing ticket splitting.

See also: Runoff Primaries

Douglas I. Hodgkin

REFERENCES

Hadley, Charles D. 1985. "The Impact of the Louisiana Open Elections System Reform." 58 *State Government* 152.

Owen Lovejoy (1811–1864)

Antislavery politician from Illinois. Owen Lovejoy was an abolitionist, an activist in the Underground Railroad, a Liberty Party candidate for Congress in 1846 and 1848, and a founding member of the Republican Party in Illinois. Under the Republican banner he was elected to the Illinois legislature in 1854 and the U.S. House of Representatives in 1856.

Lovejoy's abolitionist commitment was strengthened in 1837 when he saw his brother Elijah, editor of the Alton, Illinois, *Observer*, murdered by a proslavery mob. He vowed, "I shall never forsake the cause that has been sprinkled with my brother's blood." Lovejoy became a leader of the Underground Railroad for escaping slaves in Princeton, Illinois. In 1843 he was prosecuted for harboring two escaped slaves, but he won acquittal on technical grounds. Even when he faced conviction, Lovejoy continued to declare proudly his willingness to help fleeing slaves.

Unlike William Lloyd Garrison, Lovejoy always believed in political action against slavery. He held that the framers had deliberately avoided open references to slavery in the Constitution: thus, it was not a proslavery document. But until the late 1840s he insisted that only single-issue politics was legitimate. However, in 1848 he added support for a homestead law to his platform; then in the wake of the slavery-extending Kansas-Nebraska Act, he helped convince his fellow abolitionists to unite with antislavery Democrats like Lyman Trumbull and Whigs like Abraham Lincoln.

Lovejoy was a powerful orator. The bête noire of the Democrats, he several times disarmed or won over suspicious proslavery crowds by the reasonableness of his arguments and the strength of his speech. Aside from his *Memoir* of Elijah and one poem, his speeches are his only surviving works.

From 1856 on, Lovejoy maintained close relations with Lincoln, serving as a link between Lincoln and the abolitionist radicals. He pressed emancipation on Lincoln privately, while defending Lincoln's fundamental soundness before skeptical abolitionists. Lovejoy began the year 1864 ready to push a bill to make slave owning a criminal offense everywhere in the United States; but, stricken with liver and kidney disease, he died before he could achieve his abolitionist goal.

See also: Abolition Movement, Emancipation as a Political Issue, William Lloyd Garrison, Kansas-Nebraska Act, Liberty Party, Abraham Lincoln, Third Parties in American Elections

John C. Berg

REFERENCES

Berfield, Karen. 1980. "Three Antislavery Leaders of Bureau County." 3 *Western Illinois Regional Studies* 46.

Bohmann, George V. 1963. "Owen Lovejoy on 'The Barbarism of Slavery,' April 5, 1860." In J. Jeffrey Auer, ed. *Antislavery and Disunion, 1858–1861: Studies in the Rhetoric of Compromise and Conflict.* New York and Evanston: Harper & Row.

Magdol, Edward. 1967. *Owen Lovejoy: Abolitionist in Congress.* New Brunswick: Rutgers U. Pr.

Seth Low (1850–1916)

Anti-Tammany New York reformer. Seth Low acted upon his belief that America would never achieve its full potential for greatness without first solving its labor and racial problems. Son of a wealthy New York shipping family, Low organized the Brooklyn Bureau of Charities in 1878 and served as its first president. An active Republican and municipal reformer bent on destroying machine politics and corruption, Low served as mayor of Brooklyn from 1881 to 1885. After declining to seek a third term, Low returned to the family business, then served as president of Columbia University (1890–1901). He strove relentlessly and successfully to achieve his goal: "to build Columbia into a great university, worthy of New York."

Low was elected governor of New York on an independent, anti-Tammany "fusion" ticket in 1901. An enemy of patronage and an advocate of home rule, Low established a brilliant record of fiscal and franchise reform in his not always successful effort to clean up New York politics. His failure to be elected to a second term is in part attributed to his cold, aloof demeanor; to his dullness as a speaker; and to his general lack of political finesse. Nevertheless, his rejection by New York voters inspired President Theodore Roosevelt to observe that the voters of New York would get what they deserved, "The dog has returned to his vomit."

Following his term as governor, Low became chairman of the Tuskegee Institute's board of trustees, promoting African-American self-suf-ficiency as the path to racial acceptance and equality. In his efforts to enhance the rights of labor, he was an active member of the National Civic Federation. As the Federation's president (1908–1911), Low also worked to strengthen antitrust legislation.

See also: Theodore Roosevelt, Tammany Hall

Nancy C. Unger

REFERENCES

Kurkland, Gerald. 1971. *Seth Low: The Reformer in an Urban and Industrial Age*. Boston: Twayne.

Allard Lowenstein (1929–1980)

Anti-Vietnam War organizer. A life-long po-litical activist known for his energetic, ebullient style, Allard Lowenstein is best known for en-gineering the movement to block President Lyndon Johnson's reelection in 1968. Born in Newark, New Jersey, Lowenstein graduated from the University of North Carolina and got his law degree from Yale. He served as president of the National Student Association, chairing the Students for Adlai Stevenson in 1952. After working for a time at the United Nations, Lowenstein briefly sought a congressional seat in 1960, and then taught law and politics at Stanford and North Carolina State universities and City College of New York.

While teaching in New York in 1967 and 1968, Lowenstein canvassed the country in search of a Democratic candidate to oppose Lyndon Johnson's reelection bid; he shared the growing disenchantment with Johnson's han-dling of the Vietnam War. After refusals from Senator George McGovern and Senator Robert Kennedy, he persuaded Senator Eugene McCarthy to enter the race. Despite the fact that McCarthy lost the New Hampshire primary to Johnson, the showing of "Lowenstein's al-ternative" was sufficiently strong to persuade Johnson to bow out. Later that year, Lowenstein scored his own political success by winning election to the House of Representatives from New York's Fifth District. He was defeated in his reelection bid in 1970, however, and ran un-successfully six additional times.

Lowenstein served as an adviser to California governor Edmund G. Brown, Jr., in 1976 and was appointed by President Jimmy Carter to serve at the United Nations. In 1980 he sup-ported Senator Edward Kennedy's presidential bid. In 1980 Lowenstein was shot and killed in his New York law office by Dennis Sweeny, a longtime acquaintance with a background of mental illness.

See also: Jimmy Carter, Election of 1968, Lyndon B. Johnson, Edward M. Kennedy, Robert F. Kennedy, Eugene McCarthy, George McGovern, Adlai Stevenson II, United Nations, Vietnam War as a Political Issue

Robert J. Spitzer

REFERENCES

Chester, Lewis, Godfrey Hodgson, and Bruce Page. 1969. *An American Melodrama*. New York: Dell.

Lubin v. Panish
415 U.S. 709 (1974)

This case held that "in the absence of rea-sonable alternative ballot access, a State may not, consistent with constitutional standards, require from an indigent candidate filing fees he cannot pay."

California required that only after the filing of fees could a candidate's name be placed on the ballot. It also required a fee if a candidate wanted write-in votes to count. The filing fees in California were not nearly so high as those presented in *Bullock v. Carter*, but Donald Paul Lubin could not afford them. The Supreme Court first acknowledged that states have an interest in limiting the size of the ballot. Writing for the Court, Chief Justice Warren Burger suggested that since the Progressive era there had been a steady trend to limit the size of the ballot. He went on, "That 'laundry list' ballots discourage voter participation and confuse and frustrate those who do not participate is too obvious to call for extended discussion. The means of testing the seriousness of a given candidacy may be open to debate; the fundamental importance of ballots of reasonable size limited to serious candidates with some prospect of public support is not." The Chief Justice then noted that several states had seen movements to encourage greater access to the ballot; he saw *Lubin v. Panish* as presenting a conflict between these two worth-while goals.

The Court concluded that ways other than filing fees to demonstrate a candidate's seriousness do exist, but since California had no alternative means, its fees could not withstand constitutional challenge. The opinion ends by suggesting alternate means (e.g., requiring a substantial number of signatures on petitions). As in *Bullock*, the Court saw the restrictions on candidates as burdening the voter; however, it made much less of the voter-candidate nexus. In a concurring opinion, Justice William Douglas argued that the case should be decided on the grounds that wealth classifications are traditionally disfavored. Justice Harry Blackmun also submitted a concurring opinion, joined by Justice William Rehnquist, suggesting that it would be enough to allow write-in votes without requiring that the candidate file a fee.

Aside from its obvious importance to election law, this case provides interesting reading because of its discussions of ballot size.

H. W. Perry, Jr.

Scott W. Lucas (1892–1968)

Illinois Democratic legislator. Scott Wike Lucas's unanimous election as Senate Majority Leader in 1949 confronted him with the difficult task of enacting President Harry Truman's Fair Deal. An ostensible Senate majority of 54 Democrats was frequently strained by the defection of southern Dixiecrats on civil rights issues and by staunch anti-Communists like Pat McCarran on easing admission of displaced persons. Lucas's strength as a Democratic party regular, forged in the House (1935–1939) and the Senate (1939–1950), was insufficient to supply the kind of extraordinary leadership apparently needed in the fractious Eighty-first Congress.

Lucas's difficulties with his Senate confreres, compounded by his identification with Truman's Fair Deal, his defense of internationalism, and the coincidental outbreak of the Korean War, contributed to his own electoral defeat in 1950 by former Congressman Everett M. Dirksen. The independence that he had shown earlier in his career by bucking the Democratic Kelly-Nash Chicago machine to win the senatorial nomination, by publicly opposing President Franklin Roosevelt's plan to "pack" the Supreme Court, by objecting to the choice of Henry Wallace as Vice President, or by winning support from Illinois Republican businessmen were no longer protection against charges of being soft on socialism or too close to corrupt local politicians.

Then, in 1956, when he wanted to run against Senator Dirksen, he was blocked by Governor Adlai Stevenson and Mayor Richard J. Daley, his own party's leaders. The unfortunate Lucas may have been destined for a political career by the prescience of his father who had named him Scott Wike for a local Congressman, but it was the destiny of a small-town lawyer-politician who, thrust into a complex political arena, would eventually be defeated by forces he could neither understand nor control.

See also: Richard Daley, Everett Dirksen, Patrick McCarran, Franklin D. Roosevelt, Adlai Stevenson II, Harry S Truman, Henry Wallace

Mildred A. Schwartz

REFERENCES

Bowen, Laurel G., and Mary Michals. 1984. "The Scott Wike Lucas Collection. Manuscripts and Audiovisual Resources." 77 *Journal of the Illinois State Historical Society* 193.

Dinnerstein, Leonard. 1982. *America and the Survivors of the Holocaust.* New York: Columbia U. Pr.

Hamby, Alonzo L. 1973. *Beyond the New Deal: Harry S Truman and American Liberalism.* New York: Columbia U. Pr.

Schapsmeier, Edward L., and Frederick H. Schapsmeier. 1977. "Scott W. Lucas of Havana. His Rise and Fall as Majority Leader in the United States Senate." 70 *Journal of the Illinois State Historical Society* 302.

Shalett, Sidney. 1950. "The Senator Almost Got an Ulcer." 125 *Collier's* 28.

Georgia L. Lusk (1893–1971)

Winner of seven statewide elections in New Mexico. Georgia Lee Lusk was the most successful female politician in New Mexico history. She served 12 years as superintendent of Public Instruction, head of the state's public school system. In 1946 Lusk, a Democrat, became the only woman from her state ever to be elected to Congress when she won a seat in the House of Representatives. From 1949 to 1953 she was a member of the War Claims Commission, the appointee of President Harry Truman. That agency distributed enemy assets confiscated during World War II to prisoners of war and others who suffered at the hands of the Axis Powers.

Lusk was born on a ranch in New Mexico Territory. She attended a state normal institute and taught school briefly before marrying Dolph Lusk. In 1919 Lusk's husband died, leaving her a 26-year-old widow with three small sons. She reentered the teaching profession and subsequently ran two successful campaigns for county school superintendent before being elected to the state education post.

As state superintendent of Public Instruction, Lusk instituted tougher teacher certification standards and lobbied the legislature for increased funding for schools. During World War II, all of her sons served as officers, and one was killed in the conflict. Consequently, as a postwar member of Congress, Lusk requested appointment to the Veterans Affairs Committee where she was a staunch supporter of veterans' legislation.

See also: Harry S Truman

Roger D. Hardaway

REFERENCES

Hardaway, Roger D. 1979. *Georgia Lusk of New Mexico: A Political Biography*. Book in progress. M.A. thesis, New Mexico State University.

———. 1979. "New Mexico Elects a Congresswoman." 4 *Red River Valley Historical Review* 75.

Sicherman, Barbara, and Carol Hurd Green, eds. 1980. *Notable American Women: The Modern Period*. Cambridge: Belknap Press.

M

William G. McAdoo (1863–1941)

Unsuccessful presidential contender in 1924. Born in Marietta, Georgia, and reared in the aftermath of the Civil War, as a young adult, William Gibbs McAdoo attended the University of Tennessee. After only two years he left to become deputy clerk of the U.S. Circuit Court in Chattanooga, Tennessee. While serving in this capacity, McAdoo simultaneously studied law, and in 1885 he passed the bar. McAdoo briefly practiced law in Chattanooga yet left penniless after a soured deal to establish streetcars in Knoxville. He moved his wife and family to New York to begin a law practice.

While in New York, McAdoo saw the need for a tunnel under the Hudson River. After two unsuccessful attempts by others, McAdoo committed himself to the completion of this project. His role involved not only technical insights but also raising over $60 million to build the Lincoln and Holland tunnels, both of which opened in February 1908.

McAdoo got into politics as a result of his involvement in the building of the tunnels. Because he insisted that the women who were hired to collect tunnel tolls were to be paid an amount equal to what men would receive, he gained a certain notoriety as a liberal. He was called soon after to assist a group of teachers involved in a similar battle for equal pay.

McAdoo went on in 1912 to become Secretary of the Treasury under Woodrow Wilson. His accomplishments included the reform of the banking system, a renovation culminating in the passage of the Federal Reserve Act of 1913. This act called for the substitution of twelve district banks for one central bank and established a seven-person board of overseers for the system. In addition, during his tenure as Secretary of Treasury from 1913 to 1918, McAdoo was instrumental in the financing of America's participation in World War I. During this time, McAdoo, a widower, married his second wife, President Wilson's daughter, Eleanor.

Resigning this position after World War I, McAdoo began to practice law in California. In 1924 he unsuccessfully sought the Democratic presidential nomination. In 1932 McAdoo was a major political player when he led the California delegation that won the Democratic presidential nomination for Franklin Roosevelt.

In 1933 McAdoo again returned to public service, this time as California's U.S. Senator. He lost his Senate post six years later despite his record as a loyal supporter of FDR's New Deal. He was a practical ideologue whose service to his country was outstanding.

See also: Woodrow Wilson

Reagan Robbins

REFERENCES

Burns, James MacGregor. 1956. *Roosevelt: The Lion and the Fox.* New York: Harcourt Brace Jovanovich.

McAdoo, William G. 1931. *Crowded Years.* Boston: Houghton Mifflin.

Miller, Nathan. 1983. *FDR: An Intimate History.* Garden City, NY: Doubleday.

Synon, Mary. 1924. *McAdoo.* Indianapolis: Bobbs-Merrill.

Douglas MacArthur (1880–1964)

War hero turned presidential hopeful. Douglas MacArthur is best known for his role as commander of Allied forces in the Southwest Pacific theater during World War II and commander of United Nations forces in Korea during 1950 and 1951. Military fame brought with it political opportunities, and MacArthur drew support from many in the right wing of the Republican Party for the presidential nomination in 1944, 1948, and 1952.

First mention of MacArthur as a potential candidate came in 1942 after he gained hero status for his leadership in fighting the Japanese in the Philippines. Senator Arthur H. Vandenberg and Robert E. Wood, board chairman of Sears, Roebuck, took the lead in a secret movement to generate political support for MacArthur in hopes that he might be drafted as a presidential nominee should the 1944 Republican convention become deadlocked between the leading candidates, Wendell L. Willkie and Thomas E. Dewey. MacArthur apparently coveted the nomination and was a legitimate contender until April 1944 when, against the advice of Vandenberg, zealous supporters in Wisconsin entered his name in the primary election. The general was stung by a third place finish behind Harold E. Stassen and Thomas E. Dewey. MacArthur responded with a public statement that he was not a candidate for the presidency.

MacArthur more avidly pursued the 1948 nomination. He hoped that a conservative trend in the nation and the prestige of being a de facto head of state as supreme commander of the Allied Powers in the occupation of Japan would bring political success at home. His strongest supporter was again Robert E. Wood, and he was also favored by former President Herbert Hoover. On March 9, 1948, MacArthur made a public statement implying that he would accept the nomination if it were offered to him. Supporters then entered his name in the Wisconsin primary, which was held on April 6, where he finished a poor second behind Harold Stassen. Then, a week later, after a fifth place finish in the Nebraska primary, there was hardly any hope left for his nomination.

The general's political star rose once again in April 1951 when President Harry S Truman relieved him of assorted commands of American forces in the Far East and he returned home to a hero's welcome, particularly from conservatives who opposed Truman's policy of limited war. As in 1944 and 1948, MacArthur looked to a convention draft, but he knew that his age severely limited his chances, for if elected he would have been 72 upon taking office. In public statements he did not deny that he would accept the nomination but usually voiced support for Senator Robert Taft. By 1952, however, many Republicans looked to the less controversial General Dwight D. Eisenhower as a popular hero who could deliver victory in November. MacArthur's support was mostly limited to the far-right of the Republican Party and other extreme anti-Communists. Thus, when the convention began, Eisenhower and Taft were the only candidates still in the running for the nomination. MacArthur was afforded the role of giving the keynote speech, but played no significant part in the proceedings. On the first ballot, Eisenhower received 845 votes and the nomination. MacArthur received 4 votes and was never again a serious figure in American party politics.

See also: Dwight D. Eisenhower, Election of 1948, Harry S Truman, United Nations

Jeffrey G. Mauck

REFERENCES

James, D. Clayton. 1975. *The Years of MacArthur, Volume II, 1941–1945.* Boston: Houghton Mifflin.

———. 1985. *The Years of MacArthur, Triumph and Disaster, 1945–1964.* Boston: Houghton Mifflin.

Patrick A. McCarran (1876–1954)

Conservative Democratic member of the U.S. Senate from 1933 to 1954. Patrick Anthony McCarran was a leader of the post–World War II anti-Communist movement. The only child of Nevada homesteaders, McCarran, after attending the University of Nevada and studying law, began a long career in politics in 1902 by winning a seat in the state legislature. Ten years later he was elected to the Nevada Supreme Court and served as chief justice during the last two years of his term. McCarran failed twice in campaigns for the U.S. Senate (1916 and 1926) before winning in the Democratic landslide of 1932.

Although he was elected to the Senate in the same year that Franklin Roosevelt won the presidency, McCarran charted an independent course from the start of his career in national politics. He was, for example, an outspoken critic of much New Deal legislation, often voting with the Senate's conservative coalition. As a member of the Senate's "silver bloc" that sought repeatedly to increase the federal subsidy for silver and as an advocate of improved transportation through the establishment of the Civil Aeronautics Board and other measures,

McCarran was also careful to promote the interests of his western state.

After World War II McCarran gained national prominence when, as chairman of the Senate Judiciary Committee, he focused attention on the problem of internal subversion. In 1950 he sponsored the Internal Security Act, known popularly as the McCarran Act, requiring the registration of all Communists and Communist groups in America. Two years later, convinced that the peril to internal security was exacerbated by immigration from Communist-bloc nations, McCarran cosponsored with Congressman Francis Walter (D-Pa.) a bill to restrict immigration on the basis of national origin. Because the McCarran-Walter Act used the 1920 census to determine ethnic proportions in the population, the bill effectively limited immigration from southern and eastern Europe as well as from Asia. Both bills became law over the veto of President Harry Truman. McCarran's conservatism was influential, therefore, in shaping America's domestic and foreign policies in the tense years after World War II. His anti-Communist legacy has persisted for the rest of the century.

See also: New Deal, Franklin D. Roosevelt, Harry S Truman

John W. Malsberger

REFERENCES

Griffith, Robert. 1970. *The Politics of Fear: Joseph R. McCarthy and the Senate.* Lexington: U. Pr. of Kentucky.

McCarran, Sister Margaret Patricia. 1968. "Patrick Anthony McCarran." 11 *Nevada Historical Society Quarterly* 5.

———. 1969. "Patrick Anthony McCarran." 11 *Nevada Historical Society Quarterly* 5.

Pittman, Von. V., Jr. 1979. "Senator Patrick A. McCarran and the Politics of Containment." Ph.D. dissertation, University of Georgia.

Eugene J. McCarthy (1916–)

Reform Senator from Minnesota and maverick presidential hopeful. Eugene Joseph McCarthy sought the Democratic nomination for President in 1968, ran as an independent candidate for President in 1976, and was the presidential candidate for the Consumer Party in 1988. Additionally, McCarthy joined conservative Senator James Buckley and others to challenge the 1974 amendments to the Federal Election Campaign Act. The Supreme Court ruling in *Buckley v. Valeo* (1976) defined current rules for campaign finances.

In 1968 McCarthy surprised the media and political establishment by doing better than expected in the New Hampshire primary. Lyndon Johnson, as the incumbent, was expected to win the New Hampshire presidential primary by a wide margin. McCarthy, then known mainly as a liberal Senator from Minnesota, received 42 percent of the vote compared to Johnson's 49 percent. Although Johnson actually won the primary, the media declared McCarthy the "moral" victor. President Johnson was hurt by increasing public dissatisfaction with his Vietnam War policy and by not being listed on the primary ballot—his supporters had to write in his name. McCarthy, on the other hand, was helped by student activists who widely canvassed New Hampshire seeking support for their candidate. Johnson withdrew from the Democratic race soon after "losing" the New Hampshire primary. McCarthy lost the presidential nomination to his fellow Minnesotan Hubert Humphrey, who had been Johnson's Vice President.

In 1976 McCarthy hoped his independent candidacy for President would revitalize the Electoral College, so that it would no longer be a formality; he wanted the electors to become the deliberative body planned by the Founding Fathers. McCarthy, however, received 745,042 votes, less than 1 percent of the votes cast in 1976.

While serving Minnesota in the U.S. House from 1949 to 1959, McCarthy was a founding member of the Democratic Study Group. He was a U.S. Senator from 1959 to 1970. In 1982 McCarthy launched an unsuccessful bid to return to the Senate, losing to Mark Dayton in the Minnesota Democratic primary. In recent years, McCarthy has concentrated on writing.

See also: Buckley v. Valeo, Democratic Study Group, Election of 1976, Electoral College, Federal Election Campaign Act and Amendments, Hubert Humphrey, Lyndon B. Johnson, Vietnam War as a Political Issue

Barbara Norrander

Joseph R. McCarthy (1908–1957)

Senate demagogue from Wisconsin. Senator Joseph Raymond McCarthy was delivering a routine speech in Wheeling, West Virginia, in February 1950 when he suddenly broke from his general condemnation of communism to claim that he had a list of 205 members of the Communist Party currently employed in the State Department. This accusation, which was never documented again, initiated a period of anti-Communist hysteria that would victimize hundreds of innocent Americans.

McCarthy's popularity and power steadily grew after the Wheeling speech, despite a Senate committee report five months later that denounced McCarthy's allegations as a nefarious hoax. Communist subversion, however, became a significant issue in the 1950 congressional elections. McCarthy was the most frequently invited speaker by Republican Senators seeking reelection. McCarthyism prompted a number of laws designed to protect national security by restricting the behavior of American Communists.

McCarthy was born and raised in rural Wisconsin. Forced to quit school for financial reasons, McCarthy eventually reenrolled in high school at the age of 19. An industrious and ambitious young man, he completed a four-year curriculum with honors in one year before studying law at Marquette University, from which he graduated in 1935. He began his political career as a Democrat in 1936. Hoping to benefit from Roosevelt's coattails, McCarthy unsuccessfully sought the Democratic nomination for district attorney of Shawano County. However, in 1938 he did get elected to the Wisconsin Tenth Judicial Circuit, a nonpartisan office. McCarthy soon gained a reputation as a hard-working, efficient, and generally fair jurist.

McCarthy took a leave of absence to enlist in the United States Marine Corps in 1941. He served 30 months and gained the nickname "Tail Gunner Joe" for his alleged role as the wounded rear gunner of a dive bomber. His detractors, however, claimed that he never fired a hostile shot. His military service as an intelligence officer and an aerial photographer, not a combat officer, was routine. His only notable wound, a broken leg, occurred when he slipped on a ladder aboard a ship in the South Pacific.

McCarthy returned to partisan politics in 1944, switching to the Republican Party and unsuccessfully challenging incumbent Alexander Wiley in the primary. Telling the Wisconsin Republican congressional delegation that he was too old to climb the political ladder, McCarthy again pursued the Republican nomination for the United States Senate in 1946. Most Republican leaders in Wisconsin were either unimpressed by McCarthy or questioned the sincerity of his conversion to the Republican Party. On the other hand, they were even more suspicious and alienated about the candidacy of Robert La Follette, Jr., who along with other

Progressives had decided to rejoin the Republican Party in 1946. McCarthy skillfully managed to get the endorsement of the Republican Voluntary Committee, an extralegal organization composed of mainstream party activists. La Follette was especially vulnerable. Conservative Republicans had no enthusiasm for his candidacy, and Democrats, who could cross over and vote in the Republican primary because of Wisconsin's open primary law, resented La Follette's switch to the GOP. McCarthy narrowly won in the primary and then scored an overwhelming victory over Democratic candidate Howard McMurray in the general election. McCarthy was reelected with 54 percent of the state vote in 1952.

In 1954 McCarthy turned his attention from the State Department to the Army. His charges of Communist influence in the Army were countered by Army charges that McCarthy and his counsel, Roy Cohn, had sought preferential treatment for another McCarthy aide, G. David Schine. During the televised Army-McCarthy hearings, the Senator engaged in brutal personal attacks on participants and frequently interrupted the proceedings. The charismatic McCarthy was shown to be a shameless bully before a national television audience. Though the committee examining the charges exonerated McCarthy in a strict party-line vote, his behavior sufficiently embarrassed the Senate that his influence abated. Later in 1954 a Senate select committee was established to consider censuring McCarthy for his misbehavior. McCarthy refused to cooperate with the committee and publicly insulted its members. Censure was recommended and passed the Senate on December 2, 1954, by a vote of 67 to 22.

As McCarthy's influence waned, so too did his health and spirits. A number of reputable colleagues and friends suspected that McCarthy had become an alcoholic. He was admitted to Bethesda Naval Hospital with acute hepatitis and died there.

See also: Communism as a Political Issue, Robert La Follette, McCarthyism

Paul Haskell Zernicke

REFERENCES

Buckley, William F., and Brent L. Bozell. 1954. *McCarthy and His Enemies: The Record and Its Meaning.* Chicago: Regnery.

Reeves, Thomas C. 1982. *The Life and Times of Joe McCarthy.* New York: Stein and Day.

Rovere, Richard H. 1959. *Senator Joe McCarthy.* New York: Harcourt, Brace.

Thomas, Lately. 1973. *When Even Angels Wept: The Senator Joseph McCarthy Affair—A Story Without a Hero*. New York: Morrow.

McCarthyism

Joseph R. McCarthy (Republican of Wisconsin) gained notoriety as a U.S. Senator from 1946 to 1954 by making reckless and unproven charges—mostly alleging that various Americans in and out of public life showed sympathy or involvement with the Communist Party. These charges frequently damaged individual reputations and disrupted governmental agencies as well as the U.S. Senate. Hence, "McCarthyism" was the making of reckless and unproven charges that amounted to character assassination. McCarthy was censured by the Senate in 1954 and died of drink two and a half years later. His rise and downfall both were sudden and spectacular. The net effect of his fraudulent fight against domestic Communists in the long run was to discredit the notion that domestic communism had ever had *any* influence at all in U.S. affairs.

McCarthy accomplished all this in the very short period between February 9, 1950, when he made a Lincoln Day speech in Wheeling, West Virginia, alleging that there were 205 Communists employed in the State Department and December 2, 1954, when his colleagues in the Senate censured him in a 67 to 22 vote (all Democrats and 22 Republicans voting to censure) on two counts of conduct tending to bring the Senate into disrepute. In the intervening period McCarthy vacillated in the numbers of Communists he claimed were in the government; he also changed his story about whether they were in the government or had once been in the government as well as whether they were or had been Communists, Communist sympathizers, fellow travelers, or security risks. He urged disgruntled bureaucrats to send him material that he could fashion into charges and may at one time or another have received information from the FBI. Throughout, he received great publicity.

Following the election of 1952, the Republicans attained a majority in the Senate and McCarthy became chairman of the Senate Committee on Government Operations and its Permanent Subcommittee of Investigations. From this vantage point, aided by his well-connected and repellent young counsel, Roy Cohn, he launched investigations into the Voice of America and, notably, into alleged subversion at the U.S. Army facilities at Camp Kilmer and Fort Monmouth, New Jersey. The drafting of a young committee staff member, G. David Schine, a particular friend of Cohn's, into the Army set off a bizarre chain of events that greatly embarrassed McCarthy and caused him to self-destruct at hearings carried over nationwide television.

Behind the scenes Cohn and McCarthy made strenuous efforts to secure special treatment for Schine from the Army; the Army alternately placated McCarthy and resisted. Meanwhile McCarthy held hearings on alleged Army mismanagement and subversion at Camp Kilmer. Public charges were aired that required that a Senate committee investigate. This investigation provided the nation from April 22 to June 17, 1954, with a long, televised look at McCarthy's brutal manners, bullying tactics, and penchant for self-serving half-truths. In 1950 a Senate committee, whose proceedings were not televised, had looked into and rejected McCarthy's charges against the State Department. McCarthy campaigned strenuously against the Democratic chairman of that committee (Millard Tydings of Maryland) in the election of 1950. Tydings was defeated. From this election arose the myth, widely believed in Washington and elsewhere, that McCarthy was unusually influential with public opinion across the board. In fact he appealed mostly to conservative Republicans. But at one time or another he intimidated many public figures into silence, and he contributed greatly to an atmosphere of fear in Washington. Reluctance to deal with Joe McCarthy forthrightly was a signal failure of Dwight Eisenhower's administration. President Eisenhower could have neutralized the propensity of leading Republicans, who knew better, to treat McCarthy as a partisan political asset, as Harry Truman's administration could not.

In 1953 another Senate committee had investigated McCarthy's finances, and in August 1954 a Senate committee was formed to evaluate and recommend the resolution of censure. He denounced all four committees as obstructing the cause of anti-communism. McCarthy was censured by the Senate in December 1954; his influence and his career quickly deteriorated from the time he was first investigated until his death in 1957.

See also: Communism as a Political Issue, Dwight D. Eisenhower, Election of 1952, Joseph McCarthy

Nelson W. Polsby

REFERENCES

Anderson, Jack, and Ronald May. 1952. *McCarthy: The Man, The Senator, the "Ism."* Boston: Beacon.

Bayley, Edwin. 1981. *Joe McCarthy and the Press.* Madison: U. of Wisconsin Pr.

Fried, Richard. 1976. *Men Against McCarthy.* New York: Columbia U. Pr.

Merson, Martin. 1955. *Private Diary of a Public Servant.* New York: Macmillan.

Polsby, Nelson. 1968. "Toward an Explanation of McCarthyism." 8 *Political Studies* 250.

Rogin, Michael. 1967. *The Intellectuals and McCarthy: The Radical Specter.* Cambridge: MIT Pr.

Rovere, Richard. 1959. *Senator Joe McCarthy.* New York: Harcourt Brace Jovanovich.

Straight, Michael. 1954. *Trial by Television.* Boston: Beacon.

George B. McClellan (1826–1885)

Unsuccessful Civil War general and presidential candidate. Seeking at the polls the victory which had eluded him on the battlefield, George Brinton McClellan accepted the Democratic nomination for President in 1864. A career Army officer and railroad executive, he had been commissioned a major general at the outbreak of the Civil War and was elevated to the command of the Army of the Potomac in July 1861 after the defeat at Bull Run. For several months, he served as general in chief. A good organizer and inspirational leader, McClellan nevertheless failed to defeat the enemy, in large part because of his excessive caution and unwillingness to fight.

McClellan was all too willing to impress his political opinions on President Abraham Lincoln, most notably in the Harrison Landing letter of July 1862, an epistle that inveighed against emancipation and other aspects of total war. Ironically, his most significant battlefield success, at Antietam in September 1862, paved the way for the promulgation of the Emancipation Proclamation five days later. Frustrated by McClellan's unwillingness to assume the offensive, Lincoln removed him just after the 1862 elections. Immediately Democratic leaders courted him for the 1864 presidential contest; as expected, he was nominated at the party's Chicago convention. His campaign managers, however, finding themselves in the minority on the platform committee, were unable to prevent the inclusion of a Copperhead plank characterizing the war as a failure and calling for a negotiated peace that contemplated the possibility of disunion.

McClellan repudiated this plank in his letter accepting the nomination, although he remained silent on the fate of slavery. A series of Union victories deflated his early hopes for election, and ultimately he carried only three states and some 45 percent of the popular vote, with an overwhelming soldier vote in favor of Lincoln. A movement to nominate him again in 1868 quickly dissipated, and he had to rest content with serving a single term as governor of New Jersey (1878–1880).

See also: Copperheads, Emancipation as a Political Issue, Abraham Lincoln, Slavery

Brooks Donohue Simpson

REFERENCES

Harsh, Joseph L. 1973. "On the McClellan-Go-Round." 19 *Civil War History* 101.

McClellan, George B. 1887. *McClellan's Own Story.* New York: Charles L. Webster.

Sears, Stephen W. 1988. *George B. McClellan: The Young Napoleon.* New York: Ticknor and Fields.

Silbey, Joel H. 1977. *A Respectable Minority: The Democratic Party in the Civil War Era, 1860–1868.* New York: Norton.

William F. McCombs (1875–1921)

Democratic National Committee chairman during Woodrow Wilson's first term. When Wilson gained a reputation as a progressive during his years as president of Princeton University and governor of New Jersey, several leaders in the Southern Society of New York, including William Frank McCombs and other former students of Wilson at Princeton, began to tout Wilson for the presidency. By 1911 McCombs was at the head of a movement to win the Democratic presidential nomination for Wilson. Almost single-handedly, McCombs began raising funds and creating Wilson organizations in the states. In the latter effort, McCombs, now a prominent New York attorney, increasingly made himself the liaison between the local Democratic machines and the Wilson forces, despite Wilson's personal vendetta against party bosses in general.

Both McCombs and Wilson were extremely stubborn men, making it inevitable that substantial tension would dominate their relationship. Thus, when Wilson did win the nomination largely because of McCombs's efforts (particularly through his efforts to conciliate "the bosses"), Wilson reluctantly agreed to endorse McCombs's election as national committee chairman.

Wilson and McCombs continued to be in fundamental disagreement about the conduct of the election campaign, the handling of patronage appointments after Wilson won the presidency, and the operation of the national committee during the interim between presidential years. Hoping to get McCombs out of the way, Wilson offered him the ambassadorship to France, a post McCombs declined. Instead, the national chairman immersed himself in his law practice, in the problem of creating a permanent national party headquarters, and in the politics of New York State. In 1916 he was an unsuccessful candidate for the United States Senate.

See also: Bosses, Democratic National Committee, Woodrow Wilson

Ralph M. Goldman

REFERENCES

McCombs, William F. 1921. *Making Woodrow Wilson President.* New York: Fairview Publishing.

Tumulty, Joseph P. 1921. *Woodrow Wilson as I Know Him.* Garden City, NY: Doubleday, Page.

Ellen McCormack (1926–)

Leader of the anti-abortion movement. Ellen McCormack considered herself an ordinary suburban New York housewife before being brought into politics by the right to life (anti-abortion) movement. In 1976 McCormack sought the Democratic Party's presidential nomination on the single-plank platform of passing a constitutional amendment to reverse the 1973 Supreme Court ruling in *Roe v. Wade*, a decision that legalized abortion in the United States. She ran in 18 primaries, never garnering over 10 percent of the vote. She won a total of only 22 convention delegates.

McCormack, a Roman Catholic raised in New York City, had none of the traditional characteristics of a presidential aspirant. She was not a lawyer and had never held political office. She had been involved in neighborhood and school activities, when in 1969 her book discussion group became aware of efforts in the New York State Legislature to legalize abortion. Finding that their state legislators were not going to oppose abortion, McCormack and her friends decided to run their own candidates. Out of this group of suburban housewives, New York State's Right to Life Party was formed. The party's survival was ensured by New York's unique election law that allows candidates to run under multiple party labels.

In 1978 McCormack was the Right to Life Party's nominee for lieutenant governor, with Mary Jane Tobin as the candidate for governor.

Outpolling the Liberal Party candidates, the Right to Life ticket won 130,000 votes or 3 percent of the total. This total was large enough to ensure the Right to Life Party an automatic spot on the New York ballot for future elections.

See also: Abortion and Anti-abortion Politics, Liberal Party of New York, Right to Life Party

Barbara Norrander

REFERENCES

Carroll, Maurice. 1978. "The Unlikely Beginning of the Right to Life Party." *New York Times*, November 25.

Spitzer, Robert J. 1984. "A Political Party Is Born: Single Issue Advocacy and the New York State Election Law." 73 *National Civic Review* 321.

John W. McCormack (1891–1980)

Democratic Party leader of the U.S. House of Representatives. John William McCormack, an Irish Catholic Democrat from Boston, was Speaker of the U.S. House of Representatives from 1962 to 1971 and Democratic Majority Leader for seventeen years (Minority Whip for four) before his election as Speaker. Though a consistent supporter of the liberal domestic legislative programs of John F. Kennedy and Lyndon B. Johnson, McCormack, as Speaker, came under increasing criticism from younger liberal House members who perceived his leadership as weak and insensitive to the need for institutional reforms.

Born in South Boston, to immigrant parents, McCormack at age 13 became the family breadwinner with the death of his father. After studying law at the firm where he was employed as an office boy, McCormack passed the bar exam at age 21. As a Bostonian, McCormack's involvement in politics came naturally, and following service in the Army in World War I, McCormack was elected to the Massachusetts House of Representatives (1920–1922) and subsequently the state senate, where he became Democratic floor leader in 1925. Following an unsuccessful primary challenge to incumbent Congressman James A. Gallivan in 1926, McCormack was elected to the House seat when Gallivan died in 1928. Thereafter, McCormack was routinely reelected to the House for the next 43 years, never winning less than 70 percent of the vote.

As a young Congressman, McCormack became a protégé of Speaker John Nance Garner and his fellow Texan, Sam Rayburn. McCormack won a coveted assignment to the Ways and Means Committee after less than two terms and advanced within the leadership to the posts of secretary and chair of the Democratic Caucus in the 1930s. When Rayburn successfully sought the Majority Leader position in 1936, McCormack supported the Texan over another urban northern Democrat, corralling the votes of ten other northeastern members for Rayburn. When "Mr. Sam" assumed the speakership in 1940, McCormack received his support for the second spot in the party leadership. Working as a team with Rayburn, McCormack, though subordinate to the Speaker's personal authority, proved an effective, though at times strongly partisan, debater and vote counter. He was also a key legislative strategist for the New Deal domestic program and the war preparation policies of President Franklin D. Roosevelt. A fervent antagonist of both Nazi and Communist totalitarianism, McCormack, a devout Catholic, chaired the House Un-American Activities Committee at its inception in 1934, remaining a bitter foe of the Soviet Union throughout the postwar period.

With his election to the speakership on Rayburn's death in 1961, McCormack acted with a collegial leadership style that relied heavily on the skills of his lieutenants, Majority Leader Carl Albert and Majority Whip Hale Boggs and beyond that conciliation with committee chairmen and John Kennedy and Lyndon Johnson administration liaison officials. While the Democratic administration's legislative success record was high in the Eighty-ninth Congress (1965–1967), younger liberal Democrats under the leadership of Richard Bolling and the Democratic Study Group (DSG) grew increasingly frustrated with the conservative coalition of southern Democrats and Republicans who wielded significant power in the House and blocked civil rights and social legislation through reliance on the seniority system and apprenticeship norms. Charging that the authority of the Speaker had atrophied under McCormack, DSG members backed the unprecedented but futile challenge of Morris K. Udall to unseat the Speaker in the Democratic Caucus in 1969. For the period of slightly over one year, following the assassination of President Kennedy in 1963, Speaker McCormack at age 72 stood next in succession to the presidency, a situation that concerned some members of his own party. Following the revelation of abuse of his office by a staff aide in perpetrating fraudulent transactions without McCormack's knowledge, the Speaker announced his retirement in 1970.

Although McCormack served as Speaker for nine years, a longevity then exceeded only by Rayburn, his leadership was not enthusiastically supported by many Democrats, and as Richard Bolling noted, "his failures . . . play[ed] an important role in the development of new attitudes which were to bring about the very changes he resisted."

See also: Democratic Study Group, Lyndon B. Johnson, John F. Kennedy, New Deal, Sam Rayburn, Franklin D. Roosevelt, Speaker of the House

Richard C. Burnweit

REFERENCES

Bibby, John F., and Roger H. Davidson. *On Capitol Hill: Studies in the Legislative Process.* 2nd ed. Hinsdale, IL: Dryden Press.

Bolling, Richard. 1965. *House Out of Order.* New York: Dutton.

———. 1974. *Power in the House: A History of the Leadership of the House of Representatives.* New York: Capricorn Books.

Davidson, Roger H., David M. Kovenock, and Michael K. O'Leary. 1968. *Congress in Crisis: Politics and Congressional Reform.* Belmont, CA: Wadsworth.

MacNeil, Neil. 1963. *Forge of Democracy: The House of Representatives.* New York: David McKay.

Nelson, Garrison. 1975. "Change and Continuity in the Recruitment of U.S. House Leaders, 1789–1975." In Norman J. Ornstein, ed. *Congress in Change: Evolution and Reform.* New York: Praeger.

Peabody, Robert L. 1976. *Leadership in Congress: Stability, Succession, and Change.* Boston: Little, Brown.

Ripley, Randall B. 1969. *Majority Party Leadership in Congress.* Boston: Little, Brown.

Robert R. McCormick (1880–1955)

Chicago newspaper publisher and influential Republican. Colonel Robert McCormick, editor and publisher, was an independent Republican and chief spokesman, through his newspaper the *Chicago Tribune*, of what became known as the "Middle West viewpoint." The components of this philosophy included free enterprise; Old Guard Republican conservatism; and isolationist nationalism, as embodied in the "America First Movement," of which McCormick was a member. He was a man of paradoxes who proudly earned his military title serving in France under General Pershing in a war that he initially opposed. McCormick's early upbringing in England as a son of an American diplomat showed in his speech and mannerisms. Yet he distrusted the English and vigorously opposed Lend-Lease in 1939. He attended Groton preparatory school, as did his arch-enemies Franklin Roosevelt and Dean Acheson, and the imprint of that education appeared on them all. This fastidious, dogmatic, unpredictable, and austere individualist was most popular with the midwestern farmers, whose style of life seemed at odds with his.

A graduate of Yale University, McCormick studied law at Northwestern University, passed the bar, and practiced as an attorney until he was briefly diverted by public office. At the suggestion of the Republican boss of Chicago's Twenty-first Ward, he successfully ran for alderman in 1904. In 1905 he ran for and was elected president of the board of trustees of the Sanitary District. He served until 1910, a patrician among spoilsmen, efficiently supervising a project for digging a canal to create an outlet for Chicago's sewage. In 1910 McCormick and a cousin, Joseph Patterson, jointly gained custody of enough proxies at a stockholders' meeting to become co-editors of the *Chicago Tribune*. This strained partnership between the conservative McCormick and the liberal Patterson helped force the Republican boss of Illinois, Senator William Lorimer, from office. This odd couple also agreed to support Theodore Roosevelt for President in 1912. Greater freedom for both editors ensued in 1919 when Patterson relocated to New York to found the *Daily News*. This partner of the *Tribune* became the only newspaper to outsell McCormick's during his heyday.

The colonel's crusading newspaper focused on local targets in the 1920s by accusing Chicago's Republican mayor William Hale Thompson and other officials of theft, eventually forcing repayment of some $1.5 million. McCormick endorsed the Democrat Anton Cermak over Thompson in the election of 1931. He also opposed Governor Len Small and succeeded in getting him indicted while in office. But his most enduring target was FDR, whom McCormick regarded as a traitor to his class. Accordingly, McCormick's biggest battles were the presidential elections of 1936 and 1940.

In 1932 McCormick was lukewarmly in favor of Herbert Hoover, despite the President's internationalism and support for prohibition. But in 1936, McCormick denounced the New Deal as totalitarian and communistic. He organized volunteers to vote for Landon to save America. Strongly opposed to government-sponsored welfare programs, McCormick denounced labor unions as fascistic and instead kept his own employees happy with high wages, bonuses, and good benefits. In 1940 McCormick, a delegate to the Republican convention, supported Thomas E. Dewey to the end, unsuccessfully sought to convert Wendell Willkie to isolationism, and only reluctantly rallied to the Republican ticket. When war did come to America, McCormick endorsed it for national unity, although he considered the war as partially the result of previous misguided American policies.

More independent than a party man, McCormick opposed fellow Republicans who collaborated with the New Deal, especially his fellow Chicagoan Frank Knox, FDR's Secretary of the Navy. He carried his personal convictions onto the airwaves as well as into his editorial columns. Beginning in 1940 McCormick appeared in a weekly radio program aired by the *Tribune*'s station. In 1943 the "Republican Nationalist Revival Committee" briefly touted McCormick for President. But in 1944 he again backed Dewey, this time unenthusiastically, claiming that Dewey's nomination, like Willkie's in 1940, was influenced by Wall Street. In 1948 McCormick, as a delegate to the Republican convention, supported Robert Taft and walked out rather than vote for Dewey. Yet it was his newspaper, albeit not at McCormick's order, that rushed to proclaim "Dewey Defeats Truman" in an issue that the triumphant Truman proudly held aloft for photographers.

In 1952 McCormick opposed the nomination of Dwight Eisenhower and advised his readers to concentrate instead on electing patriotic candidates to Congress from either party. Later, he suggested that the Republican candidate was perhaps the preferable choice. After the election, McCormick suggested forming a new "American Party" for 1956. In May 1954 McCormick founded an organization in Chicago called "For America" to oppose Eisenhower's internationalist stance.

See also: Dwight D. Eisenhower, Elections of 1936 and 1940, Herbert Hoover, Isolationism in American Politics, New Deal, Prohibition, Franklin D. Roosevelt

Frederick J. Augustyn, Jr.

REFERENCES

Edwards, Jerome E. 1971. *The Foreign Policy of Col. McCormick's Tribune, 1929-1941*. Reno: U. of Nevada Pr.

Gies, Joseph. 1979. *The Colonel of Chicago*. New York: Dutton.

Vance C. McCormick (1872–1946)

Democratic National Committee chairman in Woodrow Wilson's second term. Although not a member of the Democratic National Committee, Vance Criswell McCormick was popular among progressives, and President Wilson's strong personal esteem for him led to his service as national chairman (1916–1919). McCormick was one of the first enthusiasts for a Woodrow Wilson presidency, participating as a member of Wilson's prenomination inner circle and delivering Wilson's first major state endorsement and his largest single bloc of delegate votes in the entire 1912 nominating contest. McCormick subsequently served in several capacities in the Wilson administration, initially as director of the Federal Reserve Bank at Philadelphia.

McCormick entered politics in his native Harrisburg soon after he left Yale University and was elected to the city council in 1900. At age 29 he became mayor and gave the city a vigorous reform administration. Some time after his term as mayor and as publisher of two Harrisburg newspapers—the morning *Patriot* and the evening *News*—he and A. Mitchell Palmer began a long struggle against the state's Democratic machine, on one occasion bolting the gubernatorial nomination on grounds that "it had been corruptly made." When McCormick made an unsuccessful race for governor in 1914, he was the nominee of both the Democrats and the Roosevelt Progressives.

In Wilson's second term, McCormick served as chairman of the War Trade Board and as a personal adviser during the President's historic trip to Europe. He continued his publishing enterprises and, from the late 1920s on, drifted away from his Democratic loyalties, supporting Republicans Herbert Hoover in 1928 and Wendell Willkie in 1940.

See also: Herbert Hoover, Progressive Party, Wendell Willkie, Woodrow Wilson

Ralph M. Goldman

REFERENCES

Goldman, Ralph M. 1990. *The National Party Chairmen and Committees: Factionalism at the Top.* Armonk, NY: M. E. Sharpe.

Ernest W. McFarland (1894–1984)

Two-term Democratic Senator from Arizona. Born on a farm near Earlsboro, Oklahoma, Ernest William McFarland got his baccalaureate and law degrees from Stanford University in 1921 and then moved to Arizona and practiced law in Phoenix.

McFarland was elected to the Senate in 1940 and became known as one of the most genial and friendly men in the upper chamber. His long record of party loyalty and his moderate views made him an acceptable candidate for Majority Leader. He was elected Majority Leader

as a compromise candidate in 1951 by the Democratic Steering Committee, then dominated by a group of conservative southern Senators. He served as Majority Leader until 1953 when he was defeated in his reelection bid in Arizona by Republican Barry Goldwater.

After his defeat McFarland was elected governor of Arizona for two terms. He tried again to regain his Senate seat in 1958 but was again defeated by Goldwater. In 1964 he was named associate justice of the Arizona Supreme Court and was elevated to chief justice in 1967.

After he retired from the bench in 1971, McFarland returned to Phoenix where he continued to practice law and to maintain his interest in a television station that he co-founded in 1953.

See also: Barry Goldwater

Mary Ann McHugh

REFERENCES

1984. "Ernest McFarland, Arizona Senator '41–'53." June 9 *New York Times.*

George S. McGovern (1922–)

Antiwar Democratic presidential candidate from South Dakota. George Stanley McGovern's career seems in retrospect a most unlikely one. Born in Avon, South Dakota, he served as an Army Air Corps bombardier in England during World War II (he was decorated for his service there), and after the war he received a Ph.D. in history from Northwestern University. Returning to South Dakota to teach at Dakota Wesleyan University, he was instrumental in the reinvigoration of the Democratic Party in that state, which eventually elected him to the U.S. Senate in 1962. McGovern was a strange successor to the arch-conservative Republicans who normally won Senate seats in South Dakota.

In the Senate, George McGovern usually represented progressive causes and as a member of Senate Agriculture Committee, he was a strong supporter of the Food Stamp program. By the late 1960s George McGovern, an early critic of the Vietnam War, became a rallying point for many in the Democratic Party. His antiwar activities had little effect in 1968, but by 1972, with the institution of reforms in the Democratic Party—enacted in large part because of the McGovern-Fraser Commission, a body that McGovern had earlier chaired—his candidacy became the focus of major and successful efforts by antiwar and other liberal activists leading to his nomination as the Democratic candidate for President. His campaign was beset by many problems including his choice for Vice President (Thomas Eagleton was revealed to have had psychiatric treatment). Because of Richard Nixon's highly visible incumbency and his manipulation of events (détente, the opening to China, increases in social security benefits), McGovern was able to carry only Massachusetts and the District of Columbia. Shortly thereafter, when President Nixon went down in the face of the Watergate scandal, it became a measure of pride to some that they had "voted for McGovern." Not many, however, really had; he got only 38 percent of the popular vote.

George McGovern's political career in South Dakota was cut short during the Ronald Reagan landslide of 1980 when he lost his Senate seat to James Abdnor. Since then, McGovern has lectured, taught, and been a spokesman for many liberal causes on television and elsewhere.

See also: Thomas Eagleton, Election of 1972, McGovern-Fraser Commission, Richard M. Nixon

David A. Bositis

REFERENCES

Polsby, Nelson, and Aaron B. Wildavsky. 1988. *Presidential Elections, 5th Edition*. New York: Free Press.

Price, David. 1984. *Bringing Back the Parties*. Washington: Congressional Quarterly.

White, Theodore. 1973. *The Making of the President, 1972*. New York: Atheneum.

McGovern-Fraser Commission

The Commission on Party Structure and Delegate Selection (CPSDS), also called the McGovern-Fraser Commission, was arguably the most significant reform group in the history of the Democratic Party. Chaired first by South Dakota Senator George McGovern (until he decided to run for the presidency) and then by Minnesota Congressman Donald Fraser, the Commission proposed an ambitious and dramatic set of changes in the rules governing presidential selection in the Democratic Party. The 1968 Democratic National Convention had authorized the formation of the CPSDS, and the 1972 national convention ratified its recommendations. The Commission's report, *Mandate for Change*, resulted in a substantial shift of power from the state party to the national party (and especially the national convention) as well as a dramatic change in the composition of the national party's elite and the selection of presidential nominees.

The mandate of the Commission was to devise regulations that would ensure the full, meaningful, and timely selection of delegates to the national convention. Its members were appointed in early 1969 by former Senator and then national Democratic Party chair Fred Harris from Oklahoma. The McGovern-Fraser Commission had 28 members including three U.S. Senators—McGovern, Harold Hughes (Iowa), and Birch Bayh (Ind.) and two future U.S. Senators (George Mitchell from Maine and Adlai Stevenson from Illinois), one U.S. Congressman (Fraser), two professors (Samuel Beer and Austin Ranney), one governor (Calvin Rampton of Utah), one labor leader (I. W. Abel), and an assortment of party officials, state officeholders, and political activists. The CPSDS was also advised by a number of individuals including Anne Wexler, who had been an active supporter of Eugene McCarthy. She persuaded the commission to accept the proposition that state parties would be obligated to enact the rule changes demanded by the Commission.

Under the Commission's guidelines, the state parties would have to conform to a number of new rules governing the delegate selection process. Among the provisions that the state parties would have to accept were the following: (1) written party rules regarding the delegate selection process would have to be adopted and made available; (2) numerical quotas would be required, thus ensuring representation of African-Americans, women, and youth in proportion to their numbers in the electorate; (3) delegate selection procedures would have to be timely—that is, the selection would have to be made during the calendar year of the convention; (4) proxy voting, the unit rule, and *ex officio* delegates would be eliminated; (5) no more than 10 percent of the delegates could be selected through state committees and at least 75 percent had to be selected at the congressional district level or at some more local level; (6) adequate public notice of party meetings relating to delegate selection would be required; (7) delegate meetings within a state would have to be held on the same day, except in areas where this procedure presented a genuine logistical problem; and (8) candidates would be required to state on the primary ballot the presidential candidate that they intended to support.

As important as the guidelines themselves, their eventual enforcement was essential to establishing them as party law. Fred Harris, something of a populist and very supportive of the reforms, was succeeded as party chief by Lawrence O'Brien, a figure from the John Kennedy years who was viewed as an old pol (and thus with suspicion by the reformers). O'Brien, however, proved to be as supportive of the reforms as Harris. The real test of the reforms came when the 59-member Illinois contingent to the national convention led by Richard J. Daley was refused seating at the 1972 convention because it did not conform to the new CPSDS rules. Subsequent court challenges to this decision (since the Daley "59" was elected in accordance with Illinois state law, that law was in conflict with national party law) proved unsuccessful. William Brennan, writing for the U.S. Supreme Court, noted that "the convention serves the pervasive national interest in selection of candidates for national office, and this national interest is greater than any interest of an individual state."

The McGovern-Fraser reforms have been debated endlessly since they were enacted, and some provisions have been changed by later reform commissions (Winograd, Mikulski, and Hunt). Specifically, at this writing, only women (not Blacks and not young people) retain their quota rights, and in 1984 and 1988 *ex officio* delegates were everywhere to be seen at the national conventions. These "ringers" were Walter Mondale's most enthusiastic base of support in 1984. In academic circles, this debate has been especially lively, although the losing side in the political debate—notably Jeane Kirkpatrick and Austin Ranney—has written most of the history (unlike in war where the winners get to write the history). The "restoration view" (i.e., the view of those who would return to pre–McGovern-Fraser rules) is that the reforms have created factions within the Democratic Party, thus weakening the party. Furthermore, the rules have resulted in the elevation to power of activists without reliable party ties and loyalty. Despite this dissent, there is no question that these reforms have opened up the Democratic Party to previously excluded groups, especially African-Americans and women, and thus resulted in a genuine circulation of elites.

See also: Birch Bayh, Richard Daley, Donald Fraser, Jeane Kirkpatrick, Eugene McCarthy, George McGovern, Walter Mondale, Lawrence O'Brien, Winograd Commission

David A. Bositis

REFERENCES

Baer, Denise L., and David A. Bositis. 1988. *Elite Cadres and Party Coalitions.* Westport, CT. Greenwood.

Crotty, William J. 1983. *Party Reform.* New York: Longman.

Kirkpatrick, Jeane J. 1976. *The New Presidential Elite.* New York: Russell Sage.

———. 1979. *Dismantling the Parties.* 1979. Washington: AEI Press.

Polsby, Nelson. 1983. *The Consequences of Party Reform.* New York: Oxford U. Pr.

Price, David. 1984. *Bringing Back the Parties.* Washington: Congressional Quarterly.

Ranney, Austin. 1975. *Curing the Mischiefs of Faction.* Berkeley: U. of California Pr.

Shafer, Byron. 1983. *The Quiet Revolution.* New York: Russell Sage.

J. Howard McGrath (1903–1966)

Democratic National Committee chairman in the Truman administration. James Howard McGrath was active in Democratic Party politics for most of his life. From 1930 to 1952 he continuously held public office: he was governor of and U.S. Senator from Rhode Island and Attorney General during the second Harry Truman administration. McGrath's greatest impact on American politics came during the 1948 and 1952 presidential elections.

McGrath started his public service in 1930 as city solicitor of Central Falls, Rhode Island, and from 1934 to 1940 he served as U.S. attorney for the state. In 1940 he was elected governor and in 1942 and 1944 was reelected. As Rhode Island's governor, McGrath saw the enactment of several socially progressive projects and was judged a competent administrator.

In 1944 he seconded Harry Truman's nomination for Vice President at the Democratic National Convention, and in September 1945, after Truman succeeded to the presidency, he was appointed U.S. Solicitor General. In 1946 he bucked the national Republican tide to be elected to the U.S. Senate from Rhode Island. In the Senate, McGrath built a liberal record by loyally supporting the administration of both foreign and domestic issues.

McGrath was elected chairman of the Democratic National Committee in October 1947. He was an early advocate of Truman's 1948 nomination, but he first set himself to revitalizing the party structure. McGrath then mobilized Democrats throughout the country to raise money, arouse interest in Truman, and get out the vote. His hard work was a key ingredient in Truman's upset victory in 1948.

In August 1949 McGrath resigned his U.S. Senate seat to become Truman's Attorney General, the last public office that he held. His reluctance to investigate charges of corruption within the Justice Department's tax division and his dismissal of a special assistant who had been hired to probe these charges led Truman to announce his resignation in April 1952. McGrath's actions added substance to the corruption-in-government issue, a weakness that the Republicans exploited in their successful campaign to elect Dwight Eisenhower to the presidency in 1952.

See also: Democratic National Committee, Elections of 1948 and 1952, Harry S Truman

Reed Hutner

REFERENCES

Donovan, Robert. 1982. *Tumultuous Years.* New York: Norton.

Dunar, Andrew. 1984. *The Truman Scandals and the Politics of Morality.* Columbia: U. of Missouri Pr.

Goldman, Ralph M. 1990. *The National Party Chairmen and Committees: Factionalism at the Top.* Armonk, NY: M. E. Sharpe.

Ross, Irwin. 1968. *The Loneliest Campaign.* New York: New American Library.

Norman E. Mack (1858–1932)

Chairman of the Democratic National Committee from 1908 to 1912. Norman E. Mack began his professional career as a newspaper publisher, establishing the *Buffalo Times* in 1879. The *Times* remained steadfastly loyal to the Democratic Party throughout publisher Mack's tenure, beginning with the endorsement of Grover Cleveland for President in 1884.

Mack's loyalty and his strategic position in upstate New York led to a swift rise through the ranks of the Democratic Party, although he had never once held elective office. He was first selected to attend the Democratic National Convention in 1892; in 1896, following William Jennings Bryan's nomination, Mack endorsed Bryan's candidacy in the *Times*, disregarding his own strong support of the gold standard. The endorsement established Mack's reputation as an absolute party regular, at the same time endearing him to Bryan. At Bryan's insistence, Mack was elected the national committeeman from New York in 1900. In 1908, when Bryan received his third Democratic presidential nomination, he installed Mack as the chairman of the Democratic National Committee and as the presidential campaign chairman.

The 1908 campaign was a loss for Bryan but a gain for Mack. Through the management of the Bryan campaign, he established himself as one of the inner circle of Democratic Party leaders. After he stepped down as national chairman, he was among the most vocal advocates for the presidential nominations for Bryan

in 1912, Woodrow Wilson in 1920, Alfred E. Smith in 1924, and Franklin Roosevelt in 1932. Although Mack's preferred candidate was not always nominated, he always threw his strong support behind the final nominee, helping to cement his reputation as the most "regular" of the inner-circle Democrats.

See also: William Jennings Bryan, Grover Cleveland, Democratic National Committee, Alfred E. Smith, Woodrow Wilson

Charles Stewart III

Kenneth D. McKellar (1869–1957)

Conservative Senator from Tennessee. Kenneth Douglas McKellar was born in Alabama but moved to Memphis, Tennessee, as a young man to pursue a law career. In 1908 he was a delegate from Tennessee to the Democratic National Convention. From 1911 to 1917 he served as a member of the U.S. House of Representatives from that state and then moved to the Senate in 1917 where he served for six consecutive terms until 1953. During his Senate years, McKellar maintained close ties with the Democratic political machine of Edward H. "Boss" Crump of Memphis. At the same time, he supported much New Deal legislation but opposed various social initiatives of Franklin Roosevelt, most notably the National Youth Administration.

During the 1930s McKellar's power grew; his chairmanship of the Post Office and Post Roads Committee (1933–1946) brought him considerable patronage influence. By the early 1940s McKellar was believed to have secured more federal appointments for his constituents than any other member of Congress. He also came to be considered one of the most parochial members of the Senate, that is, one who placed the interests of Tennessee before national interests. This approach to politics led him into a series of disputes with David Lilienthal, the chairman of the Tennessee Valley Authority (TVA), over that agency's operation. McKellar vigorously opposed both Lilienthal's reappointment as head of the TVA in 1946 and his nomination by President Harry Truman to chair the Atomic Energy Commission (AEC) in 1947, going so far as using "red baiting" tactics to try to discredit his liberal adversary during debate over the AEC position.

By the late 1940s, McKellar was one of the most reactionary Democrats, more closely aligned with the ideology of the Republican "Mr. Conservative," Robert A. Taft, than with

Truman's "Fair Deal." As President *pro tempore* of the Senate during most of Truman's administration, he was one of the most powerful members of Congress. Advancing age took its toll, however, and the 83-year-old McKellar finally lost his Senate seat to the much younger Albert Gore in the Democratic primary election of 1952.

See also: Edward Crump, Robert A. Taft, Harry S Truman

Jeffrey G. Mauck

Alexander P. McKenzie (1850–1922)

Boss of the turn-of-the-century Republicans of North Dakota. To Alexander P. McKenzie's supporters, "McKenzieism" (i.e., his apparent ability for 12 years, between 1894 and 1906, to rig the election of governors, state legislators, U.S. Representatives, and U.S. Senators) meant making North Dakota politically safe for rapid infrastructural investment by the Great Northern Railway and the Northern Pacific Railroad and thus for economic growth. Restless farmers needed to be controlled politically by a "boss," else enormous and risky investments would be wasted. Without "McKenzieism" these same farmers could have been condemned to poverty.

To its opponents, "McKenzieism" meant the construction of an exploitative and corrupt political economy. McKenzie's "ring" monopolized such basic organizational resources as the print media, free railroad passes, and money. That McKenzie never sought public office contributed to the reputation of "McKenzieism" as being ruled by a reclusive kingpin. He astutely used bribery and vote fraud to disorganize the legislative and electoral efforts of more radical North Dakotans to regulate corporate power for more than ten years. As a former jail keeper and sheriff, he knew enough about criminals to organize and deploy gangs occasionally. Finally, "McKenzieism" meant crooked land and financial deals in North Dakota and elsewhere, including a spectacular effort by McKenzie at an Alaskan fraud scheme that has been immortalized in a novel and in the 1942 John Wayne movie *The Spoilers*.

The transparency of McKenzie's manipulative politics in a sparsely populated, homogeneous state probably helped to set the stage for the subsequent agrarian protest of the Nonpartisan League (1915–1922). By then, however, McKenzie had long since retired from politics; indeed his retirement probably facilitated the League's rise.

See also: Bosses, Railroads

Richard M. Valelly

REFERENCES

Wilkins, Robert P. 1981. "Alexander McKenzie and the Politics of Bossism." In Thomas W. Howard, ed. *The North Dakota Political Tradition*. Ames: Iowa State U. Pr.

William McKinley (1843–1901)

Twenty-fifth President of the United States. William McKinley twice defeated William Jennings Bryan in presidential campaigns, becoming the first two-term President since Ulysses S. Grant. McKinley was a Civil War officer, an attorney, a six-term U.S. Congressman, and a governor of the pivotal state of Ohio before becoming the 1896 Republican nominee for President. During the explosive election of 1896, McKinley was a safe, traditional, solidly midwestern contrast to the fire-breathing "radical" Bryan.

In 1896 Americans feared apocalypse. Intraparty conflict, agrarian tumult, sectional tensions, and a sustained depression precipitated the despair. Myriad political disagreements were reduced to the Battle of the Standards (disputes over whether American currency should continue to be anchored in gold or expanded and cheapened by being redeemable in silver as well). Having built his career on the protective tariff, McKinley initially avoided the issue. As Speaker of the House Thomas B. Reed snorted, "McKinley isn't a silver-bug, McKinley isn't a gold-bug, McKinley is a straddle-bug." Shrewdly, albeit belatedly and halfheartedly, McKinley embraced the gold standard.

Under the expert direction of McKinley's Ohio political alter ego, Mark Hanna, the Republicans mounted a systematic, inspirational, and very expensive 1896 campaign—no party would again spend so much money until 1920. For his part, McKinley remained on his front porch in Canton, Ohio, greeting over 750,000 visitors from 30 states. This front-porch campaign was vigorous by any standards except by contrast to the grueling 18,000-mile rear-platform marathon that Bryan mounted. McKinley's victory in November was thorough enough to signal the emergence of a new, powerful, and modern Republican Party. Still, he got only 52 percent of the popular vote.

As President, McKinley led America into an era of prosperity and imperial expansion. His reelection campaign of 1900 hailed the "full dinner pail" that all Americans were enjoying under Republican rule. The second campaign also defended America's entry into war with Spain and the subsequent annexation of Puerto Rico, the Philippines, and Guam. Dismissing Bryan's tirades against McKinley's imperialism, one farmer scoffed, "What the hell do we care about the downtrodden Filipino as long as beef cattle are ten cents a pound?"

In 1900 McKinley was neither inclined nor compelled to question the tradition of presidential silence during a reelection effort. In anticipation of the campaign, he had made a two-week, eighty-speech midwestern tour in 1899. Other campaign oratory was furnished by a surprisingly eloquent Mark Hanna, bristling at the caricatures of him as a greedy manipulator, and by the vice presidential nominee, Governor Theodore Roosevelt of New York. Hanna disliked Roosevelt, the Harvard man turned Rough Rider. "Don't any of you realize that there's only one life between this madman and the presidency?" Hanna had screamed during the convention. But McKinley, who was far more independent of Hanna than many appreciated, accepted the popular governor as a running mate. Aided by Hanna and Roosevelt, McKinley's margin over Bryan was 2 percent greater than it had been in 1896. For all that, less than a year after his reelection, McKinley was assassinated by an anarchist, Leon Czolgosz, and Hanna's fears were realized: Theodore Roosevelt became President of the United States.

See also: William Jennings Bryan, Election of 1896, Marcus A. Hanna, Thomas B. Reed, Theodore Roosevelt

Gil Troy

REFERENCES

Glad, Paul W. 1964. "McKinley, Bryan, and the People." In Robert D. Cross, ed. *Critical Periods of History*. Philadelphia: Lippincott.

Hollingworth, J. Rogers. 1963. *The Whirligig of Politics: The Democracy of Cleveland and Bryan*. Chicago: U. of Chicago Pr.

Leech, Margaret. 1959. *In the Days of McKinley*. New York: Harper & Brothers.

Morgan, H. Wayne. 1969. *From Hayes to McKinley: National Party Politics, 1877–1896*. Syracuse: Syracuse U. Pr.

Morris, Edmund. 1979. *The Rise of Theodore Roosevelt*. New York: Ballantine Books.

McKinley Tariff Act of 1890

A principal incident in the "tariff wars" that characterized late-nineteenth-century politics, the McKinley Tariff was passed on October 1, 1890, and contributed to heavy Republican losses in the congressional elections the next month.

As ideological successors to the Whigs, the Republicans had long favored a protective tariff. In the post–Civil War years, as the utility of waving the "Bloody Shirt" waned, party leaders seeking success turned increasingly to economic issues. By the 1880s the protective tariff was the centerpiece of the Republican program. Presidential candidates James G. Blaine in 1884 and Benjamin Harrison in 1888 emphasized protectionism's benefits to American producers and laborers, as well as to the factory owners. Harkening to their party's formation in the fight for "free labor" in the 1850s, Republicans claimed to be carrying on that tradition by offering American workers protection from competition from "pauper labor" abroad. Moreover, the tariff revenue collected could finance internal improvements, soldiers' pensions, and other programs to stimulate the economy.

Democrats, meanwhile, generally clung to their traditional low-tariff position. Grover Cleveland's famous 1887 annual message condemned a high tariff as unnecessary taxation that kept consumer prices high and created a bloated treasury surplus that invited wasteful expenditure. Democrats argued especially that lower tariffs on raw materials would enable American producers to compete more effectively in international markets, thus bringing greater prosperity to both the factory owner and his worker.

When the Republicans won both Congress and the presidency in 1888, keeping their pledges on the tariff became their primary obligation. Complicating the task was the continuing surplus that exceeded $100 million in fiscal 1889. Moreover, party leaders—led by Secretary of State Blaine—saw the need to appeal to farmers who traditionally had doubted protectionism's benefits. After months of difficult negotiations under the direction of Ways and Means chairman William McKinley, Congress eventually produced a law designed to satisfy a variety of interests. By raising average import duties to a record peacetime high, the Republicans kept their promise of protection to American manufacturers and workers. To help eliminate the treasury surplus, they placed several items (notably sugar) on the free list and raised rates on others to levels that would discourage their importation and thereby reduce revenues. "Free sugar" also appealed to consumers. Finally, for farmers, the law placed import duties on agricultural products, while at the same time empowering the President to negotiate reciprocal treaties with foreign countries to expand the market for American farm goods.

Still, Republicans had little time to demonstrate the new law's benefits before the 1890 midterm elections; indeed, sugar was not scheduled to go on the free list for a half year. The Democrats, appealing to all Americans as consumers, lost no time in charging that high prices would be the principal result. They even paid itinerant peddlers to boost prices on such wares as tin goods (tin duties having been raised to prohibitive levels) and then to blame the McKinley Act. Although other issues affected the outcome, this tariff badly hurt the Republicans, who were reduced to 88 seats in the House while the Democrats won 235.

See also: James G. Blaine, Bloody Shirt, Grover Cleveland, Election of 1888, Benjamin Harrison, William McKinley

Charles W. Calhoun

REFERENCES

Morgan, H. Wayne. 1963. *William McKinley and His America*. Syracuse: Syracuse U. Pr.

———. 1969. *From Hayes to McKinley: National Party Politics, 1877–1896*. Syracuse: Syracuse U. Pr.

Socolofsky, Homer E., and Allan B. Spetter. 1987. *The Presidency of Benjamin Harrison*. Lawrence: U. Pr. of Kansas.

Williams, R. Hal. 1978. *Years of Decision: American Politics in the 1890s*. New York: Wiley.

Frank E. McKinney (1904–1974)

Democratic National Committee chairman in the Harry Truman era. When William M. Boyle, Jr., resigned as Democratic National Committee chairman in 1951, Indiana's national committeeman, Frank McHale, recommended his colleague Frank E. McKinney to President Harry Truman as a successor. A vocal leader of the pro-Truman faction in the Indiana Democratic Party, the wealthy and skillful fundraiser McKinney was easily elected national chairman. Although the position carried with it a salary and expenses, McKinney was able to forego all remuneration.

In the early 1930s, McKinney, a rags-to-respectability bank employee, was elected treasurer of Marion County, having already served as treasurer of the Democratic city committee of Indianapolis and of the county central committee. In 1936 he served as subtreasurer for Indiana at the Democratic National Committee. In the 1940 presidential campaign, he was vice chairman of the national committee's finance committee. His fiscal experience led to a commission as major in the Army in World War II.

At the time of his selection for the Democratic national chairmanship, McKinney was vice president of the United States Pipeline Company, president of the Fidelity Trust Company of Indianapolis, president of an Indianapolis radio station, a holder of investments in baseball clubs, and treasurer of the Democratic state central committee. Because the pipeline company then had a routine application before a federal agency, McKinney announced that he would resign as its vice president. Hoping to dissipate the negative image surrounding his tainted predecessor's resignation, McKinney made much of running a headquarters that was "clean" and free of "influence peddling." With this same objective, McKinney also publicly recommended to President Truman that internal revenue collectors, then political appointees, be brought under civil service.

When Adlai E. Stevenson, the Democratic nominee for President, failed in 1952 to choose McKinney as his national committee chairman, President Truman took strong offense. McKinney, on the other hand, seemed content to return to his political base in Indiana and to his many corporate interests.

See also: William Boyle, Democratic National Committee, Election of 1940, Adlai Stevenson II, Harry S Truman

Ralph M. Goldman

REFERENCES

Goldman, Ralph M. 1990. *The National Party Chairmen and Committees: Factionalism at the Top*. Armonk, NY: M. E. Sharpe.

Robert M. McLane (1815–1898)

Franklin Pierce's campaign organizer. Robert Milligan McLane, Democratic National Committee chairman during the Franklin Pierce campaign and administration (1852–1856), had politically distinguished forebears. His grandfather, Colonel Allen McLane, served under Lafayette and Lee in the American Revolution and was a collector of the port under every President from Washington to Jackson. His father, Louis McLane, was Andrew Jackson's minister to England in 1829, Secretary of the Treasury in 1831, and Secretary of State in 1833.

McLane was admitted to the bar in Washington in 1840 and acquired a commanding position as a public speaker. In 1845 he was elected to the Maryland legislature and two years after that to Congress. He retired from the U.S.

House to join former Secretary of the Treasury Robert J. Walker in a lucrative legal practice. The two men were instrumental in ensuring that California would be Democratic when it came into the Union. In 1852 McLane served as Maryland's Democratic national committeeman.

Since General Pierce's campaign for President was to consist mainly of dignified retirement in Concord, New Hampshire, the burden of the campaign fell to the members of the national committee and on Democratic members in Congress. Largely because he lived nearby to Washington, the national committee chose McLane as its chairman. He also happened to be an old friend of Pierce's vice presidential running mate, William R. King.

McLane's selection was not universally applauded. Some thought he lacked experience, dedication, or skill in the preparation of campaign literature. McLane limited his activities mainly to making speeches in his own state, later taking pride that national committee operations had cost less than $10,000.

President Pierce appointed McLane commissioner to China in 1853. He served as minister to Mexico under James Buchanan in 1859. He was elected governor of Maryland for the 1883–1885 term and became President Grover Cleveland's minister to France from 1885 to 1889.

See also: Democratic National Committee, Franklin Pierce

Ralph M. Goldman

REFERENCES

Goldman, Ralph M. 1990. *The National Party Chairmen and Committees: Factionalism at the Top.* Armonk, NY: M. E. Sharpe.

McLane, Robert M. 1903. *Reminiscences, 1827–1897.* Privately printed.

Straus, Oscar S. 1922. *Under Four Administrations.* Boston: Houghton Mifflin.

James McMillan (1838–1902)

Businessman, philanthropist, and Republican politician from Michigan. James McMillan entered politics late in life. Born and educated in Canada, he immigrated to Detroit in 1855 and maintained his "home" there for the remainder of his life. Involved initially in railroad car construction, he expanded his interests to shipbuilding and then to the operation of railroads and lake carrier lines. His activities eventually brought him both substantial wealth and public prominence.

Drawn into politics in the late 1870s, he became, in 1886, chairman of the Republican State Committee. In 1889 he was elected to the U.S. Senate and served until his death. He was a member of the conservative inner circle that heavily influenced Republican Party policy during the *fin de siècle* period.

McMillan's importance, however, attaches to his work on the Senate Committee on the District of Columbia. From that position, he removed the railroads from the Mall and, in general, promoted the modernization and revitalization of the District. Under his direction, a commission resurrected the comprehensive plan for the District first drafted by Pierre C. L'Enfant in 1792, but rejected and revised it extensively and spectacularly to channel the course of development in the next century and to assure Americans a capital worthy of the nation.

Although McMillan died in 1902, the McMillan plan, as it came to be called, remained the comprehensive developmental blueprint for decades afterward. In a sense, then, McMillan's most enduring monument is the present-day District of Columbia.

See also: Railroads

John F. Coleman

Charles L. McNary (1874–1944)

Republican Senator from Oregon from 1917 to 1944. Charles Linza McNary was a leading spokesman for agriculture, reforestation, land reclamation, and water power policies. The agrarian orientation of his political career was shaped by his birth on a farm carved from a homestead claim made by his grandfather near Salem, Oregon. After an active career in local and state politics, McNary was appointed to the U.S. Senate in 1917 to fill the unexpired term of Harry Lane. Except for his unsuccessful bid for the vice presidency in 1940, he remained a Senator until his death.

McNary, a member of the western Republican progressive bloc that included such Senators as George Norris, William Borah, Robert La Follette, and Hiram Johnson, gradually came to accept generally an expanded role for government in domestic issues, but he continued to be isolationist in foreign affairs. Thus, during his career he advocated such water power projects as Muscle Shoals and the Bonneville Dam. He was most well known for the McNary-Haugen bill, which sought to support domestic farm prices by subsidizing the sale of surplus crops abroad. The measure was approved by Congress in 1927 and 1928, only to be vetoed twice by Calvin Coolidge.

Following the Democratic landslide in 1932, McNary was elected Senate Minority Leader and used his influence to encourage the GOP to adopt forward-looking policies. He supported many of Franklin Roosevelt's early reforms, including the Agriculture Adjustment Act, the Securities and Exchange Commission, the Public Utility Holding Company Act, and the Works Progress Administration, seeing them as extensions of progressive reform. The New Deal's centralizing tendencies, however, and Roosevelt's increasing internationalism gradually alienated McNary, and like most other western Republican progressives, he ended his political career as an opponent of reforms that he believed were eroding the Jeffersonian agrarian bedrock of American life.

See also: William Borah, Calvin Coolidge, Election of 1940, Isolationism in American Politics, Robert La Follette, George Norris, Franklin D. Roosevelt

John W. Malsberger

REFERENCES

Feinman, Ronald L. 1981. *Twilight of Progressivism: The Western Republican Senators and the New Deal.* Baltimore: Johns Hopkins U. Pr.

Hoffmann, George C. 1951. "The Early Political Career of Charles Linza McNary, 1917–1924." Ph.D. dissertation, University of Southern California.

Johnson, Roger T. 1967. "Charles McNary and the Republican Party During Prosperity and Depression." Ph.D. dissertation, University of Wisconsin.

Nathaniel Macon (1758–1837)

Anti-Federalist opponent of the Constitution. Nathaniel Macon, an American statesman, was educated at the College of New Jersey (now Princeton). A veteran of the American Revolution, he practiced law and early on served in the North Carolina General Assembly. An advocate of states' rights and personal liberty, Macon opposed calling the Constitutional Convention and the ratification of the Constitution. Like most Anti-Federalists, he became a Republican during the partisan realignment of the early 1790s. As a member of the U.S. House of Representatives from 1791 to 1815 (Speaker, 1801–1807), he was a political confidant of Thomas Jefferson until 1806, when he joined with John Randolph of Roanoke and other southern Old Republicans in opposing the administration. In the presidential election of 1808, he supported James Monroe against James Madison. As chairman of the House Foreign Affairs Committee, Macon reported two bills that bore his name, although he opposed the second and was the author of neither. Macon's second bill imposed economic sanctions against belligerent powers that violated the neutral rights of American shipping.

As a United States Senator from 1815 to 1828 (President *pro tempore*, 1826–1828), he defended slavery and opposed the Missouri Compromise (1820). In 1824 Macon supported William H. Crawford's presidential candidacy and received Virginia's 24 electoral votes for Vice President. In 1828 he opposed both presidential candidates (John Quincy Adams and Andrew Jackson), though Adams was said to want Macon as a running mate. In retirement, he opposed nullification in 1832, declaring that secession was the only constitutional recourse for disaffected states. In 1836 he campaigned for Martin Van Buren, helping the Democrats to carry North Carolina for the last time in 12 years.

See also: John Quincy Adams, Anti-Federalists, Election of of 1824 and 1828, Thomas Jefferson, James Madison, Missouri Compromise, Nullification, Old Republicans, Speaker of the House, Martin Van Buren

Thomas A. Mason

REFERENCES

Battle, Kemp P., ed. 1902. *Letters of Nathaniel Macon, John Steele, and William Barry Grove.* Chapel Hill: U. of North Carolina.

Lester Maddox (1915–)

Ax handle–wielding governor of Georgia. Southern politics in the 1960s was a volatile mixture of social change and establishment resistance. The civil rights movement had its heroes: Martin Luther King, Jr., James Meredith, Medgar Evers, and many others. The forces of segregation had their heroes as well: Governor George Wallace and Public Safety Commissioner Bull Connor in Alabama, Senator Strom Thurmond in South Carolina, and restaurateur Lester Maddox in Georgia.

Maddox, owner of the Pickrick Restaurant in Atlanta, supplied supporters with pick handles to help keep African-Americans out of his establishment, and later he closed the restaurant rather than allow it to be integrated. Previously an unsuccessful candidate for mayor of Atlanta and lieutenant governor, in 1966 Maddox capitalized on the publicity and symbolism of his pick-wielding actions to mount a winning campaign for governor of Georgia. Though more moderate as governor than many observers expected, Maddox maintained his bitter opposition to integration, at one point referring to a federal court desegregation order as "ungodly, un-Christian, and un-American." Prohibited by the

Georgia Constitution from running for reelection in 1970, Maddox instead successfully sought election as lieutenant governor. During his tenure, Maddox often fought with Governor Jimmy Carter, at one point using his control of the state senate to block a Carter-backed progressive property tax refund.

Dismissed by many as a political court jester for his antics in office, which included riding a bicycle backward for photographers, Maddox nonetheless symbolized a particularly virulent form of public support for segregation. Opposition to integration proved to be a losing cause, however, and many southern politicians—George Wallace being the most notable—moderated their rhetoric to maintain their political appeal to an expanding multiracial electorate.

Lester Maddox underwent no such conversion and was upset in his bid for a second term as governor in 1974. He ran for President of the United States as the candidate of the States' Rights Party in 1976 and has tried his hand in later years in the real estate business, as an entertainer, and once again as a restaurant owner.

See also: Jimmy Carter, Election of 1976, Martin Luther King, Jr., Strom Thurmond, George Wallace

Tom A. Kazee

REFERENCES

Bass, Jack, and Walter De Vries. 1976. *The Transformation of Southern Politics*. New York: Basic Books.

Williams, Juan. 1988. *Eyes on the Prize*. New York: Penguin.

James Madison (1751–1836)

Fourth President of the United States. James Madison was a substantive contributor to the development of the theory and practice of early American political parties. Classically educated at plantation schools and the College of New Jersey (now Princeton), he became an effective spokesman for his state and region. In the Virginia Convention at the start of the American Revolution, he helped draft the new state constitution. He served a term in the House of Delegates but lost a reelection bid to an opponent who bribed the voters with liquor. Consequently, Madison became a more effective campaigner and never lost another election. In the Continental Congress, the Virginia House of Delegates, and the Constitutional Convention of 1787, he demonstrated wide-ranging statecraft and theoretical insight.

Although the Philadelphia Convention's final product was not entirely what Madison wished,

he skillfully advocated its ratification in essays that he anonymously contributed with Alexander Hamilton and John Jay to *The Federalist* (1788). Drawing on his wide reading in the history of the ancient Greek and Roman republics, Madison's essays discussed the necessity of union, the inadequacy of the Articles of Confederation, and the advantage of a strong federal government grounded in republican principles and providing security for the nation. At the Virginia ratifying convention, Madison successfully defended the new Constitution in debates against opponents—the Anti-Federalists—led by Patrick Henry.

While the ratification contest ended in success, Madison recognized that Henry spoke for a large national constituency. Madison was determined to win the support of the Anti-Federalists by amending the Constitution and addressing their concern for personal rights. Henry used his influence in the Virginia General Assembly to prevent the election of Madison as a United States Senator and to gerrymander his congressional district. Nevertheless, Madison so thoroughly defeated James Monroe that he was unopposed in subsequent congressional elections and served four terms in the House of Representatives. There he fulfilled a campaign pledge and rallied popular support for the new Constitution by sponsoring amendments that guaranteed fundamental liberties and came to be called the Bill of Rights.

Madison was the first example of what became a long tradition in American politics: he co-opted his adversaries' good ideas, thereby effectively neutralizing the opposition (the Anti-Federalists) as a political movement in the future. Moreover, he criticized the financial program of his former ally, Alexander Hamilton, the Federalist Secretary of the Treasury. Madison concluded that the leading Federalists were interpreting the Constitution in ways he had never intended. Although he urged President George Washington to stand for reelection in 1792, he led the congressional opposition against the Federalist administration and organized a new political party that came to be called the Republican Party. In the resulting political realignment, most former Anti-Federalists became Republicans.

The Founding Fathers distrusted political parties and did not anticipate their development. Madison had argued in *The Federalist* (Number 10) that the new Constitution was more likely than any other form of government to maintain a balance among factions and prevent any one from dominating its rivals. However, less than four years later, he abandoned that nonpartisan ideal when he began to organize the Republican Party. In 1796 he worked to secure the election as Vice President of his lifelong friend and political confidant, Thomas Jefferson. After retiring from Congress, Madison drafted the Virginia Resolutions (1798), which defended civil liberties and asserted the right of states to interpose their authority to declare unconstitutional the Federalist-sponsored Alien and Sedition Acts. For Republicans, those resolutions sharpened the issues in the 1800 election and became the foundation of states' rights doctrine in the early nineteenth century. As Secretary of State (1801–1809), Madison supported the Jefferson administration's vigorous exercise of executive power in concluding the Louisiana Purchase and imposing an embargo on foreign trade while the European powers were at war. These policies led to a split among Republicans, who had traditionally advocated legislative supremacy and a weak executive.

A caucus of congressional Republicans nominated Madison as their party's presidential candidate in 1808. He faced opposition not only from the Federalist Charles Cotesworth Pinckney but also from his own vice presidential running mate, George Clinton (nominated by New York Republicans who opposed the embargo on foreign trade) and James Monroe (supported by southern Old Republicans). To the voters, Madison had asserted American neutral rights against Great Britain and France without resorting to war. He received 122 electoral votes, Pinckney 47, and Clinton 6; Monroe withdrew from the race. Federalists, though still a minority, gained 24 House seats. The long series of legislative actions imposing economic sanctions failed to win concessions until Great Britain suspended its orders to search and seize American ships. But news of this action arrived too late to prevent the War of 1812, a conflict supported in the South but unpopular in the North.

The 1812 election became in effect a referendum on the war. The congressional caucus unanimously renominated Madison. Vice President George Clinton having died in April, the caucus nominated Elbridge Gerry to replace him. A coalition of Federalists and New York antiwar Republicans supported De Witt Clinton (George Clinton's nephew) for the presidency. Despite Madison's 128-to-89 electoral vote victory and the creation of new House seats through

reapportionment, Republicans gained only 4 seats, while the Federalists gained 32. After a series of American military reverses, resurgent New England Federalists met in the Hartford Convention (1815) and approved resolutions denouncing the war and Republican policies. But Major General Andrew Jackson's victory at New Orleans and the Treaty of Ghent discredited the Hartford Convention and its Federalist sponsors. The war's honorable conclusion achieved none of the original American war aims, but it consolidated Republican control over the executive and legislative branches. Thereafter the Federalist Party declined permanently. Monroe, who had reconciled with Madison and served as his Secretary of State, easily won the presidency in 1816.

Madison enjoyed a productive retirement, even though by the 1830s he was in declining health. Throughout a remarkably long career, he advanced the political life of his state and nation. Yet during his last years, he recognized the ominous development of conflict between North and South that eventually led to the Civil War.

See also: Alien and Sedition Acts; Anti-Federalists; Election of 1792 and 1812; Alexander Hamilton; Patrick Henry; Andrew Jackson; John Jay; Thomas Jefferson; James Monroe; Old Republicans; George Washington

Thomas A. Mason

REFERENCES

Brant, Irving. 1961. *James Madison.* Indianapolis: Bobbs-Merrill.

Hutchinson, William T., et al., eds. 1962. *The Papers of James Madison.* 17 vols. to date. Chicago: U. of Chicago Pr. and Charlottesville: U. Pr. of Virginia.

Rutland, Robert A. 1987. *James Madison: The Founding Father.* New York: Macmillan.

Warren G. Magnuson (1905–1989)

Longtime Democratic U.S. Senator from Washington State who championed consumer protection. Warren Magnuson received B.A. and J.D. degrees from the University of Washington. He first became active in politics during the 1928 presidential campaign of Al Smith. Serving as special prosecutor in Washington's King County (which includes Seattle) from 1931 to 1933, he was elected to the state legislature in 1933 and then appointed as assistant U.S. district attorney in 1934. That same year, he was elected prosecutor for King County. Regarded as a leading member of the progressive wing of the Democratic Party in his state, he was elected to the U.S. House of Representatives in 1936 and there consistently supported the policies of President Franklin Roosevelt. Magnuson also took an active role in pressing for civil rights.

He was elected to the Senate in 1944. During his early years in the Senate, Magnuson worked hardest as a member of the Appropriations Committee to channel federal money toward the development of Washington. After a close election in 1962, Magnuson shifted his attention to social legislation, and from his position as chairman of the Commerce Committee (1956–1977) and its subcommittee on consumer protection, he secured the passage of a series of bills providing federal protection for the consumer. While at times overshadowed by his popular colleague from Washington State, Henry M. Jackson, Magnuson was respected by his peers for his practical and sound judgments.

See also: Henry M. Jackson

Thomas J. Baldino

REFERENCES

Pertshuk, Michael. 1982. *Revolt Against Regulation.* Berkeley: U. of California Pr.

Redman, Eric. 1973. *The Dance of Legislation.* New York: Simon & Schuster.

Patrick Maguire (1838–1896)

Longest-reigning boss of Boston's Democratic Party. A backroom manager, never elected to important public office, Patrick Maguire ran the last citywide machine in Boston's history, controlling substantial clout in state as well as national politics. His power was rarely secure, limited as it was by challenges from restless ward bosses below him and the grim deference he had to pay to Yankee Democrats throughout his career. The collapse of Democratic cohesion in the city after his death confirmed his staying power while it lasted.

Born in Ireland, Maguire arrived in Boston at mid-century to work as a printer. By 1860 he had won his seat on the Democratic City Committee. His constant aim thereafter was to enhance his influence by aligning Irish votes behind the party's established structure. Maguire embodied the prospering immigrant's quest for respectable security through party loyalty. In 1882 he founded a weekly, *The Republic*, to guide this quest. In 1884 he helped nail down the Irish vote for Grover Cleveland, simultaneously promoting the election of Hugh O'Brien as Boston's first Irish Catholic mayor. Over the next decade Maguire nurtured a volatile alliance among the Irish, Yankee Democrats, and insurgent Mugwumps inspired by Cleveland's con-

servative reformism. Although he was obscured by flashier and more lovable demagogues, fictional and real, Maguire's prudent leadership went far to mute the early tensions surrounding Boston's most momentous power transfer—from Yankee to Irish. The *Boston Transcript*, journal of record for its elite readership, observed apprehensively on the day of Maguire's funeral, "He was a man of many admirable qualities, and the danger now is that his successor, whoever he may be, will not use the same questionable power with equal moderation, honesty, and regard for the public service." It turned out, however, that no one succeeded Maguire.

See also: Bosses, Grover Cleveland, Election of 1884, Mugwumps

Geoffrey Blodgett

REFERENCES

Blodgett, Geoffrey. 1966. *The Gentle Reformers: Massachusetts Democrats in the Cleveland Era.* Cambridge: Harvard U. Pr.

Galvin, John T. 1982. "Patrick J. Maguire: Boston's Last Democratic Boss." 55 *New England Quarterly* 392.

Mahan v. Howell
410 U.S. 315 (1973)

The Supreme Court decision in this case is significant as an early instance in which the Court permitted a nontrivial deviation from the "one person, one vote" standard in the drawing of state legislative districts. The state of Virginia, it ruled, had a "rational state policy of respecting the boundaries of political subdivisions." The Court then argued that preservation of existing political subdivisions in the construction of state legislative districts was justified in terms of insuring some voice for political subdivisions and their citizens.

In 1971 both chambers of Virginia's bicameral legislature were reapportioned. The Virginia Constitution required that electoral districts be "contiguous and compact" and "proportional to the population of the district." The plan for the house created 100 seats from 52 single-member, multimember, and floterial (i.e., at-large) districts with a maximum population range of 16.4 percent. Following *Kirkpatrick v. Preisler* and *Wells v. Rockefeller*, the district court invalidated the house plan as an "impermissible violation" of "one person, one vote" and crafted its own reapportionment plan, involving a maximum population deviation of 10 percent; this plan *did* divide political subdivisions. In earlier instances, the Court had overturned state reapportionment plans for congressional districts with much smaller maximum population deviations than those present in the Virginia case. The issue, in part, was whether the same mathematical standard had to apply to state legislative districts.

In this case the Court continued to make a distinction between national and state legislative redistricting, declaring "the latitude afforded to states in legislative redistricting is somewhat broader than that afforded to them in congressional redistricting." Rather than follow a strict equal population standard, the Court chose to use the "as nearly as is practicable" standard found in *Wesberry v. Sanders* and *Reynolds v. Sims*. This rule tolerates population variances between districts when it is "incident to the effectuation of a rational state policy." The Court ruled that the population deviations in Virginia were indeed within acceptable constitutional limits.

The case is important within the context of evolving constitutional law in the area of reapportionment for several reasons: (1) it reiterated the qualitative difference in the Court's eyes between congressional and state legislative districting; (2) it reaffirmed the unwillingness of the Court to establish a simple numerical standard by which to judge reapportionment plans; and (3) it reasserted the state's right to pursue other rational objectives, such as protecting political subdivisions, as long as the state justified the population deviations in those terms and the variance was not excessive.

See also: Kirkpatrick v. Preisler, Reynolds v. Sims, Wesberry v. Sanders

Clyde Brown

REFERENCES

Knight, Barbara B. 1976. "The States and Reapportionment: One-Man, One-Vote Reevaluated." 49 *State Government* 155.

Wollack, Andrea J., ed. 1980. *Reapportionment: Law and Technology*. Washington: National Conference of State Legislatures.

Majority Party Conflict in the Late Nineteenth Century

The central characteristic of major party competition from the mid-1870s to the mid-1890s was the national equilibrium between Republicans and Democrats. Once considered a Republican era, the period in fact was one in which the two parties were nearly equal in strength nationwide. Although the Democrats won the presidency only twice, their candidates outpolled their opponents in four of the five elections between 1876 and 1892. A substantial portion of the Democrats' popular total came form the Solid South, and Republicans had an almost equally solid bloc of states in the Northeast and upper Midwest. Because neither of these two blocs held enough electoral votes to win, presidential elections turned on the outcome in a half dozen "doubtful" states, principally New York and Indiana. The parties often looked to these two states for presidential and vice presidential nominees, and national committees were prone to send their star speakers and the bulk of their campaign funds to the doubtful states.

This party equilibrium heightened the need for thorough organization and, hence, magnified the power of state party bosses, especially in the doubtful states. A decision by a state leader to sit out an election could destroy a presidential nominee's chances of winning. Similarly, a President who narrowly won election found himself besieged by bosses who claimed responsibility and demanded patronage. The increase in the number of federal appointees from 51,000 in 1871 to 157,000 in 1891 raised the stakes enormously for state party leaders.

With the difference in national party strength so narrow, leaders felt the need to exercise caution in articulating party policy. Taking too strong a stand on some issue might offend enough members of some group—temperance advocates, wool growers, or Irish Catholics, for instance—within the party so as to bring defeat at the next election. Some historians have misinterpreted this need to treat issues in a gingerly manner as evidence that little real difference separated Republicans and Democrats, but these scholars apply an inappropriate standard. American parties generally have not followed the European model of left and right parties split inexorably and irrevocably along ideological lines. Instead, major parties in the United States traditionally are consensus organizations, both of which try to win followers from the vast middle of the political spectrum that most Americans inhabit. The equilibrium between Republicans and Democrats in the late nineteenth century underscored their need to remain within an ideological mainstream.

The even party balance also inhibited government activism at the national level. In the eleven Congresses from 1875 to 1897, each major party controlled a clear majority in both houses plus the presidency only once: the Republicans from 1889 to 1891 and the Democrats from 1893 to 1895. Typically, Congress was split, with the Democrats more often than not taking the House of Representatives, and the Republicans the Senate. Such division made the formulation of policy and the passage of legislation difficult.

In attempting to resolve the electoral stasis in its favor, each party had advantages and disadvantages. Republicans entered the era with a large fund of moral capital derived from their status as saviors of the Union and emancipators of the slaves—a moral capital they squandered to some degree in the corruption of Ulysses Grant's administration and some of the Reconstruction state governments. The Republican Party had close ties with Union veterans whom it honored with liberal pensions. For their part, Democrats argued that their party was unfairly accused of "treason," and they persistently labeled Republican denunciation of southern outrages against Blacks as "waving the bloody shirt."

The Republicans were generally better organized than the Democrats, with a consistently larger stable of well-known and capable national leaders from which to choose nominees. Although the Republican Party was riven by fights between Stalwarts and Half-Breeds, by the mid-1880s, the Half-Breed persuasion emerged supreme and succeeded in imprinting the GOP with its emphasis on economic issues. The Democrats, true to their states' rights orientation, were not so much a national party as a loose confederation of state parties whose leaders were often more interested in state or local affairs than in national party victory. Still, the Democrats retained great strength in national elections. Virtually automatically, the 15 former slave states provided the Party with more than two-thirds of the number of electoral votes required to win the presidency. Democrats had strong appeal among numerous immigrant groups turned off by sumptuary acts and English-language education laws passed by Republican state legislatures.

Perhaps most important, Democrats of the period espoused an ideology that squared with traditional American suspicion of government. As worthy successors of Thomas Jefferson and Andrew Jackson, Grover Cleveland and other Gilded Age Democrats clung to notions of limited national government and states' rights localism. Their portrayal of their opponents' activist programs as corruptly favoring special interests rang true to many Americans. The great challenge to the Republicans was to turn that deep-seated public attitude around, and by the mid-1890s they did so.

In the 1880s Republican Party leaders turned increasingly away from sectional issues and focused on a nationalistic economic program calling for a powerful national government that would give direction to the country's modernization and foster economic growth with efficiency and equity. The GOP argued that a sound national currency and banking system, a well-crafted protective tariff, careful reciprocal trade agreements, and generous subsidies were all indispensable to move the nation's economy forward. When they controlled the Fifty-first Congress (1889–1890), they put much of their program into law, only to suffer overwhelming rejection in the 1890 congressional elections by voters still enamored of the Democrats' small government ideals.

But the Democrats' negative approach to governance proved their undoing when they offered little to the nation to assuage the devastating effects of the panic of 1893. Crushing the Democrats in the 1894 congressional elections, the Republicans at last broke the 20-year stalemate between the parties. Two years later, sounding again all the components of their economic program, they billed William McKinley as the advance agent of prosperity, and he decisively defeated William Jennings Bryan in 1896. Prosperity did in fact return in the late 1890s, and the Republicans held on to their majority-party status until another great depression reversed their fortunes in the 1930s.

See also: Bloody Shirt, Bosses, William Jennings Bryan, Grover Cleveland, Ulysses S. Grant, William McKinley, Reconstruction, Stalwarts (and Half-Breeds)

Charles W. Calhoun

REFERENCES

Blodgett, Geoffrey. 1976. "A New Look at the Gilded Age: Politics in a Cultural Context." In Daniel Walker Howe, ed. *Victorian America.* Philadelphia: U. of Pennsylvania Pr.

Gould, Lewis L. 1970. "The Republican Search for a National Majority." In H. Wayne Morgan, ed. *The Gilded Age.* Syracuse: Syracuse U. Pr.

Keller, Morton. 1977. *Affairs of State: Public Life in Late Nineteenth Century America.* Cambridge: Harvard U. Pr.

Morgan, H. Wayne. 1969. *From Hayes to McKinley: National Party Politics, 1877–1896.* Syracuse: Syracuse U. Pr.

Williams, R. Hal. 1970. "'Dry Bones and Dead Language': The Democratic Party." In H. Wayne Morgan, ed. *The Gilded Age.* Syracuse: Syracuse U. Pr.

Majority Party Leadership in Congress

The importance of congressional majority party leaders and the functions they perform in the political process derive from the unique character of the U.S. Congress. For a modern legislature, the U.S. Congress is uniquely powerful. Unlike the British parliament, for example, Congress plays a significant role in policy formulation independent of the executive. Yet, during the twentieth century, the ability of the Congress to legislate has been problematical. Because the political parties are weak, numerical majorities do not automatically translate into policy majorities. In the American Congress, majorities must be constructed. Nevertheless, despite their weakness, parties have usually provided the basis upon which majorities are built. Consequently congressional party leaders, especially leaders of the majority party in a chamber, are expected to play a central role in coalition building. In fact, the attentive public—including the press—judges a party's leadership largely on the basis of its coalition-building success.

In order to satisfy the expectations of followers and of other significant actors, the sine qua non of successful legislative leadership, the congressional majority party leadership must perform two principal functions. The leadership is charged with building winning coalitions on major legislation, thereby satisfying the policy expectations of its membership and of significant actors outside the chamber, particularly interest groups allied with the party and the President if he is a fellow partisan. Second, the leadership must "keep peace in the family," as current House leaders express it. Both parties are heterogeneous; the often conflicting policy and power goals of members pose constant threats to party coherence. In addition, members' generalized dissatisfaction with the institution and their role within it can also endanger party harmony. "Keeping peace in the family" dictates that party leaders help members satisfy their expectations about their individual roles in the chamber; it requires leaders to mitigate intraparty conflicts and foster cooperative patterns of behavior among party members.

The Speaker, the Majority Leader, and the Majority Whip are the core of the majority party leadership in the modern House of Representatives. The Speaker as an officer of the House is formally elected by its full membership but is actually selected by and is the leader of the majority party in the House. As Democrats have controlled the House continuously since 1955, all recent Speakers have been Democrats. The Majority Leader and the Whip are party officials, both elected by the majority party caucus, the organization of all House members of the majority party.

The Speaker is the presiding officer of the House; as such, he recognizes members who wish to speak and decides points of order. He refers bills to committee. He appoints the members of select committees, of conference committees, of some commissions, and chairmen of the Committee of the Whole. The Majority Leader schedules legislation for floor consideration; he is the chief party spokesman on the House floor. The Whip oversees the "whip system," an organization charged with collecting and disseminating information. Conducting whip polls to determine how members stand on important legislation is the whip system's single most important function. These leadership duties provide resources useful in coalition building and party maintenance. The Speaker's influence over the interpretation of House rules, for example, can be used within the limits of fairness to his party's advantage.

Because the Constitutional Convention did not debate the nature of the speakership, we do not know what the framers envisioned. Author Mary Follett argues persuasively that the Speaker was intended to be a political leader, not simply an impartial moderator. The early Speakers, according to Follett, were "keen guardians of party interest" but not "real party leaders." Henry Clay, who served six terms as Speaker between 1811 and 1825, was the leader of his party and established the position of the Speaker as a legislative leader. Follett claims, "As a presiding officer Clay from the first showed that he considered himself not the umpire but the leader of the House; his object was clearly and expressly to govern the House as far as possible. . . . He made no attempt to disguise the fact he was a political officer." Most of the Speakers between 1825 and the Civil War did conduct the office as a political one, but not all were leaders of their party or faction. The political turmoil surrounding the slavery issue frequently made choosing a Speaker difficult, with the consequence that what Follett calls "second-rate men" or "tools in the hands of the real leaders" were sometimes chosen. Since the Civil War the Speaker has been considered to be and almost always in fact has been the leader of his party in the House.

The other party offices emerged rather late. The first formally designated House Majority Leader and Whip date from 1899 and 1897 respectively. In the Senate, a relatively permanent and formally designated floor leader did not emerge in either party until the twentieth century; the first Whips date from the same period.

The Senate Majority Leader is the leader of and is chosen by the members of the majority party in the Senate. Over the last decade five different men have held the position. George Mitchell of Maine became Majority Leader in 1989, replacing Robert Byrd of West Virginia. When Republicans took control of the chamber in 1981, Howard Baker of Tennessee, who had been Minority Leader, became Majority Leader. In 1985, after Baker's voluntary retirement from the Senate, he was succeeded by Robert Dole of Kansas. In 1986, Democrats regained a majority in the Senate and Byrd, who had served as Minority Leader during the period of Republican control, resumed the position of Majority Leader for the One Hundredth Congress. When in 1989 Byrd relinquished the position, Democratic Senators chose George Mitchell of Maine to succeed him. The Majority Whip—at this writing, Wendall Ford of Kentucky—is also elected by the members of the Senate majority party.

Political scientists increasingly agree that congressional leadership is best understood from a contextual perspective. Both the broader political context and the internal institutional environment shape and constrain leadership styles and strategies. Chamber and party rules, for example, distribute resources in the chamber, and the distribution of resources among party leaders, committee leaders, and rank-and-file members affects what strategies are feasible. The size of the party contingent in the chamber and the party affiliation of the President are other key variables affecting strategy choices and the probability of success.

In the late nineteenth century, the speakership developed into an extremely potent office. House rules gave the Speaker immense resources: he appointed the members and chairmen of all committees and chaired the Rules Committee, which controls the flow of legislation to the floor. The end of the century was a period of strong parties in the country and in the Congress. The Speaker as leader of the majority party and possessor of great institutional resources could run the House. The leadership styles and strategies of Speakers such as Thomas Reed (R-Maine) and Joseph Cannon (R-Ill.) were based on centralization and command.

The 1910–1911 revolt against Cannon stripped the Speaker of much of his power: he was removed from the Rules Committee, and the power to appoint the members and chairmen of committees was taken from him. The party system also weakened. By the 1920s, seniority had become the sole criterion for appointment to committee chairs and, as a result, chairmen became independent political barons over whom the majority party had little control. This change in context dictated a change in leadership style. Sam Rayburn (D-Tex.), the most highly regarded Speaker of the committee government period (the 1940s and 1950s), used a highly personalized and persuasion-based leadership style: he made little use of formal leadership structures, he engaged himself heavily in doing favors for members, and he relied on personal negotiation with a few key actors in building coalitions. Norms of apprenticeship and deference to senior members contributed to keeping peace in the family. So too, Rayburn believed, did his highly informal and personalized style by providing as few forums as possible for the antagonistic northern and southern factions in the party to confront each other directly.

In the late 1950s and the 1960s, junior Democrats who were predominantly liberal northerners increasingly chafed under the control of the powerful committee chairmen. These chairmen were predominantly conservative southerners, many of whom ran their committees with an iron hand and denied junior members the opportunity to participate meaningfully. In the late 1960s and early 1970s, reform forces succeeded in instituting a series of rules changes that altered the distribution of influence. Both rank-and-file members and subcommittee chairmen on the one hand and the party leadership on the other gained at the expense of committee chairmen. The chairmen's almost total control over the organization, staffing, and agenda of their committees was severely diluted when subcommittee chairmen and rank-and-file members gained significant to preponderant say. The requirement that committee chairmen must be approved by a secret ballot majority vote of the Democratic membership made chairmen more responsive to both the rank and file and to party leaders to the extent that they speak for their membership. The Speaker was given greater control over committee assignments, new powers over the referral of bills to committee, and, most significantly, the right to nominate all Democratic members of the Rules Committee subject only to ratification by the Democratic Caucus.

The desire of rank-and-file members to participate more fully in the legislative process was a major impetus for these changes. And much higher participation rates were the result. Thus, although the party leadership gained new resources, it confronted an environment made highly unpredictable by the large number of significant actors.

These changes in the House made the Rayburn's "good-old-boy" strategy obsolete. In a highly unpredictable environment, more formal and systematic ways of gathering information are necessary, and a strategy based on personal negotiation with a few key actors is obviously untenable in a House with wide participation. In the late 1970s, the newly elected leadership team of Speaker Thomas P. O'Neill (D-Mass.) and Majority Leader James Wright developed a three-pronged strategy—one that, with elaborations, is still employed in the 1990s. First, the leadership is heavily service-oriented. In addition to doing favors for individual members just as their predecessors did, the post-reform leadership is much more involved in providing services to the Democratic membership collectively. For example, the leadership provides its members with a great deal of useful information and, most importantly, in making scheduling decisions, it is sensitive to members' needs for predictability and time in the district. Given the resources now available to individual members, almost any member can cause problems for the leadership. Thus rank-and-file satisfaction or dissatisfaction is more important than it used to be. By providing services, the leaders contribute to party maintenance and develop a store of goodwill that they can draw upon in their coalition-building efforts.

Second, the leadership employs its formal powers and influence to structure the choices that members face so as to give advantage to the outcome that the leaders favor. Neither the leadership's limited resources nor current political norms make coercion of individual members a feasible basis for coalition building. Some of the resources that leaders acquired in the 1970s, especially their control over the Rules Committee, augmented their ability to shape and therefore influence the choices that members face on the floor. The leadership determines

when legislation is considered on the floor and under what ground rules. A ruling from the Rules Committee may specify the order in which major substitutes are voted on; it may allow certain amendments to be offered and not others. Decisions on timing, on order, and on the amendments allowed can all influence the outcome. Such strategies require member acquiescence, overt or tacit. A special rule from the Rules Committee requires a majority vote on the House floor. This feature limits the applicability of the strategy, but members do not then perceive the use of these rules as unreasonably coercive; consequently, the party maintenance function is not adversely affected.

The core party leadership is too small to undertake the task of successful coalition building alone. House members are independent, active, and often unpredictable in their voting. Successful coalition building, therefore, requires an extensive information-gathering and persuasion capability. To respond to this need, the party leadership has developed the strategy of inclusion; it attempts to include as many Democrats as possible in the coalition-building process. Over time the leadership has expanded and made increasing use of formal leadership structures; it also brings other Democrats into the process on an ad hoc basis.

The Steering and Policy Committee, which became the Democrats' committee on committees in 1974, is a broadly representative group. Chaired by the Speaker, it consists of twelve regionally elected members; eight others appointed by the Speaker, the chairmen of the four most important committees; and the Majority Leader, caucus chairman and secretary, Majority Whip, chief deputy whip, and chairman of the Democratic Congressional Campaign Committee. This Steering and Policy Committee has sometimes served as a forum for the exchange of information and the resolution of intraparty disagreements. It frequently endorses major legislation thereby placing the imprimatur of the Democratic Party on the legislation.

The whip system, which in the early 1970s consisted of the Whip, an assistant whip, and 18 or so regionally elected zone whips, expanded enormously during the 1970s and 1980s. In the One Hundredth Congress 82 Democrats—about 30 percent of the Democratic House membership—were part of the system. The system consists of the Majority Whip, the chief deputy whip, who has become a part of the core leadership, 10 deputy whips, 4 task-force chairmen, 44 at-large whips, and 22 zone whips.

During the speakership of Tip O'Neill in the 1970s and 1980s, the zone whips conducted the initial count of Democratic voting intentions on important legislation. The other whips, all appointed by the leadership, were used in the effort to persuade Democrats to support the leadership's position. On particularly critical legislation, the Speaker appointed a task force and charged it with engineering passage of the bill. The first task force was on President Jimmy Carter's energy legislation; being difficult to pass, budget resolutions always received task force treatment. The chairman and members of the task forces were not necessarily members of the whip system or of the committee of origin. A willingness to work on the bill at issue and the skill to do so effectively were the criteria for inclusion.

Task forces have now become the standard way of handling legislation on which any significant leadership effort is deemed necessary. The leadership selects a chairman or often two co-chairs with ties to different wings of the Democratic Party. In most cases, all the whips and Democratic committee members who support the legislation are invited to join the task force; other Democrats who are interested in working in the issue are also welcomed. Those who show up become the task force.

Through the whip system and the task forces, the leadership has enlisted a large number and a broad variety of Democrats in its efforts. The number involved in the typical task force effort makes one-on-one persuasion among a large proportion of the membership possible. The broad variety ensures that the group as a whole will have ties to all kinds of Democrats. Task forces save the leadership's time and help it to husband its resources. Clearly their contribution to successful coalition building is substantial.

The strategy of inclusion also has major payoffs for party maintenance. By involving Democrats in leadership efforts through task forces, the expanded whip system, and the Steering and Policy Committee, the leadership satisfies members' expectations of meaningful participation in the legislative process. Task forces provide an especially useful way of channeling junior members' desires for participation into activities beneficial to the leadership and the Democrats.

The 1980s brought major changes in the political context that required further leadership adaptations: the leadership has become increasingly media conscious to the extent that systematic attempts to influence opinion through the media is now considered a fourth leadership strategy. Congressional Democrats saw President Ronald Reagan make especially skillful use of the electronic media in pursuing a course that threatened their policy, reelection, and power goals. The leadership became convinced that, without a media strategy of its own, Democrats in Congress had no hope of competing.

Partisan control of the presidency, of course, influences what congressional party leaders are expected to do and their chances of success. If the President's party controls a chamber, the majority party leaders are expected to build winning coalitions on the President's legislative priorities. They do not and are not expected to serve blindly and exclusively as the President's lieutenants; leaders represent their members' views and interests to the President. They may occasionally refuse to support the President; but most of the time, they work closely with the President in attempting to pass his program. This cooperation is what their members and interest groups allied with the party expect. The President is, after all, the leader of their party.

A majority party leadership that faces a President of the other party confronts a more complex strategic situation: it can cooperate with the President and pass compromise policies, it can simply try to defeat the President's program, or it can try to pass its own program. Conditions allowing successful pursuit of the third strategy are rare but did pertain during the One Hundredth Congress.

Speaker Jim Wright and his new leadership team successfully exercised strong, policy-oriented leadership during 1987 and 1988. Wright took a lead role in agenda setting and involved himself in the substance of policy. Such leadership was made possible by the political weakening of President Reagan, the consequent belief among Democrats that policy goals stymied for six years by the Reagan administration were now attainable, and the Democrats' desire to build a record to take into the 1988 elections. Also contributing to the strong active leadership role is the increased use of very large omnibus vehicles (e.g., reconciliation bills and continuing resolutions). As the only entity that can legitimately speak for the party as a whole and that possesses integrative capability, the party leadership necessarily gets involved in such broadly encompassing legislation.

Is the stronger, more policy-oriented leadership of Wright only a function of ephemeral political conditions and thus likely to be short-lived? Or are there more permanent changes in the external context and the political environment that might provide the basis for sustained stronger leadership?

One might argue that permanent changes in House processes, especially the budget process and multiple referral, have made a coordinating, integrating entity essential if the House is to function efficiently. Given current structures, only the party leadership has the institutional resources and the legitimacy to serve as that entity.

Will majority party members (almost always Democrats for two-thirds of the twentieth century) allow their leadership to continue playing that role? That depends on the extent to which these Democrats value the passage of party-sponsored legislation over values like political independence and on the extent to which they agree on the necessity of the legislation favored by party leaders.

One can hypothesize that some contextual changes do, in fact, provide the basis for stronger leadership. Although no party realignment occurred during the Reagan years, the period did see some resurgence of party feeling, at least among elites, and a strengthening of party organizations, particularly the congressional campaign committees.

Although the fear (and hope) of a switch in party control of the House has receded, its impact may linger on, particularly so as the constituency basis for intraparty factionalism among Democrats has been declining. With the increase in voting among African-Americans and growing Republicanism in the South, the electoral constituencies of most southern Democrats are not radically different from those of their northern colleagues. The increase in party voting in the House in recent years is, scholars hypothesize, the result of this change in constituency bases and of members' perception of a greater stake in party success, in interaction with the character of the issue agenda.

Our understanding of the history and current functioning of majority party leadership in the Senate is considerably less complete than for the House. During much of the strong speakership era in the House early in the twentieth century, power in the Senate was centralized in the hands of Senators Nelson Aldrich (R-R.I.) and William Allison (R-Iowa). They "controlled the Republican party in the Senate and through it the entire Senate by influencing the committee assignment process, decisions made by the principal standing committees and scheduling decisions made by the Steering Committees," in the opinion of Randall Ripley, a political scientist. During much of the period of committee government in the House, a similar decentralized distribution of power pertained in the Senate. Thus, the literature on the Senate in the 1950s depicts a body characterized by a relatively unequal distribution of influence and constraining norms; it was committee centered, member-expertise dependent, inward looking, and relatively closed as an institution. The typical 1950s Senator was a specialist who concentrated primarily upon the issues that came before his committees. His legislative activities were largely confined to the committee room; he was seldom active on the Senate floor and made little use of the media. He was deferential to his seniors, loyal to the institution, and highly restrained in his use of the powers that Senate rules confer upon the individual.

In the 1980s Senate influence is much more equally distributed, and members are accorded very wide latitude. The Senate has become an open, staff-dependent, outward-looking institution in which significant decisions are made in multiple arenas. The typical Senator no longer specializes; he becomes involved in a broad range of issues, including ones that do not fall into the jurisdiction of his committees. Even though he serves on more committees than his predecessor in the 1950s did, he does not confine his activities to the committee room. He is also active on the Senate floor and often makes use of public arenas as well. He is less deferential to anyone and much less restrained in using the powers granted to him by the rules of Senate.

The formal powers of the Senate Majority Leader were little altered by this change, the office always having been deficient in formal powers. Certainly the resources that the Senate Majority Leader commands are far less potent than those of the Speaker of the House. He is not the chamber's presiding officer and, in any case, the presiding officer of the Senate has much less discretion than his House counterpart does. The only important resource that the Senate rules give the Majority Leader to aid him with his core tasks of scheduling legislation and floor leadership is the right to be recognized first when a number of Senators are seeking recognition on the Senate floor.

Not only do institutional rules give majority party leaders few special resources, but they also bestow great powers on rank-and-file Senators. In most cases, any Senator can offer an unlimited number of amendments to a piece of legislation on the Senate floor, and those amendments need not even be germane. A Senator can hold the Senate floor indefinitely unless cloture is invoked, a procedure requiring an extraordinary majority. As Senators in the 1980s became much more willing fully to exploit the powers inherent in the rules, the job of the Senate Majority Leader became even more difficult.

Since even a single Senator can disrupt the work of the Senate, a partisan minority of any size can bring legislative activity to a complete standstill. The Senate Majority Leader must confer with the Minority Leader on an almost continuous basis. In the House with its more constraining rules, floor scheduling is largely a Majority Leadership function; in the Senate, the Majority Leader schedules only after close consultation with the Minority Leader.

Structuring floor choices that members face so as to give an advantage to the party's position, a common House leadership strategy, is less readily available to the Senate majority leadership. The party leaders' control over the floor agenda is tenuous. By offering nongermane amendments on the floor, individual Senators can force action on issues that committee and party leaders would prefer to avoid. Rank-and-file Senators can disrupt the planned flow of business through filibusters or amending marathons, actual or threatened.

The Majority Leader does have more influence over the timing of floor consideration than anyone else in the chamber, an influence often used to strategic advantage. He is centrally involved in the negotiating of the unanimous consent agreements that are often employed to set the rules for the consideration of legislation on the Senate floor. If he is skillful, he can gain some advantage for his position, but such agreements, as their name implies, require unanimous consent. The leader's right of first recognition can sometimes be used strategically. Senate rules disallow more than second degree amendments; by using his priority in gaining recognition to offer amendments, the Majority Leader can sometimes put his opponents' amendments out of order and thereby block them.

The inclusion of a large number and broad variety of members in coalition-building efforts is less a strategy than a necessity in the Senate. If a Senator and his staff are skillful, no Senate leader can prevent him from participating in making decisions on almost any issue before the Senate. The Majority Leader must work with the significant players, and given the powers and resources of individual Senators, they will often have as much to say about the terms of the cooperative effort as the Majority Leader.

Because the Senate membership is so much smaller than that of the House, party committees and other formal structures are less important instruments of coalition building. In neither party is the whip system of much importance, although Alan Cranston, the Democratic Whip, until 1991 was renowned as an expert vote counter. On the Democratic side, the Policy Committee, which the Democratic Party leader chairs, primarily provides him with highly useful staff resources. The Republican leader does not even chair the Republican Party's Policy Committee. From the leader's perspective, the committee's weekly lunches for all Republican Senators are its most useful function; they provide a forum for the exchange of information.

If structuring the legislative agenda and inclusion are less efficacious leadership strategies in the Senate than in the House, providing services and doing favors are even more important. In making their legislative scheduling decisions, leaders attempt to accommodate the membership not only collectively but also individually.

By assiduously using the limited resources he possesses to do favors for members, the Majority Leader creates a favorable climate for coalition building. The favors he can do are often not negligible, and members generally are grateful. Yet what the Senate Majority Leader can do to or for his members is seldom decisive for the achievement of their goals. Certainly, his impact on the reelection of his members is marginal at best. Consequently, the Senate Majority Leader must rely upon persuasion; he certainly cannot command. Furthermore, lacking the powers to structure floor choices that the House Speaker has, he is even more dependent than is the House leadership upon a favorable political context for success.

See also: Individual Speakers of the House and Majority Leaders of the Senate

Barbara Sinclair

REFERENCES

Brady, David. 1973. *Congressional Voting in a Partisan Era*. Lawrence: U. Pr. of Kansas.

Clark, Joseph S. 1963. *The Senate Establishment*. New York: Hill and Wang.

Cooper, Joseph, and David W. Brady. 1981. "Institutional Context and Leadership Style: The House from Cannon to Rayburn." 70 *American Political Science Review* 411.

Davidson, Roger H. 1985. "Senate Leaders: Janitors for an Untidy Chamber?" In Lawrence C. Dodd and Bruce I. Oppenheimer, eds. *Congress Reconsidered*. 3rd ed. Washington: Congressional Quarterly.

Dodd, Lawrence C. 1979. "The Expanded Roles of the House Democratic Whip System: The 93rd and 94th Congresses." 7 *Congressional Studies* 27.

Ehrenhalt, Alan. 1987. "Changing South Perils Conservative Coalition." (Aug. 1) *Congressional Quarterly Weekly Report* 1699.

Ellwood, John W., and James A. Thurber. 1981. "The Politics of the Congressional Budget Process Re-Examined." In Lawrence C. Dodd and Bruce I. Oppenheimer, eds. *Congress Reconsidered*. 2nd ed. Washington: Congressional Quarterly.

Fenno, Richard F. 1965. "The Internal Distribution of Influence: The House." In David B. Truman, ed. *The Congress and America's Future*. Englewood Cliffs, NJ: Prentice-Hall.

———. 1973. *Congress in Committees*. Boston: Little, Brown.

———. 1978. *Home Style*. Boston: Little, Brown.

Foley, Michael. 1980. *The New Senate*. New Haven: Yale U. Pr.

Follett, Mary Parker. 1986. *The Speaker of the House of Representatives*. New York: Bert Franklin.

Huitt, Ralph K. 1965. "The Internal Distribution of Influence: The Senate." In David Truman, ed. *The Congress and America's Future*. Englewood Cliffs, NJ: Prentice-Hall.

Jones, Charles O. 1981. "House Leadership in an Age of Reform." In Frank H. Mackaman, ed. *Understanding Congressional Leadership*. Washington: Congressional Quarterly.

Loomis, Burdett A. 1981. "The 'Me' Decade and the Changing Context of House Leadership." In Frank H. Mackaman, ed. *Understanding Congressional Leadership*. Washington: Congressional Quarterly.

Matthews, Donald E. 1960. *U.S. Senators and Their World*. New York: Vintage.

Oppenheimer, Bruce I. 1981. "The Changing Relationship Between House Leadership and the Committee on Rules." In Frank H. Mackaman, ed. *Understanding Congressional Leadership*. Washington: Congressional Quarterly.

Peabody, Robert L. 1981. "Senate Party Leadership: From the 1950s to the 1980s." In Frank H. Mackaman, ed. *Understanding Congressional Leadership*. Washington: Congressional Quarterly.

Rohde, David W. 1974. "Committee Reform in the House of Representatives and the Subcommittee Bill of Rights." 41 *Annals of the American Academy of Political and Social Science* 39.

———, Norman Ornstein, and Robert Peabody. 1985. "Political Change and Legislative Norms in the U.S. Senate, 1957–1974." In Glenn Parker, ed. *Studies of Congress*. Washington: Congressional Quarterly.

Riddick, Floyd M. 1967. *Party Leaders in the House of Representatives*. Washington: Brookings.

———. 1969. *Majority Party Leadership in Congress*. Boston: Little, Brown.

———. 1969. *Power in the Senate*. New York: St. Martin's.

———. 1981. *Majority and Minority Leaders of the U.S. Senate: History and Development of the Offices of Floor Leaders*. Senate Document 97–12, 97th Congress, 1st session. Washington: U.S. Government Printing Office.

Rothman, David. 1966. *Politics and Power: The U.S. Senate 1869–1901*. Cambridge: Harvard U. Pr.

Sinclair, Barbara. 1982. *Congressional Realignment*. Austin: U. of Texas Pr.

———. 1983. *Majority Leadership in the U.S. House*. Baltimore: Johns Hopkins U. Pr.

———. 1985. "Agenda Control and Policy Success: The Case of Ronald Reagan and the 97th House." 20 *Legislative Studies Quarterly* 291.

———. 1986. "Party Leadership and Policy Change." In Gerald Wright, Leroy Rieseetbach, and Lawrence Dodd, eds. *Congress and Policy Change*. New York: Agathon Press.

———. 1986. "Senate Styles and Senate Decision-Making, 1955–80." 46 *Journal of Politics* 877.

———. 1989. "House Majority Party Leadership in the Late 1980s." In Lawrence Dodd and Bruce Oppenheimer, eds. *Congress Reconsidered*. 4th ed. Washington: Congressional Quarterly.

———. 1989. *The Transformation of the U.S. Senate*. Baltimore: Johns Hopkins U. Pr.

Charles T. Manatt (1936–)

Born in Chicago but raised on his family's 320-acre hog farm on the outskirts of Audubon, Iowa, Charles Taylor Manatt graduated from Iowa State University (B.S., 1959) and from George Washington University (J.D., 1962). From 1981 to 1985 he was chairman of the Democratic National Committee (DNC), a post he won in an unprecedentedly expensive campaign, estimated to have cost him nearly $100,000. Manatt had begun to practice law in Van Nuys, California, in 1962, and by the 1980s his very prosperous law firm was headquartered in Beverly Hills. His rise in California Democratic politics (service in Young Democrats, Young Citizens for Johnson, the California Democratic Committee) was paralleled by outstanding financial successes. At the time of his selection in 1981 as chairman of the DNC, Manatt was the multimillionaire owner of 2,500 acres of Iowa farmland and the chairman of the First Los Angeles Bank; his prosperous law practice continued to flourish during his party chairmanship.

Under Manatt's energetic leadership, the Democratic Party assiduously pursued the course of insisting on centralized regulation of state parties in the presidential nominating process, spending many thousands of dollars to establish in the federal courts the right of the national party to override the enactments of state legislatures in the matter of the procedures of delegate selection. He also raised a great deal of money for the Democratic Party through solicitation of gifts, the establishment of membership councils for various affinity groups, and loans. Manatt's chairmanship, however, was bracketed by two overwhelming defeats for the Democratic Party in presidential elections of 1980 and 1984.

See also: Democratic National Committee, Young Democrats

Nelson W. Polsby

Manifest Destiny

The ideological justification for American territorial expansion in the mid-nineteenth century. Although it contributed to the insular imperialism of the 1890s and its extreme proponents envisioned the annexation of Canada to the north and Cuba, Yucatán, and even the whole of Mexico to the south, Manifest Destiny is most closely connected to the continentalism of James Polk's administration, which acquired Texas, New Mexico, and California and settled the American claims to Oregon.

The term was promulgated by a New York Democratic editor, John L. O'Sullivan, in the summer of 1845 following Polk's election. Although the doctrine was taken up by others and echoed through the halls of Congress, O'Sullivan was the major theoretician of Manifest Destiny. In a December 1845 *New York Morning News* editorial on the Oregon Question, he succinctly stated the doctrine, insisting that American title to all of Oregon was "by the right of our manifest destiny to overspread and to possess the whole of the continent which Providence has given us for development of the great experiment of liberty and federated self government entrusted to us." Manifest Destiny was a mystical amalgam of contemporary conceptions of Anglo-Saxon "civilization, religion, and liberty"—a doctrine that assumed the inevitable expansion of the United States to the Pacific. It was God's will that the land and the natural resources of the New World be put to productive use and that the "area of human freedom" be extended so as to insure the future of humanity. Republicanism supposedly would supplant despotism, destroying monopolistic control of land and insuring religious freedom in place of the dominance of a state church.

Manifest Destiny, however, was not simply an expression of widespread public opinion nor did it represent a growing spirit of American nationalism in any conventional sense. The sentiment was too clearly confined to certain geographical areas and to certain political groups within them; it was used primarily to support a variety of very specific imperialistic goals such as securing the major ports on the Pacific Coast. The Democratic press of New York City and the Midwest disseminated the doctrine in its purest form. Yet southerners appealed to Manifest Destiny in their desire to annex Texas while shying away from expansionist demands for the northern half of Oregon and "All Mexico." Manifest Destiny and the expansionism associated with it were solely the products of the propagandists of the Democratic Party. Whigs in all sections stood opposed to what they considered "political clap trap" and the corruption of the nation's moral sense. The American voter responded by turning the Thirtieth Congress over to the Whigs. Similarly, as both O'Sullivan's writings and Polk's inaugural address show, Manifest Destiny, rather than being an expression of American nationalism, was clearly in tune with the Democrats' celebration of the rights of the states and their conception of the Union as a confederacy of "independent republics." The blessings of self-government and democracy could then be spread across space, cleansing and reforming degenerate neighbors.

See also: James K. Polk

William G. Shade

REFERENCES

Graebner, Norman, ed. 1968. *Manifest Destiny.* Indianapolis: Bobbs-Merrill.

Hietala, Thomas R. 1985. *Manifest Design.* Ithaca: Cornell U. Pr.

Merk, Frederick. 1963. *Manifest Destiny and Mission in American History.* New York: Knopf.

Weinberg, Albert K. 1935. *Manifest Destiny.* Baltimore: Johns Hopkins U. Pr.

Michael J. (Mike) Mansfield (1903–)

Low-keyed Democratic Senate Majority Leader from Montana. Michael J. "Mike" Mansfield of Montana served longer as Senate Democratic Majority Leader than any man in history—16 years (1961–1976). In the process he presided over a "quiet revolution" in Senate organization, procedures, and norms. His low-keyed, laconic personality and decentralized leadership style has often been contrasted with that of his flamboyant predecessor, Lyndon B. Johnson of Texas. For Mansfield, all Senators were equal; as leader he was their servant, a proud and dignified facilitator. In his first eight years as Majority Leader, Mansfield mainly functioned as a loyal, team leader for John Kennedy's "New Frontier" and Lyndon Johnson's "Great Society" legislative programs. However, Mansfield's relationship with President Johnson became increasingly strained in the mid-1960s, primarily over his opposition to Johnson's escalation of the Vietnam War. After 1968 Mansfield assumed the role of a loyal opposition leader to Republican Presidents Richard Nixon and Gerald Ford. Fairness, objectivity, and tolerance for the viewpoints of others were notable Mansfield characteristics. Mansfield assumed that Presidents did the best job they could; as Majority Leader, he sought accommodation, but not acquiescence, especially in his life-long love of foreign policy and a search for peace with integrity.

Born of Irish Catholic immigrants in New York City, Mansfield grew up on the Montana frontier. At the age of 14 he ran away from home to serve in the U.S. Navy and, subsequently, in the U.S. Army and Marine Corps, mainly in China. A miner and then a mining engineer, he was later to become a professor of Latin American and Far Eastern history. In 1942 Mansfield succeeded Jeannette Rankin, the first woman to be elected to the U.S. House of Representatives. Ten years later, Mansfield successfully ran for the Senate from Montana. He never lost an election, neither in running for public office nor for Senate leadership. A Senate Whip from 1957 to 1960, Mansfield's combined service on House Foreign Affairs and Senate Foreign Relations committees spanned three decades. After Mansfield left the Senate in 1976, President Jimmy Carter appointed him ambassador to Japan. Once again he set longevity records for faithful service, retiring in 1988.

See also: Gerald Ford, Lyndon B. Johnson, Richard M. Nixon, Vietnam War as a Political Issue

Robert L. Peabody

REFERENCES

Mansfield, Michael J. 1963. "The Senate and Its Leadership." *Congressional Record* (daily ed.), November 27. pp. 21754–21763.

Peabody, Robert L. 1976. *Leadership in Congress: Stability, Succession, and Change.* Boston: Little, Brown.

———. 1981. "Senate Party Leadership: From the 1950s to the 1980s." In Frank H. Mackaman, ed. *Understanding Congressional Leadership.* Washington: Congressional Quarterly.

Stewart, John G. 1971. "Two Strategies of Leadership: Johnson and Mansfield." In Nelson W. Polsby, ed. *Congressional Behavior.* New York: Random House.

Vito Marcantonio (1902–1954)

American Labor Party Congressman. Vito Marcantonio represented the East Harlem section of New York City in the U.S. House of Representatives from 1934 to 1936 and 1938 to 1950. He was elected in 1934 and defeated in 1936 as a Republican, but he subsequently won his House seat as a member of the American Labor Party (ALP). He insisted on being so designated, even though, under New York's primary system, he often won the Democratic or Republican nomination as well. Except for a few months in 1948, when fellow New York ALP member Leo Isaacson won a special election, he was the only member of his party to serve in Congress.

For much of his career Marcantonio was allied with the Communist Party. He sided with the Communists against ALP founders David Dubinsky and Alex Rose and then became state leader of the ALP after the latter withdrew to start the Liberal Party. But Marcantonio was always his own man; he resigned from the ALP the day after the 1953 New York mayoral election because of political differences with the Communists, who no longer thought it feasible to build a third party.

Marcantonio supported the New Deal, but he wanted to nationalize basic industry, not just regulate it. He was a strong supporter of labor unions, of civil rights, and of friendly relations with the Soviet Union, and he espoused the interests of Puerto Rico and Puerto Ricans, winning solid support from Puerto Rican voters in East Harlem. He admired Fiorello La Guardia (who served as a personal mentor and always endorsed him for election) for his radicalism, independence, and crusading style. He worked hard at constituent service before it became customary, spending eight to ten hours a day, three days a week meeting constituents and dealing with their problems.

Marcantonio lost the 1950 election after the law was changed to bar him from entering the Republican and Democratic primaries while also retaining his ALP nomination, that is, he could not run in more than one party's primary. Following his resignation from the ALP, he planned to run for his old seat as an Independent in 1954. He was on the way to his office to inspect the newly printed nominating petitions when a sudden heart attack left him dead in the street.

See also: Communism as a Political Movement, Fiorello La Guardia, New Deal, Alex Rose

John C. Berg

REFERENCES

LaGumina, Salvatore John. 1969. *Vito Marcantonio: The People's Politician.* Dubuque: Kendall/Hunt.

———. 1973. "Case Studies in Ethnicity and Italo-American Politicians." In Silvano M. Tomasi and Madeline H. Engel, eds. *The Italian Experience in the United States.* New York: Center for Migration Studies.

Marcantonio, Vito. 1956. *I Vote My Conscience; Debates, Speeches and Writings of Vito Marcantonio 1935–1950.* Annette T. Rubinstein and Associates, ed. New York: The Vito Marcantonio Memorial.

Meyer, Gerald. 1980. "Vito Marcantonio y el partido nacionalista puertorriqueno." *Signos.*

———. 1985. "Vito Marcantonio, Congressman for Puerto Rico: 1934–1936, 1938–1950." *Revisto Del Colegio De Abogados De Puerto Rico.*

———. 1989. *Vito Marcantonio; Radical Politician 1902–1954.* Albany: State U. of New York P.

Ojeda Reyes, Felix. 1977. *Vito Marcantonio y Puerto Rico: por los trabajadores y por la naci Rio iedras.* Ediciones Huracn.

Schaffer, Alan. 1966. *Vito Marcantonio, Radical in Congress.* Syracuse: Syracuse U. Pr.

Marchioro v. Chaney
442 U.S. 191 (1979)

In this case, the Supreme Court unanimously upheld the constitutionality of a Washington State statute that required each major political party to maintain a state committee consisting of two persons from each county in the state.

This litigation arose when the state Democratic convention amended its charter in 1976 to add one representative to the state committee from each of Washington's forty-nine legislative districts. The committee refused to seat the new members, apparently relying on the statutory definition of the composition of the committee. Some party members brought suit alleging that because the committee played a significant role in internal party affairs, Washington's restrictions on the composition of the state committee violated their rights to freedom of association secured by the First and Fourteenth amendments.

The superior court invalidated the statutory definition of the state committee. The Washington Supreme Court, however, reversed on the grounds that the members of the Democratic Party had failed to prove that the statute had imposed substantial burdens on their attempts to achieve the objectives of the Democratic Party. The U.S. Supreme Court affirmed the judgment of the state supreme court.

Justice John Paul Stevens, speaking for the Court, noted that both the Washington statute and the Charter of the Democratic Party confer power on the Democratic state committee. Washington gives the state committee the authority to fill vacancies on the ticket, call statewide conventions, and provide for the nomination of presidential electors and delegates to national conventions. The Court found these functions to be directly related to the state's legitimate interest in ensuring the fair and orderly conduct of the electoral process.

The charter of the Democratic Party of Washington had provided that the state committee act as the party's governing body when the convention is in adjournment. It also directed the committee "to organize and administer the party's administrative apparatus, raise and distribute funds to candidates, to conduct workshops, to instruct candidates on effective campaign procedures and organization, and generally to further the party's objectives of influencing policy and electing its adherents to public office."

The Court acknowledged that these activities were significantly related to the international affairs of the Democratic Party. The Court held, however, that it was the charter of the Democratic Party, not the statute, that authorized the committee's involvement in internal party decisions. The Court pointed out that the Convention could have "created an entirely new committee or one, for example, composed of members of the State Committee and such additional membership as might be desired to perform the political functions now performed by the State Committee. The fact that it did not choose such an alternative course is hardly the responsibility of the state legislature."

The Court concluded by saying that "there can be no complaint that the party's right to govern itself has been substantially burdened by statute when the source of the complaint is the party's own decision to confer critical authority on the State Committee."

Robin Bye Wolpert

REFERENCES

Tribe, Laurence. 1988. *American Constitutional Law.* 2nd ed. New York: The Foundation Press.

William L. Marcy (1786–1857)

Leader of the Albany Regency. A three-term Democratic governor of New York in the 1830s, William Learned Marcy played an important role in the presidential elections of James K.

Polk and Franklin Pierce; he went on to serve in their Cabinets. Son of a farmer from Southbridge, Massachusetts, Marcy graduated from Brown University in 1808 and soon began to practice law in Troy, New York. A leader of the famous "Albany Regency," a faction that controlled the New York Democratic Party in the 1820s and 1830s, Marcy briefly served in the U.S. Senate (1831–1832), where, in a reply to Henry Clay, he made the famous defense of political patronage "to the victor belongs the spoils of the enemy." During his years as New York governor (1833–1839), Marcy followed a fiscally cautious policy.

After Marcy and his conservative Democratic faction, nicknamed the Hunkers, carried New York for James K. Polk, the new President made him Secretary of War. His performance in that office during the Mexican War, particularly in the area of logistics, was highly competent. Marcy and the Hunkers refused to follow Martin Van Buren and his "Barnburner" followers out of the Democratic to the Free Soil Party in 1848. He later helped heal this schism among New York Democrats and then tried unsuccessfully to win the Democratic presidential nomination in 1852. Marcy went on to campaign loyally for Franklin Pierce and was rewarded with the State Department secretaryship. In that post, Marcy oversaw the purchase of land from Mexico in the Gadsden Treaty, but his efforts to annex Cuba were thwarted, in part, by the overzealousness of Pierre Soule, his ambassador to Spain.

See also: Barnburners; Henry Clay; Free Soil Party; Hunkers; Mexican War; Franklin Pierce; James K. Polk; Martin Van Buren

John R. McKivigan

REFERENCES

Hietala, Thomas R. 1985. *Manifest Destiny: Anxious Aggrandizement in Late Jacksonian America.* Ithaca, NY: Cornell U. Pr.

Nichols, Roy Franklin. 1923. *The Democratic Machine, 1850–1854.* New York: Columbia U. Pr.

Spencer, Ivor Debenham. 1959. *The Victor and the Spoils: A Life of William L. Marcy.* Providence: Brown U. Pr.

Joseph M. Margiotta (1927–)

Nassau County Republican Party leader. Joseph Michael Margiotta grew up in Brooklyn and the Long Island suburbs of Nassau County, New York. He built the strongest Republican Party machine in the country, helped select state and national tickets, fed jobs to hundreds of Republican workers, and delivered record vote margins.

In 1958 he became counsel to state senator Edward Speno, his predecessor as Nassau County chairman (1965–1968). In 1965 Margiotta was elected to the state assembly and soon became chairman of the Hempstead Republicans and then of the County Committee, championing suburban, white, middle-income, Catholic voters over emergent urban voices.

Margiotta forced the weakening of zoning powers for Governor Nelson Rockefeller's Urban Development Corporation, protected the county schools in the state budgets, and blocked the planned Oyster Bay bridge to the mainland. He delivered record New York votes to the 1972 and 1976 Richard Nixon and Gerald Ford presidential campaigns, placed Supervisor Sol Wachtler on the state court of appeals, and helped make Perry Duryea the New York assembly speaker. County workers, though, complained about having to kick back 1 percent of their salaries to the Republican Party.

Margiotta's fall stemmed from opposition to Democratic governor Hugh Carey: in 1978, the State Insurance Commission complained about insurance fee-splitting in Margiotta's Nassau County. His first trial ended with a hung jury, but a retrial convicted Margiotta on six counts of mail fraud and extortion. He resigned before serving time in 1983.

See also: Nelson Rockefeller

Jeremy R. T. Lewis

REFERENCES

Connery, Robert Howe, and Gerald Benjamin. 1979. *Rockefeller of New York: Executive Power in the Statehouse.* Ithaca: Cornell U. Pr.

Desmond, James. 1964. *Nelson Rockefeller: A Political Biography.* New York: Macmillan.

Gervasi, Frank Henry. 1964. *The Real Rockefeller: The Story of the Rise, Decline, and Resurgence of the Presidential Aspirations of Nelson Rockefeller.* New York: Atheneum.

Underwood, James E., and William J. Daniels. 1982. *Governor Rockefeller in the New York: The Apex of Pragmatic Liberalism in the United States.* Westport, CT: Greenwood.

Thomas R. Marshall (1854–1925)

Self-deprecating Vice President under Woodrow Wilson. Thomas Riley Marshall, an Indiana lawyer and politician, served eight years as Vice President of the United States. He is remembered, if at all, as a laconic humorist who said "what this country really needs is a good five-cent cigar" (an aside during a lengthy Senate debate over national priorities). Beneath the taciturn exterior of the man, however, lay a keen mind, a reformer's heart, and a loyal party spirit.

Marshall entered the political wars late in life. A native Indianan, he graduated in 1873 from Wabash College (where he had organized a Democratic Club in 1872), read law for two years in Fort Wayne, and then opened his own practice in Columbia City in 1875. Apart from an unsuccessful bid for office as a local prosecuting attorney in 1880, Marshall was content to remain a behind-the-scenes supporter of the Indiana Democratic Party until 1908, when he was nominated for governor after a bitter convention fight. The Republican Party in Indiana, however, was even more divided (over the temperance issue), and Marshall was thus able to be elected in a predominantly Republican state. His term was marked by moderate reforms and one major disappointment—a number of state constitutional amendments that he had pushed through the legislature were invalidated on procedural grounds. Still, his extraordinary luck held in 1912. Added to the national Democratic ticket with Wilson to provide geographical and ideological balance (Marshall called himself "a Progressive with the brakes on"), Marshall rejoiced in a split in the national Republican Party that paved the way for a Democratic victory; Wilson and Marshall were reelected in 1916. To his credit, in the absence of clear constitutional authority, Marshall resisted efforts to have him serve as "acting president" during Wilson's protracted illness at the end of his second term. Rather, in his typically self-deprecating manner, Marshall concluded that "the only job of the Vice President is to knock on the door of the White House and inquire as to the health of the President."

See also: Election of 1912, Woodrow Wilson

Ralph D. Gray

REFERENCES

Link, Arthur S. 1954. *Woodrow Wilson and the Progressive Era, 1910–1917.* New York: Harper & Row.

Marshall, Thomas. 1925. *Recollections of Thomas R. Marshall, Vice-President and Hoosier Philosopher: A Hoosier Salad.* Indianapolis: Bobbs-Merrill.

Smith, Gene. 1964. *When the Cheering Stopped: The Last Years of Woodrow Wilson.* New York: Morrow.

Thomas, Charles Marion. 1939. *Thomas Riley Marshall: Hoosier Statesman.* Oxford, OH: Mississippi Valley Pr.

Joseph W. Martin, Jr. (1884–1968)

Republican House leader from 1939 to 1959 and the only Republican Speaker since 1931.

Joseph William Martin, Jr., first got involved in politics at the age of 11 when he marched in a torchlight parade for presidential candidate William McKinley. In 1912 he won a seat in the Massachusetts House of Representatives; after three one-year terms, he was elected to the state senate. He returned to private life in 1917, but five years later he became executive director of the Massachusetts Republican Party. In 1924 he lost the GOP primary for a seat in the U.S. House, but when the winner died a week later, a convention gave Martin the nomination. In the autumn, he won the seat by 9,000 votes.

As a House member, he loyally supported his old friend Calvin Coolidge and then supported Herbert Hoover. Under Franklin Roosevelt, he lived by the proposition that the function of the opposition is to oppose. In his autobiography he said, "Many of the experiments of the New Deal seemed to us [Republicans] certain to undermine and destroy this society. . . . We fought them with every weapon we could lay our hands on."

The 1938 midterm election nearly doubled Republican strength in the House, making the GOP a tough obstacle to the New Deal. And with the new Congress, House Republicans elected Martin as their leader. In that role, he sided with isolationists and opposed Roosevelt social programs. In 1940 FDR extracted gleeful revenge. Noting that his House foes included Martin, arch-conservative Hamilton Fish, and advertising maven Bruce Barton, Roosevelt made "Martin, Barton and Fish" a mocking Democratic chant. From 1940 to 1942, Martin chaired the Republican National Committee.

When the 1946 elections gave the GOP control of the House, Martin became Speaker. Abandoning his earlier isolationism, he backed Greco-Turkish aid and the Marshall Plan. But his party's opposition to social programs prompted Harry Truman to rail against the "do-nothing Eightieth Congress." In 1948 the Democrats kept the White House and regained control of Congress. In 1951 Martin approvingly revealed a letter from General Douglas MacArthur criticizing President Truman, a gesture that led to the general's ouster for his insubordination.

The 1952 Dwight Eisenhower landslide returned Martin to the speakership, where he again loyally supported the administration. Despite Eisenhower's popularity, House Republicans went back to the minority in 1954; they would linger there for decades.

During the 1950s, Martin faced growing unrest within GOP ranks. In 1949 Republican backbenchers forced him to form a Policy Committee to develop Republican proposals, but Martin became chairman of the body, which did little. Younger members felt cut out from leadership decisions. After huge 1958 midterm losses, they gathered enough support to replace Martin with Charles A. Halleck of Indiana. Martin stayed in Congress until 1966.

See also: Calvin Coolidge, Dwight D. Eisenhower, Hamilton Fish, Herbert Hoover, Isolationism in American Politics, Douglas MacArthur, New Deal, Republican National Committee, Franklin D. Roosevelt, Speaker of the House, Harry S Truman

John J. Pitney, Jr.

REFERENCES

Connelly, William F., Jr. 1988. "The House Republican Policy Committee: Then and Now." Paper presented at the Annual Meeting of the American Political Science Association, Washington, DC.

Jones, Charles O. 1964. *Party and Policy-Making: The House Republican Committee.* New Brunswick: Rutgers U. Pr.

Martin, Joseph W. 1960. *My First Fifty Years in Politics.* New York: McGraw-Hill.

Marion E. Martin (1900–1987)

Founder of the National Federation of Republican Women's Clubs. Marion Elizabeth Martin began her long commitment to public service when she was elected to the Maine House of Representatives in 1931. She held her seat until 1935 when she became a state senator, serving in this capacity until 1938. Martin was active in Republican Party politics, first as a national committeewoman and then as the assistant chairman of the Republican National Committee from 1937 to 1947. As head of the Women's Division, she founded the National Federation of Republican Women's Clubs.

Martin became the commissioner of Maine's Department of Labor and Industry in 1947 and remained in that post until 1972. Her concern with safety on the job led her to membership on the board of directors of the National Safety Council (NSC), a post she held for 30 years. She advocated cooperation among government, employers, and employees to achieve safe labor conditions. As the vice president for Women's Activities for the NSC from 1952 to 1959, Martin encouraged women to become actively involved in their community by supporting public safety and accident prevention. In 1969 she became a member of the President's Task Force on Highway Safety.

In 1958 Martin was appointed adviser to the U.S. delegation attending the meeting of the International Labor Organization in Geneva, Switzerland. She was a member of the national Commission on Workmen's Compensation Laws in 1971 and 1972. Her other posts included special adviser to the New England Planning Commission, member of the American Arbitration Association, member and official in the International Association of Government Labor Officials (1949–1950), and the Association of Labor Mediation Agencies (1966–1969).

See also: Republican National Committee

Joy A. Scimé

Thomas S. Martin (1849–1919)

Boss of the Democratic Party in Virginia. Thomas Staples Martin headed Virginia's Democratic "organization" from 1893 through 1919 and laid the groundwork for the Byrd Machine, which dominated Virginia politics into the 1960s. As the "boss" of the Virginia Democrats, Martin helped restore the state's traditional politics of conservatism, efficiency, and elite control following the tumult of Reconstruction and the Readjuster movement.

Born and reared in Scottsville, Martin entered Virginia Military Institute in 1864 and fought for the Confederacy with the New Market Corps of Cadets. Following the war, he attended the University of Virginia from 1865 to 1867 and was admitted to the bar in 1869. A railroad attorney and lobbyist, he became politically active in the 1880s as a member of the Democratic state central committee and as a skilled behind-the-scenes organizer.

In 1893 he scored a major upset by winning election to the United States Senate over Civil War hero Fitzhugh Lee. Martin's victory embodied the crucial cooperation between the emerging Democratic organization and railroad and business interests. Reelected in 1899, 1905, 1911, and 1917, Martin presided over the Democratic machine's tight political control of the state. By drastically reducing the electorate by means of a new state constitution, instituting a closed party primary, and building direct lines of authority from the courthouse cliques to the state central committee, Martin and his lieutenants defeated all challenges from Populists, Republicans, and "irregular" Democrats. Although fundamentally conservative, Martin did follow state and national opinion in supporting most of the major pieces of Progressive legislation. Beginning in 1912, he chaired the Senate

Appropriations Committee, and from 1917 until his death he played a key role in the passage of war measures from his position as Majority Leader in the Senate.

See also: Bosses, Reconstruction

Joseph A. Fry

REFERENCES

Bear, James Adam, Jr. 1952. "Thomas Staples Martin: A Study in Virginia Politics, 1883–1896." M.A. thesis, U. of Virginia.

Holt, Wythe W., Jr. 1975. "The Senator from Virginia and the Democratic Floor Leadership: Thomas S. Martin and Conservatism in the Progressive Era." 83 *Virginia Magazine of History and Biography* 3.

Moger, Allen W. 1968. *Virginia: Bourbonism to Byrd, 1870–1925.* Charlottesville: U. Pr. of Virginia.

Pulley, Raymond H. 1968. *Old Virginia Restored: An Interpretation of the Progressive Impulse, 1870–1930.* Charlottesville: U. Pr. of Virginia.

George Mason (1725–1792)

The "reluctant statesman" of the American Revolution. George Mason provided much of the behind-the-scenes wisdom and intellect that set Virginia and America on the course to independence. Although he had the personal attributes and the practical local political experience that were necessary for successful election to the Virginia House of Burgesses, a defeat at the polls at age 23 and chronic ill health kept him out of legislative politics for most of the Colonial period. After serving one brief term as a burgess (1758–1761), he refused to seek reelection until revolutionary activities forced him into the public arena. Between 1775 and 1788 he served almost continuously in either state or national legislative bodies.

Mason's major contributions to the independence movement are found in a series of documents he either wrote or greatly influenced. He helped his neighbors construct the Fairfax Resolves (1774), affirming the principle that colonists were "governed by no Laws, to which they have not given their Consent, by Representatives freely chosen by themselves." His Virginia Declaration of Rights (1776) influenced the constitutions of all of the original 13 states and called for independent representatives selected by "frequent, certain, and regular elections." At the Philadelphia Constitutional Convention (1787), Mason argued for the direct election of all national offices, including the President. He refused to sign the new Constitution because it lacked a bill of rights and returned home with the growing conviction that true representation of the people would be impossible

in the proposed House of Representatives. Although his anti-Federalist stand won him considerable disfavor, his arguments greatly influenced the adoption of the federal Bill of Rights in 1791.

See also: Anti-Federalists

John G. Kolp

REFERENCES

Kolp, John G. 1988. "The Flame of Burgessing: Elections and the Political Communities of Colonial Virginia, 1728–1775." Ph.D. dissertation, U. of Iowa.

Morgan, Edmund S. 1988. *Inventing the People: The Rise of Popular Sovereignty in England and America.* New York: Norton.

Pacheco, Josephine F., ed. 1983. *The Legacy of George Mason.* Fairfax, VA: George Mason U. Pr.

Rutland, Robert A. 1961. *George Mason: Reluctant Statesman.* Williamsburg, VA: Colonial Williamsburg.

———. 1970. *The Papers of George Mason, 1725–1792.* 3 vols. Chapel Hill: U. of North Carolina Pr.

Masons

Freemasonry is one of the oldest, largest, and best-known secret fraternal societies. As such, its structure and rituals have influenced many other voluntary associations in America. Although Masonry was typically an expressive organization catering to its members' social needs, people's perception of it as an instrumentalist organization in the early nineteenth century made the Masons the center of political controversy.

Apparently originating among stone masons in medieval England, Masonry assumed its current, noncraft character in the eighteenth century. In America, to which it had spread by 1733, Masonry became an organization of middle-class, self-employed, white, Protestant men interested in social intercourse, protection from financial emergencies, moral uplift, and self-improvement. Many prominent American politicians—including George Washington, Henry Clay, and Andrew Jackson—were among its members. In a nation with high rates of geographic mobility, Masonry provided a convenient way for nomadic American middle-class men to integrate themselves quickly into a new community and feel at home there. Indeed, like a Victorian-era family, Masonry offered unconditional acceptance, mutual support, and an escape from the competitive marketplace.

Claiming to elevate initiates in their moral standing by degrees and employing rituals and symbols much as a church might, Masonry often appeared quasireligious. Yet unlike most religious sects, and perhaps reflecting its origins in eighteenth-century rationalism, Masonry was nondoctrinal and latitudinarian. All shades of Christian faith were welcome. Although they claimed 18,000 members in 1800, the Masons were already under attack from some New England Protestant ministers who saw them as a rival, heretical, even blasphemous, organization.

In upstate New York, the "Burnt Over District," an area rent by profound religious anxiety and recurrent evangelical revivals, the 1926 kidnapping and presumed murder of William Morgan, who intended to publish a book revealing the secrets of Masonry, aroused popular excitement against the Masons. Citing exclusivity, secrecy, and a tendency to unite the most prominent individuals in every community, opponents questioned the Masons' adherence to democratic, egalitarian values. The manifold difficulties encountered by investigators of Morgan's disappearance confirmed fears of a conspiracy to cover up Masonic wrongdoing. In defining the Masons' moral transgressions and uniting to oppose them, founders of the Antimasonic Party found the same kind of mutual support and sense of common interest enjoyed by Masons. Antimasonry as a political movement spread through most of the northeastern section of the country before the Civil War, ultimately becoming absorbed in other political movements.

Under this onslaught, the Masonic order lost some appeal, especially to politicians, many of whom gave up membership. But by the 1850s, with Antimasonry largely a memory, new members, including several political notables, again increased. Masonry reached its peak in the early twentieth century; by 1925, 3 million men were members. The Great Depression resulted in many lapsed memberships. Masonry also failed to do a satisfactory job in meeting the social needs of twentieth-century American males; a permanent membership decline resulted. Although Masonry has been a significant organization throughout its history, the Antimasonic episode in conjunction with the need to prevent divisions among a politically diverse membership, limited its overt political activities during much of its history to citizenship education and lobbying for those "worthy" causes that spurred little dissent among members.

See also: Antimasons, Henry Clay, Andrew Jackson, George Washington

Phyllis F. Field

REFERENCES

Demenil, Lynn. 1984. *Freemasonry and American Culture, 1880–1930.* Princeton: Princeton U. Pr.

Kutolowski, Kathleen Smith. 1982. "Freemasonry and Community in the Early Republic: The Case for Antimasonic Anxieties." 34 *American Quarterly* 543.

Lipson, Dorothy Ann. 1977. *Freemasonry in Federalist Connecticut.* Princeton: Princeton U. Pr.

Vaughn, William Preston. 1983. *The Antimasonic Party in the United States, 1826–1843.* Lexington: U. Pr. of Kentucky.

Massachusetts Office Ballot

Introduced as part of a series of election law reforms in 1888 in Massachusetts, the distinguishing characteristic of the Massachusetts Office Ballot (MOB) is that it is constructed to enable the voter to vote for candidates grouped by office, not by party slate. All candidates are grouped in alphabetical order and designated with their party affiliation under the office that they are seeking; space is also left for write-in candidates. Voters go down the ballot and under each office mark an "X" next to the name of the candidate of their choice.

In the late nineteenth century, partisan political machines had gained overwhelming power all across the country. They had achieved this power because they were able to control elections. At that time parties were responsible for printing and distributing the ballots; party functionaries would then monitor the voting in public to insure victory for their candidates.

The Australian, or secret ballot, had been created in the 1850s and brought to America in the 1880s by reformers campaigning for independence from the political machines and less fraud at the ballot box. In 1888 Massachusetts was the first state in the nation to enact election reforms with provisions that included not only a secret ballot but the office ballot as well. The ballots printed by the political machines were replaced by a standard ballot, printed and supplied by the state government at the polling place. The MOB was thus favored by reformers because it also chipped away at the power of the machines. If the secret ballot allowed voters freedom from machine intimidation, then the Massachusetts Office Ballot facilitated split-ticket voting: voters could no longer just choose a party slate; they had to vote separately for all candidates under individual office categories. Several other states have followed the successful Massachusetts Office Ballot model.

See also: Australian Ballot, Split-Ticket Voting

Mary Ann McHugh

REFERENCES

Fredman, L. E. 1968. *The Australian Ballot: The Story of an American Reform*. East Lansing: Michigan State U. Pr.

Hart, Albert Bushnell, ed. 1930. *Commonwealth History of Massachusetts*. New York: The States History Company.

League of Women Voters. 1956. *Massachusetts State Government*. Cambridge: Harvard U. Pr.

(Fontaine) Maury Maverick (1895–1954)

Texas champion of the New Deal. As a member of the U.S. House of Representatives representing a Texas district from 1935 to 1939, Maury Maverick was one of the few southern Democrats in Congress who was prominently and consistently loyal to Franklin D. Roosevelt and New Deal liberalism. Born in San Antonio, Maverick graduated from the University of Texas in 1916 and served with distinction in the Army during World War I. As a lawyer in San Antonio, Maverick helped form and lead the Citizens League in 1930, a liberal reform group opposed to San Antonio's Democratic political machine. Elected tax collector in 1930, Maverick restored honesty and efficiency to local tax collection.

Because San Antonio, like other American cities, was suffering from severe Depression-induced poverty, Maverick sought to provide adequate relief for the poor through various welfare programs, including communal-style camps for the unemployed. As an outspoken civil libertarian, he both supported the civil rights of Communist activists and sought to lessen discrimination against Mexican-Americans. Elected to Congress in 1934, Maverick was one of the few southern Democrats to support antilynching bills. He became prominent as a leading advocate of the Tennessee Valley Authority, public utilities reform, slum clearance, and conservation. Consistently loyal to Roosevelt on domestic policy, Maverick also strongly supported FDR's foreign and defense policies. In 1938 Maverick proposed expanding and modernizing American military forces especially Army Air Corps.

Defeated for reelection in 1938, Maverick served as mayor of San Antonio from 1939 to 1941. From 1941 until 1943 he was a director of the War Production Board. He was chairman of the Smaller War Plants corporation from 1943 to 1946. Until his death in 1954, Maverick concerned himself with advocating the alleviation of cold war tensions, especially in the Far East.

See also: Franklin D. Roosevelt

Sean J. Savage

REFERENCES

Henderson, Richard B. 1970. *Maury Maverick: A Political Biography*. Austin: U. of Texas Press.

Maverick, Maury. 1937. *A Maverick American*. New York: Friede.

———. 1939. *In Blood and Ink*. New York: Modern Age Books.

Media and Presidential Campaigns

Contemporary presidential election campaigns have become mass media campaigns. Clearly, the mass media do not determine all that happens in the campaign. But one need not exaggerate to say that, for the large majority of voters, the campaign has little reality apart from their media version. Moreover, the media have become the primary focus of the candidates' efforts: today's candidates try to get their messages across to the voter via the media as often and as favorably as they can

A media campaign consists of "paid" and "unpaid" communication. "Paid" communication refers to political advertising, most of which is placed on television. In recent campaigns, nearly half of all candidate spending during the general election has gone for the production and broadcast of televised political ads. Although this advertising is often criticized, it gives candidates a chance to present their campaign as they wish it to be seen. In former times, party rallies provided this opportunity; televised political ads do so now and with phenomenal reach. Millions of potential voters will see a televised political ad shown on a prime-time network entertainment program. In addition, because most Americans watch such programs at one time or another, televised ads are an answer to the perennial problem of getting the candidate's message to people who normally pay little attention to politics.

Because televised ads tend to feature clear "messages" and are usually aired again and again, they can make a strong impression on voters. A major issue of the 1988 presidential campaign—the allegation that Democratic nominee Michael Dukakis was soft on crime—was communicated chiefly through televised advertising. The George Bush advertising campaign repeatedly telecast a commercial featuring Willie Horton, a convicted murderer, who, while free on furlough from a Massachusetts prison, raped a Maryland woman. The ad insinuated that Dukakis, as governor of Massachusetts, bore part of the responsibility for Horton's crime. A few weeks after the ad began to appear on television, polls revealed a rise in voters' concern with crime and over Dukakis's ability to control it.

Although "paid" communication is important, the foundation of the modern media campaign is "unpaid" communication—the news. In order to win, a presidential candidate must have credibility, a credibility that only news coverage can bestow. The news media's influence is most evident during the nominating phase of the campaign. These preliminary races attract large fields of contenders, each of whom needs news exposure. Russell Baker of the *New York Times* aptly calls the press the "great mentioner." A candidate who is taken seriously by the news media has a chance of being taken seriously by the voters; a candidate who is ignored by the press is a certain loser.

The news media's critical role in presidential nominations is partly the result of changes that have taken place in the nominating process. As recently as the 1968 presidential election, candidates did not depend on news coverage to carry them to nomination: party leaders were the power brokers. In 1952, for example, Senator Estes Kefauver defeated President Harry Truman by a 55-to-45 margin in New Hampshire's presidential primary. Kefauver then went on to win all but one of the other twelve primaries he contested, making him the clear preference of rank-and-file Democrats in the final Gallup poll before the national convention. Yet Democratic party leaders rejected Kefauver, nominating instead Illinois governor Adlai Stevenson, who, they felt, better represented the party's traditions.

The bitter Democratic campaign of 1968 brought an end to party-controlled nominations. Against the backdrop of opposition to the Vietnam War, first Eugene McCarthy and then Robert Kennedy challenged President Lyndon Johnson's leadership, eventually driving him from the presidential race. The 1968 Democratic nominee, however, was not an antiwar candidate; instead, Johnson's Vice President, Hubert Humphrey, who had not entered a single primary, won the nomination. When Richard Nixon beat Humphrey narrowly in the fall campaign, disgruntled reform Democrats demanded changes in the nominating process. A 1970 Democratic Party commission (the McGovern-Fraser Commission) recommended that all national convention delegates be chosen in primaries or in open caucuses. (Previously, about two-thirds of the delegates had been chosen through more or less closed party pro-

cesses.) The Democrats adopted the reforms, and to a substantial degree, the Republican Party followed suit.

As a result of these party reforms, serious contenders for presidential nomination now have no choice but to appeal directly to the voters. No amount of support from "old pols" in the party leadership can substitute for support from millions of ordinary voters. One principal effect of the reforms has been to increase greatly the news media's influence on elections. The road to public support goes through the media. The press is the only means by which a candidate can hope to get the public's attention and support.

An obvious and basic question is whether the news media can do the job that the modern campaign assigns them. Can the news media do what the parties once did? Can the media bring the candidates and voters together? In purely functional terms, the answer is obviously yes. The news media have been the chief link between candidates and voters in every election since 1972. But can the media do the job well? Can they present the campaign in ways that help the American electorate to achieve a genuine understanding of the choice the candidates offer? Considerable research has been devoted to this question, and nearly everyone arrives at the same answer: the news is a poor guide to voters' choice.

Election news does not focus on questions of national policy and leadership, but on the strategic game played by the candidates in their pursuit of the presidency. The dominant themes of day-to-day election coverage are winning and losing, strategy and organization, appearances and tactics, squabbling and one-upmanship. The news, especially the television news, underplays the candidates' policy positions, their personal and leadership characteristics, their private and public histories, and their group support and commitments.

The game-like character of election news reflects the tradition in journalism that news is to be found in activity rather than in the underlying causes of that activity. "The function of news," Walter Lippmann wrote, "is to signalize an event." Because electioneering and popular support are the most salient aspects of any campaign, they are therefore the aspects most likely to be signaled by the press. Heavily emphasized are the simple mechanics of campaigning as well as voting projections and returns. Moreover, although journalists consider the campaign to have more than ritual significance, they choose not to portray it primarily as a battle over the shape of national policy. Rather, it is presented mainly as a power struggle between the candidates. "The game is a competitive one," claims Paul Weaver in describing this journalistic paradigm, "and the player's principal activities are those of calculating and pursuing strategies designed to defeat competitors. ... Public problems, policy debates, and the like ... are noteworthy only insofar as they affect, or are used by, players in pursuit of the game's rewards."

This journalistic model affects presidential campaign coverage in almost every respect. A case in point is the way that the press reports presidential primaries and caucuses. In theory, nothing is "total" about a narrow victory or even a landslide in a state's presidential primary or caucus. First, a single contest is just one indicator of the candidates' popularity in a system of fifty state contests. Second, a presidential primary or caucus lacks the finality of the general election; the difference in the popularity of one candidate who gets 51 percent of a state's vote and another who gets 49 percent is insignificant. Recognizing this, parties in recent years have discouraged "winner-take-all" contests: a state's delegates in most cases are not awarded wholly to the first-place finisher; instead they are distributed among candidates in proportion to the votes they receive.

Press coverage, however, operates from a different perspective. The press tends to interpret a single state's results as the preferences of the nation as a whole, and something close to a "winner-take-all" rule applies to its coverage. After George Bush finished behind Robert Dole and Pat Robertson in the Iowa caucuses that kicked off the 1988 campaign, a correspondent for the National Broadcasting Company flatly declared, "Bush is dead." New Hampshire's 1976 Democratic primary provides a fuller example. Jimmy Carter, the lone centrist candidate in New Hampshire's primary, received 28 percent of the vote. The remaining four candidates, all from the party's liberal wing, together received 60 percent of the vote; they were led by Morris Udall with 23 percent. Yet Carter was termed "the unqualified winner" by the press and received the balance of news coverage until the next primary. *Time* and *Newsweek* put Carter on their covers, and his story in 2,600 lines of their inside pages. The second-place finisher, Udall, received 96 lines; all of Carter's opponents to-

gether received only 300 lines. The television and newspaper coverage given Carter that week totaled four times the average amount given each of his major rivals.

In allocating coverage among the candidates on the basis of electoral success, the press is acting largely according to traditional news values. Winners are the real story—to downplay their victories would be to ignore the limited news space and the need to capture the interest of the news audience.

The press's concentration on early primary and caucus winners is not designed to promote their candidacies, but such coverage certainly has that effect. Public support in the polls for George McGovern in 1972, Jimmy Carter in 1976, George Bush in 1980, and Walter Mondale (after Iowa) and Gary Hart (after New Hampshire) in 1984 rose substantially in national polls when the media focused on their candidacies after an early primary or caucus victory.

The relationship of news coverage to popular support was also evident in 1988, as the Democratic race illustrates. Before the Iowa caucuses, a Gallup survey indicated that Hart led among Democratic voters in the South, a region that, with its "Super Tuesday" lineup of primaries (Democrats in 20 states held primaries on Super Tuesday), promised to be the crucial determinant of the nomination. After Richard Gephardt won in Iowa, a Cable News Network survey found that he had forged ahead in the South. Then, after Dukakis took New Hampshire, a Gallup poll showed that he had taken the lead in the South. What was behind such surges? Certainly not information. Democratic voters did not know appreciably more about Gephardt a few days after Iowa or about Dukakis a few days after the New Hampshire than they did before. In fact, as several studies have shown, voters are likely to know very little about their choices even at the end of the nominating campaign. In fact, ignorance, not information, fuels early shifts in vote support. When voters know very little about any of the candidates, and when one candidate is suddenly catapulted into the headlines, that candidate will pick up substantial support.

Journalistic norms also play a significant part in which issues are emphasized in election news coverage. The issues that the candidates stress most heavily are *not* those most prominent in the news. The press promotes an issue agenda based on news values rather than political ones.

Candidates ground most of their appeals to voters on government's attempts to deal with society's problems. Because candidates have differing views on the nature of these problems and the solutions they prefer, they may take opposing positions. But society's recurrent problems demand that politicians respond with a "position." These positions are translated into stump speeches that candidates repeat at nearly every campaign stop and before every audience. Yet the media seem to think that these position statements are largely meaningless, at least by journalistic standards. In the second presidential debate of 1988, George Bush became mildly angry when one of the questioners suggested that Bush was avoiding the issues. Bush noted that he had made several major policy statements on a recent day, only to find that they were ignored in the news.

Why are the candidates' policy statements not very newsworthy? Lippmann had an explanation: the underlying conditions of society, those that give rise to the public's attitudes toward policy and the candidates' appeals, are not the basis of "news." The news is an account of overt phases of events. As Lippmann said, the news is "not a first hand report of the raw material [of society . . . but] a report of that material after it has been stylized."

The nature of news helps to explain why the most memorable policy phrase of the 1988 presidential campaign was Bush's phrase "Read my lips" (i.e., "No new taxes"). Candidates' platforms become truly newsworthy only after they have assumed a stylized form. In fact, some argue that a turning point in the 1988 campaign came when Bush finally recognized that serious policy discussion would not carry him as far in news coverage as sloganeering and posturing. The press prefers clear-cut issues—those that neatly divide the candidates, provoke controversy, rest on principle rather than on complex relationships, and can be stated in simple terms, usually by reference to shorthand labels, such as "read my lips."

In addition to its preference for clear-cut issues, the press loves "campaign issues." These are issues that develop *during* the campaign, usually as a result of an error in judgment by a candidate. Examples would include Jimmy Carter's reference to lust during a *Playboy* interview in 1976 and vice presidential nominee Geraldine Ferraro's decision in 1984 not to release her family's tax returns.

The degree to which campaign issues can dominate news coverage is evident from Michael Robinson's analysis of the 1984 campaign. He used a broad definition of what constitutes such issues and found that they accounted for nearly 40 percent of total election news. Included were Ferraro's taxes and her verbal battle over abortion with Archbishop O'Connor, Walter Mondale's controversial meeting with the Soviet Union's Gromyko, and Ronald Reagan's inaccessibility to the press and his suggestion that the 1983 Beirut bombing was somehow Carter's fault.

The 1988 election also had its share of campaign issues. Two such issues dominated the period before the Iowa caucuses: Gary Hart's weekend fling with Donna Rice, and Joseph Biden's plagiarizing of a speech made by British Labour Party leader Neil Kinnock. No policy issue at any time during the campaign received headlines as bold as those accompanying the Hart affair or the Biden blunder. Another 1988 campaign issue that dominated news coverage for several days running was the revelation that Republican vice presidential nominee Dan Quayle had pulled strings to avoid being drafted for service in Vietnam by joining the Indiana National Guard. No candidate had more negative coverage in 1988 than did Quayle, who, by virtue of the newsworthiness of the military draft issue, got more than three times the election coverage of Democratic vice presidential nominee Lloyd Bentsen.

Perhaps the most revealing example of press preoccupation with campaign issues in 1988 came shortly before the Super Tuesday round of primaries, which included 20 states for the Democrats and 17 for the Republicans. Super Tuesday looked to be a decisive encounter because of the great number of delegates at stake. However, the news provided little indication of a fateful policy choice. A content analysis of network evening newscasts indicates that horserace news outpaced issue news by twenty to one in the period right before Super Tuesday. The only candidate to break through this horserace barrage was a longshot contender, televangelist Pat Robertson. He made news with his wild claim that Soviet missiles were entrenched in Cuba and his equally unfounded charge that George Bush had masterminded the recent Jimmy Swaggart scandal in order to discredit all prominent fundamentalist ministers. The only possible justification for emphasizing Robertson's issues was their news value. His charges were sensational, colorful, and unique—the stuff of headlines.

In all these news emphases, the print and television media are more alike than different. Both broadcast and print journalists emphasize the game, the "winner," the clear-cut difference, and campaign issues. However, these emphases are, in every instance, more extreme on television. It is on the network television newscasts, more than in the newspapers, that journalistic values are most evident in campaign coverage.

Of course, television's role in a presidential campaign is not confined to newscasts. Networks also feature live coverage of campaign events, most notably the party conventions and presidential debates. Although journalistic values are evident in the televised proceedings of the conventions and debates, these events also provide candidates with a fuller measure of control over how their campaigns are presented. Research indicates that televised conventions and debates do help viewers toward a better understanding of the candidates' policy and leadership agendas.

Daily news is obviously a different matter. This is not a particularly useful guide to voter choice, an insufficiency that has led critics to offer advice to the news media about how better reporting of presidential elections could lead to a better informed electorate. The assumption underlying this advice is that the media have it within their capacity to bring reason to bear on the selection of Presidents, if only they would do things somewhat differently.

However, analysis suggests that the press cannot do an adequate job as intermediary no matter how conscientiously reporters approach the task. The media are simply not designed to accept responsibility as chief intermediary between candidates and voters. The media are in the news business, not the political business; consequently, their norms and imperatives are not those required for the effective organization of electoral coalitions and debate. The media's values result in a news agenda that bears little relationship to the choices at stake in an election.

Yet the media's role in politics remains important. The press, for example, introduces a significant element of "random partisanship" into the selection of a President. Candidates are helped or hurt depending on how news values interact with campaign developments. A candidate who easily wins a primary gets more than the victory should be worth because the press blows the win out of proportion. A candidate who makes a mistake loses big because the news exaggerates that mistake.

Such realities expose the foolhardiness of the idea that the press, if it would only do things a little better, can make a presidential election into a sensible affair. The press cannot do in U.S. elections what political parties do elsewhere. As Lippmann wrote, "The press is no substitute for institutions. It is like the beam of a searchlight that moves restlessly about, bringing one episode and then another out of darkness into vision. Men cannot do the work of the world by this light alone. They cannot govern society by episodes, incidents, and interruptions."

See also: Individual presidential and vice presidential candidates, Election of 1968, George Gallup, McGovern-Fraser Commission, Vietnam War as a Political Issue

Thomas E. Patterson

REFERENCES

Bartels, Larry M. 1988. *Presidential Primaries and the Dynamics of Public Choice*. Princeton: Princeton U. Pr.

Jamieson, Kathleen Hall. 1988. *Presidential Debates: The Challenge of Creating an Informed Electorate*. New York: Oxford U. Pr.

———, and Karlyn Kohrs Campbell. 1988. *The Interplay of Influence*, 2nd ed. Belmont, CA: Wadsworth.

Keeter, Scott, and Cliff Zukin. 1984. *Uninformed Choice*. New York: Praeger.

Kern, Montague. 1989. *30-Second Politics: Political Advertising in the Eighties*. New York: Praeger.

Kraus, Sidney, ed. 1962. *The Great Debates*. Bloomington: U. of Indiana Pr.

———. 1979. *The Great Debates: Carter v. Ford, 1976*. University Park: Pennsylvania State U. Pr.

Lichter, Robert. 1988. "Media Monitor" (mimeo). Washington: Center for Media and Public Affairs.

Lippmann, Walter. 1965. *Public Opinion*. New York: Free Press.

Orren, Gary R., and Nelson W. Polsby, eds. 1989. *Media and Momentum: The New Hampshire Primary and Nomination Politics*. Chatham, NJ: Chatham House.

Page, Benjamin I. 1978. *Choices and Echoes in Presidential Elections*. Chicago: U. of Chicago Pr.

Patterson, Thomas E. 1980. *The Mass Media Election*. New York: Praeger.

———. 1989. "The Press and Its Missed Assignment." In Michael Nelson, ed. *Campaign '88*. Washington: Congressional Quarterly.

———, and Robert D. McClure. 1976. *The Unseeing Eye: The Myth of Television Power in National Elections*. New York: Putnam's.

Robinson, Michael. 1985. "The Media in Campaign '84, Part I." In Michael Robinson and Austin Ranney, eds. *The Mass Media in Campaign '84*. Washington: American Enterprise Institute.

———, and Margaret Sheehan. 1983. *Over the Wire and on TV*. New York: Russell Sage.

Seymour-Ure, Colin. 1974. *The Political Impact of Mass Media*. Beverly Hills, CA: Sage.

Andrew W. Mellon (1855–1937)

Secretary of the Treasury under three Republican Presidents. Architect of the Republican prosperity of the pro-business 1920s, Andrew Mellon served as Secretary of the Treasury for 11 years (1921–1932) under three Presidents (Warren G. Harding, Calvin Coolidge, and Herbert Hoover). Born into a prominent Pennsylvania banking family, Mellon spent the bulk of his life as a financier and industrialist, eventually accumulating one of the largest fortunes in America.

Before his appointment as Secretary of the Treasury, Mellon's political activity was confined to Pennsylvania politics where his influence was most noticeably felt in the size of his campaign contributions. In 1920, his close friend, Philander C. Knox, recommended Mellon for the position of Secretary of the Treasury to President Harding. During the next eight years this political novice created an atmosphere conducive to business and carried out his duties with such proficiency that he was touted as the "greatest Secretary of the Treasury since Alexander Hamilton." During his tenure, Mellon implemented drastic reductions in the tax rates (from a high of 73 percent in 1921 to 24 percent in 1929); reduced the national debt by decreasing governmental expenditures and requiring repayment from European debtors; raised the tariff to protect native industry; and generally restored the business community's faith in the federal government by reviving a moribund laissez faire philosophy among the upper echelons of Washington's powerful. Mellon's management of the economy proved to be a double-edged sword as credit for ushering in prosperity inevitably led to blame for the stock market crash and the Great Depression. Mellon's reputation is probably lower than deserved because of the economic cataclysm of the 1930s.

See also: Calvin Coolidge, Warren G. Harding, Herbert Hoover

David B. Raymond

REFERENCES

Love, Phillip H. 1929. *Andrew W. Mellon: The Man and His Work*. Baltimore: F. H. Coggins.

Mellon, Andrew W. 1924. *Taxation: The People's Business*. New York: Macmillan.

O'Connor, Harvey. 1933. *Mellon's Millions: The Biography of a Fortune*. New York: John Day.

Mexican War, 1846–1848

President James K. Polk declared war on Mexico, with congressional approval, on May 13, 1846. War seemed necessary because negotiations had failed to settle disputes over the boundaries and annexation of Texas, because money was owed to the United States by Mexico, because America was committed to buying California and New Mexico, and finally because Mexico had attacked American troops north of the Rio Grande.

The House of Representatives had hurriedly approved the war by a vote of 174 to 14. The nays came mainly from New Englanders or from those from New England representing western migrants; John Quincy Adams of Massachusetts led them. Similarly, many Democrats and Whigs who voted yes harbored many doubts or grew dissatisfied with their decisions within a short time. Thirty-five Representatives abstained—25 northerners and 10 southerners; 22 Democrats and 13 Whigs. The Senate vote was forty to two in favor of the war. Three Senators declined to vote. States' rights leader John C. Calhoun of South Carolina was one of them, fearing that taking Mexican land might appear to be a southern plot to spread slavery. Eleven Senators did not bother to show up for the final vote, among them Daniel Webster of Massachusetts. The 11 empty seats were divided almost equally among Democrats and Whigs. In both houses of Congress, the primary motives for accepting war combined genuine patriotism with a fear of grave political consequences if elected representatives failed to back an effort to avenge America's slain soldiers.

Having declared war, Polk next had to choose the generals who would conduct it. Very early, he concluded that Winfield Scott was an avid Whig looking primarily for a presidential nomination and therefore unworthy to command in the field. Zachary Taylor was allowed to run the operations at first; he won at Monterrey, Mexico, gained national fame, and then began also to look like a potential Whig candidate for President. Polk subsequently found Taylor's generalship wanting and late in 1846 reduced his role in the war. He chose to allow Scott to launch an attack on Mexico City from Vera Cruz. The President made this decision reluctantly, since he could find no better Democratic general to take Scott's place.

President Polk also had to deal with Congress in order to get continued support for the war effort—a difficult enterprise in the long run. Except among northern Whigs, the administration encountered little congressional opposition to the war during the early summer of 1846. But from the end of the first session of the Twenty-ninth Congress in August 1846, dissatisfaction grew apace: Whigs had never supported the war vigorously, religious groups began actively protesting, and Polk lacked the leadership qualities necessary to rally the public. By the time the second session convened in December 1846, the November elections resulted in political disaster for House Democrats; the Whigs gained 38 seats, mainly from the Northeast. This result probably reflected a growing unhappiness with the war. Subsequently, Polk had difficulty maintaining party unity, even when the Democrats had held a majority in both houses. The Democratic Party for years had been riven with dissension because of state factionalism, those unhappy with patronage decisions, and personal political rivalries among key leaders. Now the situation would be worse. Nevertheless, Whigs did approve appropriations supporting armies in the field, while at the same time denouncing the war as needless and Polk as a fool or worse.

Debates on the war conducted during the second session of the Twenty-ninth Congress showed that party loyalty was still the prevailing pattern—a trend that increased during the Thirtieth Congress, which first met in December 1847. Whigs realized that any credit in this war would probably go to the Democrats and so stepped up their criticisms, including accusations that the President wanted to seize all of Mexico. The Whigs feared that acquiring Mexican territory would only exacerbate the slavery extension problem, thus endangering both their party and the Union. Near the end of 1847, however, the public had become more sympathetic toward the war. Taylor had won a near miraculous victory at Buena Vista; Scott had pulled off a series of spectacular victories, ending in the capture of Mexico City in September 1847; and both achievements had come against much larger opposing armies. The public was also angry with Mexico for adamantly refusing to negotiate a peace treaty. Even so, the House late in 1847 narrowly passed a resolution labeling the war "unnecessary and unconstitutional."

Of all the war-related issues discussed in Congress, none was more important or more dangerous than the Wilmot Proviso. In the summer of 1846, President Polk had asked Congress for $2 million to aid peace negotiations with Mexico. Pennsylvania Democrat David Wilmot proposed an amendment to the resulting appropriations bill excluding slavery from any territory acquired from Mexico. The House passed it, but the Senate adjourned without considering Wilmot's amendment. Yet the Proviso kept reappearing and passing in the House. The motives behind this amendment came mainly from a variety of political, economic, and moral animosities harbored by northerners against Polk and the South. This issue produced a clear pattern of sectional voting behavior, as opposed to the party loyalty that had prevailed on most earlier pieces of legislation. When the Proviso was first introduced, all northern Whig Representatives and every northern Democrat, except four, voted for it. On the other hand, every southern Democrat and every southern Whig, with two exceptions, declared against it. In February 1847, after lengthy negotiations with northern Democrats, Polk got a $3 million appropriation, without the Proviso attached. However, the rancorous sectional debate on this subject continued for many years and would be a major step leading to the Civil War.

On February 2, 1848, after a tortured and prolonged process, representatives of Mexico and the United States signed the Treaty of Guadeloupe Hidalgo ending the war. Although Polk had wanted to acquire more land and to pay less money to Mexico, he concluded, for a variety of political and military reasons, that he had to send the treaty to the Senate for a decision. On March 10, 1848, the Senate approved the treaty by a vote of 38 to 14. The votes in favor formed neither a sectional nor a party pattern. Most Whigs and even the Calhoun Democrats accepted it. Though operating from different perspectives, both groups feared that a rejection of the treaty would mean the seizure of all of Mexico. Seven of the Senate dissenters on this issue were Whigs, who could not stomach taking Mexican land; five others were Democrats who wanted to shrink Mexican boundaries even more; and no one has been able to ascertain with certainty why the other two Senators voted against the treaty.

The Mexican War had cost millions of dollars and thousands of casualties. For this sacrifice, however, the United States had gained vast amounts of new land, new and lucrative trading opportunities on the Pacific Coast, and enough California gold to generate the Gold Rush in 1849. Half the new land, however, lay south of 36°30' line and had been won largely by southern Presidents, generals, and troops. The Wilmot Proviso, therefore, continued to anger the South, and many of its state legislatures and Congressmen swore to resist it. On the other hand, some 14 northern state legislatures adopted resolutions approving the Proviso, and they were increasingly supported by northern politicians in Washington. During the next 12 years, politicos would offer a variety of compromises to settle the slavery extension issue. In the end, however, this single problem would come to dominate all others in American politics and, in the wake of its virulence, would destroy the party system, harden North-South sectional lines, and produce a civil war.

See also: John Quincy Adams, John C. Calhoun, James K. Polk, Zachary Taylor, Daniel Webster, David Wilmot, Wilmot Proviso

Gerald W. Wolff

REFERENCES

Bauer, K. Jack. 1974. *The Mexican War.* New York: Macmillan.

Henry, Robert Selph. 1950. *The Story of the Mexican War.* Indianapolis: Bobbs-Merrill.

Ruiz, Ramon Eduardo, ed. 1963. *The Mexican War: Was It Manifest Destiny?* New York: Holt, Rinehart and Winston.

Singletary, Otis A. 1960. *The Mexican War.* Chicago: U. of Chicago Pr.

Smith, Justin H. 1919. *The War with Mexico.* 2 vols. New York: Macmillan.

Robert H. Michel (1923–)

Republican leader of the U.S. House of Representatives. Robert Henry Michel served as the Minority Leader in the U.S. House of Representatives throughout Ronald Reagan's presidency, helping Reagan win major House victories in spite of a large Democratic majority in that chamber. Michel came to Washington as a congressional aide in 1948 and won the Peoria, Illinois, seat in the House eight years later. Senator Everett Dirksen, a constituent, schooled him in national politics. Michel climbed the Republican ranks, distinguishing himself by fighting against liberal programs on the Appropriations Committee. He chaired the National Republican Congressional Committee during the 1974 midterms; despite severe GOP losses, he kept stature within the GOP and in December was elected Republican Whip. In 1980, he defeated Guy Vander Jagt of Michigan for the post of Republican Minority Leader.

Michel's personal style was affable, but his leadership proved more assertive than many Washington observers acknowledged. He played a crucial role in winning Democratic votes for Reagan's economic policy. In 1985 he fought the majority's effort to declare a Democrat the winner of a disputed Indiana seat.

His friendship with House Speaker Tip O'Neill (D-Mass.) caused some grumbling in Republican ranks, but his relationship with O'Neill's successor, Jim Wright, was chillier. In a 1988 floor debate, he came close to calling Wright a liar for allegedly reneging on an agreement on Central American policy. On key issues like campaign financing he maintained a partisan view, often conflicting with Wright's successor, Thomas Foley (D-Wash.), in the One-Hundred-First Congress.

See also: Everett Dirksen, Thomas Foley, Thomas O'Neill, Ronald Reagan, Jim Wright

John J. Pitney, Jr.

REFERENCES

Feulner, Edwin J., Jr. 1983. *Conservatives Stalk the House: The Story of the Republican Study Committee.* Ottawa, IL: Green Hill.

Pitney, John J., Jr. 1990. "Republican Party Leadership in the U.S. House." Paper presented at the annual meeting of the American Political Science Association, San Francisco.

Stockman, David. 1986. *The Triumph of Politics.* New York: Harper & Row.

Robert Michels (1876–1936)

Political theorist. The phrase that is perhaps the most famous in parties and organizations was first published in 1911 in Robert Michels's classic work *Political Parties*: "It is organization that gives birth to the dominion of the elected over the electors, of the mandataries over the mandators, of the delegates over the delegators. Who says organization, says oligarchy."

Robert Michels was not a scholar of the American political party. In fact, Leon Epstein has characterized American party scholars as generally adopting viewpoints sharply at variance with Michels's. Nonetheless, his influence on the study of American parties, especially of party leadership, is unparalleled. In fact, he was there (at least in spirit) at the beginning: in 1924, Charles Edward Merriam wrote, "Of great interest in the more special field of political relations is the work of Robert Michels." Michels was volubly anti-authoritarian in sentiment and passionately committed to democracy; nevertheless, after an early career on the political left, he finished his life associated with Mussolini and the Fascists. Mussolini appointed him to the faculty of the University of Perugia in 1928.

He was without question a gifted scientist and theorist, and his study of the German Social Democratic Party is a reference point from which to consider the significance of subsequent party leadership studies. Michels is famous for his "iron law of oligarchy" (organizational needs beget task specialization, which then engenders structural differentiation and a psychologically transformed leadership group distant from their followers who lose interest and are then controlled by the leadership group). His observations on the psychological transformation (metamorphosis) of leaders and the vanity and character of power (power is always conservative) also stand alone. Michels's influence is equally profound on the field of sociology as well as on a more general study of political parties. Michels serves as a reference point even for those American party scholars, such as Samuel Eldersveld, who fundamentally disagree with his positions. Eldersveld's treatment of "stratarchy" without question owes much to Michels. In fact, Eldersveld writes, "if really concerned with the development of a testable theory of party leadership, we have taken refuge in Michels. It is amazing how heavily we have relied on the iron law of oligarchy from 1915 to the present."

David A. Bositis

REFERENCES

Eldersveld, Samuel J. 1964. *Political Parties: A Behavioral Analysis.* Chicago: Rand McNally.

————. 1982. *Political Parties in American Society.* New York: Basic Books.

Epstein, Leon D. 1986. *Political Parties in the American Mold.* Madison: U. of Wisconsin Pr.

Lipset, Seymour M., Martin Trow, and James Coleman. 1956. *Union Democracy.* New York: Free Press.

Merriam, Charles E. 1924. *The American Party System.* New York: Macmillan.

Michels, Robert. 1962. *Political Parties.* New York: Collier Books.

Barbara A. Mikulski (1939–)

Liberal Maryland Democratic political leader. A spirited crusader for social justice, Barbara Ann Mikulski served five terms in the U.S. House of Representatives and then as a U.S. Senator from Maryland. Mikulski received her B.A. from Baltimore's Mount St. Agnes College and an M.S.W. from the University of Maryland. After experiences as a teacher and as a social worker in the Baltimore Department of Social Services, Mikulski won a seat on the Baltimore City Council (1971–1976). She used her position to help empower ethnic and minority groups in the city. Her activities brought her to the attention of Jean Westwood, chairwoman of the Democratic National Committee, and in 1972

Mikulski was appointed as co-chair of the Commission on Delegate Selection and Party Structure, succeeding Leonard Woodcock as chair in 1973.

In October 1973 the Mikulski Commission issued a unanimous report calling for, among other things, the replacement of the delegate quota system with a more flexible affirmative action rule so as to insure equitable representation of women, minorities, and young people to future Democratic conventions. Also recommended was the substitution of proportional primaries for winner-take-all primaries. In 1974 Mikulski ran unsuccessfully for the Senate in Maryland against the Republican incumbent, Charles Mathias, but in 1976 she defeated Republican Samuel A. Culotta for a seat in the House of Representatives. She served continuously until 1987 and was a founding member of the Congressional Women's Caucus. In 1986, after besting a crowded field in the Democratic primary, Mikulski defeated Republican Linda Chavez, a former aide to President Ronald Reagan, for the Maryland Senate seat from which Mathias retired.

See also: Democratic National Committee, Jean Westwood, Leonard Woodcock

Thomas J. Baldino

REFERENCES

Shafer, Byron E. 1983. *The Quiet Revolution.* New York: Russell Sage.

Harvey Milk (1930–1978)

First avowed homosexual elected to public office in the United States. Harvey Milk was born in New York City, the son of Russian Jewish immigrants. He graduated in 1951 from Albany State College for Teachers. Until 1969 Milk lived in New York City where he held a position as a financial analyst on Wall Street. He left the East Coast to take another position in the financial district of San Francisco and later opened a camera shop.

Harvey Milk first became politically involved in 1973, angry at what he considered the disgrace of Watergate. For Milk and for the country, two firsts occurred. Milk made his first attempt to gain a position on the San Francisco Board of Supervisors, and he became the first person in the United States to run for public office as an open homosexual. Although he lost (gathering only a token number of votes) in 1973 and again in 1975, he made a successful bid to the position of board supervisor in 1977, when he defeated 16 other candidates (with over 30 percent of the vote). Upper Market Street and Haight-Ashbury comprised his district—San Francisco's Fifth.

But Milk's service was to be cut short. Milk and San Francisco mayor George Moscone were gunned down by a former city supervisor who claimed that they had been trying to make him "the fall guy and scapegoat" in their political game.

As a politician, Harvey Milk was a liberal Democrat. Although he expanded the rights of homosexuals through his courage and conviction, Milk's platform included not only homosexual rights but also low-rent housing, free municipal transportation, expanded child care facilities, and the development of a civilian police-review board. Despite the hate and anger that were directed toward him daily because of his homosexuality, Harvey Milk lived for the chance to make a difference in the lives of all of the people he represented, including homosexuals. He considered himself a barrier breaker—like Jackie Robinson for Blacks and John F. Kennedy for Catholics—and a "hope to gays." In a recorded tape that he asked a friend to release if he was killed, Milk urged "all to work toward . . . constructive pursuits" and urged homosexuals to "come out" and no longer conceal their homosexuality.

See also: John F. Kennedy, Watergate

Joyce McPhetres Maisel

REFERENCES

"Another Day of Death." 1978. *Time,* December 11.

Crewdson, John M. 1978. "Harvey Milk, Led Coast Homosexual-Rights Fight." *New York Times,* November 27.

"Day of the Assassin." 1978. *Newsweek,* December 11.

"Gay Power." 1977. *Newsweek,* November 31.

William E. Miller (1914–1983)

Obscure GOP vice presidential candidate in 1964. William Edward Miller was a pioneer in the Republican conservative movement. The son of a factory janitor and milliner, Miller was born in Lockport, New York—a small town on the western edge of the state. Educated at the University of Notre Dame and Albany Law School, Miller practiced law from 1938 to 1942, then enlisted in the U.S. Army in World War II. Three years later he was commissioned and assigned to the judge advocate general's war crimes section where he served as an assistant prosecutor at the Nuremberg trials of Nazi war criminals. Discharged from the Army in 1946, he resumed his Lockport law practice.

Miller began his political career in 1948 when he was appointed district attorney for Niagara County. In 1950 he was elected to the U.S. House of Representatives where he served seven consecutive terms from 1951 to 1965.

Miller quickly became known for his caustic tongue, once calling John F. Kennedy "the foundering father of the New Frontier." Miller's voting record matched his reactionary rhetoric. In his last term in Congress the conservative Americans for Constitutional Action gave him a 92 percent approval rating.

Miller won recognition through appointments to key Republican Party posts. In 1960 he was named chairman of the Republican Congressional Campaign Committee. That year the GOP gained 22 seats in the House even as Republican presidential candidate Richard M. Nixon lost to John F. Kennedy. Miller was given credit for the party's strong congressional showing, and in 1961 he was named chairman of the Republican National Committee.

Miller worked closely in 1960 with Barry Goldwater, then chairman of the Republican Senatorial Campaign Committee. He subsequently supported Goldwater for the 1964 Republican presidential nomination and was chosen to be Goldwater's vice presidential candidate over Pennsylvania governor William W. Scranton and Michigan Congressman Gerald R. Ford. Goldwater reportedly selected Miller because "he drives [Lyndon] Johnson nuts."

The Goldwater-Miller ticket lost in a landslide to the Democrats Lyndon B. Johnson and Hubert H. Humphrey. After the election, Miller returned to his Lockport law practice. In 1975 Miller gained fame in television commercials as an "unknown" spokesman for American Express ("Do you know who I am?").

See also: Barry Goldwater, Hubert Humphrey, Lyndon B. Johnson, Republican National Committee

John K. White

REFERENCES

Goldwater, Barry. 1988. *Goldwater.* New York: Doubleday.

White, Theodore H. 1965. *The Making of the President 1964.* New York: Atheneum.

Wilbur Mills (1909–)

Powerful Democratic chairman of the House Ways and Means Committee. Scandal-conscious Washington may remember Wilbur Mills for his affair with stripper Fanne Fox, his alcoholism, and his subsequent fall from political grace. Students of politics, however, will look to Mills's career for clues to understanding the power of a committee chairman and how institutional changes in the U.S. House of Representatives led to the reduction of that power.

First elected to Congress from Arkansas in 1938, Mills became chairman of the Ways and Means Committee in 1958. Because Ways and Means was one of the most powerful committees in the House, Mills was to become one of the most influential members of Congress in the 1960s. Mills's power resulted from a combination of factors: the committee's jurisdiction was broad (including all tax, trade, Social Security, Medicare, and Medicaid legislation), and its Democratic members made committee assignments for all other House Democrats. Mills also was able to secure "closed" rules from the Rules Committee, procedures that prohibited floor amendments and forced the membership into all-or-nothing decisions on legislation reported from Ways and Means. Internally, the chairman's control was almost absolute. Ways and Means had no subcommittees, its staff was used only at Mills's discretion, and his close relations with ranking Republicans ensured only token opposition from the minority party. Mills even ran for the Democratic presidential nomination in 1972, though his campaign went nowhere. One wag wondered why Mills would want to "run for President and give up his grip on the country."

Mills's role as an important shaper of policy ended, however, in a series of embarrassing incidents beginning in October 1974. He was found by the National Park Police in the Washington Tidal Basin trying to prevent Fanne Fox (the "Argentine firecracker") from throwing herself in. Others alleged that one night he bought $1,400 worth of champagne at the nightclub where Fox worked, and after his 1974 reelection, he appeared on stage in Boston during her act. He eventually sought medical treatment for his alcoholism.

The Arkansas Congressman's power had peaked even before his personal problems became apparent in late 1974. As part of a broadly based set of changes in House procedures and committee powers, in 1973 House reformers stripped Ways and Means of its power to make committee assignments. And, in the wake of the Tidal Basin incident, subcommittees were created on Ways and Means, thus giving other members staff resources and added influence.

Mills was not the only powerful committee chairman affected by the congressional reform movement of the early 1970s. Ultimately, a number of chairmen were removed from their posts, a subcommittee "Bill of Rights" was passed, and committee and subcommittee meetings were opened to the public.

See also: Election of 1972.

Tom A. Kazee

REFERENCES

Dodd, Lawrence, and Bruce Oppenheimer. 1985. "The House in Transition: Partisanship and Opposition." In Lawrence Dodd and Brice I. Oppenheimer, eds. *Congress Reconsidered.* 3rd ed. Washington: Congressional Quarterly.

Reiselbach, Leroy N. 1977. *Congressional Reform in the Seventies.* Morristown, NJ: General Learning Press.

Minnesota Farmer-Labor Party

The most electorally and politically successful state-level third party in American history was the Minnesota Farmer-Labor Party (1918–1944). Its merger in 1944 with the Minnesota Democratic Party, resulting in the Minnesota Democratic Farmer-Labor Party, shaped the organization and character of postwar Democratic politics in Minnesota. Accordingly, Minnesota Democratic politicians were for several decades the most liberal in America.

The FLP's history matters for another reason. It was the most successful instance of a type of protest politics (state-level radicalism) that appeared several times in the 1910s, the 1920s, and the 1930s in north central, northwestern, western, and southwestern states. Other such protest parties were, the North Dakota Nonpartisan League, the Wisconsin Progressive Party, and End-Poverty-in-California.

The Farmer-Labor Party began as a political movement of various economic organizations. Between 1918 and 1923 the National Nonpartisan League, the Minnesota Railroad Brotherhoods, and the Minnesota State Federation of Labor all invested heavily in an effort to control several city governments, all statewide executive offices, and Minnesota's officially nonpartisan legislature. This coalition ran endorsed candidates in all relevant electoral settings. To publicize these endorsements, a daily newspaper was founded in Minneapolis, and several newspapers in county seats were taken over by the National Nonpartisan League.

In 1923 and 1924 the FLP's loose organizational structure was reformed to create a supposedly permanent infrastructure of county and ward clubs. This change resulted in part from an expectation among the state's farmer-labor elite that the party would win the governorship and that Wisconsin Progressive Robert M. La Follette would become the President. But state-level and national defeat in 1924 coupled with financial crises in the FLP's supporting organizations led to organizational and electoral weakness in the latter part of the decade.

The Great Depression revived the Farmer-Labor Party. The party's unsuccessful 1924 gubernatorial candidate, Floyd B. Olson, was able to win election as governor in 1930. He proved to be an adept politician and was reelected twice. Olson also presided over the intensive use of patronage to strengthen the FLP organizationally and financially. The party steadily increased its electoral strength in several areas, and accomplished much in the area of public policy. The FLP's strength reached its zenith in 1936 when a state bureaucrat with no electoral experience, Elmer Benson, was elected governor in a landslide.

Yet by 1938 the FLP was a shambles. It suffered a massive defeat at the hands of a Republican Party rejuvenated by generational change; astute exploitation by the Republicans of deep, long-building splits within the Farmer-Labor coalition (splits generated by the New Deal's intervention into the economy and society); and the Roosevelt recession of 1937–1938. Bitter factionalism and continuing defeat plagued the FLP until its 1944 merger with the Democratic Party, when its leaders bequeathed the FLP's sometimes effective infrastructure of ward and county clubs to the Democrats.

See also: Robert La Follette, National Nonpartisan League, New Deal, Wisconsin Progressive Party

Richard M. Valelly

REFERENCES

Gieske, Millard. 1979. *Minnesota Farmer-Laborism: The Third Party Alternative.* Minneapolis: U. of Minnesota Pr.

Valelly, Richard M. 1989. *Radicalism in the States: The Minnesota Farmer-Labor Party and the American Political Economy.* Chicago: U. of Chicago Pr.

Minority Party Leadership in Congress

Political parties in the American Congress are judged to be weak when compared to those in other nations' legislatures. However weak they may be, parties remain a dominant feature of congressional organization. In fact, since the turn of the century, the average number of members of Congress *not* identifying with one of the two major parties has been miniscule—approximately one every two years in the Senate, fewer in the House of Representatives. In the 16 Congresses between 1957 and 1989, only one House member and two Senators did not identify themselves as either a Democrat or a Republican.

Attention here is directed to the minority party in Congress, defined as the party within each chamber with the second highest number of members. It should be noted at the outset that in a two-house legislature, the minority party may not always be the same in both chambers. In fact, that situation has occurred in five Congresses in the twentieth century (62nd, 72nd, 97th, 98th, and 99th); Republicans were the minority in the House, Democrats the minority in the Senate in each of the cases.

Minority Party Leaders

Observers note two principal categories of minority party leaders: those serving their party in the chamber overall and those within each of the congressional committees. For the modern Congress, the principal leaders within the chamber are

1. The floor leader: elected by the party caucus, the floor or Minority Leader is the chief spokesman for the party. This person manages the floor strategy, makes certain appointments, and works with party leaders in the other chamber and outside Congress. The House and Senate minority floor leaders for this century are listed in Appendices 4 and 5, respectively.

2. The Whip: also elected by the caucus (though formerly appointed by the floor leader for House Democrats), the Whip assists the floor leader and manages a communication system to inform members about legislation on the floor and party positions on pending votes.

3. Caucus chairman: this person chairs meetings when all party members convene. In the case of the Senate Democrats, the floor leader serves as caucus chairman. In the other cases (Senate Republicans, House Republicans, House Democrats), a person other than the floor leader is elected by the caucus to serve in this position.

4. Chairmen of party committees: each party in each chamber has several committees, variously called Policy Committee, Steering and Policy Committee, Steering Committee, Committee-on-Committees, Research Committee. The work of these

committees varies but includes discussing party positions on legislation, scheduling of legislation, recommending committee assignments for members, and conducting research on policy issues. The chairmen are either elected by the caucus or serve by virtue of being the floor leader.

Party organization has become much more elaborate in recent decades. Party committees, in particular, were developed in the post–World War II period; those that did exist previously had few functions and no staff support. The role of the caucus, for instance, has varied over time. In general, however, the Republicans have relied more on the caucus (or conference as they call it) for policy purposes than have the Democrats. In part this reliance stems from a greater cohesion among Republicans on policy issues.

Work in the congressional committees is often less partisan than is actual action on the floor of each chamber. Yet committees and subcommittees, too, are organized along political party lines. Each committee has a chairman on the majority side and a so-called "ranking member" on the minority side. These ranking members have certain prerogatives in committee hearings, in debate, and in the mark up of legislation; they also are influential in appointments of subcommittees and staff. In recent years, party caucuses have been important within committees for organizational and policy purposes.

Minority Party Leadership in Political Context

One of the most obvious characteristics of the congressional parties seems to be the semipermanent status of the majority-minority party division. Note in Table 1 that the Democrats were in the minority most of the time during the first three decades of the century, the Republicans in the minority most of the time since 1932. Democrats had House majorities in just four Congresses and Senate majorities in just three Congresses (1901–1932). During that period they held 46 percent of the House seats and 44 percent of the Senate seats. Between 1932 and 1988, House Republicans have been in the majority in just two Congresses, Senate Republicans in just five Congresses. During this period of nearly 60 years, the Republicans have held 40 percent of the House seats and 40 percent of the Senate seats.

Unsurprising under these circumstances is the fact that those in the minority become somewhat disillusioned. Some analysts even talk of a "minority party mentality" according to which party members accommodate their status and work to serve their districts so as to be reelected. A supreme effort is necessary to achieve majority status, and members of the minority tire of the futility of such an achievement. A minority party mentality may be more characteristic of the senior members, who typically serve as leaders, thus creating tension with the more enthusiastic junior members. One House floor leader, John J. Rhodes, wrote about the frustrations of his long service in the minority in a book aptly titled *The Futile System* (1976).

A second important political condition that distinguishes minority parties is the size of the margin for the majority. Thus, for example, leading a Senate Republican Party of just 17 members out of 96 (as was the case in the 75th Congress) is vastly different from leading one with 47 members out of 96 (in the 82nd Congress). The ranges in the size of minority parties in this century have been as follows:

	Democrats		Republicans	
	from	*to*	*from*	*to*
House	132	213	89	216
	(30%)	(49%)	(20%)	(50%)
	(57th)	(83rd)	(75th)	(65th)
Senate	29	47	17	47
	(32%)	(49%)	(18%)	(49%)
	(60th)	(66%)*	(75th)	(82nd)**

*Also occurred in 70th and 72nd Congresses.
**Also occurred in 84th and 85th Congresses.

Observers note that the Republicans have dropped lower in numbers than the Democrats in both houses—primarily as a result of the landslide victories for Democrats during the Franklin Roosevelt era. The 1936 Roosevelt win decimated congressional Republicans. The point at which the House Republicans as a minority party had their greatest strength in numbers was in 1931. They actually won a narrow majority in the general election in 1930, but by the time Congress met, enough Republicans had died that the Democrats actually organized the House. This situation suggests still other important factors in determining minority party leadership—the electoral trends and the dominant issues of the time. In 1931 the trend was running against the Republicans; they would suffer a net loss of nearly 100 seats in 1932. And the dominant issue was the dire economic circumstances following the stock market crash in 1929.

As is obvious from the previous discussion, the role of the President is very important in determining the problems to be faced by minority party leaders. In particular, a pattern that has developed in recent decades is that of a Republican President having to work with Democratic majorities in one or both houses of Congress. This split in party control was characteristic of national policymaking for 22 of the 36 years between 1952 and 1988 (61 percent of the time).

Further complicating the situation for minority party leaders in Congress is that the Republican President may well have won election by a landslide in the Electoral College. Presidents Dwight Eisenhower in 1952 and 1956, Richard Nixon in 1972, and Ronald Reagan in 1980 and 1984 won with more than 80 percent of the electoral vote; Nixon and Reagan won with more than 90 percent. Under these conditions the President presumably has strong support among the American people, yet his party in Congress has been in the minority in one or both houses. The congressional Minority Leaders are then put in the position of having to take responsibility for building coalitions for the President's program while fending off majority party legislative initiatives. The Republican President cannot win without Democratic votes, even though compromises to attract these votes may alienate Republicans. Thus, coalition building by minority party leaders can be an exhausting and frustrating activity.

President Ronald Reagan had the advantage of a Senate Republican majority during his first three Congresses. He was able to initiate action in the Senate, get approval there, and then turn to the House from a position of strength. The Republican Senate could also act as a check on Democratic initiatives from the House. But Reagan's mandate was clearest in 1981. After that time House GOP Minority Leaders had to manage in a highly partisan atmosphere, particularly given the fact that the House was the only base strength for the Democrats. It was in this set of circumstances that a group of young Republicans formed a Conservative Opportunity Society (COS) to urge more aggressive policy positions for their party. The COS is a good example of an effort by younger members to overcome the disadvantage of the semipermanent status of the minority.

Summary

Minority party leadership in Congress varies according to the personal capabilities of those filling the positions and the political conditions under which they serve. The nature of the agenda may also be influential. Three broad types of minority parties are suggested by these variable factors: restricted (those with few members who face a strong President with a substantial program, e.g., the Republicans during the early years of FDR); unrestricted (those approaching 50 percent of the membership in the chamber and in a position to mount serious legislative challenges, e.g., the Democrats during the last years of Herbert Hoover); and participating (those serving a President of the same party, e.g., the Republicans with Eisenhower, Nixon-Ford, and Reagan). Finally, different types of minority parties in the two chambers, in any further complicating the strategic position of party leaders.

See also: Election of 1972, Electoral College System

Charles O. Jones

REFERENCES

Jones, Charles O. 1970. *The Minority Party in Congress.* Boston: Little, Brown.

Ornstein, Norman J., Thomas E. Mann, and Michael J. Malbin. 1990. *Vital Statistics on Congress, 1989–1990.* Washington: Congressional Quarterly.

Rhodes, John J. 1976. *The Futile System.* McLean, VA: EPM Publications.

Newton N. Minow (1926–)

Newton Norman Minow was born in Milwaukee, Wisconsin, and educated at Northwestern University (B.A., 1949; J.D., 1950). In 1950 and 1951 he clerked for Fred M. Vinson, Chief Justice of the Supreme Court of the United States, and he then followed Adlai Stevenson II into political work. As Governor Stevenson's administrative assistant in 1952, he took part in Stevenson's presidential campaign and later joined the governor's law firm. Minow's career has been divided among corporate law in Chicago in the firm of Sidley and Austin, public service as a foundation trustee (e.g., Rand Corp., Chicago Educational Television), and Washington activities mostly in the field of communication.

He is most famous for his chairmanship of the Federal Communications Commission in John Kennedy's administration (1961–1963) during which he expressed the opinion that television programming was a "vast wasteland." Since then he has served on the boards of directors of such organizations as CBS, Foote, Cone and Belding Communications, and Encyclopedia Britannica, and headed a Washington journalism center financed by Walter Annenberg and affiliated with his alma mater, Northwestern University.

See also: Federal Communications Commission, Adlai Stevenson II

Nelson W. Polsby

Mississippi Freedom Democratic Party

Formed on April 26, 1964, in Jackson, the Mississippi Freedom Democratic Party (MFDP) was designed to increase the political experience of African-Americans in the state, hitherto largely excluded from the political process. The Democratic Party ultimately claimed 60,000 Black residents as members. The MFDP started as a major goal of the Mississippi Freedom project—a project launched under the auspices of a coalition of civil rights organizations, most prominent of which was the Student Nonviolent Coordinating Committee (SNCC), an organization made up primarily of Black college students. Founders of the MFDP included Robert Moses (SNCC), Aaron Henry (NAACP), David Dennis (CORE), and Allard Lowenstein.

After African-Americans had once again been excluded from the 1964 state Democratic Party meetings to select national convention delegates, the MFDP set up a parallel delegate selection process, selecting 62 Blacks and 4 whites as national convention delegates. The MFDP delegation challenged the seating of the all-white state Democratic delegation before the national party's Credentials Committee, charging racial discrimination and segregation in the political and social environment. The committee's compromise—requiring every delegate to sign a loyalty oath to support the national party's nominees, the seating of only the two leaders of the MFDP, and the inclusion of the remaining MFDP delegation as nonvoting honored guests—was rejected by both delegations. Most importantly, the Credentials Committee report stipulated that, in the future, delegations from states that allowed racial discrimination in voting would be barred from the convention.

In early 1965 the MFDP challenged the seating of Mississippi's congressional delegation, charging that African-Americans were disenfranchised in Mississippi and that the MFDP's

candidates for Congress had been kept off of the ballot. Though the MFDP lost on a 228-to-143 vote, white Democrats began to realize that they would no longer be permitted to discriminate against Blacks. This event as well as the 1964 convention challenge contributed to passage of the landmark 1965 Voting Rights Act.

By 1965 the MFDP was split between moderates (such as Aaron Henry) who urged compromises, and young radicals from SNCC espousing Black Power and separatism (who became dominant). Henry, other NAACP leaders, white liberals, and organized labor split off to form a more moderate coalition loyal to the ideals of the national Democratic Party. In 1967 the MFDP elected Robert Clark of Holmes County to the Mississippi House of Representatives, the first Black person elected to the legislature since Reconstruction. Holmes County was the scene of a successful implementation of the MFDP's philosophy of participatory grass-roots democracy, with frequent community and monthly county MFDP meetings.

After allegations of widespread irregularities at local and state Democratic Party meetings to select national convention delegates in 1968, the moderates and the MFDP formed the Loyalist Democratic Coalition to select their own delegates and challenge the "regular" Democratic delegation. In both 1968 and 1972, the national Democratic Party recognized and seated the Loyalist delegation instead of the regular Democrats, while the regulars continued to dominate Mississippi's state government.

The split between white and Black Democrats contributed to the election of Republican Congressman Thad Cochran in 1972. Populist Democratic governor Cliff Finch successfully unified the Loyalist and regular Democrats under Black and white state party co-chairmen, and single racially integrated state delegations have been sent to the national Democratic convention since 1976.

See also: Student Nonviolent Coordinating Committee, Voting Rights Act of 1965 and Extensions

Stephen D. Shaffer

REFERENCES

Bass, Jack, and Walter DeVries. 1977. *The Transformation of Southern Politics: Social Change and Political Consequence Since 1945.* New York: New American Library.

Lamis, Alexander. 1984. *The Two-Party South.* New York: Oxford U. Pr.

Landry, David, and Joseph Parker. 1976. *Mississippi Government and Politics in Transition.* Dubuque, IA: Kendall, Hunt.

McDowell, Jennifer, and Milton Loventhal. 1971. *Black Politics: A Study and Annotated Bibliography of the Mississippi Freedom Democratic Party.* San Jose, CA: Bibliographical Information Center for the Study of Political Science.

McLemore, Leslie. 1971. "The Mississippi Freedom Democratic Party: A Case Study of Grass-Roots Politics." Ph.D. dissertation, U. of Massachusetts, Amherst.

Rothchild, Mary. 1982. *A Case of Black and White: Northern Volunteers and the Southern Freedom Summers, 1964–1965.* Westport, CT: Greenwood.

Missouri Compromise

On August 21, 1821, the Missouri Territory was admitted to the Union, ending four years of debate on issues much broader than the usual standards applied to territories petitioning for statehood. The focus of the debate was Congress' role in admitting states and the specific question of slavery in the territories.

The context behind the Missouri Compromise was one of emerging regionalism and growing sentiment for the abolition of slavery. In 1817 the territorial government of Missouri submitted its petition for statehood, noting the territory's loyalty in the War of 1812, its increased population, and its "readiness" as the primary qualifications supporting admission. Whereas these simple points might earlier have won Missouri's admission, discussions that ensued in Congress became mired down in debating the status of Missouri as a slave state or a free state.

Many northern Congressmen sought to contain the spread of slavery and deemed the admission of Missouri as a nonslaveholding state as pivotal to this end. Southerners in Congress believed that Missouri's status as a slaveholding state was a natural course for southern expansion to take and worked to preserve that course. The northern position was labeled as "restrictionist" because of the conditions it placed upon Missouri's admission as a state.

While southern territories expanded faster during the early 1800s than did northern territories, greater numbers of people lived in northern states. In Congress, northern restrictionists dominated the population-based membership of the House but could not do so in the state-based membership of the Senate. Before 1820 slave states and free states were even at 11, with Delaware counted among the slaveholding states.

With the onset of slavery as an issue of debate, admission of new states, particularly Missouri and Maine, became an extremely volatile issue. While few argued against Maine's admission as a state, Missouri became the subject of polarization in the Congress. The House continually denied Missouri admission without a conditional prohibition of slavery in that state. Nonrestrictionists argued for a state's right to self-determination and questioned the constitutionality of conditional admission. The issue was originally settled when lawmakers agreed to allow Missouri to be admitted as an unrestricted (slaveholding) state, while at the same time admitting Maine as a state restricted from slaveholding. In addition, Congress agreed that slavery in the remaining Louisiana Territory was limited to those lands south of Missouri's southern border, 36°30'.

While the compromise served initially to mollify the restrictionists, the Missouri convention submitted to Congress a constitution that included a clause prohibiting free Blacks and mulattoes from entering Missouri. This action so infuriated the restrictionists that they again blocked the entrance of Missouri into the Union. Only a second compromise—one allowing Missouri to be admitted only if no aspect of its state constitution contradicted rights granted to citizens in the national Constitution—entitled Missouri to statehood.

The substantive effect of the "second" Missouri compromise in 1821 was negligible, as the status of Blacks as citizens in slaveholding states had not yet been established. However, the Missouri Compromise stood as the main prelude to the discussion of slavery and secession in Congress before the Civil War. In this issue, voting in Congress was to become the product of a geographic region, not the result of political parties. While it served to quell discussion at the time, the Missouri Compromise only postponed a more vigorous and divisive debate in Congress years later. The balance struck by the Missouri Compromise was disrupted in 1854 when the passage of the Kansas-Nebraska Act effectively repealed the Compromise.

See also: Abolition Movement, Kansas-Nebraska Act, Slavery

Michael Heel

REFERENCES

Fegrenbacher, Don E. 1980. *The South and Three Sectional Crises.* Baton Rouge: Louisiana State U. Pr.

Nagel, Paul C. 1977. *Missouri.* New York: Norton.

———. 1954. *The Nebraska Question.* New York: Redfield.

Ray, P. Orman. 1909. *The Repeal of the Missouri Compromise.* Cleveland: Arthur H. Clark.

Rich, Louise Dickinson. 1964. *State O' Maine.* Camden, ME: Downeast Books.

Shoemaker, Floyd Calvin. 1943. *Missouri's Struggle for Statehood, 1804–1821*. New York: Russell and Russell.

George J. Mitchell (1933–)

Democratic Senate Majority Leader from Maine. George J. Mitchell is one of the latest in a long line of American politicians who have fulfilled the American dream, become successful beyond their ancestors' wildest imaginations, and repaid their nation with dedicated service. Raised in Waterville, Maine, Mitchell is the son of a Lebanese immigrant mother, who worked the night shift in a local textile mill, and an Irish immigrant father, who worked as a janitor at Colby College. Mitchell's family stressed ideals and achievements: each of his older siblings gained acclaim as an athlete and George was the most studious in the family. Mitchell graduated from Bowdoin College, served in the military, and then went through Georgetown Law School, before beginning a successful legal career.

George Mitchell's political career has been integrally linked with that of Maine Democratic Senator Edmund S. Muskie. In the early 1960s Mitchell served as Muskie's administrative assistant. Returning to Maine and a legal career, Mitchell became chair of the Democratic State Committee in 1966; he played key roles on Muskie's campaign for Vice President in 1968 and in the Senator's try for the Democratic presidential nomination in 1972. In 1974 Mitchell sought elective office in his own right. He won a divisive Democratic primary for governor but then was upset by Independent James Longley in the November general election.

Mitchell returned to the practice of law but again Muskie's influence was felt. After President Jimmy Carter won the 1976 election, Muskie suggested his former administrative assistant for the post of U.S. attorney for Maine. Two years later, again with Muskie's intervention, Mitchell was appointed as judge of the U.S. District Court. Mitchell drew high marks for his intelligence and fairness, but close friends and political allies never felt that he would be satisfied on the bench. And then Senator Muskie's career once again had an impact on Mitchell. In 1980, when President Jimmy Carter asked Muskie to become Secretary of State, Maine governor Joseph Brennan, whom Mitchell had defeated six years earlier in the Democratic gubernatorial primary, named his former rival to the Senate seat. Some were surprised that Judge Mitchell had forsaken a lifetime appointment to become Senator Mitchell, filling only two years of an unexpired term before facing the electorate in 1982.

Mitchell entered the 1982 race as a decided underdog, trailing popular First District Congressman David F. Emery by as much as 36 percent in early polls. But Mitchell put together a tight campaign organization, raised and spent over $1.2 million (the most ever spent on a Maine campaign), and demonstrated that he had learned lessons about appealing to the electorate from his 1974 defeat. He beat Emery by a three-to-two margin; six years later he won reelection, polling over 80 percent against a fundamentalist minister. Mitchell's place in Maine's delegation seems safe as long as he wants to hold it.

Mitchell's career in the United States Senate has been marked by a meteoric climb up the Senate's power ladder. In his first years Mitchell impressed his colleagues and the Washington establishment by his hard work, his intelligence, and his evenhanded approach to controversial issues. His "judicial" temperament was often cited. But observers were surprised by his political acumen, demonstrated first by his relatively easy victory over Congressman Emery and then in 1984 by his election as chair of the Democratic Senatorial Campaign Committee (DSCC). In that role Mitchell quietly and effectively revitalized an organization that had compared poorly to its Republican counterpart. Mitchell worked tirelessly to raise money for incumbents who were challenged and for challengers around the country. When the Democrats regained control of the Senate in 1986, George Mitchell was given credit for rejuvenation of the DSCC and the role that organization played in close Democratic victories. As a result, Mitchell was marked as a "comer" among the younger generation of Democratic leaders. Newly reinstated Majority Leader Robert Byrd rewarded Mitchell by granting him the largely honorific title of Deputy President *pro tempore*, a position vacant since the death of Hubert Humphrey.

Mitchell first gained national public attention through his trenchant questioning during the televised Iran-Contra hearings. Here was a Senator who was concerned and caring, intelligent and articulate, composed yet passionate. Few who heard it can forget his lecture to Oliver North on the meaning of patriotism in the United States:

> Please remember that others have [your devotion to country] and recognize that it is possible for an American to disagree with you on aid to the contras and still love God and still love this country just as much as you do. Although He is regularly asked to do so, God does not take

sides in American politics. And in America, disagreement with the policies of the Government is not evidence of lack of patriotism. . . . Indeed it is the very fact that Americans can criticize their Government openly and without fear of reprisal that is the essence of our freedom, and that will keep us free.

Mitchell's sudden prominence because of exposure after the Iran-Contra hearings, and his success in helping the Democrats regain control of the Senate led to speculation that he would be a candidate to become Majority Leader when Byrd relinquished that post. However, others were mentioned more prominently, particularly Hawaii Senator Daniel Inouye and Louisiana Senator J. Bennett Johnston. Mitchell conceded that he was interested in the leadership position but refused to campaign openly until Byrd announced that he would retire as Majority Leader after the 1988 elections. Senator Mitchell entered the three-way race as an underdog, largely because he was a very junior member of the Senate. However, again he surprised the doubters, winning the caucus vote to succeed Byrd on the first ballot. His victory was attributable to his colleagues' desire to present a leader who could compete with President George Bush on television, as Byrd had not been able to do with President Ronald Reagan, and to the debt owed to him by those Senators he had helped elect in 1986.

The early evidence is that Majority Leader Mitchell's style will be forceful and direct, but perhaps less openly partisan than that of his predecessor. His first trials as leader involved a debate over raising congressional salaries, in which he allowed the Senate to sidestep the issue so that House members took more of the public heat, and the fight over the confirmation of former Senator John Tower to be Secretary of Defense, in which he effectively mustered both the requisite number of votes and the sympathy of the public to his side. Mitchell has said that he wants to establish a "good, fair, and open relationship" with Republican leaders. He has also demonstrated that he will consult closely with Democratic colleagues, particularly those with whom he disagrees. And since his first months in office he has become the most prominent national spokesperson for the Democratic Party on policy issue after policy issue.

See also: George Bush, Robert Byrd, Jimmy Carter, Hubert Humphrey, Edmund S. Muskie, John Tower

L. Sandy Maisel

REFERENCES

Cohen, William S., and George J. Mitchell. 1988. *Men of Zeal: A Candid History of the Iran-Contra Hearings.* New York: Viking.

Dewar, Helen. 1989. "Where the Lions Lie Down with the Lambs." *Washington Post National Weekly Edition*, May 22–28.

John N. Mitchell (1913–1988)

Richard Nixon's disgraced campaign manager and Attorney General. Born into a conservative Protestant family on Long Island, New York, John Newton Mitchell earned his law degree at Fordham University and commanded PT boats in World War II. In the 1950s he specialized in municipal bonds and became a financial consultant to such politicians as New York governor Nelson Rockefeller. In 1967 his law firm merged with Richard Nixon's. Mitchell was successful in managing Nixon's "Southern Strategy" and "law and order" presidential campaign of 1968. His reward was an appointment as Attorney General in the first Nixon Cabinet.

In his new post, Mitchell called for preventive detention of those awaiting trial, life sentences for those with three felony convictions, a "No-knock" provision for police entry without warning, stiffer narcotics penalties, and more widespread legal wiretapping.

Mitchell denounced anti-Vietnam War demonstrators, both as Communist- and Nazi-inspired, and he insisted on prosecuting the Chicago Seven, the Harrisburg Seven, and Daniel Ellsberg—cases that stemmed from civil disobedience to the military draft or to the President's conduct of the war. He tried to tone down enforcement of the Civil Rights Act. President Nixon took Mitchell's advice on national security policy and urban affairs. Mitchell recommended the successful promotion of Warren Burger as Chief Justice of the Supreme Court, together with the failed appointments of Clement Haynsworth, Jr., and G. Harrold Carswell to the Supreme Court.

In 1972 Mitchell chaired the Committee to Re-Elect the President (CREEP) until several bizarre and widely disseminated media interviews by his wife Martha obliged him to resign. He denied accusations of ordering the Watergate burglary and obstruction of justice. He was acquitted of charges that he got the Securities and Exchange Commission to block investigation of financier Robert Vesco in return for a contribution to the reelection campaign. Though

Mitchell denied that he had ordered the burglary of Democratic headquarters at the Watergate and that he obstructed justice by covering up that crime, he was convicted of conspiracy, obstruction of justice, and perjury. Later disbarred, Mitchell served 19 months in federal prison, the first U.S. Attorney General to go to jail.

See also: Civil Rights Legislation and Southern Politics, Committee to Reelect the President, Richard M. Nixon, Nelson Rockefeller, Vietnam War as a Political Issue, Watergate

Jeremy R.T. Lewis

REFERENCES

Ben-Veniste, Richard, and George Frampton, Jr. 1977. *Stonewall: The Legal Case Against the Watergate Conspirators.* New York: Simon & Schuster.

Drew, Elizabeth. 1976. *Washington Journal: The Events of 1973–1974.* New York: Random House.

Harris, Richard. 1970. *Justice: The Crisis of Law, Order and Freedom in America.* New York: E. P. Dutton.

Viorst, Milton. 1971. *Hustlers and Heroes.* New York: Simon & Schuster.

Wills, Garry. *Nixon Agonistes: The Crisis of the Self-made Man.* Boston: Houghton Mifflin.

Stephen A. Mitchell (1903–1974)

Harmonizing chairman of the Democratic National Committee in the 1950s. Hoping to placate various warring faction's in the Democratic Party after his nomination for President in 1952, Adlai Stevenson II named his trusted friend, Stephen Arnold Mitchell, to the chair of the Democratic National Committee (DNC). Mitchell, a "clean amateur," was supposedly a man for all seasons. He lasted 28 months as DNC chairman.

Iowa-born, the 49-year-old Mitchell was a practicing lawyer in Chicago at the time of his election as national chairman. He attended Creighton University and received a law degree from Georgetown University in 1928. Active in civic affairs, Mitchell met Adlai E. Stevenson in 1937 when both were members of the Committee to Defend America by Aiding the Allies. The two men became close personal friends and shared common political interests. In 1947 he and others formed a Stevenson-for-Senator Committee, leading to Stevenson's first nomination for public office as candidate for governor of Illinois. In 1952 Mitchell was chief counsel for the House Judiciary subcommittee investigating irregularities in Harry Truman's Justice Department.

As national chairman, Mitchell had to contend with the organizational problems arising from two campaign headquarters, one in Springfield, Illinois, where Stevenson was still governor, and the other in Washington. After Stevenson's defeat, Mitchell made special efforts to use Stevenson's role as titular leader as the basis for providing a "loyal opposition" to Dwight Eisenhower's administration. Although the Democrats were a minority in both houses of Congress, the party's leadership there resented the Stevenson-Mitchell approach. Chairman Mitchell resigned immediately after the 1954 midterm elections. He continued, however, to chair the committee on convention rules through 1956 and subsequently served as its counsel until 1960. In later years he supported Hubert Humphrey and Eugene McCarthy's candidacies for President.

See also: Paul M. Butler, Hubert Humphrey, Eugene McCarthy, Adlai Stevenson II, Harry S Truman

Ralph M. Goldman

REFERENCES

Goldman, Ralph M. 1990. *The National Party Chairmen and Committees: Factionalism at the Top.* Armonk, NY: M. E. Sharpe.

Mobile v. Bolden
446 U.S. 55 (1980)

This case involved a claim that an at-large electoral system for city government in Mobile, Alabama, unfairly diluted the voting strength of Blacks in violation of the Fourteenth and Fifteenth amendments. The Supreme Court rejected the claim. In a plurality opinion, Justice Potter Stewart held that it is necessary to show purposeful discrimination in order to prove a violation of the Fourteenth or Fifteenth amendments. Disproportionate effects alone are not sufficient to claim unconstitutional racial vote dilution. *Bolden* was primarily a constitutional ruling, not a statutory interpretation of the Voting Rights Act. Justice Stewart declared that Section 2 of the Act added nothing to the complaint because the legislative history of Section 2 "makes clear that it was intended to have an effect no different from that of the Fifteenth Amendment itself." Largely as a result of *Bolden*, however, the Voting Rights Act was amended to ease the burden of proving discrimination under Section 2 of the Act.

Since 1911, Mobile, Alabama, had employed a commission form of municipal government. Three commissioners jointly shared executive, legislative, and administrative powers. Candidates ran at large for one of three numbered positions and were elected by a majority of the total vote. Blacks comprised about 35 percent of the population, but no African-American had ever been elected in Mobile. The federal district court upheld the plaintiffs' claim of unconstitutional vote dilution. According to Justice Stewart, the district court "based its conclusion of unconstitutionality primarily on the fact that no Negro had ever been elected to the City Commission, apparently because of the pervasiveness of racially polarized voting in Mobile. The trial court also found that city officials had not been as responsive to the interests of Negroes as to those of white persons. On the basis of these findings, the court concluded that the political processes in Mobile were not equally open to Negroes."

The Supreme Court, however, rejected the district court's position, which had been upheld in the court of appeals. Justice Stewart argued that the features of the Mobile system, such as the majority vote requirement, "tend naturally to disadvantage any voting minority . . . [t]hey are far from proof that the at large electoral scheme represents purposeful discrimination against Negro voters." He maintained that "[t]he Fifteenth Amendment does not entail the right to have Negro candidates elected." Since "there were no inhibitions against Negroes becoming candidates, and that in fact Negroes had registered and voted without hindrance," Justice Stewart found no constitutional violation (446 U.S. 55.71).

The Court issued several separate opinions. Most notably, Justice Byron White, who had written several of the previous vote dilution cases, dissented. He argued that "the absence of official obstacles to registration, voting and running for office heretofore has never been deemed to insulate an electoral system from attack under the Fourteenth and Fifteenth Amendments." He suggested that discriminatory purpose can be inferred from the totality of the relevant facts. To Justice White, the totality of the facts relied upon by the district court in *Bolden* were even more compelling than those in *White v. Regester*. He concluded that lower courts would now have little guidance as how to proceed in evaluating factors that might demonstrate purposeful discrimination.

See also: Voting Rights Act of 1965 and Extensions, *White v. Regester*

H. W. Perry, Jr.

Raymond C. Moley (1886–1975)

Central member of President Franklin D. Roosevelt's "Brains Trust." Born in Berea, Ohio, and educated at Baldwin-Wallace College, Raymond Charles Moley took his Ph.D. at Columbia University and by the late 1920s had become an influential professor of government at Columbia. He assisted in Roosevelt's 1928 campaign for governor of New York and then served in Roosevelt's state administration. Following a suggestion of Roosevelt adviser Samuel I. Rosenman, Moley in 1932 organized the so-called "Brains Trust," which also included Columbia professors Rexford G. Tugwell and Adolf A. Berle, Jr., to advise presidential candidate Roosevelt on the Depression and governmental responses to the economic crisis. The Brains Trust helped shape FDR's 1932 campaign (a Moley memorandum of May 1932 first used the term "New Deal") and helped plan early New Deal relief, reform, and recovery programs.

After Moley's key roles in the campaign and interregnum, Roosevelt named him an Assistant Secretary of State, though in fact Moley was a special presidential assistant with a charter that ran to both domestic and foreign economic policies. But his conflicts with Secretary of State Cordell Hull and FDR's seeming repudiation of him at the London Economic Conference of 1933 led Moley to leave the government in September 1933. Increasingly unhappy about what he considered the New Deal's radical and antibusiness directions, Moley became an outspoken and influential critic of the Roosevelt administration by the late 1930s and eventually aligned himself with the conservative wing of the Republican Party.

See also: Election of 1932, New Deal, Franklin D. Roosevelt

John W. Jeffries

REFERENCES

Freidel, Frank, ed. 1980. *Realities and Illusions, 1886–1931: The Autobiography of Raymond Moley.* New York: Garland.

Moley, Raymond. 1939. *After Seven Years.* New York: Harper & Bros.

———. 1966. *The First New Deal.* New York: Harcourt.

Rosen, Elliot A. 1977. *Hoover, Roosevelt, and the Brains Trust: From Depression to New Deal.* New York: Columbia U. Pr.

Walter F. Mondale (1928–)

Democratic Senator from Minnesota, Vice President, and presidential candidate. Throughout his political career, observers often wondered whether Walter Frederick Mondale—

the intellectual son of a Methodist minister—had the combination of ruthless cunning and telegenic affability that a successful late-twentieth-century politician needed. Mondale rose to political prominence, it seemed, by having public office handed to him, not by struggling to gain victories in hard-fought electoral competition. When Mondale did fight for an election, he battled from the position of an incumbent. As a result of his formative political experiences, this psychological argument goes, Mondale did not have the existential, psychic resources to be a good candidate for the presidency as the Democratic Party's nominee in 1984. His own personal limits thus contributed to his crushing defeat at the hands of President Ronald Reagan. Mondale himself has contributed to this conclusion: he said that he would not run for the presidency in 1976 because he did not have the kind of drive that it took to fight for the highest office. And he did indeed seem to fit comfortably into the role of Jimmy Carter's Vice President between 1976 and 1980, an indication to the critical observer that Mondale lacked ambition.

While this interpretation of Mondale's political psychology may have some merit, understanding Mondale's career from a different perspective is also instructive. Mondale's rise to political prominence was in many ways a reward for unswerving loyalty to the larger needs of a cohesive, social-democratic political formation, the Democratic Farmer-Labor Party of Minnesota. Within the DFL Party in the 1940s, 1950s, and 1960s, decisions about the right one to promote for public office were often made collectively in discussions involving politicians and farm and trade union leaders. Governor Orville Freeman's appointment of Mondale in 1960 to the position of Attorney General of Minnesota when the incumbent abruptly resigned and Governor Karl Rolvaag's appointment of Mondale in 1964 to the United States Senate to fill out the term of Minnesota Senator Hubert Humphrey (after Humphrey was elected Vice President in 1964) were rewards for creative service to the DFL Party. Mondale was a skilled campaign operative who both won elections and worked well in the year-round party organization. He repaid these appointments through hustling to gain voter approval; in 1960 he put together a highly successful campaign for state Attorney General in six months, winning the first of three reelections. Similarly, Mondale held on to his Senate seat first in 1966 and again in 1972.

Mondale's career would be perfectly understandable in the context of European or Canadian social-democratic politics. Indeed, few other American politicians could have gained the AFL-CIO's preconvention endorsement in 1984.

His limits as a presidential candidate stood out in part because American presidential politics turned, in the 1960s and 1970s, into a freewheeling, "candidate-centered" politics heavily dependent on business support. As trade unions rapidly weakened in these decades, they came truly to resemble the "special interest" that Senator Gary Hart of Colorado claimed them to be during the primary season in 1984. Mondale's campaign in the general election was an effort to reconcile an old and familiar social-democratic politics with the new realities of heightened business involvement in presidential elections. Unfortunately for his reputation as a politician, Mondale's 1984 effort to put together a business-labor coalition based on both lowering the budget deficit and defending the welfare programs of the Great Society proved a spectacular failure.

See also: AFL-CIO COPE, Jimmy Carter, Democratic Farmer-Labor Party of Minnesota, Hubert Humphrey

Richard M. Valelly

REFERENCES

Lewis, Finlay. 1984. *Mondale: Portrait of an American Politician.* Rev. ed. New York: Harper & Row.

James Monroe (1758–1831)

Fifth President of the United States. James Monroe was the last member of the "Virginia Dynasty" to occupy the White House. As a staunch supporter of Republican orthodoxy, his presidency was chiefly devoted to the defense of old values and traditional Jeffersonian views of government and society. Born in Westmoreland County, Virginia, he entered the College of William and Mary at age 16, leaving college in 1776 to fight in the Revolutionary War. After a distinguished military career, he resigned from the Army in 1780 to study law under Thomas Jefferson.

Two years later Monroe was elected to the Virginia assembly. Then (1783–1786) he served as a delegate to the Continental Congress. Fearing an overcentralized government, he opposed ratification of the Constitution in the Virginia convention of 1788. Monroe accepted the Federalists' victory, but he joined the opposition in 1790 and won election to the United States Senate. There he helped lead the Jeffersonian opposition to Hamilton's fiscal program. Despite his antifederalism, President George Washington in 1794 appointed Monroe as minister to France. When he subsequently refused to defend the Jay Treaty, he was recalled in 1796. A year later he published a vindication of his actions.

In 1799 Monroe began a three-year term as governor of Virginia. Early in 1803 President Jefferson sent him to Paris to cooperate with Robert R. Livingston in negotiations that resulted in the Louisiana Purchase. The following year the Jefferson administration sent Monroe to Madrid, where, confronted with Spanish intransigence, he failed in his attempts to clarify the title of West Florida and to purchase East Florida. Monroe next attempted to settle the many disputes between Great Britain and the United States. In London he and William Pinckney carried on long negotiations that resulted in a treaty (December 1806) so favorable to Britain that Jefferson refused to submit it to the Senate. Upset by the President's action, Monroe permitted his friends to enter him in the presidential election of 1808 against Jefferson's protégé, James Madison. He was decisively defeated, receiving not a single electoral vote.

In the fall of 1810 Monroe was elected to the Virginia legislature and in early 1811 he again became governor. At this time, Jefferson was able to reconcile Monroe with Madison. Subsequently, Monroe served as Madison's Secretary of State (1811–1817) and simultaneously as his Secretary of War (1814–1815). In these positions Monroe demonstrated his clear administrative talents and helped rebuild his reputation. In 1816 he narrowly won the congressional caucus's nomination for President and then easily won in the general election. Again demonstrating his administrative abilities, Monroe assembled a very distinguished Cabinet that included John Quincy Adams as Secretary of State, John C. Calhoun as Secretary of War, and William H. Crawford as Secretary of the Treasury. Owing to his personal popularity and to the decline of the Federalist Party, Monroe lost only one electoral vote in his 1820 reelection despite an economic depression that had started the previous year.

Early in his administration Monroe asserted that the Constitution did not empower Congress to create a system of internal improvements; he believed that an amendment was needed to grant that power. In this regard, he adhered to the traditional Jeffersonian view of the political economy. Slowly, however, Monroe modified his view. By 1822 he believed that the national government could appropriate funds for the general benefit of the country.

More important than the question of internal improvements was pressure to extend slavery into the territories. During the Missouri controversy of from 1819 to 1821, Monroe abstained from all intervention in the struggle since he believed it was an issue that Congress should decide. He doubted, however, that Congress had the authority to exclude slavery from states formed in the future within a territory. Nevertheless, he signed the compromise measure in the hope that it would calm the nation.

Furthermore, Monroe adhered to the Jeffersonian emphasis of territorial expansion to ensure that the United States would remain predominantly agrarian and thus a virtuous republic. Consequently, he staunchly supported the Adams-Onis Treaty. By its terms the United States acquired East Florida, a validation of the seizure of West Florida, and a clarification of the western boundary of the Louisiana Purchase that resulted in Spain's surrender to the United States of its questionable claims to the Oregon Territory.

Probably Monroe's most notable statement on foreign affairs, written in conjunction with John Quincy Adams, was embedded in his annual message to Congress, on December 2, 1823. It consisted of two widely separated passages that together came to be known as the Monroe Doctrine. In particular, he declared that the Americas were no longer open to colonization. Moreover, he asserted that the United States would refrain from intervention in European affairs, and the United States would expect the European powers to avoid intervening in Latin American wars of independence.

Monroe still retained his great popularity when his second term ended in 1825. In 1829 he presided over the Virginia Constitutional Convention, aligning himself with those delegates who opposed a broadening of the suffrage. In 1830, after the death of his wife, Monroe moved to New York City.

See also: John Quincy Adams, Anti-Federalists, John C. Calhoun, William H. Crawford, Federalist Party, Alexander Hamilton, Jay Treaty, Thomas Jefferson, James Madison, Slavery, George Washington

Steven E. Siry

REFERENCES

Ammon, Harry. 1971. *James Monroe: The Quest for National Identity.* New York: McGraw-Hill.

Moral Majority

Founded in 1979 by the Reverend Jerry Falwell, a preacher on the *Old Time Gospel Hour* television program and chancellor of Liberty Baptist College, the Moral Majority (MM) emerged as an active force in mobilizing religious conservatives during the 1980 presidential election and for several subsequent elections. In its first ten years MM spent $69 million for education and registration of voters, for lobbying Congress and state legislatures by generating thousands of supportive letters and telephone calls, and for election support of "pro-morality" candidates.

Along with other new Religious Right organizations, MM was stimulated by a perceived decline in American morality, exacerbated by the Supreme Court's abortion decisions, the gay rights movement, the battle over ratification of the Equal Rights Amendment, and the Internal Revenue Service's questions about the tax-exempt status of some private religious schools that allegedly discriminated against certain minorities. MM's basic platform includes support for national military strength to oppose godless international communism; endorsement of the free enterprise system to preserve liberty; and opposition to abortion, homosexuality, feminism, and pornography.

The organization claims a membership of 72,000 clergy and 4 million lay people and a mailing list of 6 million for fundraising. It has chapters in all 50 states, although many may be letterhead units. In the early 1980s, its newsletter went to a million households, and its radio broadcasts were heard over some 300 stations.

Although polls have indicated substantial public support for many of MM's ideological positions, the organization and Falwell have consistently received high negative evaluations. Americans seem to prefer not to mix religion and politics. In 1986 Falwell changed the organization's name formally to the Liberty Federation; in 1987 he resigned the presidency and withdrew from involvement in politics. In June 1989 Falwell disbanded the organization, declaring its success. Although it could not elect or defeat candidates at will, Moral Majority did have significant impact upon American politics through the placement of "family issues" on the agenda and through the recruitment of religious conservatives into the political process.

See also: Communism as a Political Issue, Equal Rights Amendment

Douglas I. Hodgkin

REFERENCES

Burek, Deborah M., ed. 1990. *Encyclopedia of Associations, 1991.* 25th ed. Detroit: Gale.

Dionne, E. J., Jr. 1989. "Taking Measure of the Impact That Moral Majority Has Left on America's Landscape." *New York Times*, June 15, II, 10.

Schapsmeier, Edward L., and Frederick H. Schapsmeier. 1981. *Political Parties and Civic Action Groups.* Westport, CT: Greenwood.

Walker, Richard. 1989. "Falwell Claims Victory, Dissolves Moral Majority." 33 *Christianity Today* 58.

Zwier, Robert. 1982. *Born-Again Politics: The New Christian Right in America.* Downers Grove, IL: Inter Varsity Press.

Edwin D. Morgan (1811–1883)

One of the founders of the Republican Party. A politician whose career spanned 30 years, Edwin Denison Morgan first held office in 1849 when he was elected as a Whig to the New York City Council; next, he was elected to the New York state senate in the fall of 1849. He served there until 1855, when he was appointed one of the New York commissioners of emigration, a position he held until 1858. During this period Morgan shifted his political allegiance from the Whigs to the Republican Party. With the support of his political mentor, Thurlow Weed, Morgan was elected governor and was reelected in 1860, where his most notable achievement was raising and equipping over 200,000 troops for the Union cause. In 1863, Morgan was elected to the U.S. Senate, but he was defeated for reelection in 1869 and never again held public office.

Probably Morgan's most important political service was as Republican Party chairman. After serving as chairman of the New York State Whig Party from 1853 to 1855, he was an influential participant in the 1855 conventions that merged New York's Whig and Republican parties into a greatly strengthened Republican Party. Morgan was the new party's first chairman. In 1856 Morgan was chosen chairman of the committee that made plans for the first Republican National Convention and was chairman of the Republican National Committee that conducted the John Frémont campaign. He also served as Republican national chairman during the 1860 and 1872 presidential campaigns and was an active fundraiser and organizer in 1864, 1868, and 1876.

Morgan's term in the U.S. Senate also was politically significant, for he was a moderate on Reconstruction measures during the Andrew Johnson presidency. Morgan often supported the President—most visibly in voting to sustain

Johnson's veto of the first Freedman's Bureau Bill—but on a number of important measures he voted with the Republican majority against the President. Morgan favored swift reconciliation with the South, but not without citizenship and enfranchisement for Black Americans.

See also: Andrew Johnson, Reconstruction, Republican National Committee, Thurlow Weed

Reed Hutner

REFERENCES

Benedict, Michael Les. 1974. *A Compromise of Principle.* New York: Norton.

Gienapp, William. 1987. *The Origins of the Republican Party 1852–1856.* New York: Oxford U. Pr.

Goldman, Ralph M. 1990. *The National Party Chairmen and Committees: Factionalism at the Top.* Armonk, NY: M. E. Sharpe.

Rawley, James. 1955. *Edwin D. Morgan 1811–1883: Merchant in Politics.* New York: Columbia U. Pr.

J. P. Morgan (1837–1913)

Leading financier of the late nineteenth and early twentieth centuries. John Pierpont Morgan symbolized to most Americans of his day all the woes associated with industrial capitalism. The son of a wealthy international banker, J. P. Morgan launched his career in 1856 by joining his father's financial house in London but returned to America several years later to serve as the firm's New York agent. During the post–Civil War decades Morgan's career in finance advanced steadily as the rapid industrialization of America provided abundant opportunity for a man of his enthusiasm.

Although relatively unknown to the public before the 1890s, Morgan played a major role in the reorganization of American business and industry. His initial efforts, which focused on railroads, established the pattern he followed for the rest of his life. In reorganizing such railroads as the New York Central, the Reading, and the Baltimore Ohio, Morgan sought to eliminate destructive competition through consolidation. The formation of the giant U.S. Steel Corporation in 1901 was the culmination of Morgan's consolidation efforts.

Morgan used similar strategies in 1895 and again in 1907 to address the financial panics that threatened America's economy. On both occasions he assembled syndicates of financiers to raise the capital necessary to restore public confidence in the economic system. Because both panics occurred during a time of intense concern with trusts, the autocratic control that Morgan had earlier demonstrated over the economy convinced many Americans that he was head of a powerful "Money Trust" and thus brought his actions under close scrutiny. Public concern led eventually to the Pujo Commission investigation in late 1912; despite its failure to prove the existence of a money trust, the investigation revealed the extensive control that Morgan and a handful of other bankers exerted over the American business system. Thus, these hearings confirmed the widespread public suspicion that America's economy was dominated by a willful minority of financiers. This conclusion, in turn, generated support for such Progressive reforms as the Federal Reserve Act and the Clayton Anti-Trust Act. Morgan's financial empire thus symbolized to Americans of the early 1900s the problems inherent in industrial capitalism and did much to popularize some government regulation of business.

See also: Railroads

John W. Malsberger

REFERENCES

Corey, Lewis. 1930. *The House of Morgan.* New York: Grosset & Dunlap.

Satterlee, Herbert L. 1939. *J. Pierpont Morgan: An Intimate Portrait.* New York: Macmillan.

Sinclair, Andrew. 1981. *Corsair: The Life of J. Pierpont Morgan.* Boston: Little, Brown.

John T. Morgan (1824–1907)

Five-term U.S. Senator from Alabama at the end of the nineteenth century. John Tyler Morgan was the South's and one of the Democratic Party's most vigorous economic and territorial expansionists. Although he endorsed virtually all facets of late-nineteenth-century U.S. imperialism, Morgan was most closely identified with the campaign for the construction of a canal across Nicaragua.

The Senator was convinced that the American Northeast and Great Britain combined to hold the South in colonial subservience. While pursuing domestic remedies, such as a reduced tariff, free coinage of silver, and the protection of southern racial codes, Morgan emulated his slaveholding predecessors in perceiving expansion as the key to true southern autonomy. By adding new southern states, the South would gain voting strength in Congress; by adding lucrative foreign markets for her cotton, coal, and timber, the South would gain economic leverage and independence.

Born in eastern Tennessee, Morgan migrated with his family to Alabama in 1833, where he read law and was admitted to the bar in 1845. A Whig in the 1840s, he became a Democrat and a leading secessionist in the 1850s. He served as William L. Yancey's chief lieutenant in the Alabama secession convention, rose to the rank of brigadier general in the Confederate cavalry, and played a central role in the overthrow of Republican Reconstruction. First elected to the United States Senate in 1876, Morgan was reelected five times and died in office. His fifty years in public life and three decades in the Senate made him the central figure in Alabama political history during the Gilded Age and an important representative of the New South on the national scene.

See also: Secession

Joseph A. Fry

REFERENCES

Burnette, O. Lawrence. 1965. "John Tyler Morgan and Expansionist Sentiment in the New South." 18 *Alabama Review* 163.

Fry, Joseph A. 1985. "Governor Johnston's Attempt to Unseat Senator Morgan, 1899–1900." 38 *Alabama Review* 243.

———. 1985. "John Tyler Morgan's Southern Expansionism." 9 *Diplomatic History* 329.

Radke, August C. 1959. "Senator Morgan and the Nicaragua Canal." 12 *Alabama Review* 5.

De Lesseps S. Morrison (1912–1964)

Post–World War II reform mayor of New Orleans. Born into a socially prominent southern Louisiana family, De Lesseps Story "Chep" Morrison took a law degree from Louisiana State University in 1934. Opposing the political machine of the late Governor Huey P. Long, Morrison was elected to the state legislature in 1940. At the outbreak of war, Morrison entered the Army, rising to the rank of colonel. In 1946 he waged an uphill campaign for mayor of New Orleans at the behest of the Independent Citizens' Committee opposing the Huey Long–backed administration of incumbent Robert S. Maestri. Supported by the city's Choctaw Club/Regular Democratic Organization, Maestri was vulnerable to charges of corruption and ineptitude in handling city affairs. In an upset, the war veteran defeated Maestri by a narrow margin. Morrison was subsequently reelected for four terms (1946–1961).

Morrison's tenure in city hall was marked by dynamism, controversy, and, at times, bitter infighting with then-governor Earl Long. Although Morrison revitalized the city's economic health, particularly by encouraging international trade and public works projects, critics have charged Morrison with providing only the illusion of reform. An effective employer of public relations techniques, Morrison was nonetheless denounced for his creation of a personal political "machine," the Crescent City Democratic Association, and his ambivalent leadership during the wrenching school desegregation crisis of 1960. In his three campaigns for the Louisiana governorship, Morrison, a Roman Catholic, amassed significant support from Catholics, Blacks, urbanites, and southern Louisiana voters. However, he failed to make major inroads among rural, Protestant, and northern voters throughout the state, losing in the first primary to Earl K. Long in 1956, and in the second runoff primary in 1960 and 1964, respectively, to Jimmie H. Davis and John J. McKeithen. In 1961 Morrison accepted President John Kennedy's appointment as ambassador to the Organization of American States. Morrison died in a plane crash in Mexico.

See also: Huey P. Long

Richard C. Burnweit

REFERENCES

Haas, Edward F. 1974. *De Lesseps S. Morrison and the Image of Reform: New Orleans Politics, 1946–1961.* Baton Rouge: Louisiana State U. Pr.

Morrison, De Lesseps S. 1965. Edited by Gerald Frank. *Latin American Mission: An Adventure in Hemisphere Diplomacy.* New York: Simon & Schuster.

Parker, Joseph B. 1974. *The Morrison Era: Reform Politics in New Orleans.* Gretna, LA: Pelican.

Sindler, Allan P. 1956. *Huey Long's Louisiana: State Politics, 1920–1952.* Baltimore: Johns Hopkins U. Pr.

Oliver H. P. T. Morton (1823–1877)

Leading Indiana Republican and presidential contender in 1876. Oliver Hazard Perry Throck Morton began his political life as a Democrat but switched to the nascent Republican Party over the Kansas-Nebraska issue in 1854. As Indiana's Civil War governor, he wielded virtually dictatorial power over the state in the interest of the Union war effort. Entering the U.S. Senate in 1867, he became a fervent anti-South Radical. Although denounced for his bitterly partisan "bloody shirt" oratory, he was an uncompromising champion of southern Blacks and of southern white Republicans, whose political rights were being trampled by southern white Democrats.

In 1876, presidential candidate Morton vied with New York's Roscoe Conkling to capture the retiring Grant's supporters. Besides his own Indiana, he won a considerable following among southern Republicans. But reformers and others in the party disliked his radicalism on the southern question, his spoilsmanship regarding civil service, and his inflationary views on the currency. At the national convention he started in second place behind James G. Blaine but saw his votes dwindle, until on the seventh ballot his Indiana backers, bitterly antagonistic to Blaine, led the switch to the successful Rutherford B. Hayes.

Morton campaigned vigorously that fall. During the dispute over the election's outcome he opposed the Electoral Commission Bill as a Democratic trick. He argued that the Republican president of the Senate should simply count any disputed electoral votes for Hayes.

See also: James G. Blaine, Bloody Shirt, Roscoe Conkling, Election of 1876, Ulysses S. Grant, Rutherford B. Hayes, Kansas-Nebraska Act

Charles W. Calhoun

REFERENCES

Foulke, William Dudley. 1899. *Life of Oliver P. Morton*. 2 vols. Indianapolis: Bobbs-Merrill.

Polakoff, Keith Ian. *The Politics of Inertia: The Election of 1876 and the End of Reconstruction*. Baton Rouge: Louisiana State U. Pr.

Thornbrough, Emma Lou. 1965. *Indiana in the Civil War Era, 1850–1880*. Indianapolis: Indiana Historical Bureau and Indiana Historical Society.

Walker, Charles M. 1878. *Sketch of the Life, Character, and Public Services of Oliver P. Morton*. Indianapolis: Indianapolis *Journal*.

Rogers C. B. Morton (1914–1979)

Chairman of the Republican National Committee from 1969 to 1971. While Rogers Clark Ballard Morton avoided direct White House control of party headquarters through retention of the right to name his own staff, he did work loyally in support of the policies of the Richard Nixon White House. Morton further devoted himself to exhorting Republicans to improve their image in an oft-repeated speech titled "Where the Votes Are." He warned listeners that the American people "wrote off the Republican Party" because Republicans allegedly were "writing off the Negro, writing off labor, writing off young people, writing off ethnic groups."

A graduate of Yale University, Morton helped manage his family's milling firm until it merged with Pillsbury. He then served as vice president (1951–1953) and on the board of directors (1953–1971) of that company. His political career included running his politician brother Thruston's campaigns in Kentucky, and after moving to Maryland, he won election as a U.S. Representative from the Eastern Shore District (1963–1971). His voting record in the House was moderately conservative, but he did vote for the 1964 Civil Rights Act despite his district's strong opposition. In 1968 Morton was convention floor manager for Richard Nixon's successful bid for the Republican presidential nomination. After the party chairmanship, he was Secretary of the Interior (1971–1975) and Secretary of Commerce (1975–1976) under President Nixon and President Gerald Ford.

See also: Civil Rights Legislation and Southern Politics, Gerald R. Ford, Thruston Morton, Richard M. Nixon, Republican National Committee

Douglas I. Hodgkin

REFERENCES

Goldman, Ralph M. 1990. *The National Party Chairmen and Committees: Factionalism at the Top*. Armonk, NY: M. E. Sharpe.

Thruston B. Morton (1907–1982)

Republican Congressman and U.S. Senator from Kentucky and Republican Party chairman. After graduating from Yale University in 1929, Thruston Ballard Morton worked in his family's grain and milling firm before joining the Navy in World War II. He entered electoral politics as a Republican in a Democratic state, serving three terms as a Congressman (1947–1953) and two as a U.S. Senator (1957–1969).

As a Congressman, Morton subscribed to the liberal and internationalist Republican viewpoint, demonstrated by his votes for Greek-Turkish aid, for assistance for the Tennessee Valley Authority, for federal aid to education, and against the poll tax. He served on the Post Office and Civil Service and Education and Labor committees. As a 1948 delegate to the Republican National Convention in Philadelphia, Morton's support for Harold E. Stassen was consistent with Morton's stance in world affairs. In 1949 he cosponsored a bill to allow each state to decide whether federal education funds should go to parochial and private schools as well as to public schools in states whose education standards were below the national average.

In 1952 Morton alone in Kentucky's 20-man Republican delegation supported the nomination of Dwight Eisenhower for President. He did not run for reelection that year, primarily because the Robert Taft forces, implacable foes of Eisenhower, had gained control of the Kentucky GOP. Instead, Morton managed the successful senatorial campaign of John Sherman Cooper who, like Morton, favored civil rights legislation and federal aid to education.

President Eisenhower appointed Morton Assistant Secretary of State for Congressional Relations in 1953, a post that he held until he resigned to run for the Senate in 1956. Charged with mobilizing support for Eisenhower's foreign policy, Morton fought the Bricker Amendment (designed to curtail the President's treaty-making powers), supported the reciprocal trade bill, and cogently fought the threat posed by McCarthyism. Morton enunciated Eisenhower's position that communism presented a danger to America but that opposition to it did not justify Senator Joseph McCarthy's attacks on civil liberties.

In 1956 Morton was narrowly elected to the Senate as a "modern Republican" over incumbent Senator Earle C. Clements, his victory due in part to Eisenhower's prestige and in part to a serious split among the Democrats: Governor A. B. ("Happy") Chandler had refused to support Clements. In the Senate, Morton was Eisenhower's most consistent supporter. He served on the District of Columbia and on the Post Office and Civil Service committees. Morton worked in particular with northern liberals on civil rights legislation.

Morton was chairman of the Republican National Committee from 1959 to 1961. He replaced Meade Alcorn and continued Alcorn's modern Republican positions without the imputed responsibility for the 1958 electoral rout.

As chairman during the 1960 election, Morton alleged that John Kennedy gave aid and comfort to the Communists by attacking America's pace. After Kennedy's close victory over Richard Nixon, Morton accused the Democrats of massive vote frauds and sought an investigation.

Morton, who charged his 1962 opponent, Kentucky's lieutenant governor Wilson Wyatt, with being soft on communism, won with 52.8 percent of the vote. His animosity toward Kennedy, who had actively supported Wyatt, continued; Morton backed the administration on only 35 percent of the Senate roll calls. In 1964, Morton, as chairman of the Republican Senatorial Campaign Committee, voted against most of Johnson's social welfare reforms and criticized the escalation of the Vietnam War. This antiwar position prompted Democrat Eugene McCarthy, running for President in 1968, to list Morton among those he might consider for Secretary of State should McCarthy prove successful.

Morton declined to seek reelection in 1968. He toured the country eliciting support for a Rockefeller presidential candidacy and later was Nelson Rockefeller's co-chairman when his campaign materialized. He joined his younger brother Rogers C. B. Morton in the Nixon campaign after the convention and retired from public life to become a bank director in Louisville, Kentucky.

See also: A. B. "Happy" Chandler, Communism as a Political Issue, Dwight D. Eisenhower, John F. Kennedy, Joseph McCarthy, McCarthyism, Poll Tax, Republican National Committee

Frederick J. Augustyn, Jr.

REFERENCES

Goldman, Ralph M. 1990. *The National Party Chairmen and Committees: Factionalism at the Top.* Armonk, NY: M. E. Sharpe.

Robert Moses (1888–1981)

Visionary shaper of modern New York City. Robert Moses chaired the powerful public works force of the Triborough Bridge and Tunnel Authority of New York from 1936 to 1968, but he also presided over the money-losing World's Fair of 1964 and thus lost his position as perhaps the most successful administrator in New York City's history.

Arriving in city politics as a reformer, Moses went on to build most of the major public amenities. In 1924 he headed the state Parks Department, constructing beaches on Long Island, many parks, and the commuter parkways that led to development of suburbs in Westchester and Nassau counties. In 1934 Moses took on the added responsibility for city parks and, at his peak, held 12 appointive posts, though he was never elected to office. His system of publicly issued bonds financed long-term construction and ensured Moses's longevity as an administrator, until a scandal involving slum clearance contracts obliged his resignation in 1960.

Governor Nelson Rockefeller forced Moses to resign other state posts in 1962, though he retained the Triborough Bridge and Tunnel Authority. He ran the World's Fair without the support of many European governments because of another contracting scandal, and the enthusiasm of fair goers was further hampered by coincidental demonstrations for African-American civil rights. The World Fair's subsequent losses prevented the building of more parks.

Moses managed to defeat Mayor John Lindsay's 1966 plan to subsidize the Transit Authority with the Triborough's tolls; but he was unable to block a grander scheme of Governor Rockefeller's to merge these with the Long Island and Penn Central railroads into a giant Metropolitan Transit Authority in 1968. A substantial role for Moses failed to materialize, and he effectively retired.

See also: John V. Lindsay, Railroads, Nelson Rockefeller

Jeremy R. T. Lewis

REFERENCES

Caro, Robert A. 1974. *The Power Broker: Robert Moses and the Fall of New York.* New York: Knopf.

Lewis, Eugene. 1980. *Public Entrepreneurship: Toward a Theory of Bureaucratic Political Power: The Organizational Lives of Hyman Rickover, J. Edgar Hoover, and Robert Moses.* Bloomington: Indiana U. Pr.

Moses, Robert. 1970. *Public Works: A Dangerous Trade.* New York: McGraw-Hill.

Belle Moskowitz (1877–1933)

Progressive social reformer. In her efforts to improve conditions for immigrants and workers in New York City, Belle Moskowitz developed an interest in reform politics. She helped to organize the New York Traveler's Aid Society and as representative of the Dress and Waist Manufacturers' Association, mediated labor disputes in the garment industry (1914–1916).

Moskowitz was politically active, supporting Progressive Party candidates including Theodore Roosevelt's presidential bid in 1912. In the reform administration of Mayor John P. Mitchel, she was appointed secretary to the Mayor's Committee of Women on National Defense during World War I. Her disillusionment with reformers in office led her to work for the more pragmatic Democratic candidate for governor in 1914, Alfred E. Smith. He was impressed with her campaign for the new women's vote, and she became an important adviser while he was governor (1919–1921, 1923–1929). Moskowitz proposed the New York State Reconstruction Commission and as executive secretary guided its studies of public policy, which in turn resulted in Smith's reform program. Eventually she chose to become an unofficial adviser, and as a consequence, her career flourished only as long as Smith remained in power.

As vice chairman of the Democratic National Committee, Moskowitz worked for Smith's presidential nomination first in 1924 and then more successfully in 1928. In this campaign, she became the first woman to direct national publicity.

Franklin D. Roosevelt's election as governor of New York and his refusal to give her an appointment left Moskowitz outside of government. She continued to support Smith, hoping to win him the 1932 nomination. Her political career ended when the party chose Roosevelt, but she continued her social reform activities until her death.

See also: Progressive Party, Theodore Roosevelt, Alfred E. Smith

Joy A. Scimé

REFERENCES

Perry, Elisabeth I. 1987. *Belle Moskowitz: Feminine Politics and the Exercise of Power in the Age of Alfred E. Smith.* New York: Oxford U. Pr.

James, Edward T., Janet W. James, and Paul S. Boyer. 1971. *Notable American Women 1607–1950.* Cambridge: Belknap Press.

Stewart R. Mott (1937–)

Maverick liberal political philanthropist. Stewart Rawlings Mott has developed an abiding interest in the financial aspects of political campaigning. He is both a donor and solicitor and works as an elite and direct-mail fundraiser. His interests are in issues—particularly the population explosion, the threat of nuclear war, and political finance.

Mott is an heir to a General Motors fortune, and he has carefully invested and multiplied his money in order to devote the proceeds to philanthropy. Mott first emerged in national politics as a liberal activist in presidential and congressional campaigns. In 1968 he sought an anti–Vietnam War candidate, first spending $100,000 while seeking to persuade Nelson Rockefeller, then governor of New York, to run for President; and later contributing $200,000 to Senator Eugene McCarthy's campaign for the Democratic presidential nomination. In 1972 he was a prominent supporter of George McGovern, contributing $400,000 to the Democratic candidate for President.

A civil libertarian, Mott became one of the plaintiffs in the major case relating to regulation of money in politics, *Buckley v. Valeo.* He has been in the forefront of opposition to those provisions of the Federal Election Campaign Act that unduly restrict financial activity in politics. He has utilized his direct-mail firm Mott Enterprises to generate unique credit procedures as a means of aiding candidates he favors. Independent candidate for President in 1980 John B. Anderson and Democratic candidate for President in 1984 Alan Cranston, both benefited from Mott's direct-mail campaigns, in which the proceeds from the mailings were obligated by contract to be used to pay off the initial costs of the mail campaigns. One of the issue-oriented organizations with which Mott is associated as a trustee is the Citizens' Research Foundation, an institution that studies political finance and election reform.

See also: John B. Anderson, *Buckley v. Valeo*, Direct Mail, Federal Election Campaign Act, Eugene McCarthy, George McGovern, Nelson Rockefeller

Herbert E. Alexander

Bill Moyers (1934–)

Adviser to President Lyndon Johnson and political journalist. Bill Moyers is one of America's most prominent television commentators, known both for his critical documentaries and insightful interviews with leading political figures. Born in Hugo, Oklahoma, Moyers received his undergraduate degree in journalism from the University of Texas in 1956. He later studied theology at the University of Edinburgh and received a divinity degree from Southwestern Baptist Theological Seminary in 1959. He became a personal assistant to then Texas Senator Lyndon Johnson. Shortly after Johnson became Vice President, Moyers was named associate and then deputy director of the Peace Corps. From 1963 until 1965 he served as special assistant to President Johnson and from 1965 until 1967 was his press secretary.

In 1967 Moyers left the White House and resumed his journalistic career, becoming publisher of *Newsday*. In 1971 he shifted to television and served as editor in chief of the weekly *Bill Moyers Journal* on public television until 1976 and again from 1978 to 1981. From 1976 to 1978 and again from 1981 until 1986, Moyers held a series of positions at CBS, both directing his own programs and serving as an analyst and commentator on the nightly news. In 1987 he became executive editor of Public Affairs Television. Moyers has won three Emmys and countless other awards for his work.

Among other accomplishments, Moyers moderated one of the presidential debates between Jimmy Carter and Ronald Reagan in 1980. His reporting on such issues as arms control, the plight of the poor, and the Iran-Contra affair has been widely respected and also highly controversial. Moyers has also directed a number of highly acclaimed documentaries, including *A*

Walk Through the Twentieth Century and *The Power of Myth*, a series of interviews with the late Joseph Campbell.

See also: Jimmy Carter, Lyndon B. Johnson

Charles S. Hauss

Mugwumps

Mugwump was a term widely used during the 1884 presidential campaign to characterize those who bolted from the Republican Party to protest its nomination of the controversial James G. Blaine. That bolt was the most dramatic incident in a long effort during the years between the Civil War and the Spanish-American War by political independents to impose their influence on decision-making at the highest levels of the established two-party system.

Those who led this effort were mostly well-educated urban professionals—lawyers, educators, journalists, and merchants—concentrated in New York, Boston, and other cities in the Northeast. Isolated from local politics by the growth of urban machine organizations and resentful over the new power of full-time professional politicians at all levels of government, these independents strove with uneven results to advance the reform of civil service and the tariff at the national level. After the failure of the Liberal Republican movement of 1872, their attempts to influence regular Republican presidential nominations focused on blocking the ambitions of the popular Blaine, whose political ethics they deeply mistrusted. When Blaine finally won his nomination in 1884, independents joined in a highly publicized movement to prevent his election by supporting the Democratic nominee, Grover Cleveland.

Branded as self-righteous political vagabonds in an age that prized party discipline and regularity, the Mugwump independents won more critical attention than their numbers actually merited. Their austere political idealism and invulnerability to conventional partisan reward systems infuriated party regulars in both camps.

Prominent among Mugwump spokesmen in 1884 were George William Curtis, Edwin L. Godkin, and Carl Schurz, who regarded themselves as beleaguered moral guardians of honesty, efficiency, and conservative self-restraint in the conduct of public affairs. After 1884 many of their younger Mugwump followers merged with the Cleveland wing of the Democratic Party to pursue "good government" reform causes in municipal and state politics. William Jennings Bryan's "radical" campaign of 1896 propelled many of them back toward their original home in the Republican Party. Still, the outcome of the Spanish-American War of 1898 attracted numerous aging Mugwumps to the cause of anti-imperialism, their last coherent protest against the mood of the American majority.

The Mugwumps can be understood in retrospect as members of a minority subculture of cosmopolitan elitists, at odds with the democratic impulses of their generation. Lacking a broad popular constituency, using tactics that in some ways anticipated the pressure-group techniques of the century ahead, they tried with marginal success to press the collective professional intelligence of educated men back into American politics for the first time since the age of Andrew Jackson.

See also: James G. Blaine, William Jennings Bryan, Grover Cleveland, George William Curtis, Election of 1884

Geoffrey Blodgett

REFERENCES

Blodgett, Geoffrey. 1980. "The Mugwump Reputation, 1870 to the Present." 66 *Journal of American History* 867.

McFarland, Gerald W. 1975. *Mugwumps, Morals & Politics, 1884–1920.* Amherst: U. of Massachusetts Pr.

Sproat, John G. 1982. *"The Best Men": Liberal Reformers in the Gilded Age.* New York: Oxford U. Pr.

Frederick A. C. Muhlenberg (1756–1801)

Speaker of the First and Third U.S. Congresses. Born in Trappe, Pennsylvania, and educated at the University of Halle, Frederick Augustus Conrad Muhlenberg was ordained in 1770, after which he ministered to Lutheran congregations in Stouchburg and Lebanon, Pennsylvania. In November 1773 Muhlenberg became pastor of Christ Church in New York City. As a committed patriot he fled the city in 1776, and although he continued to preach in German Pennsylvania, his religious career was increasingly usurped by political interests and commitments.

Muhlenberg was elected to the Continental Congress in 1779 and to the Pennsylvania General Assembly in 1780, where he served as speaker for three years. As president of the state's Council of Censors (1783–1784), Muhlenberg's Federalist tendencies became apparent as he campaigned for revision of the state constitution and a stronger central government. He presided over Pennsylvania's constitutional convention in 1787, was instrumental in winning ratification, and attended the First Congress as a Federalist representing Philadelphia.

Muhlenberg was reelected to the following three Congresses and was elected Speaker of the First Congress. However, his dwindling Federalist allegiances prevented his reelection as Speaker in 1791: he did, however, serve as Speaker of the Third Congress, although this time it was as a Republican in all but name.

Muhlenberg abandoned national office at the expiration of his fourth term, although his influence continued. He was instrumental in the Republican victory in Pennsylvania in 1800. Muhlenberg College founded in 1845 in Allentown, Pennsylvania, is named in his honor.

See also: Federalist Party, Speaker of the House

Simon P. Newman

REFERENCES

Follett, Mary Parker. 1896. *The Speaker of the House of Representatives.* New York: Longmans, Green.

Charles F. Murphy (1858–1924)

Leader of New York City's Tammany machine from 1902 to 1924. Charles Francis Murphy was the most powerful leader in Tammany's history; his success, however, depended upon making concessions to other influential political forces. Murphy served as a district leader in Manhattan's Gashouse District before being selected as leader of Tammany. Apart from a brief term as a Commissioner of Docks, he occupied no public offices during his career.

Under Murphy's leadership, Tammany faced no major challenge from other Democratic factions in Manhattan, and after he overcame some early resistance in Brooklyn, the Democratic organizations in New York City's four other boroughs generally followed his lead. In general elections, the Democratic Party encountered serious opposition from Progressive reformers, Socialists, and the followers of William Randolph Hearst, but its candidates won six of the seven mayoral elections during Murphy's tenure as leader.

Murphy sought to placate the reform element by distancing Tammany from police graft and, during the Progressive era, by nominating blue ribbon mayoral candidates over whom he subsequently exercised limited influence. When newspaper publisher W. R. Hearst ran for mayor in 1905, Tammany relied upon election fraud to defeat him, but it nominated the publisher for governor in 1906 and selected a mayoral candidate acceptable to him in 1917 and 1921. Most significantly, Murphy helped bring New York City's newer immigrant groups into the

Democratic Party by authorizing Democrats in the state legislature, under the leadership of Alfred E. Smith and Robert F. Wagner, to enact the nation's most comprehensive body of labor and social legislation.

See also: William Randolph Hearst, Alfred E. Smith, Tammany Hall, Robert Wagner, Sr.

Martin Shefter

REFERENCES

Henderson, Thomas McLean. 1976. *Tammany Hall and the New Immigrants.* New York: Arno Press.

Huthmacher, J. Joseph. 1965. "Charles Evans Hughes and Charles Francis Murphy: The Evolution of Progressivism." 46 *New York History* 25.

Weiss, Nancy Joan. 1968. *Charles Francis Murphy, 1858–1924: Respectability and Responsibility in Tammany Politics.* Northampton, MA: Smith College.

Frank Murphy (1890–1949)

New Dealer, Attorney General, and Associate Justice of the U.S. Supreme Court. Born and raised in Harbor Beach, Michigan, Frank Murphy attended the University of Michigan where he earned undergraduate and law degrees. After serving as an officer with the American Expeditionary Force in France, he began his public career as a U.S. attorney for the Eastern District of Michigan. Despite the notoriety he gained as a prosecutor, Murphy was defeated in his 1920 attempt to win a seat in the U.S. House of Representatives.

Murphy was more successful in his next election, becoming judge of the recorder's court in Detroit in 1923; he was reelected in 1929. He was subsequently elected mayor of Detroit in 1930 and 1932 and served as the first president of the U.S. Association of Mayors in 1933.

An early supporter of Franklin D. Roosevelt's 1932 presidential bid, Murphy was rewarded by being named governor general of the Philippine Islands. He served in that post from 1933 until 1935 when he became the first U.S. high commissioner to the Philippines, having presided over the transition of the islands to commonwealth status. Returning to Michigan, he was elected governor in 1936. His term was most noted for his early success in helping to bring an end to the wave of sit-down strikes in the automotive industry.

His strong support of Roosevelt and the New Deal was again rewarded when he was appointed Attorney General in 1939. A man of great political ambition, Murphy accepted reluctantly when he was nominated as an Associate Justice of the Supreme Court one year later. Taking his seat February 5, 1940, he became known as a strong and eloquent supporter of civil rights until his death in Detroit.

See also: Election of 1932, New Deal, Franklin D. Roosevelt

James V. Saturno

REFERENCES

Howard, J. Woodford. 1968. *Mr. Justice Murphy: A Political Biography.* Princeton: Princeton U. Pr.

Norris, Harold, ed. 1965. *Mr. Justice Murphy and the Bill of Rights.* Dobbs Ferry, NY: Oceana.

Edmund S. Muskie (1914–)

Four-term U.S. Senator from Maine, vice presidential candidate, and Secretary of State. The son of poor immigrants, Edmund Sixtus Muskie was born in the paper mill town of Rumford, Maine; despite a very successful career in politics, diplomacy, and law, Muskie never lost sight of his personal and political roots.

When Ed Muskie first became involved in Democratic politics, the conventional wisdom was that the Democratic Party of Maine could have held its convention in a telephone booth. The state was solidly Republican, with the ruling party closely linked to the dominant paper interests in the state. Muskie served in the Maine legislature for four terms, before he was asked by his colleagues among the party leaders if he would run for governor in 1954. He accepted that nomination and, in a strongly Democratic year, pulled off one of the major upsets in Maine's political history, winning election as the first Democratic governor in twenty years. A moderate by ideology and nature, Muskie was able to work effectively with the Republican majority in the legislature. He worked even harder to develop the Democratic Party as a competitive force throughout the state. In 1958, having proven himself a popular governor, Muskie was elected to the United States Senate.

In the Senate Muskie concentrated on problems of the environment and received national recognition for sponsoring legislation on clean water and clear air. While his expertise was recognized in the Senate and legendary in Maine, Muskie did not receive widespread national recognition until Hubert Humphrey, his longtime Senate colleague and the Democratic nominee for President in 1968, selected him as his running mate. Muskie's strong campaign performance in a losing effort raised his status among national leaders. Party leaders, political journalists, and his associates in the Senate not only urged him to seek the presidency in 1972, but they also installed him as the early favorite for the Democratic nomination.

Muskie's try for the presidency met with failure. The Democratic Party had altered the rules after the 1968 nomination, but the Muskie strategists never appreciated the significance of the changes implemented by the McGovern-Fraser Commission. Muskie won the endorsement of most party leaders, but Senator George McGovern understood that these endorsements no longer translated into delegate votes. When Muskie won the New Hampshire primary by fewer votes than had been expected, his campaign was in trouble. He was never able to regroup; momentum swung to McGovern and the Muskie campaign died a slow, lingering death.

Muskie remained in the Senate, a respected national spokesperson and legislative leader, until 1976 when President Jimmy Carter asked him to become Secretary of State. Muskie left the Senate, his home for 22 years, to cap his public career as the nation's top diplomat. After President Carter's defeat in the 1980 election, Muskie returned to private life as an international lawyer and consultant.

See also: Jimmy Carter, Elections of 1968 and 1972, Hubert Humphrey, George McGovern, McGovern-Fraser Commission

Kenneth P. Hayes